2018–2019 CORPORATE CONTROLLER'S HANDBOOK OF FINANCIAL MANAGEMENT

Jae K. Shim, Ph.D.

Joel G. Siegel, Ph.D., CPA

Nick Dauber, MS, CPA

Marc H. Levine, Ph.D., CPA

Wolters Kluwer

Editorial Staff

Editor . . . . Sandra Lim, Paul Mackey, C.P.A.

Production . . . . Jennifer Schencker, Vijayalakshmi Suresh, Anbarasu Anbumani

This publication is designed to provide accurate and authoritative information in regard to the subject matter covered. It is sold with the understanding that the publisher is not engaged in rendering legal, accounting, or other professional services. If legal advice or other professional assistance is required, the services of a competent professional person should be sought.

—From a *Declaration of Principles* jointly adopted by a Committee of the American Bar Association and a Committee of Publishers and Associations

In Chapter 10, FASB Accounting Standards Codification (ASC) 230, *Statement of Cash Flows,* is used with permission. Copyright by Financial Accounting Standards Board, 401 Merritt 7, P.O. Box 5116, Norwalk, Connecticut, 06856-5116, USA. Reprinted with permission. Copies of the complete document are available from the FASB.

In Chapter 46, "Deciding on Long-Term Financing," the CFA examination question on Tektronix is used with permission. It is taken from an examination of the Institute of Chartered Financial Analysts.

In Chapter 19, "Cost Allocation," the Justa Corporation example is used with permission. Materials from the Certificate in Management Accounting Examinations, Copyright 1989 by the Institute of Certified Management Accountants (ICMA), are reprinted and/or adopted with permission.

In Chapter 28, "The Internal Audit Function and Internal Control," forms from section 4400 of the AAM—Illustrative Internal Control Forms—Medium to Large Business—are used with permission. Copyright 1997 through 2004 by American Institute of Certified Public Accountants, Inc. Reprinted with permission.

ISBN: 978-0-8080-4987-6

© 2018 CCH Incorporated and its affiliates. All rights reserved.

2700 Lake Cook Road
Riverwoods, IL 60015
800-344-3734
CCHCPELink.com

No claim is made to original government works; however, within this Product or Publication, the following are subject to CCH's copyright: (1) the gathering, compilation, and arrangement of such government materials; (2) the magnetic translation and digital conversion of data, if applicable; (3) the historical, statutory and other notes and references; and (4) the commentary and other materials.

Portions of this work were published in a previous edition.

Printed in the United States of America

FSC
www.fsc.org
MIX
Paper from
responsible sources
FSC® C103525

Corporate Controller's Handbook of Financial Management

by Jae K. Shim, Joel G. Siegel, Nick Dauber, and Marc H. Levine

Highlights

The *Corporate Controller's Handbook of Financial Management* is a comprehensive source of practical solutions, strategies, techniques, procedures, and formulas covering all key aspects of accounting and financial management. Its examples, checklists, step-by-step instructions, and other practical working tools simplify complex financial management issues and give CFOs, corporate financial managers, and controllers quick answers to day-to-day questions. In addition, the handbook includes references to the relevant topics of the *FASB Accounting Standards Codification* ™.

The handbook covers important new developments in government rules, accounting procedures, taxation, and information technology. The practical, hands-on guidance helps diagnose a firm's financial health, boost financial results, avoid unpleasant surprises, cut costs, and make financial decisions with confidence.

2018–2019 Edition

This edition of the *Corporate Controller's Handbook of Financial Management* includes the following:

- Coverage of the latest statements from the Financial Accounting Standards Board (FASB) and accounting standards updates (ASUs) included in the FASB Accounting Standards Codification ™, such as:

  —Accounting Standards Update (ASU) No. 2017-12 (August 2017), *Derivatives and Hedging* (Topic 815), *Targeted Improvements to Accounting for Hedging Activities*

  —Accounting Standards Update (ASU) No. 2017-09 (May 2017), *Compensation – Stock Compensation* (Topic 718), *Scope of Modification Accounting*

  —Accounting Standards Update (ASU) No. 2017-08 (March 2017), *Receivables-Nonrefundable Fees and Other Costs* (Subtopic 310-20), *Premium Amortization on Purchased Callable Debt Securities*

  —Accounting Standards Update (ASU) No. 2017-07 (March 2017), *Compensation –Retirement Benefits (Topic 815), Improving the Presentation of Net Periodic Pension Cost and Net Periodic Postretirement Benefit Cost*

  —Accounting Standards Update (ASU) No. 2017-06 (February 2017), *Plan Accounting, Employee Benefit Master Trust Reporting*

  —Accounting Standards Update (ASU) No. 2017-05 (February 2017), *Other Income – Gains and Losses from the Deregulation of Nonfinancial Assets* (Subtopic 610-20)

—Accounting Standards Update (ASU) No. 2017-04 (January 2017), *Intangibles–Goodwill and Other* (Topic 350): *Simplifying the Test for Goodwill Impairment*

—Accounting Standards Update (ASU) No. 2017-01 (January 2017), *Business Combinations* (Topic 805), *Clarifying the Definition of a Business*

—Accounting Standards Update (ASU) No. 2016-18 (November 2016), *Statement of Cash Flows* (Topic 230), *Restricted Cash Flow*

—Accounting Standards Update (ASU) No. 2016-16 (October 2016), *Income Taxes* (Topic 740), *Intra-Entity Transfers of Assets other than Inventory*

—Accounting Standards Update (ASU) No. 2016-15 (August 2016), *Statement of Cash Flows* (Topic 230), *Classification of Certain Cash Receipts and Cash Payments*

—Accounting Standards Update (ASU) No. 2016-13 (June 2016), *Financial Instruments—Credit Losses* (Topic 326), *Measurement of Credit Losses on Financial Instruments*

—Accounting Standards Update (ASU) No. 2016-09 (March 2016), *Compensation—Stock Compensation* (Topic 718), *Improvements to Employee Share-Based Payment Accounting*

—Accounting Standards Update (ASU) No. 2016-07 (March 2016), *Investments—Equity Method and Joint Ventures* (Topic 323), *Simplifying the Transition to the Equity Method of Accounting*

—Accounting Standards Update (ASU) No. 2016-06 (March 2016), *Derivatives and Hedging* (Topic 815), *Contingent Put and Call Options on Debt Instruments*

—Accounting Standards Update (ASU) No. 2016-05 (March 2016), *Derivatives and Hedging* (Topic 815)

—Accounting Standards Update (ASU) No. 2016-04 (March 2016), *Liabilities—Extinguishment of Liabilities* (Subtopic 405-20), *Recognition of Breakage for Certain Prepaid Stored Value Products*

—Accounting Standards Update No. 2016-01 (January 2016), *Financial Instruments* (Subtopic 825-10), *Recognition and Measurement of Financial Assets and Financial Liabilities*

—Accounting Standards Update (ASU) No. 2015-17 (November 2015), *Income Taxes* (Topic 740): *Balance Sheet Classification of Deferred Taxes*

—Accounting Standards Update (ASU) No. 2015-15 (August 2015), *Interest—Imputation of Interest* (Subtopic 835-30), *Presentation and Subsequent Measurement of Debt Issuance Costs Associated with Line-of-Credit Arrangements*

—Accounting Standards Update (ASU) No. 2015-13 (August 2015), *Derivatives and Hedging* (Topic 815): *Application of the Normal Purchases and Normal Sales Scope Exception to Certain Electricity Contracts within Nodal Energy Markets*

—Accounting Standards Update (ASU) No. 2015-12 (July 2015) Part I, *Plan Accounting: Defined Contribution Pension Plans* (Topic 962)

—Accounting Standards Update (ASU) No. 2015-08 (May 2015), *Business Combinations* (Topic 805): *Pushdown Accounting – Amendments to SEC Paragraphs Pursuant to Staff Accounting Bulletin No. 115*

—Accounting Standards Update (ASU) No. 2015-04 (April 2015), *Compensation – Retirement Benefits* (Topic 715), *Practical Expedient for the Measurement Date of an Employer's Defined Benefit Obligation and Plan Assets*

—Accounting Standards Update (ASU) No. 2015-03 (April 2015), *Interest – Imputation of Interest – Simplifying the Presentation of Debt Issuance Costs*

—Accounting Standards Update (ASU) No. 2015-02 (February 2015), *Consolidation* (Topic 810) *Amendments to the Consolidation Analysis*

—Accounting Standards Update (ASU) No. 2015-01 (January 2015), *Income Statement-Extraordinary and Unusual Items* (Subtopic 225-20), *Simplifying Income Statement Presentation by Eliminating the Concept of Extraordinary Items*

—Accounting Standards Update (ASU) No. 2014-15 (August 2014), *Presentation of Financial Statements – Going Concern* (Subtopic 205-40), *Disclosure of Uncertainties About an Entity's Ability to Continue as a Going Concern*

—Accounting Standards Update (ASU) No. 2014-14 (August 2014), *Receivables – Troubled Debt, Restructurings by Creditors* (Subtopic 310-40), *Classification of Certain Government-Guaranteed Mortgage Loans Upon Foreclosure*

—Accounting Standards Update (ASU) No, 2014-12 (June 2014), *Compensation – Stock Compensation* (Topic 718), *Accounting for Stock-Based Payments When the Terms of an Award Provide That a Performance Target Could Be Achieved after the Requisite Service Period*

—Accounting Standards Update (ASU) No. 2014-11 (June 2014), *Transfers and Servicing* (Topic 860), *Repurchase-to-Maturity Transactions, Repurchase Financings, and Disclosures*

—Accounting Standards Update (ASU) No. 2014-10 (June 2014), *Development Stage Entities* (Topic 915): *Elimination of Certain Financial Reporting Requirements, Including an Amendment to Variable Interest Entities Guidance in Topic 810: Consolidation*

—Accounting Standards Update (ASU) No. 2014-09 (May 2014), *Revenue from Contracts with Customers* (Topic 606)

—Accounting Standards Update (ASU) No. 2014-08 (April 2014), *Presentation of Financial Statements (Topic 205) and Property, Plant and Equipment (Topic 360), Reporting Discontinued Operations and Disclosures of Disposals of Components of an Entity*

—Accounting Standards Update (ASU) No. 2013-11 (July 2013), *Income Taxes (ASC Topic 740), Presentation of an Unrecognized Tax Benefit When a Net Operating Loss Carryforward, a Similar Tax Loss, or Tax Credit Carryforward Exists*

—Accounting Standards Update (ASU) No. 2013-10 (July 2013), *Derivatives and Hedging (ASC Topic 815), Inclusion of the Fed Funds Effective Swap Rate as a Benchmark Interest Rate for Hedge Accounting Purposes*

—Accounting Standards Update (ASU) No. 2013-07 (April 2013), *Presentation of Financial Statements (ASC Topic 205), Liquidation Basis of Accounting*

—Accounting Standards Update (ASU) No. 2013-02 (February 2013), *Comprehensive Income (ASC Topic 220), Reporting on Amounts Reclassified Out of Accumulated Other Comprehensive Income*

—Accounting Standards Update (ASU) No. 2013-01 (January 2013), *Balance Sheet (ASC Topic 210), Clarifying the Scope of Disclosures about Offsetting Assets and Liabilities*

—Accounting Standards Update (ASU) No. 2012-02 (July 2012), *Intangibles – Goodwill and Other (ASC Topic 350), Testing Indefinite-Lived Intangible Assets for Impairment*

—Accounting Standards Update No. 2011-02 (April 2011), *Receivables (ASC Topic 310), A Creditor's Determination of Whether a Restructuring Is a Troubled Debt Restructuring*

—Accounting Standards Update No. 2011-03 (April 2011), *Transfers and Servicing (ASC Topic 860), Reconsideration of Effective Control for Repurchase Agreements*

—Accounting Standards Update No. 2011-04 (May 2011), *Fair Value Measurement (ASC Topic 820), Amendments to Achieve Common Fair Value Measurement and Disclosure Requirements in U.S. GAAP and IFRS*

—Accounting Standards Update No. 2011-05 (June 2011), *Comprehensive Income (ASC Topic 220), Presentation of Comprehensive Income*

—Accounting Standards Update No. 2011-08 (September 2011), *Intangibles—Goodwill and Other (ASC Topic 350), Testing Goodwill for Impairment*

—Accounting Standards Update No. 2011-09 (September 2011), *Compensation Retirement Benefits—Multiemployer Plans (ASC Topic 715-80), Disclosures about an Employer's Participation in a Multiemployer Plan*

—According to Accounting Standards Update (ASU) No. 2010-09 (February 2010), *Subsequent Events* (ASC Topic 855), *Amendments to Certain Recognition and Disclosure Requirements*

- New guidance and examples on goodwill impairment testing discusses the new standard ASU 2017-04, *Simplifying the Test for Goodwill Impairment* (Chapter 9)

- Updated guidance on lease accounting discusses ASC Topic 842, *Leases*, which requires entities to recognize lease assets and lease liabilities on the balance sheet and to disclose information about leasing arrangements (Chapter 12)

- Completely new section provides an indepth discussion of COSO's new *Enterprise Risk Management – Integrating with Strategy and Performance* (Chapter 34)

- Updated tax information and new sample filled-in tax forms (Chapters 59 and 60).

In addition to the above, several comparisons are made between IFRS and U.S. GAAP throughout the various chapters.

CCH Learning Center

CCH's goal is to provide you with the clearest, most concise, and up-to-date accounting and auditing information to help further your professional development, as well as a convenient method to help you satisfy your continuing professional education requirements. The CCH Learning Center* offers a complete line of self-study courses covering complex and constantly evolving accounting and auditing issues. We are continually adding new courses to the library to help you stay current on all the latest developments. The CCH Learning Center courses are available 24 hours a day, seven days a week. You'll get immediate exam results and certification. To view our complete accounting and auditing course catalog, go to: **cch.learningcenter.com.**

Accounting Research Manager™

Accounting Research Manager is the most comprehensive, up-to-date, and objective online database of financial reporting literature. It includes all authoritative and proposed accounting, auditing, and SEC literature, plus independent, expert-written interpretive guidance.

---

* CCH is registered with the National Association of State Boards of Accountancy (NASBA) as a sponsor of continuing professional education on the National Registry of CPE Sponsors. State boards of accountancy have final authority on the acceptance of individual courses for CPE credit. Complaints regarding registered sponsors may be addressed to the National Registry of CPE Sponsors, 150 Fourth Avenue North, Nashville, TN 37219-2417. Telephone: 615-880-4200.

*CCH is registered with the National Association of State Boards of Accountancy as a Quality Assurance Service (QAS) sponsor of continuing professional education. Participating state boards of accountancy have final authority on the acceptance of individual courses for CPE credit. Complaints regarding QAS program sponsors may be addressed to NASBA, 150 Fourth Avenue North, Suite 700, Nashville, TN 37219-2417. Telephone: 615-880-4200.

Our Weekly Summary e-mail newsletter highlights the key developments of the week, giving you the assurance that you have the most current information. It provides links to new FASB, AICPA, SEC, PCAOB, EITF, and IASB authoritative and proposal-stage literature, plus insightful guidance from financial reporting experts.

Our outstanding team of content experts take pride in updating the system on a daily basis, so you stay as current as possible. You'll learn of newly released literature and deliberations of current financial reporting projects as soon they occur! Plus, you benefit from their easy-to-understand technical translations.

With **Accounting Research Manager,** you maximize the efficiency of your research time while enhancing your results. Learn more about our content, our experts, and how you can request a FREE trial by visiting us at **accountingresearchmanager.com.**

06/18

© 2018 CCH Incorporated and its affiliates. All rights reserved.

*To **Chung Shim, dedicated wife;** **Roberta M. Siegel,** loving wife and colleague; and **Karen J. Dauber,** loving and devoted wife; **Katie** and **Michael Dauber,** precious children; **Margie Dauber,** dearly departed and deeply missed mother, and **Susan Dauber,** loving sister; and **Carol Levine,** devoted wife and friend, **Reva Levine,** dearly departed daughter, **Daniel and Sori Levine and Adam Fleischer,** loving children, **Jacob, Abraham, and Eli Levine,** and **Shira Fleischer,** loving* grandchildren, *and **Tessie and Samuel Levine,** dearly departed parents.*

ABOUT THE AUTHORS

JAE K. SHIM, Ph.D., is Professor of Accounting and Finance at California State University, Long Beach, and CEO of Delta Consulting Company, a management consulting and training firm. He received his M.B.A. and Ph.D. degrees from the University of California at Berkeley (Haas School of Business). Dr. Shim has been a consultant to commercial and nonprofit organizations for more than 30 years.

Dr. Shim has published numerous articles in journals, such as *Financial Management, Econometrica, Decision Sciences, Management Science, Long Range Planning, OMEGA,* and *Journal of Operational Research Society.* He has more than 50 college and professional books to his credit, including *Operations Management, Managerial Economics, Financial Management, Managerial Accounting, U.S. Master Finance Guide, Barron's Accounting Handbook, Investment Sourcebook, Dictionary of International Business Terms, The CPA Reference, CFO Fundamentals,* and *The Vest-Pocket MBA.*

Thirty-three of his publications have been translated into foreign languages, such as Spanish, Chinese, Russian, Polish, Croatian, Italian, Japanese, Indonesian, and Korean. Professor Shim's books have been published by Thomson Reuters, John Wiley, McGraw-Hill, Barron's, CCH, Prentice-Hall, the American Management Association (Amacom), and the American Institute of CPAs.

Dr. Shim has been frequently quoted by media, such as the *Los Angeles Times, Orange County Register, Business Start-ups, Personal Finance,* and *Money Radio.* Dr. Shim is the recipient of the 1982 *Credit Research Foundation* award for his article on financial modeling.

JOEL G. SIEGEL, Ph.D., CPA, is a retired Professor of Accounting and Finance at Queens College of the City University of New York.

He was previously employed by Coopers and Lybrand, CPAs, and Arthur Andersen, CPAs. Dr. Siegel has acted as a consultant in accounting and finance to many organizations, including Citicorp, International Telephone and Telegraph, United Technologies, the American Institute of CPAs, and Person/Wolinsky Associates.

Dr. Siegel is the author of 67 books and about 300 articles on accounting and financial topics. His books have been published by CCH, Southwestern, Prentice-Hall, Richard Irwin, Probus, Macmillan, McGraw-Hill, Harper and Row, John Wiley, International Publishing, Barron's, the American Management Association, and the American Institute of CPAs.

His articles have been published in many accounting and financial journals, including *Financial Executive, The Financial Analysts Journal, The CPA Journal, Practical Accountant,* and the *National Public Accountant.*

In 1972, he was the recipient of the Outstanding Educator of America Award. Dr. Siegel is listed in *Who's Where Among Writers* and *Who's Who in the World.* He served as Chairperson of the National Oversight Board.

NICK DAUBER, MS, CPA, is an accounting practitioner specializing in auditing and taxation. Prior to starting his practice more than 30 years ago, he was an audit and tax manager at a CPA firm.

Mr. Dauber has been an instructor of Auditing and Taxation at Queens College of the City University of New York for 33 years. He was the president of Person/ Wolinsky CPA Review Courses and has instructed more than 100,000 CPA Exam candidates for over 30 years. Mr. Dauber was the writer of the review course's auditing and taxation material and served as the editor of the law and financial accounting material.

In 1992, Mr. Dauber was named Professor of the Year at Queens College and was the recipient of the Golden Apple Award bestowed by the Golden Key National Honor Society. He has also served as an award-winning lecturer in auditing and taxation for the Foundation for Accounting Education at the New York State Society of CPAs as well as for the American Institute of Certified Public Accountants.

Mr. Dauber has served as a book reviewer for major book publishers and has published articles in many professional accounting journals, including *The CPA Journal* (New York), *Massachusetts CPA, Virginia Accountant Quarterly,* and *National Public Accountant.*

Books that Mr. Dauber has authored include *The Complete CPA Reference, A Complete Guide to Auditing Standards and Other Professional Standards for Accountants 2009, Barron's How to Prepare for the CPA Exam, Barron's Dictionary of Accounting Terms, and Barron's Accounting Handbook.* He has also been a contributor to professional books in accounting and auditing.

MARC H. LEVINE, Ph.D., CPA, is a financial accounting consultant and Professor of Accounting and Deputy Chairman of the Department of Accounting and Information Systems at Queens College – CUNY. Dr. Levine was previously associated with Deloitte and Touche, CPAs.

Dr. Levine is an author of CCH's *GAAP Handbook of Policies and Procedures,* and has authored seven books, including those published for Warren, Gorham and Lamont, American Management Association, and Thomson and Trentop.

In addition, he has authored 49 professional and academic articles in publications such as *The CPA Journal, Practical Accountant, National Public Accountant, Michigan CPA, Journal of Corporate Accounting, Accountants Record, Massachusetts CPA Review, Virginia Accountant Quarterly, Cost and Management, Management Accountant,* and *The Accountant.*

WHAT THIS BOOK WILL DO FOR YOU

Corporate Controller's Handbook of Financial Management is directed toward chief financial officers, corporate financial managers, controllers, treasurers, chief accountants and staff accountants, internal auditors, management accountants, and consultants. A practical reference for all areas of corporate financial management and accounting, this handbook applies to organizations of any size. It is a comprehensive, authoritative working guide that pinpoints what to look for, what to watch out for, what to do, how to do it, and how to apply it in performing the financial management and controllership functions.

The handbook is geared to the contemporary financial officer, who must follow some traditional elements common to controllership and financial management but must be cognizant of the changing financial markets and technology of today. These factors make some of the traditional techniques of financial management obsolete—new strategies and techniques are necessary in order to do an effective job that ensures financial survival. This is a true handbook containing a wealth of information, as well as the tools that make it work for the professional. The handbook focuses on the responsibilities of corporate financial managers and controllers who must meet present-day challenges in the business world. The corporate financial manager must help to maintain and even improve the company's competitive position. The handbook enlightens the corporate financial manager and controller by presenting the most current information, offering important directives, explaining technical procedures, and looking at emerging trends.

Corporate Controller's Handbook of Financial Management will help you diagnose and evaluate accounting, financial, and operating situations faced daily. The controller is more than just the chief accountant. He or she must be able to provide upper management with financial information, evaluation, and advice.

Any topic of importance can be found in this book. It covers all aspects of the controller's and financial manager's jobs, including accounting and financial reporting activities, managerial analysis and planning, tax planning, implementation of corporate policies, and treasury functions. The book includes "key" areas, such as management reports, asset management, budgeting and variance analysis, accounting principles, sources of financing, capital structure analysis, measurement of divisional and departmental performance, financial analysis, break-even analysis, forensic accounting, internal auditing, avoiding financial problems, analysis and control of costs, mergers and acquisitions, management accounting, cost management strategies, financial models and quantitative applications, computer applications, risk management, optimizing returns, investments, insurance protection, economic effects, business valuation, divestiture, failure and reorganization, and international finance.

Illustrations and step-by-step instructions are provided on what to watch out for and how to do it. This enables you to see how the techniques and procedures are applied. "Real life" examples are given of the analytical points made so you may handle everyday problems. Checklists and summaries are also provided. The book is filled with facts, explanations, commentaries, sample documents and letters, agreements, reports, flowcharts, analysis, figures, and practices. Tables, statistical data, charts, exhibits, and diagrams are provided as needed. You will find financial measures, ratios, formulas, and rules-of-thumb to help you analyze and evaluate any business-related situation. Sophisticated, up-to-date analytical techniques and managerial tools are presented.

Corporate Controller's Handbook of Financial Management provides detailed analysis of recurring problems as well as unusual situations that may crop up. It gives vital suggestions throughout. The latest developments, such as new tax laws, are also included. This reference book provides all the information you need to perform the financial management and controllership functions effectively and efficiently!

Guidelines are presented for evaluating proposals, whether they are short- or long-term, for profit potential and risk-return comparison. Tips for preparing necessary reports are also provided.

You will be able to move quickly to take advantage of favorable situations or avoid unfavorable ones. Here is the guide that will help you make smart decisions in all areas of corporate financial management and controllership. It will be your daily problem-solver for financial and accounting situations. The practical benefits of this guidebook are unlimited in that it:

- Shows you how to measure and appraise risk.
- Lists "red flags" for potential problem areas.
- Recommends proven ways to correct financial sickness and inefficiency.
- Shows you how to evaluate business proposals, operations, and activities.
- Offers tested techniques for analyzing the financial structure of the business.
- Provides interpretation of variances indicating inefficiencies in the organization.
- Gives you the tools for spotting financially strong or weak business segments.

Important questions facing the controller will be answered, such as:

- What type of reports may be prepared to enhance the decision-making process?
- How do I conform to the new pension laws?
- What should be done to achieve maximum benefit from the new income tax accounting rules?
- What should be known about recent laws and governmental regulations?
- How can inventory be managed to lower costs and better utilize production facilities?
- What factors should be considered when preparing financial forecasts?
- How can productivity and performance best be measured?

Part I (Chapters 1 through 3) looks at the responsibilities of the controller, including the types of reports that must be prepared. The use of computers to incorporate the latest technology in performing controllership functions is also discussed. SEC filings are presented.

Part II (Chapters 4 through 7) discusses the use of computers to incorporate the latest technology in performing controllership functions. Spreadsheet programs, database software, accounting packages, LANs, WANs, database management systems, the client/server environment, Web 2.0, cloud computing, and wireless technology are discussed. The AICPA's new financial reporting language, XBRL, is explained. Also explained is the use of computers in financial decision making, specifically budgeting and planning software, accounting software, forecasting and statistical software, and value chain management software (e.g., ERP, SCM, and CRM systems).

Part III (Chapters 8 through 13) covers U.S. generally accepted accounting principles (GAAP). The financial reporting requirements that must be known to the controller include important topics such as leases, pensions, and accounting for income taxes. The book includes a discussion on the convergence between U.S. GAAP and International Financial Reporting Standards (IFRS) related to specific accounting topics.

Part IV (Chapters 14 through 27) focuses on managerial accounting and cost management issues. The chapters cover what the controller should know about cost accounting, including costing systems, joint costs, cost allocation, activity-based costing and just-in-time, capital budgeting, contribution margin, budgeting and financial modeling, variance analysis, life-cycle costs and target costing, environmental costing, quality costs, break-even analysis, and segmental performance. In addition, the corporate balanced scorecard is discussed.

Part V (Chapters 28 through 30) deals with internal auditing and controls. This part covers the audit techniques involved in auditing assets, liabilities, equity, revenue, and expenses. The characteristics of sound internal control are also indicated.

Part VI (Chapters 31 through 46) is directed toward financial and risk analysis and financial forecasting, including risk/reward relationships and financial statement analysis for internal evaluation. Ways to analyze and control revenue and costs are addressed. Insurance and legal concerns are examined. Finally, economic factors are taken into account. Chapters 39 through 46 provide what must be considered in the planning, financing, and accounting for mergers and acquisitions. Acquisition criteria and objectives to be accomplished are presented. The reasons for and ways of divesting business segments are addressed. Failure and reorganization are discussed. Consideration is given to shareholder value analysis and forecasting corporate financial distress. An in-depth discussion of corporate valuations is also presented.

Part VII addresses the issue of liquidity and treasury. Chapters 47 through 58 address the proper management of assets including cash, marketable securities, accounts receivable, and inventory. Chapters 50 and 51 inform the controller what should be known about investments in securities to earn a satisfactory return while controlling risk. Chapters 52 through 58 cover how to obtain adequate financing for the business to meet its goals and requirements. Short-term, intermediate-term, and long-term financing instruments are explained and illustrated and the circumstances in which each are appropriate are given. There is also a discussion of warrants and convertibles. Cost of capital determination and dividend policy are examined. For those involved in international finance this section will be of interest.

Part VIII (Chapters 59 and 60) covers tax preparation and planning. There is a discussion of key tax topics, such as tax saving alternatives, payroll taxes, tax aspects of business combinations and leveraged buyouts, and tax effects of stock option and incentive plans.

The content of *Corporate Controller's Handbook of Financial Management* is clear, concise, and to the point. It is a valuable reference tool containing "how-tos" in controllership. The uses of this handbook are as varied as the topics presented. Keep it handy for easy, quick reference, and daily use.

Jae K. Shim, Ph.D.

Joel G. Siegel, Ph.D., CPA

Nick Dauber, MS, CPA

Marc H. Levine, Ph.D., CPA

ACKNOWLEDGMENTS

Our deepest appreciation and thanks to the staff at CCH, including Sandra Lim for her editorial advice and assistance on this book. We are grateful for their valuable contribution.

Thanks to Roberta M. Siegel, Karen J. Dauber, CPA, and Carol Ann Levine for their invaluable input and editorial assistance.

Permission has been received from the Institute of Certified Management Accountants to use questions and/or unofficial answers from past CMA examinations.

CONTENTS

SUPPLEMENTAL MATERIAL

The supplemental material for Wolters Kluwer's *2018-2019 Corporate Controller's Handbook of Financial Management* is provided at ***https://www.cchcpelink.com/ CCHFM2018-2019***

PART I
INTRODUCTION

PART II
COMPUTER APPLICATIONS

PART III
GENERALLY ACCEPTED ACCOUNTING PRINCIPLES

PART IV
MANAGEMENT ACCOUNTING AND COST MANAGEMENT

PART VIII
TAX PREPARATION AND PLANNING

PART I

INTRODUCTION

CHAPTER 1

THE RESPONSIBILITIES OF THE CONTROLLER

CONTENTS

Although the responsibilities of the controller and the treasurer may overlap between different companies, the controllership functions, themselves, remain basically similar between industries and companies. The controller may provide financial information to diverse users, including internal management, stockholders, creditors (including banks and suppliers), stock exchanges, employees, customers, the public at large, U.S. government agencies (e.g., the Securities and Exchange Commission, Internal Revenue Service, Department of Commerce, Department of Labor, and the Federal Trade Commission), and state and local tax and other agencies.

RESPONSIBILITIES

The role of the controller is changing. Businesses growing in size and complexity, intervention by the government, and more diverse means of raising capital have added to the functions and responsibilities of the controller, and these functions

We express our appreciation to Carol Klinger, MS, CPA, for her assistance in the preparation of this chapter.

continue to change rapidly. Traditionally, the controller has been thought of as the chief accounting officer and financial planner of a corporation. Indeed, *Webster's Dictionary* defines the word *controller* in just those terms. The typical controller was the executive in charge of the record keeping for a company, the preparer of financial statements, and the person responsible for internal controls. Though still responsible for these functions, controllers today have expanded responsibilities and are becoming more involved with strategic planning.

Strategic planning entails becoming involved with the decision-making processes of the organization. The controller is in the unique position to do this, as he or she has knowledge of the company plus the financial know-how that few others in the corporation possess. As more chief executive officers begin to rely on the controller's office for information and for input into planning decisions, the controller will likely become an even more valuable member of the management team. No longer is it sufficient for a controller to just add up the numbers; most executives expect more.

Controllers can do more than gather the data of past performance and pump out reports. They can use the information collected to become involved in the dynamics of running the business. Controllers have already gathered much of the information required to improve profits and operations, reduce costs, and develop strategies for the company. Moreover, they have a "hands-on" feel of the operating environment, such as the interrelationships among management, production, and sales. The accounting function, by its very nature, provides a large percentage of the information needed by executives. The trick is to put this information to use for the future and not just report on the past. Where is the company headed? Although controllers must not turn their backs on the traditionally assigned accounting tasks, they must apply a vast body of knowledge to the future prospects of the organization. It is in this regard that controllers will prove useful and valuable to any company.

The controller is usually the head officer of an accounting department whose size varies by company. He or she is responsible for the products of the accounting department as well as for running an efficient and effective department. Maintaining the company records for accounts payable, accounts receivable, inventory, and other pertinent areas has traditionally been considered the primary function of the controller. All transactions must be recorded properly and in a timely manner, either manually or using computer software. Along with record keeping, the controller is responsible for the preparation of financial statements and, if required, interpreting these statements for management. In doing so, the controller may work closely with the independent auditors to ascertain that the statements are presented fairly in accordance with generally accepted accounting principles (GAAP). The controller will also work hand-in-hand with the auditors as they perform the year-end independent audit and may require his or her staff to assist the auditors in certain tasks. Furthermore, the controller may play an important role in terms of involvement with the audit committee. In addition to assisting with the external audit, the controller is involved with internal auditing on a year-round basis: evaluating the company's internal control structure in order to determine that it is operating effectively and efficiently; making improvements in the structure if it is determined that there are deficiencies; and reporting to the audit committee or board of directors—perhaps on a regular basis—the status of the internal control structure. Addressing the needs of management is another important aspect of the controller's role. It must not be overlooked that the goal of business is to realize a profit. Without information about the costs of production and distribution, management cannot determine how to proceed in regard to marketing decisions.

The controller must construct reports relating to production costs and distribution costs. To help management determine the most profitable course to follow, the controller should be acquainted with break-even analyses, cost-volume-profit relationships, and standard cost methods. Adequate reporting to management to enable intelligent decision making requires knowledge not only of cost accounting but of responsibility accounting and exception reporting. The controller must be able to report historical data as well as develop trends and relationships from existing data. In addition, the controller should know how to make use of financial relationships, determine the trend of ratios, present the ratios in suitable form, and interpret the data in a comprehensive report.

Tax returns and other tax matters that pertain to the corporation are also handled by the controller. Although some companies refer tax matters to the public accountants, it is still the responsibility of the controller to avoid excess taxes. The controller must be fully informed about tax matters, particularly federal income taxes. Identifying and analyzing tax implications of a given transaction are important functions of the controller because the controller's role is not limited to verifying the validity of tax computations. Most important, to minimize the tax obligation, tax planning is crucial. The controller must recognize tax problems in the making—that is, before the transactions are complete.

Any statistical reports that are needed by management are usually prepared in the controller's department. Therefore, the controller must be familiar with the operational flow of the company as well as the needs of its executives so that useful information can be developed and presented. The controller must prepare a variety of reports for distribution to different levels of management, depending on their needs. These reports enable various managerial objectives to be attained and can include weekly sales reports segregated by territories, salespeople, or products, and labor reports based on actual and standard costs that can be presented by product, division, material usage, or other important variables. The annual budget, an important planning tool, is generally prepared by the controller's office. The construction of the budget and its basic guidelines are determined by the controller. The controller is expected to analyze the plan to ascertain that it is reasonable and reliable. In addition, proposing suggestions for improvements is vital to a company's growth. The budget may be flexible, fixed, or zero based and the controller must be knowledgeable in these areas. Once prepared, the budget becomes a control device, and the controller analyzes variances and advises management to take corrective action, if necessary.

The controller may also be expected to determine whether the company is carrying adequate insurance on properties and other assets. It is important to maintain adequate records of all contracts and leases and it is the controller's function to determine that they are recorded properly. The controller is also responsible for determining that the entity is satisfying all regulations prescribed by governmental agencies. If the board of directors sets any goals regarding financial transactions, these are listed in the minutes of the board, and it is the obligation of the controller's office to ensure that they are acted upon.

The passing of the Foreign Corrupt Practices Act in 1977 required corporations to maintain financial records and to establish and maintain an effective internal control structure. The controller must be aware of this Act and its requirements and realize that maintaining reasonable records and adequate controls is now a matter of law. The controller must be familiar with the mechanics of establishing a sound internal control structure as well as understand the cost/benefit relationships in establishing and monitoring the structure. Failure to do so will lead to problems such as that experienced by Enron and others.

The reporting function of the controller's job is not limited to just internal uses. The controller will be called upon to assist in the formulation of the annual report to stockholders and to prepare other reports for government agencies such as the Securities and Exchange Commission (SEC). The information in the annual report must be easily understood and well written and should frequently use graphical and other illustrative material. The financial information contained therein is typically prepared by the controller who will be responsible for its content. There should always be adequate disclosure and the information must conform to GAAP and to SEC requirements.

SKILLS

To cope with all these various tasks, the controller must possess certain skills, the most important being a knowledge of current accounting principles and practices and an ability to communicate effectively to management the impact of recent promulgations. The controller also must keep abreast of any significant changes to GAAP. This can usually be accomplished by receiving advice from the independent auditor or by referring to published sources. The controller must know how to communicate ideas both orally and through written representations. A forward-looking controller understands that information should be presented in a useful and understandable format. He or she always considers future consequences and directions.

The ability to motivate and organize subordinate staff members is essential. As the head of the accounting department, the controller must be able to direct the members of the department so that they are responsible for their own work. It is important to be fair and reasonable when dealing with subordinates.

In addition, the controller must be able to interact with people at all levels of the organization. Because the controller's position requires the providing of information to many levels of management, it is crucial that the controller possess a basic understanding of the problems faced by the business as a whole and the problems faced by individual departments within the company. Although the controller is not expected to become an expert in engineering or production, it is important to be familiar with these areas in order to anticipate the needs of all departments. To be effective, the controller has to get involved to some extent with the day-to-day operations of the company. After formulating suggestions, the controller must be able to market them. Gaining respect from other executives will enable this. If others see that the controller wants to help, they will actually seek his or her advice.

A wise controller knows the limits of his or her prescribed functions and knowledge base. The preparation of voluminous reports that are never read may make it appear that the controller is working to his or her utmost capacity, but in reality very little is being accomplished. Certain areas of reporting would more properly be done by managers with expertise in other areas, such as engineering or sales. Without the proper support staff, the controller cannot function at the level he or she would like to.

CONTROLLER VERSUS TREASURER

Unlike the controller, the treasurer's responsibility is mostly custodial in nature and involves obtaining and managing the company's capital; he or she primarily deals with "money management" activities. The treasurer's activities are *external*, primarily involving financing matters and mix; he or she is involved with creditors (e.g., bank loan officers), stockholders, investors, underwriters for equity (stock) and bond issuances, and governmental regulatory bodies (such as the SEC). The treasurer is responsible for managing corporate assets (e.g., accounts receivable and inventory), debt, credit appraisal and collection, planning the finances, planning capital expenditures, obtaining funds, dividend disbursement, managing the investment portfolio, and pension management.

In some organizations the duties of the controller and treasurer overlap, with the treasurer being, in effect, the controller's superior.

CONTROLLER'S REPORTS

A successful controller will possess the ability to communicate ideas to various interested parties through the preparation of various types of reports. Prospective financial information is often needed to enable departments and segments to plan the future effectively. In this regard, planning reports are often issued by the controller. Information reports, analytical and control reports, as well as exception reports prepared by the controller enable analysis of a diverse amount of information and situations. Reports prepared for the board of directors must address specific policy matters and general trends in revenue and profits. These reports must enable the Board to establish and attain specified goals. Reports prepared for other company employees must be useful and timely. Reports to stockholders and relevant stock exchanges must be informative and complete. The controller's role in reporting information, therefore, cannot be overstated.

GENERALLY ACCEPTED ACCOUNTING PRINCIPLES

Inasmuch as the controller is primarily responsible for the entity's accounting functions, he or she should be fully cognizant of recent promulgations in financial accounting. It is critical that the controller be able to prepare detailed and meaningful financial statements. There are a host of reporting mandates applicable to the income statement, balance sheet, and statement of cash flows. To inform readers properly, disclosures should be made of all important items not presented in the body of the financial statements.

Note: On July 1, 2009, the *FASB Accounting Standards Codification*™ (ASC) became the one source of authoritative U.S. GAAP. Effective after September 15, 2009, the Codification supercedes all present accounting standards as the single official source of authoritative U.S. GAAP.

The Codification changes the manner in which U.S. GAAP is documented, updated, referenced, and accessed. All authoritative literature applicable to a particular topic is in one place.

The Codification includes standards issued by the following standard setters:

- Financial Accounting Standards Board (FASB)
- American Institute of Certified Public Accountants (AICPA)
- Securities and Exchange Commission (SEC)
- Emerging Issues Task Force (EITF)
- Derivative Implementation Group (DIG) Issues
- Accounting Principles Board (APB) Opinions
- Accounting Research Bulletins (ARB)
- Accounting Interpretations (AIN)

The Codification does not change generally accepted accounting principles (GAAP). Rather, it takes the individual pronouncements that presently comprise GAAP and reorganizes them into approximately 90 accounting Topics and displays them using a consistent structure.

To locate information about a specific issue in the Codification:

1. Go to the Topic itself (e.g., Accounts Receivable) and expand the Topic outline to find the appropriate material.
2. Use a word search.
3. Go directly to the paragraph if the reference is known.

MANAGEMENT ACCOUNTING

The controller truly serves as a financial advisor to management. He or she must be familiar with a wide variety of managerial accounting concepts and tools.

There are many basic cost concepts, classifications, and product costing systems. Knowledge of job order costing, process costing, direct costing, standard costing, and just-in-time manufacturing may be needed. Focus is also placed on cost analysis for planning, control, and decision making.

Regression analysis and mixed cost analysis may be required. The controller should be equipped with tools for sales mix analysis and what-if analysis.

In budgeting and financial modeling, the controller should use innovative and sophisticated techniques to maximize corporate objectives.

Knowledge of responsibility accounting and cost allocation is also needed. How has the performance of the responsibility centers been? Why? It is suggested that the controller be familiar with gross profit analysis, segment reporting, and contribution analysis. How may problems be identified and corrective action taken? Transfer pricing is also needed to determine divisional profit. Once such profit has been computed, the controller can calculate and analyze return on investment and residual income. In what ways may profit be improved? There must be efficient and effective analysis of company projects, proposals, and special situations. Consideration must therefore be given to time value concepts, capital rationing, capital budgeting, and mutually exclusive investments.

Quantitative applications in managerial accounting cannot be overlooked by the controller. The controller must understand decision theory and be able to make decisions under conditions involving uncertainty. Linear programming, shadow prices, and the learning curve should not be ignored in fulfilling the role of controllership. A controller familiar with Program Evaluation and Review Techniques (PERT) and inventory planning models is in a position to further assist senior-level management. Multiple regression and correlation analysis depict previous relationships that will aid in making future predictions.

INTERNAL AUDITING AND CONTROL

The controller is often called upon to establish, monitor, and analyze the internal control structure of the company. In this regard, an internal control questionnaire may be useful. It is important to keep in mind that every company is different and, therefore, the internal control questionnaire should be tailored to the particular needs and peculiarities of each company. Internal controls should be put in place in conjunction with the outside auditors to facilitate their function and lessen audit costs.

In connection with the internal audit function, controllers must identify financial statement assertions, select appropriate audit procedures, and develop audit programs. Audit programs may be used for all accounts, including cash, receivables, inventory, fixed assets, payables, equity accounts, income, and expenses.

FINANCIAL ANALYSIS

A truly effective controller is equipped with tools for financial analysis. Risk and reward have to be considered. Techniques for analyzing and managing risk must be employed. Insurance policies must be scrutinized because proper financial management includes securing adequate insurance coverage in terms of insurance type and dollar amounts. Adequate insurance records must be kept for major assets.

Once financial statements are prepared, they must be analyzed for proper internal use. Attention should be given to horizontal and vertical analysis, evaluation of liquidity, examining corporate solvency, balance sheet analysis, and appraisal of income statement items.

Legal exposure of the firm must be monitored, and means to minimize litigation undertaken. An example is product liability insurance.

The effect of the economy on business operations always has to be considered and protective measures taken. What exposure does the company have in a depression, a recession, or an inflationary environment?

MANAGEMENT OF ASSETS

An organization's assets must be managed and used effectively to achieve the best possible return while controlling risk. Crucial assets to be managed include cash, marketable securities, accounts receivable, and inventory.

INVESTMENTS

The wealth of a service or sales organization can be strengthened by making sound investment and financing decisions. Investments in quality equity securities provide an excellent vehicle for achieving financial wealth. Controllers must measure return and risk, value securities, and make the best investment selections.

FINANCING

The optimal financing strategy has to be decided upon. Based on the particular facts, is it better to finance for the short term, intermediate term, or long term? If long-term financing is chosen, should equity or debt be issued? Of course, there are a host of factors to be considered in selecting a financing vehicle, including risk, maturity, liquidity, cost, and tax rate. The overall cost of capital must be minimized. Multinational companies have added international finance problems.

TAX PREPARATION AND PLANNING

Every business must consider the impact of payroll and income taxes. Proper corporate management involves selecting the proper form of business and minimizing the tax liability by judiciously applying relevant tax laws. Important business decisions are often based on tax factors, in addition to general business considerations. All businesses with employees must face the deposit and reporting requirements of various governmental agencies. Corporate financial managers should carefully review tax rules and use tax-planning strategies to the fullest extent. Tax planning should be done in conjunction with the outside auditors.

MERGERS AND ACQUISITIONS

Proper planning is essential in executing business combinations. Objectives of a merger should be clearly defined, acquisition criteria definitively stipulated, and pitfalls avoided. Leveraged buyouts are popular today but should be entered into with caution. Divestitures also occur in today's business world. Reasons for, and objectives of, divestitures must be established. Employee considerations should not be overlooked.

CONCLUSION

Corporate financial management clearly is predicated on a strong controllership function. The role of the controller is diverse and includes not only reporting and accounting functions but decision making. The controller must consider the financial strengths and weaknesses of the business. Current and prospective problems also must be considered, along with ways to solve them. The objectives and policies of the business and its segments must be carried out.

The controller may deal with finance, accounting, production, marketing, personnel, and operations. Cost control is directed at manufacturing, administration, and distribution. Costs must be compiled, tracked, and analyzed.

CHAPTER 2

SEC REPORTING

CONTENTS

Note: The Obama Administration recently proposed regulatory reforms that aim to modernize the financial regulatory structure and improve the SEC's ability to protect investors, concentrating on fairness, transparency, and accountability. More specifically, the proposed reforms are to improve transparency and disclosure, improve investor protection, regulate systematic risk, align executive compensation with shareholder interests, and prevent regulatory arbitrage. The Administration also proposed major corporate governance reforms, such as enhanced compensation committees and shareholder advisory votes on compensation.

The plan gives new authority to the SEC to protect investors, raise standards, improve disclosure, and increase enforcement. Any institution representing a risk to the financial system must be carefully supervised.

The Administration also proposed to create a regulator over all systemically important companies and markets. The regulator would take steps to prevent or minimize systematic risk; and legislation would regulate the entire financial system, not solely its individual components. To identify systemically important companies, the Administration would look at the following:

- Company size, leverage, off-balance sheet exposure, and extent of reliance on short-term funding.

- Financial system's interdependence with the firm.

- Importance of the company as a credit source for households, businesses, and governments as a liquidity source.

Executive compensation incentives, especially bonuses, would be aligned with shareholder interests and long-term company profitability. Bonuses would reflect actual performance and thus not be guaranteed in advance.

Compensation practices would be aligned with sound risk management. Golden parachutes and retirement packages would be reevaluated to assure they serve the interests of executives and shareholders.

The Securities and Exchange Commission (SEC) was established to protect investors by requiring full and fair disclosure in connection with the offering and sale of securities to the public. A major responsibility of the SEC is to ensure enforcement of the Securities Act of 1933 and the Securities Act of 1934.

The SEC's disclosure rules were strengthened by the Sarbanes-Oxley Act of 2002. The accounting rules of the SEC are enumerated primarily in Articles 3A through 12 of Regulation S-X, Financial Reporting Releases (FRRs), Accounting and Audit Enforcement Releases (AAERs), and Industry Guides.

SECURITIES ACT OF 1933

The Securities Act of 1933 (as amended) pertains to the initial offering and sale of securities through the mail; it does not apply to the subsequent trading of security investments. The Act requires that entities involved in a public offering file a registration statement with the SEC. Some of the more common exemptions under the registration provisions of the Act are (1) private offerings, (2) intrastate offerings, (3) governmental securities, (4) offerings of charitable institutions, and (5) bank offerings. The objective of this filing is to prevent misrepresentation, deceit, and other fraudulent activity in the sale of securities. Most of the information included in the registration statement must be provided to potential investors in a prospectus. Investor protection is provided by: (1) the imposition of stiff penalties in the event of the filing of false and misleading information, and (2) the ability of the investor to recover losses through litigation. The 1933 Act is primarily a disclosure statute. Disclosure is required of the securities to be issued, by whom, and how the securities are to be sold. The Act is concerned with securities distribution.

SECURITIES ACT OF 1934

The Securities Act of 1934 does not pertain to the initial offering and sale of securities to the public. Rather, the 1934 Act is designed to regulate the subsequent trading (secondary markets) of securities on the various national stock exchanges.

Under the 1934 Act, a scaled-down version of the 1933 Act registration statement must be filed by an entity if its securities are to be traded on a national exchange.

The 1934 Act requires the periodic filing of information reports with the SEC in order to maintain the full and fair disclosure objective of the 1933 Act. The annual Form 10-K and the quarterly Form 10-Q are the most common types of reports required by the 1934 Act. Most of the information included in these reports is available to the public. The Act is designed to prevent fraud and market manipulation. It also deals with margin trading, insider trading, and proxy solicitation.

Note: According to Accounting Standards Update (ASU) No. 2010-04 (January 2010), *Accounting for Various Topics,* when financial statements are presented to the Securities and Exchange Commission they cannot be misleading. Subsequent events must be disclosed. An earnings release does not represent financial statements being issued.

When there is a business combination accounted for as a purchase, push-down accounting should be used.

INTEGRATED DISCLOSURE SYSTEM

The complexity of the reporting requirements under the 1933 and 1934 Acts was somewhat mitigated in 1980 when the SEC adopted the Integrated Disclosure System, which requires the Basic Information Package (BIP).

The BIP consists of the following:

- Audited balance sheets for the last two years and audited statements of income, retained earnings, and cash flows for the most recent three years.

- A five-year summary containing certain selected financial data.

- Management's discussion and analysis (MD&A) of the entity's financial-condition and results of operations.

S FORMS

Form S-1

Form S-1 is normally used by any entity that desires to issue a public offering and that has been subject to the SEC reporting requirements for less than three years. Some of the more common items required to be disclosed in Form S-1 are:

- A synopsis of the business, including relevant industry and segment information, cash flows, liquidity, and capital resources.

- A listing of properties and risk factors.

- Background and financial information pertaining to the entity's directors and officers, including pending litigation involving management, and compensation arrangements.

- A description of the securities being registered.

- Identification of major underwriters.

Form S-1 also requires the disclosure of a five-year summary of selected financial data, which need not be audited by the independent certified public accountant. The data to be presented include the following items:

- Net sales or revenues.

- Total income or loss from continuing operations.

- Per-share income or loss from continuing operations.

- Total assets of the entity.

- Long-term debt, including capital leases and redeemable preferred stock.

- Declared cash dividends on a per-common-share basis.

- Disagreements with the independent certified public accounting firm.

S-1 is presented in textual form in two parts: the first is the prospectus, and the second contains supplementary and procedural information.

Form S-3

Form S-3 may generally be used by a company that passes the "float test." In other words, at least $150 million of voting stock is owned by nonaffiliates. Form S-3 may also be used if the entity has a float of $100 million accompanied by an annual trading volume of 3 million shares. Annual trading volume is the number of shares traded during a recurring 12-month period culminating within 60 days before the filing.

Form S-3 is an abbreviated form, because the public already has much of the information that would normally be required to be included. Accordingly, Form S-3 provides for incorporation by reference.

Form S-4

Form S-4 is applicable in registrations of securities in connection with such business combinations as mergers, consolidations, and asset acquisitions. Form S-4 also provides for incorporation by reference to the 1934 Act reports.

Form S-8

When registering securities to be offered to employees pursuant to an employee benefit plan, Form S-8 should be filed. Information presented in Form S-8 is normally limited to a description of the securities and the employee benefit plan. Disclosure is also made about the registrant, although this information is made available through other reports required by the 1934 Act.

Form S-18

A company whose objective is to raise capital of $7.5 million or less may file a registration statement using Form S-18. Disclosures presented in Form S-18 are quite similar to those required in Form S-1. One difference between the two forms is that management's discussion and analysis is not required. Additionally, only one year's audited balance sheet and two years' audited statements of income and cash flows are required.

MANAGEMENT'S DISCUSSION AND ANALYSIS

MD&A is an integral part of the registration filing and pertains to (1) the three years covered in the audited financial statements that are submitted as part of the registration process and (2) any interim financial statements that are also submitted. The MD&A should therefore specify the significant changes in financial condition and results of operations. To accomplish this, the following items must be disclosed:

- Liquidity.
- Capital resources.
- Results of operations.
- Positive and negative trends.
- Significant uncertainties.
- Events of an unusual or infrequent nature.
- Underlying causes of material changes in financial statement items.
- A narrative discussion of the material effects of inflation.

Though not required, forecasted information may be presented.

REGULATION S-X

Regulation S-X stipulates the accounting and reporting requirements of the SEC. It encompasses the rules pertaining to the auditor's independence, the auditor's reports, and the financial statements that must be submitted to the SEC. Regulation S-X is continually amended by the issuance of Financial Reporting Releases (FRRs). FRRs enable the SEC to present:

- New disclosure requirements.
- The required treatment for certain transaction types.
- The SEC's opinions on essential accounting issues.
- Interpretations of current rules and regulations.
- Amendments to financial statement reporting requirements.

In general, the accounting rules under Regulation S-X parallel generally accepted accounting principles (GAAP). Occasionally, however, the disclosure rules under Regulation S-X are more expansive. For instance, financial statements filed with the SEC require the following disclosures, which are not normally included in financial statements prepared in conformity with GAAP:

- Lines of credit.
- Compensating balance arrangements.
- Current liabilities if they represent in excess of 5% of the entity's total liabilities.

Regulation S-X is divided into 12 articles as follows:

- Article 1—Application of Regulation S-X.
- Article 2—Qualifications and Reports of Accountants.

- Article 3—General Instructions as to Financial Statements.
- Article 3A—Consolidated and Combined Financial Statements.
- Article 4—Rules of General Application.
- Article 5—Commercial and Industrial Companies.
- Article 6—Regulated Investment Companies.
- Article 7—Insurance Companies.
- Article 9—Bank Holding Companies.
- Article 10—Interim Financial Statements.
- Article 11—Pro Forma Information.
- Article 12—Form and Content of Schedules.

Also to be disclosed are third-party restrictions on fund transfers, inventory categorization, and redeemable preferred stock.

FORM 10-K

To comply with the Securities Act of 1934, most registrants will be required to file a Form 10-K on an annual basis. Form 10-K is due within 60 days subsequent to the closing of the registrant's fiscal year. The rules apply to companies with a market value capitalization of $75 million.

The contents of Form 10-K include general instructions; a cover page; signatures; supplemental information; and disclosures, which are divided into four parts, as follows:

Part I

- Item 1—Business.
- Item 2—Properties.
- Item 3—Legal Proceedings.
- Item 4—Submission of Matters to a Vote of Security Holders.

Part II

- Item 5—Market for the Registrant's Common Equity and Related Stockholder Matters.
- Item 6—Selected Financial Data.
- Item 7—Management's Discussion and Analysis of Financial Condition and Results of Operations.
- Item 8—Financial Statements and Supplementary Data.
- Item 9—Changes in and Disagreements with Accountants on Accounting and Financial Disclosure.

Part III

- Item 10—Directors and Executive Officers of the Registrant.
- Item 11—Executive Compensation.

- Item 12—Security Ownership of Certain Beneficial Owners and Management.
- Item 13—Certain Relationships and Related Transactions.

Part IV

- Item 14—Exhibits, Financial Statement Schedules, and Reports of Form 8-K.

In 2006, the SEC required most companies to include a footnote in the financial statements referred to as Unresolved Staff Comments. In this footnote, the company must disclose any material comments from an SEC review of its filings, issued more than 180 days before year-end, or continue unresolved by the date of Form 10-K. Examples of issues might be financial statement item restatements, procedural or disclosure questions, and accounting violations. Regulators also are increasingly disclosing the contents of correspondence with companies, which can be found under the company's name on the EDGAR search portion of the SEC Web site. Code words include *upload*, which is the SEC's staff comments, and *cover* or *corresp*, which is the company's response.

FORM 8-K

Form 8-K essentially must be filed immediately after the occurrence of a significant event (generally within 15 days) that materially affects the company's financial position or operating results. It is a current report. Form 8-K lists the following as significant events:

- Item 1—A change in control of registrant.
- Item 2—The acquisition or disposition of assets.
- Item 3—Bankruptcy or receivership.
- Item 4—Changes in registrant's certifying accountant.
- Item 5—Other events (e.g., litigation, acts of nature, new product introduction).
- Item 6—Resignation of a registrant's directors.
- Item 7—Financial statements and exhibits.

For items 4 and 7, Form 8-K must be filed within five days.

FORM 10-Q

Changes in operations and financial position since the filing of the most recent Form 10-K are disclosed in the quarterly Forms 10-Q. The quarterly Form 10-Q is due within 35 days after the end of each of the first three fiscal quarters.

Form 10-Q specifically lists the items that must be disclosed as follows:

Part I—Financial Information

- Item 1—Financial Statements.
- Item 2—Management's Discussion and Analysis of Financial Condition and Results of Operations.

Part II—Other Information
- Item 1—Legal Proceedings.
- Item 2—Changes in Securities.
- Item 3—Defaults upon Senior Securities.
- Item 4—Submission of Matters to a Vote of Security Holders.
- Item 5—Other Information.
- Item 6—Exhibits and Reports of Form 8-K.

STAFF ACCOUNTING BULLETIN

FASB Accounting Standards Codification (ASC) 250, *Accounting Changes and Error Corrections* (ASC 250-10-S99) provides guidance on quantifying material financial statement misstatements, including coverage of the impact of carryover and reversal of previous-year misstatements. Misstatements should be appraised from the prospective of their effect on the current year's income statement and balance sheet. The SEC will not object to a registrant making a one-time cumulative effect adjustment to correct errors from previous years that are qualitatively and quantitatively immaterial, based on appropriate use of the registrant's previously employed approach.

ELECTRONIC FILING

The SEC's electronic data gathering, analysis, and retrieval (EDGAR) system for public companies has registration, documents, and other information available via online databases. Thus, the controller can use EDGAR to gather for research purposes the way in which other companies have presented information to the SEC.

EDGAR will be replaced by the interactive data electronic application (IDEA) system. IDEA is a different approach than EDGAR, as it provides investors with easier and quicker access to financial information about public companies. Initially, IDEA will supplement EDGAR and then ultimately replace it.

IDEA uses data-tagging software similar to bar codes for financial data. The technology is based on the extensible business reporting language (XBRL). It allows for fast comparisons of different business entities or different time periods. The information will be available at no cost on the Internet.

TAKEOVER REGULATION

If an investor acquires in excess of 5% of a company's stock, it must file with the SEC, target business, and its stockholders the investor's identity, the financing source, and the reason for the acquisition.

CONCLUSION

It should be clear that regulation by the Securities and Exchange Commission imposes reporting and filing burdens. The controller has a vital role in ensuring that accurate data, for reporting purposes, are accumulated in a timely manner. The controller is also responsible for the timely filing of reports mandated by the SEC. Note that financial regulation still has much uncertainty given that there are so many regulations and rules yet to be legislated.

According to the 1993 Act, securities offered to the public must be registered before they can be issued. There are two parts to the registration statement. In part 1 (the prospectus), data are contained regarding the investment decision. In part 2, there is procedural and supplemental information. The *earliest* a securities issuance can occur after the registration statement becomes *effective* is *20 days*. It is *illegal* for an underwriter to deliver securities to an investor until he or she has received a final prospectus. Those involved with a defective registration statement, including the issuing company, outside CPAs, and underwriters, are legally liable. Legal liability may also fall under the RICO Act of 1970.

As amended in 1964, the 1934 Act requires registration of all unlisted companies with at least $5 million in assets and at least 500 stockholders.

A *comfort letter* may be obtained from the independent CPA furnishing specified assurances regarding financial statement information contained in the registration statement.

CHAPTER 3

CONTROLLER'S REPORTS

CONTENTS

In addition to SEC reporting (discussed in Chapter 2), the controller is responsible for communicating useful and accurate information to senior-level management, the board of directors, divisional managers, employees, and interested third parties. It is crucial that reports are issued in a timely manner and are understood by a diverse audience.

The needs of management vary from one organization to another. Management reports should be sufficiently simplistic to enable the reader to center his or her attention on problems or predicaments that may or could arise. Consistency and uniformity in report format and issuance can only enhance the organization's operational effectiveness and efficiency. The data presented in reports issued to management, employees, and third parties should be based on facts that may be corroborated by underlying financial and accounting data.

PROSPECTIVE FINANCIAL STATEMENTS

Prospective financial statements encompass financial forecasts and financial projections. Pro forma financial statements and partial presentations are specifically excluded from this category.

Financial forecasts are prospective financial statements that present the entity's expected financial position and results of operations and cash flows, based on assumptions about conditions actually expected to exist and the course of action actually expected to be taken.

A financial forecast may be given in a single monetary amount based on the best estimate, or as a reasonable range.

Caution: This range must not be chosen in a misleading manner.

Financial projections, on the other hand, are prospective statements that present the entity's financial position, results of operations, and cash flows, based on assumptions about conditions expected to exist and the course of action expected to be taken, given one or more hypothetical (i.e., what-if) assumptions.

Financial projections may be most beneficial for a limited number of users, because they may seek answers to questions involving hypothetical assumptions. These users may wish to alter their scenarios based on expected changing situations. A financial projection, like a financial forecast, may contain a range.

A financial projection may be presented to general users only when it supplements a financial forecast. Financial projections are not permitted in tax shelter offerings and other general-use documents.

Financial forecasts and financial projections may be in the form of either complete basic financial statements or financial statements containing at least the following items:

- Sales or gross revenues.
- Gross profit or cost of sales.
- Unusual or infrequently occurring items.
- Provision for income taxes.
- Discontinued operations or extraordinary items.
- Income from continuing operations.
- Net income.
- Primary and fully diluted earnings per share.
- Significant changes in financial position.
- Management's intent as to what the prospective statements present, a statement indicating that management's assumptions are predicated upon facts and circumstances in existence when the statements were prepared, and a warning that the prospective results may not materialize.
- Summary of significant assumptions.
- Summary of significant accounting policies.

PLANNING REPORTS

The controller may prepare short-term company-wide or short-term division-wide planning reports. This includes forecasted balance sheets, forecasted income statements, forecasted statements of cash flows, and projections of capital expenditures.

Special short-term planning studies of specific business segments may also be prepared. These reports may relate to the following:

- Product line expansion.
- Plant location feasibility.
- Product distribution by territory.
- Warehouse handling.
- Salesperson compensation.

Long-range planning reports include five- to ten-year projections for the company and segments therein.

INFORMATIONAL REPORTS

Informational reports may be prepared by a controller for submission to management personnel. These reports are frequently used to depict trends over long periods of time. Accordingly, informational reports may be used to report trends in sales and purchase requirements over the last five years. The format of information reports is generally left to the preparer's judgment, although graphic depiction (including charts) is popular.

ANALYTICAL AND CONTROL REPORTS

Analytical and control reports contain data derived from analytical procedures. Analytical procedures involve comparisons of financial and nonfinancial information. As a result, analytical and control reports are often utilized to disclose current-period versus prior-period changes in financial statement accounts. For example, analytical and control reports might disclose the increases and decreases in selected expense accounts over the past two years. Analytical reports are also used to summarize and describe variances from forecasts and budgets. Analyses of variances may be by revenue, expense, profit, assets, territory, product, and division.

EXCEPTION REPORTS

Exception reports are used to present detailed listings of problems that have arisen during a specified period of time. Exception reports might encompass internal control deficiencies or questionable areas pertaining to the application of generally accepted accounting principles (GAAP). This type of report may be used by or prepared by the controller. In an organization that utilizes electronic data processing, exception reports should be computer generated and should normally detail problems that may have arisen during the input, processing, and output stages of data processing.

FINANCIAL REPORTS

The controller is relied on to prepare complete and accurate financial statements that fairly present the financial position, results of operations, and cash flows of the company. The financial statements must include adequate and informative disclosures. The controller must keep in mind that the year-end financial statements must be audited by an independent certified public accountant. Accordingly, the year-end financial statements may have to include information that might not have been required had the controller prepared financial statements which were to be used solely by management.

Financial reports may also be prepared to describe operating results of individual divisions of the entity. These reports may not take the form of complete financial statements. As a result, the statements might include information that is not normally needed or used by individuals outside of the company.

REPORTS FOR THE BOARD OF DIRECTORS

The board of directors is typically interested in broad policy matters, general trends in revenue and profits, and competition. The board of directors is also concerned with short-term and long-term matters. Useful information in reports addressed to the board of directors includes company and divisional operating results, historical financial statements, prospective financial statements, status reports pertaining to capital expenditures, and special studies.

SPECIAL REPORTS TO SENIOR MANAGEMENT

Special situations and circumstances may occur that mandate separate analysis and study. For example, it may be necessary to identify the reason for a continual drop in the profitability of a particular product or territory. Another example is a feasibility study on the opening of a new plant facility. Narrative explanation of the analysis and the decision, along with proper statistical support, is crucial. Graphic presentations may also be enlightening.

REPORTS FOR DIVISIONAL MANAGERS

Reports prepared to aid divisional managers in gauging performance and improving operating results include:

- Sales and net income.
- Return on investment.
- Profitability by product line, project, or program.
- Sales by geographic area.
- Divisional contribution margin, segment margin, and short-term performance margin.
- Divisional performance relative to other divisions in the same company and to competing divisions in other companies.
- Expenses and labor performance by cost center.
- Cash flow.
- Production orders received and unfilled orders.
- Idle time.
- Comparison of operations with general indices of business conditions.

REPORTS TO EMPLOYEES

Reports may be directed toward the interests and concerns of employees. These reports may contain the following information:

- Explanation of financial condition.
- Profit per employee.
- Profit per sales dollar, units sold, and amounts invested.
- Taxes per employee relative to wages, per share of stock, dividends, and net income.
- Salaries including comparison to other industries and cost of living.
- Analytical profit and cost information.
- Investment per employee.
- Future outlook.
- Industry trends.
- Achievement in production, sales, or safety.
- Nature and importance of break-even point.
- Explanation of changes in pension, welfare, and other benefit plans.
- Need for stockholders.
- Nature of properties.
- Source of capital.
- Dividends relative to wages, per employee, and percent of investment.

An illustrative report to employees is shown in Exhibit 3-1.

Exhibit 3-1: An Illustrative Report to Employees

X COMPANY STATEMENT OF REVENUE AND EXPENSE FOR EMPLOYEES FOR THE YEAR ENDED DECEMBER 31, 20X6

	Total Amount	*Amount per Employee*	*Cents per Dollar of Receipts*
The company received:			
From customers for goods and services rendered			
Dividends			
Interest			
Total amount received			
Corporate expenses were:			
For materials, supplies, and other expenses			
Depreciation			
Taxes			
Total expenses			
Balance remaining for salaries, dividends, and reinvestment in the business			

	Total Amount	Amount per Employee	Cents per Dollar of Receipts
This was divided as follows:			
Paid to employees (excluding officers) as wages			
Paid for employee fringe benefits			
Total			
Compensation of officers			
Paid for officer fringe benefits			
Paid to shareholders as dividends			
Reinvested in the business for growth			
Total division			

REPORTS TO STOCKHOLDERS

An important role of the controller is to present useful information to stockholders. Reports to stockholders should be designed to communicate financial position, results of operations, and cash flows for a specified period of time. The annual report to stockholders is required by companies regulated by the Securities and Exchange Commission (SEC). The SEC generally permits flexibility in the format and content of the annual report to stockholders, encouraging the use of graphs and charts. Although not required by any regulatory agency, a message from the company's president is usually included in the annual report to stockholders. The president's message is usually presented before the financial statements and the report of the independent certified public accountant. It should be remembered that the president's letter is the first item normally read by the user of the annual report. As such, it primes the reader and should clearly present highlights of the company's operations and future expectations. Annual reports to shareholders also quite commonly include nonfinancial information in narrative and photographic form.

REPORTING TO THE NEW YORK STOCK EXCHANGE

The listing application to the New York Stock Exchange contains an agreement to furnish annual reports and periodic interim financial statements. Timely disclosure must be made of information that may impact security values or influence investment decisions.

CONCLUSION

The controller's role in reporting information cannot be understated. In addition to the ability to formulate useful financial and nonfinancial information, the controller must be able to communicate effectively and efficiently to management, employees, and outsiders. Reports containing data for decision-making purposes should be prepared in a timely manner.

APPENDIX I

THE SARBANES-OXLEY ACT AND CORPORATE GOVERNANCE

CONTENTS

On the heels of corporate scandals, a series of sweeping changes are being sought, such as forcing boards to have a majority of independent directors, granting audit committees power to hire and fire accountants, banning sweetheart loans to officers and directors, and requiring shareholder's approval for stock option plans. New accounting guidelines, proposals, and legislation, such as the Sarbanes-Oxley Act, have been announced and enacted in order to restore investor confidence. Their development and their implications for the financial executive are discussed in this chapter.

POINTS OF CONTROVERSY

During the past decade, the role of financial executives—primarily CFOs and controllers—has changed from that of primarily an accountant and controller to that of a business partner and strategist. Because of pressures placed on them in their emerging role as strategic partners, the CFO, controller, and finance team can also lose their objectivity and independence. This shift may have prompted some CFOs to use aggressive accounting and reporting practices. A CFO.com survey (www.cfo.com or *CFO* magazine, August 13, 2002) revealed that 17% of its 220 respondents reported being pressured to misrepresent their results by their companies' CEOs during the past five years. A key factor in recent corporate scandals was a failure of financial functions to spot the signs of malpractice. Accounting irregularities and scandals included:

- *Moving debt off the balance sheet.* The accounting technique made infamous by Enron (and the main reason for its downfall) was its use of special-purpose entities to move debt off its balance sheet. A lot of debt was carried but not reflected on its balance sheet. Much of it was collateralized with Enron stock. As the stock price fell, the house of cards came down.

Many U.S. companies have for a long time used special-purpose entities to finance projects in a way that allows tax benefits without visibly impairing balance sheets. This is perhaps the most dangerous accounting gimmick, because it is very difficult to determine from financial filings exactly when a company has entered into these agreements. The lack of disclosure makes it impossible for investors to determine how much the company must pay to fully service its debt or to fulfill other contractual obligations.

- *Earnings "management" and the use of pro forma results.* Many companies have used the "complicated accounting legerdemain" to avoid disappointing investors and brokerage analysts from quarter to quarter, potentially at the expense of a long-term focus. Companies use so-called pro forma earnings to spruce up their results. The problem with pro forma results is that they are too often promotional, eliminating the negative and emphasizing the positive. Companies in the technology sector perfected the practice, but it has spread well beyond Silicon Valley.

- *Overstated pension plan assumptions.* Pension plan accounting is complicated, esoteric, and not entirely logical. What every shareholder needs to understand is that most companies have obligations to fund their pension plan to a certain level. Any shortfall must eventually be made up by contributions from the company's coffers. During the bull market of the past few years, companies were able to cut back on contributions, as gains in the stock market helped keep pension plans healthy. However, even as stock prices stumbled, or fell dramatically, many firms kept on predicting robust growth of their pension investments to help boost their bottom line.

Some companies are using rosy projected returns for their employee pension plans to buff their financial statements. Many firms still assume 9% to 10% annual returns on their pension plans in coming years, when 5% would be more realistic. The higher the assumed long-term returns, the lower the annual pension plan contributions a company is required to make in the near term. Instead, money that would have been earmarked for a pension plan accrues to the company's bottom line.

• *Underreporting of executive compensation.* Most major companies do not treat the costs of employee stock options as an official expense on income statements. That has contributed to an overstatement of earnings in recent years. When options involve no charge to earnings, they are considered a "cheap" form of compensation—when in fact they represent a cost to shareholders. A recent survey found company after company that would have seen reported earnings slashed by as much as 200% had they been forced to expense stock option plans.

• *Revenue accounting.* Basic accounting practices must be the bedrock of every finance department and one of the most basic issues is revenue recognition—when to recognize revenue, at what amount, and the degree of provision for future reversals. Many of the recent failures stemmed from this issue. Enron, acting as a broker between sellers and buyers of energy, took sales credits for the total size of the transaction rather than only the fee involved, which made the company's size and growth rate look much stronger than it really was. Global Crossing and Qwest Communications, among other companies, bought and sold capacity from each other and took sales credit at both ends, overstating both companies' revenues.

• *Expense accounting.* The basic tenet of the matching principle in accounting is that expenses must be matched with their corresponding revenues. It does not always happen—for example, research and development expenditure is written off when incurred even though the product sales to which it relates may occur many years later. However, the accounting intent is to match. WorldCom clearly violated the matching principle by considering the fees paid for line usage bought from local carriers every month as a capital expenditure, not an operating expense.

• *Channel stuffing.* Another gray area involves inventory management. Old tricks include "channel stuffing," or shifting surplus finished goods to distributors' shelves. Nothing will destroy a company's ability to meet analysts' earnings expectations more than having a warehouse full of unsold goods. Rather than come clean and tell shareholders they have not met sales expectations, some companies are tempted to move their merchandise to the market, knowing that much of it is going to come back unsold or will have to be sold at a massive discount. Investors looking for evidence of channel stuffing should look for large changes to stated inventory levels, or an increase in the contingencies set aside for bad accounts.

The most telling example of the practice was the fall from grace of Al Dunlap, the former head of Sunbeam Corporation. He allegedly moved millions of dollars in merchandise into the hands of distributors and retailers using discounts and other inducements. That, along with the use of cash reserves to pump up the company's operating earnings, resulted in a record-breaking $189 million in reported earnings in fiscal 1992. But when the scheme was uncovered, Sunbeam was forced to restate its earnings from the fourth quarter of 1996 to the first quarter of 1998; the SEC alleges that $60 million of that record-breaking profit was the result of accounting fraud. CFO magazine (January 15, 2002) stated that Al Dunlap agreed to pay $15 million to settle a shareholder lawsuit alleging inflated stock prices. Sunbeam's auditor at the time was Arthur Andersen.

• *Auditor independence.* Auditors must recognize that their ultimate client is not management. In fact, they are supposed to serve shareholders. In practice, auditors are paid by the very companies whose books they are supposed to scrutinize, and in recent years, that relationship has become even more complicated. The Big Four routinely perform lucrative management, information technology, tax, and other consulting work for the companies they audit.

According to the Investor Responsibility Research Center (IRRC) (www.irrc.com), a Washington D.C.-based advocacy group for institutional investors, large accounting firms receive just 28% of their fees from auditing work. Non-audit fees significantly exceed the amount paid for auditing services.

• *Corporate governance.* A company's audit committee has myriad responsibilities, the most important being to oversee the presentation and honesty of financial statements. Members are appointed by the board of directors. The problem is, many company audit committees include directors who also serve on the executive team. Because management are insiders who are paid out of the funds of the company, there is a need for a check on management. Audit committees comprising directors should not be tied to management in any way. More corporations are complying in the wake of Enron—but until the guidelines become mandatory, some could continue to ignore them.

• *Stock options.* The whole premise behind expensing options is to further clarify a company's accounting, making its numbers more transparent to the public and thereby boosting investors' confidence, which has been ravaged by corporate scandals. Executives involved in those scandals were often lavished with options that made them fabulously rich and allegedly prompted the financial abuses that were aimed at keeping the companies' profits—and stock prices—as high as possible. So options came under assault, and now treating them as a cost to be deducted from earnings is seen as one solution to curbing the abuses.

FASB ISSUES CONSOLIDATION PRINCIPLES FOR SPECIAL-PURPOSE ENTITIES

ASC 810-10-05, *Consolidation of Variable Interest Entities–An Interpretation of Accounting Research Bulletin (ARB) 51*, applies to any business enterprise—whether a public or private company—that has an ownership interest, contractual relationship, or other business relationship with an SPE. The proposed guidance would not apply to not-for-profit organizations.

The objective of this proposed Interpretation is to improve financial reporting by enterprises involved with SPEs—not to restrict the use of SPEs. However, it is expected that when this proposal is implemented, more SPEs will be consolidated than in the past. Most SPEs serve valid business purposes, for example, by isolating assets or activities to protect the interests of creditors or other investors, or to allocate risks among participants. Many SPEs that were unconsolidated prior to the issuance of this proposed Interpretation were reported according to the guidance and accepted practice that existed prior to this proposed Interpretation.

The FASB's proposed rules on SPEs would cover the partnerships that Enron created, but their greatest effect would be on the "synthetic leases" used by many companies to finance property. In a synthetic lease arrangement, a financial institution sets up a special-purpose entity that borrows money to finance new construction or to purchase an existing building for a company. AOL Time Warner, for example, was a financing construction of its new Manhattan headquarters with a synthetic lease arrangement set up by Bank of America Corp.

The FASB is calling for special-purpose entities to be included on a company's balance sheet if less than 10% of the equity in an entity is from outside investors. Under existing rules, Enron was able to keep its partnerships off its books even though outsiders' capital was less than 3% of the total.

Apart from a specific percentage of outside interest, special-purpose entities should have to be consolidated on companies' books if it is evident that the entities are not truly independent.

FASB REQUIRES EXPENSING OF EMPLOYEE STOCK OPTIONS

ASC 718, *Compensation—Stock Compensation* (ASC 718-10), now requires a public entity to measure the cost of employee services received in exchange for an award of equity instruments based on the grant-date fair value of the award (with limited exceptions). That cost will be recognized over the period during which an employee is required to provide service in exchange for the award—the requisite service period (usually the vesting period). No compensation cost is recognized for equity instruments for which employees do not render the requisite service. Employee share purchase plans will not result in recognition of compensation cost if certain conditions are met; those conditions are much the same as the related conditions in ASC 718-10. A nonpublic entity, likewise, will measure the cost of employee services received in exchange for an award of equity instruments based on the grant-date fair value of those instruments, except in certain circumstances. Specifically, if it is not possible to reasonably estimate the fair value of equity share options and similar instruments because it is not practicable to estimate the expected volatility of the entity's share price, a nonpublic entity is required to measure its awards of equity share options and similar instruments based on a value calculated using the historical volatility of an appropriate industry sector index instead of the expected volatility of its share price.

The grant-date fair value of employee share options and similar instruments will be estimated using option-pricing models (e.g., the Black-Scholes or the Lattice method of valuation).

ASC 718-10 eliminates the alternative to use the intrinsic value method of accounting that was provided in ASC 718-10 as originally issued. This revised rule goes into effect for big companies on June 15, 2005, and for smaller companies (so-called SB filers) December 15, 2005. Companies must report all *new* stock-option grants immediately; options awarded during the past three years will be phased in on a prorated basis.

The Black-Scholes Problem and Other Option Models

The Black-Scholes model is widely considered to overstate the value of employee stock options by an unacceptable margin because it does not take into account the essential differences between traditional exchange-traded stock options and those granted to employees. Unlike conventional options, employee options are subject to vesting schedules and forfeiture conditions and therefore cannot be transferred. As a result, they are invariably exercised before their usual 10-year term expires. These characteristics reduce the value of an option.

The FASB does not specify a preference for a particular valuation technique or model in estimating the fair values of employee share options. It does recognize, however, that a lattice-based method can take into account assumptions that reflect the conditions under which employee options are typically granted. Though the binomial model is the most commonly used lattice-based method, other methods may be better suited to compensation programs that link vesting to specific performance objectives. The models are as follows:

- *Binomial.* Unlike Black-Scholes, the binomial method divides the time from the option's grant date to the expiration date into small increments. Because the share price may increase or decrease during any interval, the binomial model takes into account how changes in price over the term of the option would affect the employee's exercise practice during each interval. The binomial model can also consider an option grant's lack of transferability, its forfeiture restrictions, and its vesting restrictions—even for options with more-complicated terms, such as indexed and performance-based vesting restrictions.

- *Trinomial.* The trinomial model goes a step further by allowing for the underlying stock price to either remain unchanged or move up or down. This is useful for valuing performance-based options that vest only if the stock price exceeds a certain level over time.

- *Multinomial.* This model can take many more factors into account than either the binomial or trinomial framework. Such additional flexibility may be required to value options that cannot be exercised unless the underlying stock price exceeds the performance of one or more indices. However, when there are more than two such sources of uncertainty, a Monte Carlo simulation may be preferable, as it is easier to apply than lattice models.

These alternative option models are not used as much as the Black-Scholes model because users are less familiar with them and so must spend considerable time figuring out how to use them. In addition, Black-Scholes is so widely used that many software packages are available that run the model on laptops and handheld computers.

THE NEW YORK STOCK EXCHANGE'S CORPORATE GOVERNANCE RULES

The New York Stock Exchange's corporate governance rules include:

- An independent majority on a company's board.
- A stricter definition of director independence.
- Regular executive sessions of nonmanagement directors.
- The appointment of a lead director solely to run those meetings.
- Investor approval of all equity-based pay plans.
- A ban on broker votes for such plans unless they get customers' approval.

The new rules would weaken the control that management currently enjoys at many companies. Stronger governance standards will give directors better tools to empower them.

SEC APPROVES RULES TO ADDRESS ANALYST CONFLICTS

On May 8, 2002, the SEC approved proposed changes to the rules of the National Association of Securities Dealers (NASD) and the New York Stock Exchange (NYSE) to address conflicts of interest that are raised when research analysts recommend securities in public communications (www.sec.gov/news/press/2002-63.htm). These conflicts can arise when analysts work for firms that have investment banking relationships with the issuers of the recommended securities, or when the analyst or firm owns securities of the recommended issuer.

These rules include the following provisions, among others:

- *Promises of favorable research.* The rule changes prohibit analysts from offering or threatening to withhold a favorable research rating or specific price target to induce investment banking business from companies. The rule changes also impose "quiet periods" that bar a firm that is acting as manager or co-manager of a securities offering from issuing a report on a company within 40 days after an initial public offering or within 10 days after a secondary offering for an inactively traded company. Promising favorable research coverage to a company will not be as attractive if the research follows research issued by other analysts.

• *Limitations on relationships and communications.* The rule changes prohibit research analysts from being supervised by the investment banking department. In addition, investment banking personnel is prohibited from discussing research reports with analysts prior to distribution, unless staff from the firm's legal/compliance department monitor those communications. Analysts are also prohibited from sharing draft research reports with the target companies, other than to check facts after approval from the firm's legal/compliance department. This provision helps protect research analysts from influences that could impair their objectivity and independence.

• *Analyst compensation.* The rule changes bar securities firms from tying an analyst's compensation to specific investment banking transactions. Furthermore, if an analyst's compensation is based on the firm's general investment banking revenues, that fact must be disclosed in the firm's research reports. Prohibiting compensation from specific investment banking transactions significantly curtails a potentially major influence on research analysts' objectivity.

• *Firm compensation.* The rule changes require a securities firm to disclose in a research report if it managed or co-managed a public offering of equity securities for the company or if it received any compensation for investment banking services from the company in the past 12 months. A firm is also required to disclose if it expects to receive or intends to seek compensation for investment banking services from the company during the next three months. Requiring securities firms to disclose compensation from investment banking clients can alert investors to potential biases in their recommendations.

• *Restrictions on personal trading by analysts.* The rule changes bar analysts and members of their households from investing in a company's securities prior to its initial public offering if the company is in the business sector that the analyst covers. In addition, the rule changes require "blackout periods" that prohibit analysts from trading securities of the companies they follow for 30 days before and five days after they issue a research report about the company. Analysts are also prohibited from trading against their most recent recommendations. Removing analysts' incentives to trade around the time they issue research reports should reduce conflicts arising from personal financial interests.

• *Disclosures of financial interests in covered companies.* The rule changes require analysts to disclose if they own shares of recommended companies. Firms are also required to disclose if they own 1% or more of a company's equity securities as of the previous month end. Requiring analysts and securities firms to disclose financial interests can alert investors to potential biases in their recommendations.

• *Disclosures in research reports regarding the firm's ratings.* The rule changes require firms to clearly explain in research reports the meaning of all ratings terms they use, and this terminology must be consistent with its plain meaning. In addition, firms must provide the percentage of all the ratings that they have assigned to buy/hold/sell categories and the percentage of investment banking clients in each category. Firms are also required to provide a graph or chart that plots the historical price movements of the security and indicates those points at which the firm initiated and changed ratings and price targets for the company. These disclosures will assist investors in deciding what value to place on a securities firm's ratings and provide them with better information to assess its research.

• *Disclosures during public appearances by analysts.* The rule changes require disclosures from analysts during public appearances, such as television or radio interviews. Guest analysts must disclose if they or their firm have a position in the stock and if the company is an investment banking client of the firm. This disclosure will inform investors who learn of analyst opinions and ratings through the media, rather than in written research reports, of analyst conflicts. The SEC will request the NASD and NYSE to report within a year of implementing these rules on their operation and effectiveness, and whether they recommend any changes or additions to the rules.

These rules are part of an ongoing process by the SEC, NASD, NYSE, and the states to address conflicts of interest affecting the production and dissemination of research by securities firms. On April 24, 2002, the SEC announced that it had commenced a formal inquiry into market practices concerning research analysts and the conflicts that can arise from the relationship between research and investment banking. It is possible that this inquiry will indicate the need for further rulemaking by the NASD and NYSE or additional action on the part of the SEC.

SEC Approves Rules Implementing Provisions of the Sarbanes-Oxley Act, Accelerating Periodic Filings, and Other Measures

The Securities and Exchange Commission voted on August 27, 2002, to shorten the amount of time companies have to report earnings and to require stock trades by corporate insiders to be disclosed within two days (www.sec.gov/news/press/2002-128.htm). The changes, approved unanimously by the five-member Commission, come on two fronts:

1. Detailed quarterly and annual financial statements will have to be filed more quickly with the SEC. That will reduce the risk that companies will issue rosy news releases about their earnings, only to reveal problems important to investors months later in their official SEC filings.

2. The rules will require company insiders—high-ranking executives, directors, and major shareholders—to report the details of their stock trades more quickly.

THE SARBANES-OXLEY ACT

The Sarbanes–Oxley Act of 2002, also known as the Public Company Accounting Reform and Investor Protection Act or Corporate and Auditing Accountability and Responsibility Act, commonly called Sarbanes–Oxley, Sarbox or SOX, is a federal law enacted on July 30, 2002, which set new or enhanced standards for all U.S. public company boards, management, and public accounting firms. The law directly affects the following groups:

- CPAs and CPA firms auditing public companies.

- Publicly traded companies, their employees, officers, and owners, including holders of more than 10% of the outstanding common shares. This category would include CPAs employed by publicly traded companies as CFOs or in the finance department.

- Attorneys who work for or have as clients publicly traded companies.

- Brokers, dealers, investment bankers, and financial analysts who work for these companies.

The Act changes how publicly traded companies are audited and reshapes the financial reporting system. The Act adopts tough new provisions to deter and punish corporate and accounting fraud and corruption, ensures justice for wrongdoers and protects the interests of workers and shareholders.

The Act improves the quality and transparency of financial reporting, independent audits, and accounting services for public companies. It also:

- Creates a Public Company Accounting Oversight Board (www.pcaobus.org) to enforce professional standards, ethics, and competence for the accounting profession.

- Strengthens the independence of firms that audit public companies.

- Increases corporate responsibility and the usefulness of corporate financial disclosure.

- Increases penalties for corporate wrongdoing.

- Protects the objectivity and independence of securities analysts.

- Increases Securities and Exchange Commission resources.

Under the Act, CEOs and CFOs must personally vouch for the truth and fairness of their company's disclosures, which will be broader and better than ever before. Corporate officials must play by the same rules as their employees. In the periods when workers are prevented from buying and selling company stock in their pensions or 401(k)s, corporate officials will also be banned from any buying or selling.

Corporate misdeeds will be found and punished. The Act authorizes new funding for investigators and technology at the SEC to uncover wrongdoing. The SEC will now have the administrative authority to bar dishonest directors and officers from ever again serving in positions of corporate responsibility. The penalties for obstructing justice and shredding documents are greatly increased.

Public Company Accounting Oversight Board

The Act established the Public Company Accounting Oversight Board (PCAOB), consisting of five members, that is subject to SEC oversight. Though the board oversees accounting firms, only two members of the board may be CPAs. The SEC will appoint the board, whose duties include registering public accounting firms that prepare audit reports; and establishing or adopting auditing, quality control, ethics and independence standards. The board also inspects, investigates, and disciplines public accounting firms and enforces compliance with the Act. Additional information follows:

- *Registration with the board is mandatory.* For public accounting firms, foreign or domestic, that participates in the preparation or issuance of any audit report with respect to a public company. Registration and annual fees collected from each registered CPA firm will go toward the costs of processing and reviewing applications and annual reports.

- *Seven-year record retention requirement.* The PCAOB must adopt a rule to require registered CPA firms to prepare and maintain audit workpapers and other information related to an audit for at least seven years in sufficient detail to support the conclusions reached in the audit report. (A separate criminal provision requires retention of all audit and review workpapers for five years from the end of the fiscal year in which the audit or review was completed.)

- *Cooperation with CPA groups.* The board will cooperate with professional accountant groups and advisory groups to increase the effectiveness of the standards-setting process. (The PCAOB may cooperate, but authority to set standards rests with the PCAOB, subject to SEC review.)

- *Annual inspections.* Inspection of registered public accounting firms shall occur annually for every registered public accounting firm that regularly provides audit reports for more than 100 issuers (at least once every three years for registered firms that audit fewer than 100 issuers).

- *Investigations.* The board may investigate any act, omission, or practice by a registered firm or an individual associated with a registered firm for any possible violation of the Act, the board's rules, professional standards, or provisions of the securities laws relating to the preparation and issuance of audit reports. The board may require testimony or documents and information (including audit work papers) from a registered firm or individual associated with a registered firm or in the possession of any other person. Sanctions for violations that the board finds may include:

— Suspension or revocation of a registration.

— Suspension or bar of a person from further associating with any registered public accounting firm.

— Limitations on the activities of a firm or person associated with the firm.

— Penalizing the firm up to $2 million per violation, up to a maximum of $15 million.

— Individuals employed or associated with a registered firm who violate the Act can face penalties that range from required additional continuing professional education (CPE) or training to disbarment of the individual from further association with any registered public accounting firm or even a fine up to $100,000 for each violation, up to a maximum of $750,000. A portion of the penalties collected will go to accounting scholarships.

• *Funding.* The Act also provides independent funding for the Financial Accounting Standards Board. Although both the SEC and American Institute of Certified Public Accountants (AICPA) have recognized the FASB as the standards-setting body for accounting principles, federal authority to issue auditing, quality control, ethics, and independence standards may seriously affect the AICPA's role in official pronouncements. The budget for the board and the FASB will be payable from "annual accounting support fees" set by the board and approved by the Commission. The fees will be collected from publicly traded companies and will be determined by dividing the average monthly equity market capitalization of the company for the preceding fiscal year by the average monthly equity market capitalization of all such companies for that year.

Other Requirements for CPA Firms

Other requirements for CPA firms include the following:

• *Most consulting is banned for audit clients.* Title II of the Sarbanes-Oxley Act prohibits most "consulting" services outside the scope of practice of auditors. These services are prohibited even if pre-approved by the issuer's audit committee. Prohibited services include:

— Bookkeeping and related services.

— Design and implementation of financial information system.

— Appraisal or valuation services (including fairness opinions and contribution-in-kind reports).

— Actuarial services.

— Internal audit outsourcing.

— Services that provide any management or human resources.

— Investment or broker/dealer services.

— Legal and "expert services unrelated to the audit."

— Any other service that the board determines, by regulation, is impermissible. Services that are *not* prohibited are tax services (including tax planning and tax compliance) or others that are not listed, provided the firm receives pre-approval from the board. However, certain tax planning products, like tax avoidance services, may be considered prohibited nonaudit services.

• *Audit reports require concurring partner review.* Concurring or second partner's review and approval is required of all audit reports and their issuance.

• *"Revolving door" employment of CPAs with audit clients is banned.* A registered CPA firm is prohibited from auditing any SEC registered client whose chief executive, CFO, controller or equivalent was on the audit team of the firm within the past year.

• *Audit partner rotation is required.* Audit partners who either have performed audit services or been responsible for reviewing the audit of a particular client must be rotated every five consecutive years. CPAs should read carefully the requirements for rotation of both the partner-in-charge and the concurring review partner for certain organizational constraints. However, though firm rotation is *not* required, the U.S. Comptroller General will study and review the potential effects of mandatory rotation and will report its findings to the Senate Committee on Banking, Housing, and Urban Affairs and the House Committee on Financial Services.

• *CPA firms are required to report directly to the audit committee.*

• *CPA firm consolidations are to be studied.* The U.S. Comptroller General will conduct a study analyzing the impact of the merger of CPA firms to determine if consolidation leads to higher costs, lower quality of services, impairment of auditor independence, or lack of choice.

• *Corporate and criminal fraud accountability.* Changes to the securities laws can penalize anyone found to have destroyed, altered, hidden, or falsified records or documents to impede, obstruct, or influence an investigation conducted by any federal agency with fines or up to 20 years imprisonment, or both.

• *Current requirements for audit firms.* Accountants are required to maintain all audit or review workpapers for a period of five years from the end of the fiscal period in which the audit or review was concluded.

• *Additional rules and penalties.* The law requires the SEC to promulgate rules and regulations on the retention of any and all materials related to an audit, including communications, correspondence and other documents created, sent or received in connection with an audit or review. For violating the requirement or the rules that will be developed will result in a fine, or up to 10 years imprisonment, or both.

Requirements for Corporations, Their Officers, and Board Members

As indicated in Exhibit I-1, criminal penalties for violations of the Sarbanes-Oxley Act of 2002 are greatly enhanced. Requirements for corporations, their officers, and board members include the following:

• *No lying to the auditor.* The Act makes unlawful for an officer or director or anyone acting for a principal to take any action to fraudulently influence, coerce, manipulate or mislead the auditing CPA firm.

• *Code of ethics for financial officers.* The SEC is mandated to issue rules adopting a code of ethics for senior financial officers.

• *Financial expert requirement.* The SEC is required to issue rules requiring a publicly traded company's audit committee to comprise at least one member who is a financial expert.

• *Audit committee is responsible for public accounting firm.* The Act vests the audit committee of a publicly traded company with responsibility for the appointment, compensation, and oversight of any registered public accounting firm employed to perform audit services.

- *Audit committee independence.* Requires audit committee members to be members of the board of directors of the company, and to otherwise be independent.

- *CEOs and CFOs are required to affirm financials.* CEOs and CFOs must certify in every annual report that they have reviewed the report and that it does not contain untrue statements or omissions of material facts. If material noncompliance causes the company to restate its financials, the CEO and CFO forfeit any bonuses and other incentives received during the 12-month period following the first filing of the erroneous financials.

- *CEOs and CFOs must enact internal controls.* CEOs and CFOs will be responsible for establishing and maintaining internal controls to ensure they are notified of material information.

- *Penalties for fraud.* The Act also has stiffened penalties for corporate and criminal fraud by company insiders. The law makes it a crime to destroy, alter, or falsify records in a federal investigation or if a company declares bankruptcy. The penalty for those found guilty includes fines, up to 20 years' imprisonment, or both.

- *Companies affected by the Act.* Publicly traded companies affected by the Sarbanes-Oxley Act are those defined as an "issuer" under Section 3 of the Securities Exchange Act of 1934, whose securities are registered under Section 12 of the 1934 Act. An issuer also is considered a company that is required to file reports under Section 15(d) of the 1934 Act, or that files or has filed a registration statement that has not yet become effective under the Securities Act of 1933.

- *Debts are not dischargeable in bankruptcy.* The Sarbanes-Oxley Act amends federal bankruptcy law to make nondischargeable in bankruptcy certain debts that result from a violation relating to federal or state securities law, or of common law fraud pertaining to securities sales or purchases.

- *Expanded statute of limitations for securities fraud.* For a civil action brought by a nongovernment entity or individual, an action involving a claim of securities fraud, deceit or manipulation may be brought not later than the earlier of two years after discovery or five years after the violation.

- *No listing on national exchanges for violators.* The SEC will direct national securities exchanges and associations to prohibit the listing of securities of a noncompliant company.

- *No insider trading.* No insider trading is permitted during pension fund blackout periods. The insider must forfeit any profit during this period to the company.

- *SEC rules on enhanced financial disclosures:*

  — *Off-Balance-Sheet Transactions.* All quarterly and annual financial reports filed with the SEC must disclose all material off-balance-sheet transactions, arrangements, obligations (including contingent obligations), and other relationships of the issuer with unconsolidated entities. Disclosure must be made on significant aspects relating to financial condition, liquidity, capital expenditures, resources, and components of revenue and expenses.

— *Pro Forma Figures.* Pro forma financial information in any report filed with the SEC or in any public release cannot contain false or misleading statements or omit material facts necessary to make the financial information not misleading.

• *No personal loans.* No personal loans or extensions of credit to company executives either directly or through a subsidiary, except for certain extensions of credit under an open-ended credit plan or charge card, home improvement and manufactured home loans, or extensions of credit by a broker or dealer to its employee to buy, trade, or carry securities. The terms of permitted loans cannot be more favorable than those offered to the general public.

Analyst Conflicts of Interest

There are two major provisions regarding analyst conflicts of interest: (1) retaliation against analysts is not permitted, and (2) conflicts of interest must be disclosed. Brokers and dealers of securities are not allowed to retaliate or threaten to retaliate against an analyst employed by the broker or dealer as a result of an adverse, negative, or unfavorable research report on a public company. Securities analysts and brokers or dealers are required to disclose conflicts of interest, such as whether:

Exhibit I-1: Enhanced Criminal Penalties

Behavior	Sentence
The alteration, destruction, concealment of any records with the intent of obstructing federal investigation.	Fine and/or up to 10 years imprisonment.
Failure to maintain audit or review "work-papers" for at least five years.	Fine and/or up to 5 years imprisonment
Knowing execution, or attempts to execute, a scheme to defraud a purchaser of securities.	Fine and/or up to 10 years imprisonment.
Reckless violation by any CEO or CFO of his or her certification of the company's financial statements.	Fine of up to $1,000,000 and/or up to 10 years imprisonment.
If violation is willful.	Fine of up to $5 million and/or up to 20 years imprisonment.
Conspiracy by two or more persons to commit any offense against or to defraud the U.S. or its agencies.	Fine and/or up to 20 years imprisonment.

Behavior	Sentence
Corrupt alteration, destruction, or concealment of any records or documents with the intent of impairing the integrity of the record or document for use in an official proceeding.	Fine and/or up to 10 years imprisonment.
Mail and wire fraud.	Increase from 5 to 20 years imprisonment.
Violating applicable Employee Retirement Income Security Act (ERISA) provisions.	Various lengths depending on violation.

Source: Adapted from the Sarbanes-Oxley Act of 2002 and New York City Office of the Comptroller.

- The analyst has investments or debt in the company on which he or she is reporting.

- Any compensation received by the broker, dealer, or analyst is "appropriate in the public interest and consistent with the protection of investors."

- An issuer has been a client of the broker or dealer.

- The analyst received compensation with respect to a research report based on investment banking revenues.

Attorney Requirements

The SEC is required to issue rules setting forth minimum standards of professional conduct for attorneys appearing and representing a public company in any manner in front of it. As part of this requirement, the SEC will be required to issue rules requiring attorneys employed by a public company to report to the chief counsel or CEO of the company evidence of a "material" violation of securities law, breach of fiduciary duty, or similar violation by the company or its agent. Once reported, if the counsel or CEO does not appropriately respond to the evidence, the attorney must report the evidence to the board of directors or its audit committee.

Exhibit I-2 summarizes points of controversy and related proposals and legislation.

Responding to Whistle-Blowers

In theory, disgruntled ex-employees have always been able to accuse their ex-employers of misdeeds in order to claim wrongful termination, but until the passage of Sarbanes-Oxley (Section 806 provisions), most public company employees had little to gain financially if the company denied the charges and refused to settle. Since the mid-1980s, the federal government has protected whistle-blowers whose work affects public welfare, including, for example, federal employees, government contractors, power-plant operators, and airline staff. Even so, people who spoke out about financial fraud had no legal protection except for a handful of state laws—and then, often, only if the matter affected the general public.

Now, the Act states that an employee needs only "a reasonable belief" that his or her employer is violating a securities law or is in any other way imperiling shareholder value to qualify for government protection from retaliation. Retaliation encompasses everything from firing to verbal threats and missed promotions. Within 90 days of experiencing retaliation, an employee can file for protection, which means anything from reinstatement with back pay to a full federal court trial with the potential of compensation for pain and suffering. These protections apply even if the employee is wrong about his or her accusations.

Exhibit I-2: Points of Controversy and Related Proposals and Legislation

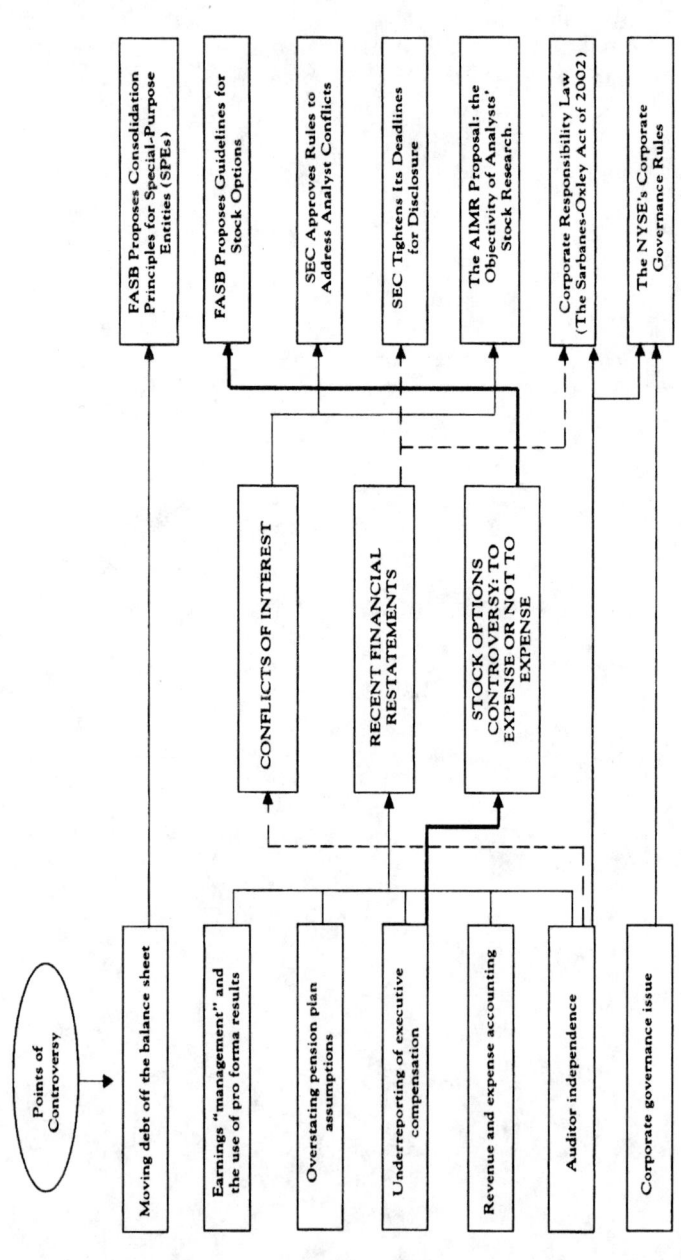

Companies must have toll-free hotlines and Web-based mechanisms that allow audit-committee members to hear directly from employees, suppliers, and customers who want to voice concerns about accounting or internal controls. According to the Sarbanes-Oxley Act and SEC rules, such systems must allow for anonymity.

Regardless, CFOs may do well to become better listeners. Most whistleblowers say they never would have gone public with their concerns about the financial statements if senior management had been more attentive to them. Opening up the lines of communication does not necessarily mean opening Pandora's box. Once a complaint is received, companies need to make every effort to protect a whistle-blower's anonymity. That task is considerably easier at big companies, where internal audits are routine. At smaller companies, the best option may be to question senior-level managers in confidence before broadening the inquiry to rank-and-file workers. Companies should also keep track of complaints, because OSHA's 90-day statute of limitations starts when the alleged retaliation occurs, not when the concerns are raised.

CORPORATE GOVERNANCE

A series of sweeping changes are being sought, such as forcing boards to have a majority of independent directors, granting audit committees power to hire and fire accountants, banning sweetheart loans to officers and directors, and requiring shareholders' approval for stock option plans. More specifically, the following five principles constitute good governance:

1. To avoid conflicts of interest, a company's board of directors should include a substantial majority of independent directors—"independent" meaning that directors do not have financial or close personal ties to the company or its executives.

2. A company's audit, nominating, and compensation committees should consist entirely of independent directors.

3. A board should obtain shareholder approval for any actions that could significantly affect the relationship between the board and shareholders, including the adoption of antitakeover measures such as "poison pills."

4. Companies should base executive compensation plans on pay for performance and should provide full disclosure of these plans.

5. To avoid abuse in the use of stock options (and executive perquisites), all employee stock option plans should be submitted to shareholders for approval.

Governance Analytics

Institutional Shareholder Services (ISS), Inc. (www.issproxy.com/), an influential proxy advisor, began scoring companies on governance issues.

ISS offers a host of database and research tools designed to augment the inhouse resources institutional investors have at their disposal. In fact, many of the world's most recognized financial institutions and plan sponsors use ISS's Corporate Governance ratings database to support their investment decision-making models.

As the foremost authority on corporate governance, ISS keeps clients informed on the latest issues, regulatory changes, and company news through a Web-based portal.

Although filing claims and recovering class action damages on behalf of shareholders is not yet mandated, it is still viewed as a fiduciary responsibility. The volume of suits continues to rise and billions of dollars in settlement dollars are at stake. For that reason, institutions look to ISS to track litigation and claim settlement awards through its Securities Class Action Services, an independent division of ISS that performs portfolio monitoring, class action advisory services and claims filing.

Corporate Governance Quotient

Provided by Institutional Shareholder Services, the leading provider of proxy voting and corporate governance data services, the Corporate Governance Quotient (CGQ) is a rating tool that assists institutional investors in evaluating the quality of corporate boards and the impact their governance practices may have on performance.

The database features corporate governance ratings on more than 5,400 U.S. companies, including the Russell 3000 index, and 2,000 non-U.S. companies. Each company is scored daily. U.S. companies are ranked relative to market capitalization and their industry peer groups. Non-U.S. companies are scored individually and ranked relative to the S&P/TSX Composite Index, MSCI EAFE Index and the MSCI World Index. Additionally, non-U.S. companies are ranked relative to their specific country index, industry, and against the ISS global universe for comparative purposes.

CGQ Rating Criteria. Ratings are calculated on the basis of eight core categories: board of directors, audit, charter and bylaw provisions, takeover practices, executive and director compensation, qualitative factors, ownership, and director education. ISS analyzes 61 data points to derive each issuer rating. The eight core categories and 61 data points are shown in Exhibit I-3. In addition, some variables are analyzed in combination with other provisions; for example, a board with a majority of independent directors and all-independent key board panels (audit, nominating, and compensation) receives a higher rating for each of these attributes than it would if it had either one of them in isolation.

Exhibit I-3: CGQ Ratings Factors

Board		6	Board Size
1	Board Composition	7	Changes in Board Size
2	Nominating Committee	8	Cumulative Voting
3	Compensation Committee	9	Boards Served On—CEO
4	Governance Committee	10	Boards Served On—Other Than CEO
5	Board Structure	11	Former CEOs

Some of the ratings factors are also looked at in combination under the premise that corporate governance is enhanced when selected combinations of these criteria are adopted.

Board Effectiveness Ratings

The Corporate Library's ratings (www.thecorporatelibrary.net/products/ratings 2003.html) are based on a small number of proven dynamic indicators of special interest to shareholders and investors. Their focus is on real-world value and risk, not best practices. The Corporate Library seeks to know which boards are most likely to enhance and preserve shareholder value, and which boards might actually increase investor risk. As such, its ratings are not intended to be used alone, but rather to enhance the effectiveness of existing investment research methods. The Corporate Library's letter-based groupings, using the common A–F scale, are derived from a combination of its proprietary rating formula, which is used to identify and highlight certain key "red flag" indicators present at any of the 2,000 + U.S. companies included in its master database, combined with a series of deeper analytics applied to specific companies, by senior staff, in certain key areas, such as CEO compensation.

STRATEGIES FOR DEALING WITH SARBANES-OXLEY

Clearly, the increased financial scrutiny required by recent legislation is going to have a major impact on business operations. The technology investment that CEOs, CFOs, and CIOs make to redefine financial processes in order to meet regulatory requirements will have significant impact on competitive stature and bottom-line success. The technology choices that enable the new processes will drive repeatability, predictability, auditability, and quality of financial processes, and will help companies achieve and maintain a world-class financial status.

Many companies that have already faced the challenges of Sarbanes-Oxley have found that the best starting point for compliance is identification of the exact regulatory requirement. With this requirement clearly specified, a company can determine the actions necessary to meet the mandate and the costs of doing so. Then it can develop a strategy to absorb these costs without diluting the earnings required to maintain investor confidence.

Three strategies are critical to successfully achieving these goals: (1) providing visibility for key stakeholders, (2) enabling compliance solutions, and (3) viewing enterprise compliance for a proposed end-state. Companies that embrace these proven concepts can move beyond merely responding to Sarbanes-Oxley. They can ultimately put in place world-class business and financial processes that will lower operational costs and risks while achieving the visibility that will support investor confidence.

Providing Visibility to Key Stakeholders

Visibility is rapidly becoming an important theme for companies as they try to provide the appropriate information to key enterprise stakeholders. Six groups must be involved in assuring effective governance: (1) management, (2) the board of directors, (3) shareholders, (4) auditors, (5) corporate counsel, and (6) regulators. To realistically meet regulatory requirements and drive greater investor confidence, companies must address the unique information needs of each of these stakeholders—as well as corporate management, the board, and shareholders—with real-time tools and easy access to appropriate content. In doing so, they will provide stakeholders with greater insight, control, and visibility, enabling them to make smarter, faster, and better decisions.

Corporate Management. Senior executives now need broad visibility to the existence and use of internal controls to assure the integrity of a wide range of financial reports, including Section 302 quarterly assertion of controls, annual

Section 404 certification by the auditors, and CEO and CFO certification for accurately reporting financials under Section 906. In addition, as responsibility and accountability is pushed throughout the organization, strategic business unit (SBU) heads must also certify their results for senior management. In other words, legislation now calls for a bottom-up approach to accountability.

As a result, under new guidelines senior executives and SBU heads must answer a series of questions, including:

- Where is there material risk in my business?

- Do we have the appropriate controls in place to mitigate this risk?

- Are these controls being universally applied in a consistent manner?

- What is compliance costing and how do we create efficiencies?

- Am I confident in attesting to the integrity of our financials on an on-going basis?

Board of Directors. The role of board members has truly been transformed by recent regulations, and their accountability will be scrutinized as never before. Although the majority of the Board will be independent, they need broad visibility across the enterprise and responsibility for various functions, such as auditing, compensation, nominating, and disclosure committees. Like CEOs, they too must respond to a number of questions that require timely information, including:

- What is the status of our internal controls and are we at risk?

- What work are our auditors proposing and what should we approve?

- What issues must the board and their subcommittees address today and tomorrow?

- What is the status of past issues now being mitigated?

Auditors and Corporate Counsel. Auditors and corporate counsel round out the initial power triangle that must be aligned prior to addressing regulators and shareholders. Both internal and external auditors are included, as the external auditors must ultimately certify annual reports. The questions they must answer include:

- Do the financial statements accurately reflect business operations?

- Are appropriate controls in place, understood, and operationalized?

- How is risk likely to vary by business unit?

Shareholders. The central purpose of the Sarbanes-Oxley Act is to restore investor confidence, and in order to meet this goal, companies must exceed regulatory requirements. They must provide greater external transparency into corporate performance and enable investors to immediately locate relevant, high-quality information required for a complete analysis of the company.

Companies that take the lead in providing this depth of information will be rewarded with investor trust and greater market capitalization. To satisfy investor needs for greater visibility and transparency, corporations need to address a series of questions, including:

- What key performance indicators do investors use to evaluate and monitor a corporation?

- How easy is it for an investor to navigate the labyrinth of financial and non-financial information to evaluate both current and future performance?

- Are public disclosures open, widely distributed, and consistent? Is Regulation FD (Fair Disclosure) met for management advisement and consistency of segmented disclosures?

Regulatory Bodies. The Sarbanes-Oxley Act provided greater resources for monitoring and enforcement by the SEC, but the role of monitoring and enforcement extends well beyond that agency to the stock exchanges; accounting bodies, such as American Institute of Certified Public Accountants (AICPA), FASB, the Public Company Accounting Oversight Board (PCAOB), the International Accounting Standards Board (IASB) and other international organizations; and even state attorneys. In most cases, the corporations' relationship with regulatory bodies is not adversarial: both have the same goal of restoring investor confidence. Corporations should thus determine how they can improve their interactions with the various regulatory bodies by:

- Creating and adjusting policies and controls according to advisements and recommendations.

- Improving procedures and processes based on recommendations.

- Effectively responding to requests for clarity or additional information.

- Participating in the shaping of regulations and standards.

With such vast and diverse information requirements, most companies are unlikely to be completely prepared to effectively manage the content and processes required to meet stakeholder and compliance needs. Corporations typically use a variety of online and offline tools and processes which, most often, are unconnected and lack security, audit, and long-term archiving capabilities. Although most corporations would agree that collaboration is critical, their collaboration efforts are based on e-mail, phone, voicemail, conference calls, and fax. These tools are necessary but insufficient to systematically and securely communicate complete responses to the kinds of questions being asked by stakeholders.

The Role of Corporate Governance and Compliance Solutions

A new set of solutions is required to address the unique needs of each stakeholder and to manage the interactions required between each group. This section introduces a series of solutions and describes the key features and associated benefits of each.

Solutions fall into two broad categories: (1) collaborative workplaces that increase visibility, collaboration, and participation; and (2) enterprise compliance solutions that deliver the underlying content and records management capabilities.

Collaborative Workplaces. Collaborative workplaces can ease compliance processes by providing greater visibility, collaboration, and training support and by maintaining a secure repository containing critical documents and records. Three examples of collaborative workplaces follow.

1. *Compliance program workplaces.* CEOs, CFOs, and SBU heads need high-level information and oversight, which requires broad communication, discussions, and coordination for which e-mail alone is not well suited. This workplace should make it easy for CEOs, CFOs, and SBU heads to:

   a. Communicate program objectives and initiatives.

   b. Manage the overall program and key activities.

   c. Provide self-assessment instruments and data analysis.

   d. Engage with business units around control gaps and remediation.

   e. Provide overall program management visibility with drill down.

2. *Control design workplace.* As companies merge, divest, introduce new products, and change business focus, they must modify or develop new internal controls. Because this is a multistep process requiring collaboration with individuals inside and outside of the organization, the workplace should enable participants to:

   a. Access controls from an internal controls repository.

   b. Create and manage workflows leading to agreement on final controls.

   c. Provide a design workplace with defined access controls and roles.

   d. Capture changes, track versions, and create alerts to ensure participation.

   e. Publish final changes to targeted audiences to assure adoption.

3. *Board of directors workplace.* Sarbanes-Oxley has had a significant impact on the role of the board and corporate governance, making them much more accountable for monitoring the corporation and driving key board sub-committees governing audit, compensation, nominating, and disclosure processes. A board of directors workplace can help to assure the effectiveness of board members by enabling them to:

   a. Access board meeting schedules, briefing documents, and issue logs.

   b. Create subcommittee workrooms designed for each specific function.

   c. Archive past board meetings and other final-form content.

   d. View the status of internal controls and key business performance indicators.

Enterprise Compliance Solutions. Collaborative workplaces depend on tight integration into an underlying platform to manage content. An internal controls repository, document and records archive, and a records management system can help ensure that internal controls, reporting, and public disclosures are managed through a single point of Web access across the organization with appropriate security and access rights. The two key solutions that facilitate fulfillment of these objectives are as follows:

1. *Internal Controls Repository.* Many companies are beginning to recognize the need to house their business controls in a central repository. Whether driven by a need to streamline the Section 404 control initiative that requires external auditor certification of annual reports, or simply as a means to improve business processes, a centralized internal controls repository can provide an infrastructure that supports controls throughout their lifecycle. Features of these repositories can be tailored to meet the specific requirements of any organization, but generally can be used to:

a. Capture internal controls, client roles, and access privileges.

b. Create workflows and lifecycles to facilitate creation, modification, and finalization.

c. Publish controls and assure widespread adoption.

d. Monitor critical controls and identify exceptions through workflows.

e. Generate workplaces to address exceptions and document resolution.

2. *Document and Records Archive.* To help ensure key content is easily and securely accessible across the enterprise, organizations turn to document and records archives. Companies had until October 31, 2003, to come up with plans for meeting 17 CFR Part 210 requirements, a mandate that requires auditors to save audit-related documents for seven years. CIOs are realizing that their organizations also need to save an equivalent set of documents, as well as audit documents, financials related to the 10K and 10Q processes, and other business-related documents. Key features of a document and records archive that expedites these tasks will allow companies to:

a. Establish policies and procedures for identifying and protecting business critical documents.

b. Capture records from a variety of physical, electronic, e-mail, and scanned image sources.

c. Retrieve and disseminate recorded information based on a set of client-defined roles and access rights.

d. Store inactive records that need to be retained for legal, fiscal, regulatory, or administrative reasons.

e. Implement procedures for the timely, secure destruction of corporate records when their prescribed retention period elapses.

Enterprise Compliance Proposed End State. As stewards of corporate responsibility, the majority of CEOs and CFOs are interested in transforming their fiscal management through better decision making and the establishment of internal controls. Corporations want to improve visibility, access, control, and collaboration of both structured content (such as balance sheets) and unstructured information (such as management disclosure and advisement) to streamline internal operations and meet regulatory requirements. At the same time, companies want to implement controls—such as the internal-control framework created by the Committee of Sponsoring Organizations of the Treadway Commission (COSO)—to create the needed structure and discipline for corporate policies and procedures.

Both PricewaterhouseCoopers (PwC) and Deloitte Touche Tohmatsu have offered white papers recommending what companies should do to comply with Sarbanes-Oxley. PwC encourages clients whose control activities are not yet designed, in place, or adequately documented to implement standardized controls. Beyond standardization, PwC recommends over the long term that the company implement an infrastructure and financial controls that can be monitored and optimized. Whereas implementing an infrastructure requires the ability to do periodic testing and management reporting, implementing financial controls focuses on real-time controls monitoring and continuous improvement by senior management. (A Deloitte Touche white paper entitled "Moving Forward" names these stages "reliable" and "optimal.")

If this is what companies need to do, what should CEOs and CFOs do in their stewardship roles? They should look to the success of other regulated industries and understand how these industries have dealt with similar mandates. For example, companies subject to the stringent mandates of the Food and Drug Administration (FDA) have turned to enterprise content management solutions to reduce the time and cost required to get new products approved and to market. Their enterprise content management infrastructures help these companies to efficiently manage, monitor, and control compliance lifecycles from a single system. To support a cradle-to-grave approach, an enterprise content management infrastructure must be built on a compliance architecture that meets the challenges of scalability, performance, integrity, and security.

Using enterprise content management—controlled repositories, process automation, collaboration, records management, and business integration corporations can better manage the risk of non-compliance and the operational costs of compliance. In short, proven technology is available today that will allow companies to achieve the internal control maturity recommended by leading audit firms and ultimately increase investor confidence. The following section addresses the issue of using computer software and various information technologies.

COMPLIANCE AIDS: SOFTWARE AND INFORMATION TECHNOLOGIES

The thickening forest of regulations enforcing corporate governance standards is enough to make any chief executive feel lost. Far-reaching legislation, such as the Sarbanes-Oxley Act and the International Accounting Standards, is imposing a considerable burden of compliance on both companies and individual executives, who can be exposed to serious penalties—including jail sentences—if they fail to put the right measures in place.

Technology would seem the obvious solution to the corporate governance and compliance problem. Much of governance is a matter of putting rules in place and ensuring that they are followed. Corporate finance systems, historically among the first business systems to be computerized, have always worked in just such a fashion. Why not tweak them to take new rules into account?

Unfortunately, it is not quite that simple. The scale of new governance standards brings many corporate systems—not just the finance function—into the picture. Customer databases, human resources systems, document management and electronic collaboration tools all can contain data relevant to corporate governance. In addition, the changing nature of regulation means that systems have to be kept up-to-date. This requires constant planning and monitoring on the part of the IT director.

The main problem for companies is documentation, including internal controls and the retention of documents. For this reason, good document management systems—which trace the history of all documents and allow for their fast retrieval—are key to any company seeking to comply with corporate governance standards. Specialized secure electronic storage areas must be established to store documents, a task made slightly less onerous thanks to the falling price of storage hardware. In addition, corporate policies on the retention of documents must be clearly articulated, whereas in the past they may have been only implicit.

Even e-mail has fallen under scrutiny. New accounting standards dictate that audit trails must be established showing exactly how executives arrived at conclusions such as the valuation of assets. As such discussions are now just as likely to take place electronically as at physical meetings, any e-mails in which valuation was discussed would also be implicated. Currently, these vital communications are simply thrown onto a server along with every other e-mail and, after a period of time, deleted to make room for more. Rooting out and keeping these documents can be an IT management nightmare.

The most important issue is trying to make the accounts that companies present as meaningful and accurate as possible so that investors and auditors can have confidence in what is being presented. In achieving this, one of the greatest difficulties that companies face is grappling with the subtle distinctions between accounting and finance systems in different countries. Companies need to put in place systems that allow them to compare apples with apples across different territories. That can be very detailed but is necessary to achieve the transparency needed.

The sheer volume of data presents further problems. Companies should try to simplify their systems, bringing more of their databases within a single overarching structure and reducing the number of points at which data enters the system. At all costs, companies must avoid rigid IT systems that will become a headache to change every time the accounting regulations are tweaked or new regulations come into force. Flexibility is key, and anything hard-coded is a dead end.

Technology is just an enabler. Once a governance structure has been agreed to at a corporate level, IT can be used to support it. Governance must not be built around a company's existing IT; the IT systems should be made to fit the business. Policies and procedures should be worked out first, in detail, to calculate the best ways of complying with all the regulations that pertain to a company. Only then should the IT department be brought in to figure out what updates need to be made to the existing systems, to decide whether new technology investments are needed, and to implement the changes and the procedures that have been deemed necessary.

To a large degree, successful corporate governance depends on people: this is a management issue. People require training around governance and must be taught the needed skills. For a company specializing in electronic invoicing, however, the real answer may not lie with people, nor with the strict implementation of dedicated compliance systems to enforce every detail of corporate governance regulation, but with eliminating manual intervention. Automation of existing processes can achieve this. Automated systems, such as enterprise resource planning applications, are more transparent than those requiring manual intervention, and less prone to fraud.

Six Technologies That Can Assist with Compliance

Much of governance is a matter of putting rules in place and ensuring that they are followed. Technology can provide the solutions to the corporate governance and compliance problem. It includes computer software for the following six functions:

1. *Business intelligence.* Because regulatory requirements stipulate real-time disclosure of factors that affect financial performance, executives need access to timely, relevant data from all areas of the business. By drilling down into financial and company data and providing sophisticated reporting and analysis tools, business intelligence software can help ensure the accessibility of information.

2. *Business process management (BPM).* Businesses have traditionally been built around functional "silos," making it difficult to share information and obtain a consistent, enterprisewide view. By extracting businesses processes from the underlying application code into an independent management layer, BPM software can help improve visibility.

3. *Document management.* Because of new corporate governance standards, companies need an efficient system for storing and retrieving important records and documents. Software packages that maintain audit trails of documents and set controls over how, where, and for how long files are stored can help companies meet these obligations.

4. *E-mail management.* As the volume of e-mail continues to soar, the logistics of storing essential e-mails and being able to retrieve them quickly become increasingly complex. And with new regulatory requirements around internal controls and disclosure obligations, the need for comprehensive e-mail management software becomes more compelling.

5. *Financing and accounting.* To help comply with new standards, such as Sarbanes-Oxley, many vendors are giving their traditional financing and accounting software a boost with additional modules that help with risk manage-

ment, more accurate budgeting and forecasting, financial analysis, and the establishment of internal financial controls.

6. *Enterprise resource planning (ERP).* ERP software can give organizations a consistent financial view across all divisions, thereby helping to maintain the accuracy of financial information. Many ERP providers are adding modules to their software to assist with compliance with Sarbanes-Oxley and other corporate governance standards.

Compliance Software

Following is a list of helpful compliance software:

1. *Trintech Unity Compliance* (www.trintech.com) manages all Sarbanes-Oxley and other compliance initiatives across the enterprise, such as quality control, IT governance, and security, as well as corporate social responsibility (CSR) initiatives, such as green and sustainability projects.

2. *Agility*™ (www.business-port.net), developed to include multiple-standard compliance, attempts to reduce Sarbanes-Oxley maintenance costs by providing the client with a sustainable method for ongoing maintenance and compliance.

3. *Ethicspoint*® (www.ethicspoint.com/en/default.asp) is a management tool for proactively addressing issues of reporting compliance with the Sarbanes-Oxley and Foreign Corrupt Practices Acts. It reduces fraud, theft, and abuse; promotes safety; identifies inappropriate behavior; reinforces the organization's ethical values; and provides reporters with a safe place to report concerns anonymously, without fear of retaliation.

4. *WB-Resources* (www.wb-resources.com/index.asp) assists companies with Sarbanes-Oxley compliance, specifically regarding Section 301(4) of the Act. WB-Resources provides a confidential, anonymous, and cost-effective solution for employees, directors, shareholders, vendors/customers, and competitors to disclose information about potential accounting and auditing matters within the company.

CORPORATE SOCIAL RESPONSIBILITY

The food industry is blamed for obesity. Mobile phone operators are challenged to protect teenagers from online pornography. Record companies are attacked when they sue music-lovers for sharing illegal files on the Internet. Fair or not, big business is being called to justify its approach to a growing array of social, environmental and ethical concerns. Despite the economic downturn, many companies are concluding that they cannot afford not to invest in being seen as responsible.

Business for Social Responsibility (BSR), a nonprofit advisory organization, reports that its membership includes many top multinational corporations. Microsoft, Lucent, and United Technologies have joined BSR this year, as has Altria, a more traditional target for pressure groups and litigation as the parent company of both Kraft Foods and Philip Morris.

More companies are focusing on a serious engagement with their stakeholders so that they can anticipate social, environmental, and ethical issues and deal with them proactively, rather than wait until these issues reach the front pages of journals and then appearing to be acting only under pressure.

The financial sector, tarnished by Wall Street's conflicts of interest and role in corporate scandals, has come under scrutiny over lending to controversial projects in the developing world. In June 2004, a group of leading banks including Citigroup, Barclays, and ABN Amro pledged to avoid loans for socially or environmentally questionable projects under banking's so-called "Equator Principles," an industry approach for determining, assessing, and managing environmental and social risks in project financing.

The concept of corporate social responsibility involves more than serving the interests of the organization and its shareholders. Rather, it is an extension of responsibility to embrace service to the public interest in such matters as environmental protection, employee safety, civil rights, and community involvement. Socially responsible behavior clearly has immediate costs to the entity, for example, the expenses incurred in affirmative action programs, pollution control, and improvements in worker safety. When one firm incurs such costs and its competitor does not, the other may be able to sell its products or services more cheaply and increase its market share at the expense of the socially responsible firm. The rebuttal argument is that in the long run the socially responsible company may maximize profits by creating goodwill and avoiding or anticipating governmental regulation.

If corporations want to stay on the right side of the global economy's growing protest movement what can they do? Here are some suggestions for corporate social responsibility (CSR):

- First and foremost, a company should match its words with deeds. CSR is not a box-ticking exercise. A CSR director should not be nominated as an afterthought and the subject forgotten about until the next annual report.

- Because it is easy to become tarnished by bad practice via a business association, suppliers and contractors should be checked to ensure that they meet standards. Any group within a company's supply chain should comply with the best CSR practice; if it does not, it could drag an otherwise ethical business into trouble.

- Remember that no business acts in isolation and all should behave as responsible members of a wider society. Employees must see themselves as part of that society. A strong lead in CSR will motivate them. The decision of South African mining company Anglo American in August 2002 to provide free HIV/AIDS drugs for its vast workforce is an example of this.

- Join forces with the CSR movement—it is not going away. The issues it raises involve too many interest groups across the world to be temporary phenomena.

- Remember Machiavelli. CSR could be a defining attribute of winning companies in the 21st century.

Executives are fond of the saying "what gets measured, gets managed," and measuring CSR performance has been a boom industry in the past few years.

Morley Fund Managers, the investment arm of Aviva, provides some help with its socially responsible investment matrix. Morley's analysts have graded FTSE100 companies according to two dimensions: the nature of the business they are in, and the level of responsibility with which the company is managed. Thus, BP and Shell are ranked D on an A to E scale, because the oil business is inherently unsustainable. However, they both gain a score of two on the one-to-five management scale because Morley thinks highly of their management vision and strategy (none of the top 100 yet merits a perfect score of one).

Specialist rating agencies have now taken this kind of approach further. Organizations, such as CoreRatings and Innovest, assign CSR ratings in the style of the debt markets, with a pinnacle of AAA, down through AA to A and on through BBB. These grades are based on in-depth analysis of the issues facing companies and how well they deal with them.

These approaches are all aimed specifically at investors. Business in the Community (BitC) has developed an index for wider consumption, which aims to create responsibility league tables, based on information supplied by the participating companies. It covers companies' impacts in the community, the environment, the market, and the workplace and aims to assess the extent to which companies translate strategy into responsible practice. Exhibit I-4 lists basic core indicators used by BitC.

The first Corporate Responsibility Index was published in 2005 and proved highly controversial, especially among companies that were ranked at the bottom of the league, despite what they regarded as important social responsibility initiatives.

Exhibit I-4: Indicators Used to Assess Corporate Social Responsibility

Marketplace indicators:

- Customer complaints

- Advertising   complaints upheld

- Upheld cases of anticompetitive behavior

- Customer satisfaction levels

- Provision for customers with special needs

Workplace indicators:

- Workforce profiles by gender, race, disability, age

- Staff absenteeism

- Number of legal noncompliances on health and safety, plus equal opportunities legislation

- Number of staff grievances

- Upheld of cases of corrupt or unprofessional behavior

- Number of recordable safety incidents (fatal and nonfatal)

- Staff turnover

- Value of training and development provided to staff

- Perception measures of the company by its employees

- Existence of confidential grievance procedures for workers

Community indicators:

• Cash value of company support as a percentage of pre-tax profit

• Individual value of staff time, gifts in kind, and management costs

Environmental indicators:

• Energy consumption

• Water usage

• Solid waste produced

• Successful environmental prosecutions

• Carbon dioxide (CO_2)/greenhouse gas emissions

• Other emissions, such as ozone, radiation, oxides of sulphur (SOx), and oxides of nitrogen (NOx)

• Net CO_2/greenhouse gas measures and offsetting effect

Business Ethics

Ethics is the "science of morals." A moral is a rule or standard of human behavior that is accepted by society insofar as the behavior in question is one that affects others in the society, even if only indirectly. The implication of this definition is therefore that private actions that have no impact on others are a matter for personal morality, which is not of business or organizational concern.

However, the distinction between personal morality and business morality may not always be so clearly defined. This is because individuals bring personal values to their jobs and to the real or perceived problems of moral choice that confront them at work. Moral choices sometimes must be made because of tensions within individuals, between individuals, or between individuals and what they believe to be the values that drive their organizations.

Furthermore, business organizations do not operate in a social vacuum. Because of the ways business organizations can and do affect the lives and livelihoods of society at large, some would argue that business organizations are kind of "moral agents" in society. Therefore, managers and members of the general public alike often wrestle with defining exactly what constitutes the ethical way of doing business, and what constitutes proper constraints on individual self-interests and by whom these constraints shall be imposed.

A further complexity results from the fact that businesses are increasingly becoming global in nature. Different countries have or seem to have vastly different customs and values. Understanding and assessing whether and how these different cultural and ethical conflicts should be taken into account is often most difficult.

Electrical-equipment conspiracy cases in 1960 caused public concern and creation of the Business Ethics Advisory Council (BEAC) in 1961 under the Secretary of Commerce. BEAC pointed out the following areas needing self-evaluation by the business community:

• General business understanding of ethical issues.

• Compliance with laws.

• Conflicts of interest.

- Entertainment and gift expenses.
- Relations with customers and suppliers, including the giving or acceptance of gifts or kickbacks.
- Social responsibilities.

BEAC's recommendations generated business interest, especially from big business, in problems of ethical behavior.

Factors That May Lead to Unethical Behavior. In any normal population, some people have less than desirable levels of ethics. If these people hold leadership positions, they will adversely influence subordinates.

Certain organizational factors may lead to unethical behavior:

- Pressures for short-run performance in decentralized return on investment (ROI) centers may inhibit ethical behavior.
- Emphasis on strict adherence to chain-of-command authority may provide excuses for ignoring ethics when following orders.
- Informal work-group loyalties may subvert ethical behavior.
- Committee decision processes may make it possible to abstain from or dodge ethical obligations.

External factors leading to unethical behavior include:

- Pressure of competition may compromise ethics in the interest of survival.
- Unethical behavior of others may force a compromise of ethics.
- Definitions of ethical behavior may vary from one culture to another. Bribes to overseas officials or buyers may be consistent with some countries' customary business practices, but such a practice is not considered ethical among U.S. purchasing agents. Bribes are now considered illegal under the Foreign Corrupt Practices Act.
- The propriety of superimposing our cultural ethical standards (by refusing to bribe) on another culture may be controversial.

General Guides to Ethics. Following are some very general guidelines to consider in assessing behavior and determining one's own actions:

- Golden Rule—Do unto others as you would have others do unto you.
- Maximize good—Act to provide the greatest good for the greatest number.
- Fairness—Act in ways that are fair or just to all concerned.
- Maximize long-run outcomes—Act to provide the best long-range benefits to society and its resources.
- General respect—Act to respect the planet all humans share and the rights of others because corporate and individual decisions affect them.

Two helpful criteria for evaluating ethical behavior are:

- Would this behavior be acceptable if people I respect knew I were doing this?

- What are the consequences of this behavior for myself, other employees, customers, and society?

Codes of Ethical Conduct. Ethics are individual and personal, influenced by life experiences (rewards for doing right, punishment for doing wrong); friendship groups (professional associations, informal groups); and organizational pressures (responsibilities to superiors and the organization). An organization's code of ethical conduct is the established general value system the organization wishes to apply to its members' activities through communicating organizational purposes and beliefs and by establishing uniform ethical guidelines for members, including guidance on behavior for members in making decisions.

Laws and written rules cannot cover all situations. However, organizations can benefit from having an established ethical code because it:

- Effectively communicates acceptable values to all members, including recruits and subcontractors.

- Provides a method of policing and disciplining members for violations:

  — Through review panels (formal).

  — Through group pressure (informal).

- Establishes high standards against which individuals can measure their own performance.

- Communicates to those outside the organization the value system from which the organization's members must not be asked to deviate.

A typical code for accounting activities (note similarities to standards such as the Standards for the Professional Practice of Internal Auditing, GAAP, and GAAS) holds that a financial manager must have:

1. Independence from conflicts of economic interest.

2. Independence from conflicts of professional interest regarding:

   a. Responsibility to present information fairly to shareholders/owners and not intentionally protect management.

   b. Responsibility to present data to all appropriate managers and not play favorites with information or cover up bad news.

   c. Responsibility to exercise an ethical presence in the conduct of professional activities:

      (1) Ensuring organizational compliance with spirit as well as letter of pertinent laws and regulations.

      (2) Conducting oneself according to the highest moral and legal standards.

      (3) Reporting to appropriate internal or external authority any illegal or fraudulent organizational act.

d. Integrity in not compromising professional values for the sake of personal goals.

e. Objectivity in presenting information, preparing reports, and making analyses.

Standards of Ethical Conduct for Financial Officers. Corporate financial officers consisting of practitioners of management accounting and financial management have an obligation to the public, their profession, the organizations they serve, and themselves, to maintain the highest standards of ethical conduct. In recognition of this obligation, the Institute of Management Accountants (IMA) has promulgated the following standards of ethical conduct for practitioners of management accounting and financial management. Adherence to these standards, both domestically and internationally, is integral to achieving the Objectives of Management Accounting. Practitioners of management accounting and financial management shall not commit acts contrary to these standards nor shall they condone the commission of such acts by others within their organizations.

Competence. Practitioners of management accounting and financial management have a responsibility to:

- Maintain an appropriate level of professional competence through ongoing development of their knowledge and skills.

- Perform their professional duties in accordance with relevant laws, regulations, and technical standards.

- Prepare complete and clear reports and recommendations after appropriate analyses of relevant and reliable information.

Confidentiality. Practitioners of management accounting and financial management have a responsibility to:

- Refrain from disclosing confidential information acquired in the course of their work except when authorized, or legally obligated to do so.

- Inform subordinates as appropriate regarding the confidentiality of information acquired in the course of their work and monitor their activities to assure the maintenance of that confidentiality.

- Refrain from using or appearing to use confidential information acquired in the course of their work for unethical or illegal advantage, either personally or through third parties.

Integrity. Practitioners of management accounting and financial management have a responsibility to:

- Avoid actual or apparent conflicts of interest and advise all appropriate parties of any potential conflict.

- Refrain from engaging in any activity that would prejudice their ability to carry out their duties ethically.

- Refuse any gift, favor, or hospitality that would influence or would appear to influence their actions.

- Refrain from either actively or passively subverting the attainment of the organization's legitimate and ethical objectives.

- Recognize and communicate professional limitations or other constraints that would preclude responsible judgment or successful performance of an activity.

- Communicate unfavorable as well as favorable information and professional judgments or opinions.

- Refrain from engaging in or supporting any activity that would discredit the profession.

Objectivity. Practitioners of management accounting and financial management have a responsibility to:

- Communicate information fairly and objectively.

- Fully disclose all relevant information that could reasonably be expected to influence an intended user's understanding of the reports, comments, and recommendations presented.

Resolution of Ethical Conflict. In applying the standards of ethical conduct, practitioners of management accounting and financial management may encounter problems in identifying unethical behavior or in resolving an ethical conflict. When faced with significant ethical issues, practitioners of management accounting and financial management should follow the established policies of the organization bearing on the resolution of such conflict. If these policies do not resolve the ethical conflict, such practitioners should consider the following courses of action:[1]

- Discuss such problems with the immediate superior except when it appears that the superior is involved, in which case the problem should be presented initially to the next higher managerial level. If satisfactory resolution cannot be achieved when the problem is initially presented, submit the issues to the next higher managerial level. If the immediate superior is the CEO, or equivalent, the acceptable reviewing authority may be a group, such as the audit committee, executive committee, board of directors, board of trustees, or owners. Contact with levels above the immediate superior should be initiated only with the superior's knowledge, assuming the superior is not involved. Except where legally prescribed, communication of such problems to authorities or individuals not employed or engaged by the organization is not considered appropriate.

- Clarify relevant ethical issues by confidential discussion with an objective advisor (e.g., IMA Ethics Counseling Service) to obtain a better understanding of possible courses of action.

- Consult your own attorney as to legal obligations and rights concerning the ethical conflict.

---

[1] *Statement on Management Accounting 1C (Revised), Objectives: Standards of Ethical Conduct for Practitioners of Management Accounting* and *Financial Management*, April 1997, pp. 69–70).

• If the ethical conflict still exists after exhausting all levels of internal review, there may be no other recourse on significant matters than to resign from the organization and to submit an informative memorandum to an appropriate representative of the organization. After resignation, depending on the nature of the ethical conflict, it may also be appropriate to notify other parties.

Conflict of Interest. Conflict of interest is a conflict between the private and the official responsibilities of a person in a position of trust, sufficient to affect judgment, independence, or objectivity in conducting the affairs of the business. Examples of conflict of interest include having a substantial financial interest in a supplier, customer, or distributor; and using privileged information gained from one's official position to enter transactions for personal gain. Some methods for control are as follows:

• Provide a code of conduct provision applying to conflicts of interest.

• Require full financial disclosure by managers.

• Require prior notification of any transaction that may raise conflict of interest.

• Prohibit financial ties to any supplier, customer, or distributor.

• Encourage adherence to strong ethical behavior through corporate actions, policies, and public communications.

Legal Aspects of Social Responsibility. The Racketeer Influenced and Corrupt Organization (RICO) Act was passed in 1970 as an attempt to combat the problem of organized crime and its infiltration of legitimate enterprises. Its goals were to eliminate organized crime by concentrating on the illegal monies through the use of civil and criminal forfeitures. RICO has been used against white-collar criminals, terrorists, Wall Street insider trading, anti-abortion protesters, local law enforcement agencies, and public accounting firms—none of which was intended by Congress when the law was passed.

RICO specifically makes the following activities unlawful:

• Using income derived from a pattern of racketeering activity to acquire an interest in an enterprise.

• Acquiring or maintaining an interest in an enterprise through a pattern of racketeering activity.

• Conducting the affairs of an enterprise through a pattern of racketeering activity.

• Conspiring to commit any of these offenses.

Criminal penalties can be levied up to $25,000 and 20 years in jail. Civil penalties include the awarding of treble damages and attorney's fees to the successful plaintiff.

The Foreign Corrupt Practices Act of 1977 (FCPA) regulates payments by U.S. firms operating in other nations. It is a reaction to publicity over questionable foreign payments. The FCPA makes it a criminal offense to make payments to a foreign government or representative thereof to secure or retain business. It prohibits payments of sales commissions to independent agents, if the commissions are knowingly passed to foreign officials. Corporations are required to establish internal accounting controls to assure that all overseas payments are proper. The FCPA applies even if payment is legal in the nation where it is made. The rationale for the FCPA is that the international reputation of the United States is affected by its international business conduct, which should reflect the best of the United States' ethics.

The SEC mandates that the composition of boards of directors include outside directors to create diversity and broaden the overview of a company's place in the market and in society.

Courts are increasingly willing to hold boards of directors and auditors liable for problems.

PART II

COMPUTER APPLICATIONS

CHAPTER 4

WHAT THE CONTROLLER MUST KNOW ABOUT INFORMATION TECHNOLOGY

CONTENTS

Information technology (IT) tools available to the controller include spreadsheet, database management, presentation, forecasting and statistical, value chain management, and accounting software packages. The controller must stay current on new IT developments, such as Web 2.0, cloud computing, and mobile computing. The next several chapters address these IT issues.

The use of IT can enhance an organization's operational efficiency and effectiveness. However, IT may have an effect on the internal control structure of the organization.

ORGANIZATIONAL CHART OF A TYPICAL IT DEPARTMENT

Segregation of functions is essential for control purposes. However, IT has an inherent lack of segregation of functions because computer systems often have a built-in authorization of transactions that eliminates human intervention. To compensate, functions within the IT department should be clearly separated.

The *director of information services* or *chief information officer (CIO)*, is the overall supervisor or manager of the department. The CIO's responsibilities include delegating responsibilities to others, reviewing reports prepared by subordinate personnel, and reconciling problems within the department.

The *systems analyst* is responsible for evaluating management's objectives in computerizing accounting and management applications. He or she is responsible for:

- Identifying management's objectives in computerizing its applications;
- Designing the system;
- Determining hardware requirements;
- Recognizing system deficiencies;
- Designing effective controls to be integrated into the system; and
- Linking human factors with technology.

The *programmer* has the often difficult task of taking the analyst's blueprints and converting them into a language that the computer can understand. Programming involves incorporating all of management's wants and needs into a complete set of instructions that can be utilized by the computer. The programmer must be able to assure management that the necessary control procedures are embodied in the program. Newly written programs include "bugs" or problems, and it is the programmer who is relied upon to eliminate them.

The *librarian* is essential for strong internal control. The librarian's function is custodial in nature. He or she is responsible for maintaining guardianship of computer programs, program and system documentation, as well as a log which tracks usage of programs and documentation.

The *data base administrator* is responsible for ensuring that data base functions are effective. A data base is a centralized accumulation of data that may be accessed by a variety of users for a variety of purposes. For example, within the organization many departments may need to access the names and addresses of thousands of customers. Rather than create many similar files containing identical information, a data base is created. This data base can then be accessed by means of a network.

A *network administrator* is responsible for ensuring that remote terminals are effectively linked to the central processing unit (i.e., the computer itself). Communication between computers is also a responsibility of the network administrator.

The *data control group* is responsible for reviewing output and ensuring that only authorized individuals have access to such output. Access is based on approved distribution lists. The data control group is also responsible for reviewing exception reports, which are detailed listings of problems that arose during the input, processing, and output phases of electronic data processing. It must be understood, though, that the data control group is normally not empowered to rectify computer problems automatically. The data control group must obtain authorization for changes from the departments responsible for the transactions involved in the problem situations.

CONTROLS AND PROCEDURES

In addition to segregating data processing functions, certain controls and procedures should be incorporated into the hardware (i.e., equipment) and the software (i.e., programs).

Input Controls

To reasonably ensure that the data entered are accurate and complete, input controls should be utilized by the IT department.

Batch totals represent the total dollars of input. In using batch totals, adding-machine totals of input items are created. These totals are then compared with computer-generated totals. Differences indicate that data have been lost during input.

Record counts represent the total number of items entered into the system. These manually derived totals are then compared with computer-generated totals. The agreement of these totals, however, does not provide absolute assurance that data has been entered correctly. For instance, dollar amounts may have been entered incorrectly, whereas the number of items entered may have been correct.

Hash totals, though used for control purposes, are meaningless in terms of financial statement effects. For example, a manual total of check numbers is obtained and compared to a similar computer-generated total. The agreement of these totals provides reasonable assurance of the accuracy of input but does not relate a dollar amount affecting the books and financial statements.

A *check digit* is a single number that is used for identification purposes. The absence of the check digit results in the rejection of input. The check digit is algebraically determined by weighting the other numbers in the input sequence.

Passwords are codes that are necessary for access to the computer room or the computer itself.

Logic tests involve comparisons of input items with software-incorporated criteria that determine the acceptability of input data. Examples of logic tests include sign, value, field size, and limit tests. A sign test is designed to accept only a positive number or only a negative number. A value test recognizes, for example, that only a "0" or a "1" is acceptable. A field size test will reject input data that includes more than a specified number of characters. A limit test, on the other hand, will reject input data above a prescribed limit. For example, when entering a number for a month, the limit test should reject the number "13."

Processing Controls

Processing controls are intended to provide reasonable assurance that the computer processing has been accomplished as intended. Accordingly, controls should prevent (1) loss, (2) corruption, (3) duplication, and (4) addition of data.

To identify files, external and internal label checks may be used. External labels are affixed to disks to enable verification that the proper file is being utilized for processing. Internal file labels are read by the computer and are matched with specific commands before processing can commence.

Limit or reasonableness tests are similar to those used as input controls.

Processing controls may also be built into the hardware. Examples include parity checks and echo checks.

Output Controls

Output controls should be designed to provide reasonable assurance that the processing of the product is accurate and the product is distributed only to authorized users.

The accuracy of output may be verified by reconciling output totals with input and processing totals. Internal control is also enhanced by generating and reviewing exception reports, which represent detailed listings of problems that arose during input processing and output stages of data processing.

The use of approved distribution lists is the primary means of ensuring limited and authorized access to output data. Furthermore, logs should be maintained that detail (1) the name of the individual receiving output, and (2) the time of receipt.

File Controls

The objectives of file controls are to ensure that (1) files are protected, (2) copies of files are maintained, and (3) reconstruction of files is possible.

Computers and the files they generate should be protected from nature's elements. Accordingly, smoking, eating, and drinking should be prohibited by employees handling computer equipment and computer disks. If possible, rugs should not be used in computer rooms as they can create magnetic fields that could possibly erase data on disks. Air conditioning should be used in computer rooms to reduce humidity, which can destroy computer components.

Although the possibility of computer failure and file destruction are always concerns faced by IT personnel, proper backup of data and off-site storage of such backup files can greatly lessen the potential for disaster. If files must be reconstructed because of computer failure and file destruction, either nondestructive or destructive IT file update is possible. Nondestructive IT file update is accomplished by maintaining three generations of data at all times; it is often referred to as the grandfather-father-son IT file update method. This technique is most often used when data is batch processed (i.e., items of a similar nature are grouped together before being processed). Destructive IT file update, on the other hand, involves the overwriting old data with new data. Accordingly, new information automatically replaces old information. This technique is most often used in online real-time situations—that is, situations in which input and output mechanisms have direct access to the central processing unit, enabling update of files at the time data is entered rather than on the delayed basis associated with batch processing. The dangers involved in destructive IT file update may be lessened by employing (1) dumping, (2) adding, and (3) checking procedures. Dumping involves transferring information from one medium to another. For instance, personnel should periodically back up data from hard disk drives to floppy disks or tape cartridges. Dumping differs from the grandfather-father-son IT file update in that it retains only one generation of data at a given point in time. In addition, before data are entered that replace existing information, checks should be performed to ensure that the new data are authorized, accurate, and complete.

SPREADSHEET PROGRAMS

The advantage of spreadsheets is that when one number is changed, every other number related to it is also altered. Spreadsheet programs can easily handle what-if assumptions, which can effortlessly be modified. A spreadsheet program is an invaluable tool to the controller because it can be useful in budgeting, forecasting, tax planning, and preparation. In addition, spreadsheet software such as Excel has a variety of financial functions (e.g., net present value (NPV), internal rate of return (IRR), and duration) and add-ins (e.g., regression, exponential smoothing). Some of the more common spreadsheet applications include:

- Any imaginable type of what-if analysis involving alternative situations (e.g., what the company's tax liability will be, assuming different tax options are taken).
- Working paper (e.g., trial balances) preparation.
- Generation of different financial reports the entity's management may require.
- Financial statement preparation.
- Budget and forecast planning.
- Payroll preparation and analysis.
- Revenue analysis by volume, price, and product/service mix.
- Analyzing expenses.
- Costs specified in terms of volume, price, and category.
- Conversion from cash to accrual basis and vice versa.
- Aging accounts receivable.
- Inventory management.
- Production forecasts.
- Economic order quantity.

- Liability valuation (such as aging accounts payable) and liability classification (such as breaking down notes payable into current and noncurrent portions).
- Expense calculations and reports such as for depreciation, amortization, leases, pensions, and accrued expenses.
- Breakdown of expenses by category (e.g., selling expenses into promotion and entertainment, commissions, and travel).
- Cash flow analysis (e.g., debt levels, interest rates) and balancing the checkbook.
- Formulation of integrated business plans in which income statements, balance sheets, statements of cash flows, and other related schedules can be integrated into one model.
- Financial statement analysis.
- Ratio computations.
- Rate of return (i.e., assets, equity).
- Cost/revenue relationship (i.e., advertising to sales).
- Input/output relationship, such as effect of volume on costs.
- Horizontal and vertical trends over the years.
- Capital expenditure analysis.
- Capital budgeting analysis.
- Present value.
- Payback.
- Internal rate of return.
- Ranking index.
- Varying assumptions (i.e., interest rate) and determining the effect.
- Future value analysis, such as with the future value table calculations.
- Break-even analysis.
- Asset management (cash, accounts receivable, inventory, and securities).
- Credit control management and analysis and means to improve credit management.
- Lease versus buy.
- Manufacture versus buy.
- Determination of the effects of inflation (i.e., the impact of price changes).
- Productivity measures.
- Loan amortization tables.
- Acquisition analyses of other companies.
- Investment selection.
- Portfolio investment transactions and balances preparation.
- Optimal financing mix (i.e., debt-equity).

- Debt covenant compliance.
- Cost and managerial accounting.
- Divisional and departmental performance evaluation (i.e., cost center).
- Product line measures.
- Overhead calculations.
- Variance determination (standard to actual, budget to actual) in dollars and percentage terms.
- Job costing.
- Tax preparation.
- Tax planning.
- Departmental control and analysis.
- Entity statistics for evaluation and reporting purposes.
- Generation of data files compatible with certain statistical packages for conducting regression analysis and other statistical procedures. (Here, a single data file may be utilized for multiple applications.).
- Marketing aspects, such as product line evaluation by market share, revenue and costs by geographic area, and sales by customer.

When utilizing spreadsheets, the controller should be concerned with the reliability of the input and output data, program support, verification methods, and ability to detect operating bugs. Even the smallest error in a spreadsheet application can mushroom into a disastrous situation. The more complicated the formula or data, the greater the likelihood of input error. Potential errors include the rounding of numbers, the incorrect order of arithmetic functions, and the incorrect order of cell calculation and recalculation. Formula development can also result in errors, as when an absolute formula should have been entered as a relative formula. Macros, in which a single keystroke invokes a series of commands, if incorrectly structured, may also result in spreadsheet problems. Similarly, problems may arise when linking or consolidating financial spreadsheets as well as when data are transferred from one source to another.

According to research from the University of Hawaii, between 78% and 97% of spreadsheets contain serious material errors with a potential to devastate the bottom line. The evidence is as follows:

- A number incorrectly recorded in a cell of a spreadsheet meant one company had to drastically reduce its fourth quarter outlook. Thus, its shares lost more than 25% of their value.
- A cut-and-paste error led to another company underbidding for an electricity supply contract.
- A missing minus sign caused a fund's projected earnings to be overstated by $2.6 billion.
- Falsely linked spreadsheets covered up a fraud totaling $700 million at one bank.

- A faulty macro delayed the introduction of a drug, savaging a pharmaceutical company's profits.

- A wrongly named spreadsheet led to the inflation of natural gas prices in the U.S. when one company submitted erroneous gas storage figures.

To avoid serious errors, such as these, spreadsheets should be the responsibility of the IT Department, so they receive the same development, testing, and control procedures as other computer applications.

In order to avoid errors or at least mitigate the effects of such errors, the controller should:

- Establish the objectives to be accomplished.

- Rectify all problems immediately upon discovery, especially those involving circular reasoning.

- Separate data from formulas.

- Specify information that is to be imported into a spreadsheet as text rather than as numbers.

- Skillfully develop a template plan including purpose, required input, and desired output.

- Place data in either a row or a column instead of both.

- Construct a template as simply as possible, creating small sections of the model and testing them before combining them with other portions of the template.

- Use parentheses in establishing the order of calculations.

- Make commands as simple as possible in order to prevent misinterpretation errors and difficulty in revision.

- Scan the entire spreadsheet, considering the formulas and the interrelationship of particular cells.

- Watch for error messages in cell references.

- Periodically test spreadsheet results by comparing them with manual calculations.

- Audit spreadsheets for mathematical errors as well as models containing judgmental errors.

- Decompose long formulas and complex macros.

- Evaluate the reasonableness of the assumptions and approach to the solution.

- Calculate sample variables to ascertain their validity.

- In a blank spreadsheet cell, test internally developed macros for reliability.

- Provide for sufficient backup.

- Avoid errors in entering data; in constructing formulas and macros, utilize pointing rather than typing. Accordingly, it is best to point to cells or ranges to indicate them in formulas and macros in lieu of typing cell addresses.

- Ensure that only authorized individuals use the spreadsheet program and the files created with the program.

- When creating or utilizing the spreadsheet, verify its validity section by section instead of checking the worksheet in its entirety at the end of its creation or use.

- Verify that the correct version of the spreadsheet is being used.

- Exercise caution with simultaneous equations and iterative calculations. The number of iterations must be accurately estimated in order to calculate a simultaneous equation reliably. Overestimation may result in wasted time; underestimation may result in an incorrect conclusion.

- When columns and rows are moved to different locations, define names for cell ranges in order to lower the probability of cell reference mistakes.

- To guard against cell destruction, consider cell protection.

- Ensure that an environmental section of the spreadsheet contains information regarding the template's configuration, such as variable names, data values, and cell locations or ranges.

- Provide for output documentation of cell locations of the report and printing guidelines.

- Have assurance that templates conform to the independent accountant's policy on structure and documentation.

- If a template uses data from other spreadsheets, provide for a proper interface between the cells of both spreadsheets.

GRAPHICS (PRESENTATION) SOFTWARE

An important attribute of a controller is the ability to communicate vital information to management, shareholders, and other interested third parties.

Presentations are more impressive when graphics are incorporated. Graphics-based presentations are often more comprehensible, more powerful, and more convincing than presentations without graphics.

Graphics software, such as *Microsoft Powerpoint and Excel*, express numeric information in graphic form, including charts, diagrams, and signs. Graphs can be converted into photographic slides, overhead transparencies, and images on paper. Absolute amounts (e.g., totals and increases, percentages, dollars, and units) can be illustrated. Rates of increase and trends can also be depicted. Presentation designed to impress the viewer may be multicolored. Software that allows freestyle drawing is more useful for imaginative enhancements. Structured programs, on the other hand, are better in clarifying a simple chart.

Accounting graphics can capture complex data collections, portray relationships between different numbers, and present them immediately and dramatically. Graphics can be used to evaluate trends and make superior decisions.

Types of graphics include the following:

- Bar graphics—stacked, horizontal, and three-dimensional.
- Line graphs.

- Area graphs.
- Pie graphs.
- High-low-close charts.
- Bubble charts, which depict the relative values of items by size and position of circles (bubbles) in a coordinate range.
- Surface area charts.
- Scatter diagrams.
- Spherical diagrams.

Graphics may be useful to controllers in creating displays for

- Charting revenue and costs by product line, market share, and customer.
- Analyzing trends in major expense categories.
- Analyzing trends in capital expenditures.
- Performing break-even analysis.
- Depicting variance between budgeted and actual amounts.
- Appraising backlog figures.
- Reflecting personnel statistics, such as the number of employees and productivity measures.

While the features included in graphics packages vary, selection of the appropriate package should be, in part, based on:

- Compatibility with other packages and applications.
- User-friendliness, including menu options and help functions.
- The maximum number of actions and symbols included.
- The maximum number of columns and rows in charts, automatic overlapped column specifications, and three-dimensional columns.
- The maximum number of bars.
- Included and available image libraries, which allow the merging of pictures with a chart or other image.
- Formatting aspects, such as screen resolution display and multiple sizes of graphs.
- The ability to modify predefined or drawn images.
- Editing abilities pertaining to titles, labels, and graph types.
- The ability to adjust plot orientation and page size.
- The ability to rotate graph axes.
- Types of graphs supported.
- Printing features such as bold type, underlining, pattern handling, and multiple copies.
- The existence of chart legends.
- Extent of color choice.

DATABASE MANAGEMENT SOFTWARE

A database is an organized collection of readily accessible related information that may be used on a recurring basis by the corporate controller.

Database management (DBM) software, such as *Microsoft Access*, may be useful in numerous applications, including accounts receivable and inventory monitoring.

Database software allows the controller to enter, manipulate, retrieve, display, extract, select, sort, edit, and index data. DBM software packages define the structure of collected data, design screen formats for data input, handle files, and generate reports. DBM software permits the creation of financial statement formats and the performance of arithmetic calculations. In essence, a database is an electronic filing cabinet providing a common core of information accessible by the programs. Programs and applications may be customized by specifying the data to be entered and what should be done to it in order to generate the desired output.

Of the different types of DBM software, the relational database manager software appears to be the most popular and useful. A relational database manager has data sets of information in a table of rows and columns (i.e., matrix). Information is stored in two-dimensional data sets or tables similar to a traditional file processing system. The reports produced from this type of database can have greater complexity and utility than those generated from other types of database systems.

A relational database allows for the access of data fields by enabling the user to ignore the traditional one-to-one relationship and permitting access to a particular grid or cell. For example, if a relational data base includes first and last names of customers as well as their street addresses, cities, states, zip codes, area codes, and telephone numbers, data can be accessed by specifying any one of these parameters.

The basic operations possible with relational DBM software include:

- Creating or deleting tables and attributes.
- Copying data from one table to another.
- Retrieving or questioning a table or attribute.
- Printing, reorganizing, or reading a table.
- Combining tables based on a value included in a table.
- Manipulating data in creative ways.

DBM software may be used by the controller for a multitude of applications, including the following:

- Retrieving information based on varied criteria. For instance, check information may be recalled based on date of issuance, payee, amount, or account posted to. This may assist in the internal audit function.

- Searching for accounting records possessing a key word or amount, such as listing accounts that are in excess of 90 days past due.
- Establishing upper and lower limits, as in the case of customer credit limits. Internal auditor selection of accounts receivable and payable for confirmation may be enhanced.
- Calculating specified fields, as in the case of footing and extending inventory listings.
- Developing statistical information, including variances.
- Preparing forecasts and projections that are often based on hypothetical assumptions.
- Performing analytical procedures when applying audit procedures.
- Generating lists to control preparation and submission of reports.
- Preparing payroll and reporting.
- Monitoring inventory.
- Preparing general and subsidiary ledgers.
- Analyzing potential investments. A database can store information on thousands of companies, which the company may want to track before making an investment.
- Creating and updating mailing lists.
- Performing tax planning and preparation.

ACCOUNTING SOFTWARE

Because the controller is responsible for the timely recording of accounting data as well as the preparation of reliable books, records, and financial statements, he or she should be concerned with the efficiency and effectiveness of the accounting system. The use of accounting software can greatly enhance the likelihood of accounting efficiency and effectiveness.

Today, a purchaser may acquire individual accounting modules or an integrated package. Smaller businesses may need only a single module, such as a general ledger package, whereas a larger business often needs several modules. Integrated accounting packages link a number of modules performing related tasks by enabling the transfer of data from one module to another, thereby eliminating the need to enter data repetitively. For example, the update of accounts payable automatically updates general ledger control accounts.

In determining the software that should be acquired, consideration should be given to the following:

- Ability to set up and integrate.
- Maximum number of accounts.
- Capability to account for separate departments, segments, and divisions.
- Versatility, reliability, and ease of use.
- Ability to produce a printed audit trail.

- Interface abilities which include on-screen prompts.
- Existence of security, including multilevel password protection.
- Ability to identify and correct errors that arise during input, processing, and output.
- Inclusion of recovery instructions.
- Accommodation for standard and customized financial and accounting reports and schedules.
- Ability to transfer files to hard disk.
- Ability to convert files to a format that is compatible with spreadsheet and data base management programs.
- Inclusion of a standardized and modifiable chart of accounts.
- Ability to prepare bank reconciliations.
- Ability to produce budgets.
- Ability to retain transaction detail as required by the entity.
- Provision for recurring monthly journal entries, thus eliminating the need to enter identical information repetitively.
- Ability to provide account history analysis.
- Recognition of out-of-balance entries, which should not be posted.
- Support for nonfinancial data such as square footage and personnel statistics that might be used in cost allocations.
- Handling of multiple open periods.
- Extra features, including but not limited to, the preparation of mailing lists and multiple inventory pricing.
- Preparation of exception reports.
- Industries accommodated by the program.

General Ledger Module

Small organizations commonly require only the general ledger module. For large organizations, this module typically represents the nucleus of the entire accounting system. The general ledger module usually produces a chart of accounts, a variety of journals, a trial balance, a general ledger, and, if report writing capabilities are incorporated, a complete set of financial statements, including the statement of cash flows. Flexibility is a key, because every company's accounting and reporting needs are different. Accordingly, it is crucial that the system and report formats be capable of being customized. As in all software, controls should be incorporated.

The controller should keep in mind that, if other modules are to be integrated presently or possibly in the future, incompatibility between software manufacturers might present a problem. In selecting a general ledger module, the controller should specifically consider:

- General ledger balancing.
- Number of accounts allowed.

- Account number format, which should provide for alpha and numeric conditions.
- Number of journal entries accepted.
- Number of clients, departments, and journals accommodated.
- Maximum dollar amount accepted.
- Ability to handle accrual and other comprehensive bases of accounting, including conversion between different bases.
- Preparation and automatic posting of recurring and reversing entries.
- Ability to keep old accounting periods open.
- Validation of account numbers, zero balances, and input data.
- Editing of journal entries and batch balancing.
- Processing of entries temporarily terminated when specified edit criteria are not satisfied.
- Preparation of exception reports.
- Provision for multilevel subsidiary accounts.
- Ability to open previously closed accounting periods.
- Online inquiry pertaining to user-designated accounts.
- Ability to perform such analytical procedures as comparison of actual amounts to budgeted and prior-period amounts.
- Report generation on demand as well as at the end of an accounting period.
- Provision for automatic backup of files.
- Allowance of departmental reporting, multicompany reporting, and consolidation.
- Allocation of designated expenses.
- Ability to interface with other programs, thereby eliminating unnecessary data entry. For example, it is important to have the ability to transfer account balances to a tax return preparation package. If this feature is not present, a bridge between the programs can often be purchased or developed.

Accounts Receivable Modules

Larger organizations often have significant amounts of sales transactions. In these cases, tracking, reconciling, and aging receivables are crucial. An accounts receivable module can easily accomplish these tasks as well as assist in cash flow planning and the granting of credit. In selecting an accounts receivable module, consideration should be given to the following:

- Types of receivables accommodated.
- Number of customers and general ledger accounts permitted.
- Customer number structure.
- Maximum dollar amount for an individual transaction.

- Number of invoices that may be generated.
- Number of payments that may be accepted.
- Number of lines per invoice and statement.
- Ability to print invoices and statements with suppression for accounts with zero balances.
- Capability of verifying customer information before processing.
- Determination of customer balances.
- Application of cash payments to appropriate accounts and invoices.
- Proper adjustment of customer accounts.
- Summarizing and detailing journal entries.
- Ability and number of recurring entries.
- Generation of a subsidiary ledger.
- Ability to generate aging analyses.
- Assignment of statement cycle codes to customers having different credit attributes; for example, a company may mail statements to corporate customers monthly as opposed to biweekly mailings for noncorporate customers.
- Comparison of individual accounts to credit limits.
- Preparation of debit and credit memos.
- Automatic calculation of finance charges, discounts, sales commissions, and late payment penalties.
- Flexible billing.
- Batch balancing and control information.
- Ability to interface with the existing general ledger module.
- Ability to forecast cash flow.
- Generation of sales analyses by salesperson, customer, and territory.
- Automatic preparation of sales tax returns.
- Ability to accept credit card charge accounts.
- Generation of mailing labels.

Accounts Payable Modules

An accounts payable module is essential when numerous checks are written. The accounts payable module should be flexible so as to permit daily, weekly, semi-monthly, or monthly check preparation. This provides assurance that all payments are made in time to secure vendor discounts.

The controller should carefully evaluate the features of an accounts payable module, which should:

- Accommodate a more-than-sufficient number of vendors, vouchers, checks, and invoices.
- List vendors alphabetically.

- Generate a vendor log.
- Provide supplier numbers.
- Create and account for debit and credit memos.
- Calculate discounts and finance charges.
- Detail and summarize journal entries.
- Accommodate recurring entries.
- Identify duplicate vendor invoices.
- Generate a check register.
- Enable printing of checks.
- List uncleared checks.
- Pinpoint frequency and amounts of payments and payables.
- Provide for entry of hand-drawn checks.
- Permit partial and automatic payments.
- Be capable of canceling an invoice approved for payment prior to payment.
- List recurring checks.
- List and account for voided checks.
- Prepare a schedule of cash requirements due on a particular date.
- Generate a due date register.
- Analyze vendors.
- Track lost discounts.
- Compare receiving reports with supplier invoices.
- Select items to be paid.
- Permit entry of purchase orders.
- Permit updating of purchase orders.
- Generate a list of open purchase orders by vendor and item.
- Require proper authorization for payments.
- Offer multilevel password protection.
- Provide a clear audit trail.
- Restrict access to checks.
- Provide a check log detailing ranges of check numbers and voided checks.
- Interface with the general ledger module.
- Satisfy tax reporting requirements.
- Provide any required miscellaneous vendor information.

Payroll Modules

The decision to utilize a payroll module should be based on the cost/benefit relationship. Unless there are numerous employees, a payroll module is usually not justified. Manual processing of a small payroll is typically accomplished efficiently and effectively. When there are few employees, and manual processing is not desired, an inexpensive alternative is to use an outside payroll preparation service.

When payroll computation and accounting become complicated, such as when there are multiple user-defined pay types and voluntary deductions, the use of a payroll module is quite feasible. Fundamental considerations in selecting a payroll module include:

- Types of payroll information provided.
- Personnel statistics.
- Maximum payroll dollar amount.
- Maximum number of employees supported.
- Types of employee information stored on master files.
- Hourly rate support.
- Pay period(s) supported.
- Payroll payment ceiling amount.
- Number and types of payroll deductions accommodated.
- Format of payroll register.
- Ability to generate check register.
- Ability to print checks and perform check reconciliation.
- Handling of voided checks.
- Treatment of payroll advances.
- Ability to modify withholding tables upon enactment of new laws.
- Detail and summary journals supported.
- Ability to handle supplemental pay provisions, such as bonuses.
- Support for overtime calculations.
- Types of payroll reports and summaries.
- Provision for sick and vacation pay.
- Support for direct deposit arrangements.
- Generation of mailing labels.
- Interface with general ledger modules.
- Ability to allocate payroll amounts to various income statement accounts.
- Support for tax calculations and reports for federal, state, and city government agencies.
- Multilevel password protection.
- Ability to set up deposits to be made at the company's bank.

Inventory Modules

Considerations pertaining to the selection of an inventory module relate to inventory management and reporting and include:

- Master files for inventory, related customers, and suppliers.
- Number of inventory items handled.

- Types of inventory records, including balances listed by item and category.
- Inventory transactions for receipts, issuances, returns, and allowances.
- Ability to interface with purchase and sales orders.
- Ability to compare packing slips to purchase orders for quantity and part verification.
- Interfacing with job cost accounting systems.
- Reflection of in-transit inventory.
- Bin location.
- Reconciliation of promised date of delivery with actual delivery date.
- Support for warehouse information.
- Generation of printed receiving stubs.
- Comparison of perpetual records to physical quantities.
- Data entry error detection.
- Variance analysis for inventory discrepancies.
- Ability to keep multiple periods open.
- Transferability of inventory items from one location to another.
- Calculation of economic order quantity and economic order point.
- Calculation of lead time in acquiring inventory items.
- Determination of safety stock.
- Preparation of shortage reports.
- Variable lot sizes.
- Calculation of inventory turnover and age of inventory items in order to identify slow-moving and obsolete inventory items.
- Monitoring of shrinkage.
- Cost accounting capabilities.
- Preparation of back-order reports.
- Reports identifying missing inventory tags.

Fixed Asset Modules

A fixed asset module should be capable of the following:

- Describing and categorizing fixed assets.
- Accepting a sufficient number and amount of fixed assets.
- Providing information pertaining to cost, estimated life, and salvage value.
- Utilizing different depreciation methods.
- Calculating depreciation and accumulated depreciation for both financial and tax reporting purposes.
- Calculating pro rata amounts.

FORECASTING AND STATISTICAL SOFTWARE

Numerous computer software packages are used for forecasting purposes. They are broadly divided into two major categories: (1) forecasting software and (2) general purpose statistical software. Some programs are templates, whereas others are spreadsheet add-ins. Still others are stand-alone. A brief summary of these three types of software follows.

Templates

A template is a worksheet or computer program that includes the relevant formulas for a particular application, but not the data. It is a blank worksheet that is saved to be filled in with the data as needed for a future forecasting and budgeting application. Most templates are spreadsheet templates used in an Excel application that produces sales and financial forecasts, even for new products with limited historical data. They offer a variety of forecasting methods (e.g., moving averages, exponential smoothing, trend analysis, decomposition of time series, regressions) for accurate forecasts. Built-in macros can be used to enter data—such as values for the first and last months of a 12-month forecast—into a forecast automatically. The compounded-growth-rate macro will automatically compute and enter values for the other ten months.

Add-Ins

Many add-ins are available that:

- Use a variety of forecasting techniques and include both automatic and manual modes.
- Eliminate the need to export or reenter data.

Add-ins can be used in either automatic or manual mode. In automatic mode, the historical data, such as sales, expenses or net income, are first highlighted in the spreadsheet. The program then tests several exponential smoothing models and picks the one that best fits the data.

Forecast results can be transferred to the spreadsheet with upper and lower confidence limits. They generate a line graph showing the original data, the forecasted values, and confidence limits. The type of trend (constant, linear, or dampened) as well as the seasonality (nonseasonal, additive, or multiplicative), can be varied.

Stand-Alone Programs

There are an abundance of stand-alone packages that are much more powerful than templates or add-ins. Some business software uses artificial intelligence. A built-in expert system examines the data and then guides the user to exponential smoothing, Box-Jenkins, or regression—whichever method suits the data best. In addition to allowing the use of all major forecasting methods, packages permit analysis of the data, suggest available forecasting methods, compare results, and provide several accuracy measures in such a way that it is easier for the user to select an appropriate method and forecast data under different economic and environmental conditions.

Numerous statistical software packages can be used to build a forecasting model. Examples are SAS, SPSS, and Minitab.

Note: A personal computer with a spreadsheet is a good beginning, but the stand-alone packages provide the most accurate forecasts and are the easiest to use.

CASH FLOW FORECASTING SOFTWARE

Computer software allows for day-to-day cash forecasting and management, determining cash balances, planning and analyzing cash flows, finding cash shortages, investing cash surpluses, accounting for cash transactions, automating accounts receivable and payable, and dial-up banking. Computerization improves availability, accuracy, timeliness, and monitoring of cash information at minimal cost. Daily cash information aids in planning how to use cash balances. It enables the integration of different kinds of related cash information, such as collections on customer accounts and cash balances, and the effect of cash payments on cash balances.

Spreadsheet program software such as *Microsoft's Excel* can help in developing cash budgets and answering a variety of what-if questions. For example, the user can see the effect on cash flow from different scenarios (e.g., the purchase and sale of different product lines).

Some computer software packages are specially designed for cash forecasting and management. These packages generally contain automatically prepared spreadsheets for profit/loss forecasts, cash flow budgets, projected balance sheet, payroll analysis, term loan amortization schedule, sales/cost of sales by product, ratio analysis, and graphs. Data is input into different categories, such as sales, cost of sales, general and administrative expenses, long-term debt, other cash receipts, inventory buildup/reduction, capital expenditures (acquisition of long-term assets, such as store furniture), and income tax. The program allows changes in assumptions and scenarios, providing a complete array of reports.

VALUE CHAIN MANAGEMENT SOFTWARE

Firms employ a wide variety of software systems to process information and improve the operation of the value chain. They are enterprise resource planning (ERP), supply chain management (SCM), and customer relationship management (CRM) systems.

Enterprise Resource Planning Systems

Enterprise resource planning (ERP) systems grew out of material requirements planning (MRP) systems, which have been used for more than 20 years. MRP systems computerized inventory control and production planning; and key features included an ability to prepare a master production schedule, a bill of materials, and generate purchase orders. ERP systems update MRP systems with better integration, relational databases, and graphical user interfaces. Features now include supporting accounting and finance, human resources, and various e-commerce applications, including SCM and CRM.

ERP Selection Criteria Checklist

Selecting an ERP application can be a time-consuming process for IT/IS managers to assess application vendors, then compare what they are offering to the organization's needs. The following checklist will help to expedite this process and ensure that all important details are addressed.

Database and network

- How many user licenses are required?
- Is the ERP designed to work with different relational database management systems (RDBMS), such as Oracle, Sybase, and Informix?
- Does the vendor have any built-in programs to handle integration?
- How will the data warehousing aspects be addressed?
- What is the maximum time required for uploading the remote data?
- What is the minimum time required for uploading the remote data?
- Does the software support distributed data processing?
- Does the software support a parallel processing option?
- Has the vendor had any problems in the past regarding concurrency?
- Does the software have an audit trail on key transactions?
- How many security layers have been incorporated into the software?
- What kind of networking protocols does the software support?
- Does the software support LONG and BLOB data types?
- What is the largest database the vendor has handled for the modules of interest?
- What is the smallest database size handled by the vendor for the modules of interest?

Implementation

- Has the vendor implemented sites in this region?
- Has the vendor implemented ERP in your industry segment?
- Has the vendor implemented the same modules that your organization needs?
- Will there be immediate delivery of the product?
- Does the vendor have a specific implementation plan?
- How long did it take for the vendor to implement the same modules elsewhere?
- How many years of experience does the vendor have with implementation?
- Does the vendor have good project plan initiatives?

- Does the vendor have a good implementation team with the required skills?
- Does the vendor have the Certification of Excellence given by other customers?
- What is the minimum implementation time for the modules you have chosen?
- What is the maximum implementation time for the modules you have chosen?

Business processes

- Does the vendor promise any reduction in lead times of those business processes in which you have some interest?
- What is the minimum processing time for material requirement planning (MRP)?
- What is the maximum processing time for MRP?
- What is the minimum processing time for master production schedule (MPS)?
- What is the maximum processing time for MPS?
- Does the software optimize the business processes after implementation?
- Does the software use a built-in business process modeler?

Hardware and software

- What kind of hardware support does the vendor offer?
- How many years of experience does the vendor have with the hardware/software that will be used for your project?
- Who are the alliance partners for the hardware support?
- What is the upgrade support for the software?
- Does the software have any interface to support the latest technology?
- How is the vendor maintaining the documentation for the software?
- Is the software Web-enabled?
- Will the software be implemented in modules?
- Will the software be purchased in modules?
- Will the software accounting adhere to international standards and to each country's standards?
- How many operating systems does the software support?
- Does the software allow transactions to be posted both in batch mode and online?
- Does the software support a multilingual operation?

Support

- What support will the vendor provide after implementation?
- If the vendor is out of the country, how is support provided?
- How much time will the vendor devote to ERP training for end users?
- Describe the user interface (UI)/graphical user interface (GUI) package support and how each will give end users ease of operation.
- Did the vendor complete any customization at any previously implemented sites? (Describe by percent and module.)
- How will the vendor complete the reports' customization?
- Does the software have any built-in programs to handle data conversions?
- Is the front-end application developed using proprietary software?
- Is the customization cost included in the ERP cost?
- Can the vendor give approval for accessing other customers' data?
- Does the vendor have any test data built into the software for proper training?
- If any bugs are found in the software during or after implementation, what is the replacement support?
- Is the vendor prepared to work with third-party tools and software?

Supply Chain Management Systems

Supply chain management (SCM) is the organization of activities between a company and its suppliers in an effort to provide for the profitable development, production, and delivery of goods to customers. By sharing information, production lead times, and inventory holding costs have been reduced, while on-time deliveries to customers have been improved. SCM software systems provide support in filling orders and tracking products and components among companies in the supply chain.

Wal-Mart and Procter & Gamble (P&G) are two companies that have become well known for their cooperation in the use of SCM. When P&G products are scanned at a Wal-Mart store, P&G receives information on the sales via satellite and, thus, is able to meet demand on a timely basis by shipping additional products as necessary to specific store locations. Related cost savings are passed on, at least in part, to Wal-Mart customers.

Customer Relationship Management Systems

Customer relationship management (CRM) systems automate customer service and support. They provide for customer data analysis and support e-commerce storefronts. In its evolution, CRM has already led to some remarkable changes in the way companies interact with customers. For example, Federal Express allows customers to track their packages on the Web. Although this service is becoming commonplace, it did not exist 10 years ago. Amazon.com uses CRM technology to offer product suggestions to customers based on their personal purchase histories. The ultimate development of CRM remains to be seen but, undoubtedly, mobile communication will play a significant role. Many companies are experimenting with systems to send messages to cell phone users, offering them special discounts and buying opportunities.

CRM systems are designed to manage all customer-related data, such as marketing, field service, and contact management. In the past year, CRM has become the primary focus of IS managers and CIOs responsible for prioritizing new systems acquisitions. CRM has also attracted ERP vendors, who realize the need to tap into this growing market and integrate CRM data with other data residing within the ERP system's database.

The concept behind CRM is that efficient customer service results in satisfied customers and increased sales, particularly repeat sales. Contact management facilitates recording and storing information related to each contact between a salesperson and a client and the context of the conversation or meeting. Information is also recorded each time a client contacts the company with queries or service help. This collection of individual client information can better equip a salesperson to provide targeted products and services to each client. These systems can also obtain additional client information such as a spouse's name, children, and hobbies, to help facilitate the salesperson's goal of making quality contact with the customer.

In addition, the software supports organizing and retrieving information on historical sales activities and promotions planning. This facilitates matching sales promotions with customer buying trends. This is a particularly crucial area for integration with an existing ERP system because much of the information necessary to support sales analyses is based on data captured during the recording of sales event data in the ERP system.

A third area that is prevalent in CRMs is customer service support, particularly for phone operators handling customer support call-in centers. For many organizations, phone operators who have not had previous contact with customers handle the majority of customer service activities. The CRM quickly provides the phone operator with the customer's historical information and usually links the operator with a database of solutions for various problems the customer may be inquiring about. These solutions may simply be warranty or contract information, or at a more complex level, solutions to operations or maintenance problems on machinery or equipment. All of this information can be efficiently stored for quick retrieval by the system's user.

Note: In today's mobile environment, phones, PDAs, and other devices will be connected by a variety of wireless technologies and will become mandatory for corporate communications with customers and employees. Mobile applications provide companies with new opportunities for interacting with customers. Adding mobility and immediacy to an application can be powerful. It offers the potential for new products and services, business process improvements, cost savings, and improved response times.

THE CFO'S VIEW OF INFORMATION TECHNOLOGY: A CURRENT SURVEY

According to a 2010 joint survey conducted by Gartner and Financial Executives Research Foundation (FERF) (www.gartner.com), more IT organizations report to the CFO than the CEO or any other executive. Forty-two percent of IT organizations surveyed said they reported to the CFO, and 53% of CFOs said that they would like to move to this reporting arrangement. In 41% of organizations, the senior financial executives (mostly CFOs) who responded to the survey viewed themselves as being the main decision maker for IT investments. This response occurred in most situations where IT reports to the CFO, but it also occurred in other reporting models. In another 34%, CFOs are among the key recommending/sponsoring executives. Thus, in 75% of firms, the CFO plays a vital role in determining IT investment. In addition, 20% of CFOs have a minor role of providing some input, and in only 5% of cases the CFO does not participate in IT decision making. In most organizations, the CFO and CIO work together to finance IT and provide information that supports financial processes, but there is also an opportunity for them to form a powerful alliance that can generate more value for their firm. "The CFO and CIO are well-positioned to work together at generating superior performance from the enterprise."

The major findings of the study are summarized below.

1. **The CFO may have more influence in technology decisions than the CIO.** Increased attention is being paid to technology investment by CFOs. Technology decisions are made by a combined team of CIO and CFO staff in 27% of organizations. The CFO is the primary decision maker in 18% of organizations, while 11% of organizations have the CIO making the majority of decisions.

2. **CFOs consider Web 2.0, Web-oriented software, cloud computing, and social networking to be leading technologies.** For the second year in a row, Web-oriented software was viewed as the top technology to affect the finance organization. Cloud computing ranked second and social networking ranked third.

3. **CFOs view ERP projects as successful.** We often hear that ERP projects are costly and have not met objectives. However, the survey shows that ERP implementations have been more positive, with 54% giving their completed ERP projects a successful rating.

4. **CFOs promote 'return to growth' projects. Eight six percent of organizations are willing to invest in technologies that demonstrate a competitive advantage.** Seventy percent are deferring some projects as a strategy to control costs in IT, 21% have stopped projects in progress, and only 8% are halting all enhancement activity.

5. **CFOs prioritize data quality.** Problems with the quality of data often negate the benefits of investment in business intelligence and analytics, leading to poor decisions. Although 51% have no formal initiatives to

improve data quality, almost all the respondents indicated they are pursuing one-off approaches to improve the integrity of their information

6. **CFOs do not see XBRL benefits.** eXtensible Business Reporting Language (XBRL) is now a requirement for all publicly traded companies in the United States. However, most companies have taken an outsourcing approach. Organizations were asked how they plan to use XBRL. Employing it for internal reporting could significantly improve results reporting. But 37% plan to use it solely for external reporting. Five percent plan to use it for internal reporting.

7. **CFOs in North America are not acting on IFRS.** Recently, the SEC announced a proposed move to international financial reporting standards (IFRS), the standard used by more than 100 countries. However, 76% have not begun planning for IFRS, despite a potential 2014-16 requirement. Most respondents (80%) do not see any benefit from conversion to IFRS. Not surprisingly, only 8% have engaged the IT organization in IFRS planning. This is a problem, because most organizations will need to do some work on their financial management systems.

8. **CFOs view profitability management as the top technological constraint.** Most organizations have difficulty understanding profitability at anything other than at an aggregate corporate level. Twenty percent of respondents viewed measuring product and customer profitability as the top constraint.

9. **CFOs improve on business intelligence and corporate performance management in 2010.** Although most organizations (72%) consider management and financial information to be consistent, 27% believe there are significant issues that require manual intervention. This was an improvement over 2009, when the results were 62 and 38%.

10. **CFOs see outsourcing and shared services opportunities.** Outsourcing of accounting services will increase 24% in the next 3-5 years, while shared services will increase 23% in the same period. As finance seeks to transform itself to a more valued business partner from a transaction processor, CFOs should look to these opportunities to improve efficiency and free resources. CFOs can use the results of this study to benchmark their organization and form a baseline for improvements to the CIO/CFO partnership.

CHAPTER 5

DATABASE MANAGEMENT SYSTEMS, THE CLIENT/SERVER ENVIRONMENT, AND CONTINGENCY PLANNING

CONTENTS

The corporate controller needs to access a database because it includes accumulated interrelated records of different types of files. The stored information provides the financial manager with sufficient data to make an informed decision. Where there is a logical order to the stored information, like data can be clustered. For example, revenue and cost data may be kept and retrieved in sequential order in department and division order. When there is simultaneous accessing of the database by more than one financial person or application, the financial manager, in looking at the database file, can view an accumulation of related records explaining a subject by using a field set.

A database management system (DBMS) refers to the software that manages and controls the database. Typically, the database is on a server. Financial managers can define, create, modify, and maintain the database. The standard query language (SQL) is typically used to create and maintain the relational databases, including their access and updating.

A systems catalog lists the data contained in a database. The data may be kept in a text file or a dictionary-like document. The financial manager should be concerned with administering financial information such as managing information resources; developing, designing, planning, and keeping standards; and maintaining policies and procedures.

A network database model comprises interrelated records and data items. The database should furnish a wide range of data to users. It should handle easy questioning, support report writing based on different desired specifications, and process very complex solutions related to decision support systems. A network database model fosters many relationships, such as the association between a vendor's database and the stocking of particular merchandise. The merchandise may be bought from different vendors, and each vendor can sell many types of merchandise.

The financial manager should schedule, in sequential order, database functions or transactions to accomplish a task in the most efficient way. In sequential access, the financial manager selects all records of a particular type.

In a leap file, financial records are in the identical order of insertion. Database files may be subdivided (fragmented) over a number of documents. In replication, there is a duplicating of key elements of the database in different locations and assurance that copies of the information are updated simultaneously.

In a computer-aided manufacturing database, manufacturing-related data is stored, such as data for the production of goods such as appliances.

Sensitivity analysis can be used to determine how output is affected by inputs. Input variables may be modified at the same time to see the impact on outcome. With sensitivity analysis, the relative importance of the various inputs can be determined. A model may be constructed to forecast multiple variables. Experimentation with different combinations of input variables may lead to better overall results. Further, the financial manager should rank variables in the order of importance.

It is possible that data on a particular topic of interest is obtained from different sources. In such cases, the controller should be careful that erroneous conclusions are not drawn when the various sources present similar data in different manners. If data are missing, the controller must be careful if he or she decides to guess at the data left out or use mean, median, or common value figures.

Data conversion software extracts information from heterogeneous sources, transfers the source information to target data, and then derives the programming codes to process it. Data must be carefully checked for consistency to ensure successful processing.

The financial manager should split the database into segments of similar financial records. An example is sales territories having a particular range of sales. In segmentation, the corporate controller may want to break down a larger project into smaller ones for analysis purposes.

In hypothesis testing, the financial manager attempts to prove or disprove an assumption. The hypothesis is proved or not by evaluating information through observation and testing.

This chapter discusses database security, classification of data, object databases, distributed databases, hierarchical databases, multidimensional databases, multimedia databases, meta-data, data warehousing, data marts, data modeling, link analysis, knowledge discovery, market basket analysis, memory-based reasoning, data mining, fuzzy searches, neural networks, online analytical processing, online transaction processing, genetic algorithms, decision trees, and personal information agents.

DATABASE SECURITY

One security solution is Kerberos, a centralized server having secured user names and passwords for all information and resources on the network. Kerberos servers have such security features as login database access and authorization codes. The Kerberos server identifies and validates a user.

It may be advisable to have a secure single login in which users log into the network rather than to each specific server or application. Access is permitted only to authorized resources.

Security of the database may be aided by referential integrity checks, which compare data among tables for appropriateness and logical relationship order. As a security control, financial managers should match the database to the transaction log file. A transaction log is a listing of database transactions, including updates for managing and control purposes.

The security analysis tool for auditing networks (SATAN) reviews the network to spot security weak points. System fault tolerances are networking aspects that safeguard the network from faults. An analytical report indicating problem areas and possible solutions is prepared.

The financial manager should hide sensitive financial information in the database so it is not revealed to unauthorized individuals. To access a database, proper identification such as a password is required. In a database lock, database data cannot be accessed or altered until a transaction has been finalized. A shared lock allows users to read data but not update it.

A time bomb is a virus activated at a particular date or time. Antivirus software must be used.

To ensure that staff are familiar with the security procedures and policies to be adhered to in a DBMS, a control plan should exist. Control-related statements should provide detailed directions to conduct procedures and explain the needs for the security system. Any policy statements should not be subject to short-term modifications. The control plan should be distributed and consistent throughout the company. The plan should have some flexibility so it may be successfully adapted to different parts of the entity that may differ to some degree from one another. The control plan should be periodically reviewed to ensure that any changes in the company's circumstances or improvements in technologies are responded to.

Access to databases containing sensitive information must be restricted to only authorized individuals. Database access should be assigned different levels of confidentiality and security, such as generally accessible data (unrestricted), internal use only, and top secret. Confidential information should not be displayed on computer screens without the appropriate access codes. Employee compliance should be periodically reviewed to ensure that individuals are honoring the controls that have been established. Each database function (e.g., payroll) should require its own password so that employees have access only to the areas that they have been approved and authorized for. Segregation of duties should also exist. For example, to prevent data manipulation, a programmer who modifies or patches a program should not have access to the computer database area or library. Thus, segregation of duties should exist between programmers, installation librarians, operators, data processing personnel, users, and control employees.

The information technology internal auditor should be concerned with the following areas when reviewing the company's database system:

- Monitoring and appraising the company's computer policy and security standards that apply to the database and network.
- Supporting internal auditing functions during operational and compliance audits.

In auditing a typical database system, the IT auditor will review and analyze the following areas of the company's information system:

- Personnel practices applying to the installation.
- Contingency planning and disaster recovery.
- Data center structure.
- Backup controls of the data center.
- Effectiveness and efficiency of operating and administrative procedures.
- Standards of developing the installation.
- Specific control practices.
- Control procedures of the database information library.

The IT auditor is responsible for ensuring that the company's database system controls are in place and properly functioning. To achieve this, the following specific control functions should be watched and appraised by the IT auditor:

- Identification and correction of errors and omissions. However, emphasis should be on preventing these problems in the first place.
- Assurance that jobs are performed in a timely manner.

- Proper approval and authorization of transactions by the appropriate level of management.

- Correctly processed transactions.

- Periodic review of functions with incompatible activities being segregated.

Transaction trails should exist of additions, deletions, or modifications of data processed by the database. Audit trails must be created or made available to provide the IT auditor information regarding (1) the date and time of the transactions, (2) who processed the transactions, and (3) where the transaction was initiated (e.g., terminal). Most database software has the ability to track database transactions.

CLASSIFICATION OF DATA

Data may be classified from the population in similar groups. The classification may be based on a training model. The classes of information are periodically appraised and updated. For example, potential clients can be classified as low risk, medium risk, or high risk. In some cases, the financial manager may start with a training set and build a predictor model on the grouping of new records. For example, credit card customers may be segmented into predefined classes to ascertain to whom to send promotional mailings.

TYPES OF DATABASES

The various types of databases include object, distributed, hierarchical, multimedia, and multidimensional databases. They are described in the following paragraphs.

Object Databases. In an object database management system, objects are stored in a multiuser client/server form. Users can have concurrent access to objects. Objects can be protected from threats and transactions can be safeguarded. The object database management system adds to the traditional database management system the functions of questioning, concurrency, locking, and protection.

Distributed Databases. A distributed database is a collection of tables spread over at least two servers in the company at different locations. With distributed transactions, one transaction gives a sequence of database requests to different remote database servers. This allows for database updating on various servers. A transaction consists of SQL statements, each allowing for the access of data at different locations. In distributed transactions processing, transactions are processed over distributed linked computers in multiple geographically separate locations.

Hierarchical Databases. In a hierarchical database, there is a family tree of related record types. Lower-level records are subordinate to higher-level ones.

Multimedia Databases. Multimedia databases contain abstract unstructured data, such as audio, graphics, video, animation, hypertext, and hypermedia. The multimedia database contains all the information needed to prepare the multimedia item. For example, if a company needs to prepare graphics depicting its sales performance, it will need a database of sales volume and dollars by geographic area, department, and division.

Multidimensional Databases. Multidimensional databases handle multiple "dimensions" of a business that include product, service, geographic locality, customer, client, guest, order, salesperson, and time period. A multidimensional database for a company's products may include time, territory, sales volume, customer, price, vendor, store, and total sales. Data may be appraised using alternative dimensions.

DATA WAREHOUSING

A data warehouse enhances productivity within the controller's department. It provides timely and accurate financial information. The data warehouse organizes and classifies information.

In data warehousing, there is a voluminous database of summarized and detailed interrelated information that may be extracted and analyzed in making financial management decisions. Detailed information may relate to sales, purchases, payables, and receivables. There is a vast accumulation of past and current data. It is updated continuously because data are reliable for a specified time period. This updating may occur through planned batch processing to foster comparative analysis. (However, in some cases, a data warehouse may not be designed to update data immediately and repetitively.) The database is subject oriented and timely. Complex, analytical, and investigative questioning of the data warehouse may solve financial problems. Data warehousing includes data pertaining to payroll, accounting, finance, marketing, and management. Information stored is usually classified by type, such as by product/service line, department, division, sales territory, marketing survey data, suppliers, customers, orders, transactions, physical resource, personnel, or financial resource. A major purpose of the data warehouse is to question a database spread over a multinational company.

The data warehouse allows the company to integrate its cumulative operational information into an accessible means so that forecasts, trends, and strategic decisions may be derived. The financial data of all departments of the company are put into a database that can be managed, controlled, and evaluated.

In data warehousing, there should be integration of extraction, retrieval, cleansing, questioning, and summarizing. For this purpose, meta-data integration software is available.

Data transformation from the data sources to the data warehouse should be well documented. Data going into the data warehouse are from numerous operational databases inside and outside the company. Thus, information is accumulated from sources in different locations. The financial manager should be abreast of the source of the information and how it was modified and transformed. Merged information should be put into a standardized and consistent format to enhance decision making and support. Therefore, there should be a derived commonality in data definition, structure, and relationships. Errors and inconsistencies in the data must be rectified to ensure information quality.

A data warehouse may be used for training purposes.

Data warehousing may be used in internal audits by providing information and analysis to appraise corporate activities and control operations. It fosters an examination of the company's efficiency. Inefficiencies may be indicated by comparing estimated to actual amounts. Areas of fraud, irregularities, and errors may readily be identified. Areas of sensitivity are highlighted.

Marketers may use a customer or guest database to profile individuals who are apt to respond to special incentives. Further, the company may accumulate information regarding buying patterns of their major customers to stimulate purchases by them.

Problems with the quality of goods may be identified by looking at the trend in product returns or allowances due to defective merchandise. An analysis may also be made of buying schedules to ascertain the appropriate times to buy merchandise to take advantage of lower prices and quantity discounts.

Data warehousing can be used by insurance companies to ascertain prospective policyholders who may be underwriting risks.

Divisions doing poorly may be identified. Then either corrective action may be taken or those divisions may be liquidated or sold.

Applications of data warehousing include:

- Measuring the impact of changing prices on product demand.
- Detailing credit standing of a new customer.
- Pricing based on inventory patterns and demand.
- Detecting insurance and warranty claims fraud.

META-DATA

Meta-data describe data kept in the data warehouse, including where they came from, content, and importance. Information flow in and out of the data warehouse is indicated. Therefore, the history of any data may be reconstructed. Meta-data reveal what data are available in the system and their location. As such, meta-data enable financial managers to comprehend the logical data model of the data warehouse. Meta-data allow tracking the data components of the data warehouse, data content, integration and transformation of data, and from where the data were derived. Meta-data involve a review and analysis of where information was extracted, indexing process, statistical analysis, data aggregations, and patterns. For control purposes, meta-data should be well defined, updated, secured, integrated, comprehendible, and documented. Retrieval policies should be specified.

DATA MARTS

A data mart is a data file consisting of logical records. It is an element of a data warehouse furnishing summarized information that can be used in decision making by a department or division manager. The data mart may be either tied to or separated from the entity's centralized data warehouse. Because data marts have much less data than a data warehouse, a data mart is simpler to understand and utilize.

Data marts service the data requirements of particular departments within the organization. A data mart is a subset of a data warehouse that accumulates the information required by a particular department or other responsibility unit, such as a product or service line. Also, a given data mart might be used solely by two or more departments on a shared basis for common requirements.

Information for the data mart is obtained directly from the data warehouse of the overall company. (However, it is possible to construct a data mart as an independent unit with departmental information accumulated just for it.) With a data mart, information may be available more quickly because of a substantially lower transaction volume. Further, the information may be better customized to meet the department's needs. Another benefit of a data mart is that its cost is much lower than that of a data warehouse.

Data marts may be transportable personal warehouses on a laptop to be used by internal auditing staff when auditing branches.

DATA MODELING

Data modeling involves designing and planning a database. In an entity's data model, there is shown important financial information, key relationships between financial data, and the impact of the information on the firm. The financial manager should make use of a data model in explaining information, their interrelations, and limitations. The financial manager wants to fully understand the database. Noted are cases in which data are shared.

In modeling, an output(s) is derived from inputs. In a time series model, the effect of a factor is shown over time, such as the market price of the company's stock based on various changes associated with the company's financial health. In a clustering model, financial records are grouped in terms of similarity. This model would be used, for example, to determine what similar financial characteristics divisions of the company have in common. In a classification model, a record is classified according to some predetermined criteria. New classifications may emerge in addition to old classifications. A prediction model forecasts future results, based on past and current information. The correctness of the model as a predictor should be assessed by comparing what is expected to what actually happens. What is the degree of deviation? The model should be tested over time, any changes should be incorporated as needed.

LINK ANALYSIS

The financial manager should engage in link analysis, which entails looking at the relationship between fields, such as in relating departmental profit to departmental assets. In link appraisal, the financial manager looks at how financial records are related to see what patterns exist. For example, the financial manager may want to know the likelihood that merchandise or services will be purchased together. Also, how are vendors associated and what effect will that have on the company if there is a shortage of raw material? What is the link between customers, lenders, and employee unions?

In link analysis, the corporate controller may find new characteristics associated with financial data. However, the controller should note that link analysis is not as reliable with large data sets as with smaller ones.

KNOWLEDGE DISCOVERY

Knowledge discovery does not involve prior assumptions. The financial manager searches database information so as to draw new views or management conclusions. A knowledge base is a set of information to answer queries and solve business problems. What patterns are evident? There is an emphasis on finding meaningful information. Data are chosen, refined, and put into a useful form. The data are then evaluated to determine what should be investigated further. Based on the results, management will undertake steps to control a problem situation or eliminate a problem. For example, is there a way to attract additional business? Special attention should be given to unusual associations. However, files marked "secure" may not be transferred.

Knowledge discovery helps the financial manager determine who is apt to purchase certain kinds of merchandise.

MARKET BASKET ANALYSIS

The market basket analysis (MBA) method classifies item groupings that take place together in a transaction. MBA is particularly appropriate for numeric and categorical data. The financial manager should examine the likelihood of different goods or services being bought together in some logical order. Thus, MBA can be used to examine multiple buys by a customer or a sales catalog of numerous types of merchandise. Guidelines for this process should be enumerated. Why do customers purchase certain products? Which customers buy multiple products simultaneously and why? MBA also aids in establishing a good advertising and promotion plan.

With MBA, financial managers can better compare sales derived from different geographic areas, such as urban versus suburban. Seasonal differences may be taken into account.

An unexpected combination of insurance claims over a short time period may point to fraud.

MEMORY-BASED REASONING

Under memory-based reasoning (MBR), cases of known events or occurrences are used to predict unknown events or instances. Similar events (neighbors) in prior years are looked at to predict what will happen now. The number of neighbors to use for analysis depends on information distribution and the nature of the problem being evaluated. What was an insurance company's historical experience with the types of claims being submitted now? Did fraud occur in prior years? Were the claims legitimate and immediately paid? MBR can also be used to predict how customers will react to a particular advertisement.

The degree of similarity or dissimilarity between the historical records and current records must be ascertained. What is the distance between the two? The less distance, the more reliable the conclusions drawn.

The training set is the historical records that enable the financial manager to find the nearest neighbors to an unknown (current) record. For useful results to occur, an adequate amount of records by category is necessary. The more neighbors used, the more accurate the conclusions.

The training set should include a sufficient number of occurrences for all possible classifications. Rare instances, such as fraud, should also be included for analytical purposes to arrive at a good balance of usual and unusual occurrences for all categories. Better results are achieved when the training set is voluminous and representative.

DATA MINING

Data mining involves software examining a database to identify patterns, relationships, and trends to assist in financial management decision making. Past and current information are extracted from a voluminous database for analysis. Are there any problem areas requiring corrective action? To be effective, data mining relies on the source data to be accurate, consistent, and integrated. Data mining looks both to confirm expected patterns and to uncover new patterns. Anything unusual, hidden, or unexpected should be investigated.

Data mining allows financial managers to evaluate integrated consistent information for future strategic decisions. However, over time, data mining results may change owing to, say, changing economic and political factors. Data mining results should be reviewed by the controller for common sense and reasonableness. The controller may be able to come up with new ideas, guidelines, yardsticks, and rules. Data mining assists in improving corporate operations and the resulting bottom line.

A data warehouse stores data, while data mining extracts, cleanses, and appraises the information for management decision making. Data mining provides intelligence to a database.

In deciding on the appropriate data mining method suitable in a given situation, the corporate controller should take into account the circumstances, tasks to be performed, nature of input in terms of quality and amount, reliability required, type of output, importance, training desired, available software and data, scalability, and accuracy and understandability of the model.

In actuality, data mining is most advantageous when there is a vast amount of sophisticated and complex information. In data mining, large databases are searched for useful patterns, relationships, and trends. Some of the results ensuing will be expected; others will be unexpected. The corporate controller will continually question the database until a complete financial picture emerges. Any unanticipated patterns should be verified through repeated questioning and evaluation. The controller can refine his or her search by extracting only key information.

Artificial intelligence or statistical methods may be used when searching and evaluating the data warehouse or data marts. Data mining involves clusters, segmentation, grouping, linking, predicting, explaining, and highlighting variances between expected and actual financial figures.

Managerial and financial applications for which data mining may be applied include:

- Determining whether a bank should grant a loan to a particular borrower (and, if so, how much).
- Spotting insurance fraud.
- Noting fraudulent warranty claims and credit card fraud.
- Creating advertising and promotional efforts to maximize sales (including gauging which prospective customers will react best to a specified promotion, or which products or services are most favored by customers in a particular geographic area).
- Evaluating and selecting vendors.
- Analyzing financial statements, including the appraisal of profitability and liquidity.
- Profiling customers based on factors such as buying behavior.
- Selecting stocks and bonds in portfolio management.
- Establishing a credit rating for a loan applicant or customer.
- Pricing products or services.
- Ascertaining the risk level for a new project or proposal.
- Predicting sales.
- Controlling inventory.
- Managing production.
- Detecting questionable patterns of internal funds transfers.
- Ascertaining the degree of customer confidence and commitment.
- Providing customer service.
- Determining which products or services to cross-sell.
- Performing marketing research and planning.
- Finding the reasons products or services sell better in certain markets or to certain customer types.

Other applications include:

- Appraising seasonality issues.
- Deciding on which products to push and when.
- Arranging merchandise in a branch store or sales catalog to generate the most orders.
- Deciding how to best package merchandise.
- Profiling clients and hotel guests.

- Uncovering forgeries in documents.
- Performing quality control, including identifying defective goods purchased from a supplier.
- Determining products a particular class of customer is likely to buy (e.g., young people are more apt to buy sporting merchandise than older individuals).
- Predicting future prices in commodities.
- Forecasting foreign currency exchange rates.
- Performing direct marketing.
- Predicting employee theft.
- Deriving optimal selling techniques.
- Approving credit.
- Developing and retaining employees.
- Deciding on whether to offer discounts for certain products to promote sales.
- Planning store layout to promote business.
- Assessing the possibility of a product or service line failing.
- Determining the merchandise mix in a retail store.
- Projecting profit of a new product or service.
- Forecasting expected profit from a new customer.
- Predicting trading patterns of securities.
- Estimating which hotel guests are likely to return.
- Grouping and classifying customers.
- Selecting the best location for a new store.
- Improving product design.
- Determining customer retention.
- Appraising suppliers.
- Deciding which customers should receive incentives so they do not switch to competitors.
- Efficiently allocating resources.
- Deciding on advertising approaches to maximize orders.
- Determining the best piggyback products.
- Reducing risk.
- Performing demographic analysis.

Numeric variables are good for data mining purposes because they may be totaled and sorted in mathematical computations. An example is costs.

There are many considerations to take into account when selecting data mining software. These include how many data records exist, database access, reporting aspects and requirements, network functioning, simplicity, documentation, graphic support, operating systems, data compatibility, scalability in product and users, technical support, interfaces supported, and organizational fit.

ONLINE ANALYTICAL PROCESSING

Online analytical processing (OLAP) helps financial executives gain a clear perspective on financial information so as to facilitate decision making. It shows patterns and trends evident in financial data.

OLAP techniques are used in accessing voluminous databases, including data stored in a centralized data warehouse, operational system, or virtual distributed warehouse. OLAP extracts information from a data warehouse that is relevant and timely. Many OLAP tools are capable of drilling down into the initial database. The controller is able to get interactive access to a large variety of data views.

In OLAP, why and what-if questions can be asked and answered to improve financial decision making. For instance, the financial manager may wish to find out how the entity's new products have affected its sales over the past three years by major geographic region. There are significant analytical attributes. Data may be evaluated by some predetermined criteria. OLAP is mostly a decision support technique with such beneficial characteristics as links, dimensions, and formulas. With OLAP, the controller is provided with the records answering his or her queries as well as with scenario settings.

Factors that need to be considered in choosing a suitable OLAP tool for a given application include type of software used, conformity to the company's environment, future needs, scalability, questioning capabilities and evaluative techniques, operations to be conducted, performance, and ability to add, delete, or modify data.

In OLAP, multidimensional aggregate data provide fast access to key financial information so it can be properly appraised by the corporate controller. In most cases, corporate controllers examine financial information by product or service line, scenario, geographic area, and time. It is essential that financial executives can appraise data by dimension, function, or aggregation level. Multidimensional OLAP is suitable for financial applications where detailed computations are needed for different products, services, business segments, responsibility units, divisions, and departments of the company. With multidimensional information, financial executives may obtain budgeted compared to actual amounts as well as summarized financial data by product/service line, time, and organization. Sales may be noted by time, product, service, sales price, geographic area, distribution channel, and customer. A typical query in OLAP is, "What are the sales by product, service, customer, quarter, and store?" OLAP can go across various domains—for example, presenting sales in stores and credit card charges.

Financial applications of OLAP include financial forecasting (e.g., sales), retrieval of relevant financial information for decision making from large data sets, budgeting, operating performance analysis, financial modeling, and activity-based costing. In production, OLAP assists in manufacturing planning and uncovering assembly line problem areas. In marketing, OLAP assists with marketing research, market segmentation, customer appraisal, and advertising and promotion.

In evaluating the company compared to competitors, OLAP can be helpful to financial managers by looking at the percentage growth in accounts such as revenue, costs, and assets. Complex and sophisticated relationships can be modeled.

Advantages of OLAP include fast computation and response time, flexibility, interactivity, and easy application. Also, it considers multidimensional data, supplies timely information, and is sound in analyzing time series. Unfortunately, continuous variables are not handled well.

ONLINE TRANSACTION PROCESSING

With online transaction processing (OLTP), transactions are immediately entered. Information has to be accurate and consistent. The nature of processing is repetitive with continual updates. Database integrity should have proper controls. Numerous applications exist, such as inventory control, management control, and collections. OLTP is mostly structured for transactional, repetitive processing instead of unstructured investigative processing. By using OLTP, the financial manager can optimize his or her transaction processing capability associated with such applications as manufacturing, accounting, marketing, and sales. OLTP is application and event driven. Data in OLTP are changing and volatile.

In OLTP, the nature of questioning involves such day-to-day operations as the updating of inventory for buys and sells. At a certain inventory level, a reorder occurs.

THE CLIENT/SERVER ENVIRONMENT

The corporate controller should have some basic familiarity with the client/server environment. There should be a list of authorized users with specified identifications to access certain equipment or information files. Different layers of authorization should exist, depending on the activities to be performed.

A network should be designed to meet corporate goals and purposes. In a client/server arrangement, computers are connected by a network in which some computers (clients) process applications while other computers (servers) provide services (e.g., Internet hosting, file storage) to the clients. Depending on need, it is possible to combine various clients and servers. In-process servers execute in the same processing space as clients.

In a client/server environment, the corporate controller is primarily concerned with issues of functioning, decision making, and security.

FUNCTIONING

Does transparency exist, and if so, to what extent? Transparency is the ability of distributed processing systems to merge clients and servers of different operating systems and protocols into a logical framework that processes distributed applications.

Middleware is the software layer enabling the communication and accessing of information between servers and clients. If differences or irregularities are found, they should be reconciled.

Network traffic may be appraised with a network analyzer. An example is the decoding of data packets. A work flow manager facilitates and monitors multistep data movement through the network. Transaction processing (TP) monitors and polices client/server traffic. It manages transactions from the initiation point, typically on the client, across servers, and then back to the initiating client. TP monitors can run transactions, route and execute transactions, and restart them after failure. If a network management issue needs to be resolved, point products software may be written.

On a periodic basis, equipment and software should be checked as to their proper functioning, including making comparisons to norms. To safeguard the system, one server should substitute for another one that has malfunctioned.

The financial manager may want to make use of a remote procedure call allowing software running on the client to use the services of a program running on the server.

A network management platform (framework) enables integration between a shared database and modules to which alerts and warnings are stored.

There should be global services in which the network operating system can locate a particular user, resource, or server, regardless of location.

With a peer-to-peer network, any computer on the network can act as a server. Local area networks (LANs) accommodate network activities for departments and divisions. To access shared network services and resources, LAN resource management software should be used.

Point-to-point protocol clients are remote clients that are linked to servers operating in different network operating systems.

Financial managers should make use of groupware so that staff can communicate and work together in electronic form, enhancing productivity regardless of location or time.

For the distribution of code and data across clients and servers, mobile agents are used.

DECISION MAKING

An executive information system furnishes data on how the entity is currently conducting its financial and operating functions. It gives management up-to-date information to make better decisions.

The financial manager should be aware of performance metrics, which compare actual performance to established standards. A significant variance is examined for corrective action.

The financial manager should engage in what-if analysis, which is a simulation approach predicting the outcome of changing inputs relative to alternative network scenarios. What-if analysis is undertaken to derive optimal solutions. Network simulation and modeling software are used to look at what-if possibilities associated with the network. Decision support system software allows managers to derive better decisions based on available information. Customization of reports occurs.

In packetizing, management information is added to raw data so that it is properly delivered.

Personal information agents represent mobile applications on the data warehouse. Questions are asked to uncover patterns and unexpected events. Agents are usually rule based and warn if something unusual occurs. A financial manager may use personal information management software to maximize his or her productivity.

SECURITY CONCERNS

The number of data breaches at businesses, government agencies, and educational institutions in the United States increased by nearly 50% in 2011 compared with the number of data breaches occurring in 2010, according to the Identity Theft Resource Center (ITRC) (www.idtheftcenter.org/artman2/publish/lib_survey/ITRC_2008_Breach_List.shtml). The ITRC is a nonprofit organization that supports victims of identity theft and broadens public awareness of the problem. The ITRC has found that hacking accounted for the largest number of breaches in 2011. Almost 37% of breaches were due to malicious attacks on computer systems. This is more than double the amount of targeted attacks reflected in the 2010 ITRC Breach List (17.1%). The most significant key to security is the institutionalization of an enterprise risk management committee composed of leadership from every line of business.

The financial manager should be assured that protective steps have been taken to protect the computer system, such as financial database files. Access to information on the network can be restricted by having a nonprivileged mode.

Encryption equipment can be used to ensure proper security during transmission. Encryption safeguards a message so it cannot be comprehended except if the receiver has a "key" to decipher it. A private key is a shared confidential key used to encrypt or decrypt a message or transmission. In encryption, the plain text of the initial uncoded message is scrambled with an algorithm that has a key to derive unintelligible ciphertext. Further, check sums should be used to provide confidence that data have not been improperly changed while being processed over the network.

There should be a security server keeping security data, such as names and passwords. A password authentication protocol repeatedly transmits user identifications and passwords for authentication reasons. A digital signature (electronic identification) ensures the author's authenticity and the integrity of the communication or message. A digital signature is attached to documents being transferred electronically for security to guarantee that a sender is actually who he or she purports to be. The signature gives assurance that the document has not been changed improperly. Digital signature encryption is public key encryption in reverse. Further, security can be enhanced by using network auditing tools that highlight which users accessed which network files.

Before a server acts on an important client request, the server should substantiate the appropriateness of the request.

There is network filtering software that examines source and destination addresses to determine access. Internal firewalls are filters on the network to ascertain if corporate transmissions on the internal network are authorized. Filter tables list those individuals authorized to proceed through the firewall server into the entity's network. Filter tables may have different levels of access to different file types. With application-level filters, there is additional security by evaluating the whole data request rather than just the source and destination addresses.

There should be workstation-based security software. To monitor suspicious behavior of employees and outside users, intrusion detection software can be used. The financial manager should make use of performance monitoring software, which sets limits for which an overage indicates a problem to be appraised and corrected. There is usually an audit trail.

The financial manager should note the proper values applicable to various data fields. Decoy files may be used and allowed to become infected so as to identify, monitor, and control viruses. In preemptive monitoring, a problem is run on a recurring basis to diagnostically test network traffic and to alert the financial manager if a malfunction is detected. Financial managers must be on guard against polymorphic viruses—those that change their appearance each time infected software is run to make detection more difficult. A Trojan horse is a virus hidden in a legitimate program. Unknown viruses can be identified by running an emulation program. Antivirus software must be used to safeguard data files and programs.

Any out-of-the-ordinary occurrences should be investigated. Event-detection software is used to identify and filter data for such unexpected events.

Security penetration/vulnerability analysis should be conducted periodically to uncover any possible problems. Penetration tools, such as the security analysis tool for auditing networks (SATAN), should be used to try to break into a system to uncover weaknesses in the firewall and router configurations. Automated tools exist to audit the computer system and report potential security weaknesses. Vulnerabilities, such as poor passwords or failure to update software with security patches, are identified.

Vulnerability testing tools search for potential weaknesses that may allow an attacker to gain unauthorized access. Vulnerability tests may audit the system or launch a mock attack. Vulnerability testing programs may be classified according to scope. Their focus may be narrow and they may examine just a single vulnerability, or their emphasis may be broad and they may appraise the whole system.

Access controls should exist to use a specific terminal or application. Data and time constraints along with file usage should be enumerated. Unauthorized use should deactivate or lock a terminal.

DISASTER RECOVERY

Tsunamis, hurricanes, earthquakes, fires, floods, criminal and terrorist acts, and human error can all severely damage an organization's computing resources, and thus the health of the organization. Many companies, especially online e-commerce retailers and wholesalers, airlines, banks, and Internet service providers, for example, are crippled by losing even a few hours of computing power. That is why it is important for organizations to develop *disaster recovery* procedures and formalize them in a *disaster recovery plan.* The plan specifies which employees will participate in disaster recovery and what their duties will be; what hardware, software, and facilities will be used; and the priority of applications that will be processed. Arrangements with other companies for use of alternative facilities that serve as a disaster recovery site and offsite storage of an organization's databases are also part of an effective recovery effort. The purpose of computer security is to protect the information services of the organization as a whole. Information should not be lost, damaged, or modified; it should be readily available to authorized users. It should not be possible to accidentally or intentionally disable the computer system. Contingency planning is a must to minimize a variety of business risks a company may encounter.

CONTINGENCY PLANNING

Contingency planning is a strategy to minimize the effect of disturbances and to allow for timely resumption of activities. The aim of contingency planning is to minimize the effects of a disruption on your organization. A disruption is any security violation, man-made or natural, intentional or accidental, that affects normal operations. Disruptions in computer processing can be classified into three categories:

1. *Malfunction*—Minor disruptions that affect hardware, software, or data files. They are usually narrow in scope, and it is usually possible to recover from them quickly.

2. *Disasters*—Disruptions to the entire facility. They typically require the use of alternate offsite processing facilities to recover operations. Entire facilities may be disrupted for a significant period of time.

3. *Catastrophes*—The most serious type of disruption. In a catastrophe, the facilities may have been destroyed. Alternate facilities are always needed to process data. It may be necessary to rebuild or establish new or permanent facilities.

Rarely will a company face either a disaster or a catastrophe. Malfunctions or other minor failures are likely to be the norm. For minor malfunctions, it is generally more convenient to use onsite backup facilities.

A contingency plan should focus on the continuity of a business. The plan's primary purpose is to reduce the risk of financial loss and enhance an organization's ability to recover from a disruption promptly, at least cost. It should apply to all facets of an organization (i.e., its staff, computer programs, data, workspace, production, and vital records). Contingency planning for an organization's information systems should examine all critical areas, including LANs and WANs, client-server systems, distributed databases, and personal computers.

A common mistake in contingency planning is an excessive focus on *computer* recovery when a *business* recovery plan is needed. Undue emphasis on the technology, rather than the business, is counterproductive. Quick recovery of computer technology is useless if an organization cannot recover its business. Excessive focus on computer technology results in committing too many resources to redundant processing facilities.

A contingency is an event that may or may not occur. The focus of computer security contingency planning is to provide options in case disruption strikes. Recovery from loss of key personnel is usually accomplished through succession planning and backup training. Computer facilities that are typically covered by insurance policies and businesses can generally recover their investment in computers and equipment. But losses in a disaster or catastrophe typically exceed what is recoverable through insurance policies. Some types of losses are uninsurable.

The primary focus of computer security should always be preventive rather than corrective action, though it is impossible to anticipate every problem; even if a problem can be anticipated, the cost/benefit ratio may not justify taking preventive measures. Sometimes precautionary measures may prove ineffective because of human or other error. Productivity and efficiency may also be sacrificed if precautionary measures are too extreme.

Emergency procedures are necessary for each type of potential disaster. One must consider how a disaster may affect data processing and business operations (e.g., how long would service be interrupted or at what level would the company be able to operate).

Organizations are sometimes hesitant about using resources to develop a disaster or catastrophe recovery plan. The probability of a disaster or catastrophe is generally low, and the high costs associated with developing a detailed contingency plan may be a deterrent. Many organizations may feel that the costs exceed the benefits. However, while the probability of a disaster or catastrophe may be low, the cost of being unprepared is high. Most businesses are heavily dependent on computer technology; even a minor interruption could have serious financial consequences.

Contingency planning should provide an organized way to make decisions if there is a disruption. Its purpose is to reduce confusion and enhance the ability of the staff to deal with the crisis. When a disruption occurs, a company does not have the time to deliberate, plan, and organize its recovery. The organization needs to recover quickly. A well-tested, comprehensive recovery plan can save critical time (and therefore money).

CHAPTER 6

USING COMPUTERS IN FINANCIAL DECISION MAKING

CONTENTS

Exhibits

Global competition demands that companies increase their use of computer technology in all areas of financial management, including financial modeling, forecasting, budgeting, and activity-based costing (ABC). Controllers and CFOs are often leading the charge. Because client/server technology increases productivity and improves accessibility to information, more than 40 vendors now offer client/server financial software to meet increased demands on the part of CFOs.

Selecting and implementing the "best" software is a major investment. It has to be the right decision, beginning with the definition of the company's vendor, critical factors, and software critical requirements. Many CFOs and controllers hire a financial software consultant. However, finding a well-versed consultant may be a difficult task. Controllers should try to find unbiased consultants who work full-time in the business of software selection and who make recommendations only.

The Internet, of course, is an ever-increasing phenomenon. FIN*Web*, RISK*Web*, and A-*Net* are popular Internet resources of journals and databases for finance, risk and insurance, and accounting, respectively. CFOs and accountants may want to utilize ample information resources available on the Internet to their advantage, including financial data, SEC information, tax information, and information on professional societies.

Financial forecasting and planning can be done using a microcomputer with a powerful spreadsheet program, such as Excel, templates, add-ins, or stand-alone software. Besides using spreadsheet programs, more and more companies are developing computer-based models for financial planning and budgeting through the use of powerful yet easy-to-use financial modeling languages, such as Centage's *Budget Maestro*. The models help to build a budget for profit planning and answer a variety of what-if scenarios. The resultant calculations provide a basis for choice among alternatives under conditions of uncertainty. In recent years, spreadsheet software and computer-based financial modeling software have been developed and utilized for budgeting and planning in an effort to speed up the budgeting process and allow CFOs to investigate the effects of changes in budget assumptions and scenarios. These languages do not require any knowledge of computer programming on the part of the financial officers. They are all English-like languages. Some of the well-known budgeting and planning system packages are described in the following section.

PLANNING AND BUDGETING SOFTWARE

The following are a variety of popular computer software packages designed specifically for planning, budgeting, optimization, and simulation:

1. *Business Plan, Sales and Marketing Plan* (Palo Alto Software)

   www.paloalto.com

   This software provides projections of cash inflow and cash outflow. Data is input into seven categories: sales, cost of sales, administrative expense, long-term debt, other cash receipts, inventory build-up/reduction, and capital expenditures (acquisition of long-term assets, such as equipment). The program allows changes in assumptions and scenarios and provides a complete array of reports.

2. *@Risk* (Palisade Corporation)

   www.palisade.com

   How will a new competitor affect market share? @RISK calculates the likelihood of changes and events affecting the bottom line. @RISK's familiar @ functions are used to define the risk in a worksheet. The program then runs thousands of what-if tests using Monte Carlo simulation. A clear, colorful graph shows the likelihood of every possible bottom-line value. The model's results can be viewed from hundreds or even thousands of what-if scenarios. Answers are provided to such questions as, "What is the chance of a negative result?", "What is the chance of a result over one million?" Controllers can determine, at a glance, whether a risk is acceptable or a contingency plan is needed.

3. *What's Best!* (Lindo Systems, Inc.)

www.lindo.com

If resources are limited—for example, people, inventory, materials, time, or cash—What's Best! lets the controller decide how to allocate these resources in order to maximize or minimize a given objective, such as profit or cost. What's Best! uses proven methods—linear programming (LP), integer programming, and nonlinear programming—to solve a variety of business problems that cut across every industry at every level of decision making. What's Best! also has sensitivity analysis, extensive error handling, full solution report capabilities, and user interface via Excel or Lotus. (Stand-alone)

4. *SIMUL8* (Visual8 Corporation)

www.visual8.com

SIMUL8 is a full-features simulation package. Fully integrated with Excel, it uses easy-to-enter graphics to represent both the objects in the company's system—such as machines and workers—and the process flows that describe their interaction. It can simulate many business processes, such as invoice and order flow, hospital process design, and any other situations where flows and processes can be redesigned and optimized.

5. *ILOG Inventory and Product Flow Analyst*

www.ibm.com

ILOG's Inventory and Product Flow Analyst is a Web-based, multi-echelon inventory optimization solution that provides end-to-end functionality for manufacturers, retailers, and distributors. Inventory Analyst handles both inbound/outbound and distribution-focused business models allowing companies to answer a broad range of business questions from determining the right inventory policies and strategic positioning of inventory to the ongoing setting of safety stocks and inventory levels in operational environments. LogicTools' advanced inventory optimization technology enables companies to transform supply chains into drivers of profitability, efficiency, and growth.

6. *Oracle Crystal Ball*

www.oracle.com/crystalball

Oracle Crystal Ball automatically calculates thousands of different 'what-if' cases with Monte Carlo simulation, saving the inputs and results of each calculation as individual scenarios. It is a spreadsheet-based software unit for predictive modeling, forecasting, and optimization.

FORECASTING AND STATISTICAL SOFTWARE

Numerous computer software packages are used for forecasting purposes. They are broadly divided into two major categories: forecasting software and general-purpose statistical software. Some programs are stand-alone, whereas others are spreadsheet add-ins or templates. Some popular programs are as follows:

1. *Forecast Pro*

   Business Forecast Systems, Inc.

   www.forecastpro.com

   Forecast Pro is business software that uses artificial intelligence. A built-in expert system examines the data and guides the user to state-of-the-art forecasting techniques—exponential smoothing, Box-Jenkins, dynamic regression, Croston's model, event models, and multiple-level models—that best suit the data.

2. *Autobox*

   Automatic Forecasting Systems

   www.autobox.com

   Autobox 6.0 for Windows uses the Box-Jenkins forecasting methodology.

3. *Demand Solutions*

   Demand Management, Inc.

   www.demandsolutions.com

   Demand Solutions is a forecasting engine and data warehouse for effective supply chain management. It delivers detailed information to front-line inventory managers and top-level sales forecasts to front-office executives. It is compliant with Microsoft SQL Server ODBC.

4. *ForecastX Wizard*

   John Galt Solutions, Inc.

   www.forecastxperttoolkit.com

   Fully integrated with Excel, ForecastX Wizard software provides customizable reports, ad-hoc planning and analysis with what-if scenarios, and best-and-worst-case analysis.

5. *Smoothie*™

   Demand Works Co.

   www.demandworks.com

   The demand forecast is the critical element in a supply chain plan. Smoothie improves the business planning function by maximizing forecast accuracy. It leverages demand history, current sales orders, promotions, events, and user judgment to arrive at an optimal estimate of future demand and required safety stocks.

6. *SmartForecasts*

   Smart Software, Inc.

   www.smartcorp.com

SmartForecasts combines automatic forecasting with rapid batch processing to enable manufacturers, distributors, and retailers to create accurate demand forecasts for each product item in inventory along with item-specific estimates of safety stock requirements that significantly reduce inventory costs. The Enterprise Edition features direct connectivity and easy integration with corporate databases (including major client/server systems, such as Oracle, IBM DB2, and SQL Server), as well as enterprise resource planning, disaster recovery planning, supply chain, and other planning systems. Its expert system selects the best forecasting method for the data and handles all of the mathematics, incorporating trends, seasonal patterns, and the effects of promotions and other special events. Forecast results can be adjusted directly on-screen, based on business knowledge, for more realistic forecasts and informed planning decisions. Results also can be arranged from the top down or from the bottom up—by product group/item or item/region—for large groups containing hundreds or thousands of items.

7. *EViews 8*

Quantitative Micro Software

www.eviews.com

EViews 8 software provides the tools most frequently used in practical econometric and forecasting work. It covers estimation, forecasting, statistical analysis, graphics, simulation, and data management all in a powerful, graphical object-oriented interface.

PROJECT MANAGEMENT SOFTWARE

Most current project management applications use computers extensively. The management of projects is enhanced by tools such as Gantt charting, Fish-bone diagram, the program evaluation and review technique (PERT), and critical path method (CPM). These tools are easily computerized and there are dozens of commercial packages on the market. The user inputs activity time estimates and procedure information, program output slack for each activity, duration and variance for critical paths, and other useful project management information. Many project management software packages, such as Microsoft Project, allow planners to enter defined activities, events, and times only once, and then present either a Gantt or a PERT chart—or both—on the computer's monitor. The project manager can then view how changing parameters will alter the charts and completion times. Some managers prefer using Gantt charts, some prefer PERT charts, and others use both, for the same projects. The preference depends on the personality of the manager and on presentation needs rather than on the nature of the project.

Types of project management software are as follows:

- *Project- and Resource-Tracking Software*—enables the assignment of entered tasks, subtasks, and subprojects to defined resources (such as employees and contractors). Most of these tools allow the user to define priorities and set the order in which subprojects or individual parts of the project must be done. While many good specialized project-tracking tools are available, spreadsheets, and even text editors, can do the job in a pinch. The quality of project management depends more on skill and attentiveness than on the tools used.

- *Time-Tracking Software*—enables detailed tracking of the amount of time it takes to implement a project which, over time, will aid in the improvement of estimating skills.
- *Bug-Tracking and Source-Code Version-Control Software*—in addition to being used for software-development projects, can be used to control changes to documentation, keep on top of the versions of vendor software in the standard desktop image, and track problems at every stage of a project.

Following is a list of project management software:

1. *Project and Portfolio Management*
   Computer Associates International
   www.ca.com/us/project-portfolio-management.aspx
2. *iPlan Project and Quality Management*
   Integrated Strategies Information Systems Pvt. Ltd.
   www.iPlanEnterprise.com
3. *Microsoft Project*
   Microsoft Corp.
   www.microsoft.com/project
4. *Marina Project and Portfolio Management*
   Serena
   www.serena.com
5. *Planview Project Portfolio Management*
   PlanView
   www.planview.com
6. *Deltek Enterprise Project Management*
   Deltek
   www.deltek.com

CASH FLOW FORECASTING SOFTWARE

Computer software allows for day-to-day cash forecasting and management, determining cash balances, planning and analyzing cash flows, finding cash shortages, investing cash surpluses, accounting for cash transactions, automating accounts receivable and payable, and dial-up banking. Computerization improves availability, accuracy, timeliness, and monitoring of cash information at minimal cost. Daily cash information aids in planning how to use cash balances and enables the integration of different kinds of related cash information, such as collections on customer accounts and cash balances and the effect of cash payments on cash balances.

Spreadsheet program software such as *Lotus 1-2-3, Microsoft's Excel,* and *Quattro Pro* can assist in the development of cash budgets and answering a variety of what-if questions. For example, the user can see how cash flow will be affected by different actions and decisions (e.g., the purchase and sale of different product lines).

Software packages specially designed for cash forecasting and management generally contain automatically prepared spreadsheets for profit/loss forecasts, cash flow budgets, projected balance sheet, payroll analysis, term loan amortization schedules, sales/cost of sales by product, ratio analysis, and graphs. Data are input into different categories, such as sales, cost of sales, general and administrative expenses, long-term debt, other cash receipts, inventory build-up/reduction, capital expenditures (i.e., acquisition of long-term assets such as store furniture), and income tax. The program allows changes in assumptions and scenarios providing a complete array of reports.

Four popular software packages are:

1. *Quicken (quicken.intuit.com)*. This fast, easy-to-use, inexpensive accounting program can help a small business manage its cash flow. Bills can be recorded as postdated transactions when they arrive. The program's *Billminder* feature automatically reminds the payer when bills are due. Checks can be printed for bills that are due with a few mouse clicks and/or keystrokes. Invoices can be recorded and aged receivables can be tracked, which can help maximize cash on hand.

2. *Up Your Cash Flow XT (www.cashplan.com)*. Up Your Cash Flow XT creates financial forecasts for small to mid-sized businesses. It automatically prepares spreadsheets for profit/loss forecasts, cash flow budgets, projected balance sheets, payroll analysis, term loan amortization schedules, sales/cost of sales by product, ratio analysis, and graphs. It can be used by accountants and consultants to provide management advice, secure financing, assist troubled businesses, and offer other valuable services. Up Your Cash Flow XT is used by CFOs, controllers, and financial managers to quickly create company budgets, manage cash flow, and reach desired levels of profitability. More than 30 reports show the impact of sales, expenses, cost of sales, financing, payroll, inventory, and more. What-if scenarios can be run to show how changes in business activity affect the bottom line, compare plan to actual data to measure how closely goals have been met, and predict any cash shortfalls before they occur.

3. *Cashflow Plan—Cashflow Forecast Software (www.planware.org/cashflowforecastsoftware.htm)*. Cashflow Plan is a range of software packages for preparing comprehensive, monthly cashflow projections for as far ahead as 12 months. It can be used by burgeoning and established businesses of all sizes and types for cashflow planning, budgets, business planning, and fund raising. A roll-forward facility allows for quick updating

of projections every month. More powerful versions also include a tool for consolidating projections. Cashflow Plan will aid in planning a business's cash requirements, improving control over cash flows, and conserving cash resources. It is especially useful when cash flows must be forecast in the context of:

    a. Tight cash/profit margins.

    b. Limited financial resources.

    c. Planning for growth or radical change.

    d. Compiling cash budgets.

    e. Preparing business improvement plans.

Cashflow Plan is preformatted to handle the wide range of the variables and functions normally encountered when preparing cash flow and financial projections. Based on the assumptions input, it compiles detailed, fully integrated financial projections for the coming year on a monthly basis and, for the initial three months, on a weekly basis. It automatically produces more than 20 pro-forma financial and management reports together with numerous graphs for key variables.

   4. *Budget Maestro (www.centage.com)*. Budget Maestro is cash flow forecasting software that provides managers with what-if capabilities by which to model and test alternative budgeting or financing scenarios. A limitless number of what-if scenarios can be created to gauge the impact of projected changes of operations on cash flow, balance sheets, and income statements. Rolling forecasts—monthly or several years out—can be used to predict the impact on operations and cash flow based on changing variables.

ACCOUNTING SOFTWARE PACKAGES

Several software applications are of particular interest to accountants. The following discussion includes the major players in the area, and some important features to look for when considering a particular type of software.

Many factors must be weighed when selecting a computer software package. Besides determining the software features currently needed and required in the future, the buyer must have a thorough understanding of the firm's existing system, and whether proposed software will integrate with all areas of that system and business. Some of the basic considerations include features and capabilities, compatibility and integration, ease of customization, ease of use, written documentation and technical support, price, and vendor's reputation and stability.

Vendors began to compete by improving integration and customization. With Windows interfaces, data can more easily be linked and exchanged with all types of applications, such as spreadsheets, databases, and even e-mail. Thus, compatibility with existing systems and data is an extremely important consideration when selecting new software. Likewise customization of input screens and reports to conform to a firm's needs can more easily be done, and capabilities vary between packages.

Although the price of a system is an important consideration, it should never be the deciding factor. Often, the cost of software is relatively insignificant when compared to the costs of implementation, training, ongoing maintenance, and support. Training costs can be reduced if the program has good context-sensitive online help. Installation will be much simpler if the program has a checklist or "wizard" that actually walks the user through the installation procedure.

Before buying any package, financial managers should try calling the customer support department of the vendor. Customer support can provide detailed information about the features of a package. Vendors typically offer a demo or a free or low cost trial of their computer software product. Information about specials or discounts is also available to professionals such as practicing accountants.

Accounting Software

The fundamental task of accounting software is to automate the routine chore of entering and posting accounting transactions. This information is organized in an electronic format so as to produce financial statements and can be accessed immediately to assist in the management of the firm.

An accounting software package consists of a series of highly integrated modules. Each module corresponds to a specific accounting function (e.g., payroll, accounts receivable, and accounts payable). In an integrated system, after the details of the transaction are entered in one of the modules, the chart of accounts from the general ledger is "read." The transaction is then automatically posted to the accounts in the general ledger. For example, when a sale on account is entered in the accounts receivable module, a debit is automatically made to the accounts receivable account in the general ledger and an offsetting credit made to the general ledger sales account.

Module Descriptions. The basic modules typically required by a firm and often integrated in an accounting software package include general ledger, accounts receivable and invoicing, accounts payable and purchase order processing, inventory, payroll, job costing, and fixed assets.

General Ledger. The general ledger is the heart of the accounting system. It contains the chart of accounts of the business. A general ledger module should contain a sample chart of accounts that can be customized to a particular business. In addition, it should contain predefined reports that support budget data and prior-year comparisons, which can be tailored to a firm's specific needs. Other essential features include the capability of generating automatic reversing and recurring journal entries, the capability of having at least 13 periods open at one time, and the ability to make prior-period adjustments or post entries to another year without closing the current year.

Accounts Receivable and Invoicing. The accounts receivable and invoicing functions are often combined in the same module. This module allows the controller to enter sales data and permits extensive sales analysis. It provides customer receivables management by tracking customers' balances and generates invoices, monthly statements, and aging reports. It should allow for setting up credit limits for each customer, provide for flexible billing options, and be able to apply partial payments to specific invoices or to the oldest balance. For faster processing, online inquiry should show the complete customer record at a glance, including balances and unpaid invoices, and allow the controller to make changes "on the fly."

Accounts Payable and Purchase Order Processing. Accounts payable and purchase order processing can also be combined in a single module. The module tracks obligations to vendors and determines a best payments schedule, prints checks, and provides for the distribution to accounts. It should allow for enhanced management of order processing by tracking orders from the start to the receipt of goods. It should be able to detect supply problems and thus permit early planning for alternate sources. To analyze vendor performance, it must track the complete purchase and delivery history of vendors and allow for easy access to this information.

Inventory. This module automatically tracks inventory as purchases or sales are made and maintains cost and price data for each inventory item. In an integrated system, the Inventory main file, which stores the product's number, is checked when a sales invoice is created in the accounts receivable module. If sufficient inventory is on hand, the amount of the sale is reduced from the balance. Likewise, when inventory is purchased, the inventory quantity is automatically increased. The module should help improve inventory management by alerting the user when to reorder, identifying slow moving items and analyzing performance by item and category.

Payroll. The payroll module maintains default information for each employee (e.g., rate of pay and income tax withholding information). The module calculates the wages to be paid, prints checks, and keeps track of deductions, sick and vacation days, and other such information. It maintains information for government reporting (e.g., 941, W-2, unemployment, and state tax forms). For cost control, it should be able to provide for expense distribution or integrate with a costing module.

Job Costing. A job costing module allows the user to track and report on the costs, income, and profitability of individual jobs or projects. This is done by assigning a job ID number to purchases, sales, and employee hours. A job cost module should provide for an accurate audit trail, detailed income, expenses and committed costs, as well as the tracking of other user-defined categories.

Fixed Assets. Fixed assets usually represent a significant investment by a firm. Thus, it is essential to keep track of them, but extremely tedious to do so. Tracking fixed assets and the repetitive calculation of depreciation is well suited for the computer. Most accounting software packages include a fixed asset module or capabilities to control fixed assets. It is also possible to purchase dedicated standalone fixed asset packages.

Fixed asset software can handle large amounts of data and a variety of depreciation methods for financial accounting and tax purposes. It should be able to maintain detailed information about each asset, including a description of the asset, its location, date placed in service, and estimated useful life. It should also be able to track additions and disposal, as well as basis adjustments. An example of a fixed asset package is Decision Support Technology's BASSETS Fixed Asset System.

Before purchasing an accounting package, the controller should determine if it has a fixed asset module or capabilities sufficient for his or her needs. If not, the controller should ask if the vendor produces a stand-alone version, or would recommend a third party vendor. Before purchasing a stand-alone fixed asset software package, the controller should make sure that it allows for easy sharing of information with his or her general ledger, tax packages, and other data repositories.

Market Leaders. The various accounting software products can be categorized as high-end, mid-level, and low-end packages. TechRepublic—http://techrepublic.com—provides a list of the various software packages.

High-End Packages. High-end applications serve both mid-sized, regional companies and large, multinational corporations. They are flexible, easy to implement, and can be modified to meet users' needs. Although the software products in this category are not inexpensive, they are not as expensive as AS/400 or ERP installations. Some high-end packages are as follows:

AccountMate Software—for SQL, Express, and LAN

http://www.accountmate.com

Client/server software available to almost any size business.

Sage 300 ERP

http://na.sage.com/sage-300-erp/

Multi-tier business management system, multi-currency and multilingual support, e-business and sales force automation capabilities, customization options.

MS Dynamics AX

http://www.microsoft.com/en-us/dynamics/default.aspx

Designed for mid-size and large companies, Microsoft® Dynamics AX (formerly Microsoft Axapta) is a multi-language, multi-currency enterprise resource planning (ERP) solution. Its core strengths are in manufacturing and e-business, and it includes strong functionality for the wholesale and services industries.

Epicor—Enterprise and iscala

http://www.epicor.com

Integration between front office and back office applications, customization options.

Infor Financial Management

http://www.infor.com

Freestyle reporting capabilities; multinational, multi-currency processing of payments, invoices, and receivables; Web-enabled accounts receivable function.

Sage 50

http://na.sage.com/sage-50-accounting-us/?isnow=sage50us

Designed for small to medium-sized businesses; features multi-user capabilities.

Sage DacEasy

http://na.sage.com/sage%20daceasy

Designed to meet the needs of small- and medium-size businesses. DacEasy offers extensive functionality that lends itself to a wide range of industries. Its powerful reporting increases users' knowledge of their business. Its fully integrated modular design allows companies to choose cost-effective solutions for their accounting, payroll, order entry, and point-of-sale needs.

Mid-Level Packages. Purchasers of mid-level programs, although tough to define by revenue, usually include four or five accounting users and have needs that are technically sophisticated. These buyers generally require more robust, multi-user features and management reporting while still retaining tools that are required for a small business. Essential features of a package include client/server architectures, custom report design, and Internet/intranet-enabled functions. Some mid-level packages are as follows:

AccountMate Software—AccountMate

http://www.accountmate.com

Client/server software available to almost any size business.

CheckMark Software—MultiLedger

http://www.checkmark.com

Integrated, cross-platform accounting program combining general ledger, accounts receivable/payable, and inventory.

PC Accountant—ProBooks

http://pcaccountant.com

Features integrated, point-and-click accounting.

Sage BusinessWorks Accounting

http://na.sage.com/sage%20businessworks

Features 10 fully integrated modules; can support up to 48 concurrent users.

Low-End Packages. Products in this category are not short on capabilities or features. Rather, they are made for sole proprietorships, partnerships, and corporations that are closely held with only a few employees. Users of these products need a package that will help them balance checkbooks, prepare payroll reports and deposits, and keep track of bills and customer invoices; they want features such as single points of entry for data, on-the-fly updating, tight integration with the

Internet, sophisticated customized reporting, built-in job costing, and electronic payroll and bill paying services. Some low-end packages are as follows:

Aatrix Software—P&L Accounting for Mac and Windows

http://www.aatrix.com

Full suite of applications at low cost, including general ledger, payroll, and inventory management.

SAGE

http://na.sage.com/sage-na/products-solutions/by-small-business

Entry-level package for the small office/home office user.

Intuit—QuickBooks

http://quickbooks.intuit.com

Features include time tracking, job costing, and estimations; integrated with Microsoft Excel, Word, Outlook, and Symantec ACT!

Account Edge for Mac and Windows

http://www.accountedge.com

Features more than 100 accounting and financial management reports; supports multiple-currency accounting.

Selecting Accounting Software. When selecting accounting software, consider the following:

1. *Customization.* Can the package be customized? Can it be customized enough to meet user requirements? Can it customize items such as reports, forms, input screens, and source codes?

2. *Vendor reliability.* Is the vendor reliable? Does the vendor have sufficient resources? Is the vendor profitable and supported by sufficient, knowledgeable staff?

3. *Reporting.* Can the package produce required financial statements in a timely and accurate manner? Do the reports include the required ratios? Do the reports include graphical output? Do the reports incorporate third-party products FRx (offers reporting capabilities for the general ledger module) and Crystal Reports (extracts and reports event data from all modules)?

4. *Database.* Do the databases available with the package—Btrieve, Microsoft SQL Server, Oracle, and IBM DB2—match the user's needs? The user's number of transactions is a typical determinant of the database required.

5. *Client/Server.* Does the package come with a client/server version (i.e., a version that allows the user to save the bandwidth and time on the LAN and to distribute single processes across multiple computers throughout the organization)?

6. *Account number structure.* Does the account number structure accommodate the number of segments—subsidiaries, divisions, accounts, subac-

counts, departments, programs, and funds—and total number of characters required by the user?

7. *Internet.* Does the pack include Internet-related features that will allow such functions as publication of web catalogs directly from, and making links to, the software's inventory module; retrieval of orders directly from the web site and the import of the orders to the sales module; printing reports to a web page (HTML) format; allowing users to access reports and accounting data across the web; and the support of remote data entry across the web?

8. *International.* Does the package process multiple currencies? Does the package support foreign languages?

9. *User friendliness.* Does the package contain user-friendly features such as graphical guidance, default-rich settings, and clear, simple, and intuitive screens and labels?

10. *Other features.* Does the package include pivot tables and hotlinking? Does the package alert users when certain conditions, such as cash on hand, gross margin, and inventory balances, reach user-defined levels?

Note: For more in-depth analysis of various accounting packages, consult the following professional organizations and manuals, some of which offer advice on purchasing software:

- CPA Practice Advisor (www.cpapracticeadvisor.com).
- 411AccountingSoftware.com   (http://accountingsoftware411.com/AS411Home.aspx).
- Institute of Management Accountants (www.imanet.org).
- The American Institute of Certified Public Accountants (www.aicpa.org).

Web-Based Accounting Systems. Web-based software packages are transforming business. Functions such as accounting, cash-flow management, customer relationship management (CRM), inventory control, and marketing can be performed electronically anytime and anywhere for a low monthly fee. For example, a small business can use ePeachtree (www.accountingweb.com) or QuickBooks Online (http://search.quickbookonline.com) to process transactions. Intuit offers payroll services on the Web, and a small business can outsource its payroll function. Not only can a business owner view and manage employee compensation via the Internet, but the outsourced services allow employees to access personal information, including earnings, income tax withholdings, retirement plans, and vacation days, without placing an added burden on the company.

Reliable and efficient access to information has become a must for business firms to stay competitive. To embrace web-based software and to stay competitive, small businesses must first set up a computer network. With networking technology, staff members or users at any location can share information simultaneously. The fast pace of advances in information technology (IT) makes it difficult for accounting professionals to stay current.

Implementing Web-Based Accounting Systems. Implementing a web-based accounting system that will leverage current IT tools to improve profitability and efficiency involves setting up a system network; selecting and subscribing to software; customizing the accounting system; and preparing system documentation.

Set up a system network. To connect local and remote computers for sharing information and resources, Ethernet networking is a good choice for small business local area networks (LAN) because it is inexpensive and reliable. Ethernet networking strikes a good balance between cost and speed, is built into most newer PCs, and can support nearly all popular network protocols. For older computers, installing a network interface card (NIC) is easy, and all major networking manufacturers (e.g., D-Link, Linksys, and Netgear) offer reliable and inexpensive NICs. Fast Ethernet, based on the same protocol as traditional Ethernet, can enable small businesses to affordably realize significant boosts to network performance.

Ethernet networks, however, have practical limits. A primary concern is the length of the shared cable. Though data can travel on the cable quickly, signals weaken as they travel. In addition, electrical interference from the surrounding devices may interfere with the signals, which limits the maximum distance between two devices on an Ethernet network. Although distance is seldom an issue for small business networks, if a company has several branch offices with some distance between them, one option is to set up a virtual private network (VPN). Additionally, if the structure of the office makes it economically infeasible to run Ethernet cables, a company may prefer to set up a wireless network.

Small businesses with 50 employees or less can use Microsoft Windows Small Business Server, Windows 7, or Windows 8 to function as either a dedicated or a nondedicated server. With Windows 7 or 8, the network administrator can manage the access to data, files, printers, and other resources on a small network. If the business lacks qualified IT staff or wants to set up more complicated networks, another option is to hire a consultant or value-added reseller (VAR) to do the wiring and system configuration. Linux is a growing alternative in the server software market. Linux's low cost, reliability, and high performance make it a promising choice; however, setting up a Linux server may require employing an individual with extensive networking and Linux-specific experience.

A business must also have the bandwidth capacity that broadband Internet access provides in order to use web-based accounting packages effectively. The process of choosing the right ISP can be complicated, and a company must consider several factors, including price, performance, access numbers (for alternative dial-up service), and technical support/services.

Select and subscribe to software. Businesses should make sure that the provider offers all the required features before subscribing to the service. A business should select a web-based accounting package based on the company's information needs and the software's features. For example, QuickBooks Online cannot provide detailed inventory information and, thus, is not suitable for most retailers. Although neither QuickBooks Online nor ePeachtree can handle product costing, both packages allow the user to accumulate service or manufacturing costs by project. **Note:** All web-based accounting packages listed offer free trial periods of from 14 to 30 days.

Customize the accounting system. Web-based accounting packages are general-purpose software, and a company needs to use and customize only the features required for its business. Working from the predefined chart of accounts, forms, and reports, a small business can set up and customize its accounting system in hours.

Prepare system documentation. Companies need to prepare system documentation so that new staff can learn how to use the system. System documentation should provide detailed procedures, including system activation and deactivation, a chart of accounts, a sales cycle, a purchase cycle, employee and payroll cycles, cash receipts, cash disbursements, journal entries, inventory, financial reports and queries, and error corrections. The system designer should copy the predefined forms, screens, and reports and include them within the system documentation.

Good system documentation should be easy to read, make it easy for users to find specific information (i.e., include a table of contents, page numbers, and an index), and be well organized (i.e., by cycles or accounts). The procedures should be complete and easy to follow (i.e., showing all relevant forms, screens, and reports). The overall presentation should be professional, and the system documentation should be kept in a safe place.

Outsourcing. Web-based (or cloud-based) accounting makes the data easily accessible to multiple remote users at one time, and offers the usual benefits of web-based software: server-side upgrades; maintenance; and backups. The general ledger, accounts payable and receivable, invoicing, and reports functions can be outsourced to companies such as the following:

- SAGE *(http://na.sage.com/sage-300-erp/)*. SAGE accounting solutions sells what it calls a complete business management system integrating an electronic storefront with a complete back-office system. It serves businesses doing e-commerce with a system connecting everything from inventory to invoicing. The SAGE system automates inventory control, purchase orders, Web site orders, credit checking, fraud protection, accounts payable and receivable, general ledger, and payroll.

- *Intacct (http://us.intacct.com)*. Intacct, of Los Gatos, California, views itself as "an accounting utility company." The company serves businesses employing up to 500 people with a full-function package—general ledger, financial reporting, budgeting, accounts payable and receivable, invoicing, expense reporting, human resources reporting, and payroll services.

A small operation interested in low cost and ease of use may be interested in the following:

- *Intuit QuickBooks.* While Quickbooks may be the market leader in small-business accounting software, the company has lagged in developing a Web-based version. QuickBooks for the Web—http://quickbooks.intuit.com—is a significantly stripped-down version of the desktop product. Oddly, one thing it lacks is the ability to import QuickBooks data (something NetLedger offers). Other no-shows in the Web incarnation include estimates, graphs, online banking or bill paying, custom fields, time tracking, and the ability to export data into a spreadsheet or other file format. However, the Web version is easy to set up, and allows for the billing of customers via e-mail.

A small or medium-sized operation interested in functionality and scalability may be interested in the following:

- *SAGE 50.* The online offering—http://na.sage.com/sage-50-accounting-us/ services/hosting-providers is more robust than QuickBooks for the Web. It can import a Peachtree Office Accounting file, though some features from the desktop version have been altered or dropped. For example, customized reports are not imported. However, reports and forms can be exported to Excel, Word, Rich Text, or Crystal Reports format. A wireless service allows the user to check inventory as well as customer and vendor information from various Web-enabled cell phones or from a Palm.

Advice and Caveats. A recent survey published by Financial Executives International (FEI) (www.financialexecutives.org) revealed that outsourcing would continue to be a solution for areas where management does not believe that in-house efforts can be cost-effective. The same survey also revealed that financial executives' satisfaction levels with shared services are as high as 90%. Web-based accounting packages enable small businesses to outsource their accounting function at an affordable price and web-based inventory control software allows small businesses to track their inventories in real time. Web-based software has the added bonus of always being up-to-date because providers continuously provide incremental upgrades and new features.

To embrace web-based software, a small business must first develop a technology plan. This plan should be based on a thorough review of the company's existing computing resources, and focus on what the business plans to do with technology. The plan should clearly state the goals, prioritize the goals, and tie the goals to a budget and a timetable. The firm must complete this prioritizing process before making any purchase decisions.

Once the company completes the technology plan, it must then match software products to the company's goals and objectives. The business should be flexible regarding the technologies and should consider all available products in the market. At this point, the company can either handle the process with its own staff or use consultants to expedite the process.

Purchasing equipment can be overwhelming when facing all the choices in the market. Categorizing the available products can simplify this process. When evaluating competing services, the value-added features—unlimited free nationwide dial-up, robust Web-based e-mail, and hosting web content—can be extremely beneficial. For example, outsourcing the tasks of maintaining a Web server, managing the associated traffic, and maintaining the continuous server uptime may result in savings of $2,000 to $3,000 per year.

Write-Up Software

With the development of easy-to-use and inexpensive accounting software, many companies that previously relied on CPAs to keep their books are doing it themselves. CPA firms can counter this trend with dedicated write-up software, which is easy-to-use and provides more features so as to add value to their write-up services.

Write-up software should allow the controller to do more than just record transactions. One of the biggest features to look for is the ability to easily create an array of printouts and reports that a client might need. This includes being able to link and transfer data from other software packages and applications.

Another important feature is the ability to customize the input screen so that it is consistent with the layout of the client's source documents, thereby reducing unneeded keystrokes. Easy setup is another means of reducing the cost of write-up service. The package should contain sample company data and the ability to copy common information and make changes to default information included in the setup "on the fly." WebCPA (http://www.webcpa.com) provides a comprehensive review of write-up software.

Exhibit 6-1 lists four write-up software products.

Exhibit 6-1: Write-Up Software

Client Write-Up System	*Write-Up CS*
Pro Systems, Inc.	Creative Solutions
www.prosystems.com/writeup.htm	http://cs.thomsonreuters.com/ cs-accounting/write-up.aspx
CYMA Client Write-Up	*Client Write-Up*
CYMA Systems, Inc.	CertiflexDimension
www.cyma.com	www.clientwrite-up.com

Compliance Software

The Sarbanes-Oxley Act, passed by Congress in July 2002, is the most significant change to U.S. business regulations in 70 years. The Act creates tough new penalties for corporate fraud, prevents accounting firms from offering consulting services to audit clients, and places restrictions on financial analysts. Section 404, *Management Assessment of Internal Controls*, requires each annual report of an issuer to contain an "internal control report" that shall:

(1) State the responsibility of management for establishing and maintaining an adequate internal control structure and procedures for financial reporting; and

(2) Contain an assessment, as of the end of the issuer's fiscal year, of the effectiveness of the internal control structure and procedures of the issuer for financial reporting.

Much of compliance is a matter of putting rules in place and ensuring that they are followed. Technology can provide the solutions to the corporate governance and compliance problem. It includes computer software for the following six areas:

1. *Business intelligence.* Regulatory requirements for "real-time" disclosure of factors that affect financial performance mean that executives need access to timely, relevant data from all areas of the business. Business intelligence software can help ensure the accessibility of information by drilling down into financial and company data and providing sophisticated reporting and analysis tools.

2. *Business process management (BPM).* Businesses have traditionally been built around functional "silos," making it difficult to share information and obtain a consistent, enterprise-wide view. By extracting businesses processes from the underlying application code into an independent management layer, BPM software can help improve visibility.

3. *Document management.* New corporate governance standards mean that companies need an efficient system for storing and retrieving important records and documents. Software packages that maintain audit trails of documents and set controls over how, where, and for how long files are stored can help companies meet these obligations.

4. *E-mail management.* As the volume of e-mail continues to soar, the logistics of storing essential e-mails and being able to retrieve them quickly become increasingly complex. With new regulatory requirements around internal controls and disclosure obligations, the need for comprehensive e-mail management software becomes increasingly compelling.

5. *Financial and accounting software.* To help comply with new standards such as Sarbanes-Oxley, many vendors are giving their traditional financing and accounting software a boost with additional modules that help with risk management, more accurate budgeting and forecasting, financial analysis, and the establishment of internal financial controls.

6. *Enterprise resource planning (ERP).* ERP software can provide organizations with a consistent financial view across all divisions, thereby helping to maintain the accuracy of financial information. Many ERP providers are adding modules to their software to assist with compliance with Sarbanes-Oxley and other corporate governance standards.

Tax Preparation Software

Computer technology has had a significant impact on the way tax returns are prepared. Computerized tax return preparation enables the user to prepare a return quickly and accurately and to quickly analyze different tax planning strategies. Some software packages have built-in tools for tax research and permit for the electronic filing of tax returns. The software also lets the user easily do what-if planning and then quickly makes all the necessary changes. Furthermore, data can be imported directly from accounting packages or electronic spreadsheets into tax preparation software.

Although tax preparation software can help with tax planning, financial executives should consider a dedicated tax research package for serious tax research. Most Compact Disc (CD)-based tax services can effectively replace the printed version of tax services. A major advantage of using CD-based tax services is having the ability to do electronic key-word searches. This can greatly facilitate the tax research process and make it much more efficient. In addition, it is easier to maintain and store all this information on a CD, thereby saving a good deal of library storage space.

The tax software industry is fiercely competitive and continues to go through consolidations and shakeouts. Thus, it makes sense to deal with the larger, better-known vendors whose products are more likely to be supported in the future.

Market Leaders. The leading tax software packages can be categorized into the three segments that follow.

Lower-Cost Alternatives. The price for this category is generally under $1,000. In spite of their low price, their features compare favorably with the higher priced products. The five products included in this category, are listed in Exhibit 6-2.

Mainstream Packages. These packages are suitable for mainstream tax practices. They are generally easy to use and learn, but are not intended to handle every situation that may arise. The packages in this category, listed in Exhibit 6-2, are generally more powerful than those in the lower-cost category.

High-End Packages. This group is marketed for use by multistate regional and national firms. These packages, listed in Exhibit 6-2, are able to handle the most complex returns and track their progress through large offices.

Exhibit 6-2: Tax Software

Lower-Cost Alternatives

Drake Tax Software
  Drake Software
  www.drakesoftware.com
ProSeries Tax
  Intuit
  http://accountants.intuit.com/
tax/proseries

Turbotax
  Intuit
  www.turbotax.com
H&R Block At Home
  www.hrblock.com

Mainstream Packages

Lacerte Tax Planner
  Lacerte Software
  Corporation
  http://accountants.intuit.com/
tax/lacerte

TaxWorks
  www.taxworks.com
Fast Tax
  http://tax.thomsonreuters.com

High-End Packages

Go Systems
  Thomson Reuters
  www.tax.thomsonreuters.com

Prosystem fx
  CCH, Inc.
  http://www.cchgroup.com/webapp/
wcs/stores/servlet/category_ProSystem-
fx-Suite-Solutions_10151_-1_10053_
50005702_10151_N_Y

Audit Software

Audit software is used by accountants to perform audits efficiently and effectively. Software audit tools include automated workpapers, data extraction software, and trial balance software.

Products such as APG (Audit Program Generator) by the American Institute of Certified Public Accountants (AICPA) and the optional add-on modules allow the user to prepare customized audit programs. It eliminates the photocopying, cutting, and pasting usually required when creating the audit program and guides users through the engagement.

Data extraction software, such as IDEA (Interactive Data Extraction and Analysis), also by the AICPA, allows auditors to access clients' files for audit testing. The auditor can either access the client's live data or obtain a copy of the company's data files on tape or disk. Data extraction software allows the auditor to audit "through the computer." The auditor can, for example, select a sample of accounts receivable for confirmations or perform analytical reviews and do ratio analysis. Transactions may be compared to predetermined criteria. Linton Shafer's The Number—Audit Sampling software packages select random numbers and dates. It handles multiple ranges and evaluates results and performs compliance and substantive testing.

Trial Balance software, such as the AICPA's ATB (Accountant's Trial Balance) helps the auditor organize client's general ledger balances into a working trial balance. The auditor can then perform adjustments and update account balances. The calculation of financial ratios is extremely simple with trial balance software. This type of software aids in the preparation of financial statements. While trial balance software is designed primarily for audits, it can be used instead of write-up software for compilation and review services.

CCH's TeamMate is an electronic working paper system that helps automate the working paper preparation, review, reporting, and storage process. It includes standard and free form schedule templates, an automatic tick mark system, and powerful cross referencing capability. CCH's TeamMate also integrates popular spreadsheet, word processing, and imaging software. Hypertext links between documents and applications enable the auditor to jump backward through related numbers in reports or spreadsheets to the original data. The search, cross referencing, and retrieval capabilities allow the auditor to automatically correct errors in all affected documents. The working paper review features include automatic exception reporting, a working paper navigation system, and text and voice annotation. For example, the auditor can obtain a directory of all review notes pertaining to a document. The reporting features include key audit point summarization, report drafting, audit status reports, and time summaries. Financial data are quickly accessed by the sorting and filtering tools. A standard index provides a branch and node system for all papers. A simultaneous multiuser feature enables auditors/reviewers to work with the same document set even if they are working in various locations. CCH's TeamMate improves the quality, productivity, and effectiveness of the auditor's work.

Exhibit 6-3 contains a number of audit software packages, which contain one or more features previously discussed. Visit http://auditsoftware.net for more details.

Exhibit 6-3: Audit Software

ACL	*CaseWare Working Papers*
ACL Services Ltd.	Case Ware International
www.acl.com	www.caseware.com
The Pentana Audit Work System (PAWS)	
Pentana America	
www.pentana.com	

Spreadsheets

The electronic spreadsheet has done more than any other product to make the capabilities of microcomputers evident to the business community. An electronic spreadsheet allows the user to work with data in a huge number of rows and columns. The user works with this data in a columnar spreadsheet, a format familiar to accountants. A major advantage of the spreadsheet is that it eliminates the need to perform manual calculations and can perform powerful computer-aided operations.

The spreadsheet has become a valuable tool in business planning because it permits the user to perform what-if scenarios. Inputs can be continuously changed and the results will automatically be recalculated throughout the spreadsheet.

Thus, the effect of alternative decisions is easily determined and planning greatly facilitated. The use of templates is another important feature of spreadsheets. Templates provide the format and contain the formulas that are used to repeatedly solve various business applications. Because the user does not have to be a programmer to construct a template, all firms can now more easily use the vast power of the computer to help make better decisions in the management of a firm.

Activity-Based Costing and Activity-Based Management Software

An activity-based costing (ABC) system accumulates costs on the basis of production or service activities at a firm. Basically, it assigns costs by activity and links them to specific products. It is argued that the resulting cost data is much more realistic and precise as compared to the data obtained from a traditional costing system. ABC helps in determining what a product or process should cost, areas of possible cost reduction, and value-added versus non-value-added aspects. Activity-based costing is beneficial in appraising value-chain functions. Further, costs are a function of their consumption factors, such as number of employees, units produced, and labor hours. Aided by computer software designed for ABC, the controller can more easily and accurately accumulate cost information and perform what-if testing. With this data, management is in a better position to evaluate and make decisions regarding its operations and products. There is a good deal of software that the management accountant can use to aid in accumulating cost data. Some software are actually spreadsheet applications; others are modules of mainframe packages. Exhibit 6-4 lists popular cost management software packages, all of which are for use on a personal computer, most being designed for activity-based costing or activity-based management (ABM). Some products include consulting support as part of the overall package.

Exhibit 6-4: ABC and ABM Software

Cost Management	Activity-Based Management
Decimal Technologies, Inc. www.decimal.ca	http://www.oracle.com/us/ products/applications/peoplesoft- enterprise/financial- management/053702.html
Acorn Systems ABC/M Acorn Systems, Inc. www.acornsys.com	*Prodacapo ABC/M* Prodacapo www.prodacapo.com
Activity Analyzer Lead Software, Inc. www.leadsoftware.com	*SAS Activity-Based Management* SAS Institute, Inc. http://www.sas.com/solutions/abm

Lead Software's Activity Analyzer (www.leadsoftware.com) assigns activities to cost objects and calculates by activity costs and profitability. Profitability may be determined by product, service, customer, and territory. Acorn Systems Cost

Analyzer (www.acornsys.com) provides an accurate, accessible, actionable, and maintainable measurement of cost so the controller can better set transfer pricing, allocate cost, and price and charge back for shared services. Lawson Software (www.lawson.com) is based on installation of the Strategic General Ledger concept and ABC. This is client/server technology.

Note: Online advisors are also useful sources of information, such as The CPA Practice Advisor site (www.cpapracticeadvisor.com) for reviews of various accounting-related software, Accounting Software Advisor (www.accountingsoftwareadvisor.com), and 411AccountingSoftware.com (http://accountingsoftware411.com/AS411Home.aspx). Exhibit 6-5 captures Accounting-Software411.com home screen and provides a listing of software and its uses.

Exhibit 6-5: AccountingSoftware411.com Home Page

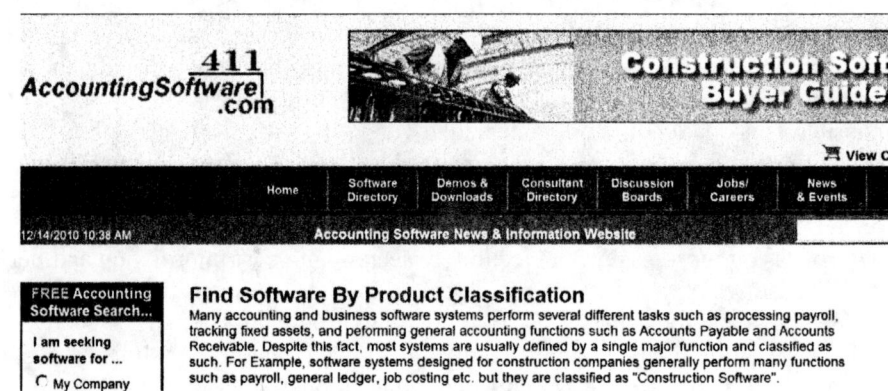

Reprinted with permission from Accountingsoftware411.com.

This site offers a list of software in the following areas:

Personal Finance	Medical Billing
Low-End Accounting	Non Profit
Mid-Range Accounting	Offer In Compromise
High-End Accounting	Payroll
Enterprise Resource Planning (ERP)	Physician Practice Management
Business Intelligence	Point of Sale
Business Activity Monitoring	Practice Management
Checks & Forms Solutions	Project Management
Client Write-Up	Property Management
Construction	Purchasing
Customer Relationship Management	Revenue Accounting
Document Management	Service Management
E-Business	Shipping
Estimating	Supply Chain Management
Expense Control	Tax Preparation

Financial Planning	Tax Research
Government Contractors	Taxes—Estate Trust & Retirement
Fixed Assets / Depreciation	Taxes—Payroll & 1099
Human Resource	Taxes—Property Tax
Inventory Management	Taxes—Sales & Use
Loan Service/Amortization	Trial Balance
Manufacturing	Other

CHAPTER 7

XBRL, Cloud Computing, and Wireless Technology

CONTENTS

Accountants and financial professionals need to be familiar with three important developments in information technology that significantly affect their financial reporting practices and the way they communicate with each other and clients as well: (1) extensible business reporting language (XBRL), (2) cloud computing, and (3) wireless technology (mobile computing). XBRL represents a major step in the preparation, publication, exchange, and analysis of financial data. XBRL results in a simpler process for issuing financial reports and making investment and credit decisions. XBRL standardizes financial reports by clearly specifying and defining each item of data, using clearly defined tags. This allows computers to accurately read and understand the figures.

The precise definitions, or tags, are necessary because terms such as "revenue," "income," "fees," "stock," and "inventory" can have a variety of meanings depending on the organization. Humans use judgment to interpret financial data, but for computers to make sense of it, they need precise definitions. The SEC has been adopting a three-year phased approach in the United States, where XBRL was voluntary for public companies in 2009 and will be mandatory by 2013, with an increasing number of data elements required.

The accountant must also stay current on the latest developments in cloud computing and mobile computing to properly advise client companies. This requires becoming familiar with the various business applications of wireless networks, the benefits, the drawbacks, and getting the most out of the system to enhance efficiency, productivity, timeliness, and profitability. The use of wireless networks will optimize computer operations and corporate activities.

XBRL

Many data formats on the Internet prevent users from analyzing financial information without labor-intensive conversions. Excessive time is devoted to extracting useful information from available accounting and financial data. Further time is wasted rekeying the same information into a spreadsheet. The Securities and Exchange Commission's (SEC's) database, referred to as EDGAR (Electronic Data Gathering, Analysis, and Retrieval System), for example, performs automated collection, validation, indexing, acceptance, and forwarding of submissions by companies and others who are required by law to file forms with the SEC. The comparison of numbers and ratios requires significant effort and time-consuming rekeying, and EDGAR's data cannot be imported directly into spreadsheets.

XBRL does not require additional disclosure from companies to outside audiences. It was developed to provide the financial community with a standards-based method to prepare, publish in a variety of formats, reliably extract, and *automatically exchange* financial statements of publicly held companies and the information they contain. XBRL uses a framework based on the Extensible Markup Language (XML) to make available financial information in an easy-to-use format on the Internet, its objective being to enhance the usability of existing accounting standards and allow the financial community to communicate in a universal language. Simple examples are associating numbers with variables and matching a name to a picture.

XBRL is an *intelligent* Internet language that can be used in business by preparers and users of financial statements including corporate accountants, CPAs, financial analysts, business managers (in reviewing reports), loan officers at banks, investors, suppliers, securities exchanges (e.g., New York Stock Exchange), over-the-counter market members of NASDAQ, and federal and local governmental agencies (e.g., the SEC and Internal Revenue Service). By comparison, the Hyper Text Markup Language (HTML) format is not intelligent enough as a language to understand and reveal relationships in accounting and financial data. HTML is not designed to be aware of the information it presents. XBRL closes the "communication gap" between the preparers and users of financial data on the Internet. Because it is based on XML, content and relationships may easily be understood.

XML is a general-purpose markup standard for creating languages to standardize the data exchange between different computing platforms and applications. XML uses tags to identify (i.e., mark up) pieces of data but leaves the interpretation of the data to the user, such as one who is reviewing the financial numbers and their significance for a database management application. A tag is a command inserted into a document that specifies how the document, or a portion of it, should be formatted. Tags are used by all format specifications that store documents as text files, including SGML and HTML.

XML is extensible and platform independent and it supports both internationalization and localization. It is self-describing. Like HTML, XML files are also text files that users should not have to read but may when the need arises. XML enables users to define new document formats by combining and reusing other formats to exchange in environments that do not share common platforms. It has the capability to retrieve information from any computer (e.g., PC, Macintosh, or mainframe) with any operating system (e.g., Windows or Unix). XML adds structure and context to unstructured information.

Today, XML is accepted as the standard data interchange tool for the Internet. Yet implementing XML-based projects can be confusing, especially when the same term is ascribed different meanings across different industries.

CFOs and CPAs should refer to the following Web sites to learn more about XML:

- Oasis: http://xmlcoverpages.org/xml.html

- Microsoft: http://msdn.microsoft.com/en-us/data/bb190600.aspx

- IBM: http://www.ibm.com/developerworks/xml/

The following Web sites post a complete list of XML applications:

- http://xml.coverpages.org/siteIndex.html

- http://xml.coverpages.org/xmlApplications.html

XBRL as a Universal Business Reporting Language

The XBRL working group was initiated by the American Institute of Certified Public Accountants (AICPA). The current XBRL Consortium comprises more than 140 of the world's largest accounting, technology, governmental, and financial services bodies. Members of XBRL International include the International Accounting Standards Board, PricewaterhouseCoopers, Deloitte & Touche, Ernst & Young, KPMG, BDO Seidman, Grant Thornton, Bank of America, Deutsche Bank, CCI-1 Tax Compliance, Institute of Management Accountants, Canadian Institute of Chartered Accountants, Institute of Chartered Accountants of Australia, NASDAQ Stock Market, Morgan Stanley Dean Witter, Microsoft, General Electric, Oracle, and IBM.

As a cross-industry XML-based language, XBRL defines a set of vocabulary for the electronic interchange of financial information. XBRL "tags" specific information with a precise contextual description. This improves both the validity of reported data as per generally accepted accounting principles (GAAP) and investor access to that information. The goal of XBRL is to facilitate the reporting of business information, not to capture data at the transaction level. Consequently, the financial information includes such data as annual and quarterly reports, SEC filings, general ledger information, net revenue, and accountancy schedules.

The components of XBRL are as follows:

- *XBRL specification.* Explains what XBRL is and how to build XBRL instance documents and XBRL taxonomies. The XBRL specification explains XBRL in technical terms and is intended for a technical audience.

- *XBRL schema.* Made up of the core low-level components of XBRL, that is, the physical XML Schema Definition (XSD) and Document Type Definition (DTD) files that express how instance documents and taxonomies are to be built.

- *XBRL taxonomy.* A "dictionary" created by a group compliant with the XBRL specification to exchange business information.

- *XBRL instance document.* A business report, such as a financial statement prepared to the XBRL specification. The meaning of the values in the instance document is explained by the taxonomy. An instance document is somewhat useless unless the taxonomy to which it is prepared is known.

The primary problems solved by XBRL are in the preparation and use of business reports. A report currently not prepared in XBRL cannot be used for multiple purposes. The same report, if prepared in XBRL format, however, can be used for printing (word processing), filing (EDGAR), or posting on a Web site (HTML). That is, the information is entered once and used many times. For example, a report originally prepared for EDGAR may be used for banking and other regulatory reports. Extracting specified detailed information from a financial statement published on the Internet, even an electronic financial statement such as an EDGAR filing, is a difficult and time-consuming task. A user cannot, for example, obtain inventory turnover ratios of one or more corporations from the EDGAR Web site. However, if a financial statement is prepared with XBRL standards, numerous computer programs can easily extract every piece of information to that statement.

To enable companies to create XBRL statements, accounting software vendors will put XBRL tags in their accounting systems that allow users to cross-reference their accounts to this framework. Some of the most popular accounting software companies have already announced their plans to provide XBRL output in the financial statements; the list includes SAP, Oracle, Great Plains, and ACCPAC. On March 5, 2002, Microsoft became the first major corporation to publish its financial statements on the Internet using the XBRL framework. SEC requires that by 2011 all public companies must be onboard.

Companies will have to use XBRL for the three primary financial statements as well as for footnotes, which can be presented in a "block" format in the first year but must be in a more detailed format in subsequent years. Companies will be allowed to file their first XBRL-coded submissions 30 days after they conduct a more traditional filing on the SEC's EDGAR database system. But all subsequent financial results must be filed on EDGAR and with XBRL tagging at the same time.

Applications of XBRL

The many accounting, financial, and business applications of XBRL include:

- Automating business reporting.
- Financial statement preparation and analysis. For example, XBRL financial statements on a company's Web site can go directly into Microsoft Excel so rekeying is not required.
- Auditing of financial statements.
- Managing and distributing accounting data.
- Consolidating and reporting data to regulatory bodies.
- Collecting and updating financial data on borrowers, such as by accessing the borrower's Web page.
- Assessing credit risk.
- Integrating investment information.
- Communicating financial performance to users of financial statements.
- Internal management reporting, such as cost control and analysis.

In addition, companies can measure their performance more accurately against their competitors. For regulators, the advantages of XBRL are clear. The ability to receive files via the Internet and read them with computers is a big attraction; and being able to manipulate the data automatically offers huge cost-savings. Regulators can run instantaneous analyses of trends and ratios that might be indicative of underpayment of tax. They can divide tax returns into high risk and low risk to help inspectors decide where to focus resources.

XBRL-enabled applications include:

- Federal Deposit Insurance Corporation's (FDIC's) new Call Report System. The FDIC believes this system will result in better information quality, more flexibility, and improved timeliness. It will result in about 10,000 U.S. banks submitting quarterly financial information in XBRL.
- One Source Information Services (www.onesource.com) is the first provider to deliver a fully Internet-enabled Web service for XBRL information on U.S. companies.
- The Tokyo Stock Exchange accepts company financial summary filings in XBRL.

XBRL vendors include Decision Soft (http://xbrl.decisionsoft.com), Semansys Technologies (www.semansys.com), Universal Business Matrix (http://www.ubmatrix.com), Oracle (www.oracle.com), SAP (www.sap.com), CaseWare International (www.caseware.com), SYSPRO (www.americassyspro.com), and XBI Software (www.xbisoftware.com).

Benefits of XBRL

Accountants spend a great deal of time creating and formatting reports. The XBRL framework will help speed up financial reporting and user access to that information, reduce financial reporting costs by eliminating redundancies in financial report production, reduce the potential of manual re-entry error, streamline the process of publishing the financial data to the external or internal users, and provide greater flexibility to investment and credit professionals. With XBRL, accountants will be able to render the basic financial information once and deliver it in whatever format is needed, whether for the company's Web site, regulatory reporting and disclosure, or internal management use. XBRL will also benefit authoritative accounting literature and internal accounting and business reports. Authoritative literature published by the AICPA and Financial Accounting Standards Board (FASB) will describe accounting terminology and accounting related issues clearly and more efficiently; for instance, accounting for foreign exchange transactions may be explained in a drill-down format. Internal accounting reports (e.g., cost reports) and business reports are used for managerial decisions and to capture financial transactions (e.g., purchase requisition forms, purchase orders, and sales invoices).

Those who will benefit from XBRL include:

- *Companies and accountants who prepare financial statements.* They can prepare financial statements more efficiently by imputing information one time and with the same information, creating printing financial statements, Web site financial statements, EDGAR SEC filings and other regulatory filings, and tax returns. For closely held companies, the task of using different accounting software is neutralized as all software programs can be easily linked to each other. For example, a company that uses QuickBooks can download the information through XBRL to an accountant who uses ATB software.

- *Analysts, investors, and regulators.* They will be able to receive financial information in the format they want, and have access to automated analysis from the financial information with less re-keying of information from one form to another.

- *Financial publishers and aggregators.* They will be able to collect data more efficiently by not having to re-key information and will be able to utilize more expanded diagnostic data analysis.

- *Independent software vendors.* Virtually any software product that manages financial information can use XBRL for its data export and import formats, thus increasing its interactivity with other financial and analytical applications.

The AICPA has published the following scenarios to illustrate how XBRL can benefit its users:

- *Financial statements.* XBRL-based financial statements will allow the linking of financial statements with authoritative literature, detailed transactions, audit working papers, and other documents. An audit partner could more easily review financial statements, and CFOs and their staff could better answer questions in board meetings regarding financial statements.

- *Financial analysis.* XBRL can be used for general financial reporting and for comparing information from one company with that of another. This is achieved by using "type" elements to identify in a common way, the varying "labels" used to describe similar information on a financial statement. That is, because XBRL has a universal "chart of accounts," it facilitates financial analysis among companies.

- *Extracting financial information.* XBRL makes it easy to extract information from a financial statement into a model such as an Excel spreadsheet.

- *Audits and assurance services.* If all accounting software is in the same XBRL format, it is much simpler to extract data for use in a financial statement audit. The current inefficient approach of each auditor customizing a system to dump data from an accounting system and then importing data into an audit tool is eliminated. Further, when companies change auditors or accounting systems, their data export infrastructure will still work.

- *Accounting research tools online.* Because all financial data is in a standard format, the ability to extract that data into online versions of tools, such as *Accounting Trends and Techniques,* is possible.

During the next couple of years, virtually any software product that manages or uses financial information could use XBRL for its data export and import formats, thereby increasing its potential for full interoperability with other financial and analytical applications. In addition, given the advantages for companies and their accountants who prepare financial statements, and users of the financial information, the XBRL framework will be the future standard for the delivery and use of financial information over the Web.

XBRL Products and Services

From mainstream software companies to newer niche software creators, XBRL products and services are beginning to proliferate.

- *Cartesis*—The XBRL module pulls tagged data into the company's Cartesis 10 products for benchmarking and M&A analysis and contains an XBRL Publication module that enables companies to self-tag data and generate XBRL documents.

- *CoreFiling*—XBRL provides consulting and tags companies' reported data for SEC filings and press releases (in conjunction with *BusinessWire*).

- *Edgar Online*—Edgar Online tags companies' reported data and validates the accuracy of XBRL self-tags for SEC filing. This product offers *I-Metrix,* a financial-data feed in XBRL format.

- *Fujitsu*—The Interstage XW allows companies to create custom tags, as well as tag basic documents. In addition, it can tag internal data and unify data across enterprise resource planning (ERP) systems.

- *Oracle-Hyperion Solutions*—The System 9 Financial-Reporting Module includes an XBRL component that permits users to consolidate, analyze, and report financial results in XBRL formats.

- *Microsoft*—Excel 2003 and 2007 both support custom-defined XML schemas, such as XBRL, allowing users to construct, publish, and analyze XBRL data. In addition, FRX allows users to convert internal numeric data into XBRL.

- *Oracle*—Releases have supported XBRL and have been updated for most recent taxonomies. Customers can convert internal general-ledger data into XBRL and publish rolled-up data in XBRL for external-reporting purposes.

- *Rivet Software*—*DragonTag* assists in tagging Word and Excel documents in XBRL for reporting purposes. The *Crossfire Analyst* (in beta) collects and analyzes XBRL data; and *Rivet* tags companies' reported data for SEC filings.

- *RR Donnelley*—Along with *Edgar Online*, this product tags documents for clients and validates self-tagged data from companies.

- *SAS*—Risk Intelligence and Financial Intelligence products allow users to analyze XBRL data and publish results with XBRL tags.

- *SavaNet*—SavaNet tags company data for reporting purposes.

- *Semansys Technologies*—*XBRL Taxonomy Builder, XBRL Composer*, and *XBRL Integrator* allow companies to create custom tags, as well as tag basic documents. In addition, companies can tag internal data and unify data across ERP systems.

- *UBmatrix*—*XBRL Taxonomy Designer* and *UBmatrix Report Builder* tools assist companies in creating custom tags, as well as tagging basic documents. The tools can tag internal data and unify data across ERP, CRM, and other systems.

CLOUD COMPUTING AND COMPETITIVE ADVANTAGE

Mobile communication and cloud computing are the two prevailing technological trends today. In many businesses, desktop computers are fast becoming obsolete with the advent of ever smaller laptops, netbooks, smartphones, and other compact mobile devices. Furthermore, virtual private networks (VPN) offer secure access to company information from any location in the world that provides an Internet connection. If one uses Flickr, Gmail, or Facebook, to name a few, he or she is already participating in cloud computing. Photos and other data are stored in a remote location that can be accessed by using a PC, laptop, netbook, or smartphone.

Most IT departments are forced to spend a significant portion of time on frustrating implementation, maintenance, and upgrade projects that too often add no significant value to the company's bottom line. Increasingly, IT teams are turning to cloud computing technology to minimize the time spent on lower-value activities and allow IT to focus on strategic activities with greater impact on the business. Cloud computing requires no management of hardware and software. It has a shared infrastructure that causes it to function like a utility: Payment is required for only what is needed, upgrades are automatic, and scaling up or down is easy. A cloud can be private or public. A *public cloud* sells services to anyone on the Internet. (Currently, Amazon Web Services is the largest public cloud provider followed by Microsoft Azure.) A *private cloud* is a proprietary network or a data center that supplies hosted services to a limited number of people. When a service provider uses public cloud resources to create their private cloud, the result is called a virtual private cloud. Private or public, the goal of cloud computing is to provide easy, scalable access to computing resources and IT services.

Lately, the concept of a hybrid cloud has become popular. A hybrid cloud is a combination of at least one private cloud and one public cloud. Although the characteristics of the hybrid cloud are combined together, the two remain unique and as a result offer users the benefits of both. That is, hybrid clouds provide users with private cloud security combined with the benefits of cost-effective usage and scalability characteristics of the public cloud.

Instead of running applications personally, clouds run on a shared data center (i.e., remote network clusters, or "clouds"). Once an application is accessed by logging in with the requested ID and password, it can be customized and used.

Businesses are running all types of applications in the clouds these days, such as CRM, HR, accounting, and custom-built applications. Unlike traditional business software, cloud-based applications can be operating in a few days. Cloud computing technology has the competitive advantage of being less expensive, because it does not require the support of staff, products, and facilities to function. In addition, cloud-based applications are more scalable, secure, and reliable than most other applications, with the latest versions of security and performance upgrades auto-matically installed. CFOs are seeing capital requests decrease because cloud computing (or SaaS, in general) is captured as an *operating expense*, not as a capital expenditure.

The Service Models of the Cloud

The National Institute of Standards and Technology (NIST)[1] of the U.S. Depart-ment of Commerce defined the following service models provided by cloud computing:

- Software as a Service (SaaS) – This capability enables a client company to run the provider's applications on a cloud infrastructure accessible through a client device such as a web browser or other program interface. The client company does not control or manage the cloud infrastructure of network, servers, operating systems, storage, or specific available applications. How-ever, the client company may set specific application configuration settings pertinent to its usage.

- Platform as a Service (PaaS) – This service enables the client company to put into use client created or acquired applications that were created using the provider's cloud programming languages, libraries, services, and tools.

---

[1] Peter Mell and Timothy Grance, National Institute of Standards and Technology, U.S. Department of Com-merce, *The NIST Definition of Cloud Computing, Recom-mendations of the National Institute of Standards and Technology.* NIST Special Publication, 800-145, September 2011.

These provider capabilities may also be obtained from other sources. In this service, as in SaaS, the client company does not control or manage the cloud infrastructure of network, servers, operating systems, or storage but is able to control the specific applications that it has put into use as well as any configurations of the application(s) in the cloud environment.

- Infrastructure as a Service (IaaS) – In this service the client company is provided with processing, storage, networks, and other computing resources so that it is able to run and use operating systems and applications. The client company does not control the cloud infrastructure but is given the right to control its specific operating systems, storage, and applications.

Companies are lured to cloud computing by the promise of greater efficiency, lower costs, and higher profits that the aforementioned services provide. In fact, reduction of cost is a compelling factor for the use of cloud computing. In addition to its cost advantages, cloud services provide a "single source of truth" across the globe, provide up-to-the-minute and painless software upgrades, and are a step ahead of constantly altering global accounting standards and other technical regulations. This compares with customers of on premises models paying hundreds of thousands of dollars to upgrade the software in their systems.

Huge Opportunities and Security Risks

The shift from storing information on isolated machines to information sharing in digital and social networks is seen by some as the largest growth opportunity since the Internet boom. The market for cloud products and services will likely soar. However, companies should be cautious about the risks of convenience. Concerns may include the security of transferred confidential data or accessibility and reliability of data stored on these networks or clouds. That cloud disruption is just one in a series of recent incidents: the breach of online marketing provider Epsilon that exposed e-mail addresses and customer names held by about 50 companies, including JPMorgan Chase, Citigroup, and Hilton Hotels; the hacks of Sony's PlayStation Network; the Microsoft BPOS (Business Productivity Online Services) hiccup that also shut down its Outlook portal; Google's software glitch that allowed unauthorized access to a certain percentage of user files and left some Gmail customers unable to use their online applications. Cloud computing is flexible and cost-efficient. But without proven public cloud protection and trusted compliance codes, security remains its largest hurdle. Exhibit 7-1 lists seven cloud security risks.

Exhibit 7-1: Cloud Security Risks

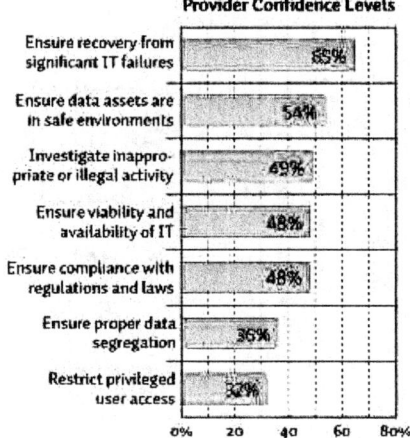

Provider Confidence Levels

Source: Ponemon Institute, "Security of Cloud Computing Providers Study," April 2011, *CFO Magazine*, September 2011 and CFO.com.

ACCOUNTANTS HEAD TO THE CLOUDS

The meteoric growth of cloud computing (see statistics below) has not gone unnoticed by accountants. The literature indicates several significantly appealing benefits for an entity to switch their accounting system to a cloud environment[2]. These include:

- Ease of implementation – Cloud processing applications can be up and running very quickly because there is no software to install. This also applies to companies that have multiple and or remote locations because all of these locations will simultaneously gain access to the application.

- Access to the application(s) from anywhere by an Internet connection ensures that employees may work remotely and have the same processing capabilities as if they were working at their company's business location.

- Upfront costs may be less than paying for an annual license fee. Many cloud vendors allow their clients to pay monthly, although some may require annual contracts. Because cloud servers are designed to accommodate many customers that share the cloud infrastructure, including networks, servers, storage, and programs, accounting costs are minimized.

- There are minimal or no maintenance or hardware costs – Because maintenance, software, and hardware are maintained by the cloud vendor, the vendor is responsible for the costs of these items. As a result, fees are minimized for the user entity, and the cost of doing business is generally less than doing so "in-house."

---

[2] Alexandra Defelice, "Cloud Computing: What Accountants Need to Know," *Journal of Accountancy* (AICPA); October 1, 2010. (Comments by Donny C. Shimamoto, Founder and Managing Director of Intraprise techKnowlogies, have been included).

- The need for IT "in-house" professionals is minimized – Payroll costs for the consumer entity are minimized because the cloud vendor supplies all IT support needed for the applications used by the cloud environment.

- Better more effective use of IT professionals – Because of the use of cloud applications, professionals who are on payroll are not needed for support of in-house accounting processing, maintenance, and program updating, and may now be deployed for more strategic IT planning and projects.

- Upgrades to software applications are made seamlessly and automatically – Customers are alerted to upgrades that occur automatically in the background without disrupting customer processing. In addition, customers are given the option to turn on or ignore upgraded new features.

- Benefit from the backup and disaster recovery capabilities of a cloud environment – One of the most sensitive and risky issues facing an entity who maintains data files "on-premises" is backing them up to protect against loss. Commonly, this is done by creating back-up files or utilizing a back-up provider. Although there are security and risk issues related to cloud computing (see Exhibit 7-1 above), commonly, cloud vendors have reliable redundant backup systems so that customer data may be replicated in a separate data center in case of a disaster such as, for example, a fire, a flood, tornado damage. In general, when a backup is launched, another replication is automatically created.

The use of cloud computing to lower accounting costs has gained a strong foothold among small and medium-size companies. There is practically limitless room for growth in this market. Recent studies have found that 78% of all U.S. small businesses will have fully adopted cloud computing by 2020. This more than doubles the current percentage of 37% that exists today. In addition, American small- and medium-cloud computing is expected to grow from $43 billion in 2015 to $55 billion in 2016. Compass Intelligence estimates an annual growth rate increase of 40% from 2011 to 2016 in this area.[3]

The American Institute of Certified Public Accountants (AICPA) is strengthening its endorsement of software-as-a-service solutions for small and midsize businesses, citing lower costs and competitive advantages. It is essentially pushing to accelerate adoption of cloud solutions among its 350,000 members, focusing especially on small and midmarket companies as well as CPA firms. The AICPA's first official endorsement of a cloud vendor, payroll-solutions provider **Paychex,** came several years ago. But the institute has rolled out more such partnerships with increasing frequency, including partnering with bill.com for invoice management and payment in 2008, financial management and accounting software maker **Intacct** a year ago, and tax-automation supplier **Copanion** at year-end 2009. Another cloud vendor that will receive the AICPA's approval this spring is **CPA2Biz,** an AICPA subsidiary that provides the parent with technology and marketing services and advocates the use of accounting automation by small businesses.

---

[3] "Roundup of Small and Medium Business Cloud Computing Forecasts and Market Estimates," 2015, *Forbes*, May 4, 2015, Louis Columbus, contributor.

FUTURE TRENDS IN CLOUD COMPUTING

In recent years, cloud adoption is fast becoming indispensable for those entities wanting to maintain a competitive edge. A recent study by technology and media giant, International Data Group, provides important insights about what to expect in 2017[4]:

Investment in cloud computing will continue to increase with companies in the United States planning to spend an average of $1.77 million on cloud computing, while companies in Europe and the rest of the world plan to spend $1.3 million. Larger companies (with over 1,000 employees) intend to spend an average of $3 million with one in ten intending to spend at least $330 million. In addition, it is predicted that in 2017, companies will spend 28% of their information technology (IT) budgets on cloud computing with 45% on Software as a Service (SaaS), 30% on Infrastructure as a Service (IaaS), and 19% on Platform as a Service (PaaS) for development.

1. Most companies in 2017 will be using the cloud to run their applications. Currently, at least 70% of all organizations have a cloud-run application. In comparison, in 2011 only 51% of companies utilized cloud-run applications. For larger companies, the numbers are more pronounced with 75% using the cloud to run applications. Current predictions are that by 2020, this number will grow to 90% with an upward trend continuing into the future. In addition, by the end of 2017, most IT departments will have both the majority of their applications and platforms on cloud systems.

2. In 2017-18, companies plan to increase their use of cloud computing. Specifically, over the next 18 months, companies surveyed indicated an increase in cloud computing from 45% to 60% with the following classification augmentations: private cloud: 23% to 28%, public cloud: 15% to 22%, and hybrid cloud 7% to 10%. It is apparent that not only are companies relying more on the cloud for their computing operations but that private and public clouds will experience the greatest increases. Currently, 62% of all companies use private clouds, 60% use public clouds, and 26% use hybrid clouds, thus indicating that all three cloud configurations are being used to satisfy companies' IT demands.

3. The use of the cloud to perform big data analytics for both large and small size entities will be a significant reason for cloud adoption in 2017. Big data analytics consist of evaluating large amounts of data for unexpected correlations, trends, market relationships, unexpected patterns, and analytic demands. The poll showed that 22% of companies indicated that big data analytics would be the main reason for their migration to the cloud in 2017 followed by 21% for data storage and management.

The survey also found that there was a difference between large and medium/small companies regarding how money was authorized for cloud adoption expenditures. In large companies, chief information officers, IT architects, and IT network-

---

[4] http://idgenterprise.com/resource/research/2016/-cloud-computing-executive-summary/ cited in https:// www.eukhost.com/blog/webhosting/6-predictions-for-cloud–computing-in-2017/

ing management individuals control cloud budgets. In medium/small businesses, such spending is directed by chief executives and chief financial officers. This distinction is significant because those organizations with IT architects (large companies), that is, those that have personnel with IT clout, are more likely to push for cloud adoption when compared to medium/small organizations that do not have IT officers and must first seek the approval of senior financial officers for such expenditures. The survey found that one of the biggest differences between large and medium/small entities was the influence of an organization's chief IT security officer. It was found that the person in this position has cloud IT spending influence in 80% of large businesses but only 59% in medium/small businesses.

Although the adoption of cloud services in 2017 is expected to significantly rise, it is important to note that companies have reservations about cloud usage. The survey indicated concerns relating to:

- Where data is stored,
- Cloud security, and
- Vendor lock-ins.

Data Storage

Data storage issues relate to privacy regulations that a nation may have relating to its citizens' data. A country may have laws that require information about its citizens be stored on servers physically based within its geographical borders. Therefore, a French company might be precluded from choosing vendors in the United States with American-based servers. In fact, the survey predicted that as a result of such geographical constraints, many companies in the future will choose only those vendors based in the same country as the client company.

Cloud Security

The authors of the survey noted that data security issues should not be a concern because generally cloud vendors have much better security procedures than private data centers with much stronger control standards and procedures. In addition, cloud vendors utilize professional IT staff that are experts in data security, as well as cutting-edge software and hardware minimizing the chance of a data security breach.

Vendor Lock-ins

Regarding over reliance on cloud vendors (vendor lock-ins), companies should develop IT skills from within to privately manage clouds rather than be dependent on a specific cloud vendor. It is predicted that many companies will increase their IT funding for hiring and training company personnel to ensure the development of such clouds. Accordingly, it is expected that next year will see an increase in the use of private and hybrid cloud computing.

WIRELESS TECHNOLOGY (MOBILE COMPUTING)

Mobile computing is fast becoming a feasible alternative for companies that can utilize the advantages it provides: enhanced connectivity and flexibility for companies seeking to expand a computer network or make their employees more mobile.

Major technology companies have adopted its standards and the price and choice of products should only improve.

Wireless fidelity (Wi-Fi) and Bluetooth, two major developing technologies, are changing the computer networking landscape—and can change the entire infrastructure of business networks. The Bluetooth Special Interest Group (SIG; www.bluetooth.com) and the Wi-Fi Alliance (www.weca.net) formed to help effectively develop, integrate, and implement these wireless technologies globally. These two groups have created global standards for each technology, which must be met by any company producing hardware or software to operate with Bluetooth or Wi-Fi, and many new hardware and software products produced by many big name technology companies are equipped for use with Bluetooth and Wi-Fi.

Bluetooth

Bluetooth is a radio frequency specification for short-range data transfer. Any device containing Bluetooth technology, whether it be a handheld PC, cell phone, laptop, or standard PC, receives the signal broadcasted by the network. The Bluetooth SIG was formed to develop and maintain a global standard for Bluetooth wireless technology that facilitates interoperability, advancement, and development of the technology. More than 2,000 companies from around the globe are members of this industry group, which consists of leaders in telecommunications and computing, including Agere, Ericsson, IBM, Intel, Microsoft, Motorola, Nokia, and Toshiba. The Bluetooth-specified standard contains the information necessary to ensure that all devices supporting Bluetooth are able to communicate with each other globally. In other words, no matter who manufactured a device, as long as it has the Bluetooth logo or label on it, it can be fully synchronized with any other Bluetooth device. This is a huge step toward full integration: Instead of using many independently operating devices to accomplish one task, businesses may utilize these devices as one tool by integrating their performance. Using Bluetooth can also give a business many more options in terms of purchasing new hardware and upgrades in the future. Because all Bluetooth devices are fully interoperable, businesses are not forced to go back to the same manufacturer; they can look for the best prices, as long as the alternative device supports Bluetooth.

The current Bluetooth-specified standard calls for the support of several elements. First, there must be general access among devices—they must be able to link, synchronize, and communicate with each other. Next, cordless telephony must be supported, enabling cell phones with Bluetooth to operate as cordless phones when they are in proximity to their base station (i.e., a laptop or desktop PC). The serial ports on Bluetooth-supportive devices will act similar to wire serial ports: Each device will also be able to receive and transmit voice data as well as send faxes. Dial-up networking between a cell phone and a laptop computer are also part of the standard. Bluetooth devices will have full wireless personal area network (WPAN) access, with the ability to transfer files.

Bluetooth Networks. Bluetooth provides a 10-meter personal bubble for the simultaneous transmission of information and voice data. A network of Bluetooth devices is called a piconet. Each piconet can support a maximum of eight devices and a minimum of two. All devices containing Bluetooth can be potentially networked with each other. Each piconet has a master unit and slave units. The master unit synchronizes all of the slave units. The slave units are all of the networked devices other than the master unit. Piconets may be integrated to form a scatter-net by setting up a master device to synchronize several piconet master devices. Therefore, the master device of a piconet can also be a slave in a scatternet. The gross data transfer of Bluetooth devices is 1 megabyte per second (MB/s), whereas the actual data rate is 432 kilobytes per second (KB/s). Bluetooth technology is as secure as a wire with up to 128-bit public/private key authentication. Furthermore, it supports good encryption. As mentioned earlier, Bluetooth transmits its signal for up to 10 meters—that is, when only a 0 dBm radio is used. Using a +20 dBm radio, the link range can be increased to up to 100 meters.

Practical Uses. The most attractive feature of Bluetooth is that all products containing this technology will work together. All manufacturers implementing Bluetooth into their products must get them tested and certified so as to ensure interoperability. Accordingly, this feature is perhaps the most advantageous for a client's business. All of a company's hardware can be integrated and can share information. Employees will be able to synchronize their mobile computer with their desktop simply by placing the mobile computer near the desktop, and thus save much of the time wasted plugging and unplugging. This technology is also useful outside of the office. An employee can leave his or her cell phone in a pocket or purse and, using a laptop, dial up to the Internet, as opposed to lining up the phone's infrared port with that of the mobile computer. The best part is that this synchronization will be automatic when the devices are within a certain range of each other.

Currently, Bluetooth's most practical uses are wireless synchronization of devices and serving as small networks. Its range limits its ability to serve the needs of large networks. However, for small business or sole practitioners who require smaller networks, Bluetooth can serve this purpose. The main advantage of Bluetooth, though, is the ability a CPA and businessperson has when making use of this technology. A person can coordinate each piece of his or her equipment to create a more powerful and efficient business tool.

Wireless Fidelity

Wireless fidelity (Wi-Fi), also known as 802.11b, has a transmission range that is longer than that of Bluetooth. Wi-Fi transfers data at 11 MB/s. (Wireless-G operates at speeds almost five times faster than 802.11b and is compatible with 802.11b products.) Many large corporations use Wi-Fi wireless devices to extend standard wired networks to such areas as training classrooms and large public spaces. In addition, many companies make use of Wi-Fi to provide wireless networks to their employees. These wireless networks may also be accessed remotely from employees' homes or other offices. Wi-Fi is also used to bridge the information flow between two or more offices in different buildings.

Wi-Fi networks are also found in public places such as hotels and airports. When in an area that supports Wi-Fi, a Wi-Fi-certified product is automatically linked to the network when the device is turned on. Wi-Fi is ideal for mid-sized and large companies. It enables businesses to boost productivity and efficiency through constant real-time flow of information, full sharing of data, and constant, uninterrupted communication. People are able to continue to work on projects or prepare for meetings in the airport while they are waiting to board their flight. With wireless technologies such as Wi-Fi, companies can keep their employees, whether they are in or out of the office, up to date at all times. In time, Wi-Fi networks will be just about everywhere. Members of the Wi-Fi Alliance—all major players in their respective markets—plan to bring Wi-Fi to urban areas, central cities, and even some major highways.

Another advantage of Wi-Fi is mobility. Having a wireless network affords client companies many options. Other wireless computers are easily added to a Wi-Fi network by plugging in the user's card or universal serial bus (USB) connection. After doing so, the computer is instantly networked. Computers can just as easily be removed. Furthermore, if a client's business needs to move, the company will not have to abandon its network infrastructure or hire someone to rewire its new office location. To assemble a wireless network, all that needs to be done is to simply unplug at the old office and plug in the base station to a power outlet at the new office, and then turn on the other devices.

Range and Security. When a Wi-Fi computer is close to the base station, it can transfer and receive data at a rate of up to 11 MB/s. As the Wi-Fi device is moved further away from the base station, the data rate will drop to around 5.5 MB/s. Generally, the lowest data transfer rate at the maximum range from a base station will not drop below 1 MB/s or 2 MB/s. This is a drastic deterioration from the 11 MB/s maximum transfer rate. However, transferring information at 1 MB/s is still an acceptable performance level, as compared to other connection types. For instance, 1 MB/s is faster than most digital service line (DSL) and cable connections. Therefore, it is still an above-average high-speed transmission and adequate for sending and receiving e-mail, browsing the Internet, and entering data from a mobile computer. A standard Wi-Fi antenna broadcasts from 750 to 1,000 feet outdoors, in open spaces. In an office or other workplace setting, which has other stimuli that could interfere with the signal, the standard antenna broadcasts from 150 to 350 feet. Dense materials such as certain metals may affect the transmission of radio waves, and therefore affect a Wi-Fi broadcast. If the walls in an office are heavily reinforced with such materials as metal, heavy wood, brick, or stone, Wi-Fi devices may have difficulty transmitting from one room to another.

Wired Equivalent Privacy (WEP) is 802.11's encryption standard. WEP works by encrypting the data transferred between the Wi-Fi computer and the Wi-Fi access point. A Wi-Fi access point is a hardware device or software that acts as a communication hub for wireless devices to connect to a wired local area network (LAN). WEP and 802.11 provide wireless security while extending the service range that a user of wireless technology can access. When data is sent to the access point, it is done so via the public Internet. Therefore, unless it is encrypted, the data is unprotected during its transmission. When the data reaches the access point, it is encrypted and transferred to a Wi-Fi device by WEP. However, there have been several security problems with WEP. Consequently, other wireless technology standards with better security are consequently also in development, such as IEE 802.1X, which is a more secure wireless access that makes use of an Extensible Authentication Protocol (EAP). The Wi-Fi Alliance is planning on implementing a new security standard called Wi-Fi Protected Access (WPA), which implements 802.1X and the EAP to provide better security.

Many corporations use Virtual Private Networks (VPNs) to protect remote access to their WLANs. The VPNs also protect their connections. A VPN creates a secure virtual tunnel from the user's computer all the way to the corporation's server. This means that a secure connection is established from the user's Wi-Fi hardware, through his or her Wi-Fi access point, over the public Internet, through the corporation's access point, to the corporation's hardware. Existing systems can be modified to make use of VPN as to support a Wi-Fi network. There are many different types of VPNs, some of which are very expensive. Microsoft, however, provides a very basic VPN technology that is free. The VPN is provided with Microsoft's advanced server operating systems.

A VPN works through a company's server. It encrypts any data transferred to company computers from outside the office. VPN software also operates on remote computers and laptops. VPNs enable the transfer of data while protecting that data from being viewed by intruding parties. Setting up a VPN gives a company mobility, supporting communications from areas such as airports and hotels, thus enabling people to stay abreast of developing situations, which may be crucial to a client company. Through VPNs, individuals can access information in company networks from anywhere and companies can expand their networks to the homes of their employees. Therefore, through the use of a WLAN with a VPN, part-time employees can do more from the personal computers in their homes. In addition, full-time employees can spend more time with their families, due to the fact that they can perform a variety of tasks from their homes. Another important aspect of Wi-Fi security is its ability to provide different levels of access. For example, a company can provide top-notch security while allowing open access to the Internet and e-mail accounts for guests on the network. This is accomplished by granting network access at different levels. Therefore, a company's visitors can still have unlimited access to the Internet and e-mail while the VPN access is given only to authorized employees.

In addition to a VPN, wireless networks have a standard technology called Remote Access Dial-Up User Service (RADIUS). RADIUS is used to protect access to wireless networks. Remote Access Dial-Up User Service is security that allows only approved users to access the network. In order for someone to access the network and the corresponding files contained on the network, he or she must input a user name and password. The RADIUS server then verifies the name and password and, if correct, allows that person to access the network. A key feature to RADIUS is that it may be used to provide different levels of access. A company may use a RADIUS server to provide access to the Internet, another level of access for network databases, and yet another for e-mail. Microsoft provides a basic RADIUS server with its advanced server operating systems for free. Other RADIUS servers may be purchased in the forms of software and hardware, but can be rather pricey.

One of the most formidable lines of system defense is the firewall. Firewalls work by blocking unwanted and unauthorized people from viewing company databases. Many Wi-Fi access points have built-in firewalls. In addition, all Wi-Fis include a network capability enabling a group of devices to share one Internet provider (IP) address, regardless of whether the IP is from a dial-up, cable, or DSL connection. This capability is called Network Address Translation (NAT). NAT works by creating new IP addresses for each computer of the group from the original single IP address. Therefore, the new IP addresses are invisible to users of the public Internet. The new IP addresses function separately "under the cover" of the original one.

Public Wi-Fi. Wireless networks are making their way into today's businesses and are steadily becoming a reality in many public areas. Companies such as Wayport, a company that provides Wi-Fi to hotels, airports, and other public areas around the country, are teaming up with major companies such as Sony, Sharp, and other members of the Wi-Fi Alliance to provide wireless fidelity. The Four Seasons, Holiday Inn, Hampton Inn, Ramada, and other major hotels are also teaming up to provide wireless fidelity, through Wayport, in their hotel chains. With members of industry groups such as the Bluetooth SIG and Wi-Fi Alliance pushing the development and advancement of a global wireless infrastructure, more hardware will be built on this standard. Cellular phones and laptops equipped with Bluetooth and Wi-Fi certification are already on the market. Eventually, wired connections will be a thing of the past. With hotels and airports around the world upgrading to wireless, companies that go wireless will be a step ahead. They will have the up-to-the-minute information needed, full integration of technological equipment, full access to their network databases, and the infrastructure to make it possible from anywhere in the world. An interested party's best bet is to begin researching the benefits and detriments of going wireless. The benefits of going wireless are:

- It is cost-effective because there are no costs to wire or for the labor to do so (it requires only setting up a software protocol).
- The network is portable—computers can be moved around the wireless router (a radio transmitter).
- It has peer-to-peer flexibility because of the absence of wires, so a traditional wired router is not needed.

The detriments of going wireless are:

- Transmission time is slower than the fastest wired networks.
- Radio frequency transmission is believed by some to cause health problems similar to those caused by microwaves (this is controversial).
- There may be security problems.

With the use of a *bridge*, a wireless network may be hooked up to a wired network. Therefore, a company's system may have an integration of wired and wireless networks. Beginning to upgrade now may be beneficial in the long run.

WiMAX, 3G, 4G, and LTE Technologies

Worldwide Interoperability for Microwave Access (WiMAX) is a wireless metropolitan area network based on the 802.16 family of standards. It covers a much wider area than a Wi-Fi wireless network, has a long-range radio with a reach of up to 50kms, and has the potential for speeds of up to 70 mbps.

The third generation of cellular wireless (3G) is faster at displaying and sending content than the second generation of cellular wireless (2G), the mobile standard used by most people in Europe. Yet, unlike Wi-Fi or broadband, 3G only offers download speeds of up to 384 kilobits per second. However, 3G will operate faster on a laptop (or other device) if a 3G/high-speed downlink packet access (HSDPA) card is added.

The fourth generation of cellular wireless and a successor to 3G and 2G standards is 4G, which can upgrade existing communication networks. It is expected to provide a comprehensive and secure IP-based solution where facilities such as voice, data, and streamed multimedia will be provided to users on an anytime, anywhere basis and at much higher data rates compared to previous generations.

LTE (Long-Term Evolution, for short), marketed as 4G LTE, is a standard for wireless communication of high-speed data for mobile phones and data terminals. It aims to increase the capacity and speed of sending and receiving data using a different radio interface together with core network improvements.

Wireless versus Wired

Mobility and efficiency are the advantages of using wireless technology. Using other network technologies, such as wired, phone line, or power-line-based networks, requires connections through wire or cable. Wireless uses radio waves that are capable of traveling through walls and floors. Furthermore, connections can be made from anywhere, regardless of whether a person is indoors or outdoors. Wireless networks do not require phone jacks to be close to the devices for them to be networked with the rest of the system. This completely eliminates the inefficient and expensive task of hiring people to rewire an office to support a wired network. Furthermore, wireless technology simply eradicates the clutter of wires around offices. In addition, power line networks are generally more expensive than Wi-Fi networks. Plus, transformers, large appliances, and surge protectors may interfere with power line networks (a type of wired network). Lastly, no wired network is portable.

An employee at an office with a wired network cannot pick up his or her laptop and go to another part of the office to continue his or her work unless there is an available connection. With wireless networks, having a limited number of connections in an office is not an issue because everywhere is a connection. For a company already having an expensive wired network in the office, adding wireless components would not be a problem. Many wireless access points and gateways allow users to connect to wired equipment, and corporations frequently do this. Companies can extend their wired networks by adding Wi-Fi networks. By connecting wireless access points to an existing wired network, a company can provide wireless access to all areas of its office.

The major problem with wireless technology is its price tag. The components for wired networks are still cheaper than wireless network components. Access points can cost up to $1,000 each. Therefore, the cost of hardware that supports wireless connections can be easily two to four times more expensive than wired network components. The opposing argument, however, is that this higher cost for hardware is offset by the ease of installation and maintenance. Accordingly, long-run costs to maintain the equipment are lower. There will be no expenditures to replace old wires. Furthermore, companies using wireless will never have to hire an electrician to run electrical wiring or install outlets to make a part of the office "networkable." If the company is wireless, all that need be done is to power on the new hardware, and it is instantly networked. For a wireless network, the major expenditures will be for new hardware to add to the network, but companies will not have to drill holes or run wires through floors and ceilings when installing a wireless network.

Access points are a bit pricey; however, in most instances, the purchases of additional access points will be few and far between. The only foreseeable instance in which the purchase of a new access point will be necessary is when a company needs to significantly expand its network. As more hardware is produced to support wireless communication, more people will switch to this newer technology. Therefore, as demand grows, the price will decline. Also offsetting the higher costs of wireless are the savings the technology generates. As a result of lower maintenance costs, companies will spend less on information technology. This, coupled with greater efficiency and a higher level of productivity (generated through the use of wireless), will result in higher bottom lines.

The Accountant's Role

The accountant must stay abreast of the latest developments in wireless networks to properly advise client companies. This requires becoming familiar with the various business applications of wireless networks, the benefits, the drawbacks, and getting the most out of the system to enhance efficiency, productivity, timeliness, and profitability. The use of wireless networks will optimize computer operations and corporate activities. In a wireless network, a wireless network adapter is installed in each computer so there is no need to drill holes and run cables. However, the further the wirelessly networked computer is from a wireless access point, and the greater the number of solid objects standing in the way, the slower the connection will be. To optimize network speed and range, the wireless access point should be at least a few feet above the floor and *not* close to metal objects. It is suggested to position the access point in the center of the coverage area; however, another approach is to position the access point so it is as close to the largest number of computers as is feasibly possible. With larger areas, or those with many obstructions, multiple access points are needed. CPAs should advise clients to make sure the access points have the same settings. Almost all wireless network adapters support "roaming." When access point coverage areas overlap, the adapter will latch onto the strongest signal.

Because reliability, performance, and range depend on signal quality, an *extra* antenna should be added to the network adapter and access point in order to materially improve the quality of the signal. Signal strength—a card's ability to receive data under different conditions—is crucial to successful transmission. The farther away from the gateway, the more degraded the signal strength and performance. The measure of gateway performance is the combination of range and throughput. *Range* is a term that means how far a wireless user can go from the gateway and still have an acceptable signal. *Throughput* measures the amount of work performed by a computer system over a specified time period, and it decreases dramatically when several users access the gateway simultaneously. The card in the gateway has a fixed bandwidth that all client cards must share. For security reasons, numbers should be combined with letters in the wireless network's Service Set Identifier, which each wireless device on the network uses to log in.

Considerations for CFOs, CIOs, and Users

Wireless technology raises specific concerns and challenges for CFOs, CIOs, and users.

CFOs. Mobile working can dramatically boost productivity and improve an organization's responsiveness and flexibility. It also poses challenges for the CFO. However, as the trend toward mobile working gathers momentum, these are issues that CFOs cannot afford to ignore. As wired and wireless network-enabled notebook PCs and smart phones proliferate, mobile working is becoming a reality, not just for the select few corporate "road warriors," but for a much larger group of employees.

This expansion has significant advantages—and risks—for corporate managements. On the positive side, mobile and remote access to corporate systems, such as e-mail, enterprise portals, and such applications as contact management and customer relationship management systems often provide a competitive edge for companies while improving both customer and employee satisfaction. On the other hand, mobile technologies and services tend to come with premium price tags, pushing costs up at a time when chief executives are still under pressure to improve margins and show rapid returns on investments.

Mobile systems are also notoriously difficult to manage and control and perhaps, most seriously, ad-hoc arrangements can represent a real threat to enterprise system security. Balancing the risks and rewards of mobile working and establishing a corporate policy framework to cover, for example, remote access to corporate networks, has become an important issue for CFOs—an issue that they ignore at their peril.

CFOs will want to ensure that they are getting value for money when they invest in mobile working infrastructure. Therefore, they will probably want to see estimates—and subsequently evidence—of productivity gains and other tangible improvements. They also will want to see investment return projections and will probably be involved in making choices about competing projects.

Most likely, CFOs also will be concerned about how to ensure that mobile and remote workers are earning their keep when they are out of the office. Trust plays a key role in enabling a mobile workforce, but it is important to lay down guidelines and keep a watch on costs to ensure they do not spiral out of control. Given the growing threat posed by e-mail viruses, spyware, and other unwelcome network intrusions, most CFOs are well advised to take steps to ensure that the benefits of mobile working are not negated by the threat it can pose to corporate security. Although it may be tempting to use security as an excuse for inaction, the competitive and financial risks of not adopting mobile working practices when competitors are pushing forward may be even greater.

CIOs. Like it or not, mobile devices ranging from Wi-Fi-enabled notebook PCs and smartphones to data-centric communicators such as the Treo 600 or RIM's Blackberry are finding their way into the corporate environment. Sometimes they are part of a corporate roll-out and can therefore be planned and controlled. More often than not, however, they are surreptitiously introduced by individuals who have tasted the benefits of remote access and mobile working as consumers and now want to use the same devices and services at work. One of the key challenges for CIOs in either case is to find ways to accommodate a diverse group of mobile devices while protecting the corporate IT infrastructure and minimizing the network security threat they can pose.

Given the fast pace of change in the technology industry, particularly in the mobile device sector, it is also often a challenge for a CIO to keep up with hardware, software, and service developments and to provide the level of support—often with reduced resources—that users have come to expect. One way to minimize the support overhead is to standardize on a set of devices such as notebook PCs, smartphones, mobile phones, and communicators. However, this often delays deployment and can lead to end-user frustration. Another option is to outsource the provision of devices and services. For example, U.S.-based Aruba, which supplies secure Wi-Fi networks for corporate customers, says many customers also want it to manage the deployment and maintenance of the Wi-Fi system.

One of the fastest growing areas in the mobile technology sector is security. Typically, larger companies will deploy virtual private networks to facilitate secure access for mobile and remote users (e.g., home office workers) to a corporate network. However, there are secure alternatives, including remote access programs such as LapLink and the GoToMyPC remote access service that can be rolled out across an enterprise or made available to a few users. There is also a growing market for software and hardware, such as mini-USB drives, and biometric devices, such as fingerprint readers designed to protect confidential or sensitive data stored on a portable PC. Other vendors have developed systems designed to enable secure access to e-mail and other corporate services from Internet public access points such as hotels, conference centers, or even Wi-Fi hotspots.

Most CIOs have already discovered that the trend toward mobile working cannot be stopped. So while it makes sense to lay down guidelines about which mobile devices are supported and how they should be used, ultimately the CIO has to deal with the realities of mobile working.

Users. The rapid growth of mobile working and the proliferation of new hardware devices, software, and services designed to enable mobile employees to do their jobs from virtually anywhere poses both great opportunities and challenges. For many employees, the availability of basic tools, such as portable PCs, pocket-sized smartphones, and the now nearly ubiquitous mobile phone, gives them much greater freedom and flexibility. For example, salespeople can use mobile technologies to update customer profiles, download price quotes, and provide their audiences with dazzling multimedia presentations. Executives can send and receive e-mail messages, peer into the corporate enterprise resource planning (ERP) system, or check share prices and competitors' Web sites while traveling using Wi-Fi or WLAN wireless connections. For mobile professionals in particular, as a recent study conducted by Intel, the U.S. chipmaker, showed, technology has dramatically changed their lives, making it much easier to stay in touch while traveling and respond to colleagues and customers in a more timely fashion. Meanwhile, a growing number of employees now have broadband Internet access at home or work in remote local offices and yet can tie back into corporate headquarters securely via a virtual private network connection. However, while more and more employees have "always-on" wired and wireless Internet access, they are also finding that they need to set boundaries in order to ensure that they retain a balance between home and office lives and that they are the masters of technology rather than its slave.

Individual attitudes toward mobile technology also vary. For example, while some employees relish the idea of being able to deal with the overnight flood of e-mail using a wireless device on the train before they reach the office, others balk at the idea of work intruding into another part of their life. Balancing the demands of work and private lives in the age of mobile technology—when the pressure for greater productivity is often unrelenting—has become one of the more interesting questions probed by sociologists.

Fortunately, with the wide range of technologies available, most employees can choose which technologies to adopt and just how much they should intrude into their home lives. Arguably, portable PCs, tablets, and smartphones enable employees to work more flexibly and at times that best suit them. Provided a balance is kept, mobile devices and technologies can be valuable tools that enrich both work and private lives.

HANDHELD DEVICE SECURITY AND CONTINGENCY PLANNING

While these mobile devices provide productivity benefits, they also pose new risks to an organization for the following reasons:

- Because of their small size and use outside the office, handheld devices can be easier to misplace or to have stolen than a laptop or notebook computer.

If they do fall into the wrong hands, gaining access to the information they store or are able to access remotely can be relatively easy.

- Communications networks, desktop synchronization, and tainted storage media can be used to deliver malware to handheld devices. Malware is often disguised as a game, device patch, utility or other useful third-party application available for download. Once installed, malware can initiate a wide range of attacks and spread itself onto other devices.

- Similar to desktop computers, tablets, cell phones, and other mobile phones are subject to spam, but this can include text messages and voice mail, in addition to electronic mail. Besides the inconvenience of deleting spam, charges may apply for inbound activity. Spam can also be used for phishing attempts.

- Electronic eavesdropping on phone calls, messages, and other wirelessly transmitted information is possible through various techniques. Installing spy software on a device to collect and forward data elsewhere, including conversations captured via a built-in microphone, is perhaps the most direct means, but other components of a communications network, including the airwaves, are possible avenues for exploitation.

Handheld device security (also called: mobile device security, wireless handheld device security, enterprise device security, handheld security, device security, PDA security, wireless data security) and the corresponding contingency plans must be addressed in the company's overall contingency planning. The National Institute of Standards and Technology (NIST) issued two of its publications. The first one, *Guidelines on Cell Phone and Smartphone Security* (www.itbusinessedge.com/cm/docs/DOC-1371), provides an overview of cell phone and other mobile devices currently in use and offers insights into making informed IT security decisions on their treatment. The document gives details about the threats and technology risks associated with the use of these devices and the available safeguards to mitigate them. Organizations can use this information to enhance security and reduce incidents involving cell phone and smartphone devices.

The second document is *NIST Contingency Planning Guide for IT Systems* (www.itbusinessedge.com/cm/docs/DOC-1370). This in-depth guide provides instructions, recommendations, and considerations for government IT contingency planning. Contingency planning refers to interim measures to recover IT services following an emergency or system disruption. Interim measures may include the relocation of IT systems and operations to an alternate site, the recovery of IT functions using alternate equipment, or the performance of IT functions using manual methods.

PART III

GENERALLY ACCEPTED ACCOUNTING PRINCIPLES

CHAPTER 8

FINANCIAL STATEMENT REPORTING: THE INCOME STATEMENT[*]

CONTENTS

---

[*] Adrian P. Fitzsimons Ph.D., CPA (St. John's University, NY), and Biagio Pilato, LL.M., CPA (St. John's University, NY), contributed to the updates in this chapter.

Income statement preparation involves proper revenue and expense recognition. There are many methods available to recognize revenue, including specialized methods for particular industries. Extraordinary and nonrecurring items require separate presentation. The income statement format is highlighted along with the earnings-per-share computation.

INCOME STATEMENT FORMAT

The format of the income statement, starting with income from continuing operations follows:

Income from continuing operations before tax		$XXX
Less: Taxes		XXX
Income from continuing operations		XXX
Discontinued operations:		
Income for discontinued operations (net of tax)	$XXX	
Loss or gain on disposal of a division (net of tax)	XXX	XXX
Net income		$XXX

Note: Earnings per share is shown on these items as well.

Comprehensive Income

ASC 220, *Comprehensive Income,* requires companies to report comprehensive income and its elements in a full set of financial statements. ASC 220 keeps the current reporting requirements for net income, but it considers net income a major element of comprehensive income. A restatement of previous years' financial statements is needed when presented for comparative purposes.

Comprehensive income applies to the change in equity (net assets) arising from either transactions or other occurrences with nonowners. Excluded are investments and withdrawals by nonowners. Comprehensive income is made up of two components (1) net income and (2) other comprehensive income. Other comprehensive income relates to all items of comprehensive income excluding net income. Thus, net income plus other comprehensive income equals total comprehensive income. Other comprehensive income includes the following:

- Foreign currency items, including translation gains and losses, and gains and losses on foreign currency transactions designated as hedges of a net investment in a foreign entity.

- Unrealized losses or gains on available-for-sale securities.

- Minimum pension liability adjustments applying to the amount by which the additional pension liability exceeds the unrecognized prior service cost.

- Changes in market value of a futures contract that is a hedge of an asset reported at fair value.

ASC 220 provides flexibility on how comprehensive income may be shown in the financial statements. Two allowable options for reporting other comprehensive income and its components are as follows:

1. Below the net income figure in the income statement, or

2. In a separate statement of comprehensive income beginning with net income.

Options 1 and 2 are income-statement-type formats.

A sample presentation under option 1 within the income statement follows.

Statement of Income and Comprehensive Income

Net income		$600,000
Other comprehensive income:		
Foreign currency translation loss	($50,000)	
Unrealized gain on available-for-sale securities	70,000	
Minimum pension liability adjustment	(10,000)	
Total other comprehensive income		10,000
Total comprehensive income		$610,000

Under option 2, a separate statement of comprehensive income is presented. The reporting follows.

Income Statement

Net income	$600,000

Statement of Comprehensive Income

Net income		$600,000
Other comprehensive income:		
Foreign currency translation loss	($50,000)	
Unrealized gain on available-for-sale securities	70,000	
Minimum pension liability adjustment	(10,000)	
Total other comprehensive income		10,000
Total comprehensive income		$610,000

The components of other comprehensive income for the period may be presented on a before-tax basis with one amount for the tax impact of all the items of other comprehensive income.

A reclassification adjustment may be required so as not to double-count items reported in net income for the current period when they have also been considered as part of other comprehensive income in a prior period. An example is the realized gain on an available-for-sale security sold in the current year when a holding gain was also included in other comprehensive income in a prior year. Reclassification adjustments may also apply to foreign currency translation. The reclassification adjustment applicable to a foreign exchange translation applies only to translation gains and losses realized from the sale or liquidation of an investment in a foreign entity.

Reclassification adjustments may be presented with other comprehensive income or in a footnote. The reclassification adjustment may be shown on a gross or net basis (except that the minimum pension liability adjustment must be presented on a net basis).

EXAMPLE 1: On January 1, 2X11, a company purchased 1,000 shares of available-for-sale securities having a market price per share of $100. On December 31, 2X11, the available-for-sale securities had a market price of $150 per share. On January 1, 2X12, the securities were sold at a market price of $130 per share. The tax rate is 30%.

The unrealized gain or loss included in other comprehensive income is determined as follows:

	Before Tax	Tax Effect at 30%	Net of Tax
20X5 (1,000 × $50*)	$50,000	$15,000	$35,000
20X6 (1,000 × $20**)	(20,000)	(6,000)	(14,000)
Total gain	$30,000	$9,000	$21,000

* $150 – $100 = $50
** $150 – $130 = $20

The presentation in the income statement for 2X11 and 2X12 is as follows:

	20X5	20X6
Net income:		
Gross realized gain on available-for-sale securities		$30,000
Tax expense		9,000
Net realized gain		$21,000

	20X5	20X6
Other comprehensive income:		
Unrealized gain or loss after tax	$35,000	$(14,000)
Reclassification adjustment net of tax		(21,000)
Net gain included in other comprehensive income	$35,000	$(35,000)
Total effect on comprehensive income	$35,000	$(14,000)

According to Accounting Standards Update (ASU) No. 2011-05 (June 2011), *Comprehensive Income* (ASC Topic 220), *Presentation of Comprehensive Income*, a company has the option to present total comprehensive income, the components of net income, and the components of other comprehensive income either in a single continuous statement of comprehensive income or in two separate but consecutive statements.

The company must present reclassification adjustments for items reclassified from other comprehensive income to net income in the statement(s) where the components of net income and other comprehensive income are presented.

Tax effects must also be presented in the statement or related footnotes.

Companies no longer have the option to present the components of other comprehensive income as part of the statement of changes in stockholders' equity. This ASU eliminates that option.

In interim financial statements issued to the public, ASC 220 requires a business to present total comprehensive income. However, it is not required for interim reporting to present the individual components of other comprehensive income.

U.S. GAAP allows for both multi-step and single-step income statement formats, while IFRS does not permit the single-step format. U.S. GAAP has four elements in the income statement: revenue, expenses, gains and losses. IFRS has two elements: income and expenses. Under IFRS, all items are reported as income from operations, ignoring unusual or irregular activity. IFRS prohibits the reporting of extraordinary items, but the reporting of discontinued operations is allowed.

Extraordinary Items

In January 2015, the FASB issued Accounting Standards Update (ASU) 2015-01, *Income Statement-Extraordinary and Unusual Items*, as part of its initiative to reduce complexity in accounting standards. It determined that events may no longer be classified as extraordinary under generally accepted accounting principles (GAAP). Under the old guidance, an entity was required to present separately extraordinary items, net of taxes, including related earnings per share disclosures. This presentation is no longer allowed under GAAP. The update aligns GAAP income statement presentation more closely with International Accounting Standard 1 (IAS 1), *Presentation of Financial Statements*, which also prohibits the presentation and disclosure of extraordinary items. ASU 2015-1 is effective for fiscal years, and interim periods within those fiscal years, beginning after December 15, 2015.

Unusual or Infrequently Occurring Items

ASU 2015-01 also requires that a material event or transaction that is unusual nature or occurs infrequency, or both, should be reported as a separate component of income from continuing operations or, alternatively, should be disclosed in the notes to the financial statements. Such items should not be reported on the face of the income statement net of income taxes. In addition, the earnings per share effects of these items should not be presented on the face of the income statement. ASU 2015-01 provides the following examples of items that are unusual in nature or occur infrequently:

1. A large portion of a tobacco manufacturer's crop is destroyed by a hail storm. Severe damage from hailstorms in the locality where the manufacturer grows tobacco is rare.

2. An earthquake destroys one of the oil refineries owned by a large multinational oil company.

3. A steel manufacturer sells the only land it owns. The land was acquired 10 years ago for future expansion, but shortly, thereafter, the entity abandoned all plans for expansion and held the land for appreciation.

Discontinued Operations

A business segment is a major line of business or customer class. A discontinued operation is an operation that has been discontinued during the year or will be discontinued shortly after year-end. A discontinued operation may be a segment that has been sold, abandoned, or spun off. Even though it may be operating, there exists a formal plan to dispose. Footnote disclosure regarding the discontinued operation should include an identification of the segment, the disposal date, the manner of disposal, and a description of remaining net assets of the segment at year-end.

ASC 360, *Impairment or Disposal of Long-Lived Assets* (ASC 360-10-05-4), requires the following accounting and presentation to report discontinued operations:

- In a year in which a *component* of a company either has been disposed of or is considered held for sale, the income statement for the current and previous years must separately present the profit (loss) of the component, including any gain or loss recognized in discontinued operations.

- The profit (loss) of a component classified as held for sale is presented in discontinued operations in the year(s) in which they take place. Thus, phase-out operating losses are *not* accrued.

- The net of tax effect of the results of discontinued operations are reported as a separate component of income before extraordinary items and the cumulative effect of a change in accounting principle.

- The profit (loss) of a component of a company that either has been disposed of or is held for sale is reported in discontinued operations only if *both* of the following criteria are satisfied:

  — The company will not have any material continual involvement in the operations of the component subsequent to the disposal transaction.

— The cash flows and operations of the component have been (or will be) eliminated from the continual operations of the company because of the disposal transaction.

In general, gain or loss from operations of the discontinued component should include operating gains or losses incurred and the gain or loss on disposal of a component incurred in the current year. Gains should not be recognized until the year actually realized.

EXAMPLE 2: Davis Company produces and sells consumer products. There are a number of product groups, each with different product lines and brands. For this company, a product group is the lowest level at which the operations and cash flows can be clearly distinguished, operationally and for financial reporting purposes, from the rest of the company. Thus, each product group is a component of the company.

The company has incurred losses in its beauty care products group and has decided to exit it. Therefore, Davis Company is committed to a plan to sell this group. The product group is classified as held for sale. The cash flows and operations of the beauty care products group will be eliminated from the ongoing operations because of the sale transaction, and the company will not have any continuing involvement in the operations of the product group once sold.

As a result of the aforementioned, Davis Company should present in discontinued operations the operations of the product group while it is classified as held for sale.

Assume the company decided to continue in the beauty care business but discontinued the brands with which the losses are associated. Because the brands are part of a larger cash-flow-generating product group and, in the aggregate, do not constitute a group that on its own is a component of Davis Company, the conditions for reporting in discontinued operations the losses associated with the brands that are discontinued would not be satisfied.

ASC 205, *Presentation of Financial Statements* (ASC 205-20-55-4; 360-10-05-4), provides guidance as to when a component of a company should be shown in discontinued operations if the business will have cash flows from, or continuing involvement in, the component that is disposed of or held for sale. Classification of a disposed component is suitable only if the ongoing entity has no continuing direct cash flows and does not retain an interest, contract, or other arrangement to allow it to have material influence over the disposed component's operating and financial policies subsequent to the disposal transaction.

According to IFRS, a discontinued operation must be a major business line or geographic segment. Separate disclosure is also required of the cash flows associated with the discontinued operation.

Accounting Standards Update (ASU) No. 2014-08 (April 2014), *Presentation of Financial Statements* (ASC Topic 205) *and Property, Plant and Equipment* (ASC Topic 360), *Reporting Discontinued Operations and Disclosures of Disposals of Com-*

ponents of an Entity, requires the following additional disclosures about discontinued operations:

- Major classes of line items of the discontinued operations;
- Total operating and investing cash flows of the discontinued operation;
- Depreciation, amortization, capital expenditures, and significant operating and investing noncash items of the discontinued operation; and
- Amount of any cash inflows (outflows) from (to) the discontinued operation after its disposal.

REVENUE RECOGNITION

Revenue, which is associated with a gross increase in assets or decrease in liabilities, may be recognized under different methods, depending on the circumstances. (Special revenue recognition guidelines exist for franchisers and in sales involving a right of return. A product financing arrangement may also exist.) The basic methods of recognition include:

- Realization.
- Completion of production.
- During production.
- Cash basis.

Realization. Revenue is recognized when goods are sold or services are performed. It results in an increase in net assets. This method is used almost all of the time. At realization, the earnings process is complete. Further, realization is consistent with the accrual basis, meaning that revenue is recognized when earned rather than when received. Realization should be used when the selling price is determinable, future costs can be estimated, and an exchange that can be objectively measured has taken place. There must exist a reasonable basis to determine expected bad debts. There are exceptional situations where another method of revenue recognition should be used. These are now discussed.

Completion of Production. Revenue is recognized prior to sale or exchange. There must exist a stable selling price, absence of material marketing costs to complete the final transfer, and interchangeability in units. This approach is used with agricultural products, by-products, and precious metals when the aforementioned criteria are met. It is also used in accounting for construction contracts under the completed contract method.

During Production. Revenue recognition is made in the case of long-term production situations where an assured price for the completed item exists by contractual agreement and a reliable measure of the degree of completion at various stages of the production process is possible. An example is the percentage-of-completion method used in accounting for long-term construction contracts.

Cash Basis. In the case of a company selling inventory, the accrual basis is used. However, when certain circumstances exist, the cash basis of revenue recognition is used. Namely, revenue is recognized upon collection of the account.

The cash basis instead of the accrual basis must be used when one or more of the following exist:

- The selling price is not objectively determinable at the time of sale.
- Expenses cannot be estimated at the time of sale.
- Risk exists as to collections from customers.
- Collection period is uncertain.

Revenue recognition under the installment method equals the cash collected times the gross profit percent. Any gross profit not collected is deferred on the balance sheet until collection occurs. When collections are received, realized gross profit is recognized by debiting the deferred gross profit account. The balance sheet presentation is:

Accounts receivable (cost + profit)

Less: deferred gross profit

Net accounts receivable (cost)

Note: A service business that does not deal in inventory has the option of using either the accrual basis or cash basis.

In the case of construction contracts, revenue is recognized by the completed contract method, the percentage-of-completion method, or the cost-to-cost method.

Under the completed contract method, revenue should not be recognized until completion of a contract. The method should be used only when the use of the percentage of completion method is inappropriate.

Under the percentage-of-completion method, revenue is recognized as production activity is occurring. The gradual recognition of revenue levels out earnings over the years and is more realistic since revenue is recognized as performance takes place. This method is preferred over the completed contract method and should be used when reliable estimates of the extent of completion each period are possible. If not, the completed contract method should be used. Percentage-of-completion results in a matching of revenue against related expenses in the benefit period.

Using the cost-to-cost method, revenue recognized for the period equals:

$$\frac{\text{Actual costs to date}}{\text{Total estimated costs}} \times \text{Contract price} = \text{Cumulative revenue}$$

Revenue recognized in prior years is deducted from the cumulative revenue to determine the revenue in the current period. An example follows:

Cumulative revenue (1–4 years)

Revenue recognized (1–3 years)

Revenue (year 4–current year)

Revenue less expenses equals profit

EXAMPLE 3: In year 4 of a contract, the actual costs to date were $50,000. Total estimated costs are $200,000. The contract price is $1,000,000. Revenue recognized in the prior years (years 1–3) were $185,000.

$$\frac{\$50,000}{\$200,000} \times \$1,000,000 = \$250,000 \text{ Cumulative Revenue}$$

Cumulative revenue	$250,000
Prior-year revenue	185,000
Current-year revenue	$ 65,000

Regardless of whether the percentage-of-completion method or the completed contract method is used, conservatism dictates that an obvious loss on a contract should immediately be recognized even before contract completion.

Journal entries under the construction methods using assumed figures follow:

	Percentage of Completion		Completed Contract	
Construction in progress (CIP)	100,000		100,000	
Cash		100,000		100,000
Construction costs				
Progress billings receivable	80,000		80,000	
Progress billings on CIP		80,000		80,000
Periodic billings				
Construction in progress	25,000		No entry	
Profit		25,000		
Yearly profit recognition				

In the last year when the construction project is completed, the following additional entry is made to record the profit in the final year:

	Percentage of Completion	Completed Contract
Progress billings on construction in progress	Total billings	Total billings
Construction in progress	Cost & profit	Cost
Profit	Incremental Profit for last year	Profit for all the years

Construction in progress less progress billings is shown net. Usually, a debit figure results and is shown as a current asset. Construction in progress is an inventory account for a construction company. If a credit balance occurs, the net amount is shown as a current liability.

In most cases, when using IFRS, revenue is recognized when there is reliable measurement and probable economic benefit. With IFRS, gains are included with revenue, while with GAAP, gains are segregated from revenue. IFRS only allows the percentage-of-completion construction method. In the event that revenues and costs are too difficult to estimate, the company should recognize revenue only to the extent of costs incurred referred to as the zero-profit method.

Revenue Recognition When a Right of Return Exists

When a buyer has a right of returning the merchandise bought, the seller can recognize revenue only at the time of sale in accordance with ASC 605, *Revenue Recognition* (ASC 605-15-45), provided that all of the following conditions are satisfied:

- The selling price is known.

- The buyer has to pay for the goods even if unable to resell them. An example is the sale of a good from a manufacturer to a wholesaler. No provision must exist that the wholesaler has to be able to sell the item to the retailer.

- If the buyer loses the item or it is damaged in some way, the buyer still has to pay for it.

- Purchase by the buyer of the item has economic feasibility.

- The seller does not have to render future performance in order that the buyer will be able to resell the goods.

- Returns may be reasonably estimated.

In the case that any one of the previously mentioned criteria is not met, revenue must be deferred along with related expenses until all criteria have been satisfied or the right of return provision has expired. An alternative to deferring the revenue would be to record a memo entry as to the sale.

The ability of a company to predict future returns involves consideration of the following:

- Predictability is lessened when there is a risk that the product may become technologically obsolete or when there are uncertain product demand changes or other material external factors.

- Predictability is lessened when a long-time period is involved for returns.

- Predictability is enhanced when a large volume of similar transactions exists.

- The seller's previous experience in estimating returns for similar products.

- The nature of customer relationship and types of product involved.

A reasonable estimate of returned merchandise may be impaired if the products are not similar, there is a lack of previous experience in estimating returns because the product is new or circumstances have changed, a long time period exists for returns, and the product has a high degree of obsolescence.

EXAMPLE 4: On March 1, 2X11, product sales of $1,000,000 were made. The cost of the goods is $600,000. A 60-day return privilege exists. The anticipated return rate of goods is 10%. On April 15, 2X11, a customer returns goods having a selling price of $80,000. The criteria to recognize revenue when the right of return exists have been satisfied. The journal entries follow:

March 1, 2X11

Accounts receivable	1,000,000	
Sales		1,000,000
Cost of sales	600,000	
Inventory		600,000
Sales returns	100,000	
Allowance for sales returns		100,000

$1,000,000 × 10% = $100,000

Inventory	60,000	
Cost of sales		60,000

$100,000 × 60% (1 − gross profit rate) = $60,000

April 15, 2X11

Allowance for sales returns	80,000	
Accounts receivable		80,000
Cost of sales	12,000	
Inventory		12,000*
* Inventory assumed returned ($100,000 × 60%)		$60,000
Less: amount returned ($80,000 × 60%)		48,000
Adjustment to inventory		$12,000

ASC 605-15-45 does not apply to dealer leases or real estate transactions or to service industries.

ASC 605-50 specifies that when the vendor provides a customer something to buy the vendor's product, such consideration reduces the vendor's revenue applicable to that sale. The vendor's consideration constitutes a cost if the vendor receives a benefit and *both* of the following conditions are satisfied:

- The vendor receives products or services from the customer related to the arrangement representing an identifiable benefit. For example, the vendor would have purchased the product or service from a third party if not provided by the customer.
- There is a determinable fair value to the benefit.

Multiple Deliverables

Accounting Standards Update (ASU) No. 2009-13 (October 2009), *Revenue Recognition* (ASC Topic 605), *Multiple-Deliverable Arrangements*, discusses revenue recognition policy (ASC Topic 205) and provides amendments to ASC Subtopic 605-25, *Revenue Recognition—Multiple-Element Arrangements*, for separating consideration in multiple-deliverable arrangements. A selling price hierarchy is established to determine the selling price of a deliverable. The selling price used for each deliverable is based on vendor-specific evidence if available, third-party evidence if vendor-specific objective evidence is not available, or estimated selling price if neither of the two aforementioned evidence is unavailable.

Arrangement consideration should be allocated at the inception of the arrangement to all deliverables using the relative selling price method. This method allocates any discount in the arrangement proportionally to each deliverable on the basis of each deliverable's selling price.

A vendor must determine its best estimate of selling price consistent with that used to determine the price to sell the deliverable on a stand-alone basis.

The following should be disclosed by similar types of arrangement:

- Timing of revenue recognition for separate units of accounting.
- Description of multiple-deliverable arrangements including nature and terms.
- Factors and estimates used to determine vendor-specific objective evidence, third-party evidence, or estimated selling price.
- Significant deliverables within its arrangements.
- General timing of delivery or performance.

Single Unit of Accounting

According to ASC 605-25, a company may agree to revenue arrangements that stipulate multiple payment streams for a single unit of accounting. For instance, a service provider may get an upfront payment when signing a service contract and then receive additional payments as services are provided to the customer.

If delivery of a single unit of accounting covers multiple accounting periods, a company must determine how to allocate the multiple payment streams applicable to the unit of accounting to those accounting periods.

Delivery or performance of a deliverable is deemed to have taken place when the seller has fulfilled its obligations applicable to that deliverable and the customer has realized the value of the deliverable.

Reimbursements Received

ASC 605-45-15 mandates that companies record the recovery of reimbursable expenses as revenue. An example is travel costs on service contracts. **Note:** These costs are *not* to be netted as a reduction of cost.

Other Revenue

Staff Accounting Bulletin No. 101, *Revenue Recognition in Financial Statements*, provides guidance on the recognition, presentation, and disclosure of revenue.

ASC 605, *Revenue Recognition* (ASC 605-20-25-14), requires barter transactions to be recorded at the fair value of the advertising surrendered. A company can record advertising barter revenue only up to the amount of similar previous cash transactions and can use only cash-based advertising with like features (e.g., time length, positioning, Web page). With respect to Internet barter transactions, each transaction should be treated individually.

ASC 605-45-45-19 stipulates that all shipping and handling costs billed to customers be recorded as revenue.

Accounting Standards Update (ASU) No. 2010-17 (April 2010), *Revenue Recognition—Milestone Method* (ASC Topic 605), applies to recognizing revenue for research and development efforts based on the achievement of a milestone or event happening. The milestone method is when a company records a milestone payment as revenue. A payment may be contingent on the happening of a future event. A company can record as revenue a substantive contingent consideration when a milestone is achieved if it satisfies the following conditions (ASC 605-28-25-2):

1. The vendor has accomplished the milestone.

2. The earned consideration applies to prior performance.

3. The consideration is reasonable.

A milestone should be deemed substantive in full. There may be multiple milestones involved, and if so, each milestone should be appraised separately to ascertain whether it is substantive. It is possible that a situation can exist when there are substantive and nonsubstantive milestones.

Disclosure should be made of the arrangement, each contingent milestone, whether the milestone is substantive or not, and the amount of revenue recorded for the milestone. (ASC 605-28-50-2)

Product Financing Arrangements

As per ASC 470, *Debt* (ASC 470-40), the arrangement involving the sale and repurchase of inventory is in substance a financing arrangement. It mandates that the product financing arrangement be accounted for as a borrowing instead of a sale. In many cases, the product is stored on the company's (sponsor's) premises. Often, the sponsor will guarantee the debt of the other entity.

Types of product financing arrangements include:

- The sponsor sells a product to another business and agrees to reacquire the product or one basically identical to it. The established price to be paid by the sponsor typically includes financing and holding costs.

- The sponsor has another company buy the product for it and agrees to repurchase the product from the other entity.

- The sponsor controls the distribution of the product that has been bought by another company in accordance with the aforementioned terms.

In all situations, the company (sponsor) either agrees to repurchase the product at given prices over specified time periods or guarantees resale prices to third parties.

When the sponsor sells the product to the other firm and in a related transaction agrees to repurchase it, the sponsor should record a liability when the proceeds are received to the degree the product applies to the financing arrangement. A sale should not be recorded and the product should be retained as inventory on the sponsor's book.

In the case where another firm buys the product for the sponsor, inventory is debited and liability credited at the time of purchase.

Costs of the product, except for processing costs, in excess of sponsor's original production cost or acquisition cost, or the other company's purchase cost, constitute finance and holding costs. The sponsor accounts for these costs according to its typical accounting policies. Interest costs will also be incurred in connection with the financing arrangement. These should be separately shown and may be deferred.

EXAMPLE 5: On January 1, 2X11, a sponsor borrows $100,000 from another company and gives the inventory as collateral for the loan. The entry is:

Cash	100,000	
Liability		100,000

Note that a sale is not recorded and the inventory remains on the books of the sponsor. In effect, inventory serves as collateral for a loan.

On December 31, 2X11, the sponsor pays back the other company. The collateralized inventory item is returned. The interest rate on the loan was 8%. Storage costs were $2,000. The entry is:

Liability	100,000	
Deferred interest	8,000	
Storage expense	2,000	
Cash		110,000

Typically, most of the product in the financing arrangement is eventually used or sold by the sponsor. However, in some cases, small amounts of the product may be sold by the financing entity to other parties.

The entity that gives financing to the sponsor is usually an existing creditor, nonbusiness entity, or trust. It is also possible that the financier may have been established only for the purpose of providing financing for the sponsor.

Footnote disclosure should be made of the particulars of the product financing arrangement.

Sales Incentives

According to ASC 605, *Revenue Recognition* (ASC 605-50-45-16), resellers are allowed to report as a deduction from cost of sales the value of the consideration received for *all* sales incentive agreements associated with the vendor. Further, footnote disclosure is required by the reseller of the vendor's accounting policies with respect to sales arrangements. **Note:** ASC 605-50-15 shifted vendor allowances from advertising expense to cost of sales. Thus, cash consideration received by a customer from a vendor is assumed to reduce the prices of the vendor's products or services and thus reduce cost of sales when recognized. However, this presumption is overcome in the following two cases:

1. The customer should record the cash consideration received from the vendor as *revenue* if the consideration is for payment for assets or services delivered to the vendor by the customer.

2. The customer should record the consideration received by the vendor as a *reduction of cost of sales* if the receipt is because of a reimbursement of costs.

SERVICE SALES REVENUE

A transaction often involves the sale of both a product and a service. It is thus necessary to determine if the transaction should be classified primarily as a product transaction or a service transaction, or a combination of both. For transactions having both a product and service element, the following applies:

- A transaction should be classified as primarily a service transaction if the inclusion or exclusion of the product would not change the total price of the transaction.

- If the inclusion or exclusion of the service would not alter the total transaction price, the transaction should be classified as primarily a product transaction.

- If the inclusion or exclusion of the service or product would change the total transaction price, the transaction should be split and the product component should be accounted for separately from the service element.

The following four methods should be used to recognize revenue from service activities:

1. *The specific performance method.* This method is used when performance involves a single action and the revenue is recognized when that action occurs.

2. *The proportional performance method.* This method is used when performance relates to a series of actions. If the transaction involves an unspecified number of actions over a stated time period, an equal amount of revenue should be recognized at fixed intervals. If the transaction relates to a specified number of similar actions, an equal amount of revenue should be recorded when each action is completed. If the transaction relates to a given number of dissimilar or unique actions, revenue should be recognized based upon the following ratio: direct costs involved in a single action, total estimated direct costs of the transaction × total revenue for the entire transaction.

3. *The completed performance method.* This method is used to recognize revenue when completing the final action is so critical that the entire transaction should be considered incomplete without it.

4. *The collection method.* This method is used to recognize revenue when there is significant uncertainty with regard to the collection of revenue. Revenue is not recognized until cash is received.

The three major cost categories that arise from service transactions are:

1. *Initial direct costs.* These costs are incurred to negotiate and obtain a service agreement. They include commissions, credit investigation, legal fees, and processing fees.

2. *Direct costs.* These costs arise from rendering the service, such as labor charges and the cost of materials.

3. *Indirect costs.* These costs are all costs needed to perform the service that cannot be classified as either initial direct costs or direct costs. Indirect costs include rent, depreciation, selling and administrative costs, allowance for bad debts, and the costs to negotiate transactions that are not consummated.

Indirect costs are expensed as incurred. Initial direct costs and direct costs are expensed only when the related revenue is recognized, using either the specific performance or completed performance method. In other words, initial direct costs and direct costs should be recorded as prepaid assets and expensed once the service has been rendered. The same accounting treatment is used to expense initial direct costs under the proportional performance method; that is, initial direct costs are recorded as prepaid assets and expensed when the revenue is recognized. On the other hand, direct costs should be expensed as incurred when the proportional performance method is used. This is done because of the close relationship between the direct costs incurred and the completion of the service. If the collection method is used, both initial direct costs and direct costs are expensed as incurred.

A loss may be incurred in a service transaction. A loss should be recognized when initial direct costs and estimated total direct costs exceed the estimated revenue. The loss is first applied to reduce the prepaid asset and any remaining loss is charged against the estimated liability account.

A service transaction may involve initiation and/or installation fees. The fees are usually nonrefundable. If one can objectively determine the value of the right or privilege granted by the initiation fees, the fees should be recognized as revenue and the associated direct costs should be expensed on the initiation date. On the contrary, if the value cannot be determined, the fees should initially be deemed unearned revenue, a liability account. Revenue should be recognized from such initiation fees using one of the service revenue recognition methods.

The accounting afforded to equipment installation fees depends upon whether the customer can buy the equipment independent of the installation. If equipment may be bought independent of installation, the transaction is considered a product transaction and installation fees are treated as part of the product transaction. On the contrary, if both the equipment and installation are essential for service and the customer cannot buy the equipment separately, the installation fees should be treated as unearned revenue. Unearned revenue should be recognized and the cost of installation and equipment should be amortized over the estimated service period.

As per ASC 605-45-15, service revenues also include reimbursable expenses billed to customers, such as travel expenses. Further, ASC 605-50-05 requires that consideration, including warrants issued to a customer, should be classified by the vendor as an offset to the amount of cumulative revenues recognized from that customer.

FRANCHISE FEE REVENUE

According to ASC 952, *Franchisors*, the franchiser can record revenue from the initial sale of the franchise only when all significant services and obligations applicable to the sale have been substantially performed. This has occurred when:

- There is an absence of intent to give cash refunds or relieve the accounts receivable due from the franchisee.
- Nothing material remains to be done by the franchiser.
- Initial services have been rendered.

The earliest date that substantial performance can occur is the franchisee's commencement of operations unless special circumstances can be shown to exist. In the case where it is probable that the franchiser will ultimately repurchase the franchise, the initial fee must be deferred and treated as a reduction of the repurchase price.

If revenue is deferred, the related expenses must be deferred for later matching in the year in which the revenue is recognized, as illustrated:

Year of initial fee:

Cash

 Deferred revenue

Deferred expenses

 Cash

Year when substantial performance takes place:

Deferred revenue

 Revenue

Expenses

 Deferred expenses

In the case where the initial fee includes both initial services and property (real or personal), there should be an appropriate allocation based on fair market values.

When part of the initial franchise fee applies to tangible property (e.g., equipment, signs, inventory), revenue recognition is based on the fair value of the assets. Revenue recognition may take place prior to or after recognizing the portion of the fee related to initial services. For instance, part of the fee for equipment may be recognized at the time title passes with the balance of the fee being recorded as revenue when future services are performed.

Recurring franchise fees are recognized as earned and receivable. Related costs are expensed. There is an exception to this revenue recognition practice: If the price charged for the continuing services or goods to the franchisee is below the price charged to third parties, it indicates that the initial franchise fee was in essence a partial prepayment for the recurring franchise fee. In this situation, part of the initial fee has to be deferred and recognized as an adjustment of the revenue from the sale of goods and services at bargain prices.

When there is a probability that continuing franchise fees will not cover the cost of the continuing services and provide for a reasonable profit to the franchiser, the part of the initial franchise fee should be deferred to satisfy the deficiency and amortized over the life of the franchise. The deferred amount should be adequate to meet future costs and generate an adequate profit on the recurring services. This situation may occur if the continuing fees are minimal relative to services provided or the franchisee has the privilege of making bargain purchases for a particular time period.

Unearned franchise fees are recorded at present value. Where a part of the initial fee constitutes a nonrefundable amount for services already performed, revenue should be recognized accordingly.

The initial franchise fee is not typically allocated to specific franchiser services before all services are performed. This practice can only be followed if actual transaction prices are available for individual services.

If the franchiser sells equipment and inventory to the franchisee at no profit, a receivable and payable are recorded. No revenue or expense is recognized.

In the case of a repossessed franchise, refunded amounts to the franchisee reduce current revenue. If there is no refund, the franchiser books additional revenue for the consideration retained that was not previously recorded. In either situation, prospective accounting treatment is given for the repossession. Warning: Do not adjust previously recorded revenue for the repossession.

Indirect costs of an operating and recurring nature are expensed immediately. Future costs to be incurred are accrued no later than the period in which related revenue is recognized. Bad debts applicable to expected uncollectibility of franchise fees should be recorded in the year of revenue recognition.

Installment or cost recovery accounting may be employed to account for franchise fee revenue only if a long collection period is involved and future uncollectibility of receivables cannot be accurately predicted.

Footnote disclosure is required of:

- Outstanding obligations under agreement.
- Segregation of franchise fee revenue between initial and continuing.

SOFTWARE REVENUE RECOGNITION

Accounting Standards Update (ASU) No. 2009-14 (October 2009), *Software* (ASC Topic 985), *Certain Revenue Arrangements Include Software Elements,* relates to the accounting for revenue arrangements consisting of tangible products and software. A vendor must sell a particular element separately to assert vendor-specific objective evidence for that element. If a vendor does not have vendor-specific objective evidence for the undelivered element in an arrangement, the revenue for both the delivered and undelivered elements are combined into one unit of accounting. Any revenue associated to the delivered products is then deferred and recognized at a later date, which in most instances is as the undelivered elements are delivered by the vendor.

The Update does not affect software revenue arrangements that do not include tangible products. In addition, the Update changes the accounting model for revenue arrangements that include both tangible products and software elements.

If software contained on the tangible product is essential to the tangible products' functionality, the software is excluded from the scope of the software revenue guidance. This exclusion includes essential software that is sold with the product and undelivered software elements that relate to the tangible product's essential software.

This update is effective for fiscal years beginning on or after June 15, 2010.

As per ASC 985, *Software* (ASC 985-605), revenue should be recorded when the software contract does not involve major production, change, or customization, as long as the following four conditions exist:

1. The contract is enforceable.
2. The software has been delivered.
3. Receipt of payment is probable.
4. The selling price is fixed or known.

Separate accounting is required for the service aspect of a software transaction if the following two conditions exist:

1. The services are required for the software transaction.
2. A separate provision exists in the contract covering services, so that a price for such services is provided for.

A software contract may include more than one component, such as upgrade, customer support subsequent to sale, add-ons, and return or exchange provision. The total selling price of the software transaction should be allocated to the contractual components based on their fair values. If fair value is not ascertainable, revenue should be deferred until it is determinable or when all components of the transaction have been delivered. **Note:** The four revenue criteria previously stipulated must be met before any allocation of the fee to the contractual elements may be made. Additionally, the fee for a contractual component is ascertainable if the element is sold separately.

WARRANTY AND MAINTENANCE REVENUE

Extended warranty and product maintenance contracts are often provided by retailers as separately priced services in addition to the sale of their products. Any warranty or maintenance agreements that are not separately priced should be accounted for as contingencies. Services under contracts may be provided at fixed intervals, a certain number of times, or as required to keep the product operational.

Revenues and incremental direct cost from separately priced extended warranty and product maintenance contracts should be initially deferred. Revenue should be recorded on a straight-line basis over the contract period. The associated incremental direct costs should be expensed proportionately to the revenue recognized. Incremental direct costs arise from obtaining the contract. Other costs, such as the cost of services rendered, general and administrative costs, and the costs of contracts not consummated, should be expensed as incurred.

Losses from these contracts should be recognized when the anticipated costs of rendering the service plus the unamortized portion of acquisition cost exceeds the corresponding deferred revenue. To ascertain loss, contracts should be grouped in a consistent manner. Losses are not recognized on individual contracts but instead apply to a grouping of similar contracts. Loss is recognized by initially reducing unamortized acquisition costs. If this is insufficient, a liability is recorded.

REVENUE RECOGNITION[1]

This section provides an overview of the new revenue recognition accounting standard issued by the Financial Accounting Standards Board (FASB) on May 28, 2014. This Accounting Standards Update (ASU) No. 2014-09 creates ASC 606, *Revenue from Contracts with Customers,* which supersedes most existing U.S. GAAP contained within ASC 605, *Revenue Recognition,* discussed in the prior revenue recognition section.

The guidance is a result of a joint project by the FASB and the International Accounting Standards Board (IASB) to unify U.S. and international revenue recognition guidance and provide a framework that entities could apply consistently in any industry, legal jurisdiction, or capital market. Therefore, ASC 606 will also supersede most industry-specific revenue recognition guidance contained within the industry's ASC Codification.

During August 2015, the FASB issued an amendment, ASU No. 2015-14, to defer the initial effective dates. Public business, certain not-for-profit entities, and certain employee benefit plans should apply ASC 606 to annual reporting periods beginning after December 15, 2017, including interim reporting periods within that initial reporting period. Earlier application is permitted, but only as of annual reporting periods beginning after December 15, 2016, including interim reporting periods within that annual reporting period. All other entities should apply ASC 606 to annual reporting periods beginning after December 15, 2018, and interim reporting periods within annual reporting periods beginning after December 15, 2019. All other entities have two options to apply ASC 606 early, at an annual reporting period beginning after December 15, 2016, including interim reporting periods within that reporting period, or at an annual reporting period beginning after December 15, 2016, and interim reporting periods within annual reporting periods beginning one year later.

---

[1] The section on ASC Topic 606, *Revenue from Contracts with Customers,* was contributed by Renee Weiss, Ph.D., Assistant Professor, Queens College, CUNY.

The FASB has also added a project to its technical agenda to improve ASC 606 with respect to identifying performance obligations and resolving licensing implementation issues. At the time of this writing, the FASB's proposed ASU is still in the comment period. Therefore, the following section will address ASC 606, as issued on May 28, 2014.

ASC 606 provides five steps to achieve the core principle of revenue recognition with customers: "to depict the transfer of promised goods or services to customers in an amount that reflects the consideration to which the entity expects to be entitled in exchange for those goods or services" (ASC 606-10-25-1). The five steps to achieve the core revenue recognition principle are:

- Step 1: Identify the contract with a customer.
- Step 2: Identify the performance obligations that the contract includes.
- Step 3: Determine the transaction price.
- Step 4: Allocate the transaction price to the performance obligations the entity identified in Step 2.
- Step 5: Recognize revenue at a point in time, or over a period of time in which the entity satisfies a performance obligation.

The following discussion and illustrative examples pertain to each of the above steps.

Step 1: Identify the Contract with a Customer

A contract is an agreement between at least two parties, with a party expecting some right "consideration" in exchange for fulfilling some obligation to the other with the "transfer of a promised good or service." If a party fails to receive the right to which that party is entitled by the terms of the contract, that party can obtain enforcement of the contract through the courts. An agreement does not have to be in writing, adhere to some format, or even be prepared by an attorney as a contract (unless it is the entity's customary practice or is required by the jurisdiction of the contract) as long as it is legally enforceable.

EXAMPLE 1: A bookseller did not have a particular book in stock that a prospective customer wanted. The bookseller offered to order the book and notify the customer when it would be available. The customer agreed to return to the bookstore at that time. The customer promised to pay for the book upon pick up. The agreement represents a customary arrangement of booksellers that reflects a legally enforceable (unexecuted) contract.

Not only must the agreement be a contract, it must also be a contract with a customer. A customer is one who contracts with an entity to obtain goods or services that the entity provides through its ordinary activities.

EXAMPLE 2: Suppose the bookseller agreed to provide a neighboring business with the right to exclusive use of its forklift truck in exchange for consideration because the bookseller planned to purchase a new forklift truck. This agreement would not be a contract with a customer because the lease of equipment is not part of the bookseller's primary activities.

ASC 808 provides guidance on contracts in which two or more participants agree to become involved in a joint operating activity. If the participants in the joint operating activity are active and the participants are exposed to significant risks and rewards that depend on the commercial success of the activity, the contract is a collaborative arrangement. A collaborator would not meet the definition of a customer under ASC 606.

EXAMPLE 3: Two pharmaceutical companies enter into a worldwide agreement to market and develop a portfolio of drug treatments based on a certain class of compounds. The companies will share equally in the cost and profits from the collaboration and implement a joint development and commercialization strategy. As each pharmaceutical company is engaged in carrying out the development and commercialization activities of the agreement, each company is an active participant. In this example, the participants are in a collaborative agreement that is within the scope of ASC 808. The collaborator does not meet the definition of a customer under ASC 606.

Having identified a contract with a customer, the entity must also determine, at the contract's inception, whether the following conditions are met before the entity can apply the revenue recognition guidance to this contract: (1) the parties to the contract have approved the contract and are committed to performing their obligations; (2) the entity can identify each party's rights regarding the goods or services to be transferred; (3) the entity can identify the payment terms; (4) the entity determines that collectability of payment is probable; and (5) the contract must have commercial substance; that is, the entity expects that the risk, timing, or amount of its future cash flows will change as a result of the contract. If the contract with a customer did not meet these conditions, the entity could not fully assert that the contract established enforceable rights and obligations.

If the entity receives consideration from a customer, the entity would not recognize revenue until either one of the following events occurred (ASC 606-10-25-7):

1. The entity has no remaining obligations to transfer goods or services to the customer, and all, or substantially all, of the consideration promised by the customer has been received by the entity and is nonrefundable.

2. The contract has been terminated, and the consideration received from the customer is nonrefundable.

EXAMPLE 4: A food service company enters into franchise or license agreements with third-party restaurant operators. The agreements specify the terms of the arrangement with the franchisee or licensee. The agreements typically require the franchisee or licensee to pay an initial, non-refundable deposit toward the franchise fee and the remainder of the fee when the franchisee opens the restaurant. The food service company enters into a franchise agreement with a new operator for one restaurant and receives payment of the initial franchise fee. The franchisee is responsible for capital to purchase or lease the land, equipment, signs, and seating to establish the restaurant. The franchisee has one other restaurant location and intends to finance the construction of the new restaurant using profits from its existing restaurant.

The entity notes there is increasing competition in the present location of the existing restaurant of its newest operator and that restaurants in the area are experiencing declining sales. The entity also notes that the franchisee is experiencing significant delays and added costs in building the new restaurant. The entity concludes it is not probable that it will collect the remainder of the franchise fee. The entity did not substantially receive the entire promised franchise fee, and it has not terminated the agreement (conditions (a) or (b) above are not met). Therefore, the entity will continue to account for the initial deposit as a liability. The entity will continue to assess the agreement: either the entity determines that collectability is probable or that either condition (a) or (b) is met.

If, on the other hand, the contract met all of the criteria, the entity would employ the revenue recognition guidance of ASC 606. Under this scenario, the guidance does not require the entity to reassess its initial determination unless some significant change occurred. In that case, the entity must reconsider its assessment because the change might indicate that the remaining rights and obligations under the contract are no longer enforceable.

ASC 606 specifically excludes certain contracts with customers that are addressed in other topics, which are leases, insurance contracts, financial instruments, and other contractual rights or obligations. In the event that a contract includes elements within the scope of another topic as well as this topic, the entity should first apply guidance from the other (more specific) topic.

Step 2: Identify the Performance Obligations That the Contract Includes

A performance obligation is a promise to transfer goods or services in the contract with a customer (similar to the concept of deliverables in earlier revenue guidance). Because a contract may contain more than one such promise, at the inception of the contract, the entity must identify the separate performance obligations included in the contract. The entity must also consider whether its customary business practices imply certain promises, causing the customer to expect that the entity will transfer certain goods or services not explicitly stated. The entity would then identify such implied promises as performance obligations.

A separate performance obligation is a promise to transfer a good or service that is distinct or a promise to transfer a series of distinct goods or services that are substantially the same and have the same pattern of transfer to the customer. The promise is distinct if it meets **both** of the following criteria:

1. The good or service provides a benefit to the customer on its own or together with other resources that are readily available to the customer (*capable of being distinct*).

2. The entity can separately identify a promise to transfer the good or service to the customer that is distinct from other promises included in the contract (***distinct within the context of the contract***). The entity is not integrating promised goods and services (inputs) to produce some combined output. This provision requires that the entity recognizes revenue when it provides **and** uses the inputs to perform the promised transfer of goods and services in the contract.

A separate performance obligation is therefore a unit of account that is the basis of the individual pattern by which the entity recognizes revenue. The pattern of revenue recognition differs from that of other separate performance obligations in the contract. A series of distinct goods or services could be an ongoing service arrangement providing hourly cleaning services. Requiring the entity to identify multiple distinct services and to allocate the transaction price to each hour of service would not be cost effective. The ability to identify a promise to transfer a series of distinct goods or services that are substantially the same and have the same pattern of transfer to the customer allows the entity to determine one measure of revenue that it can apply to one performance obligation.

If a promised good or service is not distinct, the entity combines this promise with other promises until it identifies a bundle of goods or services that is distinct. It is possible that all promised goods or services in the contract are connected to a single performance obligation.

EXAMPLE 1: A Construction Management Company (CMC) enters into a contract with a data analytic company that has leased a floor of an office building to accommodate its administrative and research staff. CMC will provide all of the materials and services to construct the office space, including electrical power, heating and air conditioning, network capability, ceiling, partitions, painting, and flooring. CMC is responsible for managing and coordinating all aspects of the construction project.

CMC will account for all of the goods and services it will provide to the data analytic company as a single performance contract, because the goods and services are not distinct. Although certain goods and services may be capable of being distinct, CMC's promise to transfer certain goods and services is not inseparable from the transfer of the other promised goods and services (distinct within the context of the contract). CMC is providing significant services to integrate all of the different goods and services promised (inputs) into a finished office space (output).

EXAMPLE 2: (ASC 606-10-55-141) A software developer enters into a contract with a customer to first transfer a software license, perform an installation service (modify the web screen based on the type of user), and provide unspecified software updates and technical support (online and telephone) for a two-year period. The entity sells the license, installation service, and technical support separately. Other entities routinely perform the installation service, which does not significantly modify the software. The customer may fully use the software without the updates or technical support.

The entity considers whether each good or service to be transferred to the customer is distinct (i.e., can the customer benefit from the goods or services independently, or with other goods and services that are readily available). The customer can benefit from the software without the updates or technical support. The entity also considers whether each promise to transfer a good or service is separately identifiable from each of the other promises. As the installation service does not significantly modify or customize the software, software and installation service are each separate outputs rather than inputs to produce one integral output (the risk the entity assumes to provide the software license and installation to make a minor modification to the software are separable). The entity identifies four separate performance obligations: (1) transfer of the license, (2) provision of installation services, (3) provision of software updates, and (4) provision of technical support.

EXAMPLE 3:[2]

An entity agrees to design an experimental new product for a customer and to manufacture 10 prototype units of that product. The product specifications document a certain expected functionality. The entity must make design revisions and run tests of the prototypes to achieve the expected functionality. The entity will implement ongoing revisions to the design of the product during the construction and testing of the prototypes. The entity further expects that it will need to rework most or all of the units it will produce because of design changes made during the production process.

In this example, the entity's risk of providing the design service is inseparable from the manufacturing service. Thus, although each promise may provide benefit on its own (capable of being distinct), each promise is not separately identifiable (distinct within the context of the contract). This is because the entity determines that each promise is highly dependent on, and highly interrelated with, the other promises in the contract.

Thus far, the discussion about identifying the performance obligation(s) included within the contract with a customer reflected one entity having an agreement with a customer. If this entity has control over the promised good or service before transfer to the customer, and is satisfying the performance obligation by itself, the entity is acting as a principal. If the entity that satisfies the performance obligation is a principal, that entity recognizes revenue at the gross amount of the consideration it expects to have a right to for transferring the goods or services. Alternatively, the entity may hire another party to satisfy some or the entire performance obligation (an agent). If the entity that satisfies the performance obligation is an agent, that entity recognizes revenue in the amount of the fee or commission (the net amount of consideration) that the entity retains after paying the other party the consideration in exchange for the goods or services that party provides to the customer.

---

[2] Accounting Standards Update 2014-09, Section C, "Background Information and Basis for Conclusions," BC112.

EXAMPLE 4: An entity sells unique home furnishings on the Internet. The entity employs experienced designers to locate sources for antiques, carpets, bedding, furniture, and other decorative items. Customers place their order online. The entity and the supplier jointly determine the price for the merchandise the customer orders. When the entity receives payment from the customer, the entity instructs the particular supplier to ship the ordered product directly to the customer. The entity pays the supplier when the customer receives the merchandise. The entity retains a fee that is a fixed percentage of the selling price. The entity works with the customer to resolve any complaints that may arise with the supplier, though it is the supplier's responsibility to provide first quality merchandise and honor any claims for defects.

In this case, the supplier is primarily responsible for fulfilling the contract. The supplier is shipping the merchandise to the customer so that the entity does not incur inventory risk. The entity does not have full discretion in setting prices for the merchandise and, as the customer must pay for the merchandise prior to shipment by the supplier, neither the entity nor the supplier incur credit risk. The entity's consideration is a commission. The entity is an agent in the transaction and recognizes revenue as the net amount of the consideration (the selling price less payment to the supplier).

Step 3: Determine the Transaction Price

The entity determines the transaction price based on the terms of the contract and its customary business practices. The transaction price is the amount of consideration the entity expects to have a right to in exchange for transferring the promised goods or services to a customer. The following five factors can have an effect on the transaction price:

1. Certain performance obligations may require estimates of variable consideration.

2. The likelihood of a constraint upon the estimate of variable consideration.

3. Whether a performance obligation includes a significant financing component.

4. Noncash consideration.

5. Consideration payable to a customer.

The following additional information and examples illustrate the effect of the five factors above on the transaction price.

1. Estimates of variable consideration.

Common types of variable consideration are discounts, rebates, refunds, price concessions, incentives, performance bonuses, or penalties.

At the inception of the contract certain facts or circumstances may imply that the entity intends to offer a price concession. The customer may form a valid expectation that the company will provide a price concession on the basis of the entity's usual business practices, policies, or disclosures. In this case, the transaction price reflects an implied price concession that is variable consideration. The entity estimates the amount of the variable consideration and reflects this amount as a component of the transaction price.

EXAMPLE 1: A bookseller agreed to provide 100 books each to a new business that offers tutoring services to high school students and is about to open 20 new tutoring centers in the bookseller's geographic region. The bookseller does not expect to collect the full amount of the stated consideration of $200,000 because the tutoring company is a new business that initially may not attract enough high school students as clients. However, the bookseller made certain representations to the tutoring company that it will extend a price concession in the hope that, when successful, the tutoring company will participate in future agreements for books for its centers.

Although the bookseller concludes that collectability of the $200,000 consideration is not probable, its offer of a price concession makes the promised consideration variable. The bookseller determines that the agreement meets all other criteria and estimates the variable consideration to be $150,000. The bookseller accounts for this agreement according to the guidance in ASC 606.

The following examples illustrate the allowable methodologies to estimate the amount of variable consideration. The first example illustrates use of the most likely amount method in a contract that includes a fixed transaction price and a bonus. In this case, the bonus is variable consideration; the entity's right to the bonus is contingent upon the occurrence or nonoccurrence of a future event.

EXAMPLE 2: Pharmaceutical Company A (PCA), the developer of a regulatory approved drug treatment for pulmonary hypertension, entered into an agreement to make its drug treatment available to Pharmaceutical Company B (PCB), which will obtain the right to market and sell the product in certain geographic regions. PCA will provide a $1 million payment to PCB each year for five years, which includes a $450,000 bonus if PCB exceeds an agreed-upon sales threshold each year.

PCB has a well-established sales structure in the geographic regions that are part of this agreement and a strong base of existing hospital, urgent care, and medical practice accounts. PCB estimates that it is 90% likely that it will exceed the first-year sales threshold and, therefore, estimates the transaction price to be $1 million, which includes the $450,000 variable consideration. PCB uses the *most likely amount method* to estimate the variable consideration.

EXAMPLE 3: An equipment manufacturer enters into an agreement providing the right to sell its reciprocating engines to a distributor with an international sales network. Production of this equipment is highly competitive, prompting the equipment manufacturer to agree to provide the distributor with a bonus at the end of each year based on the dollar amount that the distributor sold during the year. The distributor estimates the probability that it will receive a performance bonus as follows:

Dollar Amount Sold	Percent of Sales Bonus	Expected Probability
100,000	10%	70%
200,000	12%	20%
250,000	15%	10%

The distributor determines that it is most appropriate to use the *probability-weighted method* to estimate variable consideration. Using this method, the distributor estimates the amount of variable consideration to be $15,550 (($100,000 × 10% × 70%) + ($200,000 × 12% × 20%) + ($250,000 × 15% × 10%)) and will include this as part of the transaction price. This estimate does not reflect the possibility that the distributor could be constrained from recognizing the variable consideration.

2. Constraint upon the estimate of variable consideration.

Despite best efforts to measure the amount of variable consideration to include in the transaction price, uncertainty remains about whether the future outcome giving rise to the consideration will confirm the amount initially estimated. An entity is permitted to include variable consideration only to the extent it is probable that the future outcome will confirm the estimated amount of consideration (constraint on the estimate of variable consideration). Once included in the transaction price and allocated to the entire contract or part of a contract (see ASC 606-10-32-39 to ASC 606-10-32-41), the entity recognizes revenue when it satisfies performance obligations (fixed plus variable). Hence, the need for the entity's assessment of whether estimated variable consideration exceeds the probable threshold is to avoid a significant reversal of cumulative revenue recognized. The entity must assess whether it is probable that in the future as uncertainties are resolved or new information about remaining uncertainties becomes available that a significant reversal of the amount of cumulative revenue (fixed plus variable) that the entity recognizes will **not** occur. Examples of factors that could increase the likelihood of a revenue reversal include (ASC 606-32-12):

a. The amount of consideration is highly susceptible to factors outside the entity's influence. Those factors may include volatility in a market, the judgment or actions of third parties, weather conditions, and a high risk of obsolescence of the promised good or service.

b. The uncertainty about the amount of consideration is not expected to be resolved for a long period of time.

c. The entity's experience (or other evidence) with similar types of contracts is limited, or that experience (or other evidence) has limited predictive value.

d. The entity has a practice of either offering a broad range of price concessions or changing the payment terms and conditions of similar contracts in similar circumstances.

e. The contract has a large number and broad range of possible consideration amounts.

The standard requires the entity to update its estimate of the transaction price in the event that the price includes variable consideration at the end of each reporting period. The entity shall also update its assessment of whether its estimate of variable consideration is constrained.

3. Performance obligation includes a significant financing component.

If the terms of the contract with a customer indicate that the entity is providing the customer with a significant benefit of financing (whether explicitly stated or implied), the entity must adjust the amount of promised consideration to reflect the effect of the time value of money. To do so, the entity applies a discount rate as if there is a separate financing transaction between the entity and the customer at inception of the contract. The entity considers the credit characteristics of the customer as well as any collateral or security the customer may provide (ASC 606-10-32-19).

> **EXAMPLE 4:** An entity enters into a contract to sell equipment to a customer. The entity transfers control of the equipment to the customer when the parties sign the contract. The contract states a selling price of $200,000. In addition, the terms of the contract require the customer to make annual payments of $57,718 each, which reflect a 6% annual interest rate. However, the entity determines that it would impose an 8% rate of interest because of the specific credit attributes of the customer. The entity determines that the transaction price is $191,170 based on four annual contract payments discounted at 8%. The entity recognizes revenue of $191,170 and a loan receivable when it transfers control of the equipment to the customer. The entity follows the guidelines of ASC 310 and ASC 835-30 to account for the receivable and interest revenue over the period of the contract.

4. Noncash consideration.

If the contract with a customer includes noncash consideration, the entity measures this consideration at fair value. If the entity cannot reliably measure the fair value of the noncash consideration, then the entity measures this component of the transaction price at the stand-alone selling price of the goods or services it promises to transfer to the customer.

> **EXAMPLE 5:** A consulting company enters into an agreement with a merchandising company to devise a marketing strategy for a new product launch. The entity determines that the promised provision of consulting services is distinct and is a single performance obligation. The merchandising company agrees to pay consideration of 1,000 shares of its common stock upon receipt of the detailed marketing plan. The entity measures the fair value of the 1,000 shares of common stock it receives upon furnishing the marketing plan to the merchandising company. The entity does not reflect any subsequent changes in the fair value of the common stock as a new receivable or additional revenue.

5. Consideration payable to a customer.

The entity may agree to provide consideration to the customer or third parties that purchase the entity's goods or services from the customer. The consideration may be in the form of cash payments, credits, coupons, or vouchers. The entity must determine whether the consideration payable represents a payment for a distinct good or service. If so, the entity accounts for the consideration payable as a purchase from suppliers. If not, the entity accounts for the consideration payable as a reduction of the transaction price. The entity recognizes the reduction of the transaction price at the later of the time that the entity recognizes revenue for the transfer of the related promised goods or services or the entity pays or promises to pay the consideration.

> **EXAMPLE 6:** An organic produce farm and a food specialty store enter into an agreement whereby the food specialty store commits to purchase $35,000 fruits and vegetables over the upcoming three-month summer season. The produce farm agrees to make a non-refundable payment of $8,000 to the food specialty store for special display cases that accommodate the produce. Should the parties decide not to renew the agreement, control of the display cases reverts to the produce farm. In this case, the produce farm's cash payment is for a distinct good (display cases) purchased from a supplier because the produce farm obtains control of the rights to the display cases.

Step 4: Allocate the Transaction Price to the Performance Obligations the Entity Identified in Step 2

The entity allocates the transaction price to each performance obligation it had identified in the contract with a customer on the basis of the relative standalone selling price. A standalone selling price is the price an entity would charge if it were to sell the promised good or service separately to a customer. If the entity does not have an observable price from selling a good or service separately, it should estimate the standalone selling price. However, the entity should maximize its use of observable inputs when it is estimating standalone selling prices. The objective of allocating the transaction price to the various performance obligations is to depict the amount of consideration that the entity expects to have a right to in exchange for transferring each promised good or service to the customer.

> **EXAMPLE 1:** An entity sells a 3D printer to a customer with a one-year service contract for telephone support. The total transaction price is $4,800. The entity examines its recent sales history for this printer model, and focuses on sales made that are in the same market segment as this customer. The entity determines that the observable standalone price of the 3D printer in this contract is $4,500. The entity must estimate the standalone selling price of the telephone support because it does not sell this service separately. The following provides estimates of the standalone selling price of the telephone support using each of three different allowable methods: *adjusted market assessment approach, expected cost plus margin approach, and residual approach.* (ASC 606-10-32-34).
>
> Using the *adjusted market assessment approach,* the entity considers the market in which it sells the goods or services and estimates a price that a customer in that market would be willing to pay. The entity might also use a benchmark price from one of its competitors and make adjustments to reflect its own costs and required margins. In this case, the entity's competitors in this

market segment that provide telephone support services on a standalone basis, offer one-year support contracts at prices between $450 and $550. The entity considers the characteristics of this market segment, its market share, and distribution capability and estimates a standalone selling price of $500. The entity allocates the total transaction price using the adjusted market assessment approach as follows:

Product or Service	Standalone Selling Price	Transaction Price Allocation
3D printer	4,500	(4,500/5,000) × 4,800 = 4,320
Telephone support service	500	(500/5,000) × 4,800 = 480
Total	$5,000	$4,800

Using the *expected cost plus margin approach* the entity estimates the costs it expects to incur to satisfy the performance obligation and adds an appropriate margin for the good or service. If the entity uses this approach, it would identify all of the costs to provide telephone support services such as personnel, telephone lines, computers, and work stations. Suppose these costs amounted to $360 and the entity's usual margin for this market is 25%. The estimated standalone selling price using this approach would amount to $450. Allocation of the total transaction price based on the expected cost plus a margin approach would be as follows:

Product or Service	Standalone Selling Price	Transaction Price Allocation
3D printer	4,500	(4,500/4,950) × 4,800 = 4,364
Telephone support service	450	(450/4,950) × 4,800 = 436
Total	$4,950	$4,800

Using the *residual approach*, the entity estimates the standalone selling price as the total transaction price less the sum of the observable standalone selling prices of other goods or services promised in the contract. However, the entity must meet one of the following criteria in order to use the residual approach:

1. The entity cannot determine a representative selling price from past transactions or other observable evidence.

2. The entity has not yet sold the goods or services on a standalone basis.

Allocation of the total transaction price based on the residual approach would be as follows:

Product or Service	Standalone Selling Price	Transaction Price Allocation	
Total transaction price	4,800		
3D printer	− 4,500	3D printer	4,500
Residual	$300	Telephone support service	300
Total			$4,800

Step 5 Recognize Revenue at a Point in Time, or Over a Period of Time in Which the Entity Satisfies a Performance Obligation

The entity shall recognize revenue when (or as) it has satisfied its performance obligation by transferring *control* of the good or service (asset) underlying the performance obligation to the customer. The entity should assess control from the perspective of the customer. The guidance defines control as the customer's ability to direct the use of, and obtain substantially all of the remaining benefits from, the asset.[3] The customer obtains substantially all of the benefits from the asset through potential cash flows that the customer obtains (through use, consumption, sale, or exchange of the asset). The guidance recognizes that in certain service contracts the customer simultaneously consumes the service asset as the entity creates it. This is also true of construction-type contracts. Though certain construction-type contracts may include a recognizable asset, it may be difficult to assess the timing of transfer of control to the customer as the seller creates the asset. As a result, the standard provides guidance on the timing of when an entity satisfies the performance obligation in its contract with a customer.

An entity transfers control of a good or service over time (satisfies its performance obligation) and recognizes revenue over time, if one of the following criteria is met (ASC 610-10-25-27 to ASC 610-10-25-29):

1. The customer simultaneously receives and consumes the benefits provided by the entity's performance as the entity performs.

2. The entity's performance creates or enhances an asset (e.g., work in process) that the customer controls as the asset is created or enhanced.

3. The entity's performance does not create an asset with an alternative use to the entity, and the entity has an enforceable right to payment for performance completed to date.

The following examples depict contracts with customers with respect to meeting or failing to meet criterion 1-3 above:

EXAMPLE 1: A catering company provides dining services to a customer who uses a suite of offices within its corporate headquarters to hold weekly executive management meetings. The customer benefits from these services as the catering company provides the dining services, as required by condition (1) above.

---

[3] Accounting Standards Update 2014-09, Section C, "Background Information and Basis for Conclusions," BC120.

EXAMPLE 2: A construction company agrees to perform substantial renovations to a customer-owned manufacturing plant. As the construction company performs phases of the renovation work, the customer obtains and controls the resulting enhancements to its asset, the manufacturing plant, meeting condition (2) above.

EXAMPLE 3: In a contract to provide a standard inventory-type item, the entity has the ability to substitute the inventory item across contracts with different customers. As a result, the customer does not have control of the asset as the entity creates it because the customer cannot restrict the entity from allocating that asset to another customer thus failing to meet condition (3) above.

If the entity does not meet any one of the conditions to indicate it has satisfied a performance obligation over time, then the entity satisfies the performance obligation at a point in time when the entity transfers the promised good or service and the customer obtains control.

Indicators of the transfer of control of an asset include, but are not limited to (ASC 606-10-25-30):

- The entity has a present right to payment for the asset.
- The customer has legal title to the asset.
- The entity has transferred physical possession of the asset.
- The customer has the significant risks and rewards of ownership of the asset.
- The customer has accepted the asset.

The entity measures progress toward satisfaction of a performance obligation over time by applying a single method to the performance obligation and to other similar performance obligations. The entity is required to remeasure its progress toward complete satisfaction of a performance obligation satisfied over time at the end of each reporting period. The entity may use output methods (e.g., surveys of performance completed to date, appraisals of results achieved, milestones reached, time elapsed, units produced or delivered). However, output methods based on units produced or units delivered may not appropriately depict the progress toward satisfaction of a performance obligation if the value of work-in-process or finished goods controlled by the customer is material or if the contract includes both design and production services (ASC 606-10-55-17).

The entity may also use input methods (e.g., resources consumed, labor hours expended, costs incurred, time elapsed, or machine hours used) to measure progress toward satisfaction of a performance obligation over time. However, it may be necessary for the entity to make an adjustment to the measure of progress when using a cost-based input method if:

1. The entity incurs a cost that does not contribute to the entity's progress toward satisfying the performance obligation (e.g., costs of an unexpected amount of wasted material).
2. The entity incurs a cost that is not proportionate to the entity's progress toward satisfying the performance obligation.

The following example illustrates measuring progress using costs incurred (an input method), when a cost incurred is not proportionate to the entity's progress toward satisfying the performance obligation (ASC 606-10-65-1):

EXAMPLE 4: A construction company contracts with a customer to renovate a multi-story retail mall and install new escalators for total consideration of $5 million. The promised renovation service, including the installation of escalators, is a single performance obligation satisfied over time. Total expected costs are $4 million, including $1.5 million for the escalators. The construction company determines that it acts as a principal with respect to the installation of escalators because the construction company obtains control of the escalators before it transfers them to the customer. The transaction price and expected costs are as follows:

Expected costs:

Escalators	$1,500,000
Other costs	2,500,000
Total Expected costs:	$4,000,000
Transaction Price:	$5,000,000

The construction company evaluates whether its use of a cost-incurred input method warrants an adjustment to its measure of progress, based on criterion (2) above. The customer has obtained control of the escalators (the construction company has delivered them to the site), but the construction company will not complete the installation for another four months. By the date of delivery of the escalators, the construction company has incurred $500,000 of the $2,500,000 other costs.

The construction company determines that the cost of purchasing the escalators is not proportionate to the costs the entity has incurred in its progress as of the date of the escalator delivery. The construction company excludes the $1,500,000 cost of the escalators from the costs incurred and from the transaction price. The construction company therefore considers costs incurred to date ($500,000) to expected total costs excluding the cost of the escalators ($4,000,000 - $1,500,000= $2,500,000) as a measure of progress, which is 20%.

At the date of delivery, the construction company recognizes the following:

Revenue	$2,200,000	(20% × adjusted transaction price of $3,500,000) = 700,000 + 1,500,000
Cost of Goods Sold	2,000,000	(500,000 other costs + escalator procurement of 1,500,000)
Profit	200,000	

The following example depicts revenue recognition at a point in time:

EXAMPLE 5: A manufacturer of expresso machines enters into a contract to furnish its newest model to a restaurant for consideration in the amount of $3,500. The manufacturer will ship the machine to the restaurant and the restaurant agrees to make payment to the manufacturer upon receipt of the machine. If the restaurant cancels the contract, the manufacturer can allocate this inventory item to another customer. The restaurant does not cancel the order, the manufacturer ships the expresso machine, and the restaurant accepts the machine. On the day of delivery and customer acceptance, the manufacturer has satisfied its performance obligation and recognizes revenue of $3,500. The agreement did not meet any one of three criteria for revenue recognition over time. The restaurant did not simultaneously receive and consume the benefits concurrent with the manufacturer's performance. The manufacturer's performance did not create or enhance an asset over which the restaurant obtained control during the creation or enhancement of the asset. Finally, the manufacturer's newest model expresso machine has alternative use to the entity; the entity could supply this machine to another customer if the restaurant cancels its order.

Additional Issues

Combination of Contracts:

An entity may combine two or more contracts with the same customer (or a related party of the customer) if the entity entered into these contracts at or near the same time and the contracts meet one of more of the following conditions:

1. The entity and customer negotiated the contracts as a single commercial package.

2. Consideration in one contract depends on the other contract.

3. Some or all of the goods or services are a single performance obligation.

Contract Modifications:

A contract modification occurs when the entity and the customer approve additional enforceable rights and obligations or approve changes to the existing enforceable rights and obligations in the contract. The entity may treat the modification as a new, separate contract if it meets the following conditions:

1. The modification adds a distinct performance obligation.

2. The approved price change reflects the standalone selling price of the additional performance obligation.

If the modification does not meet the above conditions, the accounting for the modification depends on whether the remaining goods or services under the modified contract are distinct from the goods or services that the entity transferred to the customer before the modification:

- If distinct, the entity considers the existing contract to be terminated and creates a new contract.

- If not distinct, the entity combines the modification with the existing contract.

EXAMPLE 1: A skin care products company promises to sell a specialty store 300, five-ounce tubes of an anti-aging face cream at a price of $200 per tube. The skin care products company will ship 100 tubes to the customer each month, for three months. The entity transfers control of each product at a point in time. After two months, the skin care products company and its customer agree to a contract modification to transfer an additional 50, five-ounce tubes of the anti-aging face cream. The parties agree to a price of $180 per tube for the additional tubes, which is the entity's standalone selling price at this time.

In this example, the contract modification adds a distinct performance obligation (transfer of 50 tubes of cream). The approved unit price change for the additional units is equal to the standalone selling price of the cream at the time of the contract modification. Therefore, the modification meets the conditions to be treated as a new, separate contract. The entity recognizes revenue for the remaining 100 units of the product at $200 per unit specified in the existing contract and each of the 50 units under the new contract at $180 per unit.

EXAMPLE 2: A skin care products company promises to sell a specialty store 300, five-ounce tubes of an anti-aging face cream at a price of $200 per tube. The skin care products company will ship 100 tubes to the customer each month, for three months. The entity transfers control of each product at a point in time. After two months, the skin care products company and its customer agree to a contract modification to transfer an additional 50, five-ounce tubes of the anti-aging face cream. At the time of the modification, the parties agree to a reduced price of $150 per tube for the additional tubes. The price was not the entity's standalone selling price at the time of modification.

In this example, the contract modification adds a distinct performance obligation (transfer of 50 tubes of cream) but the approved unit price change for the additional units is not equal to the entity's standalone selling price at the time of the modification. The entity accounts for the 100 remaining units to be transferred and the additional units from the contract modification as a new contract. The entity accounts for revenue under this new contract as it transfers control of the products to its customer at a weighted average price of $183.33 ((100 units × $200 per unit) + (50 units × $150 per unit))/150 units.

Sale with a Right of Return:

An entity may transfer control of a product to a customer and provide that customer with the right to return the product. If the customer exercises that right, the customer may be entitled to a full or partial refund for the consideration paid, a credit applied to the remaining amount the customer may owe, or another product in lieu of the returned product. In the case of a sale with the right of return, the entity limits the amount of revenue it recognizes to the amount the entity expects to be entitled to, which excludes an estimate of the amount of products the entity expects the customer to return. The entity further recognizes a refund liability to be equal to the entity's estimate of products that it expects the customer to return. Finally, the entity recognizes an asset (and a corresponding adjustment to the cost of sales) for its right to recover products from customers when settling the refund liability.

Warranties:

The entity should account for a warranty as a separate performance obligation if the entity provides the customer with an option to purchase a warranty separately; in this case, the warranty is a distinct service. The entity should allocate a portion of the transaction price to the separate performance obligation. If the entity does not provide the customer with an option to purchase a warranty separately, the entity should account for a warranty according to ASC 460-10, unless all or part of the warranty provides the customer assurance in addition to the assurance that the product complies with agreed-upon specifications. A warranty that the entity does not make available to the customer under an option, but provides additional assurance, is a performance obligation (the additional assurance is a distinct service). In the case of additional warranty assurance that is a performance obligation, the entity should allocate the transaction price to the product and the service.

Customer Options for Additional Goods or Services:

These options may afford the customer the opportunity to acquire additional goods or services for free or at a discount (e.g., sales incentives, award credits or points, contract renewal options). The entity would consider such options to be a performance obligation only if the option requires the customer to enter into the contract in order to receive the right associated with the option. If the option provides a material right to the customer, in essence the customer is paying the entity in advance for the future goods or services. The entity would recognize revenue when it transfers those goods or services to the customer in the future or when the option expires. The entity determines the amount of revenue it will recognized by allocating the transaction price to the performance obligations in the contract on the basis of the relative standalone selling prices.

Incremental Costs of Obtaining a Contract:

These are costs the entity would not have incurred if it did not obtain the contract with a customer (e.g., sales commissions). The entity would recognize an asset for the incremental costs of obtaining a contract with a customer if the entity expects to recover those costs.

Disclosure:

The overall objective of the disclosure requirements is that the entity provides sufficient information to enable financial statement users to understand the nature, amount, timing, and uncertainty of revenue and cash flows created from contracts with customers. The standard requires the entity to provide qualitative and quantitative information regarding the entity:

- Its contracts with customers.

- The significant judgments, and changes to these judgments that the entity makes as it applies the guidance of ASC 606 to its contracts with customers.

- Any assets the entity recognizes from the costs to obtain or to fulfill contracts with its customers.

Additional Implementation Rulings[4]

Reporting Revenue Gross versus Net

Accounting Standards Update (ASU) No. 2016-08 clarifies the implementation guidance on principal versus agent considerations. ASU 2016-08 states that when another party is involved in providing goods or services to a customer, an entity is required to determine whether the nature of its promise is to provide the specified good or service itself (i.e., the entity is a principal) or to arrange for that good or service to be provided by the other party (i.e., the entity is an agent).

ASU 2016-08 states that when (or as) an entity that is:

- A principal satisfies a performance obligation, the entity recognizes revenue in the gross amount of consideration to which it expects to be entitled in exchange for the specified good or service transferred to the customer.

- An agent satisfies a performance obligation, the entity recognizes revenue in the amount of any fee or commission to which it expects to be entitled in exchange for arranging for the specified good or service to be provided by the other party.

ASU 2016-08 states that an entity is a principal if it controls the specified good or service before that good or service is transferred to a customer. ASU 2016-08 includes indicators to assist an entity in determining whether it controls a specified good or service before it is transferred to the customer.

ASU 2016-08 states that the indicators do not override the assessment of control, should not be viewed in isolation, do not constitute a separate or additional evaluation, and should not be considered a checklist of criteria to be met in all scenarios. ASU 2016-08 states that:

- Considering one or more of the indicators often will be helpful in determining whether the entity controls the specified good or service before it is transferred to the customer.

- Depending on the facts and circumstances, the indicators may be more or less relevant to the assessment of control.

- One or more of the indicators may be more persuasive to the assessment than the other indicators.

ASU 2016-08 is intended to improve the operability and understandability of the implementation guidance on principal versus agent considerations by clarifying the following:

  1. An entity determines whether it is a principal or an agent for each specified good or service promised to the customer. A specified good or service is a distinct good or service (or a distinct bundle of goods or services) to be provided to the customer. If a contract with a customer includes more than

---

[4] The section on ASC Topic 606, *Revenue from Contracts with Customers,* was contributed by Adrian P. Fitzsimons, Ph.D., Professor, St. John's University, and Biagio Pilato, Assistance Professor, St. John's University.

one specified good or service, an entity could be a principal for some specified goods or services and an agent for others.

2. An entity determines the nature of each specified good or service (e.g., whether it is a good, a service, or a right to a good or service).

3. When another party is involved in providing goods or services to a customer, an entity that is a principal obtains control of:

    a. A good or asset from the other party that it then transfers to the customer;

    b. A right to a service that will be performed by another party, which gives the entity the ability to direct that party to provide the service to the customer on the entity's behalf; or

    c. A good or service from the other party that it combines with other goods or services to provide the specified good or service to the customer.

4. The purpose of the indicators in ASC paragraph 606-10-55-39 is to support or assist in the assessment of control. The amendments in ASC paragraph 606-10-55-39A clarify that the indicators may be more or less relevant to the control assessment and that one or more indicators may be more or less persuasive to the control assessment, depending on the facts and circumstances.

Identifying Performance Obligations

ASU 2016-10 states that before an entity can identify its performance obligations in a contract with a customer, the entity first identifies the promised goods or services in the contract. The guidance in ASU 2016-10 expects to reduce the cost and complexity of applying ASC 606 on identifying promised goods or services by adding the following:

-   An entity is not required to assess whether promised goods or services are performance obligations if they are immaterial in the context of the contract with the customer.

-   An entity is permitted, as an accounting policy election, to account for shipping and handling activities that occur after the customer has obtained control of a good as an activity to fulfill the promise to transfer the good rather than as an additional promised service.

ASU 2016-10 states that to identify performance obligations in a contract, an entity evaluates whether promised goods and services are distinct. ASC 606 includes two criteria for assessing whether promises to transfer goods or services are distinct. One of those criteria is that the promises are separately identifiable. ASU 2016-10 improves the guidance on assessing that criterion by:

1. Better articulating the principle for determining whether promises to transfer goods or services to a customer are separately identifiable by emphasizing that an entity determines whether the nature of its promise in the contract is to transfer each of the goods or services or whether the

promise is to transfer a combined item (or items) to which the promised goods and/or services are inputs.

2. Revising the related factors and examples to align with the improved articulation of the separately identifiable principle.

Licensing Implementation Guidance

ASC 606 includes implementation guidance on determining whether an entity's promise to grant a license provides a customer with either a right to use the entity's intellectual property (which is satisfied at a point in time) or a right to access the entity's intellectual property (which is satisfied over time). ASU 2016-10 improves the operability and understandability of the licensing implementation guidance by clarifying the following:

- An entity's promise to grant a customer a license to intellectual property that has significant standalone functionality (e.g., the ability to process a transaction, perform a function or task, or be played or aired) does not include supporting or maintaining that intellectual property during the license period. Rather, the nature of the entity's promise is to provide a right to use the entity's intellectual property as that intellectual property exists at the point in time the license is granted unless the entity is expected to undertake activities (that do not transfer a promised good or service to the customer) that will change the functionality of the intellectual property to which the customer has rights. An entity's promise to provide a customer with a right to use the entity's intellectual property is satisfied at the point in time the customer is able to use and benefit from the license, because the entity's promise in granting the license is solely to make the underlying intellectual property available for the customer's use and benefit. Functional intellectual property includes software, biological compounds or drug formulas, and completed media content (e.g., films, television shows, or music).

- An entity's promise to grant a customer a license to symbolic intellectual property (i.e., intellectual property that does not have significant standalone functionality) includes supporting or maintaining that intellectual property during the license period. Therefore, the nature of the entity's promise to the customer is both to:

  — Grant the customer rights to use and benefit from the entity's intellectual property and make that underlying intellectual property available for the customer's use and benefit; and

  — Support or maintain the intellectual property during the license period (or over the remaining economic life of the intellectual property, if shorter).

- Consequently, a license to symbolic intellectual property is satisfied over time. Symbolic intellectual property includes brands, team or trade names, logos, and franchise rights.

- An entity considers the nature of its promise in granting a license, regardless of whether the license is distinct, in order to apply the other guidance in

ASC 606 to a single performance obligation that includes a license and other goods or services (in particular, the guidance on determining whether a performance obligation is satisfied over time or at a point in time and the guidance on how best to measure progress toward the complete satisfaction of a performance obligation satisfied over time).

ASC 606 includes implementation guidance on when to recognize revenue for a sales-based or usage-based royalty promised in exchange for a license of intellectual property. ASU 2016-10 clarifies the scope and applicability of the implementation guidance as follows:

1. An entity should not split a sales-based or usage-based royalty into a portion subject to the recognition guidance on sales-based and usage-based royalties and a portion that is not subject to that guidance. That requirement does not affect allocation of the transaction price to performance obligations.

2. The implementation guidance on sales-based and usage-based royalties applies to a sales-based or usage-based royalty whenever the predominant item to which the royalty relates is a license of intellectual property.

ASU 2016-10 clarifies that contractual provisions that, explicitly or implicitly, require an entity to transfer control of additional goods or services to a customer (e.g., by requiring the entity to transfer control of additional rights to use or rights to access intellectual property that the customer does not already control) should be distinguished from contractual provisions that, explicitly or implicitly, define the attributes of a single promised license (e.g., restrictions of time, geographical region, or use). ASU 2016-10 clarifies that attributes of a promised license define the scope of a customer's right to use or right to access an entity's intellectual property and, therefore, do not define whether the entity satisfies its performance obligation at a point in time or over time and do not create an obligation for the entity to transfer any additional rights to use or access its intellectual property.

Assessing the Collectability Criterion

ASU 2016-12 states that one criterion in Step 1 of the revenue model provided in ASC 606, *Revenue from Contracts with Customers*, is that it is probable that an entity will collect the consideration to which it will be entitled in exchange for the goods or services that will be transferred to the customer. ASU 2016-12 states that some stakeholders have narrowly interpreted that guidance related to collectability in a manner that would result in more contracts not meeting the collectability criterion.

ASU 2016-12 states that if a contract fails to meet the collectability criterion at contract inception, an entity continues to assess the contract to determine whether that criterion is subsequently met. If the criterion is not subsequently met, an entity only recognizes consideration received as revenue when the criteria in ASC paragraph 606-10-25-7 have been met. ASU 2016-12 states that some stakeholders expressed the view that it is unclear when the criteria in ASC paragraph 606-10-25-7 would be met for certain arrangements.

ASU 2016-12 clarifies that the objective of the collectability criterion in Step 1 is to determine whether the contract is valid and represents a substantive transaction on the basis of whether a customer has the ability and intention to pay the promised consideration in exchange for the goods or services that will be transferred to the customer.

ASU 2016-12 also adds a new criterion to ASC paragraph 606-10-25-7 to clarify when revenue would be recognized for a contract that fails to meet the criteria in Step 1. That criterion allows an entity to recognize revenue in the amount of consideration received when the entity has transferred control of the goods or services, the entity has stopped transferring goods or services (if applicable) and has no obligation under the contract to transfer additional goods or services, and the consideration received from the customer is nonrefundable.

Presentation of Sales Taxes and Other Similar Taxes Collected from Customers

In Step 3 of the revenue recognition model, an entity determines the transaction price of the contract. The transaction price is the amount of consideration to which an entity expects to be entitled in exchange for transferring promised goods or services to a customer, excluding amounts collected on behalf of third parties (e.g., some sales taxes).

To determine whether amounts are collected on behalf of third parties, ASU 2016-12 states that an entity would need to identify and analyze taxes on a jurisdiction-by-jurisdiction basis to determine which amounts should be reported gross and which should be reported net. ASU 2016-12 notes that compliance with that aspect of ASC 606 could be complex and costly for many entities because of the number of jurisdictions in which an entity would have to determine which party is primarily obligated for payment of the tax and because of the variation of, and changes in, tax laws among federal, state, and local jurisdictions.

ASU 2016-12 permits an entity, as an accounting policy election, to exclude amounts collected from customers for all sales (and other similar) taxes from the transaction price.

Noncash Consideration

In Step 3 of the revenue recognition model, an entity determines the transaction price of the contract. Some contracts include promises of consideration in a form other than cash (i.e., noncash consideration). ASC 606 states that noncash consideration is measured at fair value. However, ASC 606 does not specify the measurement date for noncash consideration. ASU 2016-12 specifies that the measurement date for noncash consideration is contract inception.

Additionally, some stakeholders indicated that it is unclear how the constraint on variable consideration is applied in circumstances in which the fair value of noncash consideration varies both because of the form of the consideration and for reasons other than the form of consideration. ASU 2016-12 also clarifies that the variable consideration guidance applies only to variability resulting from reasons other than the form of the consideration.

Contract Modifications at Transition

ASC 606 includes two transition methods:

1. Retrospectively to each prior reporting period presented in accordance with ASC 606, and

2. Retrospectively with the cumulative effect of initially applying the guidance in ASC 606 at the date of initial application.

In applying either method, ASU 2016-12 states that an entity is required to evaluate contract modifications that occurred before the beginning of the earliest period presented. ASU 2016-12 notes that this analysis may be complex and costly in instances in which an entity has a significant volume of contract modifications or when the modifications have occurred over a long period of time.

ASU 2016-12 provide a practical expedient that permits an entity to reflect the aggregate effect of all modifications that occur before the beginning of the earliest period presented when identifying the satisfied and unsatisfied performance obligations, determining the transaction price, and allocating the transaction price to the satisfied and unsatisfied performance obligations.

Completed Contracts at Transition

The two transition methods for ASC 606 include practical expedients related to completed contracts. The transition guidance in ASC 606 explains that a completed contract is "a contract for which the entity has transferred all of the goods or services identified in accordance with revenue guidance that is in effect before the date of initial application."

ASU 2016-12 notes that it is unclear when a contract should be considered "completed" for purposes of applying the transition guidance. ASU 2016-12 clarifies that a completed contract for purposes of transition is a contract for which all (or substantially all) of the revenue was recognized under legacy U.S. GAAP before the date of initial application. Accounting for elements of a contract that do not affect revenue under legacy U.S. GAAP are irrelevant to the assessment of whether a contract is complete.

In addition, ASU 2016-12 permits an entity to apply the modified retrospective transition method either to all contracts or only to contracts that are not completed contracts.

Retrospective Application

ASU 2016-12 states that an entity that retrospectively applies the guidance in ASC 606 to each prior reporting period is required to provide the accounting change disclosures in ASC paragraphs 250-10-50-1 through 50-3 in the period of adoption. ASC paragraph 250-10-50-1(b)(2) requires an entity to disclose current-period financial information in the period of adoption under former U.S. GAAP. Stakeholders reported that this requirement would significantly increase transition costs because an entity would have to account for contracts with customers under former U.S. GAAP and ASC 606 for one additional year.

ASU 2016-12 clarifies that an entity that retrospectively applies the guidance in ASC 606 to each prior reporting period is not required to disclose the effect of the accounting change for the period of adoption. However, an entity is still required to disclose the effect of the changes on any prior periods retrospectively adjusted.

Loan Guarantee Fees

ASU 2016-20 notes that ASC 606 specifically identifies a scope exception for guarantees (other than product or service warranties) within the scope of ASC 460, *Guarantees*. Stakeholders indicated that a few consequential amendments included in ASU 2014-09 are inconsistent on whether fees from financial guarantees are within the scope of ASC 606. ASU 2016-20 clarifies that guarantee fees within the scope of ASC 460 (other than product or service warranties) are not within the scope of ASC 606. In addition, entities should see ASC 815, *Derivatives and Hedging*, for guarantees accounted for as derivatives.

Contract Costs—Impairment Testing

ASU 2016-20 states the ASC Subtopic 340-40, *Other Assets and Deferred Costs— Contracts with Customers*, includes impairment guidance for costs capitalized in accordance with the recognition provisions of that subtopic. ASU 2016-20 clarifies that when performing impairment testing an entity should:

- Consider expected contract renewals and extensions, and
- Include both the amount of consideration it already has received but has not recognized as revenue and the amount it expects to receive in the future.

ASU 2016-20 clarifies that impairment testing first should be performed on assets not within the scope of ASC 340.

Provisions for Losses on Construction-Type and Production-Type Contracts

ASU 2016-20 require that the provision for losses be determined at least at the contract level. However, it allows an entity to determine the provision for losses at the performance obligation level as an accounting policy election.

Removal of Term "Insurance" from Scope of ASC 606

ASU 2016-20 remove the term *insurance* from the scope exception to clarify that all contracts within the scope of ASC 944 are excluded from the scope of ASC 606.

Disclosure of Remaining Performance Obligations

ASU 2016-20 provide optional exemptions from the disclosure requirement for remaining performance obligations for specific situations in which an entity need not estimate variable consideration to recognize revenue. ASU 2016-20 also expands the information that is required to be disclosed when an entity applies one of the optional exemptions.

Disclosure of Prior-Period Performance Obligations

ASU 2016-20 clarifies that the disclosure of revenue recognized from performance obligations satisfied (or partially satisfied) in previous periods applies to all performance obligations and is not limited to performance obligations with corresponding contract balances.

Advertising Costs

ASU 2016-20 reinstate the guidance on when to recognize a liability in the accrual of advertising costs and also move the guidance to ASC 720, *Other Expenses*.

Fixed-Odds Wagering Contracts in the Casino Industry

ASU 2016-20 creates a new ASC Subtopic 924-815, *Entertainment—Casinos—Derivatives and Hedging,* which includes a scope exception from derivatives guidance for fixed-odds wagering contracts; and includes a scope exception within ASC 815 for fixed-odds wagering contracts issued by casino entities.

Cost Capitalization for Advisors to Private Funds and Public Funds

ASU 2016-20 aligns the cost-capitalization guidance for advisors to both public funds and private funds in ASC 946, *Financial Services—Investment Companies.*

CONTRIBUTIONS

ASC 720, *Other Expenses* (ASC 720-25, 958-605-05-25), applies to the accounting and reporting for contributions received and contributions made. Cash, other monetary and nonmonetary assets, services, or unconditional promises to give assets or services qualify as contributions. Contributions may involve either donor-imposed restrictions or donor-imposed conditions. If the donor restricts the way a contribution is to be used (such as to build a research laboratory), it is considered a restriction and the revenue from such a contribution and any associated costs are recognized immediately. However, if the donor imposes a condition, such as the donee must obtain matching funds, that condition must be met before revenue may be recognized.

A donor may make an unconditional or conditional promise. An unconditional promise exists if the donor has no right to take back the donated asset and the contribution would be available after some stated time period or on demand. Unconditional promises to give contributions are recognized immediately. A conditional promise is contingent upon the happening of a future occurrence. If that event does not take place, the donor is not obligated by the promise. A vague promise is considered conditional. Conditional promises are recorded only when their terms are met. A conditional promise may be treated as an unconditional promise if the possibility that the condition will not be satisfied is remote.

There must be supporting evidence to substantiate that a promise has been made. Such evidence includes information about the donor (e.g., donor's name and address), the amount the donor commits to give (e.g., in a public announcement), when the amount promised will be given, and to whom the promise to give was made. The donor may have taken certain actions relying on the promise. The donor may have made partial payments. A recorded promise should be at the fair market value of the consideration. If the amount will be collected beyond one year, a discounted cash flow calculation may be made. If discounting is done, the interest is accounted for as contribution income, not interest income.

Contributed services should be recognized if specialized skills are rendered by the donor and those skills would have been purchased by the donee if they were not donated. Contributions received should be recorded at fair value by debiting the asset and crediting revenue. Quoted market prices or market prices for similar assets, appraisal by independent experts, or valuation techniques, such as discounted cash flows, should be used to compute fair value. The value of contributed services should be based on quoted market prices for those services.

Disclosures are required in the financial statements of recipients of contributions. For unconditional promises to give, the amount of receivables due within one year, in one to five years, and in more than five years should be disclosed along with the amount expected to be uncollected. For conditional promises to give, disclosure is required of promised amounts along with a description of the promise. Promises with similar characteristics may be grouped. Disclosure should be made of the nature and degree of contributed services, limitations or conditions set by the donor, and the programs or activities benefiting from contributed services. Companies are encouraged to disclose the fair value of services received but not recorded as revenue.

The donor should record an expense and a corresponding decrease in assets, or an increase in liabilities, at fair value, in the year in which the contribution is made. If fair value differs from carrying value, a loss or gain on disposition is recorded.

CONTRACTS

Contract Types

There are various types of construction contracts, including time-and-materials, unit price, fixed price, and cost-type. Time-and-materials contracts reimburse the contractor for direct labor and direct material costs. Unit price contracts provide payment to the contractor based on the amount of units completed. Fixed-price contracts are not usually subject to adjustment such as due to increasing construction costs. Cost-type contracts may be either cost without a fee or cost plus a fee. The fee is usually based on a profit margin. However, the fee may be based on some other factor such as total expected costs, uncertainty in estimating costs, project risk, or economic conditions. The contract cost should never be more than its net realizable value; otherwise the contract would not be financially feasible. A loss is recognized when accumulated cost exceeds net realizable value.

Contracts that are very similar may be grouped for accounting purposes. Similarity may be indicated by a similar project management, single customer, conducted sequentially or concurrently, interrelated, and negotiated as a package deal. The segmenting of a contract is segregating the larger unit into smaller ones for accounting purposes. By breaking up a unit, revenues are associated with different components or phases. In consequence, different profitability margins may apply to each different unit or phase. Segmenting of a project may be indicated when all of the following criteria are satisfied:

- The project may be segregated into its components.
- A contract bid price exists for the entire project and its major components.
- Customer approval is received.

Even if all of these conditions are not met, the project may still be segmented if all of the following exist:

- Segregation is logical and consistent.
- Risk differences are explainable.

- Each segment is negotiated.
- Cost savings arise.
- Stability exists.
- Similarity exists in services and prices.
- Contractor has a track record.

An addition or modification made to an existing contract arising from an option clause is accounted for as a separate contract if any of the following applies:

- Price of the new product or service is distinct.
- Product or service is similar to that in the original contract but differences do exist in contract pricing and cost.
- Product or service is materially different from the product or service provided for in the initial contract.

A claim is an amount above the contract price that a contractor wants customers to pay because of customer errors in specifications, customer delays, or other unanticipated causes resulting in higher costs to the contractor. The contractor may recognize additional revenue because of these claims if justification exists and the amount is determinable. The revenue is recognized only to the extent that contract costs related to the claim have been incurred. As per ASC 605, *Revenue Recognition* (ASC 605-35), the following benchmarks exist to establish the ability to record the additional revenue:

- Additional costs incurred were not initially expected when the contract was signed.
- The claim has a legal basis.
- The claim is verifiable and objective.
- Costs are determinable.

If the previous conditions are not met, a contingent asset should be disclosed.

Contract Costs

Costs incurred to date on a contract include precontract costs and costs incurred after the contract date. Precontract costs include learning costs for a new process, design fees, and any other expenditures likely to be recouped after the contract is signed. After the contract, the precontract costs are considered contract costs to date.

Some precontract costs, such as for materials and supplies, may be deferred to an asset called Deferred Contract Costs in anticipation of a specific contract, as long as recoverability is probable. If recoverability is not probable, the precontract costs must be immediately expensed. If excess goods are produced in anticipation of future orders, related costs may be deferred to inventory if the costs are considered recoverable.

After the status of a contract bid has been determined (accepted or rejected), a review of the precontract costs should be conducted. If the contract has been approved, the deferred precontract costs are included in contract costs. If the contract is rejected, the precontract costs are immediately expensed unless there are other related contracts pending that might recoup these costs.

Back charges are billable costs for work performed by one party that should have been performed by the party billed. Such an agreement is usually stipulated in the contract. Back charges are accounted for by the contractor as a receivable from the subcontractor with a corresponding reduction in contract costs. The subcontractor accounts for the back charge as contract costs and as a payable.

Government Contracts

The percentage method to account for contracts should be used when financial soundness exists on the part of the buyer. ASC 605-35 specifies that the company should apply profit rates to all contracts costs, including general and administrative expenses, to determine sales and operating earnings. A company should periodically assess earnings rates to ascertain any needed adjustment in contract values and estimated costs at completion. Any adjustment in profit rates should be made over current and future years.

On cost-plus-fixed-fee government contracts, fees should typically be accrued as billable. If an advance payment is received, it should not offset receivables unless the payment is for work in process. If any amounts are offset, disclosure is required.

If a government contract is subject to renegotiation, a renegotiation claim for which the contractor is accountable should be charged to sales and credited to a current liability. Disclosure must be provided of the basis used to compute the anticipated refund.

If the government terminates a contract, contract costs included in inventory should be transferred to receivables. The claim against the government should be shown under current assets unless a long delay in payment is expected. A termination claim should be accounted for as a sale. A subcontractor's claim arising from the termination should be included in the contractor's claim against the government. For example, a contractor has a termination claim receivable of $800,000, of which $200,000 applies to the contractor's obligation to the subcontractor. In this situation, a liability should be accrued for $200,000. The termination claim is reduced by any inventory applying to the contract that the contractor is retaining. Disclosure should be provided of the terms of terminated contracts.

Direct costs are included in contract costs, such as material, labor, and subcontracting costs. Indirect costs are allocated to contracts on an appropriate basis. Allocable costs include quality control, insurance, contract supervision, repairs and maintenance, tools, and inspection. Learning and start-up costs should be charged to existing contracts. The entry for an expected loss on a contract is to make a loss provision.

RESEARCH AND DEVELOPMENT COSTS

Research is the testing done in searching for a new product, service, process, or technique. Research can also be aimed at deriving a material improvement to an existing product or process. Development is the translation of the research into a design for the new product or process. Development may also result in material improvement in an existing product or process. As per ASC 730, *Research and Development,* research and development (R&D) costs are expensed as incurred. However, R&D costs incurred under contract for others that are reimbursable are charged to a receivable account rather than expensed. Further, materials, equipment, and intangibles purchased from others that have alternative future benefit in R&D activities are capitalized. The depreciation or amortization on such assets is classified as R&D expense. If no alternative future use exists, the costs should be expensed.

R&D cost includes the salaries of personnel involved in R&D activities. R&D cost also includes a rational allocation of indirect (general and administrative) costs. If a group of assets is acquired, allocation should be made to those that relate to R&D efforts. When a business combination is accounted for as a purchase, R&D costs are assigned their fair market value.

Expenditures paid to others to conduct R&D activities for the company are expensed.

Examples of R&D activities include:

- Formulation and design of product alternatives and testing thereof.
- Laboratory research.
- Engineering functions until the point the product satisfies operational requirements for manufacture.
- Design of tools, molds, and dies involving new technology.
- Preproduction prototypes and models.
- Pilot plant cost.

Examples of activities that are not associated with R&D include:

- Quality control.
- Seasonal design changes.
- Legal costs of obtaining a patent.
- Market research.
- Identifying breakdowns during commercial production.
- Engineering follow-up in the initial stages of commercial production.
- Rearrangement and start-up activities, including design and construction engineering.
- Recurring and continuous efforts to improve the product.
- Commercial use of the product.

ASC 730 does not apply to regulated industries and to the extractive industries (e.g., mining).

According to ASC 985, *Software* (ASC 985-20), costs incurred for computer software to be sold, leased, or otherwise marketed are expensed as R&D costs until technological feasibility exists as indicated by the development of a detailed program or working model. After technological feasibility exists, software production costs should be deferred and recorded at the lower of unamortized cost or net realizable value. Examples of such costs include debugging the software, improvements to subroutines, and adaptions for other uses. Amortization begins when the product is available for customer release. The amortization expense should be based on the higher of:

- The percent of current revenue to total revenue from the product.
- The straight line amortization amount.

As per ASC 810, *Consolidation* (ASC 810-30), if a business enters into an arrangement with other parties to fund the R&D efforts, the nature of the obligation must be determined. In the case where the entity has an obligation to repay the funds irrespective of the R&D results, a liability has to be recognized with the related R&D expense. The journal entries are:

Cash

    Liability

Research and development expense

    Cash

A liability does not exist when the transfer of financial risk involved to the other party is substantive and genuine. If the financial risk applicable with R&D is transferred because repayment depends only on the R&D possessing future economic benefit, the company accounts for its obligation as a contract to conduct R&D for others. In this case, R&D costs are capitalized and revenue is recognized as earned and becomes billable under the contract. Footnote disclosure is made of the terms of the R&D agreement, the amount of compensation earned, and the costs incurred under the contract.

When repayment of loans or advances to the company depends only on R&D results, such amounts are deemed R&D costs incurred by the company and charged to expense.

If warrants or other financial instruments are issued in an R&D arrangement, the company records part of the proceeds to be provided by the other parties as paid-in capital based on their fair market value on the arrangement date.

According to ASC 730, *Research and Development* (ASC 730-20-25-13), nonrefundable advance payments for goods or services that will be used for future research and development activities should be deferred and capitalized. Such amounts should be recognized as an expense as the related goods are delivered or the associated services are performed. If an entity does not anticipate the goods to be delivered or services to be rendered, the capitalized advance payment should be charged to expense.

According to ASC 805, *Business Combinations,* research and development costs acquired in a business combination should be recorded at fair market value, even if alternative future use is nonexistent. In subsequent years, the R&D costs are subject to a yearly impairment test. Supplies used in R&D operations that are bought in a business combination are also measured at fair market value.

As per IFRS, development costs incurred subsequent to technological feasibility are capitalized. This matches U.S. GAAP for software development costs, but not for ordinary research and development.

ADVERTISING COSTS

ASC 720, *Other Expenses* (ASC 720-35), requires the expensing of advertising as incurred when the advertising program first occurs. However, the cost of direct-response advertising may be deferred if the major purpose of the promotion is to elicit sales to customers who respond specifically to the advertising and for which future benefit exists. For example, the former condition is satisfied if the response card is specially coded. The latter condition is met if the resulting future revenues exceed the future costs to be incurred. The deferred advertising is amortized over the expected benefit period using the revenue method (current year revenue to total revenue). The cost of a billboard should also be capitalized and amortized. Advertising expenditures incurred after revenue is recognized should be accrued. These advertising costs should be expensed when the related revenues are recognized.

Disclosures for advertising include:

- Accounting policy to account for advertising.

- Total advertising expense for each year.

- For direct-response advertising, description, amortization period, and amount capitalized each period.

RESTRUCTURING CHARGES

ASC 420, *Exit or Disposal Cost Obligations* (ASC 420-10-599), requires restructuring charges to be expensed and presented as a component in computing income from operations.

In general, an expense and liability should be accrued for employee termination benefits in a restructuring. Disclosure should be made of the group and number of workers laid off.

An exit plan requires the recognition of a liability for the restructuring changes incurred if there is no future benefit to continuing operations. The expense for the estimated costs should be made on the commitment date of the exit plan. Expected gains from assets to be sold in connection with the exit plan should be recorded in the year realized. These gains are not allowed to offset the accrued liability for exit costs. Exit costs incurred are presented as a separate item as part of income from continuing operations. Disclosures associated with an exit plan include the terms of the exit plan, description and amount of exit costs incurred, activities to be exited from, method of disposition, expected completion date, and liability adjustments.

ENVIRONMENTAL COSTS

ASC 410, *Asset Retirement and Environmental Obligations* (ASC 410-30-25-16), provides that environmental contamination costs generally must be expensed. However, in the following cases only, the company may elect either to expense or capitalize the costs:

- The expenditures are made to prepare the property for sale.
- The expenditures prevent or lessen environmental contamination that may result from *future* activities of property owned.
- The expenditures either extend the life or capacity of the asset or enhance safety of the property.

WEB SITE DEVELOPMENT COSTS

As per ASC 350, *Intangibles—Goodwill and Other* (ASC 350-50), Web site development is segregated into three stages that affect the accounting treatment for expenditures incurred. The initial stage is planning, in which the costs incurred are expensed. Development is the second stage, and Web application and infrastructure as well as graphics development costs are capitalized and then amortized once the Web site is ready for its intended use. However, costs to develop the content for the Web site may be capitalized or expensed, depending on the circumstances. In the third stage, postimplementation, work is performed after the site is put into service (e.g., security, training, administration). These costs are expensed as incurred. Also in the third stage, there are expenditures for additional upgrades and features once the Web site is launched; these costs are capitalized if the upgrades and enhancements furnish *additional functionality*.

INSURANCE

As per ASC 720, *Other Expenses* (ASC 720-20), amounts paid for retroactive insurance should be immediately expensed, and a receivable should be recorded at the same time for anticipated recoveries applicable to the underlying event.

ORGANIZATION COSTS

Organization costs (e.g., legal and accounting fees to start a business) must be expensed as incurred.

Start-Up Costs

Under ASC 720, *Other Expenses* (ASC 720-15), start-up (preoperating, preopening) costs must be expensed as incurred. Start-up costs include the one-time costs of opening a new business, introducing a new product or service, conducting business in a new territory, or having business with a new class of customer.

Costs to Develop or Obtain Computer Software for Internal Use

ASC 350, *Intangibles—Goodwill and Other* (ASC 350-40), deals with software development or purchase for internal (not external) use. The company has no plan to sell the software.

The three stages of computer development are:

1. *Preliminary project stage.* This stage may involve such activities as structuring an assembly team, appraising vendor proposals, and thinking about reengineering efforts. A software development strategy or vendor has not yet been decided upon. During this stage, all costs should be expensed as incurred without separate presentation in the income statement.

2. *Application development stage.* A determination has been made as to how the software development work will be carried out. Costs incurred during this stage are capitalized, provided it is probable the project will be completed successfully. Typical costs that should be capitalized include direct material or services contributing to the project, payroll costs, and any interest costs incurred during the development process, testing, and installation. General and administrative costs, overhead, and training costs are not deferred.

3. *Postimplementation/operation stage.* The stage begins when the internal use software is put in service. Capitalized costs should be amortized on a straight-line basis over the estimated useful life of the internally used software. Because the estimated life is typically short, it should be reappraised periodically. Capitalized costs of any existing software that is to be replaced by newly developed software should be expensed when the new software is ready for use.

Costs for upgrades or enhancements should be capitalized only if they result in additional functionality beyond the original software.

Manual data conversion costs should be expensed. However, costs to develop bridging software should be capitalized.

If internally developed computer software is used in R&D activities, it should be accounted for under ASC 730. The software development costs included as R&D expenditures are (1) software acquired to be used in R&D activities where the software has no alternative future use, and (2) software applicable to a specific pilot R&D project.

In the event it is later decided to sell computer software initially developed for internal use, the sales proceeds (in excess of direct incremental costs) should be netted against the book value of the deferred software costs. When book value is reduced to zero, profit is recognized on the excess amount. Under ASC 720, *Other Expenses* (ASC 720-45), business process reengineering costs are expensed irrespective of whether such reengineering efforts are performed as a separate project or as an element of a larger project encompassing software development.

EARNINGS PER SHARE

ASC 260, *Earnings per Share*, covers the computation, reporting, and disclosures associated with earnings per share. The pronouncement makes some major changes in the computation of earnings per share as previously existed under Accounting Principles Board Opinion No. 15, *Earnings per Share*. Presentation of both basic and diluted earnings per share is mandated.

Basic earnings per share takes into consideration only the actual number of outstanding common shares during the period (and those contingently issuable in certain cases).

Diluted earnings per share includes the effect of common shares actually outstanding and the effect of convertible securities, stock options, stock warrants, and their equivalents. Diluted earnings per share should not assume the conversion, exercise, or contingent issuance of securities having an antidilutive effect (increasing earnings per share or decreasing loss per share) because it violates conservatism.

BASIC EARNINGS PER SHARE

Basic earnings per share equals net income available to common stockholders divided by the weighted average number of common shares outstanding. Common stock equivalents are no longer presented in this computation. When a prior period adjustment occurs that causes a restatement of previous years' earnings, basic EPS should be restated.

EXAMPLE 6:

The following data are presented for a company:

Preferred stock, $10 par, 6% cumulative, 30,000 shares issued and outstanding		$300,000
Common stock, $5 par, 100,000 shares issued and outstanding		$500,000
Net income	$400,000	

The cash dividend on the preferred stock is $18,000 (6% × $300,000).

Basic EPS equals $3.82 as computed below.

Earnings available to common stockholders:

Net income	$400,000
Less: Preferred dividends	(18,000)
Earnings available to common stockholders	$382,000

Basic EPS = $382,000/100,000 shares = $3.82

EXAMPLE 7:
On January 1, 2X11, David Company had the following shares outstanding:

6% Cumulative preferred stock, $100 par value	150,000 shares
Common stock, $5 par value	500,000 shares

During the year, the following took place:

- On April 1, 2X11, company issued 100,000 shares of common stock
- On September 1, 2X11, the company declared and issued a 10% stock dividend.
- For the year ended December 31, 2X11, the net income was $2,200,000.

Basic earnings per share for 2X11 equals $2.06 ($1,300,000/632,500 shares) computed below

Earnings available to common stock holders:

Net income	$2,200,000
Less: preferred dividend (150,000 shares × $6)	(900,000)
Earnings available to common stockholders	$1,300,000

Weighted-average number of outstanding common shares is determined as follows:

1/1/2X11 – 3/31/2X11 (500,000 × 3/12 × 110%)	137,500
4/1/2X11 – 8/31/2X11 (600,000 × 5/12 × 110%)	275,000
9/1/2X11 – 12/31/2X11 (660,000 × 4/12)	220,000
Weighted-average outstanding common shares	632,500

DILUTED EARNINGS PER SHARE

If potentially dilutive securities exist that are outstanding, such as convertible debt, convertible preferred stock, stock options, or stock warrants, both basic and diluted earnings per share must be shown.

If options are granted as part of a stock-based compensation agreement, the assumed proceeds from the exercise of the options under the treasury stock method include deferred compensation and the ensuing tax benefit that would be credited to paid-in capital arising from the exercise of the options.

The denominator of diluted earnings per share equals the weighted average outstanding common shares for the period plus the assumed issue of common shares arising from convertible securities plus the assumed shares issued because of the exercise of stock options or stock warrants, or their equivalent.

Exhibit 8-1 shows in summary form the earnings-per-share fractions.

Exhibit 8-1: Earnings-per-Share Fractions

BASIC EARNINGS PER SHARE = Net Income Available to Common Stockholders/Weighted Average Number of Common Shares Outstanding

DILUTED EARNINGS PER SHARE = Net Income Available to Common Stockholders + Net of Tax Interest and/or Dividend Savings on Convertible Securities/Weighted Average Number of Common Shares Outstanding + Effect of Convertible Securities + Net Effect of Stock Options

EXAMPLE 8: The same information as in the prior example dealing with basic earnings per share for David Company is assumed. Potentially diluted securities outstanding includes 5% convertible bonds (each $1,000 bond is convertible into 25 shares of common stock) having a face value of $5,000,000. There are options to buy 50,000 shares of common stock at $10 per share. The average market price for common shares is $25 per share for 2X11. The tax rate is 30%. Diluted earnings per share for 2X11 is $1.87 ($1,475,000/787,500 shares) as computed below.

Income for diluted earnings per share:

Earnings available to common stockholders		$1,300,000
Interest expense on convertible bonds		
($5,000,000 × .05)	$250,000	
Less: tax savings ($250,000 × .30)	(75,000)	
Interest expense (net of tax)		175,000
Income for diluted earnings per share		$1,475,000
Shares outstanding for diluted earnings per share:		
Weighted average outstanding common shares		632,500
Assumed issued common shares from convertible bonds (5,000 bonds × 25 shares)		125,000
Assumed issued common shares from exercise of option	50,000	
Less: assumed repurchase of treasury shares (50,000 × $10 = $500,000/$25)	(20,000)	30,000
Shares outstanding for diluted earnings per share		787,500

Basic earnings per share and diluted earnings per share (if required) must be disclosed on the face of the income statement. A reconciliation is required of the numerators and denominators for basic and diluted earnings per share.

EXAMPLE 9: On January 1, 2X12, 10,000 shares were issued. On April 1, 2X12, 2,000 of those shares were bought back by the company. The weighted-average common stock outstanding is:

$$(10,000 \times 3/12) + (8,000 \times 9/12) = 8,500 \text{ shares}$$

When shares are issued because of a stock dividend or stock split, the computation of weighted-average common stock shares outstanding mandates retroactive adjustment as if the shares were outstanding at the beginning of the year.

The common stock equivalency of options and warrants is determined using the treasury stock method. Options and warrants are assumed exercised at the beginning of the year (or at time of issuances, if later).

Convertible securities are accounted for using the if-converted method. The convertible securities are assumed converted at the beginning of the earliest year presented or date of security issuance. Interest or dividends on them are added back to net income since the securities are considered part of equity in the denominator of the EPS calculation.

To accomplish the fullest dilution in arriving at fully diluted EPS, an assumption is made that all common stock issuances on exercise of options or warrants during the period were made at the start of the year. The higher of the closing price or the average price of common stock is used in determining the number of shares of treasury stock to be purchased from the proceeds received upon issuance of the options. If the ending market price exceeds the average market price, the assumed treasury shares acquired will be lessened resulting in higher assumed outstanding shares with the resulting decrease in EPS.

Net income less preferred dividends is in the numerator of the EPS fraction representing earnings available to common stockholders. On cumulative preferred stock, preferred dividends for the current year are subtracted out whether or not paid. Further, preferred dividends are only subtracted out for the current year. Thus, if preferred dividends in arrears were for five years, all of which were paid, plus the sixth year dividend, only the sixth year dividend (current year) is deducted. Preferred dividends for each of the prior years would have been deducted in those years.

In computing EPS, preferred dividends are subtracted out only on preferred stock that was not included as a common stock equivalent. If the preferred stock is a common stock equivalent, the preferred dividend would not be subtracted out since the equivalency of preferred shares into common shares is included in the denominator.

If convertible bonds are included in the denominator of EPS, they are considered as equivalent to common shares. Thus, interest expense (net of tax) has to be added back in the numerator.

Disclosure of EPS should include information on the capital structure, explanation of the computation of EPS, identification of common stock equivalents, assumptions made, and number of shares converted. Rights and privileges of the securities should also be disclosed. Such disclosure includes dividend and participation rights, call prices, conversation ratios, and sinking fund requirements.

A stock conversion occurring during the year or between year-end and the audit report date may have materially affected EPS if it had taken place at the beginning of the year. Thus, supplementary footnote disclosure should be made reflecting on an "as-if" basis what the effects of these conversions would have had on EPS if they were made at the start of the accounting period.

If a subsidiary has been acquired during the year, the weighted-average shares outstanding for the year are used from the purchase date.

When comparative financial statements are presented, there is a retroactive adjustment for stock splits and stock dividends. Assume in 2X11 a 10% stock dividend occurs. The weighted-average shares used for previous years' computations have to be increased by 10% to make EPS data comparable.

When a prior-period adjustment occurs that causes a restatement of previous years' earnings, EPS should also be restated.

According to ASC 260, *Earnings per Share* (ASC 260-10-45-60), under the two-class method, the presentation of basic and diluted EPS for all participating securities is *not* required. A participating security may participate in undistributed earnings with common stock, regardless of whether the participation is conditional upon an event.

ASC 260-10-45-28 provides guidance in calculating earnings per share for share-based payment awards with dividend rights. Unvested share-based payment awards that have nonforfeitable rights to dividends or dividend equivalents (whether paid or unpaid) are considered participating securities and are includable in the earnings per share calculation under the two-class method.

ASC 260-10-45-43 provides that issued securities with embedded conversion features contingently exercisable upon the occurrence of a market-price condition should be part of the computation of diluted EPS, irrespective of whether the market price trigger has been satisfied.

According to Accounting Standards Update (ASU) No. 2010-05 (January 2010), *Compensation—Stock Compensation* (ASC Topic 718), *Escrowed Share Arrangements and the Presumption of Compensation*, in the case of a contract for escrowed stock that is forfeited if employees no longer work is deemed compensation. Escrowed shares may be given back to stockholders when certain conditions as to performance are satisfied. In some cases, major stockholders may be involved in escrow stock contracts.

DISCLOSURES ASSOCIATED WITH OPERATIONS

Disclosure should be made of a company's major products and services, including principal markets by geographic area. The information enables a proper evaluation of the entity's nature of operations. Further, ASC 275, *Risk and Uncertainties*, mandates disclosure of major risks and uncertainties facing the entity. ASC 275 also requires disclosure in the significant accounting policies footnote that the financial information presented is based on management's estimates and assumptions. Reference should be made that actual results may differ from such estimates.

CHAPTER 9

FINANCIAL STATEMENT REPORTING: THE BALANCE SHEET*

CONTENTS

* Adrian P. Fitzsimons Ph.D., CPA (St. John's University, NY), and Biagio Pilato, LL.M., CPA (St. John's University, NY), contributed to the updates in this chapter.

On the balance sheet, the financial officer is concerned with the accounting for and reporting of assets, liabilities, and stockholders' equity.

According to Accounting Standards Update (ASU) No. 2013-01 (January 2013), *Balance Sheet* (Topic 210), *Clarifying the Scope of Disclosures about Offsetting Assets and Liabilities*, this pronouncement specifies that ASU No. 2011-11 relating to disclosures about offsetting assets and liabilities also applies to financial derivatives and repurchase agreements.

ASSETS

An asset is recorded at the price paid plus related costs of placing the asset in service (e.g., freight, insurance, installation). If an asset is bought in exchange for a liability, the asset is recorded at the present value of the payments.

> *EXAMPLE 1:* A machine was acquired by taking out a loan requiring ten $10,000 payments. Each payment includes principal and interest. The interest rate is 10%. While the total payments (principal and interest) are $100,000, the present value will be less since the machine is recorded at the present value of the payments. The asset would be recorded at $61,450 ($10,000 × 6.145). The factor is obtained from the present value of annuity table for $n = 10$, $i = 10\%$.

Note: The asset is recorded at the principal amount excluding the interest payments. If an asset is acquired for stock, the asset is recorded at the fair value of the stock issued. If it is impossible to ascertain the fair market value of the stock (e.g., from a closely held company), the asset will be recorded at its appraised value.

Unearned discounts (except for quantity or cost), finance charges, and interest included in the face of receivables should be subtracted to obtain the net receivable.

Some of the major current and noncurrent assets include:

- Accounts receivable.
- Inventory.
- Fixed assets.
- Intangibles.

Under IFRS, the format of asset presentation is not based on the order of liquidity as is the case under GAAP.

Cash

IFRS allows the offsetting of cash overdrafts, while GAAP does not.

Accounts Receivable

When accounts receivable are assigned, the owner of the receivables borrows cash from a lender in the form of a note payable. The accounts receivable act as collateral. New receivables substitute for receivables collected. The assignment of accounts receivable typically requires the incurrence of a financing charge as well as interest expense on the note.

At a particular date, the transferer's equity in the assigned receivables equals the difference between the accounts receivable assigned and the balance of the line ($5,000). When payments on the receivables are received, they are remitted by the company to the lending institution to reduce the liability. Assignment is on a nonnotification basis to customers. It is made with recourse, where the company has to make good for uncollectible customer accounts.

EXAMPLE 2: On April 1, 2X11, X Company assigns accounts receivable totaling $600,000 to A Bank as collateral for a $400,000 note. X Company will continue to receive customer remissions because the customers are not notified of the assignment. There is a 2% finance charge of the accounts receivable assigned. Interest on the note is 13%. Monthly settlement of the cash received from assigned receivables is made. During the month of April, there were collections of $360,000 of assigned receivables less cash discounts of $5,000. Sales returns were $10,000. On May 1, 2X11, April remissions were made plus accrued interest. In May, the balance of the assigned accounts receivable was collected less $4,000 that were uncollectible. On June 1, 2X11, the balance due was remitted to the bank plus interest for May. The journal entries follow:

4/1/2X11

Cash	388,000	
Finance charge (2% × $600,000)	12,000	
Accounts receivable assigned	600,000	
Notes payable		400,000
Accounts receivable		600,000

During April:

Cash	355,000	
Sales discount	5,000	
Sales returns	10,000	
Accounts receivable assigned		370,000

5/1/2X11

Interest expense	4,333*	
Notes payable	355,000	
Cash		359,333

*$400,000×.13×1112 = $4,333

During May:

Cash	226,000	
Allowance for bad debts	4,000	
Accounts receivable assigned ($600,000 – $370,000)		230,000

6/1/2X11

Interest expense	488*	
Notes payable ($400,000 – $355,000)	45,000	
Cash		45,488

*$45,000×.13×1112 = $488

In a factoring of accounts receivable, the receivables are in effect sold to a finance company. The factor buys the accounts receivable at a discount from face value, usually at a discount of 6%. Customers are typically notified. Factoring is usually done without recourse, where the risk of uncollectibility of the customer's account rests with the financing institution. Billing and collection is typically done by the factor. On a factoring arrangement, the factor charges a commission of from ¾% to ½% of the net receivables acquired. The entry is:

Cash (proceeds)

Loss on sale of receivables

Due from factor (proceeds kept by factor to cover possible adjustments such as sales discounts, sales returns and allowances) accounts receivable (face amount of receivables)

Factoring is normally a continuous process. The seller of the goods receives orders and transmits the purchase orders to the factor for approval; on approval, the goods are shipped; the factor advances the money to the seller; the buyers pay the factor when payment is due; and the factor periodically remits any excess reserve to the seller of the goods. Once a routine is established, a continuous circular flow of goods and funds takes place among the seller, the buyers, and the factor. Once the agreement is in force, funds from this source are spontaneous.

EXAMPLE 3: T Company factors $200,000 of accounts receivable. There is a 4% finance charge. The factor retains 6% of the accounts receivable. Appropriate journal entries are:

Cash	180,000	
Loss on sale of receivables (4% × $200,000)	8,000	
Due from factor (6% × $200,000)	12,000	
Accounts receivable		200,000

Factors provide a needed and dependable source of income for small manufacturers and service businesses.

EXAMPLE 4: A company needs an additional $100,000. The company is considering a factoring arrangement. The factor is willing to buy the accounts receivable and advance the invoice amount less a 4% factoring commission on the receivables purchased. Sales are on 30-day terms. A 14% interest rate will be charged on the total invoice price and deducted in advance. With the factoring arrangement, the credit department will be eliminated, reducing monthly credit expenses by $1,500. Also, bad debt losses of 8% on the factored amount will be avoided.

To net $100,000, the amount of accounts receivable to be factored would be:

$$\frac{\$100,000}{1 - (0.04 + 0.14)} = \frac{\$100,000}{0.82} = \$121,951$$

The effective interest rate on the factoring arrangement is:

$$\frac{0.14}{0.82} = 17.07\%$$

The annual total dollar cost is:

Interest (0.14 × $121,951)	$17,073
Factoring (0.04 × $121,951)	4,878
Total cost	$21,951

According to ASC 860, *Transfers and Servicing* (ASC 860-20), a sale is recorded for the transfer of receivables with recourse if all of the following criteria are satisfied:

- The transferer gives up control of the future economic benefits applicable to the receivables (e.g., repurchase right).
- The liability of the transferer under the recourse provisions is estimable.
- The transferee cannot require the transferer to repurchase receivables unless there is a recourse provision in the contract.

When the transfer is treated as a sale, gain or loss is recognized for the difference between the selling price and the net receivables. The selling price includes normal servicing fees of the transferer and appropriate probable adjustments (e.g., debtor's failure to pay on time, effects of prepayment, and defects in the transferred receivable). Net receivables equal gross receivables plus finance and service charges minus unearned finance and service charges.

When selling price varies during the term of the receivables because of a variable interest rate provision, the selling price is estimated with the use of an appropriate "going market interest rate" at the transfer date. Later changes in the rate cause a change in estimated selling price, not in interest income or interest expense.

If one of the aforementioned criteria is not satisfied, a liability is recognized for the proceeds received.

Footnote disclosure includes:

- Amount received by transfer.

- Balance of the receivables at the balance sheet date.

With IFRS, receivables are initially presented at fair market value.

Loans Receivable

ASC 310, *Receivables* (ASC 310-20), applies to both the incremental direct costs of originating a loan and internally incurred costs directly related to loan activity. Loan origination fees are netted with the related loan origination costs and are accounted for in the following manner:

- For loans held for resale, the net cost is capitalized and recognized at the time the loan is sold.

- For loans held for investment, the net cost is capitalized and amortized over the loan period using the interest method.

Loan commitment fees are initially deferred and recognized in earnings as follows:

- If the commitment is exercised, the fee is recognized over the loan period by the interest method.

- If the commitment expires, the fee is recognized at the expiration date.

- If, based upon previous experience, exercise of the commitment is remote, the fee is amortized over the commitment period using the straight-line method.

Accounting Standards Update (ASU) No. 2017-08 (March 2017), *Receivables–Nonrefundable Fees and Other Costs* (Subtopic 310-20), *Premium Amortization on Purchased Callable Debt Securities*, reduces the amortization period for certain callable debt securities held at a premium. The premium must be amortized to the earliest call date; however, the discount continues to be amortized to maturity.

Impairment of Loans. ASC 310, *Receivables* (ASC 310-10-50-15), provides that a loan is a contractual obligation to receive money either on demand or at a fixed or determinable date. Loans include accounts receivable and notes if their maturity dates exceed one year. If it is probable that some or all of the principal or interest is uncollectible, the loan is deemed impaired. A loss on an impaired loan is recorded immediately by debiting bad debt expense and crediting a valuation allowance.

Determining the Value of an Impaired Loan. The loss on an impaired loan is the difference between the investment in the loan and the discounted value of future cash flows using the effective interest rate on the original loan. In general, the investment in the loan is the principal plus accrued interest. In practical terms, the value of a loan may be based on its market price, if available. The loan value may also be based on the fair value of the collateral, less estimated selling costs, if the loan is collateralized and the security is expected to be the only basis of repayment.

EXAMPLE 5: On December 31, 2X11, Debtor Inc. issues a five-year, $100,000 note at an annual interest rate of 10% payable to Creditor Inc. The market interest rate for the loan is 12%. The discounted value of the principal is $56,742 (based on a principal of $100,000 discounted at 12% for five years). The discounted value of the interest payments is $36,048 (based on annual interest of $10,000 for five years discounted at 12%). Thus, the discounted value of the loan is $92,790 ($56,742 plus $36,048). Discount on Notes Receivable is $7,210 ($100,000 less $92,790). The discount will be amortized using the effective interest method. Creditor Inc. records the note as follows:

Notes receivable	100,000	
Discount on notes receivable		7,210
Cash		92,790

On December 31, 2X13, Creditor Inc. determines that it is probable that Debtor Inc. will be able to repay interest of only $8,000 per year (rather than $10,000 per year) and $70,000 (rather than $100,000) of face value at maturity. This loan impairment requires the immediate recognition of a loss. The discounted value of future cash flows discounted for three years at 12% for $70,000 is $49,824, and for $8,000 is $19,215. Therefore, the total present value of future cash flows is $69,039 ($49,824 plus $19,215). On December 31, 2X13, the carrying value of the investment in loan is $95,196. As a result, the impairment loss is $26,157 ($95,196 less $69,039). The journal entry to record the loss is:

Bad debts	26,157	
Allowance for bad debts		26,157

Interest income from an impaired loan may be recognized using several methods, including cash basis, cost recovery, or a combination.

If the creditor's charging off of some part of the loan results in recording an investment in an impaired loan below its present value of future cash flows, no additional impairment is to be recorded.

In determining the collectibility of a loan, consideration should be given to:

- Financial problems of borrower.
- Borrower in an unstable or unhealthy industry.
- Regulatory reports.

- Compliance exception reports.
- Amount of loan.
- Prior loss experience.
- Lack of marketability of collateral.

A loan is not considered impaired when the delay in collecting is insignificant.

Disclosures. The following should be disclosed either in the body of the financial statements or in the footnotes:

- The creditor's policy of recognizing interest income on impaired loans, including the recording of cash receipts.
- The average recorded investment in impaired loans, the related interest revenue recognized while the loans were impaired, and the amount of interest revenue recognized using the cash basis while the loans were impaired.
- The total investment in impaired loans including (1) the amount of investments for which a related valuation allowance exists, and (2) the amount of investments for which a valuation allowance does not exist.

Lending to or Financing the Activities of Others. ASC 945, *Financial Services—Depository and Lending,* specifies that a business has a loan or trade receivable not held for sale when the expectation is to hold the loan or receivable for the foreseeable future or until the maturity date. These loans and receivables are to be shown at the principal balance after adjustment for any chargeoffs, bad debt provisions, deferred loan fees, and unamortized discounts or premiums for purchased loans.

A company must record credit losses arising from off-balance-sheet exposures by debiting loss and crediting the associated liability.

A nonmortgaged loan held for sale is reported at the lower of cost or fair value.

Footnote disclosure is made of the entity's accounting policies for its loans and trade receivables along with its policies for doubtful accounts and credit losses, measurement and recognition for loan losses, gain or loss on the sale of loans and trade receivables, recognition methods for interest revenue on loans and trade receivables, collateralized assets along with their carrying values, accounting treatment for nonaccrual and past due loans and trade receivables, foreclosed or repossessed assets, classification policies, and lease financings.

A purchased loan may have poor credit quality. In this case, according to Accounting Standards Update (ASU) No. 2010-18 (April 2010), *Receivables* (ASC Topic 310), *Effect of a Loan Modification When the Loan Is Part of a Pool That Is Accounted for as a Single Asset,* if an acquired asset has similar risk attributes (e.g., credit risk), it may be treated as a pool, which is considered an accounting unit. The pooled loans do not involve the allocation of the purchase discount to the specific loans. In addition, one pool rate applies to all of the loans. The loan pool is also evaluated for any impairment.

In some cases, a modification of a loan may be considered a reworking of troubled debt. A loan modification for a pool does not constitute a loan removal from the pool even when the loan restructuring is deemed troubled debt. In determining if a loan impairment exists, anticipated future cash flows should be taken into account.

The cost of purchased assets should be allocated based on fair market value at the time of acquisition. If a loan is refinanced, except for a troubled debt restructuring, that loan is not considered to be a new loan. A loan is only taken out of a pool if it is written-off or if assets are obtained in exchange for the loan; a removal of a loan should be at book value. A troubled debt restructuring does not apply to a modification of a worker contract or lease modification. (ASC 310-30-15-6; 310-30-35-13; 310-30-40-1; 310-40-15-11)

Accounting Standards Update (ASU) No. 2010-20 (July 2010), *Receivables* (ASC Topic 310), *Disclosures about the Credit Quality of Financing Receivables and the Allowance for Credit Losses,* specifies that disclosures should be made of the provision for credit losses from the beginning to end of the year, investment in financing receivables, nonaccrual of financing receivables, financing receivables that have defaulted, indicators of credit quality, major purchases and sales of financing receivables, and troubled debt restructurings and their impact on the provision for credit losses.

According to Accounting Standards Update (ASU) No. 2011-02 (April 2011), Receivables (ASC Topic 310), *A Creditor's Determination of Whether a Restructuring Is a Troubled Debt Restructuring,* in appraising if a restructuring is of troubled debt, the creditor must conclude that both the restructuring is a concession and the debtor is having financial problems.

Inventory

Inventories consist of merchandise purchased by a retailer or wholesaler for resale or inventories of a manufacturing entity that consist of raw materials, work in process (partially completed goods), finished goods, operating supplies, and ordinary maintenance parts.

Inventories are generally presented on the Balance Sheet as current assets. However, if inventory consists of slow-moving items or excessive amounts that will not be sold within the normal operating cycle of the business, such excess amounts should be classified as noncurrent assets.

Inventory includes direct and indirect costs associated with preparing inventory for sale or use. Therefore, the cost of inventory to a retail store includes the purchase price, taxes paid, delivery charges, storage, and insurance. A manufacturer includes in its cost of inventory, the direct materials (including the purchase price and freight-in), direct labor, and factory overhead (including factory utilities, rent, and insurance).

Lower of Cost and Net Realizable Value. U.S. GAAP (ASU 2015-11) requires that an entity's inventory be reported at the lower of cost and net realizable value (LCANRV) (net realizable value [NRV] is defined in the next paragraph) for all methods of inventory valuation other than last-in, first-out (LIFO) or the retail inventory method. Accordingly, inventory valued at first-in, first out (FIFO) or average cost must be reported at LCANRV. Inventories valued at LIFO and the retail inventory method, on the other hand, are reported at the lower of cost or market (LCM). This directive is a result of the FASB's ongoing Simplification Initiative in which the rule-making body concluded using LCANRV would reduce costs and increase comparability for inventory measurements such as first-in, first-out (FIFO) or average cost. Correspondingly, because of their complexity, the Board decided that the use of LCANRV for LIFO and retail inventory methods would generate significant transition costs that did not justify the benefits of this use and thus were excluded from the LCANRV requirement. LIFO is commonly applied using Dollar Value LIFO (DVL) or retail LIFO methods. Both of these methodologies are illustrated in other sections of this chapter.

Net realizable value (NRV) is defined as the estimated selling price of the inventory in the ordinary course of business, less reasonably predictable costs of completion, disposal, and transportation. Disposal and transportation costs are viewed as the necessary costs that must be incurred to sell the inventory. The LCANRV concept is illustrated in the following example.

EXAMPLE 6:

Product	Estimated Selling Price	Predictable Costs of Completion Disposal and Transportation	Net Realizable Value
1	$75	$12	$63
2	60	10	50
3	45	9	36
4	80	16	64
5	110	23	87

Then, compare the net realizable value (NRV) of each product item to cost.

Each item is valued at the lower of these two amounts.

Product	Cost	Net Realizable Value	Inventory Value (Lower of Cost and Net Realizable Value)
1	$59	$63	$59
2	75	50	50
3	43	36	36
4	61	64	61
5	92	87	87

The application of LCANRV may be applied on an individual items basis, a logical category of inventory basis, or a total inventory basis. The individual items basis is the most frequently chosen because it generates the most conservative valuation of inventory and it is the only one of the three that is acceptable for tax purposes. Whichever approach is chosen must be applied consistently. The reduction of inventory to LCANRV may be charged to cost of goods sold and credited to inventory directly. Alternatively, if it is desired to separately record the inventory holding loss, a loss account and inventory valuation account must be utilized. The loss account, known as "Loss to reduce inventory to lower of cost or net realizable value," is shown separately on the income statement, if material. A contra assets account, termed "Allowance to reduce inventory to net realizable value," is credited for the loss and is presented on the Balance Sheet as a reduction to inventory.

Lower of Cost or Market. As indicated in the last section, the FASB decided that companies using LIFO or retail inventory methods were excluded from the LCANRV requirement because using them in this manner would not simplify the inventory valuation process. These inventory valuation methodologies use the lower of cost or market (LCM) reporting approach. A comprehensive discussion of this concept follows.

Inventory valued at LCM, such as LCANRV, may be applied on a total inventory basis, a category basis, or an individual items basis. In this area, as well as in LCANRV, the individual items basis is the most popular because it generates the most conservative valuation of inventory and is the only basis acceptable for tax purposes. Whichever approach is chosen, it must be applied consistently.

In the LCM approach, market is defined as replacement cost. Replacement cost is the cost to "replace" the product at a given point in time; for example, the cost to buy or manufacture the product at fiscal year-end. However, in computing the lower-of-cost-or-market valuation, replacement cost is constrained by an "upper limit" and "lower limit" (see the steps below).

The lower-of-cost-or-market valuation is computed by applying the following steps:

1. Market is initially viewed as the replacement cost of the product. (See Example 7)

2. Market cannot exceed the upper limit of net realizable value (net realizable value equals selling price less costs to complete and dispose) shown in Example 7. If it does, the upper limit is selected.

3. Market cannot be less than the lower limit of net realizable value less a normal profit margin. If it is, the lower limit is selected.

4. Replacement cost is selected as market when it lies between the upper and lower limits.

5. After the market value is selected, compare it to cost. The lower of the two constitutes the lower-of-cost-or-market valuation.

EXAMPLE 7:

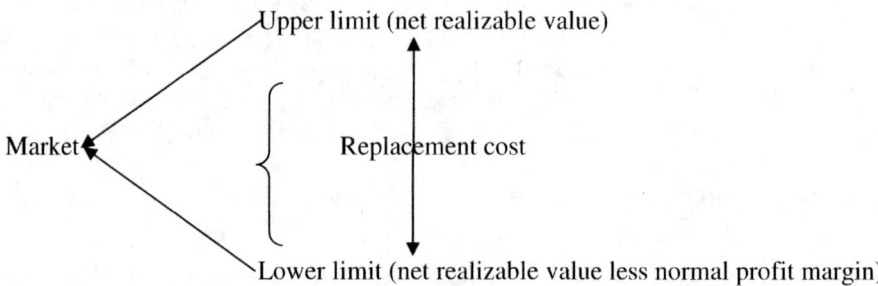

Company ABC uses the lower of cost or market value method on an item-by-item basis. The valuation of each product follows:

Product	Cost	Replacement Cost	Upper Limit	Lower Limit	LCM
M	$10	$14	$18	$12	$10
N	28	24	22	14	22
O	36	30	32	24	30
P	40	24	36	32	32
Q	12	10	24	14	12

With respect to Q, replacement cost is initially selected as the market value. However, as the replacement cost of $10 is below the lower limit, the lower limit of $14 is chosen as the market value. This value ($14) is then compared to cost and the lower of the two ($12) is selected as the final lower-of-cost-or-market valuation.

The recording of inventory to LCM is handled similarly to the recording of inventory to LCANRV.

Retail Method. The retail method is used by department stores and other large retail businesses. These businesses usually carry inventory items at retail selling price. The retail method is used to estimate the ending inventory at cost by employing a cost to retail (selling price) ratio. The ending inventory is first determined at selling price and then converted to cost. Markups and mark-downs are both considered in arriving at the cost-to-retail ratio resulting in a higher ending inventory than the retail-lower-of-cost-or-market-value method.

Retail-Lower-of-Cost-or-Market-Value (Conventional Retail) Method. This is a modification of the retail method and is preferable to it. In computing the cost-to-retail ratio, markups but not markdowns are considered, resulting in a lower inventory figure.

The following example illustrates the accounting difference between the retail method and the retail-lower-of-cost-or-market-value method.

EXAMPLE 8:

	Cost	Retail	
Inventory 1/1	16,000	30,000	
Purchases	30,000	60,000	
Purchase returns	(5,000)	(10,000)	
Purchase discount	(2,000)		
Freight in	1,000		

	Cost		Retail	
Markups	25,000			
Markup cancellations	5,000		20,000	
Total		40,000	100,000	(40%)
Markdowns	22,000			
Markdown cancellations	2,000		20,000	
Cost of goods available		40,000	80,000	(50%)
Deduct:				
Sales	55,000			
Less: Sales returns	5,000		50,000	
Inventory—retail			30,000	
Retail method:				
At cost 50% × 30,000			15,000	
Retail-lower-of-cost-or-market-value method: 40% × 30,000			12,000	

Retail LIFO. In computing ending inventory, the mechanics of the retail method are basically followed. Beginning inventory is excluded and both markups and markdowns are included in computing the cost-to-retail ratio. A decrease in inventory during the period is deducted from the most recently added layer and then subtracted from layers in the inverse order of addition. A retail price index is used in restating inventory.

EXAMPLE 9: Retail price indices follow:

2X11 100
2X12 104
2X13 110

2X12	Cost	Retail
Inventory—Jan. 1 (base inv.)	80,000	130,000
Purchases	240,000	410,000
Markups		10,000

2X12	Cost	Retail				
Markdowns		(20,000)				
Total (exclude beg. inv.)	240,000	400,000	60%			
Total (include beg. inv.)	320,000	530,000				
Sales		389,600				
2X12 Inv.—end at retail		140,400				

Cost Basis

	Cost	Retail				
2X12 Inventory in terms of 2X11 prices 140,400 ÷ 1.04		135,000				
2X11 base	80,000	130,000	– 130,000	×	1.04	135,200
2X12 layer in 2X11 prices		5,000				
2X13 layer in 2X12 prices		5,200	5,000	×	1.04	5,200
						140,400
2X12 LIFO cost 60% × 5,200	3,120					
	83,120	140,400				

2X13	Cost	Retail				
Inventory—Jan. 1	83,120	140,400				
Purchases	260,400	430,000				
Markups		20,000				
Markdowns		(30,000)				
Total (exclude beg. inv.)	260,400	420,000	62%			
Total (include beg. inv.)	343,520	560,400				
Sales		408,600				
2X13 inventory—end at retail		151,800				

Cost Basis

	Cost	Retail				
2X13 Inventory in terms of 2X11 prices 151,800 ÷ 1.10		138,000				
2X11 base	80,000	130,000	130,000	×	1.10	143,000
Excess over base year		8,000				
2X12 layer in 2X12 prices	3,120	5,000	5,000	×	1.10	5,500
2X13 layer in 2X11 prices		3,000				

2X13	Cost	Retail				
2X13 increase in 2X13 prices		3,300	3,000	×	1.10	3,300
2X13 increase in 2X13 prices LIFO cost 62% × 3,300	2,046					
	85,166	151,800				151,800

Dollar Value LIFO. Dollar value LIFO is an extension of the historical cost principle. The method aggregates dollars instead of units into homogeneous groupings. The method assumes that an inventory decrease came from the last year.

The procedures under dollar value LIFO are as follows:

1. Restate ending inventory in the current year into base dollars by applying a price index.

2. Subtract the year 0 inventory in base dollars from the current year's inventory in base dollars.

3. Multiply the incremental inventory in the current year in base dollars by the price index to obtain the incremental inventory in current dollars.

4. Add to the year 0 inventory, in base dollars, the incremental inventory for the current year in current dollars to obtain the reportable inventory for the current year.

EXAMPLE 10: At December 31, 2X11, the ending inventory is $130,000 and the price index is 1.30. The base inventory on January 1, 2X11, was $80,000. The January 31, 2X11, inventory is computed thus:

12/31/2X11 inventory in base dollars $130,000/1.30	$100,000
1/1/2X11 beginning base inventory	80,000
2X11 increment in base dollars	$20,000
2X11 increment in current year dollars	× 1.3
	$26,000
Inventory in base dollars	$80,000
Increment in current year dollars	26,000
Reportable inventory	$106,000

Losses on Purchase Commitments. Significant net losses on purchase commitments should be recognized at the end of the reporting period.

EXAMPLE 11: In 2X12, ABC Company committed itself to buy raw materials at $1.20 per pound. At the end of the year, before fulfilling the purchase commitment, the price of the materials dropped to $1.00 per pound. Conservatism dictates that a loss on purchase commitment of $.20 per pound be recognized in 2X12. Loss on Purchase Commitment is debited and Allowance for Purchase Commitment Loss is credited.

Inventory Valuation Difficulties. Whereas the basics of inventory cost measurement are easily stated, difficulties arise because of cost allocation problems. General and administrative expenses are inventoried when they specifically relate to production activity.

ASC 330, *Inventory* (ASC 330-10-30), requires the immediate expensing of abnormal amounts of idle facility expense, freight, handling, and wasted material (spoilage). Further, allocation of fixed production overhead to the costs of conversion must be based on the normal capacity of the manufacturing facilities.

Inventory Stated at Market Value in Excess of Cost. In unusual circumstances, inventories may be stated in excess of cost. This may occur when there is no basis for cost apportionment (e.g., meat packing industry). Market value may also be used when immediate marketability exists at quoted prices (e.g., certain precious metals or agricultural products). Disclosure is necessary when inventory is stated above cost.

ASC 845, *Nonmonetary Transactions* (ASC 845-10-05-8), deals with the situation in which one company both sells inventory to and buys inventory from another company in the same line of business. Such purchase and sale arrangements may be under single or separate contracts.

Two or more sell and buy transactions between two entities should be combined and accounted for as one transaction.

Nonmonetary exchange transactions of finished goods for work-in-process or raw materials in the same line of business are *not* exchange transactions with commercial substance according to ASC 845, *Nonmonetary Transactions*. However, a transaction should be recognized at fair value if reasonable determination of fair value is possible and the transaction has commercial substance. All other nonmonetary exchanges of inventory in the same line of business (e.g., work-in-process for raw materials or exchange of raw materials) should be accounted for at the carrying amount of the transferred inventory.

Under IFRS, inventory valuation using the LIFO method is not allowed. FIFO and average cost are the only allowed cost flow assumptions under IFRS. Both U.S. GAAP and IFRS permit the specific identification method. In the lower of cost or market value test for inventory valuation, IFRS defines market value as net realizable value. IFRS does not use a ceiling or a floor to determine market value. Marketing costs are not includable in cost of sales under GAAP but are includable in cost of sales using IFRS.

Fixed Assets

A fixed asset is recorded at its fair market value or the fair market value of the consideration given, whichever is more clearly evident.

The cost of buying an asset includes all costs necessary to put that asset into existing use and location, including insurance, taxes, installation, freight, and breaking-in costs (e.g., instruction).

Using IFRS, fixed assets are shown at fair market value less accumulated depreciation.

Additions to an existing building (such as constructing a new garage for the building) are capitalized and depreciated over the shorter of the life of the addition or the life of the building. Rearrangement and reinstallation costs are capitalized when future benefit is created. If not, they should be expensed. Obsolete fixed assets should be reclassified from property, plant, and equipment to other assets and shown at salvage value reflecting a loss.

When two or more assets are bought for one price, cost is allocated to the assets based on their relative fair market values. If an old building is demolished to make way for the construction of a new building, the costs of demolishing the old building are charged to the land account.

Self-constructed assets are recorded at the incremental costs to build assuming idle capacity; however, they should not be recorded at more than the outside price.

A deposit on a fixed asset to be purchased within one year is still presented as a long-term asset.

EXAMPLE 12: Incremental costs to self-construct equipment are $12,000. The equipment could have been bought outside for $9,000. The journal entry is:

Equipment	9,000	
Loss	3,000	
Cash		12,000

A fixed asset donated to the company should be reflected at fair market value. The entry is to charge fixed assets and credit contribution revenue.

Note: Fixed assets cannot be written up, except in the case of a discovery of a natural resource or in a purchase combination. In a discovery of a natural resource (e.g., oil), the land account is debited at appraised value and then depleted by the units of production method.

Land improvements (e.g., driveways, sidewalks, fencing) are capitalized and depreciated over useful life. Land held for investment purposes or for a future plant site should be classified under investments and not fixed assets.

Ordinary repairs to an asset (e.g., tune-up for a car) are expensed because they have a life of less than one year.

Extraordinary repairs are capitalized because they benefit a period of one year or more (e.g., new motor for a car). Extraordinary repairs add to an asset's life or make the asset more useful. Capital expenditures improve the quality or quantity of services to be derived from the asset.

Depreciation is the allocation of the historical cost of a fixed asset into expense over the period benefited to result in matching expense against revenue.

Fractional year depreciation is computing depreciation when the asset is acquired during the year. A proration is required.

EXAMPLE 13: On October 1, 2X11, a fixed asset costing $10,000 with a salvage value of $1,000 and a life of 5 years is acquired.

Depreciation expense for 2X12 using the sum-of-the-years' digits method is:

1/1/2X12 – 9/30/2X12 5/15 × $9,000 × 9/12	$2,250
10/1/2X12 – 12/31/2X12 4/1 × $9,000 × 3/12	600
	$2,850

Depreciation expense for 2X12 using double declining balance is:

Year	Computation	Depreciation	Book Value
0			$10,000
10/1/20X4– 12/31/20X4	3/12 × $10,000 × 40%	$1,000	9,000
1/1/20X5– 12/31/20X5	$9,000 × 40%	(3,600)	5,400

Group and composite depreciation methods involve similar accounting. The group method is used for similar assets while the composite method is used for dissimilar assets. Both methods are generally accepted. There is one accumulated depreciation account for the entire group. The depreciation rate equals:

$$\frac{\text{Depreciation}}{\text{Gross cost}}$$

Depreciation expense for a period equals:

$$\text{Depreciation rate} \times \text{Gross Cost}$$

The depreciable life equals:

$$\frac{\text{Depreciation cost}}{\text{Depreciation}}$$

When an asset is sold in the group, the entry is:

Cash (proceeds received)

Accumulated depreciation (plug figure)

    Fixed asset (cost)

Note: Upon sale of a fixed asset in the group, the difference between the proceeds received and the cost of the fixed asset is plugged to accumulated depreciation. No gain or loss is recognized upon the sale. A gain or loss would only be recognized if the entire assets were sold.

EXAMPLE 14: Calculations for composite depreciation follow:

Asset	Cost	Salvage	Depreciable Cost	Life	Depreciation
A	$25,000	$5,000	$20,000	10	$2,000
B	40,000	2,000	38,000	5	7,600
C	52,000	4,000	48,000	6	8,000
	$117,000	$11,000	$106,000		$17,600

Composite rate:

$$\frac{\$17,600}{\$117,000} = 15.04\%$$

Composite life:

$$\frac{\$106,000}{\$17,600} = 6.02 \text{ years}$$

The entry to record depreciation is:

Depreciation	17,600	
Accumulated depreciation		17,600

The entry to sell asset B for $36,000 is:

Cash	36,000	
Accumulated depreciation	4,000	
Fixed asset		40,000

Capitalized Interest. Disclosure should be given of the interest capitalized and expensed. Interest incurred on borrowed funds is expensed.

However, interest on borrowed funds is capitalized to the asset account and then amortized in the following cases:

- Self-constructed assets for the company's own use. To justify interest capitalization, a time period must exist for assets to be prepared for use.

- Assets for sale or lease constructed as discrete, individual projects (e.g., real estate development).

- Assets purchased for the entity's own use by arrangements requiring a down payment and/or progress payments.

Interest is not capitalized for:

- Assets in use or ready for use.
- Assets not in use and not being prepared for use.
- Assets produced in large volume or on a recurring basis.

Interest capitalized is based on the average accumulated expenditures for that asset. The interest rate used is either:

- Interest rate on the specific borrowing.
- Weighted-average interest rate of corporate debt.

EXAMPLE 15: In the purchase of a qualifying asset, a company expends $100,000 on January 1, 2X11, and $150,000 on March 1, 2X11. The average accumulated expenditures for 2X11 are computed as follows:

Expenditure	Number of Months	Average Expenditure
$100,000	12	$100,000
150,000	10	125,000
$250,000		$225,000

The interest capitalization period begins when the following exist:

- Interest is being incurred.
- Expenditures have been incurred.
- Work is taking place to make the asset ready for intended use. These activities are not restricted to actual construction but may also include administrative and technical activities prior to the time of construction. Included are costs of unforeseen events occurring during construction, such as labor unrest and litigation.

The capitalization period ends when the asset is substantially complete and usable. When an asset consists of individual elements (e.g., condominium units), the capitalization period of interest costs applicable to one of the separate units ends when the particular unit is materially finished and usable. Capitalization of interest is not continued when construction ends, except for brief or unanticipated delays.

When the total asset must be finished to be useful, interest capitalization continues until the total asset is substantially finished, such as for a manufacturing plant where sequential production activities must take place.

Under ASC 835, *Interest* (ASC 835-20), an investor's qualifying assets for capitalizing interest purposes include loans, equity funds, and advances to investees accounted for by the equity method. Thus, an investor (parent and/or consolidated subsidiaries) must capitalize interest costs on such qualifying assets if, during that period, the investee begins planned significant operations and such activities include funds used to buy qualifying assets for its operations. No capitalization of interest occurs by the investor on or after the date the investor begins its planned major operations.

Nonmonetary Exchange of Assets. ASC 845 deals with nonmonetary transactions and covers the accounting for exchanges or distributions of fixed assets. It states that, typically, an exchange of nonmonetary assets should be based on the fair market value of the asset given or received, whichever is more clearly evident. As a result, there should be immediate recording of any gain or loss arising from the exchange. The reasoning is that there is commercial substance to the transaction. Thus, fair market value is the measurement basis for the asset received in a nonmonetary exchange *when commercial substance exists*. There is commercial substance when future cash flows change because of the transaction arising from a change in economic positions of the two parties.

EXAMPLE 16: X Company exchanges machinery for Y Company's land. It is probable that the timing and dollar amount of cash flows from the land received will be materially different from the equipment's cash flows. Hence, both companies now have different economic positions indicating an exchange with commercial substance.

Even in the case of a similar exchange of assets (machine for machine) there may arise a change in economic position. For example, when the life of the machine received is much longer than that of the machine given up, the cash flows for the machines can be materially different. In consequence, there is commercial substance to the transaction and fair market value should be used as the measurement basis for the machine received in the exchange. On the other hand, if the difference in cash flows is not significant, the company is still in the same economic position as previously and, therefore, no gain or loss would be recognized on the exchange.

When fair market value is used, a gain or loss typically will be recorded on the exchange. As a result, business entities must appraise the cash flow features of the assets exchanged to ascertain whether there is commercial substance to the transaction. In determining whether future cash flows change, it is required to either (1) analyze if cash flows are affected from the exchange versus without it, or (2) determine whether the timing, amount, and risk of cash flows resulting from the asset received is different from the cash flows applicable with the asset given up.

In the exchange situation in which fair market value is determinable and commercial substance exists, the asset obtained is recorded at fair market value with a gain or loss recognized. If the exchange lacks commercial substance, the asset given up is recorded at book value with no recognition of gain or loss.

Commercial Substance Exists. The cost of a nonmonetary asset received in exchange for another nonmonetary asset is typically recorded at the fair market value of the asset given up with a gain or loss recognized. The fair market value of the asset acquired should be used only if it is more clearly evident than the fair market value of the asset given up.

EXAMPLE 17: XYZ Company exchanged automobiles plus cash for land. The automobiles have a fair market value of $100,000. They cost $130,000 with accumulated depreciation of $50,000, so the book value is $80,000. Cash paid is $35,000. The cost of the land to XYZ equals:

Fair market value of automobiles exchanged	$100,000
Cash paid	35,000
Cost of land	$135,000

The journal entry for the exchange transaction is:

Land	135,000	
Accumulated depreciation—automobiles	50,000	
Automobiles		130,000
Cash		35,000
Gain on disposal of automobiles		20,000

The gain equals the fair market value of the automobiles less their book value computed as follows:

Fair market value of automobiles	$100,000	
Book value		
Cost of automobiles	$130,000	
Less: accumulated depreciation	50,000	80,000
Gain		$20,000

However, if the automobiles had a fair market value of $78,000 rather than $100,000, there would be a loss recognized of $2,000 ($80,000 less $78,000). In either situation, the company is in a different economic position and thus the transaction has commercial substance. Hence, a gain or loss is recognized.

EXAMPLE 18: ABC Company exchanges its old equipment for new equipment. The used equipment has a book value of $40,000 (cost $60,000 less accumulated depreciation of $20,000) with a fair market value of $30,000. The list price of the new equipment is $80,000; the trade-in allowance is $45,000; and commercial substance exists. Cash to be paid equals:

List price of new equipment	$80,000
Less: trade-in allowance	45,000
Cash to be paid	$35,000

Cost of the new equipment equals:

Fair market value of old equipment	$30,000
Cash due	35,000
Cost of new equipment	$65,000

The journal entry to record this exchange transaction is:

Equipment	65,000
Accumulated depreciation	20,000
Loss on disposal of equipment	10,000

Equipment—old	60,000
Cash	35,000

The loss is computed as follows:

Fair market value of old equipment	$30,000
Book value of old equipment	40,000
Loss	$10,000

Because assets should not be valued in excess of their cash equivalent price, the loss is recognized immediately instead of being added to the cost of the newly acquired asset.

Commercial Substance Does Not Exist. Exchanges lacking commercial substance may exist such as in the real estate industry. In real estate, for example, there may be a "swap" of real estate properties.

EXAMPLE 19: A Company and B Company both have undeveloped land for which the cash flows from the land properties to be exchanged are not materially different. A gain cannot be recognized because commercial substance does not exist. Both companies are in the same economic position after the swap as before. Thus, the asset acquired is recorded at book value without gain recognition. **Caution:** The asset given up may be impaired. In consequence, if the book value is more than fair market value, an impairment is recorded provided the impairment test is satisfied.

EXAMPLE 20: Avis Car Rental has mostly Chrysler automobiles. Avis contracts with Hertz Car Rental to exchange a group of Chrysler automobiles that are basically similar to Hertz's General Motors models. The Chrysler automobiles to be exchanged have a fair market value of $320,000 and a book value of $270,000 (cost $300,000 less accumulated depreciation of $30,000). The General Motors automobiles have a fair market value of $340,000. Avis pays $20,000 cash besides the Chrysler models exchanged. Avis has an *unrecognized* total gain of:

Fair market value of Chrysler automobiles exchanged	$320,000
Book value of Chrysler automobiles exchanged	270,000
Total unrecognized gain	$ 50,000

In this situation, Avis still has an automobile fleet essentially of the same cash flows as the automobiles given up even though they are different models. Thus, the transaction does not have commercial substance. In consequence, the total gain is deferred, and the basis for the GM automobiles is decreased. The computation of the basis of the GM automobiles follows:

Book value of Chrysler automobiles	$270,000
Cash paid	20,000
Basis of GM automobiles	$290,000

An alternative calculation is:

Fair market value of GM automobiles	$340,000
Less: unrecognized gain	50,000
Basis of GM automobiles	$290,000

Avis prepares the following journal entry to record this transaction:

Automobiles (GM)	290,000	
Accumulated depreciation	30,000	
Automobiles (Chrysler)		300,000
Cash		20,000

The gain that lowered the basis of the new automobiles will be recorded when they are sold to an external party. The reduced basis means higher net income because of lower depreciation expense in later years while the automobiles are held.

Note: Fair market value is the basis on which to measure an asset received in a nonmonetary exchange when the transaction has commercial substance. The gain or loss equals the difference between the book value of the asset given up and the fair market value of the asset received. However, if fair market values for either the asset received or the asset given up are *not* reasonably determinable, the book value of the asset given up (plus cash paid) is recorded at the cost of the asset received. Another exception to the fair market value rule is for an exchange that facilitates customer sales. An example is when a business exchanges its inventory for that of another business because of same features (e.g., size, color) to make the inventory items easier to sell to an outside customer. In this situation, the earnings process for the inventory is not deemed complete, and there will be *no* recognition of gain.

> **EXAMPLE 21:** Because of a change in product processing, X Company trades its outdated machinery for new machinery that can be used in the new product processing. Because of the specialized nature of the machinery being exchanged, the fair market values of the assets being exchanged is not readily determinable. The old machinery has a book value of $19,000 (cost $32,000 less accumulated depreciation $13,000). The new machinery has a list price of $32,000. The trade-in allowance on the old machinery is $25,000. The cash to be paid equals:

List price of new machinery	$32,000
Less: trade-in allowance for used machinery	25,000
Cash to be paid	$ 7,000

The cost of the new machinery equals:

Cash to be paid	$ 7,000
Book value of old machinery	19,000
Cost of new machinery	$26,000

The journal entry for the exchange follows:

Machinery—new	26,000	
Accumulated depreciation	13,000	
Machinery—old		32,000
Cash		7,000

Reminder: If fair market values for either the asset obtained or relinquished are *not* reasonably determinable, the business uses the book value of the old asset plus the cash paid as the cost basis for the new asset.

Footnote disclosure required for nonmonetary exchanges are as follows:

- Nature of the transaction.
- Method to account for transferred assets.
- Gain or loss on the exchange.

In conclusion, the asset received in a nonmonetary exchange is recorded at fair market value when the transaction has commercial substance. A gain or loss is recognized for the difference between the book value of the asset given up and the fair market value of the asset received. However, if commercial substance does *not* exist, the exchange is recorded based on book values with no gain or loss recorded.

Involuntary Conversion. There may arise an involuntary conversion of non-monetary assets into monetary assets, followed by replacement of the involuntarily converted assets. For example, a warehouse is destroyed by a fire and the insurance proceeds received are used to purchase a similar warehouse. According to ASC 605, *Revenue Recognition* (ASC 605-40-25), gain or loss is recognized for the difference between the insurance recovery and the book value of the destroyed asset. The new warehouse replacing the destroyed one, therefore, is recorded at its purchase price. Caution: A contingency arises if the old fixed asset is damaged in one period but the insurance recovery is not received until a later period. A contingent gain or loss is reported in the period the old fixed asset was damaged. The gain or loss may be recognized for book and tax purposes in different years, resulting in a temporary difference for income tax allocation purposes.

Donation of Fixed Assets. ASC 720, *Other Expenses* (ASC 720-25; 958-605-05-25), requires a donated fixed asset to be recorded at its fair market value by debiting the fixed asset and crediting contribution revenue.

According to ASC 720-25; 958-605-05-25, the company donating a nonmonetary asset recognizes an expense for the fair value of the donated asset. The difference between the carrying value and the fair value of the donated asset is a gain or loss.

EXAMPLE 22: Hartman Company donates land costing $100,000 with a fair value of $130,000. The journal entry is:

Contribution expense	130,000	
Land		100,000
Gain on disposal of land		30,000

If a company pledges unconditionally to give an asset in the future, contribution expense and a payable are accrued. However, if the pledge is conditional, an entry is not made until the asset is transferred.

Barter Transactions. A barter transaction may relate to an exchange of goods or services or barter credits. With respect to the latter, for example, the asset inventory may be exchanged for barter credits. (ASC 845, *Nonmonetary Transactions* (ASC 845-10-05-9).

ASC 845-10-05-9 stipulates that APB 29, *Accounting for Nonmonetary Transactions*, should be applied to an exchange of a nonmonetary asset for barter credits. With respect to barter credits, it is assumed that the fair market value of the asset exchanged is more clearly evident than the fair market value of the barter credits received. As a result, the barter credits received should be recorded at the fair market value of the asset exchanged. In ascertaining the fair market value of the asset surrendered, it is assumed that the fair market value of the asset does not exceed its book value.

In the event that the fair market value of the asset surrendered is below its book value, an impairment should be recorded before making the entry for the exchange. For example, inventory being exchanged in a barter transaction should be reflected at the lower of cost or market value before recording the barter transaction.

At year-end, the recorded amount of barter credits should be appraised for impairment. An impairment loss is recognized when the fair market value of any remaining barter credits is below its book value, or in the event that it is probable that what is left of the barter credits will not be used.

Impairment of Fixed Assets. ASC 360-10-05-4 discusses the accounting, reporting, and disclosure requirements for impaired long-term assets to be held and used, and for long-lived assets to be disposed of. ASC 360-10-05-4 continues in effect the requirements of ASC 360-10-05-4 with respect to the recognition and measurement of impaired long-term assets.

ASC 360-10-05-4 is applicable to a company's long-term assets to be retained or to be disposed of, including noncurrent prepaid assets, lessor long-term assets leased under operating leases, lessee capital leases, and deferred exploration costs under the successful efforts method.

If a long-term asset is a part of a group of other assets or debt, ASC 360-10-05-4 is applicable to the group. In this event, the group is the accounting unit for the long-term asset.

With regard to long-term assets to be kept and utilized, this asset group constitutes the minimum level at which identifiable cash flows are mostly not connected to the cash flows of other asset and liability groups. With regard to long-term assets to be disposed of, this disposal group refers to the net assets (assets less liabilities) to be disposed of in one transaction. An example of a liability associated with the disposed asset is a pollution-related obligation of a disposed plant.

ASC 360-10-05-4 does not change the accounting for individual assets not included in asset groups falling under this Statement, such as inventory, accounts receivable, accounts payable, and noncurrent debt.

Long-Term Assets to Be Retained and Used. ASC 360-10-05-4 provides GAAP for long-lived assets to be held and used with regard to recognizing and measuring impairment loss; recoverability tests; asset grouping; formulating the new cost basis; estimating future cash flows to test the recoverability of a long-lived asset; fair value determination; and reporting and disclosure requirements.

Recognizing and Measuring the Impairment Loss. An impairment exists when the fair value of a long-term asset group is less than its book (carrying) value. The impairment loss is recorded only when the carrying value of the asset group is unrecoverable and is more than its fair value. A lack of recoverability is evident when the book value of the asset group is more than the total undiscounted cash flows expected to result from the use and eventual disposition of the asset group. This evaluation of carrying value should be made on the date of the recoverability test (which could be made on a date other than the end of a reporting period). The impairment loss equals the carrying value of the asset group less its fair value.

EXAMPLE 23: The following information is provided for an asset group:

Carrying value	$200,000,000
Fair value	160,000,000
Sum of the undiscounted cash flows	190,000,000

Because the sum of the undiscounted cash flows is below the carrying value, a non-recoverability situation is evident. The impairment loss to be recognized equals $40,000,000 ($200,000,000 – $160,000,000). **Note:** The impairment loss is not $10,000,000 ($200,000,000 – $190,000,000) or $30,000,000 ($190,000,000 – $160,000,000).

EXAMPLE 24: The following data is given for an asset group:

Carrying value	$200,000,000
Fair value	212,000,000
Sum of the undiscounted cash flows	186,000,000

Because the sum of the undiscounted cash flows is below the carrying value, a nonrecoverability situation exists. However, an impairment loss is not recognized, because the fair value is more than the carrying value of the asset group.

EXAMPLE 25:

Carrying value	$200,000,000
Fair value	184,000,000
Sum of the undiscounted cash flows	208,000,000

Because the sum of the undiscounted cash flows exceeds the carrying value, a recoverability situation exists. As such, no impairment loss has occurred.

Recoverability Tests. A recoverability test must be performed when the carrying value of the asset group may lack recoverability, as when:

- An operating or cash flow loss for the reporting period has occurred coupled with either a prior history of such losses or expected future losses for the asset group.

- There is a significant adverse development in how the asset group is being used.

- A major impairment occurs in the physical condition of the asset group.

- A probability exceeding 50% exists that the asset group will be sold or disposed of much earlier than its anticipated useful life.

- There is a drastic decline in the market value of the asset group.

- The total costs incurred for the asset group (e.g., actual construction costs) far exceed the expected costs.

- A major business-related government or legal development could have a material adverse effect on the value of the asset group. An example is new government regulations limiting the business use of the long-lived assets.

In conducting a recoverability test, controllers may need to evaluate the existing depreciation method and estimates for fixed assets as well as amortization periods for intangibles.

A change in useful life arising from such appraisal should be considered in formulating estimates of future cash flows to test the asset group for recoverability. **Caution:** A change in the accounting method for an asset arising from this review can occur only after this test has been applied.

Asset Grouping. To determine and record an impairment loss, the asset group should be based on the minimum level that identifiable cash flows are predominant independent of the cash flows of other assets and liabilities.

In a few situations, a long-lived asset may not have identifiable cash flows predominantly independent of the cash flows of other assets and liabilities and other asset groups. An example is the central administrative office of the business entity. In such a case, the long-term asset group should encompass all of the company's assets and liabilities.

Goodwill may be considered for impairment in the asset group only if such group is or includes a reporting unit. Thus, goodwill must be tested for impairment at the reporting unit level (a reporting unit is the same level as one level below an operating segment). It can be tested only subsequent to the other assets of the reporting unit being tested for impairment based on other authoritative pronouncements.

It is prohibited that goodwill be part of a lower-level asset group that incorporates only a segment of a reporting unit. Even so, future cash flow projections used to test the recoverability of the lower-level asset group cannot be modified for the impact of the goodwill omission from the group.

With the exception of goodwill, the carrying values of net assets in the group not falling under the dictates of ASC 360-10-05-4 must be adjusted based on relevant GAAP before testing for the recoverability of the asset group.

The impairment loss for the asset group should be proportionately allocated to the specific assets of the group, based on relative carrying values. However, a particular asset in the group cannot be reduced for an amount that will bring it below its fair market value, provided such value is ascertainable without unreasonable effort and cost.

EXAMPLE 26: Travis Manufacturing Company is testing its plant with other assets for recoverability purposes as an asset group. This group includes long-lived assets W, X, Y, Z, inventory (at lower of cost or market value), and other current assets and liabilities not falling under ASC 360-10-05-4. The total carrying value of the asset group of $6,000,000 is not recoverable. The market value of the asset group is $5,200,000. The impairment loss of $800,000 ($6,000,000 – $5,200,000) is allocated to the long-term assets of the group as follows:

Asset Group (Dollars in Thousands)	Carrying Value	Proportionate Allocation Percentage	Allocated Impairment Loss	Adjusted Carrying Value
Current assets	$1,700			$1,700
Liabilities	(400)			(400)
Long-lived assets:				
Asset W	1,400	30%	$(240)	1,160
Asset X	1,500	32%	(256)	1,244
Asset Y	1,200	25%	(200)	1,000
Asset Z	600	13%	(104)	496
Total long-lived assets	4,700	100%	(800)	3,900
Total	$6,000	100%	$(800)	$5,200

EXAMPLE 27: In the event that the fair market value of a specific long-lived asset of the asset group is ascertainable without undue effort, and cost and the fair value is more than the adjusted carrying value of that particular asset after an impairment loss is initially allocated, the excess impairment loss initially allocated to that asset would be reallocated to the other long-lived assets of the group. Assume the fair market value of asset Y is $1,030,000. The excess impairment loss of $30,000 ($1,030,000 – $1,000,000) initially allocated to that asset (based on the adjusted carrying value of $1,000,000) is reallocated to the other long-lived assets of the group proportionately based on the adjusted carrying amounts of those assets as follows:

Long-Lived Assets (Dollars in Thousands)	Adjusted Carrying Value	Reallocation Proportionate Percentage	Reallocation of Excess Impairment Loss	Adjusted Carrying Value after Reallocation
Asset W	$1,160	40%	$(12)	$1,148
Asset X	1,244	43%	(13)	1,231
Asset Z	496	17%	(5)	491
Subtotal	2,900	100%	(30)	2,870
Asset Y	1,000		30	1,030
Total	$3,900		$0	$3,900

Formulating the New Cost Basis. After the impairment loss is recorded, the adjusted carrying value becomes the new cost basis of the long-term asset. A later recovery in market value of the impaired asset cannot be recorded, because the asset cannot be written up above its cost basis. A written-down fixed (intangible) asset should be depreciated (amortized) based on its new cost basis over the period of benefit.

Estimating Future Cash Flows to Test the Recoverability of a Long-Lived Asset. The estimation of future cash flows for testing the recoverability of the asset group represents the net cash flows directly related to, and resulting from, the utilization and ultimate disposition of the asset group. Interest expense is excluded from this calculation.

In cash flow estimation, the company should take into account its reasonable assumptions and evidence about how the asset group will be used. If alternative steps to recover the carrying value of an asset group are being thought of, or if there is a range of projected cash flows tied to a likely considered action, the business must take into account the probability of possible outcomes. In this regard, a probability-weighted method should be used in assessing the likelihood of potential results. This approach is explained in the following example. **Note:** A range of possible projected cash flows may take into account future sales price, quantity sold, volume produced, and production costs. Varying scenarios are considered. Management assessments should take into account the probabilities of the best, worst, and most likely courses of action.

EXAMPLE 28: At December 31, 2X11, a production plant having a carrying value of $100,000,000 is being evaluated for recoverability. The two alternative action strategies for recovering the carrying value of the plant are to sell either in three years or at the end of its remaining useful life of 12 years. Cash flows applicable to the production plant are clearly identifiable from cash flows of other assets. The following information is provided:

Course of Action: Sell in 3 Years ($ in Millions)

Projected Cash Flow (Use)	Projected Cash Flow (Disposition)	Estimated Cash Flow	Probability	Probability-Weighted Cash Flows
$15	$65	$80	25%	$20
20	65	85	60%	51
25	65	90	15%	13.5
Total				$84.5

Course of Action: Sell in 12 Years ($ in Millions)

Projected Cash Flow (Use)	Projected Cash Flow (Disposition)	Estimated Cash Flow	Probability	Probability-Weighted Cash Flows
$70	$2	$72	25%	$18
100	2	102	60%	61.2
120	2	22	15%	18.3
Total				$97.5

In deriving the future cash flows used to test the plant for recoverability, it is decided that there is a 70% likelihood that the plant will be sold after 3 years but a 30% probability that it will be used for its remaining estimated life of 12 years. The probability computation to derive the final estimated future cash flows considering the weighted-average probabilities of the alternative scenarios is as follows:

(Cash flows in millions)

Course of Action	Probability-Weighted Cash Flows	Probability Assessment	Expected Cash Flows
Sell in 3 years	$84.5	70%	$59.2
Sell in 12 years	97.5	30%	29.3
			88.5

The undiscounted future cash flows using probability analysis of the alternative scenarios is $88,500,000. Hence, the plant's carrying amount of $100,000,000 is not recoverable.

Note: The alternatives of selling or using an asset are not necessarily independent of each other. Consequently, a business might opt for the action resulting in a much higher future cash flow. If such is the case, management typically will use the probable future cash flows applicable just to that particular scenario. In the preceding example, that option would be to sell in 12 years because its probability weighted cash flows of $97,500,000 is higher than the other option of selling in 3 years of $84,500,000.

The company must make cash flow projections to test recoverability of a long-term asset for its remaining useful life. The remaining useful life of an asset group is based on that of the primary asset in the group. The primary asset is defined as the major long-term depreciable tangible asset or the intangible asset being amortized that is the most important component asset in the asset group in terms of cash flow generation. (Thus, the primary asset cannot be land or an intangible asset not subject to amortization.) To determine the primary asset, consideration should be given to:

- The remaining useful life of the asset compared to other group assets.
- The replacement cost of the asset.
- The likelihood that other assets would have been bought without the primary asset. In the case that the primary asset does not have the longest remaining life of the group assets, future cash flow projections for the group are based on the assumed sale of the group at the end of the remaining useful life of the primary asset.

Projected cash flows applied to the recoverability test for long-term assets in use (including significantly constructed or developed assets) is based on the current service potential of the asset on the test date. Service potential considers in addition to remaining useful life, cash-flow-generating capacity, and, if applicable, output potential. The estimates include cash flows related to future costs required to upkeep the existing service potential of the long-term asset, including any component parts. Excluded from the estimates of cash flows are future capital expenditures to increase service potential.

Future cash flow estimates for recoverability testing of long-lived assets being developed should depend on the anticipated service potential when development is significantly finished. Deferred interest costs for self-construction should be included. The capitalization period should end when the asset is substantially finished and available for use.

Fair Value Determination. The fair value of an asset (liability) is the purchase (settlement) price in an arm's-length transaction currently made. If an active market price does not exist, other reasonable valuation approaches may be used, such as the prices of similar assets. A present value approach is often suitable in fair value estimation. Two present value approaches are used to derive the fair value of an asset (liability). In the first approach, expected present value is derived based on multiple cash flow scenarios applying to a range of potential outcomes and a risk-free interest rate. In the second approach, one set of estimated cash flows and one interest rate based on the risk level are used in fair value determination. **Note:** The first approach is preferred when timing and amount uncertainties exist.

If individuals in the market make certain assumptions regarding fair value estimation, that should be incorporated. If not, the company should use its own assumptions.

Reporting and Disclosure Requirements. The impairment loss on a long-term asset held and used is a component of income from continuing operations before income taxes in the income statement. The following should be footnoted for an impairment loss:

- A description of the impaired asset along with impairment circumstances.
- The technique used to compute fair value.
- If not shown by itself in the income statement, the amount of the impairment loss and where such loss is included in the income statement.
- The business segment associated with the impaired asset.

Intangibles

Intangible assets have a life of one year or more and lack physical substance (e.g., goodwill), or represent a right granted by the government (e.g., patent) or another company (e.g., franchise fee). Accounting Principles Board Opinion No. 17, *Intangible Assets*, and ASC 350, *Intangibles—Goodwill and Other*, cover the accounting for intangible assets whether purchased or internally developed. The costs of intangibles acquired from others should be reported as assets. The cost equals the cash or fair market value of the consideration given. The individual intangibles that can be separately identified must be costed separately. If not separately identified, the intangibles are assigned a cost equal to the difference between the total purchase price and the cost of identifiable tangible and intangible assets. **Note:** "goodwill" does not include identifiable assets.

The cost of developing and maintaining intangibles should be charged against earnings if the assets are not specifically identifiable, have indeterminate lives, or are inherent in the continuing business (e.g., goodwill). An example of internally developed goodwill that is expensed is the costs incurred in developing a name (e.g., Burger King).

Intangible assets having limited lives are amortized over the period benefited using the straight-line method. Factors in estimating useful lives include:

- Legal, contractual, and regulatory provisions.
- Renewal or extension provisions. If a renewal occurs, the life of the intangible may be increased.
- Obsolescence and competitive factors.
- Product demand.
- Service lives of essential employees within the organization.

For example, an intangible may be enhanced because of good public relations staff.

Footnote disclosure is made of the amortization period and method.

Companies must disclose information about how recognized intangible assets would aid financial statement users to determine how a company's ability to renew or extend an arrangement impacts the company's anticipated cash flows associated with the asset.

Disclosure should be made of:

- Weighted-average period at acquisition or renewal before the next renewal or extension.
- Accounting policy for costs incurred to renew or extend an intangible asset's term.
- In the event renewal or extension costs are capitalized, the total cost incurred to renew or extend the term of a recognized intangible asset.

If a firm buys, on a step-by-step basis, an investment using the equity method, the fair value of the acquired assets and the goodwill for each step purchased must be separately identified.

When the purchase of assets results in goodwill, later sale of a separable portion of the entity acquired mandates a proportionate reduction of the goodwill account. A portion of the unamortized goodwill is included in the cost of assets sold.

Goodwill is recorded in a business combination accounted for under the purchase method when the cost to the acquirer exceeds the fair market value of the net assets acquired. Goodwill may be determined by an individual appraiser or a purchase audit done by the acquiring company's public accounting firm, for example. Goodwill is tested for impairment at least yearly. If the cost to the acquirer is less than the fair market value of the net assets acquired, a credit arises, called negative goodwill, which is reported as an extraordinary gain for the portion in excess of allocating to certain assets.

Goodwill is theoretically equal to the present value of future excess earnings of a company over other companies in the industry. However, it is difficult to predict the length of time superior earnings will occur. Some factors involved in the makeup of goodwill are superior sales force, outstanding management talent, effective advertising, strategic location, and dependable suppliers.

In buying a new business, a determination must often be made as to the estimated value of the goodwill. Two possible methods that can be used are (1) capitalization of earnings and (2) capitalization of excess earnings.

EXAMPLE 29: The following information is available for a business that is a potential acquisition:

Expected average annual earnings	$10,000
Expected future value of net assets exclusive of goodwill	$45,000
Normal rate of return	20%

Using the capitalization of earnings approach, goodwill is estimated at:

Total asset value implied ($10,000/20%)	$50,000
Estimated fair value of asset:	45,000
Estimated goodwill	$ 5,000

Assuming the same facts as stated previously, except a capitalization rate of excess earnings of 22%, and using the capitalization of excess earnings method, goodwill is estimated at:

Expected average annual earnings	$10,000
Return on expected average assets ($45,000 × 20%)	9,000
Excess earnings	$ 1,000

Goodwill ($1,000/.22) = $4,545

EXAMPLE 30: The net worth of ABC Company excluding goodwill is $800,000 and profits for the last four years were $750,000. Included in the latter figure are nonrecurring gains of $50,000 and nonrecurring losses of $30,000. It is desired to determine a selling price of the business. A 12% return on net worth is deemed typical for the industry. The capitalization of excess earnings is 45% in determining goodwill.

Net Income for 4 years	$750,000
Less: Nonrecurring gains	50,000
Add: Nonrecurring losses	30,000
Adjusted 4-year earnings	$730,000
Average earnings ($730,000/4)	$182,500
Normal earnings ($800,000 × .12)	96,000
Excess annual earnings	$86,500

Excess earnings capitalized at 45%:

$$\frac{\$86,500}{.45} = \$192,222$$

Internally generated costs to derive a patented product, such as R&D incurred in developing a new product, are expensed. The patent is recorded at the registration fees to secure and register it, legal fees to successfully defend it in court, and the cost of acquiring competing patents from outsiders. The patent account is amortized over its useful life not exceeding 20 years. If an intangible asset is deemed worthless, it should be written off recognizing a loss.

Organization costs are the costs incurred to incorporate a business (e.g., legal fees). They are immediately expensed as incurred.

Leaseholds are rent paid in advance and are amortized over the life of the lease.

If the amortization expense of an intangible is not tax deductible, a permanent difference arises. Thus, no interperiod tax allocation is involved.

ASC 805, *Business Combinations*, provides that an intangible asset related to customer relationship intangibles may exist even though the relationship is not evident by a contract.

ASC 350 relates to financial accounting and reporting for intangibles purchased individually or with a group of other assets, but not to those bought in a business combination (because they are covered in ASC 805. These intangibles are initially measured and recorded at fair value. The optimal measure of fair value is quoted market prices in active markets. If such is not available, valuation may be based on multiples of revenue or profits or a similar performance measure, if appropriate. The pronouncement also provides GAAP to account and report good-will and other intangibles subsequent to purchase. Goodwill and intangible assets with unlimited lives are not amortized; they tested for impairment at least once a year. In the event there is no factor (e.g., legal, economic, regulatory, competition) that limits an intangible's useful life, such intangible is considered to have an indefinite life. Intangible assets having finite useful lives are amortized over their useful lives. However, the arbitrary limitation of 40 years no longer applies. If the amount paid is less than the fair value of the net identifiable assets purchased, a bargain purchase results. This excess is recorded as a gain by the purchaser.

Goodwill for each reporting unit must be tested each year for impairment. A reporting unit is defined as an operating segment or one level below an operating segment. If certain events occur, more than one annual impairment test is required. An impairment test can be performed at any date, as long as it is consistently used each year. However, different reporting units may be tested for impairment at different dates.

There are two steps in applying the impairment test. The initial step is to determine whether there is potential impairment. The book value of the reporting unit (including goodwill) is compared to its fair value. The fair value of the reporting unit is derived by ascertaining the amount for which the reporting entity could be sold. No impairment exists if fair value exceeds book value. If this is the case, the second step is not undertaken. However, if the reporting unit's fair value is below its book value, there is an impairment and step 2 must be followed.

EXAMPLE 31:

Step 1
Book value	$150
Fair value	190

No impairment exists because the fair value exceeds the book value.
Do not proceed to step 2.

If, on the other hand, the fair value is less than the book value, step 2 would have to performed to ascertain the possible impairment.

In the second step, the amount of impairment, if any, is measured. A comparison is made between the book value of goodwill and to the "implied fair value of goodwill." The implied fair value of goodwill may be obtained by comparing the fair value of the reporting unit to the fair value of all net identifiable assets excluding goodwill. In order to do this, GAAP requires that the fair value of the reporting unit be allocated to all the net identifiable assets (which excludes goodwill) as if the reporting unit was being acquired. Goodwill is not an identifiable asset. The difference between the fair value of the reporting unit and the fair value allocated to all the net identifiable assets (which excludes goodwill) of the reporting unit is the implied fair value of goodwill. If the implied fair value of goodwill is more than book value, no impairment loss exists and no entry is made. However, if the implied fair value of goodwill is below book value of the entity's goodwill, an impairment loss must be recognized for the difference. After an impairment loss for goodwill is recorded, the downwardly adjusted book value becomes the intangible's new cost basis, which means the new accounting basis cannot be written up for a recovery in fair value. The following example illustrates the requirements of step 2.

EXAMPLE 32:

Step 2

The following are the net assets of the Levine Enterprises Division (in millions). Levine Enterprises is a division of the Marc Company:

Cash	$100
Accounts Receivable	400
Property, plant, and equipment (net)	5,200
Goodwill	400
Less: Bonds Payable	5,400
Net Assets	$700

Recently, the Marc Company received an offer to purchase Levine Enterprises for $670 million. Assume that the fair value and book value of all identifiable assets and liabilities are the same except for the property, plant and equipment (net) whose fair value is $10 million more than its carrying value.

Determine if there is an impairment of goodwill and, if so, prepare the journal entry to record it.

Because the fair value of the reporting entity is $670, which is less than its book value of $700, there may be an impairment of goodwill and step 2 must be carried out to determine the possible impairment. This step determines the implied value of the goodwill and compares it to its book value to determine the amount of the impairment loss, if any.

Fair value of the Levine Enterprise Division	$670
Less: Fair value of the identifiable net assets (which excludes goodwill) ($710- $400)	310
Implied value of goodwill	$360
Less: Book value of goodwill	400
Loss on impairment of goodwill	$40

The entry for the impairment loss is shown below:

Loss on Impairment	40	
Goodwill		40

The new carrying value of goodwill is $360 ($400 – $40). If there is a recovery of fair value in a subsequent period, it may not be recorded.

Note that, steps 1 and 2 may be completely avoided [to be explained in detail in ASU 2011-08 below] if a company chooses to perform a qualitative assessment and ascertains that it is more likely than not (more than a 50% probability) that the fair value of a reporting unit is greater than its carrying value. Then, performing the goodwill impairment assessment (step 1 and 2 in this case) need not be done. The performance of a qualitative assessment, however, is optional. Therefore, the example above illustrates the requirements of step 1 and 2 under an implied assumption that either a qualitative assessment was voluntarily not performed or failed (i.e., it is more likely than not that the fair value of the Levine Enterprises Division is less than its carrying value).

If goodwill and another asset of a reporting unit are tested for impairment at the same time, the other asset shall be tested for impairment before goodwill. Accordingly, before tests for goodwill impairment are performed, all other assets of the reporting entity should be tested for impairment and written down if required.

Goodwill should be tested for impairment at least annually. However, ASC 350-20-35-30 notes that if an event, circumstance, or occurrence results in a probability that would make it more likely than not that a reporting unit's fair value would be below its book value, then the reporting units should be tested between annual tests. The following are examples of such events:

- Adverse economic or political developments.
- Drastic actions by competitors.
- Serious lawsuits filed against the company.
- Key senior executives quit.
- Anticipation that a reporting unit will be sold or disposed of.
- Recently issued government regulations or laws having a negative effect on the company.
- Applying the recoverability test of a major "asset group" within a reporting unit.
- Accounting for a goodwill impairment loss by a subsidiary that is part of a reporting unit. (Subsidiary goodwill is tested for impairment at the subsidiary level using the subsidiary's reporting unit.)

If only a part of goodwill is assigned to a business to be sold or disposed of, the remainder of the goodwill in the reporting unit must be tested for impairment using the adjusted carrying value. Goodwill impairment losses are presented as a separate line item in the income statement.

Accounting Standards Update (ASU) No. 2011-08 (September 2011), *Intangibles—Goodwill and Other* (ASC Topic 350), *Testing Goodwill for Impairment*, specifies that a company has the option to first evaluate qualitative information to ascertain if the existence of circumstances results in a determination that it is more likely than not that the fair value of a business unit is below its carrying value. If the company determines it is not more likely than not that the fair value of a reporting unit is less than its carrying value, then using the two-step impairment test is not needed. However, if the company decides otherwise, then it must conduct the first step by computing the fair value of the reporting unit and comparing the fair value with the carrying value of the business unit. If the carrying amount is more than the fair value, the entity must do the second step of the goodwill impairment test to measure any impairment loss. **Note:** A company has the option to bypass the qualitative appraisal for any reporting unit in any year and go directly to conducting the first step of the two-step goodwill impairment test. A company may resume doing the qualitative evaluation in any later year.

Accounting Standards Update (ASU) No. 2017-04 (January 2017), *Simplifying the Test for Goodwill Impairment,* further simplifies the measurement of goodwill impairment by completely removing step 2 of the impairment test. In step 2, a reporting entity was required to compute the implied fair value of goodwill by performing procedures to determine the fair value of the entity's assets and liabilities (net assets) in an assumed acquisition of the reporting entity.

Under the new standard, the reporting entity will be required to perform an annual or interim goodwill impairment test by comparing the fair value of the reporting entity with its carrying value. An impairment charge would then be recognized for the amount by which the carrying amount of the reporting entity exceeds its fair value with the added requirement that the loss recognized could not exceed the total amount of goodwill allocated to the reporting entity. Under the old guidance, it was possible that there might be no impairment loss even though step 1 failed. However, under the new guidance, there will always be an impairment if step 1 fails.

In addition, the update eliminates the requirements for a reporting entity with a zero or negative carrying value to perform a qualitative assessment test with the added proviso that if it fails that test, then step 2 of the impairment computative process would have to be performed. Under the new standard, the same impairment test, previously noted, applies to all reporting entities. The new standard also now requires that an entity disclose the amount of goodwill allocated to each of its reporting entities that has a zero or negative carrying amount of net assets.

In addition, note that under the new standard, a reporting entity still has the option of first performing a qualitative assessment to determine if a goodwill impairment computation is needed.

ASU 2017-04 parameters note that this new guidance should be applied on a prospective basis and should be adopted for annual or any interim goodwill impairment tests in fiscal years beginning after December 15, 2019. Early adoption is permitted, however, for interim or annual goodwill impairment tests performed on testing dates after January 1, 2017.

> **EXAMPLE 33:** Using the data from the last example, the requirements for the impairment computation under ASU 2017-04 would consist of the following ($ are stated in millions):

Fair value of the Levine Enterprises Reporting entity:	$670
Book value:	$700
Goodwill:	$400

The impairment loss is the amount by which the carrying value of the reporting entity exceeds its fair value, not to exceed the amount of goodwill allocated to the reporting entity.

Accordingly, the impairment loss to be recognized under the new rule would be computed as follows: $700 – $670=$30. The $30 is appropriate because this amount does not exceed the $400 of goodwill carrying value allocated to this reporting entity.

The entry for the recognition of the loss is:

Loss on impairment	30	
Goodwill		30

The new carrying value of goodwill is $370 ($400 – $30). If there is a recovery of fair value in a subsequent period, it may not be recorded. As noted above, under the new standard a reporting entity still has the option of first performing a qualitative assessment to determine if a goodwill impairment computation is needed.

Under Accounting Standards Update (ASU) No. 2012-02 (July 2012), *Intangibles—Goodwill and Other* (ASC Topic 350), *Testing Indefinite-Lived Intangible Assets for Impairment*, a company has the option first to evaluate qualitative factors to ascertain if circumstances indicate it is more likely than not that the indefinite-lived intangible asset is impaired. If the company determines it is not more likely than not that such intangible asset is impaired, further action is not required. On the other hand, if the business concludes otherwise, the company must ascertain the fair value of the indefinite-lived intangible asset and conduct the quantitative impairment test by comparing the fair value with the book value.

As per ASC 350, *Unit of Accounting for Purposes of Testing for Impairment of Intangible Assets Not Subject to Amortization* (ASC 350-30-35-21), acquired or internally developed intangible assets having indefinite lives that have been separately recognized and are inseparable from each other due to being operated as a single unit should be combined in one accounting unit when the impairment test is applied.

The following are footnote disclosures for goodwill and other intangible assets:

- Amortization period and expected amortization expense for the next five years.
- Amount of any significant residual value.
- Amount of goodwill included in the gain or loss on disposal of all or a part of a reporting unit.
- Method in deriving fair value.
- The book values of intangible assets by major class for intangibles subject to amortization and separately for those not subject to amortization. An intangible asset class is a group of similar intangibles either based on their use in the company's operations or by their nature. .
- Description of impaired intangible assets and the causes for such impairment.
- Information relating to the changes in the carrying values of goodwill over the year both in total and by reporting unit.
- Total amount of impairment losses.

IFRS allows for the recovery of impairment losses on intangible assets in subsequent periods if a change in economic circumstances arises.

ASC 840, *Leases* (ASC 840-10-35-6), mandates that leasehold improvements acquired in a business combination or purchase subsequent to the inception of the lease should be amortized over the lesser of the asset's useful life or the term of the lease, which includes reasonably assured lease renewals as provided on the purchase date of the leasehold improvement. However, leasehold improvements not considered at the start of a lease and put in service well after lease inception should be amortized over the shorter of the asset's life or a term that includes required lease periods and renewals that are assured when the leasehold improvements are purchased.

Accounting for a Cloud Computing Arrangement

Accounting Standards Update No. 2015-05, *Intangibles—Goodwill and Other—Internal-Use Software* (Subtopic 350-40): *Customer's Accounting for Fees Paid in a Cloud Computing Arrangement,* provides new guidance on accounting for cloud computing arrangements purchased by customer entities. If such an arrangement includes a software license and certain criteria are satisfied, the software license should be accounted for as an acquired intangible asset and treated comparably to other acquired intangible licenses.

Examples of cloud computing activities are software-as-a-service (SaaS), which include applications such as payroll, invoicing and payments, marketing, and more sophisticated usage such as large data analytics and high-end graphics applications. It also includes platform-as-a-service (PaaS), which allows an entity, among other things, to create new applications, efficient testing, and development methods without concerns regarding servers, storage, and other services that would be required to support the application. This significantly reduces an entity's IT costs while increasing its application potential. (An in-depth discussion of cloud computing may be found in Chapter 7, "XBRL, Cloud Computing, and Wireless Technology.")

ASU No. 2015-05 now requires an entity to ascertain whether an acquired cloud computing arrangement includes a software license. If it does include a software license, the entity must account for the software license element of the arrangement as an intangible asset. This is consistent with accounting for the acquisition of other intangible licenses. If it does not include a software license, the entity should account for the cloud computing arrangement as a service contract. The guidance applies to internal-use software that an entity gains access to in a hosting arrangement. A hosting arrangement is defined by the FASB as an arrangement in which an end user of software does not take possession of the software. Instead, the software application resides on the vendor's or a third party's hardware. The end user accesses and uses the software on an as-needed basis over the Internet or through a dedicated line.

The cloud computing arrangement that an end user acquires includes an internal-use software license as part of the hosting arrangement if the following criteria are met. If so, then a software license should be recognized: (1) The entity has the contractual right to take possession of the software at any time during the hosting period without significant penalty; and (2) The entity can either run the software on its own hardware or contract with another party unrelated to the vendor to host the software. "Without significant penalty" is defined by the ASU as having the following two parameters: (1) having the ability to take delivery of the software without incurring significant cost and (2) having the ability to use the software without a significant diminution in utility or value. Cloud computing arrangements that satisfy these criteria must allocate the cost of the arrangement between the software license and hosting components. Fair value is a common basis for such an allocation. Hosting arrangements that do not satisfy the aforementioned criteria are simply service contracts that do not represent the purchase of a software license.

This determination is very important because it affects not only the way cloud computing arrangements are accounted for but how they are presented on the financial statements. Price Waterhouse Coopers (PWC) recently noted in an evaluation of this pronouncement[*] how accounting for an upfront fee paid in a cloud computing arrangement that has a software license could have a significant influence on the financial statements of an entity. For example, if an entity purchases a cloud computing arrangement that contains a software license, the license would be recognized as an intangible asset on the balance sheet and amortized as an expense over its useful life. On the other hand, if the acquisition is viewed as a service contract, the cost should be accounted for as a prepaid asset and accounted for as an operating expense. In addition, from the perspective of the Statement of Cash Flows, the former would be considered an investing activity, while the latter would be classified as an operating activity.

Financial Assets

ASC 860, *Transfers and Servicing*, requires additional information about transfers of financial assets such as securitization transactions, and where business entities have continuing exposure to the risks associated with transferred financial assets. It eliminates the concept of a "qualifying special-purpose entity." It changes other requirements for derecognizing financial assets, and requires additional disclosures. There is greater transparency about transfers of financial assets and the company's continued involvement in transferred financial assets.

A purpose is to determine if a transferor has surrendered control over transferred financial assets.

A participating interest is to establish specific conditions for reporting a transfer of part of a financial asset as a sale. If the transfer does not satisfy those conditions, a transferor should account for the transfer as a sale only if it transfers an entire financial asset or a group of entire financial assets and surrenders control over the entire transferred assets.

---

[*] Price Waterhouse Coopers, In Depth-A Look at Current Financial Reporting Issues, *Cloud Computing Fees-*   *FASB Issues Guidance on Customer Accounting*, No. 2015-09, May 1, 2015.

A transferor must recognize and initially measure at fair value all assets obtained and liabilities incurred due to a transfer of financial assets accounted for as a sale.

ASC 860 clarifies the principle that the transferor must appraise whether it, its consolidated affiliates, or its agents effectively control the transferred financial assets directly or indirectly.

According to Accounting Standards Update (ASU) No. 2009-16 (December 2009), *Transfers and Servicing* (ASC Topic 860), *Accounting for Transfers of Financial Assets*, there may be a removal-of-accounts stipulation in credit card securitizations that permits the seller to withdraw receivables from a group. To allow for sale accounting, an entire financial asset cannot be broken down into components prior to a transfer unless all of the components satisfy the criteria of a participating interest. A company cannot account for a transfer of an entire financial asset in part as a sale and in part as a secured debt. If the transferor gives up control, it is recorded as a sale.

Certain financial instruments such as forward contracts have the potential to be financial assets or financial liabilities. A transferor discloses how similar transfers are combined and differentiates between transfers treated as secured borrowings versus those accounted for as sales. The transfer of part of an entire financial asset may result in a gain or loss if the contractual interest rate and the market rate differ at the time of transfer.

In Accounting Standards Update (ASU) No. 2016-13 (June 2016), *Financial Instruments—Credit Losses* (Topic 326), *Measurement of Credit Losses on Financial Instruments*, a financial asset measured on the amortized cost basis must be shown as the net amount expected to be collected. The allowance for credit losses is a valuation account that is subtracted from the amortized cost basis of the financial asset to present its net carrying value at the amount to be received.

The income statement shows the credit losses for new financial assets as well as the change (increases or decreases) in expected credit losses for the year on already existing financial assets. Credit losses applying to available-for-sale debt securities are recorded through an allowance for credit losses.

In Accounting Standards Update (ASU) No. 2017-05 (February 2017), *Other Income–Gains and Losses from the Deregulation of Nonfinancial Assets* (Subtopic 610-20), if most of the fair value of assets promised to a counterparty in a contract is concentrated in nonfinancial assets, then all of the financial assets promised to the counterparty are in substance nonfinancial assets for purposes of subtopic 610-20. The scope of this subtopic may also include nonfinancial assets transferred within a legal entity to a counterparty. An example is when a parent transfers ownership control in a consolidated subsidiary.

A firm should identify each distinct nonfinancial asset promised to a counterparty and derecognize each asset when a counterparty obtains control of it. Once a business transfers control of a distinct financial asset, it must measure any noncontrolling interest received at fair value.

If a company transfers ownership interests in a consolidated subsidiary and continues having a controlling financial interest in the subsidiary, it should not derecognize the subsidiary's assets and liabilities and it must account for the transaction as an equity transaction. Thus, gain or loss is not recognized.

This ASU requires an entity to record a full gain or loss on transfers of nonfinancial assets to equity method investees.

LIABILITIES

In accounting for liabilities, the corporate financial officer must take into account many reporting and disclosure responsibilities:

- Bonds payable may be issued between interest dates at a premium or discount.
- Bonds may be amortized using the straight-line method or effective interest method.
- Debt may be extinguished prior to the maturity date when the company can issue new debt at a lower interest rate.
- Estimated liabilities must be recognized when it is probable that an asset has been impaired or liability has been incurred by year-end, and the amount of loss is subject to reasonable estimation.
- An accrued liability may also be made for future absences, for example sick leave or vacation time.
- Special termination benefits, such as early retirement, may also be offered to and accepted by employees.
- Short-term debt may be rolled over to long-term debt, requiring special reporting.
- A callable obligation by the creditor may also exist.
- Long-term purchase obligations have to be disclosed.

In Accounting Standards Update (ASU) No. 2015-15 (August 2015), *Interest—Imputation of Interest* (Subtopic 835-30), *Presentation and Subsequent Measurement of Debt Issuance Costs Associated with Line-of-Credit Arrangements*, a company can defer and present debt issuance costs as an asset and amortize the deferred issuance costs ratably over the life of the line-of-credit agreement, irrespective of whether any outstanding borrowings exist on the line-of-credit agreement.

Bonds Payable

The cost of a corporate bond is expressed in terms of yield. Two types of yield calculations are:

1. *Simple Yield:*

$$\frac{\text{Nominal Interest}}{\text{Present Value of Bond}}$$

It is not as accurate as yield to maturity.

2. *Yield to Maturity (Effective Interest Rate):*

$$\frac{\text{Nominal Interest} + \dfrac{\text{Discount}}{\text{Years}} - \dfrac{\text{Premium}}{\text{Years}}}{\dfrac{\text{Present Value} + \text{Maturity Value}}{2}}$$

EXAMPLE 34: A $100,000, 10%, five-year bond is issued at $96,000. The simple yield is:

$$\frac{\text{Nominal Interest}}{\text{Present Value of Bond}} = \frac{\$10,000}{\$96,000} = 10.42\%$$

The yield to maturity is:

$$\frac{\text{Nominal Interest} + \dfrac{\text{Discount}}{\text{Years}}}{\dfrac{\text{Present Value} + \text{Maturity Value}}{2}} = \frac{\$10,000 + \dfrac{\$4,000}{5}}{\dfrac{\$96,000 + \$100,000}{2}}$$

$$\frac{\$10,800}{\$98,000} = 11.02\%$$

When a bond is issued at a discount, the yield (effective interest rate) is greater than the nominal (face, coupon) interest rate.

When a bond is issued at a premium, the yield is less than the nominal interest rate.

The two methods of amortizing bond discount or bond premium are:

1. *The straight-line method,* which results in a constant dollar amount of amortization but a different effective rate each period.

2. *The effective interest method,* which results in a constant rate of interest but different dollar amounts each period. This method is preferred over the straight-line method. The amortization entry is:

Interest expense (Yield – Carrying value of bond at the beginning of the year)

Discount

Cash (Nominal interest × Face value of bond)

In the early years, the amortization amount under the effective interest method is lower, relative to the straight-line method (either for discount or premium).

EXAMPLE 35: On January 1, 2X11, a $100,000 bond is issued at $95,624. The yield rate is 7%, and the nominal interest rate is 6%. The following schedule is the basis for the journal entries to be made:

Date	Debit Interest Expense	Credit Cash	Credit Discount	Carrying Value
1/1/2X11				$95,624
12/31/2X11	$6,694	$6,000	$694	$96,319
12/31/2X12	6,742	6,000	742	97,060

The entry on 12/31/2X11 is:

Interest expense	6,694	
Cash		6,000
Discount		694

At maturity, the bond will be worth its face value of $100,000. When bonds are issued between interest dates, the entry is:

Cash

    Bonds payable

    Premium (or debit discount)

    Interest expense

EXAMPLE 36: A $100,000, 5% bond having a life of five years is issued at 110% on April 1, 2X11. The bonds are dated 1/1/2X11. Interest is payable on 1/1 and 7/1. Straight-line amortization is used. The journal entries are:

4/1/2X11 cash (110,000 + 1,860)	111,250.00	
Bonds payable		100,000.00
Premium on bonds payable		10,000.00
Bond interest expense (100,000 × 5% × 3/12)		1,250.00
7/1/2X11 bond interest expense	2,500.00	
Cash		2,500.00
100,000 × 5% × 6/12		
Premium on bonds payable	526.50	
Bond interest expense		526.50

4/1/2X11– 1/1/2X16= 4 years

9 months = 57 months

$$\frac{\$10,000}{57} = \$175.50 \text{ per month}$$

$175.50 × 3 months = $526.50

12/31/2X11 bond interest expense	2,500.00	
Interest payable		2,500.00
Premium on bonds payable	1,053.00	
Bond interest expense		1,053.00
1/1/2X12 interest payable	2,500.00	
Cash		2,500.00

Bonds Payable is shown on the balance sheet at its carrying value in the following manner:

Bonds payable

Add: premium

Less: discount

Less: bond issue costs

Carrying value

Bond (Debt) issue costs are the expenditures incurred in issuing the bonds, such as legal, registration, and printing fees. ASU No. 2015-03, *Interest – Imputation of Interest – Simplifying the Presentation of Debt Issuance Costs*, requires that debt issuance costs related to a bond or other debt liability shall be reported in the balance sheet as a direct deduction from the face amount of the liability and should not be classified as a deferred charge. It should be accounted for in the exact same manner as a discount relating to the bond. In addition, the amortization of debt issuance costs should be reported as interest expense and is accordingly accounted for in the exact same manner as the amortization of a bond discount. Also, debt issuance costs reduce the proceeds of borrowing thereby increasing the effective interest rate of the debt instrument. That interest rate together with a description of the bond and the face amount of the bond should be disclosed in either the financial statements or in the notes. This update is effective for financial statements issued for fiscal years beginning after December 15, 2015. However, in ASU No. 2015-15, *Imputation of Interest*, the SEC staff announced that in light of ASU No. 2015-03 (see paragraph above), the SEC would not object when a public entity presents debt issuance costs related to a revolving debt arrangement (line-of-credit) as an asset (deferred charge), which would be amortized ratably over the life of the debt arrangement. This would apply regardless of whether there is an outstanding balance on the revolving debt arrangement.

In determining the price of a bond, the face amount is discounted using the Present Value of $1 table. The interest payments are discounted using the Present Value of Annuity of $1 table. The yield rate is used as the discount rate.

EXAMPLE 37: A $50,000, 10-year bond is issued with interest payable semiannually at an 8% nominal interest rate. The yield rate is 10%. The present value of $1 table factor for n = 20, i = 5% is .37689. The present value of annuity of $1 table factor for n = 20, i = 5% is 12.46221. The price of the bond should be:

Present value of principal $50,000 × .37689	$18,844.50
Present value of interest payments $20,000 × 12.46221	24,924.42
	$43,768.92

The method used to account for a conversion of a bond into stock is the book value of bond method. Under this method, no gain or loss on bond conversion will result because the book value of the bond is the basis to credit equity.

EXAMPLE 38: A $100,000 bond with an unamortized premium of $8,420.50 is converted to common stock. There are 100 bonds ($100,000/$1,000). Each bond is converted into 50 shares of stock. Thus, 5,000 shares of common stock are involved. Par value is $15 per share. The market value of the stock is $25 per share. The market value of the bond is 120. Using the book value method, the entry for the conversion is:

Bonds payable	100,000.00	
Premium on bonds payable	8,420.50	
Common stock (5,000 × 15)		75,000.00
Premium on common stock		33,420.50

Accounting Standards Update (ASU) No. 2009-15, *Accounting for Own-Share Lending Arrangements in Contemplation of Convertible Debt Issuance or Other Financing*, provides information on the following:

- ASC 470-20-05-1 provides accounting and reporting advice for bonds and other types of preferred stock with conversion attributes. These include convertible bonds, bonds with detachable warrants, forfeiture of interest, and conversions that are induced.

- ASC 470-20-05-12A is applicable in the following instance. A firm that has a high cost of borrowed shares may contract for share lending separately transacted but along with a convertible bond issuance. The share lending contract allows investors to hedge the conversion option.

- ASC 470-20-05-12B offers guidance when, in a share-lending contract, the firm issues loaned shares to an investment bank for a small charge. This fee typically equals the par value of the common stock, which is usually below the market value of the loaned securities. At maturity, the loaned shares are returned to the company.

- ASC 470-20-25-20A provides information for properly recording a share-lending contract. When issued, a share-lending contract is recorded at market value and recorded at issuance cost with an adjustment to paid-in capital.

Early Extinguishment of Debt

Long-term debt may be called back early when new debt can be issued at a lower interest rate. It can also occur when the company has excess cash and wants to avoid paying interest charges and having the debt on its balance sheet. The gain or loss on the early extinguishment of debt is an ordinary item. Debt may be construed as being extinguished in the case where the debtor is relieved of the principal liability and it is probable the debtor will not have to make future payments.

EXAMPLE 39: A $100,000 bond payable with an unamortized premium of $10,000 is called at 85. The entry is:

Bonds payable	100,000	
Premium on bonds payable	10,000	
Cash (85% × 100,000)		85,000
Gain		25,000

Footnote disclosures regarding extinguishment of debt follow:

- Description of extinguishment transaction including the source of funds used

- Per-share gain or loss net of tax

If convertible debt is converted to stock in connection with an inducement offer in which the debtor alters conversion privileges, the debtor recognizes an expense. The amount is the fair value of the securities transferred in excess of the fair value of securities issuable according to the original conversion terms. This fair market value is measured at the earlier of the conversion date or date of the agreement. An inducement offer may be accomplished by giving debt holders a higher conversion ratio, payment of additional consideration, or other favorable changes in terms.

According to ASC 470, *Debt* (ASC 470-50), if the debtor puts cash or other assets in a trust to be utilized only for paying interest and principal on debt on an irrevocable basis, disclosure should be made of the particulars, including a description of the transaction and the amount of debt considered to be extinguished.

ASC 470-20-30, 27-28 states that interest costs associated with convertible debt instruments recognized in periods subsequent to their initial recognition should constitute the borrowing rate a company would have incurred had it issued a comparable debt instrument without the embedded conversion option. That objective is achieved by requiring issuers to separately account for the liability and equity components of convertible debt instruments.

The following steps should be used to initially measure the convertible debt:

1. Determine the carrying value of an instrument's liability component using a fair value measurement of a similar liability (including embedded features, if any, other than the conversion option) that has no related equity component.

2. Determine the carrying value of the instrument's equity component corresponding to the embedded conversion option by subtracting the liability component's fair value from the initial proceeds applicable to the total convertible debt instrument.

3. Appraise the total convertible debt instrument if its embedded features, other than the conversion option, are substantive at the issuance date. If, at issuance, the company concludes that it is probable that a convertible instrument's embedded feature will not be exercised, that embedded feature is considered to be nonsubstantive and would not impact the initial measurement of an instrument's liability component.

Transaction costs incurred with third parties except the investors that directly relate to convertible debt issuance should be allocated to the liability and equity components in the same proportion as the allocation of proceeds and accounted for as costs of issuing debt and equity, respectively.

A temporary tax basis difference associated with the liability component may occur. Additional paid-in-capital should be adjusted when deferred taxes are initially recognized for the tax impact of the temporary difference.

The principal amount of the liability component over its initial fair value must be amortized to interest cost using the interest method.

A liability component's anticipated life is not impacted by embedded features determined to be nonsubstantive when the convertible debt was issued.

If a conversion option has to be reclassified from stockholders' equity to a liability measured at fair value, the difference between the amount that has been recognized in equity and the fair value of the conversion option at the date of reclassification should be accounted for as an adjustment to stockholders' equity. On the other hand, when a conversion option accounted for in stockholders' equity is reclassified as a liability, gains or losses recognized to account for that conversion option at fair value while classified as a liability should not be reversed if later the conversion option is reclassified back to stockholders' equity. The reclassification of a conversion option does not impact the accounting for the liability component.

The following should be disclosed:

- Conversion price and the number of shares used to calculate the total consideration to be delivered on conversion.

- Effective interest rate on the liability component.

- Amount of interest cost applicable to both the contractual interest coupon and discount amortization on the liability component.

- Carrying value of the equity component.

- Principal amount of the liability component, its amortized discount, and its carrying value.

- Remaining years for which the discount on the liability will be amortized.

- Amount by which the instrument's if-converted value is more than the principal amount, irrespective of whether the instrument is currently convertible.

- Term of derivative transactions, reasons to enter into derivative transactions, and number of shares underlying derivative transactions.

Accounting Standards Update (ASU) No. 2016-04 (March 2016), *Liabilities— Extinguishment of Liabilities* (Subtopic 405-20), *Recognition of Breakage for Certain Prepaid Stored Value Products Liabilities,* related to the sale of prepaid store-valued products, are financial liabilities. Prepaid store-value products are in physical and digital forms with stored monetary values that are issued to be commonly accepted as payment for goods or services.

Estimated Liabilities (Contingencies)

A loss contingency should be accrued if both of the following criteria exist:

- At year-end, it is probable (likely to occur) that an asset was impaired or a liability was incurred.
- The amount of loss is subject to reasonable estimation.

The loss contingency is booked because of the principle of conservatism. The entry for a probable loss is:

Expense (loss)

    Estimated liability

A probable loss that cannot be estimated should be footnoted.

    EXAMPLE 40: On December 31, 2X11, warranty expenses are estimated at $20,000. On March 15, 2X12, actual warranty costs paid for were $16,000. The journal entries are:

12/31/2X11 warranty expense	20,000	
Estimated liability		20,000
3/15/2X12 estimated liability	16,000	
Cash		16,000

If a loss contingency exists at year-end but no asset impairment or liability incurrence exists (e.g., uninsured equipment), footnote disclosure may be made.

A probable loss occurring after year-end but before the audit report date requires only subsequent event disclosure.

Examples of probable loss contingencies may be:

- Warranties.
- Lawsuits.
- Claims and assessments.
- Expropriation of property by a foreign government.
- Casualties and catastrophes (e.g., fire).

If the amount of loss is within a range, the accrual is based on the best estimate within that range. However, if no amount within the range is better than any other amount, the minimum amount (not maximum amount) of the range is booked. The exposure to additional losses should be disclosed. IFRS accrues the estimated loss at the mid-point of the range.

In the case of a reasonably possible loss (more than remote but less than likely), no accrual is made but rather footnote disclosure is required. The disclosure includes the nature of the contingency and the estimate of probable loss or range of loss. If an estimate of loss is not possible, that fact should be stated.

A remote contingency (slight chance of occurring) is usually ignored and no disclosure is made. There are exceptions when a remote contingency would be disclosed in the case of guarantees of indebtedness, standby letters of credit, and agreements to repurchase receivables or properties.

General (unspecified) contingencies are not accrued. Examples are self-insurance and possible hurricane losses. Disclosure and/or an appropriation of retained earnings can be made for general contingencies. To be booked as an estimated liability, the future loan must be specific and measurable, such as parcel post and freight losses.

Gain contingencies cannot be booked because doing so violates conservatism. However, footnote disclosure can be made.

Accounting for Compensated Absences

Compensated absences include sick leave, holiday, and vacation time. ASC 710, *Compensation—General* (ASC 710-10-05-5), is not applicable to severance or termination pay, postretirement benefits, deferred compensation, stock option plans, and other long-term fringe benefits (e.g., disability insurance).

The employer shall accrue a liability for employee's compensation for future absences when all of the following criteria are met:

- Employee rights have vested.

- Employee services have already been performed.

- Probable payment exists.

- Amount of estimated liability can reasonably be determined. **Note:** If the criteria are met except that the amount is not determinable, only a footnote can be made because an accrual is not possible.

Accrual for sick leave is required only when the employer allows employees to take accumulated sick leave days off regardless of actual illness. No accrual is required if employees may take accumulated days off only for actual illness, since losses for these are usually immaterial.

> **EXAMPLE 41:** Estimated compensation for future absences is $30,000. The entry is:

Expense	30,000	
Estimated liability		30,000

> If at a later date a payment of $28,000 is made, the entry is:

Estimated liability	28,000	
Cash		28,000

Accounting for Special Termination Benefits to Employees

An expense should be accrued when an employer offers special termination benefits to an employee, he or she accepts the offer, and the amount is subject to reasonable estimation. The amount equals the current payment plus the discounted value of future payments.

When it can be objectively measured, the effect of changes on the employer's previously accrued expenses applicable to other employee benefits directly associated with employee termination should be included in measuring termination expense.

EXAMPLE 42: On January 1, 2X11, as an incentive for early retirement, the employee receives a lump-sum payment today of $50,000 plus payments of $10,000 for each of the next 10 years. The discount rate is 10%. The journal entry is:

Expense	111,450	
Estimated liability		111,450
Present value $10,000 \times 6.145 =$	$ 61,450	
Current payment	50,000	
Total	$111,450	

*Present value factor for n = 10, i = 10% is 6.145

Refinancing of Short-Term Debt to Long-Term Debt

A short-term obligation shall be reclassified as a long-term obligation in two cases:

1. After the year-end of the financial statements but before the audit report is issued, the short-term debt is rolled over into a long-term obligation or an equity security is issued in substitution.

    OR

2. Prior to the audit report date, the company enters into a contract for refinancing the current obligation on a long-term basis and all of the following are met:

    a. Agreement does not expire within one year.

    b. No violation of the agreement exists.

    c. The parties are financially capable of meeting the requirements of the agreement.

The proper classification of the refinanced item is under long-term debt and not stockholders' equity even if equity securities were issued in substitution of the debt. When short-term debt is excluded from current liabilities, a footnote should describe the financing agreement and the terms of any new obligation to be incurred.

If the amounts under the agreement for refinancing vary, the amount of short-term debt excluded from current liabilities will be the minimum amount expected to be refinanced based on conservatism. The exclusion from current liabilities cannot be greater than the net proceeds of debt or security issuances, or amounts available under the refinancing agreement.

Once cash is paid for the short-term debt even though the next day long-term debt of a similar amount is issued, the short-term debt shall be shown under current liabilities since cash was disbursed.

Obligations Callable by the Creditor

Included as a current liability is a long-term debt callable by the creditor because of the debtor's violation of the debt agreement, except if one of the following conditions exists:

- The creditor waives or lost the right to require repayment for a period in excess of one year from the balance sheet date.

- There is a grace period in the terms of the long-term debt issue that the debtor may cure the violation that makes it callable, and it is probable that the violation will be rectified within the grace period.

Disclosure of Long-Term Purchase Obligations

An unconditional purchase obligation is an obligation to provide funds for goods or services at a determinable future date. An example is a take-or-pay contract obligating the buyer to pay specified periodic amounts for products or services. Even when the buyer does not take delivery of the goods, periodic payments must still be made.

When unconditional purchase obligations are recorded in the balance sheet, disclosure is still made of the following:

- Payments made for recorded unconditional purchase obligations.

- Maturities and sinking fund requirements for long-term borrowings.

Unconditional purchase obligations that are not reflected in the balance sheet should usually be disclosed if they:

- Cannot be cancelled except upon a remote contingency.

- Were negotiated to arrange financing to provide contracted goods or services.

- Are for a term in excess of one year.

The disclosure needed for unconditional purchase obligations, when not recorded in the accounts, are:

- Nature and term.

- Fixed and variable amounts.

- Total amount for the current year and for the next five years.

- Purchases made under the obligation for each year presented.

Optional disclosure exists of the amount of imputed interest required to reduce the unconditional purchase obligation to present value.

Asset Retirement Obligations

ASC 410, *Asset Retirement and Environmental Obligations* (ASC 410-20), requires companies to record a liability when a retirement obligation is incurred, provided fair value can be reasonably estimated even though it is years before the asset's planned retirement. The asset retirement obligation must be measured and recorded along with its associated asset retirement cost. However, the requirements of ASC 410-20 do not apply to a liability arising from an asset's improper operation or functioning. An example is a machine resulting in environmental remediation. Asset retirements may be from sale, recycling, abandonment, or disposal. However, if the entity only has the intent or a plan for an asset disposal, that in and of itself does not require recognition.

ASC 410-20 applies to tangible long-term assets, including individual ones, similar asset groups, and major parts of assets. A company may be legally liable for the purchase, development, construction, or usual operation of the fixed asset.

A company must record the fair value of a liability for an asset retirement obligation as incurred. When the initial obligation arises, the company books a liability and defers the cost to the long-term asset for the same amount. After the initial recognition, the liability will change over time so the obligation must be accreted to its present value each year. The long-term asset's capitalized cost is depreciated over its useful life. When the liability is settled, the company either settles the liability for the amount recorded or will have a settlement gain or loss.

The asset retirement obligation is recorded at its fair value. In determining the fair value, the first valuation (provided it is ascertainable) is the amount by which the obligation could be settled in a current transaction in an active market between willing parties (not in a forced or liquidating transaction). Quoted market prices are the best basis for fair value measurement. If quoted market prices are unavailable, fair value can be estimated based on the best data available. Examples are the prices of similar liabilities and the use of present value techniques.

Fair value also can be estimated based on an alternative market value valuation, such as the discounted (present) value of projected future cash flows needed to pay the obligation. Projected cash flows are based on various assumptions, such as technology and the inflation rate. The present value technique is typically the best method to use when quoted market prices are unavailable.

The long-lived asset is charged with the asset retirement costs. Thus, the entry consists of debiting the long-term asset and crediting the asset retirement obligation. The asset is then depreciated, including the deferred (capitalized) retirement costs and interest attributable to the accretion of the asset retirement obligation arising from the passage of time.

There will be an increase in the carrying value of long-term assets because of the inclusion of asset retirement costs. Closure costs may be incurred during the asset's life. Further, carrying values of the assets will increase because assets bought with a related retirement obligation will be shown on a gross rather than net basis.

Any incremental liability incurred in a later year is an additional layer of the original obligation. Each layer is initially measured at fair value. For example, the contamination-related costs each year of a nuclear plant represent a separate layer for measurement and recognition.

In years after initial measurement, a business recognizes the yearly change in the asset retirement obligation owing to the passage of time, and modifications to the timing and original projection of undiscounted cash flows.

The entity may experience retirement obligations at the beginning of the asset's life or during its operating life. An example of the former is a production facility that experiences a removal obligation when it starts operations (e.g., oil production facility). An example of the latter is a mine that experiences a reclamation obligation gradually over its life as digging in the mine takes place over the years. Further, an asset retirement obligation may arise because of new govern-mental regulations or laws affecting the asset, such as newly enacted environmental restrictions.

The interest method of allocation is used to reflect changes in the asset retirement obligation. The interest rate is multiplied by the liability balance at the beginning of the year. The interest rate used is the one existing when the liability, or part thereof, was *initially* measured. The ensuing *accretion expense* increases the carrying value of the liability each year. Accretion expense is presented in the income statement as an operating item.

Changes in the timing or initial estimated undiscounted cash flows shall be recognized as an addition or reduction of the asset retirement obligation and the associated asset retirement cost deferred to the long-lived asset. Upward adjust-ments to the undiscounted estimated cash flows are discounted based on the current credit-adjusted risk-free rate. However, downward revisions are discounted using the rate existing when the initial liability was recognized. If asset retirement costs change because of revised estimated cash flows, we must adjust the asset retirement cost allocated to expense in the year(s) affected.

If an asset has an indeterminate service life, sufficient data to estimate a range of potential settlement dates for the obligation might not be available. In such cases, the liability is initially recognized in the year in which adequate information exists to estimate a range of potential settlement dates required to use a present value approach to estimate fair value.

Uncertainty of whether performance will be required does not defer recogniz-ing a retirement obligation. Instead, that uncertainty is considered in the measure-ment of the fair value of the liability through assignment of probabilities to cash flows.

Any difference between the actual retirement costs and the asset retirement obligation is a gain or loss on retirement presented in the income statement.

According to ASC 410, *Asset Retirement and Environmental Obligations* (ASC 410-20), a company should identify its asset retirement obligations. If the company has sufficient information to reasonably estimate the fair value of an asset retire-ment obligation, it must recognize the liability as incurred. Reasonable estimation to an asset retirement obligation arises if:

- An active market exists for the obligation's transfer.
- Fair value of the obligation is incorporated in the asset's purchase price.
- Sufficient information exists to use a present value method.

Present Value Method. In using the present value method, the company must discount future estimated cash flows based on a credit-adjusted risk-free rate (e.g., rate on a zero-coupon U.S. Treasury Security) increased for the company's actual credit risk. After the final rate is decided on, the present value of cash flow calculation must reflect any relevant probabilities, uncertainties, and assumptions. Multiple cash flow and probability scenarios are used based on a range of possible outcomes.

EXAMPLE 43: A long-lived asset's carrying cost includes a $250,000 original cost plus the capitalized retirement cost of $53,426, which equals the initial liability amount. The business entity incurs an obligation to retire the asset upon installation. The asset retirement obligation is based on the following data:

Original cost	$250,000
Credit-adjusted risk free rate at date of installation	8%

Depreciation is based on the straight-line method for a five-year period of benefit.

The four possible alternative estimated market-based cash flows in year 5 to settle the obligation along with their related probabilities are:

Scenario	Projected Cash Outflow (Year 5)	Probability
1	$100,000	30%
2	80,000	35%
3	70,000	15%
4	50,000	20%
Total probability		100%

The computation of the capitalized retirement cost of $53,426 is as follows:

Computation of Capitalized Retirement Cost

Scenario	Projected Cash Outflow (Year 5)	Probability	Weighting
1	$100,000	30%	$30,000
2	80,000	35%	28,000
3	70,000	15%	10,500
4	50,000	20%	10,000
Expected cash outflow			$78,500
Present value for year 0 at 8%*			$53,426

*$78,500 × present value of $1 factor for n = 5, i = 8%
$78,500 × .68058 = $53,426

The retirement entry for the long-term asset based on the assumption that actual cash flows to settle the retirement liability are the same as those projected is as follows:

Accumulated depreciation	303,426	
Asset retirement liability	78,500	
Long-term asset		303,426
Cash		78,500

The annual accounting for the long-lived asset and the asset retirement obligation is as follows:

Computation of the Long-Term Asset and Obligation

Installment	Asset	Accumulated Depreciation	Book Value	Liability	Net Balance Sheet
Install	$303,426	—	$303,426	$53,426	$250,000
1	303,426	$ 60,685[a]	242,741	57,700[b]	185,041
2	303,426	121,370	182,056	62,316	119,740
3	303,426	182,055	121,371	67,301	54,070
4	303,426	242,740	60,686	72,685	(11,999)
5	303,426	303,426	0	78,500	(78,500)
Retirement (303,426) (303,426)					

[a] $303,426 ÷ 5 years = $60,685
[b] $53,426 × 1.08 = $57,700

The depreciation expense and interest expense (accretion) are as follows:

Computation of Depreciation and Interest Expense

Year	Depreciation	Interest Expense	Net Income Statement
1	$60,685	$4,274[c]	$64,954
2	60,685	4,616	65,301
3	60,685	4,985	65,670
4	60,685	5,384	66,069
5	60,686	5,815	66,501
Total	$303,426	$25,074	$328,500

[c] $53,426 × 8% = $4,274

Asset Impairment. The carrying value of an asset being analyzed for impairment includes the deferred asset retirement costs. Projected future cash flows for the asset retirement obligation shall exclude the undiscounted cash flows used to test the asset for recoverability and the discounted cash flows used to derive the asset's fair value. If the fair value of the asset is based on a quoted market price and such price reflects the costs to retire the asset, the market price shall be increased by the fair value of the asset retirement obligation when measuring for impairment.

Disclosures. The following footnote disclosures are required:

- A description and valuation of legally restricted assets to settle the obligation.

- A description of both the asset retirement liability and the associated long-term asset.

- If the fair value of an asset retirement liability is not subject to reasonable estimation, that fact should be noted along with the reasons.

- Reconciliation of the asset retirement obligation balance for the year. This reconciliation shows the beginning and ending carrying values of the asset retirement obligation presenting separately the changes related to the liability incurred as well as settled in the current year, accretion expense, and adjustments made to projected cash flows.

The fair value of a conditional asset retirement obligation must be recognized before the event that either mandates or waives performance occurs. Further, a clear requirement that gives rise to an asset retirement debt coupled with a low likelihood of required performance still requires liability recognition.

Liability Associated with Exit or Disposal Activities

ASC 420, *Exit or Disposal Cost Obligations*, relates to costs associated with a restructuring, discontinued operation, plant closing, or other exit or disposal activity. (Restructurings include altering the management structure, relocating business operations, closing a location, and ceasing a business line.) Examples of such costs are operating lease termination costs and one-time termination benefits to current employees and costs to consolidate facilities or relocate workers. These costs are recognized as incurred (*not* at the commitment date to an exit plan) based on fair value along with the related liability. Therefore, the company must actually incur the liabilities before recognition may be made. If fair value cannot reasonably be estimated, recognizing the liability must be postponed until it can.

The fair value of a liability is the amount the liability can be settled for in a current transaction between willing parties; that is, other than in a forced or liquidated transaction. The best reflection of fair value is quoted market prices in active markets. If such data are unavailable, fair value should be estimated on the best data available.

The initiation date of an exit or disposal activity is when management obligates itself to a plan to do so or to otherwise dispose of a long-lived asset, and if the activity includes worker termination.

In years following initial measurement, changes to the liability should be measured on the basis of the credit-adjusted risk-free rate that was used to initially measure the liability. The cumulative effect of a change due to revising either the timing or the amount of estimated cash flows shall be recognized as an adjustment to the liability in the year of change and reported in the same line item(s) in the income statements used when the related costs were recognized initially. Changes due to the passage of time shall be recognized as an increase in the carrying value of the liability and as an expense (e.g., accretion expense).

Examples of costs attributable to exit or disposal activities are included in income from continuing operations unless they apply to discontinued operations.

If an event arises that discharges a company's obligation to settle a liability for a cost associated with an exit or disposal activity recognized in a prior year, the liability and the related costs are reversed.

The liability to end a lease or other legal agreement prior to the end of its term is measured at its fair value when the company cancels the contract. A liability for future costs under a contract for its remaining years without benefiting the entity is recorded and measured at its fair value when the business no longer uses its right under the contract such as using rented property. In the case of an operating lease, the obligation's fair value at the date the entity no longer uses the property is computed based on the balance of the lease payment, less any expected sublease rentals. However, the remaining rentals cannot be reduced to less than zero.

When and how much a liability for one-time termination benefits is based on whether employees are obligated to work until they are let go in order to be eligible for termination benefits and, if such is the case, whether workers will be kept to work beyond a minimum retention period. The minimum retention period cannot be more than the legal notification period or, in the event none exists, 60 days. In the situation where workers do not have to work until they are let go to obtain termination benefits or if workers will not be retained to work beyond a minimum retention period, the obligation for termination benefits is recorded at fair value at the date of communication. If workers must work until they are terminated so as to obtain benefits and will be kept to work beyond the minimum retention period, the liability is initially measured at the communication date based on fair value as of the termination date but is recorded ratably over future service years.

The following should be footnoted:

- A description of the exit or disposal activity and the expected completion date.

- Where exit or disposal costs are presented in the income statement or statement of activities.

- When a liability for a cost is not recorded because fair value is not reasonably estimated, that should be noted along with the reasons.

- For each major kind of cost attributable to the exit activity, the total cost expected, the amount incurred in the current year, and the cumulative amount to date.

- A reconciliation of the beginning and ending liability balances presenting the changes during the year associated with costs incurred and charged to expense, costs paid or otherwise settled, and any adjustments of the liability along with the reasons for doing so.

Third-Party Credit Enhancement

As per ASC 820, *Fair Value Measurements and Disclosures* (ASC 820-10-05-3), debt securities may be issued with a third-party credit enhancement. An example is a financial guarantee from an unrelated third party, who guarantees the issuer's payment obligations. That guarantee may be purchased by the issuer, who combines it with the debt and issues the combined security to an investor. In issuing debt combined with the guarantee, the issuer can obtain a lower interest rate and receive higher proceeds.

This ASC applies to an issuer's accounting for debt issued with an inseparable third-party credit enhancement that is measured or disclosed at fair value. An issuer should not include the effect of the third-party credit enhancement in the fair value measurement of the liability. Therefore, the fair value measurement is determined taking into account the issuer's credit standing (without considering the third-party guarantor's credit standing). The unit of accounting for the debt does not include the guarantee (or other third-party credit enhancement), and the guarantee does not represent an asset of the issuer. The guarantee is for the investor's benefit.

There should be disclosure of the credit enhancement.

Fair Value Measurements

ASC 820, *Fair Value Measurements and Disclosures*, provides the definition of fair value, offers guidance on fair value measurements, and indicates appropriate disclosures in the financial statements of the measures of fair value used. Fair value is a market-based measurement that reflects current market participant assumptions with respect to future inflows of the asset and future outflows of the liability. A fair value measurement should consider characteristics of a specific asset or liability, such as its condition or location.

In determining fair value, the *exchange price* is considered. The exchange price is the market price at the measurement date in an *orderly transaction* between the parties to sell the asset or transfer the liability. The focus is on the price at the measurement date that would be received to sell the asset or paid to transfer the liability (an exit price), *not* the price that would be paid to purchase the asset or received to assume the liability (an entry price).

The asset or liability may be by itself, such as a financial instrument or an operating asset, or there may be a group of assets or liabilities, such as an asset group or a reporting unit.

Taking into account the assumptions made by market participants in fair value measurements, ASC 820 sets forth a hierarchy of fair value that distinguishes between (1) assumptions based on market information derived from independent outside sources to the reporting entity (observable inputs) and (2) assumptions by the reporting entity itself (unobservable inputs). The use of unobservable inputs allows for cases in which there is minimal or no market activity for the asset or liability at the measurement date. Under these circumstances, the reporting company need not conduct all possible efforts to obtain data concerning market participant assumptions. However, the entity must *not* ignore data regarding market participant assumptions that is reasonably available. Valuation techniques used to measure fair value shall maximize the use of observable inputs and minimize the use of unobservable inputs.

Market participant assumptions include *risk* considerations, such as the risk involved in a specific valuation method to measure fair value (pricing model) or input risks to the valuation technique. There should be an adjustment for risk in a fair value measurement when market participants would include risk in the pricing of the asset or liability.

Market participant assumptions should take into account assumptions concerning the affect of a *restriction* on the sale or use of an asset that influences the *price* of that asset.

A fair value measurement for a liability should consider the risk that the obligation will not be fulfilled (nonperformance risk). In assessing this risk, the reporting company's credit risk should be noted.

The fair value of a position in a financial instrument, including a block that is actively traded, should be measured by multiplying the quoted price of the instrument by the quantity held (within Level 1 of the fair value hierarchy). Quoted price should *not* be adjusted according to the size of the position compared to trading volume (blockage factor).

A fair value measurement assumes the transaction occurs in the *principal market* for the asset or liability. The principal market is the one in which the reporting company would sell the asset or transfer the liability with the greatest volume and activity level. If a principal market does *not* exist, the most advantageous market should be used. The most advantageous market is one in which the reporting entity would sell the asset or transfer the liability with the price that maximizes the amount that would be received for the asset or minimizes the amount that would be paid to transfer the liability, taking into account any transaction costs.

The price in the principal (or most advantageous) market used to measure fair value should *not* be adjusted for transaction costs. On the other hand, transportation costs for the asset or liability should be included in the fair value measurement.

In measuring fair value, valuation techniques in conformity with the market, income, and cost approaches should be used. Under the *market approach*, the prices for market transactions applying to identical or comparable assets or liabilities are used. Matrix pricing is an example of a market approach. It is a mathematical method used mainly to value debt securities by relying not solely on quoted prices for the particular securities, but rather on the relationship of the securities to other benchmark quoted securities. Under the *income approach*, valuation techniques are used to convert future amounts (e.g., cash flows or profits) to a present value amount. For example, future cash flows are discounted to their present value amount using the present value tables. The measurement is based on the value indicated by prevailing market expectations regarding future amounts. Examples of these valuation techniques are present value determination, option-pricing models, and the multi-year excess earnings method (to value goodwill). The *cost approach* is based on the amount that currently would be needed to replace an asset's service capability (current replacement cost). An example is the cost to buy or construct a substitute asset of comparable utility after adjusting for obsolescence.

Depending on the situation, a single or multiple valuation technique may be required. For example, a single valuation method would be used to value an asset using quoted prices in an active market for identical assets, while a multiple valuation method would be needed to value a reporting unit.

Input availability and reliability applicable to the asset or liability may affect the selection of the appropriate valuation method.

The fair value hierarchy prioritizes the *inputs* to valuation techniques used to measure fair value into three broad levels. The highest priority (Level 1) is assigned to inputs that are quoted prices (unadjusted) in active markets for identical assets or liabilities, while the lowest priority (Level 3) represents unobservable inputs.

Middle priority (Level 2) inputs do not include quoted prices but are included within Level 1 if they are observable for the asset or liability, either directly or indirectly. In a situation where the asset or liability has a specified (contractual) term, a Level 2 input must be observable for substantially the full term of the asset or liability. Included as Level 2 inputs are:

- Quoted prices for similar assets or liabilities in active markets.

- Quoted prices for similar or identical assets or liabilities in markets that are not active namely because of few transactions, noncurrent prices, significantly varied price quotations, or limited public information.

- Inputs excluding quoted prices that are observable for the asset or liability. Examples are interest rates observable at often quoted intervals, credit risks, default rates, volatilities, loss severities, and prepayment speeds.

- Inputs derived mostly from observable market information by correlation or other means.

Adjustments to Level 2 inputs vary depending on factors specific to the asset or liability. Those factors include the location or condition of the asset or liability, the volume and activity level in the markets, and the degree to which the inputs relate to comparable items to the asset or liability. A major adjustment to the fair value measurement might result in a Level 3 measurement.

Level 3 inputs, which are unobservable for the asset or liability, are used to measure fair value to the degree that observable inputs are unavailable. This allows for situations in which there is little or no market activity for the asset or liability at the measurement date. Unobservable inputs shall reflect the reporting company's own assumptions about the assumptions that market participants would use in pricing the asset or liability (i.e., including risk assumptions).

In the event that an input used to measure fair value is based on bid and ask prices, the price within the bid-ask spread that is most representative of fair value shall be used to measure fair value irrespective of where in the fair value hierarchy the input falls.

Numerous disclosures are required for fair value measurements to enhance financial statement user comprehension. Quantitative disclosures using a tabular format are required in all periods (annual and interim). Qualitative (narrative) disclosures are required about the valuation methods used to measure fair value. Disclosures of fair value in measuring assets and liabilities concentrates on the inputs used to measure fair value and the effect of fair value measurements on profit or change in net assets.

For assets and liabilities measured at fair value on a *recurring* basis in periods after initial recognition (e.g., trading securities), disclosures should be made to allow financial statement users to evaluate the inputs used to formulate fair value measurements. To accomplish this, the following should be disclosed in annual and interim periods for each major category of asset and liability:

1. Fair value measurements at the reporting date.

2. The level within the fair value hierarchy in which the fair value measurements in their entirety fall, segregating the fair value measurements using quoted prices in active markets for identical assets or liabilities (Level 1), major other observable inputs (Level 2), and significant unobservable inputs (Level 3).

3. For fair value measurements using major unobservable inputs (Level 3), a reconciliation of the beginning and ending balances, separately presenting changes during the period attributable to the following:

   a. Total gain or loss (realized and unrealized), segregating those gains or losses included in earnings (or changes in net assets), as well as where those gains or losses are reported in the financial statements.

   b. Purchases, sales, issuances, and settlements (net).

   c. Transfers into or out of Level 3. An example is a transfer because of a change in the observability of major inputs.

4. For annual reporting only, the valuation techniques used to measure fair value and a discussion of any changes in those techniques.

For assets and liabilities that are measured at fair value on a *nonrecurring* basis in periods after initial recognition, such as impaired assets, disclosure should be made of:

1. Fair value measurements recorded during the period and the reasons for those measurements.

2. The level within the fair value hierarchy in which the fair value measurements fall.

3. For fair value measurements using significant unobservable inputs (Level 3), a description of the inputs and the data used to develop them.

4. For annual reporting only, the valuation methods used and any changes in them to measure similar assets and liabilities in previous years.

Accounting Standards Update (ASU) No. 2009-05 (August 2009), *Fair Value Measurements and Disclosures* (Topic 820), *Measuring Liabilities at Fair Value*, provides information on the following:

- ASC 820-10-35-41 offers guidance for identifying fair value in an active market. The best indication of fair value is the price in an active market. The quoted price is a Level 1 measurement. If a quoted priced for an identical liability is not present, fair value may be measured based on the prevailing price for an identical liability traded as an asset. An income method using present value or a market method may also be used.

- ASC 820-10-35-16A discusses the measurement of fair value. In measuring fair value, there is a presumption of an exchange of a debt in an orderly way. In reality, the transfer of liabilities is rare; certain liabilities are traded as assets.

- ASC 820-10-35-16C states that observable inputs should be maximized and unobservable inputs should be minimized.

- ASC 820-10-35-16D specifies that in measuring the fair value of a liability, the quoted price of the asset should not be adjusted for any limitation on its sale.

- ASC 820-10-35-16E states that in valuing a liability, an independent input applicable to a limitation on liability transfer should not be included.

- ASC 820-10-35-41A explains that a Level 1 valuation for a liability is the quoted price in an active market. If the quoted price is adjusted, the liability has a lower level measured fair value associated with it.

- ASC 820-10-35-50 discusses Level 2 inputs, which, when modified, vary based on asset or liability characteristics. Factors include asset or liability status and location, activity and volume levels, and comparability of inputs.

According to Accounting Standards Update (ASU) No. 2011-04 (May 2011), *Fair Value Measurement* (ASC Topic 820), *Amendments to Achieve Common Fair Value Measurement and Disclosure Requirements in U.S. GAAP and IFRSs,* the concepts of highest and best use and valuation in fair value measurement are only relevant in measuring the fair value of nonfinancial assets not financial assets or liabilities. A business should measure the fair value of its own equity instrument from the perspective of a holder of that instrument. A business should also disclose quantitative information regarding unobservable inputs used in measuring fair value classified in Level 3. The application of discounts or premiums in a fair value measurement relates to the unit of account for the asset or liability being measured at fair value.

In the case of a Level 3 fair value hierarchy, disclosure should be made of the valuation processes, as well as the sensitivity of the fair value measurement to changes in unobservable inputs and any interrelationships between them.

FAIR VALUE OF FINANCIAL ASSETS

ASC 820-10-35-15A and 820-10-35-55 (AB) states that irrespective of the valuation technique, a company must include suitable risk adjustments that market participants would use for nonperformance and liquidity risks. When markets are not active, brokers may rely on models with inputs based on information available to the broker. An income approach (e.g., present value) may be used to maximize the use of relevant observable inputs to value a financial asset that is not actively traded. A discount rate adjustment technique may be used to determine fair value of a financial asset at the measurement date. Risks considered in the discount rate include liquidity risk (e.g., difficulty selling an asset under present market conditions) and nonperformance risk (e.g., collateral value risk, default risk).

Fair Value Accounting

The SEC Office of the Chief Accountant and FASB staff clarified fair value accounting in a news release. It states that management may use internal assumptions such as expected cash flows including appropriate risk premiums to measure fair value when suitable market evidence is non-existent. In some cases, unobservable inputs (level 3) may be more appropriate then observable inputs (level 2). An example is when significant adjustments are needed to available observable inputs it may be better to use an estimate based mostly on unobservable inputs. Fair value determination often involves judgment. In some situations, multiple inputs from different sources may give the best indication of fair value. In this case, expected cash flows may be taken into account with other relevant data.

Broker quotes may be an input to measure fair value. However, they are not necessarily determinative if an active market does not exist for the security. When markets are less active, brokers may rely more on models with inputs based on information available to the broker. Less reliance should be placed on quotes not reflecting market transactions. The nature of the quote should also be considered such as if it indicates a price or binding offer.

Disorderly transactions are not determinative in measuring fair value. Fair value measurement assumes orderly transactions among market participants. Distressed or forced liquidation sales are not orderly transactions.

If prices in an inactive market are not reflective of current prices for similar assets, adjustments may be needed to determine fair value.

In determining if a market is inactive, consider the spread between the asking price of sellers and the bid price of buyers as well as the number of "bidding" parties. A significant increase in the spread and a small number of bidders indicate an inactive market.

In determining if an other-than-temporary impairment of the financial asset exists examine the following:

- Intent and ability of the holder to keep its investment in the issuer for a time period adequate to allow for a recovery in market value.
- How long and degree to which the market value has been less than cost.
- The issuer's financial condition and short-term prospects.
- The expected recovery period must be taken into account.

LEEWAY IN VALUING FINANCIAL ASSETS

In determining whether a market is not active and a transaction is not distressed, the FASB has given companies greater leeway in valuing assets and reporting losses on bank's balance sheets and income statements. The bank's assets may now be valued at what they could be sold for in an "orderly" sale in an inactive market between market participants at the measurement date as distinguished from a forced liquidation or distressed sale. The new guidelines will allow banks to avoid reporting some losses on securities. The change in how companies record impaired assets they do not currently plan to sell allows for the splitting off of credit losses from non-credit losses arising from such reasons as fluctuating interest rates. The latter will not have to be counted toward net income or loss. Banks will benefit because their asset values would be higher and so would earnings.

Assets would be valued at what banks project they might sell for in the future, instead of the current distressed environment. In effect, the mark-to-market rules are relaxed for banks' toxic assets.

To avoid a write-down as an impairment loss on an asset, management must assert it has the intent and ability to hold on to an asset until its value recovers. Under new rules, a company could avoid a write-down by stating it intends to hold the asset and it is more likely than not it will.

Once an asset is other than temporarily impaired, only losses related to the underlying creditworthiness would impact earnings and regulatory capital. Losses associated with market conditions would be disclosed and accounted for elsewhere.

More weight should be given when transactions are in a market operating in an orderly manner and less weight given to an inactive market.

The effective date for the pronouncement is the second quarter of 2009. Early adoption for the first quarter of 2009 is allowed.

FASB Staff Position FAS 157-4, *Determining Fair Value When the Volume and Level of Activity for the Asset or Liability Have Significantly Decreased and Identifying Transactions That Are Not Orderly,* provides guidance for estimating fair value in accordance with ASC 820, *Fair Value Measurements and Disclosures,* when the volume and activity level for the asset or liability have significantly decreased. This FSP includes guidance on identifying circumstances that indicate a transaction is not orderly. Fair value is the price that would be received to sell an asset or paid to transfer a liability in an orderly transaction (i.e., not a forced liquidation or distressed sale) between market participants at the measurement date under current market conditions.

If the reporting entity decides there has been a major decrease in the volume and level of activity for the asset or liability relative to normal market activity for the asset or liability, transactions or quoted prices may not be determinative of fair value. Further analysis is needed, and a significant adjustment to the transaction or quoted prices may be necessary to estimate fair value. Significant adjustments also may be needed in other situations (e.g., when a price for a similar asset requires significant adjustment to make it more comparable to the asset being measured or when the price is old).

Even in cases where there has been a significant decrease in the volume and level of activity for the asset or liability regardless of the valuation technique used, the objective of a fair value measurement remains the same. Determining the price at which willing market participants would transact at the measurement date under current market conditions if there has been a significant decrease in the volume and level of activity for the asset or liability depends on the facts and circumstances and requires the use of judgment. However, a reporting entity's intention to hold the asset or liability is not relevant in estimating fair value. Fair value is a market-based measurement, not an entity-specific measurement.

Even if there has been a significant decrease in the volume and level of activity for the asset or liability, it is not appropriate to conclude that all transactions are not orderly (i.e., distressed or forced).

INVESTMENTS IN CERTAIN ENTITIES THAT CALCULATE NET ASSET VALUE PER SHARE (OR ITS EQUIVALENT)

An investor may invest in entities (investees) that allow the investor to redeem its investments directly with the investee. Many of these investments do not have readily determinable fair values. Examples of these investees (also called alternative investments) are hedge funds, private equity funds, real estate funds, and venture capital funds. Many of these investees provide their investors with a net asset value per share (or its equivalent).

The net asset value per share (or its equivalent) provided by the investee may not represent fair value of the investor's investment in all cases. Certain aspects of the investment and transaction prices from principal-to-principal or brokered transactions may require adjustments to net asset value per share to estimate fair value of the investment.

Accounting Standards Update (ASU) No. 2015-07 (May 2015), *Fair Value Measurement* (Topic 820), removed the requirement to categorize investments for which fair values are measured using the net asset per share practical expedient. Previously, investments valued using the practical expedient were categorized within the fair value hierarchy on the basis of whether the investment was: (a) redeemable with the investee at net asset value on the measurement date, (b) never redeemable with the investee at net asset value, or (c) redeemable with the investee at a future date.

Disclosure should be made of any restrictions on the investor's ability to redeem its investment on the measurement date. Disclosure is required of unfunded commitments and the investment strategies of investees. An example of an unfunded commitment is a contract by the investor to invest additional capital at a later date to fund investments that the investee will make.

The amendment to this Update improves financial reporting by allowing use of a practical expedient, with appropriate disclosures, when measuring the fair value of an alternative investment that does not have a readily determinable fair value.

The amendments to this Update apply to all reporting entities holding an investment required or allowed to be measured or disclosed at fair value on a recurring or nonrecurring basis and, as of the reporting entity's measurement date, if the investment satisfies both of the following conditions:

1. The investment does not have a readily determinable fair value.

2. The investment is in an entity that has all of the attributes specified in paragraph 946-10-15-2 or, if one or more of the attributes specified in that paragraph are not present, is an entity for which industry practice is to issue financial statements using the measurement principles in Topic 946. An example is certain investments in real estate funds that measure investment assets at fair value on a recurring basis. Paragraph 946-10-15-2

limits the scope of Topic 946 to investment companies having the following attributes:

a. Unit of ownership is in the form of units of investments, such as shares of stock.

b. Pooling of funds exist.

c. Reporting entity is the primary one.

Investment activity is primarily investment in assets, usually in securities of other entities not under common management.

ASC 270, *Interim Reporting*, states that disclosures are required about fair value of financial instruments for interim periods of public companies. A company must disclose in the body or notes to the summarized financial information the fair value of all financial instruments for which it can practically estimate fair value, whether recognized or not recognized in the balance sheet.

Fair value information disclosed in the notes shall be presented along with the related carrying amount of the asset or liability. Disclosure shall also be made of the method(s) and major assumptions used to estimate fair value of financial instruments and describe any changes in method(s) and significant assumptions.

FAIR VALUE OPTION FOR FINANCIAL ASSETS AND FINANCIAL LIABILITIES

ASC 825, *Financial Instruments* (ASC 825-10), allows companies to measure many financial instruments and other items at fair value. The pronouncement is effective as of the beginning of the company's first fiscal year beginning after November 15, 2007. Most provisions of the pronouncement apply solely to businesses that choose the fair value option. The eligible items for the fair value measurement option are:

1. Recognized financial assets and financial liabilities excluding

   a. Financial assets and financial liabilities recognized under leases.

   b. Financial instruments classified by the issuer as an element of stockholders' equity such as a convertible bond with a noncontingent beneficial conversion feature.

   c. Investment in a subsidiary or variable interest entity that must be consolidated.

   d. Deposit liabilities that can be withdrawn on bank demand.

   e. Employers' plan obligations or assets for pension and postretirement benefits.

2. Nonfinancial insurance contracts and warranties that can be settled by the insurer by paying a third party for goods or services.

3. Firm commitments applying to financial instruments such as a forward purchase contract for a loan not readily convertible to cash.

4. Written loan commitment.

5. Host financial instruments arising from separating an embedded nonfinancial derivative instrument from a nonfinancial hybrid instrument.

ASC 825-10 permits a company to measure eligible items at fair value at stipulated election dates. Included in earnings at each reporting date are the unrealized (holding) gains and losses on items for which the fair value option has been elected.

The fair value option is irrevocable (except if a new election date occurs) and is applied solely to *entire* instruments (*not* portions of those instruments or specified risks or specific cash flows). In most cases, the fair value option may be applied instrument-by-instrument including investments otherwise accounted for under the equity method.

ASC 825-10's amendment to ASC 320, *Investments—Debt and Equity Securities* (ASC 320), applies to all companies with trading and available-for-sale securities.

Upfront costs and fees applicable to items for which the fair value option is selected are expensed as incurred.

Electing the Fair Value Option

A company may elect the fair value option for all eligible items only on the date that one of the following occurs:

1. The company first recognizes the eligible item.
2. The company engages in an eligible firm commitment.
3. There is a change in the accounting treatment for an investment in another company because the investment becomes subject to the equity method or the investor no longer consolidates a subsidiary because a majority voting interest no longer exists, although the investor retains an ownership interest.
4. The specialized accounting treatment no longer applies for the financial assets that have been reported at fair value such as under an AICPA Audit and Accounting Guide.
5. An event that mandates an eligible item to be measured at fair value on the event date but does not require fair value measurement at each subsequent reporting date.

Events

Some events that require remeasurement of eligible items at fair value, initial recognition of eligible items, or both, and thus create an election date for the fair value option are:

- Consolidation or deconsolidation of a subsidiary or variable interest entity.
- Business combination.
- Major debt modification.

Instrument Application

The fair value option may be selected for a single eligible item without electing it for other identical items except for the following:

1. If the fair value option is selected for an eligible insurance contract, it must be applied to all claims and obligations under the contract.

2. If the fair value option is selected for an investment under the equity method, it must be applied to all of the investor's financial interests in the same entity that are eligible items.

3. If multiple advances are made to one borrower under a single contract (e.g., construction loan) and the individual advances lose their identity and become part of the larger loan, the fair value option must be applied to the larger loan balance but not to the individual advances.

4. If the fair value option is selected for an insurance contract for which integrated or nonintegrated contract features or riders are issued at the same time or later, the fair value option also must be applied to those features or coverage.

The fair value option does not usually have to be applied to all financial instruments issued or bought in a single transaction. For example, an investor in stock or bonds may apply the fair value option to some of the stock shares or bonds issued or acquired in a single transaction. In this case, an individual bond is considered the minimum denomination of that debt security. A financial instrument that is a single contract cannot be broken down into parts when using the fair value option. However, a loan syndication may be in multiple loans to the same debtor by different creditors. Each of the loans is a separate instrument, and the fair value option may be selected for some of the loans but not others.

An investor in an equity security may choose the fair value option for its entire investment in that security including any fractional shares.

According to Accounting Standards Update No. 2010-06 (January 2010), *Fair Value Measurements and Disclosures* (ASC Topic 820), *Improving Disclosures about Fair Value Measurements,* ASC 820-10 provides that a transfer between Levels 1 and 2 must be footnoted along with the reasons. Gross information should be furnished for Level 3 items such as for sales. Each type of asset and liability must have a disclosure as to how fair value was determined. Valuation methods should be disclosed including the inputs used.

Balance Sheet

Companies must report assets and liabilities measured at the fair value option in a way that separates those reported fair values from the book (carrying) values of similar assets and liabilities measured with a different measurement attribute. To achieve this, a company must either:

- Report the aggregate fair value and nonfinancial fair value amounts in the same line items on the balance sheet and, in parentheses, disclose the amount measured at fair value included in the aggregate amount.

- Report two separate line items to display the fair value and nonfair value carrying amounts.

Accounting Standards Update No. 2016-01 (January 2016), *Financial Instruments* (Subtopic 825-10)*, Recognition and Measurement of Financial Assets and Financial Liabilities,* requires equity investments (excluding those accounted for under the equity method or those resulting from the consolidation of the investee) to be measured at fair market value. Any changes to fair market value are to be recognized in net income. However, a company may elect to measure equity investments not having a readily available fair market value at cost less any impaired loss, and adjusted (plus or minus) for changes in price from orderly transactions for similar investments of the same issuer.

The impairment evaluation of equity investments not having determinable fair values should be based on a qualitative assessment to identify impairment. If that assessment shows impairment, the investment should be measured at fair value.

ASU 2016-01 eliminates the mandate for companies to disclose the methods and assumptions used in fair value estimation for financial instruments measured at amortized cost in the balance sheet.

Companies are required to use the exit price notion in measuring fair value of financial instruments for disclosure purposes.

A company must show separately in "other comprehensive income" the portion of the total change in a liability's fair value caused by a change in its credit risk when the company measures the liability at its fair value.

There should be a separate presentation of financial assets and financial liabilities by measurement category and form.

A company should appraise the need for a valuation allowance on a deferred tax asset applicable to available-for-sale securities in conjunction with its other deferred tax assets.

Statement of Cash Flows

Companies must classify cash receipts and cash payments for items measured at fair value based on their nature and purpose.

Disclosures

Disclosures of fair value are required in annual and interim financial statements.

When a balance sheet is presented, the following must be disclosed:

1. The reasons why the company selected the fair value option for each allowable item or group of similar items.

2. In the event the fair value option is chosen for some but not all eligible items within a group of similar items, management must describe those similar items and the reasons for partial election. Further, information must be provided so that financial statement users can comprehend how the group of similar items applies to individual line items on the balance sheet.

3. For every line item on the balance sheet that includes an item or items for which the fair value option has been selected, management must provide information on how each line item relates to major asset and liability categories. Further, management must provide the aggregate carrying amount of items included in each line item that are not eligible for the fair value option.

4. To be disclosed is the difference between the aggregate fair value and the aggregate unpaid principal balance of loans, long-term receivables, and long-term debt instruments with contractual principal amounts for which the fair value option has been chosen.

5. In the case of loans held as assets for which the fair value option has been selected, management should disclose the aggregate fair value of loans past due by 90 days or more. If the company recognizes interest revenue separately from other changes in fair value, disclosure should be made of the aggregate fair value of loans in the nonaccrual status. Disclosure should also be made of the difference between the aggregate fair value and aggregate unpaid principal balance for loans that are 90 days or more past due or in nonaccrual status.

6. Disclosure should be made of investments that would have been reported under the equity method if the company did not elect the fair value option.

When an income statement is presented, the following must be disclosed:

1. An enumeration of how dividends and interest are measured and where they are presented in the income statement.

2. Gains and losses from changes in fair value included in profit and where they are shown.

3. For loans and other receivables, the estimated amount of gains and losses (including how they were calculated) included in earnings associated with changes in instrument-specific credit risk.

4. For liabilities with fair values that have been materially impacted by changes in the instrument-specific credit risk, the estimated amount of gains and losses from fair value changes (including how they were calculated) applicable to changes in such credit risk, and the reasons for those changes.

Other disclosures include the methods and assumptions used in fair value estimation. Also to be disclosed is qualitative information about the nature of the event, as well as quantitative information, including the impact on earnings of initially electing the fair value option for an item.

Eligible Items at the Effective Date

A company may select the fair value option for eligible items at the effective date. The difference between the book (carrying) value and the fair value of eligible items chosen for the fair value option at the effective date must be removed from the balance sheet and included in the cumulative-effect adjustment. These differences include (1) valuation allowances (e.g., loan loss reserves); (2) unamortized deferred costs, fees, discounts, and premiums; and (3) accrued interest associated with the fair value of the eligible item.

A company that selects the fair value option for items at the effective date must provide in financial statements that include the effective date the following:

1. Impact on deferred tax assets and liabilities of selecting the fair value option.

2. Reasons for choosing the fair value option for each existing eligible item or group of similar items.

3. Amount of valuation allowances removed from the balance sheet because they applied to items for which the fair value option was selected.

4. Schedule presenting the following by line items in the balance sheet:

    a. Before-tax portion of the cumulative-effect adjustment to retained earnings for the items on that line.

    b. Fair value at the effective date of eligible items for which the fair value option is selected and the book (carrying) amounts of those same items immediately before opting for the fair value option.

5. In the event the fair value option is selected for some but not all eligible items within a group of similar eligible items, there should be a description of similar items and the reasons for the partial election. Further, information should be provided so financial statement users can comprehend how the group of similar items applies to individual items on the balance sheet.

Available-for-Sale and Held-to-Maturity Securities

Available-for-sale and held-to-maturity securities held at the effective date are eligible for the fair value option at that date. In the event that the fair value option is selected for any of those securities at the effective date, cumulative holding (unrealized) gains and losses must be included in the cumulative-effect adjustment. Separate disclosure must be made of the holding gains and losses reclassified from accumulated other comprehensive income (for available-for-sale securities) and holding gains and losses previously unrecognized (for held-to-maturity securities).

OFFSETTING

Offsetting is the reporting of assets and liabilities on a net basis on the balance sheet. An entity is permitted to offset certain assets and liabilities that are recognized in the balance sheet when a "right of setoff" exists. Under ASC Subtopic 210-20, *Balance Sheet—Offsetting*, a right of setoff exists when all of the following conditions are met:

1. Each of the two parties owes the other a determinable amount, thus, only bilateral netting is permitted.

2. The party has the right to set off the amount owed with the amount owed by the other party.

3. The party intends to set off. This condition does not have to be met for fair value amounts recognized for conditional or exchange contracts that have been executed with the same counterparty under a master netting arrangement.

4. The right of setoff is enforceable at law.

Under ASC Subtopic 210-20, the party needs to consider legal constraints to determine whether the right of setoff is enforceable (*i.e.*, the right of setoff is required to be upheld in bankruptcy or receivership). Offsetting is only appropriate if the available evidence (both positive and negative), indicates that there is reasonable assurance that the right of setoff would be upheld in bankruptcy or receivership.

According to ASC Subtopic 210-20, for forwards, options, interest rate swaps, currency swaps, and other derivative contracts, a master netting arrangement exists if the entity has multiple contracts (whether for the same type of derivative contracts or for different types of contracts) with a single counterparty that are subject to a contractual agreement that provides for the net settlement of all contracts through a single payment in a single currency in the event of default or termination of any one contract.

Offsetting assets and liabilities recognized for derivative contracts outstanding with a single counterparty result in a net position between the two counterparties and is reported as either an asset or a liability on the balance sheet. Offsetting of the following assets and liabilities is permitted by other accounting pronouncements: leveraged leases, pension plan and other postretirement benefit plan assets and liabilities, and deferred tax assets and liabilities. If an entity elects to offset or not to offset its payables and receivables, that decision must be applied consistently.

STOCKHOLDERS' EQUITY

In accounting for stockholders' equity, consideration is given to preferred stock characteristics, conversion of preferred stock to common stock, stock retirement, appropriation of retained earnings, treasury stock, quasi-reorganization, dividends, fractional share warrants, stock options, stock warrants, and stock splits.

The stockholders' equity section of the balance sheet includes major categories for:

- Capital stock (stock issued and stock to be issued).

- Paid-in capital.

- Retained earnings.

- Cumulative unrealized loss or gain on available-for-sale securities.

- Cumulative gains or losses on foreign currency translation.

- Treasury stock.

Note: Disclosure should be made for required redemptions of capital stock redeemable at given prices on specific dates.

Preferred Stock

Although participating preferred stock rarely exists, if it does, it may be partially or fully participating. In the case of partially participating, preferred stockholders participate in excess dividends over the preferred dividend rate proportionately with common stockholders, but there is a maximum additional rate. For example, an 8% preferred stock issue may permit participating up to 12% so that an extra 4% dividend may be tacked on. In the case of fully participating preferred stock, there is a distribution for the current year at the preference rate plus any cumulative preference. Further, the preferred stockholders share in dividend distributions in excess of the preferred stock rate on a proportionate basis using the total par value of the preferred stock and common stock. For instance, a 10% fully participating preferred stock will get the 10% preference rate plus a proportionate share based on the total par value of the common and preferred stock of excess dividends once common stockholders have obtained their matching 10% of par of the common stock.

EXAMPLE 44: For this example, 5% preferred stock, $20 par, and 5,000 shares are assumed. The preferred stock is partially participating up to an additional 2%. Common stock is $10 par, 30,000 shares. A $40,000 dividend is declared. Dividends are distributed as follows:

	Preferred	*Common*
Preferred stock, current year ($100,000 × 5%)	$5,000	
Common stock, current year ($300,000 × 5%)		$15,000
Preferred stock, partial ($100,000 × 2%)	2,000	
Common stock, matching ($300,000 × 2%)		6,000
Balance to common stock		12,000
Total	$7,000	$33,000

For cumulative preferred stock, if no dividends are paid in a given year, the dividends accumulate and must be paid before any dividends can be paid to noncumulative stock.

The liquidation value of preferred stock is the value preferred stockholders will receive, in the event of corporate liquidation, before any funds may be distributed to common stockholders.

Disclosure for preferred stock includes liquidation preferences, call prices, and cumulative dividends in arrears.

When preferred stock is converted to common stock, the preferred stock and paid-in capital accounts are eliminated and the common stock and paid-in capital accounts are credited. If a deficit results, retained earnings would be charged.

EXAMPLE 45: Preferred stock having a par value of $300,000 and paid-in capital (preferred stock) of $20,000 are converted into common stock. There are 30,000 preferred shares having a $10 par value per share. Common stock issued is 10,000 shares having a par value of $25. The journal entry is:

Preferred stock	300,000	
Paid-in capital (preferred stock)	20,000	
Common stock ($10,000 × $25)		250,000
Paid-in capital (common stock)		70,000

Preferred securities redeemable for cash or other assets are to be classified outside of permanent capital if they are redeemable (1) at a fixed or determinable price on a fixed or determinable date, (2) at the holder's option, or (3) upon the occurrence of an event that is not solely within the control of the issuer. There is a major difference between a security with mandatory redemption or whose redemption is outside the control of the issuer and conventional equity capital. The SEC believes future cash obligations attached to this type of security should be highlighted to distinguish it from permanent capital.

Equity instruments with redemption features that are not solely within the control of the issuer must be classified as "temporary equity."

According to the SEC, the initial carrying amount of a redeemable equity instrument should be its issuance date fair value.

For share-based payment arrangement with employees, the amount presented in temporary equity at each balance sheet date should be based on the redemption provisions of the instrument and should take into consideration the proportion of consideration received in the form of employee services.

Disclosures are required for redeemable equity instruments as follows:

- For a redeemable equity instrument that is not adjusted to its redemption amount, the reasons why it is not probable that the instrument will be redeemable.

- Description of the accounting method used to adjust the redemption amount of a redeemable equity instrument.

- If the registrant decides to accrete changes in the redemption amount of a redeemable equity instrument the redemption amount of the equity instrument as if it were currently redeemable.

- Amount credited to equity of the parent upon the subsidiary's deconsolidation.

Stock Retirement

A company may elect to retire its stock. If common stock is retired at par value, the entry is:

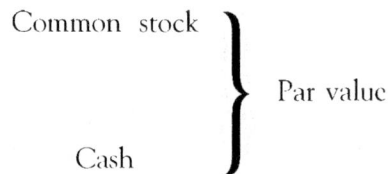

If common stock is retired for less than par value, the entry is:

Common stock

    Cash

    Paid-in capital

If common stock is retired for more than par value, the entry is:

Common stock

Paid-in capital (original premium per share)

Retained earnings (excess over original premium per share)

    Cash

Note: In retirement of stock, retained earnings can only be debited, not credited.

Appropriation of Retained Earnings (Reserve)

The appropriation of retained earnings is the setting aside of retained earnings, making them unavailable for dividends. It indicates the need to restrict asset disbursements to stockholders because of expected major uses or contingencies. Examples include appropriations for sinking fund, plant expansion, debt retirement, and general contingencies (e.g., self-insurance).

    The entry to record an appropriation is:

Retained earnings

    Appropriation of retained earnings

    When the contingency actually takes place, the preceding entry is reversed.

Treasury Stock

Treasury stock is issued shares that have been bought back by the company. The two methods of accounting for treasury stock are:

  1. *Cost Method.* Treasury stock is recorded at the cost to purchase it. If treasury stock is later sold above cost, the entry is:

    Cash

    Treasury stock

    Paid-in capital

If treasury stock is sold instead below cost, the entry is:

Cash

    Paid-in capital—treasury stock (up to amount available)

    Retained earnings (if paid-in capital is unavailable)

      Treasury stock

If treasury stock is donated, only a memo entry is required. When the treasury shares are subsequently sold, the entry based on the market price at that time is:

Cash

    Paid-in-capital—donation

Note: In some states, the corporation laws require an appropriation of retained earnings equal to the cost of treasury stock on hand.

    Treasury stock is shown as a reduction from total stockholders' equity.

  2. *Par Value Method.* Treasury stock is recorded at its par value when bought. If treasury stock is purchased at more than par value, the entry is:

Treasury stock—par value

Paid-in capital—original premium per share

Retained earnings—if necessary

    Cash

If treasury stock is purchased at less than par value, the entry is:

Treasury stock—par value

  Cash

  Paid-in capital

Upon sale of the treasury stock above par value, the entry is:

Cash

  Treasury stock

  Paid-in capital

Upon sale of the treasury stock at less than par value, the entry is:

Cash

Paid-in capital (amount available)

Retained earnings (if paid-in capital is insufficient)

  Treasury stock

An appropriation of retained earnings equal to the cost of the treasury stock on hand is required.

Treasury stock is shown as a contra account to the common stock it applies to under the capital stock section of stockholders' equity.

Quasi-Reorganization

A quasi-reorganization provides a "fresh start" for a financially troubled company with a deficit in retained earnings. A quasi-reorganization is implemented to avoid bankruptcy. Assets are revalued and the deficit is eliminated by reducing paid-in capital:

- Stockholders and creditors must agree to the quasi-reorganization.
- Net assets are reduced to fair market value. If fair value is not readily determinable, then conservative estimates of such value may be made.
- Paid-in capital is reduced to eliminate the deficit in retained earnings. If paid-in capital is insufficient, then capital stock is charged.
- Retained earnings becomes a zero balance. Retained earnings will bear the quasi-reorganization date for 10 years after the reorganization.

The retained earnings account consists of the following components:

Retained Earnings—Unappropriated	
Dividends	Net income
Appropriations	
Prior-period adjustments	

Retained Earnings—Unappropriated	
Quasi-reorganization	

The entry for the quasi-reorganization is:

Paid-in capital

Capital stock (if necessary)

    Assets

    Retained earnings

Caution: If potential losses exist at the readjustment date but the amounts of losses cannot be determined, there should be a provision for the maximum probable loss. If estimates used are later shown to be incorrect, the difference goes to the paid-in capital account.

Note: New or additional common stock or preferred stock may be issued in exchange for existing indebtedness. Thus, the current liability account would be charged for the indebtedness and the capital account credited.

EXAMPLE 46: A business having a $3,500,000 deficit undertakes a quasi-reorganization. There is an overstatement in assets of $800,000 compared to fair market value. The balances in capital stock and paid-in capital are $5,000,000 and $1,500,000 respectively. The following entry is made to effect the quasi-reorganization:

Paid-in capital	1,500,000
Capital stock	2,800,000
Assets	800,000
Retained earnings	3,500,000

Note that the paid-in capital account has been fully wiped out, so the residual debit goes to capital stock.

Dividends

Dividends represent distributions paid out by the company to stockholders. After the date of declaration of a dividend is the date of record. In order to qualify to receive a dividend, a person must be registered as the owner of the stock on the date of record. Several days prior to the date of record, the stock will be selling "ex-dividend." This is done to alert investors that those owning the stock before the record date are eligible to receive the dividend, and that those selling the stock before the record date will lose their rights to the dividend.

A dividend is usually in the form of cash or stock. A dividend is based on the outstanding shares (issued shares less treasury shares).

EXAMPLE 47: Issued shares are 5,000, treasury shares are 1,000, and outstanding shares are therefore 4,000. The par value of the stock is $10 per share. If a $.30 dividend per share is declared, the dividend is:

$$4,000 \times \$.30 = \underline{\$1,200}$$

If the dividend rate is 6%, the dividend is:

4,000 shares × $10 par value =	$40,000
	× .06
	$2,400

Assuming a cash dividend of $2,400 is declared, the entry is:

Retained earnings	2,400	
Cash dividend payable		2,400
No entry is made at the record date.		
The entry at the payment date is:		
Cash dividend payable	2,400	
Cash		2,400

A property dividend is a dividend payable in assets of the company other than cash. When the property dividend is declared, the company restates the distributed asset to fair market value, recognizing any gain or loss as the difference between the fair market value and carrying value of the property at the declaration date.

EXAMPLE 48: A company transfers investments in marketable securities costing $10,000 to stockholders by declaring a property dividend on December 16, 2X11, to be distributed on 1/15/2X12. At the declaration date, the securities have a market value of $14,000. The entries are:

Declaration:

12/16/2X11 investment in securities	4,000	
Gain on appreciation of securities		4,000
Retained earnings	14,000	
Property dividend payable		14,000

Note that the net reduction is still the $10,000 cost of the asset.

Distribution:

1/15/2X12 property dividend payable	14,000	
Investment in securities		14,000

A stock dividend is issued in the form of stock. Stock dividend distributable is shown in the capital stock section of stockholders' equity. It is not a liability. If the stock dividend is less than 20% to 25% of outstanding shares at the declaration date, retained earnings is reduced at the market price of the shares. If the stock dividend is in excess of 20% to 25% of outstanding shares, retained earnings is charged at par value. Between 20% and 25% is a gray area.

EXAMPLE 49: A stock dividend of 10% is declared on 5,000 shares of $10 par value common stock having a market price of $12. The entry at the declaration and issuance dates is as follows:

Retained earnings (500 shares × $12)	6,000	
Stock dividend distributable (500 shares × $10)		5,000
Paid-in capital		1,000
Stock dividend distributable	5,000	
Common stock		5,000

Assuming instead that the stock dividend was 30%, the entries would be:

Retained earnings (5000 × $10)	5,000	
Stock dividend distributable		5,000
Stock dividend distributable	5,000	
Common stock		5,000

A liability dividend (scrip dividend) is payable in the form of a liability (e.g., notes payable). A liability dividend sometimes occurs when a company has financial problems.

EXAMPLE 50: On January 1, 2X11, a liability dividend of $20,000 is declared in the form of a one-year, 8% note. The entry at the declaration date is:

| Retained earnings | 20,000 | |
| Scrip dividend payable | | 20,000 |

When the scrip dividend is paid, the entry is:

Scrip dividend payable	20,000	
Interest expense	1,600	
Cash		21,600

A liquidating dividend can be deceptive as it is not actually a dividend. It is a return of capital and not a distribution of earnings. The entry is to debit paid-in capital and credit dividends payable. The recipient of a liquidating dividend pays no tax on it.

According to Accounting Standards Update (ASU) No. 2010-01 (January 2010), *Equity,* (ASC Topic 505), *Accounting for Distributions to Shareholders with Components of Stock and Cash,* the stock part of a stockholder distribution that permits them to receive stock or cash with a possible restriction of the cash to be received is deemed an issuance of shares. It is not considered a stock dividend. EPS computation will include these distributions. The effective date for this accounting is December 15, 2009.

Stock Splits

In a stock split, the shares are increased and the par value per share is decreased. However, total par value is the same.

Only a memo entry is needed.

EXAMPLE 51: Before: 1,000 shares, $10 par value = $10,000 total par value

2-for-1 stock split declared

After: 2,000 shares, $5 par value = $10,000 total par value

If there were a reverse split, it would have the opposite effect.

Stock-Based Compensation

ASC 718, *Compensation—Stock Compensation*, applies to stock option plans, nonvested stock, employee stock purchase plans, and stock compensation awards that are to be settled by cash payment.

Stock Option Plans. Employers must account for stock option plans using the fair value method as required by ASC 718. The pronouncement improves a company's accounting for its equity-based employee compensation agreements, including share options, restricted share plans, performance-based awards, share appreciation rights, and employee share purchase plans. The pronouncement sets standards to account for transactions in which a company issues its equity instruments for goods or services. ASC 718, *Compensation—Stock Compensation*, concentrates primarily on accounting for transactions in which a company receives employee services in share-based payment transactions.

A company must measure the cost of employee services obtained in exchange for an award of equity instruments based on the grant date fair value of the award using an option-pricing model. That cost is recognized over the period employees render services in exchange for the award (typically the vesting period).

A company will initially measure the cost of employee services in exchange for an award of liability instruments based on its current fair value. The fair value of that award will be remeasured subsequently at each reporting date through the settlement date. Changes in fair value during the requisite service period will be recognized as compensation costs over that period.

Incremental compensation cost for modified terms of an award is measured by comparing the fair value of the modified award with the fair value of the award immediately prior to the modification.

Under the fair value method, fair value is computed by using an option-pricing model that takes into account several factors. A popular option-pricing model is Black-Scholes. It is used to compute the equilibrium value of an option. The model provides insight into the valuation of debt relative to equity, and may be programmed into computer spreadsheets and some pocket calculators. The Black-Scholes model makes it possible to determine the present value of hypothetical financial instruments. Some assumptions of this model are that (1) the stock options are freely traded and (2) the total return rate (considering the change in price plus dividends) may be determined based on a continuous compounding over the life of the option. Under ASC 718, the option life is the expected time period until the option is exercised, rather than the contractual term. By reducing the option's life, its value is reduced. It is a random variable derived from a normal bell curve distribution. The Black-Scholes model was developed based on European-style options exercisable only at expiration. However, most employee stock options are American-style and are exercisable at any time during the options life once vesting has taken place. The Black-Scholes model uses the volatility expected for the option's life. Note: Difficulties arise in determining option values when there is an early option exercise and variability in stock price and dividends. The Black-Scholes model may also be used in valuing put options by modifying computations. See Chapter 38, "Financial Derivative Products and Financial Engineering," for additional information on Black-Scholes.

Other models may be used for option pricing, such as the more complicated binomial model.

Before the current value of an option may be computed, consideration must be given to its expiration value.

Note: Noncompensatory stock option plans may also exist. Such plans are characterized by having stock offered to employees on some basis (e.g., equally, percentage of salary), participation by full-time employees, a reasonable time period for the exercise of the options, and the discount to employees to buy the stock is not better than that afforded to company stockholders. If any of these criteria are not satisfied, the plan is compensatory in nature. The objective of a noncompesatory plan is to obtain funds and to have greater widespread ownership in the company among employees. It is not primarily designed to provide compensation for services performed. Therefore, no compensation expense is recognized.

Nonvested Stock. Nonvested stock is stock that cannot be sold currently because the employee who was granted the shares has not yet satisfied the vesting requirements to earn the right to the shares. The fair value of a share of nonvested stock awarded to an employee is measured at the market price per share of nonrestricted stock on the grant date unless a restriction will be imposed after the employee has a vested right to it, in which case the fair value is approximated considering the restriction.

Employee Stock Purchase Plans. An employee stock purchase plan allows employees to buy stock at a discount. It is noncompensatory if the discount is minor (5% or less), most full-time employees may participate, and the plan has no option features.

Stock Compensation Awards Required to Be Settled by Cash Payment. Some stock-based compensation plans require an employer to pay an employee, either on demand or at a particular date, a cash amount based on the appreciation in the market price of the employer's stock. A ceiling stock price may be established depending on the plan. The compensation cost applicable to the award is the amount of change in stock price.

Accounting Standards Update (ASU) No. 2010-13 (April 2010), Compensation–Stock Compensation (ASC Topic 718), *Effect of Denominating the Exercise Price of a Share-Based Payment Award in the Currency of the Market in Which the Underlying Equity Security Trades,* specifies that liability classification is mandated in the case of a share-based payment award when the condition does not apply to service or performance. A worker share-based award having an exercise price in a currency where a significant amount of the company's stock trades is not deemed a service or performance condition. Hence, liability presentation is not appropriate for the award when equity classification is required. Footnote disclosure should be made of the particulars of the award.

Accounting Standards Update (ASU) No. 2017-09 (May 2017), *Compensation–Stock Compensation (Topic 718), Scope of Modification Accounting*, provides guidance on which changes to the conditions of a share-based payment award require a company to use modification accounting. A firm should use modification accounting unless all of the following are met:

1. The fair value of the modified award is the same as the fair value of the original award.

2. The vesting conditions of the modified award are the same as the original award.

The classification of the modified award as an equity (or liability) instrument is the same as the original award.

Disclosures. The following should be disclosed regarding the fair value method to account for stock options as well as for stock-based compensation plans in general:

- Weighted-average grant date fair value of options and other equity instruments granted during the year.

- A description of the method and assumptions used to estimate fair value of options.

- Major changes in the terms of stock-based compensation plans.

- Amendments to outstanding awards.

Footnote disclosure should be made to help those who use financial statements to understand the nature of share-based payment transactions and the impact of such transactions.

ASC 718, *Compensation—Stock Compensation* (ASC 718-10-50), permits two alternative transition approaches for a voluntary change to the fair value method. These additional methods avoid the ramp-up effect resulting from prospective application of the fair value method. ASC 718-10-50 mandates prominent disclosure in annual and quarterly financial statements about the method to account for stock-based employee compensation and the effect of the method used on net profit. A specific tabular format of information must be presented and disclosed. The three methods encompassed by this pronouncement are (1) prospective, (2) modified prospective, and (3) retroactive restatement.

Accounting Standards Update (ASU) No, 2014-12 (June 2014), *Compensation – Stock Compensation (Topic 718), Accounting for Stock-Based Payments When the Terms of an Award Provide That a Performance Target Could Be Achieved after the Requisite Service Period*, mandates that a performance target that affects vesting and could be accomplished subsequent to the requisite service period should be treated as a performance condition. The performance target should not be reflected in estimating the fair value of the award at the grant date. Compensation cost should be reflected in the year when it becomes probable that the performance target will be accomplished and should represent the compensation cost attributable to the year(s) for which the associated service has already been performed. The total amount of compensation cost recognized during and after the service period should take into account the number of awards anticipated to vest and should be adjusted to consider those awards that ultimately vest. The requisite service period ends when the worker can stop rendering service and still be eligible to vest In the award if the performance target is accomplished.

Tax Aspects. Compensation expense is deductible for tax reporting when paid but deducted for financial reporting when accrued. This results in interperiod income tax allocation involving a deferred income tax credit. If for some reason reversal of the temporary difference does not occur, a permanent difference exists which does not impact profit. The difference should adjust paid-in capital in the year the accrual occurs.

Debt Issued with Stock Warrants. If bonds are issued along with detachable stock warrants, the portion of the proceeds applicable to the warrants is credited to paid-in capital. The basis for allocation is the relative values of the securities at the time of issuance. In the event that the warrants are not detachable, the bonds are accounted for solely as convertible debt. There is no allocation of the proceeds to the conversion feature.

EXAMPLE 52: A $20,000 convertible bond is issued at $21,000 with $1,000 applicable to stock warrants. If the warrants are not detachable, the entry is:

Cash	21,000	
Bonds payable		20,000
Premium on bonds payable		1,000

If the warrants are detachable, the entry is:

Cash	21,000	
Bonds payable		20,000
Paid-in capital-stock warrants		1,000

In the event that the proceeds of the bond issue were only $20,000 instead of $21,000 and $1,000 could be attributable to the warrants, the entry is:

Cash	20,000	
Discount	1,000	
Bonds payable		20,000
Paid-in capital-stock warrants		1,000

Reverse Spinoffs. According to ASC 505, *Equity* (ASC 505-60), a transaction should be treated as a reverse spinoff if the substance of the transaction is most realistic for shareholders by treating a legal spinnee as the accounting spinnor.

Fractional Share Warrants. Fractional share warrants may be issued.

EXAMPLE 53: There are 1,000 shares of $10 par value common stock. The common stock has a market price of $15. A 20% dividend is declared resulting in 200 shares (20% × 1,000). Included in the 200 shares are fractional share warrants. Each warrant equals one-fifth of a share of stock. There are 100 warrants resulting in 20 shares of stock (100/5). Thus, 180 regular shares and 20 fractional shares are involved.

The journal entries follow:

At the declaration date:

Retained earnings (200 shares × 15)	3,000	
Stock dividends distributable (180 shares × 10)		1,800
Fractional share warrants (20 shares × 10)		200
Paid-in capital		1,000

At time of issuance:

Stock dividend distributable	1,800	
Common stock		1,800
Fractional share warrants	200	
Common stock		200

If, instead of all the fractional share warrants being turned in, only 80% were turned in, the entry is:

Fractional share warrants	200	
Common stock		160
Paid-in capital		40

Conversion Spread. As per ASC 470, *Debt* (ASC 470-20-40-12), an issuer should take into account only the *cash* payment when calculating a gain or loss on extinguishment of a liability or convertible debt if the accreted value is settled in cash and the embedded equity instrument (excess conversion spread) are *not* taken into account in calculating the gain or loss.

Indexed to Stock. ASC 815, *Derivatives and Hedging* (ASC 815-40), provides that if an instrument (or embedded feature) that has the characteristics of a derivative instrument is indexed to an entity's own stock, it is still needed to appraise whether it is classified in stockholders' equity (or would be classified in stockholders' equity if it were a freestanding instrument).

A company shall appraise if an equity-linked financial instrument (or embedded feature) is indexed to its own stock using the following two-step approach:

- *Step 1.* Appraise the instrument's contingent exercise provisions, if any.
- *Step 2.* Evaluate the instrument's settlement provisions.

According to Accounting Standards Update (ASU) No. 2010-21 (August 2010), *Accounting for Technical Amendments to Various SEC Rules and Schedules,* in a note or statement, an evaluation should be made of the changes in other stockholders' equity and noncontrolling interests. The opening balance should be reconciled to the closing balance for each year. Disclosure should be made of the change in ownership interest in a subsidiary. (ASC 505-10-S99-1)

In addition, the parent company should provide its investment in its subsidiaries based on its proportionate share of a subsidiary's net assets. (ASC 470-10-S99-1)

A company should consolidate majority-owned entities. In the case of redeemable preferred stock, there should be a description of its redemption provisions (e.g., sinking fund) and the rights. Disclosure should be made of noncontrolling interests in consolidated subsidiaries.

Under IFRS, the issuer of convertible debt issued with stock warrants must record the liability and equity components separately.

Under IFRS, a company has the option of either preparing a statement of stockholders' equity similar to U.S. GAAP or preparing a statement of recognized income and expense (SoRIE). The SoRIE reports the items that were charged directly to equity (e.g., revaluation surplus), and then adds the net income for the year to obtain total recognized income and expense. In this instance, footnote disclosure is made to provide reconciliations of other equity items.

CHAPTER 10

FINANCIAL STATEMENT REPORTING: THE STATEMENT OF CASH FLOWS

CONTENTS

As per ASC 230, *Statement of Cash Flows*, a statement of cash flows is required in the annual report. The objective of the statement is to furnish useful data regarding a company's cash receipts and cash payments for a period. There should exist a reconciliation between net income and net cash flow from operations. In addition, separate reporting is mandated for certain information applicable to noncash investments and financing transactions. This chapter discusses how the statement may be prepared as well as the analytical implications for the financial manager.

PREPARATION OF THE STATEMENT

The statement of cash flows explains the change in cash for the period. The statement of cash flows classifies cash receipts and cash payments as arising from investing, financing, and operating activities.

Investing Activities

Investing activities involve cash flows generally applicable to changes in long-term asset items. Investing activities include purchasing debt and equity securities in other entities, buying and selling fixed assets, and making and collecting loans. Cash inflows from investing comprise (1) receipts from sales of equity or debt securities of other companies, (2) amounts received from disposing of fixed assets, and (3) collections or sales of loans made by the company principal portion. Cash outflows for investing activities include (1) disbursements to buy equity or debt securities of other companies, (2) payments to buy fixed assets, and (3) disbursements for loans made by the company.

Note: Activities related to acquisition or sale of a business or part thereof are investing items.

Caution: Gains or losses on sales of noncurrent assets are included as investing activities along with the assets to which they relate. These gains or losses are not included in net cash flow from operating items. Thus, they are an adjustment to net income in obtaining cash flow from operations.

Financing Activities

Financing activities include cash flows generally resulting from changes in long-term liabilities and stockholders' equity items. Included in financing activities are receiving equity funds, furnishing owners with a return on their investment, debt financing, and repayment or settlement of debt. Another element is obtaining and paying for other resources derived from creditors on noncurrent credit. Cash inflows from financing activities are composed of (1) funds received from the sale of stock and (2) funds obtained from the incurrence of debt. Cash outflows for financing activities include (1) paying off debt, (2) repurchase of stock, (3) dividend payments, and (4) other principal payments to long-term creditors.

Note: Stock dividends, stock splits, and appropriations of retained earnings are not included as financing activities because they do not use cash. They are intra-stockholder equity transactions.

Caution: Gains or losses from the early extinguishment of debt are part of the cash flow related to the repayment of the amount borrowed as a financing activity. Such gains or losses are not an element of net cash flow from operating activities.

Operating Activities

Operating activities relate to manufacturing and selling goods or the rendering of services. They do not apply to investing or financing functions.

Cash flow derived from operating activities typically applies to the cash effects of transactions entering into profit computations. Cash inflows from operating activities include:

- Cash sales or collections on receivables arising from the initial sale of merchandise or rendering of service; Cash receipts from returns on loans, debt securities (e.g., interest income), or equity securities (e.g., dividend income) of other entities;

- Cash received from licensees and lessees;
- Receipt of a litigation settlement; and
- Reimbursement under an insurance policy.

Cash outflows for operating activities include:

- Cash paid for raw material or merchandise for resale;
- Principal payments on accounts payable arising from the initial purchase of goods;
- Payments to suppliers of operating expense items (e.g., office supplies, advertising, insurance);
- Wages;
- Payments to governmental agencies (e.g., taxes, penalties);
- Interest expense;
- Lawsuit payment;
- Charitable contributions; and
- Cash refunds to customers for defective merchandise.

Additional breakdowns of operating cash receipts and disbursements may be made to enhance financial reporting. For example, a manufacturing company may divide cash paid to suppliers into payments applicable to inventory acquisition and payments for selling expenses.

ASC 410, *Asset Retirement and Environmental Obligations* (ASC 410-20), provides that a cash payment to pay off an asset retirement obligation should be presented under operating activities.

Other Considerations

There should be a separate presentation within the statement of cash flows of cash inflows and cash outflows from investing and financing activities. For example, the purchase of fixed assets is an application of cash, whereas the sale of a fixed asset is a source of cash. Both are shown separately to aid analysis by readers of the financial statements. Debt incurrence would be a source of cash, but debt payment would be an application of cash. Thus, cash received of $800,000 from debt incurrence would be shown as a source, and the payment of debt of $250,000 would be presented as an application. The net effect is $550,000.

Separate disclosure shall be made of investing and financing activities impacting upon assets or liabilities that do not affect cash flow. Examples of noncash activities of an investing and financing nature are bond conversion, purchase of a fixed asset by the incurrence of a mortgage payable, capital lease, and nonmonetary exchange of assets. This disclosure may be footnoted or shown in a schedule. An illustrative presentation is as follows:

Net increase in cash	$980,000
Noncash investing and financing activities:	
Purchase of land by the issuance of common stock	$400,000

Conversion of bonds payable to common stock	<u>200,000</u>
	<u>$600,000</u>

If a cash receipt or cash payment applies to more than one classification (investing, financing, operating), classification is made as to the activity that is the main source of that cash flow. For instance, the purchase and sale of equipment to be used by the company is typically construed as an investing activity.

In the case of foreign currency cash flows, the exchange rate at the time of the cash flow should be used in reporting the currency equivalent of foreign currency cash flows. The effect of changes in the exchange rate on cash balances held in foreign currencies should be reported as a separate element of the reconciliation of the change in cash and cash equivalents for the period.

Cash flow per share shall not be shown in the financial statements because it will detract from the importance of the earnings-per-share statistic.

As per Accounting Standards Update (ASU) No. 2016-15 (August 2016), *Statement of Cash Flows* (Topic 230), *Classification of Certain Cash Receipts and Cash Payments,* cash paid to repay debt or for debt extinguishment costs are classified in the financing activities section.

Cash payments made shortly after the acquisition date of a business combination by the acquirer to satisfy a contingent liability consideration should be shown in the investing section. If the cash paid is not made soon after the acquisition date for such contingent consideration, the cash paid should be separated for financing and operating activities.

Cash received from an insurance settlement should be classified based on the related insurance coverage tied to the nature of the loss.

Cash received from settling a company-owned life insurance policy should be presented in the operating section.

Regarding distributions received from equity method investees, the cumulative earnings approach provides generally that distributions received are considered returns on investment and are classified as cash inflows from operating activities.

A transferor's beneficial interest obtained in a securitization of financial assets should be disclosed as a noncash activity. Cash received due to payments on the beneficial interests in securitization trade receivables should be shown as cash inflows from investing activities.

According to Accounting Standards Update (ASU) No. 2016-18 (November 2016), *Statement of Cash Flows* (Topic 230), *Restricted Cash Flow,* a Statement of Cash Flows must explain the change during the year in total cash, cash equivalents, and amounts generally described as restricted cash or restricted cash equivalents.

Direct Method versus Indirect Method

The direct method is preferred in that companies should report cash flows from operating activities by major classes of gross cash receipts and gross cash payments and the resulting net amount in the operating section. A reconciliation of net income to cash flow from operating activities should be shown in a separate schedule after the body of the statement.

Note: This schedule has the same net result as gross cash receipts and cash payments from operating activities.

Although the direct method is preferred, a company has the option of using the indirect (reconciliation) method. In practice, most companies are using the indirect method because of its easier preparation. Under the indirect method, the company reports net cash flow from operating activities indirectly by adjusting profit to reconcile it to net cash flow from operating activities. This is shown in the operating section within the body of the statement of cash flows or in a separate schedule. If presented in a separate schedule, the net cash flow from operating activities is presented as a single line item. The adjustment to reported earnings for noncash revenues and expenses involves:

- Effects of deferrals of past operating cash receipts and cash payments (e.g., changes in inventory and deferred revenue) and accumulations of expected future operating cash receipts and cash payments (e.g., changes in receivables and payables).

- Effects of items whose cash impact applies to investing or financing cash flows (e.g., depreciation, amortization expense, gain or loss on the retirement of debt, and gain or loss on the sale of fixed assets).

The basic difference in statement presentation between the direct and indirect method relates solely to the operating section. Under the direct method, the operating section presents gross cash receipts and gross cash payments from operating activities with a reconciliation of net income to cash flow from operations in a separate schedule. Under the indirect method, gross cash receipts and gross cash payments from operating activities are not shown. Instead, only the reconciliation of net income to cash flow from operations is shown in the operating section or in a separate schedule with the final figure of cash flow from operations presented as a single line item in the operating section.

The indirect method is the one commonly used in practice. Exhibit 10-1 presents the reconciliation process of net income to cash flow from operating activities.

Exhibit 10-2 shows a skeleton outline of the indirect method.

Exhibit 10-1: Indirect Method of Computing Cash Provided by Operations

	Add (+) or deduct (–) to adjust net income
Net income	$XXX
Adjustments required to convert net income to cash basis:	
Depreciation, depletion, amortization expense, and loss on sale of noncurrent assets	+
Amortization of deferred revenue, amortization of bond premium, and gain on sale of noncurrent assets	–

	Add (+) or deduct (−) to adjust net income
Add (deduct) changes in current asset accounts affecting revenue or expenses (a)	
Increase in the account	−
Decrease in the account	+
Add (deduct) changes in current liability accounts affecting revenue or expense (b)	
Increase in the account	+
Decrease in the account	−
Add (deduct) changes in the deferred income	
Taxes account	
Increase in the account	+
Decrease in the account	−
Cash provided by operations	$XXX

(a) Examples include accounts receivable, accrued receivables, inventory, and prepaid expenses.

(b) Examples include accounts payable, accrued liabilities, and deferred revenue.

Exhibit 10-2: Format of the Statement of Cash Flows (Indirect Method)

Net cash flow from operating activities:		
Net income	x	
Adjustments for noncash expenses, revenues, losses, and gains included in income:	x	
	(x)	
Net cash flow from operating activities		x
Cash flows from investing activities:	x	
	(x)	
Net cash flows provided (used) by investing activities		x
Cash flows from financing activities:	x	
	(x)	
Net cash provided (used) by financing activities		x
Net increase (decrease) in cash		—
Schedule of noncash investing and financing activities:		xx
	x	
	x	

FINANCIAL ANALYSIS OF THE STATEMENT

An analysis of the statement of cash flows will provide financial managers with essential information about the company's cash receipts and cash payments for a period as they apply to operating, investing, and financing activities. The statement assists in the appraisal of the effect on the firm's financial position of cash and noncash investing and financing transactions.

Comparative statements of cash flows must be analyzed in detail because they hold clues to a company's earnings quality, risk, and liquidity. Comparative statements show the degree of repeatability of the company's sources of funds, their costs, and whether such sources may be relied upon in future years. Uses of funds for growth as well as for maintaining competitive share are revealed. An analysis of comparative statements of cash flows holds the key to a full and reliable analysis of corporate financial health in the present and future. It aids in planning future ventures and financing needs. Comparative data help managerial accountants identify abnormal or cyclical factors as well as changes in the relationships among each flow component.

The statement serves as a basis to forecast earnings based on plant, property, and equipment posture. It assists in evaluating growth potential and incorporates cash flow requirements, highlighting specific fund sources and future means of payment. Will the company be able to meet its obligations and pay cash dividends?

The statement reveals the type and degree of financing required to expand long-term assets and to bolster operations.

The financial executive should calculate for analytical purposes cash flow per share equal to net cash flow divided by the number of shares. A high ratio is desirable because it indicates the company is in a very liquid position.

A discussion of the analysis of the operating, investing, and financing sections of the statement of cash flows follows.

Operating Section

An analysis of the operating section of the statement of cash flows enables the financial manager to determine the adequacy of cash flow from operating activities to satisfy company requirements. Can the firm obtain positive future net cash flows? The reconciliation tracing net income to net cash flow from operating activities should be examined to see the effect of noncash revenue and noncash expense items.

An award under a lawsuit is a cash inflow from operating activities that results in a nonrecurring source of revenue.

An operating cash outlay for refunds given to customers for deficient goods indicates a quality problem with the firm's merchandise.

Payments of penalties, fines, and lawsuit damages are operating cash outflows that show poor management in that a problem arose that required a nonbeneficial expenditure to the organization.

Investing Section

An analysis of the investing section of the statement of cash flows enables identifying an investment in another company that may point to an attempt for eventual control for diversification purposes. It may also indicate a change in future direction or change in business philosophy.

An increase in fixed assets indicates capital expansion and growth. The financial executive should determine which assets have been bought. Are they assets for risky (specialized) ventures or are they stable (multipurpose) ones? This provides a clue as to risk potential and expected return. The nature of the assets signals future direction and earning potential of product lines, business segments, and dimensions of the business. Are these directions sound and viable?

The financial manager should ascertain whether there is a contraction in the business arising from the sale of fixed assets without adequate replacement. Is the problem corporate (e.g., product line is weakening) or industrywide (e.g., industry is on the downturn)? If corporate, management is not optimistic regarding the future. Nonrecurring gains may occur because of the sale of low-cost-basis fixed assets (e.g., land). Such gains cause temporary increases in profits above normal levels and represent low quality of earnings sources. They should be discounted by the analyst.

Financing Section

An appraisal of the financing section will help the financial manager form an opinion of the company's ability to obtain financing in the money and capital markets as well as its ability to satisfy its obligations. The financial mixture of equity, bonds, and long-term bank loans impact the cost of financing. A major advantage of debt is the tax deductibility of interest. However, dividends on stock are not tax deductible. In inflation, paying debt back in cheaper dollars will result in purchasing power gains. The risk of debt financing is the required repayment of principal and interest. Will the company have the needed funds at maturity? The financial manager must evaluate the stability of the fund source to ascertain whether it may be relied upon in the future, even in a tight money market. Otherwise, there may be problems in maintaining corporate operations in a recession. The question is: Where can the company go for funds during times of cash squeeze?

By appraising the financing sources, the financing preferences of management are revealed. Is there an inclination toward risk or safety? Creditors favor equity issuances because they protect their loans. Excessive debt may be a problem during economic downturn.

The ability of a company to finance with the issuance of common stock on attractive terms (high stock price) indicates that investors are positive about the financial health of the entity.

The issuance of preferred stock may be a negative indicator because it may mean the company has a problem issuing common stock.

An appraisal should be made of the company's ability to meet debt. Excessive debt means greater corporate risk. The problem is acute if earnings are unstable or dropping. On the contrary, the reduction in long-term debt is favorable because it lessens corporate risk.

A financing cash outflow for the early extinguishment of debt will result in a gain or loss resulting in a one-time earnings impact.

The financial manager should appraise the firm's dividend-paying ability. Stockholders favor a company with a high dividend payout.

Is there a purchase of treasury stock resulting in an artificial increase in earnings per share?

Schedule of Noncash Financing and Investing Activities

A bond conversion is a positive signal about the entity's financial health since it indicates that bondholders are optimistic about the firm's financial well-being and/ or the market price of stock has increased. A conversion of preferred stock to common stock is also favorable because it shows preferred stockholders are impressed with the company's future and are willing to have a lower priority in liquidation.

Bond and preferred stock conversions affect the existing position of long-term creditors and stockholders. For example, a reduction in debt by conversion to stock protects to a greater degree the loans of the remaining bond holders and banks.

COMPREHENSIVE EXAMPLES

Current profitability is only one important factor for corporate success. Also essential are the current and future cash flows. In fact, a profitable company may have a cash crisis.

Management is responsible for planning how and when cash will be used and obtained. When planned expenditures necessitate more cash than planned activities are likely to produce, managers must decide what to do. They may decide to obtain debt or equity financing or to dispose of some fixed assets or a whole business segment. Alternatively, they may decide to cut back on planned activities by modifying operational plans, such as ending a special advertising campaign or delaying new acquisitions. Or, they may decide to revise planned payments to financing sources, such as delaying bond repayment or reducing dividends. Whatever is decided, the managers' goal is to balance, over the short and the long term, the cash available, and the needs for cash.

Managerial planning is aided by evaluating the statement of cash flows in terms of coordinating dividend policy with other corporate activities, financial planning for new products and types of assets needed, strengthening a weak cash posture and credit availability, and ascertaining the feasibility and implementation of existing top management plans.

The analysis and evaluation of the statement of cash flows is essential if the analyst is to properly appraise an entity's cash flows from operating, investing, and financing activities. The company's liquidity and solvency positions as well as future directions are revealed. Inadequacy in cash flow has possible serious implications, as it may lead to declining profitability, greater financial risk, and even bankruptcy.

EXAMPLE 1: X Company provides the following financial statements:

X Company
Comparative Balance Sheets
December 31
(In Millions)

	20X6	20X5
Assets:		
Cash	$ 40	$ 47
Accounts receivable	30	35
Prepaid expenses	4	2
Land	50	35
Building	100	80
Accumulated depreciation	(9)	(6)
Equipment	50	42
Accumulated depreciation	(11)	(7)
Total assets	$254	$228
Liabilities and stockholders' equity:		
Accounts payable	$ 20	$ 16
Long-term notes payable	30	20
Common stock	100	100
Retained earnings	104	92
Total liabilities and stockholders' equity	$254	$228

X Company
Income Statement
for the Year Ended December 31, 2X12
(In Millions)

Revenue		$300
Operating expenses (excluding depreciation)	$200	
Depreciation	7	207
Income from operations		$ 93
Income tax expense		32
Net income		$ 61

Additional Information:

1. Cash dividends paid: $49.
2. The company issued long-term notes payable for cash.
3. Land, building, and equipment were acquired for cash.

We can now prepare the Statement of Cash Flows under the indirect method as follows:

X Company
Statement of Cash Flows
for the Year Ended December 31, 2X12
(In Millions)

Income from operations		$ 93
Cash flow from operating activities		
Net income		$ 61
Add (deduct) items not affecting cash		
Depreciation expense	$ 7	
Decrease in accounts receivable	5	
Increase in prepaid expenses	(2)	
Increase in accounts payable	4	14
Net cash flow from operating activities		$ 75
Cash flow from investing activities		
Purchase of land	($15)	
Purchase of building	(20)	
Purchase of equipment	(8)	(43)
Cash flow from financing activities		
Issuance of long-term notes payable	$ 10	
Payment of cash dividends	(49)	(39)
Net decrease in cash		$ (7)

A financial analysis of the statement of cash flows reveals that the profitability and operating cash flow of X Company improved. This indicates good earnings performance as well as the fact that earnings are backed up by cash. The decrease in accounts receivable may reveal better collection efforts. The increase in accounts payable is a sign that suppliers are confident in the company and willing to give interest-free financing. The acquisition of land, building, and equipment points to a growing business undertaking capital expansion. The issuance of long-term notes payable indicates that part of the financing of assets is through debt. Stockholders will be happy with the significant dividend payout of 80% (dividends divided by net income, or $49/$61). Overall, there was a decrease in cash of $7. However, this should not cause alarm because of the company's profitability and the fact that cash was used for capital expansion and dividend payments. The dividend payout should be reduced from its high level and the funds reinvested in the profitable business.

Also, the curtailment of dividends by more than $7 would result in a positive net cash flow for the year. Cash flow is needed for immediate liquidity needs.

EXAMPLE 2: Y Company presents the following statement of cash flows:

Y Company
Statement of Cash Flows
for the Year Ended December 31, 2X11

Cash flows from operating activities		
Net income		$134,000
Add (deduct) items not affecting cash		
Depreciation expense	$21,000	
Decrease in accounts receivable	10,000	
Increase in prepaid expenses	(6,000)	
Increase in accounts payable	35,000	60,000
Net cash flow from operating activities		$194,000
Cash flows from investing activities		
Purchase of land	$(70,000)	
Purchase of building	(200,000)	
Purchase of equipment	(68,000)	
Cash used by investing activities		(338,000)
Cash flows from financing activities		
Issuance of bonds	150,000	
Payment of cash dividends	(18,000)	
Cash provided by financing activities		132,000
Net decrease in cash		$(12,000)

An analysis of the statement of cash flows reveals that the company is profitable. Also, cash flow from operating activities exceeds net income, which indicates good internal cash generation. The ratio of cash flow from operating activities to net income is a solid 1.45 ($194,000/$134,000). A high ratio is desirable because it shows that earnings are backed up by cash. The decline in accounts receivable could indicate better collection efforts. The increase in accounts payable shows the company can obtain interest-free financing. The company is definitely in the process of expanding for future growth as evidenced by the purchase of land, building, and equipment. The debt position of the company has increased, indicating greater risk. The dividend payout was 13.4% ($18,000/$134,000). Stockholders look positively on a firm that pays dividends. The decrease in cash flow for the year of $12,000 is a negative sign.

EXAMPLE 3: Summarized below is financial information for the current year for Company M, which provides the basis for the statements of cash flows:

Company M
Consolidated Statement of Financial Position

	1/1/2X11	*12/31/2X11*	*Change*
Assets:			
Cash	$ 600	$ 1,665	$1,065
Accounts receivable (net of allowance for losses of $600 and $450)	1,770	1,940	170
Notes receivable	400	150	(250)
Inventory	1,230	1,375	145
Prepaid expenses	110	135	25
Investments	250	275	25
Property, plant, and equipment, at cost	6,460	8,460	2,000
Accumulated depreciation	(2,100)	(2,300)	(200)
Property, plant, and equipment, net	4,360	6,160	1,800
Intangible assets	40	175	135
Total assets	$8,760	$11,875	$3,115
Liabilities:			
Accounts payable and accrued expenses	$1,085	1,090	$5
Interest payable	30	45	15
Income taxes payable	50	85	35
Short-term debt	450	750	300
Lease obligation	–	725	725
Long-term debt	2,150	2,425	275
Deferred taxes	375	525	150
Other liabilities	225	275	50
Total liabilities	4,365	5,920	1,555
Stockholders' equity:			
Capital stock	2,000	3,000	1,000
Retained earnings	2,395	2,955	560
Total stockholders' equity	4,395	5,955	1,560
Total liabilities and stockholders' equity	$8,760	$11,875	$3,115

Source: Statement of Financial Accounting Standards No. 95, *Statement of Cash Flows,* 1987, Appendix C, Example 1, pp. 44–51. Reprinted with permission of the Financial Accounting Standards Board.

Company M
Consolidated Statement of Income
for the Year Ended December 31, 2X11

Sales	$13,965
Cost of sales	(10,290)
Depreciation and amortization	(445)
Selling, general, and administrative expenses	(1,890)
Interest expense	(235)
Equity in earnings of affiliate	45
Gain on sale of facility	80
Interest income	55
Insurance proceeds	15
Loss from patent infringement lawsuit	(30)
Income before income taxes	1,270
Provision for income taxes	(510)
Net income	$ 760

The following transactions were entered into by Company M during 2X11 and are reflected in the preceding financial statements:

a. Company M wrote off $350 of accounts receivable when a customer filed for bankruptcy. A provision for losses on accounts receivable of $200 was included in Company M's selling, general, and administrative expenses.

b. Company M collected the third and final annual installment payment of $100 on a note receivable for the sale of inventory and collected the third of four annual installment payments of $150 each on a note receivable for the sale of a plant. Interest on these notes through December 31 totaling $55 was also collected.

c. Company M received a dividend of $20 from an affiliate accounted for under the equity method of accounting.

d. Company M sold a facility with a book value of $520 and an original cost of $750 for $600 cash.

e. Company M constructed a new facility for its own use and placed it in service. Accumulated expenditures during the year of $1,000 included capitalized interest of $10.

f. Company M entered into a capital lease for new equipment with a fair value of $850. Principal payments under the lease obligation totaled $125.

g. Company M purchased all of the capital stock of Company S for $950. The acquisition was recorded under the purchase method of accounting. The fair values of Company S's assets and liabilities at the date of acquisition are as follows:

Cash	$ 25
Accounts receivable	155
Inventory	350
Property, plant, and equipment	900
Patents	80
Goodwill	70
Accounts payable and accrued expenses	(255)
Long-term note payable	(375)
Net assets acquired	$950

h. Company M borrowed and repaid various amounts under a line-of-credit agreement in which borrowings are payable 30 days after demand. The net increase during the year in the amount borrowed against the line-of-credit totaled $300.

i. Company M issued $400 of long-term debt securities.

j. Company M's provision for income taxes included a deferred provision of $150.

k. Company M's depreciation totaled $430, and amortization of intangible assets totaled $15.

l. Company M's selling, general, and administrative expenses included an accrual for incentive compensation of $50 that has been deferred by executives until their retirement. The related obligation was included in other liabilities.

m. Company M collected insurance proceeds of $15 from a business interruption claim that resulted when a storm precluded shipment of inventory for one week.

n. Company M paid $30 to settle a lawsuit for patent infringement.

o. Company M issued $1,000 of additional common stock of which $500 was issued for cash and $500 was issued upon conversion of long-term debt.

p. Company M paid dividends of $200.

Based on the financial data from the preceding example, the following computations illustrate a method of indirectly determining cash received from customers and cash paid to suppliers and employees for use in a statement of cash flows under the direct method:

Cash received from customers during the year:

Customer sales	$13,965
Collection of installment payment for sale of inventory	100

Gross accounts receivable at beginning of year		
Accounts receivable acquired in		$ 2,370
purchase of Company S		155
Accounts receivable written off		(350)
Gross accounts receivable at end of year		(2,390)
Excess of new accounts receivable over collections from customers		(215)
Cash received from customers during the year		$13,850

Cash paid to suppliers and employees during the year:

Cost of sales		$10,290
General and administrative expenses		$ 1,890
Expenses not requiring cash outlay (provision for uncollectible accounts receivable)		(200)
Net expenses requiring cash payments		1,690
Inventory at beginning of year		(1,230)
Inventory acquired in purchase of Company S		(350)
Inventory at end of year		1,375
Net decrease in inventory from Company M's operations		(205)
Adjustments for changes in related accruals:		
Account balances at beginning of year		
Accounts payable and accrued expenses	$ 1,085	
Other liabilities	225	
Prepaid expenses	(110)	
Total		1,200
Accounts payable and accrued expenses acquired in purchase of Company S		255
Account balances at end of year		
Accounts payable and accrued expenses	1,090	
Other liabilities	275	
Prepaid expenses	(135)	
Total		(1,230)
Additional cash payments not included in expense		225
Cash paid to suppliers and employees during the year		$12,000

Following is a statement of cash flows for the year ended December 31, 2X11 for Company M. This statement of cash flows illustrates the direct method of presenting cash flows from operating activities.

Company M
Consolidated Statement of Cash Flows
for the Year Ended December 31, 2X11
Increase (Decrease) in Cash and Cash Equivalents

Cash flows from operating activities:		
Cash received from customers	$13,850	
Cash paid to suppliers and employees	(12,000)	
Dividend received from affiliate	20	
Interest received	55	
Interest paid (net of amount capitalized)	(220)	
Income taxes paid	(325)	
Insurance proceeds received	15	
Cash paid to settle lawsuit for patent infringement	(30)	
Net cash provided by operating activities		$1,365
Cash flows from investing activities:		
Proceeds from sale of facility	600	
Payment received on note for sale of plant	150	
Capital expenditures	(1,000)	
Payment for purchase of Company S, net of cash acquired	(925)	
Net cash used in investing activities		(1,175)
Cash flows from financing activities:		
Net borrowings under line-of-credit agreement	300	
Principal payments under capital lease obligation	(125)	
Proceeds from issuance of long-term debt	400	
Proceeds from issuance of common stock	500	
Dividends paid	(200)	
Net cash provided by financing activities		875
Net increase in cash and cash equivalents		1,065
Cash and cash equivalents at beginning of year		600
Cash and cash equivalents at end of year		$1,665

Reconciliation of net income to net cash provided by operating activities:

Net income	$ 760	
Adjustments to reconcile net income to net cash provided by operating activities:		
Depreciation and amortization	$ 445	
Provision for losses on accounts receivable	200	
Gain on sale of facility	(80)	
Undistributed earnings of affiliate	(25)	
Payment received on installment note receivable for sale of inventory	100	
Change in assets and liabilities net of effects from purchase of Company S:		
Increase in accounts receivable	(215)	
Decrease in inventory	205	
Increase in prepaid expenses	(25)	
Decrease in accounts payable and accrued expenses	(250)	
Increase in interest and income taxes payable so		
Increase in deferred taxes	150	
Increase in other liabilities	50	
Total adjustments		605
Net cash provided by operating activities		$1,365

Supplemental schedule of noncash investing and financing activities:

The Company purchased all of the capital stock of Company S for $950. In conjunction with the acquisition, liabilities were assumed as follows:

Fair value of assets acquired	$1,580
Cash paid for the capital stock	(950)
Liabilities assumed	$ 630

A capital lease obligation of $850 was incurred when the Company entered into a lease for new equipment.

Additional common stock was issued upon the conversion of $500 of long-term debt.

Disclosure of accounting policy:

For purposes of the statement of cash flows, the Company considers all highly liquid debt instruments purchased with a maturity of three months or less to be cash equivalents.

Following is Company M's statement of cash flows for the year ended December 31, 2X11, prepared using the indirect method.

Company M
Consolidated Statement of Cash Flows
for the Year Ended December 31, 2X11
Increase (Decrease) in Cash and Cash Equivalents

Cash flows from operating activities:		
Net income		$ 760
Adjustments to reconcile net income to net cash provided by operating activities:		
Depreciation and amortization	$ 445	
Provision for losses on accounts receivable	200	
Gain on sale of facility	(80)	
Undistributed earnings of affiliate	(25)	
Payment received on installment note receivable for sale of inventory	100	
Change in assets and liabilities net of effects from purchase of Company S:		
Increase in accounts receivable	(215)	
Decrease in inventory	205	
Increase in prepaid expenses	(25)	
Decrease in accounts payable and accrued expenses	(250)	
Increase in interest and income taxes payable	50	
Increase in deferred taxes	150	
Increase in other liabilities	50	
Total adjustments		605
Net cash provided by operating activities		$1,365
Cash flows from investing activities:		
Proceeds from sale of facility	600	
Payment received on note for sale of plant	150	
Capital expenditures	(1,000)	
Payment for purchase of Company S, net of cash acquired	(925)	
Net cash used in investing activities		(1,175)
Cash flows from financing activities:		
Net borrowings under line-of-credit agreement	300	
Principal payments under capital lease obligation	(125)	
Proceeds from issuance of long-term debt	400	
Proceeds from issuance of common stock	500	
Dividends paid	(200)	
Net cash provided by financing activities		875

Net increase in cash and cash equivalents	1,065
Cash and cash equivalents at beginning of year	600
Cash and cash equivalents at end of year	$1,665

Supplemental disclosures of cash flow information:

Cash paid during the year for:

Interest (net of amount capitalized)	$ 220
Income taxes	325

Supplemental schedule of noncash investing and financing activities:

The Company purchased all of the capital stock of Company S for $950. In conjunction with the acquisition, liabilities were assumed as follows:

Fair value of assets acquired	$ 1,580
Cash paid for the capital stock	(950)
Liabilities assumed	$ 630

A capital lease obligation of $850 was incurred when the Company entered into a lease for new equipment.

Additional common stock was issued upon the conversion of $500 of long-term debt.

Disclosure of accounting policy:

For purposes of the statement of cash flows, the Company considers all highly liquid debt instruments purchased with a maturity of three months or less to be cash equivalents.

INTERNATIONAL FINANCIAL REPORTING STANDARDS

IFRS mandates a statement of cash flows with classifications for operating, investing, and financing. In certain instances, bank overdrafts are deemed part of cash and cash equivalents (which is not the case under U.S. GAAP). U.S. GAAP considers bank overdrafts to be financing activities.

Under IFRS, interest and dividends received as well as interest payments are considered operating or investing activities, but U.S. GAAP only considers them to be operating activities. Dividends paid are considered to be operating or financing activities under IFRS but are only deemed financing activities under U.S. GAAP. Finally, income taxes paid are considered operating, investing, or financing activities under IFRS but are only considered operating activities for U.S. GAAP.

IFRS mandates that noncash investing and financing activities be excluded from the statement of cash flows. Instead, these noncash activities are disclosed in the footnotes. Under U.S. GAAP this information may appear either at the bottom of the cash flow statement or in a separate note.

CHAPTER 11

ACCOUNTING AND DISCLOSURES

CONTENTS

This chapter discusses the accounting for changes in principle, estimate, and reporting entity. Corrections of errors are also delved into. The accounting requirements for development stage companies are mentioned. In a troubled debt situation, the debtor wants relief from the creditor. Noninterest-bearing notes and futures contracts are presented. Disclosure about financial instruments with off-balance- sheet risk are discussed.

ACCOUNTING CHANGES

The types of accounting changes provided for in ASC 250, *Accounting Changes and Error Corrections*, are principle, estimate, and reporting entity. Proper disclosure of accounting changes is necessary.

Change in Accounting Principle

Once adopted, it is presumed that an accounting principle should not be changed for events or transactions of a similar nature. A method used for a transaction that is being terminated or was a single, nonrecurring event in the past should not be changed. Only where necessary should a change in principle be made.

Footnote disclosure should be made of the nature and justification of a change in principle and should include an explanation of why the new principle is preferred. Proper justification may take the form of a new FASB pronouncement, new tax law, new AICPA recommended practice, a change in circumstances, and a change to conform more readily to industry practice.

If an accounting change in principle is deemed immaterial in the current year but is expected to be material in later years, disclosure is necessary.

Not considered changes in accounting principle are:

- A principle adopted for the first time on new or previously immaterial events or transactions.

- A principle adopted or changed owing to events or transactions that are clearly different in substance.

ASC 250 mandates retrospective application of changes in accounting principle to previous years' financial statements, unless either the cumulative effect of the change or the period-specific effect cannot be determined. Retrospective application is the application of a different accounting method to prior years as if that new principle had always been used. If it is not practical to ascertain the period-specific impact of a change in accounting principle on previous periods, the newly adopted accounting method must be applied to the beginning balances of assets or liabilities of the earliest period for practical retrospective application. Additionally, a corresponding adjustment must be made to the beginning balance of retained earnings (or other appropriate equity components or net assets) for that period; it is not to be reported in the income statement. In the event that the cumulative dollar impact of applying an accounting principle change to previous periods is impractical, the new accounting method must be applied as if it were adopted prospectively from the earliest practical date.

It is deemed impractical to apply the effect of a change in principle retrospectively only when any of the following three conditions exists:

1. After a good faith effort, the entity is unable to apply the pronouncement's requirement.

2. The entity is unable to verify management's presumptive intent in a prior year.

3. Management is unable to objectively estimate amounts required that:

a. Would have been available in the previous year, and

b. Provides proof of circumstances that existed on the date(s) when the amounts would be recognized, measured, or disclosed under retrospective application.

Note: If any of the three conditions exists, it is not practical to use the retrospective approach. Rather, the new accounting method is applied prospectively as of the earliest date that it is practical to do so.

An example of an impractical situation is the change to the LIFO method. In this event, the base-year inventory for all later LIFO computations is the beginning inventory in the year the method is adopted. It is impractical to restate prior years' income. A LIFO restatement has assumptions—which usually result in computing a number of different earnings figures—as to the different years the layers occurred. The only adjustment needed may be to restate the beginning inventory to a cost basis from a lower of cost or market value approach. Therefore, disclosure is limited to showing the effect of the change on the operating results in the year of change.

ASC 250 requires that retrospective application to a change in accounting principle be limited to the direct effects of the change (e.g., net of tax). An example of a change in accounting principle is switching from the average cost inventory method to the FIFO method. Indirect effects of a change in principle are recognized in the year of change. An example of indirect effects of a change in principle is changing profit-sharing payments because of an accounting change.

A change in amortization, depreciation, or depletion is treated as a change in estimate effected by a change in principle.

The retained earnings statement after a retroactive change for a change in accounting method is as follows:

Retained earnings—1/1, as previously reported

Add: Adjustment for the cumulative effect on prior years of applying, retrospectively, the new accounting principle for long-term construction contracts

Retained earnings—1/1, as adjusted

Following is an example of the retrospective accounting approach when previous years are presented.

EXAMPLE 1: Prior to 2X11, ABC Construction Company used the completed contract method for construction contracts. In 2X11, the company changed to the percentage-of-completion method. The tax rate is 30%. The following data are given:

| | Before Tax Income from | |
	Percentage-of-Completion	Completed Contract
Before 2X11	$600,000	$400,000
In 2X11	180,000	160,000

| | Before Tax Income from | |
	Percentage-of-Completion	Completed Contract
Total at beginning of 2X11	780,000	560,000
Total in 2X11	200,000	190,000

The basis for the journal entry to record the change in 2006 is:

	Difference	Tax (30%)	Net of Tax
Before 2X11	$200,000	$60,000	$140,000
In 2X11	20,000	6,000	14,000
Total at beginning of 2X11	220,000	66,000	154,000
Total in 2X11	10,000	3,000	7,000

The journal entry to record the change in 2X11 is:

Construction-in-Progress	220,000	
Deferred Tax Liability		66,000
Retained Earnings		154,000

Footnote disclosures for a change in accounting method are as follows:

- The cumulative effect of the change on retained earnings as of the start of the earliest period presented.

- New principle used.

- Per share amounts for the current year and prior years retrospectively adjusted.

- Description of previous year data that were retrospectively adjusted.

- The effect of the change on income from continuing operations, net income, and any other impacted financial statement line item.

- With respect to indirect effects of a change in accounting method, a description of such indirect effects, including the amounts that have been recognized in the current year and the related per-share amounts. Also, make a disclosure of the amount of the total of recognized indirect effects and the related per-share amounts for each previous year presented.

- In the case where it is impractical to derive retrospective application to previous years, provide a disclosure of the reasons along with a description of the alternative method used to report the change.

A change in accounting principle should be recognized by a retroactive adjustment of previous years' financial statements recast with the newly adopted method. Any cumulative effect of the change for years before those presented is recorded as an adjustment to the beginning retained earnings of the earliest year presented. Thus, under the mandated retrospective approach, the prior year(s) income numbers are restated under the newly adopted method in the current year, resulting in comparability over the years.

Change in Accounting Estimate

A change in accounting estimate is caused by new circumstances or events requiring a revision in the estimates, such as a change in salvage value or life of an asset. A change in accounting estimate is accounted for prospectively over current and future years. There is no restatement of prior years. A footnote should describe the nature of the change. Disclosure is required in the period of the change for the effect on income before extraordinary items, net income, and earnings per share. However, such disclosure is not required for estimate changes in the ordinary course of business when immaterial. Examples are revising estimates of uncollectible accounts or inventory obsolescence. If a change in estimate is coupled with a change in principle and the effects cannot be distinguished, it is accounted for as a change in estimate. For instance, a change may be made from deferring and amortizing a cost to expensing it as incurred because future benefits may be doubtful. This should be accounted for as a change in estimate.

EXAMPLE 2: Equipment was bought on January 1, 2X11, for $40,000, having an original estimated life of 10 years with a salvage value of $4,000. On January 1, 2X11, the estimated life was revised to eight remaining years, with a new salvage value of $3,200. The journal entry on December 31, 2X15, for depreciation expense is:

Depreciation	2,800	
Accumulated depreciation		2,800

Computations follow:

Book value on 1/1/2X15:

Original cost		$40,000
Less: accumulated depreciation		

$$\frac{\$40,000 - \$4,000}{10} = \$3,600 \times 4 \qquad \underline{14,400}$$

Book value	$25,600

Depreciation for 2X15:

Book value	$25,600
Less: new salvage value	3,200
Depreciable cost	$22,400

$$\frac{\text{Depreciable cost } \$22,400}{\text{New life } 8} = \$2,800$$

Change in Reporting Entity

A change in reporting entity (e.g., two previously separate companies combine) is accounted for by restating prior years' financial statements as if both companies were always combined. Restatement for a change in reporting entity is necessary to show proper trends in comparative financial statements and historical summaries. The effect of the change on income before extraordinary items, net income, and per-share amounts is reported for all periods presented. The restatement process does not have to go back more than five years. Footnote disclosure should be made of the nature of and reason for the change in reporting entity only in the year of change. Examples of changes in reporting entity are:

- Presentation of consolidated statements instead of statements of individual companies.
- Change in subsidiaries included in consolidated statements or those included in combined statements.

PRIOR-PERIOD ADJUSTMENTS

A prior-period adjustment consists of the correction of an error made in a prior period in the fiscal year it is discovered.

When a single year is presented, prior-period adjustments adjust the beginning balance of retained earnings. The presentation is as follows:

Retained earnings—1/1 unadjusted

Prior-period adjustments (net of tax)

Retained earnings—1/1 adjusted

Add: net income

Less: dividends

Retained earnings—12/31

Errors may be due to mathematical mistakes, errors in applying accounting principles, or misuse of facts existing when the financial statements were prepared. Further, a change in principle from one that is not GAAP to one that is GAAP is an error correction. Disclosure should be made of the nature of the error and the effect of correction on earnings.

When comparative statements are prepared, a retroactive adjustment for the error is made as it affects the prior years. The retroactive adjustment is disclosed by showing the effects of the adjustment on previous years' earnings and component items of net income.

EXAMPLE 3: In 2X11, a company incorrectly charged furniture for promotion expense amounting to $30,000. The error was discovered in 2X12. The correcting journal entry is:

Retained earnings	30,000	
Furniture		30,000

EXAMPLE 4: At the end of 2X11 a company failed to accrue telephone expense that was paid at the beginning of 2X12. The correcting entry on December 31, 2X12, is:

Retained earnings	16,000	
Telephone expense		16,000

EXAMPLE 5: On January 1, 2X11, an advance retainer fee of $50,000 was received covering a 5-year period. In error, revenue was credited for the full amount. The error was discovered on December 31, 2X13, before closing the books. The correcting entry is:

12/31/20X5 Retained earnings	30,000	
Revenue		10,000
Deferred revenue		20,000

EXAMPLE 6: A company bought a machine on January 1, 2X11, for $32,000 with a $2,000 salvage value and a five-year life. Repairs expense was mistakenly charged. The error was discovered on December 31, 2X14, before closing the books. The correcting entry is:

Depreciation expense	6,000	
Machine	32,000	
Accumulated depreciation		24,000
Retained earnings		14,000

Accumulated depreciation of $24,000 is calculated below:

$$\frac{\$32,000 - \$2,000}{5} = \$6,000 \text{ per year } \times 4 \text{ years} = \$24,000$$

The credit to retained earnings reflects the difference between the erroneous repairs expense of $32,000 in 2X11 versus showing depreciation expense of $18,000 for three years (2X11-2X13).

EXAMPLE 7: At the beginning of 2X11, a company bought equipment for $300,000 with a salvage value of $20,000 and an expected life of 10 years. Straight-line depreciation is used. In error, salvage value was not deducted in computing the depreciation. The correcting journal entries on December 31, 2X12, are:

	2X11	and	2X12
Depreciation taken $300,000/10 × 2 years			$60,000
Depreciation correctly stated $280,000/10 × 2 years			$56,000
			$ 4,000
Depreciation			28,000
Accumulated depreciation			28,000
Depreciation for current year			
Accumulated depreciation	4,000		
Retained earnings			4,000
Correct prior-year depreciation misstatement			

Under IFRS, a prior-period error has to be corrected by restatement. A change in accounting policy can only be made if a new standard requires it or results in more reliable and relevant information about financial performance, financial condition, cash flows, or transactions.

DISCLOSURE OF ACCOUNTING POLICIES

Accounting policies of a business entity are the specific accounting principles and methods of applying them that are selected by management. Accounting policies used should be those that are most appropriate in the circumstances to fairly present financial position and results of operations for the period. Accounting policies can relate to reporting and measurement methods as well as disclosures. They include:

- A selection from generally accepted accounting principles.
- Practices unique to the given industry.
- Unusual applications of generally accepted accounting principles.

The first footnote or section preceding the notes to the financial statements should be a description of the accounting policies followed by the company.

The application of GAAP requires the use of judgment where alternative acceptable principles exist and where varying methods of applying a principle to a given set of facts exist. Disclosure of these principles and methods is vital to the full presentation of financial position and operations so that rational economic decisions can be made.

Examples of accounting policy disclosures are the depreciation method used, consolidation bases, amortization period for patents, construction contract method, and inventory pricing method.

Note: Financial statement classification methods and qualitative data (e.g., litigation) are not accounting policies.

Note: Some types of financial statements need not describe the accounting policies followed. Examples are quarterly unaudited statements when there has not been a policy change since the last year-end, and statements solely for internal use.

A company shall disclose information to assist readers of its financial statements of the impact of netting arrangements such as rights of set off of its assets and liabilities.

DEVELOPMENT-STAGE COMPANIES

A development-stage entity concentrates on establishing a new business; either major operations have not begun or principal operations have started but no significant revenue has been derived. Some types of activities of a development stage enterprise are establishing sources of supply, developing markets, obtaining financing, financial and production planning, research and development, buying capital assets, and recruiting staff. The same generally accepted accounting principles for an established company must be followed by a development-stage enterprise. A balance sheet, income statement, and statement of cash flows are prepared. The balance sheet shows the accumulated net losses as a deficit. The income statement presents cumulative amounts of revenues and expenses since inception of the business. Similarly, the statement of cash flows presents the operating, investing, and financing cash receipts and cash payments. The stockholders' equity statement shows, for each equity security from inception, (1) date and number of shares issued and (2) dollar figures per share applicable to cash and noncash consideration. The nature and basis to determine amounts for noncash consideration must also be provided.

Financial statements must be headed "development-stage enterprise." A footnote should describe the development-stage activities. In the first year the entity is no longer in the development stage, it should disclose that in previous years it was.

Accounting Standards Update No. 2014-10 (June 2014), *Development Stage Entities (Topic 915): Elimination of Certain Financial Reporting Requirements, Including an Amendment to Variable Interest Entities Guidance in Topic 810: Consolidation*, removes the financial reporting distinction between development stage entities and other reporting entities. The update also eliminates the requirements of development stage companies to present inception-to-date financial information, label the statements as a development stage entity, and disclose developmental stage activities.

TROUBLED DEBT RESTRUCTURING

When a troubled debt restructuring occurs, the debtor, because of his or her financial problems, is relieved of part or the entire amount owed the creditor. The concession arises from the debtor-creditor agreement or law, or applies to foreclosure and repossession. The types of troubled debt restructurings are as follows:

- The debtor transfers to creditor receivables from third parties or other assets.
- The debtor gives creditor equity securities to satisfy the debt.
- Modifications are made of the debt terms, including reducing the interest rate, extending the maturity date, or reducing the principal of the obligation.

The debtor books an extraordinary gain (net of tax) on the restructuring, and the creditor recognizes a loss. The loss may be ordinary or extraordinary, depending on whether the arrangement by the creditor is unusual and infrequent. Typically, the loss is ordinary.

Debtor

The gain to the debtor equals the difference between the fair value of assets exchanged and the book value of the debt including accrued interest. Further, there may arise a gain on disposal of assets exchanged equal to the difference between the fair market value and the book value of the transferred assets. The latter gain or loss is not a gain or loss on restructuring, but instead an ordinary gain or loss in connection with asset disposal.

> **EXAMPLE 8:** A debtor transfers assets having a fair market value of $70 and a book value of $50 to settle a payable having a carrying value of $85. The gain on restructuring is $15 ($85 – $70). The ordinary gain is $20 ($70 – $50).

A debtor may provide the creditor with an equity interest. The debtor records the equity securities issued based on fair market value and not the recorded value of the debt extinguished. The excess of the recorded payable satisfied over the fair value of the issued securities represents an extraordinary item.

A modification in terms of an initial debt contract is accounted for prospectively. A new interest rate may be determined based on the new terms. This interest rate is then used to allocate future payments to lower principal and interest. When the new terms of the agreement result in the sum of all the future payments being less than the carrying value of the payable, the payable is reduced and a restructuring gain recorded for the difference. Future payments are deemed a reduction of principal only. Interest expense is not recorded.

A troubled debt restructuring may result in a combination of concessions to the debtor. This may take place when assets or an equity interest is given in partial satisfaction of the obligation and the balance is subject to a modification of terms. Two steps are involved. First, the payable is reduced by the fair value of the assets or equity transferred. Second, the balance of the debt is accounted for as a "modification of terms" type restructuring.

Direct costs, such as legal fees, incurred by the debtor in an equity transfer reduce the fair value of the equity interest. All other costs reduce the gain on restructuring. If there is no gain involved, they are expensed.

EXAMPLE 9: The debtor owes the creditor $200,000 and has expressed that, owing to financial problems, there may be difficulty in making future payments. Footnote disclosure of the problem should be made by both debtor and creditor.

EXAMPLE 10: The debtor owes the creditor $80,000. The creditor relieves the debtor of $10,000. The balance of the debt will be paid at a subsequent time.

The journal entry for the debtor is:

Accounts payable	10,000	
Gain from forgiveness of debt		10,000

The journal entry for the creditor is:

Ordinary loss	10,000	
Accounts receivable		10,000

EXAMPLE 11: The debtor owed the creditor $90,000. The creditor agrees to accept $70,000 in full satisfaction of the obligation.

The journal entry for the debtor is:

Accounts payable	20,000	
Gain from forgiveness of debt		20,000

The journal entry for the creditor is:

Loss	20,000	
Accounts receivable		20,000

The debtor should disclose the following in the footnotes:

- Particulars of the restructuring agreement.

- The aggregate and per share amounts of the gain on restructuring.

- Amounts that are contingently payable, including the contingency terms.

Creditor

The creditor's loss is the difference between the fair value of assets received and the book value of the investment. When terms are modified, the creditor recognizes interest income to the degree that total future payments are greater than the carrying value of the investment. Interest income is recognized using the effective interest method. Assets received are reflected at fair market value. When the book value of the receivable is in excess of the aggregate payments, an ordinary loss is recognized for the difference. All cash received in the future is accounted for as a recovery of the investment. Direct costs of the creditor are expensed.

The creditor does not recognize contingent interest until the contingency is removed and interest has been earned. Further, future changes in the interest rate are accounted for as a change in estimate.

The creditor discloses the following in the footnotes:

- Loan commitments of additional funds to financially troubled companies.

- Loans and/or receivables by major type.

- Debt agreements in which the interest rate has been downwardly adjusted, including an explanation of the circumstances.

- Description of the restructuring terms.

Accounting Standards Update (ASU) No. 2014-14 (August 2014), *Receivables – Troubled Debt, Restructurings by Creditors* (Subtopic 310-40), *Classification of Certain Government-Guaranteed Mortgage Loans Upon Foreclosure*, states that a mortgage loan should be derecognized and a separate other receivable should be recognized upon foreclosure if the following exist: (1) it is a government guaranteed loan, (2) at foreclosure the creditor intends to convey the real estate properties to the guarantor, and (3) the claim amount based on the fair value of the real estate is fixed. Upon foreclosure, the receivable should be based on the loan balance anticipated to be received.

IMPUTING INTEREST ON NOTES

When the face amount of a note does not represent the consideration given or received in the exchange, an interest calculation is needed to avoid the misstatement of profit. Interest is imputed on non-interest-bearing notes, notes that provide for an unrealistically low interest rate relative to interest rates, and notes with face value significantly different from the "going" selling prices of such notes.

If a note is issued only for cash, the note should be recorded at the cash exchanged irrespective of whether the interest rate is reasonable. The note has a present value at issuance equal to the cash transacted. When a note is exchanged for property, goods, or services, a presumption exists that the interest rate is fair and reasonable. Where the stipulated interest rate is not fair and adequate, the note has to be recorded at the fair value of the merchandise or services or at an amount that approximates fair value. If fair value is not determinable for the goods or services, the discounted present value of the note has to be used.

The imputed interest rate is the one that would have resulted if an independent borrower or lender had negotiated a similar transaction. For example, it is the prevailing interest rate the borrower would have paid for financing. The interest rate is based on economic circumstances and events.

Factors to be considered in deriving an appropriate discount rate include:

- Prime interest rate.
- "Going" market rate for similar quality instruments.
- Issuer's credit standing.
- Collateral.
- Restrictive covenants and other terms in the note agreement.
- Tax effects of the arrangement.

ASC 835, *Interest* (ASC 835-30), applies to long-term payables and receivables. Short-term payables and receivables are typically recorded at face value because the extra work of amortizing a discount or premium on a short-term note is not worth the information benefit obtained. ASC 835-30 is not applicable to:

- Security deposits.
- Usual lending activities of banks.
- Amounts that do not mandate repayment.
- Receivables or payables occurring within the ordinary course of business.
- Transactions between parent and subsidiary.

The difference between the face value of the note and the present value of the note represents discount or premium that must be accounted for as an element of interest over the life of the note. Present value of the payments of the note is based on an imputed interest rate.

The interest method is used to amortize the discount or premium on the note. The interest method results in a constant rate of interest. Under the method, amortization equals:

$$\text{Interest rate} \quad \times \quad \frac{\text{Present value of the liability}}{\text{Receivable at the beginning of the year}}$$

Interest expense is recorded for the borrower, whereas interest revenue is recorded for the lender. Issuance costs are treated as a deferred charge.

The note payable and note receivable are presented in the balance sheet as follows:

Notes payable (face amount)

Less: discount

Present value (principal)

Notes receivable (face amount)

Add: premium

Present value (principal)

EXAMPLE 12: On January 1, 2X11, equipment is acquired in exchange for a one-year note payable of $1,000 maturing on December 31, 2X11. The imputed interest rate is 10% resulting in the present value factor for $n = 1$, $i = 10\%$ of .91.

Relevant journal entries are as follows:

1/1/2X11 Equipment	910	
Discount		90
Notes payable		1,000
12/31/2X11		
Interest expense	90	
Discount		90
Notes payable	1,000	
Cash		1,000

EXAMPLE 13: On January 1, 2X12, a machine is bought for cash of $10,000 and the incurrence of a $30,000, five-year, non-interest-bearing note payable. The imputed interest rate is 10%. The present value factor for $n = 5$, $i = 10\%$ is .62.

Appropriate journal entries are as follows:

1/1/2X12		
Machine (10,000 + 18,600)	28,600	
Discount	1,400	
Notes Payable		30,000
Cash		10,000

Present value of note equals $30,000 × .62 = $18,600

On January 1, 2X12, the balance sheet shows:

1/1/2X12	
Notes payable	$30,000
Less: discount	11,400
Present value	$18,600

12/31/2X12		
Interest expense	1,860	
Discount		1,860

10% × $18,600 = $1,860

1/1/2X13	
Notes payable	$30,000
Less: discount (11,400 – 1,860)	9,540
Present value	$20,460
12/31/2X13	
Interest expense	2,046
Discount	
10% × $20,460 = $2,046	2,046

CAPITAL STRUCTURE INFORMATION

ASC 505, *Equity* (ASC 505-10-50), requires footnote disclosure regarding the rights and privileges of common and preferred stockholders, such as dividend preferences, participation privileges, conversion terms, unusual voting rights, sinking fund requirements, and terms for additional issuances. In a liquidation situation, footnote information must be made of liquidation preferences, such as dividend arrearages and liquidation values for preferred stock. In the case of redeemable stock, disclosure must be made of redemption requirements for each of the next five years.

As per ASC 505-10-50, companies must disclose "key" conversion features of contingently convertible securities and the possible conversion effect. Disclosures include:

- Conversion price and number of shares to be converted.
- Conversion timing and rights.
- Description of events that would cause conversion.
- Reasons for an adjustment to a contingency.
- How a conversion is settled (e.g., shares, cash).
- Manner of including convertible securities in calculating diluted EPS.
- Enumeration of derivative transactions emanating from the issuance of contingently convertible securities (such as number of shares underlying the derivatives and terms of derivative transactions).

RELATED-PARTY DISCLOSURES

ASC 850, *Related Party Disclosures*, deals with disclosures for related-party transactions. Such transactions occur when a transacting party can significantly influence or exercise control of another transaction party because of a financial, common ownership, or familial relationship. It may also arise when a nontransacting party can significantly impact the policies of two other transacting parties. Related-party transactions include those involving:

- Joint ventures.
- Activities between a subsidiary and parent.
- Activities between affiliates of the same parent company.
- Relationships between the company and its principal owners, management, or their immediate families.

Related-party transactions often occur in the ordinary course of business and may include such activities as granting loans or incurring debt, sales, purchases, services performed or received, guarantees, allocating common costs as the basis for billings, compensating balance requirements, property transfers, rentals, and filing of consolidated tax returns.

Related-party transactions are presumed not to be at arm's length. They are usually not derived from competitive, free-market dealings. Some possible examples follow:

- A "shell" company (with no economic substance) purchases merchandise at inflated prices.
- A lease at "bargain" or excessive prices.
- Unusual guarantees or pledges.
- A loan at an unusually low or high interest rate.
- Payments for services at inflated prices.

Related-party disclosures include:

- Nature and substance of the relationship.
- Amount of transaction.
- Terms of transaction.
- Year-end balances due or owed.
- Any control relationships that exist.

A significant related-party relationship to an R&D arrangement exists when 10% or more of the entity providing the funds is owned by related parties.

DISCLOSURES FOR DERIVATIVES

The SEC requires certain disclosures for the accounting and reporting for derivatives, including financial instruments and commodities. Derivative commodity instruments include futures, forwards, options, and swaps. These disclosures include:

- The types and nature of derivative instruments to be accounted for.
- The accounting method used for derivatives, such as the fair value method, accrual method, and deferral method. Disclosure should be made where gains and losses associated with derivatives are reported.
- The risks associated with the derivatives.
- Distinguishment of derivatives used for trading or nontrading purposes.
- Derivatives used for hedging purposes, including explanation.

ASC 815, *Derivatives and Hedging*, requires enhanced disclosures about the company's derivative and hedging activities, thereby improving the transparency of financial reporting.

Under the statement, a company must provide enhanced disclosures about (1) how and why a company uses derivative instruments, (2) how derivative instruments and related hedged items are accounted for, and (3) how derivative instruments and related hedged items impact a company's financial position, financial performance, and cash flows. Disclosure is required of the objective for using derivative instruments with respect to underlying risk and accounting designation. Further, disclosure is made of fair value of derivative instruments and their gains or losses in tabular format. Finally, there should be disclosure of credit risk-related contingent features to assess the company's liquidity from using derivatives.

The statement is effective for fiscal years beginning after November 15, 2008.

INFLATION INFORMATION

ASC 255, *Changing Prices,* permits an entity to voluntarily disclose inflation information so management and financial statement readers can better evaluate the impact of inflation on the business. Selected summarized financial information should be presented based on current costs and adjusted for inflation (in constant purchasing power) for a five-year period. The Consumer Price Index for All Urban Consumers may be used. Inflation disclosures include those for sales and operating revenue stated in constant purchasing power, income from continuing operations (including per-share amounts) on a current cost basis, cash dividends per share in constant purchasing power, market price per share restated in constant purchasing power, purchasing power gain or loss on net monetary items, inflation-adjusted inventory, restated fixed assets, foreign currency translation based on current cost, net assets based on current cost, and the Consumer Price Index used.

SUBSEQUENT EVENTS

The purpose of ASC 855, *Subsequent Events,* is to set forth standards for accounting and disclosure for events taking place between the balance sheet date and the date the financial statements are issued or available to be issued.

The Statement provides for the following information:

1. The period subsequent to the date of the financial statements during which management should appraise events or transactions that may occur for possible recognition or disclosure in the financial statements.

2. The circumstances in which a company should recognize events or transactions taking place after the balance sheet date.

3. The disclosures that should be made for subsequent events or transactions.

The Statement applies to interim and annual financial periods.

Subsequent events are events or transactions that take place after the balance sheet date but before the financial statements are issued or available to be issued. The two types of subsequent events are:

1. Event or transaction that provides additional evidence about conditions that existed at the balance sheet date, including the estimates inherent in the process of preparing financial statements.

2. Event providing evidence about conditions that did not exist at the balance sheet date but arose after that date. This is a nonrecognized subsequent event.

A company shall recognize in the financial statements the effect of a subsequent event that provides additional evidence about conditions existing at the balance sheet date. Recognized subsequent events of this nature include a settlement amount in a lawsuit different from that estimated at the balance sheet date and a customer's bankruptcy filing after year-end but before the issue date of the financial statements.

A company should not recognize subsequent events providing evidence about conditions that did not exist at the balance sheet date but arose after the balance sheet date but before the financial statements are issued. Examples are the sale of stocks or bonds after the balance sheet date but before the financial statements are issued, a business combination taking place after the balance sheet date, fire loss on fixed assets and inventory after the balance sheet date, and issuing significant guarantees after the balance sheet date but before the statements are issued.

Disclosure should be made of the date through which subsequent events have been appraised, and whether that date is the date the financial statements were issued or available to be issued.

Some nonrecognized subsequent events may need to be disclosed to keep the financial statements from being misleading. For this type of event, the company should disclose the nature of the event, and an estimate of its financial effect, or a statement that such an estimate cannot be made.

A company should consider supplementing the historical financial statements with pro forma financial information. In some cases, a nonrecognized subsequent event may be so material that disclosure can best be made by way of pro forma financial data. Such data shall give effect to the event as if it had taken place on the balance sheet date.

According to Accounting Standards Update (ASU) No. 2010-09 (February 2010), *Subsequent Events* (ASC Topic 855), a company must appraise subsequent events up to the time of the issuance of the balance sheet and income statement.

A revised financial statement includes one resulting from an error correction or restatement of previous years because of the adoption of a new accounting method.

COLLABORATIVE ARRANGEMENTS

According to ASC 808, *Collaborative Arrangements*, a collaborative arrangement is a contractual agreement in which the parties are active participants and have significant risks and rewards that depend on the eventual commercial success of the endeavor. Many collaborative arrangements apply to developing and commercializing intellectual property. A collaborative arrangement can start at any point in the endeavor's life cycle.

According to ASC 808, transactions with third parties (i.e., revenue generated and cost incurred by participants from transactions with parties outside of a collaborative arrangement), should be shown gross or net on the appropriate line item in each participant's respective financial statements. For example, a participant in a collaborative arrangement that is considered to be the principal for a given transaction should record that transaction on a gross basis in its financial statements. Further, the equity method should not be applied to an arrangement that is performed by the participants without creating a separate legal entity for the arrangement.

If one party to an arrangement must make a payment to the other party to reimburse a part of that party's research and development (R&D) cost, that portion of the net payment may be an R&D expense in the payor's financial statements.

A participant in a collaborative arrangement should disclose the following:

- Amounts owed to or due from other participants.
- Accounting policy for collaborative arrangements.
- Rights and obligations under collaborative arrangements.
- Nature and purpose of the arrangement.
- Life cycle stage.
- Classification in the income statement and amounts attributable to transactions between participants.

ENVIRONMENTAL REPORTING AND DISCLOSURES

Companies are faced with federal and local compliance requirements regarding environmental issues. Environmental laws provide rigorous specifications with which companies must comply. The costs of compliance could significantly increase a company's expected cost of projects and processes. Failure to abide by environmental dictates could result in substantial costs and risks, including civil and criminal prosecution and fines. The company must police itself to avoid legal defense fees and penalties. An effective compliance program, such as having preventive and detective controls, is crucial in minimizing environmental risks. The corporate manager must be assured that appropriate accounting, reporting, and disclosures for environmental issues are being practiced by the firm.

Legislation

The Environmental Protection Agency (EPA) enforces federal laws regulating pollution, solid waste disposal, water supply, pesticide and radiation control, and ocean dumping. EPA regulations require adherence to specific pollution detection procedures, such as leak testing, and installation of corrosion protection and leak detection systems applicable to underground storage tanks.

The Clean Air Act of 1963 concentrates on issues such as acid rain, urban smog, airborne toxins, ozone-depleting chemicals, and other air pollution problems. The Clean Water Act established controls of water pollution and wetlands preservation.

The Environmental Response Compensation and Liability Act (Superfund) relates to uncontrolled or abandoned hazardous waste disposal sites. Companies must disclose emergency planning, spills or accidents of hazardous materials, and when chemicals are released into surrounding areas. The chemicals must be disclosed to prospective buyers, employees, and tenants.

To go from a reactive position (the company just complies with regulations) to a proactive policy (the company envelops environmental concerns into its daily business practices), the entity must formulate financial information to complement technical and scientific data. Further, environmental expenditures have to be segregated so as to improve decision making and accountability for environmental responsibilities. There should be an appraisal model for setting priorities as the basis for resource allocations.

Accounting and Reporting

ASC 450, *Contingency* (ASC 450-20), deals with how environmental liabilities are determined, future contingencies, "key" environmental factors, and disclosures of environmental problems. Depending on the circumstances, a liability and/or footnote disclosure would be required. Examples are:

- Information on site remediation projects, such as current and future costs and remediation trends. Site remediation includes hazardous waste sites.
- Contamination caused by environmental health and safety problems.
- Legal and regulatory compliance issues, such as with regard to cleanup responsibility.
- Water or air pollution.

Environmental problems should be addressed immediately to avoid significant future costs, including additional cleanup costs, penalties, and legal fees.

Environmental costs should be compared to budgeted amounts, and variances may be computed and tracked. Forecasted information should be changed as new information is available. Internal controls must be established over the firm's environmental responsibility, including internal checks, safeguarding of assets, and segregation of duties.

A financial analysis of environmental costs should be conducted by analyzing cost trends over the years within the company, comparisons to competing companies, and comparisons to industry averages. Additionally, comparisons should be made between projects within the company.

Environmental costs should be allocated across departments, products, and services. Environmental cost information is useful in product and service mix decisions, pricing policies, selecting production inputs, appraising pollution prevention programs, and evaluating waste management policies.

Business Interruption Insurance Disclosure

ASC 225, *Income Statement* (ASC 225-30), mandates disclosure of the event causing losses arising from business interruption as well as the total amount received from insurance and where such amounts are reported in the income statement.

Insurance Contracts

ASC 944, *Financial Services—Insurance*, requires that an insurance company record a claim liability before a default (insured event) when evidence exists of credit deterioration occurring in an insured financial obligation. The statement is limited to financial guarantee insurance and reinsurance contracts, and is effective for financial statements issued for fiscal years beginning after December 15, 2008.

ASC 944 relates to recognizing and measuring premium revenue and claim liabilities and disclosures. The premium revenue recognition approach for a financial guarantee insurance contract links premium revenue recognition to the amount of insurance protection and the period to which it applies. The amount of insurance protection provided is a function of the insured principal amount outstanding.

The recognition approach for a claim liability applying to a financial guarantee insurance contract mandates that an insurance company record a claim liability when the insurance company anticipates that a claim loss will be more than unearned premium revenue. The claim loss is based on the present value of anticipated net cash outflows to be paid discounted using a risk-free rate.

GOING CONCERN

Accounting Standards Update (ASU) No. 2014-15 (August 2014), *Presentation of Financial Statements – Going Concern* (Subtopic 205-40), *Disclosure of Uncertainties About an Entity's Ability to Continue as a Going Concern*, states that management should ascertain if there exists substantial doubt about the company's ability to continue as a going concern within one year of the date the financial statements are issued. A going concern problem is indicated if it is probable that the company will not be able to pay its obligations due within one year after the issuance of the financial statements. If management's plans are expected to alleviate or remove the substantial doubt of the company's ability to continue as a going concern, disclosure should be made of the following: major conditions or events that raise substantial doubt, management's appraisal of the significance of those conditions or events relative to the entity's ability to satisfy its obligations, and management's plans that alleviate such substantial doubt. However, if the substantial doubt is not alleviated, the company should provide a footnote stating that there is in fact a going concern problem within one year of the date of the financial statements. Disclosure should also be made of the major circumstances causing substantial doubt, management's appraisals and evaluations, and management's plans.

CHAPTER 12

KEY FINANCIAL ACCOUNTING AREAS*

CONTENTS

* Adrian P. Fitzsimons Ph.D., CPA (St. John's University, NY), and Biagio Pilato, LL.M., CPA (St. John's University, NY), contributed to the updates in this chapter.

This chapter discusses the accounting requirements for major financial areas, including consolidation, investing in stocks and bonds, leases, pension plans, post-retirement benefits excluding pensions, profit-sharing plans, tax allocation, and foreign currency translation and transactions.

This chapter was coauthored by Leonard Lederich, JD, MBA, CPA, professor of accounting and business administration at Hostos Community College (CUNY), Bronx, NY.

CONSOLIDATION

Consolidation occurs when the parent owns in excess of 50% of the voting common stock of the subsidiary. The major objective of consolidation is to present as one economic unit the financial position and operating results of a parent and subsidiaries. It shows the group as a single company with one or more branches or divisions rather than as separate companies. It is an example of theoretical substance over legal form. The companies making up the consolidated group keep their individual legal identity. Adjustments and eliminations are for the sole purpose of financial statement reporting. Consolidation is still appropriate even if the subsidiary has a material amount of debt. Disclosure should be made of the firm's consolidation policy in footnotes or by explanatory headings.

A consolidation is negated, even if more than 50% of voting common stock is owned by the parent, in the following cases:

- The parent is not in actual control of a subsidiary—for example, the subsidiary is in receivership, or it is in a politically unstable foreign country.

- The parent has sold or contracted to sell a subsidiary shortly after year-end. The subsidiary is a temporary investment.

- Minority interest is very large in comparison to the parent's interest, thus individual financial statements are more meaningful.

Intercompany elimination includes those for intercompany payables and receivables, advances, and profits. However, for certain regulated companies, intercompany profit does not have to be eliminated if the profit represents a reasonable return on investment. Subsidiary investment in the parent's shares is not consolidated outstanding stock in the consolidated balance sheet. Consolidated statements do not reflect capitalized earnings in the form of stock dividends by subsidiaries subsequent to acquisition.

Minority interest in a subsidiary is the stockholders' equity of those outside compared to the parent's controlling interest in the partially owned subsidiaries. Minority interest should be shown as a separate component of stockholders' equity. When losses applicable to the minority interest in a subsidiary exceed the minority interest's equity capital, the excess and any subsequent losses related to the minority interest are charged to the parent. If profit subsequently occurs, the parent's interest is credited to the degree of prior losses absorbed.

If a parent acquires a subsidiary in more than one block of stock, each purchase is on a step-by-step basis and consolidation does not occur until control exists.

When the subsidiary is acquired within the year, the subsidiary should be included in consolidation as if it had been bought at the beginning of the year with a subtraction for the preacquisition part of earnings applicable to each block of stock. An alternative, but less preferable, approach is to include in consolidation the subsidiary's earnings subsequent to the acquisition date.

The retained earnings of a subsidiary at the acquisition date are not included in the consolidation financial statements.

When the subsidiary is disposed of during the year, the parent should always be consolidated.

Consolidation is still permissible without adjustments when the fiscal year-ends of the parent and subsidiary are three months or less apart. Footnote disclosure is needed of material events occurring during the intervening period.

The equity method of accounting is used for unconsolidated subsidiaries unless there is a foreign investment or a temporary investment. In a case where the equity method is not used, the cost method is followed. The cost method recognizes the difference between the cost of the subsidiary and the equity in net assets at the acquisition date. Depreciation is adjusted for the difference as if consolidation of the subsidiary were made. There is an elimination of intercompany gain or loss for unconsolidated subsidiaries to the extent the gain or loss exceeds the unrecorded equity in undistributed earnings. Unconsolidated subsidiaries accounted for with the cost method should have adequate disclosure of assets, liabilities, and earnings. Such disclosure may be in footnote or supplementary schedule form.

There may be instances when combined rather than consolidated financial statements are more meaningful, such as where a person owns a controlling interest in several related operating companies (e.g., brother-sister corporation).

There are cases in which parent company statements are required to properly provide information to creditors and preferred stockholders. In this event, dual columns are needed—one column for the parent and other columns for subsidiaries.

With respect to a consolidation, GAAP mandates a parent company to prepare consolidated financial statements, while IFRS allows exemptions if a parent is wholly owned.

ASC 810, *Consolidation* (ASC 810-10-30), requires variable interest entities to be consolidated by the primary beneficiary. The primary beneficiary is the entity that holds the majority of the beneficial interests in the variable interest entity.

The accounting for business combinations is discussed in "Mergers and Acquisitions" in Part XI.

Although the FASB provides significant guidance on how consolidated financial statements are prepared under the acquisition method, little attention has been given to how an acquired subsidiary should present its assets and liabilities on the books. One perspective is that the subsidiary should retain its prior recording basis (e.g., historical cost, market value). Under that view, fair value adjustments to prepare consolidated financial statements would only be shown on the worksheet and not posted to the subsidiary's general ledger.

Under another perspective, the change in ownership arising from buying the subsidiary results in a new measurement basis, fair value, for that company. The balances on the subsidiary's general ledger are adjusted to fair value. Thus, there is no need for consolidated worksheet adjustments, as these are made directly to the accounts of the subsidiary on its books. This process is called "push down accounting." Under this perspective, the acquired company generally will have higher asset and liability values on the acquisition date because the net assets of the acquired entity have been increased to fair value. In addition, goodwill will have been recognized.

Recently issued Accounting Standards Update (ASU) No. 2014-08 (November 2014), *Pushdown Accounting*, eliminates previously issued SEC staff guidance, which required that acquired entities either use, or be prohibited from using, pushdown accounting based on the percentage of ownership change of an acquired company (e.g., SEC required push down accounting when ownership was greater than 95% and objected to it when ownership was less than 80%). In addition, the update now makes the use of pushdown accounting by an acquired entity optional.

The decision to utilize pushdown accounting generally is made in the reporting period in which an acquirer obtains control of another company (acquiree). This is referred to as a change-in-control event. When the pushdown accounting option is chosen, the acquired company will record its assets and liabilities at fair value. In general, this is the value used by the acquiring company for the acquiree in a business combination. In addition, goodwill should be recognized by the acquiree because it is purchased by the acquirer in the combination. A bargain purchase gain, on the other hand, should not be recognized in the acquired company's income statement. Instead, the gain should be recognized in the acquiree's equity section as additional paid-in capital.

It is also important to note that the choice to use push down accounting by an acquired company under ASU 2014-08 is irrevocable. However, if an acquired entity has not made the election in the accounting period in which a change-in-control event has taken place, then it may make such an election in a later period. In this case, the election would be considered a change in accounting principle requiring a retrospective adjustment of the acquired company's financial statement back to the period in which the change-in-control event took place.

Accounting Standards Update (ASU) No. 2010-02 (January 2010), *Consolidation* (ASC Topic 810), *Accounting and Reporting for Decreases in Ownership of a Subsidiary—a Scope Clarification*, provides the following amendment.

A deconsolidation of a subsidiary by a parent is when the parent no longer has a controlling financial interest. An ensuing gain or loss is recognized by the parent; and a change in a parent's ownership interest is treated as an equity transaction. As a result, gain or loss is not recorded. A parent's ownership changes if it buys, sells, or reacquires shares in the subsidiary.

A deconsolidation should include disclosure of the nature of activities, any related-party transaction, valuation method to determine fair value, fair value inputs, and resulting gain or loss.

Disclosure for a business combination includes the date of purchase, identification and description of acquiree, percentage of ownership bought, way in which control of the targeted company occurred, accounting treatment for the combination, reasons for the combination, transaction description, issuance costs, when a combination occurs in stages, fair value measurements, acquisition costs, valuation method, acquiree's profit after the purchase date, and profit for the combined company for a comparable previous period.

Accounting Standards Update (ASU) No. 2010-10 (February 2010), *Consolidation* (ASC Topic 810), *Amendments for Certain Investment Funds,* specifies the following.

The mandates of FASB Statement No. 167 are deferred for a company's interest in an investment firm. However, this deferral is not applicable in the case of a company that is required to fund substantial losses in the situation where securitization exists. The deferral also does not relate to special purpose companies. In applying this ASU, related-party relationships should be taken into account to ascertain if there exists a variable interest. A mathematical computation should not be the only foundation for appraisal. This ASU is effective for periods after November 15, 2009. The difference between the amount shown in the statement of financial position and the amount of the prior interest in the resulting variable interest entity should be reported as an adjustment to retained earnings. Disclosure should be made of the fair value option applied as well as the major beneficiary of the variable interest entity.

Noncontrolling Interests in Consolidated Financial Statements

ASC 810, *Consolidation* (ASC 810-10-65), specifies that a noncontrolling (minority) interest is the part of equity in a subsidiary that is not attributable to the parent. ASC 810-10-65 applies to all companies preparing consolidated financial statements and is effective for fiscal years beginning on or after December 15, 2008.

Ownership interests in subsidiaries held by parties other than the parent should be identified and presented in the consolidated balance sheet within equity, but separate from the parent's equity. The consolidated net income attributable to the parent and the noncontrolling interest should be identified and presented in the consolidated income statement. The computation of earnings-per-share amounts in consolidated financial statements is based on amounts attributable to the parent.

Changes in a parent's ownership interest in a subsidiary, such as when the parent buys additional equity interest or sells ownership interest, represents an equity transaction if the parent keeps the controlling financial interest in the subsidiary. An equity transaction is also when a subsidiary reacquires or issues additional ownership interests.

If a subsidiary is deconsolidated, any retained noncontrolling equity investment in the former subsidiary should initially be recorded at fair value. The gain or loss on the deconsolidation of the subsidiary is measured based on the fair value of any noncontrolling equity investment instead of the carrying amount of the retained investment. A parent deconsolidates a subsidiary at the date the parent no longer has a controlling financial interest in the subsidiary.

A subsidiary may incur losses with its ensuing negative financial impact on noncontrolling interests. If the noncontrolling interest in the subsidiary's net assets has been reduced to zero due to losses, the noncontrolling interest will continue to be charged for its share of additional losses, even if that causes a deficit balance in the noncontrolling interest account.

Disclosures are made to identify and distinguish between the interests of the parent and the noncontrolling owners of the subsidiary. There should be reconciliation at the beginning and ending balances of the equity associated with the parent and the noncontrolling owners, as well as a schedule that presents the impact of changes in a parent's ownership interest in a subsidiary on the equity related to the parent.

ASC 810, *Consolidation*, changes how a company determines when an entity that is inadequately capitalized or is not controlled through voting should be consolidated. The determination is based on factors such as the company's purpose and design and its ability to direct activities that impact its economic performance.

The Statement amends Interpretation 46R to replace the quantitative-based risks and rewards calculation to determine which company, if any, has a controlling financial interest in a variable interest entity with an approach based on identifying which company has the power to direct activities of a variable interest entity that mostly affects the entity's economic performance and (a) the obligation to absorb the entity's losses or (b) the right to receive benefits from the entity. A qualitative approach will be more effective.

ASC 810 requires a company to provide additional disclosures about its involvement with variable interest entities and any major changes in risk exposure because of that involvement. Disclosure is made of how the involvement impacts the company's financial statements.

The pronouncement is effective January 1, 2010, for companies reporting earnings on a calendar-year basis.

Accounting Standards Update (ASU) No. 2009-17 (December 2009), *Consolidations* (Topic 810), *Improvements to Financial Reporting by Enterprises Involved with Variable Interest Entities*, provides the following information.

Variable interest entities (VIEs) are usually designed for one particular reason, such as for leasing and research and development. The typical condition to set up a controlling financial interest as a majority voting interest does not apply to VIEs. As a result, a consolidation that mandates ownership of voting stock is not relevant. The initial determination of whether a legal entity is a VIE is made when the reporting entity becomes associated with the legal entity.

The consolidation of a VIE occurs when the business has a variable interest that provides a controlling financial interest. The firm that consolidates a VIE is called a primary beneficiary.

In Accounting Standards Update (ASU) No. 2015-02 (February 2015), *Consolidation* (Topic 810) *Amendments to the Consolidation Analysis*, a variable interest that has a controlling financial interest in a variable interest entity results in consolidation of the legal entity. In the case of single decision makers, related party arrangements must be considered indirectly on a proportionate basis.

INVESTMENTS IN SECURITIES

Investments in stock may be accounted for and reported under ASC 946, *Investments—Debt and Equity Securities* (ASC 946-320), or ASC 323, *Investments—Equity Method and Joint Ventures,* depending on the percentage of ownership in voting common stock.

Market Value Adjusted (ASC 320)

Securities are defined as either held to maturity, trading, or available for sale.

Held-to-maturity treatment applies just to debt securities because stock does not have a maturity date. Held-to-maturity debt securities are reported at amortized cost. Amortized cost equals the purchase price adjusted for the amortization of discount or premium. Held-to-maturity securities are not adjusted to market value. Held-to-maturity categorization applies to debt securities only if the company has the intent and ability to hold the securities to the maturity date.

Trading securities can be either debt or equity. The intent is to sell them in a short time period. Trading securities are often bought and sold to earn short-term gain. Trading securities are recorded at market value with the unrealized (holding) loss or gain presented separately in the income statement. Trading securities should be reported as current assets on the balance sheet.

EXAMPLE 1: On December 31, 2X11, the trading securities portfolio had a cost and market value of $500,000 and $520,000, respectively. The journal entry to account for this portfolio at market value is:

Market adjustment	20,000	
Unrealized gain		20,000

The Market Adjustment account has a debit balance and is added to the cost of the portfolio in the current asset section of the balance sheet as follows:

Trading securities (cost)	$500,000
Add: market adjustment	20,000
Trading securities (market value)	$520,000

The unrealized (holding) gain is presented in the income statement under "other income."

Available-for-sale securities may be either debt or equity. These securities are not held for trading reasons or until maturity. They are reported at market value with the cumulative unrealized loss or gain shown as a separate item in the stockholders' equity section of the balance sheet. The portfolio of available-for-sale securities may be presented in the current asset or noncurrent asset sections of the balance sheet, depending on how long these securities are intended to be held.

EXAMPLE 2: On December 31, 2X11, the available-for-sale securities portfolio had a cost and market value of $300,000 and $285,000, respectively. The journal entry to recognize the portfolio at market value is:

| Unrealized loss | 15,000 | |
| Market adjustment | | 15,000 |

The portfolio is presented in the balance sheet at $285,000 net of the Market Adjustment account of $15,000. The unrealized loss is presented separately in the stockholders' equity section of the balance sheet.

When securities are sold, irrespective of the type, the realized gain or loss is reported in the income statement. If the decline in market value of either available-for-sale or held-to-maturity securities is deemed permanent, a realized loss is presented in the income statement. When the security is written down, market value at that date becomes the new cost basis.

EXAMPLE 3: On December 31, 2X12, a company presented the following accounts before adjustment:

| Available-for-sale securities | $300,000 |
| Market adjustment | 25,000 |

It was determined on December 31, 2X12, the portfolio's market value was $290,000. The journal entry needed to bring the portfolio up to date is:

| Market adjustment | 15,000 | |
| Unrealized gain | | 15,000 |

If two or more securities are purchased at one price, the cost is allocated among the securities based on their relative fair market value. In the exchange of one security for another, the new security received in the exchange is valued at its fair market value.

EXAMPLE 4: Preferred stock costing $10,000 is exchanged for 1,000 shares of common stock having a market value of $15,000. The entry is:

Investment in common stock	15,000	
Investment in preferred stock		10,000
Gain		5,000

A stock dividend involves a memo entry reflecting more shares at no additional cost. As a result, the cost per share decreases.

EXAMPLE 5: Fifty shares are owned at $12 per share for a total cost of $600. A 20% stock dividend is declared amounting to 10 shares. A memo entry is made reflecting the additional shares as follows:

		Investment
50	$12	$600
10		0
60	$10	$600

If shares are later sold at $15, the entry is:

Cash	150	
Long-term investment		100
Gain		50

A stock split has the effect of increasing the shares and reducing the cost basis on a proportionate basis. A memo entry is made. Assuming 100 shares costing $20 per share were owned, a two-for-one split would result in 200 shares at a cost per share of $10. Total par value remains at $2,000.

Under IFRS, securities are classified as either available-for-sale or held-to-maturity.

IMPAIRMENT GUIDANCE

ASC 325-40-65-1 deals with whether a company's investments should be considered "other-than-temporarily" impaired. This applies when a company holds corporate debt, equities, or structural investment securities (e.g., CDOs, mortgage-backed and other asset-backed securities). Companies must make a subjective evaluation in ascertaining when impairment is "other than temporary," and if such is the case, to write down the impaired asset to its fair value recognizing a loss. After the realized loss is recognized, a new cost basis is established for the security. A later recovery in fair value cannot be recognized unless the security is later sold.

The ASC provides disclosure requirements for securities with fair values below recorded cost. Companies must disclose in tabular form the amount of unrealized losses and the total fair value of investments with unrealized losses in investment securities having a fair value below book value and for which an other-than-temporary impairment charge has not been taken. The rationale for considering impairment as temporary should be presented. Disclosure should be made of the amounts of unrealized losses and the aggregated fair value of investments with unrealized losses. Companies must disclose in narrative form their rationale for considering existing impairment temporary including the following:

- Reasons for the impairment.
- Length and severity of the impairment.
- Nature of the investments.
- Number of investment positions that are considered unrealized.
- Other evidence in concluding the investment is not other-than-temporarily impaired.

Factors indicating a security's value is other-than-temporarily impaired include:

- Issuer's financial health.
- Investee's cash position.
- Credit rating of the security and any credit downgrading.
- Length of time and degree to which the market value has been below cost.
- Issuer's short-term prospects.
- Failure to make required interest payments.

- Decline in fair value is applicable to negative conditions specifically related to, for example, security, location, industry, economy, or politics.
- Dividend reduction or elimination.
- Information about collectibility of the security such as present conditions, reasonable forecasts, prior events, and estimates of future cash flows.

If there is default by the issuer on principal and/or interest payments on debt, it is very probable that there is other-then-temporary impairment. If the investor does not plan or is unable to hold the security long enough to realize the recorded amount, an impairment charge should be made.

The following is suggested:

- Document the factors for each security evaluated.
- Examine the inability to hold a security to maturity.
- Quarterly appraise impairment.
- Look at credit-related issues.
- Apply methodology consistently.
- Look at the nature of collateral including the kind of assets and date of origination.
- Consider illiquidity.

Equity Method

The investor company is the owner, and the investee company is being owned. If an investor owns between 20% to 50% of the voting common stock of an investee, the equity method is used. The equity method is also employed when the holder owns less than 20% of the voting common stock but possesses significant influence (effective control). The equity method would also be used if more than 50% of the voting common stock were owned but one of the negating factors for consolidation existed. Further, investments in joint ventures have to be accounted for under the equity method.

As per ASC 323, *Investments—Equity Method and Joint Ventures*, when an investor has the ability to exercise significant influence over the operating and financial policies of an investee, the equity method should be applied only when the investor has an investment in common stock.

As per ASC 323, *Investments—Equity Method and Joint Ventures*, the following circumstances may imply that the investor is *unable* to exercise significant influence:

- The written agreement exists between the parties that there is *no* effective control.
- The investor cannot obtain financial information needed to account under the equity method.
- The investor is not included on the investee's board of directors.

- The investee is against the investment such as by filing a lawsuit or a complaint to the SEC.
- Significant influence exists by a small group of stockholders excluding the investor representing majority ownership of the investee.

The accounting under the equity method can be illustrated by examining the following "T-accounts" (which will be described in more detail shortly):

Investment in Investee

Cost	Dividends
Ordinary profit	
	Depreciation on excess of fair market value less book value of specific assets
	Permanent decline

Equity in Earnings of Investee

Depreciation	Ordinary profit

	Loss
Permanent decline	

The cost of the investment includes brokerage fees. The investor recognizes his or her percentage ownership interest in the ordinary profit of the investee by debiting investment in investee and crediting equity in earnings of investee. The investor's share in the investee's earnings is computed after deducting cumulative preferred dividends, whether or not declared. The investor's share of the investee's profit should be based on the investee's most recent income statement applied on a consistent basis. Prior period adjustments are also picked up as shown on the investee's books. Dividends reduce the carrying value of the investment account.

The excess paid by the investor for the investee's net assets is first assigned to the specific assets and liabilities and depreciated. The unidentifiable portion of excess is considered goodwill. Depreciation on excess value of assets reduces the investment account and is charged to equity in earnings. Temporary decline in price of the investment in the investee is ignored. Permanent decline in value of the investment is reflected by debiting loss and crediting investment in investee.

When the investor's share of the investee's losses is greater than the balance in the investment account, the equity method should be discontinued at the zero amount unless the investor has guaranteed the investee's obligations or where immediate profitability is assured. A return to the equity method is made only after offsetting subsequent profits against losses not recorded.

When the investee's stock is sold, a realized gain or loss will arise for the difference between selling price and the cost of the investment account.

The mechanics of consolidation essentially apply with the equity method. For example, intercompany profits and losses are eliminated. Investee capital transactions impacting the investor's share of equity should be accounted for as in a consolidation. Investee's capital transactions should be accounted for as if the investee were a consolidated subsidiary. For example, when the investee issues its common stock to third parties at a price in excess of book value, there will be an increase in the value of the investment and a related increase in the investor's paid-in capital.

Interperiod income tax allocation will occur because the investor shows the investee's profits for book reporting, but dividends for tax reporting. This results in a deferred income tax credit account.

If the ownership goes below 20%, or the investor for some reason is unable to control the investee, the investor should cease recognizing the investee's earnings. The equity method is discontinued but the balance in the investment account is maintained. The fair value method should then be applied.

If the investor increases ownership in the investee to 20% or more, the equity method should be used for current and future years. Further, the effect of using the equity method rather than the fair value method on prior years at the old percentage (e.g., 15%) should be recognized as an adjustment to retained earnings and other accounts so affected, such as investment in investee. The retroactive adjustment on the investment, earnings, and retained earnings should be applied in the same manner as a step-by-step acquisition of a subsidiary.

Disclosures of the following should be made by the investor in footnotes, separate schedules, or parenthetically: percentage owned, name of investee, investor's accounting policies, material effects of possible conversions and exercises of investee common stock, and quoted market price (for investees not qualifying as subsidiaries). Further, summarized financial data as to assets, liabilities, and earnings should be given in footnotes or separate schedules for material investments in unconsolidated subsidiaries. Material realized and unrealized gains and losses relating to the subsidiary's portfolio occurring between the dates of the financial statements of the subsidiary and parent must also be disclosed.

EXAMPLE 6: On January 1, 2X12, X Company bought 30,000 shares for a 40% interest in the common stock of AB Company at $25 per share. Brokerage commissions were $10,000. During 2X12, AB's net income was $140,000 and dividends received were $30,000. On January 1, 2X13, X Company received 15,000 shares of common stock as a result of a stock split by AB Company. On January 4, 2X13, X Company sold 2,000 shares at $16 per share of AB stock. The journal entries are as follows:

1/1/2X12 investment in investee	760,000	
Cash		760,000
12/31/2X12 investment in investee	56,000	
Equity in earnings of investee		56,000

40% × $140,000 = $56,000

Cash		30,000
Investment in investee		30,000

1/1/2X13 Memo entry for stock split

1/4/2X13 Cash (2,000 × $16)	32,000	
Loss on sale of investment	2,940	
Investment in investee (2,000 × $17.47)		34,940

$$\frac{\$786,000}{45,000} = \$17.47 \text{ per share}$$

Investment in Investee

1/1/2X12	760,000	12/31/2X12	30,000
12/31/2X12	56,000		
	816,000		
	786,000		

EXAMPLE 7: On January 1, 2X13, an investor purchased 100,000 shares of the investee's 400,000 shares outstanding for $3,000,000. The book value of net assets acquired was $2,500,000. Of the $500,000 excess paid over book value, all of it is attributable to undervalued tangible assets. The depreciation period is 20 years. In 2X13, the investee's net income was $1,000,000. Dividends of $75,000 were paid on June 1, 2X13. The following journal entries are necessary for the acquisition of the investee by the investor accounted for under the equity method:

1/1/2X13 Investment in investee	3,000,000	
Cash		3,000,000
6/1/2X13 Cash	18,750	
Investment in Investee		18,750

25% × $75,000

12/31/2X13

Investment in investee	250,000	
Equity in earnings of investee		250,000

$1,000,000 × 25% = $250,000

Equity in earnings of investee	25,000	
Investment in investee		25,000

Computation follows:

Undervalued depreciable assets

$300,000/20 years	25,000	

Note: Under ASC 825, *Financial Instruments* (ASC 825-10-25), a company using the equity method can elect to use the fair value option. If that option is selected, the Investment in Investee account will reflect temporary changes in market value of the investee. The resulting unrealized (holding) loss or gain will be presented as a separate item in the income statement. For example, if the fair market value of the investee decreases, the investor will debit unrealized loss and credit the Investment in Investee account (or a Valuation Allowance account) for the decrease in value. On the other hand, if there is an increase in fair market value, the Investment in Investee account (or Valuation Allowance) would be debited and unrealized gain credited for the increase in fair market value.

Accounting Standards Update (ASU) No. 2016-07 (March 2016), *Investments— Equity Method and Joint Ventures* (Topic 323), *Simplifying the Transition to the Equity Method of Accounting*, eliminates the mandate that an investment qualifies for the equity method of accounting because of the increase in ownership percentage that the investor retroactively adjust on a step-by-step basis as if the equity method had been in effect for prior years. Instead, the equity method investor should add the cost of buying the additional interest in the investee to the current basis of the investor's previously held interest and adopt the equity method when the investment becomes qualified for this method.

A company having an available-for-sale equity security that becomes qualified for the equity method must recognize through earnings the unrealized holding gain or loss in "accumulated other comprehensive income."

Held-to-Maturity Bond Investments

The difference between the cost of a held-to-maturity security and its face value is discount or premium. Discount or premium is amortized over the life of the bond from the acquisition date.

The bond investment account is usually recorded net of the discount or premium. If bonds are acquired between interest dates, accrued interest should be recorded separately.

The market price of the bond takes into account:

• The financial health of the issuer.
• "Going" interest rates in the market.
• The maturity period.

The market price is computed by discounting the principal and interest payments using the yield rate.

> **EXAMPLE 8:** An investor buys $100,000, 6%, 20-year bonds on March 1, 2X14. Interest is payable on January 1 and June 30. The bonds are bought at face value.

3/1/2X14

Investment in bonds	100,000	
Accrued bond interest receivable	1,000	
Cash		101,000

$100,000 × 6% = $6,000 per year
$6,000 × 2/12 = $1,000

6/30/2X14

Cash	3,000	
Accrued bond interest receivable (2 months)		1,000
Interest Income (4 months)		2,000

$6,000 × 6/12 = $3,000

12/31/2X14

Accrued bond interest receivable	3,000	
Interest income		3,000

1/1/2X15

Cash	3,000	
Accrued bond interest receivable		3,000

6/30/2X15

Cash	3,000	
Interest income		3,000

EXAMPLE 9: On January 1, 2X11, $10,000 of ABC Company 6%, 10-year bonds are bought for $12,000. Interest is payable 1/1 and 6/30. On April 1, 2X12, the bonds are sold for $11,000. There is a commission charge on the bonds of $100. Applicable journal entries are:

1/1/2X11

Investment in bonds	12,000	
Cash		12,000

6/30/2X11

Interest income	100	
Investment in bonds		100

Amortization of premium computed as follows:

$2,000 ÷ 110 years = $200 per year × 6/12 = $100

Cash	300	
Interest income		300

6% × $10,000 × 6/12 = $300

12/31/2X11

Accrued bond interest receivable	300	
Interest income		300
Interest Income	100	
Investment in bonds		100

4/1/2X12

Accrued bond interest receivable	150	
Interest Income		150

6% × $10,000 × 3/12 = 150

Interest Income	50	
Investment in bonds		50

Amortization of premium computed as follows:

$200 per year × 3/12 = $50

Cash (11,000 + 150 − 100)	11,050	
Loss on sale of investments	850	
Investments in bonds (12,000 − 100 − 100 − 50)		11,750
Accrued bond interest receivable		150

Held-to-maturity securities are classified as a noncurrent asset. If pledged as collateral, they still are classified as long-term if the company intends and anticipates it will be able to repay the borrowing and recover access to its collateral.

Note: Under ASC 825-10-25, a company can elect to value held-to-maturity securities at fair market value in the balance sheet with the unrealized gain or loss reported separately in the income statement.

Under IFRS, the equity method is not required if:

- Investment classification is held-for-sale.

- Investment is only purchased to be disposed of within one year or there are circumstances similar to those that would exempt a company from preparing consolidated statements.

FAIR VALUE OF FINANCIAL ASSETS

ASC 820, *Fair Value Measurements and Disclosures*, states that irrespective of the valuation technique, a company must include suitable risk adjustments that market participants would use for nonperformance and liquidity risks. When markets are not active, brokers may rely on models with inputs based on information available to the broker. An income approach (e.g., present value) may be used to maximize the use of relevant observable inputs to value a financial asset that is *not* actively traded. A discount rate adjustment technique may be used to determine fair value of a financial asset at the measurement date. Risks considered in the discount rate include liquidity risk (e.g., difficulty selling an asset under present market conditions) and nonperformance risk (e.g., collateral value risk, default risk).

The SEC's Office of the Chief Accountant and FASB Staff clarified fair value accounting in a news release. It states that management may use internal assumptions, such as expected cash flows including appropriate risk premiums, to measure fair value when suitable market evidence is non-existent. In some situations, unobservable inputs (level 3) may be more appropriate than observable inputs (level 2). For example, when significant adjustments to available observable inputs are required, it may be better to use an estimate based mostly on unobservable inputs. Fair value determination often involves judgment. In some situations, multiple inputs from different sources may offer the best indication of fair value. In this case, expected cash flows may be taken into account with other relevant data.

Broker quotes may be used as an input to measure fair value. However, they are not necessarily determinative if an active market does not exist for the security. When markets are less active, brokers may rely more on models with inputs based on information available to the broker. Less reliance should be placed on quotes not reflecting market transactions. The nature of the quote should also be considered such as if it indicates a price or binding offer.

Disorderly transactions are not determinative in measuring fair value. Fair value measurement assumes orderly transactions among market participants. Distressed or forced liquidation sales are not orderly transactions.

If prices in an inactive market are not reflective of current prices for similar assets, adjustments may be needed to determine fair value. In determining if a market is inactive, consider the spread between the asking price of sellers and the bid price of buyers, as well as the number of bidding parties. A significant increase in the spread and a small number of bidders indicate an inactive market.

In determining if an other-than-temporary impairment of the financial asset exists, the following should be examined:

- The intent and ability of the holder to keep its investment in the issuer for a time period adequate to allow for a recovery in market value.

- The length of time and degree to which the market value has been less than cost.

- The issuer's financial condition and short-term prospects.

- The expected recovery period must be considered.

According to ASC 320, *Investments—Debt and Equity Securities*, an investment is impaired if the fair value is less than the amortized cost. This FSP applies to debt securities classified as available-for-sale and held-to-maturity that are subject to other-than-temporary impairment guidance.

If the fair value of a debt security is less than amortized cost at year-end, the company shall assess if impairment is other than temporary. If a company intends to sell the debt security, an other-than-temporary impairment has taken place. If a company is more likely than not to be required to sell the security before there is a recovery in its amortized cost, an other-than-temporary impairment has occurred.

If the company does not anticipate recovering the full amortized cost of the security, the company would be unable to assert it will recover its amortized cost. In this case, an other-than-temporary impairment has occurred. If the present value of cash flows expected to be collected is less than amortized cost, credit loss still exists, and an other-than-temporary impairment has occurred. To determine whether a credit loss exists, factors such as the time period and degree to which fair value has been less than amortized cost should be considered.

If a company intends to sell the debt security or more likely than not will be required to sell the security before recovery of its amortized cost basis less any current period credit losses, the other-than-temporary impairment shall be recognized in earnings equal to the difference between the investment's amortized cost basis and its fair value on the balance sheet date. If the entity does not intend to sell the security, the other-than-temporary impairment shall be separated into the (1) credit loss and (2) amount related to other factors. The amount of impairment related to the credit loss is recognized in earnings, while the impairment related to other factors is recognized in other comprehensive income.

LEASES

ASC Topic 842, *Leases*, requires entities to recognize lease assets and lease liabilities on the balance sheet and to disclose information about leasing arrangements. ASC Topic 842 concludes that the economics of leases can vary for a lessee and that those economics should be reflected in the financial statements. Therefore, ASC Topic 842 distinguishes between finance leases and operating leases. ASC Topic 842 notes that the classification criteria for distinguishing between finance leases and operating leases are substantially similar to the classification criteria for distinguishing between capital leases and operating leases in the previous leases guidance. The result of retaining the distinction between finance leases and operating leases is that under the lessee accounting model in ASC Topic 842, the effect of leases in the statement of comprehensive income and the statement of cash flows is largely unchanged from previous GAAP.

Lessee Accounting

ASC Topic 842 requires a lessee to recognize in the statement of financial position a liability to make lease payments (the lease liability) and a right-of-use asset representing its right to use the underlying asset for the lease term. When measuring assets and liabilities arising from a lease, ASC Topic 842 requires a lessee (and a lessor) to include payments to be made in optional periods only if the lessee is reasonably certain to exercise an option to extend the lease or not to exercise an option to terminate the lease. Similarly, ASC Topic 842 requires optional payments to purchase the underlying asset to be included in the measurement of lease assets and lease liabilities only if the lessee is reasonably certain to exercise that purchase option. ASC Topic 842 notes that *reasonably certain* is a high threshold that is consistent with and intended to be applied in the same way as the *reasonably assured* threshold in the previous leases guidance. In addition, also consistent with the previous leases guidance, ASC Topic 842 states that a lessee (and a lessor) should exclude most variable lease payments in measuring lease assets and lease liabilities, other than those that depend on an index or a rate, or are in substance fixed payments.

For leases with a term of 12 months or less, ASC Topic 842 permits a lessee to make an accounting policy election by class of underlying asset not to recognize lease assets and lease liabilities. If a lessee makes this election, it should recognize lease expense for such leases generally on a straight-line basis over the lease term.

Under ASC Topic 842, the recognition, measurement, and presentation of expenses and cash flows arising from a lease by a lessee have not significantly changed. ASC Topic 842 continues the differentiation between finance leases and operating leases; however, the principal difference from previous guidance is that the lease assets and lease liabilities arising from operating leases should be recognized in the statement of financial position.

ASC Topic 842 requires a lessee to do the following for finance leases:

- Recognize a right-of-use asset and a lease liability, initially measured at the present value of the lease payments, in the statement of financial position;

- Recognize interest on the lease liability separately from amortization of the right-of-use asset in the statement of comprehensive income; and
- Classify repayments of the principal portion of the lease liability within financing activities and payments of interest on the lease liability and variable lease payments within operating activities in the statement of cash flows.

ASC Topic 842 also requires a lessee to do the following for operating leases:

- Recognize a right-of-use asset and a lease liability, initially measured at the present value of the lease payments, in the statement of financial position;
- Recognize a single lease cost, calculated so that the cost of the lease is allocated over the lease term on a generally straight-line basis; and
- Classify all cash payments within operating activities in the statement of cash flows.

Lessor Accounting

ASC Topic 842 leaves the accounting applied by a lessor largely unchanged from that applied under previous GAAP. For example, the vast majority of operating leases will remain classified as operating leases, and lessors will continue to recognize lease income for those leases on a generally straight-line basis over the lease term; however, some changes to the lessor accounting guidance were made by ASC Topic 842 to align both of the following:

- The lessor accounting guidance with specific changes made to the lessee accounting guidance. For example, certain glossary terms that are applied by lessees and lessors and that will affect a lessee applying the lessor guidance as a sub-lessor were updated so that lessees and lessors apply the same terms.
- ASC Topic 842 retains alignment in key respects between the lessor accounting guidance and the revenue recognition guidance in ASC Topic 606, *Revenue from Contracts with Customers*.

The FASB states that leasing is fundamentally a revenue-generating activity for lessors, and many aspects of the previous lessor accounting guidance aligned with, or were derived from, the revenue recognition guidance that preceded ASC Topic 606. For example, whether a lease is similar to a sale of the underlying asset depends on whether the lessee, in effect, obtains control of the underlying asset as a result of the lease, and a lessor is precluded from recognizing selling profit or sales revenue at lease commencement for a lease that does not transfer control of the underlying asset to the lessee. In addition, the lessor accounting model in ASC Topic 842 does not differentiate between leases of real estate and leases of other assets.

Definition of a Lease

At inception of a contract, an entity should determine whether the contract is or contains a lease. ASC Topic 842 defines a lease as a contract, or part of a contract, that conveys the right to control the use of identified property, plant, or equipment (an identified asset) for a period of time in exchange for consideration. Control over the use of the identified asset means that the customer has both:

- The right to obtain substantially all of the economic benefits from the use of the asset, and

- The right to direct the use of the asset.

Under ASC Topic 842, the entity is required to determine whether a contract is or contains a lease because a lessee is required to recognize lease assets and lease liabilities for all leases, whether they are finance or operating leases other than short-term leases (i.e., if the entity elects the short-term lease recognition and measurement exemption).

Components

ASC Topic 842 requires an entity to separate the lease components from the non-lease components (e.g., maintenance services or other activities that transfer a good or service to the customer) in a contract.

ASC Topic 842 requires the consideration in the contract to be allocated to the lease and non-lease components on a relative standalone price basis (for lessees) or in accordance with the allocation guidance in ASC Topic 606 (for lessors). ASC Topic 842 notes that consideration attributable to non-lease components is not a lease payment and, therefore, is not included in the measurement of lease assets or lease liabilities. ASC Topic 842 states that entities should account for non-lease components in accordance with other applicable Topics. ASC Topic 842 notes that activities that do not transfer a good or service to the lessee or amounts paid solely to reimburse costs of the lessor are not components in a contract and are not allocated any of the consideration in the contract.

ASC Topic 842 provides a practical expedient for lessees as it relates to separating lease components from non-lease components. Lessees may make an accounting policy election by class of underlying asset not to separate lease components from non-lease components. If an entity makes that accounting policy election, it is required to account for the non-lease components together with the related lease components as a single lease component.

Sale and Leaseback Transactions

For a sale to occur in the context of a sale and leaseback transaction, ASC Topic 842 requires the transfer of the asset to meet the requirements for a sale in ASC Topic 606. If there is no sale for the seller-lessee, the buyer-lessor also does not account for a purchase. According to ASC Topic 842, any consideration paid for the asset is accounted for as a financing transaction by both the seller-lessee and the buyer-lessor.

ASC Topic 842 notes that there are circumstances in which a transaction that qualified for a sale under the previous leases guidance does not qualify for a sale under ASC Topic 606, or vice versa. For example, some sale and leaseback transactions involving real estate may now qualify for sale and leaseback accounting that previously did not qualify for that treatment. In contrast, some sale and leaseback transactions involving assets other than real estate that previously qualified for sale and leaseback accounting may no longer qualify for that treatment.

ASC Topic 842 specifies that if the leaseback is classified as a finance/sales-type lease, no sale has occurred. ASC Topic 842 also specifies that a repurchase option (i.e., for the seller-lessee to repurchase the asset from the buyer-lessor) precludes sale accounting unless:

- The asset is nonspecialized, and
- The exercise price of the option is the fair value of the asset on the date the option is exercised.

Transactions that were previously accounted for as a sale and a leaseback are not required to be reassessed as to whether the transaction would qualify as a sale and a leaseback in accordance with ASC Topic 842.

Disclosures

ASC Topic 842 requires disclosures by lessees and lessors to meet the objective of enabling users of financial statements to assess the amount, timing, and uncertainty of cash flows arising from leases. ASC Topic 842 also requires qualitative disclosures along with specific quantitative disclosures to supplement the amounts recorded in the financial statements so that users can understand more about the nature of an entity's leasing activities.

Transition

In transition, ASC Topic 842 requires lessees and lessors to recognize and measure leases at the beginning of the earliest period presented using a modified retrospective approach. The modified retrospective approach includes a number of optional practical expedients that entities may elect to apply. These practical expedients relate to:

- The identification and classification of leases that commenced before the effective date,
- Initial direct costs for leases that commenced before the effective date, and
- The ability to use hindsight in evaluating lessee options to extend or terminate a lease or to purchase the underlying asset.

ASC Topic 842 provides that an entity that elects to apply the practical expedients will, in effect, continue to account for leases that commence before the effective date in accordance with previous GAAP unless the lease is modified, except that lessees are required to recognize a right-of-use asset and a lease liability for all operating leases at each reporting date based on the present value of the remaining minimum rental payments that were tracked and disclosed under previous GAAP.

The transition guidance in ASC Topic 842 also provides specific guidance for sale and leaseback transactions, build-to-suit leases, leveraged leases, and amounts previously recognized in accordance with the business combinations guidance for leases.

PENSION PLANS

ASC 715, *Compensation—Retirement Benefits* (ASC 715-30). Under ASC 715, a company is not required to have a pension plan. If it does, the firm must conform to FASB and governmental rules regarding the accounting and reporting for the pension plan. ASC 715-30 requires accounting for pension costs on the accrual basis. Pension expense is reflected in the service periods using a method that considers the benefit formula of the plan. On the income statement, pension expense is presented as a single amount. The pension plan relationship between the employer, trustee, and employee is depicted in Exhibit 12-1.

Exhibit 12-1: Pension Plan Relationship

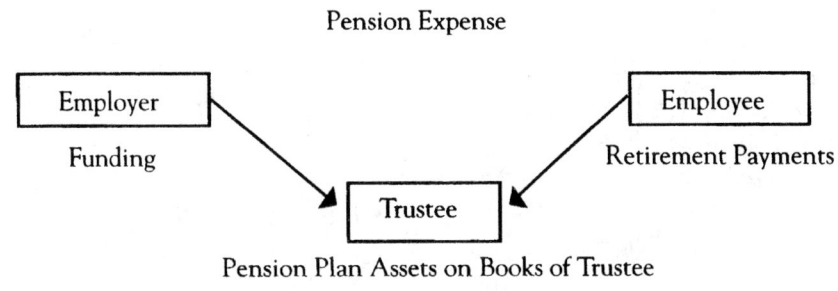

Pension Expense

Employer — Funding → Trustee ← Retirement Payments — Employee

Pension Plan Assets on Books of Trustee

Pension accounting is divided and treated separately between the employer's accounting and the accounting for the pension fund. The employer incurs the cost and makes contributions to the pension fund. The fund (plan) is the entity that receives the contributions, administers pension assets, and makes benefit payments to retirees. The assets and liabilities of a pension plan are not included in the employer's financial statements. The pension fund is a separate legal and accounting entity.

The two types of pension plans are:

1. *Defined contribution.* In a defined contribution plan, the annual contribution amount by the employer is specified instead of the benefits to be paid.

2. *Defined benefit.* In a defined benefit plan, the determinable pension benefit to be received by participants upon retirement is specified. In determining amounts, consideration is given to such factors as age, salary, and years of service. The employer has to provide plan contributions so that sufficient assets are accumulated to pay for the benefits when due. Typically, an annuity of payments is made. Pension expense applicable to administrative staff is expensed. Pension expense related to factory personnel is inventoriable.

The following pension plan terminology should be understood:

- *Actuarial assumptions.* Actuaries make assumptions as to variables in determining pension expense and related funding. Examples of estimates are disability rate, mortality rate, employee turnover, compensation levels, rate of return, length of paid benefits, rate of salary increases, salary amounts, and retirement rate.

- *Actuarial cost (funding) method.* The method used by actuaries in determining the employer contribution to ensure sufficient funds will be available at employee retirement. The method used determines the pension expense and related liability.

- *Actuarial present value of accumulated plan benefits.* The discounted amount of money that would be required to satisfy retirement obligations for active and retired employees.

- *Benefit information date.* The date the actuarial present value of accumulated benefits is presented.

- *Vested benefits.* Employee vests when he or she has accumulated pension rights to receive benefits upon retirement. The employee no longer has to remain in the company to receive pension benefits.

- *Projected benefit obligation.* The projected benefit obligation is the year-end pension obligation that measures the deferred compensation amount. It is the actuarial present value of vested and nonvested benefits for services performed before a particular actuarial valuation date based on expected *future* salaries.

- *Accumulated benefit obligation.* The accumulated benefit obligation is the year-end obligation based on current salaries. It is the actuarial present value of benefits (vested and nonvested) attributable to the pension plan based on services performed before a specified date based on current salary levels. The accumulated and projected benefit obligation figures will be the same in the case of plans having flat-benefit or non-pay-related pension benefit formulas.

- *Net assets available for pension benefits.* Net assets represent plan assets less plan liabilities. The plan's liabilities exclude participants' accumulated benefits.

Defined Contribution Pension Plan

In a defined contribution plan, only the employer's contribution is defined; therefore, there is no assurance of the benefits to be paid to retirees.

Pension expense equals the employer's cash contribution for the year. There is no deferred charge or deferred credit arising. If the defined contribution plan stipulates contributions are to be made for years subsequent to an employee's rendering of services (e.g., after retirement), there should be an accrual of costs during the employee's service period.

Footnote disclosure includes:

- Description of the plan, including employee groups covered.
- Basis of determining contributions.

- Nature and effect of items affecting interperiod comparability.

- Cost recognized for the period.

According to Accounting Standards Update (ASU) No. 2010-25 (September 2010), *Plan Accounting Defined Contribution Pension Plans* (ASC Topic 962), *Reporting Loans to Participants,* participant loans should be presented as notes receivable and are to be segregated from plan investments and valued at their unpaid principal amount plus any accrued but unpaid interest.

Fully Benefit-Responsive Investment Contracts

Fully benefit-responsive investment contracts may be issued to defined benefit plans. These contracts provide contract value protection to plan participants for certain permitted transactions defined by the contract. Permitted transactions include, for example, transfers initiated by participants to other funds within the plan, withdrawals for benefits, and loans. ASC Topic 962, *Plan Accounting: Defined Contribution Pension Plans,* required that fully benefit-responsive investment contracts be valued at contract value. It also required that if this measurement was different from fair value, an adjustment was to be made to reconcile contract value to fair value on the face of the plan financial statements. As part of the FASB's ongoing Simplification Intiative, ASU No. 2015-12 Part I, *Plan Accounting: Defined Contribution Pension Plans* (Topic 962), now requires that contract value should be the sole measure to value fully benefit-responsive investment contracts. Contract valuation was chosen as the sole measure because it represents the amount that participants would receive if they were to execute permitted transactions under the defined benefit plan. In addition, fully benefit-responsive investment contracts are reported at contract value for regulatory purposes.

Defined Benefit Pension Plan

ASC 715 applies only to single-employer plans, not multiemployer plans. The pronouncement makes it easier for financial statement users to comprehend an employer's financial position and its ability to fulfill its obligations under its benefit plans. ASC 715 is intended to communicate the funded status of defined benefit postretirement plans in a clear and comprehensive way. Although the pronouncement changes the recognition and disclosure requirements for defined benefit postretirement plans, it does *not* change the measurement of pension or other postretirement expense. ASC 715 is expected to have a pronounced effect on corporations. Upon adoption, most companies will report a very significant increase in liabilities as well as a reduction in stockholders' equity. This is because most companies are underfunded. The affect on pension expense from ASC 715 is expected to be none or very little, because the amortization requirements for actuarial gains and losses and prior-service costs are *not* changed. Further, the computation of other components of pension expense, including service cost and interest on projected benefit obligation, remain intact.

Upon initially applying ASC 715 and in later periods, an employer should continue to follow the dictates of FASB Statement Nos. 87, 88, and 106 in measuring plan assets and benefit obligations as of the balance sheet date and in determining the net periodic benefit cost.

The components of pension expense in a defined benefit pension plan are as follows:

- Service cost.
- Amortization of any prior-service cost or credit included in "accumulated other comprehensive income."
- Expected return on plan assets (reduces pension expense).
- Interest cost on projected benefit obligation.
- Net gain or loss.
- Amortization of net transition assets or obligation existing at the adoption date of ASC 715 and remaining in accumulated other comprehensive income.

Service Cost. Service cost is based on the present value of future payments under the benefit formula for employee services of the current period. It is recognized in full in the current year. The calculation involves actuarial assumptions, such as promotion and early retirement service cost increases pension expense.

Employers must incorporate future salary levels in measuring pension expense and the present obligation if the plan benefit includes them. ASC 715 adopts the benefits/years-of-service actuarial method, which computes pension expense based on future compensation levels. The employer is required to fund at least the annual service cost computed under the plan.

Accounting Standards Update (ASU) No. 2017-07 (March 2017), *Compensation – Retirement Benefits (Topic 815), Improving the Presentation of Net Periodic Pension Cost and Net Periodic Postretirement Benefit Cost,* states that an employer must report the service cost component in the same line item or items as other compensation costs for employee services performed. The other components of net benefit cost must be shown in the income statement separately from the service cost component and outside a subtotal of income from operations.

Prior-Service Cost. Prior-service cost is the pension expense applicable to services rendered before the adoption or amendment date of a pension plan. The cost of the retroactive benefits is the increase in the projected benefit obligation at the date of amendment. It involves the allocation of amounts of cost to future service years. Prior-service cost determination involves actuarial considerations. Amortization is accomplished by assigning at the amendment date an equal amount to each service year of active employees who are expected to receive plan benefits. The amortization of prior-service cost may take into account future service years, any change in the projected benefit obligation, the period employees will receive benefits, and any decrement in employees receiving benefits each year. "Other comprehensive income" is adjusted as a result of amortizing prior-service cost. Amortization of prior-service cost usually increases pension expense.

A plan modification that retroactively increases benefits increases the projected benefit obligation. The cost of the benefit improvement is recognized as a charge to other comprehensive income at the amendment date. On the other hand, a plan amendment that retroactively reduces benefits decreases the projected benefit obligation. The reduction in benefits is recognized as a credit (prior-service credit) to other comprehensive income that is used first to reduce any remaining prior-service cost included in accumulated other comprehensive income. Any remaining credit is amortized as a component of pension cost on the same basis as the cost of a benefit increase.

The employer initially records the prior-service cost as an adjustment to other comprehensive income and then recognizes the prior-service cost as a component of pension expense over the remaining service lives of employees covered by the plan. ASC 715 prefers a years-of-service amortization method consisting of the following steps: (1) the total number of service years to be worked by all participating employees is computed; (2) prior-service cost is divided by the total number of service years to derive a cost per service year (unit cost); and (3) the number of service years each year is multiplied by the cost per service year to compute the annual amortization charge. Employers may also use the straight-line method of amortization in which prior-service cost is amortized over the average remaining service life of employees.

Prior-service cost is reported as a component of accumulated other comprehensive income in the stockholders' equity section of the balance sheet.

With respect to defined benefit pension plans, both IFRS and U.S. GAAP recognize the net of the pension assets and liabilities on the balance sheet. The following differences exist:

- As opposed to U.S. GAAP, which recognizes prior-service cost on the balance sheet as a component of accumulated other comprehensive income, IFRS does not recognize prior-service cost on the balance sheet. However, similar treatment is given to the amortization of prior-service costs into income over the anticipated employee service years.

- Under U.S. GAAP, actuarial gains and losses (and prior-service costs) are recognized in accumulated other comprehensive income and amortized to income over remaining service lives. This differs from IFRS, which gives the company a choice of recognizing actuarial gains and losses in income immediately or amortizing them over the expected remaining service lives of workers.

EXAMPLE 10: On January 1, 2X11, a company amends its pension plan and grants $800,000 of prior-service cost to employees. The employees are expected to provide 4,000 service years in the future with 500 service years in the year 2X11. The amortization of prior-service cost for the year 2X11 is:

Cost per service year = $800,000/4,000 = $200

2X11 amortization = 500 × $200 = $100,000

EXAMPLE 11: A company decides to amortize prior-service cost under the years-of-service method. There are 400 employees and the prior-service cost is $105,000. Workers are grouped based on anticipated years of retirement as follows:

Grouping	Number of Employees	Expected Retirement on December 31
1	100	2X11
2	60	2X12
3	130	2X13
4	110	2X14
	400	

The computation of the service years per year and the total service years follows:

Year	Service Years 1	2	3	4	Total
2X11	100	60	130	110	400
2X12		60	130	110	300
2X13			130	110	240
2X14				110	110
Total	100	120	390	440	1,050

Because prior-service cost is $105,000 and there are a total of 1,050 service years for all years, the cost per service year is $100 ($105,000/1,050 service years). The annual amount of amortization based on a $100 cost per service year is computed below:

Year	Total Service Years		Cost per Service Year	Annual Amortization
2X11	400	×	$100	$ 40,000
2X12	300	×	100	30,000
2X13	240	×	100	24,000
2X14	110	×	100	11,000
	1,050			$105,000

EXAMPLE 12: X Company changes its pension formula from 2% to 5% of the last three years of pay multiplied by the service years on January 1, 2X12. This results in the projected benefit obligation being increased by $500,000. Employees are anticipated to receive benefits over the next 10 years.

$$\text{Total future service years equals: } \frac{n(n+1)}{2} \times P$$

n is the number of years services are to be made

P is the population decrement each year

$$\frac{10(10+1)}{2} \times 9 = 495$$

Amortization of prior-service cost in 2X12 equals:

$$\$500,000 \times \frac{10 \times 9}{495} = \$90,909$$

Return on Plan Assets. The expected return on plan assets (e.g., stocks, bonds) typically reduces pension expense. Plan assets are valued at the moving average of asset values for the accounting period.

The expected return is the anticipated increase in plan assets arising from investment activities. The FASB mandates that expected return on plan assets be included as a component of pension expense.

The annual pension expense is adjusted for dividends and interest earned by the pension fund in addition to the appreciation or decline in the market value of the fund assets.

Pension assets are increased from employer contributions and actual returns, but pension assets are decreased from benefit payments to retirees. Actual return on plan assets increases the fund balance and reduces the employer's net cost of providing employees' pension benefits. Again, return increases pension funds from dividends, interest, and realized and unrealized gains in the fair market value of plan assets. Using hypothetical numbers, actual return on plan assets is computed as follows:

Fair market value of plan assets—end of year		$600,000
Less: Fair market value of plan assets—beginning of year		400,000
Increase in fair market value of plan assets		$200,000
Less: Employer contributions	$70,000	
Deduct retiree benefit payments	20,000	50,000
Actual return on plan assets		$150,000

An alternative way to calculate the actual return follows:

Fair market value of plan assets—beginning of year	$400,000
Add: Contributions	70,000
Less: Benefit payments	(20,000)
Add: Actual return	?
Fair market value of plan assets—end of year	$600,000

Actual return must be $150,000 (the missing number).

Note: Actual return reduces pension expense. However, if there is an actual loss (such as when there is a significant decline in the fair market value of plan assets during the year because of a sharp stock market decline), pension expense increases.

Interest is on the projected benefit obligation (PBO) at the beginning of the year. Interest on the PBO increases pension expense. The settlement rate is employed representing the rate that pension benefits could be settled for. Interest equals:

Interest Rate × Projected Benefit Obligation at the Beginning of the Year

Because a pension is a deferred compensation arrangement, a time value of money factor exists. The assumed interest (discount) rate should reflect the rate companies can settle pension benefits. In ascertaining these settlement rates, return rates on high-quality fixed-income investments, whose cash flows match the amount and timing of the anticipated benefit payments should be considered. The purpose is to derive a discount rate to measure an amount that, if invested in a high-quality debt portfolio, generates the needed future cash flows to pay the pension benefits when due.

Accounting Standards Update (ASU) No. 2017-06 (February 2017), *Plan Accounting, Employee Benefit Master Trust Reporting*, requires that for each master trust, a plan's interest in the master trust and any change in that interest should be shown in separate line items in the statement of changes in net assets available for benefits. There should be disclosure of the master trust's balances in each general type of investments. Disclosure is also required of a master trust other asset and liability balances.

Gains and Losses. Actuarial gains and losses are the differences between estimates and actual experience. For example, if the assumed interest rate is 10% and the actual interest rate is 12%, an actuarial gain results. There may also be a change in actuarial assumptions regarding the future. Actuarial gains and losses are deferred and amortized as an adjustment to pension expense over future years. Actuarial gains and losses related to a single event not related to the pension plan and not in the ordinary course of business are immediately recognized in the current year's income statement. Examples are plant closing and segment disposal.

Gains and losses are changes in the amount of either the projected benefit obligation or pension plan assets because of experience different from that assumed from changes in assumptions. Gains and losses that are *not* recognized immediately as a component of pension expense shall be recognized as increases or decreases in other comprehensive income as they arise.

Under ASC 715, the gains and losses and prior-service costs or credits that occur during the period but that are not recognized as elements of net periodic benefit cost, as per ASC 715, are recognized as a component of other comprehensive income, net of tax.

Amounts recognized in accumulated other comprehensive income, including the gains and losses and prior-service costs or credits, are adjusted as they are later recognized as components of net periodic benefit cost in accordance with the recognition and amortization provisions of ASC 715.

Actuarial Gains and Losses/Prior-Service Costs. Actuarial gains and losses not recognized as a component of pension expense are recognized as increases and decreases in other comprehensive income. The same is true for prior-service costs.

EXAMPLE 13: DEF Company provides the following information for the year 2X11:

Net income for 2X11	$250,000
Actuarial liability loss for 2X11	40,000
Prior-service cost adjustment to provide additional benefits in December 2X11	10,000
Accumulated other comprehensive income— 1/1/2X11	80,000

Assume that none of the accumulated other comprehensive income should be amortized in 2X11. Therefore, accumulated other comprehensive income (1/1/2X11 in this example) is *not* adjusted for actuarial gains and losses and prior-service cost amortization that would change pension expense. However, these items will be amortized to pension expense in subsequent years.

Both the actuarial liability loss and the prior-service cost adjustment reduce the funded status of the plan on the balance sheet. However, neither the actuarial liability loss nor the prior-service cost adjustment affects pension expense in 2X11. In later years, though, these items will affect pension expense through amortization.

The computation of other comprehensive income for 2X11 equals:

Actuarial liability loss	$40,000
Prior-service cost benefit adjustment	10,000
Other comprehensive loss	$50,000

Comprehensive income for 2X11 is presented as:

Net income	$250,000
Other comprehensive loss	50,000
Comprehensive income	$200,000

It is *not* required to present earnings per share for comprehensive income.

The comprehensive income statement for the year ended 12/31/2X11 follows:

Net income		$250,000
Other comprehensive loss		
Actuarial liability loss	$40,000	
Prior-service cost	10,000	50,000
Comprehensive loss		$200,000

The computation of accumulated other comprehensive income to be presented in the stockholders' equity section of the balance sheet on 12/31/2X11 follows:

Accumulated other comprehensive income—1/1/2X11	$80,000
Other comprehensive loss	50,000
Accumulated other comprehensive income—12/31/2X11	$30,000

Looking more closely at prior-service costs or credits, assume XYZ Company modifies its defined benefit plan and gives additional service years to workers after plan initiation. This increases the projected benefit obligation. ASC 715 mandates that the prior-service cost arising in the amendment year (which increases the projected benefit obligation) be reflected by an offsetting debit to other comprehensive income. This recognition conforms with that afforded to actuarial gains and losses.

EXAMPLE 14: Travis Company presents the following data for the year 2X12:

Net Income	$600,000
Actuarial liability loss for 2X12	180,000
Prior-service cost adjustment during 2X12	45,000
Accumulated other comprehensive income	520,000

The actuarial liability loss and the prior-service cost adjustment will reduce the funded status of the plan on the balance sheet because the projected benefit obligation increases. However, the actuarial liability loss and the prior-service cost adjustment will *not* affect pension expense in 2X12. In later years, though, these two items usually affect pension expense through amortization.

Other comprehensive income for 2X12 equals:

Actuarial liability loss	$(180,000)
Prior-service cost adjustment	(45,000)
Other comprehensive loss	$(225,000)

The computation of comprehensive income for 2X12 is:

Net Income	$600,000
Other comprehensive loss	(225,000)
Comprehensive income	$375,000

The computation of accumulated other comprehensive income to be shown in the stockholders' equity section of the balance sheet at 12/31/2X12 follows:

Accumulated other comprehensive income—1/1/2X12	$520,000
Other comprehensive loss	(225,000)
Accumulated other comprehensive income—12/31/2X12	$295,000

Note: Assumed in this example is that accumulated other comprehensive income at 1/1/2X12 is *not* adjusted for any actuarial gains or losses and any prior-service cost that would change pension expense. However, these items will be amortized into pension expense in future years.

Gain or Loss

Companies may experience uncontrollable fluctuation in pension expense arising from: (1) sudden and unexpected changes in the fair market value of plan assets and (2) changes in actuarial assumptions affecting the projected benefit obligation (which can occur when actuaries change assumptions or when actual experience is different from expected experience). The gain or loss consists of two components: (1) the difference between actual return and expected return on plan assets and (2) amortization of the net gain or loss from prior years. Thus, ASC 715 elected to reduce the fluctuation in pension expense by using *smoothing techniques* to reduce such volatility.

Smoothing Unexpected Gains and Losses on Plan Assets. Actual return on plan assets reduces pension expense. Because a very significant return rate can substantially affect pension expense, actuaries use an expected return rate as a component of pension expense. The expected return equals the expected rate of return times the market-related value of plan assets at the beginning of the period. *Unexpected gain or loss* is the difference between the expected return and actual return. The FASB simply calls this *asset gains and losses*. If actual return is more (less) than expected return, there is an asset gain (loss). The employer records asset gains and losses in other comprehensive income, combining them with gains and losses accumulated in previous years. (This is treated in a similar fashion to prior-service cost). An unexpected asset loss is debited to other comprehensive income and credited to pension expense, while an unexpected asset gain is debited to pension expense and credited to other comprehensive income.

Smoothing Unexpected Gains and Losses on the Pension Liability. Actuarial assumptions are used to estimate the projected benefit obligation (PBO). Any change in actuarial assumptions affects the amount of the PBO. Actual experience is typically different from actuarial predictions. *Liability gains and losses* are the unexpected gains and losses arising from changes in the PBO. An unexpected reduction in the PBO is a liability gain, while an unexpected increase in the PBO is a liability loss. Liability gains and losses are reported in other comprehensive income.

Note: Liability gains and losses as well as asset gains and losses are shown in the *same* other comprehensive income account. The employer accumulates the asset and liability gains and losses over the years that are *not* amortized in accumulated other comprehensive income, which is shown in the stockholders' equity section of the balance sheet.

Summary. An asset gain or loss occurs on plan assets when the expected return differs from the actual return.

Asset gain = actual return > expected return

Asset loss = actual return < expected return

A liability gain or loss arises when actuarial assumptions differ from actual experiences applicable to the computation of the projected benefit obligation.

Liability gain = unexpected decrease in the PBO

Liability loss = unexpected increase in the PBO

Asset gains and losses are combined with liability gains and losses to find the *net* gain or loss. Net gain or loss is the change in the fair market value of plan assets and the amount of change in the projected benefit obligation.

Corridor Amortization. Asset gains and losses and liability gains and losses can offset each other. The FASB has adopted the *corridor method* to amortize the accumulated other comprehensive income account balance when it becomes too large in amount. The FASB established a limit of 10% of the *greater* of the beginning balances of the market-related value of plan assets or the projected benefit obligation. Above the 10% limit, the accumulated other comprehensive income account related to gains and losses is too large and must be amortized.

EXAMPLE 15:

Projected benefit obligation	$600,000
Market-related asset value	$500,000

Corridor = 10% × $600,000 = $60,000

Any amount exceeding $60,000 would be amortized; thus, if the accumulated other comprehensive income account balance was $80,000 the amount to be amortized would be $20,000 ($80,000 – $60,000). However, if the balance of the accumulated net gain or loss account remains within the upper and lower limits of the corridor, no amortization is made. Therefore, if the accumulated other comprehensive income account had a balance of $60,000 or below, no amortization is required.

If amortization is required, the *minimum* amortization is the excess ($20,000) divided by the average remaining service years of active employees to receive benefits. Assuming a service life of 10 years, the amortization for the year would be $2,000 ($20,000/10 years).

The amortization of a loss increases pension expense, while the amortization of a gain reduces pension expense.

Note: A company can use any amortization method for gains and losses as long as it is greater than the minimum amount.

An employer can only include the amortization of net gain or loss as a component of pension expense if, at the beginning of the year, the net gain or loss in accumulated other comprehensive income exceeds the corridor. The following example illustrates the amortization of net gains and losses.

EXAMPLE 16: In the years 2X11 and 2X12, a company has actuarial losses of $1,200 and $900, respectively, in other comprehensive income. The average remaining service life is 20 years. The beginning market-related asset values and projected benefit obligations for 2X11, 2X12, and 2X13 were:

	2X11	2X12	2X13
Market-related asset value	$7,800	$8,400	$8,100
Projected benefit obligation	6,300	7,800	8,700

The amortization schedule (Schedule 1) for the net gain or loss follows:

Schedule 1

Year	Plan Assets	PBO	Corridor	Accumulated OCI[1] (G/L) – 1/1	Amortization of Loss
2X11	$7,800	$6,800	$780	$ 0	$ 0
2X12	8,400	7,800	840	1,200	18[2]
2X13	8,100	8,700	870	2,082[3]	60.6[3]

[1] OCI = Other comprehensive income
[2] $1,200 – $840 = $360: 360/20 years = $18
[3] $1,200 – $18 + $900 = $2,082; $2,082 – $870 = $1,212; $1,212/20 years = $60.6

Note: Employers determine the amortized net gain or loss by amortizing the accumulated other comprehensive income account related to net gain or loss at the beginning of the year subject to the corridor limitation. In other words, if the accumulated gain or loss exceeds the corridor, these net gains and losses are subject to amortization.

When the current-year unexpected gain or loss is combined with the amortized net gain or loss, the current-year gain or loss is determined as follows:

Current-year unexpected gain or loss (current-year actual return less current-year expected return)

Plus: Current-year amortized net gain or loss (accumulated other comprehensive income (G/L) less corridor = Balance; Balance divided by average remaining service years)

Total current-year gain or loss

EXAMPLE 17: A company has a pension plan for its employees. On January 1, 2X11, the following information is presented:

Accumulated other comprehensive loss (prior- service cost)	$37,500
Fair market value of plan assets	50,000
Projected benefit obligation	87,500

The average remaining service period for employees is 10 years. For the year 2X11, service cost was $13,000, actual return on plan assets was $2,750, and contributions were $16,250. No benefit payments were made. On December 31, 2X11, the projected benefit obligation was $113,000 and the fair market value of plan assets was $69,000. The return rate on plan assets and the interest (settlement) rate on the projected benefit obligation were both 10%.

Pension expense for 2X11 equals:

Service cost	$13,000
Interest on projected benefit obligation (10% × $87,500)	8,750
Actual return on plan assets	(2,750)
Unexpected loss on plan assets	(2,250)*
Amortization of prior-service cost ($37,500/10 years)	3,750
Pension expense	$20,500

* Unexpected loss on plan assets = expected return – actual return = $5,000 – $2,750 = $2,250.

Expected return = rate of return × plan assets (beginning of year) = 10% × $50,000) = $5,000.

The journal entry for 2X11 is:

Other comprehensive income (G/L)	6,000*	
Pension expense	20,500	
Cash		16,250
Pension liability		6,500
Other comprehensive income (prior-service cost)		3,750

* Other comprehensive income (G/L) is debited for $6,000 as computed below:

Asset loss:		
Fair market value of plan assets—12/31/2X11		$69,000
Less: Fair market value of plan assets—1/1/2X11	$50,000	
Expected return	5,000	
Contributions	16,250	71,250
Asset loss		$ 2,250

Liability loss:

Projected benefit obligation—12/31/2X11		$113,000
Less: Projected benefit obligation—1/1/2X11	$87,500	
Interest	8,750	
Service cost	13,000	109,250
Liability loss		$3,750

Other comprehensive income (G/L):

Asset loss	$2,250
Liability loss	3,750
Net loss at 12/31/2X11	$6,000

The $6,000 net loss in the accumulated other comprehensive income (G/L) account becomes the beginning balance in 2X12.

The corridor at 1/1/2X12 is computed below:

Corridor = 10% of the greater of PBO as of 12/31/2X11 ($113,000) or the fair market value of plan assets as of 12/31/2X11 ($69,000).

Corridor = 10% × $113,000 = $11,300.

Because the corridor of $11,300 exceeds the accumulated other comprehensive income (G/L) account of $6,000, no gain or loss will be amortized in the year 2X12.

Note: No amortization occurs in the year 2X11 because no balance existed in the accumulated other comprehensive income (G/L) account on 1/1/2X11.

Pension expense will not usually equal the employer's funding amount. Pension expense and related liability are based on estimating future salaries for total benefits to be paid.

If pension expense > Cash paid = Pension liability

If pension expense < Cash paid = Pension asset

EXAMPLE 18: Mr. A has six years of service prior to retirement. The estimated salary at retirement is $50,000. The pension benefit is 3% of final salary for each service year payable at retirement. The retirement benefit is computed as follows:

Final annual salary	$50,000
Formula rate	× 3%
	$1,500
Years of service	× 6
Retirement benefit	$9,000

EXAMPLE 19: On 1/1/2X13, a company adopts a defined benefit pension plan. Expected return and interest rate are both 10%. Service cost for 2X13

and 2X14 are $100,000 and $120,000, respectively. The funding amount for 2X13 and 2X14 are $80,000 and $110,000, respectively.

The entry for 2X13 is:

Pension expense	100,000	
Cash		80,000
Pension liability		20,000

The entry in 2X14 is:

Pension expense	122,000	
Cash		110,000
Pension liability		12,000

Computation:

Service cost	$120,000
Interest on projected benefit obligation 10% × $100,000	10,000
Expected return on plan assets 10% × $80,000	
	(8,000)
	$122,000

At 12/31/2X14:

Projected benefit obligation $230,000 ($100,000 + $120,000 + $10,000)

Pension plan assets $198,000 ($80,000 + $110,000 + 8,000)

EXAMPLE 20: The following information is presented:

Service cost	$6,000
Return on plan assets	700
Interest on projected benefit obligation	1,000
Amortization of net loss	200
Amortization of prior service cost	2,000

Pension expense equals:

Service cost	$6,000
Interest on projected benefit obligation	1,000
Return on plan assets	(700)
Amortization of net loss	200
Amortization of prior service cost	2,000
Pension expense	$8,500

Note: If there was in this example an amortization of net gain (instead of amortization of net loss), then it would be a deduction.

EXAMPLE 21: Company X has a defined benefit pension plan for its 100 employees. On January 1, 2X12, pension plan assets have a fair value of $230,000, and the projected benefit obligation is $420,000. Ten employees are expected to resign each year for the next 10 years. They will be eligible to receive benefits. Service cost for 2X12 is $40,000. The expected return on plan assets and the interest rate are both 8%. No actuarial gains or losses occurred during the year. Cash funded for the year is $75,000.

Pension expense equals:

Service cost	$ 40,000
Interest on projected benefit obligation	
8% × $420,000	33,600
Expected return on plan assets 8% × $230,000	(18,400)
Amortization of actuarial gains and losses	–
Amortization of unrecognized transition amount	34,545
Pension expense	$ 89,745
Projected benefit obligation	$420,000
Fair value of pension plan assets	230,000
Initial net obligation	$190,000

$$\text{Amortization} \quad \frac{\$190,000}{5.5 \text{ years}} \quad = \quad 34,545$$

$$\frac{n(n+1)}{2} \times P = \frac{10(10+1)}{2} \times 10 = 550$$

$$\frac{550}{100} = 5.5 \text{ years (average remaining service period)}$$

The journal entry to record pension expense December 31, 2X12, follows:

Pension expense	89,745	
Cash		75,000
Deferred pension liability		14,745

As per ASC 715-30, *Compensation—Retirement Benefits*, a cash balance plan should be considered a defined benefit plan.

Financial Statement Presentation. The reporting of the funded position of the plan in the balance sheet arises because actuarial gains and losses and prior-service costs are now recognized in other comprehensive income. As a result of ASC 715, actuarial gains and losses and prior-service costs are reflected in the projected benefit obligation and plan assets, with corresponding entries in other comprehensive income. However, there is no or little effect on pension expense because the amortization provisions for actuarial gains and losses and prior-service costs remain intact as that required under ASC 715. Further, the computation of other components of pension expense (e.g., service cost or interest on the projected benefit obligation) still adheres to the requirements of ASC 715.

The change in the fair market value of pension plan assets equals:

Fair market value of plan assets—beginning of year

Plus: Actual return on plan assets

Plus: Contributions

Minus: Benefits paid

Fair market value of plan assets—end of year

The change in the projected benefit obligation equals:

Projected benefit obligation—beginning of year

Plus: Service cost

Plus: Interest cost

Plus: Amendments (prior-service cost)

Plus: Actuarial loss

Minus: Benefits paid

Projected benefit obligation—end of year

ASC 715 requires an employer to recognize overfunded or underfunded status of a single-employer defined benefit postretirement plan in the balance sheet instead of the footnotes (which was previously done). Thus, a reconciliation of funded status in the footnotes is eliminated. Further, the pronouncement requires an employer to recognize all transactions and events affecting the overfunded or underfunded status of a defined benefit postretirement plan in comprehensive income in the year they take place. The employer must measure the funded status (assets and liabilities) of a plan at its fiscal year end date used for financial reporting. However, the following two exceptions exist.

1. The plan is sponsored by a subsidiary that is consolidated using a fiscal year different from its parent, as allowed under ASC 810, *Consolidation*.

2. The sponsor of the plan is an investee accounted for using the equity method, using financial statements of the investee for a fiscal year different from the investor, allowable under APB Opinion No. 18.

In situations (1) or (2) above, the employer should measure the subsidiary's plan assets and benefit obligations as of the date used to consolidate the subsidiary's balance sheet and should measure the investee's plan assets and benefit obligations as of the date of the investee's financial statements used to apply the equity method.

With respect to the net funded status of the defined benefit pension plan, the employer is required to recognize on its balance sheet the full underfunded or overfunded amount.

EXAMPLE 22: ABC Company has a projected benefit obligation of $500,000 and a fair market value of plan assets of $400,000. Thus, the pension plan is underfunded by $100,000 and must report a pension liability of $100,000.

EXAMPLE 23: DEF Company has a fair market value of plan assets of $600,000 and a projected benefit obligation of $460,000. Therefore, the pension plan is overfunded by $140,000 and must report a pension asset of $140,000.

The reporting of the funded status of the pension plan in the balance sheet arises because ASC 715 mandates that actuarial gains and losses and prior-service costs are to be recognized in other comprehensive income.

There should be an aggregation of the status of all overfunded plans and the amount should be recognized as an asset. The excess of the fair market value of plan assets over the projected benefit obligation is shown as a noncurrent asset. (**Note:** No part of a pension asset is reported as a current asset.) The reasoning for the noncurrent classification is that the pension plan assets are *restricted.* Specifically, pension assets are used to fund the projected benefit obligation and, in consequence, the noncurrent classification is appropriate. There should be an aggregation of the status of all underfunded plans and the amount should be recorded as a liability. The liability for an underfunded plan may be classified as a current liability, noncurrent liability, or a combination of both. The current portion is the amount by which the actuarial present value of benefits included in the benefit obligation payable within the year or normal operating cycle of the business, if longer, exceeds the fair market value of plan assets.

All overfunded plans should be combined and presented as a pension plan asset. Similarly, all underfunded plans should be combined and presented as a pension plan liability. (**Note:** It is prohibited to combine all plans and show a net amount as a single net asset or net liability.)

EXAMPLE 24: Mavis Company has four pension plans as follows:

Plan	Fair Value of Plan Assets	Projected Benefit Obligation	Pension Asset/ Liability
1	$500,000	$450,000	$50,000 Asset
2	600,000	500,000	100,000 Asset
3	700,000	900,000	200,000 Liability
4	640,000	750,000	110,000 Liability

Pension plan assets are reported as $150,000, whereas pension plan liabilities are separately reported as $310,000.

Summary of Accounting for Pension Plans. Exhibit 12-2 presents a summary of the accounting for pension plans as per ASC 715.

Exhibit 12-2: Pension Plan Accounting

Item	Journal Entry Account	Memo Account
1. Prior-service cost	Other comprehensive income—prior-service cost Dr.	Projected benefit obligation Cr.
2. Service cost	Pension expense Dr.	Projected benefit obligation Cr.
3. Interest on projected benefit obligation	Pension expense Dr.	Projected benefit obligation Cr.
4. Actual return	Pension expense Cr.	Plan assets Dr.
5. Amortization of prior-service cost	Pension expense Dr., other comprehensive income—prior-service cost Cr.	
6. Contributions	Cash Cr.	Plan assets Dr.
7. Benefit payments		Projected benefit obligation Dr., plan assets Cr.
8. Unexpected loss (expected return on plan assets exceeds actual return)	Other comprehensive income (G/L) Dr., pension expense Cr.	
9. Unexpected gain (actual return on plan assets exceeds expected return)	Pension expense Dr., other comprehensive income (G/L) Cr.	
10. Liability (projected benefit obligation) increase	Other comprehensive (G/L) income Dr.	Projected benefit obligation Cr.
11. Liability (projected benefit obligation) decrease	Other comprehensive (G/L) income Cr.	Projected benefit obligation Dr.
12. Amortization of excess loss over the corridor	Pension expense Dr., other comprehensive income (G/L) Cr.	
13. Amortization of excess gain over the corridor	Other comprehensive income (G/L) Dr., pension expense Cr.	

Application Examples. The following application examples enhance an understanding of the pension requirements provided for in ASC 715.

EXAMPLE 25: The following information is presented of Harris Company's pension plan:

	1/1/2X12	12/31/2X12
Projected benefit obligation	$ 1,000	$1,040
Fair market value of plan assets	400	565
Accumulated other comprehensive income (G/L)—net gain	0	200

On January 1, 2X12, the pension liability was $600 ($1,000 – $400).

Service cost for 2X12	$140
Amortization of prior-service cost for 2X12	$ 60
Contributions for 2X12	$125
Return rate on plan assets	10%
Interest rate of projected benefit obligation	10%

On January 1, 2X12, accumulated other comprehensive income (prior-service cost) had a balance of $600. No benefit payments to retirees were made in 2X12.

Pension expense equals:

Service cost	$140
Interest on projected benefit obligation (10% × $1,000)	100
Expected return on plan assets (10% × $400)	(40)
Amortization of prior-service cost	60
Pension expense	$260

The journal entry to record pension expense and the employer's contribution to the plan in 2X12 follows:

Pension expense	260	
Pension asset	125	
Other comprehensive income (prior-service cost)		60
Other comprehensive income (G/L)		200
Cash		125

The 12/31/2X12 balance sheet shows a balance in pension liability of $475 computed as follows:

Projected benefit obligation—12/31/2X12	$1,040
Less: Pension assets—12/31/2X12	565
Pension liability	$ 475

An alternative calculation for the pension liability year-end balance is:

Pension liability 1/1/2X12	$600 Cr.
Journal entry in 2X12	125 Dr.
Pension liability	$ 475 Cr.

The 12/31/2X12 presentation of stockholders' equity on the balance sheet shows:

Stockholders' Equity:

Accumulated other comprehensive income (prior-service cost) ($600 – $60)	$540
Accumulated other comprehensive income (G/L)	$100

EXAMPLE 26: ABC Company provides the following information:

Employer contributions	$4,000
Benefit payments to retirees	3,500
Fair market value of plan assets—1/1/2X16	50,000
Projected benefit obligation—1/1/2X16	50,000
Service cost	4,500
Actual return on plan assets	5,000
Interest rate	10%

Because the fair market value of plan assets and the projected benefit obligation are the same at 1/1/2X16, the pension asset/liability has a zero balance on 1/1/2X16.

Interest cost = interest rate x projected benefit obligation – 1/1/2X16
= 10% × $50,000 = $5,000

WORKSHEET A

	Journal Entries			Memo	
Item	Pension Expense	Cash	Pension Asset/ Liability	PBO	Plan Assets
Balance— 1/1/2X16				50,000 Cr.	50,000 Dr.
1. Service cost	4,500 Dr.			4,500 Cr.	
2. Interest cost	5,000 Dr.			5,000 Cr.	
3. Actual return	5,000 Cr.				5,000 Dr.
4. Contributions		4,000 Cr.			4,000 Dr.
5. Benefit payments				3,500 Dr.	3,500 Cr.
Journal entry for year 2X16	4,500 Dr.	4000 Cr.	500 Cr.		
Balance— 12/31/2X16			500 Cr.	56,000 Cr.	55,500 Dr.

Note: Service cost and interest cost increase pension expense and the projected benefit obligation. Actual return decreases pension expense and increases plan assets. Contributions decrease cash and increase plan assets. Benefit payments decrease plan assets and the projected benefit obligation.

The journal entry on 12/31/2X16 is:

Pension expense	4,500	
Cash		4,000
Pension liability		500

There is a pension liability because the plan is underfunded (the amount funded is less than the pension expense). (If the plan was overfunded, there would be a pension asset.

The pension liability of $500 can also be derived by comparing the projected benefit obligation and plan assets as indicated in the memo columns of Worksheet A as follows:

Projected benefit obligation (Cr.)	$56,000
Fair market value of plan assets (Dr.)	55,500
Pension liability (Cr.)	$ 500

Note: If the fair market value of plan assets (Dr.) exceeded the projected benefit obligation (Cr.), there would be a pension asset (Dr.).

EXAMPLE 27: This is a continuation of Example 26 for ABC Company for the year 2X17. On 1/1/2X17, the company has a prior-service cost of $40,000 because it amended its pension plan. Amortization of prior-service cost is assumed to be $13,600. Additional information follows:

Contributions	$10,050
Benefit payments to retirees	4,000
Accumulated other comprehensive income— 12/31/2X16	0
Service cost	4,750
Actual return on plan assets	5,550
Interest rate	10%

Notes:

- Interest cost = interest rate × PBO (beginning of year) = 10% × $96,000 = $9,600.

- The granting of the prior-service cost increases the projected benefit obligation and decreases other comprehensive income by $40,000.

- Amortization of prior-service cost requires debiting pension expense and crediting other comprehensive income for $13,600.

The journal entry on 12/31/2X17 is:

Pension expense	22,450	
Other comprehensive income (PSC)	26,400	
Cash		10,050
Pension liability		38,800

Worksheet B

Items	Journal Entries				Memo	
	Pension Expense	Cash	Other Comprehensive Income Prior-Service Cost	Pension Asset/Liability	Projected Benefit Obligation	Plan Assets
Balance - 12/31/20X8				500 Cr.	56,000 Cr.	55,500 Dr.
1 Prior-service cost			40,000 Dr.		40,000 Cr.	
Balance - 1/1/20X9					96,000 Cr.	55,500 Dr.
2 Service cost	4,750 Dr.				4,750 Cr.	
3 Interest cost	9,600 Dr.				9,600 Cr.	
4 Actual return	5,500 Cr.					5,500 Dr.
5 Amortization of prior-service cost	13,600 Dr.		13,600 Cr.			
6 Contributions		10,050 Cr.				10,050 Dr.
7 Benefit payments					4,000 Dr.	4,000 Cr.
Journal entry for 20X9	22,450 Dr.	10,050 Cr.	26,400 Dr.	38,800 Cr.		
Accumulated other comprehensive income - 12/31/20X8			0			
Balance - 12/31/20X9			26,400 Dr.	39,300 Cr.	106,350 Cr.	67,050 Dr.

The balance in the pension liability shown in the balance sheet on 12/31/2X17 equals $39,300 ($500 + $38,800). The balance of the pension liability can also be derived as follows:

Projected benefit obligation (Cr.)	$106,350
Fair market value of plan assets (Dr.)	67,050
Pension liability (Cr.)	$ 39,300

EXAMPLE 28: This is a continuation of Example 27 for ABC Company for the year 2X18. The following information is presented for 2X18:

Contributions	$12,000
Benefit payments to retirees	5,250
Amortization of prior-service cost	10,400
Service cost	6,500
Actual return on plan assets	6,000
Interest rate	10%
Expected return rate	10%

Changes in actuarial assumptions resulted in a year-end balance of $132,500 in the projected benefit obligation.

* Accumulated other comprehensive income (prior-service cost)	$16,000 Dr.
Accumulated other comprehensive income (G/L)	26,855 Dr.
Accumulated other comprehensive income— 12/31/2X18	$42,855 Dr.

Notes:

- Interest cost = interest rate × projected benefit obligation (beginning of year) = 10% × $106,350 = $10,635.

- Unexpected loss = (expected return – actual return). The expected return equals return rate × plan assets (beginning of year).

  Expected return = 10% × $67,050 = $6,705.

  Expected return ($6,705) – actual return ($6,000) = $705

  ABC Company defers the unexpected loss of $705 by debiting other comprehensive income (G/L) and crediting pension expense. Because of this adjustment the expected return on plan assets is the amount actually used to compute pension expense.

- Liability increase = projected benefit obligation (end of year) – projected benefit obligation (beginning of year)

  $132,500 – $106,350 = $26,150

Worksheet C

Items	Pension Expense	Cash	Other Comprehensive Income — Prior-Service Cost	Other Comprehensive Income — Gains/Losses	Pension Asset/Liability	Projected Benefit Obligation	Plan Assets
			Journal Entries			Memo	
Balance - 1/1/201X					39,300 Cr.	106,350 Cr.	67,050 Dr.
1 Service cost	6,500 Dr.					6,500 Cr.	
2 Interest cost	10,635 Dr.					10,635 Cr.	
3 Actual return	6,000 Cr.						6,000 Dr.
4 Unexpected loss	705 Cr.			705 Dr.			
5 Amortization of prior-service cost	10,400 Dr.		10,400 Cr.				
6 Contributions		12,000 Cr.					12,000 Dr.
7 Benefit payments						5,250 Dr.	5,250 Cr.
8 Liability increase				26,150 Dr.		26,150 Cr.	
Journal entry for 201X	20,830 Dr.	12,000 Cr.	10,400 Cr.	26,855 Dr.	25,285 Cr.		
Accumulated OCI - 12/31/20X9			26,400 Dr.	0			
Balance - 12/31/201X*			16,000 Dr.	26,855 Dr.	64,585 Cr.	144,385 Cr.	79,800 Dr.

Entry 8 in Worksheet C records the change in the projected benefit obligation due to the change in actuarial assumptions. The actuary computed the ending balance of $132,500. The projected benefit obligation balance at 12/31/2X18 is computed below:

Projected benefit obligation—1/1/2X18	$106,350
Service cost	6,500
Interest cost	10,635
Benefits paid	(5,250)
Projected benefit obligation—12/31/2X18 (before liability increase)	$118,235

The difference between the projected benefit obligation ending balance of $144,385 and the balance of the projected benefit obligation (before the liability increase) is $26,150 ($144,385 – $118,235). The increase of $26,150 in the employer's liability is an unexpected loss.

The $64,585 balance in the pension liability account at 12/31/2X18 equals the net of the balances in the memo accounts as indicated below:

Projected benefit obligation	$144,385 Cr.
Fair market value of plan assets	79,800 Dr.
Pension liability	$ 64,585 Cr.

The journal entry on 12/31/2X18 is:

Pension expense	20,830	
Other comprehensive income (G/L)	26,855	
Cash		12,000
Other comprehensive income (prior-service cost)		10,400
Pension liability		25,285

EXAMPLE 29: This is a continuation of Example 28 for ABC Company for the year 2X19. The following information is given for 2X19:

Contributions	$13,500
Benefit payments to retirees	9,000
Amortization of prior-service cost	8,800
Service cost	8,000
Actual return on plan assets	11,000
Interest rate	10%
Expected return rate	10%
Average service life of eligible workers	10 years

Worksheet D

	Journal Entries					Memo	
			Other Comprehensive Income				
Items	Pension Expense	Cash	Prior-Service Cost	Gains/Losses	Pension Asset/Liability	Projected Benefit Obligation	Plan Assets
Balance - 1/31/201Y					64,585 Cr.	144,385 Cr.	79,800 Dr.
1 Service cost	8,000 Dr.					8,000 Cr.	
2 Interest cost	14,439 Dr.					14,439 Cr.	
3 Actual return	11,000 Cr.						11,000 Dr.
4 Unexpected gain	3,020 Dr.			3,020 Cr.			
5 Amortization of prior-service cost	8,800 Dr.		8,800 Cr.				
6 Contributions		13,500 Cr.					13,500 Dr.
7 Benefit payments						9,000 Dr.	9,000 Cr.
8 Amortization of loss	1,242 Dr.			1,242 Cr.			
Journal entry for 201Y	24,501 Dr.	13,500 Cr.	8,800 Cr.	4,262 Cr.	2,061 Dr.		
Accumulated OCI - 12/31/201X			16,000 Dr.	26,855 Dr.			
Balance - 12/31/201Y			7,200 Dr.	22,593 Dr.	62,524 Cr.	157,824 Cr.	95,300 Dr.

Notes:

- Interest cost = interest rate × projected benefit obligation (beginning of year) = 10% × $144,385 = $14,439.

- Unexpected gain = (actual return–expected return). Expected return equals the return rate multiplied by the plan assets (beginning of year).

  Expected return = 10% × $79,800 = $7,980

  (Actual return $11,000 – expected return $7,980) = $3,020

  ABC Company defers the unexpected gain of $3,020 by crediting other comprehensive income (G/L) and debiting pension expense. Because of this adjustment, the expected return on plan assets is the amount actually used to compute pension expense. By netting the gain of $3,020 against the actual return of $11,000, pension expense is affected only by the expected return of $7,980.

ABC begins the year 2X19 with a balance in the net loss account of $26,855. The corridor test is applied in 2X19 to ascertain whether the balance is excessive and should be amortized. The corridor equals 10% of the greater of the beginning balances of plan assets ($79,800) or projected benefit obligation ($144,385). Therefore, the corridor equals $14,439 (10% × $144,385). Because the balance in the accumulated other comprehensive income account is a net loss of $26,855, the excess over the corridor equals $12,416 ($26,855 – $14,439). This excess ($12,416) is amortized over the average remaining service life of employees (10 years), so that the amortization for 2X19 is $1,242 ($12,416/10 years). The company debits pension expense and credits other comprehensive income for $1,242.

A schedule for the year 2X19 corridor test follows:

Net loss at the beginning of year in accumulated other comprehensive income	$26,855
10% of greater of plan assets or projected benefit obligation (10% × $144,385)	14,439
Amount to be amortized	$12,416
Average service life	10 years
Amortization for 2X19 ($12,416/10 years) = $1,242	

The journal entry to record pension expense for 2X19 is:

Pension expense	24,501	
Pension asset/liability	2,061	
Cash		13,500
Other comprehensive income (G/L)		4,262
Other comprehensive income (prior-service cost)		8,800

The balance on 12/31/2X19 of $62,524 in pension liability equals:

Projected benefit obligation (Cr.)	$157,824
Fair market value of plan assets (Dr.)	95,300
Pension liability	$ 62,524

Disclosures. Footnote disclosures for a pension plan are as follows:

- A description of the plan including benefit formula, funding policy, employee groups covered, and retirement age.
- Components of pension expense.
- Pension assumptions (e.g., interest rate, mortality rate, employee turnover).
- Amounts in accumulated other comprehensive income that have not yet been recognized as components of net periodic benefit costs, showing separately the net gain or loss, net prior-service cost or credit, and net transition asset or obligation.
- Present value of vested and nonvested benefits.
- The weighted-average assumed discount rate in measuring the projected benefit obligation. At each measurement date, the employer must ascertain the appropriate discount rate used to measure the pension liability, based on current interest rates.
- The weighted-average expected return rate on pension plan assets.
- Amounts and types of securities included in pension plan assets.
- Amount of approximate annuity benefits to employees.

A company that has one or more benefit plans should disclose the following in the footnotes, separately for pension plans and other postretirement plans:

1. Amounts recognized in other comprehensive income in the income statement, presenting separately the net gain or loss and net prior-service cost or credit. Those amounts shall be separated into amounts arising during the year and reclassification adjustments of other comprehensive income as a result of being recognized as components of net periodic benefit cost for the year.
2. For each annual statement of income, the net transition asset or liability recognized as a reclassification adjustment of other comprehensive income as a result of being recognized as a component of net periodic benefit cost.
3. The amount and timing of any plan assets anticipated to be returned to the company during the 12-month period, or operating cycle, if longer.
4. The nature and amount of changes in pension plan assets and benefit obligations recognized in net income and in other comprehensive income.
5. The accumulated amount of changes in pension plan assets and benefit obligations that have been recognized in other comprehensive income and would be recycled into net profit in future years. This information indicates pension and related balances recognized in stockholders' equity, which will have an impact on future income.

6. The amount of anticipated net actuarial gain or loss and prior-service costs or credits that will be amortized from accumulated other comprehensive income into net income over the next fiscal year. This data aids in predicting the effect of deferred pension expense items on next year's income.

7. The amortization method used for the excess of the accumulated other comprehensive income balance over the corridor amount.

8. The effects on net periodic benefit cost for the next fiscal year that arises from delayed recognition of the gains and losses and prior-service costs or credits.

9. A reconciliation of how the fair market value of pension plan assets and the projected benefit obligation changed from the beginning to end of the year.

10. The rates used to measure benefit amounts, such as discount rate, expected return rate on plan assets, and rate of compensation.

11. A schedule showing the allocation of pension plan assets by category (e.g., equity securities, debt securities, and real estate) and indicating the percentage of the fair value to total plan assets. Further, the employer must have a narrative discussion of investment policies, including any target allocation percentage.

12. An estimate of the anticipated contributions to be funded to the plan next year.

13. The expected benefit payments to retirees for each of the next five years and in total for the five years thereafter.

Practical Expedient for the Measurement Date of an Employer's Defined Benefit Obligation and Plan Assets

ASU No. 2015-04, *Practical Expedient for the Measurement Date of an Employer's Defined Benefit Obligation and Plan Assets,* amends Section 715, *Compensation-Retirement Benefits,* by providing for a practical expedient when an entity's fiscal year does not coincide with the month end of the year used to measure its defined benefit plan assets and obligations (measurement date). This may occur, for example, when an entity defines its fiscal year end as the first Friday of January each year. In such a situation, this update permits the entity to measure its defined benefit plan assets and obligations using the month end that is closest to the entity fiscal year end. (e.g., December 31 measurement date versus January 3, fiscal year end, in the next calendar year). If a contribution or other significant event such as a curtailment, settlement, or plan amendment occurs between the month end being used to measure the entity's plan assets and obligations and its fiscal year end, then the plan assets and obligations must be adjusted for these amounts. However, the entity should not adjust the fair value of each class of plan assets for the effects of the contribution but rather should simply disclose in its notes the amount of the contribution that would reconcile the *total* fair value for all of the classes of plan assets to the ending balance of its fair value.

This update was approved as part of the FASB's initiative to reduce complexity in accounting standards. It enables entities to reduce their costs by using measurements of fair value of their plan assets and liabilities at the month end provided by consultants and actuaries at December 31, for example, rather than having to adjust this information to the entity's fiscal year end date (i.e., in this example, first Friday of the following January).

An illustration of how a contribution by an employer after the plan asset measurement date would be disclosed is shown below. Assume for this illustration that the measurement date of the defined benefit plan assets is December 31, 20X1, and a contribution is made by the employer to the plan on January 2, 20X2. In addition, assume the entity's fiscal year end is January 3, 20X2.

ILLUSTRATION

Disclosure of Fair Value Measurements of Plan Assets at January 3, 20X2

| | | Fair Value Measurements at January 3, 20X2 (in thousands) | | |
	Total	Quoted Prices in Active Markets for Identical Assets (Level 1)	Significant Observable Inputs (Level 2)	Significant Unobservable Inputs (Level 3)
Classes of Assets				
Cash	$ 10,221	$ 10,221		
Stocks				
US Companies	35,651	35,000		$ 651
International Companies	23,313	19,563	$ 2,200	1,550
Mortagage-backed securities	3,645		1,722	854
Fair value of assets-Measurement date 12/31/20X1	72,830	$ 64,784	$ 3,922	$ 3,055
Contributions after measurement date	9,576			
Total assets reported at January 3, 20X2	$ 82,406			

Settlement in a Pension Plan

ASC 715 amends ASC 712, *Compensation—Retirement Benefits; and Compensation—Nonretirement Postemployment Benefits.* As per ASC 712, a settlement is discharging some or all of the employer's pension benefit obligation. Excess plan assets can revert to the employer. A settlement must satisfy *all* of the following criteria:

- It is irrevocable.
- It relieves pension benefit responsibility.
- It materially curtails risk related to the pension obligation.

The amount of gain or loss recognized in the income statement when a pension obligation is settled is limited to the unrecognized net gain or loss from realized or unrealized changes in either the pension benefit obligation or plan assets caused from actual experiences being different from original assumptions. All or a pro rata share of the unrecognized gain or loss is recognized when a plan is settled. If full settlement occurs, all unrecognized gains or losses are recognized. If only a part of the plan is settled, a pro rata share of the unrecognized net gain or loss is recognized.

An example of a settlement is when the employer furnishes employees with a lump-sum amount to give up pension rights. The gain or loss resulting is included in the current year's income statement.

Curtailment in a Pension Plan

As per ASC 712, a curtailment occurs when an event significantly reduces future service years of present employees or eliminates for most employees the accumulation of defined benefits for future services. An example is a plant closing ending employee services prior to pension plan expectations. The gain or loss is recognized in the current year's income statement and contains the following elements:

- Prior-service cost attributable to employee services no longer needed.
- Change in pension benefit obligation due to the curtailment.

The projected benefit obligation may be decreased (gain) or increased (loss) by a curtailment. To the degree that such a gain (loss) exceeds any net loss (gain) included in accumulated other comprehensive income, it is a curtailment gain (loss).

The amount of net periodic benefit cost should include the gain or loss recognized because of settlements or curtailments.

Termination in a Pension Plan

When termination benefits are offered by the employer, and accepted by employees, and the amount can reasonably be determined, an expense and liability are recognized. The amount of the accrual equals the down payment plus the present value of future payments to be made by the employer. The entry is to debit loss and credit cash (down payment) and liability (future payments). Footnote disclosure should be given of the arrangement.

Employers Having More Than One Defined Benefit Plan

If an employer has more than one pension plan, it has to prepare separate calculations of pension expense, fair value of plan assets, and liabilities for each plan.

The employer is prohibited from offsetting assets or liabilities of different pension plans unless a legal right exists to use the assets of one plan to pay the debt or benefits of another plan.

Disclosures may be combined for all pension plans kept by the employer with the following exception:

- U.S. pension plans may not be aggregated with foreign pension plans unless there exist similar assumptions.

Multiemployer Plans

A multiemployer plan typically includes participation of two or more unrelated employers. It often arises from a collective-bargaining contract with the union. The plan is typically administered by a Board of Trustees. In this instance, plan assets contributed by one employer may be used to pay employee benefits of another participating employer. Hence, the assets are combined for all employers and are available and unrestricted to pay benefits to all employees irrespective of by whom they are employed. In other words, there is no segregation of assets in a particular employer's account or any restrictions placed on that employer's assets. An example is a plan contributed to by all employers employing the members of a particular union regardless of for whom the employees work. Retirees of different employers receive payment from the same combined fund. An example is the Teamsters' union.

In a multiemployer plan, the employer's pension expense equals its contribution to the plan for the year. If a contribution is accrued, the employer must record a liability.

If an employer withdraws from the multiemployer plan, it may incur a liability for its share of the unfunded benefit obligation of the plan. If an employer would probably incur a liability if it withdraws from the plan and the amount is reasonably ascertainable, a loss must be accrued with a concurrent liability. However, if the loss is reasonably possible, only footnote disclosure is needed.

Footnote disclosures for employers involved with a multiemployer plan include:

- A description of the plan, including employees covered.
- The benefits to be provided.
- Nature of matters affecting the comparability of information for the years presented.
- Pension expense for the period.

Accounting Standards Update (ASU) No. 2011-09 (September 2011), *Compensation Retirement Benefits—Multiemployer Plans (ASC Topic 715-80), Disclosures about an Employer's Participation in a Multiemployer Plan*, requires that companies give additional quantitative and qualitative disclosures for multiemployer pension plans and other postretirement benefit plans. The disclosures include identifying names and numbers, plan benefits, employer contributions, funded status, surcharges on contributions, and employer commitments and obligations.

Multiple-Employer Plans

These plans have similarities to multiemployer plans. They also consist of two or more unrelated employers. However, multiple-employer plans are in effect aggregated single-employer plans that are combined so that assets of all may be totaled to lower administrative costs. The assets are merged to improve the overall rate of return from investing them. In many instances, participating employers may use different benefit formulas for their respective pension contributions. Each employer in the plan accounts for its particular interest separately. An example of such an arrangement is when businesses in an industry have their trade group handle the plans of all the companies. Each company retains its responsibilities only for its own workers. Multiple-employer plans are typically not associated with collective-bargaining agreements.

Annuity Contracts

An employer may sign a valid and irrevocable insurance contract to pay benefit obligations arising from a defined benefit plan. Annuity contracts are used to transfer the risk of providing employee benefits from the employer to the insurance company.

If the annuity contracts are the basis to fund the pension plan and to pay plan obligations, the employer's insurance premium is the pension expense for the period covering all currently earned benefits. In this instance, the company and plan do not report plan assets, accumulated benefit obligation, or a projected benefit obligation. On the contrary, if the annuity contracts only cover part of the benefit obligation, the employer is liable for the uncovered obligation.

In a participating annuity contract, the insurer pays the employer part of the income earned from investing the insurance premiums. In most instances, income earned (e.g., interest, dividends) reduces pension expense. A disadvantage to the employer of a participating contract is that it costs more than one that is nonparticipating owing to the participation privilege. This additional cost applicable to the participation right should be recognized as a pension plan asset. Therefore, except for the cost of participation rights, pension plan assets exclude the cost of annuity contracts. In later years, fair value should be used in valuing the participation right included in plan assets. In the event that fair value may not be reasonably determined, the asset should be recorded at cost with amortization based on the dividend period stipulated in the contract. However, unamortized cost cannot exceed the net realizable value of the participation right. If the terms of the participating annuity contract are such that the employer retains all or most of the risk applicable to the benefit obligation, the purchase of this contract does not constitute a settlement of the employer's obligations under the pension plan.

Insurance contracts other than annuity contracts are considered investments. They are reported as pension plan assets and reported at fair value. Fair value may be in terms of conversion value, contract value, or cash surrender value, for example, depending on the circumstances.

The definition of an annuity contract is *not* met if either or both of the following is true:

- There exists uncertainty as to whether the insurance company, because of financial difficulties, will be able to pay its debts.

- There is a captive insurance company, meaning that the insurance entity has as its major client the employer or any of its associated parties.

An employer has to record a loss when it assumes the obligation to pay retirees because the insurance company is financially unable to do so. The loss is recorded at the lower of any gain associated with the original insurance contract or the amount of benefit assumed. An unrecognized additional loss should be treated as an amendment to the pension plan.

Employee Retirement Income Security Act (ERISA)

The Act generally provides for full vesting of pension benefits if an employee has worked for 15 years. Past service costs must be funded over a period of not more than 40 years.

Trustee Reporting for a Defined Benefit Pension Plan

ASC 960, *Plan Accounting—Defined Benefit Pension Plans*, deals with the reporting and disclosures of the trustee of a defined benefit pension plan. Generally accepted accounting principles must be followed. Financial statements are not required to be issued by the plan. If they are issued, reporting guidelines have to be followed. The prime objective is to assess the plan's capability to meet retirement benefits.

The balance sheet presents pension assets and liabilities as an offset. Operating assets are at book value. In determining net assets available, accrual accounting is followed. An example is accruing for interest earned but not received. Investments are shown at fair market value. An asset shown is "contributions receivable due from employer." In computing pension plan liability, participants' accumulated benefits are excluded. In effect, plan participants are equity holders rather than creditors of the plan.

Disclosure is required of:

- Net assets available for benefits.
- Changes in net assets available for benefits, including net appreciation in fair value of each major class of investments.
- Actuarial present value of accumulated plan benefits. Accumulated plan benefits include benefits anticipated to be paid to retired employees, beneficiaries, and present employees.
- Changes in actuarial present value of accumulated plan benefits.
- Description of the plan, including amendments.
- Accounting and funding policies.

Unlike U.S. GAAP, IFRS permits companies the choice to report the funded status of the pension plan on the balance sheet.

There may exist an annuity contract by which an insurance company agrees to give specified pension benefits in return for receiving a premium.

POSTRETIREMENT BENEFITS EXCLUDING PENSIONS

ASC 715 requires the recognition for the first time of the postretirement liability.

ASC 712 deals with all types of postretirement benefits, but *concentrates* on postretirement health care benefits. However, brief references are made to long-term care, tuition assistance, legal advisory services, and housing subsidies.

The major differences between pension benefits and postretirement benefits (e.g., health care or welfare) are:

- Pension benefits are usually funded, whereas postretirement benefits are not.

- Pension benefits are well-defined within a level dollar amount, whereas postretirement benefits are typically uncapped and show significant fluctuation.

Postretirement benefits for current and future retirees represent deferred compensation. The time period the postretirement benefit cost accrues is referred to as the *attribution period.*

ASC 712 requires *accrual* of the expected cost of postretirement benefits during the years in which active employee services are rendered. These expected postretirement benefits may be paid to employees, employees' beneficiaries, and covered dependents.

The employer's obligation for postretirement benefits expected to be provided must be *fully accrued* by the date that the employee attains full eligibility for all of the benefits expected to be received (the full eligibility date), even if the employee is expected to perform additional services beyond that date.

The beginning of the accrual (attribution) period is the *date of employment* unless the plan grants credit for service only from a later date, in which instance benefits are generally attributed from the beginning of that credited service period. An equal amount of the anticipated postretirement benefit is attributed to each year of service unless the plan provides a disproportionate share of the expected benefits to early years of service.

ASC 712 requires a single measurement approach to spread costs from the date of hire to the date the employee is *fully* eligible to receive benefits (vesting date). If information on gross charges is not available, there is a measurement approach based on net claims cost (e.g., gross charges less deductibles, copayments, Medicare). There is a projection of future retiree health care costs based on a health care cost trend assumption to current costs.

The *accumulated postretirement benefit obligation* (APBO) is the actuarial present value of future benefits assigned to employees' services performed up to a particular date. The *expected postretirement benefit obligation* (EPBO) is the actuarial present value, as of a particular date, of all benefits a company anticipates to pay after retirement to employees. The APBO equals the EPBO for retirees and active employees fully eligible for benefits at the end of the attribution period. Before full eligibility is reached, the APBO is a portion of the EPBO. Thus, the difference between the APBO and the EPBO is the future service costs of active employees who are not yet fully eligible.

Components

Net periodic postretirement benefit cost is made up of the following components:

- *Service cost*—actuarial present value of benefits applicable to services performed during the current year.

- *Interest cost*—interest on the accumulated postretirement benefit obligation at the beginning of the period, adjusted for benefit payments during the year.

- *Actual return on plan assets*—return based on the fair value of plan assets at the beginning and end of the period, adjusted for contributions and benefit payments.

- *Amortization expense on prior-service cost*—expense provision for the current year due to amortization of the prior-service cost arising from adoption or amendment to the plan. Prior-service cost applies to credited services before adoption or amendment, and is accounted for over current and future years. The usual amortization period, starting with the amendment date, is the remaining service years to the full eligibility date. There should be amortization of any prior-service cost or credit included in accumulated other comprehensive income.

- *Gain or loss component*—gains and losses apply to changes in the amount of either the accumulated postretirement benefit obligation or plan assets resulting from actual experience being different from the actuarial assumptions. The gains and losses may also apply to changes in actuarial assumptions. Gains and losses may be realized (i.e., sale of securities) or unrealized. Gains and losses that are not recognized immediately as a component of net periodic postretirement benefit cost are recognized as increases or decreases in other comprehensive income as they arise.

EXAMPLE 30: On January 1, 2X11, Levine Company adopts a health care benefit plan and provides the following information for the year 2X11:

Service cost	$1,350
Contribution	950
Benefit payments	700

The service cost of $1,350 increases postretirement expense and the accumulated postretirement benefit obligation (APBO). The contribution of $950 reduces cash and increases plan assets. The benefit payments to retirees of $700 reduce the APBO and the plan assets.

Postretirement Schedule A

Item	Journal Entries (JEs)			Memo	
	Postretirement Expense	Cash	Postretirement Asset/Liability	APBO	Plan Assets
Bal.— 1/1/2X11					
1. Service cost	1,350 Dr.			1,350 Cr.	
2. Contribution		950 Cr.			950 Dr.
3. Benefit payments				700 Dr.	700 Cr.
JE for 2X11	1,350 Dr.	950 Cr.	400 Cr.		
Bal.— 12/31/2X11			400 Cr.	650 Cr.	250 Dr.

	Journal Entries (JEs)			Memo	
Item	**Postretirement Expense**	**Cash**	**Postretirement Asset/Liability**	**APBO**	**Plan Assets**

The journal entry on 12/31/2X11 is:

Postretirement expense	1,350				
Cash			950		
Postretirement liability			400		

The credit to postretirement liability can also be calculated as:

APBO (Cr.)	$650
Fair market value of plan assets (Dr.)	250
Postretirement liability	400

The postretirement liability means the plan is underfunded by $400.

Plan Amendment. A plan amendment that retroactively increases benefits increases the accumulated postretirement benefit obligation. The cost of the benefit improvement is recognized as a charge to other comprehensive income at the date of the amendment. On the other hand, a plan modification that retroactively reduces the benefits decreases the accumulated postretirement benefit obligation. The reduction in benefits is recognized as a corresponding credit (prior-service credit) to other comprehensive income that is first used to reduce any remaining prior-service cost included in accumulated other comprehensive income and then reduces any transition obligation remaining in accumulated other comprehensive income. The excess, if any, is amortized as a component of net periodic postretirement benefit cost. It is prohibited to immediately recognize the excess.

Corridor. As with pensions, employers amortize the gains and losses in accumulated other comprehensive income as an element of postretirement expense assuming, at the beginning of the year, the gains and losses exceed the corridor. In the case of postretirement plans, the corridor equals 10% of the greater of the APBO or market-related value of plan assets.

The minimum amortization amount is the excess of the gains or losses over the corridor amount. The excess is amortized over the average remaining service life of active employees. The employer must recompute the amount of gains or losses in accumulated other comprehensive income each year and amortize the excess gains or losses.

EXAMPLE 31: This is a continuation of Example 30 for Levine Company for the year 2X12. The company provides the following information for 2X12:

Actual return on plan assets	$ 15
Expected return on plan assets	$ 20
Interest rate	8%

Increase in APBO because of change in actuarial assumptions	$1,500
Service cost	$ 650
Contributions	$ 450
Benefit payments	$ 125
Average remaining service period	20 years

Postretirement Schedule B

	Journal Entries (JEs)				Memo Item	
	Postretire-ment Expense	Cash	OCI[1] (G/L)	Postretire-ment Asset/ Liability	APBO	Plan Assets
Bal.—1/1/2X12				400 Cr.	650 Cr.	250 Dr.
1. Service cost	650 Dr.				650 Cr.	
2. Interest cost[2]	52 Dr.				52 Cr.	
3. Actual return	15 Cr.					15 Dr.
4. Unexpected loss[3]	5 Cr.		5 Dr.			
5. Contributions		450 Cr.				450 Dr.
6. Benefit payments					125 Dr.	125 Cr.
7. Increase in the APBO (loss)			1,500 Dr.		1,500 Cr.	
JE for 2X12	682 Dr.	450 Cr.	1,505 Dr.	1,737 Cr.		
Accumulated OCI— 12/31/2X11			0			
Bal.— 12/31/2X12			1,505 Dr.	2,137 Cr.	2,727 Cr.	590 Dr.

[1] Other comprehensive income
[2] Interest Cost = interest rate × APBO beginning of year = 8% × $650 = $52
[3] Unexpected loss = actual return – expected return = $15 – $20 = $5
The unexpected loss of $5 is deferred by debiting other comprehensive income (G/L) and crediting postretirement expense. Because of this adjustment, the expected return on plan assets is the amount actually used to compute postretirement expense.

The increase in the APBO due to a change in actuarial assumptions of $1,500 is an unexpected loss, which is debited to other comprehensive income (G/L) and credited to APBO.

The journal entry for postretirement expense for 2X12 follows:

Postretirement expense	682	
Other comprehensive income (G/L)	1,505	
Cash		450
Postretirement liability		1,737

The postretirement liability at 12/31/2X12 is $2,137. This balance may also be computed as follows:

APBO (Cr.)	$2,727
Fair market value of plan assets (Dr.)	590
Postretirement liability	$2,137

The amortization of net gain or loss in the year 2X13 follows, based on the corridor approach:

Accumulated other comprehensive income— beginning of year	$1,505
10% of the greater of APBO or market-related value of plan assets (10% × $2,727)	273
Amount to be amortized	$1,232
Average remaining service period	20 years

Amortization of loss for 2X13 ($1,232/20 years) = $62

Disclosures

Footnote disclosure includes:

- A description of the postretirement plan including employee groups covered, type of benefits provided, funding policy, types of assets held, and liabilities assumed.
- The funded status of the plans.
- The components of net periodic postretirement cost.
- The fair value of plan assets.
- Accumulated postretirement benefit obligation showing separately the amount applicable to retirees, other fully eligible participants, and other active plan participants.
- The amount of net postretirement benefit asset or liability recognized in the balance sheet.
- The assumed health care cost trends used to measure the expected postretirement benefit cost for the next year.
- The discount rate used to determine the accumulated postretirement benefit obligation. A company should consider return rates on high-quality fixed-income securities in deriving the assumed discount rate. The assumed discount rate should be reappraised at each measurement date. In the event

that the general level of interest rates rises or declines, the assumed discount rate changes in a similar fashion.

- The return rate used on the fair value of plan assets.
- The cost of providing termination benefits recognized during the period.

Interim Periods. With respect to interim periods, it should be noted that unless a company remeasures both its plan assets and benefit obligations during the fiscal year, the funded status it reports in its interim balance sheet shall be the same asset or liability recognized in the prior year-end balance sheet adjusted for (1) subsequent accruals of net periodic postretirement benefit cost excluding the amortization of amounts previously recognized in other comprehensive income (e.g., subsequent accruals of service cost, interest, and return on plan assets) and (2) contributions to a funded plan, or benefit payments. Upon remeasurement, a company shall adjust its balance sheet in a later interim period to take into account the underfunded or overfunded status of the plan consistent with that measurement date.

Note: Sometimes a company remeasures both plan assets and benefit obligations during the fiscal year. An example is when a major event occurs, such as plan modification, curtailment, or settlement.

Individual deferred compensation contracts must be fully *accrued* by the date the employee is fully eligible to receive benefits.

Postemployment Benefits

ASC 712, *Compensation—Nonretirement Postemployment Benefits,* provides authoritative guidance in accounting and reporting for postemployment benefits. ASC 712 relates to benefits to former or inactive employees, their beneficiaries, and dependents after employment, but before retirement. Former or inactive employees include individuals on disability and those who have been laid off. However, individuals on vacation or holiday or who are ill are not considered inactive.

Postemployment benefits are different from postretirement benefits. Postemployment benefits may be in cash or in kind and include salary continuation benefits, supplemental unemployment benefits, severance benefits, disability related benefits, job training and counseling benefits, life insurance benefits, and health care benefits.

An accrual is made for postemployment benefits if the following conditions are met:

- The amount of benefits is reasonably determinable.
- Benefits apply for services already rendered.
- Payment of benefits is probable.
- Benefit obligations vest or accumulate.

PROFIT-SHARING PLANS

A profit-sharing plan may be discretionary (contributions are at the discretion of the board of directors) or nondiscretionary (contributions are based on a predetermined formula and depend on attaining a specified earnings level). In a discretionary plan, an accrual of expense is made when set by the board. The entry is to debit profit-sharing expense and credit accrued profit-sharing liability. In a nondiscretionary arrangement, an accrual is made when required under the plan terms.

TAX ALLOCATION

ASC 740, *Income Taxes*, applies to income tax allocation. Temporary differences occur between book income and taxable income. The deferred tax liability or asset is measured at the tax rate under *current* law that will exist when the temporary difference reverses. Further, the deferred tax liability or asset must be adjusted for changes in tax law or in tax rate. Consequently, the *liability method* must be used to account for deferred income taxes. Comprehensive deferred tax accounting is practiced. Tax expense equals taxes payable plus the tax effects of all temporary differences.

Interperiod tax allocation is used to account for temporary differences impacting the current year's results. Tax effects of *future* events should be reflected in the year they occur. It is improper to anticipate them and recognize a deferred tax liability or asset in the current year.

Temporary Differences

Temporary differences arise from the following four kinds of transactions:

1. Revenue includable on the tax return after being reported on the financial records (e.g., installment sales).

2. Expenses deductible on the tax return after being deducted on the financial records (e.g., bad debts provision).

3. Revenue includable on the tax return before being recognized in the financial records (e.g., unearned revenue).

4. Expenses deductible on the tax return before being deducted on the financial records (e.g., accelerated depreciation).

Footnote reference is made to the types of temporary differences.

If tax rates are graduated based on taxable income, aggregate calculations may be made using an estimated average rate.

Permanent Differences

Permanent differences do not reverse and thus do not require tax allocation. Examples are penalties and fines, which are not tax deductible, and interest on municipal bonds, which is not taxable.

Financial Statement Presentation

Deferred tax assets and liabilities must be offset and presented as a single amount. ASU No. 2015-17, *Income Taxes* (Topic 740): *Balance Sheet Classification of Deferred Taxes* (effective for financial statements issued after December 15, 2016, and interim periods within those annual periods), requires that deferred tax assets and liabilities should be netted and classified as noncurrent on an entity's classified balance sheet. This will result in an entity presenting its balance sheet classification of deferred taxes as either a noncurrent deferred tax asset or a noncurrent deferred tax liability. Because IFRS has the same requirement, ASU No. 2015-17 aligns GAAP and IFRS with respect to this presentation parameter.

Intraperiod Tax Allocation

Intraperiod tax allocation takes place when tax expense is shown in different parts of the financial statements for the current year. The income statement presents the tax effect of income from continuing operations, of income from discontinued operations, other comprehensive income, and items charged directly to shareholders equity. In the statement of retained earnings, prior-period adjustments are presented net of tax.

Loss Carrybacks and Carryforwards

The tax effects of net operating *loss carrybacks* are allocated to the loss period. A business may carry back a net operating loss two years and receive a tax refund for taxes paid in those years. The loss is first applied to the earliest year; any residual loss is carried forward up to 20 years.

A *loss carryforward* may be recognized to the degree that there exist net taxable amounts in the carryforward period (deferred tax liabilities) to absorb them. A loss carryforward benefit may also be recognized if there is more than a 50% probability of future realization.

Footnote disclosure should be provided of the amount and expiration dates of operating loss carryforwards.

Deferred Tax Liability versus Deferred Tax Asset

If book income is more than taxable income, then tax expense exceeds tax payable, causing a deferred tax credit. If book income is below taxable income, then tax expense is less than tax payable, resulting in a deferred tax charge.

EXAMPLE 32: Book income and taxable income are both assumed to be $10,000. Depreciation for book purposes is $1,000 using the straight-line method, and depreciation for tax purposes is $2,000 based on the modified accelerated cost recovery system (ACRS) method. Assuming a 40% tax rate, the entry is:

Income tax expenses ($9,000 × .40)	3,600	
Income tax payable ($8,000 × .40)		3,200
Deferred tax liability ($1,000 × .40)		400

At the end of the asset's life, the deferred tax liability of $400 will be fully reversed.

A deferred tax asset may be recognized when it is more likely than not that the tax benefit will be realized in the future. The phrase "more likely than not" means at least slightly more than a 50% probability of occurring. The deferred tax asset must be reduced by a valuation allowance if it is more likely than not that some or all of the deferred tax asset will not be realized. The net amount is the amount likely to be realized. The deferred tax asset would be shown in the balance sheet as presented in the following table, assuming a temporary difference of $200,000, the tax rate of 30%, and $140,000 of the tax benefit has a probability in excess of 50% of being realized.

Deferred tax asset (gross) ($200,000 × .30)	$60,000
Less: valuation allowance ($60,000 × .30)	18,000
Deferred tax asset (net) ($140,000 × .30)	$42,000

EXAMPLE 33: In 2X11, a business sold a fixed asset at a gain of $35,000 for book purposes, which was deferred for tax purposes (installment method) until 2X12. Further, in 2X11, $20,000 of unearned revenue was received. The income was recognized for tax purposes in 2X11 but was deferred for book purposes until 2X12.

The deferred tax asset may be recognized, because the deductible amount in the future ($20,000) offsets the taxable amount ($35,000). Using a 40% tax rate and income taxes payable of $50,000, the entry in 2X11 is:

Income tax expense (balancing figure)	56,000	
Deferred tax asset ($20,000 × .40)	8,000	
Deferred tax liability ($35,000 × .40)		14,000
Income tax payable		50,000

A deferred tax asset can also be recognized for the tax benefit of deductible amounts realizable by carrying back a loss from future years to reduce taxes paid in the current or a previous year.

According to Accounting Standards Update (ASU) No, 2013-11 (July 2013), *Income Taxes* (Topic 740), *Presentation of an Unrecognized Tax Benefit When a Net Operating Loss Carryforward, a Similar Tax Loss, or a Tax Credit Carryforward Exists*, an unrecognized tax benefit should generally be shown in the financial statements as a reduction of a deferred tax asset for a net operating loss carryforward, a similar tax loss, and a tax credit forward.

Tax Rates

Deferred taxes are presented at the amounts of settlement when the temporary differences reverse.

EXAMPLE 34: A total temporary difference of $100,000 in 2X11 that will reverse in the future, is assumed. It will generate the following taxable amounts and tax rate:

	2X12	2X13	2X14	Total
Reversals	$30,000	$50,000	$20,000	$100,000
Tax rate	×.40	×.35	×.33	
Deferred tax liability	$12,000	$17,500	$ 6,600	$ 36,100

On December 31, 2X14, the deferred tax liability is recorded at $36,100.

A change in tax rate must immediately be accounted for by adjusting tax expense and deferred tax.

EXAMPLE 35: At the end of 2X11, a law is passed lowering the tax rate from 34% to 32% beginning in 2X13. In 2X11, the company has a deferred profit of $200,000 and presents a deferred tax liability of $68,000. The gross profit is to be reflected equally in 2X12, 2X13, 2X14, and 2X15. Therefore, the deferred tax liability at the end of 2X11 is $65,000 computed as follows:

	2X12	2X13	2X14	2X15	Total
Reversals	$50,000	$50,000	$50,000	$50,000	$200,000
Tax rate	×.34	×.32	×.32	×.32	
Deferred tax liability	$17,000	$16,000	$16,000	$16,000	$ 65,000

The required journal entry in 2X11 is:

Deferred Tax Liability	3,000	
Income Tax Expense		3,000

Indefinite Reversal

As per ASC 740, *Income Taxes,* no interperiod tax allocation is needed for indefinite reversal situations. Indefinite reversal is when undistributed earnings of a foreign subsidiary will indefinitely be postponed as to remission back to the United States or when profit will be remitted in a tax-free liquidation. If a change in circumstances takes place and the assumption of indefinite reversal is no longer applicable, tax expense should be adjusted. Disclosure should be made not only of the declaration to reinvest indefinitely or to remit tax free but also of the cumulative amount of undistributed earnings.

Multiple Tax Jurisdictions

The determination for federal reporting purposes may differ from that of local reporting requirements. As a result, temporary differences, permanent differences, and loss carrybacks or carryforwards may differ between federal and state and/or city reporting. If temporary differences are significant, separate deferred tax computations and recording will be required.

Intra-Entity Transfers

According to Accounting Standards Update (ASU) No. 2016-16 (October 2016), *Income Taxes* (Topic 740), *Intra-Entity Transfers of Assets Other Than Inventory,* a company should recognize the income tax consequences of an intra-entity transfer of an asset except inventory at the time of the transfer. Examples of such assets are fixed assets and intellectual property.

Tax Status Changes

The impact of any change in tax status affecting a business requires an immediate adjustment to deferred tax liabilities (or assets) and to income tax expense. An example of a tax status change requiring an adjustment on the accounts is a company opting for C corporation status. There should be a footnote describing the nature of the status change and its impact on the accounts.

Intra-entity transactions in a consolidated group may occur when the selling/distribution entity is part of that consolidated group but different from the legal entity originally producing (or acquiring) those goods. The acquirer should also account for other possible tax impact of temporary differences, carryforwards, or other tax uncertainties of the acquirer.

Business Combinations

In a business combination accounted for under the purchase method, the costs assigned to the acquired entity's net assets may differ from the valuation of those net assets on the tax return. This may cause a temporary difference in either a deferred tax liability or deferred tax asset reported on the acquirer's consolidated financial statements.

A company may have unrecognized tax benefits applicable to operating losses or tax credits arising from a purchase business combination. This may give rise to other similar tax advantages after the combination date. The tax benefits realized should be apportioned for book reporting between pre- and postacquisition tax benefits.

Separate Financial Statements of a Subsidiary

If separate financial statements are prepared, the consolidated income tax expense should be allocated to each of the subsidiaries.

Employee Stock Ownership Plans

Retained earnings is increased for the tax benefit arising from deductible dividends paid on unallocated shares held by an ESOP. However, dividends paid on allocated shares are includable in income tax expense.

Quasi-Reorganization

The tax benefits applicable to deductible temporary differences and carryforwards on the date of a quasi-reorganization should usually be recorded as an increase in paid-in-capital if the tax benefits will occur in later years.

Share-Based Payment Awards

According to ASC 718, *Compensation—Stock Compensation* (ASC 718-740-45-8), unrealized income tax benefits from dividends on equity-classified employee share-based payment awards should be excluded from the pool of excess tax benefits available to absorb tax deficiencies on share-based payment awards.

As per Accounting Standards Update (ASU) No. 2016-09 (March 2016), *Compensation—Stock Compensation* (Topic 718), *Improvements to Employee Share-Based Payment Accounting,* in accounting for income taxes, any excess tax benefits and tax deficiencies should be recognized as income tax expense or benefit in the income statement. Tax effects of exercised or vested awards should be recognized in the year they occurred.

In the Statement of Cash Flows, excess tax benefits should be shown along with other income tax cash flows in the operating section. Employer cash paid for tax withholding reasons should be classified in the financing section.

FOREIGN CURRENCY TRANSLATION AND TRANSACTIONS

ASC 830, *Foreign Currency Matters*, applies to foreign currency transactions, such as exports and imports denominated in other than a company's functional currency. It also relates to foreign currency financial statements of branches, divisions, and other investees incorporated in the financial statements of a U.S. company by combination, consolidation, or the equity method.

A purpose of translation is to furnish data of expected impacts of rate changes on cash flow and equity. Also, it provides data in consolidated financial statements relative to the financial results of each individual foreign consolidated entity.

Covered in ASC 830 are the translation of foreign currency statements and gains and losses on foreign currency transactions. Translation of foreign currency statements is typically needed when the statements of a foreign subsidiary or equity-method investee having a functional currency other than the U.S. dollar are to be included in the financial statements of a domestic enterprise (e.g., through consolidation or using the equity method). Generally, the foreign currency statements should be translated using the exchange rate at the end of the reporting year. Resulting cumulative translation gains and losses are shown as a separate item in the stockholders' equity section under "accumulated other comprehensive incomes."

Also important is the accounting treatment of gains and losses emanating from transactions denominated in a foreign currency. These are presented in the current year's income statement.

Foreign Currency Terminology

Key definitions to be understood by the practitioner are as follows:

- *Conversion*—an exchange of one currency for another.
- *Currency swap*—an exchange between two companies of the currencies of two different countries as per an agreement to re-exchange the two currencies at the same rate of exchange at a specified future date.
- *Denominate*—pay or receive in that same foreign currency. It can be denominated only in one currency (e.g., pounds). It is a real account (asset or liability) fixed in terms of a foreign currency, irrespective of exchange rate.
- *Exchange rate*—ratio between a unit of one currency and that of another at a particular time. If there is a *temporary lack of exchangeability* between two currencies at the transaction date or balance sheet date, the first rate available thereafter at which exchanges could be made is used.
- *Foreign currency*—a currency other than the functional currency of the business. (For instance, the dollar could be a foreign currency for a foreign entity).
- *Foreign currency statements*—financial statements using a functional currency that is not the reporting currency of the business.
- *Foreign currency transactions*—transactions whose terms are denominated in a currency other than the entity's functional currency. Foreign currency

transactions take place when a business: buys or sells on credit goods or services whose prices are denominated in foreign currency; borrows or lends funds and the amounts payable or receivable are denominated in foreign currency; is a party to an unperformed forward exchange contract; or acquires or disposes of assets or incurs or settles liabilities denominated in foreign currency.

- *Foreign currency translation*—expressing in the reporting currency of the company those amounts that are denominated or measured in a different currency.

- *Foreign entity*—an operation (e.g., subsidiary, division, branch, joint venture) whose financial statements are prepared in a currency other than the reporting currency of the reporting entity.

- *Functional currency*—the currency of the primary economic environment in which the business operates. It is typically the currency of the environment in which the business primarily obtains and uses cash. This is usually the foreign country. The functional currency of a foreign operation may be the same as a related affiliate in the case where the foreign activity is an essential component or extension of the related affiliate.

Prior to translation, the foreign country figures are remeasured in the functional currency. For instance, if a company in Italy is an independent entity and received cash and incurred expenses in Italy, the Italian currency is the functional currency. However, in the event the Italian company was an extension of a Canadian parent, the functional currency is the Canadian currency. The functional currency should be used consistently except if material economic changes necessitate a change. However, previously issued financial statements are not restated for an alteration in the functional currency.

If a company's books are not kept in its functional currency, remeasurement into the functional currency is mandated. The remeasurement process occurs before translation into the reporting currency takes place. When a foreign entity's functional currency is the reporting currency, remeasurement into the reporting currency obviates translation. The remeasurement process is intended to generate the same result as if the entity's books had been kept in the functional currency.

Guidelines are referred to in determining the functional currency of a foreign operation. The "benchmarks" apply to the following:

- *Selling price.* The functional currency is the foreign currency when the foreign operation's selling prices of products or services are primarily because of local factors, such as government law and competition, not due to changes in exchange rate. The functional currency is the parent's currency when the foreign operation's sales prices mostly apply in the short run to fluctuation in the exchange rate resulting from international factors (e.g., worldwide competition).

- *Market.* The functional currency is the foreign currency when the foreign activity has a strong local sales market for products or services even though a significant amount of exports may exist. The functional currency is the parent's currency when the foreign operation's sales market is mostly in the parent's country.

- *Cash flow.* The functional currency is the foreign currency when the foreign operation's cash flows are primarily in foreign currency not directly affecting the parent's cash flow. The functional currency is the parent's currency when the foreign operation's cash flows directly impact the parent's cash flows. They are usually available for remittance via intercompany accounting settlement.

- *Financing.* The functional currency is the foreign currency if financing the foreign activity is in foreign currency and funds obtained by the foreign activity are sufficient to meet debt obligations. The functional currency is the parent's currency when financing for the foreign activity is provided by the parent or occurs in U.S. dollars. Funds obtained by the foreign activity are insufficient to satisfy debt requirements.

- *Expenses.* The functional currency is the foreign currency when foreign operation's production costs or services are usually incurred locally. However, some foreign imports may exist. The functional currency is the parent's currency when foreign operation's production and service costs are primarily component costs obtained from the parent's country.

- *Intercompany transactions.* The functional currency is the foreign currency when minor interrelationship occurs between the activities of the foreign entity and parent except for competitive advantages (e.g., patents). There is a restricted number of intercompany transactions. The functional currency is the parent's currency when material interrelationship exists between the foreign entity and parent. Many intercompany transactions exist.

Consistent use of the functional currency of the foreign entity must exist over the years unless changes in circumstances warrant a change. If a change in the functional currency takes place, it is accounted for as a change in estimate.

Foreign exchange terms are as follows:

- *Local currency*—the currency of the particular foreign country.

- *Measure*—translation into a currency other than the original reporting currency. Foreign financial statements are measured in U.S. dollars by using the applicable exchange rate.

- *Reporting currency*—the currency in which the business prepares its financial statements. It is usually U.S. dollars.

- *Spot rate*—exchange rate for immediate delivery of currencies exchanged.

- *Transaction gain or loss*—transaction gains or losses occur because of a change in exchange rates between the functional currency and the currency in which a foreign currency transaction is denominated. They represent an increase or decrease in the actual functional currency cash flows realized upon settlement of foreign currency transactions and the expected functional currency cash flows on unsettled foreign currency transactions.

- *Translation adjustments*—translation adjustments arise from translating financial statements from the entity's functional currency into the reporting currency.

Translation Process

Translation of Foreign Currency Statements When the U.S. Dollar Is the Functional Currency. The foreign entity's financial statements in a highly inflationary economy are not stable enough and should be remeasured as if the functional currency were the reporting currency. Thus, the financial statements of those entities should be remeasured into the reporting currency (the U.S. dollar becomes the functional currency). In effect, the reporting currency is used directly.

A highly inflationary environment is one that has cumulative inflation of about 100% or more over a three-year period. In other words, the inflation rate must be increasing at a rate of about 35% a year for three consecutive years.

Tip: The International Monetary Fund of Washington, D.C. publishes monthly figures on international inflation rates.

Translation of Foreign Currency Statements When the Foreign Currency Is the Functional Currency. Balance sheet items are translated through the current exchange rate. For assets and liabilities, use the rate at the balance sheet date. If a current exchange rate is not available at the balance sheet date, the first exchange rate available after that date is used. The current exchange rate is also used to translate the statement of cash flows, except for those items found in the income statement that are translated using the weighted-average rate. For income statement items (revenues, expenses, gains, and losses), the exchange rate at the dates those items are recognized should be used. Because translation at the exchange rates at the dates the many revenues, expenses, gains, and losses are recognized is almost always impractical, a weighted-average exchange rate should be used for the period in translating income statement items.

A material change occurring between the date of the financial statements and the audit report date should be disclosed as a subsequent event. Disclosure should also be made of the effects on unsettled balances pertaining to foreign currency transactions.

Translation Adjustments. The steps involved in translating the foreign country's financial statements into U.S. reporting requirements are as follows:

1. Conform the foreign country's financial statements to U.S. GAAP.
2. Determine the functional currency of the foreign entity.
3. Remeasure the financial statements in the functional currency, if necessary. Gains or losses from remeasurement are includable in remeasured current net income.
4. Convert from the foreign currency into U.S. dollars (reporting currency).

If a company's functional currency is a foreign currency, translation adjustments arise from translating that company's financial statements into the reporting currency. Translation adjustments are unrealized, are reported as "other comprehensive income," and are shown separately and accumulated in a separate component of equity. However, if remeasurement from the recording currency to the functional currency is required before translation, the gain or loss is reflected in the income statement.

Upon sale or liquidation of an investment in a foreign entity, the amount attributable to that entity and accumulated in the translation adjustment component of equity is removed from the stockholders' equity section and considered a part of the gain or loss on sale or liquidation of the investment in the income statement for the period during which the sale or liquidation occurs.

As per ASC 830, *Foreign Currency Matters* (ASC 830-30), a sale of an investment in a foreign entity may include a partial sale of an ownership interest. In that case, a pro rata amount of the cumulative translation adjustment reflected as a stockholders' equity component is includable in arriving at the gain or loss on sale. For example, if a business sells a 40% ownership interest in a foreign investment, 40% of the translation adjustment applicable to it is included in calculating gain or loss on sale of that ownership interest.

Foreign Currency Transactions

Foreign currency transactions are those denominated in a currency other than the company's functional currency. Foreign currency transactions may result in receivables or payables fixed in terms of the amount of foreign currency to be received or paid.

A foreign currency transaction requires settlement in a currency other than the functional currency. A change in exchange rates between the functional currency and the currency in which a transaction is denominated increases or decreases the expected amount of functional currency cash flows upon settlement of the transaction. This change in expected functional currency cash flows is a foreign currency transaction gain or loss that typically is included in arriving at earnings in the income statement for the period in which the exchange rate is altered. An example of a transaction gain or loss is when a British subsidiary has a receivable denominated in pounds from a French customer.

Similarly, a transaction gain or loss (measured from the transaction date or the most recent intervening balance sheet date, whichever is later) realized upon settlement of a foreign currency transaction usually should be included in determining net income for the period in which the transaction is settled.

EXAMPLE 36: An exchange gain or loss occurs when the exchange rate changes between the purchase date and sale date.

Merchandise is bought for 100,000 euros. The exchange rate is four euros to one dollar. The journal entry is:

Purchases	$25,000	
Accounts payable		$25,000

100,000/4 = $25,000

When the merchandise is paid for, the exchange rate is five to one. The journal entry is:

Accounts payable	$25,000	
Cash		$20,000
Foreign exchange gain 100,000/5 = $20,000		5,000

The $20,000, using an exchange rate of five to one can buy 100,000 euros. The transaction gain is the difference between the cash required of $20,000 and the initial liability of $25,000.

Note that a foreign transaction gain or loss has to be determined at each balance sheet date on all recorded foreign transactions that have not been settled.

EXAMPLE 37: A U.S. company sells goods to a customer in England on November 15, 2X12, for 10,000 euros. The exchange rate for one euro is $.75. Thus, the transaction is worth $7,500 (10,000 euros × .75). Payment is due two months later. The entry on November 15, 2X12, is:

Accounts receivable—England	$7,500	
Sales		$7,500

Accounts receivable and sales are measured in U.S. dollars at the transaction date employing the spot rate. Even though the accounts receivable is measured and reported in U.S. dollars, the receivable is fixed in euros. Thus, there can occur a transaction gain or loss if the exchange rate changes between the transaction date (November 15, 2X12) and the settlement date (January 1, 2X13).

Because of the financial statements are prepared between the transaction date and settlement date, receivables that are denominated in a currency other than the functional currency (U.S. dollar) have to be restated to reflect the spot rate on the balance sheet date. On December 31, 2X12, the exchange rate is one euro equals $.80. Hence the 10,000 euros are now valued at $8,000 (10,000 × $.80). Therefore, the accounts receivable denominated in pounds should be upwardly adjusted by $500. The required journal entry on December 31, 2X12, is:

Accounts receivable—England	$500	
Foreign exchange gain		$500

The income statement for the year ended December 31, 2X12, shows an exchange gain of $500. Note that sales are not affected by the exchange gain, because sales relates to operational activity.

On January 15, 2X13, the spot rate is one euro = $.78. The journal entry is:

Cash	$7,800	
Foreign exchange loss	200	
Accounts receivable—England		$8,000

The 2X13 income statement shows an exchange loss of $200.

Transaction Gains and Losses to Be Excluded from Determination of Net Income.   Gains and losses on the following foreign currency transactions are not included in earnings but rather reported as translation adjustments:

- Foreign currency transactions designated as *economic hedges* of a net investment in a foreign entity, beginning as of the designation date.

- Intercompany foreign currency transactions of a long-term investment nature (settlement is not planned or expected in the foreseeable future), when the entities to the transaction are consolidated, combined, or accounted for by the equity method in the reporting company's financial statements.

A gain or loss on a forward contract or other foreign currency transaction that is intended to *hedge* an identifiable foreign currency commitment (e.g., an agreement to buy or sell machinery) should be deferred and included in the measurement of the related foreign currency transaction. Losses should not be deferred if it is anticipated that deferral would cause recognizing losses in subsequent periods. A foreign currency transaction is considered a hedge of an identifiable foreign currency commitment provided both of the following criteria are satisfied:

1. The foreign currency transaction is designated as a hedge of a foreign currency commitment.

2. The foreign currency commitment is firm.

Forward Exchange Contracts

A forward exchange contract is an agreement to exchange different currencies at a given future date and at a specified rate (forward rate). A forward contract is a foreign currency transaction. A gain or loss on a forward contract that does not meet the conditions described in the following is includable in net income.

Note: Currency swaps are accounted for in a similar fashion.

A gain or loss (whether or not deferred) on a forward contract, except a speculative forward contract, should be computed by multiplying the foreign currency amount of the forward contract by the difference between the spot rate at the balance sheet date and the *spot rate* at the date of inception of the forward contract.

The *discount or premium on a forward contract* (i.e., the foreign currency amount of the contract multiplied by the difference between the contracted forward rate and the spot rate at the date of inception of the contract) should be accounted for separately from the gain or loss on the contract and typically should be included in computing net income over the life of the forward contract.

A gain or loss on a *speculative forward contract* (a contract that does not hedge an exposure) should be computed by multiplying the foreign currency amount of the forward contract by the difference between the forward rate available from the remaining maturity of the contract and the contracted forward rate (or the forward rate last used to measure a gain or loss on that contract for an earlier period). No separate accounting recognition is given to the discount or premium on a speculative forward contract.

Hedging. Foreign currency transactions, gains and losses on assets, and liabilities, denominated in a currency other than the functional currency, can be hedged if the U.S. company enters into a forward exchange contract.

A hedge can occur even when a forward exchange contract does not exist. For instance, a foreign currency transaction can serve as an economic hedge offsetting a parent's net investment in a foreign entity when the transaction is entered into for hedging purposes and is effective.

> **EXAMPLE 38:** A U.S. parent completely owns a French subsidiary having net assets of $3 million in euros. The U.S. parent can borrow $3 million euros to hedge its net investment in the French subsidiary. The French euro is the functional currency and the $3 million obligation is denominated in euros. Variability in the exchange rate for euros does not have a net impact on the parent's consolidated balance sheet, because increases in the translation adjustments balance arising from translation of the net investment will be netted against decreases in this balance emanating from the adjustment of the liability denominated in euros.

ASC 830, *Foreign Currency Matters* (ASC 830-30-45-13), stipulates that a business that plans to dispose of an equity method investment in a foreign operation or a consolidated foreign subsidiary should include in the book value of the investment both the foreign currency translation adjustments associated with the foreign entity's disposal and the part of the gain or loss from the hedge of the company's net investment in the foreign operation.

DERIVATIVES

Derivatives are commonly used by entities to manage (position or hedge) their exposure to market risk (including interest rate risk and foreign exchange risk), cash flow risk, and other risks in their operations and for trading. The accounting and reporting standards for derivatives, including certain derivatives embedded in other contracts, and for hedging activities are provided in ASC Topic 815, *Derivatives and Hedging*. ASC Topic 815 requires all derivatives to be recognized on the balance sheet as either assets or liabilities at their fair value.

ASC 815 defines a derivative as a financial instrument or contract having the following three components:

1. The derivative has one or more underlying price or rate (*i.e.*, specified interest rate, security price, commodity price, foreign exchange rate, index of prices or rates, or other variable) and one or more notional amounts (*i.e.*, number of currency units, shares, bushels, pounds, or other units specified in the contract) or payment provisions or both. The derivative's terms determine the amount of the settlement or settlements, and in some cases, whether or not a settlement is required.

2. The derivative requires no initial net investment or an initial net investment that is smaller than would be required for other types of contracts that would be expected to have similar response to changes in market factors.

3. The terms of the derivative: require or permit net settlement, can be readily settled net by a means outside the contract, or provides for delivery of an asset that puts the recipient in a position not substantially different from net settlement.

ASC Topic 815 specifically excludes from its scope certain contracts that may meet the definition of a derivative. These include:

- Regular-way securities trades that are completed within the time period generally established by regulations and conventions in the marketplace or by the exchange on which the trade is executed;

- Normal purchases and sales of an item other than a financial instrument or a derivative (*e.g.*, a commodity) that will be delivered in quantities expected to be used or sold by the entity over a reasonable period in the normal course of business;

- Traditional life insurance and property and casualty contracts; and

- Certain financial guarantee contracts.

ASU No. 2015-13, *Derivatives and Hedging*, clarifies that the use of locational marginal pricing by an independent system operator to determine the transmission charge (or credit) does not constitute net settlement of a contract for the purchase or sale of electricity on a forward basis that necessitates transmission through, or delivery to a location within, a nodal energy market. Consequently, the use of locational marginal pricing by the independent system operator does not cause that contract to fail to meet the physical delivery criterion of the normal purchases and normal sales scope exception.

Types of Derivatives

The most common types of freestanding derivatives are forwards, futures, swaps, and options (including caps, floors, and collars).

- A *Forward contract* is an agreement that obligates two parties to purchase (long) and sell (short) a specific financial instrument, foreign currency, or commodity at a price specified now with delivery and settlement at a specified future date. A forward contract can only be terminated, other than by receipt of the underlying asset, by agreement of both buyer and seller. A forward contract can be traded over the counter and its terms are not standardized. Forward contracts include:

  — A forward rate agreement is a forward contract that specifies a reference interest rate and an agreed on interest rate (one to be paid and one to be received), an assumed principal amount (the notional amount), and a specific maturity and settlement date.

- A *Futures contract* is a standardized forward contract that is traded on an organized exchange (in the U.S., futures contracts and futures exchanges are registered with and regulated by the Commodity Futures Trading Commission). Futures contracts include:

— Interest-rate future contracts require the delivery of an underlying financial instrument of a specified investment-grade, such as U.S. Treasury security.

— Foreign currency futures contracts require the delivery of a specified amount of a particular foreign currency.

— Commodity futures contracts require the delivery of a specified amount, and grade of commodities, such as gold bullion.

— Equity futures contracts have a portion of their return linked to the price of a particular equity or to an index of equity prices, such as the Standard and Poor's 500.

- A *Swap contract* is a forward-based agreement that enables two parties to swap streams of payments over a specified period. The payments are based on an agreed upon notional principal amount. Swap contracts include:

— An interest rate swap involves no exchange of principal at inception or maturity; instead, the notional amount is used to calculate the payment streams to be exchanged.

— A foreign exchange swap involves the exchange of principal determined in two different currencies at the current (spot) rate, under an agreement to repay the principal at a specified price at a specified future date.

— A mortgage swap involves an exchange of the difference between a fixed-rate payment and a floating-rate payment on a notional principal amount that declines in proportion to the monthly payments and prepayments of an indexed pool of mortgage-backed securities for a specified period.

- An *Option contract* may be traded on an exchange or over the counter. An option contract grants the right, but not the obligation, to the purchaser (holder) to buy (call) or sell (put) a specific or standard security, money market instrument, futures contract, other financial instrument, or commodity at a specified price during a specified period (American option) or at a specified date (European option). Option contracts include:

— A purchased option is a contract in which the buyer has paid a fee or premium to acquire the right to sell or purchase an instrument at a stated price on a specified future date.

— A written option obligates the option seller to purchase or sell the instrument at the option of the buyer of the contract.

— An interest rate cap is an option contract in which the cap seller, in return for a premium, agrees to limit the cap holder's risk associated with an increase in an interest rate. If the rate goes above a specified interest-rate level (the strike price or cap rate), the cap holder is entitled to receive cash payments equal to the excess of the market rate over the strike price multiplied by the notional principal amount.

— An interest rate floor is an option contract in which the floor seller, in return for a premium, agrees to limit the risk associated with a decline in interest rates based on a notional amount. If the rate falls below an agreed rate, the floor holder will receive cash payments from the floor writer equal to the difference between the market rate and an agreed rate, multiplied by the notional principal amount.

— An interest rate collar is an option contract that combines a cap and a floor (one held and one written). An interest rate collar enables a user with a floating rate contract to lock into a predetermined interest-rate range.

Embedded Derivatives

ASC Topic 815 defines an embedded derivative as an implicit or explicit term within a contract that affects some or all of its cash flows or the value of other exchanges required by the contract in a manner similar to a derivative. ASC 815 notes that the effect of embedding a derivative in another type of contract (host contract) is that some or all of the cash flows or other exchanges that otherwise are required by the host contract, whether unconditional or contingent upon the occurrence of a specified event, are modified based on one or more of the underlyings.

ASC Topic 815 requires an embedded derivative instrument to be separated from the host contract and accounted for as a derivative (*i.e.*, bifurcated), if and only if all of the following three conditions are met:

1. The economic characteristics and risks of the embedded derivative instrument are not clearly and closely related to the economic characteristics and risks of the host contract (see below);

2. The contract (hybrid instrument) that embodies the embedded derivative instrument and the host contract are not remeasured at fair value under otherwise applicable GAAP with changes in fair value reported in earnings as they occur; and

3. A separate instrument with the same terms as the embedded derivative instrument would be a considered a derivative.

ASC Topic 815 requires an embedded derivative in which the underlying is an interest rate or interest rate index that alters net interest payments that otherwise would be paid or received on an interest-bearing host contract as being clearly and closely related to the host contract unless either of the following conditions exist:

1. The hybrid instrument can contractually be settled in such a way that the investor (holder) would not recover substantially all of its initial recorded investment; or

2. The embedded derivative could at least double the investor's initial rate of return on the host contract and could also result in a rate of return that is at least twice what otherwise would be the market return for a contract that has the same terms as the host contract and that involves a debtor with a similar credit quality.

According to Accounting Standards Update (ASU) No. 2010-08 (February 2010), *Technical Corrections to Various Topics,* a hybrid financial instrument that is in the form of a host contract may be accounted for under the fair value option. In other words, the contract is measured at fair market value with any change in fair value recorded as a gain or loss.

Some types of embedded derivative products are:

- *Pay-in-kind (PIK) preferred stock*—the issuing company postpones paying cash dividends to holders and instead issues more preferred stock to them. The entry is to charge retained earnings and credit preferred stock.

- *Dual-currency bonds*—debt paying interest in one currency but paying the principal amount in another currency. The interest is usually paid in a currency having a low interest rate. Foreign exchange risk may be curtailed through hedging.

- *Bunny bond*—a bond in which interest is reinvested into comparable bonds. The issuing entity charges interest expense and credits debt payable for the reinvested funds.

- *Variable-coupon redeemable notes (VCRs)*—notes repriced periodically. The initial maturity date is one year but the interest rate changes weekly. Interest expense is charged at the actual interest rate for the period.

- *Dutch auction notes*—notes for which the nominal interest rate is adjusted periodically (e.g., quarterly) based on new, low bids for the notes. Interest expense is recorded based on the interest rate set by the Dutch auction.

- *Increasing-rate debt*—an obligation maturing in the short term that may be extended periodically. Interest expense is based on the average interest rate for the anticipated time period of the debt.

- *Zero-coupon bond*—a bond having no interest rate issued at a substantial discount. Interest is accrued each year irrespective of the fact that interest is not paid until the maturity date.

- *Covered option securities (COPs)*—short-term, dollar-denominated debt, which the issuer may pay at maturity in either dollars or a specified foreign currency. A higher-yield rate exists owing to the flexibility provided the issuer. Unrealized gains and losses on the foreign currency are presented in the income statement.

- *European currency bonds (ECUs)*—a type of Eurobond specified in the ten currencies of the countries that make up the European Economic Community. The interest and principal is payable in ECUs or another currency preferred by the investor. The effect of a change in exchange rates is recognized each year in net income.

Hedge Accounting

An entity must report derivatives at fair value as either assets or liabilities. Depending on the circumstances, a derivative must be a hedge against exposure to:

- Changes in the fair value of a recognized asset or liability or an unrecognized firm commitment.

- Variable cash flows applicable to a forecasted transaction.

- Foreign currency risk of a net investment in a foreign operation, foreign currency denominated forecasted transaction, available-for-sale security, or unrecognized firm commitment.

How the change in fair value of a derivative (gain or loss) is accounted for varies with the planned use of the derivative as follows:

- A derivative designed to hedge vulnerability to changes in the fair value of a recognized asset or liability or firm commitment will have the gain or loss included in net income in the year of change coupled with the offsetting loss or gain on the hedged item associated with the hedged risk. The net impact of this accounting is to include in net income the degree to which the hedge is not effective in offsetting changes in fair value.

- A derivative hedging exposure to variable cash flows of a forecasted transaction (cash flow hedge) will have the effective part of the derivatives gain or loss initially presented as an element of other comprehensive income (outside of earnings) and later reclassified into earnings when the forecasted transaction impacts earnings. The ineffective part of the gain or loss is immediately presented in earnings. If a cash flow hedge is discontinued because it is probable that the initial forecasted transaction will not take place, the net gain or loss in accumulated other comprehensive income shall be immediately reclassified into earnings.

- A derivative whose purpose is to hedge foreign currency exposure of a net investment in a foreign activity will have the gain or loss presented under other comprehensive income as an element of the cumulative translation adjustment. The hedge of the foreign currency exposure may apply to an unrecognized firm commitment or an available-for-sale security.

Note: If a derivative is not to hedge an instrument, the gain or loss is included in net income in the period of change.

A company opting to use hedge accounting must disclose the method it will use to evaluate the success of the hedging derivative and the measurement means to ascertain the ineffective part of the hedge. The methods chosen must conform to the company's risk management policy.

Accounting for the change in fair value (gain or loss) of a derivative depends on whether it qualifies as part of a hedging arrangement and, if such is the case, the purpose of holding the derivative. Either all or a proportion of a derivative may be considered a hedging instrument. The proportion must be stated as a percentage of the whole derivative so that the risk in the hedging part of the derivative is the same as the entire derivative.

Two or more derivatives, or parts thereof, may be considered in combination and jointly designated as a hedging instrument.

If an impairment loss is recorded on an asset or liability associated with a hedged forecasted transaction, any offsetting net gain associated with that transaction in accumulated other comprehensive income should be reclassified immediately into net income of the period. In a similar manner, a recovery of the asset or liability resulting in a reduction of the net loss should be shown in earnings.

Required disclosures include identifying derivatives, time period for intended hedging, risk management policies of the company, where net gain or loss associated with derivatives are presented in the financial statements, and description of transactions or other events that will result in reclassification into earnings of gain and loss reported in accumulated other comprehensive income.

According to Accounting Standards Update (ASU) No. 2016-05 (March 2016), *Derivatives and Hedging* (Topic 815), a change in the counterparty to a derivative instrument designated as the hedging instrument does not by itself require a redesignation of the hedging relationship.

Accounting Standards Update (ASU) No. 2017-12 (August 2017), *Derivatives and Hedging (Topic 815), Targeted Improvements to Accounting for Hedging Activities,* allows hedge accounting for risk components in hedging relationships for nonfinancial risk and interest rate risk. This update allows a company to:

1. Measure the change in fair value of the hedged item based on the benchmark rate component of the contractual coupon cash flows determined at hedge inception; and

2. Measure the hedged item in a partial-term fair value hedge of interest rate risk by assuming the hedged item term reflects only the cash flows being hedged.

A company also must present the earnings impact of a hedging instrument in the same income statement line item in which the earnings impact of the hedged item is reported. The company can exclude the components of a hedging instrument's change in fair value from the evaluation of hedge effectiveness, and can exclude the part of the change in fair value of a currency swap applicable to a cross-country basis spread from the evaluation of hedge effectiveness.

Tabular disclosure should be made of the impact on the income statement of fair value and cash flow hedges. Disclosure is also required of cumulative basis adjustments for fair value hedges.

According to Accounting Standards Update (ASU) No. 2016-06 (March 2016), *Derivatives and Hedging* (Topic 815), *Contingent Put and Call Options on Debt Instruments,* when a call (put) option is contingently exercisable, a company need not have to assess whether the event triggering the ability to exercise the option is related to interest rates or credit risks.

ACCOUNTING FOR TRANSFERS AND SERVICING OF FINANCIAL ASSETS AND EXTINGUISHMENTS OF LIABILITIES

According to ASC 860 and 470, *Transfers and Servicing; and Debt* (ASC 860; 470-50), once financial assets are transferred, the company recognizes the financial and servicing assets it controls and the debt it has incurred, derecognizes financial assets when control has been given up, and derecognizes liabilities when extinguished. A distinction must be made between transfers of financial assets that are sales from those that are secured borrowings.

A transfer of financial assets in which the transferor gives up control over those assets is accounted for as a sale to the extent that consideration except for the beneficial interests in the transferred assets is received in exchange. It is considered that the transferor has given up control over transferred assets if all of the following criteria are met:

- Each transferee has the right to pledge or exchange the assets it received.
- The transferor does not retain effective control over the transferred assets.
- The transferred assets have been isolated from the transferor, for instance, the assets are out of the reach of the transferor or its creditors even if bankruptcy takes place.

Obligations and derivatives incurred or obtained by transferors as part of a transfer of financial assets are measured at fair value. The allocation values between servicing assets sold and retained should be based on relative fair values at the transfer date.

Servicing assets and obligations should be later measured by:

1. Amortization proportional to the period of estimated net service income or loss, and
2. Assessment for asset impairment or liability incurrence based on their fair values.

A liability is derecognized only if the debtor provides payment or is legally released from the obligation (e.g., judicial order). A liability is *not* extinguished by an in-substance defeasance.

Assets collateralized should be disclosed if they are not reported in the balance sheet. Disclosure includes the fair value of the collateral, amount of collateral sold or repledged, and the sources and uses of the collateral.

A company with securitized financial assets should disclose accounting policies, volume, cash flows, assumptions made to estimate fair values, principal amount outstanding, amount derecognized, and credit losses.

ASC 825, *Financial Instruments*, requires an issuing company to classify the following financial instruments as liabilities or, where applicable, assets:

- A financial instrument, not in the form of an outstanding share, that, when issued, represents a commitment to reacquire the issuer's stock or is indexed to such an obligation and requires that the issuer satisfy that obligation by transferring assets. An example is a written put option on the issuing company's equity shares that is to be paid in cash.
- A financial instrument of mandatorily redeemable shares involving an unconditional obligation by requiring the issuing entity to redeem it by transferring assets.

Forward contracts to reacquire a company's equity securities that must be settled in cash are initially recorded at the fair value of the shares at inception.

ASC 825 is not applicable to features embedded in a financial instrument that is not fully derivative.

Disclosure should be made of the provisions of the financial instruments and alternative settlement arrangements.

ASC 480, *Distinguishing Liabilities from Equity* (ASC 480-10-55), provides that freestanding warrants and other similar instruments on shares that are puttable or mandatorily redeemable include obligations to transfer assets, which should be recognized as a liability. With puttable shares, the issuer is contingently obligated to transfer assets if the warrant is exercised and the shares are put to the issuer. In the case of mandatorily redeemable shares, the issuer is contingently liable to transfer assets when the holder exercises the warrant. In both situations, the warrant should be accounted for as a liability.

ASC 860, *Transfers and Servicing* (ASC 860-50), amends ASC 860 and 470-50 with respect to accounting for separately recognized servicing assets and liabilities. A servicing asset (liability) is a contract to service financial assets under which the estimated future revenues from specified servicing fees, late charges, and other ancillary revenues are (not) expected to more than compensate for performing services.

ASC 860-50 requires that a company recognize a servicing asset or liability each time it is obligated to service a financial asset by agreeing to a service contract in any of the following three situations:

1. A transfer of the servicer's financial assets that meets the requirements for sale accounting.

2. An acquisition or commitment to an obligation to service a financial asset that does not apply to financial assets of the servicer or its consolidated affiliates.

3. A transfer of the servicer's financial assets to a special-purpose entity in a guaranteed mortgage securitization in which the transferor retains all of the securities and classifies them as either trading or available-for-sale. (Securitization is the process by which financial assets are transformed into securities).

ASC 860-50 requires separate presentation of servicing assets and liabilities subsequently measured at fair value on the balance sheet. Appropriate disclosures should be provided for separately recognized servicing assets and liabilities.

A change that utilizes derivatives to reduce the risks associated with servicing assets and liabilities must account for those derivative instruments at fair value.

A transfer is the conveyance of a noncash financial asset by and to someone other than the issuer of that financial asset. Therefore, a transfer includes selling a receivable, collateralizing a receivable, or putting the receivable into a securitization trust. However, the term *transfer* excludes the origination of a receivable, the settlement of a receivable, or the restructuring of a receivable into a securitization in a troubled debt restructuring.

CHAPTER 13

INTERIM AND SEGMENTAL REPORTING

CONTENTS

This chapter discusses the requirements for the preparation of interim financial statements and segmental disclosures included in the annual report.

INTERIM REPORTS

Interim reports may be issued at periodic reporting intervals (e.g., quarterly or monthly). Complete financial statements or summarized data may be provided to financial statement users, but interim financial statements do not have to be certified by the outside auditors.

Interim balance sheets and cash flow information should be given to investors and creditors. If these statements are not presented, significant changes in liquid assets, cash, long-term debt, and stockholders' equity should be disclosed.

Usually, interim reports include results of the current interim period and the cumulative year-to-date figures. Typically, comparisons are made to results of comparable interim periods for the prior years.

Interim results should be based on the accounting principles used in the last year's annual report unless a change has been made in the current year.

A gain or loss cannot be deferred to a later interim period except if such deferral would have been permissible for annual reporting.

Revenue from merchandise sold and services performed should be accounted for as earned in the interim period in the same way as accounted for in annual reporting. If an advance is received in the first quarter and benefits the entire year, it should be allocated ratably to the interim periods affected.

Costs and expenses should be matched to related revenue in the interim period. If a cost cannot be associated with revenue in a future interim period, it should be expensed in the current period. Yearly expenses, such as administrative salaries, insurance, pension plan expense, and year-end bonuses, should be allocated to the quarters. The allocation may be based on such factors as the time expired, benefit obtained, and activity.

The gross profit method can be used to estimate interim inventory and cost of sales. Disclosure should be made of the method, assumptions made, and material adjustments by reconciliations with the annual physical inventory.

A permanent inventory loss should be reflected in the interim period in which it occurs. A subsequent recovery is treated as a gain in the later interim period. However, if the change in inventory value is temporary, no recognition is given in the accounts.

When there is a temporary liquidation of the LIFO base with replacement expected by year-end, cost of sales should be based on replacement cost.

EXAMPLE 1: The historical cost of an inventory item is $10,000 with replacement cost expected at $15,000. The entry is:

Cost of sales	15,000	
Inventory		10,000
Reserve for liquidation of LIFO base		5,000

Note the Reserve for Liquidation of LIFO Base account is shown as a current liability.

When replenishment is made at year-end the entry is:

Reserve for liquidation of LIFO base	5,000	
Inventory	10,000	
Cash		15,000

Volume discounts given to customers tied into annual purchases should be apportioned to the interim period based on the ratio of:

$$\frac{\text{Purchases for the interim period}}{\text{Total estimated purchases for the year}}$$

When a standard cost system is used, variances expected to be reversed by year-end may be deferred to an asset or liability account.

With regard to income taxes, the income tax provision includes current and deferred taxes. Federal and local taxes are provided for. The tax provision for an interim period should be cumulative (e.g., total tax expense for a nine-month period is shown in the third quarter based on nine months' income). The tax expense for the three-month period based on three months' revenue may also be presented (e.g., third-quarter tax expense based on only the third quarter). In computing tax expense, the estimated annual effective tax rate should be used. The effective tax rate should be based on income from continuing operations. If a reliable estimate is not practical, the actual year-to-date effective tax rate should be used.

At the end of each interim period, a revision to the effective tax rate employing the best current estimates of the annual effective tax rate may be necessary. The projected tax rate includes adjustment for net deferred credits. Adjustments should be contained in deriving the maximum tax benefit for year-to-date figures.

The estimated effective tax rate should incorporate all available tax credits (e.g., foreign tax credit) and available alternative tax methods in determining ordinary earnings. A change in tax legislation is reflected only in the interim period affected.

Income statement items after income from continuing operations (e.g., income from discontinued operations, extraordinary items) should be presented net of the tax effect. The tax effect on these unusual line items should be reflected only in the interim period in which they actually occur. For example, items should not be predicted before they occur. Prior-period adjustments in the retained earnings statement are also shown net of tax when they take place.

The tax implication of an interim loss is recognized only when realization of the tax benefit is assured beyond reasonable doubt. If a loss is expected for the remainder of the year, and carryback is not possible, the tax benefits typically should not be recognized.

The tax benefit of a previous year operating loss carryforward is recognized as an extraordinary item in each interim period to the extent that income is available to offset the loss carryforward.

ASC 250, *Accounting Changes and Error Corrections*, addresses the reporting of accounting changes in interim financial reports. A change in accounting method made in an interim period is presented by retrospective application. In the case where retrospective application to prechange interim periods is impractical, the accounting principle change may only be made as of the beginning of a subsequent fiscal period.

Disclosure should be made of seasonality aspects affecting interim results and contingencies. When a change in the estimated effective tax rate occurs, it should be disclosed. Further, if a fourth quarter is not presented, any material adjustments to that quarter must be commented on in the footnotes to the annual report. If an event is immaterial on an annual basis but material in the interim period, it should be disclosed. Purchase transactions should be noted.

For prior-period adjustments, the financial statement presentation must:

- Include in net income for the current period the portion of the effect related to current operations.
- Restate earnings of affected prior interim periods of the current year to include the portion related thereto.
- Include any prior-period adjustment affecting prior years in the earnings of the first interim period of the current year.

The criteria to be met for prior-period adjustments in interim periods are as follows:

- Materiality.
- Estimability.
- Identification to a prior interim period.

Examples of prior-period adjustments for interim reporting are:

- Error corrections.
- Settlement of litigation or claims.
- Adjustment of income taxes.
- Renegotiation proceedings.
- Utility revenue under rate-making processes.

Earnings per share is computed for interim purposes the same way as for annual purposes.

Segmental disposal is shown separately in the interim period in which it occurs.

SEGMENTAL DISCLOSURES

ASC 280, *Segment Reporting,* requires that the amount reported for each segment item should be based on what is used by the "chief operating decision maker" to determine the amount of resources to assign to a segment and how to appraise the performance of that segment. The term "chief operating decision maker" may apply to the chief executive officer or chief operating officer or to a group of executives; it also may apply to a function and not necessarily to a specific person.

Revenue, gains, expenses, losses, and assets should be allocated to a segment only if the chief operating decision maker considers it in measuring a segment's earnings for purposes of making a financial or operating decision. The same is true with regard to allocating to segments eliminations and adjustments applying to the company's general-purpose financial statements. Any allocation of financial items to a segment should be rationally based.

In measuring a segment's earnings or assets, the following should be disclosed for explanatory purposes:

- Measurement or valuation basis used.
- Differences in measurements used for the general-purpose financial statements relative to the financial information of the segment.
- A change in measurement method relative to prior years.
- A symmetrical allocation (i.e., an allocation of depreciation or amortization to a segment without a related allocation to the associated asset).

Segmental information is required in annual financial statements. Some segmental disclosures are required in interim financial statements.

Segmental Attributes

An operating segment is a distinct revenue-producing component of the business for which internal financial data are produced. Expenses are recognized as incurred in that segment. **Note:** A start-up operation would qualify as an operating segment even though revenue is not being earned. An operating segment is periodically reviewed by the chief operating decision maker to evaluate performance and to determine what and how much resources to allocate to the segment.

A reportable segment requiring disclosure is an operating segment that meets certain percentage tests discussed in the following section.

An aggregation may be made of operating segments if they are similar in terms of products or services, customer class, manufacturing processes, distribution channels, legal entity, and regulatory control.

Percentage Tests

A reportable segment satisfies one of the following criteria:

- Revenue, including unaffiliated and intersegment sales or transfers, is 10% or more of total (combined) revenue of all operating segments.

- Operating profit or loss is 10% or more of total operating profit of all operating segments.

- Assets are 10% or more of total assets of all operating segments.

After the 10% tests have been satisfied, additional segments may be reported on if they do not satisfy the 10% tests until at least 75% (constituting a substantial portion) of total revenue of all operating segments have been included. As a practical matter, no more than 10 segments (upper limit) should be reported because to do otherwise would result in too cumbersome or detailed reporting. In this case, combined reporting should be of those operating segments most closely related.

If a segment does not meet the 10% test for reportability in the current year but met the 10% test in prior years and is expected to be reportable in future years, it should still be reported in the current year.

If a segment passes the 10% test in the current year because of some unusual and rare occurrence, it should be excluded from reporting in the current year.

Reconciliation

A company does not have to use the same accounting principles for segmental purposes as that used to prepare the consolidated financial statements. There must be a reconciliation between segmental financial data and general-purpose financial statements. The reconciliation is for revenue, operating profit or loss, and assets. Any differences in measurement approaches between the company as a whole and its segments should be explained. If measurement practices have changed over the years regarding the operating segments, that fact should be disclosed and explained. The business must describe its reasoning and methods in deriving the composition of its operating segments.

Restatement

If the business structure changes, this may require a restatement of segmental information presented in prior years to aid in comparability. If restatement occurs, appropriate footnote disclosure should be made.

Disclosures

Disclosure of major sources of foreign revenue constituting 10% or more of total revenue should be provided. Further, disclosure is necessary if a foreign area constitutes 10% or more of total operating profit or loss, or of total assets. The foreign area and the percentage derived therein should be disclosed.

Disclosure should exist of the dollar sales to major customers making up 10% or more of total revenue. A single customer may refer to more than one customer if under common control (e.g., subsidiaries of a parent). A single customer may also be defined as government agencies.

Information about foreign geographic areas and customers is required even if this information is not used by the business in formulating operating decisions.

As per ASC 280, *Segment Reporting* (ASC 280-10-50), operating segments that do not meet the qualitative thresholds can be aggregated into a reportable segment if aggregation is consistent with the purpose and principles of ASC 280-10-50, the segments share a majority of the other aggregation criteria, and the segments have similar economic features.

Disclosure should be made of major contracts to other entities and governments.

Disclosure should be made of how reporting segments were determined (e.g., customer class, products or services, geographic areas). Disclosure should be given identifying those operating segments that have been aggregated. The following should be disclosed for each reportable segment:

- Types of products and services.
- Revenue to outside customers as well as intersegment revenue.
- Operating profit or loss.
- Total assets.
- Capital expenditures.
- Depreciation, depletion, and amortization.
- Major noncash revenues and expenses excluding those immediately above.
- Interest revenue and interest expense.
- Unusual items.
- Equity in earnings of investee.
- Tax effects.

EXAMPLE 2: A company reports the following information for its reportable segments:

Segment	Total Revenue	Operating Profit	Identifiable Assets
1	$ 500	$ 50	$ 200
2	250	10	150
3	3,500	200	1,950
4	1,500	100	900
Total	$5,750	$360	$3,200

The revenue test is 10% × $5,750 = $575. Segments 3 and 4 satisfy this test.

The operating profit (loss) test is 10% × $360 = $36. Segments 1, 3, and 4 satisfy this test.

The identifiable assets test is 10% × $3,200 = $320. Segments 3 and 4 satisfy this test.

Therefore, the reportable segments are 1, 3, and 4.

PART IV

Management Accounting and Cost Management

CHAPTER 14

COST CONCEPTS, CLASSIFICATIONS, AND PRODUCT COSTING SYSTEMS

CONTENTS

Management accounting as defined by the Institute of Management Accountants (IMA) is the process of identification, measurement, accumulation, analysis, preparation, interpretation, and communication of financial information, which is used by management to plan, evaluate, and control within an organization. It ensures the appropriate use of, and accountability for, an organization's resources. Management accounting also relates to the preparation of financial reports for nonmanagement groups, such as regulatory agencies and tax authorities. Simply stated, management accounting is the accounting for the planning, control, and decision-making activities of an organization.

COST ACCOUNTING VERSUS MANAGEMENT ACCOUNTING

The difference between cost accounting and management accounting is a subtle one. The IMA defines cost accounting as "a systematic set of procedures for recording and reporting measurements of the cost of manufacturing goods and performing services in the aggregate and in detail. It includes methods for recognizing, classifying, allocating, aggregating and reporting such costs and comparing them with standard costs." From this definition of cost accounting and the IMA's definition of management accounting, one thing is clear: the major function of cost accounting is cost accumulation for inventory valuation and income determination. Management accounting, however, emphasizes the use of the cost data for planning, control, and decision-making purposes.

COST CONCEPTS, TERMS, AND CLASSIFICATIONS

In financial accounting, the term *cost* is defined as a measurement, in monetary terms, of the amount of resources used for some purposes. In managerial accounting, the term *cost* is used in many ways. That is, different types of costs are used for different purposes. Some costs are useful and required for inventory valuation and income determination. Some costs are useful for planning, budgeting, and cost control. Still others are useful for making short-term and long-term decisions. Costs can be classified into various categories, according to:

1. Management function:
   a. Manufacturing costs.
   b. Nonmanufacturing costs (operating expenses).
2. Ease of traceability:
   a. Direct costs.
   b. Indirect costs.

3. Timing of charges against sales revenue:
   a. Product costs.
   b. Period costs.
4. Behavior in accordance with changes in activity:
   a. Variable costs.
   b. Fixed costs.
   c. Mixed (semivariable) costs.
5. Degree of averaging:
   a. Unit (average) costs.
   b. Total costs.
6. Relevance to planning, control, and decision making:
   a. Controllable and noncontrollable costs.
   b. Standard costs.
   c. Incremental (differential) costs.
   d. Sunk costs.
   e. Out-of-pocket (outlay) costs.
   f. Relevant costs.
   g. Opportunity costs.

Each of the cost categories is discussed in the remainder of this chapter.

Costs by Management Function

In a manufacturing firm, costs are divided categorically by the functional activities with which they are associated: (1) manufacturing costs and (2) non-manufacturing costs (operating expenses).

Manufacturing Costs. Manufacturing costs are those costs associated with the manufacturing activities of the company. Manufacturing costs are subdivided into three categories: (1) direct materials, (2) direct labor, and (3) factory overhead. Direct materials are all materials that become an integral part of the finished product. Examples are the steel used to make an automobile and the wood to make furniture. Glues, nails, and other minor items are called indirect materials (or supplies) and are classified as part of factory overhead, which is explained below.

Direct labor is the labor directly involved in making the product. Examples of direct labor costs are the wages of assembly workers on an assembly line and the wages of machine tool operators in a machine shop. Indirect labor, such as wages of supervisory personnel and janitors, is classified as part of factory overhead. Factory overhead can be defined as including all costs of manufacturing except direct materials and direct labor. Some of the many examples include depreciation, rent, taxes, insurance, fringe benefits, payroll taxes, and cost of idle time. Factory overhead can be defined as including all costs of manufacturing except direct materials and direct labor. Some of the many examples include depreciation, rent, property taxes, insurance, fringe benefits, payroll taxes, setup costs, waste control costs, quality costs, engineering, workers' compensation, and cost of idle time. Factory overhead is also called *manufacturing overhead, indirect manufacturing expenses, factory expense,* and *factory burden.*

Many costs overlap within their categories. For example, direct materials and direct labor, when combined, are called *prime costs.* Direct labor and factory overhead, when combined, are termed *conversion costs* (or *processing costs*).

One important category of factory overhead is that of quality costs. Quality costs are costs that occur because poor quality may exist or actually does exist. These costs are significant in amount, often totaling 20% to 25% of sales. The subcategories of quality costs are prevention, appraisal, and failure costs. *Prevention costs* are those incurred to prevent defects. Amounts spent on quality training programs, researching customer needs, quality circles, and improved production equipment are considered in prevention costs. Expenditures made for prevention will minimize the costs that will be incurred for appraisal and failure. *Appraisal costs* are costs incurred for monitoring or inspection; these costs compensate for mistakes not eliminated through prevention. *Failure costs* may be internal (e.g., scrap and rework costs and reinspection) or external (e.g., as product returns or recalls owing to quality problems, warranty costs, and lost sales due to poor product performance).

Nonmanufacturing Costs. Nonmanufacturing costs (or operating expenses) are subdivided into selling expenses and general and administrative (G & A) expenses. Selling expenses are all the expenses associated with obtaining sales and the delivery of the product. Examples are advertising and sales commissions. G & A expenses include all the expenses that are incurred in connection with performing general and administrative activities. Examples are executives' salaries and legal expenses. Many other examples of costs by management function and their relationships are found in Exhibit 14-1.

Direct Costs and Indirect Costs

Costs may be viewed as either direct or indirect in terms of the extent that they are *traceable* to a particular cost object. A *cost object* is any item for which the manager wishes to measure cost. Jobs, product lines, departments, divisions, sales territories, or units produced are typical cost objects. *Direct costs* can be directly traceable to the costing object. For example, if the object of costing under consideration is a product line, then the materials and labor involved in the manufacture of the line would both be direct costs.

Factory overhead items are all indirect costs, as they are not directly identifiable to any particular product line. Costs shared by different departments, products or jobs, called *common costs* or *joint costs* are also *indirect costs.* National advertising that benefits more than one product and sales territory is an example of an indirect cost. Accountants may *allocate* them on some *arbitrary* basis to specific products or departments.

The following examples illustrate a cost object and its related direct costs for nonmanufacturing firms:

- In a *retail firm,* such as a department store, costs can be traced to a department. For example, the direct costs of the shoe department include the costs of shoes and the wages of employees working in that department. Indirect costs include the costs of utilities, insurance, property taxes, storage, and handling.

- In a *service organization,* such as an accounting firm, costs can be traced to a specific service, such as tax return preparation. Direct costs for tax return preparation services include the costs of tax return forms, computer use, and labor to prepare the return. Indirect costs include the costs of office rental space, utilities, secretarial labor, telephone expenses, and depreciation of office furniture.

Product Costs and Period Costs

By their timing of charges against revenue or by whether they are inventoriable, costs are classified as product costs or period costs.

Product costs are inventoriable costs, identified as part of inventory on hand. They are therefore assets until they are sold. Once they are sold, they become expenses (i.e., cost of goods sold). All manufacturing costs are product costs.

Exhibit 14-1: Costs by Management Function

Direct Materials

plus

Direct Labor

plus

Indirect Materials		Indirect Labor		Factory Overhead Costs		Factory Overhead
	plus		plus		equals	

Indirect Materials	Indirect Labor	Factory Overhead Costs	
Factory supplies	Supervision	Rent	
Glues and nails	Inspection	Insurance	
Small tools	Security guards	Property tax	
	Factory clerks	Depreciation—factory	
	Janitors	Maintenance and repair	equals
		Utilities	
		Employer payroll taxes—factory labor	
		Overtime premium	
		Cost of idle time	
		Setup costs	
		Quality costs	

Manufacturing Costs

plus

Selling Expenses		General & Administrative Expenses		Nonmanufacturing Expenses (or operating expenses)
	plus		equals	

Selling Expenses	General & Administrative Expenses
Sales salaries and commissions	Administrative and office salaries
	Employer payroll taxes—office
Employer payroll taxes—sales	Rent
Advertising	Depreciation—office
Samples	Property tax—office
Entertainment and travel	Auditing expense
Rent	Legal expense
Depreciation—sales	Bad debts
Property tax on sales office	
Freight out	Travel and entertainment

Total Cost

Period costs are not inventoriable and, hence, are charged against sales revenues in the period in which the revenue is earned. Selling and general and administrative expenses are period costs.

Exhibit 14-2 shows the relationship of product and period costs and other cost classifications presented thus far.

Variable Costs, Fixed Costs, and Mixed (Semivariable) Costs

From a planning and control standpoint, perhaps the most important way to classify costs is by how they behave in accordance with changes in volume or some measure of activity. By behavior, costs can be classified as variable, fixed, or mixed.

Variable costs vary in total in direct proportion to changes in activity. Examples are direct materials and gasoline expense based on mileage driven. Fixed costs remain constant in total, regardless of changes in activity. Examples are rent, insurance, and taxes. Mixed (or semivariable) costs vary with changes in volume but, unlike variable costs, do not vary in direct proportion. In other words, these costs contain both a variable component and a fixed component. Examples are the rental of a delivery truck, where a fixed rental fee plus a variable charge based on mileage is made; and power costs, where the expense consists of a fixed amount plus a variable charge based on consumption. Costs by behavior will be examined further in a later chapter. The breakdown of costs into their variable components and their fixed components is very important in many areas of management accounting, such as flexible budgeting, break-even analysis, and short-term decision making.

Exhibit 14-2: Various Classifications of Costs

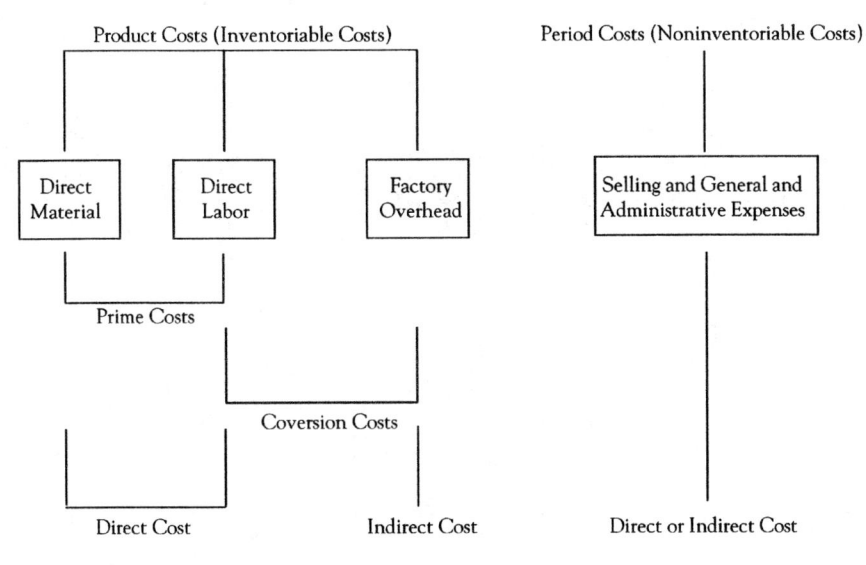

Unit (Average) Costs and Total Costs

For external reporting and pricing purposes, accountants are frequently interested in determining the unit (average) cost per unit of product or service. The unit cost is simply the average cost, which is the total cost divided by the volume in units. Alternatively, the unit cost is the sum of (a) the variable cost per unit and (b) the fixed cost per unit. It is important to realize that the unit cost declines as volume increases because the total fixed costs that are constant over a range of activity are being spread over a larger number of units.

EXAMPLE 1: Fixed costs are $1,000 per period, and variable costs are $.10 per unit. The total and unit (average) costs at various production levels are as follows:

Volume in Units (a)	Total Fixed Costs (b)	Total Variable Costs (c)	Total Costs (b) + (c) = (d)	Variable Cost per Unit (c)/(a) = (a)	Fixed Cost per Unit (b)/(a) = (f)	Unit (Average) Cost (d)/(a) or (e) + (f)
1,000	$1,000	$100	$1,100	$.10	$1.00	$1.10
5,000	1,000	500	1,500	.10	.20	.30
10,000	1,000	1,000	2,000	.10	.10	.20

The increase in total costs and the decline in unit costs are illustrated in Exhibit 14-3. The relationships for variable and fixed costs per unit are:

Behavior as Volume Changes from 5,000 to 10,000

	Total Cost	Unit Cost
Variable cost	Change ($500 to $1,000)	No change ($.10)
Fixed cost	No change ($1,000)	Change ($.20 to $10)

Costs for Planning, Control, and Decision Making

Controllable and Noncontrollable Costs. A cost is said to be controllable when the amount of the cost is assigned to the head of a department and the level of the cost is significantly under the manager's influence. Noncontrollable costs are those costs not subject to influence at a given level of managerial supervision.

Exhibit 14-3: Total and Unit (Average) Costs

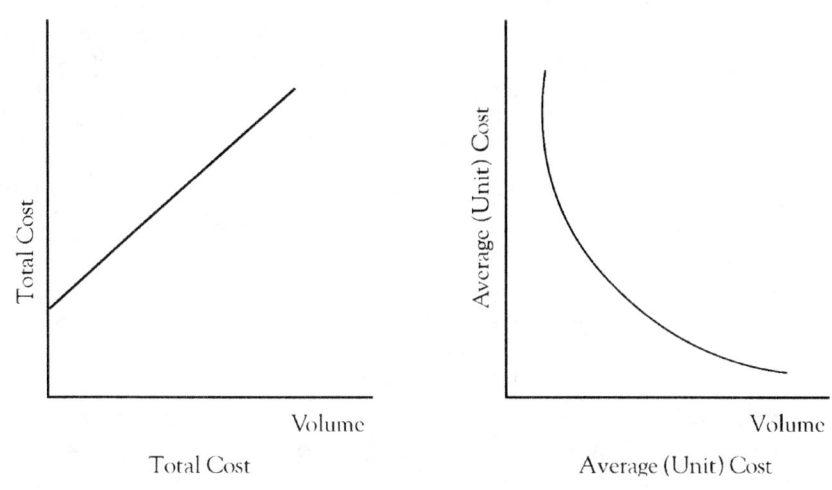

Total Cost   Average (Unit) Cost

EXAMPLE 2: All variable costs, such as direct materials, direct labor, and variable overhead are usually considered controllable by the department head. Further, a certain portion of fixed costs can also be controllable. For example, depreciation on the equipment used specifically for a given department would be an expense controllable by the head of the department.

Standard Costs. Standard costs are the costs established in advance to serve as goals, norms, or yardsticks to be achieved and, after the fact, to determine how well those goals were met. They are based on the quantities and prices of the various inputs (e.g., direct materials, direct labor, and factory overhead) needed to produce output efficiently. Standard costs can also be set for service businesses.

EXAMPLE 3: The standard cost of materials per pound is obtained by multiplying standard price per pound by standard quantity per unit of output in pounds as follows:

Purchase price	$3.00
Freight	0.12
Receiving and handling	0.02
Less: purchase discounts	(0.04)
Standard price per pound	$3.10
Per bill of materials in pounds	1.2
Allowance for waste and spoilage in lbs.	0.1
Allowance for rejects in lbs.	0.1
Standard quantity per unit of output	1.4 lbs.

The standard cost of material is 1.4 pounds × $3.10 = $4.34 per unit.

Incremental (Differential) Costs. The incremental cost is the difference in costs between two or more alternatives. Incremental costs are increases or decreases in total costs; or changes in specific elements of cost (e.g., direct labor cost), that result from any variation in operations. Incremental costs will be incurred (or saved) if a decision is made to proceed with (or to stop) some activity, but not otherwise.

EXAMPLE 4: The costs for alternatives A and B are as follows:

	A	B	Difference (B – A)
Direct materials	$10,000	$10,000	$ 0000
Direct labor	10,000	15,000	5,000

The incremental costs are simply B – A (or A – B) as shown in the last column. The incremental costs are relevant to future decisions.

Sunk Costs. Sunk costs are the costs of resources that have already been incurred, whose total will not be affected by any decision made now or in the future. Sunk costs are considered irrelevant to future decisions because they are past or historical costs.

EXAMPLE 5: An asset was acquired for $50,000 three years ago and is now listed at a book value of $20,000. The $20,000 book value is a sunk cost that does not affect a future decision.

Out-of-Pocket (Outlay) Costs. These costs require future expenditures of cash or other resources and are usually relevant to a particular decision.

EXAMPLE 6: A capital investment project requires $120,000 in cash outlays; $120,000 is an out-of-pocket cost.

Relevant Costs. Relevant costs are expected future costs that will differ between alternatives.

EXAMPLE 7: The incremental cost is said to be relevant to the future decision. The sunk cost is considered irrelevant.

Opportunity Costs. An opportunity cost is the net benefit forgone by rejecting an alternative. There is always an opportunity cost involved in making a choice or decision. It is a cost incurred relative to the alternative given up and does not appear on the formal accounting records.

EXAMPLE 8: A company has a choice of using its capacity to produce an extra 10,000 units or renting it out for $20,000. The opportunity cost of using the capacity is $20,000.

Income Statements and Balance Sheets—Manufacturer

Exhibit 14-4 illustrates the income statement of a manufacturer. The important characteristic of the income statement is that it is supported by a schedule of cost of goods manufactured shown in Exhibit 14-5. This schedule shows the specific costs (i.e., direct materials, direct labor, and factory overhead) that have gone into the goods completed during the period. Because the manufacturer carries three types of inventory—raw materials, work-in-process, and finished goods)—all three items must be incorporated into the computation of the cost of goods sold. These inventory accounts also appear on the balance sheet for a manufacturer, as shown in Exhibit 14-6.

Exhibit 14-4: Manufacturer's Income Statements for the Year Ended December 31, 2X15

Sales		$320,000
Less: cost of goods sold		
Finished goods, Dec. 31, 2X14	$18,000	
Cost of goods manufactured (see Schedule, Exhibit 14-5)	121,000	
Costs of goods available for sale	$139,000	
Finished goods, Dec. 31, 2X15	21,000	
Cost of goods sold		$118,000
Gross margin		$202,000
Less: selling and administrative expenses		60,000
Net income		$142,000

Exhibit 14-5: Manufacturer's Schedule of Cost Goods Manufactured

Direct materials:		
Inventory, Dec. 31, 2X14	$23,000	
Purchases	64,000	
Cost of direct materials available for use	$87,000	
Inventory, Dec. 31, 2X15	7,800	
Direct materials used		$79,200
Direct labor		25,000
Factory overhead		
Indirect labor	$3,000	
Indirect material	2,000	
Factory utilities	500	
Factory depreciation	800	
Factory rent	2,000	
Miscellaneous	1,500	9,800
Total manufacturing costs incurred during 2X15		$114,000

Add: work-in-process inventory, Dec. 31, 2X14	9,000
Manufacturing costs to account for	$123,000
Less: work-in-process inventory, Dec. 31, 2X15	2,000
Cost of goods manufactured (to Income Statement (Exhibit 14-4))	$121,000

Exhibit 14-6: Manufacturer's Current Asset Section of the Balance Sheet

December 31, 2X15

Current assets:		
Cash		$25,000
Accounts receivable		78,000
Inventories:		
Raw materials	$ 7,800	
Work-in-process	2,000	
Finished goods	21,000	30,800
Total		$133,800

COST ACCUMULATION SYSTEMS

A cost accumulation system is a product costing system, which is the process of accumulating manufacturing costs such as materials, labor, and factory overhead and assigning them to cost objectives, such as finished goods and work-in-process. Product costing is necessary, not only for inventory valuation and income determination but also for establishing the unit selling price. The cost accumulation system that is used to measure the manufacturing costs of products is essentially a two-step process: (1) the measurement of costs that are applicable to manufacturing operations during a given accounting period and (2) the assignment of these costs to products.

The two basic approaches to cost accounting and accumulation are:

1. Job order costing.

2. Process costing.

Job order costing and process costing differ largely in the manner in which product costing is accomplished. With job order costing, the focus is to apply costs to specific jobs, which may consist of either a single physical unit or a few like units. Under process costing, accounting data are accumulated by the production department (or cost center) and averaged over all of the production that occurred in the department. There is mass production of like units that are manufactured on a continuous basis through a series of uniform production steps known as *processes*. Exhibit 14-7 summarizes the basic differences between the two costing methods.

Exhibit 14-7: Differences Between Job Order Costing and Process Costing

	Job Order Costing	Process Costing
Cost unit:	Job, order, or contract	Physical unit
Costs accumulated:	By jobs	By departments
Subsidiary record:	Job cost sheet	Cost of production report
Used by:	Custom manufacturers	Processing industries
Permits computation of:	(a) A unit cost for inventory costing purposes (b) A profit or loss on each job	A unit cost to be used to compute the costs of goods completed and each job work in process

Job Order Costing

Job order costing is the system under which costs are accumulated by jobs, orders, or contracts. This costing method is appropriate when the products are manufactured in identifiable lots or batches, or when the products are manufactured to customer specifications. Job order costing is widely used by custom manufacturers such as printing, aircraft, and construction companies. It may also be used by service businesses such as auto repair shops and professional services. Job order costing keeps track of costs by tracing direct material and direct labor to a particular job. Costs not directly traceable—factory overhead—are applied to individual jobs using a predetermined overhead (application) rate.

A *job cost sheet* is used to record various production costs for work-in-process inventory. A separate cost sheet is kept for each identifiable job, accumulating the direct materials, direct labor, and factory overhead assigned to that job as it moves through production. The form varies according to the needs of the company. The basic records or source documents used for job costing, shown in Exhibit 14-8, include the following:

- *Job cost sheet.* This is the key document in the system. It summarizes all of the manufacturing costs—direct materials, direct labor, and applied factory overhead (discussed in detail later)—of producing a given job or batch of products. One sheet is maintained for each job, and the file of job cost sheets for unfinished jobs is the subsidiary record for the Work-in-Process Inventory account. When the jobs are completed and transferred, the job order sheets are transferred to a completed jobs file and the number of units and their unit costs are recorded on inventory cards supporting the Finished Goods Inventory account.

- *Materials requisition form.* This form shows the types, quantities, and prices of each type of material issued for production.

- *Work ticket.* Also called a *time ticket,* the work ticket shows who worked on what job for how many hours as well as the wage rate.

- *Factory overhead cost sheet.* Provides a summary of the various factory overhead costs incurred.
- *Memo for applied factory overhead.* This memorandum shows how the factory overhead applied rate has been developed.
- *Finished goods record.* This is a record maintained for each type of product manufactured and sold. Each record contains a running record of units and costs of products received, sold, and on hand.

The general flow of costs through a job cost system is shown in Exhibit 14-9.

Exhibit 14-8: Basic Records in a Job Cost System

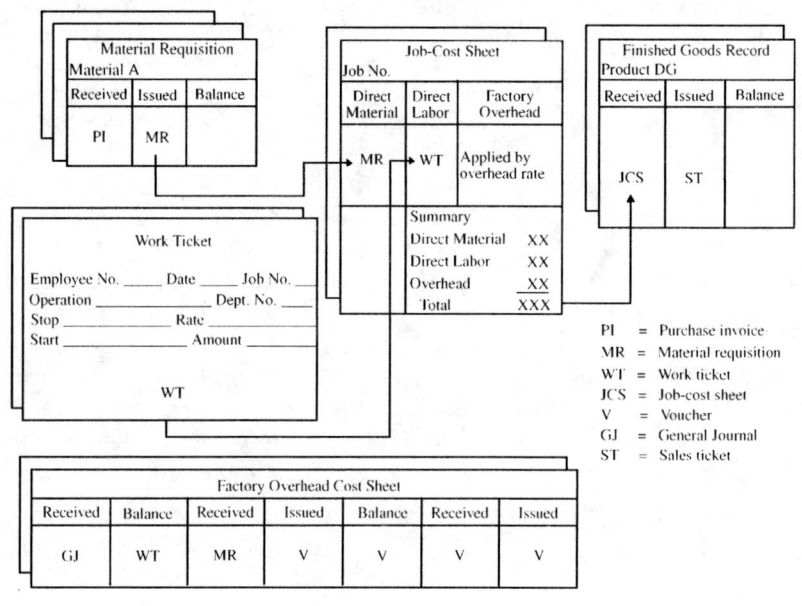

PI = Purchase invoice
MR = Material requisition
WT = Work ticket
JCS = Job-cost sheet
V   = Voucher
GJ = General Journal
ST = Sales ticket

Exhibit 14-9: Job Cost System—Flow Chart of Ledger Relationship

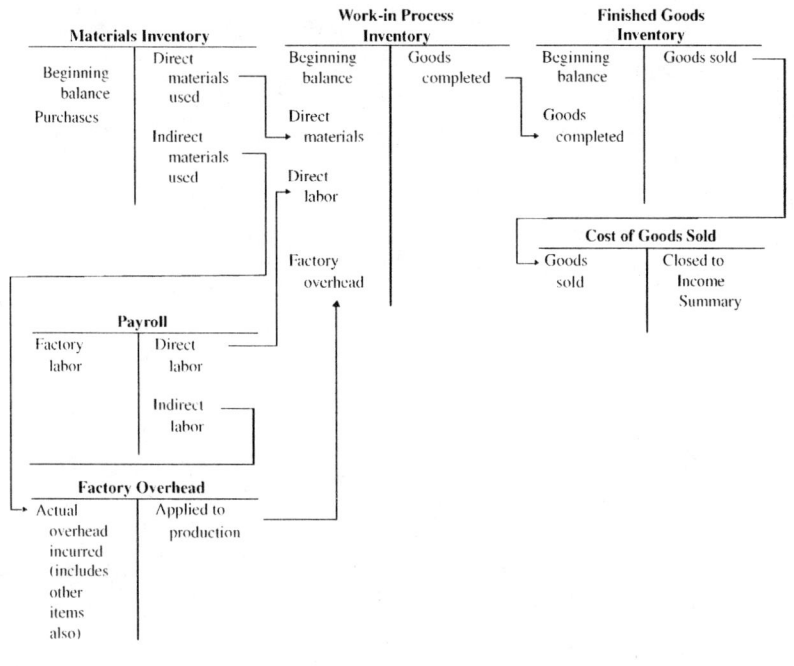

Following is an example of the tie-in between the general ledger accounts and the subsidiary records in a job order cost system.

> **EXAMPLE 9:** In June, the beginning inventories were as follows:

Materials inventory (Material A, $10,000; Material B, $6,000; indirect materials $4,000)	$20,000
Work-in-process inventory (Job No. 310; direct materials, $4,200; direct labor, $5,000; and overhead, $4,000)	13,200
Finished goods inventory (500 units of Product X at a cost of $11 per unit)	5,500

Assume that Job No. 310 was completed in June, and that, of the two jobs started in June—320 and 510—only Job No. 510 was incomplete at the end of June. The transactions, and the associated journal entries, would be as follows:

1. Purchased $10,000 of Material A and $15,000 of Material B on account.

Materials inventory	$25,000	
Accounts payable		$25,000

   To record purchase of direct materials.

2. Direct materials issued: Material A to Job No. 310: $1,000; to Job No. 320: $8,000; and to Job No. 510: $2,000. Material B to Job No. 310: $2,000; to Job No. 320: $6,000; and to Job No. 510: $4,000. Indirect materials issued to all jobs: $1,000.

Work-in-process inventory	$23,000	
Factory overhead	1,000	
Material inventory		$24,000

To record direct and indirect materials issued.

3. Factory payroll for the month: $25,000. Social security and income taxes withheld: $4,000.

Payroll summary	$25,000	
Various liability accounts for taxes withheld		$ 4,000
Accrued wages payable		21,000

To record factory payroll for June.

4. Factory payroll paid: $19,000.

| Accrued wages payable | $19,000 | |
| Cash | | $19,000 |

To record cash paid to factory employees in June.

5. Payroll costs distributed: Direct labor: $20,000 (Job No. 310, $5,000; Job No. 320, $12,000; and Job No. 510, $3,000). Indirect labor: $5,000.

Work-in-process inventory	$20,000	
Factory overhead	5,000	
Payroll summary		$25,000

To distribute factory labor costs incurred.

6. Other factory overhead costs incurred:

Payroll taxes accrued	$3,000
Repairs (on account)	1,000
Property taxes accrued	4,000
Heat, light, and power (on account)	2,000
Depreciation	5,000
	$15,000

Factory overhead	$15,000	
Accounts payable		3,000
Accrued payroll taxes		3,000
Accrued property taxes payable		4,000
Accumulated depreciation		5,000

To record factory overhead costs incurred.

7. Factory overhead applied to production (at rate of 80% of direct labor cost):

| Job No. 310, Product Y (0.80 × $5,000) | $4,000 |
| Job No. 320, Product Z (0.80 × $12,000) | 9,600 |

Job No. 510, Product W (0.80 × $3,000)		2,400
		$16,000

Work-in-process inventory	$16,000	
Factory overhead		$16,000

To record application of overhead to production.

Note: As factory overhead costs are incurred, they are recorded in a subsidiary ledger and debited to the factory overhead account (as shown in journal entries nos. 2, 5, and 7). The factory overhead costs applied to production are periodically credited to the factory overhead account and debited to the work-in-process account (as shown in journal entry no. 7).

8. Jobs completed and transferred to finished goods inventory (see Exhibit 14-10 for details):

Job No. 310 (4,000 units of Product Y at $6.30)	$25,200
Job No. 320 (10,000 units of Product Z at $3.56)	35,600
	$60,800

Finished goods inventory	60,800	
Work-in-process inventory		60,800

To record completed production for June.

9. Sales on account for the month: 500 units of Product X for $8,000, cost: $5,500. 10,000 units of Product Z for $62,000, cost: $35,600 (Job No. 320).

Accounts Receivable	$70,000	
Sales		$70,000

To record sales on account ($8,000 + $62,000) for June.

Cost of goods sold	$41,100	
Finished goods inventory		$41,100

To record cost of goods sold ($5,500 + $35,600) for June.

After the above entries have been posted to the accounts of the company, the Work-in-Process Inventory and Finished Goods Inventory accounts would appear (in T-account form) as follows:

Work-in-Process Inventory

June 1 balance	13,200	Completed	60,800
Direct materials used	23,000		
Direct labor cost incurred	20,000		
Overhead applied	16,000		

Finished Goods Inventory

June 1 balance	5,500	Sold	41,100
Completed	60,800		

The Work-in-Process Inventory account has a balance at June 28 of $11,400, which agrees with the total costs charged thus far to Job No. 510, as shown in Exhibit 14-10. These costs consist of direct materials, $6,000; direct labor, $3,000; and factory overhead, $2,400. The Finished Goods Inventory account has a balance at June 28 of $25,200. The finished goods inventory card for Product Y supports this amount (see Exhibit 14-10), showing that there are indeed units of Product Y on hand having a total cost of $25,200.

Note: The entries in the ledger accounts given above are often made from summaries of costs and are thus entered only at the end of the month. To keep management informed as to costs incurred, the details of the various costs incurred may be recorded more frequently, often daily.

The preceding example makes clear the real advantages of using overhead rates (including predetermined rates). Three jobs were worked on during the month. Job No. 310 was started before June and was completed in June. Job No. 320 was both started and completed in June. Job No. 510 was started in June but was not completed in June. Each required different amounts of direct materials and direct labor (and, perhaps, different types of direct labor). Under these conditions, there is simply no way to apply overhead to products without the use of a rate based on some level of activity.

The use of a predetermined overhead rate permits the computation of unit costs of Job Nos. 310 and 320 at the time of their completion rather than waiting until the end of the month. However, this advantage is secured only at the cost of keeping more detailed records of the costs incurred. As will be clear below, the other major cost system—process costing—requires far less record keeping, but the computation of unit costs is more complex.

Factory Overhead Application. Many items of factory overhead cost are incurred for the entire factory and for the entire accounting period and cannot be specifically identified with particular jobs. Furthermore, the amount of actual factory overhead costs incurred is not usually available until the end of the accounting period. However, it is often critical to make cost data available for pricing purposes as each job is completed. Therefore, in order for job costs to be available on a timely basis, it is customary to apply factory overhead by using a *predetermined factory overhead rate.*

Note: Although an actual rate is simple to compute, the results are misleading because overhead rates may fluctuate significantly from month to month. When these fluctuations occur, similar jobs completed in different months will have differing overhead costs and total costs.

Predetermined Factory Overhead Rate. Regardless of the cost accumulation system used (i.e., job order or process), factory overhead is applied to a job or process. Companies use *predicted* levels of activity and cost rather than *actual* levels. The successful assignment of factory overhead costs depends on a careful estimate the total overhead costs and a good forecast of the activity used as the cost driver.

Exhibit 14-10: Job Cost Sheets and Supporting Inventory Cards

Material Requisition		
Material A		
Received	Issued	Balance
		$10,000
$10,000		20,000
	$1,000	19,000
	8,000	11,000
	2,000	9,000

Material Requisition		
Material B		
Received	Issued	Balance
		$ 6,000
$15,000		21,000
	$2,000	19,000
	6,000	13,000
	4,000	9,000

Job Cost Sheet (Product Y) Job No. 310

Date	Direct Materials	Direct Labor	Factory Overhead Applied
June	$4,200	$ 5,000	$4,000
	A 1,000	5,000	4,000
	B 2,000	$10,000	$8,000
	$7,200		
Job completed (4,000 units of Product Y @ $6.30). Total cost, $25,200.			

Job Cost Sheet (Product Z) Job No. 320

Date	Direct Materials	Direct Labor	Factory Overhead Applied
June	A 8,000	$12,000	$9,600
	B 6,000		
	$14,000		
Job completed (10,000 units of Product Z @ $3.56). Total cost, $35,600.			

Job Cost Sheet (Product W) Job No. 510

Date	Direct Materials	Direct Labor	Factory Overhead Applied
June	A 2,000	$3,000	$2,400
	B 4,000		
Job completed (4,000 units of Product W). Cost to date, $11,400.			

Finished Goods Record		
Product X		
Received	Issued	Balance
		$5,500
	$5,500	– 0 –

Finished Goods Record		
Product Y		
Received	Issued	Balance
$25,200		$25,200

Finished Goods Record		
Product Z		
Received	Issued	Balance
$35,600		$35,600
	$35,600	– 0 –

The predetermined overhead rate is determined as follows:

$$\text{Predetermined overhead rate} = \frac{\text{Budgeted annual factory overhead costs}}{\begin{array}{c}\text{Budgeted annual activity units}\\ \text{(e.g., direct labor hours, machine hours)}\end{array}}$$

Budgeted activity units used in the denominator of the formula, more often called the *denominator activity* level or *cost driver,* are measured in:

- Direct labor hours;
- Machine hours;
- Direct labor costs;
- Direct material dollars; or
- Production units.

Deposition of Under- and Overapplied Overhead. Actual overhead cost incurred and during a period and factory overhead costs applied will inevitably differ. Conventionally, at the end of the year, the difference between actual overhead and applied overhead is close to cost of goods sold if it is immaterial. On the other hand, if a material difference exists, work-in-process, finished goods, and cost of goods sold are adjusted on a proportionate basis based on units or dollars at year-end for the deviation between actual and applied overhead. Underapplied overhead and overapplied overhead results are as follows:

Underapplied overhead = Applied overhead < Actual overhead

Overapplied overhead = Applied overhead > Actual overhead

Process Costing

Process costing is a cost accumulation system that aggregates manufacturing costs by departments or by production processes. Total manufacturing costs are accumulated in two major categories: (1) direct materials and (2) conversion costs (the sum of direct labor and factory overhead applied). Unit cost is determined by dividing the total costs charged to a cost center by the output of that cost center. In that sense, the unit costs are averages. Process costing is appropriate for companies that produce a continuous mass of like units through a series of operations or processes. Process costing is generally used in such industries as petroleum, chemicals, oil refinery, textiles, and food processing.

Identification of System and Problems and Choice of a System. Because the unit costs under process costing are averages, the process costing system requires less bookkeeping than a job order costing system. A lot of companies prefer to use a process costing system for this reason. However, before any particular system is chosen, the principal system problem must be identified in a broader perspective. Typically, the method of costing chosen depends more on the characteristics of the production process and the types of products manufactured. If the products are alike and move from one processing department to another in a continuous chain, a process costing method is desirable. If, however, there are significant differences among the costs of the various products, a process costing system would not provide adequate product cost information and thus a job order costing method would be more appropriate. For example, a job order costing system would invariably be used if the customer paid for the specific item, production order, or service on the basis of its cost, which is often the case in repair shops and custom work.

Some companies might find it necessary to use a hybrid of the job order and process costing systems, depending on how a product flows through the factory. For example, in a parallel processing situation, which is discussed later, some type of hybrid system has proven to be the optimal system choice.

Industries that are most suitable for process costing have the following characteristics:

- Production quantity is uniform.
- A given order does not affect the production process.
- Customer orders are filled from the manufacturer's stock.
- There is continuous mass production through an assembly line approach.
- There exists a standardization of the process and product.
- There is a desire to implement cost control on a departmental basis rather than on a customer or product basis.
- There is continuity of demand for the output.
- Quality standards can be implemented on a departmental basis, such as online inspection, as processing proceeds.

Product Flow. The three types of product (processing) flow in processing—sequential, parallel, and selective—are shown in Exhibit 14-11. In a sequential flow, each product item manufactured goes through the same set of operations. For example, in a textile industry, a typical plant operates a dyeing department as well as a spinning department. The dyeing department receives yarn from the spinning department and dyes it, then transfers it to finished goods. Thus, the product flow in textile operations is sequential.

In a parallel flow, certain portions of work are done simultaneously and then brought together in a particular process in chain form. The portions of work done simultaneously may require a job order type of costing, as this may be needed to keep track of the differences in costs between the portions of work done simultaneously. Canned food processing industries employ this type of system. In manufacturing fruit cocktail products, different kinds of fruits are peeled and processed simultaneously in different locations in a factory. They are then brought together in a final process or processes for canning and transfer to finished goods inventory.

Exhibit 14-11: Types of Processing Flow

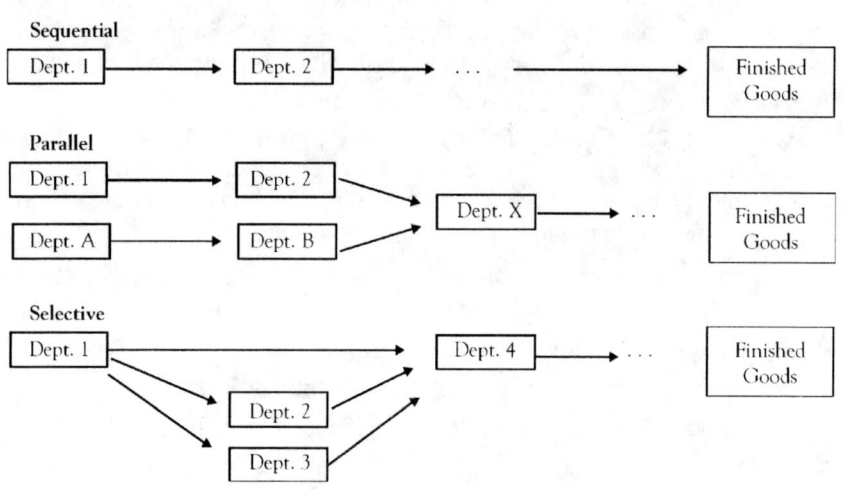

Finally, in a selective flow, the product goes through a selected set of processing departments within a factory, depending on the desired final product. Meat processing and petroleum refining falls in this category. Take meat processing, for example. After initial butchering, some of the meat product goes to grinding, then to packing, and then to finished goods; and some goes to smoking, packaging, and finished goods in that order. The selected flows may take a wide variety of forms.

Steps in Process Costing Calculations. The four steps involved in accounting for process costs are as follows:

Step 1: Summarize the Flow of Physical Units. The first step of the accounting provides a summary of all units on which some work was done in the department during the period. Input must equal output. This step helps to detect units lost during the process. The basic relationship may be expressed in the following equation:

Beginning inventory + Units started for the period = Units completed
and transferred out + Ending inventory

Step 2: Compute Output in Terms of Equivalent Units. In order to determine the unit costs of the product in a processing environment, it is important to measure the total amount of work done during an accounting period. A special problem arises in processing industries in connection with how to deal with work still in process (i.e., the work partially completed at the end of the period). The partially completed units are measured on an equivalent whole-unit basis for process costing purposes.

Equivalent units are a measure of how many whole units of production are represented by the units completed plus the units partially completed. For example, 100 units that are 60% completed are the equivalent of 60 completed units in terms of processing costs.

Step 3: Summarize the Total Costs to Be Accounted for and Compute the Unit Costs per Equivalent Unit. This step summarizes the total costs assigned to the department during the period. Then the unit cost per equivalent is computed as follows:

$$\text{Unit cost} = \frac{\text{Total costs incurred during the period}}{\text{Equivalent units of production during the period}}$$

Step 4: Apply Total Costs to Units Completed and Transferred Out and to Units in Ending Work in Process. The process costing method uses what is called the cost of production report. It summarizes both total and unit costs charged to a department, and indicates the allocation of total costs between work-in-process inventory and the units completed and transferred out to the next department or the finished goods inventory.

The cost of production report covers all four steps previously described. It is also the source for monthly journal entries and is a convenient compilation from which cost data may be presented to management.

Weighted-Average versus FIFO. When there is a beginning inventory of work in process, the production completed during the period comes from work partially completed in a prior period and from new units started in the current period. Because costs tend to vary from period to period, each batch may carry different unit costs. Costs of the beginning inventory are treated either with weighted-average costing or with first-in-first-out costing.

Under the weighted-average method of costing, both units' costs of work in process at the beginning of the period are combined with current production units started in the current period and their costs and an average cost is computed. In determining equivalent production units, no distinction is made between work partially completed in the prior period and the units started and completed in the current period. Thus, there is only one average cost for goods completed.

Equivalent units under weighted-average costing may be computed as follows:

Units completed + [Ending work-in-process × Degree of completion (%)]

Under FIFO, on the other hand, beginning work-in-process inventory costs are separated from added costs applied in the current period. Thus, there are two unit costs for the period: (1) beginning work-in-process units completed and (2) units started and completed in the same period. Under FIFO, the beginning work in process is assumed to be completed and transferred first. Equivalent units under FIFO costing may be computed as follows:

Units completed + [Ending work-in-process × Degree of completion (%)]
    – [Beginning work-in-process × Degree of completion (%)]

EXAMPLE 10: To illustrate, the following data relate to the activities of Department A during the month of January:

	Units
Beginning work in process (100% complete as to materials; 2/3 complete as to conversion)	1,500
Started this period	5,000
Completed and transferred	5,500
Ending work in process (100% complete as to materials; 6/10 complete as to conversion)	1,000

Equivalent production in Department A for the month is computed, using weighted-average costing, as follows:

	Materials	Conversion Costs
Units completed and transferred	5,500	5,500
Ending work in process		
Materials (100%)	1,000	
Conversion costs (60%)		600
Equivalent production	6,500	6,100

Equivalent production in Department A for the month is computed, using FIFO costing, as follows:

	Materials	Conversion Costs
Units completed and transferred	5,500	5,500
Ending work in process		
Materials (100%)	1,000	
Conversion costs (60%)		600
Equivalent production	6,500	6,100
Minus: beginning work in process		
Materials (100%)	1,500	
Conversion costs (2/3)		1,000
	5,000	5,100

The following example illustrates, step-by-step, the weighted-average and FIFO methods.

EXAMPLE 11: The Portland Cement Manufacturing Company, Inc. manufactures cement. Its processing operations involve quarrying, grinding, blending, packing, and sacking. For cost accounting and control purposes, there are four processing centers: Raw Material No. 1, Raw Material No. 2, Clinker, and Cement. Separate cost-of-production reports are prepared in detail with respect to the foregoing cost centers. The following information pertains to the operation of Raw Material No. 2 Department for July 2X15:

	Materials	Conversion
Units in process July 1		
800 bags	complete	60% complete
Costs	$12,000	$56,000
Units transferred out		
40,000 bags		
Current costs	$41,500	$521,500
Units in process July 31		
5,000 bags	complete	30% complete

Using weighted-average costing and FIFO costing, the following are computed:

(a) Equivalent production units and unit costs by elements.

(b) Cost of work in process (WIP) for July.

(c) Cost of units completed and transferred.

Computation of Output in Equivalent Units

	Physical Flow		Materials	Conversion
WIP, beginning	800		(60%)	
Units transferred in	44,200			
Units to account for	45,000			
Units completed and transferred out	40,000	40,000	40,000	
WIP, end	5,000	(30%)	5,000	1,500
Units accounted for	45,000			
Equivalent units used for weighted average			45,000	41,500
Less: old equivalent units for work done on beginning inventory in prior period			800	480
Equivalent units used for FIFO			44,200	41,020

Cost of Production Report—Weighted Average Raw Material No. 2 Department for the Month Ended July 31, 2X15

	WIP Beginning	Current Costs	Total Costs	Equivalent Units	Average Unit Cost
Materials	$12,000	$ 41,500	$ 53,500	45,000	$ 1.1889
Conversion costs	56,000	521,500	577,500	41,500	13.9156
	$68,000	563,000	631,000		$15.1045

	WIP Beginning	Current Costs	Total Costs	Equivalent Units	Average Unit Cost
Cost of goods completed 40,000 × $15.1045		$604,180			
WIP, end:					
Materials 5,000 × $1.1889		$5,944.50			
Conversion 1,500 × 13.9156		20,873.40	$26,817.90		
Total costs accounted for			$631,000	(rounded)	

Cost of Production Report—FIFO Raw Material No. 2 Department for the Month Ended July 31, 2X15

		Total Costs	Equivalent Units	Unit Costs
WIP, beginning		$ 68,000.00		
Current costs:				
Materials		41,500.00	44,200.00	$ .9389
Conversion costs		521,500.00	41,020.00	12.7133
Total costs to account for		$631,000.00		$13.6522
WIP, end:				
Materials 5,000 × $.9389	$ 4,694.50			
Conversion 1,500 × 12.7133	19,069.95	23,764.45		
Cost of goods completed, 40,000 units:				
• WIP, beginning to be transferred out first	68,000.00			
• Additional costs to complete 800 × (1 – .6) × $12.7133	4,068.26			
• Cost of goods started and completed this month 39,200 $13.652				
	535,166.24	$607,234.50		
Total costs accounted for		$631,000.00	(rounded)	

Answers are summarized as follows:

	Weighted Average		FIFO	
	Materials	*Conversion*	*Materials*	*Conversion*
(a) Equivalent units	45,000	41,500	44,200	41,020
Unit costs	$1.1889	$13.9156	$.9389	$12.7133
(b) Cost of WIP	$26,817.90		$23,764.45	
(c) Cost of units completed and transferred	$604,180		$607,234.50	

Estimating Degree of Completion. Estimating the degree of completion for work in process is critical. Inaccurate estimates will undoubtedly lead to inaccurate computation of unit costs especially for conversion. Estimating the degree of completion is usually easier for materials than for processing or conversion costs. The degree of completion for materials is normally 100% unless the material is added during or at the end of any given process. On the other hand, the stage of completion for conversion costs requires specific knowledge about the conversion sequence. The sequence consists of a standard number of processing operations or a standard number of days, weeks, or months for mixing, refining, aging, and finishing.

Thus, in order to estimate the degree of completion for conversion, the proportions of the total effort (in terms of direct labor and overhead) needed to complete one unit or one batch of production must be determined. Industrial engineers should be able to measure the proportion of conversion needed with reasonable accuracy. In practice, instead of putting effort into estimating the actual stage of completion, the assumption is often made that work still in process at the end of the accounting period is 50% complete. At the other extreme, some firms ignore the work in process completely and show no work-in-process inventory account. This approach is acceptable only if the work-in-process inventory is insignificant in amount or remains relatively constant in size.

Application of Factory Overhead Using Predetermined Rates. As discussed previously, it is common to charge factory overhead to work in process using a predetermined overhead application rate, because the actual overhead is not available until the end of the period. In process costing, the overhead is usually applied only at the end of the period; however, in many cases, the duration of the time period desired for product costing and control information is not the same as the time period considered satisfactory for financial reporting. When the time periods are equal and actual overhead costs can be obtained on a timely basis, the application of overhead to each processing unit's production is unnecessary, and using actual overhead is preferable. When production and overhead costs vary significantly from period to period, however, it is desirable to apply overhead using predetermined application rates. This provides representative unit costs, especially if dealing with a seasonal business. The rates may be based on such measures as direct labor hours, machine hours, direct labor costs, direct material costs, or production volume. The use of departmental rates reflecting the different characteristics of different processing departments is certainly desirable. For example, it may be most realistic to apply overhead on a direct labor basis in one department and on a machine hours basis in another department.

Managerial Use of Process Cost Data. A process costing system, just like a job order costing system, is essentially a cost accumulation system that produces the unit manufacturing cost for a given process. Per-unit manufacturing costs are used primarily for product costing, inventory valuation, and income determination. Equally important, however, are the per-unit cost data vital for pricing purposes. They are used not only for pricing finished products but also for product mix strategies to maximize profits and for determining optimal production methods. Perhaps the most effective way to fully utilize process cost data is to integrate the output into the standard costing system of the firm. Blended with standard costing, the process cost data provide the basis on which management can judge the cost performance of a processing department as a cost center in all categories of costs, such as direct material, direct labor, and overhead. An increase in any one of these cost components is a "red flag" to management, indicating a possible inefficient operation in a given department. This topic is explored in further detail in Chapter 21, "Using Variance Analysis as a Financial Tool."

The process cost data also aid management in many processing decisions. In situations involving multiple or joint products, management is often faced with the decision as to whether to sell the product at what is called the split-off point or process it further in the hope of increased revenues. In addition, for external reporting purposes, process cost data, whether in total or in units, will help management allocate joint manufacturing costs to different joint products so that they can produce income statements by products.

In designing the system to meet the needs of both product costing and cost control, management should identify the cost centers. Cost centers may be assigned to each division, department, or section. The number of processing departments as cost centers will depend on the detail desired by management. Cost centers should typically be set up along organizational lines for control purposes. Management must weigh the cost/benefit relationship in deciding on the number of cost centers desired.

Process Costing and Decision Making. Process costing has many advantages for management decision making, including:

- It monitors production of component parts and subassemblies.

- It provides good inventory management by retaining accurate records of the amount of materials, labor, and overhead on an equivalent unit basis.

- It assists management in the evaluation of the performance of processing departments and product managers.

- It helps to determine the most efficient or least costly alternative production methods or processes. The information may assist management in deciding to invest in a new plant or new machinery, or to repair existing machinery.

- It reveals to management the number of unfinished period-end units so management can anticipate how quickly those units will be completed the next period.

Although process costing requires less paperwork and detail, it has certain drawbacks. Under a process costing system, management is unable to explicitly identify actual costs with individual items. Therefore, if a particular product incurs any unusual costs, such as excessive spoilage or rework, its costs would be averaged with the other products' costs. Averaging simplifies, but makes cost loss specific and less informative.

More on Factory Overhead Application. Regardless of the cost accumulation system used (i.e., job order, process, or standard costing), factory overhead is applied to a job or process, using a predetermined overhead rate that is determined based on budgeted factory overhead cost and budgeted activity. The rate is calculated as follows:

$$\text{Predetermined overhead rate} = \frac{\text{Budgeted yearly total factory overhead cost}}{\text{Budgeted yearly activity (e.g., direct labor hours)}}$$

Budgeted activity units (capacity) used in the denominator of the formula, more often called the denominator level, are measured in direct labor hours, machine hours, direct labor costs, production units, or any other surrogate of production activity.

EXAMPLE 12: Assuming that two companies have prepared the following budgeted data for the year 2X15:

	Company X	Company Y
Predetermined rate based on	Machine hours	Direct labor cost
Budgeted overhead	$200,000 (1)	$240,000 (1)
Budgeted machine hours		100,000 (2)
Budgeted direct labor cost		$160,000 (2)
Predetermined overhead rate (1)/(2)	$2 per machine hour	150% of direct labor cost

It is further assumed that actual overhead costs and the actual level of the activity for 2X15 for each firm are:

	Company X	Company Y
Actual overhead costs	$198,000	$256,000
Actual machine hours	96,000	
Actual direct labor cost		$176,000

Note that for each company, the actual cost and activity data differ from the budgeted figures used in calculating the predetermined overhead rate. The computation of the resulting underapplied and overapplied overhead for each company is as follows:

	Company X	Company Y
Actual overhead costs	$198,000	$256,000
Factory overhead applied to work in process during 2X15:		
96,000 actual machine hours × $2	192,000	
$176,000 actual direct labor cost × 150%		264,000
Underapplied (overapplied) factory overhead	$6,000	($ 8,000)

Selecting the Denominator (Capacity) Measures. It is important to define different denominator (capacity) measures because they affect underapplied or overapplied factory overhead. Capacity is the ability to produce during a given time period, with an upper limit imposed by the availability of space, machinery, labor, materials, or capital. It may be expressed in units, weights, size, dollars, labor hours, or labor cost, for example. There are typically four concepts of capacity:

1. *Theoretical capacity*—the volume of activity that could be attained under ideal operating conditions, with minimum allowance for inefficiency. It is the largest volume of output possible, also called ideal capacity, engineered capacity, or maximum capacity.

2. *Practical capacity*—the highest activity level at which the factory can operate with an acceptable degree of efficiency, taking into consideration unavoidable losses of productive time (i.e., vacations, holidays, repairs to equipment). Also called maximum practical capacity. Two variations of the practical capacity concept are widely used as the denominator volume. They are normal capacity and expected annual activity.

3. *Normal capacity*—the average level of operating activity that is sufficient to fill the demand for the company's products or services for a span of several years, taking into consideration seasonal and cyclical demands and increasing or decreasing trends in demand.

4. *Expected annual activity*—similar to normal capacity except it is projected for a particular year. Also called planned capacity.

The choice of activity level used in determining the overhead application rate potentially will have a large effect on overapplied or underapplied overhead. The aforementioned four capacity measures may be 100,000, 95,000, 70,000, and 80,000 units of activity, respectively. If the actual level of activity were 85,000 units, over- or underapplication would result.

ALLOCATION OF SERVICE DEPARTMENT COSTS TO PRODUCTION DEPARTMENTS

The two basic types of departments in a manufacturing company are (1) production departments and (2) service departments. A production department (such as assembly or machining) is where the production or conversion occurs. A service department (such as engineering or maintenance) provides support to production departments. Before departmental factory overhead rates are developed for product costing, the costs of a service department should be allocated to the appropriate production departments (as part of factory overhead).

Basis of Assigning Service Department Costs

Some service department costs are direct. Examples are the salaries of the workers in the department. Other service department costs are indirect; that is, they are incurred jointly with some other department. An example is depreciation of building. These indirect costs must be allocated on some arbitrary basis.

The problem is that of selecting appropriate bases for assigning the indirect costs of service departments to other departments. Service department costs should be allocated on a basis that reflects the type of activity in which the service department is engaged. The ideal basis should be logical, have a high cause-and-effect relationship between the service provided and the costs of providing it, and be easy to implement. The basis selected may be supported by physical observation, by correlation analysis, or by logical analysis of the relationships between the departments. A list of some service departments and possible bases for allocation follows.

Service Departments	*Allocation Basis*
Supplies	Number of requisitions
Power	Kilowatt-hours used
Buildings and grounds	Number of square or cubic feet
Maintenance and repairs	Machine hours or number of calls
Personnel	Number of employees
Cafeteria	Number of employees
Purchasing	Number of orders

Procedure for Service Department Cost Allocation

Once the service department costs are known, the next step is to allocate the service department costs to the production departments. This may be accomplished by one of the following procedures:

- Direct method.

- Step method.

- Reciprocal method.

Direct Method

The direct method is used to allocate the costs of each service department directly to production departments, with no intermediate allocation to other service departments. That is, no consideration is given to services performed by one service department for another. This is perhaps the most widely used method because of its simplicity and ease of use.

EXAMPLE 13: The following data are assumed:

	Service Departments		Production Departments	
	General Plant (GP)	Engineering (E)	A Machining	B Assembly
Overhead costs before allocation	$20,000	$10,000	$30,000	$40,000
Direct labor hours by General Plant (GP)	15,000	20,000	60,000	40,000
Engineering hours by Engineering (E)	5,000	4,000	50,000	30,000

Using the direct method yields:

	Service Departments		Production Departments	
	(GP)	(E)	A	B
Overhead costs	$20,000	$10,000	$30,000	$40,000
Reallocation:				
GP (0, 0, 60%, 40%)*	($20,000)		12,000	8,000
E (0, 0, 5/8, 3/8)#		($10,000)	6,250	3,750
	0	0	$48,250	$51,750

* Base is (60,000 + 40,000 = 100,000); 60,000/100,000 = .6; 40,000/100,000 = .4
\# Base is (50,000 + 30,000 = 80,000); 50,000/80,000 = 5/8, 30,000/80,000 = 3/8

Step Method

The step method (also called the step-down method and the sequential method) is used to allocate services rendered by service departments to other service departments using a sequence of allocation. The sequence normally begins with the department that renders service to the greatest number of other service departments; the sequence continues in a step-by-step fashion and ends with the allocation of costs of service departments that provide the least amount of service. After a given service department's costs have been allocated, that department will not receive any charges from the other service departments.

Using the same data, the step allocation method yields the following:

	Service Departments		Production Departments	
	(GP)	*(E)*	*A*	*B*
Overhead costs	$20,000	$10,000	$30,000	$40,000
Reallocation:				
GP (0, 1/6, 1/2, 1/3)*	($20,000)	3,333	10,000	6,667
E (0, 0, 5/8, 3/8)#		($13,333)	8,333	5,000
	0	0	$48,333	$51,667

* Base is (20,000 + 60,000 + 40,000 = 120,000); 20,000/120,000 = 1/6; 60,000/120,000 = 1/2; 40,000/120,000 = 1/3
\# Base is (50,000 + 30,000 = 80,000); 50,000/80,000 = 5/8; 30,000/80,000 = 3/8

Reciprocal Method

The reciprocal method (also known as the reciprocal service method, the matrix method, and the simultaneous allocation method) is used to allocate service department costs to production departments, where reciprocal services are allowed between service departments. The method sets up simultaneous equations to determine the allocable cost of each service department.

Using the same data, the following equations are set up:

$$GP = \$20,000 + 50/85 \; E$$
$$E = \$10,000 + 1/6 \; GP$$

Substituting *E* from the second equation into the first:

$$GP = \$20,000 + 50/85 \; (\$10,000 + 1/6 \; GP)$$

Solving for *GP* gives *GP* = $28,695. Substituting *GP* = $28,695 into the second equation and solving for *E* gives *E* = $14,782.

Using these solved values, the reciprocal method yields:

	Service Departments		Production Departments	
	(GP)	*(E)*	*A*	*B*
Overhead costs	$20,000	$10,000	$30,000	$40,000
Reallocation:				
GP (0, 1/6, 1/2, 1/3)	($28,695)	4,782	14,348	9,565
E (50/85, 0, 30/85, 5/85)	8,695	($14,782)	5,217	870
	0	0	$49,565	$50,435

Solving Simultaneous Equations with Lotus 1-2-3 and Microsoft Excel

Solving simultaneous equations with more than three unknowns is a time-consuming and difficult task. It uses, typically, the matrix operation procedure. Using algebra, the solution for simultaneous equations $Ax = b$ is $x^* = A^{-1}b$. Matrix inversion and multiplication can be done quickly, utilizing a spreadsheet program, such as Lotus 1-2-3 or Microsoft Excel.

More specifically, solving simultaneous equations involves the following three steps:

1. Rearrange the equations in the form of $Ax = b$

Given:

$$GP = \$20,000 + 50/85\ E$$
$$E = \$10,000 + 1/6\ GP$$

Transforming them into the form of $Ax = b$ yields:

$$GP{-}50/85E = 20000$$
$$-1/6GP + E = 10000$$

or

$$\begin{pmatrix} 1 & -0.58823 \\ -0.16666 & 1 \end{pmatrix} \begin{pmatrix} GP \\ E \end{pmatrix} = \begin{pmatrix} 20000 \\ 10000 \end{pmatrix}$$

which is in the form of $Ax = b$

2. Invoke/Data Matrix Invert to find the inverse of matrix A to obtain the following:

$$A^{-1} = \begin{pmatrix} 1.108695 & 0.652173 \\ 0.184782 & 1.108695 \end{pmatrix}$$

3. Multiply A^{-1} by b, invoke/Data Matrix Multiply to obtain the following solution x^*:

$$x^* = \begin{pmatrix} GP \\ E \end{pmatrix} = \begin{pmatrix} 28695.65 \\ 14782.60 \end{pmatrix}$$

Note: Microsoft Excel has similar routines: MINVERSE(array) returns the inverse for the matrix in any array, and MMULT(array1,array2) returns the matrix product of two arrays. Because MINVERSE and MMULT produce an array as a result, this function must be entered as an array formula by (1) *selecting a square range of cells* of equivalent size, (2) typing the formula, and then (3) pressing F2 and then *Shift* + Ctrl + *Enter*. It is strongly recommended that managerial accountants take advantage of the reciprocal service method for their cost allocation.

CHAPTER 15

JOINT PRODUCTS AND BY-PRODUCTS

CONTENTS

Joint products are two or more products produced simultaneously by a common manufacturing process. The common manufacturing costs are called *joint costs* and must be allocated on some basis to these products. Each joint product is relatively significant to total revenue. By-products are two or more products produced from a common source that are not significant to the makeup of total revenue. By-products have a relatively low sales value in relation to the firm's other products.

ALLOCATION OF COSTS TO JOINT PRODUCTS

A joint product, unlike a by-product, has a high sales value and is marketable. For example, gasoline, heating oil, and kerosene are joint products in oil refining.

Note: An item's classification status can change from joint product to by-product as technology and market conditions change.

Joint cost allocations may be necessary for inventory valuation, determination of cost of goods sold, deriving selling prices, meeting regulatory agency requirements, and taxation.

Some ways to allocate costs among joint products are:

- Market value at the split-off point.
- Net realizable value (final sales price less separable costs).
- Final sales price.
- Physical measure (e.g., units, feet, pounds).

- Unit cost.
- Gross margin.
- Chemical property.
- Energy potential.
- Weighted average.
- Opportunity cost.
- Arbitrary mathematical techniques.
- Judgmental allocation.

The most commonly used allocation methods are net realizable value and physical measure. The net realizable value method is widely used because of the desire to value inventory based on the relative income-generating ability of the inventory items. Joint cost allocation using a physical measure is feasible when there is homogeneity of units in physical terms, the market potential of the products is similar, and there are new products. A major limitation of the physical measure method is that it bears no relationship to the revenue-producing ability of the products. Also, there is a distortion in the gross profit computation any time the sales price per unit of quantity is not the same for the joint products.

The market value at split-off point method is recommended when market values are available for raw materials at the separation point. The market value allocation ratio equals:

$$\frac{\text{Market value of each item}}{\text{Market value of all items}} \times \text{Joint cost}$$

The use of final selling price as a basis for joint cost allocation is feasible when a close relationship exists between cost and selling price. It may be advisable when the company must justify its selling prices, based on price/cost relationships, to governmental agencies. It may also be used when there is a rapid inventory turnover or a low normal profit percentage.

Note: When there is wide vacillation in selling price, average anticipated prices for the period may be used.

The amount of each joint product to be produced depends on manufacturing technology, product salability, and the expected future market. Short-term factors such as inventory levels also need to be considered.

Joint cost information is helpful in assessing the effect of altering the output mix on costs and profitability, establishing a selling price for the product, determining the relative profitability between products, and controlling and evaluating the production and distribution processes.

Processing efficiency may be appraised by determining the physical yield for each product. In this regard, an index of production (i.e., a weighted-average index) may be computed to evaluate output efficiency.

COMPARING THE METHODS OF JOINT COST ALLOCATION

The allocation of joint costs by physical units results in an equal price per unit for each product.

EXAMPLE 1: A refining process results in two products, A and B, in quantities of 2,000 gallons of product A and 4,000 gallons of product B. Because product A contains 2,000 gallons of the total 6,000 gallons, product A would be assigned one-third of the joint costs of the process of refining; product B would be assigned the other two-thirds. If the process costs $36,000, product A would be charged one-third of these joint costs, or $12,000. Product B would be assigned the remaining $24,000, or two-thirds of the joint costs. Because 2,000 gallons of product A were produced at a cost of $12,000, the unit cost is $6 per gallon. The 4,000 gallons of product B were produced at a cost of $24,000, giving the same unit cost of $6 per gallon.

EXAMPLE 2: It is assumed that product A could be sold at $14 per gallon and product B could be sold at $5 per gallon at the split-off point. Because the costs of products A and B were $6 per gallon each, product A shows a profit of $8 per gallon whereas product B shows a loss of $1 per gallon. It seems less than desirable to sell a product for considerably less than its cost.

The allocation of joint costs by the physical units method is appropriate if the net realizable values of the products are approximately the same. In many cases in which the net realizable values of the products are not close, joint costs could be allocated according to the ability of a product to absorb these joint costs.

EXAMPLE 3: Once again, it is assumed that product A could be sold for $14 per gallon and product B for $5 per gallon after the joint refining process. Therefore, the 2,000 gallons of product A could be sold for $28,000, and the 4,000 gallons of product B could be sold for $20,000. Product A would absorb $28,000 divided by the $48,000 total sales value, or seven-twelfths of the joint costs. Product B would absorb $20,000 divided by the cost of the $48,000 total sales value, or five-twelfths of the joint costs. The total joint cost was $36,000. Product A would absorb seven-twelfths of $36,000, or $21,000. Product B would absorb five-twelfths of $36,000, or $15,000. This results in product A selling for $28,000 and costing $21,000, for a profit of $7,000. This is 25% of the sales price. Product B sells for $20,000 and costs $15,000 for a profit of $5,000. This is also 25% of its sales price.

The method of allocation of joint costs according to the ability of each product to absorb these costs will result in the same gross profit margin for each product when there are no separable costs. This is generally called the relative sales value method.

It is very possible that a market for the joint products at the split-off point does not exist. The joint products must then be operated on further before there is a market for them. The net realizable value at the split-off point is determined by subtracting the separable costs from the sales value.

EXAMPLE 4: As in Example 3, it is assumed that the 2,000 gallons of product A could be sold for $14 per gallon and the 4,000 gallons of product B could be sold for $5 per gallon. However, after the split-off point, product A undergoes further processing and incurs $4 per gallon of separable costs. Product B undergoes no further processing and therefore incurs no separable costs. To determine the net realizable value of product A at the split-off point, the $4-per-gallon separable cost is subtracted from the $14-per-gallon sale price. Therefore, the net realizable value of product A at the split-off point is $10 per gallon for the 2,000 gallons. Product A has a total net realizable value of $20,000 at the split-off point. The 4,000 gallons of product B selling for $5 per gallon at the split-off point also has a total net realizable value of $20,000. Because products A and B have the same net realizable value at the split-off point, they will share equally in the $36,000 of joint costs. Products A and B are each allocated $18,000 of the joint costs.

The profit margin would no longer be the same for the two products. Product A has separable costs of $4 per gallon, or $8,000, and joint costs of $18,000. The total cost is $26,000 with a sales value of $28,000, giving a profit of $2,000. This is only a 7% gross profit margin. Product B has only the joint costs of $18,000 and sells for $20,000. The profit of the same $2,000 is just a coincidence. The gross profit margin of product B is 10% larger than the 7% gross profit margin of product A. The reasons for the profit margin of product B being less than it was in Example 3 is that product B is absorbing a larger share of the joint costs than before.

UNIT COST AND WEIGHTED-AVERAGE UNIT COST METHODS

The unit cost of a joint product will have to be determined based upon a simple unit cost or weighted-average unit cost.

EXAMPLE 5: The joint cost of manufacturing products X, Y, and Z is $150,000. The units produced are product X, 20,000; product Y, 25,000; and product Z, 30,000.

The cost per unit is:

$$\frac{\$150,000}{75,000} = \$2$$

Using the unit cost method, the joint cost is allocated in the following manner:

Product X = $2 × 20,000 =	$40,000
Product Y = $2 × 25,000 =	50,000
Product Z = $2 × 30,000 =	60,000
Total	$150,000

The weighted-average unit cost method should be used when complexities such as production problems, time required to produce, and the quality of materials or labor, exist regarding the joint products. Taking these complexities into account requires weighing the factors in order to arrive at a reasonable allocation basis.

EXAMPLE 6: Products X, Y, and Z are weighted per unit as follows: 2.8, 2.3, and 3.5.

Using the weighted-average method, the allocation of the joint cost is as follows:

$$\text{Product X} = 20,000 \times 2.8 = \frac{56,000}{218,500} \times \$150,000 = \$38,444$$

$$\text{Product Y} = 25,000 \times 2.3 = \frac{57,500}{218,500} \times \$150,000 = \$39,474$$

$$\text{Product Z} = 30,000 \times 3.5 = \frac{105,000}{218,500} \times \$150,000 = \underline{\$72,082}$$

Total $150,000

JOINT COST ALLOCATION BASED ON BOTH PHYSICAL AND NET REALIZABLE VALUE

The following examples show the allocation of joint costs using both physical measure and net realizable value.

EXAMPLE 7: The Audio Processing Company refines two products by a joint process, product A and product B, in quantities of 2,000 gallons and 4,000 gallons, respectively. The joint costs are $36,000.

1. To determine the portion each product will absorb, the allocation by physical units method is used:

	Number of Units	**Fractional Part of Total Units**	**Joint Costs to Be Allocated**	**Allocated Joint Costs**
Product A	2,000 gal	1/3	36,000	$12,000
Product B	4,000 gal	2/3	36,000	24,000
Total	6,000 gal			$36,000

The allocated joint costs for products A and B are $6 per gallon.

2. Assuming that product A sells for $14 per gallon and product B for $5 per gallon at the split-off point, the gross profit for each product is found:

	Number of Units	**Sale Price per Gallon**	**Total Sale Price**	**Allocated Joint Costs**	**Gross Margin**
Product A	2,000 gal	$14	$28,000	$12,000	$16,000
Product B	4,000 gal	5	20,000	24,000	(4,000)

The gross margin of Product A is $8 per gallon.

The gross margin of Product B is a loss of $1 per gallon.

3. Assuming the same information in 2, the net realizable value at split-off method is used to determine the allocated costs and gross profit for each product:

	Net Realizable Value	Fractional Part of Total Realizable Value	Joint Costs to Be Allocated	Allocated Joint Costs
Product A	$28,000	7/12	$36,000	$21,000
Product B	20,000	5/12	36,000	15,000
	$48,000			$36,000

	Sales Price	Allocated Joint Costs	Gross Margin	Gross Margin Percentage
Product A	$28,000	$21,000	$7,000	25%
Product B	20,000	15,000	5,000	25%

4. The same information as in 2, above, is assumed, except that product A must undergo $4 per gallon in separable costs before it can be sold for $14 per gallon. The net realizable value at the split-off point method is used to allocate the joint costs and find the gross profit as follows:

	Sales Price	Separable Costs	Net Realizable Value	Fractional Part of Total Net Realizable Value	Joint Costs to Be Allocated	Allocated Joint Costs
Product A	$28,000	$8,000	$20,000	1/2	$36,000	$18,000
Product B	20,000	-0-	20,000	1/2	36,000	18,000
			$40,000			$36,000

	Sales Price	Separable Costs	Allocated Joint Costs	Total Costs	Gross Margin
Product A	$28,000	$8,000	$18,000	$26,000	$2,000
Product B	20,000	-0-	18,000	18,000	2,000

The gross margin of product A is $1 per gallon.

The gross margin of product B is $.50 per gallon.

EXAMPLE 8: A machine of the Berry Machine Shop cuts nails of two different sizes, small and large, and then packages them. A box of large nails sells for $1.75 and a box of small nails sells for $1.30. During the month of June, the machine cut and boxed 10,000 boxes of small nails and 8,000 boxes of large nails. The cost of running the machine for the month was $9,000.

The allocated joint costs for each type of box of nails are determined using the number of units and the net realizable value method of costing for joint products:

1.

Berry Machine Shop
Allocation of Joint Costs
Physical Units Method
for the Month of June

Type Units	Number of Joint Cost	Fractional Part Joint Cost	Total Joint Cost	Allocated
Small nails	10,000	5/9	$9,000	$5,000
Large nails	8,000	4/9	9,000	4,000
Total	18,000		$9,000	

The number of units of each type is divided by the total number of units.

The total joint cost to be allocated is multiplied by the fractional part of joint costs.

Thus, $5,000 has been allocated to the boxes of small nails or $.50 per box, and $4,000 to the boxes of large nails, or also $.50 per box.

2.

Allocation of Joint Costs
Net Realizable Value Method
for the Month of June

Type	Sales Value or Net Realizable Value	Fractional Part of Joint Costs	Total Joint Costs	Allocated Joint Costs
Large nails	$14,000	14/27	$9,000	$4,667
Small nails	13,000	13/27	9,000	4,333
Total	$27,000			$9,000

The sales value, or net realizable value is determined as follows:

$1.75 × 8,000 = $14,000

$1.30 × 10,000 = $13,000

The net realizable value of each product is then divided by the total net realizable value.

The total joint costs are multiplied by the fractional part of joint costs to arrive at the answer: $4,667 for the boxes of large nails, or $.58 each box, and $4,333 for the boxes of small nails, or $.43 per box.

EXAMPLE 9: The M.J.H. Company manufactures three products—M, J, and H—using the same machinery. Product J is sold at the split-off point, and M and H are processed further. For the month of November, the joint costs for the three products are $48,000, and the costs after the split-off for M are $6,000 and for H are $10,000. Product M sells for $36,000, product J for $20,000, and product H for $20,000.

1. The net realizable value at split-off is used to allocate the joint costs:

M.J.H. Company
Allocation of Joint Costs
Net Realizable Value Method
for the Month of November

Product	Sales Value	Separable Costs	Net Realizable Value	Fractional Part of Joint Cost	Total Joint Cost	Allocated Joint Cost
M	$36,000	$ 6,000	$30,000	1/2	$48,000	$24,000
J	20,000	–	20,000	1/3	48,000	16,000
H	20,000	10,000	10,000	1/6	48,000	8,000
Total			$60,000			$48,000

2. The gross margin for each product is then determined:

		M	J	H		
Sales value		$36,000	$20,000	$20,000		
Costs:						
Joint	$24,000		$16,000		$8,000	
Separable	6,000	30,000	–	16,000	10,000	18,000
Gross margin		$ 6,000		$ 4,000		$ 2,000

MULTIPLE SPLIT-OFF POINTS

When more than one split-off point exists, management should:

1. Diagram the physical flow and cost incurrence of products.

2. Determine the net realizable values at each split-off point.

3. Allocate joint costs based on relative net realizable value.

EXAMPLE 10: The following data are given for a manufacturer for the month of December:

In Department 1, 5,000 feet of A are converted into 4,000 feet of B and 1,000 feet of C. In Department 2, 3,000 feet of X were added to the 1,000 feet of

C to manufacture 1,000 feet of D, 2,000 feet of E, and 1,000 feet of waste. Before sale, D had to be further processed in Department 3.

Production costs were:

	Department		
	1	2	3
Material	$50,000	$10,000	–
Labor	20,000	8,000	$ 5,000
Overhead	20,000	3,000	6,000
	$90,000	$21,000	$11,000

Unit selling prices per foot are:

B	$20
D	45
E	15

The diagramming of the process follows.

The relative net realizable values are:

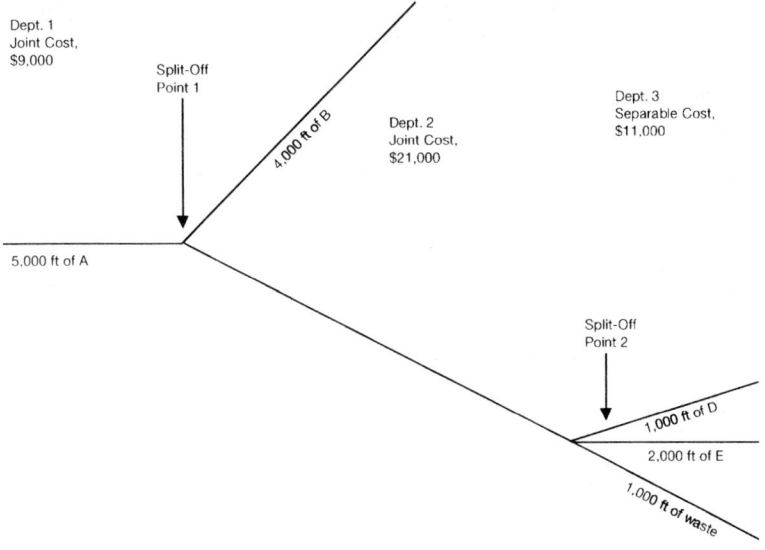

	Sales Value	Separable Cost	=	Net Realizable Value	Relative Net Realizable Value
Split-Off Point 2					
D	(1,000 × $45)	$11,000	=	$ 34,000	53.1%
E	(2,000 × $15)	0		30,000	46.9%
				$ 64,000	100.0%
Split-Off Point 1					
B	(4,000 × $20) –	0	=	$ 80,000	65.0%
C	64,000 –	$21,000		$ 43,000	35.0%
				$ 123,000	100.0%

The allocation of joint costs is:

	Allocated Joint Cost	+	Additional Joint Cost	=	Total	Relative Net Realizable Value	Allocation of Joint Cost
Split-Off Point 1:							
B } C	0	+	$90,000	=	$90,000	65.0%	$58,500
						35.0%	31,500
							$90,000
Split-Off Point 2:							
D } E	$31,500	+	$21,000	=	$52,500	53.1%	$27,878
						46.9%	24,622
							$52,500

The final total and per foot product costs are:

		Total Cost	Feet	Cost per Foot
B		$ 58,500	4,000	$14.63
D	$27,878 + $11,000	38,878	1,000	38.88
E		24,622	2,000	12.31
		$122,000		

MANUFACTURING JOINT PRODUCTS IN DIFFERENT PROPORTIONS

In the case of two or more joint products being manufactured in different proportions, the differential cost of each may be determined by varying the output of these products. An example involving alternative products follows.

> **EXAMPLE 11:** The total cost of manufacturing joint products A and B is $10,000 in the proportions of 40 to 60, respectively. A change in the proportion to 50 to 50 will increase the joint cost by $2,000. The total $12,000 cost assigned to A and B will now be:

Differential cost of 10 more As = $2,000 + 10Bs
Total cost is:
50 As + Bs = $12,000

Therefore,
50 As = 5 (10As) = 5 ($2,000 + 10Bs)

Therefore,
5 ($2,000 + 10 Bs) + 50 Bs – $12,000
$10,000 + 50 Bs + 50 Bs = $12,000
100 Bs = $2,000
50 Bs cost = $1,000
50 As cost = $11,000

DECIDING WHETHER A JOINT PRODUCT SHOULD BE PROCESSED FURTHER OR SOLD AT SPLIT-OFF POINT

A joint product should be processed further when the incremental revenue exceeds the incremental costs. Some considerations regarding the decision to sell or process further are the impact on profitability, the market for the intermediate product versus the final product, sales volume, the advertising effort needed, time required and risk involved of additional processing, and the ability to obtain materials or labor for further processing.

> **EXAMPLE 12:** Production of joint product A is 200 units having a selling price of $.90 per unit. Product A may be further processed into 200 units of product AB having a selling price of $1.05. The additional processing cost is $35.

Should product A be sold at the split-off point or processed further?

Additional revenue 200 × $.15	$30
Additional cost	35
Loss	$ 5

Product A should be sold at the split-off point.

EXAMPLE 13: Company T has five products produced from a joint process. The joint cost is allocated based on the sales value of each product at the split-off point. Waste arises from the joint process, which is discarded. However, the company's research division has now found that the waste could be salable as fertilizer with additional processing at a cost of $200,000. The sales value of fertilizer is $280,000. Management has decided to allocate the joint cost based on relative sales value at split-off of the five products and the waste. As a result of this allocation, the waste product was assigned a joint cost of $110,000. The fertilizer thus showed a net loss of $30,000:

Sales value	$280,000
Assignable	310,000
Loss	$30,000

Because of the loss, management decided not to process the waste further. However, management has made the wrong decision. The joint cost is the same whether or not the waste product is further processed. In other words, the joint process involves the same total cost for the five products. It is, in fact, financially advantageous to process the waste further as fertilizer because there exists an incremental profit of $80,000 ($280,000 – $200,000).

Management must recognize that joint product costs incurred up to the point of splitoff are sunk costs and, thus, are irrelevant in decisions regarding what should be done subsequent to the split-off point.

EXAMPLE 14: A manufacturer produces three products from a process involving a vat and a furnace. A diagram of the flow process follows:

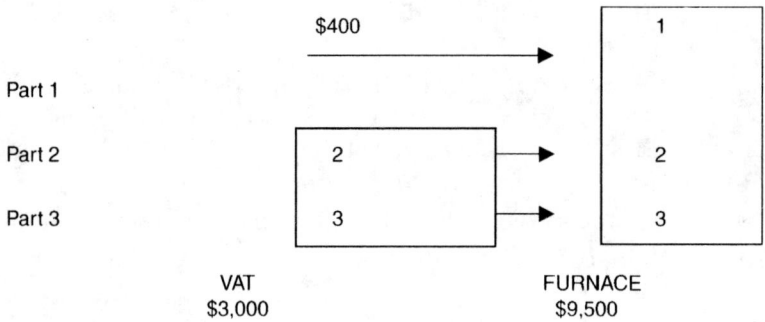

Before going into the furnace, Part 1 has a separable cost of $400. Parts 2 and 3 go through a vat prior to being put in the furnace. In addition to the $3,000 vat costs, parts 2 and 3 require "dipping" in the vat at $.30 per cubic foot. The volume of cubic feet per unit of parts 2 and 3 are .6 and .8, respectively. Information regarding selling price per unit and production follows:

Part	Selling Price	Production
1	$4	800
2	5	1,000
3	7	1,200

Management decides to allocate the vat cost based on cubic feet and the furnace cost based on the relative sales value before the parts are placed in the furnace.

1. The profitability of parts 1, 2, and 3 is determined:

Part	Sales Value	Separable Costs and Allocated VAT Costs	=	Sales Value before Furnace	Allocated Furnace Cost	=	Profit
1 ($4 × 800)	= $ 3,200	$400	=	$ 2,800	$2,090	=	$ 710
		(*DIP + **VAT)					
2 ($5 × 1,000)	= 5,000	($180 + $1,154)	=	3,666	2,735	=	931
3 ($7 × 1,200)	= 8,400	(288 + 1,846/2)	=	6,266	4,675	=	1,591
	$16,600	3,868	=	$12,732	$9,500	=	$3,232

2. Management has an opportunity to sell Part 2 undipped at $4.60. Should management sell Part 2 undipped or fully processed?

Part	Dip and Vat Costs Cubic Volume		*Dip Cost at $30[a]	**Allocated VAT Cost[b]
2	1,000 × .6	600	$180	$1,154
3	1,200 × .8	960	288	1,846
Total		1,560	$468	$3,000

[a] 600 × $.30 = $180

[b]

$$\frac{600}{1,560} \times \$3,000 = \$1,154$$

Reduction in selling price if Part 2 is sold undipped	$.40
Savings in dip cuts if Part 2 is sold undipped ($180/1,000)	.18
Decline in profitability	$.22

Part 2 should be processed further because profitability per unit will decline by $.22 if it is sold undipped. **Note:** The vat and furnace costs are still the same even if Part 2 is sold undipped.

COSTS ASSIGNED TO BY-PRODUCTS

Generally speaking, if a product's value is too small to affect the decision to produce, it is a by-product. By-products are produced in limited quantity and result from the manufacture of main products. Examples of by-products are sawdust in lumber mills and bone in meat-packing plants.

The method used for by-product valuation depends on whether:

- The by-product's value is uncertain when produced.
- There is an established market for the by-product. Market stability and the reliability of market values determine whether a value should be placed on the by-product before sale. If there is a very unstable market, the sale of the by-product should be reflected in income with no value assigned to the by-product inventory.
- The by-product can be used as a substitute for other raw materials.
- The by-product is a possible alternative to the main product.
- The by-product can be used as an energy source for the firm.
- The external outlet for by-products cannot be used internally.
- The market is characterized as a long-term rather than a temporary short-term situation.

Note: An abnormal increase in by-products may indicate that production inefficiencies may exist.

When there is an internal transfer of a by-product, the transfer price should preferably be its market value at the separation point.

By-products may be accounted for in the following ways:

- Income from by-products may be reported as "other income."
- Income from by-products may reduce cost of sales or the manufacturing cost of the main product.
- Income from by-products is reflected as in the foregoing methods except that the by-product income is reduced by appropriate expenses, such as marketing and administrative costs.

The replacement method is suggested for a by-product when it is used in the production process rather than sold. Under this method, the production cost of the principal product is reduced by the replacement cost of the by-product materials.

When a by-product is both sold and used as a raw material for other products, it should be valued at the market price, less costs and less a profit provision.

When a by-product is used internally (e.g., for fuel or as a new raw material for the main product), it may be valued at net realizable value or replacement cost.

ACCOUNTING FOR BY-PRODUCTS

Because by-products are incidental to the manufacturing process, they usually do not share in the joint costs. The net realizable value of a by-product is the sales value less any separable or disposal costs. This value is either accounted for as other income on the income statement or subtracted from the joint costs of the production process before these joint costs are allocated among the joint products. If a profit were recognized on by-product sales, the net realizable value could be reduced by an allowance for the profit. The result would be subtracted from the joint costs.

EXAMPLE 15: It is assumed that 6,500 gallons of a product are refined to produce 2,000 gallons of product A, 4,000 gallons of product B, and 500 gallons of product C. The revenue produced by product C is insignificant relative to the revenue produced by products A and B; product C is therefore a by-product. Product C could be sold for $1.50 per gallon at the split-off point. The net realizable value of the 500 gallons of product C at $1.50 per gallon is $750. The refining process costs $36,000.

Under the first method, the entire $36,000 joint costs would be allocated between products A and B. The $750 would be recorded as other income on the income statement.

Under the second method, the $750 would be subtracted from the $36,000 joint costs, and the remaining $35,250 would be allocated between products A and B. The method used to allocate the joint costs between A and B does not affect, and is not affected by, the method chosen to account for by-product revenue.

Under the third method, a normal profit margin of 30% in sales is assumed. (30% of $750 is $225.) The $225 would be recognized as profit from the sales of the by-product. The remaining $525 would be deducted from the $36,000 joint costs. The difference of $35,475 would be allocated between products A and B. This assumes no identifiable separable costs for the by-products.

If a by-product has separable or disposal costs, these are subtracted from the sales revenue to reach the net realizable value. Assuming that the 500 gallons of product C could be sold for $4 per gallon after separable costs of one dollar are incurred, the net realizable value would be $3 per gallon, giving a total net revenue of the by-product as $1,500. This $1,500 net revenue could be shown as other income or subtracted from the $36,000 joint costs. If subtracted, the sum of $36,000 less the $1,500 revenue from the by-product gives $34,500 to be allocated between the joint products. The net realizable value of $1,500 could be further reduced by a profit margin. Taking the same 30% of the sales price as before, the profit margin is $600, 30% of $2,000. The separable costs were $500. The sum of the two, $1,100, would be subtracted from the sales value of $2,000 to get a remainder of $900. This $900 would be subtracted from the joint costs. The $36,000 minus $900, or $35,100, would be allocated between the joint products A and B.

The net revenue of the by-product could be recognized when produced or when sold. If the net revenue is recognized when the by-product is produced, an estimated sales value is used as the sales price. If the actual price is different, an account called gain or loss on sales of by-product could be used to record the difference. If the net revenue is recognized as sold, the actual sales price would be used. When the salability of the by-product is uncertain, or the price is unstable, it would be better to defer revenue recognition until sold.

The value of the inventory of the by-product could be found by calculating the cost per unit, using any of the foregoing methods, and assigning this amount times the number of units in inventory to get the inventory value. Also, if the value of the inventory were so small as to be immaterial, it could simply be ignored.

Certain by-products are not sold but are used in the manufacturing process within the plant. In these cases, the value assigned to the by-product would be its replacement value. This value would be equal to the price the company would have to pay to purchase the by-product in the open market.

The most popular accounting method is to subtract the net realizable value of the by-product from the joint costs. A variation would be to subtract this amount from the cost of sales. The inventory of the joint products would then be unaffected by this reduction. It is possible that the costs of production are used as a control device, and the company may be advised to consider by-product revenue as other income. In this way, by-product yields and revenue do not affect costs. However, in most cases, the revenue should be inconsequential.

Scrap metal is actually a by-product that is disposed of at the split-off point. It usually has a very minor sales value and would follow one of the previous accounting methods described for the by-product.

Recommendation: The method to choose is the one that is most feasible and logical and that would also enhance the profits of the company. Because in most cases by-products are relatively insignificant, the most convenient method may be used. If the values associated with the by-product are significant, it is possible that the by-product has moved into a position where it should be considered a joint product.

EXAMPLE 16: Dart Refinery produces 2,000 gallons of product A, 4,000 gallons of product B, and 500 gallons of product C. The revenue produced by product C is insignificant relative to the revenue produced by products A and B. Therefore, product C is a by-product. Product C sells for $1.50 per gallon at the split-off point, and products A and B sell for $14 per gallon and $5 per gallon, respectively. The refining process costs $36,000.

1. The joint costs are allocated if the revenue from product C is listed as other income. The net realizable value of the split-off point method is used to allocate joint costs:

Joint Products	Number of Gallons	Net Realizable Value	Fractional Part of Total Net Realizable Value	Joint Costs to Be Allocated	Allocated Joint Costs
A	2,000	$28,000	7/12	$36,000	$21,000
B	4,000	20,000	5/12	36,000	$15,000
		$48,000			$36,000
C	500	$750			

$750 listed as Other Income.

2. The joint costs are allocated if the revenue from product C is used to reduce the costs of the joint process. The net realizable value at the split-off point method is used to allocate the joint costs. In this case, product C's 500 gallons are priced at $1.50 per gallon, total revenue $750. Subtract $750 from the joint costs of $36,000, leaving $35,250 to be allocated.

Products	Net Realizable Value	Fractional Part of Total Net Realizable Value	Joint Costs to Be Allocated	Allocated Joint Costs
A	$28,000	7/12	$35,250	$20,562.50
B	20,000	5/12	35,250	14,687.50
	$48,000			$35,250.00

3. Assuming a 30% profit on the sale of by-products, the joint costs are allocated using the net realizable value at the split-off point method. The remainder of the sales price of the by-product is subtracted from the joint costs:

$ 750	sales price for the by-product
30%	profit on by-product
$ 225	profit recognized as Other Income on sale of by-products
$ 525	is subtracted from $36,000 joint costs
$35,475	joint costs must be allocated between Products A and B

Products	Net Realizable Value	Fractional Part of Total Net Realizable Value	Joint Costs to Be Allocated	Allocated Joint Costs
A	$28,000	7/12	$35,475	$20,693.75
B	20,000	5/12	35,475	14,781.25
	$48,000			$35,475.00

4. Product C undergoes $1 per gallon of separable costs and can then be sold for $4 per gallon. Also, product A undergoes $4 per gallon of separable costs before it can be sold for $14 per gallon. The joint costs are allocated, and the gross profit is determined when the joint costs are allocated using the net realizable value at the split-off point and when the revenue from the by product is:

(a) Subtracted from the joint costs,

(b) Considered as other income, and

(c) Subtracted from the joint costs after a 30% profit is recognized for the by-product.

The total sales price for product C is $4 per gallon times 500 gallons, or $2,000. The only costs to consider are the separable costs of $1 per gallon, or $500. The net realizable value of the by-product is $1,500.

a. The $1,500 would be subtracted from the $36,000 joint costs leaving $34,500 to be allocated as follows:

Product	Sales Value	Separable Costs	Net Realizable Value	Fractional Part of Total Net Realizable Value	Joint Costs to Be Allocated	Allocated Joint Costs	Gross Profit
A	$28,000	$ 8,000	$20,000	1/2	$34,500	$17,250	10,750
B	20,000	-0-	20,000	1/2	34,500	17,250	2,750
			$40,000			$34,500	

b. The $1,500 is recognized as "other income." The joint costs are allocated as in 4a, except that $36,000 is split 50/50 over products A and B (i.e., $18,000 each), yielding a gross profit of $11,500 and $3,500, respectively.

c.

$ 1,500	net realizable value for the by-product
30%	profit on by-product
$ 450	profit recognized as Other Income
$ 1,050	is subtracted from the $36,000 joint costs
$ 34,950	joint costs must be allocated between Products A and B, yielding a gross profit of $10,525 and $2,525, respectively.

Product	Sales Value	Separable Costs	Net Realizable Value	Fractional Part of Total Net Realizable Value	Joint Costs to Be Allocated	Allocated Joint Costs
A	$28,000	$ 8,000	$20,000	1/2	$34,950	$17,475
B	20,000	-0-	20,000	1/2	34,950	17,475
			$40,000			$34,950

EXAMPLE 17: The L.J. Company manufactures ice cream pop sticks and tongue depressors by a joint process. The scrap wood is turned into toothpicks and is classified as a by-product. The policy of the company is to reduce the joint costs by the expected revenue of the toothpicks manufactured.

During the second quarter of 2X15, the company incurred $37,000 of joint costs to manufacture 40,000 boxes of ice cream pop sticks and 80,000 boxes of tongue depressors. Five thousand boxes of toothpicks were also produced. A box of toothpicks sells for $.20. The ice cream pop stick boxes sell for $.50 per box after $2,000 of additional costs for packaging and selling. The tongue depressors sell for $.75 per box after the additional cost of $3,000 for packaging and selling. The toothpick boxes do not require any additional costs.

There was no beginning inventory, and the inventory is valued at allocated costs with the exception of the toothpicks. These are valued at the sales price. The company uses the net realizable value method to allocate costs.

The value of the inventory on hand is determined if 38,000 boxes of ice cream pop sticks, 75,000 boxes of tongue depressors, and 4,500 boxes of the toothpicks were sold.

The company reduces its joint costs by the expected sales revenue of the by-product, toothpicks:

Joint costs	$37,000
Expected sales value of by-product (5,000 × .20)	1,000
Joint costs to be allocated	$30,000

L.J. Company
Allocation of Joint Costs
Net Realizable Value Method
for the 2nd Quarter, 2X15

Product	Sales Value	Separable Costs	Net Realizable Value	Fractional Part of Joint Cost	Total Joint Costs	Allocated Joint Cost
Tongue depressors	$60,000	$3,000	$57,000	19/25	$36,000	$27,360
Ice cream pop sticks	20,000	2,000	18,000	6/25	36,000	8,640
			$75,000			$36,000

Total Costs

	Tongue Depressors	Ice Cream Pop Sticks
Separate costs	3,000	2,000
Joint costs	27,360	8,640
Total costs	30,360	10,640
Total number of boxes produced	80,000	40,000
Cost per box	$ .3795	$ .266

Inventory

	Number of Boxes	Cost per Box	Total Value in Inventory
Tongue depressors	5,000	$.3795	$1,897.50
Ice cream pop sticks	2,000	.266	532.00
Toothpicks			-0-

Note: The by-product (toothpicks) should have no inventory value because the expected sales value ($1,000) is treated as a reduction of the manufacturing joint costs. There are two cost accounting alternatives here: the company should either credit the cost of goods sold account or adjust the inventory value of the principal product(s).

CHAPTER 16

ANALYSIS OF COST BEHAVIOR

CONTENTS

Not all costs behave in the same way. There are certain costs that vary in proportion to changes in volume or activity, such as labor hours and machine hours. There are other costs that do not change even though volume changes. An understanding of cost behavior is helpful:

- For break-even and cost-volume-profit analysis.
- To appraise divisional performance.
- For flexible budgeting.
- To make short-term choice decisions.
- To make transfer decisions.

A FURTHER LOOK AT COSTS BY BEHAVIOR

As discussed in Chapter 14, depending on how a cost will react or respond to changes in the level of activity, costs may be viewed as variable, fixed, or mixed (semivariable). This classification is made within a specified range of activity, called the relevant range. The relevant range is the volume zone within which the behavior of variable costs, fixed costs, and selling prices can be predicted with reasonable accuracy.

Variable Costs

As previously discussed, variable costs vary in total with change in volume or level of activity. Examples include the costs of direct materials, direct labor, and sales commissions. The following factory overhead items fall in the variable cost category:

Variable Factory Overhead

Supplies	Receiving costs
Fuel and power	Overtime premium
Spoilage and defective work	

Fixed Costs

As previously discussed, fixed costs do not change in total, regardless of the volume or level of activity. Examples include advertising expense, salaries, and depreciation. The following factory overhead items fall in the fixed cost category:

Fixed Factory Overhead

Property taxes	Rent on factory building
Depreciation	Indirect labor
Insurance	Patent amortization

Mixed (Semivariable) Costs

Mixed costs contain both a fixed element and a variable one. Salespersons' compensation, including salary and commission is an example. The following factory overhead items may be considered mixed costs:

Mixed Factory Overhead

Supervision	Maintenance and repairs
Inspection	Compensation insurance
Service department costs	Employer's payroll taxes
Utilities	Rental of delivery truck
Fringe benefits	

Note: Factory overhead, taken as a whole, would be a perfect example of mixed costs. Exhibit 16-1 displays how each of these three types of costs varies with changes in volume.

TYPES OF FIXED COSTS—COMMITTED OR DISCRETIONARY

Strictly speaking, there is no such thing as a fixed cost. In the long run, all costs are variable. In the short run, however, some fixed costs, called discretionary (or managed or programmed) fixed costs, will change. These costs change because of managerial decisions, not because of changes in volume. Examples of discretionary types of fixed costs are advertising, training, and research and development. Another type of fixed costs, called committed fixed costs, do not change and are the results of commitments previously made. Fixed costs such as rent, depreciation, insurance, and executive salaries are considered committed types of fixed costs because management has committed itself for a long period of time regarding the company's production facilities and manpower requirements.

Exhibit 16-1: Cost Behavior Patterns

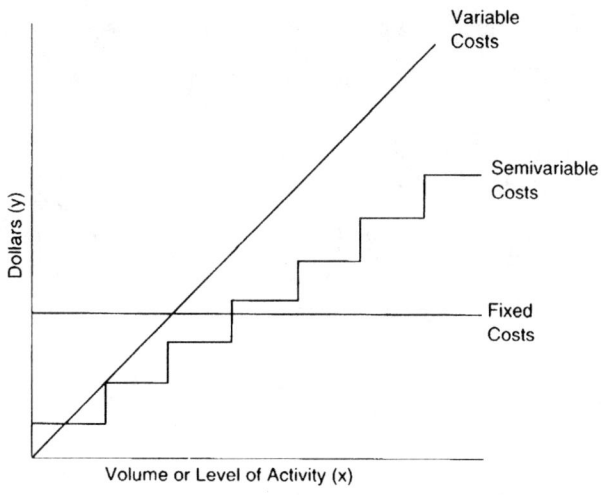

ANALYSIS OF MIXED (SEMIVARIABLE) COSTS

For planning, control, and decision-making purposes, mixed costs need to be separated into their variable and fixed components. Because the mixed costs contain both fixed and variable elements, the analysis takes the following mathematical form, which is called a cost-volume formula (flexible budget formula or cost function):

$$y = a + bx$$

where:

y = the mixed cost to be broken up

x = any given measure of activity such as direct labor hours, machine hours, or production volume

a = the fixed cost component

b = the variable rate per unit of x

Separating the mixed cost into its fixed and variable components is the same as estimating the parameter values a and b in the cost-volume formula. The various methods that can be used for this purpose are discussed in the following subsections.

High-Low Method

The high-low method, as the name indicates, uses two extreme data points to determine the values of a (the fixed cost portion) and b (the variable rate) in the equation $y = a + bx$. The extreme data points are the highest representative $x - y$ pair and the lowest representative $x - y$ pair. The activity level x, rather than the mixed cost item y, governs their selection.

The high-low method is explained, step by step, as follows:

1. The highest pair and the lowest pair are selected.

2. The variable rate b is computed using the formula:

$$\text{Variable rate} = \frac{\text{Difference in cost } y}{\text{Difference in activity } x}$$

3. The fixed cost portion is computed as:

Fixed cost portion = Total mixed cost – Variable cost

EXAMPLE 1: Flexible Manufacturing Company decided to relate total factory overhead costs to direct labor hours (DLH) to develop a cost-volume formula in the form of $y = a + bx$. Twelve monthly observations are collected. They are listed and plotted as follows:

Month	Direct Labor Hours (x) (000 omitted)	Factory Overhead (y) (000 omitted)
January	9 hours	$15
February	19	20
March	11	14
April	14	16
May	23	25
June	12	20
July	12	20
August	22	23
September	7	14
October	13	22

Month	Direct Labor Hours (x) (000 omitted)	Factory Overhead (y) (000 omitted)
November	15	18
December	17	18
Total	174 hours	$225

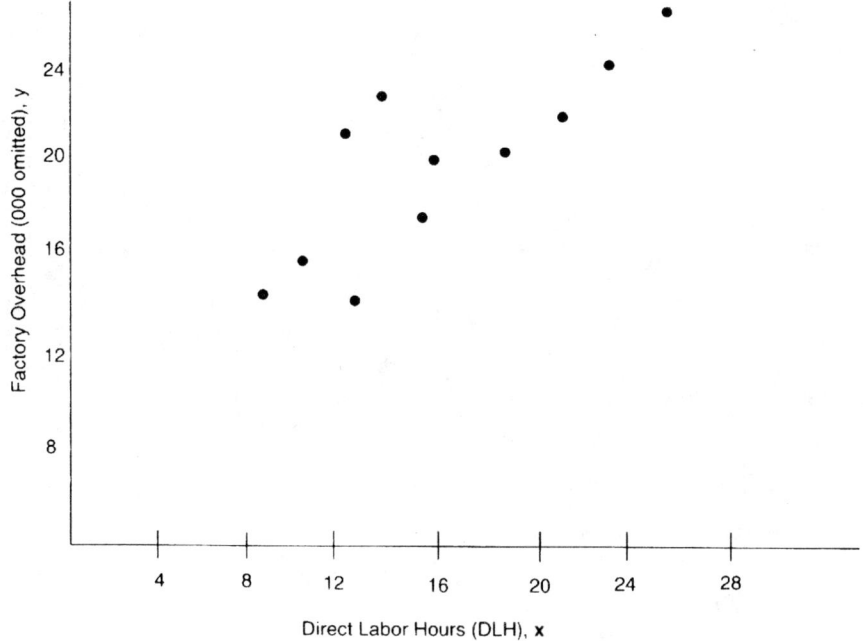

The high-low points selected from the monthly observations are:

	x	y	
High	23 hours	$25	(May pair)
Low	7	14	(September pair)
Difference	16 hours	$11	

Thus

$$\text{Variable rate } b = \frac{\text{Difference in } y}{\text{Difference in } x} = \frac{\$11}{16 \text{ hours}} = \$0.6875 \text{ per DLH}$$

The fixed cost portion is computed as:

	High	Low
Factory overhead (*y*)	$25	$14
Variable expense ($0.6875/DLH)	(15.8125)	(4.8125)
	$9.1875	$9.1875

Therefore, the cost-volume formula for factory overhead is $9.1875 fixed plus $0.6875 per DLH.

The high-low method is simple and easy to use. It has the disadvantage, however, of using two extreme data points, which may not be representative of normal conditions. The method may yield unreliable estimates of *a* and *b* in the formula. In such a case, it would be wise to drop them and choose two other points that are more representative of normal situations.

Least-Squares Method (Regression Analysis)

One popular method for estimating the cost-volume formula is regression analysis. Regression analysis is a statistical procedure for estimating mathematically the average relationship between the dependent variable and the independent variable(s). Simple regression involves one independent variable (e.g., DLH or machine hours alone) whereas multiple regression involves two or more activity variables. For this discussion, a simple linear regression is assumed, which means that the $y = a + bx$ relationship is maintained.

Unlike the high-low method, in an effort to estimate the variable rate and the fixed cost portion, the regression method includes all the observed data and attempts to find a line of best fit. To find this line, a technique called the least-squares method is used.

To explain the least-squares method, the error is defined as the difference between the observed value and the estimated value of some mixed cost and is denoted with *u*.

$$\text{Symbolically, } u = y - y'$$

where:

y = observed value of a semivariable expense

y' = estimated value based on $y' = a + bx$

The least-squares criterion requires that the line of best fit be such that the sum of the squares of the errors (or the vertical distance in Exhibit 16-2 from the observed data points to the line) is a minimum—that is:

$$\text{minimum: } \Sigma u^2 = \Sigma (y - y')^2$$

Using differential calculus, the following equations, called normal equations, are obtained:

$$\Sigma y = na + b\Sigma x$$
$$\Sigma xy = a\Sigma x + b\Sigma x^2$$

Solving the equations for *b* and *a* yields:

$$b = \frac{n\Sigma xy - (\Sigma x)(\Sigma y)}{n\Sigma x^2 - (\Sigma x)^2}$$

$$a = \bar{y} - b\bar{x}$$

where $\bar{y} = \Sigma y/n$ and $x = \Sigma x/n$.

Exhibit 16-2: *y* and *y'*

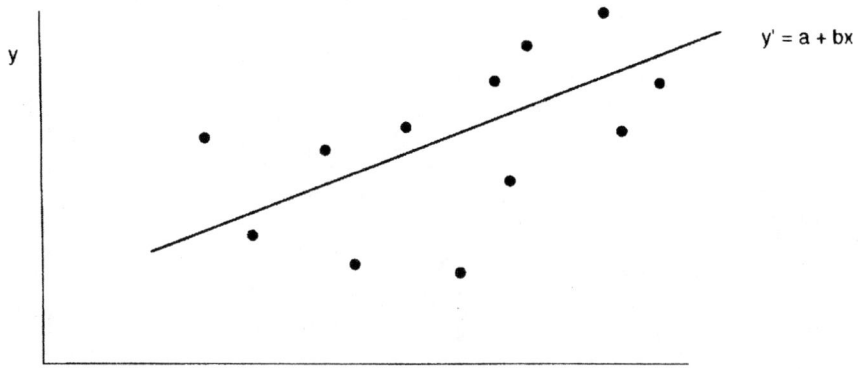

EXAMPLE 2: The data in Example 1 are used to illustrate the computations of *b* and *a*. All the sums required are computed and shown as follows:

DLH(x)	Factory Overhead (y)	xy	x^2	y^2
9 hours	$ 15	135	81	225
19	20	380	361	400
11	14	154	121	196
14	16	224	196	256
23	25	575	529	625
12	20	240	144	400
12	20	240	144	400
22	23	506	484	529
7	14	98	49	196
13	22	286	169	484
15	18	270	225	324
17	18	306	289	324
174 hours	$225	3,414	2,792	4,359

From the preceding table:

$\Sigma x = 174$ $\Sigma y = 225$ $\Sigma xy = 3{,}414$ $\Sigma x^2 = 2{,}792$

$\bar{X} = \Sigma x/n = 174/12 = 14.5$ $\bar{y} = \Sigma y/n = 225/12 = 18.75$

Substituting these values into the formula for b first:

$$ b = \frac{n\Sigma xy - (\Sigma x)(\Sigma y)}{n\Sigma x^2 - (\Sigma x)^2} $$

$$ = \frac{(12)(3{,}414) - (174)(225)}{(12)(2{,}792) - (174)^2} = \frac{1{,}818}{3{,}228} = 0.5632 $$

$$ a = \bar{y} - b\bar{x} = 18.75 - (0.5632)(14.5) = 18.75 - 8.1664 = 10.5836 $$

Note Σy^2 is not used here but rather is computed for future use.

Regression Statistics

Unlike the high-low method, regression analysis is a statistical method. It uses a variety of statistics to tell about the accuracy and reliability of the regression results. They include:

1. Correlation coefficient (r) and coefficient of determination (r^2).

2. Standard error of the estimate (S_e).

3. Standard error of the regression coefficient (S_b) and t-statistic.

Correlation Coefficient (r) and Coefficient of Determination (r^2). The correlation coefficient r measures the degree of correlation between y and x. The range of values it takes on is between -1 and $+1$. More widely used, however, is the coefficient of determination, designated r^2 (read as r-squared). Simply put, r^2 indicates how good the estimated regression equation is. In other words, it is a measure of "goodness of fit" in the regression. Therefore, the higher the r^2, the more confidence can be placed in the estimated cost formula.

More specifically, the coefficient of determination represents the proportion of the total variation in y that is explained by the regression equation. It has the range of values between 0 and 1.

EXAMPLE 3: The statement "Factory overhead is a function of machine hours with r^2 of 70%," can be interpreted as "70% of the total variation of factory overhead is explained by the regression equation or the change in machine hours and the remaining 30% is accounted for by something other than machine hours."

The coefficient of determination is computed as:

$$r^2 = 1 - \frac{\Sigma(y - y')^2}{\Sigma(y - y')^2}$$

In a simple regression situation, a shortcut method is available:

$$r^2 = \frac{[n\Sigma xy - (\Sigma x)(\Sigma y)]^2}{[n\Sigma x^2 - (\Sigma x)^2][n\Sigma y^2 - (\Sigma y)^2]}$$

In comparing this formula with the one for *b*, the only additional information that must be computed is r^2 is Σy^2

EXAMPLE 4: From the table prepared in Example 2, $\Sigma y^2 = 4{,}359$

Using the shortcut method for r^2,

$$r^2 = \frac{(1{,}818)^2}{(3{,}228)[(12)(4{,}359) - (225)^2]} = \frac{3{,}305{,}124}{(3{,}228)(52{,}308 - 50{,}625)}$$

$$= \frac{3{,}305{,}124}{(3{,}228)(1{,}683)} = \frac{330{,}305{,}124}{5{,}432{,}724} = 0.6084 = 60.84\%$$

This means that about 60.84% of the total variation in total factory overhead is explained by DLH and the remaining 39.16% is still unexplained. A relatively low r^2 indicates that there is a lot of room for improvement in the estimated cost-volume formula ($y¢ = \$10.5836 + \$0.5632x$). Machine hours or a combination of DLH and machine hours might improve r^2.

Notes:

1. r^2 is a measure of goodness of fit. Even though the line, obtained by the use of the least-squared error rule, is supposed to be the line of best fit, it may still be inaccurate. The least-square line may have been the best among the *linear* lines. The observed data, however, may exhibit a *curvilinear* pattern, which cannot be visualized especially in multiple regressions. In other words, because it is impossible to draw the scatter diagram in a multivariable situation, a statistic such as r^2 must be relied on to determine the degree of the goodness of fit. Note that low values of r^2 indicate that the cost driver does not fully explain cost behavior.

2. A low r^2 is an indication that the model is inadequate for explaining the *y* variable. The general causes for this problem are use of a wrong functional form; poor choice of an *x* variable as the predictor; and the omission of some important variable or variables from the model.

Standard Error of the Estimate (S_e). The standard error of the estimate, designated S_e is defined as the standard deviation of the regression. It is computed as:

$$S_e = \sqrt{\frac{\Sigma(y - y')^2}{n - 2}} = \sqrt{\frac{\Sigma y^2 - a\Sigma y - b\Sigma xy}{n - 2}}$$

The statistics can be used to gain some idea of the accuracy of the predications.

EXAMPLE 5: Going back to the example data, S_e is calculated as:

$$S_e = \sqrt{\frac{4{,}359 - (10.5836)(225) - (0.5632)(3{,}414)}{12 - 2}}$$

$$= \sqrt{\frac{54.9252}{10}} = 2.3436$$

If the managerial accountant wants to be 95% confident in the prediction, the confidence interval would be the estimated cost + –2(2.3436).

Standard Error of the Regression Coefficient (S_b) and the *t*-statistic. The standard error of the regression coefficient, designated, S_b, and the *t*-statistic are closely related. S_b is calculated as:

$$S_b = \frac{S_e}{\sqrt{\Sigma(x - \bar{x})^2}}$$

or, in short-cut form:

$$S_b = \frac{S_e}{\sqrt{\Sigma x^2 - \bar{x}\Sigma x}}$$

S_b gives an estimate of the range in which the true coefficient will "actually" fall. The *t*-statistic shows the statistical significance of an independent variable x in explaining the dependent variable y. It is determined by dividing the estimated regression coefficient b by its standard error S_b. Thus, the *t*-statistic measures how many standard errors the coefficient is away from zero. Generally, any *t* value greater than +2 or less than –2 is acceptable. The higher the *t* value, the greater is the confidence in the coefficient as the predictor.

EXAMPLE 6: The S_b for this example is:

$$S_b = \frac{2.3436}{\sqrt{2,792 - (14.5)(174)}}$$

$$= \frac{2.3436}{\sqrt{2,792 - 2,523}} = \frac{2.3426}{\sqrt{269}} = .143$$

Thus, *t*-statistic = b/S_b = .5632 = 3.94

Because t = 3.94 > 2, it can be concluded that the *b* coefficient is statistically significant.

Notes:

1. *t*-statistic is more relevant to multiple regressions, which have more than one *b*.

2. r^2 represents the overall fit of all variables, while t-statistic represents each independent variable.

3. In summary, the table *t* value, based on a degree of freedom and a level of significance, is used:

    a. To set the prediction range—upper and lower limits—for the predicted value of the dependent variable.

    b. To set the confidence range for regression coefficients.

    c. As a cutoff value for the *t*-test.

Use of a Spreadsheet Program for Regression

A spreadsheet program, such as Microsoft Excel, can be used to develop a model and estimate most of the statistics discussed thus far. This involves several steps. To utilize Excel for regression analysis:

1. Enter the data on *x* and *y*, as shown:

2. Under the Tools menu, click Data Analysis and then Regression.

Month	Direct Labor Hours (*x*)	Factory Overhead (*y*)
January	9 hours	$15
February	19	20
March	11	14
April	14	16
May	23	25
June	12	20
July	12	20
August	22	23
September	7	14

Month	Direct Labor Hours (*x*)	Factory Overhead (*y*)
October	13	22
November	15	18
December	17	18

3. Define the *x* and *y* ranges.

4. Define the output range.

5. Define the confidence level.

6. Click OK.

Exhibit 16-3 presents the output for simple regression.

Exhibit 16-3: Excel Output for Simple Regression

SUMMARY OUTPUT

Regression Statistics

Multiple *r*	0.7800
r-Squared	0.6084
Adjusted *r* squared	0.5692
Standard error	2.3436
Observations	12

ANOVA

	df	SS	MS	F	Significance F
Regression	1	85.3243	85.3243	15.5345	0.0028
Residual	10	54.9257	54.9257		
Total	11	140.25			

	Coefficients	Standard Error	t-Stat	*P*-value*	Lower 95%	Upper 95%
Intercept	10.583643	2.1796	4.8558	0.0007	5.7272	15.4401
DLH	0.563197	0.1429	3.9414	0.0028	0.2448	0.8816

* The *p*-value for *x* variable = .0028 indicates that there is a 0.28% chance that the true value of the variable coefficient is equal to 0, implying a high level of accuracy about the estimated value of 0.563197.

The results show:

$$y = 10.583643 + 0.563197x$$

with:

(1) r-squared ($r^2 = 0.6084 = 60.84\%$)

(2) Standard error of the estimate ($S_e = 0.1429$)

(3) Standard error of the coefficient ($S_b = 0.1429$)

(4) t-value $= 3.9414$

All of the preceeding are the same as the results manually obtained.

Note: To obtain a scattergraph, use Excel's Chart Wizard.

Multiple Regression

The least-squares method (regression analysis) provides the opportunity for the managerial accountant to consider more than one independent variable. In case a simple regression is not good enough to provide a satisfactory cost-volume formula (as indicated typically by a low r-squared), the managerial accountant should use multiple regression. Following is an example of multiple regression and a spreadsheet printout.

EXAMPLE 7: The following data are assumed:

Month	Factory Overhead (y)	Direct Labor Hours (x_1)	Machine Hours (x_2)
1	2,510	82	88
2	2,479	84	101
3	2,080	74	88
4	2,750	113	99
5	2,330	77	93
6	2,690	91	109
7	2,480	95	77
8	2,610	117	102
9	2,920	116	122
10	2,730	103	107
11	2,760	120	101
12	2,109	76	65

First two simple regression results are presented (one variable at a time):

Simple regression result 1:	Simple regression result 2:
$Y = b_0 + b_1 x_1$	$Y = b_0 + b_2 x_2$

Then the following multiple regression result is presented:

Multiple regression result:

$$Y = b_0 + b_1 x_1 + b_2 x_2$$

Exhibit 16-4 shows simple and multiple regression results (Excel output) for cost prediction.

Exhibit 16-4: Simple and Multiple Regression Results for Cost Prediction

SUMMARY OUTPUT

Regression Statistics

Multiple r	0.84489
r-Squared	0.71384
Adjusted r-squared	0.68522
Standard error	145.759
Observations	12

ANOVA

	df	SS	MS
Regression	1	529979.3889	529979.389
Residual	10	212455.6111	21245.5611
Total	11	742435	

	Coefficients	Standard Error	t-Stat
Intercept	133.84	244.0486934	5.47367233
DLH	12.5504	2.512829835	4.99453875

SUMMARY OUTPUT

Regression Statistics

Multiple r	0.7989
r-Squared	0.63825
Adjusted r-squared	0.60207
Standard error	163.884
Observations	12

ANOVA

	df	SS	MS
Regression	1	473856.0063	473856.006
Residual	10	268578.9937	26857.8994
Total	11	742435	

	Coefficients	Standard Error	t-Stat
Intercept	1220.08	316.9563584	3.84936576
MH	13.7127	3.264643407	4.20036638

SUMMARY OUTPUT
Regression Statistics

Multiple r	0.91977
r-Squared	0.84598
Adjusted r-squared	0.81176
Standard error	112.717
Observations	12

ANOVA

	df	SS	MS
Regression	2	628088.7656	314044.383
Residual	9	114346.2344	12705.1372
Total	11	742435	

	Coefficients	Standard Error	t-Stat
Intercept	975.155	229.0522564	4.25734521
DLH	8.47915	2.433626337	3.48416437
MH	7.8143	2.81206043	2.77885304

As can be seen, simple regression 1 (overhead cost versus DLH) yielded:

$$y = 1335.84 + 12.55x \qquad \text{with } r^2 = 71.38\%$$
$$S_e = 145.76$$

Because of a low r^2, trying the second regression (overhead cost versus MH) yielded:

$$y = 1220.08 + 13.71x \qquad \text{with } r^2 = 63.83\%$$
$$S_e = 163.88$$

It shows that MH did not fare any better. In fact, r^2 and S_e were worse. When machine hours (MH) are added to the simple regression model, the result is as follows:

$$y' = 975.16 + 8.48x_1 + 7.81x_2$$
$$r^2 = 84.59\%, \; S_e = 112.72$$

The explanatory power (r^2) of the regression has increased dramatically to 84.59%, and the standard error of the regression has decreased to 112.72.

Use of Dummy Variables

In many cost analyses, an independent variable may be discrete or categorical. For example, in estimating heating and fuel bills, the season will make a big difference. To control this effect, a dummy variable can be included in the regression model. This variable has a value equal to 1 during the winter months and 0 during all the other months.

A dummy variable can also be used to account for jumps or shifts in fixed costs. This situation is well illustrated by the following data for nonstationary factory overhead costs:

Month	Factory Overhead (y)	Direct Labor Hours (x_1)	Shift Dummy (x_2)
1	2,234	105	1
2	2,055	89	1
3	2,245	99	1
4	2,110	85	1
5	2,377	118	1
6	2,078	89	1
7	2,044	101	0
8	2,032	112	0
9	2,134	107	0
10	2,090	100	0
11	2,078	109	0
12	2,007	93	0

A simple regression of overhead versus DLH yields the following:

$$y' = 1614 + 5.06x_1 \qquad r^2 = 22.42\%, \; S_e = 100.33$$
$$(2.98)$$

Exhibit 16-5 shows the resulting output.

Exhibit 16-5: Excel Output for Overhead versus Direct Labor Hours

SUMMARY OUTPUT
Regression Statistics

Multiple r	0.47354
r-Squared	0.22424
Adjusted r-squared	0.14666
Standard error	100.362
Observations	12

ANOVA

	df	SS	MS
Regression	1	29094.33565	29094.3357
Residual	10	100652.331	10065.2331
Total	11	129746.6667	

	Coefficients	Standard Error	t-Stat
Intercept	1614.84	300.67525558	5.37072665
DLH	5.05871	2.97541537	1.70016982

The explanatory power of the model is extremely low, and the coefficient of DLH is barely statistically significant (i.e., $t = 5.06/2.98 = 1.7 < 2$). The data suggests that there might be a decrease around the end of the sixth month. To test this hypothesis, a dummy variable, x_2 is defined as a shift or jump, where:

$$x_2 = \begin{cases} 1 \text{ if } t=1,2,\ldots 6 \\ 0 \text{ if } t = 7,8,\ldots 12 \end{cases}$$

Rerunning the regression with the shift variable leads to the printout shown in Exhibit 16-6.

Exhibit 16-6: Excel Output for a Shift Variable

SUMMARY OUTPUT
Regression Statistics

Multiple r	0.89667
r-Squared	0.80402
Adjusted r-squared	0.76047
Standard error	53.1539
Observations	12

ANOVA

	df	SS	MS
Regression	2	104318.6442	52159.3221
Residual	9	25428.02251	2825.33583
Total	11	129746.6667	

	Coefficients	Standard Error	*t*-Stat
Intercept	1258.13	173.6557749	7.24495057
DLH	7.7753	1.662006058	4.67826055
Shift Dummy	166.948	32.35461912	5.15993301

$$y' = 1258.13 + 7.78x_1 + 166.95x_2 \qquad r^2 = 80.40\%, \ S_e = 53.15$$
$$(1.66) \quad (32.35)$$

The explanatory power of the model is quite good, and both the DLH shift variables are highly significant (*t*-values are 4.68 and 5.16, respectively).

Cost Prediction. To predict costs for the first six months of the following year, the predicted equation is:

$$y' = 1258 + 7.78x_1 + 166.95x_2$$
$$= 1258 + 7.78x_1 + 166.95(1)$$
$$= 1424.95 + 7.78x_1$$

To predict costs for the second six months of the following year, the predicted model becomes:

$$y' = 1258 + 7.78x_1 + 166.95x_2$$
$$= 1258 + 7.78x_1 + 166.95(0)$$
$$= 1258 + 7.78x_1$$

The Contribution Income Statement

The traditional (absorption) income statement for external reporting shows the functional classification of costs; that is, manufacturing costs versus nonmanufacturing expenses (or operating expenses). An alternative format of income statement, known as the contribution income statement organizes the costs by behavior rather than by function. It shows the relationship of variable costs and fixed costs, regardless of the functions a given cost item is associated with.

Conclusion

The contribution approach to income determination provides data that are useful for managerial planning and decision making. For example, the contribution approach is useful:

- For break-even and cost-volume-profit analysis.
- In evaluating the performance of the division and its manager.
- For short-term and nonroutine decisions.

The contribution income statement is not acceptable, however, for income tax or external reporting purposes, because it ignores fixed overhead as a product cost.

The statement highlights the concept of contribution margin, which is the difference between sales and variable costs. The traditional format, on the other hand, emphasizes the concept of gross margin, which is the difference between sales and cost of goods sold. These two concepts are independent and have nothing to do with each other. Gross margin is available to cover nonmanufacturing expenses, whereas contribution margin is available to cover fixed costs. The concept of contribution margin has numerous applications for internal management, which will be discussed in later chapters.

A comparison is made between the traditional format and the contribution format:

<table>
<tr><td colspan="3" align="center">*Traditional Format*</td></tr>
<tr><td>Sales</td><td></td><td>$15,000</td></tr>
<tr><td>Less: cost of goods sold</td><td></td><td>7,000</td></tr>
<tr><td>Gross margin</td><td></td><td>$ 8,000</td></tr>
<tr><td>Less: operating expenses</td><td></td><td></td></tr>
<tr><td> Selling</td><td>$2,100</td><td></td></tr>
<tr><td> Administrative</td><td>1,500</td><td>3,600</td></tr>
<tr><td>Net income</td><td></td><td>$ 4,400</td></tr>
</table>

Contribution Format

Sales		$15,000
Less: variable expenses		
Manufacturing	$4,000	
Selling	1,600	
Administrative	500	6,100
Contribution margin		$8,900
Less: fixed expenses		
Manufacturing	$3,000	
Selling	500	
Administrative	1,000	4,500
Net income		$4,400

CHAPTER 17

COST-VOLUME-PROFIT ANALYSIS AND LEVERAGE

CONTENTS

Exhibits

Cost-volume-profit (CVP) analysis, together with cost behavior information, helps managerial accountants perform many useful analyses. CVP analysis deals with how profit and costs change with a change in volume. More specifically, it looks at the effects on profits of changes in such factors as variable costs, fixed costs, selling prices, volume, and mix of products sold. By studying the relationships of costs, sales, and net income, management is better able to cope with many planning decisions. Break-even analysis, a branch of CVP analysis, determines the break-even sales. Breakeven point—the financial crossover point when revenues exactly match costs—does not show up in corporate earnings reports, but financial officers find it an extremely useful measurement in a variety of ways.

QUESTIONS ANSWERED BY COST-VOLUME-PROFIT ANALYSIS

Cost-Volume-Profit (CVP) analysis is used to answer the following questions:

- What sales volume is required to break even?
- What sales volume is necessary to earn a desired profit?
- What profit can be expected on a given sales volume?
- How would changes in selling price, variable costs, fixed costs, and output affect profits?
- How would a change in the mix of products sold affect the break-even and target income volume and profit potential?

Contribution Margin

For accurate CVP analysis, a distinction must be made between costs as being either variable or fixed. Mixed costs must be separated into their variable and fixed components.

The following concepts play an important role in computing the break-even point and performing various CVP analyses.

Contribution Margin (CM). The contribution margin is the excess of sales (*S*) over the variable costs *(VC)* of the product. It is the amount of money available to cover fixed costs *(FC)* and to generate profits. Symbolically, $CM = S - VC$.

Unit CM. The unit CM is the excess of the unit selling price (*p*) over the unit variable cost (*v*). Symbolically, unit $CM = p - v$.

CM Ratio. The CM ratio is the contribution margin as a percentage of sales—that is:

$$\text{CM ratio} = \frac{CM}{S} = \frac{S - VC}{S} = 1 - \frac{VC}{S}$$

The CM ratio can also be computed using per-unit data as follows:

$$\text{CM ratio} = \frac{\text{Unit CM}}{p} = \frac{p - v}{p} = 1 - \frac{v}{p}$$

Note: The CM ratio is 1 minus the variable cost ratio. For example, if variable costs account for 70% of the price, the CM ratio is 30%.

EXAMPLE 1: The following data for company Z illustrate the various concepts of CM:

	Total	Per Unit	Percentage
Sales (1500 units)	$37,500	$25	100%
Less: variable costs	15,000	10	40
Contribution margin	$22,500	$15	60%
Less: fixed costs	15,000		
Net income	$ 7,500		

From the data just listed, CM, unit CM, and the CM ratio are computed as:

$$CM = S - VC = \$37,500 - \$15,000 = \$22,500$$

$$\text{Unit } CM = p - v = \$25 - \$10 = \$15$$

$$CM \text{ ratio} = \frac{CM}{S} = \frac{\$22,500}{\$37,500} = 60\%$$

$$\text{or Unit } \frac{CM}{p} = \frac{\$15}{\$25} = 0.6 = 60\%$$

Break-Even Analysis

The break-even point represents the level of sales revenue that equals the total of the variable and fixed costs for a given volume of output at a particular capacity use rate. Examples are the break-even occupancy rate (or vacancy rate) for a hotel or the break-even load rate for an airliner. Generally, the lower the breakeven point, the higher the profits and the less the operating risk, other things being equal. The break-even point also provides managerial accountants with insights into profit planning. It can be computed using the following formulas:

$$\text{Break-even point in units} = \frac{\text{Fixed costs}}{\text{Unit CM}}$$

$$\text{Break-even point in dollars} = \frac{\text{Fixed costs}}{\text{CM ratio}}$$

EXAMPLE 2: Using the same data given in Example 1, where unit CM = $25 – $10 = $15 and CM ratio = 60%:

Break-even point in units = $15,000/$15 = 1,000 units

Break-even point in dollars = 1,000 units × $25 = $25,000 or, alternatively,

$15,000/0.6 = $25,000

Graphical Approach in a Spreadsheet Format

The graphical approach to obtaining the break-even point is based on the so-called break-even chart as shown in Exhibit 17-1. Sales revenue, variable costs, and fixed costs are plotted on the vertical axis and volume x is plotted on the horizontal axis. The chart can be easily produced in a spreadsheet format. The break-even point is the point where the total sales revenue line intersects the total cost line. The chart can also effectively report profit potentials over a wide range of activity and therefore be used as a tool for discussion and presentation. The profit-volume (PV) chart, as shown in Exhibit 17-2, focuses directly on how profits vary with changes in volume. Profits are plotted on the vertical axis, and units of output are shown on the horizontal axis. The PV chart provides a quick condensed comparison of how alternatives on pricing, variable costs, or fixed costs may affect net income as volume changes. The slope of the chart is the unit CM.

Exhibit 17-1: Break-Even Chart

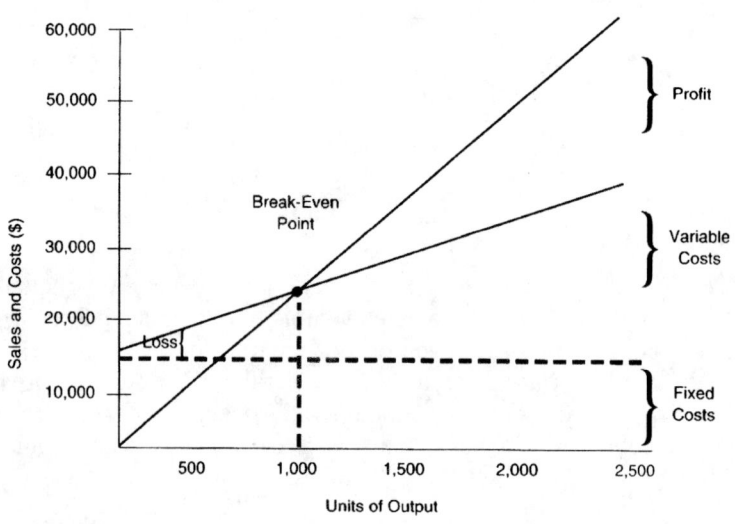

EXAMPLE 3: The data given in Example 1 are assumed. Company Z wishes to attain a target income of $15,000 before tax.

The target income volume required would therefore be:

$$\frac{\$15,000 + \$15,000}{\$25 - \$10} = \frac{\$30,000}{\$15} = 2,000 \text{ units}$$

Exhibit 17-2: Profit-Volume (PV) Chart

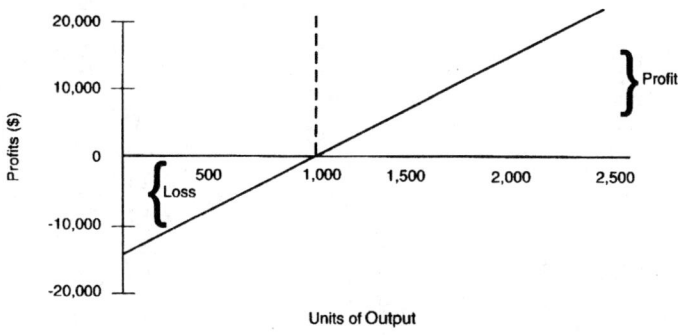

Determination of Target Income Volume

Besides determining the break-even point, CVP analysis determines the sales required to attain a particular income level or target net income. The formula is:

$$\text{Target income sales volume} = \frac{\text{Fixed costs plus target income}}{\text{Unit CM}}$$

Cash Break-Even Point

If a company has a minimum of available cash or the opportunity cost of holding excess cash is too high, management may want to know the volume of sales that will cover all cash expenses during a period. This is known as the cash break-even point. Not all fixed operating costs involve cash payments. For example, depreciation expenses are noncash fixed charges. To find the cash break-even point, the noncash charges must be subtracted from fixed costs. Therefore, the cash break-even point is lower than the usual break-even point. The formula is:

$$\text{Cash break-even point} = \frac{\text{Fixed costs} - \text{Depreciation}}{\text{Unit CM}}$$

EXAMPLE 4: It is assumed from Example 1 that the total fixed costs of $15,000 include depreciation of $1,500. The cash break-even point is therefore:

$$\frac{\$15,000 - \$1,500}{\$15 - \$10} = \frac{\$13,500}{\$15} = 900$$

Company Z has to sell 900 units to cover only the fixed costs involving cash payments of $13,500 and to break even.

Impact of Income Taxes

If target income is given on an after-tax basis, the target income volume formula becomes:

$$\text{Target income volume} \ = \ \frac{\text{Fixed costs} + [\text{Target after-tax income}/(1 - \text{Tax rate})]}{\text{Unit CM}}$$

EXAMPLE 5: From Example 1, company Z wants to achieve an after-tax income of $6,000. The tax rate is 40%. Therefore:

$$\text{Target income volume} \ = \ \frac{\$15,000 + [\$6,000/(1 - 0.4)]}{\$15}$$

$$= \ \frac{\$15,000 + \$10,000}{\$15} \ = \ 1,667 \text{ units}$$

Margin of Safety

The margin of safety is a measure of difference between the actual sales level and the break-even sales. It is the amount by which sales revenue may drop before losses begin, and is expressed as a percentage of expected sales:

$$\text{Margin of safety} \ = \ \frac{\text{Expected sales} - \text{Break-even sales}}{\text{Expected sales}}$$

The margin of safety is often used as a measure of operating risk. The larger the ratio, the safer the situation is, because there is less risk of reaching the break-even point.

EXAMPLE 6: Company Z projects sales of $35,000, with a break-even sales level of $25,000. The projected margin of safety is:

$$\frac{\$35,000 - \$25,000}{\$35,000} \ = \ 28.57\%$$

Company Z's sales can drop 28.57% before they lose money.

Some Applications of CVP and What-If Analysis

The concepts of contribution margin and the contribution income statement have many applications in profit planning and short-term decision making. Many what-if scenarios can be evaluated using them as planning tools, especially utilizing a spreadsheet program, such as Microsoft Excel. Some applications are illustrated in Examples 7 through 10 using the same data as in Example 1.

EXAMPLE 7: As in Example 1, Company Z has a CM of 60% and fixed costs of $15,000 per period. Assuming that the company expects sales to go up by $10,000 for the next period, how much will income increase?

The CM concepts can be used to quickly compute the impact of a change in sales on profits. The formula for computing the impact is:

Change in net income = Dollar change in sales × CM ratio

Thus:

Increase in net income = $10,000 × 60% = $6,000

Therefore, the income will go up by $6,000, assuming there is no change in fixed costs.

If there is a change in unit sales instead of dollars, the formula becomes:

Change in net income = Change in unit sales × Unit CM

EXAMPLE 8: What net income is expected on sales of $47,500?

The answer is the difference between the CM and the fixed costs:

CM: $47,500 × 60%	$28,500
Less: fixed costs	15,000
Net income	$13,000

EXAMPLE 9: Company Z is considering increasing the advertising budget by $5,000, which would increase sales revenue by $8,000. Should the advertising budget be increased?

The answer is no, because the increase in the CM is less than the increased cost.

Increase in CM: $8,000 × 60%	$4,800
Increase in advertising	5,000
Decrease in net income	$(200)

EXAMPLE 10: The original data are considered and it is assumed again that Company Z is currently selling 1,500 units per period. In an effort to increase sales, management is considering cutting its unit price by $5 and increasing the advertising budget by $1,000. If these two steps are taken, management feels that unit sales will go up by 60%. Should the two steps be taken?

A $5 reduction in the selling price will cause the unit CM to decrease from $15 to $10. Thus,

Proposed CM: 2,400 units × $10		$24,000
Present CM: 1,500 units × $15		22,500
Increase in CM		$1,500
Increase in advertising outlay		1,000
Increase in net income		$500

The answer, therefore, is yes. Alternatively, the same answer can be obtained by developing comparative income statements in a contribution format:

	Present (1,500 units)		Proposed (2,400 units)		Difference
Sales	$37,500	(@ $25)	$48,000	(@ $20)	$10,500
Less: variable cost	15,000		24,000		9,000
CM	$22,500		$24,000		$1,500
Less: fixed costs	15,000		16,000		1,000
Net income	$7,500		$8,000		$500

Sales Mix Analysis

Break-even and cost-volume-profit analysis requires some additional computations and assumptions when a company produces and sells more than one product. In multiproduct firms, sales mix is an important factor in calculating an overall company break-even point.

Different selling prices and different variable costs result in different unit CM and CM ratios. As a result, the break-even points and cost-volume-profit relationships vary with the relative proportions of the products sold, called the sales mix. In break-even and CVP analysis, it is necessary to predetermine the sales mix and then compute a weighted-average unit CM. It is also necessary to assume that the sales mix does not change for a specified period. The break even formula for the company as a whole is:

$$\text{Break-even sales in units (or in dollars)} = \frac{\text{Fixed costs}}{\text{Weighted-average unit CM (or CM ratio)}}$$

EXAMPLE 11: Company X has two products with the following unit CM data:

	Deluxe	Standard
Selling price	$ 15	$10
Variable cost per unit	12	5
Unit CM	$3	$5

	Deluxe	Standard
Sales mix	60%	40%
Fixed costs	76,000	

The weighted average unit CM = ($3)(0.6) + ($5)(0.4) = $3.80. Therefore, the company's break-even point in units is:

$$\$76,000/\$3.80 = 20,000 \text{ units}$$

which is divided as follows:

Deluxe: 20,000 units × 60% = 12,000 units
Standard: 20,000 units × 40% = 8,000

20,000 units

An alternative is to build a package containing three deluxe models and two standard models (3:2 ratio). By defining the product as a package, the multiple-product problem is converted into a single-product one, and then the following steps are followed:

Step 1: The package CM is computed as follows:

	Deluxe	Standard
Selling price	$15	$10
Variable cost per unit	12	5
Unit CM	$3	$5
Sales mix	3	2
Package CM	$9	$10
	$19 package total	

$76,000/$19 per package = 4,000 packages

Step 2: This number is multiplied by the packages' respective mix units:

Deluxe: 4,000 packages × 3 units = 12,000 units
Standard: 4,000 packages × 2 units = 8,000

20,000 units

EXAMPLE 12: Company Y produces and sells three products with the following data:

	A	B	C	Total
Sales	$30,000	$60,000	$10,000	$100,000
Sales mix	30%	60%	10%	100%
Less: VC	24,000*	40,000	5,000	69,000
CM	$6,000	$20,000	$5,000	$31,000

	A	B	C	Total
CM ratio	20%	33⅓%	50%	31%
Fixed costs				$18,600
Net income				$12,400

* 24,000 = 30,000 × 80%

The CM ratio for company Y is $31,000/$100,000 = 31%. Therefore, the break-even point in dollars is:

$$\$18,600/0.31 = \$60,000$$

which will be split in the mix ratio of 3:6:1 to give the following break-even points for the individual products A, B, and C:

A: $60,000 × 30% = $18,000
B: $60,000 × 60% = 36,000
C: $60,000 × 10% = 6,000
$60,000

One of the most important assumptions underlying CVP analysis in a multiproduct firm is that the sales mix will not change during the planning period. However, if the sales mix changes, the break-even point will also change.

EXAMPLE 13: Total sales from Example 11 remain unchanged at $100,000, but a shift is expected in mix from product B to product C, as follows:

	A	B	C	Total
Sales	$30,000	$30,000	$40,000	$100,000
Sales mix	30%	30%	40%	100%
Less: VC	24,000	20,000*	20,000	64,000
CM	$6,000	$10,000	$20,000	$36,000
CM ratio	20%	33%	50%	36%**
Fixed costs				$18,600
Net income				$17,400

* $20,000 = 30,000 × 66%
** $36,000/$100,000 = 36%

The shift in sales mix toward the more profitable line C has caused the CM ratio for the company as a whole to go up from 31% to 36%. The new break-even point will be $18,600/0.36 = $51,667. The break-even dollar volume has decreased from $60,000 to $51,667. The improvement in the mix caused net income to increase. Generally, the shift of emphasis from low-margin products to high-margin products will increase the overall profits of the company.

IMPORTANCE OF IDENTIFYING VARIABLE AND FIXED COSTS—CVP-BASED STRATEGIES

Why is it important to segregate costs into variable and fixed elements? The answer may become apparent by considering the following four business decisions:

1. If American Airlines is to make a profit when it reduces all domestic fares by 30%, what reduction in costs or increase in passengers will be required?

Answer: To make a profit when it cuts domestic fares by 30%, American Airlines will have to increase the number of passengers or cut its variable costs for those flights. Its fixed costs will not change.

2. If Ford Motor Company meets the United Auto Workers' demands for higher wages, what increase in sales revenue will be needed to maintain current profit levels?

Answer: Higher wages to UAW members at Ford Motor Company will increase the variable costs of manufacturing automobiles. To maintain present profit levels, Ford will have to cut other variable costs or increase the price of its automobiles.

3. If USX Corp.'s program to modernize plant facilities through significant equipment purchases reduces its workforce by 50%, what will be the effect on the cost of producing one ton of steel?

Answer: The modernizing of plant facilities at USX Corp. changes the proportion of fixed and variable costs of producing one ton of steel. Fixed costs increase because of higher depreciation charges, whereas variable costs decrease due to the reduction in the number of steelworkers.

4. What happens if Kellogg Company increases its advertising expenses but cannot increase prices because of competitive pressure?

Answer: Sales volume must be increased to cover the increase in fixed advertising costs.

COST-VOLUME-REVENUE ANALYSIS AND NONPROFIT ORGANIZATIONS

Cost-volume-profit (CVP) analysis and break-even analysis are not limited to for-profit firms. CVP is appropriately called cost-volume-revenue (CVR) analysis, when it pertains to nonprofit organizations. The CVR model not only calculates the break-even service level but helps answer a variety of what-if decision questions.

> *EXAMPLE 14:* A county has a $1,200,000 lump-sum annual budget appropriation for an agency to help rehabilitate mentally ill patients. On top of this, the agency charges each patient $600 a month for board and care. All of the appropriation and revenue must be spent. The variable costs for rehabilitation activity average $700 per patient per month. The agency's annual fixed costs are $800,000. The agency manager wishes to know how many patients can be served. Let x = number of patients to be served.

$$\text{Revenue} = \text{Total expenses}$$

$$\text{Revenue} = \text{Variable expenses} + \text{Fixed costs}$$

$$\$1,200,000 + \$7,200x = \$8,400x + \$800,000$$
$$(\$7,200 - \$8,400)x = \$800,000 - \$1,200,000$$
$$-\$1,200x = -\$400,000$$
$$x = \$400,000/\$1,200$$
$$x = 333 \text{ patients}$$

The manager is concerned that the total budget for the coming year will be cut by 10% to a new amount of $1,080,000. All other data remain unchanged. The manager wants to know how this budget cut affects the next year's service level.

$$\$1,080,000 + \$7,200x = \$8,400x + \$800,000$$
$$(\$7,200 - \$8,4000)x = \$800,000 - \$1,080,000$$
$$-\$1,200x = -\$280,000$$
$$x = \$280,000/\$1,200$$
$$x = 233 \text{ patients}$$

The manager does not reduce the number of patients served despite a budget cut of 10%. All other factors remain unchanged. How much more does he or she have to charge his/her patients for board and care? In this case, x = board and care charge per year.

$$\$1,080,000 + 333x = \$8,400 (333) + \$800,000$$
$$333x = \$2,797,200 + \$800,000 - \$1,080,000$$
$$333x = \$2,517,200$$
$$x = \$2,517,200/333 \text{ patients}$$
$$x = \$7,559$$

Thus, the monthly board and care charge must be increased to $630 ($7,559/12 months).

ASSUMPTIONS UNDERLYING BREAK-EVEN AND CVP ANALYSIS

The basic break-even and CVP models are subject to the following limiting assumptions:

- The behavior of both sales revenue and expenses is linear throughout the entire relevant range of activity.
- All costs are classified as fixed or variable.
- There is only one product or a constant sales mix.
- Inventories do not change significantly from period to period.
- Volume is the only factor affecting variable costs.

CVP ANALYSIS UNDER CONDITIONS OF UNCERTAINTY

The CVP analysis discussed so far assumed that all variables determining profit or contribution margin—the selling price, variable costs, sales volume, and fixed costs—are known with certainty. This is not a realistic assumption. If one or more of these variables are subject to uncertainty, management should analyze the potential impact of this uncertainty. This additional analysis is required in evaluating alternative courses of action and in developing contingency plans. If management must choose between two products, expected profitability and risk should be considered before a choice is made. For example, if both products have the same expected profits, management might want to select the less risky product (less variation in profits).

One way of handling the conditions of uncertainty is to use sensitivity analysis (what-if analysis), which was already discussed.

Statistical Method

Another approach to dealing with uncertainty is to use a statistical (probability) model. When sales volume is subject to uncertainty and, in fact, normally distributed, the standard statistical method can be used to summarize the effect of this uncertainty on a dependent variable, such as profit or contribution margin. In addition, the following planning questions can be answered:

- What is the probability of breaking even?
- What is the chance that profits from the proposal would be at least a certain amount?
- What are the chances that the proposal would cause the company to lose as much as a specified amount?

Any uncertainty in sales volume affects the total contribution margin (CM) and profits (P). The expected contribution margin E(CM), is the unit CM times the expected volume, $E(x)$:

$$
\begin{aligned}
E(CM) \quad &= \quad \text{unit } CM \times E(x) \\
&= \quad (p - v)\, E(x)
\end{aligned}
$$

The expected profit E(n) is the expected contribution minus the fixed costs (FC):

$$ E(\pi) = E(CM) - FC = (p - v)\, E(x) - FC $$

Because of the uncertainty in sales volume, the expected contribution margin and profits are also uncertain. The standard deviation of the expected contribution margin and profits is equal to the unit CM times the standard deviation of the sales volume. In equation form,

$$ \sigma_\pi = (p - v)\, \sigma_x $$

where:

σ_p = standard deviation of expected profits

σ_p = standard deviation of sales volume

EXAMPLE 15: ABC Corporation has annual fixed costs of $1,500,000 and variable costs of $4.50 per unit. The selling price per unit is stable at $7.50, but the annual sales volume is uncertain and normally distributed with mean expected sales of 600,000 units and a standard deviation of 309,278 units. Management expects this pattern to continue in the future. The normal distribution of profits is illustrated in Exhibit 17-3.

The expected contribution is $1,800,000:

$$E(CM) = (\$7.50 - \$4.50) \times 600,000 \text{ units}$$
$$= \$3 \times 600,000 = \$1,800,000$$

The expected profits are $300,000:

$$E(\pi) = \$1,800,000 - \$1,500,000 = 300,000$$

The standard deviation of the expected profits is $927,834:

$$\sigma_\pi = \$3 \times 309,278 = \$927,834$$

Exhibit 17-3: Probability Distribution of Profits

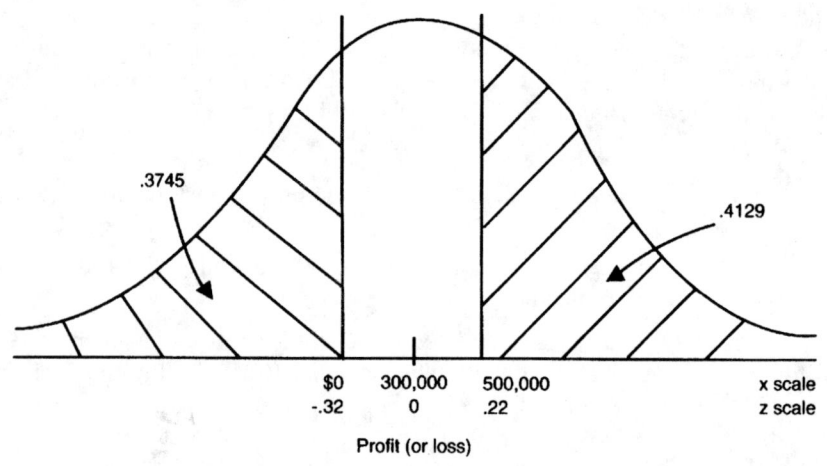

| $0 | 300,000 | 500,000 | x scale |
| -.32 | 0 | .22 | z scale |

Profit (or loss)

EXAMPLE 16: From the results obtained in Example 15, the following questions can be answered:

1. What is the probability of breaking even?
2. What is the probability of obtaining a profit of $500,000 or more?
3. What is the probability of losing as much as $250,000?

In each case, the standard normal variate must be determined. The standard normal variate, better known as z, is the number of standard deviations from any profit to the expected (mean) profit.

To determine the probability of at least breaking even, z must first be determined as follows:

$$z = \frac{0 - E(n)}{\sigma_\pi} = \frac{\$0 - \$300,000}{\$927,834} = -.32$$

In Table 1 of the Appendix (Normal Distribution), the probability of obtaining a z value of $-.32$ or less is $.3745 (1 - 6255 = .3745)$, which means there is only a

37.45% chance that the company would lose money or about a 62.55% chance the company will at least break even.

To find the probability of obtaining at least a profit of $500,000, the number of standard deviations $500,000 is from the expected profit is determined:

$$z = \frac{\$500,000 - \$300,000}{\$927,834} = \frac{\$200,000}{\$927,834} = .22$$

According to Exhibit 17-4, the chances are only .5871 of earning less than $500,000; therefore, the chances of bettering a $500,000 profit are .4129 or 41.29% (1 – .5871 = .4129).

To find the probability of losing as much as $250,000, the value for z is calculated:

$$z = \frac{-\$250,000 - \$300,000}{\$927,834} = \frac{-\$550,000}{\$927,834} = -.59$$

Exhibit 17-4 indicates that there is only a 2.776 (1 – .7224 = .2776) chance of losing $250,000 or more.

To summarize:

1. The chance of breaking even is better than 62.55%.

2. The chance of making at least $500,000 is 41.29%.

3. The chance of losing $250,000 or more is only about 27.76%.

Exhibit 17-3 depicts the probability distribution of profits for this example.

Caution: In the previous example, sales volume was considered to be subject to uncertainty—random variable. It is also possible to consider fixed costs, variable costs, and selling price as random variables to test the effects of their uncertainty on profits. When one of these four variables—sales volume, price, variable cost, or fixed cost—is allowed to be uncertain, the analysis is accomplished exactly as illustrated previously. However, if they become random variables simultaneously, the analysis is complicated and reserved for a more advanced statistical text.

Exhibit 17-4: Normal Distribution Table

Areas under the Normal Curve

Z	0	1	2	3	4	5	6	7	8	9
.0	.5000	.5040	.5080	.5120	.5160	.5199	.5239	.5279	.5319	.5359
.1	.5398	.5438	.5478	.5517	.5557	.5596	.5636	.5675	.5714	.5753
.2	.5793	.5832	.5871	.5910	.5948	.5987	.6026	.6064	.6103	.6141
.3	.6179	.6217	.6255	.6293	.6331	.6368	.6406	.6443	.6480	.6517
.4	.6554	.6591	.6628	.6664	.6700	.6736	.6772	.6808	.6844	.6879

Areas under the Normal Curve

.5	.6915	.6950	.6985	.7019	.7054	.7088	.7123	.7157	.7190	.7224
.6	.7257	.7291	.7324	.7357	.7389	.7422	.7454	.7486	.7517	.7549
.7	.7580	.7611	.7642	.7673	.7703	.7734	.7764	.7794	.7823	.7852
.8	.7881	.7910	.7939	.7967	.7995	.8023	.8051	.8078	.8106	.8133
.9	.8159	.8186	.8212	.8238	.8264	.8289	.8315	.8340	.8365	.8389
1.0	.8413	.8438	.8461	.8485	.8508	.8531	.8554	.8577	.8599	.8621
1.1	.8643	.8665	.8686	.8708	.8729	.8749	.8770	.8790	.8810	.8830
1.2	.8849	.8869	.8888	.8907	.8925	.8944	.8962	.8980	.8997	.9015
1.3	.9032	.9049	.9066	.9082	.9099	.9115	.9131	.9147	.9162	.9177
1.4	.9192	.9207	.9222	.9236	.9251	.9265	.9278	.9292	.9306	.9319
1.5	.9332	.9345	.9357	.9370	.9382	.9394	.9406	.9418	.9430	.9441
1.6	.9452	.9463	.9474	.9484	.9495	.9505	.9515	.9525	.9535	.9545
1.7	.9554	.9564	.9573	.9582	.9591	.9599	.9608	.9616	.9625	.9633
1.8	.9641	.9648	.9656	.9664	.9671	.9678	.9686	.9693	.9700	.9706
1.9	.9713	.9719	.9726	.9732	.9738	.9744	.9750	.9756	.9762	.9767
2.0	.9772	.9778	.9783	.9788	.9793	.9798	.9803	.9808	.9812	.9817
2.1	.9821	.9826	.9830	.9834	.9838	.9842	.9846	.9850	.9854	.9857
2.2	.9861	.9864	.9868	.9871	.9874	.9878	.9881	.9884	.9887	.9890
2.3	.9893	.9896	.9898	.9901	.9904	.9906	.9909	.9911	.9913	.9916
2.4	.9918	.9920	.9922	.9925	.9927	.9929	.9931	.9932	.9934	.9936
2.5	.9938	.9940	.9941	.9943	.9945	.9946	.9948	.9949	.9951	.9952
2.6	.9953	.9955	.9956	.9957	.9959	.9960	.9961	.9962	.9963	.9964
2.7	.9965	.9966	.9967	.9968	.9969	.9970	.9971	.9972	.9973	.9974
2.8	.9974	.9975	.9976	.9977	.9977	.9978	.9979	.9979	.9980	.9981
2.9	.9981	.9982	.9982	.9983	.9984	.9984	.9985	.9985	.9986	.9986
3.0	.9987	.9990	.9993	.9995	.9997	.9998	.9998	.9999	.9999	1.0000

LEVERAGE

Leverage is the portion of the fixed costs that represents a risk to the firm. Operating leverage, a measure of operating risk, refers to the fixed operating costs found in the firm's income statement. Financial leverage, a measure of financial risk, refers to financing a portion of the firm's assets, bearing fixed financing charges in hopes of increasing the return to the common stockholders. The higher the financial leverage, the higher the financial risk, and the higher the cost of capital. Cost of capital rises because it costs more to raise funds for a risky business. Total leverage is a measure of total risk.

Operating Leverage

Operating leverage is a measure of operating risk and arises from fixed operating costs. A simple indication of operating leverage is the effect that a change in sales has on earnings. The formula is:

Operating leverage at a given level of sales (x)

$$= \frac{\text{Percentage change in EBIT}}{\text{Percentage change in sales}} = \frac{(p-v)x}{(p-v)x - FC}$$

where EBIT earnings before interest and taxes $= (p-v)x - FC$

EXAMPLE 17: The Wayne Company manufactures and sells doors to home builders. The doors are sold for $25 each. Variable costs are $15 per door, and fixed operating costs total $50,000. The Wayne Company is currently selling 6,000 doors per year. Its operating leverage is:

$$\frac{(p-v)x}{(p-v)x - FC} = \frac{(\$25 - \$15)(6,000)}{(\$25 - \$15)(6,000) - \$50,000} = \frac{\$60,000}{10,000} = 6$$

which means if sales increase by 1%, the company can expect its net income to increase by six times that amount, or 6%.

Financial Leverage

Financial leverage is a measure of financial risk and arises from fixed financial costs. One way to measure financial leverage is to determine how earnings per share are affected by a change in EBIT (or operating income):

Financial leverage at a given level of sales (x)

$$= \frac{\text{Percentage in change in EPS}}{\text{Percentage in change in EBIT}} = \frac{(p-v)x - FC}{(p-v)x - FC - IC}$$

where *EPS* is earnings per share, and *IC* is fixed finance charges (i.e., interest expense or preferred stock dividends). (Preferred stock dividends must be adjusted for taxes (i.e., preferred stock dividend/$(1-t)$).)

EXAMPLE 18: Using the data in Example 17, the Wayne Company has total financial charges of $2,000, half in interest expense and half in preferred stock dividend. The corporate tax rate is 40%. First, the fixed financial charges are:

$$IC = \$1,000 + \frac{\$1,000}{(1 - 0.4)} = \$1,000 + \$1,667 = \$2,667$$

Therefore, Wayne's financial leverage is computed as follows:

$$\frac{(p-v)x - FC}{(p-v)x - FC - IC} = \frac{(\$25 - \$15)(6,000) - \$50,000}{(\$25 - \$15)(6,000) - \$50,000 - \$2,667}$$

$$= \frac{\$10,000}{\$7,333} = 1.36$$

which means that if EBIT increases by 1%, Wayne can expect its EPS to increase by 1.36 times, or by 1.36%.

Total Leverage

Total leverage is a measure of total risk. The way to measure total leverage is to determine how FPS is affected by a change in sales.

$$\text{Total leverage at a given level of sales } (X) = \frac{\text{Percentage in change in EPS}}{\text{Percentage in change in sales}}$$

$$= \text{Operating leverage} \times \text{Financial leverage}$$

$$= \frac{(p-v)x}{(p-v)x - FC} \times \frac{(p-v)x - FC}{(p-v)x - FC - IC}$$

$$= \frac{(p-v)x}{(p-v)x - FC - IC}$$

EXAMPLE 19: From Examples 17 and 18, the total leverage for Wayne Company is:

Operating leverage × financial leverage = 6 × 1.36 = 8.16

or

$$\frac{(p-v)x}{(p-v)x - FC - IC} = \frac{(\$25 - \$15)(6,000)}{(\$25 - \$15)(6,000) - \$50,000 - \$2,667}$$

$$= \frac{\$60,000}{\$7,333} = 8.18 \text{ (because of a rounding error)}$$

CONCLUSION

The cost-volume-profit analysis is useful as a frame of reference for analysis, as a vehicle for expressing overall managerial performance, and as a planning device via break-even techniques and what-if scenarios. The following points highlight the analytical usefulness of CVP analysis as a tool for profit planning:

- A change in either the selling price or the variable cost per unit alters CM or the CM ratio and thus the breakeven point.

- As sales exceed the break-even point, a higher unit CM or CM ratio will result in greater profits than a small unit CM or CM ratio.

- The lower the break-even sales, the less risky the business is, and the safer the investment, other things being equal.

- A large margin of safety means lower operating risk because a large decrease in sales can occur before losses are suffered.

- Using the contribution income statement model and a spreadsheet program such as Microsoft Excel, a variety of what-if planning and decision scenarios can be evaluated.

- In a multiproduct firm, sales mix is often more important than overall market share. The emphasis on high-margin products tends to maximize overall profits of the firm.

- If one of the variables that enter into the determination of profit is a random variable and normally distributed, the standard statistical procedure can be introduced to summarize the effect of this uncertainty on contribution margin or profit.

- Leverage is that portion of the fixed costs representing a risk to the firm. Operating leverage, a measure of operating risk, refers to the fixed operating costs found in the firm's income statement. CVP analysis and operating leverage are closely related.

CHAPTER 18

CONTRIBUTION MARGIN ANALYSIS FOR SHORT-TERM AND NONROUTINE DECISIONS

CONTENTS

In the short run, financial management is faced with many nonroutine, nonrecurring types of decisions. Contribution margin analysis is an important tool the financial manager can use in making such decisions. It can be used to appraise the performance of department managers, their departments, and particular programs. When performing the manufacturing and selling functions, financial management is constantly faced with the problem of choosing between alternative courses of action. Typical questions to be answered include what to make, how to make it, where to sell the product, and what price to charge.

CONTRIBUTION MARGIN INCOME STATEMENT

In the contribution margin approach, expenses are categorized as either fixed or variable. The variable costs are deducted from sales to obtain the contribution margin. Fixed costs are then subtracted from contribution margin to obtain net income. The contribution margin income statement looks at cost behavior. It shows the relationship between variable and fixed cost, irrespective of the functions a given cost item is associated with. This information helps the manager to (1) decide whether to drop or push a product line; (2) evaluate alternatives arising from production, or special advertising; and (3) appraise performance. For instance, contribution margin analysis indicates how to optimize capacity utilization, how to formulate a bid price on a contract, and whether to accept an order even if it is below the normal selling price.

The format of the contribution margin income statement is as follows:

Sales

Less variable cost of sales

Manufacturing contribution margin

Less variable selling and administrative expenses

Contribution margin

Less fixed cost

Net income

The contribution margin income statement provides an advantage by facilitating decision making, for example regarding:

- Whether to drop or push a product line.
- Whether to ask a selling price that is below the normal price.

Tip: When idle capacity exists, an order should be accepted at below the normal selling price as long as a contribution margin is earned, because fixed cost will not change.

The disadvantages of a contribution margin income statement are that it:

- Is not accepted for financial reporting or tax purposes.
- Ignores fixed overhead as a product cost.
- Does not allow for easy segregation of fixed cost and variable cost.

EXAMPLE 1: The following information is assumed:

Selling price	$15
Variable manufacturing cost per unit	$7
Variable selling cost per unit	$2
Fixed manufacturing overhead	$150,000
Fixed selling and administrative expenses	$ 60,000
Sales volume	600,000
Beginning inventory	50,000 units
Ending inventory	70,000 units

Production is:

Sales	600,000
Add ending inventory	70,000
Need	670,000

Less beginning inventory	50,000		
Production	620,000		
Contribution margin income statement follows:			
Sales (600,000 × $15)			$9,000,000
Less variable cost of sales			
Beginning inventory (50,000 × $7)		$ 350,000	
Variable cost of goods manufactured (620,000 × $7)		4,340,000	
Variable cost of goods available		$4,690,000	
Less ending inventory (70,000 × $7)		490,000	
Total variable cost of sales			4,200,000
Manufacturing contribution margin			$4,800,000
Less variable selling and administrative expenses (600,000 × $2)			1,200,000
Contribution margin			$3,600,000
Less fixed costs			
Fixed overhead	$ 150,000		
Fixed selling and administrative	60,000		
Total fixed costs			210,000
Net income			$3,390,000

RELEVANT COSTS

Not all costs are of equal importance in decision making, and managers must identify the costs that are relevant to a decision. *Relevant costs* are the expected future costs (and also revenues) that differ between the decision alternatives. *Sunk costs* (past and historical costs), therefore, are not considered relevant in the decision at hand. What is relevant are the incremental or differential costs. To make the best decision, financial managers must:

1. Gather all costs associated with each alternative.

2. Drop the sunk costs.

3. Drop those costs that do not differ between alternatives.

4. Select the best alternative based on the remaining cost data.

FURTHER PROCESSING OF A PRODUCT

Managers must often decide whether to process an item further. The decision is based on whether further processing will result in incremental profitability.

EXAMPLE 2: Product X may be sold at split-off or processed further. Relevant data are as follows:

Production	Sales Value at Split-Off	Additional Cost and Sales Value for Further Processing	
		Sales	Cost
5,000	$95,000	$120,000	$18,000
Incremental revenue ($120,000 – $95,000)			$25,000
Incremental cost			18,000
Incremental gain			$7,000

This product should be processed further because it results in incremental earnings.

UTILIZATION OF CAPACITY

Contribution margin analysis can be used to ascertain the best way of utilizing capacity. In general, the emphasis on products with higher contribution margin maximizes the company's total net income, even though total sales may decrease. This is not true, however, where there are constraining factors and scarce resources. Constraining factors, such as machine hours, labor hours, or cubic feet of warehouse space, restrict or limit the production or sale of a given product. In the presence of these constraining factors, maximizing total profits depends on getting the highest contribution margin per unit of the factor (rather than the highest contribution margin per unit of product output).

EXAMPLE 3: Company R can make a raw metal that can either be sold at this stage or worked on further and sold as an alloy. Relevant data are as follows:

	Raw Metal	Alloy
Selling price	$200	$315
Variable cost	90	120

Total fixed cost is $400,000, and 100,000 hours of capacity are interchangeable between the products. There is unlimited demand for both products. Three hours are required to produce the raw metal, and five hours are needed to make the alloy.

Contribution margin per hour follows:

	Raw Metal	Alloy
Selling price	$200	$315
Less variable cost	90	120
Contribution margin	$110	$195

	Raw Metal	Alloy
Hours per ton	3	5
Contribution margin per hour	$36.67	$39

Based on the contribution margin analysis, only the alloy should be sold because it results in the highest contribution margin per hour. Fixed costs are not considered because they are constant and are incurred irrespective of which product is manufactured.

ACCEPTING AN ORDER BELOW THE NORMAL SELLING PRICE

A short-term, special order may be received for products at lower prices than usual. In normal times, such an order may be refused because it will not yield a satisfactory profit. If times are bad, however, such an order should be accepted if the incremental revenue obtained from it exceeds the incremental costs involved. Fixed costs are constant at idle capacity. The company is better off receiving some revenue above its variable costs than receiving nothing at all. Such a price—that is, one lower than the regular price—is called a contribution price. This approach is more appropriate under the following conditions:

- When operating in a distress situation.

- When there is idle capacity.

- When faced with sharp competition or in a competitive bidding situation.

EXAMPLE 4: A company currently sells 8,000 units at $30 per unit. Variable cost per unit is $15. Fixed costs are $60,000 (fixed cost per unit is thus $7.50; $60,000/8,000). Idle capacity exists. A potential customer is willing to purchase 500 units at $21 per unit.

This order should be accepted because it increases profitability.

Sales (500 × $21)	$10,500
Less variable costs (500 × $15)	7,500
Contribution margin	$ 3,000
Less fixed costs	0
Net income	$ 3,000

Note: If idle capacity exists, the acceptance of an additional order does not increase fixed cost. If fixed cost were to increase, say by $1,200, to buy a special tool for this job, it still is financially attractive to accept this order because a positive profit of $1,800 ($3,000 – $1,200) would arise.

EXAMPLE 5: Company X manufactures a product. It can produce 200,000 units per year at a total variable cost of $800,000 and a total fixed cost of $500,000. It is estimated that 150,000 units can be sold at a normal selling price of $4 each. Further, a special order has been placed by a customer for 60,000 units at a 25% discount.

Profit will rise by $50,000 because of this special order.

Variable cost per unit   = $\dfrac{\$800,000}{200,000}$ $4

Special order price 0.75 × $4   3

Incremental profit per unit $1

Incremental earnings $1 × 50,000 units = $50,000

EXAMPLE 6: Financial data for a department are as follows:

Selling price	$15
Direct material	$2
Direct labor	$1.90
Variable overhead	$0.50
Fixed overhead ($100,000/20,000 units)	$5

Selling and administrative expenses are fixed except for sales commissions, which are 14% of the selling price. Idle capacity exists.

The department receives an additional order for 1,000 units from a potential customer at a selling price of $9.

Even though the offered selling price of $9 is much less than the current selling price of $15, the order should be accepted.

Sales (1,000 × $9)	$9,000
Less variable manufacturing costs (1,000 × $4.40)*	4,400
Manufacturing contribution margin	$4,600
Less variable selling and administrative expenses (14% × $9,000)	1,260
Contribution margin	$3,340
Less fixed cost	0
Net income	$3,340

---

* Variable manufacturing cost = $2 + $1.90 + $0.50 = $4.40

EXAMPLE 7: A markup of 40% over cost is desired on a product. Relevant data regarding the product are:

Direct material	$ 5,000
Direct labor	12,000
Overhead	4,000
Total cost	$21,000

Markup on cost (40%)	8,400
Selling price	$29,400

Total direct labor for the year is $1,800,000. Total overhead for the year is 30% of direct labor. The overhead consists of 25% fixed and 75% variable. A customer offers to buy the item for $23,000. There is idle capacity. The incremental order should be accepted because additional profitability arises.

Selling price		$23,000
Less variable costs		
Direct material	$5,000	
Direct labor	12,000	
Variable overhead ($12,000 × 22.5%) *	2,700	19,700
Contribution margin		$ 3,300
Less fixed cost		0
Net income		$ 3,300

---

* Total overhead 0.30 × $1,800,000 = $540,000

Variable overhead = 22.5% of direct labor, computed as follows:

$$\frac{\text{Variable overhead}}{\text{Direct labor}} = \frac{0.75 \times \$540,000}{\$1,800,000} = \frac{\$405,000}{\$1,800,000} = 22.5\%$$

BID PRICE DETERMINATION

Pricing policies using contribution margin analysis may be helpful in contract negotiations for a product or service. Often, such business is sought during the slack season, when it may be financially beneficial to bid on extra business at a competitive price that covers all variable costs and makes some contributions to fixed costs plus profits. Knowledge of variable and fixed costs is necessary to make an accurate bid price determination.

EXAMPLE 8: An order for 10,000 units is received. What is the minimum bid price that will result in a $20,000 increase in profits? The current income statement is as follows:

Sales (50,000 units × $25)		$1,250,000
Less cost of sales		
Direct material	$120,000	
Direct labor	200,000	
Variable overhead ($200,000 × 0.30)	60,000	
Fixed overhead	100,000	480,000
Gross margin		$770,000

Less selling and administrative expenses
Variable (includes freight costs of $0.40 per
  unit) $ 60,000
Fixed   30,000   90,000

Net income $680,000

In the event the contract is awarded, cost patterns for the incremental order are the same except that:

- Freight costs will be borne by the customer.
- Special tools of $8,000 will be required for this order and will not be reused again.
- Direct labor time for each unit under the order will be 20% longer.

Preliminary computations:

	Per Unit Cost
Direct material ($120,000/50,000)	$2.40
Direct labor ($200,000/50,000)	4.00
Variable selling and administrative expense ($60,000/50,000)	1.20

A forecasted income statement is as follows:

Forecasted Income Statement

	Current	Forecasted	Explanation
Units	50,000	60,000	
Sales	$1,250,000	$1,372,400	[a]Computed last
Cost of Sales			
Direct material	$120,000	$144,000	($2.40 × 60,000)
Direct labor	200,000	248,000	($200,000 + [10,000 × $4.80[b]])
Variable overhead	60,000	74,400	($248,000 × .30)
Fixed overhead	100,000	108,000	
Total	$480,000	$574,000	
Selling and Administrative Expenses			
Portable	$60,000	$68,000	($60,000 + [10,000 × $.80][c])
Fixed	30,000	30,000	
Total	$90,000	$ 98,000	
Net income	$680,000	$700,000[d]	

^a Net income + Selling and administrative expenses + Cost of sales = Sales
  $700,000 + $98,000 + $574,400 = $1,372,400
^b $4 × 1.2 = $4.80
^c $1.20 – $.40 = $.80
^d $680,000 + $20,000 = $700,000

The contract price for the 10,000 units should be $122,400 ($1,372,400 – $1,250,000), or $12.24 per unit ($122,400/10,000).

The contract price per unit of $12.24 is below the $25 current selling price per unit. Note that total fixed cost is the same except for the $8,000 expenditure on the special tool.

ADDING OR DROPPING A PRODUCT LINE

The decision to drop an old product line or to add a new one must take into account both qualitative and quantitative factors. However, any final decision should be based primarily on the impact the decision will have on contribution margin or net income.

EXAMPLE 9: The ABC Company has three major product lines: P, M, and C. The company is considering the decision to drop the M line because the income statement shows it is being sold at a loss. The income statement for these product lines is as follows:

	P	M	C	Total
Sales	$10,000	$15,000	$25,000	$50,000
Less variable costs	6,000	8,000	2,000	
Contribution margin	$4,000	$7,000	$13,000	$24,000
Less: Fixed costs				
Direct	$2,000	$6,500	$4,000	$12,500
Allocated	1,000	1,500	2,500	5,000
Total	$3,000	$8,000	$6,500	$17,500
Net income	$1,000	($1,000)	$6,500	$6,500

Direct fixed costs are those costs that are identified directly with each of the product lines, whereas allocated fixed costs are the amount of common fixed costs allocated to the product lines using some base, such as space occupied. The amount of common fixed costs typically continues regardless of the decision, and thus cost cannot be saved by dropping the product line to which it is distributed.

If product M is dropped:

Sales revenue lost		$15,000
Gains:		
Variable cost avoided	$8,000	
Direct fixed costs avoided	6,500	14,500
Increase (decrease) in net income		$ (500)

By dropping product M, the company will lose an additional $500. Therefore, the M product line should be kept. One of the great dangers in allocating common fixed costs is that such allocations can make a product line look less profitable than it really is. Because of such an allocation, the M product line showed a loss of $1,000, but in effect contributes $500 ($7,000 – $6,500) to the recovery of the company's common fixed costs.

THE MAKE-OR-BUY (OUTSOURCE) DECISION

Often, companies purchase subcomponents used to make their products instead of making them in their in-house manufacturing facilities. Buying services, products, or components of products from outside vendors instead of producing them is called *outsourcing*. The decision whether to produce a subcomponent in-house or to buy it externally from an outside vendor is called a "make-or-buy (outsource)" decision. Examples include:

- Processing payroll in-house versus outsourcing it to an outside service bureau.

- Developing a training program in-house versus sending employees outside for training.

- Providing data processing and network services internally versus buying them (the benefits of which would be access to technology and cost savings).

Other strong candidates for outsourcing include managing fleets of vehicles, sales and marketing, and custodial services.

EXAMPLE 10: Assume that Company Q has prepared the following cost estimates for the manufacture of a subassembly component based on an annual production of 8,000 units:

	Per Unit	Total
Direct materials	$ 5	$ 40,000
Direct labor	4	32,000
Variable factory overhead applied	4	32,000
Fixed factory overhead applied (150% of direct labor cost)	6	48,000
Total cost	$19	$152,000

The supplier has offered to provide the subassembly at a price of $16 each. Two-thirds of fixed factory overhead, which represents executive salaries, rent, depreciation, and taxes, continues regardless of the decision. Should Company Q buy or make the product?

The key to the decision lies in the investigation of those relevant costs that change between the make-or-buy alternatives. Assuming that the productive capacity will be idle if not used to produce the subassembly, the analysis takes the following form:

Schedule of Make or Buy

	Per Unit		Total of 8,000 Units	
	Make	**Buy**	**Make**	**Buy**
Purchase price		$16		$128,000
Direct materials	$5		$40,000	
Direct labor	4		32,000	
Variable overhead	4		32,000	
Fixed overhead that can be avoided by not making	2	—	16,000	—
	$15	$16	$120,000	$128,000
Difference in favor of making	$1		$8,000	

The make-or-buy decision must be investigated, along with the broader perspective of considering how best to utilize available facilities. The alternatives are:

- Leaving facilities idle.
- Buying the parts and renting out idle facilities.
- Buying the parts and using idle facilities for other products.

MAINTAINING SOME PROFIT WITH A LOWER SALES BASE

Contribution margin analysis assists in determining how to derive the same profit as last year even though there is a drop in sales volume.

EXAMPLE 11: In 2X11, sales volume was 200,000 units, selling price was $25, variable cost per unit was $15, and fixed cost was $500,000.

In 2X12, sales volume is expected to total 150,000 units. As a result, fixed costs have been slashed by $80,000. On 4/1/2X12, 40,000 units have already been sold. The contribution margin that has to be earned on the remaining units for 2X12 must be computed.

Net income computation for 2X11:
$$S = FC + VC + P$$
$$\$25 \times 200{,}000 = \$500{,}000 + (\$15 \times 200{,}000) + P$$
$$\$1{,}500{,}000 = P$$

Contribution margin to be earned in 2X12:

Total fixed cost ($500,000 – $80,000)	$420,000
Net income	1,500,000
Contribution margin needed for year	$1,920,000
Contribution margin already earned:	
(Selling price – variable cost) × units ($25 – $15) = $10 × 40,000 units	400,000
Contribution margin remaining	$1,520,000

$$\frac{\text{Contribution margin}}{\text{Per unit needed}} = \frac{\text{Contribution margin remaining}}{\text{Units remaining}}$$

$$= \frac{\$1{,}520{,}000}{110{,}000} = \$13.82$$

LIFE-CYCLE COSTS AND WHOLE LIFE COST

Life-cycle costing tracks and accumulates all product costs in the value chain from research and development and design of products and processes through production, marketing, distribution, and customer service. The value chain is the set of activities required to design, develop, produce, market, and service a product (or service). The phrases "cradle-to-grave costing" and "womb-to-tomb costing" convey the sense of fully capturing all costs associated with the product.

Life-cycle costing focuses on minimizing locked-in costs, for example, by reducing the number of parts, promoting standardization of parts, and using equipment that can make more than one kind of product. The product life cycle is simply the time a product exists—from conception to abandonment. *Life-cycle costs* are all costs associated with the product for its entire life cycle. These costs include development (planning, design, and testing), manufacturing (conversion activities), and logistics support (advertising, distribution, warranty).

Because total customer satisfaction has become a vital issue in the new business setting, whole-life cost has emerged as the central focus of life-cycle cost management. *Whole-life cost* is the life-cycle cost of a product plus after-purchase (or post-purchase) costs that consumers incur, including operation, support, maintenance, and disposal. Because the costs a purchaser incurs after buying a product can be a significant percentage of whole-life costs and thus an important consideration in the purchase decision, managing activities so that whole-life costs are reduced can provide an important competitive advantage. **Note:** Cost reduction, not cost control, is the emphasis. Moreover, cost reduction is achieved by judicious analysis and management of activities.

Studies show that 90% or more of a product's costs are committed during the development stage. Thus, it makes sense to emphasize management of activities during this phase of a product's existence. Every dollar spent on pre-manufacturing activities is known to save $8 to $10 on manufacturing and post-manufacturing activities. The real opportunities for cost reduction occur before manufacturing begins. Managers need to invest more in pre-manufacturing assets and dedicate more resources to activities in the early phases of the product life cycle so that overall whole-life costs can be reduced.

TARGET COSTING VERSUS COST-PLUS PRICING

Life-cycle and whole-life cost concepts are associated with target costing and target pricing. A firm may determine that market conditions require that a product sell at a given target price. Hence, target cost can be determined by subtracting the desired unit profit margin from the target price. The cost reduction objectives of life-cycle and whole-life cost management can therefore be determined using target costing.

Thus, *target costing* becomes a particularly useful tool for establishing cost reduction goals. Toyota, for example, calculates the lifetime target profit for a new car model by multiplying a target profit ratio times the target sales. It then calculates the estimated profit by subtracting the estimated costs from target sales. Usually, at this point, target profit is greater than estimated profit. The cost reduction goal is defined by the difference between the target profit and the estimated profit. Toyota then searches for cost reduction opportunities through better design of the new model. Toyota's management recognizes that more opportunities exist for cost reduction during product planning than in actual development and production.

The Japanese developed target costing to enhance their ability to compete in the global marketplace. This approach to product pricing differs significantly from the cost-based methods described. Instead of first determining the cost of a product or service and then adding a profit factor to arrive at its price, target costing reverses the procedure. Target costing is a pricing method that involves (1) identifying the price at which a product will be competitive in the marketplace, (2) defining the desired profit to be made on the product, and (3) computing the target cost for the product by subtracting the desired profit from the competitive market price. The formula is:

Target price – Desired profit = Target cost

Target cost is then given to the engineers and product designers, who use it as the maximum cost to be incurred for the materials and other resources needed to design and manufacture the product. It is their responsibility to create the product at or below its target cost.

Exhibit 18-1 compares the cost-plus philosophy with the target costing philosophy.

Exhibit 18-1: Cost-Plus Pricing versus Target Costing

	Formula	**Implications**
Cost-plus pricing	Cost base + Markup = Selling price	• Cost is the base (given) • Markup is added (given) • The firm puts the product on the market and hopes the selling price is accepted
Pricing based on target costing	Target selling price – Desired Profit = Target cost	• Markets determine prices (given) • Desired profit must be sustained for survival (given) • Target cost is the residual, the variable to be managed

EXAMPLE 12: A salesperson at Diva Products Company has reported that a customer is seeking price quotations for two electronic components: a special-purpose battery charger (Product X101) and a small, transistorized machine computer (Product Y101). Competing for the customer's order are one French company and two Japanese companies. The current market price ranges for the two products are as follows:

Product X101 $310–$370 per unit

Product Y101 $720–$820 per unit

The salesperson feels that if Diva could quote prices of $325 for Product X101 and $700 for Product Y101, the company would get the order and gain a significant share of the global market for those goods. Diva's usual profit markup is 25% of total unit cost. The company's design engineers and cost accountants put together the following specifications and costs for the new products:

Activity-based cost rates:

Materials handling activity	$1.30 per dollar of raw materials and purchased parts cost
Production activity	$3.50 per machine hour
Product delivery activity	$24.00 per unit of X101 $30.00 per unit of Y101

	Product X101	Product Y101
Projected unit demand	26,000	18,000
Per unit data:		
Raw materials cost	$30.00	$65.00
Purchased parts cost	$15.00	$45.00
Manufacturing labor		
Hours	2.6	4.8
Hourly labor rate	$12.00	$15.00
Assembly labor		
Hours	3.4	8.2
Hourly labor rate	$14.00	$16.00
Machine hours	12.8	28.4

The company wants to address the following three questions:

1. What is the target cost for each product?

  Product X101 = $325.00 ÷ 1.25 = $260.00*

  Product Y101 = $700.00 ÷ 1.25 = $560.00

  *Target Price – Desired Profit = Target Cost

  $325.00 – .25X = X

  $325.00 = 1.25X

$$X = \frac{\$325.00}{1.25} = \$260.00$$

2. What is the projected total unit cost of production and delivery?

	Product X101	Product Y101
Raw materials cost	$30.00	$65.00
Purchased parts cost	15.00	45.00
Total cost of raw materials and parts	$45.00	$110.00
Manufacturing labor		
X101 (2.6 hours × $12.00)	31.20	
Y101 (4.8 hours × $15.00)		72.00
Assembly labor		
X101 (3.4 hours × $14.00)	47.60	
Y101 (8.2 hours × $16.00)		131.20

	Product X101	Product Y101
Activity-based costs		
Materials handling activity		
X101 ($45.00 × $1.30)	58.500	
Y101 ($110.00 × $1.30)		143.00
Production activity		
X101 (12.8 machine hours × $3.50)	44.80	
Y101 (28.4 machine hours × $3.50)		99.40
Product delivery activity		
X101	24.00	
Y101		30.00
Projected total unit cost	$251.10	$585.60

3. Using the target costing approach, should the company produce the products?

	Product X101	Product Y101
Target unit cost	$260.00	$560.00
Less: projected unit cost	251.10	585.60
Difference	$8.90	($25.60)

Product X101 can be produced below its target cost, so it should be produced. As currently designed, Product Y101 cannot be produced at or below its target cost; either it needs to be redesigned or the company should drop plans to make it.

CONCLUSION

Contribution margin analysis aids in making sound departmental decisions. Is an order worth accepting even though it is below the normal selling price? Which products should be emphasized? What should the price of a product or service be? What should the bid price be on a contract? Is a proposed agreement advantageous? What is the incremental profitability? What is the best way of using departmental capacity and resources?

In some cases, a manager's bonus may be based on the contribution margin earned for the department. Thus, an understanding of the computation of contribution margin is necessary.

CHAPTER 19

COST ALLOCATION

CONTENTS

One important aspect of controllership and financial management deals with the problem of allocating costs to various parts (segments) of an organization. The segment can be products, divisions, departments, or sales territories. Cost allocation (assignment) is necessary to provide useful data for (1) product costing and establishment of selling price, (2) evaluation of managerial performance and control, and (3) making special decisions.

ASPECTS OF COST ALLOCATION

The three aspects of cost allocation are (1) choosing the object of costing, (2) choosing and accumulating the costs related to that object, and (3) choosing a method of identifying the accumulated costs with the object. A *cost objective* (i.e., object) is an activity for which a separate measure of cost is needed, such as activities for departments, products, processes, jobs, contracts, customers, and sales territories. Costs related to the cost object include manufacturing expenses, selling and administrative expenses, joint costs, common costs, service department costs, and fixed costs. The method of attributing costs to the object is the cost allocation base, which in the case of manufacturing costs, for example, would typically be labor hours, machine hours, or production units.

The allocation of revenues and variable costs is typically straightforward because they can be traced directly to a specific segment of activity. Direct costs are directly chargeable to the product or territory. Semidirect costs (e.g., advertising) cover several products. Indirect costs are not directly identified and thus must be allocated to the cost objective on a logical basis, such as allocating rent based on square footage in a department.

COST ALLOCATION GUIDELINES

Cost accumulation determines actual cost by program, cost center, or account number for accounting and planning purposes.

Cost allocation assigns a common cost to two or more departments or products. The costs are allocated in proportion to the relative responsibility for their incurrence. Although allocation methods are arbitrary, some allocation plans make more sense than others. Possible allocation bases include units produced, direct labor cost, direct labor hours, machine hours, number of employees, floor space, and replacement cost of equipment.

The guiding criteria in choosing proper allocation bases are as follows:

- *Benefits obtained.* Costs are allocated based on benefits received. Corporate advertising may be allocated, for example, based on divisional sales. The higher the sales, the greater the benefit received from the advertising. Heating can be allocated to user departments based on space occupied. Although the management of the user department does not control heating cost, the department must have heat to operate.
- *Equity.* Costs are allocated based on fairness. The "equity basis" is often used in government contracting to come up with a mutually agreeable price.
- *Cause-effect relationship.* Costs are allocated based on services provided. It is easy to formulate this relationship when dealing with direct manufacturing costs (e.g., direct material, direct labor). Relationships aid in relating the cost objective to the cost incurred. A preferable relationship assists in predicting changes in total costs.
- *Ability to bear.* Costs are allocated based on the cost objective's ability to bear. An example is allocating corporate executive salaries based on divisional profitability. It is assumed that a more profitable division can absorb more costs.

The Institute of Management Accountants (IMA) (formerly, the National Association of Accountants) favors the allocation of centralized costs only if they satisfy one or more of the following four criteria:[1]

1. The costs can be influenced by a division manager's actions, even if just indirectly.

2. The costs reflect the amount of resources that headquarters gives as divisional support.

3. The allocated costs enhance comparability of the division's performance with that of an independent firm that incurs such costs directly.

4. The costs are the basis for pricing decisions.

Besides using the most representative basis, other considerations in selecting a basis are cost/benefit, ease of use, and common industry practice.

An equitable basis should be selected to allocate common costs among divisions, products, territories, and other cost objectives. If no demonstrable relationship exists between a cost and benefit, guidelines for allocation may include:

- Cost Accounting Standards Board (CASB) guidelines for allocating costs to cost objectives.

- Scatter charts used to measure an activity and related costs.

Tip: A factor that acts as a sound measure of activity in controlling cost is often a good basis for allocating that cost.

- Time studies and job analyses of specific employee activities may give insight into the factors affecting costs and the relationship to individual segment activities.

- Searching inquiries about the factors affecting the costs of the function.

Allocation techniques favored by the CASB are:

- Activity measure of the cause of the pool of cost, such as labor hours, machine hours, or space occupied.

- Measure of the functions output, such as number of purchase orders processed.

- Measure of activity based on service received, such as number of employees served by personnel.

Beware: Sales dollars is typically a poor allocation base because sales vary each period, whereas allocated costs are usually fixed in nature. The use of a variable base to allocate costs may result in inequity between departments because the costs being allocated to one department depend largely on what occurs in another department. For instance, less selling effort in one department will move more allocated costs into another, more productive department.

---

[1] National Association of Accountants, Statement of Management Accounting No. 4B, "Allocation of Service and Administrative Costs," June 13, 1985, paragraph 20.

Recommendation: Sales dollars should be used as a basis of allocation only when a direct causal relationship exists between sales dollars and the allocated service department costs.

Cost Accounting Standard (CAS) No. 418, *Allocation of Direct and Indirect Costs*, applies to cost allocation methods used by government contractors. It states that indirect costs should be allocated to cost objectives in a "reasonable proportion to the beneficial or causal relationship of the pooled costs to cost objective."

A segment should be allocated the fixed costs that the company could save if it were to withdraw from that segment.

Material should be used as an allocation basis when overhead is closely related to the value of that material.

Because most administrative expenses are budgeted as fixed for a budget period, adequate accuracy in reporting is accomplished when budgeted rather than actual costs are allocated to product lines. Some administrative expenses may be allocated directly to products, others to factories, and others to sales divisions.

Fringe benefits should be allocated based on the percentage of related total salary. A refinement may be to allocate some fringe-related costs (e.g., pension plan, payroll taxes) based on salaries with the other costs (e.g., dental insurance) based on number of employees.

Divisions would require financing if they were separate entities so the company may charge them an allocable fee for that service. The fee may be a percentage of revenue, total divisional assets, or other reasonable basis.

CAUTIONS REGARDING COST ALLOCATION

Arbitrary cost allocations should not be made because they may lead to wrong decisions. However, such allocations may be used with care under certain circumstances, as follows:

- The arbitrary allocation is done so that employees will act in a certain desired way according to upper management preferences. For example, central R&D costs may be charged to a division so the manager becomes interested in helping central research efforts.

- A retainer fee should be charged for essential services, such as legal or internal auditing, so the user department is motivated to use the important service even though it may not feel it necessary. If the manager is being charged for the service, why not use it?

ALLOCATION OF SERVICE DEPARTMENT COSTS TO PRODUCTION DEPARTMENTS

The two basic types of departments in a manufacturing company are (1) production departments and (2) service departments. A production department (such as assembly or machining) is where the production or conversion occurs. A service department (such as engineering or maintenance) provides support to production departments.

Before developing departmental overhead rates for product costing, service department costs must first be assigned to production departments.

In allocating service department costs, there are two general approaches that may be followed:

1. *Single-rate method.* Departmental costs are accumulated into a single-cost pool. There is no distinction between variable costs and fixed costs.

2. *Dual-rate method.* Departmental costs are accumulated into two or more cost pools. One pool may be the fixed costs; the other pool may be the variable costs.

Service costs (e.g., computer, accounting and legal, printing, management consulting) should preferably be allocated based on usage, such as through a competitive hourly rate charged by outsiders.

An allocation base, once chosen, typically remains unchanged for a long time period because it represents a major policy. It is usually reviewed only infrequently or when an inequity is evident.

The allocation base should be straightforward because complexity may result in the computational cost and time exceeding the benefits to be derived. Further, clarity is needed so that managers can easily understand the allocation formulas and rationale.

Other than product costing, the reasons to allocate service department costs include:

- To accomplish control and aid in efficiency evaluation.
- To provide superior income and asset measurement for external parties.
- To remind production department managers of the existence of indirect costs they have to absorb. Users benefit from service department costs and should have to pay for them. Without allocation, there is an understatement in the full costs of the operating center. Managers being charged for service department costs will ensure that managers in the service departments are properly controlling those costs.
- To encourage department managers to use services wisely. If the service department costs were not allocated, production managers would perhaps overuse what they consider to be "free" services. For instance, without allocating computer service time, user managers would inefficiently use computer time because they are not paying for it. If a service is underused, allocating the costs for such services would prompt managers to utilize the service to a greater extent.
- To have in place a basis for cost justification or reimbursement. An example of cost justification is to derive an "equitable" price, such as when a defense contractor wants to obtain cost reimbursement.

Note: Although most service departments are cost centers generating no revenue, a few may in fact obtain some revenues (e.g., cafeteria). In such a case, the revenues should be netted against the costs, and the net cost should be allocated to other departments. In this way, the other departments do not have to absorb costs for which the service department has already been reimbursed.

The three basic methods of allocating service department costs to production departments are:

1. The direct allocation method.
2. The step-down method.
3. The reciprocal service method.

These methods are discussed in Chapter 14, "Cost Concepts, Classifications, and Product Costing Systems."

Variable Costs versus Fixed Costs

Generally, variable costs should be charged to user departments using the activity base for the incurrence of the cost involved. For example, variable costs of the maintenance department should be charged to production departments based on machine hours. Thus, departments responsible for the incurrence of service costs must bear them in proportion to actual usage of services.

The fixed costs of service departments constitute the cost of having long-run service capacity available. An equitable allocation basis for the consuming departments is predetermined lump-sum amounts. Predetermined lump sums represent amounts to be charged to consuming departments that have been determined in advance and will be the same each period. Usually, the lump-sum amount charged to a department is based either on the department's peak-period or long-term average servicing needs. Budgeted fixed costs, not actual fixed costs, should be allocated.

Budgeted service department costs are allocated to production departments at the beginning of the period in order to derive the production department's predetermined overhead application rate.

During the accounting period, actual service department costs are allocated to production departments. Thus, a comparison can be made at the end of the reporting period between budgeted costs and actual costs. The allocation of service department costs to production departments is essentially an imposed form of transfer pricing.

Often, multistage allocations are made when service departments serve each other as well as production departments. Complex interrelationships may therefore arise. In a simple relationship, management is costing a product requiring two hours of machine time in product department C. Department C utilizes department A's services, which in turn needs the services of department B. Hence, part of B's cost may be allocated to A and part of A's cost to C so that A and B costs are proportionately included in the cost of product Z. This relationship is depicted in Exhibit 19-1. With this approach, the unit cost of a department's output includes direct labor of that department, part of the costs of departments furnishing the services, and part of the untraceable costs of the entire factory. The output may be in volume of either product or service.

Exhibit 19-1: Cost Allocation Sequence

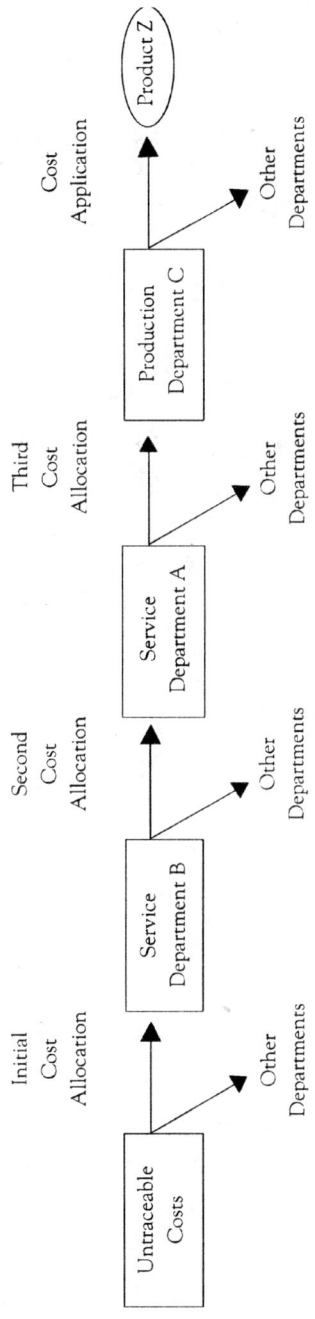

Exhibit 19-1 Cost Allocation Sequence

When it is impractical to distinguish between variable costs and fixed costs of a service department, departmental costs should be allocated to consuming departments according to the base reflecting the optimal measure of benefits received. In general, all service department costs incurred to perform specific services to operating departments should be allocated. The allocated costs are used in determining overhead rates and measuring profitability.

Cost Pools and Allocation Bases

A cost pool is homogeneous when the activity whose costs are included have a similar cause-effect relationship to the cost objective as other activities whose costs are included in the cost pool. Exhibit 19-2 presents corporate headquarter cost pools.

Exhibit 19-3 presents cost items and the basis for their allocation.

Exhibit 19-2: Corporate Headquarter Cost Pools

Department	Allocation Basis
Payroll	Number of employees or dollar salaries
Personnel	Number of employees
Purchasing	Dollar amount of purchases
Accounts payable	Number of vendor invoices paid
Internal audit	Audit time reports
Central cost and budget	Dollar of factory cost and selling expenses
Traffic	Number of freight bills
Central stenographic	Hours spent or number of pages typed
Marketing	Sales
Laundry	Pounds of laundry or number of items processed
Cafeteria	Number of employees
Medical facilities	Number of employees or hours spent
Custodial services (building and grounds)	Square footage occupied
Engineering	Periodic evaluation of service rendered or direct labor hours
Production planning and control	Periodic evaluation of services performed or direct labor hours
Receiving and shipping	Volume handled, number of requisition and issue slips, or square footage occupied
Factory administration	Labor hours

Department	Allocation Basis
Bookkeeping	Number of sales invoices or lines per invoice for each product
Accounting	Volume of transactions or labor hours
Tax	Dollar of tax paid
Legal	Research hours for particular case
Tabulating	Number of punched cards processed
Property	Cost of fixed assets
Credit	Number of accounts in division
Billing	Number of invoices
Accounts receivable	Number of customer accounts or number of postings to customer accounts
Treasury	Identifiable assets

Exhibit 19-3: Common Bases of Cost Allocation

Cost	Allocation Basis
Plant management (including area management and general supervisor)	Number of plants or number of hourly employees
Heat and light (energy)	Square footage
Depreciation on building	Square footage
Maintenance and repairs in building	Square footage
Rent	Square footage
Property taxes	Square footage
Insurance	Square footage
Taxes and insurance on equipment	Book value of equipment
Laboratory	Number of jobs performed or time spent on jobs
Power	Horsepower of equipment
Inspection	Number of units inspected
Maintenance and repairs for machinery and equipment	Machine hours or value of equipment
Plant superintendent	Direct labor dollars
Credit and collection	Sales value of products
Administrative expenses received for each product	Sales value of products or the number of orders
Corporate executive salaries	Sales
Office space	Square footage
Corporate income taxes	Determinants of taxable income

EXAMPLE 1: ARC Company produces inexpensive merchandise. The three production departments are molding, filing, and packing. There are two service departments—administration and maintenance. The direct factory costs of these cost centers follow:

| | Service Departments | | Production Departments | | |
	Administration	Maintenance	Molding	Filing	Packing
Materials		$ 500	$4,000	$10,000	$6,000
Salaries	$8,000	4,000	7,000	6,000	9,000
Depreciation	200	800	3,000	2,000	200
Rent	14,000				
Power		1,500			
Other	4,000	700	2,000	3,000	1,000
Total	$27,700	$6,000	$16,000	$21,000	$16,200

Material costs in a cost center are proportional to volume. Salaries are 10% fixed and 90% variable with volume in the production centers, and 100% fixed in the service centers. Depreciation is fixed. Power is 70% fixed and 30% variable. Other costs are 75% fixed and 25% variable in factory administration, and 50% fixed and 50% variable in the other cost centers. Six thousand units were manufactured.

The variable cost per unit is computed below.

	Administration	Maintenance	Molding	Filing	Packing
Materials		$500	$4,000	$10,000	$6,000
Salaries			6,300	5,400	8,100
Power	$450	—	—	—	—
Other	1,000	350	1,000	1,500	500
Total	$1,450	$850	$11,300	$16,900	$14,600
Variable cost per unit	$.24[a]	$.14	$1.88	$2.82	$2.43

[a] $1,450/6,000 = $.24

EXAMPLE 2: XYZ Company has three divisions operating as profit centers and three central administrative departments operating as service centers. Data for the three profit centers follow:

	Western Division	Central Division	Eastern Division	Total
Sales	$3,000,000	$6,000,000	$4,000,000	$13,000,000
Profit contribution	400,000	1,800,000	1,000,000	3,200,000

	Western Division	Central Division	Eastern Division	Total
Investment	2,000,000	3,000,000	1,000,000	6,000,000
Number of employees	1,000	2,000	1,500	4,500

The operating costs of the administrative departments are as follows:

Accounting	$400,000
Marketing	200,000
Executive offices	300,000

The allocation bases are:

Accounting—number of employees

Marketing—sales

Executive offices—investment

The income before tax for each division follows:

	Western Division	Central Division	Eastern Division
Profit contribution	$400,000	$1,800,000	$1,000,000
Allocations:			
Accounting $400,000	$88,888[a]	$ 177,778	$ 133,333
Marketing $200,000	46,154[b]	92,308	61,538
Executive offices $300,000	100,000[c]	150,000	50,000
Total	$235,042	$420,086	$ 244,871
Income before tax	$164,958	$1,379,914	$755,129

[a]
$$\$400,000 \ \times \ \frac{1,000}{4,500} \ = \ \$88,888$$

[b]
$$\$200,000 \ \times \ \frac{\$3,000,000}{\$13,000,000} \ = \ \$46,154$$

[c]
$$\$300,000 \ \times \ \frac{\$2,000,000}{\$6,000,000} \ = \ \$100,000$$

SEGMENTAL REPORTING AND THE CONTRIBUTION APPROACH TO COST ALLOCATION

A segment is any part or activity of the entity about which the managerial accountant seeks to obtain cost data.

Cost allocation is an important issue in managerial accounting for segmental reporting purposes. Segmental reporting is the process of reporting activities of various segments of an organization, such as divisions, product lines, or sales territories. Segmental information is useful for many purposes. Some product lines may be profitable while others are not. Some sales territories may have a poor sales mix or may be failing to take advantage of opportunities. Some salespersons may be doing a good job while others are not. Some production divisions may not be utilizing their resources properly. These are just some examples of the usefulness of segmental reporting. Segmental reports may be prepared for activity at different levels of the business and in varying formats, depending on the needs of the managerial accountant.

The contribution approach is valuable for segmental reporting because it emphasizes the cost behavior patterns and the controllability of costs that are generally useful for evaluating performance and making decisions. Specifically, the contribution approach to cost allocation is based on the following:

- Fixed costs are much less controllable than variable costs.
- Direct fixed costs and common fixed costs must be clearly distinguished. Direct fixed costs can be identified directly with a particular segment of an organization, whereas common fixed costs cannot be identified directly with a particular segment.
- Common fixed costs should be clearly identified as unallocated in the contribution income statement by segments. Any attempt to allocate these types of costs, on some arbitrary basis, to the segments of the organization would simply destroy the value of responsibility accounting. It would lead to unfair evaluation of performance and misleading managerial decisions.

Exhibit 19-4 presents a contribution margin income statement by division with a further breakdown into product lines.

DISTRIBUTION COSTS

Distribution cost analysis aids in planning sales effort. Distribution costs relate to the distribution of the product to the customer. They include the costs of storing, handling, packaging, advertising and promotion, selling, transportation (shipping costs to the customer and paying for the delivery of returned goods), and market research. Some companies include credit and administrative costs. Distribution costs may be analyzed by product, department, branch, territory, class of customer, distribution outlet, and method of sale. Distribution costs are typically controllable by the marketing and sales department.

Exhibit 19-4: Contribution Margin Income Statement by Segments

	Entire Company	Divisional Breakdown		Unallocable	Breakdown of Division Y			
		Division X	Division Y		Product 1	Product 2	Product 3	Product 4
Sales	1,200	300	900		300	100	200	300
Variable manufacturing cost of sales	700	200	500		100	50	100	250
Manufacturing contribution margin	500	100	400		200	50	100	50
Variable selling and administrative costs	200	50	150		40	40	40	30
Contribution margin	300	50	250		160	10	60	20
Controllable fixed costs by segment managers	180	40	140	40	30	5	50	15
Contribution controllable by segment managers	120	10	110	(40)	130	5	10	5
Fixed costs controllable by others	70	6	64	20	20	15	5	4
Segmental contribution	50	4	46	(60)	110	(10)	5	1
Unallocated costs	23							
Net income	27							

Note: Only those costs logically traceable to a product line should be allocated.

Distribution cost standards may be set jointly by the sales executives and the controller. Distribution cost standards may be either (1) generally applicable to overall distribution functions as a whole or by major division, or (2) in units that measure individual performance. Some illustrative standards that may be used for distribution costs are cost per sales order, cost per customer account, cost per call, cost per mile traveled, cost per day, cost per dollar of gross profit, selling expense as a percent of net sales, and selling expense per unit sold.

Distribution cost data may be analyzed in terms of number of new customers obtained, number of miles or days a salesperson travels, number of sales demonstrations, number of trucking miles, volume of goods handled in warehouse, and number of shipments handled.

Unlike manufacturing, for which there is typically only one standard cost for a product, many standard costs exist for distribution of the same item. For example, the cost per call may vary by territory. Further, even in one territory the standard cost to sell may vary, depending on the class of customers. Standards will vary because of different distribution channels, products, departments, territories, and customer classes. The conditions in each are not the same.

Distribution costs may be analyzed by size of order. Costs are segregated by factor of variability. Some costs will be recognized as fixed for all order sizes, and other costs may vary depending on volume (e.g., money volume, physical volume).

Although many distribution costs may be allocated based on sales, some distribution costs vary with factors other than sales volume itself, such as weight.

When distribution costs are to be prorated and determined based on products or territories, the predetermined distribution cost rate should be based on estimated sales by products or territories. The manager must establish standards for the activities of order getting and order filling.

When distribution costs are determined based on customers, costs should be allocated based on the amount of services received by each customer. This information will also help in determining which customers are entitled to price concessions and discounts.

The allocation of distribution expenses may be based on the credit terms associated with sales such as based on cash sales, credit sales, and installment sales.

Marketing costs may be evaluated based on distribution methods, such as direct selling to retailers and wholesalers as well as mail order sales.

Allocation of Costs to Products

In allocating distribution costs to products, some guidelines that may be used are:
- Actual costs may be allocated based on actual activity.
- Budgeted costs may be allocated based on budgeted activity.
- Budgeted costs may be used because distribution costs for product lines are typically fixed and do not significantly change from actual costs. At the end of the year, the variance between budgeted and actual may be allocated to the product lines.

- Sales-effort costs (e.g., advertising samples) may be allocated on planned activity, and sales-service costs may be allocated based on actual activity. For example, when salespeople are required to report their time by product line, their salaries and related expenses should be allocated on this basis.

Recommendation: The preceding approaches will typically provide better product line costs than the generally used method of allocating total distribution costs on actual sales dollars or units.

Exhibit 19-5 presents different distribution costs and how they may be allocated to product lines.

In determining the amount of sales office expense assigned by dollar of sale groupings (e.g., sales less than 10,000 or sales between 10,000 and 20,000), the managerial accountant should consider the cost of taking an order, entering the order, billings, and accounting for the sale.

In evaluating a product line, consideration should be given to profitability, growth, competition, and capital employed. Accurate cost information aids in determining whether to drop unprofitable products or substantially raise prices.

Exhibit 19-5: Distribution Costs and Allocation Bases to Products

Distribution Cost	*Allocation Basis*
Warehousing	Units or tonnage handled
Sales-service costs	Orders and invoices for each product
Direct selling costs (salespersons' salaries, commissions, and bonuses as well as sales or branch office expenses)	Sales value of product
Samples	Specific cost of each product sample
General corporate advertising	Sales value of products
Direct product advertising, newspaper, magazine, and direct mail	Directly to product being advertised
Shipping department sales and weight of product sales	Sales value of each product or relative
Delivery expenses	Size of product weighted by quantity sold

The purpose of allocating departmental overhead costs to products is similar to the purpose of allocating service department costs to production departments. A "fair share" of departmental overhead should be assigned to each product manufactured in the department.

An economic decision to allocate resources may have to be made, such as the allocation of capacity among products. This is especially important in the case of introducing a new product line.

When specific products have associated with them a greater portion of indirect costs, it may be preferable to allocate indirect costs to product lines. This approach may be feasible in pricing, and decisions whether to continue producing a product based on profit margins.

Caution: Care must be taken in allocating a cost to a specific product because an inappropriate allocation may make a profitable product look bad, and vice versa.

Exhibit 19-6 shows the contribution of a company's product lines to the total. It should be determined whether the company is making money on a particular account. Customer classes may be analyzed in terms of geographic location, type of agent (i.e., wholesaler, retailer), call frequency, annual volume of business, order size, and credit rating.

Exhibit 19-6: Contribution by Products

	Entire Company	Product A	Product B
Projected sales	$100,000	$60,000	$40,000
Variable costs			
Goods sold	$30,000	$10,000	$20,000
Marketing	5,000	4,000	1,000
Total variable costs	$35,000	$14,000	$21,000
Contribution margin	$65,000	$46,000	$19,000
Direct fixed costs			
Production	$4,000	$2,000	$2,000
Marketing	3,000	2,000	1,000
Total direct fixed costs	$7,000	$4,000	$3,000
Profit contribution	$58,000	$42,000	$16,000
Common fixed costs			
Production	$10,000		
Marketing	8,000		
Administrative and general	5,000		
Total common costs	$ 23,000		
Income before tax	$ 35,000		

An illustrative profit and loss statement by customer class is presented in Exhibit 19-7.

EXAMPLE 3: The Justa Corporation produces and sells three products—A, B, and C—which are sold in a local market and in a regional market. At the end of the first quarter of the current year, the following income statement was prepared:

	Total	Local	Regional
Sales	$1,300,000	$1,000,000	$300,000
Cost of goods sold	1,010,000	775,000	235,000
Gross margin	$290,000	$225,000	$65,000
Selling expenses	$105,000	$60,000	$45,000
Administrative expenses	52,000	40,000	12,000
Total	$157,000	$100,000	$57,000
Net Income	$133,000	$125,000	$8,000

Management has expressed special concern with the regional market because of the extremely poor return on sales. This market was entered a year ago because of excess capacity. It was originally believed that the return on sales would improve with time, but after a year no noticeable improvement can be seen from the results as reported in the preceding quarterly statement.

In attempting to decide whether to eliminate the regional market, the following information has been gathered:

	Products		
	A	B	C
Sales	$500,000	$400,000	$400,000
Variable manufacturing expenses as a percentage of sales	60%	70%	60%
Variable selling expenses as a percentage of sales	3%	2%	2%

Exhibit 19-7: Profit and Loss Statement by Customer Class

	Total Sales	Retail Sales	Mail Order Sales
		Percent of Sales	Percent of Sales
Gross sales			
Less: sales discount and returns			
Net sales			
Less: cost of sales			
Gross profit			

	Total Sales	Retail Sales	Mail Order Sales
		Percent of Sales	Percent of Sales

Less: direct customer distribution
  costs
Profit after direct distribution costs
Indirect customer distribution costs
Net profit after distribution costs

Sales by Markets

Product	Local	Regional
A	$400,000	$100,000
B	300,000	100,000
C	300,000	100,000

All administrative expenses and fixed manufacturing expenses are common to the three products and the two markets and are fixed for the period. Remaining selling expenses are fixed for the period and separable by market. All fixed expenses are based upon a prorated yearly amount.

1. The quarterly income statement showing contribution margins by markets is prepared.
2. Assuming there are no alternative uses for the Justa Corporation's present capacity, would dropping the regional market be recommended? Why or why not?
3. The quarterly income statement showing contribution margins by products is prepared.
4. It is believed that a new product can be ready for sale next year if the Justa Corporation decides to go ahead with continued research. The new product can be produced by simply converting equipment currently used in producing product C. This conversion will increase fixed costs by $10,000 per quarter. What must be the minimum contribution margin per quarter for the new product to make the changeover financially feasible?

(CMA, adapted)

end of the first quarter of the current year, the following income statement was prepared:

	Total	Local	Regional
Sales	$1,300,000	$1,000,000	$300,000
Cost of goods sold	1,010,000	775,000	235,000
Gross margin	$290,000	$225,000	$65,000
Selling expenses	$105,000	$60,000	$45,000
Administrative expenses	52,000	40,000	12,000
Total	$157,000	$100,000	$57,000
Net Income	$133,000	$125,000	$8,000

Management has expressed special concern with the regional market because of the extremely poor return on sales. This market was entered a year ago because of excess capacity. It was originally believed that the return on sales would improve with time, but after a year no noticeable improvement can be seen from the results as reported in the preceding quarterly statement.

In attempting to decide whether to eliminate the regional market, the following information has been gathered:

	Products		
	A	B	C
Sales	$500,000	$400,000	$400,000
Variable manufacturing expenses as a percentage of sales	60%	70%	60%
Variable selling expenses as a percentage of sales	3%	2%	2%

Exhibit 19-7: Profit and Loss Statement by Customer Class

	Total Sales	Retail Sales	Mail Order Sales
		Percent of Sales	Percent of Sales
Gross sales			
Less: sales discount and returns			
Net sales			
Less: cost of sales			
Gross profit			

	Total Sales	Retail Sales	Mail Order Sales
		Percent of Sales	Percent of Sales

Less: direct customer distribution
  costs
Profit after direct distribution costs
Indirect customer distribution costs
Net profit after distribution costs

Sales by Markets		
Product	**Local**	**Regional**
A	$400,000	$100,000
B	300,000	100,000
C	300,000	100,000

All administrative expenses and fixed manufacturing expenses are common to the three products and the two markets and are fixed for the period. Remaining selling expenses are fixed for the period and separable by market. All fixed expenses are based upon a prorated yearly amount.

1. The quarterly income statement showing contribution margins by markets is prepared.

2. Assuming there are no alternative uses for the Justa Corporation's present capacity, would dropping the regional market be recommended? Why or why not?

3. The quarterly income statement showing contribution margins by products is prepared.

4. It is believed that a new product can be ready for sale next year if the Justa Corporation decides to go ahead with continued research. The new product can be produced by simply converting equipment currently used in producing product C. This conversion will increase fixed costs by $10,000 per quarter. What must be the minimum contribution margin per quarter for the new product to make the changeover financially feasible?

(CMA, adapted)

Note: Items 1 through 4 following correspond to the aforementioned four items.

1.

Justa Corporation
Quarterly Income Statement

	Total	Local	Regional
Sales	$1,300,000	$1,000,000	$300,000
Variable expenses:			
Manufacturing (Schedule A)	$ 820,000	$ 630,000	$190,000
Selling (Schedule B)	31,000	24,000	7,000
Total variable expenses	$ 851,000	$ 654,000	$197,000
Contribution margin	$ 449,000	$ 346,000	$103,000
Separable fixed selling expenses	74,000	36,000	38,000
Net market contributions	$ 375,000	$ 310,000	$ 65,000
Common fixed expenses:			
Manufacturing	$ 190,000		
Administrative	52,000		
Total common fixed expenses:	$ 242,000		
Net income	$ 133,000		

Schedule A—Variable Manufacturing Expenses

(1)	(2)	(3)	(4)	(5)	(6)	(7)
			Local Variable		Regional Variable	Total Variable
		Local	Expenses	Regional	Expenses	Expenses
Product	%	Sales	(2) × (3)	Sales	(2) × (5)	(4) + (6)
A	60	$400,000	$240,000	$100,000	$ 60,000	$300,000
B	70	300,000	210,000	100,000	70,000	280,000
C	60	300,000	180,000	100,000	60,000	240,000
Totals			$630,000		$190,000	$820,000

Schedule B—Variable Selling Expenses

A	3	$400,000	$12,000	$100,000	$3,000	$15,000
B	2	300,000	6,000	100,000	2,000	8,000
C	2	300,000	6,000	100,000	2,000	8,000
Totals			$24,000		$7,000	$31,000

Separable fixed selling expense computation:

	Local	Regional
Total selling expense	$60,000	$45,000
Less: variable (Schedule B)	24,000	7,000
Fixed selling expense	$36,000	$38,000

2. The answer is no; the regional market should not be dropped. The regional market sales are adequate to cover variable expenses and separable fixed expenses of the regional market and contribute $65,000 toward the recovery of the $242,000 common fixed expenses and net income.

If the regional market is dropped, the local market contribution margin must absorb its separable fixed selling expenses plus all common fixed expenses, as shown:

Contribution margin	$346,000
Separable fixed selling expenses	36,000
Net market contribution	$310,000
Total common fixed expenses	242,000
Net income	$ 68,000

The corporation net income thus declines from $133,000 to $68,000. This $65,000 is the amount of the contribution loss from the regional market.

3.

Justa Corporation
Quarterly Income Statement

	Total	Product A	Product B	Product C
Sales	$1,300,000	$500,000	$400,000	$400,000
Variable expenses:				
Manufacturing (Schedule A)	$820,000	$300,000	$280,000	$240,000
Selling (Schedule B)	31,000	15,000	8,000	8,000

Justa Corporation
Quarterly Income Statement

	Total	Product A	Product B	Product C
Total variable expenses	$ 851,000	$315,000	$288,000	$248,000
Contribution margin	$ 449,000	$185,000	$112,000	$152,000
Fixed expenses:				
Manufacturing	$ 190,000			
Selling	74,000			
Administrative	52,000			
Total fixed expenses	$ 316,000			
Net income	$ 133,000			

4. When the new product replaces product C, the minimum contribution margin per quarter must be at least $162,000 (the present contribution margin of product C + $10,000 of new fixed expenses) in order for Justa Corporation to be no worse off financially than it is currently. This contribution margin will still provide a net income of $133,000.

Allocation of Costs to Territories

Distribution costs should be analyzed by territories because each territory may have its own particular characteristics. For example, the cost to sell in a populated area, such as California, is different than to sell in a less densely populated area, such as Texas.

In allocating costs by territory, the following guidelines exist:

Cost	Allocation Base
Salesperson's wages and expenses	Hours spent in each territory
Billing and office expenses charge	Number of billing items or direct
Advertising	Territory covered by media
Transportation	Direct or based on mileage
Credit and collection	Number of customer accounts or sales dollars in territory

Exhibit 19-8 reveals the contribution of a company's sales territories to overall profits.

Exhibit 19-8: Contribution by Sales Territory (000 omitted)

| | Company | | Sales Territories | | | | | |
| | | | Eastern | | Central | | Western | |
	Amount	Percent	Amount	Percent	Amount	Percent	Amount	Percent
Net sales	$6,000	100	$3,000	100	$2,000	100	$1,000	100
Variable cost of sales								
Production	$1,000	17	$300	10	$500	25	$200	20
Marketing	500	8	400	13	50	3	50	5
Total variable cost of sales	$1,500	25	700	23	$550	28	$250	25
Contribution margin	$4,500	75	$2,300	77	$1,450	72	$750	75
District territory costs								
Advertising and promotion	$600	10	$300	10	$200	10	$100	10
District sales office	400	7	200	7	100	5	100	10
Travel and entertainment	800	13	400	13	350	18	50	5
Total direct territory costs	$1,800	30	$900	30	$650	33	$250	25
Territory contribution	$2,700	45	$1,400	47	$800	39	$500	50
Common fixed costs								
Production	$600	10						
Marketing	400	7						
General and administrative	200	3						
Total common fixed costs	$1,200	20						
Net income	$1,500	25						

CONCLUSION

Costs may be allocated to divisions, products, contracts, customers, territories, or any other logical cost objective. Many allocation methods may be used such as by benefits received, equity, and cause-effect. Proper allocation is needed to derive accurate cost figures for product costing, pricing, control, and decision-making purposes.

In appraising the distribution effort, consideration should be given to number of calls on existing and new customers, number of deliveries, and number of samples distributed.

CHAPTER 20

BUDGETING AND FINANCIAL MODELING

CONTENTS

Exhibits

A budget is a detailed quantitative plan outlining the acquisition and use of financial and other resources of an organization over some given time period. It is a tool for planning. If properly constructed, it is used as a control device. This chapter shows step by step, how to formulate a master budget. The process of developing an annual budget or interim financial forecast should provide a company with the opportunity to integrate its strategic objectives with the budget proposals of its business units and functions. The process begins with the development of a sales budget and proceeds through a number of steps that ultimately lead to the cash budget, the budgeted income statement, and the budgeted balance sheet.

In recent years, computer-based models and spreadsheet software have been utilized for budgeting in an effort to speed up the process and allow budget analysts to investigate the effects of changes in budget assumptions. Financial models constitute a functional branch of a general corporate planning model. They are essentially used to generate pro forma financial statements and financial ratios—the basic tools for budgeting and profit planning. Also, the financial model is a technique for risk analysis and what-if scenarios. The financial model is also needed for day-to-day operational and tactical decisions for immediate planning problems.

Rolling budgeting has received considerable attention recently as a new approach to budgeting as an alternative to incremental budgeting.

THE MASTER BUDGET

A comprehensive (master) budget is a formal statement of management's expectation regarding sales, expenses, volume, and other financial transactions of an organization for the coming period. Simply put, a budget is a set of pro forma (projected or planned) financial statements. It consists basically of a pro forma income statement, a pro forma balance sheet, and a cash budget.

A budget is a tool for both planning and control. At the beginning of the period, the budget is a plan or standard; at the end of the period, it serves as a control device to help management measure its performance against the plan so that future performance may be improved.

With the aid of computer technology, budgeting can be used as an effective device for evaluation of what-if scenarios. This way management should be able to move toward finding the best course of action among various alternatives through simulation. If management does not like what it sees on the budgeted financial statements in terms of various financial ratios such as liquidity, activity (turnover), leverage, profit margin, and market value ratios, it can always alter its contemplated decision and planning set.

The budget is classified broadly into two categories:

1. Operating budget, reflecting the results of operating decisions.
2. Financial budget, reflecting the financial decisions of the firm.

The operating budget consists of:

- Sales budget.
- Production budget.
- Direct materials budget.
- Direct labor budget.
- Factory overhead budget.
- Selling and administrative expense budget.
- Pro forma income statement.

The financial budget consists of:

- Cash budget.
- Pro forma balance sheet.

The major steps in preparing the budget are:

1. Prepare a sales forecast.
2. Determine expected production volume.
3. Estimate manufacturing costs and operating expenses.
4. Determine cash flow and other financial effects.
5. Formulate projected financial statements.

Exhibit 20-1 shows a simplified diagram of the various parts of the comprehensive (master) budget, the master plan of the company.

Exhibit 20-1: Types of Processing Flow

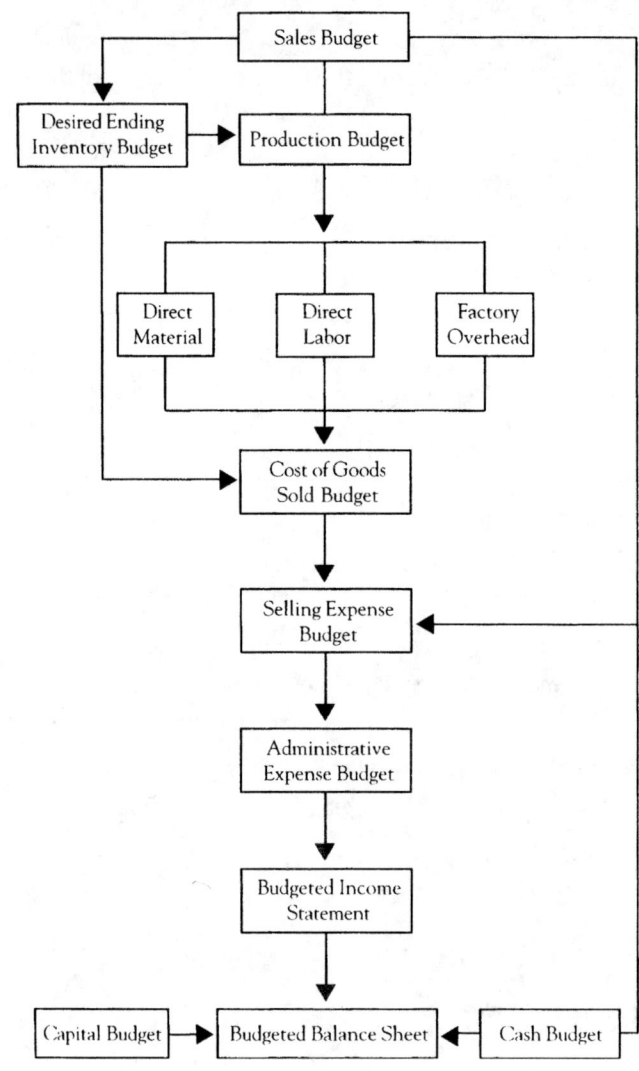

ILLUSTRATION

To illustrate how these budgets are put together, this chapter focuses on a *manufacturing* company called the Johnson Company, which produces and markets a single product. The following is assumed:

- The company uses a single material and one type of labor in the manufacture of the product.

- It prepares a master budget on a *quarterly* basis.

- Work-in-process inventories at the beginning and end of the year are negligible and are ignored.

- The company uses a single cost driver—direct labor hours (DLH) as the allocation base for assigning all factory overhead costs to the product.

THE SALES BUDGET

The sales budget is the starting point in preparing the master budget, because estimated sales volume influences nearly all other items appearing throughout the master budget. The sales budget should show total sales in quantity and value. The expected total sales can be break-even or target income sales or projected sales. It may be analyzed further by product, territory, customer and, of course, seasonal pattern of expected sales. Generally, the sales budget includes a computation of expected cash collections from credit sales, which will be used later for cash budgeting.

EXAMPLE 1:

The Johnson Company
Sales Budget
for the Year Ended December 31, 2X15

	Quarter				
	1	2	3	4	Year as a Whole
Expected sales in units*	1,000	1,800	2,000	1,200	6,000
Unit sales price*	× $150	× $150	× $150	× $150	× $150
Total sales	$150,000	$270,000	$300,000	$180,000	$900,000

* Given.

Schedule of Expected Cash Collections

	1	2	3	4	Year as a Whole
Accounts receivable, 12/31/2X14	$100,000*				$100,000
1st quarter sales ($150,000)	60,000†	$90,000‡			150,000
2d quarter sales ($270,000)		108,000	$162,000		270,000
3d quarter sales ($300,000)			120,000	$180,000	300,000
4th quarter sales ($180,000)				72,000	72,000
Total cash collections	$160,000	$198,000	$282,000	$252,000	$892,000

* All $100,000 accounts receivable balance is assumed to be collectible in the first quarter.
† 40% of a quarter's sales are collected in the quarter of sale.
‡ 60% of a quarter's sales are collected in the quarter following.

MONTHLY CASH COLLECTIONS FROM CUSTOMERS

Frequently, there are time lags between monthly sales made *on account* and their related monthly cash collections. For example, in any month, credit sales are collected as follows: 15% in month of sale, 60% in the following month, 24% in the month after, and the remaining 1% are uncollectible.

	April-Actual	May-Actual	June-Budgeted	July-Budgeted
Credit sales	$320	200	300	280

The budgeted cash receipts for June and July are computed as follows:

For June:

From April sales	$320 × .24	$ 76.80
From May sales	200 × .6	120.00
From June sales	300 × .15	45.00
Total budgeted collections in June		$241.80

For July:

From May sales	$200 × .24	$48
From June sales	300 × .6	180
From July sales	280 × .15	42
Total budgeted collections in July		$270

THE PRODUCTION BUDGET

After sales are budgeted, the production budget can be determined. The production budget is a statement of the output by product and is generally expressed in units. It should take into account the sales budget, plant capacity, whether stocks are to be increased or decreased, and outside purchases. The number of units expected to be manufactured to meet budgeted sales and inventory requirements is set forth in the production budget. In the Just-in-Time (JIT) firm, there are no inventory requirements, as a customer triggers production. Note that the production budget is expressed in terms of units. At this juncture, there is no indication of how much they will cost.

Expected production volume = Planned sales + Desired ending inventory – beginning Inventory

The production budget is illustrated as follows:

EXAMPLE 2:

THE JOHNSON COMPANY
Production Budget
For the Year Ended December 31, 2X15
QUARTER

	1	2	3	4	Year as a Whole
Planned sales (Example 1)	1,000	1,800	2,000	1,200	6,000
Desired ending inventory*	180	200	120	300**	300
Total Needs	1,180	2,000	2,120	1,500	6,300
Less: Beginning inventory	200**	180***	200	120	200
Units to be produced	980	1,820	1,920	1,380	6,100

*   10% of the next quarter's sales. (For example, 180 = 10% × 1,800).
**   Given.
***   The same as the previous quarter's ending inventory.
Note: (1.) The beginning inventory for one quarter is always equal to the ending inventory in the previous quarter. (2.) The column for the year is not simply the addition of the amounts for the four quarters. Notice that the desired ending inventory for the year is 300, which is equal to the desired ending inventory for the fourth quarter.

INVENTORY PURCHASES — MERCHANDISING FIRM

Johnson Company is a manufacturing firm that prepares a *production budget*, as shown in Example 2. If it were a merchandising (retailing or wholesaling) firm, then it would develop a merchandise purchase budget showing the amount of goods to be purchased from its suppliers during the period. The merchandise purchases budget is in the same basic format as the production budget, except that it shows goods to be purchased rather than goods to be produced, as shown below:

Budgeted cost of goods sold (in units or dollars)	$560,000
Add: Desired ending merchandise inventory	120,000
Total needs	$680,000
Less: Beginning merchandise inventory	(80,000)
Required purchases (in units or in dollars)	$600,000

Note:

1. Cost of goods sold = beginning inventory + purchases – ending inventory. Hence, purchases = cost of goods sold + ending inventory – beginning inventory.

2. Gross profit (margin) = sales – cost of goods sold (or cost of sales). For example, as a percent, 30% = 100% – 70%. For example, sales is $800,000, then the cost of goods sold is $800,000 × 70% = $560,000.

3. The merchandise purchase budget can be prepared in *units* as well as in dollars.

THE DIRECT MATERIAL BUDGET

When the level of production has been computed, a direct material budget should be constructed to show how much material will be required for production and how much material must be purchased to meet this production requirement. It also provides the cost of direct materials to purchase, which is needed later for cash budgeting purposes.

The purchase will depend on both expected use of materials in production and the materials inventory needs of the firm. The formula for computation of the purchase is:

$$\text{Purchase in units} = \text{Usage} + \text{Desired ending material inventory units} - \text{Beginning inventory units}$$

The desired ending inventory is determined by the firm's inventory policy. The direct material budget is usually accompanied by a computation of expected cash payments for materials.

EXAMPLE 3:

THE JOHNSON COMPANY
Direct Material Budget
For the Year Ended December 31, 2X15
QUARTER

	1	2	3	4	Year as a Whole
Units to be produced (Ex.2)	980	1,820	1,920	1,380	6,100
Material needs per unit (lbs)*	× 2	× 2	× 2	× 2	× 2
Production needs (usage)	1,960	3,640	3,840	2,760	12,200*****
Desired ending inventory of materials**	910	960	690	520 ****	520
Total needs	2,870	4,600	4,530	3,280	12,720
Less: Beginning inventory of materials	490 **	910***	960	690	490
Materials to be purchased	2,380	3,690	3,570	2,590	12,230
Unit price*	× $5	× $5	× $5	× $5	× $5
Purchase cost	$11,900	$18,450	$17,850	$12,950	$61,150

* Given
** 25% of the next quarter's units needed for production. For example, the second quarter production needs are 3,640 lbs. Therefore, the desired ending inventory for the first quarter would be 25% × 3,640 lbs. = 910 lbs. Also note: 490 lbs = 25% × 1,960 = 490 lbs.
*** The same as the prior quarter's ending inventory.
**** Assume that the budgeted production needs in lbs. for the first quarter of 20C = 2,080 lbs. So, 25% × 2,080 lbs. = 520 lbs.
***** The cost of direct materials used is therefore $61,000 (12,200 units × $5 per unit).

Schedule of Expected Cash Disbursements

Accounts payable, 12/31/20A	$6,275*				$6,275
1st quarter purchases ($11,900)	$5,950**	$5,950**			11,900
2d quarter purchases ($18,450)		9,225	9,225		18,450
3d quarter purchases ($17,850)			8,925	8,925	17,850
4th quarter purchases ($12,950)				6,475	6,475
Total disbursements	$12,225	$15,175	$18,150	$15,400	$60,950

* All of the $6,275 accounts payable balance (from the balance sheet, 2X14) is assumed to be paid in the first quarter.
** 50% of a quarter's purchases are paid for in the quarter of purchase; the remaining 50% are paid for in the following quarter.

THE DIRECT LABOR BUDGET

The production requirements as set forth in the production budget also provide the starting point for the preparation of the direct labor budget. To compute direct labor requirements, expected production volume for each period is multiplied by the number of direct labor hours required to produce a single unit. The direct labor hours to meet production requirements is then multiplied by the (standard) direct labor cost per hour to obtain budgeted total direct labor costs.

EXAMPLE 4:

The Putnam Company
Direct Labor Budget
For the Year Ended December 31, 2X15

	Quarter				Year as a Whole
	1	2	3	4	
Units to be produced (Ex. 2)	980	1,820	1,920	1,380	6,100
Direct labor hours per unit*	× 5	× 5	× 5	× 5	× 5
Total hours	4,900	9,100	9,600	6,900	30,500
Direct labor cost per hour*	× $10	× $10	× $10	× $10	× $10
Total direct labor cost	$49,000	$91,000	$96,000	$69,000	$305,000

* Both are given.

THE FACTORY OVERHEAD BUDGET

The factory overhead budget should provide a schedule of all manufacturing costs other than direct materials and direct labor, namely indirect manufacturing costs. Unlike direct materials and direct labor, there is no readily identifiable input-output relationship for overhead items. Recall, however, factory overhead consists of two types of costs: variable and fixed. Past experience in can be used as a guide. To illustrate the factory overhead budget, assume the following:

- Total factory overhead budgeted = $18,300 fixed (per quarter), plus $2 per hour of direct labor. This is one example of a cost-volume (or flexible budget) formula (y = a + bx), developed via the *least-squares method (regression)* with a high r^2. (see Chapter 16).

- Depreciation expenses are $4,000 each quarter. Note that depreciation does not entail a cash outlay and therefore must be deducted from the total factory overhead in computing cash disbursement for factory overhead.

- Overhead costs involving cash outlays are paid for in the quarter incurred.

   EXAMPLE 5: To illustrate the factory overhead budget, assume that:
   - Total factory overhead budgeted = $6,000 fixed (per quarter), plus $2 per hour of direct labor.
   - Depreciation expenses are $3,250 each quarter.
   - All overhead costs involving cash outlays are paid for in the quarter incurred.

The Johnson Company Factory Overhead Budget
for the Year Ending December 31, 2X15

	Quarter				
	1	2	3	4	Year as a Whole
Budgeted direct labor hours	4,900	9,100	9,600	6,900	30,500
Variable overhead rate	× $2	× $2	× $2	× $2	× $2
Variable overhead budgeted*	$9,800	$18,200	$19,200	$13,800	$61,000
Fixed overhead budgeted**	18,300	18,300	18,300	18,300	73,200
Total budgeted overhead	$28,100	$36,500	$37,500	$32,100	$134,200
Less: depreciation***	4,000	4,000	4,000	4,000	16,000
Cash disbursement for Factory overhead	$24,100	$32,500	$33,500	$28,100	$118,200

* Includes supplies and utilities. Many companies use direct labor hours as the driver for overhead.
** The overhead costs that do not vary with direct labor hours are pooled into fixed overhead, such as rent, property taxes, and insurance.
*** Depreciation does not require a cash outlay.

THE ENDING FINISHED GOODS INVENTORY BUDGET

The ending finished goods inventory budget provides us with the information required for the construction of budgeted financial statements. After completing Examples 1-5, sufficient data will have been generated to compute the per-unit manufacturing cost of finished product. This computation is required for two reasons: (1) to help compute the cost of goods sold on the budgeted income statement; and (2) to give the dollar value of the ending finished goods inventory to appear on the budgeted balance sheet. The unit manufacturing cost and the dollar value of the desired ending inventory are shown below.

   EXAMPLE 6:

The Johnson Company
Ending Finished Goods Inventory Budget
Ending Inventory

Units	Unit Product Cost	Total
300 units (Example 2)	$82*	$24,600

* The unit variable cost of $82 is computed as follows:

	Unit Cost	Units	Total
Direct materials	$5 per lbs	2 pounds	$10
Direct labor	10 per hr.	5 hours	50
Factory overhead**	4.40 per hr.	5 hours	22
Unit product cost			$82

** Predetermined factory overhead applied rate = Budgeted annual factory overhead/budgeted annual activity units = $134,200/30,500 DLH = $4.40 (see Chapter 14).

THE COST OF GOODS SOLD BUDGET

Assuming that the beginning finished goods inventory is valued at $26,400 (Example 11), the budgeted cost of goods sold schedule can be prepared using Examples 3, 4, 5, and 6. This cost of goods sold Example 7 will be used as an input for the budgeted income statement.

EXAMPLE 7:

The Johnson Company Costs of Goods Sold Budget
For the Year Ended December 31, 2X15

	From Example	
Direct materials used	3	$ 61,000
Direct labor	4	305,000
Factory overhead	5	134,200
Total manufacturing costs		500,200*
Beginning finished goods inventory	11	16,400
Cost of goods available for sale		516,600
Less: Ending finished goods inventory	6	24,600
Budgeted cost of goods sold		492,000

* *Cost of goods manufactured* = total manufacturing cost + beginning work in process inventory – ending work in process inventory. Because there are no work in process inventories in this illustration, cost of goods manufactured = total manufacturing cost. Thus, cost of goods manufactured = direct materials used + direct labor + factory overhead = $61,000 (12,200 lbs. @$5 per lbs. from Example 3) + $305,000 (Example 4) + $134,200 (Example 5) = $500,200.

THE SELLING AND ADMINISTRATIVE EXPENSE BUDGET

The selling and administrative expense budget lists the nonmanufacturing (operating) expenses involved in selling the products and in managing the business. Similar to the factory overhead budget, selling and administrative expenses can be broken down into variable and fixed components. Such items as sales commissions, freight, and supplies vary with sales activity. As with factory overhead, this budget can be developed using the coat-volume (*flexible budget*) formula in the form of $y = a + bx$.

If the number of expense items is very large, separate budgets may be needed for the selling and administrative functions.

EXAMPLE 8:

The Johnson Company
Selling and Administrative Expense Budget
For the Year Ending December 31, 2X15

	Quarter				
	1	2	3	4	Year as a Whole
Expected sales in units	1,000	1,800	2,000	1,200	6,000
Variable selling and admin. expense per unit*	× $3	× $3	× $3	× $3	× $3
Budgeted variable expense	$3,000	$5,400	$6,000	$3,200	$18,000
Fixed selling and administrative expenses:**					
Advertising	20,000	20,000	20,000	20,000	80,000
Insurance		12,600			12,600
Office salaries	40,000	40,000	40,000	40,000	160,000
Taxes				7,400	7,400
Total budgeted selling and administrative expenses***	$63,000	$78,000	$66,000	$71,000	$278,000

* Assumed. It includes sales agents' commissions, shipping, and supplies.
** Scheduled to be paid.
*** Paid for in the quarter incurred.

THE CASH BUDGET

The cash budget is prepared for the purpose of cash planning and control. It presents the expected cash inflow and outflow for a designated time period. The cash budget helps management keep cash balances in reasonable relationship to its needs. It aids in avoiding unnecessary idle cash and possible cash shortages. The cash budget consists typically of four major sections:

1. The *cash receipts* section, which is cash collections from customers and other cash receipts such as royalty income and investment income.

2. The *cash disbursements* section, which comprises all cash payments made by purpose.

3. The *cash surplus* or *deficit* section, which simply shows the difference between the total cash available and the total cash needed including a *minimum cash balance* if required. If there is surplus cash, loans may be repaid or temporary investments made.

4. The *financing* section, which provides a detailed account of the borrowings, repayments, and interest payments expected during the budgeting period.

5. The *investments* section, which encompasses investment of excess cash and liquidation of investment of surplus cash.

EXAMPLE 9: To illustrate, assume the following:

- Johnson Company has an open line of credit with its bank that can be used as needed to bolster the cash position.

- The company desires to maintain a $10,000 minimum cash balance at the end of each quarter. Therefore, borrowing must be sufficient to cover the cash shortfall and to provide for the minimum cash balance of $10,000.

- All borrowings and repayments must be in multiples of $1,000 amounts, and interest is 10% per annum.

- Interest is computed and paid on the principal as the principal is repaid.

- All borrowings take place at the beginning of a quarter, and all repayments are made at the end of a quarter.

- No investment option is allowed in this example. The loan is *self-liquidating* in the sense that the borrowed money is used to obtain resources that are combined for sale, and the proceeds from sales are used to pay back the loan.

Note: To be useful for cash planning and control, the cash budget must be prepared on a *monthly* basis.

The Johnson Company
Cash Budget
for the Year Ending December 31, 2X15

	From Example	Quarter 1	2	3	4	Year as a Whole
Cash balance beginning		$19,000*	$10,675	$10,000	$10,350	$19,000
Add: receipts:						
Collection from customers	1	160,000	198,000	282,000	252,000	892,000
Total cash available (a)		$179,000	$208,675	$292,000	$262,350	$911,000

	From Example	Quarter 1	2	3	4	Year as a Whole
Less: disbursements:						
Direct materials	3	$12,225	$15,175	$18,150	$15,400	$60,950
Direct labor	4	49,000	91,000	96,000	69,000	305,000
Factory overhead	5	24,100	32,500	33,500	28,100	118,200
Selling and admin.	8	63,000	78,000	66,000	71,000	278,000
Equipment purchase	Given	30,000	12,000	0	0	42,000
Dividends	Given	5,000	5,000	5,000	5,000	20,000
Income tax	11	15,000	15,000	15,000	15,000	60,000
Total disbursements (b)		$198,325	$248,675	$233,650	$203,500	$884,150
Minimum cash balance		$10,000	$10,000	$10,000	$10,000	$10,000
Total cash needed (c)		$208,325	$258,675	$243,650	$213,500	$894,150
Cash surplus (deficit) (a) – (c)		$(29,325)	$(50,000)	$48,350	$48,850	$16,850
Financing:						
Borrowing		$30,000**	$50,000	0	0	$80,000
Repayment		0	0	$(45,000)	$(35,000)	$(80,000)
Interest		0	0	(3,000)***	(2,625)+	(5,625)
Total effects of financing (d)		30,000	50,000	$(48,000)	(37,625)	$(5,625)
Cash balance, ending [(a) – (b) + (d)]		$10,675	$10,000	$10,350	$21,225	$21,225

* $19,000 (from the balance sheet 2X14 – Example 11).

** The company desires to maintain a $10,000 minimum cash balance at the end of each quarter. Therefore, borrowing must be sufficient to cover the cash shortfall of $19,325 and to provide for the minimum cash balance of $10,000, for a total of $29,325.

*** The interest payments relate only to the principal being repaid at the time it is repaid. For example, the interest in quarter 3 relates only to the interest due on the $30,000 principal being repaid from quarter 1 borrowing and on the $15,000 principal being repaid from quarter 2 borrowing. Total interest being paid is $3,000, shown as follows:

$30,000 × 10% × 3/4 = $2,250
$15,000 × 10% × 2/4 = 750
+$35,000 × 10% × 3/4 = $2,625

THE BUDGETED INCOME STATEMENT

The budgeted income statement summarizes the various component projections of revenue and expenses for the budgeting period. However, for control purposes the budget can be divided into quarters or even months depending on the need.

EXAMPLE 10:

The Johnson Company
Budgeted Income Statement
for the Year Ended December 31, 2X15

	From Example	
Sales (6,000 units) @$150)	1	$900,000
Less: Cost of goods sold	7	492,000
Gross margin		408,000
Less: Selling and administrative expenses	8	278,000
Operating income		130,000
Less: Interest expense	9	5,625
Net income before taxes	6	124,375
Less: Income taxes		60,000*
Net income after taxes		$64,365

* Estimated

THE BUDGETED BALANCE SHEET

The budgeted balance sheet is developed by beginning with the balance sheet for the year just ended and adjusting it, using all the activities that are expected to take place during the budgeting period. Some of the reasons why the budgeted balance sheet must be prepared are:

• It could disclose some unfavorable financial conditions that management might want to avoid.

• It serves as a final check on the mathematical accuracy of all the other Examples.

- It helps management perform a variety of ratio calculations.
- It highlights future resources and obligations.

We can construct the budgeted balance sheet by using:

- The December 2X14 balance sheet (Example 11).
- The cash budget (Example 9).
- The budgeted income statement (Example 10).

Johnson's budgeted balance sheet for December 31, 2X15, is presented below. Supporting calculations of the individual statement accounts are also provided.

EXAMPLE 11: To illustrate, the following balance sheet is used for the year 2X14:

The Johnson Company
Balance Sheet
December 31, 2X14

Assets

Current Assets:		
Cash	$ 19,000	
Accounts receivable	100,000	
Materials inventory (490 lbs.)	2,450	
Finished good inventory (200 units)	16,400	
Total current assets		$137,850
Plant and equipment:		
Land	30,000	
Buildings and equipment	250,000	
Accumulated depreciation	(74,000)	
Plant and equipment, net		206,000
Total assets		$343,850

Liabilities and Stockholders' Equity

Current Liabilities:		
Accounts payable (raw materials)	$ 6,275	
Income tax payable	60,000	
Total current liabilities		$66,275
Stockholders' equity:		
Common stock, no par	$200,000	
Retained earnings	77,575	
Total stockholders' equity		277,575
Total liabilities and stockholders; equity		$343,850

The Johnson Company
Balance Sheet
December 31, 2X15

Assets

Cash	$ 21,225 (a)	
Accounts receivable	108,000 (b)	
Materials inventory (520 lbs.)	2,600 (c)	
Finished good inventory (300 units)	24,600 (d)	
Total current assets		$156,425
Plant and equipment:		
Land	30,000 (e)	
Buildings and equipment	292,000 (f)	
Accumulated depreciation	(90,000) (g)	
Plant and equipment, net		232,000
Total assets		$388,425

Liabilities and Stockholders' Equity

Current Liabilities:		
Accounts payable (raw materials)	$ 6,275 (h)	
Income tax payable	60,000 (i)	
Total current liabilities		$66,475
Stockholders' equity:		
Common stock, no par	$200,000 (j)	
Retained earnings	121,950 (k)	
Total stockholders' equity		321,950
Total liabilities and stockholder's equity		$388,425

Supporting computations:

(a) From Example 8 (cash budget).

(b) $100,000 (accounts receivable, 12/31/20A) + $900,000 (credit sales from Example 1) $892,000 (collections from Example 1) = $108,000, or 60% of fourth quarter credit sales, from Example 1 ($180,000 × 60% = $108,000).

(c) Direct materials, ending inventory = 520 pounds × $ 5 = $2,600 (from Example 3).

(d) From Example 6 (ending finished goods inventory budget).

(e) From the 2X14 balance sheet and Example 8 (no change).

(f) $250,000 (building and equipment, 12/31/2X14) + $42,000 (purchases from Example 8) = $292,000.

(g) $74,000 (accumulated depreciation, 12/31/2X14) + $16,000 (depreciation expense from Example 5) = $90,000.

(h) Note that all accounts payable relate to material purchases. $6,275 (accounts payable, 12/31/2X14) + $61,150 (credit purchases from Example 3) - $60,950 (payments for purchases from Example 3) = $6,475, or 50% of fourth quarter purchase = 50% ($12,950) = $6,475.

(i) From Example 10.

(j) From the 2X14 balance sheet and Example 8 (no change).

(k) $77,575 (retained earnings, 12/31/2X14) + $64,375 (net income for the period, Example 9) – $20,000 (cash dividends from Example 9) = $121,950.

SOME FINANCIAL CALCULATIONS

To see what kind of financial condition the Johnson Company is expected to be in for the budgeting year, a sample of financial ratio calculations are in order: (Assume 2X14 after tax net income was $45,000)

	2X14	2X15
Current ratio (Current assets/current liabilities)	$137,850/$66,275 = 2.08	$156,425/$66,475 =2.35
Return on total assets (Net income after taxes/total assets)	$45,000/$343,850 = 13.08%	$64,375/$388,425 = 16.57%

Sample calculations indicate that the Johnson Company is expected to have better liquidity as measured by the current ratio. Overall performance will be improved as measured by return on total assets. This could be an indication that the contemplated plan may work out well.

THE BUDGET MANUAL

The budget manual describes how a budget is prepared. It includes a planning calendar and distribution instructions for all budget schedules. Distribution instructions are important for ensuring that all designated departments within the organization receive a budget schedule in order to prepare their own budgets.

The budget manual communicates throughout the company the policies and procedures for budget preparation and explains how the budget is to be used by managers and those responsible for different aspects of the budgeting process, such as preparation, presentation, reporting, evaluation, and approval. The manual:

- Lists positions rather than names to avoid unnecessary updating.
- Contains a preparation chart listing the budgeting steps to aid in cooperation and coordination throughout each department.
- Specifies the procedures to be followed to revise the budget based on changing conditions and goals (e.g., revisions may be necessary because of changing objectives, new methods, changing economic environment, and errors).
- Receives participation from all affected managerial levels.

The budget manual stipulates authority, responsibility, and duties; fosters standardization; documents procedures; simplifies the budget process; provides communication; answers users' questions; enhances supervision; and fosters training.

It includes:

- Standardized forms, lists, and reports.
- Instructions.
- Format and coverage of performance reports.
- Administrative details.
- Follow-up procedures.
- Budget objectives, purposes, procedures, guidelines, and policies.
- Desired accomplishments.
- Data descriptions.
- Personnel duties (i.e., those assigned to prepare, review, approve, and revise the budget).
- Individuals with authority and responsibility for budget items (There should be a designated manager or subordinate to perform the activity).
- Approval requirements.
- Individuals assigned to evaluate the difference between budget and actual figures, and those assigned to take corrective action.
- Budget timetable.
- Glossary of terminology.
- Instructions to complete budget activities.
- Uses of budget information.
- Policies for modifying the budget and updating the calendar.
- Communication between upper management and subordinates.
- Coordination between departments of the budget.
- Explanatory footnotes.

The budget manual is organized with each department included in a separate section, separated by an index tab. Department managers and employees contribute important information, such as operating problems, constraints, and limitations in their departments, to the manual's development. The manual includes a standard cost table for different types of expenses used by managers of various departments throughout the organization, which allows for consistency and uniformity throughout the company.

It is in looseleaf form so pages may be substituted for updates. The manual's layout enhances its clarity and conciseness; it does not contain complex, technical language, which makes it easy for nonaccountants to understand; and it is arranged logically and orderly with a user-friendly index and updated as conditions warrant.

There are many advantages to the budget manual, including simplification and standardization of budget procedures. It acts as a reference and provides an organized approach to the budget process. It promotes consistency between departments and provides job description guidance to new employees, while assisting current employees with adjusting to new positions when transferred or promoted.

THE BUDGET CALENDAR

The budget planning calendar is the first step in the budget process, as it presents an overall view of each sequential step in budget preparation. It provides a schedule of activities for the development and adoption of the budget. The calendar serves as a timetable for operating managers, who must submit their proposed budgets so the overall company budget may be prepared on time. It provides a list of realistic and attainable dates, which indicate and track the delivery of specific information, such as documents and reports, between sources.

Accompanying the calendar is a draft of the time schedule in which the budgeting process will be implemented, which identifies the deadlines, the personnel responsible, and those designated to send and receive the information. The plan furnishes the structure of the budgeting process and the overall objectives. These items are crucial for the budgeting process and must be completed before the process can proceed. An illustrative budget calendar for a company is presented in the following example.

>*EXAMPLE 12:* ABC Company Budget Preparation Calendar Fiscal 2X13
>
>1.   *General Guidelines* issued to senior management staff by the president provides the company's broad objectives for the ensuing year. These objectives must be specific enough to provide divisions with adequate direction, yet broad enough to allow for creativity. A general indication of gross margins, operating profit, net profit, and productivity are some of the areas to be addressed.
>
>2.   *New Products Forecast* provides an indication of new and improved products to be available next year. This includes estimated availability dates and likely segments, as applicable.
>
>3.   *Discussion of Action Plans* involving the president and senior management occurs with particular emphasis on achieving objectives (on an

individual basis) for the coming year. Each senior vice president produces, in writing, and justifies, in detail, his or her plan for meeting the year's objectives. For example, Sales and Marketing provides expected sales by regions supported by level of sales force and related promotional expenses (e.g., advertising or conventions and product giveaways).

a. *Headcount* by department or division to support objectives are justified by each senior vice president.

b. *C.E. Projections* outline the major projects to be executed in the budget year, as determined by the department managers and Facilities Engineering. Projects are ranked in order of priority with an explanation of their benefits and drawbacks.

c. *Inventory Projections*, as furnished by the vice president of the respective user department (e.g., Film, Chemistry, and Equipment), indicates the levels of the inventory by major product lines. Where applicable, a desired minimum and maximum level of support to production and sales is given.

4. *Fringe Benefits Package*, including payroll increases prepared by the Human Resources Department, outlines the basis of the company's contribution of the major programs and fringes. Both quantitative and qualitative factors are presented. Major areas to be covered are incentives, medical, dental, retirement, life insurance, and workmen's compensation. Other expenditures, such as FICA and unemployment tax, are computed by Corporate Planning.

5. *Budget Package*, issued to departmental managers by Corporate Planning, contains the necessary forms and instructions to prepare the budget.

6. *Preliminary Profit & Loss (P&L) Fiscal 2X13*, based on sales forecast and assumptions in 2-4, is prepared by Corporate Planning. This indicates the likely outcome of the actions contemplated. Major directions and proactive measures are then taken to keep the budget process in line with the president's guidelines.

7. *Final Sales Forecast*, as issued to senior management staff by Sales and Marketing, provide sales volume and dollars by major product lines (e.g., film and paper [sq. ft. & $], chemistry [quantity & $] and equipment [unit & $]). Film and paper is analyzed by region, international, dealers, national accounts, and others. New products are clearly identified. An adequate explanation is given for any significant changes (over the current year) in volume or price.

8. *Departmental Expense Budgets* are prepared (on a monthly basis) by department managers and approved by the respective senior management. These include all the operating expenses (i.e., excluding payroll, fringes, depreciation, and facilities cost), as prepared in the Basic Budget Worksheet.

9.   *Preliminary Budget* incorporates data and payroll, fringes, depreciation, and facilities cost, as computed by Corporate Planning. The preliminary data is returned to managers for their review.

10.   *Revisions* made by managers to the preliminary budget are sent to Corporate Planning on a timely basis.

11-13.   *Budgets* are sent to the senior vice president, and meetings are held to review them. Senior vice presidents present their budgets and negotiate the necessary changes to bring budgets in line with corporate objectives.

14.   *Preparation of Budgeted P&L, Cash Flow, Balance Sheet* is performed by Corporate Planning and the Finance Division. This provides management with a financial picture of the budget year.

15-16.   *Budget Package* is sent to senior management for review and approval prior to its presentation to ABC Company.

17.   *Presentation of Budget Package* by Corporate Planning and the president is made to ABC Company for its approval.

18.   *Approved Budgets* are issued to the respective departments. The budgets then serve as a guide for the upper limit of expenditures for the coming year.

BUDGETING THROUGH FINANCIAL MODELING

Many companies are increasingly using financial modeling to develop their budgets. Using financial modeling effectively requires understanding:

- What a financial model is.
- Some typical uses of financial models.
- The types of financial modeling.
- How widespread the use of financial modeling is in practice.
- How to go about building a financial model.
- Spreadsheets and financial modeling languages.

A Financial Model

A financial model, narrowly called a budgeting model, is a system of mathematical equations, logic, and data that describes the relationships among financial and operating variables. A financial model can be viewed as a subset of broadly defined corporate planning models or a stand-alone functional system that attempts to answer a certain financial planning problem. A financial model is one in which:

- One or more financial variables appear (e.g., expenses, revenues, investment, cash flow, taxes, earnings).
- The model user can manipulate (set and alter) the value of one or more financial variables.
- The purpose of the model is to influence strategic decisions by revealing to the decision maker the implications of alternative values of these financial variables.

The two types of financial models are simulation models (better known as what-if models) and optimization models. What-if models attempt to simulate the effects of alternative management policies and assumptions about the firm's external environment. They are basically a tool for management's laboratory. Optimization models are used to maximize or minimize an objective, such as present value of profit or cost. Multi-objective techniques, such as goal programming, are being experimented with. Models can be deterministic or probabilistic. Deterministic models do not include any random or probabilistic variables, whereas probabilistic models incorporate random numbers and/or one or more probability distributions for variables, such as sales and costs. Financial models can be solved and manipulated computationally to derive from them the current and projected future implications and consequences. Owing to technological advances in computers (such as spreadsheets, financial modeling languages, graphics, data base management systems, and networking), more companies are using modeling.

Budgeting and Financial Modeling

Basically, a financial model is used to build a comprehensive budget—that is, projected financial statements, such as the income statement, balance sheet, and cash flow statement. Such a model can be called a budgeting model, it is being used, in this case, develop a master budget. Applications and uses of the model, however, go beyond developing a budget. They include:

- Financial forecasting and analysis.
- Capital expenditure analysis.
- Tax planning.
- Exchange rate analysis.
- Analysis for mergers and acquisitions.
- Labor contract negotiations.
- Capacity planning.
- Cost-volume-profit analysis.
- New venture analysis.
- Lease/purchase evaluation.
- Appraisal of performance by segments.
- Market analysis.
- New product analysis.
- Development of long-term strategy.
- Planning financial requirements.
- Risk analysis.
- Cash flow analysis.
- Cost and price projections.

Use of Financial Modeling in Practice

The use of financial modeling, especially a computer-based financial modeling system, is rapidly growing. The reasons are quite simple: the wide and easy availability of computer hardware and software and a growing need for improved and quicker support for management decisions, such as a decision support system (DSS).

Some of the functions currently served by financial models, as described by the users, are:

- Projecting financial results under any given set of assumptions; evaluating the financial impact of various assumptions and alternative strategies; and preparing long-range financial forecasts.

- Computing income, cash flow, and ratios for five years by months, as well as energy sales, revenue, power generation requirements, operating and manufacturing expenses, manual or automatic financing, and rate structure analysis.

- Providing answers and insights into financial what-if questions, and producing financial scheduling information.

- Forecasting the balance sheet and income statement with emphasis on alternatives for the investment securities portfolio.

- Projecting operating results and various financing needs, such as plant and property levels and financing requirements.

- Computing manufacturing profit, given sales forecasts, and any desired processing sequence through the manufacturing facilities; simulating effect on profits of inventory policies.

- Generating profitability reports of various cost centers.

- Projecting financial implications of capital investment programs.

- Showing the effect of various volume and activity levels on budget and cash flow.

- Forecasting corporate sales, costs, and income by division by month.

- Providing sales revenue for budget, a basis for evaluating actual sales department performance, and other statistical comparisons.

- Determining pro forma cash flow for alternative development plans for real estate projects.

- Analyzing the impact of acquisition on company earnings.

- Determining economic attractiveness of new ventures (e.g., products, facilities, and acquisitions).

- Evaluating alternatives of leasing or buying computer equipment.

- Determining corporate taxes as a function of changes in price.

- Evaluating investments in additional capacity at each major refinery.

- Generating income statements, cash flow, present value, and discounted rate of return for potential mining ventures, based on production and sales forecasts.

Supported by the expanded capabilities provided by models, many companies are increasingly successful in including long-term strategic considerations in their business plans, thus enabling them to investigate the possible impact of their current decisions on the long-term welfare of the organization.

Quantitative Methods Used in Financial Models

In view of the development of sophisticated quantitative models for analysis in business planning and decision making, there is a rapid growing trend for their use, certainly with the aid of computer technology. The techniques used by the model builders are as follows:

- Econometric and statistical methods:
  - Simple and multiple regressions.
  - Econometric modeling.
  - Time series models.
  - Exponential smoothing.
  - Risk analysis.
  - Simulation.
- Optimization models:
  - Linear programming.
  - Goal programming.
  - Integer programming.
  - Dynamic programming.

Developing Financial Models

Development of financial models essentially involves three steps: (1) definition of variables, (2) input parameter values, and (3) model specification. Regarding model specification, this section concentrates only on the simulation-type model. Generally speaking, the model consists of three important components:

1. Variables.
2. Input parameter values.
3. Definitional and/or functional relationships.

Definition of Variables. Fundamental to the specification of a financial model is the definition of the variables to be included in the model. The three types of variables are as follows:

1. Policy variables (Z). The policy variables (often called control variables) are those management can exert some degree of control over. Examples of policy variables are cash management, working capital, debt management, depreciation, tax, merger-acquisition decisions, the rate and direction of the firm's capital investment programs, the extent of its equity and external

debt financing and the financial leverage represented thereby, and the size of its cash balances and liquid asset position. Policy variables are denoted by the symbol z in Exhibit 20-2.

2. External variables (X). The external variables are the environmental variables that are external to the company, influence the firm's decisions from outside the firm, and are generally exogenous in nature. Generally speaking, the firm is embedded in an industry environment. This industry environment, in turn, is influenced by overall general business conditions. General business conditions exert influences upon particular industries in several ways. Total volume of demand, product prices, labor costs, material costs, money rates, and general expectations are among the industry variables affected by the general business conditions. The symbol x represents the external variables in Exhibit 20-2.

Exhibit 20-2: Financial Model Variables

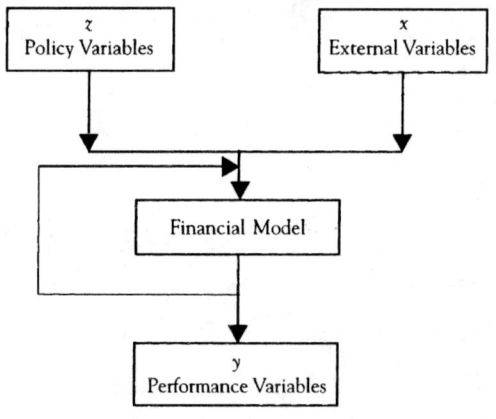

3. Performance variables (Y). The performance variables measure the firm's economic and financial performance, which are usually endogenous. The symbol y is used in Exhibit 20-2. The y s are often called output variables. The output variables of a financial model would be the line items of the balance sheet, cash budget, income statement, or statement of cash flows. How to define the output variables of the firm will depend on the goals and objectives of management. They basically indicate how management measures the performance of the organization or some segments of it. Management is likely to be concerned with (1) the firm's level of earnings; (2) growth in earnings; (3) projected earnings; (4) growth in sales; and (5) cash flow.

Frequently when a financial model is set up, risk or uncertainty is associated with particular projections. In a case such as this, some of these variables, such as sales, are treated as random variables with given probability distributions. The inclusion of random variables in the model transforms it from a deterministic model to a risk analysis model. However, the use of the risk analysis model in practice is rare because of the difficulty involved in modeling and computation.

Input Parameter Values. The model includes various input parameter values. For example, in order to generate the balance sheet, the model needs to input beginning balances of various asset, liability, and equity accounts. These input and parameter values are supplied by management. The ratio between accounts receivable and such financial decision variables as the maximum desired debt-equity ratio would be good examples of parameters.

Model Specification. Once various variables and input parameters for the financial model are developed, a set of mathematical and logical relationships linking the input variables to the performance variables must be specified. The relationships usually fall into two types of equations: (1) definitional equations and (2) behavioral equations. Definitional equations take the form of accounting identities. Behavioral equations involve theories or hypotheses about the behavior of certain economic and financial events. They must be empirically tested and validated before they are incorporated into the financial model.

Definitional Equations. Definitional equations are exactly what the term refers to—mathematical or accounting definitions. For example,

$$\text{Assets} = \text{Liabilities} + \text{Equity}$$

$$\text{Net Income} = \text{Revenues} - \text{Expenses}$$

These definitional equations are fundamental definitions in accounting for the balance sheet and income statement, respectively. Two more examples follow.

$$\text{CASH} = \text{CASH}(-1) + \text{CC} + \text{OCR} + \text{DEBT} - \text{CD} - \text{LP}$$
$$\text{INV} = \text{INV}(-1) + \text{MAT} + \text{DL} + \text{MO} - \text{CGS}$$

The first equation is a typical cash equation in a financial model. It states that ending cash balance (CASH) is equal to the beginning cash balance (CASH(-1)) plus cash collections from customers (CC) plus other cash receipts (OCR) plus borrowings (DEBT) minus cash disbursements (CD) minus loan payments (LP). The second equation states that ending inventory (INV) is equal to the beginning inventory (INV(-1)) plus cost of materials used (MAT) plus cost of direct labor (DL) plus manufacturing overhead (MO) minus the cost of goods sold (CGS).

Behavioral Equations. Behavioral equations describe the behavior of the firm regarding the specific activities that are subject to empirical testing and validation. The classical demand function in economics is:

$$Q = f(P) \text{ or more specifically } Q = a - bP$$

It simply says that the quantity demanded is negatively related to the price. That is to say, the higher the price, the lower will be the demand.

However, the firm's sales are more realistically described as follows:

$$SALES = f(\text{P, ADV, I, GDP, Pc, and so on}) \text{ or}$$

assuming linear relationship among these variables, the model can be specified as follows:

$$SALES = a + b(P) + c(ADV) + d(I) + e(GDP) + f(Pc)$$

which says that the sales are affected by such factors as price (P), advertising expenditures (ADV), consumer income (I), gross domestic product (GDP), and prices of competitive goods (Pc).

With the data on *SALES, P, ADV, I, GDP*, and *Pc*, parameter values $a, b, c, d, e,$ and f can be estimated using linear regression. The statistical significance of each of the parameter estimates can be tested, and the overall explanatory power of the model can be evaluated, measured by the *t*-statistic and *r*-squared, respectively. This allows identification of the most influential factors that affect the sales of a particular product. With the best model chosen, management can simulate the effects on sales of alternative pricing and advertising strategies. It can also experiment with alternative assumptions regarding the external economic factors such as GDP, consumer income, and prices of competitive goods.

Model Structure. A majority of financial models that have been in use are recursive and/or simultaneous models. In recursive models, each equation can be solved one at a time by substituting the solution values of the preceding equations into the right-hand side of each equation. An example of a financial model of the recursive type follows.

1. SALES   = A – B*PRICE + C*ADV
2. REVENUE   = SALES*PRICE
3. CGS   = .70*REVENUE
4. GM   = SALES – CGS
5. CIE   = \$10,000 + .2*SALES
6. EBT   = GM – CIE
7. TAX   = .46*EBT
8. EAT   = EBT – TAX

In this example, the selling price (PRICE) and advertising expenses (ADV) are given. A, B, and C are parameters to be estimated, and:

SALES	= sales volume in units
REVENUE	= sales revenue
CGS	= cost of goods sold
GM	= gross margin
OE	= operating expenses
EBT	= earnings before taxes
TAX	= income taxes
EAT	= earnings after taxes

Simultaneous models are frequently found in econometric models, which require a higher level of computational methods, such as matrix inversion. An example of a financial model of this type is:

1. INT	= .10*DEBT
2. EARN	= REVENUE – CGS – OE – INT – TAX – DIV
3. DEBT	= DEBT(– 1) + BOW
4. CASH	= CASH(– 1) + CC + BOW + EARN – CD – LP
5. BOW	= MBAL – CASH

Earnings (EARN) in equation 2 is defined as sales revenue (REV) minus CGS, OE, interest expense (INT), TAX, and dividend payment (DIV). INT is a percentage interest rate on total debt in equation 1. Total debt in equation 3 is equal to the previous period's debt (DEBT(– 1)) plus new borrowings (BOW). New debt is the difference between a minimum cash balance (MBAL) minus cash in equation 5. The ending cash balance in equation 4 is defined as the sum of the beginning balance (CASH (– 1)), cash collections, new borrowings, and earnings minus cash disbursements and loan payments of the existing debt (LP). Even though the model presented here is a simple variety, it is still simultaneous in nature, which requires the use of a method capable of solving simultaneous equations. Very few of the financial modeling languages have the capability to solve this kind of system.

Decision Rules. The financial model may, in addition to the ones previously discussed (e.g., definitional equations and behavioral equations), include basic decision rules specified in a very general form. The decision rules are not written in the form of conventional equations. They are described algebraically using conditional operators, consisting of statements of the type: "IF . . . THEN . . . ELSE." For example, the decision rule "If X is greater than 0, then Y is set equal to X multiplied by 5. Otherwise, Y is set equal to 0" is expressed as follows:

$$Y = \text{IF } X \text{ GT } 0 \text{ THEN } X*5 \text{ ELSE } 0$$

Suppose the company wishes to develop a financing decision problem based upon alternative sales scenarios. To determine an optimal financing alternative, managers might want to incorporate some decision rules into the model for a what-if or sensitivity analysis. Some examples of these decision rules are:

- The amount of dividends paid is determined on the basis of targeted earnings available to common stockholders and a maximum dividend pay-out ratio specified by management.

- After calculating the external funds needed to meet changes in assets as a result of increased sales, dividends, and maturing debt, the amount of long-term debt to be floated is selected on the basis of a prespecified leverage ratio.

- The amount of equity financing to be raised is chosen on the basis of funds needed that are not financed by new long-term debt, but it is constrained by the responsibility to meet minimum dividend payments.

In the model just described, simultaneity is quite evident. A sales figure is used to generate earnings and this in turn leads to, among other items, the level of long-term debt required. Yet the level of debt affects the interest expense incurred within the current period and, therefore, earnings. Furthermore, as earnings are affected, so is the price at which new shares are issued, the number of shares to be sold, and, thus, earnings per share. Earnings per share then "feeds back" into the stock price calculation.

Lagged Model Structure. Lagged model structure is common in financial modeling. Virtually all balance sheet equations or identities are of this type. For example:

Capital = capital(-1) + net income + contributions − cash dividends

More interestingly,

$$CC = a*SALES + b*SALES(-1) + c*SALES(-2)$$

where:

CC = cash collections from customers

a = percent received in the month of sale

b = percent received in the month following sale

c = percent received in the second month following sale

This indicates that the realization of cash lags behind credit sales. Exhibit 20-3 illustrates a sample financial (budgeting) model.

Exhibit 20-3: A Corporate Financial Model

Balance Sheet Equation

$$Cash_t = Cash_{t-1} + Cash\ receipts_t - Cash\ disbursements_t$$

$$\text{Accounts receivable}_t = (i-a)\ \text{Sales} + (1-b-a)\ \text{Sales}_{t-1} + (1-c-b-a)\ \text{Sales}_{t-2}$$

$$\text{Inventory}_t = \text{Inventory}_{t-1} + \text{Inventory purchase}_t$$

$$-\text{Variable cost per unit}\left(\frac{\text{Sales}_t}{\text{Selling price per unit}}\right)$$

Plant = Initial value

Accounts payable$_t$ = (m) Variable selling/administrative expenses$_{t-1}$

+ (n) Variable selling/administrative expenses$_t$

+ Inventory purchase$_t$ + Fixed expenses$_t$

Bank loan$_t$ = Bank loan$_{t-1}$ + Loan, − Loan repayment$_t$

Common stock = Initial value

Retained earnings$_t$ = Retained earnings$_{t-1}$ + Net income$_t$

Income Statement and Cash Flow Equations

Cash receipts$_t$ = (a) Sales$_t$ + (b) Sales$_{t-1}$ + (c) Sales$_{t-2}$ + Loan$_t$

Cash disbursements$_t$ = Accounts payable$_{t-1}$ + Interest$_t$ + Loan repayments$_t$

Inventory purchase$_t$ [≥0] = Variable cost per unit

$$\left(\frac{\text{Sales}_t + \text{Sales}_{t-1}^t + \text{Sales}_{t-2} + \text{Sales}_{t-3}}{\text{Selling price per unit}} \right) - \text{Inventory}_{t-1}$$

Interest$_t$ = (*i*) Bank loan$_t$

$$\text{Variable cost of sales}_t = \text{Sales}_t \left(\frac{\text{Variable cost per unit}}{\text{Selling price per unit}} \right)$$

Variable selling/administrative expenses$_t$ + (*v*) Sales$_t$

Net income before taxes$_t$ = Sales$_t$ – Variable cost of sales$_t$

+ Variable selling/administrative expenses$_t$

– Fixed expenses$_t$ – Depreciation$_t$

Tax expense$_t$ [≥0] = (*t*) Net income before taxes$_t$

Net income$_t$ = Net income before taxes$_t$ – Tax expenses$_t$

Input variable (dollars)

Sales$_{t-1, t-2, t-3}$

Loan$_t$

Loan repayment$_t$

Fixed expense$_t$

Depreciation$_t$

Selling price per unit

Variable cost per unit

Input Parameters

Accounts receivable collection patterns

a—Percent received within current period

b—Percent received with one-period lag

c—Percent received with two-period lag

$$a + b + c < 1$$

Lag in accounts payable cash flow

m—Percent paid from previous period

n—Percent paid from current period

$$m + n = 1$$

t = Tax rate

i = Interest rate

v = Variable selling/administrative expense ratio to sales

Initial values (dollars)

Plant

Common stock

$Cash_{t-1}$

$Sales_{t-1, t-2}$

$Inventory_{t-1}$

$Retained\ earnings_{t-1}$

$Bank\ loan_{t-1}$

$Variable\ selling/administrative\ expenses_{t-1}$

$Accounts\ payable_{t-1}$

Assumptions: time interval equals one month; accounts payable paid in full in next period; no lag between inventory purchase and receipt of goods; and no dividends paid.

USE OF A SPREADSHEET PROGRAM AND SOFTWARE FOR BUDGETING

Budgeting and profit planning can be done using a microcomputer with a powerful spreadsheet program, such as Excel. Or it can be done using specific financial modeling software, such as Centage's Budget Maestro.

Spreadsheet Programs

This section discusses how to use spreadsheet programs, such as Excel. Three examples of projecting an income statement are presented.

EXAMPLE 13: Sales for the first month of XYZ Company are $60,000. The cost of sales is 42% of sales, all variable. Operating expenses are $10,000 fixed plus 5% of sales; taxes equal 30% of net income; and sales increase by 5% each month. Based on this information, Exhibit 20-4 presents a spreadsheet for the contribution income statement for the next 12 months and in total. Exhibit 20-5 shows the same spreadsheet, assuming that sales increase by 10% and operating equal $10,000 plus 10% of sales; this is an example of what-if scenarios.

EXAMPLE 14: Delta Gamma Company wishes to prepare a three-year projection of net income. The 2X14 base year amounts are as follows:

Sales revenues	$4,500,000
Cost of sales	2,900,000
Selling and administrative expenses	800,000
Net income before taxes	800,000

Exhibit 20-4: A Projected Income Statement

	1	2	3	4	5	6	7	8	9	10	11	12	Total	Percentage
Sales	$60,000	$63,000	$66,150	$69,458	$72,930	$76,577	$80,406	$84,426	$88,647	$93,080	$97,734	$102,620	$955,028	100%
Less: VC Cost of sales	$25,200	$26,460	$27,783	$29,172	$30,631	$32,162	$33,770	$35,459	$37,232	$39,093	$41,048	$43,101	$401,112	42%
Operating ex.	$3,000	$3,150	$3,308	$3,473	$3,647	$3,829	$4,020	$4,221	$4,432	$4,654	$4,887	$5,131	$47,751	5%
CM	$31,800	$33,390	$35,060	$36,812	$38,653	$40,586	$42,615	$44,746	$46,983	$49,332	$51,799	$54,389	$506,165	53%
Less: FC Op. expenses	$10,000	$10,000	$10,000	$10,000	$10,000	$10,000	$10,000	$10,000	$10,000	$10,000	$10,000	$10,000	$120,000	13%
Net income	$21,800	$23,390	$25,060	$26,812	$28,653	$30,586	$32,615	$34,746	$36,983	$39,332	$41,799	$44,389	$386,165	40%
Less: Tax	$6,540	$7,017	$7,518	$8,044	$8,596	$9,176	$9,785	$10,424	$11,095	$11,800	$12,540	$13,317	$115,849	12%
NI after tax	$15,260	$16,373	$17,542	$18,769	$20,057	$21,410	$22,831	$24,322	$25,888	$27,533	$29,259	$31,072	$270,315	28%

Exhibit 20-5: A Projected Income Statement—What-If Scenario

	1	2	3	4	5	6	7	8	9	10	11	12	Total	Percentage
Sales	$60,000	$66,000	$72,600	$79,860	$87,846	$96,631	$106,294	$116,923	$128,615	$141,477	$155,625	$171,187	$1,283,057	134%
Less: VC														
Cost of sales	$25,200	$27,720	$30,492	$33,541	$36,895	$40,585	$44,643	$49,108	$54,018	$59,420	$65,362	$71,899	$538,884	56%
Operating ex.	$6,000	$6,600	$7,260	$7,986	$8,785	$9,663	$10,629	$11,692	$12,862	$14,148	$15,562	$17,119	$64,153	7%
CM	$28,800	$31,680	$34,848	$38,333	$42,166	$46,383	$51,021	$56,123	$61,735	$67,909	$74,700	$82,170	$615,867	64%
Less: FC														
Op. expenses	$10,000	$10,000	$10,000	$10,000	$10,000	$10,000	$10,000	$10,000	$10,000	$10,000	$10,000	$10,000	$120,000	13%
Net income	$18,800	$21,680	$24,848	$28,333	$32,166	$36,383	$41,021	$46,123	$51,735	$57,909	$64,700	$72,170	$495,867	52%
Less: Tax	$5,640	$6,504	$7,454	$8,500	$9,650	$10,915	$12,306	$13,837	$15,521	$17,373	$19,410	$21,651	$148,760	16%
NI after tax	$13,160	$15,176	$17,394	$19,833	$22,516	$25,468	$28,715	$32,286	$36,215	$40,536	$45,290	$50,519	$347,107	36%

The following assumptions are used:

- Sales revenues increase by 6% in 2X15, 7% in 2X16, and 8% in 2X17.
- Cost of sales increase by 5% each year.
- Selling and administrative expenses increase only 1% in 2X15 and will remain at the 2X16 level thereafter.
- The income tax rate = 46%.

A spreadsheet for the income statement for the next three years follows.

	2X14	*2X15*	*2X16*	*2X17*
Sales	$4,500,000	$4,770,000	$5,103,900	$5,512,212
Cost of sales	$2,900,000	$3,045,000	$3,197,250	$3,357,113
Gross margin	$1,600,000	$1,725,000	$1,906,650	$2,155,100
Selling, general & administrative expenses	$ 800,000	$ 808,000	$ 808,000	$ 808,000
Earnings before tax	$ 800,000	$ 917,000	$1,098,650	$1,347,100
Income tax	$ 368,000	$ 421,820	$ 505,379	$ 619,666
Earnings after tax	$ 432,000	$ 495,180	$ 593,271	$ 727,434

Budgeting Software

According to *2004 Budgeting and Forecasting Survey Report of KPMG*, spreadsheets are the technology mainstay for most companies (85%), and about half use more than one tool—which may impede integration of budget-oriented data. However, in recent years, the focus has been on moving away from spreadsheets to enterprise budgeting applications in order to make the planning and budgeting process more efficient and the data more reliable. The underlying process, however, remains fundamentally unchanged—it is still about capturing and consolidating line item expenses. Several popular budgeting applications are described briefly in the paragraphs that follow.

Budget Maestro and Planning Maestro. Centage's Budget Maestro (www.centage.com) guides the financial executive through budgeting, planning, modeling, forecasting, resource management, consolidation, analysis, and reporting. With Budget Maestro, CFOs and budget managers can plan, analyze, and manage, in new ways, at a user's screen and make changes directly without ever being there; deliver budget models and deploy reconfigured software updates to many users at once; and manage budgetary information, even enterprise-wide information systems, with a single consistent interface. As an alternative to spreadsheets, Budget Maestro automates many of the complex and repetitive tasks in the budgeting process while eliminating the need for creating complicated formulas and manual consolidation of multiple worksheets.

Microsoft Dynamics. This is Web-based budgeting and planning solution from MS (www.microsoft.com) that helps organizations perform the ongoing dynamics budgeting and planning processes necessary to keep business performance on target, and avoid financial surprises and consequent sacrifices that negatively affect strategic objectives.

Host Budget. Host Budget (www.hostanalytics.com) is an integrated budgeting and planning software that provides streamlined budgeting, forecasting, reporting, and analysis. Modules are used to automatically manage, consolidate, and change information for planning and replanning. The modules included with Host's performance measurement scorecard are SG&A budgeting, human resources budgeting, sales and operation planning, capital expenditure budgeting, and sales forecasting. Host Budget is designed for the Web so that users can either work online, directly with the database, for queries and updates or work offline and easily upload the Excel file later or submit it via e-mail.

Because of the streamlined effects of Host Budget on an organization's budgeting process, budgets and forecasts can be refined on an ongoing basis. Managers can consider what has happened so far and can regularly look into the future aided by actual versus budgeted information, along with current forecast projections, in their effort to meet financial goals. Executive Managers can create top-down budgets and "push down" the budget to lower levels of the organization. Line managers and department heads can create budgets from the bottom up and submit budgets for approval.

SAP BusinessObjects Budgeting and Consolidation. BusinessObjects Budgeting (www.sap.com) leverages the power of Microsoft Excel embedded in an enterprise application to create detailed, flexible plans and budgets. It improves accountability, reduces cycle time, and facilitates top-down adjustments.

The Latest Generation of Budgeting and Planning Software

The new budgeting and planning (B & P) software represents a giant step forward for financial managers. Finance managers can use these robust, Web-enabled programs to scan a wide range of data, radically speed up the planning process, and identify managers who have failed to submit budgets. More often known as active financial planning software, these packages include applications and the new level of functionality that combine budgeting, forecasting analytics, business intelligence, and collaboration. Exhibit 20-6 lists popular B&P software.

Exhibit 20-6: Active Financial Planning Software—Next-Generation Budgeting and Planning Software.

Companies	Websites	Software
ActiveStrategy	www.activestrategy.com	ActiveStrategy Enterprise
Actuate	www.actuate.com	e.Reporting Suite
IBM Cognos	www.cognos.com	Cognos Finance, Cognos Visualizer, Cognos Enterprise, Business Intelligence
Rocket CorVu	www.rocketsoftware.com	CorPlanning, CorStrategy, CorBusiness, CorPortfolio
Epicor	www.epicor.com	Epicor e.Intelligence Suite
Infor	www.geac.com	Infor Smartstream Financials, Enterprise Solutions Expert Series, FRx
Lawson Software	www.lawson.com	Enterprise Budgeting SEA Applications—including E-Scorecard; Analytic Extensions
Oracle	www.oracle.com	Oracle Strategic Enterprise Management (SEM), Hyperion Planning
SAP	www.sap.com	SAP Strategic Enterprise Management (SEM), SAP Financial Analyzer Business Intelligence with mySAP.com
SAS Institute	www.sas.com	SAS Total Financial Management, Strategic Vision, SAS/Warehouse Administrator, SAS Enabling Technology (OLAP), SAS BusinessObjects Portfolio, Oros Products
Silvon	www.silvon.com	Stratum

CONSTRUCTION OF A ROLLING BUDGET

A *rolling budget*, often called a *continuous* or *perpetual budget*, is a 12-month (four-quarter) budget that rolls forward one month (or quarter) as the current month (or quarter) is completed. In other words, one month (or quarter) is added to the end of the budget as each month (or quarter) comes to a close. This approach keeps managers focused at least one year ahead so that they do not become too narrowly focused on short-term results.

In addition, markets are changing so fast that the traditional budget is often out of date within weeks of its publication. Many companies adopt a rolling-forecast process so that budget allocations can be constantly adjusted to meet changing market conditions and increased uncertainty. In fact, an increasing number of companies are abandoning the annual plan or budget in favor of rolling forecasts. A 2011 Key Issues Study by the Hackett Group (www.thehackettgroup.com/re-search/key2011nafn and www.cfo.com/article.cfm/14570220/ c_14570395?f=magazine_coverstory) attributes this trend to the increase in various forms of economic volatility—from pre-financial crisis to post-financial crisis. Exhibit 20-7 lists these forms of economic volatility.

Exhibit 20-7: Forms of Economic Volatility

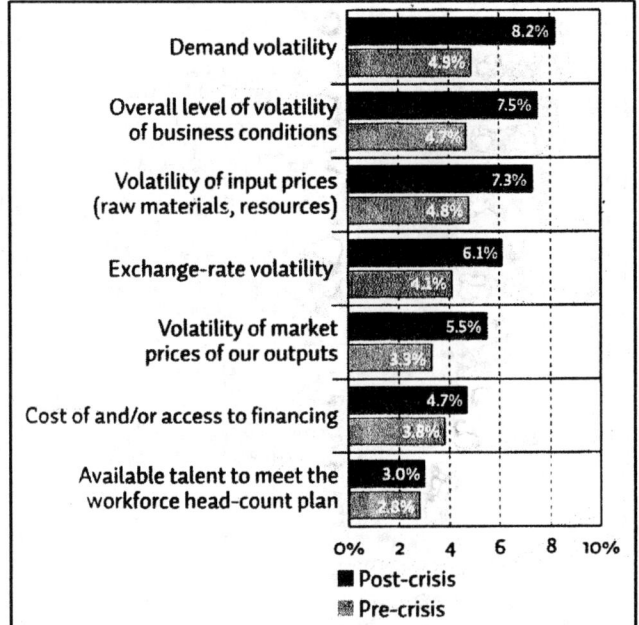

Source: The Hackett Group—A 2011 Key Issues Study.

Moreover, because budgets are typically used to control and evaluate the performance of managers, they are subject to considerable gaming behavior that tends to reduce their accuracy and usefulness. Because the rolling forecasts of financial results are not used to control spending or to evaluate managers' performance, managers have little incentive to game the system, and hence the forecasts are more accurate than those obtained through the traditional budgeting process. Example 3 illustrates how rolling budgeting plans work.

EXAMPLE 15: Handy Retail Company uses a rolling profit plan covering a six-month period. The plan is revised monthly. Summary budget plan data for one six-month period are shown in Exhibit 20-8.

Exhibit 20-8: Six-Month Budget (March through August)

	March	April	May	June	July	August	Total
Sales	$210,000	$216,000	$224,000	$208,000	$190,000	$180,000	$1,228,000
Cost of goods sold	84,000	86,400	89,600	83,200	76,000	72,000	$491,200
Gross margin	126,000	129,600	134,400	124,800	114,000	108,000	$736,800
Selling expenses	52,000	53,000	55,000	51,000	49,000	47,000	307,000
G&A expenses	26,000	27,000	27,000	25,000	24,000	24,000	153,000
Operating income	48,000	49,600	52,400	48,800	41,000	37,000	276,800
Interest expenses	1,000	1,000	1,200	1,200	900	900	6,200
Income (before taxes)	47,000	48,600	51,200	47,600	40,100	36,100	270,600
Income taxes (40%)	18,800	19,440	20,480	19,040	16,040	14,440	108,240
Net income	$28,200	$29,160	$30,720	$28,560	$24,060	$21,660	$162,360

The month of March has just ended. Therefore, the March column will be dropped and a column for September will be added. In conformity with company planning procedures, the following decision inputs are developed by the management and given to the budget director:

1. Marketing departments revised estimates: Sales-April, $220,000; May, $225,000; June, $210,000; July, $192,000; August, $182,000; September, $195,000. Selling expense- September estimate, $50,100.

2. Executive vice-president's estimates—G&A expenses for September, $25,000; no changes in prior months.

3. Treasurer's estimates-interest expenses for July through September, $1,100 per month.

4. Accounting department's estimates—cost of goods sold (CGS) will stay at 40% for the new budget, for each month; September CGS estimate, $78,000.

Based on the concept of rolling budgeting, a revised profit plan can be prepared, incorporating the new plans (estimates), as shown in Exhibit 20-9.

Exhibit 20-9: Revised Six-Month Rolling Budget (April through September)

	April	May	June	July	August	September	Total
Sales	$220,000	$225,000	$210,000	$192,000	$182,000	$195,000	$1,224,000
Cost of goods sold	88,000	90,000	84,000	76,800	72,800	78,000	$489,600
Gross margin	132,000	135,000	126,000	115,200	109,200	117,000	$734,400
Selling expenses	53,000	55,000	51,000	49,000	47,000	50,100	305,100
G&A expenses	27,000	27,000	25,000	24,000	24,000	25,000	152,000
Operating income	52,000	53,000	50,000	42,200	38,200	41,900	277,300
Interest expenses	1,000	1,000	1,200	1,100	1,100	1,100	6,500
Income (before taxes)	51,000	52,000	48,800	41,100	37,100	40,800	270,800
Income taxes (40%)	20,400	20,800	19,520	16,440	14,840	16,320	108,320
Net income	$30,600	$31,200	$29,280	$24,660	$22,260	$24,480	$162,480

CHAPTER 21

USING VARIANCE ANALYSIS AS A FINANCIAL TOOL

CONTENTS

A standard cost is a predetermined cost of manufacturing, servicing, or marketing an item during a given future period. It is based on current and projected future conditions. The norm is also dependent upon quantitative and qualitative measurements. Standards may be based on engineering studies looking at time and motion. Although the development of standards is primarily the responsibility of the industrial engineer, the managerial accountant should work closely with the engineer to ensure that the formulated standard is accurate and useful for control purposes.

Standards are set at the beginning of the period. They may be in physical and dollar terms. Standards assist in the measurement of both effectiveness and efficiency. Examples are sales quotas, standard costs (e.g., material price and wage rate), and standard volume. Variances are not independent, so a favorable variance in one responsibility area may result in an unfavorable one in other segments of the business.

Variance analysis compares standard to actual performance. It could be done by department, program, or cost center. When more than one department is used in a production process, individual standards should be developed for each department in order to assign accountability to department managers. Variances may be as detailed as necessary considering the cost/benefit relationship. Evaluation of variances may be done yearly, quarterly, monthly, daily, or hourly, depending on the importance of identifying a problem quickly. Because actual figures (e.g., hours spent) are not known until the end of the period, variances can be determined only at this time. A material variance requires highlighting who is responsible and taking corrective action. Insignificant variances need not be looked into further unless they recur repeatedly or reflect potential difficulty. Generally, a variance should be investigated when the inquiry is expected to result in corrective action that will reduce costs by an amount exceeding the cost of the inquiry.

When the production cycle is long, variances that are computed at the time of product completion may be too late for prompt corrective action to be taken. In such a case, inspection may be undertaken at "key" points during the processing stage. This allows for spoilage, labor inefficiency, and other costs associated with problems to be recognized before product completion.

One measure of materiality is to divide the variance by the standard cost. A variance of less than 5% may be deemed immaterial. A 10% variation may be more acceptable to a company using tight standards than 5% variation to a company employing loose standards. In some cases, materiality is looked at in terms of dollar amount or volume level. For example, the financial executive may set a policy looking into any variance that exceeds $10,000 or 20,000 units, whichever is less. Guidelines for materiality also depend upon the nature of the particular element as it affects performance and decision making. For example, where the item is critical to the future functioning of the business (e.g., critical part, promotion, repairs), limits for materiality should be such that reporting is encouraged. Further, statistical techniques can be used to ascertain the significance of cost and revenue variances. The managerial accountant must establish an acceptable range of tolerance for management (e.g., percent). Even if a variance never exceeds a minimum allowable percentage or minimum dollar amount, the managerial accountant may want to bring it to management's attention if the variance is consistently close to the prescribed limit each year. Perhaps this may indicate the standard is out of date and proper adjustment to current levels is mandated so as to improve overall profit planning. It could also indicate lax cost control requiring a check by the supervisor as to operations. Because of the critical nature of costs such as advertising and maintenance, materiality guidelines are more stringent.

Often, the reason for the variance is out-of-date standards or a poor budgetary process. Thus, it may not be due to actual performance. By questioning the variances and trying to find answers, the managerial accountant can make the operation more efficient and less costly. It must be understood, however, that quality should be maintained. If a variance is out of management's control, follow-up action by management is not called for. For instance, utility rates are not controllable internally.

Standards may change at different operational volume levels. Further, standards should be periodically appraised, and when they no longer realistically reflect conditions, they should be modified. Standards may not be realistic any longer because of internal events (e.g., product design) or external conditions, such as management and competitive changes. Standards should be revised, for example, when prices, material specifications, product designs, labor rates, labor efficiency, and production methods change to such a degree that present standards no longer provide a useful measure of performance. Changes in the methods or channels of distribution, or basic organizational or functional changes, would require changes in selling and administrative activities.

Note: Significant favorable variances should also be investigated and should be further taken advantage of. Those responsible for good performance should be rewarded.

For variable and semivariable costs, the accuracy of standards developed depends on the ability of the method to measure the correlation between cost incurrence and output bases. Regression analysis may provide reliable association.

Variances are interrelated and, hence, the net effect has to be examined. For example, a favorable price variance may arise when lower-quality materials are bought at a cheaper price, but the quantity variance will be unfavorable because more production time is required to manufacture the goods from poor-quality material.

In the case of automated manufacturing facilities, standard cost information can be integrated with the computer that directs operations. Variances can then be identified and reported by the computer system and necessary adjustments made as the operation proceeds.

In appraising variances, consideration should be given to information that may have been, for whatever reason, omitted from the reports. Have there been changes in the production processes that have not been reflected in the reports? Have new product lines increased setup times that necessitate changes in the standards?

USEFULNESS OF VARIANCE ANALYSIS

Standards, and variance analyses resulting therefrom, are essential in financial analysis and decision making.

Advantages of Standards and Variances

The advantages of standards and variances are as follows:

- Aid in inventory costing.
- Assist in decision making.
- Facilitate selling price formulation based on what costs should be.
- Aid in coordinating by having all departments focus on common goals.
- Facilitate setting and evaluation of corporate objectives.
- Aid in cost control and performance evaluation by comparing actual to budgeted figures. The objective of cost control is to produce an item at the lowest possible cost according to predetermined quality standards.
- Highlight problem areas through the "management by exception" principle.
- Pinpoint responsibility for undesirable performance so that corrective action may be taken. Variances in product activity (cost, quality, quantity) are typically the supervisor's responsibility. Variances in sales orders and market share are often the responsibility of the marketing manager. Variances in prices and methods of deliveries are the responsibility of purchasing personnel. Variances in profit usually relate to overall operations. Variances in return on investment relate to asset utilization.
- Help in motivating employees to accomplish predetermined goals.

- Facilitate communication within the organization such as between top management and supervisors.
- Assist in planning by forecasting needs (e.g., cash requirements).
- Establish bid prices on contracts.
- Simplify bookkeeping procedures by keeping the records at standard cost.

Standard costing is not without some drawbacks (e.g., the possible biases in deriving standards and the dysfunctional effects of establishing improper norms and standards).

When a variance has multiple causes, each cause should be cited.

STANDARD SETTING

Standards may be set by such individuals as engineers, production managers, purchasing managers, personnel administrators, and managerial accountants. Depending on the nature of the cost item, computerized models can be used to corroborate what the standard costs should be. Standards may be established through test runs or mathematical and technological analysis.

Standards are based on the particular situation being appraised. Some examples follow.

Situation	Standard
Cost reduction	Tight
Pricing policy	Realistic
High-quality goods	Perfection

Capacity may be expressed in such terms as units, weight, size, dollars, selling price, and direct labor hours. It may be expressed in different time periods (e.g., weekly, monthly, yearly).

Types of Standards

The four types of standards are as follows:

1. *Basic.* These are not changed from period to period and are used in the same way as an index number. They form the basis to which later period performance is compared. What is unrealistic about it is that no consideration is given to a change in the environment.

2. *Maximum efficiency.* These are perfect standards assuming ideal, optimal conditions, allowing for no losses of any kind even those considered unavoidable. They will always result in unfavorable variances. Realistically, certain inefficiencies will occur, such as materials not always arriving at work stations on time and tools breaking. Ideal standards cannot be used in forecasting and planning because they do not provide for normal inefficiencies.

3. *Currently attainable (practical).* These refer to the volume of output possible if a facility operated continuously, but after allowing for normal and unavoidable losses such as vacations, holidays, and repairs. Currently

attainable standards are based on efficient activity. They are possible, but difficult to achieve. Considered are normal occurrences such as anticipated machinery failure and normal materials shortage. Practical standards should be set high enough to motivate employees and low enough to permit normal interruptions. Besides pointing to abnormal deviations in costs, practical standards may be used in forecasting cash flows and in planning inventory. Attainable standards are typically used in practice.

4. *Expected.* These are expected figures based on foreseeable operating conditions and costs. They come very close to actual figures.

Standards should be set at a level that is realistic to accomplish. Those affected by the standards should participate in formalizing them so there will be internalization of goals. When reasonable standards exist, employees typically become cost conscious and try to accomplish the best results at the least cost. If standards are too tight, they will discourage employee performance. If they are too loose, they will result in inefficient operations. If employees receive bonuses for exceeding normal standards, the standards may be even more effective as motivation tools.

A standard is not an absolute and precise figure. Realistically, a standard constitutes a range of possible acceptable results. Thus, variances can and do occur within a normal upper-lower limit. In determining tolerance limits, relative magnitudes are more important than absolute values. For instance, if the standard cost for an activity is $100,000, a plus or minus range of $4,000, may be tolerable.

Variance analysis is usually complicated by the problem of computing the number equivalent units of production.

Variances may be controllable, partly controllable, or uncontrollable. It is not always easy to assign responsibility even in the case of controllable variances. The extent to which a variance is controllable depends on the nature of the standard, the cost involved, and the particular factors causing the variance.

> **EXAMPLE 1:** Manufacturing, service, food, and not-for-profit entities use standards (costs or quantities) to some degree. For instance, auto service centers establish labor time standards for the completion of certain tasks, such as for a tune-up, and then measure actual results against the standards. Fastfood stores (e.g., Burger King) have standards as to the amount of meat for a sandwich, as well as standards for the cost of the meat. Hospitals have standards (e.g., food, laundry) for each patient per day, as well as standard times to perform certain typical activities, such as laboratory testing.

PLANNING VARIANCE

The planning variance arises when expected industry or other environmental factors do not materialize. For example, at the beginning of the period, the sales projection may be based on reviewing supply and demand. However, because of actual conditions in the industry, the actual sales may be much less. This sales unit variance may then be deemed a planning error, and not a performance problem. Industry sales are typically considered beyond management control.

SALES VARIANCES

Sales standards may be established to control and measure the effectiveness of the marketing operations as well as for other relevant purposes such as stimulating sales, reallocating sales resources, and providing incentive awards. The usual standard set for a salesperson, branch, or territory is a sales quota. The sales quota, typically expressed in dollars, may also be expressed in volume. Other types of standards that may be set to evaluate sales efforts are number of calls, order size, gross profit obtained, new customers obtained, and number of regular customers retained.

Sales variances are computed to gauge the performance of the marketing function.

EXAMPLE 2:

Western Corporation's budgeted sales for 2X15 were:

Product A 10,000 units at $6.00 per unit	$ 60,000
Product B 30,000 units at $8.00 per unit	240,000
Expected sales revenue	$300,000
Actual sales for the year were:	
Product A 8,000 units at $6.20 per unit	$ 49,600
Product B 33,000 units at $7.70 per unit	254,100
Actual sales revenue	$303,700

There is a favorable sales variance of $3,700, consisting of the sales price variance and the sales volume variance.

The sales price variance =
(Actual selling price versus budgeted selling price) × Actual units sold

Product A ($6.20 versus $6.00 × 8,000)	$ 1,600	Favorable
Product B ($7.70 versus $8.00 × 33,000)	9,900	Unfavorable
Sales price variance	$ 8,300	Unfavorable

The sales volume variance =
(Actual quantity versus budgeted quantity) × Budgeted selling price

Product A (8,000 versus 10,000 × $6.00)	$12,000	Unfavorable
Product B (33,000 versus 30,000 × $8.00)	24,000	Favorable
Sales volume variance	$12,000	Favorable

The sales price variance indicates if the product is being sold at a discount or premium. Sales price variances may be due to uncontrollable market conditions or managerial decisions. However, a sales price variance is not recorded in the books.

The analysis of sales volume includes consideration of budgets, standards, sales plans, industry comparisons, and manufacturing costs. High sales volume does not automatically mean high profits. There may be high costs associated with the products.

An unfavorable sales volume variance may arise from poor marketing or from price cuts by competing companies. If the unfavorable volume variance is coupled with a favorable price variance, a company may have lost sales by raising its prices.

The sales volume variance reflects the effect on the total budgeted contribution margin that is caused by changes in the total number of units sold. The variance can be caused by unpredictable product demand, lack of product demand, or from poor sales forecasting. The sales volume variance is not recorded in the accounts.

An unfavorable total sales variance may signal a problem with the marketing manager because he or she has control over sales, advertising, and often pricing. Another possible cause of the unfavorable sales situation may be a lack in quality control, substitution of poorer quality components due to deficient purchasing, or deficient product design emanating from poor engineering.

The sales variances (price and volume) are prepared only for the product sales report and the sales district report.

The sales vice president is responsible for sales variances and must explain deviations to the president.

COST VARIANCES

When a product is made or a service is performed, the following three measures must be determined:

1. Actual cost equals actual price times actual quantity, where actual quantity equals actual quantity per unit of work times actual units of work produced.

2. Standard cost equals standard price times standard quantity, where standard quantity equals standard quantity per unit of work times actual units of work produced.

3. Total (control) variance equals actual cost less standard cost. Total (control) variance has the following elements:

   a. Price (rate, spending) variance:

      (Standard Price versus Actual Price) × Actual Quantity

   b. Quantity (usage, efficiency) variance:

      (Standard Quantity versus Actual Quantity) × Standard Price

These are computed for both material and labor.

Exhibit 21-1 depicts the variance analysis. A variance is unfavorable when actual cost is higher than standard cost.

Exhibit 21-1: Variance Analysis

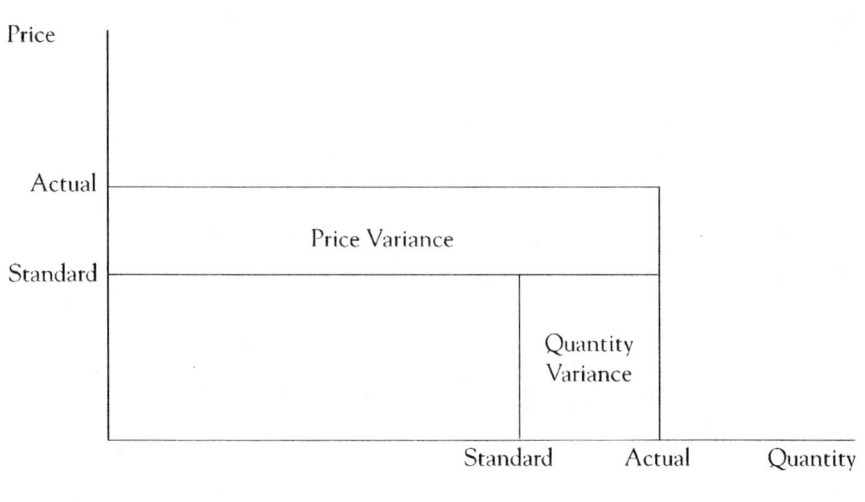

MATERIAL VARIANCES

Quantity and delivery standards have to be established before a standard price per unit can be determined. Material price standards are set by the cost accounting department and/or purchasing department because they have knowledge of price data and market conditions. The company should increase the initial standard price per unit to a standard weighted-average price per unit to incorporate expected price increases for the period. The standard price should reflect the total cost of buying the material, which includes the basic price less discounts plus freight, receiving, and handling. The standard price must coincide with the specific quality material. In setting the material price standard, the price should be in accord with the firm's inventory policies regarding the most economical order size and/or frequency of ordering. It is further assumed that buying, shipping, and warehousing will occur on favorable terms. Special bargain prices are ignored unless they are readily available. The material price standard should include normal or unavoidable spoilage allocations.

The material price variance can be used to evaluate the activity of the purchasing department and to see the impact of raw material cost changes on profitability. A material price variance may be isolated at the time of purchase or usage.

The material quantity variance is the responsibility of the production supervisor. Material quantity standards should include not only the raw materials but also purchased parts, cartons, and packing materials that are visible in, or can be directly related to, the product. Material quantity standards are basically determined from material specifications prepared by engineers based on product design and production flow. The standard quantity should be based on the most economical size and quality of product. It should be increased to take into account normal waste, rejections, and spoilage. The standard should consider prior experience for the same or similar operation. Test runs may be made under controlled conditions. Material standards may be aided by analyzing previous experiences using descriptive statistics and/or test runs under controlled conditions. Physical standards for materials are based on determination of kind and quality specifications, quantity specifications, and assembly specifications.

When many different types of raw materials are needed for a product, the types and standard quantities of each raw material are itemized on the *standard bill of materials.*

> **EXAMPLE 3:** The standard cost of one unit of output (product or service) was $15: three pieces at $5 per piece. During the period, 8,000 units were made. Actual cost was $14 per unit; two pieces at $7 per piece.

Total Material Variance

Standard quantity times standard price (24,000 × $5)	$120,000
Actual quantity times actual price (16,000 × $7)	112,000
	$ 8,000 F

Material Price Variance

(Standard price versus actual price) times actual quantity ($5 versus $7 × 16,000)	$32,000 U

Material Quantity Variance

(Standard quantity versus actual quantity) times standard price (24,000 versus 16,000 × $5)	$40,000 F

When the amount of material purchased is different from the amount issued to production, the stores account should be carried at standard cost and a price variance determined at the time of purchase. When material is issued, a quantity (usage) variance is determined. In this case, the variances are determined as follows:

Material price variance = (Actual price versus standard price) × actual quantity bought

Material quantity variance = (Actual quantity issued versus standard quantity issued) × standard price

> **EXAMPLE 4:** Material purchased was 20,000 pounds. Material issued to production was 15,000 pounds. Material budgeted per unit is one pound. Budgeted price is $2.50 per pound while actual price is $3.00 per pound. Production was 10,000 units.

Material Price Variance

(Actual price versus standard price) × quantity purchased ($3.00 versus $2.50) × 20,000	$10,000 U

Material Quantity Variance

(Actual quantity issued versus standard quantity) × standard price (15,000 versus 10,000) × $2.50	$12,500 U

Material price variances can not be controlled when higher prices are due to inflation or shortage situations, or when rush orders are required by the customer, who will bear the ultimate cost increase.

If the material price variance is favorable, one would expect higher quality material is being acquired. Thus, a favorable usage variance should be forthcoming. If it is not, there is an inconsistency. A favorable material price variance may result from other causes, such as when actual price is less than expected because of excess supply of the raw material in the industry.

The controllable portion of a price variance should be segregated from the uncontrollable in management reports. Exhibit 21-2 presents a daily material price variance report.

Exhibit 21-2: Daily Material Price Variance Report

Date ———————— Prepared by ———————— Approved by ————————

Voucher No.	Item No.	Item Name	Vendor No.	Quantity Purchased	Standard Cost		Actual Cost		Variance		Percent from Standard	Explanation
					Per Unit	Total	Per Unit	Total	Per Unit	Total		

Generally, the material quantity variance is the responsibility of the production department. However, the purchasing department will be responsible for purchasing inferior goods to economize on cost.

The reason and responsible party for an unfavorable material variance follows.

Reason	Responsible Party
Overstated price paid, failure to take discounts, improper specifications, insufficient quantities, use of a lower grade material purchased to economize on price, uneconomical size of purchased orders, failure to obtain an adequate supply of a needed variety, purchase at an irregular time, or sudden and unexpected purchase required	Purchasing
Poor mix of materials, poorly trained workers, improperly adjusted machines, substitution of nonstandard materials, poor production scheduling, poor product design or production technique, lack of proper tools or machines, carelessness in not returning excess materials to storeroom, or unexpected volume changes	Production Manager
Failure to detect defective goods	Receiveing
Inefficient labor, poor supervision, or waste on the production line	Foreman
Inaccurate standard price	Budgeting
Excessive transportation charges or too small a quantity purchased	Traffic management
Insufficient quantity bought because of lack of funds	Financial

To correct an unfavorable material price variance, consider increasing the selling price, substituting chapter materials, changing a production method or specification, or engaging in a cost reduction program.

An unfavorable price variance does not automatically mean the purchasing department is not performing well. It may point to a need for new pricing, product, or buying decisions. For these purposes, price variances may be broken down by product, vendor class, or other appropriate distinction. When several types of raw materials are used, it might be better to break down the price variance by major category of material used (e.g., steel, paint).

Tip: You should examine the variability in raw material costs. Look at price instability in trade publications. Emphasize vertical integration to reduce the price and supply risk of raw materials.

To aid in identifying material usage variances, if additional material is required to complete the job, additional materials requisitions could be issued in a different color with a distinctive code number to show that the quantity of material is above standard. This approach brings attention to the excessive usage of materials while production is in process and allows for the early control of a developing problem. When material usage is recorded by flow meters, such as in chemical operations, usage variances can be identified on materials usage forms in a similar manner as excess labor hours are identified on labor time tickets.

Managers should have the option to acquire cheaper raw materials or to combine available resources so that overall corporate costs are minimized. For instance, slightly inferior raw materials (i.e., lower grade of metals) may intentionally be purchased at a bargain price. The material price variance may thus be quite favorable. However, such raw material component may cause above average defective finished items and/or excessive productive labor hours resulting in an unfavorable efficiency variance. The manager may have permission to engage in this tradeoff if it results in a significant net reduction in total manufacturing costs. A standard cost system should not be rigid in the sense that an unfavorable variance is always regarded as bad. One should look to see if overall corporate objectives have been accomplished. Since many interdependencies exist, one should look at the entire picture rather than at just the fact that a given variance is unfavorable.

When computing material price variances, it may be good to eliminate increasing costs due to inflation, which are not controllable by management.

Illustration of How Inflationary Cost Increases May Be Isolated
from the Material Price Variance

Assume the following data for Charles Company for 2X15.

Standard price of material per foot	$3.00
Actual price of material per foot	3.80
Actual material used	10,000 ft.

The inflation rate for the year is 16%.

The direct material price variance can be broken down into the inflation aspect and the controllable element.

Price variance due to inflation
(Standard price versus inflation-adjusted price) × actual quantity
$3.00 versus $3.80 × 10,000 ft $4,800

Controllable price variance
(Inflation-adjusted price versus actual price) × actual quantity
$3.48 versus $3.80 × 10,000 ft $3,200

Proof—material price variance
(Standard price versus actual price) × actual quantity
$3.00 versus $3.80 × 10,000 ft $8,000

It is important to have prompt reporting to lower managerial levels. Production managers should immediately be informed of variances so problems are identified and corrections made at the production level.

Exhibit 21-3 presents a daily material usage report. Exhibit 21-4 presents a monthly material variance report.

Exhibit 21-3: Daily Material Usage Report

		Cost Center Material Type	Unit Date				
		Daily		Month		Year	
Date	Variance	Variance Percent	Explanation	Variance	Variance Percent	Variance	Variance Percent

Exhibit 21-4: Monthly Material Variance Report

	Month		Year to Date	
Department	Variance	Percent	Variance	Percent

LABOR VARIANCES

Standard labor rates may be computed based on the current rates adjusted for future changes in such variables as:

- Union contracts.
- Changes in operating conditions.
- Changes in the mix of skilled versus unskilled labor.
- The average experience of workers.

The wage system affects the standard cost rates. The basic rates are (1) daily or hourly, (2) straight piece rate, and (3) multiple piece rates or bonus systems. Wage incentive systems can be tied to a standard cost system once standards have been formulated.

While direct labor quantities may be obtained from engineering estimates, line supervisors can corroborate the estimates by observing and timing employees.

When salary rates are set by union contract, the labor rate variance will usually be minimal. For planning purposes, the rate standard should be the average rate expected to prevail during the planning period.

Note: Labor rates for the same operation may vary due to seniority or union agreement.

Labor time standards should include only the elements controllable by the worker or work center. If the major purpose of a cost system is control, there should be a tight labor time standard. If costing or pricing is the major purpose of the cost system, looser labor standards are needed. Labor efficiency standards are typically estimated by engineers on the basis of an analysis of the production operation. The standard time may include allowances for normal breaks, personal needs, and machine downtime.

Labor variances are determined in a manner similar to that in which material variances are determined. Labor variances are isolated when labor is used for production.

EXAMPLE 5: The standard cost of labor is 4 hours times $9 per hour, or $36 per unit. During the period, 7,000 units were produced. The actual cost is 6 hours times $8 per hour, or $48 per unit.

Total Labor Variance

Standard quantity times standard price (28,000 × $9)	$252,000
Actual quantity times actual price (42,000 × $8)	336,000
	$84,000 U

Labor Price Variance

(Standard price versus actual price) × actual quantity
($9 versus $8 × 42,000) $42,000 F

Labor Quantity Variance

(Standard quantity versus actual quantity) × standard price
(28,000 versus 42,000 × $9) $126,000 U

Possible causes of unfavorable labor variances are:

For a labor price (rate) variance:

- Increase in wages
- Poor scheduling of production resulting in overtime work
- Use of workers commanding higher hourly rates than expected

For a labor efficiency variance:

- Poor supervision
- Use of unskilled workers paid lower rates or the wrong mixture of labor for a given job
- Use of poor quality machinery
- Improperly trained workers
- Poor quality of materials requiring more labor time in processing
- Machine breakdowns
- Employee unrest
- Production delays due to power failure

Possible reasons for a labor price variance and the responsible party follow.

Reason	Responsibility Party
Use of overpaid or excessive number of Workers	Production manager or union contract
Poor job descriptions or excessive wages	Personnel
Overtime and poor scheduling of production	Production planning

In the case of a shortage of skilled workers, it may be impossible to avoid an unfavorable labor price variance.

Price variances due to external factors are beyond management control (e.g., a new minimum wage established by the government).

The cause and the responsible party for an unfavorable labor efficiency variance follow.

Cause	Responsible Party
Poor quality workers or poor training	Personnel or training
Inadequate supervision, inefficient flow of materials, wrong mixture of labor for a given job, inferior tools, or idle time from production delays	Supervisor
Employee unrest	Personnel or supvr.
Improper functioning of equipment	Maintenance
Insufficient material supply or poor quality	Purchasing

To control against an unfavorable labor efficiency variance due to inadequate materials or sales orders, a daily direct labor report should be prepared.

An unfavorable labor efficiency variance may indicate that better machinery is needed, plant layout should be revised, improved operating methods are needed, and better employee training and development are required.

If a permanent change occurs in the amount of labor required or the labor wage rate for the various types of employee help, the company may wish to switch to using more capital assets than labor.

Variances interrelate. A favorable labor efficiency variance coupled with an unfavorable labor rate variance may mean that higher skilled labor was employed than was necessary. However, the supervisor would be justified in doing this if a rush order arose in which the selling price was going to be upwardly adjusted.

Exhibit 21-5 presents a daily labor mix report. Exhibit 21-6 presents a labor performance report, a review of which aids in evaluating labor effectiveness and coming up with a revision in labor policies. A graph of weekly labor efficiency is presented in Exhibit 21-7.

OVERHEAD VARIANCES

Management is concerned with the tradeoff between fixed and variable costs. As the output level increases, the capital intensive business will be more efficient. The cost associated with a wrong decision is the variance between the total costs of operating the given plant and the total costs of operating the most efficient one based on the actual output level.

Exhibit 21-5: Daily Labor Mix Report

Department Skill Level	Actual Hours	Actual Hours in Standard Proportions	Output Variance
I			
II			
III			

Exhibit 21-6: Labor Performance Report

Department

	Day		Date	
Machine Operator	Achieved in Percent	Explanation	Month to Date in Percent	Year to Date in Percent

Overhead variances may be determined by department and by cost center. Fixed and variable overhead variances should be analyzed independently. In many firms, variances are expressed in both dollars and physical measures.

Variable Overhead Variances

The two variances associated with variable overhead are (1) price (spending) and (2) efficiency.

Variable overhead price (spending) variance =
Actual variable overhead versus budget adjusted to actual hours
(Actual hours × Standard variable overhead rate)

Variable overhead efficiency variance =
Budget adjusted to actual hours versus budget adjusted to standard hours
(Standard hours × Standard variable overhead rate)

Exhibit 21-7: Labor Efficiency by Week

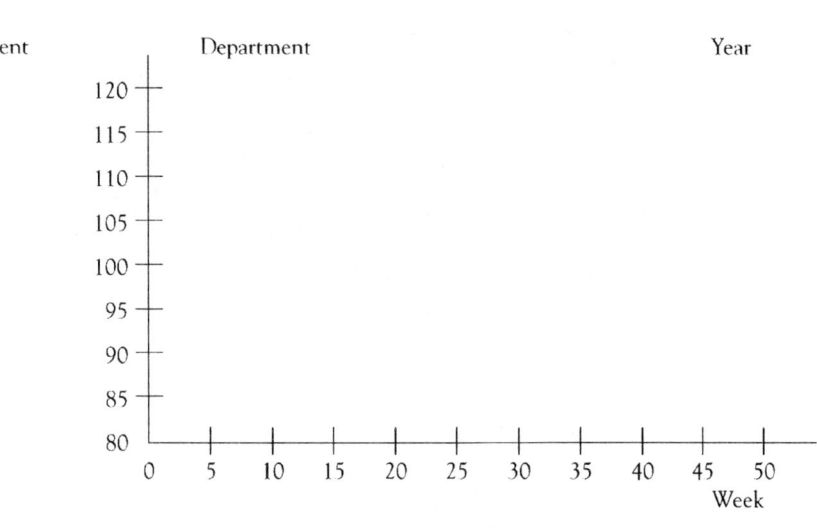

Variable overhead variance information is helpful in arriving at the output level and output mix decisions. The production department is usually responsible for any variable overhead variance that might occur. It also assists in appraising decisions regarding variable inputs.

> **EXAMPLE 6:** The standard hours are three hours per unit. The standard variable overhead rate is $12 per hour. Actual variable overhead is $13,000. There are 2,500 actual hours. Production is 1,000 units. The variable overhead variances are:

Variable Overhead Price Variance

Actual variable overhead	$13,000
Budget adjusted to actual hours (2,500 × $4)	10,000
Price variance	$ 3,000 U

Variable Overhead Efficiency Variance

Budget adjusted to actual hours	$10,000
Budget adjusted to standard hours (3,000 × $4)	12,000
Efficiency variance	$ 2,000 F

Fixed Overhead Variances

Fixed overhead may be analyzed in terms of the budget (flexible budget, spending) variance and volume (production volume) variances. The volume variance may be further broken down into the efficiency and pure volume variances.

Fixed overhead budget variance =
Actual fixed overhead versus budgeted fixed overhead
(Denominator or budget hours × Standard fixed overhead rate)

Note: Budgeted fixed overhead may also be referred to as a lump sum amount.

Fixed overhead volume variance =
Budgeted fixed overhead versus standard overhead
(Standard hours × Standard fixed overhead rate)

The breakdown of the volume variance follows:

Fixed overhead efficiency variance =
(Actual hours versus standard hours) × Standard fixed overhead rate

Fixed overhead pure volume variance =
(Actual hours versus budgeted hours) × Standard fixed overhead rate

Fixed overhead variance data provide information about decision-making astuteness when buying some combination of fixed plant size variable production inputs. However, variances for fixed overhead are of questionable usefulness for control purposes, since these variances are usually beyond the control of the production department.

The volume variance is a measure of the cost of deviating from denominator (budgeted) volume used to set the fixed overhead rate. When actual volume is less than budgeted volume, the volume variance will be unfavorable. In the opposite case, the volume variance is favorable because it is considered as a benefit of better-than-anticipated utilization of facilities.

EXAMPLE 7: Standard hours are two hours per unit. Standard fixed overhead rate is $20 per hour. Actual hours per unit are two. Total production is 9,500 units. Actual hours are 20,200. Actual fixed overhead is $420,000. The denominator activity is 10,000 units. The fixed overhead variances are:

Fixed Overhead Budget Variance

Actual fixed overhead	$420,000
Budgeted fixed overhead (10,000 × 2 = 20,000 × $20)	400,000
Budget variance	$ 20,000 U

Volume Variance

Budgeted fixed overhead	$400,000
Standard fixed overhead (9,500 × 2 = 19,000 × $20)	380,000
Volume variance	$ 20,000 U

The production volume variance of $20,000 is now broken down into the efficiency and pure volume variances.

Fixed Overhead Efficiency Variance

(Actual hours versus standard hours) × Standard fixed overhead rate	
(20,200 versus 19,000) × $20	$ 24,000 U

Fixed Overhead Pure Volume Variance

(Actual hours versus budget hours) × Standard fixed overhead rate

(20,200 versus 20,000) × $20 $ 4,000 F

Variances for Total Overhead

One-way, two-way, and three-way analysis may be used for total overhead.

One-Way Method. The total (control, net) variance is:

Total Overhead Variance

Actual overhead

Standard overhead (standard hours × standard overhead rate)

Two-Way Method. Under the two-variance method, the overhead variance comprises the controllable (budget, flexible-budget, spending) and volume (capacity, idle capacity, activity, denominator) variances.

Controllable Variance

Actual overhead

Budget adjusted to standard hours

    Fixed overhead (denominator hours × standard fixed overhead rate)

    Variable overhead (standard hours × standard variable overhead rate)

Volume (Production) Variance

Standard overhead

Budget adjusted to standard hours

The controllable (budget) variance may indicate changes in the amount charged for overhead services or in the correlation between overhead items and the variable used to measure output. If such changes are of a permanent nature, output levels may have to be revised.

Management uses the overhead budget variance as a basis for determining the extent to which the cost centers were within their budgeted cost levels. Such variances are useful in formulating decisions regarding cost center operations.

The controllable variance is the responsibility of the supervisor, since he or she influences actual overhead incurred. An unfavorable variance may be due to price increases, a lack of control over costs, and waste.

The volume variance is the responsibility of management executives and production managers, since they are involved with plant utilization. **Note:** A consistently unfavorable volume variance may be due to having purchased the incorrect size plant. An unfavorable volume variance may arise from controllable factors such as poor scheduling, lack of orders, shortages or defectiveness in raw materials, inadequate tooling, lack of employees, machine breakdowns, long operating times, and incompetent workers. Uncontrollable factors for the overhead volume variance are decrease in customer demand, excess plant capacity, and calendar fluctuations (e.g., differences in number of working days in a month).

Overhead capacity variances can bring to a manager's attention the existence of slack resources. Idle capacity may imply long-term operating planning deficiencies.

The volume of activity is often determined outside the factory based on customer orders. If this is the case, volume variances may not be controllable by the department head or even by the plant manager. They should still be reported to plant managers to help in explaining the total overhead variance to higher management.

Responsibility for the factory overhead volume variance rests with those responsible for generating volume. In some cases marketing managers, rather than manufacturing managers, bear this responsibility.

Possible reasons for a recurring unfavorable overhead volume variance are:

* Buying the wrong size plant.
* Improper scheduling.
* Insufficient orders.
* Shortages in material.
* Machinery failure.
* Long operating time.
* Inadequately trained workers.

When idle capacity exists, this may indicate long-term operating planning problems.

Note: A favorable variance may be causing an unfavorable one. For example, lower maintenance expenditures for equipment may lower the overhead budget variance, but lead to machinery breakdowns causing an unfavorable volume variance.

Three-Way Method. The three-variance method involves further analysis of the two-variance method. The three-way approach consists of the spending, efficiency, and volume variances.

Note: The volume variance is identical under the three-way and two-way approaches. The controllable variance under the two-way method is broken down into the spending and efficiency variances under the three-way method:

Spending Variance

Actual overhead

Budget adjusted to actual hours

Fixed overhead (denominator hours × standard fixed overhead rate)

Variable overhead (actual hours × standard variable overhead rate)

Efficiency Variance

Budget adjusted to actual hours

Budget adjusted to standard hours

Volume (Production) Variance

Budget adjusted to standard hours

Standard overhead

The efficiency variance is the responsibility of the supervisor and arises from inefficiencies or efficiencies in the production process. The variance is unfavorable when actual hours exceed standard hours charged to production. Inefficiencies may arise from such factors as unskilled labor, modification of operations, deficient machinery, and inferior quality materials.

Spending and efficiency variances are the responsibility of the department supervisor. The volume variance is attributable to executive management since the decision as to the degree of plant utilization rests with them. Idle capacity may be due to the lack of a proper balance between production facilities and sales. It may also arise from a favorable selling price that recovers fixed overhead at an exceptionally low production level.

EXAMPLE 8:

The standards for total overhead are:

Variable overhead 2 hrs. @ $6 = $12 per unit

Fixed overhead 2 hrs. @ $20 = $40 per unit

The actual figures are:

Production 9,500 units

Denominator activity 10,000 units

Variable overhead $115,000

Fixed overhead $420,000

Actual hours 20,200

Part 1: One-Way Analysis

Control Variance

Actual overhead ($115,000 + $420,000)	$535,000	
Standard overhead (9,500 × 2 = 19,000 × $26)	494,000	
Control variance	$41,000	U

Part 2: Two-Way Analysis

Controllable Variance

Actual overhead		$535,000	
Budget adjusted to standard hours			
Fixed overhead (10,000 × 2 = 20,000 × $20)	$400,000		
Variable overhead (19,000 × $6)	114,000		
		514,000	
Controllable variance		$21,000	U

Volume (Production) Variance

Budget adjusted to standard hours	$514,000
Standard overhead	494,000
Volume variance	$20,000 U

OR

Budgeted hours	20,000
Standard hours	19,000
Difference in hours	1,000
× Fixed overhead rate	× $20
Volume Variance	$ 20,000 U

Part 3: Three-Way Analysis
Spending Variance

Actual overhead		$535,000
Budget adjusted to actual hours		
Fixed overhead (10,000 × 2 = 20,000 × $20)	$400,000	
Variable overhead (20,200 × $6)	121,200	
		521,200
Spending Variance		$13,800 U

Efficiency Variance

Budget adjusted to actual hours	$521,200
Budget adjusted to standard hours	514,000
Efficiency variance	$7,200 U

OR

Actual hours	20,200
Standard hours	19,000
Difference in hours	1,200
× Standard variable overhead rate	× $6
Efficiency variance	$7,200 U

Volume Variance

Budget adjusted to standard hours	$514,000
Standard overhead	494,000
Volume variance	$20,000 U

Comprehensive Illustration. A comprehensive example showing all the variances for material, labor, and overhead follows.

EXAMPLE 9: The following standards are given:

		Per Unit
Direct material	5 lbs. @ $ 4 per lb.	$ 20
Direct labor	3 hrs. @ $12 per hr.	36
Variable overhead	3 hrs. @ $ 7 per hr.	21
Fixed overhead	3 hrs. @ $20 per hr.	60
		$137

Actual data are:

Production 9,800 units
Denominator (budget) activity 11,000 units
Purchases 50,000 lbs. @ $150,000
Direct material used 44,000 lbs.
Direct labor 22,000 hrs. @ $220,000
Variable overhead $125,000
Fixed overhead $450,000

Part 1: Material
Material Price Variance

(Actual price versus standard price) × Actual quantity
  bought
($3 versus $4) × 50,000 $50,000 F

Material Quantity Variance
(Actual quantity issued versus standard quantity) × Standard price
(44,000 versus 49,000) × $4 $20,000 F

Part 2: Labor
Control Variance

Standard quantity × Standard price (29,400 × $12)	$352,800
Actual quantity × Actual price (22,000 × $10)	220,000
Control variance	$132,800 F

Labor Price Variance

(Actual price versus standard price) × Actual quantity $ 44,000 F
  ($10 versus $12) × 22,000

Labor Quantity Variance
(Actual quantity versus standard quantity) × Standard price
(22,000 versus 29,400*) × $12 $ 88,800 F

(9,800 × 3 = 29,400)

Part 3: Variable Overhead
Variable Overhead Price Variance
Actual variable overhead $125,000

Budget adjusted to actual hours (22,000 × $7)	154,000	
Price variance	$ 29,000	F

Variable Overhead Efficiency Variance

Budget adjusted to actual hours	$154,000	
Budget adjusted to standard hours (9,800 × 3 = 29,400 × $7)	205,800	
Efficiency variance	$ 51,800	F

Part 4: Fixed Overhead
Fixed Overhead Budget Variance

Actual fixed overhead	$450,000	
Budgeted fixed overhead (11,000 × 3 = 33,000 × $20)	660,000	
Budget variance	$210,000	F

Fixed Overhead Volume Variance

Budgeted fixed overhead	$660,000	
Standard overhead (9,800 × 3 = 29,400 × $20)	588,000	
Volume variance	$ 72,000	U

The fixed overhead volume variance is broken down into the fixed overhead efficiency variance and fixed overhead pure volume variance.

Fixed Overhead Efficiency Variance
(Actual hours versus standard hours) × Standard fixed overhead rate

(22,000 versus 29,400) × $20	$148,000	F

Fixed Overhead Pure Volume Variance
(Actual hours versus budgeted hours) × Standard fixed overhead rate

(22,000 versus 33,000) × $20	$220,000	U

Part 5: One-Way Analysis
Total Overhead Variance

Actual overhead	$575,000	
Standard overhead (29,400 × $27)	793,800	
Total overhead variance	$218,800	F

Part 6: Two-Way Analysis
Controllable Variance

Actual overhead		$575,000	
Budget adjusted to standard hours			
Fixed overhead (11,000 × 3 = 33,000 × $20)	$660,000		
Variable overhead (9,800 × 3 = 29,400 × $7)	205,800	865,800	
Controllable variance		$290,800	F

Volume Variance

Budget adjusted to standard hours		$865,800
Standard overhead		793,800
Volume variance		72,000 U

Part 7: Three-Way Analysis

Spending Variance

Actual overhead		$575,000
Budget adjusted to actual hours		
Fixed overhead (11,000 × 3 = 33,000 × $20)	$660,000	
Variable overhead (22,000 × $7)	154,000	814,000
Spending variance		$239,000 F

Efficiency Variance

Budget adjusted to actual hours	$814,000
Budget adjusted to standard hours	865,800
Efficiency variance	$ 51,800 F

Volume Variance

Budget adjusted to standard hours	$865,800
Standard overhead	793,800
Volume variance	$ 72,000 U

DISPOSITION OF VARIANCES

Variance accounts are closed out at the end of the reporting period so that the financial statements are reflected at actual cost. Cost Accounting Standards Board requirements, applicable to defense contractors dealing with governmental units, specify that significant cost variances should be adjusted to work-in-process, finished goods, and cost of sales on a pro rata basis according to the number of units or dollars associated with these accounts. Where immaterial variances exist, cost of sales may be adjusted for the net effect of the variances. In cases where a variance is considered a managerial cost rather than a manufacturing one, a loss account may be charged.

With regard to Internal Revenue Service requirements, inventories must include an allocated portion of significant variances. If immaterial, such a method is not required unless the allocation approach has been used for book reporting. However, idle capacity variances may be expensed for tax purposes.

Variances that exist at the end of each quarter may be deferred if they are expected to reverse at year-end. If they are not, they should be disposed of immediately.

INTERRELATIONSHIP OF VARIANCES

With regard to variance analysis for all production costs (direct material, direct labor, and overhead), each variance does not represent a separate and distinct problem to be handled in isolation. All variances in one way or another are interdependent. For example, the labor rate variance may be favorable because lower-paid workers are being used. This could lead to (1) an unfavorable material usage variance because of a higher incidence of waste, (2) an unfavorable labor efficiency variance because it takes longer hours to make the equivalent number of products, (3) an unfavorable overhead efficiency variance because the substandard work causes more hours to be spent for a specified output, and (4) an unfavorable overhead volume variance arising from abnormally high machine breakdowns because of lower-skilled operators.

A tradeoff between variances may be a managerial objective. For example, a material price variance may be favorable because of a bargain purchase opportunity or because of a combination of available resources designed to save overall corporate costs. However, the raw material acquired may be somewhat inferior in quality to that which is usually purchased. In processing, use of this material may lead to greater waste or more labor hours in producing a finished item that will satisfy product quality guidelines. The company goal here may be to minimize total production costs through the tradeoff of a favorable price variance and an unfavorable quantity variance. The net effect of the variances, in this case, is what counts.

MIX AND YIELD VARIANCES FOR MATERIAL AND LABOR

Mix refers to the relative proportion of various ingredients of input factors such as materials and labor. *Yield* is a measure of productivity.

Material and Labor Mix Variances

The material mix variance indicates the impact on material costs of the deviation from the standard mix. The labor mix variance measures the impact of changes in the labor mix on labor costs.

Formulas

$$\text{Material mix variance} = \left(\begin{array}{c} \text{Actual units used at standard mix} \end{array} - \begin{array}{c} \text{Actual units used at actual mix} \end{array} \right) \times \begin{array}{c} \text{Standard unit price} \end{array}$$

$$\text{Labor mix variance} = \left(\begin{array}{c} \text{Actual firs. used at standard mix} \end{array} - \begin{array}{c} \text{Actual hrs. used at actual mix} \end{array} \right) \times \begin{array}{c} \text{Standard hourly rate} \end{array}$$

Recording Mix Variances

The material and labor mix variances are isolated and recorded when materials and labor are used for production. They are debited if they are unfavorable, credited if they are favorable.

Mix and Yield Variances

The material quantity variance is divided into a material mix variance and a material yield variance. The material mix variance measures the impact of the deviation from the standard mix on material costs, while the material yield variance reflects the impact on material costs of the deviation from the standard input material allowed for actual production. The material mix variance is computed by holding the total input units constant at their actual amount.

The material yield variance is computed by holding the mix constant at the standard amount. The computations for labor mix and yield variances are the same as those for materials. If there is no mix, the yield variance is the same as the quantity (or usage) variance.

Formulas

$$\text{Material yield variance} = \left(\begin{array}{l} \text{Actual units} \\ \text{used at} \\ \text{standard mix} \end{array} - \begin{array}{l} \text{Actual units} \\ \text{used at} \\ \text{actual mix} \end{array} \right) \times \begin{array}{l} \text{Standard} \\ \text{unit} \\ \text{price} \end{array}$$

$$\text{Labor yield variance} = \left(\begin{array}{l} \text{Actual hrs.} \\ \text{used at} \\ \text{standard mix} \end{array} - \begin{array}{l} \text{Actual hrs.} \\ \text{used at} \\ \text{actual mix} \end{array} \right) \times \begin{array}{l} \text{Standard} \\ \text{hourly} \\ \text{rate} \end{array}$$

Probable Causes of Unfavorable Mix Variances

- When capacity restraints force substitution.
- Poor production scheduling.
- Lack of certain types of labor.
- Certain materials are in short supply.

Probable Causes of Unfavorable Yield Variances

- The use of low-quality materials and/or labor.
- The existence of faulty equipment.
- The use of improper production methods.
- An improper or costly mix of materials and/or labor.

EXAMPLE 10 (Mix Variances): J Company produces a compound composed of materials Alpha and Beta which is marketed in 20-lb. bags. Material Alpha can be substituted for material Beta. Standard cost and mix data have been determined as follows:

	Unit Price	Standard Unit	Standard Mix Proportions
Material Alpha	$3	5 lbs.	25%
Material Beta	4	15	75
		20 lbs.	100%

Processing each 20 lbs. of material requires 10 hrs. of labor. The company employs two types of labor, "skilled" and "unskilled," working on two processes, assembly and finishing. The following standard labor cost has been set for a 20-lb. bag:

	Standard Hrs.	Standard Wage Rate	Total	Standard Mix Proportions
Unskilled	4 hrs.	$2	$8	40%
Skilled	6	3	18	60
	10 hrs.	$2.60	$26	100%

At standard cost, labor averages $2.60 per unit. During the month of December, 100 20-lb. bags were produced with the following labor costs:

	Actual Hrs.	Actual Rate	Actual Wages
Unskilled	380 hrs.	$2.50	$ 950
Skilled	600	3.25	1,950
	980 hrs.		$2,900

Material records show:

	Beginning Inventory	Purchase	Ending Inventory
Material Alpha	100 lbs.	800 @ $3.10	200 lbs.
Material Beta	225	1,350 @ $3.90	175

We now want to determine the following variances from standard costs:

1. Material purchase price.
2. Material mix.
3. Material quantity.
4. Labor rate.
5. Labor mix.
6. Labor efficiency.

We will show how to compute these variances in a tabular form as follows:

1. *Material Purchase Price Variance*

Material Price per Unit

	Standard	Actual	Difference	Actual Quantity Purchased	Variance ($)
Material Alpha	$3	$3.10	$.10 U	800 lbs.	$ 80 U
Material Beta	4	3.90	.10 F	1,350	135 F
					$ 55 F

2. *Material Mix Variance*

	Units That Should Have Been Used at Standard Mix*	Actual Units at Actual Mix**	Diff.	Standard Unit Price	Variance ($)
Material Alpha	525 lbs.	700 lbs.	175 U	$3	$525 U
Material Beta	1,575	1,400	175 F	4	700 F
	2,100 lbs.	2,100 lbs.			$175 F

* This is the standard mix proportions of 25% and 75% applied to the actual material units used of 2,100 lbs.

** Actual units used = Beginning inventory + Purchases – Ending inventory. Therefore,
Material Alpha: 700 lbs. = 100 + 800 – 200
Material Beta: 1,400 lbs. = 225 + 1,350 – 175

The material mix variance measures the impact on material costs of the deviation from the standard mix. Therefore, it is computed holding the total quantity used constant at its actual amount and allowing the material mix to vary between actual and standard. As shown above, due to a favorable change in mix, we ended up with a favorable material mix variance of $175.

3. *Material Quantity Variance*

	Units That Should Have Been Used at Standard Mix	Standard Units at Standard Mix	Diff.	Standard Unit Price	Variance ($)
Material Alpha	525 lbs.	500 lbs.	25 U	$3	$ 75 U
Material Beta	1,575	1,500	75 U	4	300 U
	2,100 lbs.	2,000 lbs.			$375 U

The total material variance is the sum of the three variances:

Purchase price variance	$ 55 F
Mix variance	175 F
Quantity variance	375 U
	$145 U

The increase of $145 in material costs was due solely to an unfavorable quantity variance of 100 pounds of material Alpha and Beta. The unfavorable quantity variance, however, was compensated largely by favorable mix and price variances. J Company must look for ways to cut down waste and spoilage.

The labor cost increase of $300 ($2,900 – $2,600) is attributable to three causes:

a. An increase of $.50 per hour in the rate paid to skilled labor and $.25 per hour in the rate paid to unskilled labor.

b. An unfavorable mix of skilled and unskilled labor.

c. A favorable labor efficiency variance of 20 hours.

Three labor variances are computed below.

4. *Labor Rate Variance*

Labor Rate per Hr.

	Standard	Actual	Diff.	Actual Hrs. Used	Variance ($)
Unskilled	$2	$2.50	$ .5 U	380 hrs.	$190 U
Skilled	3	3.25	.25 U	600	150 U
					$340 U

5. *Labor Mix Variance*

	Actual Hrs. at Standard Mix*	Actual Hrs. at Actual Mix	Diff.	Standard Rate	Variance ($)
Unskilled	392 hrs.	380 hrs.	12 F	$2	$24 F
Skilled	588	600	12 U	3	36 U
	980 hrs.	980 hrs.			$12 U

* This is the standard proportions of 40% and 60% applied to the actual total labor hours used of 980.

6. *Labor Efficiency Variance*

	Actual Hrs. at Standard Mix	Standard Hrs. at Standard Mix	Diff.	Standard Rate	Variance ($)
Unskilled	392 hrs.	400 hrs.	8 F	$2	$16 F
Skilled	588	600	12 F	3	36 F
	980 hrs.	1,000 hrs.			$52 F

The total labor variance is the sum of these three variances:

Rate variance	$340 U
Mix variance	12 U
Efficiency variance	52 F
	$300 U

which is proved to be:

Total Labor	Variance Actual Hrs. Used	Actual Rate	Total Actual Cost	Standard Hrs. Allowed	Standard Rate	Total Standard Cost	Variance ($)
Unskilled	380 hrs.	$2.50	$ 950	400	$2	$ 800	$150 U
Skilled	600	3.25	1,950	600	3	1,800	150 U
			$2,900			$2,600	$300 U

The unfavorable labor variance, as evidenced by the cost increase of $300, may be due to:

    a. Overtime necessary because of poor production scheduling resulting in a higher average labor cost per hour; and/or

    b. Unnecessary use of more expensive skilled labor. J Company should put more effort into better production scheduling.

    EXAMPLE 11 (Yield Variances): The Giffen Manufacturing Company uses a standard cost system for its production of a chemical product. This chemical is produced by mixing three major raw materials, A, B, and C. The company has the following standards:

36 lbs. of Material A	@	$1.00	=	$ 36.00
48 lbs. of Material B	@	2.00	=	96.00
36 lbs. of Material C	@	1.75	=	63.00
120 lbs. of standard mix	@	$1.625	=	$195.00

The company should produce 100 lbs. of finished product at a standard cost of $1.625 per lb. ($195.00/120 lbs.)

    To convert 120 pounds of materials into 100 pounds of finished chemical requires 400 DLH at $3.50 per DLH, or $14.00 per pound. During the month of December, the company produced 4,250 pounds of output with the following direct labor: 15,250 hrs.@ $3.50.

	Materials Purchased During the Month	Materials Used During the Month
Material A	1,200 @ $1.10	1,160 lbs.
Material B	1,800 @ 1.95	1,820
Material C	1,500 @ 1.80	1,480

The material price variance is isolated at the time of purchase. We want to compute the material purchase price, quantity, mix, and yield variances.

We will show the computations of variances in a tabular form as follows:

Material Purchase Price Variance

| | **Material Price per Unit** | | | | |
	Standard	**Actual**	**Diff.**	**Actual Quantity Purchased**	**Variance ($)**
Material A	$1.00	$1.10	$.10 U	1,200 lbs.	$120 U
Material B	2.00	1.95	.05 F	1,800	90 F
Material C	1.75	1.80	.05 U	1,500	75 U
					$105 U

The material quantity variance computed in the following results from changes in the mix of materials as well as from changes in the total quantity of materials. The standard input allowed for actual production consists of 1,275 pounds of Material A, 1,700 pounds of Material B, and 1,275 pounds of Material C—a total of 4,250 pounds. The actual input consisted of 1,160 pounds of Material A, 1,820 pounds of Material B, and 1,480 pounds of Material C, a total of 4,460 pounds. To separate these two changes, the material quantity variance is subdivided into a material mix variance and a material yield variance, as shown in the following.

Material Quantity Variance

	Actual Units Used at Actual Mix	**"Should Have Been" Inputs Based upon Actual Output**	**Diff.**	**Standard Unit Price**	**Variance ($)**	
Material A	1,160 lbs.	1,275 lbs.	115 F	$1.00	$115	F
Material B	1,820	1,700	120 U	2.00	240	U
Material C	1,480	1,275	205 U	1.75	358.75	U
	4,460 lbs.	4,250 lbs.			$483.75	U

The computation of the material mix variance and the material yield variance for the Giffen Manufacturing Company is as follows:

Material Mix Variance

	"Should Have Been" Individual Inputs Based upon Total Actual Throughput*	**Actual Units Used at Actual Mix**	**Diff.**	**Standard Unit Price**	**Variance ($)**	
Material A	1,338 lbs.	1,160 lbs.	178 F	$1.00	$178	F
Material B	1,784	1,820	36 U	2.00	72	U

	"Should Have Been" Individual Inputs Based upon Total Actual Throughput*	Actual Units Used at Actual Mix	Diff.	Standard Unit Price	Variance ($)	
Material C	1,338	1,480	142 U	1.75	248.5	U
	4,460 lbs.	4,460 lbs.			$142.5	U

* This is the standard mix proportions of 30%, 40%, and 30% applied to the actual material units used of 4,460 pounds.

Material Yield Variance

	Expected Input Units at Standard Mix	"Should Have Been" Inputs Based upon Actual Output*	Diff.	Standard Unit Price	Variance ($)	
Material A	1,338 lbs.	1,275 lbs.	63 U	$1.00	$63	U
Material B	1,784	1,700	84 U	2.00	168	U
Material C	1,338	1,275	63 U	1.75	110.25	U
	4,460 lbs.	4,250 lbs.			$341.25	U **

 * This is the standard mix proportions of 30%, 40%, and 30% applied to the actual throughput of 4,460 pounds or output of 4,250 pounds.

** The material yield variance of $341.25 U can be computed alternatively as follows:

Actual input quantity at standard prices

Material A	1,338 lbs.	@	$1.00	=	$1,338	
Material B	1,784 lbs.	@	2.00	=	3,568	
Material C	1,338 lbs.	@	1.75	=	2,341.5	$7,247.50

Actual output quantity at standard price

	4,250 lbs.	@	1.625			$6,906.25

Hence, $7,247.5 – $6,906.25 = $341.25 U

The material mix and material yield variances are unfavorable, indicating that a shift was made to a more expensive (at standard) input mix and that an excessive quantity of material was used. Poor production scheduling requiring an unnecessarily excessive use of input materials and an undesirable mix of Materials A, B, and C was responsible for this result. To remedy the situation, the company must ensure that:

    a. The material mix is adhered to in terms of the least cost combination without affecting product quality.

    b. The proper production methods are being implemented.

c. Inefficiencies, waste, and spoilage are within the standard allowance.

d. Quality materials, consistent with established standards, are being used.

Employees seldom complete their operations according to standard times. Two factors should be brought out in computing labor variances if the analysis and computation will be used to fix responsibility:

1. The change in labor cost resulting from the efficiency of the workers, measured by a labor efficiency variance. (In finding the change, allowed hours are determined through the material input.)

2. The change in labor cost due to a difference in the yield, measured by a labor yield variance. (In computing the change, actual output is converted to allowed input hours.)

For the Giffen Manufacturing Company, more efficient workers resulted in a savings of 383.33 hours (15,250 hrs. – 14,866.67 hrs.). Priced at the standard rate per hour, this produced an unfavorable labor efficiency variance of $1,341.66 as shown below.

Labor Efficiency Variance

Actual hrs. at standard rate	$53,375
Actual hrs. at expected output	
(4,460 hrs. × 400/120 = 14,866.67 hrs. @ $3.5)	52,033.34
	$ 1,341.66 U

With a standard yield of 831/3% (= 100/120), 4,250 pounds of finished material should have required 17,000 hours of direct labor (4,250 lbs. × 400 DLH/100). Comparing the hours allowed for the actual input, 14,866.67 hours with the hours allowed for actual output, 17,000 hours, we find a favorable labor yield variance of $7,466.66, as shown below.

Labor Yield Variance

Actual hrs. at expected output	$52,033.34
Actual output (4,250 lbs. × 400/100	
17,000 hrs. @ $3.5 or 4,250 lbs. @ $14.00)	59,500
	$ 7,466.66 F

The labor efficiency variance can be combined with the yield variance to give us the traditional labor efficiency variance, which turns out to be favorable as follows:

Labor efficiency variance	$ 1,341.66 U
Labor yield variance	7,466.66 F
	$ 6,125 F

This division is necessary when there is a difference between the actual yield and standard yield, if responsibility is to be fixed. The producing department cannot be rightfully credited with a favorable efficiency variance of $6,125. However, a favorable yield variance, which is a factor most likely outside the control of the producing department, more than offsets the unfavorable labor efficiency variance of $1,341.66, for which the producing department rightfully should have been responsible.

PROFIT VARIANCE ANALYSIS

Gross profit analysis is determining the causes for the change in gross profit. Any variances that impact upon gross profit are reported to management so corrective steps may be taken.

Causes of Profit Variance

- Changes in unit sales price and cost.
- Changes in the volume of products sold.
- Changes in sales mix.

Analysis of the changes furnishes data needed to bring actual operations in line with budgeted expectations. Comparisons should be made between budgeted and actual operations for the current year or between actual operations for the previous year and those for the current year. Changes in gross profit may be looked at in terms of the entire company or by product line.

In an effort to improve profitability, the change in character of sales or mix of sales is just as important as the increase in total volume. For example, if the total volume in the budget is constant, but a larger proportion of high-margin products are sold than were budgeted, then higher profits will result. For instance, in the furniture business, there is an increasing trend toward more expensive and durable pieces carrying a higher margin per unit, although volume may not be all that great. Computations and analysis of sales mix variances are a very important part of profit analysis. It provides additional insight into: (a) what caused the increase or decrease in profit over the previous year, and (b) why the actual profit differed from the original expectation.

Gross profit (or contribution margin) is usually the joint responsibility of the managers of the sales department and the production department; the sales department manager is responsible for the sales revenue component, and the production department manager is accountable for the cost-of-goods-sold component. However, it is the task of top management to ensure that the target profit is met. The sales department manager must hold fast to prices, volume and mix; the production department supervisor must control the costs of materials, labor and factory overhead, and quantities; the purchasing manager must purchase materials at budgeted prices; and the personnel manager must employ the right people at the right wage rates. The internal audit department must ensure that the budgetary figures for sales and costs are being adhered to by all the departments that are, directly or indirectly, involved in contributing to making profit.

The computation of the production mix variance is very similar to that of the sales mix variance. While the sales mix variance is part of profit analysis, the production mix variance for materials and labor is an important part of cost variance analysis. However, the analysis of standard cost variances should be understood as part of what is broadly known as profit analysis. In industries where each cost element is substituted for each other and production is at or near full capacity, the manner in which different types of materials and different classes of labor are combined will affect the extent to which the costs are controlled and gross profit maximized. The production volume variance must be further analyzed to separate the effect on costs of a change in mix of the production inputs such as materials and labor.

The yield variances for materials, labor, and overhead are useful in managerial control of material consumption. In some cases, the newly found mix is accompanied by either a favorable or unfavorable yield of the finished product. Usually, the favorable mix variance may be offset by an unfavorable yield variance, or vice versa. It is the responsibility of the laboratory or the engineering department to make sure that no apparent advantage created by one type of variance is canceled out by another.

Taken as a whole, the analysis of profit involves careful evaluation of all facets of variance analysis (i.e., sales variances and cost variances). The effect of changes in mix, volume, and yield on profits must be separated and analyzed. The analysis of these variances provides management with added dimensions to responsibility accounting since it provides additional insight into what caused the increase or decrease in profits or why the actual profit deviated from the target profit. Analyzing the change in gross profit via an effective responsibility accounting system based on the control of costs and sales variances is a step toward maximization of profits.

Profit Variance Analysis for a Single Product. Profit variance analysis is simplest in a single product firm—there is only one sales price, one set of costs (or cost price), and a unitary sales volume. An unfavorable profit variance is composed of: (a) sales price variance, (b) cost price variance, (c) sales volume variance, and (d) cost volume variance. The total volume variance is the difference between the sales volume variance and the cost volume variance.

(a) Sales price variance
  = (Actual cost – Budget or standard cost) × Actual sales
(b) Cost price variance
  = (Actual cost – Budget or standard cost) × Actual sales
(c) Sales volume variance
  = (Actual sales – Budget or standard sales) × Budget or standard price
(d) Cost volume variance
  = (Actual sales – Budget or standard sales) × Budget or standard cost per unit
(e) Total volume variance
  = Sales volume variance – Cost volume variance

Profit Variance Analysis for Multiple Products. The total volume variance in a multiple product situation is composed of: (a) sales mix variance, and (b) sales quantity variance.

(a) Sales mix variance

$$= \left(\begin{array}{c} \text{Actual sales at budget} \\ \text{or standard mix} \end{array} - \begin{array}{c} \text{Budget or standard sales} \\ \text{at budget or standard mix} \end{array} \right) \times \begin{array}{c} \text{Budget or} \\ \text{standard} \\ \text{CM (or GM)} \\ \text{per unit} \end{array}$$

CM = Contribution margin and GM = Gross margin

(b) Sales quantity variance

$$= \left(\begin{array}{c} \text{Actual sales at budgeted} \\ \text{or standard mix} \end{array} - \begin{array}{c} \text{Actual sales at budgeted or} \\ \text{standard mix} \end{array} \right) \times \begin{array}{c} \text{Budget or} \\ \text{standard} \\ \text{CM (or GM)} \\ \text{per unit} \end{array}$$

(c) Total value variance

= Sales mix variance + Sales quantity variance

$$\text{or} = \left(\begin{array}{c} \text{Actual sales} \\ \text{at actual mix} \end{array} - \begin{array}{c} \text{Budgeted or standard sales} \\ \text{at budgeted or standard mix} \end{array} \right) \times \begin{array}{c} \text{Budget or} \\ \text{standard} \\ \text{CM (or GM)} \\ \text{per unit} \end{array}$$

The sales price variance and the cost price variance are calculated the same way as for a single product.

Frequently, a contribution margin approach is superior to the gross profit approach. That is because "gross profit" has a deduction for fixed costs that may be beyond the control of a particular level of management. A simple example follows.

	Budget (00) Omitted		*Actual (00) Omitted*		*Variance*	
	Unit A	*Unit B*	*Unit A*	*Unit B*	*Unit A*	*Unit B*
Sales Price	$10	$5	$11	$6	$1 F	$1
Units	10	8	10	8	–0–	–0–
Variable Manufacturing Costs	$4	$3	$6	$4	$2 U	$1
Fixed Manufacturing Costs	$3	$1	$4	$2	$1 U	$1

	Budget (00) Omitted		Actual (00) Omitted		Variance	
	Unit A	Unit B	Unit A	Unit B	Unit A	Unit B
Manufacturing Contribution Margin per unit	$6	$2	$5	$2	$1 U	$-0-
Gross profit per unit	$3	$1	$1	$0	$2 U	$1

Using the foregoing data, an unfavorable manufacturing contribution margin Variance of $10 for Unit A and $0 for Unit B is more meaningful than the $20 and $8 unfavorable gross profit variance if local management had no control over fixed costs.

EXAMPLE 12 (Profit Variance Analysis): The Lake Tahoe Ski Store sells two ski models, Model X and Model Y. For the years 2X14 and 2X15, the store realized a gross profit of $246,640 and only $211,650, respectively. The owner of the store was astounded since the total sales volume in dollars and in units was higher for 2X15 than for 2X14 yet the gross profit achieved actually declined. Given below are the store's unaudited operating results for 2X14 and 2X15. No fixed costs were included in the cost of goods sold per unit.

	Model X				Model Y			
Year	Selling Price	Cost of Goods Sold per Unit	Sales (in units)	Sales Revenue	Selling Price	Cost of Goods Sold per Unit	Sales (in units)	Sales Revenue
1	$150	$110	2,800	$420,000	$172	$121	2,640	$454,080
2	160	125	2,650	424,000	176	135	2,900	510,400

We explain why the gross profit declined by $34,990. We include a detailed variance analysis of price changes and changes in volume both for sales and cost. Also, we subdivide the total volume variance into changes in price and changes in quantity.

Sales price and sales volume variances measure the impact on the firm's CM (or GM) of changes in the unit selling price and sales volume. In computing these variances, all costs are held constant in order to stress changes in price and volume. Cost price and cost volume variances are computed in the same manner, holding price and volume constant. All these variances for the Lake Tahoe Ski Store are computed below.

Sales Price Variance

Actual sales for 2X15:

Model X 2,650 × $150 = $424,000

Model Y 2,900 × 176 = 510,400 $934,400

Actual 2X15 sales at 2X14 prices:

Model X 2,650 × $150 = $397,500

Model Y 2,900 × 172 = 498,800   896,300

$ 38,100 F

Sales Volume Variance

Actual 2X15 sales at 2X14 prices:	$896,300
Actual 2X14 sales (at 2X14 prices):	
Model X 2,800 × $150 = $420,000	
Model Y 2,640 × 172 = 454,080	874,080
	$ 22,220 F

Cost Price Variance

Actual cost of goods sold for 2X15:	
Model X 2,650 × $125 = $331,250	
Model Y 2,900 × 135 = 391,500	$722,750
Actual 2X15 sales at 2X14 costs:	
Model X 2,650 × $110 = $291,500	
Model Y 2,900 × 121 = 350,900	642,400
	$ 80,350 U

Cost Volume Variance

Actual 2X15 Sales at 2X14 costs:	$642,400
Actual 2X14 sales (at 2X14 costs):	
Model X 2,800 × $110 = $308,000	
Model Y 2,640 × 121 = 319,440	627,440
	$ 14,960 U

$$\begin{aligned}\text{Total volume variance} &= \text{Sales volume variance} - \text{Cost volume variance} \\ &= \$22,250\text{ F} - \$14,960\text{ U} = \$7,260\text{ F}\end{aligned}$$

The total volume variance is computed as the sum of a sales mix variance and a sales quantity variance as follows:

Sales Mix Variance

	2X15 Actual Sales at 2X14 Mix*	2X15 Actual Sales at 2X15 Mix	Diff.	2X14 Gross Profit per Unit	Variance ($)
Model X	2,857	2,650	207 U	$40	$ 8,280 U
Model Y	2,693	2,900	207 F	51	10,557 F
	5,550	5,550			$ 2,277 F

* This is the 2X14 mix (used as standard or budget) proportions of 51.47% (or 2,800/5,440 = 51.47%) and 48.53% (or 2,640/5,440 = 48.53%) applied to the actual 2X15 sales figure of 5,550 units.

Sales Quantity Variance

	2X15 Actual Sales at 2X14 Mix	2X14 Actual Sales at 2X14 Mix	Diff.	2X14 Gross Profit per Unit	Variance ($)
Model X	2,857	2,800	57 F	$40	$2,280 F
Model Y	2,693	2,640	53 F	51	2,703 F
	5,550	5,440			$4,983 F

A favorable total volume variance is due to a favorable shift in the sales mix (that is, from Model X to Model Y) and also to a favorable increase in sales volume (by 110 units) which is as follows:

Sales mix variance	$2,277 F
Sales quantity variance	4,983 F
	$7,260 F

However, there remains the decrease in gross profit. The decrease in gross profit of $34,990 can be explained as follows:

	Gains	Losses
Gain due to increased sales price	$38,100 F	
Loss due to increased cost		80,350 U
Gain due to increase in units sold	4,983 F	
Gain due to shift in sales mix	2,277 F	
	$45,360 F	$80,350 U
Hence, net decrease in gross profit = $80,350 – $45,360 =		$34,990 U

Despite the increase in sales price and volume and the favorable shift in sales mix, the Lake Tahoe Ski Store ended up losing $34,990 compared to 2X15. The major reason for this comparative loss was the tremendous increase in cost of goods sold, as indicated by an unfavorable cost price variance of $80,350. The costs for both Model X and Model Y went up quite significantly over 2X15. The Store has to take a close look at the cost picture. Even though only variable costs were included in cost of goods sold per unit, both variable and fixed costs should be analyzed in an effort to cut down on controllable costs. In doing that, it is essential that responsibility be clearly fixed to given individuals. In a retail business like the Lake Tahoe Ski Store, operating expenses such as advertising and payroll of store employees must also be closely scrutinized.

EXAMPLE 13 (Sales Mix and Quantity Variances): Shim and Siegel, Inc. sells two products, C and D. Product C has a budgeted unit CM (contribution margin) of $3 and Product D has a budgeted unit CM of $6. The budget for a recent month called for sales of 3,000 units of C and 9,000 units of D, for a total of 12,000 units. Actual sales totaled 12,200 units, 4,700 of C and 7,500 of D. We compute the sales volume variance and break this variance down into: (a) the sales quantity variance and (b) the sales mix variance.

Shim and Siegel's sales volume variance is computed below. While total unit sales increased by 200 units, the shift in sales mix resulted in a $3,900 unfavorable sales volume variance.

Sales Volume Variance

	Actual Sales at Actual Mix	Standard Sales at Budget Mix	Difference	Budgeted CM per Unit	Variance ($)
Product C	4,700	3,000	1,700 F	$3	$5,100
Product D	7,500	9,000	1,500 U	6	9,000
	12,200	12,000			$3,900

In multiproduct firms, the sales volume variance is further divided into a sales quantity variance and a sales mix variance. The computations of these variances are shown below.

Sales Quantity Variance

	Actual Sales at Budgeted Mix	Standard Sales at Budget Mix	Difference	Standard CM per Unit	Variance ($)
Product C	3,050	3,000	50 F	$3	$150 F
Product D	9,150	9,000	150 F	6	900 F
	12,200	12,000			$1,050 F

Sales Mix Variance

	Actual Sales at Budgeted Mix	Actual Sales at Actual Mix	Difference	Standard CM per Unit	Variance ($)
Product C	3,050	4,700	1,650 F	$3	$4,950 F
Product D	9,150	7,500	1,650 U	6	9,900 U
	12,200	12,200			$4,950 U

The sales quantity variance reflects the impact on the CM or GM (gross margin) of deviations from the standard sales volume, whereas the sales mix variance measures the impact on the CM of deviations from the budgeted mix. In the case of Shim and Siegel, Inc., the sales quantity variance came out to be favorable (i.e., $1,050 F), and the sales mix variance came out to be unfavorable (i.e., $4,950 U). These variances indicate that, while there was favorable increase in sales volume by 200 units, it was obtained by an unfavorable shift in the sales mix—that is, a shift from Product D, with a high margin, to product C, with a low margin.

Note that the sales volume variance of $3,900 U is the algebraic sum of the following two variances:

Sales quantity variance	$1,050 F
Sales mix variance	4,950 U
	$3,900 U

In conclusion, the product emphasis on high-margin sales is often a key to success for multiproduct firms. Increasing sales volume is one side of the story; selling the more profitable products is another.

In view of the fact that Shim and Siegel, Inc. experienced an unfavorable sales volume variance of $3,900 due to an unfavorable (or less profitable) mix in the sales volume, the company is advised to put more emphasis on increasing the sale of Product D.

In doing that the company might wish to:

a. Increase the advertising budget for succeeding periods to boost Product D sales

b. Set up a bonus plan in such a way that the commission is based on quantities sold rather than higher rates for higher-margin items such as Product D, or revise the bonus plan to consider the sale of Product D

c. Offer a more lenient credit term for Product D to encourage its sale

d. Reduce the price of Product D enough to maintain the present profitable mix while increasing the sale of product. This strategy must take into account the price elasticity of demand for Product D.

STANDARD COSTING INTEGRATED WITH OTHER COST SYSTEMS

Standard costing is an "accessory" that may be added to either job order costing or process costing to aid these basic cost systems.

Job Order Costing and Standard Costing

With job order costing, individual jobs consist of a single complex unit or a small batch of complex units. The units are customized to meet particular specifications. Thus, standard setting may be used in formulating "custom made" direct material, direct labor, and factory overhead standards prior to starting each unique job.

Process Costing and Standard Costing

Process costing can be combined with standard costing and variances determined. Certain requirements exist issued by the Cost Accounting Standards Board.

EXAMPLE 14: The Curry Quality Products, Inc. manufactures fabrics for a variety of uses including automotive, furniture, belts, shoe, garter, suspenders, and industrial applications. A substantial percentage of the company's operations embrace the manufacture of a variety of webbings for the foregoing purposes. The company has the following standard cost at a normal monthly volume of 10,000 units for the Weaving Department:

Direct materials—yarn (2 lbs. @ $15)	$30.00
Direct labor (1 DLH @ $9)	9.00
Factory overhead:	
Variable (1 DLH @ $6)	6.00
Fixed (1 DLH @ $5)	5.00
Total standard cost	$50.00

Budgeted fixed factory overhead is $50,000. Material is introduced at the beginning of the process. Data for the month of September 2X15 include the following:

Work-in-process, beginning	3,000 units, 1/3 complete as to conversion
Units started during September	10,000 units
Units completed and transferred to finished goods inventory	12,000 units
Materials purchased	20,000 lbs. @ $14.00/lb. 25,000/lb. placed into production
Work-in-process, end	1,000 units, 112 complete
Actual September conversion costs were:	
Direct labor (12,000 hours @ $9)	$108,000
Variable overhead	78,000
Fixed overhead	51,000
	$237,000

The Curry Company uses a standard cost system. Raw materials are inventoried at standard. Costs in process on September 1 were recorded at standard. A separate variance account is maintained for record keeping purposes. Separate control and applied accounts for variable overhead and fixed overhead are maintained for control purposes.

    1. The equivalent units used for standard costing purposes are:

	Physical	Flow	Materials	Conversion
WIP, beginning	3,000	(1/3)		
Units started	10,000			
Units to account for	13,000			

	Physical	Flow	Materials	Conversion
Units completed and transferred	12,000		12,000	12,000
WIP, end	1,000	(1/2)	1,000	500
Units accounted for	13,000			
Total work done			13,000	12,500
Less: old equivalent units on beginning WIP			3,000*	1,000**
Equivalent units produced			10,000	11,500

* 3,000 units, 100% complete as to materials

** 3,000 units, 2/3 complete as to conversion are equivalent to 1,000 fully completed units

2. To compute all the variances, we will use a three-column worksheet for direct materials and direct labor and a four-column worksheet for factory overhead.

Variance Analysis for Direct Materials

(1)	(2)		(3)
Actual Quantity × Actual Price	Actual Quantity × Standard Price		Standard Quantity Allowed × Standard Price
(purchase) 20,000 × $14 = $280,000	(purchase) 20,000 × $15 = $300,000	(usage) 25,000 × $15 = $375,000	20,000 × $15 = $300,000
	Material purchase Price variance = $20,000 (F)	Material quantity Variance = $75,000 (U)	

In the above, F and U stand for favorable and unfavorable, respectively. The standard material quantity allowed was computed on the basis of equivalent units produced for materials (i.e., 1,000 units), multiplied by 2 lbs. = 20,000 units.

Since the responsibility for the material purchase price variance does not rest with the Weaving Department, it does not appear on its cost of production report and also on its performance report. It would appear on the performance report of the purchasing department.

Variance Analysis for Direct Labor

(1) Actual Hours × Actual Rate	(2) Actual Hours × Standard Rate	(3) Standard Hours Allowed × Standard Rate
12,000 hrs. × $9 = $108,000	12,000 × $9 = $108,000	11,500 × $9 = $103,500
Labor rate var.		Labor efficiency variance
= $0		= $4,500 (U)

The standard hours allowed for actual equivalent units produced were computed on the basis of equivalent units manufactured for direct labor—that is, 11,500 units of equivalent production for direct labor, multiplied by 1 DLH =11,500 hours.

Variance Analysis for Variable Overhead and Fixed Overhead

Before we perform variance analysis for factory overhead, it is necessary to develop (1) a flexible budget formula used for cost control purposes and (2) applied rates for variable overhead and fixed overhead used for product costing. In this illustrative case, they are

(1) Flexible budget formula

Variable overhead rate: $6 per DLH

Budgeted fixed overhead: $50,000, which is 10,000 units

of normal volume × 1 DLH × $5 = 50,000

(2) Applied rates:

Variable overhead rate: $6 per DLH

Fixed overhead rate: $5 per DLH

Now we are in a position to isolate spending, efficiency, and volume variances for factory overhead. We will use a four-column worksheet approach.

	(1) Actual Hours × Actual Price = Actual Overhead Incurred *(12,000 hrs.)*	*(2)* Actual Hours × Standard Price = Flexible Budget Based on Actual Hours Worked *(12,000 hrs.)*	*(3)* Standard Hours Allowed × Standard Price = Flexible Budget Based on Standard Hours Allowed *(11,500 hrs.)*	*(4)* Applied *(11,500 hrs.)*
Variable	$78,000	$72,000 (12,000 hrs. × $6)	$69,000 (11,500 hrs. × $6)	$69,000 (11,500 hrs. × $6)
Fixed	51,000	50,000	50,000	57,500 (11,500 hrs × $5)
	$129,000	$122,000	$119,000	$126,500

Spending Variance:		Efficiency Variance:		Volume Variance:	
Variable	$6,000(U)	Variable	$3,000(U)	Variable	not applicable
Fixed	1,000(U)	Fixed	not applicable	Fixed	$7,500(F)
	$7,010(U)		$3,000(U)		$7,500(U)

In summary,

Variable overhead spending variance	$6,000(U)
Fixed overhead spending variance	1,000(U)
Variable overhead efficiency variance	3,000 (U)
Fixed overhead volume variance	7,500 (U)
	$2,500(U)

3. The *favorable* material purchase price variance of $20,000 may be due to taking advantage of the $1 cash discount on the quantity purchase (@ $14 vs. @ $15). The *unfavorable* material quantity variance results from the fact that the Weaving Department used 5,000 pounds more of materials than the standard quantity, which may be explained by controllable factors such as use of inefficient workers, poor equipment, changes in production methods, or faulty blueprints. Controllable causes must be detected before any corrective action can be taken. There may also exist uncontrollable factors such as the use of faulty materials, the responsibility for which rests with the purchasing department rather than with the Weaving Department.

There was no labor rate variance. The unfavorable labor efficiency variance of $4,500 could be due to a variety of reasons including materials being in short supply, the use of poor equipment or inefficient workers, and poor production scheduling resulting in overtime work. The undesirable efficiency variance could be explained by such factors as machine breakdown, which is usually outside the responsibility of the Weaving Department. In the Curry Company, the unfavorable variable overhead spending variance may be explained in the same way as the unfavorable labor efficiency variance. An unfavorable spending variance for both variable overhead and fixed overhead must be studied carefully on a cost-by-cost basis. The difference between actual spending and budgeted amounts is usually caused by higher prices paid for supplies, indirect labor, maintenance and repair, and unexpected increases in such committed types of fixed overhead expenses as rent, insurance, and taxes, which are not controllable by the department head. The Weaving Department's performance report should distinguish between controllable items and uncontrollable items so that the entire system of responsibility accounting functions properly and efficiently. Perhaps a certain uncontrollable item might safely be dropped from the report of the department. For example, the material purchase price variance should not appear on the performance report of the Weaving Department; it should be charged to the purchasing manager.

A favorable overhead volume income variance indicates that the Weaving Department operated at more than average capacity and the fixed costs "attached" to better-than-average utilization of capacity amounted to $7,500 (F). However, this factor may be beyond the control of the manager of the Weaving Department. Whether or not the favorable variance should appear on his or her performance report will require further investigation.

4. Here is the cost of production report.

Cost of Production Report
Weaving Department
for the Month Ended September 30, 2X15

WIP, beginning at standard:		
Materials (3,000 × $30)	$ 90,000	
Conversion (1,000 × $20)	20,000	$110,000
Current costs assigned to Weaving Department:		
Materials (25,000 × $15)	$375,000	
Direct labor (12,000 × $9)	108,000	
Factory overhead	129,000	612,000
Total costs to account for		$722,000
WIP, end at standard		
Materials (1,000 × $30)	$ 30,000	
Conversion (500 × $20)	10,000	40,000
Goods completed and transferred at standard 12,000 × $50		600,000
Variances:		
Material quantity	75,000 (U)	

Cost of Production Report
Weaving Department
for the Month Ended September 30, 2X15

Labor efficiency	4,500 (U)	
Variable overhead spending	6,000 (U)	
Fixed overhead spending	1,000 (U)	
Variable overhead efficiency	3,000 (U)	
Fixed overhead volume	(7,500) (F)	82,000
Total costs accounted for		$722,000

* Note that the costs assigned to Weaving Department include the standard cost of materials used ($375,000 = 25,000 units × $15 standard cost) and the actual costs of direct labor and factory overhead. Also note that material purchase price variance is assumed to be assigned to the purchasing department.

5. The Cost Accounting Standards Board requirement for the use of standard costs would not greatly affect the company's present standard costing system. Some of the things that are affected are the following:

   a. Since material purchase price variances are recognized at the time the materials are purchased, and valued at standard costs, they must be accumulated separately by homogeneous groupings and may be included in appropriate indirect cost pools.

   b. Labor rate variances and labor efficiency variances may be combined to form a single labor cost variance account.

   c. These variances (presumably including various overhead variances) must be allocated at least annually between inventory and production units based on various criteria described in the Standard. For example, they may be allocated in proportion to the related standard costs in each account.

EXAMPLE 15: CPA Manufacturing Company produces a product in two processing departments: Finishing Department and Cutting Department. The Finishing Department assembles and puts a finishing touch on the product it receives from the Cutting Department. Materials are introduced at the start of the Cutting Department, while conversion costs are applied uniformly throughout the department. The company has the following standard cost at a normal monthly production volume of 1,300 direct labor hours:

Raw materials (2 units @ $5)	$10
Direct labor (1 hour @ $6)	6

Factory overhead:

Variable (1 hour @ $2)	2
Fixed (1 hour @ $5)	5
	$23

Fixed overhead budgeted is $6,500 per month. The Finishing Department has work-in-process at the beginning and end of March as follows:

	Units	Percentage of Completion as to Conversion
Beginning	400	1/2
End	200	3/4

In addition to the work-in-process inventory at the beginning, the Finishing Department also received 1,100 units from the Cutting Department and processed them during the month of March. During the process, no units were lost. During the month of March, the following events occurred:

Actual overhead costs:

Variable	$2,853
Fixed	6,725
Materials (@ $5.20 per unit):	
Purchased	2,600 units
Used	2,500 units
Direct labor hours used @ $6.50/hr	1,350 hours

1. Equivalent units produced for the month of March are:

	Physical Flow	Materials	Conversion
WIP, beginning	400(1/2)		
Units started	1,100		
Units to account for	1,500		
Units completed	1,300	1,300	1,300
WIP, end	200(3/4)	200	150
Units accounted for	1,500		
Total work done		1,500	1,450
Less: old equivalent units on beginning WIP		400	200
Equivalent units produced		1,100	1,250

2.   *Variance analysis for materials*

(1) **Actual Quantity** **× Actual Price**		(2) **Actual Quantity** **× Standard Price**	(3) **Standard Quantity** **Allowed × Standard Price**	
(purchase) 2,600 units × $5.20 = $13,520	(purchase) 2,600 × $5 $13,000	(usage) 2,500 × $5 = $12,500	2,200* × $5 = $11,000	

Material purchase price

variance = $520 (U)

Material quantity variance

= $1,500 (U)

*The standard input quantity allowed, 2,200 units = 1,100 × 2

Variance Analysis for Direct Labor

(1) **Actual Hours** **× Actual Price**	(2) **Actual Hours** **× Standard Price**	(3) **Standard Hours Allowed** **× Standard Price**
1,350 hrs. × $ 6.50 = $8,775	1,350 × $6 = $8,100	1,250* × $6 = $7,500

Labor rate variance

= $675 (U)

Labor efficiency variance

= $600 (U)

*Standard hours allowed, 1,250 hours = 1,250 equivalent units for conversion × 1 hour.

Variance Analysis for Variable Overhead and Fixed Overhead Combined

(1)   Flexible budget formula: variable overhead rate, $2 per DLH
                                     fixed overhead budgeted, $6,500

(2)   Applied rates: variable, $2 per
      DLH fixed, $5 per DLH

Variance Analysis for Variable Overhead and Fixed Overhead Combined

(1)   Flexible budget formula: variable overhead rate, $2 per DLH
                                     fixed overhead budgeted, $6,500

(2)   Applied rates: variable, $2 per
      DLH fixed, $5 per DLH

(1)	(2) Flexible Budget Based on Actual Hours Worked (1,350 hrs.)	(3) Flexible Budget Based on Standard Hours Allowed (1,250 hrs.)	(4)
Actual Overhead Incurred (1,350 hrs.)			Applied (1,250 hrs.)
Variable $2,853	$2,700 (1,350 × $2)	$2,500 (1,250 × $2)	$2,500
Fixed 6,725	6,500	6,500	6,250
$9,578	$9,200	$9,000	$8,750

	Spending Var. Variable $153 (U) Fixed 225 (U)	Efficiency Var. $200 (U) not applicable	Volume Var. not applicable $250 (U)
	$378 (U)	$200 (U)	$250 (U)

3.

Cost of Production Report
Finishing Department
for the Month of March

WIP, beginning at standard:		
Materials (400 × $10)	$4,000	
Conversion (200 × $13)	2,600	$6,600
Current costs charged to Finishing Dept.:		
Materials (2,500 × $5)	12,500	
Direct labor (1,350 hrs × $6.50)	8,775	
Factory overhead:		

Variable	$2,853		
Fixed	6,725	9,578	30,853
Total costs to account for			$37,453

WIP, end at standard:		
Materials (200 × $10)	$2,000	
Conversion (150 × $13)	1,950	3,950
Goods completed and transferred at standard. 1,300 × $23		29,900
Variances:		
Material quantity	$1,500 (U)	
Labor rate	675 (U)	
Labor efficiency	600 (U)	
Variable overhead spending	153 (U)	
Fixed overhead spending	225 (U)	

Cost of Production Report
Finishing Department
for the Month of March

Variable overhead efficiency	200 (U)	
Fixed overhead volume	250 (U)	3,603
		$37,453

Note that the materials are valued at standard—that is, $12,500 = 2,500 units used × $5 standard price per unit. The material purchase price variance does not appear on the cost of production report.

EXAMPLE 16: The Fernandez Company uses a standard process costing system. The following are the March performance reports for the purchasing department and the Production Department B:

Schedule 1 Performance Report—Purchasing Dept.

	Actual		Standard		
	Units	Amount	Units	Amount	Variance (F or U)
Purchased materials	5,400	$36,720	5,400	$37,800	$1,080 (F)
Variance					
Analysis			$37,800 − $38,720 = $1,080 (F)		

Evaluation: The purchasing department purchased materials for $6.80, which is $.20 lower than the standard price. It was due to the quantity purchase which resulted in a $.20 per unit discount.

Schedule 2 Performance Report—Department B

	Actual	Budget (or standard) Adjusted for Actual Output	Variance (F or U)
Production volume	2,400 units		
Actual direct labor hours worked	2,800 hrs.		
Standard DLH		2,400 hrs.	
Direct materials	5,200 units	5,000 units	
	$36,400	$35,000	1,400 (U)*
Direct labor	$23,800	$21,600	2,200 (U)**

  * 200 units × $7.00

** Labor efficiency = (2,800 − 2,400) ($9) = $3,600 (U)

$$\text{Labor rate} = (9.00 - 8.50) \ (2,800) = \frac{1,400 \ (F)}{2,200 \ (U)}$$

Departmental overhead:

Variable:			
Indirect materials	$4,200	$3,900	$300 (U)
Indirect labor	5,500	4,950	550 (U)
Utilities	800	750	50 (U)
Fixed:			
Depreciation	3,300	3,300	—
Insurance and taxes	700	700	—
Utilities	500	500	—
Total overhead	$15,000	$14,100	$900

Budgeted annual output in hours: 30,000
Budgeted annual overhead: Variable: $120,000
Budgeted annual overhead: Fixed: 54,000

We now calculate and evaluate the variances for each cost item.

Direct materials:

Material quantity variance: $36,400 – $35,000 = $1,400 (U) or
(5,200 units – 5,000) × $7 = $1,400 (U)

Evaluation: The $1,400 unfavorable overall variance is due solely to excess usage. Department B used 200 units more than it should have in producing 2,400 units of output. Note that the material price variance, based on units purchased, is reflected on the performance report of the purchasing department.

Direct labor:

Wage rates: Actual, $23,800/2,800 hrs. = $8.50

Standard, $21,600/2,400 hrs. = $9

Actual Hours × Actual Rate	Actual Hours × Standard Rate	Standard Hours Allowed × Standard Rate
(1)	(2)	(3)
2,800 hrs. × $8.5 = $23,800	2,800 × $9 = $25,200	2,400 × $9 = $21,600

Labor rate var.
= $1,400 (F)

Labor efficiency variance
= $3,600 (U)

Evaluation: The labor efficiency variance should be investigated further to determine the cause. It may be due to such factors as use of faulty equipment and improper production methods. Since there is a favorable rate variance of $1,400, however, it may be that the foreman used low-quality, lower-wage workers with a consequent drop in efficiency.

Factory overhead:

Flexible budget formula: variable $120,000/30,000 units = $4/hr.

                     fixed $54,000/12 = $4,500

         Applied rates: variable $4/hr.

                     fixed $54,000/30,000 units = $1.8/hr.

	Actual Overhead (2,800 hrs.) (1)	Budget Based on Actual Hrs. (2,800 hrs.) (2)	Budget Based on Standard Hrs. (2,400 hrs.) (3)	Applied (2,400 hrs.) (4)
Variable	$10,500	11,200 (2,800 hrs. × $4)	9,500 (2,400 hrs. × $4)	9,600
Fixed	4,500	4,500	4,500	4,320
				(2,400 hrs. × $1)
	$15,000	$15,700	$14,100	$13,920

	Spending var.	Efficiency var.	Volume var.
Variable:	$700 (F)	$1,600 (U)	not applicable
Fixed:	0	not applicable	$180 (U)
	$700	$1,600 (U)	$180 (U)

Evaluation: The $900 unfavorable variance is explained as follows:

Favorable spending variance	$ 700 (F)
Unfavorable efficiency variance	1,600 (U)
	$ 900 (U)

This may be the result of the use of low quality labor and materials coupled with a consequent drop in efficiency. It appears that indirect materials and indirect labor should be investigated further. The $180 unfavorable fixed overhead volume variance is an indication of below-average utilization of capacity. The department operated 100 hours below its normal capacity of 2,500 hours (30,000 hrs./12). If below-capacity operation is demand-related, this variance is not controllable by the department supervisor and therefore should not appear on his or her performance report. However, it could also be the result of inefficient operations, in which case the supervisor should be held accountable.

NONMANUFACTURING ACTIVITIES

When nonmanufacturing activities repeat and result in a homogeneous product, standards may be used. The manner of estimating and employing standards can be similar to that applicable with a manufactured product. For instance, standards may be used for office personnel involved in processing sales orders, and a standard unit expense for processing a sales order may be derived. The variance between the actual cost of processing a sales order with the standard cost can be appraised by management and corrective steps taken. The number of payroll checks prepared should be a reliable measure of the activity of the payroll department. The number of invoices or vouchers prepared applies to billing and accounts payable. In these two cases, a standard cost per unit could be based on the variable expenses involved.

Variance analysis is used in non-production-oriented companies such as service businesses. Since a product is not dealt with, a measure of volume other than units is necessary (e.g., time spent). The measure of revenue is fee income.

The cost variances are still the same as in a manufacturing concern, namely budgeted costs versus actual costs. The gross margin or contribution margin variance can also be derived as the difference between that budgeted and that actually obtained. The profitability measures are expressed as a percent of sales rather than as dollars per unit. The relationship between costs and sales is often highlighted.

Service firms typically have numerous variances expressed in physical, rather than dollar, measures. Examples of physical measures are number of customers serviced and turnover rate in customers.

AN ILLUSTRATIVE VARIANCE ANALYSIS REPORT FOR A SERVICE BUSINESS

For a service business, cost variances may be reported to management in special reports. For example, the variance in time and cost spent for processing payments to creditors may be analyzed. An illustrative format follows.

	Variance in Time	*Variance in Cost*
Function		
Processing purchase orders		
Processing receiving reports		
Processing vendors' invoices		
Preparing checks		
Filing paid vouchers and supporting documents		

Variances for these functions are useful only for large companies where the volume of activity allows for the arrangement and analysis of such repetitive tasks.

VARIANCES TO EVALUATE MARKETING EFFORT

Prior to setting a marketing standard in a given trade territory, prior, current, and forecasted conditions for the company itself and the given geographical area should be examined. Standards will vary depending upon geographical location. In formulating standard costs for the transportation function, minimum cost traffic routes should be selected on the basis of the given distribution pattern.

Standards for advertising cost in particular territories will vary depending upon the types of advertising media needed, which are in turn based on the type of customers the advertising is intended to reach, as well as the nature of the competition.

Some direct selling costs can be standardized, such as product presentations for which a standard time per sales call can be established. Direct selling expenses should be related to such items as distance traveled and frequency of calls made. If sales commissions are based on sales generated, standards can be based on a percentage of net sales.

Time and motion studies are usually a better way of establishing standards than prior performance, since the past may include inefficiencies.

Cost variances for the selling function may pertain to the territory, product, or personnel.

Variances in Selling Expenses

The control of selling expenses is not as significant for a company manufacturing a standard line of products with a limited number of established customers as for a manufacturer of custom products in a very competitive market. For the latter, significant advertising and salesperson costs are mandated. The variance in selling costs is equal to the actual cost versus the flexible budgeted cost.

Assume actual cost is $88,000 and the flexible budget is:

$40,000 + (5% × Sales revenue) + ($.03 per unit shipped)

If sales revenue is $500,000 and 100,000 units are shipped, the flexible budgeted cost is:

$40,000 + (5% × $500,000 + ($.03 × 100,000 units) = $68,000

The variance is unfavorable by $20,000. Perhaps advertising and travel should be further investigated. These costs are highly discretionary in that they may easily be altered by management.

Further refinement of the selling expense variance is possible. Each element of selling expense (i.e., advertising, travel, commissions, shipping costs) could be looked at in terms of the difference between budgeted cost and actual cost.

Sales Personnel Performance

Actual sales may not be the best measure of sales personnel performance. It does not take into account differing territory potentials. Also, a high-volume salesperson may have to absorb high selling cost, making the profit generated by him or her low. Profit is what counts, not sales.

The evaluation of sales personnel based on the trend in their sales generated over the years shows signs of improvement. However, not considered here are customer's market demand, potential markets as defined by the company, product mix, and cost incurrence.

Travel expense standards are often formulated based on distance traveled and the frequency of customer calls. Standards for salesperson automobile expense may be in terms of cost per mile traveled and cost per day. Entertainment and gift expenditures can be based on the amount, size, and potential for customers. The standard might relate to cost per customer or cost per dollar of net sales. Selling expense standards are frowned upon by sales managers because they may create ill will among sales personnel. The standards also do not take into account sales volume or product mix.

Profitability per salesperson may be a good measurement yardstick. Sales, less variable product costs, less selling expenses, per salesperson will give us the relevant profitability. Not considered here, however, are territory expectations or territory demand.

Standard costing procedures and performance measures should be used to control sales personnel costs and compute earnings generated by salesperson category. Further, revenue, cost, and profit by type of sales solicitation (i.e., personal visit, telephone call, mail) should be determined.

A break-even analysis for individual salespeople may also be performed.

Sales commissions should be higher for higher-profit merchandise. Any quotas established should be based on a desired sales mix.

Consideration of fixed versus variable costs for a function is critical in marketing cost control and in deciding whether to add or drop sales regions and product lines.

Fixed marketing costs include administrative salaries, wages of warehousing and shipping personnel, rent, and insurance. Variable marketing costs comprise processing, storing, and shipping goods, which tend to fluctuate with sales volume. Also of a variable nature are sales personnel salaries and commissions as well as travel and entertainment.

It is difficult to project marketing costs because they may materially change as market conditions are altered. An example is a modification in the channels of distribution. Also, customer brand loyalty is difficult to predict. The point here is that it is more difficult to forecast and analyze marketing costs than manufacturing costs. Thus, standards established in this area are quite tentative and very difficult to manage.

ILLUSTRATIVE MARKETING PERFORMANCE REPORT

An illustrative format for a marketing performance report designed for the vice president of marketing follows.

	Budget	*Percent*	*Actual*	*Percent*	*Variance*
Sales					
Less: standard variable cost of sales					
Manufacturing margin					
Less: variable distribution costs					
Contribution margin					
Less: regional fixed charges					
Controllable regional contribution margin					

	Budget	Percent	Actual	Percent	Variance
Less: marketing fixed charges (i.e., central) marketing administration costs, national advertising)					
Marketing contribution margin					

An illustrative format for a marketing performance report designed for the regional sales manager follows.

	Budget	Percent	Actual	Percent	Variance
Sales					
Less: standard variable cost of sales					
Manufacturing margin					
Less: variable distribution costs (i.e., sales personnel commissions, freight out)					
Contribution margin					
Less: regional fixed charges (i.e., salesperson salaries, travel and entertainment, local advertising)					
Controllable regional contribution margin					

The marketing manager should be responsible for standard variable cost of sales, distribution costs (i.e., packing, freight out, marketing administration), and sales. The reason standard variable cost of sales is used is not to have the marketing area absorb manufacturing efficiencies and inefficiencies. An illustrative format follows.

Sales

Less: standard variable cost of sales

Less: distribution costs

Profitability

The profit figure constitutes the marketing efforts contribution to fixed manufacturing costs and administration costs.

How to Analyze Salesperson Variances

Sales force effectiveness within a territory, including time spent and expenses incurred, should be appraised.

EXAMPLE 17:

Sales data for your company follow.

Standard cost	$240,000
Standard salesperson days	2,000

Standard rate per salesperson day	$ 120
Actual cost	$238,000
Actual salesperson days	1,700
Actual rate per salesperson day	$140
Total Cost Variance	
Actual cost	$238,000
Standard cost	240,000
	$ 2,000 F

The control variance is broken down into salesperson days and salesperson costs.

Variance in Salesperson Days

Actual days versus standard days times standard rate per day
  (1,700 versus 2,000 × $120) $ 36,000 F

The variance is favorable because the territory was handled in fewer days than expected.

Variance in Salesperson Costs

Actual rate versus standard rate times actual days
  ($140 versus $120 × 1,700) $ 34,000 U

An unfavorable variance results because the actual rate per day is greater than the expected rate per day.

EXAMPLE 18: A salesperson called on 55 customers and sold each an average of $2,800 worth of merchandise. The standard number of calls is 50, and the standard sales is $2,400. Variance analysis looking at calls and sales follows.

Total Variance

Actual calls × actual sale 55 × $2,800	$154,000
Standard calls × standard sale 50 × $2,400	120,000
	$ 34,000

The elements of the $34,000 variance are:

Variance in Calls

Actual calls versus standard calls × standard sale
  (55 versus 50 × $2,400) $ 12,000

Variance in Sales

Actual sale versus standard sale × standard calls
  ($2,800 versus $2,400 × 50) $ 20,000

Joint Variance

(Actual calls versus standard calls) × (Actual sale versus
standard sale) (55 versus 50) × ($2,800 versus $2,400) $ 2,000

Additional performance measures of sales force effectiveness include meeting sales quotas, number of orders from existing and new customers, profitability per order, and the relationship between salesperson costs and revenue obtained.

The trend in the ratios of selling expense to sales, selling expense to sales volume, and selling expense to net income should be computed. Are selling expenses realistic in light of revenue generated? Are selling expenses beyond limitations pointing to possible mismanagement and violation of controls?

Variances in Warehousing Costs

In warehousing, standards for direct labor may be in terms of cost per item handled, cost per pound handled, cost per order filled, and cost per shipment.

Variances in warehousing costs can be calculated by looking at the cost per unit to store the merchandise and the number of orders anticipated.

EXAMPLE 19: The following information applies to a product:

Standard cost	$ 12,100
Standard orders	5,500
Standard unit cost	$ 2.20
Actual cost	$ 14,030
Actual orders	6,100
Actual unit cost	$ 2.30
Total Warehousing Cost Variance	
Actual cost	$ 14,030
Standard cost	12,100
	$1,930 U

The total variance is segregated into the variance in orders and variance in cost.

Variance in Orders

Actual orders versus standard orders × standard unit cost
6,100 versus 5,500 × $2.20 $ 1,320 U

Variance in Cost

Actual cost per unit versus standard cost per unit × actual
orders $2.30 versus $2.20 × 6,100 $ 610 U

VARIANCES IN ADMINISTRATIVE EXPENSES

As business expands, there is a tendency for administrative expenses to increase proportionately and get out of line. However, central general and administrative expenses typically are of a fixed cost nature and hence there is less need to monitor these types of costs. Here, comparison of budgeted to actual costs can be made quarterly, or even yearly. These comparisons should be done by department or unit of responsibility. Suggested standards for administrative expenses follow.

Administrative Function	Unit of Standard Measurement
Handling orders	Number of orders handled
Billing	Number of invoices
Check writing	Number of checks written
Clerical	Number of items handled
Customer statements	Number of statements
Order writing	Number of orders
Personnel	Number of employees hired
Payroll	Number of employees

Selling and administrative variances for nonoperating items are the responsibility of top management and staff. Such items include taxes and insurance. Performance reports may be prepared for the administrative function such as the salaries of top executives and general department service costs such as data processing. Performance measures may also be of a nonmonetary nature, such as the number of files processed, the number of phone calls taken, and the number of invoices written. Variances between the dollar and nondollar factors can be determined and analyzed.

CAPITAL EXPENDITURES

Variance reports are useful in controlling capital expenditures by looking at the actual versus budgeted costs as well as actual versus budgeted times for proposals at each stage of activity. Such reports enable management to take corrective cost-saving action such as changing the construction schedule. The director of the project is held accountable for the construction cost and time budget. Component elements within the project should also be analyzed. The expected payback period and actual payback period can also be compared. This assists in measuring operational results and budgeting efficiency. Also, estimated cash flows of the project can be compared with actual cash flows.

VARIANCE ANALYSIS REPORTS

Performance reports may be prepared looking at the difference between budgeted and actual figures for: (1) production in terms of cost, quantity, and quality; (2) sales; (3) profit; (4) return on investment; (5) turnover of assets; (6) income per sales dollar; (7) market share; and (8) growth rate. Variance reports raise questions rather than answering them. For example, is sales volume down because of deficiencies in sales effort or the manufacturer's inability to produce?

Variance analysis reports may be expressed in dollars, percentages, ratios, graphs, and in narrative form.

Performance reports are designed to motivate managers and employees to change their activities and plans when variances exist. They should be terse and should concentrate on potential difficulties and opportunities. A section for comments should be provided so that explanations may be given for variances.

The timeliness of performance reports and detail supplied depends upon the management level to which the report is addressed and the nature of the costs whose performance is being measured. A production supervisor may need daily information on the manufacturing operations, the plant superintendent may need only weekly data from his or her supervisor, and the vice president for manufacturing may be satisfied with monthly performance figures for each plant. As the distance from the actual operation increases, the time interval for performance evaluation lengthens. Also, performance reports from those high up in the organization contain data in increasingly summarized form.

Since performance reports depend upon the organizational structure, they should be designed based on the company's organization chart. Performance reports designed for a senior vice president might deal with the entire business operations of the firm and the earnings derived from them; the vice president of manufacturing would look at the efficiency of the production activity; the vice president of marketing would evaluate the selling and distribution function; a plant head would be concerned with the output and earnings generated from his or her plant; a department head within the plant would be concerned with cost control.

Performance reports should contain analytical information. To obtain it, source data such as work orders, material requisitions, and labor cards should be evaluated. Reasons for inefficiency and excessive costs, such as those due to equipment malfunction and low-quality raw materials, should be noted.

For labor, the productivity measurement ratio of volume output per direct labor hour should be computed. Further, the output of the individual or machine should be compared to the "normal" output established at the beginning of the reporting period. Operating efficiency can thus be measured. A labor efficiency ratio can also be computed which is the variation between actual hours incurred and standard hours.

With regard to the evaluation of the divisional manager, fixed costs are generally not controllable by him or her, but variable costs are. There are instances, however, where variable costs are controllable by those above the division manager's level. An example is fringe benefits. These items should be evaluated independently since the division manager has no responsibility for them. The opposite may also be true—that is, the department manager may have control over certain fixed expenses such as lease costs. In such cases he or she should similarly be assigned responsibility, although a successor not involved in the lease negotiation may not be assigned responsibility.

Appraisal of Marketing Department

Revenue, cost, and profitability information should be provided by product line, customer, industry segment, geographic area, channel of distribution, type of marketing effort, and average order size. New product evaluations should also be undertaken balancing risk with profitability. Analysis of competition in terms of strengths and weaknesses should be made. Sales force effectiveness measures should also be employed for income generated, by salesperson, call frequency, sales incentives, sales personnel costs, and dollar value of orders generated per hour spent. Promotional effectiveness measures should be employed for revenue; marketing costs; and profits prior to, during, and subsequent to promotional efforts, including a discussion of competitive reactions. Advertising effectiveness measures, such as sales generated based on dollar expenditure per media, and media measures (i.e., audience share) are also useful. Reports discussing product warranty complaints and disposition should also be provided.

Marketing costs may be broken down into the following areas: selling, promotion, credit evaluation, accounting, and administration (i.e., product development, market research). Another element is physical distribution inventory management, order processing, packaging, warehousing, shipping, outbound transportation, field warehousing, and customer services.

Control of marketing cost is initiated when such costs are assigned to functional groups such as geographic area, product line, and industry segment. Budgeted costs and rates should be provided and comparisons made between standard costs and actual costs at the end of the reporting period.

NONFINANCIAL PERFORMANCE MEASURES

Standard costs are widely used in manufacturing, service, and not-for-profit organizations. The list of companies using standards as a method for controlling costs and measuring performance continues to grow. For a firm to improve, managers should encompass nonfinancial (or operational) measures as well as financial measures, especially those that track factors required for world-class status. In an automated environment, labor is a smaller proportion of product cost, often less than 5%. Thus, traditional labor variances are of little value to management. Also, the manufacturing process is more reliable in an automated environment, and the traditional variances are usually minimal.

The new performance measures tend to be nonfinancial and more subjective than standard costs. Exhibit 21-8 presents five sets of *nonfinancial performance measures*. They include statistics for such activities as quality control, on-time delivery, inventory, machine downtime, and material waste. Measures such as *quality control and delivery performance* are customer oriented, and are useful in all organizations, particularly service organizations in which the focus is on services, not goods. A general model for measuring the relative success of an activity compares number of successes with total activity volume. For example, delivery performance could be measured as follows:

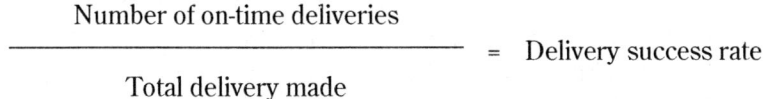

$$\frac{\text{Number of on-time deliveries}}{\text{Total delivery made}} = \text{Delivery success rate}$$

The percentage of external failures may be monitored for quality control.

Other performance measures may be production oriented. *Reducing material waste, inventory, and machine downtime* have been shown to improve quality and efficiency. These nonfinancial performance measures and measures of performance using standard costs are not mutually exclusive. Reducing materials waste would eliminate an unfavorable materials usage variance, for example. Measures such as inventory turnover and days of inventory can be used, however. Exhibit 21-8 illustrates nonfinancial performance measures.

Exhibit 21-8: Nonfinancial Performance Measures

Task	Objective
Inventory:	
Inventory levels	Decrease inventory levels
Number of inventoried items	Curtail number of different items
Quality control:	
Number of customer complaints	Reduce complaints
Number of defects	Reduce defects
Delivery performance:	
Delivery success rate	Increase on-time deliveries
Materials waste:	
Scrap and waste as a percentage of total cost	Decrease scrap and waste
Machine downtime:	
Percentage of machine downtime	Reduce downtime

CONCLUSION

Variance analysis is essential in the organization for the appraisal of all aspects of the business, including manufacturing, marketing, and service.

Variances should be investigated if the benefits outweigh the costs of analyzing and correcting the source of the variance. Variance analysis reports should be in dollars and percentages.

Significant unfavorable variances must be examined to ascertain whether they are controllable by management or uncontrollable because they relate solely to external factors. When controllable, immediate corrective action must be undertaken to handle the problem. The managerial accountant should provide his or her recommendations. If a variance is favorable, an examination should be made of the reasons for it so that corporate policy may include the positive aspects found. Further, the entity responsible for a favorable variance should be recognized and rewarded.

Different degrees of significance of variances may be present, including:

- The variance is within tolerable and normal range and thus no remedial steps are necessary.
- The variance is intolerable and thus either performance must be improved or new standards formulated in light of the current environment.
- The decision model was inappropriate considering the goal to be achieved, and thus a more relevant model should be developed.

Reports on operating performance should show where performance varies from standard, the trend of performance, and the reasons for the variances, including the manager's explanation.

Reporting systems differ among companies regarding the frequency and timeliness of reports, details presented, arrangement of data, employee distribution, and size of variances necessitating follow-up. Variances can be evaluated by divisions, subdivisions, departments, and cost centers. Variance analysis should be made to the point that additional savings from cost control justify the additional cost of appraisal and reporting.

If responsibility for a variance is joint, corrective action should also be joint. If correction of an unfavorable variance involves a conflict with a corporate policy, the policy should be reevaluated and perhaps changed. If the policy is not changed, the variance should be considered uncontrollable.

Even if a variance is below a cut-off percent or dollar figure, management may still want to investigate it if the variance is consistently unfavorable because it may reveal a problem (e.g., poor supervision, wasteful practice). The cumulative impact of a repeated small unfavorable variance may be just as damaging as an occasional one.

CHAPTER 22

THE USE OF CAPITAL BUDGETING IN DECISION MAKING

CONTENTS

Capital budgeting relates to planning for the best selection and financing of long-term investment proposals. Capital budgeting decisions are not equally essential to all companies; the relative importance of this essential function varies with company size, the nature of the industry, and the growth rate of the firm. As a business expands, problems regarding long-range investment proposals become more important. Strategic capital budgeting decisions can turn the tide for a company.

The types of scarce resources that may be committed to a project include cash, time of key personnel, machine hours, and floor space in a factory. When estimating costs for a proposed project, the allocation of the company's scarce resources must be converted in terms of money.

The two broad categories of capital budgeting decisions are (1) screening decisions and (2) preference decisions. Screening decisions relate to whether a proposed project satisfies some present acceptance standard. For instance, your company may have a policy of accepting cost reduction projects only if they provide a return of 15%. On the other hand, preference decisions apply to selecting from competing courses of action. For example, a company may be looking at four different machines to replace an existing one in the manufacture of a product. The decision as to which of the four machines is best is referred to as a preference decision.

The basic types of investment decisions are selecting between proposed projects and replacement decisions. Selection requires judgments concerning future events about which there is no direct knowledge. Timing and risk must be considered. The task is to minimize the chances of being wrong. To help deal with uncertainty, the risk-return tradeoff method may be used. Discounted cash flow methods are more realistic than methods not taking into account the time value of money in appraising investments. Consideration of the time value of money becomes more essential in inflationary periods. Capital budgeting can be used in profit and nonprofit settings.

Planning for capital expenditures requires that a determination be made regarding the "optimal" proposal, the number of dollars to be spent, and the amount of time required for completion. An appraisal is needed of current programs evaluation of new proposals, and coordination of interrelated proposals within the company. In planning a project, consideration should be given to time, cost, and quality, which all interact. For control, a comparison should be made between budgeted cost and time compared to actual cost and time.

Capital budgeting decisions must conform to the company's cash position, financing strategy, and growth rate. Will the project provide a return exceeding the long-range expected return of the business? Projects must be tied into the company's long-range planning, taking into account corporate strengths and weaknesses. The objectives of the business and the degree to which they depend on economic variables (e.g., interest rate, inflation), production (e.g., technological changes), and market factors must be established. Also, the capital budget may have to be adjusted after considering financial, economic, and political concerns. However, consideration should be given to sunk and fixed costs, which are difficult to revise once the initial decision is made.

Recommendation: Use cost-benefit analysis. Is there excessive effort for the proposal? Can it be performed internally or must it be done externally (e.g., make or buy)? Is there a more efficient means and less costly way of accomplishing the end result? Further, problem areas must be identified. An example is when long-term borrowed funds are used to finance a project where sufficient cash inflows will not be able to meet debt at maturity.

Suggestion: Measure cash flows of a project using different possible assumed variations (e.g., change in selling price of a new product). By modifying the assumptions and appraising the results, the sensitivity of cash flows to applicable variables can be seen. An advantage is the appraisal of risk in proposals based on varying assumptions. An increase in risk should result in a higher return rate.

Taxes have to be considered in making capital budgeting decisions because a project that looks good on a before-tax basis may not be acceptable on an after-tax basis. Taxes have an effect on the amount and timing of cash flows.

What-if questions are often the most crucial and difficult with regard to the capital expenditure budget and informed estimates of the major assumptions are needed. Spreadsheets can be used to analyze the cash flow implications of acquiring fixed assets.

Practices to improve the capital budgeting process to achieve sustained corporate value include optimizing project value, accounting for intangibles, managing downside risks, timing cash flows, and using project portfolio information systems.

Once an investment proposal is approved, there has to be an implementation of controls over expenditures and a reporting system regarding the project's status. Expenditures should be traced to the project and controls in place assuring the expenditures are in conformity with the approved investment proposal. Continuous monitoring should be made of how well the project is doing relative to the original plan.

DETERMINING CAPITAL EXPENDITURES

When determining capital expenditures, consider the following factors:

- Rate of return.
- Budget ceiling.
- Probability of success.
- Competition.
- Tax rate.
- Dollar amounts.
- Time value of money.
- Risk.
- Liquidity.
- Tax credits.
- Long-term business strategy.
- Forecasting errors.

TYPES OF CAPITAL BUDGETING DECISIONS TO BE MADE

As part of the capital budgeting process, decisions regarding the following must be made:

- Cost reduction program.
- Undertaking an advertising campaign.
- Replacement of assets.
- Obtaining new facilities or expanding existing ones.
- Merger analysis.

- Refinancing an outstanding debt issue.

- New and existing product evaluation.

- No profit investments (e.g., health and safety).

Exhibit 22-1 shows a typical project application form while Exhibit 22-2 presents an advice of project change form, and Exhibit 22-3 shows an appropriation request form.

Exhibit 22-1: Project Application Form

Powers Chemco, Inc.
Capital Planning and Control System
Project Application

DEPARTMENT NAME	APPLICATION NO.
DEPARTMENT CODE _____ FUNCTION CODE _____	OFFENSIVE ☐ DEFENSIVE ☐

PROJECT TITLE

DESCRIPTION/OBJECTIVES

EXPENDITURE AMOUNTS

FISCAL YEAR	1st Qtr.	2nd Qtr.	3rd Qtr.	4th Qtr.	TOTAL
20					
20					
20					
20					
20					
TOTAL					

DATE   SUBMITTED BY

COMMENTS

_____
For the Division

Exhibit 22-2: Advice of Project Change Form

Powers Chemco, Inc.
Capital Planning and Control System
Advice of Project Charge

DEPARTMENT NAME	DATE
DEPARTMENT CODE	APPROPRIATION REQUEST NO.

PROJECT TITLE

EXPENDITURE AMOUNTS

	ORIGINAL AUTHORIZED	LATEST ESTIMATE	INCREASE (DECREASE)
CAPITAL			
EXPENSE			
TOTAL			

AMOUNT SPENT TO DATE $____   AMOUNT COMMITTED TO DATE $____

WHY IS THIS NEW AMOUNT BEING REQUESTED?

PROJECT SPONSOR	DEPARTMENT / AREA SUPERVISOR

PROJECT TO BE CONTINUED   ☐
REVISED REQUEST REQUIRED   ☐
SEE COMMENT ON REVERSE SIDE   ☐   FINAL APPROVER _____
                                        DATE _____

Following is a discussion of the various capital budgeting methods: accounting (simple) rate of return; payback period; payback reciprocal; discounted payback period; net present value; profitability (ranking) index; and internal (time-adjusted) rate of return. Also discussed are contingent proposals, capital rationing, and nondiscretionary projects, as well as the incorporation of risk into the analysis.

ACCOUNTING (SIMPLE) RATE OF RETURN

Accounting rate of return (ARR) measures profitability from the conventional accounting standpoint by comparing the required investment (sometimes average investment) to future annual earnings. **Rule of Thumb:** Select the proposal with the highest ARR.

Exhibit 22-3: Appropriation Request Form

Powers Chemco, Inc. Appropriation Request
(See Reverse Side for Instruction)

ORIG. DEPT. NAME	DEPT. CODE	APPROPRIATION NO.
BUDGET CAPITALIZED ☐ EXPENSED ☐	PROJECT APPLIC. NO.	
ACCOUNTING CODE	PROJECT APPL. TOT. EXP. $	APPROPRIATION TOTAL $
DESCRIPTION		
PURPOSE		
CURRENT FACILITIES		
PROPOSED FACILITIES		
COST JUSTIFICATION (SAVINGS / BENEFITS)		

PROPOSED EXPENDITURES		APPROVALS		DATE
Equipment Cost	_____	Originator	_____	____
Material Cost	_____		_____	____
Installation Costs:	_____		_____	____
External Services	_____	Dept/Area Suprv.	_____	____
Internal Services	_____	V. President	_____	____
Miscellaneous Costs	_____	Controller	_____	____
Freight	_____	Division Head	_____	____
Taxes	_____	C.E.O	_____	____
Total	_____	Bd. Of Dir.	_____	____

EXAMPLE 1:

Initial investment	$8,000
Life	15 years
Cash inflows per year	$1,300

$$\text{Depreciation} = \frac{\text{Cost} - \text{Salvage value}}{\text{Life}} = \frac{\$8,000 - 0}{15} = \$533$$

$$\text{ARR} = \frac{\text{Cash inflows per year} - \text{Depreciation}}{\text{Initial Investment}}$$

$$\frac{\$1,300 - \$533}{\$8,000} = \frac{\$767}{\$8,000} = 9.6\%$$

If you use average investment, ARR is:

$$\text{ARR} = \frac{\$767}{\$8,000/2} = \frac{\$767}{\$4,000} = 19.2\%$$

Note: When average investment is used rather than the initial investment, ARR is doubled.

The advantages of ARR are:

- Easy to comprehend and calculate.
- Considers profitability.
- Numbers relate to financial statement presentation.
- Considers full useful life.

The disadvantages of ARR are:

- Ignores time value of money.
- Uses income data rather than cash flow data.

Note: In an automated environment, the cost of the investment would include engineering, software development, and implementation.

PAYBACK PERIOD

Payback is the number of years it takes to recover the initial investment. Payback assists in evaluating a project's risk and liquidity, faster rate of return, and earlier recoupment of funds. A benefit of payback is that it permits companies that have a cash problem to evaluate the turnover of scarce resources in order to recover earlier those funds invested. In addition, there is likely to be less possibility of loss from changes in economic conditions, obsolescence, and other unavoidable risks when the commitment is short term.

Supporters of the payback period point to its use where preliminary screening is more essential than precise figures, in situations where a poor credit position is a major factor, and when investment funds are exceptionally scarce. Some believe that payback should be used in unstable, uncertain industries subject to rapid technological change because the future is so unpredictable that there is no point in guessing what cash flows will be more than two years from now.

A company may establish a limit on the payback period beyond which an investment will not be made; a majority of executives want payback in three years or less. Another business may use payback to choose one of several investments, selecting the one with the shortest payback period.

The advantages of payback are:

- Easy to use and understand.
- Effectively handles investment risk.
- Good approach when a weak cash-and-credit position influences the selection of a proposal.
- Can be used as a supplement to other, more sophisticated techniques since it does indicate risk.

The disadvantages of payback are:

- Ignores the time value of money.
- Does not consider cash flows received after the payback period.
- Does not measure profitability.
- Does not indicate how long the maximum payback period should be.
- Penalizes projects that result in small cash flows in their early years and heavy cash flows in their later years.

Warning: Do not select a proposal simply because the payback method indicates acceptance. The discounting methods, such as present value and internal rate of return, will still have to be used.

EXAMPLE 2: You are considering a new product. It will initially cost $250,000. Expected cash inflows are $80,000 for the next five years. You want your money back in four years.

$$\text{Payback period} \;=\; \frac{\text{Initial investment}}{\text{Annual cash inflow}} \;=\; \frac{\$250,000}{\$80,000} \;=\; 3.125$$

Because the payback period (3.125) is less than the cutoff payback period (4), you should accept the proposal.

EXAMPLE 3: You invest $40,000 and receive the following cash inflows:

Year 1 $15,000

Year 2 $20,000

Year 3 $28,000

If there are unequal cash inflows each year, to determine the payback period, add up the annual cash inflows to come up with the amount of the cash-out lay. The result will reveal how long it will take to recover the investment.

Manufacturers usually use an unadjusted payback period of between two and four years when appraising advanced manufacturing equipment.

PAYBACK RECIPROCAL

Payback reciprocal is the reciprocal of the payback time. This often gives a quick, accurate estimate of the internal rate of return (IRR) on an investment when the project life is more than twice the payback period and the cash inflows are uniform every period.

> **EXAMPLE 4:** ABC Company is contemplating three projects, each of which would require an initial investment of $10,000, and each of which is expected to generate a cash inflow of $2,000 per year. The payback period is five years ($10,000/$2,000), and the payback reciprocal is 1/5, or 20%. The table of the present value of an annuity of $1 shows that the factor of 5.00 applies to the following useful lives and internal rates of return:

Useful Life	IRR
10 years	15%
15	18
20	19

> It can be observed that the payback reciprocal is 20% as compared with the IRR of 18% when the life is 15 years, and 20% as compared with the IRR of 19% when the life is 20 years. This shows that the payback reciprocal gives a reasonable approximation of the IRR if the useful life of the project is at least twice the payback period.

DISCOUNTED PAYBACK PERIOD

Before looking at discounted cash flow methods, it is important to realize that less reliability exists with discounted cash flow analysis where there is future uncertainty, the environment is changing, and cash flows are hard to predict.

The time value of money can be taken into account by using the discounted payback method. The payback period will be longer using the discounted method because money is worth less over time.

How to Do It: Discounted payback is computed by adding the present value of each year's cash inflows until they equal the investment.

> **EXAMPLE 5:** Assume the same facts as in Example 3 and a cost of capital of 10%.

$$\text{Discounted payback} = \frac{\text{Initial cash outlay}}{\text{Discounted annual cash inflows}}$$

	$40,000	
Year 1	**Year 2**	**Year 3**
$15,000 +	$20,000 +	$28,000
× .9091 +	× .8264 +	× .7513
$13,637 +	$16,528 +	$21,036

$$\$30,165 \qquad + \quad \$\ 9,835$$
$$\$21,036$$
$$2\ \text{years} \qquad + \quad .47 \qquad = 2.47\ \text{years}$$

EXAMPLE 6: Assume a machine purchased for $18,000 yields cash inflows of $4,000, $5,000, $6,000, $6,000, and $8,000. The cost of capital is 10%. Use Table A-3 in the Appendix. Then we have:

Year	Cash Flow	(Table A-3) = T3(10%, *n*) PV Factor at 10%	PV of Cash Flow
1	$4,000	.909	$3,636
2	5,000	.826	4,130
3	6,000	.751	4,506
4	6,000	.683	4,098
5	8,000	.621	4,968

The number of years required to recoup the $18,000 investment is:

Year	1	$ 3,636
	2	4,130
	3	4,506
	4	4,098
		$16,370

Balance in year 5: ($18,000 – $16,370) = $1,630

Therefore, the discounted payback period is: 4 years + $1,630/$4,968 = 4.33 years.

The discount payback rule recognizes the time value of money, but still ignores all cash flows after that date.

NET PRESENT VALUE

The present value method compares the present value of future cash flows expected from an investment project to the initial cash outlay for the investment. Net cash flows are the difference between forecasted cash inflow received because of the investment to the expected cash outflow of the investment. The minimum rate of return earned by the company on its money should be used as a discount rate.

A company should use as the discount rate its cost of capital. **Rule of Thumb:** Considering inflation, the cost of debt, and so on, the anticipated return should be about 10%–13%.

Note: The net present value method discounts all cash flows at the cost of capital, thus implicitly assuming that these cash flows can be reinvested at this rate.

Tip: If a proposal is supposed to provide a return, invest in it only if it provides a positive net present value. If two proposals are mutually exclusive (acceptance of one precludes the acceptance of another), accept the proposal with the highest present value. An advantage of net present value is that it considers the time value of money. A disadvantage is the subjectivity in determining expected annual cash inflows and expected period of benefit.

Note: In an advanced automated environment, the terminal value requires managerial accountants to forecast technological, economic, operational, strategic, and market developments over the investment's life so that a reasonable estimate of potential value may be made.

Warning: Using the return rate earned by the company as the discount rate may be misleading in certain cases. It may be a good idea to also look at the return rate investors earn on similar projects. If the hurdle rates selected are based on the company's return on average projects, an internal company decision will occur that helps to increase the corporate return. Yet if the company with a very limited budget is earning a very high rate of return, some good projects will be selected and some will be rejected. What if the project left would really enhance value?

If the corporate return rate is below what investors can earn elsewhere, the tendency is to believe that the investment is attractive. The project may involve below-normal profitability or lower per-share value, and result in lower creditor and investor ratings of the firm.

The net present value method typically provides more reliable signals than other methods. By employing net present value and using best estimates of reinvestment rates, the most advantageous project can be selected.

EXAMPLE 7: You are considering replacing Executive 1 with Executive 2. Executive 2 requires a payment of $200,000 upon contract signing. She will receive an annual salary of $300,000. Executive 1's current annual salary is $140,000. Because Executive 2's performance is superior, you expect there will be an increase in annual cash flows from operations (ignoring salary) of $350,000 for each of the next ten years. The cost of capital is 12%.

As indicated in the following calculations, since there is a positive net present value, Executive 2 should replace Executive 1.

Year	Explanation	Amount	×	Factor	=	Present Value
0	Contract signing bonus	– $200,000	×	1		– $ 200,000
1–10	Increased salary: ($300,000 – $140,000)	– $160,000	×	5.6502*		– $ 904,032
1–10	Increase in annual cash flow from operations	+ $350,000	×	5.6502*		$1,977,570
	Net present value					$ 873,538

* Present value of an ordinary annuity factor for 10 years and an interest rate of 12% = T4 (12%, 10 years) from Table A-4 in the Appendix.

Use of Financial Calculators and Excel Spreadsheet Program

There are many financial calculators that contain pre-programmed formulas to perform many present value applications. Furthermore, spreadsheet software such as Excel has built-in financial functions to perform many such applications. Excel financial functions include:

1. PV(rate, nper, pmt, [fv], [type])—calculates the present value of an investment

2. NPV(rate,value1,[value2])—calculates the net present value of an investment by using a discount rate and a series of future payments (negative values) and income (positive values).

3. IRR(values, [guess])—calculates the internal rate of return for a series of cash flows represented by the numbers in values. These cash flows do not have to be even.

4. MIRR(values, finance rate, reinvest rate)—returns the modified internal rate of return (MIRR) for a series of periodic cash flows. MIRR considers both the cost of the investment and the interest received on reinvestment of cash.

For numerical examples, click f_x, select the function you want to use, and then click "help on this function."

EXAMPLE 8: You own a business for which you have received a $1,000,000 offer. If you do not sell, you will remain in business for eight years and will invest another $50,000 in your firm. If you stay, you will sell your business in the eighth year for $60,000.

You expect yearly sales to increase by 50% from the present level of $500,000. Direct material is proportional to sales. Direct labor is proportional to sales, but will increase by 30% for all labor. Variable overhead varies with sales, and annual fixed overhead will total $70,000, including depreciation. Straight-line depreciation will increase from $7,000 to $10,000. At the end of eight years, all fixed assets will be fully depreciated. Selling and administrative expenses are assumed to remain constant. The cost of capital is 14%.

Your current year's income statement is:

Sales		$500,000
Less: cost of sales		
Direct material	$100,000	
Direct labor	120,000	
Variable overhead	50,000	
Fixed overhead	65,000	335,000
Gross margin		$165,000
Less: selling and administrative expenses*		40,000
Net income		$125,000

* Includes your salary of $20,000

Your forecasted income statement for each of the next eight years is:

Sales: $500,000 × 1.5		$750,000
Less: cost of sales		
Direct material $100,000 × 1.5	$150,000	
Direct labor $120,000 × 1.5 × 1.3	234,000	
Variable overhead $50,000 × 1.5	75,000	
Fixed overhead	70,000	529,000
Gross margin		$221,000
Less: selling and administrative expenses		40,000
Net Income		$181,000

Your annual cash flow from operations is:

Net income	$181,000	
Add: depreciation		10,000
Salary		20,000
Annual cash flow from operations		$211,000

A comparison of your alternatives is:

Sell business	+ $1,000,000

Stay in business:

Year	Explanation	Amount	×	Factor	=	Present Value
0	Investment in assets	– $ 50,000	×	1		– $ 50,000
1–8	Annual cash inflow	+ $211,000	×	4.6389		+ $ 987,808
8	Sales price of business	+ $ 60,000	×	0.3506		+ $ 21,036
Net present value						+ $ 949,844

Since the net present value is higher for selling the business ($1,000,000) than for staying in business ($949,844), you should sell now.

EXAMPLE 9: You are considering replacing an old machine with a new one. The old machine has a book value of $800,000 and a remaining life of 10 years. The expected salvage value of the old machine is $50,000, but if you sold it now you would obtain $700,000. The new machine costs $2,000,000 and has a salvage value of $250,000. The new machine will result in annual savings of $400,000. The tax rate is 50%, tax credit is 10%, and the cost of capital is 14%. Use straight line depreciation. You have to determine whether to replace the machine.

The net increase in annual cash flow is:

	Net Income	Cash Flow
Annual savings	$400,000	$400,000

Less: incremental depreciation

$$\text{New machine} \quad \frac{\$2,000,000 - \$250,000}{10} = \$175,000$$

$$\text{Old machine} \quad \frac{\$800,000 - \$50,000}{10} = \$75,000$$

	Net Income	Cash Flow
Incremental depreciation		100,000
Income before tax		$300,000
Tax (50%)	150,000	150,000
Income after tax		$150,000
Net cash inflow		$250,000

The net present value is:

Year	Explanation	Amount	× Factor	=	Present Value
0	Cost of new machine	− $2,000,000	× 1.000		$2,000,000
0	Sale of old machine	700,000	× 1.000		700,000
1	Tax credit	200,000	× 0.877		175,400
1	Tax benefit from loss on sale of old machine	50,000	× 0.877		43,850
1–10	Yearly increase in cash flows	250,000	× 5.216		1,304,000
10	Incremental salvage value	200,000	× 0.270		54,000
					$ 277,500

The replacement of the old machine with a new machine should be made because of the resulting positive net present value.

PROFITABILITY INDEX

The profitability (ranking) index (also called excess present value index, cost-benefit ratio) is a net rather than an aggregate index and is employed to differentiate the initial cash investment from later cash inflows. If there are budget constraints, proposals of different dollar magnitude can be ranked on a comparative basis. Use the index as a means of ranking the project in descending order of attractiveness. Rank the projects in descending order using the profitability index. The profitability index is:

$$\text{Profitability index} \ = \ \frac{\text{Present value of cash inflows}}{\text{Present value of cash outflows}}$$

Rule of Thumb: Accept a proposal with a profitability index equal to or greater than 1.

Warning: A higher profitability index does not always coincide with the project with the highest net present value.

Tip: The internal rate of return and the net present value approaches may give conflicting signals when competing projects have unequal times. The profitability index gives the correct decision, however, and is superior under these circumstances.

Capital rationing takes place when a business is not able to invest in projects having a net present value greater than or equal to zero. Typically, the firm establishes an upper limit to its capital budget based on budgetary constraints.

Special Note: With capital rationing, the project with the highest ranking index rather than net present value should be selected for investment.

Exhibit 22-4 shows the capital rationing decision process.

EXAMPLE 10: You have the following information regarding two proposals:

	Proposal A	Proposal B
Initial investment	$100,000	$10,000
Present value of cash inflows	$500,000	$90,000

The net present value of proposal A is $400,000 and that of proposal B is $80,000. Based on net present value, proposal A is better. However, this is very misleading when a budget constraint exists. In this case, proposal B's profitability index of 9 far surpasses proposal A's index of 5. Thus, profitability index should be used in evaluating proposals when budget constraints exist. The net result is that proposal B should be selected over proposal A.

EXAMPLE 11:

Projects	Investment	Present Value	Profitability Index	Ranking
A	$ 70,000	$112,000	1.6	1
B	100,000	145,000	1.45	2
C	110,000	126,500	1.15	5
D	60,000	79,000	1.32	3
E	40,000	38,000	0.95	6
F	80,000	95,000	1.19	4

The budget constraint is $250,000. You should select projects A, B, and D, as indicated by the following calculations:

Exhibit 22-4: Capital Rationing Decision Process

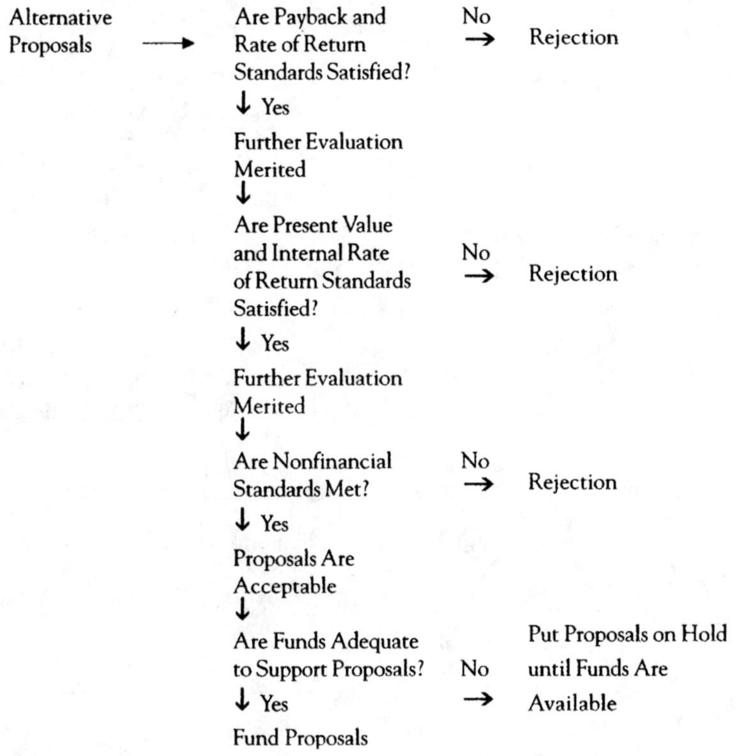

Alternative Proposals	→	Are Payback and Rate of Return Standards Satisfied?	No →	Rejection
		↓ Yes		
		Further Evaluation Merited		
		↓		
		Are Present Value and Internal Rate of Return Standards Satisfied?	No →	Rejection
		↓ Yes		
		Further Evaluation Merited		
		↓		
		Are Nonfinancial Standards Met?	No →	Rejection
		↓ Yes		
		Proposals Are Acceptable		
		↓		
		Are Funds Adequate to Support Proposals?	No →	Put Proposals on Hold until Funds Are Available
		↓ Yes		
		Fund Proposals		

Project	Investment	Present Value
A	$ 70,000	$112,000
B	100,000	145,000
D	60,000	79,000
	$ 230,000	$336,000

where net present value = $336,000 – $230,000 = $106,000

Unfortunately, the profitability index method has some limitations. One of the more serious limitations is that it breaks down whenever more than one resource is rationed.

A more general approach to solving capital rationing problems is the use of mathematical (or zero-one) programming. Here, the objective is to select the mix of projects that maximizes the net present value subject to a budget constraint.

EXAMPLE 12: Using the data given in Example 11, we can set up the problem as a mathematical programming one. First we label project A as X_1, B as X_2, and so on. The problem can be stated as follows:

Maximize

NPV = $42,000 X_1 + $45,000 X_2 + $16,500 X_3 + $19,000 X_4 – $2,000 X_5 + $15,000 X_6

subject to

$70,000 X_1 + $100,000 X_2 + $110,000 X_3 + $60,000 X_4 + $40,000 X_5 + $80,000 X_6 ≤ $250,000;

X_1 = 0, 1 (i = 1, 2, ..., 6)

Using the mathematical program solution routine, the solution to this problem is:

$$X_1 = 1, X_2 = 1, X_4 = 1$$

and the net present value is $106,000. Thus, projects A, B, and D should be accepted.

CONTINGENT PROPOSALS

A contingent proposal is one that requires acceptance of another related one. Hence, the proposals must be looked at together. A profitability index for the group is computed.

EXAMPLE 13:

Proposal	Present Value of Cash Outflow	Present Value of Cash Inflow
A	$160,000	$210,000
B	60,000	40,000
Total	$220,000	$250,000

$$\text{Profitability index} = \frac{\$250,000}{\$220,000} = 1.14$$

INTERNAL (TIME-ADJUSTED) RATE OF RETURN

The internal rate of return (IRR), also known as the time-adjusted rate of return, is the return earned on a given proposal. It is the discount rate equating the net present value of cash inflows to the net present value of cash outflows to zero. The internal rate of return assumes cash inflows are reinvested at the internal rate.

This method involves trial-and-error computations. However, the use of a computer or programmable calculator simplifies the internal rate of return process.

The internal rate of return can be compared with the required rate of return (cutoff or hurdle rate).

Rule of Thumb: If the internal rate of return equals or exceeds the required rate, the project is accepted. The required rate of return is typically a company's cost of capital, sometimes adjusted for risk.

The internal rate of return considers the time value of money, and is more realistic and accurate than the accounting rate of return method. It does not consider the varying size of investment in competing projects and their respective dollar profitabilities. Further, in limited cases, when there are multiple reversals in the cash flow stream, the project could yield more than one IRR.

To solve for internal rate of return where unequal cash inflows exist, the trial-and-error method can be used while working through the present value tables. Guidelines in using trial and error are:

- Compute net present value at the cost of capital, denoted here as r_1.
- See if net present value is positive or negative.
- If net present value is positive, use a higher rate than r_1.
- If net present value is negative, use a lower rate than r_1. The exact internal rate of return at which net present value equals zero is somewhere between the two rates.
- Compute net present value using r_1 and the other rate chosen.
- Perform interpolation for exact rate.

   EXAMPLE 14: A project costing $100,000 is expected to produce the following cash inflows:

Year	
1	$50,000
2	30,000
3	20,000
4	40,000

Using trial and error, you can calculate the internal rate as follows:

Year	10%	Present Value (PV)	16%	PV	18%	PV
1	0.909	$ 45,450	0.862	$ 43,100	0.847	$ 42,350
2	0.826	24,780	0.743	22,290	0.718	21,540
3	0.751	15,020	0.641	12,820	0.609	12,180
4	0.683	27,320	0.552	22,080	0.516	20,640
		+ $112,570		+ $100,290		+ $96,710
Investment		– 100,000		– 100,000		– 100,000
NPV		+ $ 12,570		+ $290		– $ 3,290

The internal rate of return on the project is a little more than 16% because at that rate the net present value of the investment is approximately zero.

If the return on the investment is expected to be in one lump sum after a period of years, you can use the Present Value of $1 table to find the internal rate.

EXAMPLE 15: You are considering two mutually exclusive investment proposals. The cost of capital is 10%. Expected cash flows are as follows:

Project	Investment	Year 1	Year 6
A	$10,000	$12,000	
B	$10,000		$20,000

Internal rates of return are:

$$\text{Project A} \quad \frac{\$10,000}{\$12,000} \ = \ 0.8333$$

Looking across one year on the table, 0.8333 corresponds to an internal rate of 20%.

$$\text{Project B} \quad \frac{\$10,000}{\$20,000} \ = \ .5000$$

Looking across six years on the table, 0.5000 corresponds to an internal rate of 12%.

Project A should be selected because it has a higher internal rate of return than Project B.

If the cash inflows each year are equal, the internal rate of return is computed first by determining a factor (which happens to be the same as the payback period) and then looking up the rate of return on the present value of an annuity of one table.

EXAMPLE 16: You invest $100,000 in a proposal that will produce annual cash inflows of $15,000 a year for the next 20 years.

$$\text{Internal rate of return} \ = \ \frac{\$100,000}{\$15,000} \ = \ 6.6667$$

Now we go to the Present Value of an Annuity of $1 table (Table A-4 in the Appendix). Looking across 20 years, we find that the factor closest to 6.6667 is 6.6231, in the 14% column. Hence the internal rate is about 14%.

EXAMPLE 17:

Initial investment	$ 12,950
Estimated life	10 years
Annual cash inflows	$ 3,000
Cost of capital	12%

The internal rate of return (IRR) calculation follows, including interpolation to get the exact rate.

$$\text{T4 } (i, \ 10 \text{ years}) = \text{PV of annuity factor} \ = \ \frac{\$12,950}{\$3,000} \ = \ 4.317$$

The value 4.317 is somewhere between 18% and 20% in the 10-year line of the PV of Annuity table. Using interpolation you get:

	Present Value of Annuity Factor	
18%	4.494	4.494
IRR		4.317
20%	4.192	
Difference	0.302	0.177

$$\text{Therefore, IRR} \ = \ 18\% \ + \ \frac{0.177}{0.302} \ (20\% - 18\%)$$

$$= \ 18\% + 0.586(2\%) = 18\% + 1.17\% = 19.17\%$$

Because the internal rate of return (19.17%) exceeds the cost of capital (12%), the project should be accepted.

CAN A COMPUTER HELP?

Spreadsheet programs can be used in making IRR calculations. For example, Microsoft's Excel has a function IRR (values, guess). Excel considers negative numbers as cash outflows (such as the initial investment) and positive numbers as cash inflows. Many financial calculators have similar features. Suppose there is a need to calculate the IRR of a $12,950 investment (the value – 12950 entered in year 0) that is followed by 10 monthly cash inflows of $3,000 (3,000 in year 1 through year 10). Using a guess of 12% (the value of 0.12), which is in effect the cost of capital, the formula would be @IRR (values, 0.12), and Excel would return 19.15%, as follows:

Year 0	1	2	3	4	5	6	7	8	9	10
12,950	3,000	3,000	3,000	3,000	3,000	3,000	3,000	3,000	3,000	3,000

IRR = 19.15%
NPV = $4,000.67

Note: The Excel formula for NPV is NPV (discount rate, cash inflow values) + *I*, where *I* is given as a negative number.

MULTIPLE INTERNAL RATES OF RETURN

In nonconventional (mixed) projects that have one or more periods of cash outflows (inflows) with periods of cash inflows (outflows), there may be multiple internal rates of return.

> ***EXAMPLE 18:*** Consider a strip-mining project with the following cash flows:

0	1	2
–$60,000	155,000	–100,000

This project yields two internal rates of return (IRRs) = 25% and 33.33%. Unfortunately, financial calculators and spreadsheet software are not aware of this problem and solely report the first IRR. Descartes's rule of signs states that in a capital budgeting context, the number of IRRs is equal to the number of variations in the sign of the cash flow series or is less than that number by an even integer. For example, according to the rule, if the series of cash flows has three variations in sign, this series must have either three or one value of IRRs.

NONDISCRETIONARY PROJECTS

Some investments are made out of necessity rather than profitability (e.g., pollution control equipment, safety equipment). In this case, you will have solely a negative cash flow. Hence, the discretionary projects must earn a return rate in excess of the cost of capital to make up for the losses on nondiscretionary projects.

EXAMPLE 19: A company's cost of capital is 14% and $30 million of capital projects, 25% of which are nondiscretionary projects. It thus has to earn $4.2 million per year (14% × $30 million). The $22.5 million of discretionary projects ($30 million less 25%) must earn 18.7% ($4.2 million/$22.5 million) rather than 14% to achieve the overall corporate earnings goal of $4.2 million.

COMPARISON OF METHODS

In general, the discounting cash flow methods (net present value, internal rate of return, and profitability index) yield the same conclusions for competing proposals, but these methods can give different rankings to mutually exclusive proposals in certain cases. Any one of the following conditions can cause contradictory rankings:

- Project lives differ.

- There is a higher cost for one project relative to another.

- The trend in cash flow of one project is the reverse of that of another.

One of the following characteristics of the company may also produce conflicting rankings:

- Future investment opportunities are expected to be different than at present, and the investor knows whether they will be better or worse.

- There is capital rationing, (a maximum level of funding for capital investments).

The major cause for different rankings of alternative projects under present value and internal rate of return methods relates to the varying assumptions regarding the reinvestment rate employed for discounting cash flows. The net present value method assumes cash flows are reinvested at the cost of capital rate. The internal rate of return method assumes cash flows are reinvested at the internal rate.

Tip: The net present value method typically provides a correct ranking because the cost of capital is a more realistic reinvestment rate.

The determination as to which method is best for a business really depends on which reinvestment rate is nearest the rate the business can earn on future cash flows from a project.

Note: The Board of Directors typically reviews the company's required rate of return each year, and may increase or decrease it depending on the company's current rate of return and cost of capital.

The minimum rate of return required for a proposal may be waived in a situation where the proposal has significant future benefit (e.g., research and development), applies to a necessity program (e.g., safety requirement), and has qualitative benefit (e.g., product quality).

EXAMPLE 20: Assume the following:

Cash Flows

Project	0	1	2	3	4	5
A	$(100)	$120				
B	(100)					$201.14

Computing IRR and NPV at 10% gives the different rankings as follows:

	IRR	NPV
A	20%	9.09
B	15%	24.89

The general rule is to go by NPV ranking. Thus project B would be chosen over project A.

The difference in ranking between the two methods is caused by the methods' reinvestment rate assumptions. The IRR method assumes project A's cash inflow of $120 is reinvested at 20% for the subsequent four years, and the NPV method assumes $120 is reinvested at 10%. The correct decision is to select the project with the higher NPV (project B), because the NPV method assumes a more realistic reinvestment rate—that is, the cost of capital (10% in this example).

THE MODIFIED INTERNAL RATE OF RETURN

When the IRR and NPV methods produce a contradictory ranking for mutual exclusive projects, the modified IRR (MIRR) overcomes the disadvantage of IRR.

The MIRR is defined as the discount rate that forces I to equal PV of terminal (future) value compounded at the cost of capital.

The MIRR forces cash flow reinvestment at the cost of capital rather than the project's own IRR, which was the problem with the IRR. MIRR avoids the problem of multiple IRRs. Conflicts can still occur in ranking mutually exclusive projects with differing sizes. NPV should again be used in such a case.

In Example 20, project A's MIRR is:

First, compute the project's terminal value at a 10% cost of capital.

$$120 \ T1_{4.10} = 120 \times 1.4641 = 175.69$$

where Tl = FV of $1 (from Table A-1 in the Appendix)

Next, find the IRR by setting:

$$100 = 175.69 \ T3 \ (MIRR, 5)$$

$$T3 = 100/175.69 = 0.5692, \text{ which gives MIRR} = \text{about } 12\%$$

where T3 = PV of $1 (from Table A-3 in the Appendix)

Now we see the consistent ranking from both the NPV and MIRR methods.

	MIRR	NPV at 10%
A	12%	$9.09
B	15	24.89

Note: Microsoft Excel has a function MIRR (values, finance rate, reinvest rate). The following shows Excel calculations on IRR, NPV, and MIRR.

| | Cash Flows | |
Period	A	B
0	$(100.00)	$(100.00)
1	120	0
2	0	0
3	0	0
4	0	0
5	0	201.14
IRR =	20%	15%
NPV =	$9.09	$24.89

Finance rate   0.12
Reinvest rate   0.1

MIRR =	12%	15%

COMPARING PROJECTS WITH UNEQUAL LIVES

A replacement decision typically involves two mutually exclusive projects. When the two mutually exclusive projects have significantly different lives, an adjustment is necessary. The two approaches discussed are: (1) the replacement chain (common life) approach and (2) the equivalent annual annuity approach.

The Replacement Chain (Common Life) Approach

This procedure extends one, or both, projects until an equal life is achieved. For example, project A has a six-year life, whereas Project B has a three-year life. Under this approach, the projects would be extended to a common life of six years. Project B would have an adjusted NPV equal to the NPV_B plus the NPV_B discounted for three years at the project's cost of capital. Then the project with the higher NPV would be chosen.

> **EXAMPLE 21:** Sims Industries, Inc. is considering two machines to replace an old machine. Machine A has a life of ten years, will cost $24,500, and will produce net cash savings of $4,800 per year. Machine B has an expected life of five years, will cost $20,000, and will produce net cash savings in operating costs of $6,000 per year. The company's cost of capital is 14%. Project A's NPV is

$$NPV_A = PV - I = \$4,800 \text{ T4 } (14\%, 10) - \$24,500$$
$$= \$4,800(5.2161) - \$24,500 = \$25,037.28 - \$24,500$$
$$= \$537.28$$

where T4 = PV of an annuity (from Table A-4 in the Appendix)

Project B's extended time line can be set up as follows:

0	1	2	3	4	5	6	7	8	9	10
−20000	6000	6000	6000	6000	6000	6000	6000	6000	6000	6000
					−20000					

Adjusted NPV_B $= PV - I = \$6,000 \text{ T4 } (14\%, 10) - \$20,000 \text{ T3 } (14\%, 5) - \$20,000$
$= \$6,000(5.2161) - \$20,000(0.5194) - \$20,000$
$= \$31,296.60 - \$10,388.00 - \$20,000$
$= \$908.60$

Or, alternatively:

$NPV_B = PV - I = \$6,000 \text{ T4 } (14\%, 5) - \$20,000$
$= \$6,000(3.4331) - \$20,000$
$= \$20,598.60 - \$20,000$
$= \$598.60$

Adjusted NPV_B $= NPV_B + NPV_B$ discounted for five years
$= \$598.60 + \$598.60 \text{ T3 } (14\%, 5)$
$= \$598.60 + \$598.60(0.5194)$
$= \$598.60 + \$310.91$
$= \$909.51$ (due to rounding errors)

The Equivalent Annual Annuity Approach

It is often cumbersome to compare projects with different lives. For example, one project might have a four-year life versus a ten-year life for the other. This would require a replacement chain analysis over 20 years, the lowest common denominator of the two lives. In such a case, it is often simpler to use an alternative approach—the *equivalent annual annuity (EAA) method.*

This procedure involves three steps:

1. Determine each project's NPV over its original life.
2. Find the constant annuity cash flow or EAA, using

$$\frac{NPV \text{ of each project}}{\text{T4 } (i, n)}$$

3. Assuming infinite replacement, find the infinite horizon (or perpetuity) NPV of each project, using

$$\frac{\text{EAA of each}}{\text{Cost of capital}}$$

EXAMPLE 22: From Example 21, NPV_A = $537.28 and NPV_B = $598.60.

To obtain the constant annuity cash flow or EAA, we do the following:

EAA_A = $537.28/T4 (14%,10) = $537.28/5.2161 = $103.00

EAA_B = $598.60/T4 (14%,5) = $598.60/3.4331 = $174.36

Thus, the infinite horizon NPVs are as follows:

Infinite horizon NPV_A = $103.00/0.14 = $735.71

Infinite horizon NPV_B = $174.36/0.14 = $1,245.43

THE CONCEPT OF ABANDONMENT VALUE

The notion of abandonment value recognizes that abandonment of a project before the end of its physical life can have a significant impact on the project's return and risk. This distinguishes between the project's economic life and physical life. Two types of abandonment can occur:

1. Abandonment of an asset that is unprofitable.

2. Sale of the asset to some other party who can extract more value than the original owner.

EXAMPLE 23: ABC Company is considering a project with an initial cost of $5,000 and net cash flows of $2,000 for next three years. The expected abandonment cash flows for years 0, 1, 2, and 3 are $5,000, $3,000, $2,500, and $0. The firm's cost of capital is 10%. We will compute NPVs in three cases.

Case 1. NPV of the project if kept for 3 years.

NPV = PV – I = $2,000 T4 (10%, 3) = $2,000 (2.4869) – $5,000

= –$26.20

Case 2. NPV of the project if abandoned after year 1

NPV = PV – I = $2,000 T3 (10%, 1) + $3,500 T3 (10%, 2) – $5,000

= $2,000 (0.9091) + $3,000 (0.9091) – $5,000

= $1,818.20 + $2,717.30 – $5,000 = –$454.50

Case 3. NPV of the project if abandoned after year 2

NPV = PV – I = $2,000 T3 (10%, 1) + $2,000 T3 (10%, 2) + $1,500 T3 (10%, 2) – $5,000

= $2,000 (0.9091) + $2,000 (0.8264) + $2,500 (0.8264) – $5,000

= $1,818.20 + $1,652.80 + $2,066.00 – $5,000 = $537

The company should abandon the project after year 2.

HOW INCOME TAXES AFFECT INVESTMENT DECISIONS

Income taxes make a difference in many capital budgeting decisions. The project that is attractive on a before-tax basis may have to be rejected on an after-tax basis and vice versa. Income taxes typically affect both the amount and the timing of cash flows. Because net income, not cash inflows, is subject to tax, after-tax cash inflows are not usually the same as after-tax net income.

How to Calculate After-Tax Cash Flows

Following is an example of the calculation of after-tax cash flows.

Let us define

S = Sales

E = Cash operating expenses

d = Depreciation

t = Tax rate

Then, before-tax cash inflows (or cash savings) = $S - E$ and net income = $S - E - d$.

By definition,

$$\text{After-tax cash inflows} = \text{Before-tax cash inflows} - \text{Taxes}$$
$$= (S - E) - (S - E - d)\,(t)$$

Rearranging gives the short-cut formula:

$$\text{After-tax cash inflows} = (S - E)\,(1 - t) + (d)\,(t) \text{ or}$$
$$= (S - E - d)\,(1 - t) + d$$

As can be seen, the deductibility of depreciation from sales in arriving at taxable net income reduces income tax payments and thus serves as a *tax shield.*

Tax shield = Tax savings on depreciation = $(d)\,(t)$

> ***EXAMPLE 24:*** Assume:
>
> S = $12,000
>
> E = $10,000
>
> d = $500 per year using the straight line method
>
> t = 30%
>
> Then,

$$\text{After-tax cash inflow} = (\$12{,}000 - \$10{,}000)\,(1 - .3) + (\$500)\,(.3)$$
$$= (\$2{,}000)\,(.7) + (\$500)\,(.3)$$
$$= \$1{,}400 + \$150 = \$1{,}550$$
$$\text{Note that a tax shield} = \text{tax savings on depreciation} = (d)\,(t)$$
$$= (\$500)\,(.3) = \$150$$

Because the tax shield is dt, the higher the depreciation deduction, the higher the tax savings on depreciation. Therefore, an accelerated depreciation method (such as double-declining balance) produces higher tax savings than the straight-line method. Accelerated methods produce higher present values for the tax savings, which may make a given investment more attractive.

EXAMPLE 25: The Navistar Company estimates that it can save $2,500 a year in cash operating costs for the next ten years if it buys a special-purpose machine at a cost of $10,000. No residual value is expected. Depreciation is by the straight-line method. Assume that the income tax rate is 30%, and the after-tax cost of capital (minimum required rate of return) is 10%. After-tax cash savings can be calculated as follows:

Note that depreciation by the straight-line method is $10,000/10 = $1,000 per year. Thus,

$$\text{After-tax cash savings} = (S - E)(1 - t) + (d)(t)$$
$$= \$2,500(1 - .3) + \$1,000(.3)$$
$$= \$1,750 + \$300 = \$2,050$$

To see if this machine should be purchased, the net present value can be calculated.

$$PV = \$2,050 \ T4_{10,10} = \$2,050 \ (6.145) = \$12,597.25$$

Thus, $NPV = PV - I = \$12,597.25 - \$10,000 = \$2,597.25$

Because NPV is positive, the machine should be bought.

CAPITAL BUDGETING DECISIONS AND THE MODIFIED ACCELERATED COST RECOVERY SYSTEM

Although the traditional depreciation methods still can be used for computing depreciation for book purposes, 1981 saw a new way of computing depreciation deductions for tax purposes. The current rule is called the *modified accelerated cost recovery system* (MACRS) rule, enacted by Congress in 1981 and modified somewhat in 1986 under the Tax Reform Act of 1986. This rule is characterized as follows:

- It abandons the concept of useful life and accelerates depreciation deductions by placing all depreciable assets into one of eight age property classes. It calculates deductions, based on an allowable percentage of the asset's original cost (see Exhibits 22-5 and 22-6).

  With a shorter asset tax life than useful life, the company would be able to deduct depreciation more quickly and save more in income taxes in the earlier years, thereby making an investment more attractive. The rationale behind the system is that this way the government encourages the company to invest in facilities and increase its productive capacity and efficiency. (Remember that the higher the *d,* the larger the tax shield $(d)(t)$).

- Because the allowable percentages in Exhibit 22-5 add up to 100%, there is no need to consider the salvage value of an asset in computing depreciation.

- The company may elect the straight-line method. The straight-line convention must follow what is called the *half-year convention.* This means that the company can deduct only half of the regular straight-line depreciation amount in the first year. The reason for electing to use the MACRS optional straight-line method is that some firms may prefer to stretch out depreciation deductions using the straight-line method rather than to accelerate them. Those firms are the ones that just start out or have little or no income and wish to show more income on their income statements.

• If an asset is disposed of before the end of its class life, the half-year convention allows half the depreciation for that year (early disposal rule).

EXAMPLE 26: Assume that a machine falls under a three-year property class and costs $3,000 initially. The straight line option under MACRS differs from the traditional straight-line method in that, under this method, the company would deduct only $500 depreciation in the first year and the fourth year ($3,000/3 years = $1,000; $1,000/2 = $500). The following table compares the straight-line with half-year convention and the MACRS.

Year	Straight-Line (half-year) Depreciation	Cost		MACRS %	MACRS Deduction
1	$ 500	$ 3,000	×	33.3%	$ 999
2	1,000	3,000	×	44.5	1,335
3	1,000	3,000	×	14.8	444
4	500	3,000	×	7.4	222
	$3,000				$3,000

EXAMPLE 27: A machine costs $10,000. Annual cash inflows are expected to be $5,000. The machine will be depreciated using the MACRS rule and will fall under the three-year property class. The cost of capital after taxes is 10%. The estimated life of the machine is five years. The salvage value of the machine at the end of the fifth year is expected to be $1,200. The tax rate is 30%. Should you buy the machine? Use the NPV method.

The formula for computation of after-tax cash inflows $(S - E)(1 - t) + (d)(t)$ needs to be computed separately. The NPV analysis can be performed as follows:

					Present Value Factor @ 10%	Present Value
(S − E)(1 − t):						
	$5,000	$5,000 (1 − .3)	=	**$3,500**	3.791(a)	$13,268.50
(d)(t):						
Year	Cost	MACRS %	d	(d) (t)		
1	$10,000 ×	33.3%	$3,330	$999	.909(b)	908.09
2	$10,000 ×	44.5	4,450	1,335	.826(b)	1,102.71
3	$10,000 ×	14.8	1,480	444	.751(b)	333.44
4	$10,000 ×	7.4	740	222	.683(b)	151.63

Salvage value:

$1,200 in	$1,200(1 – .3) = **$840**(c)	$840	.621 (b)	521.64
year 5	in year **5**			
	Present value (PV)			$16,286.01

(a) T4 at 10% for 4 years = T4 (10%, 4) = 3.170 (from Table A-4 in the Appendix).

(b) T3 values (year 1, 2, 3, 4, 5) = T3 (10%, *n*) obtained from Table A-3 in the Appendix.

(c) Any salvage value received under the MACRS rules is a *taxable gain* (the excess of the selling price over book value, $1,200 in this example), because the book value will be zero at the end of the life of the machine.

Since NPV = PV – I = $16,286.01 – $10,000 = $6,286.01 is positive, the machine should be bought.

EXAMPLE 28: A firm is considering the purchase of an automatic machine for $6,200. The machine has an installation cost of $800 and zero salvage value at the end of its expected life of five years. Depreciation is by the straight-line method with the *half-year convention*. The machine is considered a five-year property. Expected cash savings before tax is $1,800 per year over the five years. The firm is in the 40% tax bracket. The firm has determined the cost of capital (or minimum required rate of return) of 10% after taxes.

	Year(s) Having Cash Flows	Amount of Cash Flows	10% PV Factor	PV
Initial investment	Now	$(7,000)	1.000	$(7,000)
Annual cash inflows:				
$1,800				
× 60%				
$1,080	1–5	1,080	3.791	4,094

Depreciation deductions:

Year	Depreciation	Tax Shield at 40%				
1	$700	$280	1	280	0.909	255
2	1,400	560	2	560	0.826	463
3	1,400	560	3	560	0.751	421
4	1,400	560	4	560	0.683	382
5	1,400	560	5	560	0.621	348
6	700	280	6	280	0.564	158
Net present value						$(879)

The firm should not buy the automatic machine because its NPV is negative.

EXAMPLE 29: The Wessels Corporation is considering installing a new conveyor for materials handling in a warehouse. The conveyor will have an initial cost of $75,000 and an installation cost of $5,000. Expected benefits of the conveyor are: (a) Annual labor cost will be reduced by $16,500, and (b) breakage and other damages from handling will be reduced by $400 per month. Some of the firm's costs are expected to increase as follows: (a) Electricity cost will rise by $100 per month, and (b) annual repair and maintenance of the conveyor will amount to $900.

Assume the firm uses the MACRS rules for depreciation in the five-year property class. No salvage value will be recognized for tax purposes. The conveyor has an expected useful life of eight years and a projected salvage value of $5,000. The tax rate is 40%. We will determine the projects NPV at 10%. Should the firm buy the conveyor?

Annual cash inflows are computed as follows:

$16,500	Reduction in labor cost
4,800	Reduction in breakage
– 1,200	Increase in electricity costs
– 900	Increase in repair and maintenance cost
$19,200	

Initial amount of investment is:

$$\$75,000 + \$5,000 = \$80,000$$

			Year(s) Having Cash Flows	Amount of Cash Flows	10% PV Factor	PV
Initial investment			Now	$(80,000)	1.000	$(80,000)
Annual cash inflow:	$19,200					
	× 60%					
After-tax cash inflow:	$11,520		1–8	11,520	5.335	61,459.20

Depreciation deductions:

Year	Cost	MACRS	Depre-ciation	Tax Shield				
1	$80,000	20%	$16,000	$ 6,400	1	6,400	0.909	5,817.60
2	80,000	32	25,600	10,240	2	10,240	0.826	8,458.24
3	80,000	19.2	15,360	6,144	3	6,144	0.751	4,614.14
4	80,000	11.5	9,200	3,680	4	3,680	0.683	2,513.44
5	80,000	11.5	9,200	3,680	5	3,680	0.621	2,285.28
6	80,000	5.8	4,640	1,856	6	1,856	0.564	1,046.78
								$24,735.48

Salvage value, fully taxable because book value will be zero:

$5,000				
× 60%				
$3,000	8	3,000	0.467	1,401.00
Net present value				$ 7,595.68

The JKS Corporation should buy and install the conveyor because it brings a positive NPV.

Exhibit 22-5: MACRS Classification of Assets

			Property Class			
Year	3-year	5-year	7-year	10-year	15-year	20-year
1	33.3%	20.0%	14.3%	10.0%	5.0%	3.8%
2	44.5	32.0	24.5	18.0	9.5	7.2
3	14.8[a]	19.2	17.5	14.4	8.6	6.7
4	7.4	11.5	12.5	11.5	7.7	6.2
5		11.5	8.9	9.2	6.9	5.7
6		5.8	8.9	7.4	6.2	5.3
7			8.9	6.6	5.9[a]	4.9
8			4.5	6.6	5.9	4.5
9				6.5	5.9	4.5
10				6.5	5.9	4.5
11				3.3	5.9	4.5
12					5.9	4.5
13					5.9	4.5
14					5.9	4.5
15					5.9	4.5
16					3.0	4.4
17						4.4
18						4.4
19						4.4
20						4.4
21						2.2
Total	100%	100%	100%	100%	100%	100%

[a] Denotes the year of changeover to straight-line depreciation.

Exhibit 22-6: MACRS Tables by Property Class

MACRS Property Class & Depreciation Method	*Useful Life (ADR Midpoint Life)*[a]	*Examples of Assets*
3-year property 200% declining balance	4 years or less	Most small tools are included; the law specifically excludes autos and light trucks from this property class.
5-year property 200% computers, declining balance	More than 4 years to less than 10 years	Autos and light trucks, duplicating typewriters, copiers, equipment, heavy general-purpose trucks, and research and experimentation equipment are included.
7-year property 200% and declining balance	10 years or more to less than 16 years	Office furniture and fixtures, most items of machinery and equipment used in production are included.
10-year property 200% declining balance	16 years or more to less than 20 years	Various machinery and equipment, such as that used in petroleum distilling and refining and in the milling of grain, are included.
15-year property 150% declining balance	20 years or more to less than 25 years	Sewage treatment plants, telephone and electrical distribution facilities, and land improvements are included.
20-year property 150% declining balance	25 years or more	Service stations and other real property with an ADR midpoint life of less than 27.5 years are included.

MACRS Property Class & Depreciation Method	Useful Life (ADR Midpoint Life)ᵃ	Examples of Assets
27.5-year property straight-line	Not applicable	All residential rental property is included.
31.5-year property straight-line	Not applicable	All nonresidential property is included.

ᵃ The term *ADR midpoint life* means the "useful life" of an asset in a business sense; the appropriate ADR midpoint lives for assets are designated in the tax Regulations.

CAPITAL BUDGETING PROCESS—QUESTIONS TO BE ASKED

As part of the capital budgeting process, the following questions must be asked:

- How is risk incorporated into the analysis?
- Is risk versus return considered in choosing projects?
- Prior to making a final decision, are all the results of the capital budgeting techniques considered and integrated?
- In looking at a proposal, are both dollars and time considered?
- Is the proposal consistent with long-term goals?
- Does each project have a cost-benefit analysis?
- Is there knowledge as to which proposals and products are most profitable?
- How much business is in each proposal/product?
- Are there projects of an unusual nature?
- Is the performance of current programs in terms of original expectations tracked periodically?
- In the capital budgeting process, are qualitative factors also considered, such as marketing, production, and economic and political variables?
- Has the proposal been considered incorporating the company's financial health?
- What is the quality of the project?
- Given the current environment, are capital investments adequate?
- Are you risk prone or risk averse?
- Is the discounted payback method being used?
- How are probable cash flows computed?
- How is the expected life determined?

To look at the entire picture of the capital budgeting process, a comprehensive example is provided.

EXAMPLE 30: You are deciding whether to buy a business. The initial cash outlay is $35,000. You will receive annual net cash inflows (excluding depreciation) of $5,000 per year for 10 years. The cost of capital is 10%. The tax rate is 50%. You want to evaluate whether you should buy this business. The annual cash inflow follows:

	Years 1–10	
	Net Income	**Cash Flow**
Annual cash savings	$5,000	+$5,000
Depreciation ($35,000/10)	3,500	
Income before tax	$1,500	
Tax (50%)	750	– 750
Net income	$ 750	
Net cash inflow		+$4,250

Average rate of return on investment:

$$\frac{\text{Net income}}{\text{Average investment}} = \frac{\$750}{\$35,000/2} = \frac{\$750}{\$17,500} = 4\%$$

Payback period:

$$\frac{\text{Initial investment}}{\text{Annual net cash inflow}} = \frac{\$35,000}{\$4,250} = 8.2 \text{ years}$$

Net present value:

Year	Explanation	Amount	×	Factor	=	Present Value
0	Initial investment	–$35,000	×	1		–$35,000
1–10	Annual net cash inflow	+ 4,250	×	6.1446		26,095
	Net present value					–$ 8,905

Profitability index:

$$\frac{\text{Present value of cash inflow}}{\text{Present value of cash outflow}} = \frac{\$26,095}{\$35,000} = 0.74$$

Internal rate of return:

$$\text{Factor} = \frac{\text{Initial outlay}}{\text{Annual cash inflow}} = \frac{\$35,000}{\$4,250} = 8.2$$

Going to the Present Value of Annuity table (Table A-4 in the Appendix), we look for the intersection of 10 years and a factor of 8.2. Looking up the column we find 4%, which is the internal rate.

Conclusion: The business should not be bought for the following reasons:

- An average rate of return of 4% is low.
- The payback period is long.
- The net present value is negative.
- The internal rate of return of 4% is less than the cost of capital of 10%.

CAPITAL BUDGETING AND INFLATION

The accuracy of capital budgeting decisions depends on the accuracy of the data regarding cash inflows and outflows. For example, failure to incorporate price-level changes due to inflation in capital budgeting situations can result in errors in the predicting of cash flows and thus in incorrect decisions. Typically, the managerial accountant has two options dealing with a capital budgeting situation with inflation: (1) restate the cash flows in nominal terms and discount them at a nominal cost of capital (minimum required rate of return) or (2) restate both the cash flows and cost of capital in constant terms and discount the constant cash flows at a constant cost of capital. The two methods are basically equivalent.

EXAMPLE 31: A company has the following projected cash flows estimated in real terms:

	Real Cash Flows (000s)			
Period	0	1	2	3
	−100	35	50	30

The nominal cost of capital is 15%. Assume that inflation is projected at 10% a year. Then the first cash flow for year 1, which is $35,000 in current dollars, will be 35,000 × 1.10 = $38,500 in year one dollars. Similarly the cash flow for year two will be 50,000 × $(1.10)^2 = \$60,500$ in year two dollars, and so on. If we discount these nominal cash flows at the 15% nominal cost of capital, we have the following net present value (NPV):

Period	Cash Flows	T3	Present Values
0	−100	1,000	−100
1	38.5	.870	33.50
2	60.5	.756	45.74
3	39.9	.658	26.25
			NPV = 5.49 or $5,490

Instead of converting the cash flow forecasts into nominal terms, we could convert the cost of capital into real terms by using the following formula:

$$\text{Real cost of capital} = \frac{1 + \text{normal cost of capital}}{1 + \text{inflation rate}} - 1$$

In the example, this gives

Real cost of capital = $(1 + .15)/(1 + .10) = 1.15/1.10 = 0.045$ or 4.5%

We will obtain the same answer except for rounding errors ($5,490 versus $5,580).

Period	Cash Flows	T3^n	Present Values
0	−100	1.000	−100
1	35	.957	33.50
2	50	.916	45.80
3	30	.876	26.28
		NPV =	5.58 or $5,580

POSTAUDIT PROJECT REVIEW

The postaudit (postcompletion) project review is a second aspect of reviewing the performance of the project. A comparison is made of the actual cash flow from operations of the project with the estimated cash flow used to justify the project. There are several reasons why the postaudit project review is helpful. First, managers proposing projects will be more careful before recommending a project. Second, it will identify those managers who are repeatedly optimistic or pessimistic regarding cash flow estimates. How reliable are the proposals submitted and approved (perhaps additional investments can be made to result in even greater returns)? Top management will be better able to appraise the bias that may be expected when a certain manager proposes a project.

The postaudit review also gives an opportunity to reinforce successful projects, to strengthen or salvage "problem" projects, to cease unsuccessful projects before excessive losses occur, and to enhance the overall quality of future investment proposals.

In conducting a postaudit, the same technique should be employed as was used in the initial approval process to maintain consistency in evaluation. For example, if a project was approved using present value analysis, the identical procedure should be implemented in the postaudit review.

As per the "management by exception" principle, the managers responsible for the original estimates should be asked to furnish a complete explanation of any significant differences between estimates and actual results.

For control reasons, project performance appraisal should not be conducted by the group that proposed the project. Rather, internal auditors should be given this responsibility to maintain independence. A review report should be issued. Typically, only projects above a specified dollar amount require postaudit and/or periodic evaluation.

REAL OPTIONS

Almost all capital budgeting proposals can be viewed as *real options*. In addition, projects and operations contain implicit options, such as the option of when to take a project, the option to expand, the option to abandon, and the option to suspend or contract operations. Deciding when to take a project is called the *investment timing option*.

   EXAMPLE 32: A project costs $100 and has a single future cash flow. If it is taken today, the cash flow will be $120 in one year. If it is not taken for one year, the project will still cost $100, but the cash flow the following year (i.e., two years from now) will be $130 because the potential market is bigger. If these are the only two options, and the relevant discount rate is 10%, it is necessary to compute the two NPVs to find the optimal time to begin the project. If the project is taken today, the NPV = –$100 + 120/1.1 = $9.09. If the project is taken in one year, the NPV at that time would be NPV = –$100 + 130/1.1 = $18.18. $18.18 is the NPV one year from today. To obtain the value today, it is necessary to discount back $18.18/1.1 = $16.53.

   If the project is not taken immediately, the NPV is $16.53 today compared to $9.09 if the project is started immediately, so the optimal time to begin the project is one year from now. A project that does not have to be taken immediately is referred to as an "option to wait."

   In this example, the value of the option to wait is the difference in NPVs, $16.53 – 9.09 = $7.44. This $7.44 is the extra value created by deferring the start of the act as opposed to taking it today.

   EXAMPLE 33: A project costs $200 and has a future cash flow of $42 per year forever. If there is a one-year wait to start the project, the project will cost $240 because of inflation, but the cash flows will be $48 per year forever. If these are the only two options, and the relevant discount rate is 12%, it is necessary to determine the value of the option to wait.

   In this case, the project is a simple perpetuity. If the project is taken today, the NPV is: NPV = –$200 + 42/1.12 = $150.

   If the project is taken in one year, the NPV at that time would be: NPV = –$240 + 48/1.12 = $160.

   Therefore, $160 is the NPV one year from now, but it is necessary to know the value today. Discounting back one period: NPV = $160/1.12 = $142.86.

If the project is not taken immediately, the NPV is $142.86 today compared to $150 if the project is started immediately, so the optimal time to begin the project is now. In addition, the value of the option to wait is not $142.86 – $150 = –$7.14. Because an option can never have a negative value, the option to wait has a zero value.

CAPITAL BUDGETING AND NONPROFIT ORGANIZATIONS

With regard to nonprofit institutions, the only real problem in using capital budgeting is the selection of an appropriate discount rate. Some nonprofit entities employ the interest rate on special bond issues (e.g., building a school) as the discount rate. Other nonprofit organizations employ the interest rate that could be earned by putting money in an endowment fund instead of spending it on capital improvements. Other nonprofit institutions use discount rates that are arbitrarily established by governing boards.

A pitfall to watch out for is using an excessively low discount rate. This may result in accepting projects that will not be profitable. To guard against this problem, the Office of Management and Budget promulgates a discount rate of at least 10% on all projects to be considered by federal government units (source: Office of Management and Budget Circular No. A-94, March 1972). In the case of nonprofit units such as schools and hospitals, the discount rate should be the average rate of return on private sector investments. The average discount rate will provide more meaningful results than using a specific interest rate on a special bond issue or the interest return on an endowment fund.

THE LEASE OR PURCHASE DECISION

The lease or purchase decision is one commonly confronting firms considering the acquisition of new assets. It is a hybrid capital budgeting decision that forces a company to compare the leasing and financing (purchasing) alternatives.

There are tax benefits of leasing equipment rather than financing it with a term loan. Depending on the needs of the company and the nature of the business, the entire lease payment may be fully deductible as a business expense, thereby reducing the taxable income. With a loan, only the interest and depreciation can be used for deductions. Another benefit a lease offers is 100% financing plus an additional 10% of the equipment's costs to cover "soft costs," such as taxes, shipping and installation. Some term loans offer 100% financing but, typically, they cover the cost of equipment only.

A lease can help with cash flow management. The payments are usually lower than for a term loan. Because a lease payment requires no down payment or deposit, the equipment needed can be purchased without depleting the reserve capital. The types of business that most often lease equipment to generate revenue are manufacturing, transportation, printing, and professional corporations, such as medical, law, or accounting firms. Leasing works well for such companies because equipment can be kept current without having to dip into capital. Because the business' capital is not being used for equipment, capital can be used for business development and expansion.

A loan is the best means by which to keep the equipment and build equity quickly. Loans can be structured so that the equipment can be owned outright at the end of the term. **Note:** If a company wishes to retain the equipment beyond the lease term, to find out the full cost of financing up front, a lease purchase option may be chosen. As the name implies, this option requires no additional payment to own the equipment at the end of the lease.

To make an intelligent financial decision on a lease purchase, an after-tax, cash outflow, *present value* comparison is needed. There are special steps to take when making this comparison. When considering a lease, take the following steps:

1. Find the annual lease payment. Because the annual lease payment is typically made in advance, the formula used is:

$$\text{Amount of lease} = A + A.T4(i, n - 1) \text{ or } A = \frac{\text{Amount of lease}}{1 + T4(i, n - 1)}$$

Notice we use $n - 1$ rather than n.

2. Find the after-tax cash outflows.
3. Find the present value of the after-tax cash outflows.

When considering a purchase, take the following steps:

1. Find the annual loan amortization by using:

$$A = \frac{\text{Amount of loan for the purchase}}{T4(i, n - 1)}$$

Note: This step may not be necessary since this amount is usually available.

2. Calculate the interest. The interest is segregated from the principal in each of the annual loan payments because only the interest is tax deductible.
3. Find the cash outflows by adding interest and depreciation (plus any maintenance costs), and then compute the after-tax outflows.
4. Find the present value of the after-tax cash outflows, using Table A-3 in the Appendix.

EXAMPLE 34: A firm has decided to acquire a computer system costing $100,000 that has an expected life of five years, after which the system is not expected to have any residual value. The system can be purchased by borrowing or it can be leased. If leasing is used, the lessor requires a 12% return. As is customary, lease payments are made in advance, that is, at the end of the year prior to each of the 10 years. The tax rate is 50% and the firm's cost of capital, or after-tax cost of borrowing, is 8%.

First compute the present value of the after-tax cash outflows associated with the leasing alternative.

Step 1: Find the annual lease payment:

$$A = \frac{\text{Amount of lease}}{1 + T4\ (i,\ n-1)}$$

$$= \frac{\$100,000}{1 + T4\ (12\%,\ 4\ \text{years})} = \frac{\$100,000}{1 + 3.037} = \frac{\$100,000}{4.037} = \$24,769\ (\text{rounded})$$

Steps 2 and 3 can be done in the same schedule, as follows:

Year	(1) Lease Payments ($)	(2) Tax Savings ($)	(3) = (1) – (2) After-Tax Cash Outflow ($)	(4) PV at 8%	(5) = (3) × (4) PV of Cash Outflow ($, Rounded)
0	24,769		24,769	1.000	24,769
1–4	24,769	12,385[a]	12,385	3.3121[b]	41,019
5	24,769	12,385	(12,385)	0.6806[c]	(8,429)
					57,359

[a] $24,769 × 50%
[b] From Table A-4 in the Appendix.
[c] From Table A-3 in the Appendix.

If the asset is purchased, the firm is assumed to finance it entirely with a 10% unsecured term loan. Straight-line depreciation is used with no salvage value. Therefore, the annual depreciation is $20,000 ($100,000/5 years). In this alternative, first find the annual loan payment by using:

$$A = \frac{\text{Amount of loan}}{T4\ (i,\ n)}$$

$$A = \frac{\$100,000}{T4(10\%,\ 5\ \text{years})} = \frac{\$100,000}{3.7906} = \$26,381\ (\text{rounded})$$

Step 2: Calculate the interest by setting up a loan amortization schedule.

Year	(1) Loan Payment ($)	(2) Beg-of-Yr Principal ($)	(3) = (2)(10%) Interest ($)	(4) = (1) – (3) Principal ($)	(5) = (2) – (4) End-of-Yr Principal
1	26,381	100,000	10,000	16,381	83,619
2	26,381	83,619	8,362	18,019	65,600
3	26,381	65,600	6,560	19,821	45,779

Year	(1) Loan Payment ($)	(2) Beg-of-Yr Principal ($)	(3) = (2)(10%) Interest ($)	(4) = (1) – (3) Principal ($)	(5) = (2) – (4) End-of-Yr Principal
4	26,381	45,779	4,578	21,803	23,976
5	26,381	23,976[a]	2,398	23,983[a]	

[a] Because of rounding errors, there is a slight difference between (2) and (4).

Steps 3 and 4: Steps 3 (cash outflows) and 4 (present values of those outflows) can be done as shown below:

Lease Versus Purchase Evaluation Report

	Leasing		Purchase/Borrow					Discounted Cash Flow	
Year	Lease Payments	Net After- Tax Cash Flow	Loan Payments	Interest Expense	Depre- ciation Expense	Net After- Tax Cash Flow	Present Value Factor	Leasing	Purchase
0	$24,769	$24,769					1	$24,769	
1	24,769	12,385	$26,381	$10,000	$20,000	$11,381	0.9259	11,467	10,538
2	24,769	12,385	26,381	8,362	20,000	12,200	0.8573	10,617	10,459
3	24,769	12,385	26,381	6,560	20,000	13,101	0.7938	9,831	10,400
4	24,769	12,385	26,381	4,578	20,000	14,092	0.735	9,103	10,358
5		(12,385)	26,381	2,398	20,000	15,182	0.6806	(8,429)	10,333
	$99,076	$61,923	$131,905	$31,898	$100,000	$65,956		$57,358	$52,087

	Lease Purchase	Purchase Proposal
Cost of machine	$100,000	$100,000
Terms of payment	5 years	5 years
Interest rate	12%	10%
Down payment		
Monthly lease payment at the end of the year	$24,769	
Monthly loan payment		$26,381
Depreciation		Straight line
Residual purchase price	0	0
Corporate tax bracket	50%	50%
After-tax cost of capital	8%	8%

The sum of the present values of the cash outflows for leasing and purchasing by borrowing shows that purchasing is preferable because the PV of borrowing is less than the PV of leasing ($52,087 versus $57,358). The incremental savings is $5,271.

ECONOMIC FEASIBILITY STUDY FOR A NEW INFORMATION SYSTEM

Determining economic feasibility requires a careful investigation of the costs and benefits of a proposed information system. The basic framework for feasibility analysis is the *capital budgeting* model in which cost savings and other benefits, as well as initial outlay costs, operating costs, and other cash outflows, are translated into dollar estimates.

The estimated benefits are compared with the costs to determine whether the system is cost beneficial. Where possible, benefits and costs that are not easily quantifiable should be estimated and included in the feasibility analysis. If they cannot be accurately estimated, they should be listed and the likelihood of their occurring and the expected impact on the organization evaluated. Some of the tangible and intangible benefits a company might obtain from a new system are cost savings; improved customer service, productivity, decision making, and data processing; better management control; and increased job satisfaction and employee morale.

Equipment costs are an initial outlay cost if the system is purchased and an operating cost if rented or leased. Equipment costs vary from a few thousands for microcomputer systems to millions of dollars for enormous mainframes. Equipment costs are usually less than the cost of acquiring software and maintaining, supporting, and operating the system. Software acquisition costs include the purchase price of software as well as the time and effort required to design, program, test, and document software. The personnel costs associated with hiring, training, and relocating staff can be substantial. Site preparation costs may be incurred for large computer systems. There are costs involved in installing the new system and converting files to the appropriate format and storage media.

The primary operating cost is maintaining the system. There may be significant annual cash outflows for equipment replacement and expansion and software updates. Human resource costs include the salaries of systems analysts, programmers, operators, data entry operators, and management. Costs are also incurred for supplies, overhead, and other operating costs. Initial cash outlay and operating costs are summarized in Exhibit 22-7.

Exhibit 22-7: Initial Cash Outlay and Operating Costs for a New Information System

Hardware
  Central processing unit
  Peripherals
  Special input/output devices
  Communications hardware
  Upgrade and expansion costs

Software
:   Application, system, general-purpose, utility, and communications
    software
    Updated versions of software
    Application software design, programming, modification, and testing

Installation
:   Freight and delivery charges
    Setup and connection fees

Conversion
:   Systems testing
    File and data conversions
    Parallel operations

Documentation
:   Systems documentation
    Training program documentation
    Operating standards and procedures

Site preparation
:   Air conditioning, humidity, and dust controls
    Physical security (access)
    Fire and water protection
    Cabling, wiring, and outlets
    Furnishing and fixtures

Staff
:   Supervisors
    Analysts and programmers
    Computer operators
    Input (data conversion) personnel
    Recruitment and staff training

Maintenance/backup
:   Hardware/software maintenance
    Backup and recovery operations
    Power supply protection

Supplies and overhead
:   Preprinted forms
    Data storage devices
    Supplies (paper, ribbons, toner)
    Utilities and power

Others
:   Legal and consulting fees
    Insurance

During systems design, several alternative approaches to meeting system requirements are developed. Various feasibility measures, such as technical, operational, legal, and scheduling feasibility measures, are then used to narrow the list of alternatives. Economic feasibility and capital budgeting techniques, which were discussed earlier, are used to evaluate the benefit-cost aspects of the alternatives.

EXAMPLE 35: Sophie, an information systems (IS) project manager for the MYK chain of discount stores, is contemplating installation of a new IS system that is flexible, efficient, timely, and responsive to user and customer needs. The new system aims to improve the company's business processes. After the analysis, Sophie's IS project team decided that it wanted the corporate office to gather daily sales data from each store. Analyzing the prior day's sales will help the company adapt quickly to customer needs. Providing sales data to suppliers will help avoid stockouts and overstocking.

Coordinating buying at the corporate office will help MYK to minimize inventory levels and negotiate lower wholesale prices. Stores will send orders electronically the day they are prepared. Based on store orders, the previous day's sales figures, and warehouse inventory, MYK will send purchase orders to suppliers. Suppliers will process orders and ship goods to regional warehouses or directly to the stores the day orders are received. Each store will have the flexibility to respond to local sales trends and conditions by placing local orders. Accounts payable will be centralized so the firm can make payments electronically.

Sophie's team conducted an economic feasibility study and determined that the project makes excellent use of funds. As shown in Exhibit 22-8, the team estimated that initial outlay costs for the system are $4.32 million (initial systems design and new hardware $1.8 million each, software $375,000, and training, site preparation, and conversion $250,000 each).

The team estimated the cost to operate the system for its estimated six-year life, as well as the savings. The following recurring costs were identified: hardware expansion, additional software and software updates, systems maintenance, added personnel to operate the system, communication charges, and overhead. The system will also save the company money by eliminating clerical jobs, generating working capital savings, increasing sales and profits, and decreasing warehouse costs. The costs and savings for years 1 through 6, which are expected to rise from year to year, are shown below.

Sophie calculated the annual savings minus the recurring additional costs and then calculated the annual after-tax cash savings under the MACRS tax rule. The $4.66 million system can be depreciated over the six-year period. For example, the depreciation in year 1 of $932,000 reduces net income by that amount. Since the company does not have to pay taxes on the $1 million, at their tax rate of 34% they end up saving an additional $316,880 in year 1. Finally, Sophie calculated the net savings for each year.

Sophie used MYK's cost of capital of 10% to calculate the net present value (NPV) of the investment, which is over $3 million. The internal rate of return (IRR) is a respectable 26%. Sophie realized how advantageous it would be for the company to borrow the money (at 10% interest rates) in order to produce a 26% return on that borrowed money. In addition, payback (the point at which the initial cost is recovered) occurs in the fourth year. NPV and IRR are calculated as shown in Exhibit 22-8.

Sophie presented the system and its cost-benefit calculations to top management. Challenges to her estimates (various what-if scenarios) were plugged into the Excel model so that management could see the effect of the changed assumptions. This spreadsheet analysis was intended to ensure a positive return of the new system under future uncertainty.

Exhibit 22-8: Economic Feasibility Study for a New Information System

	Initial Outlay	Years				
	0	1	2	3	4	5
Initial outlay costs (1)						
Initial system design	$ 800,000					
Hardware	1,800,000					
Software	375,000					
Training	185,000					
Site preparation	250,000					
Conversion	250,000					
Total	$ 4,660,000					
Recurring costs						
Hardware expansion			$ 250,000	$ 290,000	$ 330,000	$ 370,000
Software			160,000	210,000	230,000	245,000
Systems maintenance		$ 70,000	120,000	130,000	140,000	150,000
Personal costs		485,000	800,000	900,000	1,000,000	1,100,000
Communication charges		99,000	160,000	180,000	200,000	220,000
Overhead		310,000	420,000	490,000	560,000	600,000
Total		$ 964,000	$ 1,910,000	$ 2,200,000	$ 2,460,000	$ 2,685,000
Cash savings						
Clerical cost savings		$ 500,000	$ 1,110,000	$ 1,350,000	$ 1,500,000	$ 1,700,000
Working capital savings		1,000,000	1,200,000	1,500,000	1,500,000	1,500,000
Increased sales and profits			500,000	900,000	1,200,000	1,500,000
Reduced warehouse costs			400,000	800,000	1,200,000	1,600,000
Total		$ 1,500,000	$ 3,210,000	$ 4,550,000	$ 5,400,000	$ 6,300,000
Cash savings minus recurring costs		536,000	1,300,000	2,350,000	2,940,000	3,615,000
Less income taxes (34%)	34%	(182,240)	(442,000)	(799,000)	(999,600)	(1,229,100)
Cash savings (net of tax)		$ 353,760	$ 858,000	$ 1,551,000	$ 1,940,400	$ 2,385,900
Tax shield from depreciation		316,880	507,008	304,205	182,206	182,206
Net cash inflows (net savings) after taxes	$ (4,660,000)	$ 670,640	1,365,008	1,885,205	2,122,606	$ 2,568,106

RISK AND UNCERTAINTY

Risk analysis is important in making capital investment decisions because of the significant amount of capital involved and the long-term nature of the investments being considered. The higher the risk associated with a proposed project, the greater the return rate that must be earned on the project to compensate for that risk.

The interrelation of risk among all investments should be considered. By properly diversifying, you can obtain the best combination of expected net present value and risk can be obtained.

Tip: Do not automatically reject a high-risk project. For example, a new product with much risk may be accepted if there is a chance of a major break-through in the market. The business may be able to afford a few unsuccessful new products if one is developed for extraordinary return.

Probabilities can be assigned to expected cash flows based on risk. The probabilities are multiplied by the monetary values to derive the expected monetary value of the investment. A probability distribution function can be generated by computer.

Special Note: The tighter the probability distribution of expected future returns, the lower the risk associated with a project.

Several methods to incorporate risk into capital budgeting are probability distributions, risk-adjusted discount rate, standard deviation and coefficient of variation, certainty equivalent, semivariance, simulation, sensitivity analysis, and decision (probability) trees. Other means of adjusting for uncertainty are to de-crease the expected life of an investment, use pessimistic estimates of cash flow, and compare the results of optimistic, pessimistic, and best-guess estimates of cash flows.

Tax savings from depreciation deduction

Year	MACRS	Depreciation	Tax savings
1	20.00%	$932,000	$316,880
2	32.00%	1,491,200	507,008

Tax savings from depreciation deduction

Year	MACRS	Depreciation	Tax Savings
3	19.20%	894,720	304,205
4	11.50%	535,900	182,206
5	11.50%	535,900	182,206
6	5.80%	270,280	91,895

Net present value calculations @ a cost of capital of 10%

Year	Net savings	PV factor	PV
0	$ (4,660,000)	$ 1.0000	$ (4,660,000)
1	670,640	0.9091	609,679
2	1,365,008	0.8265	1,128,179
3	1,855,205	0.7513	1,393,815
4	2,122,606	0.6830	1,449,740
5	2,568,106	0.6209	1,594,537
6	2,896,895	0.5645	1,635,297
		NPV	$ 3,151,248
		IRR	26.26%

Probability Distributions

Expected values of a probability distribution may be computed. Before any capital budgeting method is applied, compute the expected cash inflows or, in some cases, the expected life of the asset.

EXAMPLE 36: A company is considering a $30,000 investment in equipment that will generate cash savings from operating costs. The following estimates regarding cash savings and useful life, along with their respective probabilities of occurrence, have been made:

Annual Cash Savings		Useful Life	
$6,000	0.2	4 years	0.2
$8,000	0.5	5 years	0.6
$10,000	0.3	6 years	0.2

Then, the expected annual savings is:

$$\$6,000 \ (0.2) \ = \ \$1,200$$
$$\$8,000 \ (0.5) \ = \ 4,000$$
$$\$10,000 \ (0.3) \ = \ \$3,000$$
$$\$8,200$$

The expected useful life is:

$$4 \ (0.2) \ = \ 0.8$$
$$5 \ (0.6) \ = \ 3.0$$
$$6 \ (0.2) \ = \ 1.2$$
$$5 \ \text{years}$$

The expected NPV is computed as follows (assuming a 10% cost of capital):

NPV = PV − I = $8,200 T4 (10%, 5 years) − $30,000

= $8,200 (3,7908) − $30,000 = $31,085 − $30,000

= $1,085

The expected IRR is computed as follows:

By definition, at IRR,

$$I = PV$$

$$\$30,000 = \$8,200 \text{ T4 } (r, 5 \text{ years})$$

$$\text{T4 } (r, 5 \text{ years}) = \frac{\$30,000}{\$8,200} = 3.6585$$

which is about halfway between 10% and 12% in Table A-4, so we can estimate the rate to be 11%. Therefore, the equipment should be purchased, since (1) NPV = $1,085, which is positive, and/or (2) IRR = 11%, which is greater than the cost of capital of 10%.

Risk-Adjusted Discount Rate

Risk can be included in capital budgeting by computing probable cash flows on the basis of probabilities and assigning a discount rate based on the riskiness of alternative proposals.

Using this approach, an investment's value is determined by discounting the expected cash flow at a rate allowing for the time value of money and for the risk associated with the cash flow. The cost of capital (discount rate) is adjusted for a project's risk. A profitable investment is indicated by a positive net present value. Using the method, the risk class of the proposed capital investment and the risk-adjusted discount rate appropriate for that class is judged.

Tip: If there is any doubt about the results, check them by estimating the cost of capital of other companies specializing in the type of investment under consideration.

EXAMPLE 37: You are evaluating whether to accept proposal A or B. Each proposal mandates an initial cash outlay of $12,000 and has a three-year life. Annual net cash flows along with expected probabilities are as follows:

Proposal A:

Expected Annual Cash Inflow	Probability
$5,800	.4
6,400	.5
7,000	1

Proposal B:

Expected Annual Cash Inflow	Probability
$3,400	.3
8,000	.5
11,000	.2

The inflation rate and interest rate are estimated at 10%. Proposal A has a lower risk since its cash flows show greater stability than those of Proposal B. Since Proposal A has less risk, it is assigned a discount rate of 8%, while Proposal B is assigned a 10% discount rate because of the greater risk.

Proposal A:

Cash Flow	Probability	Probable Cash Flow
$5,800	.4	$2,320
6,400	.5	3,200
7,000		700
Expected annual cash inflow		$6,220

Proposal B:

Cash Flow	Probability	Probable Cash Flow
$3,400	.3	$1,020
8,000	.5	4,000
11,000	.2	2,200
Expected annual cash inflow		$7,220

Proposal A:

Year	Explanation	Amount	×	Factor	=	Present Value
0	Initial investment	−$12,000	×	1		−$ 12,000
1–3	Annual cash flow	+ 6,220	×	2.5771*		+ 16,030
	Net present value					+$ 4,030

* Using an 8% discount rate

Proposal B:

Year	Explanation	Amount	×	Factor	=	Present Value
0	Initial investment	−$12,000	×	1		−$ 12,000
1–3	Annual cash flow	+ 7,220	×	2.4869**		+ 17,955
	Net present value					+$ 5,955

** 10% discount rate

Even though Project B has more risk, it has a higher risk-adjusted net present value. Project B should thus be selected.

Standard Deviation and Coefficient of Variation

Risk is a measure of dispersion around a probability distribution. It is the variability of cash flow around the expected value. Risk can be measured in either absolute or relative terms. First, the expected value, A, is

$$\bar{A} = \sum_{i-1}^{n} A_i p_i$$

where

A_i = the value of the ith possible outcome

p_i = the probability that the ith outcome will take place

n = the number of possible outcomes

Then, the absolute risk is determined by the standard deviation:

$$\sigma = \sqrt{\sum_{i-1}^{n}(A_i - \bar{A})^2 p_i}$$

The relative risk is expressed by the coefficient of variation:

$$\frac{\sigma}{\bar{A}}$$

EXAMPLE 38: You are considering investing in one of two projects. Depending on the state of the economy, the projects would provide the following cash inflows in each of the next five years:

Economic Condition	Probability	Proposal A	Proposal B
Recession	.3	$1,000	$ 500
Normal	4	2,000	2,000
Boom	.3	3,000	5,000

We now compute the expected value $(\bar{A})$, the standard deviation (σ), and the coefficient of variation ($\sigma/\bar{A}$).

Proposal A:

A_1	P_1	A_1P_1	$(A_1-\bar{A})$	$(A_1-\bar{A})^2$	$(A_1-\bar{A})^2p_1$
$1,000	.3	$ 300	-$1,000	$1,000,000	$300,000
2,000	.4	800	0	0	0
3,000	.3	900	1,000	1,000,000	300,000
	$\bar{A} =$	$2,000	$\sigma^2 =$		$600,000

Because $\sigma^2 = \$600,000$, $\sigma = \$755$. Thus

$$\sigma = \frac{\$775}{2,000} = 0.39$$

Proposal B:

A_1	P_1	A_1P_1	$(A_1-\bar{A})$	$(A_1-\bar{A})^2$	$(A_1-\bar{A})^2p_1$
$ 500	.3	$ 150	-$1,950	$3,802,500	$1,140,750
2,000	.4	800	-450	202,500	81,000
5,000	.3	1,500	2,550	6,502,500	1,950,750
	$\bar{A} =$	$2,450	$\sigma^2 =$		$3,172,500

Because $\sigma^2 = \$3,172,500$, $\sigma = \$1,781$. Thus

$$\frac{\sigma}{\bar{A}} = \frac{\$1,781}{\$2,450} = 0.73$$

Therefore, proposal A is relatively less risky than proposal B, as measured by the coefficient of variation.

Certainty Equivalent

The certainty equivalent approach relates to utility theory. The point at which the company is indifferent to the choice between a certain sum of dollars and the expected value of a risky sum is specified. The certainty equivalent is multiplied by the original cash flow to obtain the equivalent certain cash flow. Then, normal capital budgeting is used. The risk-free rate of return is employed as the discount rate under the net present value method and as the cutoff rate under the internal rate of return method.

EXAMPLE 39: A company's cost of capital is 14% after taxes. Under consideration is a four-year project that will require an initial investment of $50,000. The following data also exist:

Year	After-Tax Cash Flow	Certainty Equivalent Coefficient
1	$10,000	.95
2	15,000	.80

Year	After-Tax Cash Flow	Certainty Equivalent Coefficient
3	20,000	.70
4	25,000	.60

The risk-free rate of return is 5%.

Equivalent certain cash inflows are:

Year	After-Tax Cash Inflow	Certainty Equivalent Coefficient	Equivalent Certain Cash Inflow	×	Present Value Factor at 5%	=	Present Value
1	$10,000	.95	$9,500		.9524		$9,048
2	15,000	.80	12,000		.9070		10,884
3	20,000	.70	14,000		.8638		12,093
4	25,000	.60	15,000		.8227		12,341
							$44,366

Net Present Value:

Initial Investment	–$50,000
PV of Cash Inflows	+ 44,366
Net Present Value	–$ 5,634

Using trial and error, an internal rate of 4% is obtained.

The proposal should be rejected because of the negative net present value and an internal rate (4%) less than the risk-free rate (5%).

Semivariance

Semivariance is the expected value of the squared negative deviations of the possible outcomes from an arbitrarily chosen point of reference. Semivariance appraises risks applicable to different distributions by referring to a designated fixed point. In computing semivariance, positive and negative deviations contribute differently to risk, whereas in computing variance, equivalent positive and a negative deviations contribute to risk. In effect, there is an opportunity cost of tying up capital measured by the prospect of failure to earn the return.

Simulation

A simulation enables probability distributions for a number of variables (e.g., investment outlays, unit sales) to be obtained. Selecting these variables from the distributions at random results in an estimated net present value. Since a computer is used to generate many results using random numbers, project simulation is expensive.

Simulation can be useful in budgeting and planning, improving effectiveness through examining risk tolerance in complex relationships. In addition, forecasts can be developed in causal models using alternative assumptions or with causal variables treated as random variables. Simulation allows for the approximation through the interaction of random variables in "what-if" scenarios. This method helps to determine approximate costs.

Historical simulation can be used in computing value at risk in financial scenarios. This approach generates scenarios by sampling historical data associated with each risk factor, which may improve accuracy. The financial manager can modify the parameters in the data simulation to compare outcomes. For example, the financial manager can simulate certain production costs to see the impact on total units produced.

Monte Carlo simulation is a computerized random probability sampling of inputs to obtain solutions to financial problems, and aids in risk analysis. Simulated values are used in a predictive model to generate an outcome. It allows for the defining of feasible values for key inputs and their likelihood of occurrence. The result is a range of possible outcomes based on different inputs.

It can be used to analyze the uncertainty in predictive and forecasting models. The financial manager simulates data based on specified parameters.

The simulation enables the financial manager to approximate risk while the values of risk variables are generated randomly based on specified probability distributions. Bias may exist when an estimate departs from the parameter for which it is designed, thus increasing the range of error.

Sensitivity Analysis

Forecasts of many calculated net present values and internal rates of return under various alternatives are compared to identify how sensitive net present value or internal rate of return is to changing conditions. Shown is whether one or more than one variable significantly affects net present value once that variable is changed. If net present value is materially changed, a much riskier asset than was originally forecast is being dealt with. Sensitivity analysis provides an immediate financial measure of possible errors in forecasts. It focuses on decisions that may be sensitive.

Sensitivity analysis can take various forms. For example, a managerial accountant may want to know how far annual sales will have to decline to break even on the investment. Sensitivity analysis could also be used to test the sensitivity of a decision to estimates of selling price and per-unit variable cost.

Sensitivity analysis provides managers with an idea of the degree to which unfavorable occurrences, such as lower volumes, shorter useful lives, or higher costs, are likely to impact the profitability of a project. It is employed due to the uncertainty in dealing with real-life situations. The analysis measures potential gain or loss and allows for "what-if" evaluation. The most likely results will be the basis for most financial managers' decisions.

Sensitivity analysis is the mathematical recomputing of outcomes with alternative assumptions to assess the impact of variables. This analysis is also useful for testing the results of a financial model, as it shows the relationships between input and output variables. This may uncover unexpected relationships within the variables. Examples of variables include budgeting staff levels, operating costs, inflation rates, interest rates, and future tax rates.

A financial model is a series of equations, input variables, and parameters used in making financial decisions. Because many inputs are uncertain, quantification of the uncertainty in the model should be determined.

Projected results will have some risk level and uncertainty that should be evaluated. Risk evaluation should include measures of outcomes such as likelihood, worst case, and best case leading to reduced risk; therefore, this analysis should result in risk minimization.

When many input variables exist, models built from sensitivity analysis foster improved quality assurance. Sensitivity analysis closely relates to uncertainty appraisal through the recognition of which sources of uncertainty weigh more on the study's results and conclusions.

The analysis predicts what happens when variables deviate from expectations and which factors result in the largest deviations. Monte Carlo filtering identifies ranges of input variables corresponding to the high and low values of the output. The total-order sensitivity index shows the impact of the interactions, which occurs when multiple inputs result in output variation greater than that of the individual inputs.

Variance-based sensitivity analysis are probabilistic approaches. Output sensitivity to an input factor is measured by the amount of variance caused by that input. Screening can be used as a preliminary step to eliminate benign variables before applying a more sophisticated evaluation.

Regression analysis in the context of sensitivity analysis involves a linear regression for the financial model. Using gradient boosting or successive simple regressions to weigh data can sequentially reduce error.

In meta-analysis, sensitivity analysis tests if the results are sensitive to restrictions on the included data. Multi-criteria decision making examines how to prioritize the best alternatives.

There are some difficulties in sensitivity evaluation including:

- Insufficient data exists to build probability distributions of inputs. The subjectivity of probability distributions or ranges will have an important effect on sensitivity analysis.
- There may be excessive inputs to analyze.
- Piecewise sensitivity analysis is when the financial manager conducts sensitivity analysis on one subject model at a time. However, this approach may miss interactions among variables in submodels.
- Variables are often interdependent, so examining each factor individually may be unrealistic. For example, changing one factor (e.g., unit sales) will impact other factors (e.g., selling price).
- Assignment of an optimistic (maximum) or pessimistic (minimum) value is subject to subjectivity.
- Assumptions based on past information that may not hold in the future.

Decision Trees

A decision (probability) tree graphically shows the sequence of possible outcomes. The capital budgeting tree shows cash flows and net present value of the project under different possible circumstances. Advantages of this approach are that it shows possible outcomes of the contemplated project, heightens awareness of adverse possibilities, and depicts the conditional nature of later years' cash flows. The disadvantage is that many problems are too complex to allow for a year-by-year depiction. For example, a three-year project with three possible outcomes following each year, has 27 paths. A 10-year project with three possible outcomes following each year has about 60,000 paths.

EXAMPLE 40: You want to introduce one of two products. The probabilities and present values of expected cash inflows are

Product	Investment	PV of Cash Inflows	Probability
A	$225,000		
		$450,000	.4
		200,000	.5
		−100,000	.1
B	80,000		
		320,000	.2
		100,000	.6
		−150,000	.2

	Initial Investment (1)	Probability (2)	PV of Cash Inflows (3)	PV of Cash Inflows (2) × (3) = (4)
		.40	$450,000	$180,000
		.50	200,000	100,000
Product A	$225,000	.10	−100,000	−10,000
				$270,000
or				
		.20	$320,000	$ 64,000
Product B	$ 80,000	.60	100,000	60,000
		.20	−150,000	−30,000
				$ 94,000

Net present value:

$$\text{Product A} \quad \$270,000 - \$225,000 = \$45,000$$

$$\text{Product B} \quad \$ 94,000 - \$ 80,000 = \$14,000$$

Product A should be selected.

EXAMPLE 41: A firm has an opportunity to invest in a machine which will last two years, initially cost $125,000, and has the following estimated possible after-tax cash inflow pattern: In year one, there is a 40% chance that the after-tax cash inflow will be $45,000, a 25% chance that it will be $65,000, and a 35% chance that it will be $90,000. In year two, the after-tax cash inflow possibilities depend on the cash inflow that occurs in year one; that is, the year two after-tax cash inflows are conditional probabilities. Assume that the firm's after-tax cost of capital is 12%. The estimated conditional aftertax cash inflows (ATCI) and probabilities follow.

If ATCI1 = $45,000		If ATCI1 = $65,000		If ATCI1 = $90,000	
ATCI2($)	Probability	ATCI2($)	Probability	ATCI2($)	Probability
30,000	0.3	80,000	0.2	90,000	0.1
60,000	0.4	90,000	0.6	100,000	0.8
90,000	0.3	100,000	0.2	110,000	0.1

Then the decision tree which shows the possible after-tax cash inflow in each year, including the conditional nature of the year two cash inflow and its probabilities, can be depicted as follows:

Time 0	Time 1	Time 2	NPV at 12%	Joint Probability	Expected NPV
		$ 30,000	−$60,905[a]	0.120[b]	−$7,309
	$45,000	$ 60,000	−$36,995	0.160	−5,919
		$ 90,000	−$13,085	0.120	−1,570
		$ 80,000	−$ 3,195	0.050	−160
−$125,000	$65,000	$ 90,000	$ 4,775	0.150	716
		$100,000	$12,745	0.050	637
		$ 90,000	$27,100	0.035	949
	$90,000	$100,000	$35,070	0.280	9,820
		$110,000	$43,040	0.035	1,506
				1.000	−$1,330

a. $\text{NPV} = \text{PV} - 1 = \dfrac{\$45,000}{(1 + 0.12)} + \dfrac{\$30,000}{(1 + 0.12)^2} - \$125,000$

= $45,000 T3(12%, 1 year) + $30,000 T3(12%, 2 years) − $125,000

= $45,000(0.893) + $30,000(0.797) − $125,000

= $40,185 + $23,910 − $125,000 = $60,905

b. Joint Probability = (0.4)(0.3) = 0.120

The last column shows the calculation of expected NPV, which is the weighted average of the individual path NPVs where the weights are the path probabilities. In this example, the expected NPV of the project is –$1,330, and the project should be rejected.

Correlation of Cash Flows Over Time

When cash inflows are independent from period to period, it is fairly easy to measure the overall risk of an investment proposal. In some cases, however, especially with the introduction of a new product, the cash flows experienced in early years affect the size of the cash flows in later years. This is called the *time dependence of cash flows,* and it has the effect of increasing the risk of the project over time.

EXAMPLE 42: Janday Corporation's after-tax cash inflows (ATCI) are time dependent, so that year one results ($ATCI_1$) affect the cash flows in year two ($ATCI_2$) as follows:

If $ATCI_1$ is $8,000 with a 40% probability, the distribution for $ATCI_2$ is

0.3	$5,000
0.5	10,000
0.2	15,000

If $ATCI_1$ is $15,000 with a 50% probability, the distribution for $ATCI_2$ is

0.3	$10,000
0.6	20,000
0.1	30,000

If $ATCI_1$ is $20,000 with a 10% chance, the distribution for $ATCI_2$ is

0.1	$15,000
0.8	40,000
0.1	50,000

The project requires an initial investment of $20,000, and the risk-free rate of capital is 10%.

The company uses the expected NPV from decision tree analysis to determine whether the project should be accepted. The analysis is as follows:

Time 0		Time 1	Time 2	NPV at 10%	Joint Probability	Expected NPV
			0.3 $5,000 –	$8,595[a]	0.12[b]	–$1,031
		$8,000	0.5 $10,000	– 4,463	0.20	– 893
	0.4		0.2 15,000	–33	0.08	– 26
			0.3 $10,000	$1,901	0.15	285
–$20,000	0.5	$15,000	0.6 20,000	10,165	0.30	3,050
	0.1		0.1 30,000	18,429	0.05	921
			0.1 $15,000	$10,596	0.01	106
		$20,000	0.8 40,000 3	1,238	0.08	2,499
			0.1 50,000	39,502	0.01	395
					1.00	$5,306

(a) NPV = PV – I = $8,000 T3(10%, 1) + $5,000 T3(10%,1) – $20,000 = $8,000(0.9091) – $5,000(0.8264) – $20,000 = – $8,595

(b) Joint probability of the first path = (0.4)*(0.3) = 0.12

Since the NPV is positive (5,306), Janday Corporation should accept the project.

NORMAL DISTRIBUTION AND NPV ANALYSIS— STANDARDIZING THE DISPERSION

With the assumption of independence of cash flows over time, the expected NPV would be

$$NPV = PV - I$$

$$= \sum_{t=1}^{n} \frac{\bar{A}_t}{(1 + r)^t} - I$$

The standard deviation of NPV is

$$\sigma = \sqrt{\sum_{t=1}^{n} \frac{\sigma_t^2}{(1 + r)^{2t}}}$$

The expected value (A) and the standard deviation (s) give a considerable amount of information by which to assess the risk of an investment project. If the probability distribution is normal, some probability statement regarding the project's NPV can be made. For example, the probability of a project's NPV providing an NPV of less or greater than zero can be computed by standardizing the normal variate x as follows:

$$z = \frac{x - NPV}{\sigma}$$

where

x	=	the outcome to be found
NPV	=	the expected NPV
z	=	the standardized normal variate whose probability value can be found in Exhibit 22-9.

Exhibit 22-9: Normal Probability Distribution Table

Area of normal distribution that is z standard deviations to the left or right of the mean.

Number of Standard Deviations from Mean (z)	Area to the Left or Right (One tail)	Number of Standard Deviations from Mean (z)	Area to the Left or Right (One tail)
0.00	.5000	1.55	.0606
0.05	.4801	1.60	.0548
0.10	.4602	1.65	.0495
0.15	.4404	1.70	.0446
0.20	.4207	1.75	.0401
0.25	.4013	1.80	.0359
0.30	.3821	1.85	.0322
0.35	.3632	1.90	.0287
0.40	.3446	1.95	.0256
0.45	.3264	2.00	.0228
0.50	.3085	2.05	.0202
0.55	.2912	2.10	.0179
0.60	.2743	2.15	.0158
0.65	.2578	2.20	.0139
0.70	.2420	2.25	.0122
0.75	.2264	2.30	.0107
0.80	.2119	2.35	.0094
0.85	.1977	2.40	.0082
0.90	.1841	2.45	.0071
0.95	.1711	2.50	.0062
1.00	.1577	2.55	.0054
1.05	.1469	2.60	.0047
1.10	.1357	2.65	.0040
1.15	.1251	2.70	.0035

Number of Standard Deviations from Mean (z)	Area to the Left or Right (One tail)	Number of Standard Deviations from Mean (z)	Area to the Left or Right (One tail)
1.20	.1151	2.75	.0030
1.25	.1056	2.80	.0026
1.30	.0968	2.85	.0022
1.35	.0885	2.90	.0019
1.40	.0808	2.95	.0016
1.45	.0735	3.00	.0013
1.50	.0668		

EXAMPLE 43: Assume an investment with the following data:

	Period 1	Period 2	Period 3
Expected cash inflow (A)	$5,000	$4,000	$3,000
Standard deviation (σ)	1,140	1,140	1,140

Assume that the firm's cost of capital is 8% and the initial investment is $9,000. Then the expected NPV is:

NPV = PV – 1

$$= \frac{\$5,000}{(1 + 0.08)} + \frac{\$4,000}{(1 + 0.08)^2} + \frac{\$3,000}{(1 + 0.08)^3} - \$9,000$$

$= \$5,000 T3(8\%, 1) + \$4,000 T3(8\%, 2) + \$3,000 T3(8\%, 3) - \$9,000$

$= \$5,000(0.9259) + \$4,000(0.8573) + \$3,000(0.7983) - \$9,000$

$= \$4,630 + \$3,429 + \$2,381 - \$9,000 = \$1,440$

The standard deviation about the expected NPV is

$$\sigma = \sqrt{\sum_{t=1}^{\pi} \frac{\sigma_t^2}{(1+r)^{2t}}}$$

$$= \sqrt{\frac{\$1,140^2}{(1+0.08)^2} + \frac{\$1,140^2}{(1+0.08)^4} + \frac{\$1,140^2}{(1+0.08)^6}}$$

$$= \sqrt{\$2,888,411} = \$1,670$$

The probability that the NPV is less than zero is then:

$$z = \frac{x - \text{NPV}}{\sigma} = \frac{0 - \$1,440}{\$1,670} = -0.862$$

The area of normal distribution that is z standard deviations to the left or right of the mean may be found in Exhibit 22-9. A value of z equal to –0.862 falls in the area between 0.1977 and 0.1841 in Exhibit 22-9. Therefore, there is approximately a 19% chance that the project's NPV will be zero or less. Putting it another way, there is a 19% chance that the internal rate of return of the project will be less than the risk-free rate.

CAPITAL ASSET PRICING MODEL IN CAPITAL BUDGETING

Portfolio considerations play an important role in the overall capital budgeting process. Through diversification, a firm can stabilize earnings, reduce risk, and thereby increase the market price of the firm's stock. The beta coefficient can be used for this purpose.

The capital asset pricing model (CAPM) can be used to determine the appropriate cost of capital. The NPV method uses the cost of capital as the rate to discount future cash flows. The IRR method uses the cost of capital as the cutoff rate. The required rate of return, or cost of capital according to the CAPM, or security market line (SML), is equal to the risk-free rate of return (r_f) plus a risk premium equal to the firm's beta coefficient (b) times the market risk premium. That is:

$$r_j = r_f + b(r_m - r_f)$$

EXAMPLE 44: A project has the following projected cash flows:

Year 0	Year 1	Year 2	Year 3
$(400)	$300	$200	$100

The estimated beta for the project is 1.5. The market return is 12%, and the risk-free rate is 6%. Then the firm's cost of capital or required rate of return is

$$r_j = r_f + b(r_m - r_f) = 6\% + 1.5(12\% - 6\%) = 15\%$$

The project's NPV can be computed using 15% as the discount rate:

Year	Cash Flow ($)	T3 = PV at 15%	PV ($)
0	(400)	1.000	(400)
1	300	0.870	261
2	200	0.756	151
3	100	0.65	66
NPV			78

The project should be accepted since its NPV is positive—that is, $78. Also, the project's IRR can be computed by trial and error. It is almost 30%, which exceeds the cost of capital of 15%. Therefore, by that standard also the project should be accepted.

EXAMPLE 45 (An Integrated Case): CoinToss Foods, Inc. is considering expansion in the fruit cocktail cannery business. The required equipment would cost $200,000, plus an additional $40,000 for shipping and installation. In addition, inventories would rise by $25,000, while accounts payable would increase by $5,000. The machinery will be depreciated under the MACRS system as three-year property. The applicable MCRS depreciation rates are 33.3%, 44.5%, 14.8%, and 7.4%.

The project is expected to operate for four years, at which time it will be terminated. The cash inflows are assumed to begin one year after the project is undertaken, and to continue to the fourth year. At the end of the project's life, the equipment is expected to have a salvage value of $25,000. Unit sales are expected to total 100,000 cans per year, and the expected sales price is $2.00 per can now and to increase by 5% annually thereafter. Cash total costs for the project (total manufacturing and operating costs less depreciation) are expected to total 60% of dollar sales. CoinToss's tax rate is 40%, and its cost of capital is 10% after taxes. The analysis is as follows:

INPUT DATA

Initial Costs:

Equipment	$200,000
Shipping and installation	$40,000
Expected salvage value	$25,000
Changes in working capital	
Inventories	$25,000
Accounts payable	$5,000

MACRS 3-year depreciation
deduction:

Year	1	2	3	4
Rate	33.3%	44.5%	14.8%	7.4%

Expected unit sales	100,000
Price per unit	$2.00
Price increase	5%
Total costs (% of sales)	60%

Tax rate	40%
Cost of capital	10%

		Year			
	0	1	2	3	4
Initial outlay:					
Equipment cost	($200,000)				
Installation	(40,000)				
Increase in inventory	(25,000)				
Increase in A/P	5,000				
Initial net investment					
Operating cash flows:					
Units sales		100,000	100,000	100,000	100,000
Price per unit		$2.10	$2.21	$2.32	$2.43
Total revenues		$210,000	$220,500	$231,525	$243,101
Total cash costs		$126,000	$132,300	$138,915	$145,861
Depreciation deduction		79,920	106,800	35,520	17,760
Total costs		$205,920	$239,100	$174,435	$163,621
Operating income		$4,080	($18,600)	$57,090	$79,481
Taxes on operating income		1,632	(7,440)	22,836	31,792
Operating income after taxes		$2,448	($11,160)	$34,254	$47,688
Depreciation		79,920	106,800	35,520	17,760
Operating cash flow		$82,368	$95,640	$69,774	$65,448
Terminal year cash flows:					
Recovery of net working capital					20,000
Salvage value					25,000
Tax on salvage value					(10,000)
Total termination cash flow					$35,000
Net cash flows:					
Net cash flows	($260,000)	$82,368	$95,640	$69,774	$100,448
Cumulative cash flows for payback	(260,000)	(177,632)	(81,992)	(12,218)	88,230
Compounded inflows for MIRR		109,632	115,724	76,751	100,448
Terminal value of inflows:					402,556

Results	
NPV	$14,951
IRR	12.59%
MIRR	11.55%
Payback	3.12

Based on the analysis, the project should be undertaken, as NPV>0 and both IRR and MIRR are greater than 10%.

Sensitivity Analysis

A sensitivity analysis is now performed on unit sales, salvage value, and cost of capital for the project. Assume that each of these variables deviates from its base-case, or expected, value by plus and minus 10%, 20%, and 30%. Using Excel yields the following sensitivity results:

	Unit sales	NPV		Salvage	NPV		Cost of capital	NPV
				Sensitivity Analysis Results				
0%		$14,951			$14,951			$14,951
-30%	70,000	-$36,394		$17,500	$11,878		7.0%	$34,103
-20%	80,000	-$19,279		$20,000	$12,902		8.0%	$27,484
-10%	90,000	-$2,164		$22,500	$13,927		9.0%	$21,104
0%	100,000	$14,951		$25,000	$14,951		10.0%	$14,951
10%	110,000	$32,066		$27,500	$15,976		11.0%	$9,016
20%	120,000	$49,181		$30,000	$17,000		12.0%	$3,287
30%	130,000	$66,296		$32,500	$18,025		13.0%	-$2,244

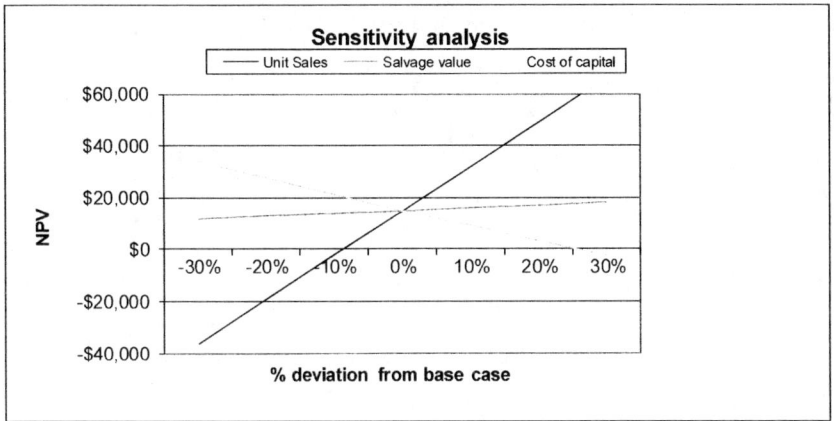

The plots for unit sales and salvage value are upward sloping, indicating that higher variable values lead to higher NPVs. Conversely, the plot for cost of capital is downward sloping, because a higher cost of capital leads to a lower NPV. The plot of unit sales is much steeper than that for salvage value. This indicates that NPV is more sensitive to changes in unit sales than to changes in salvage value.

CONCLUSION

Net present value, internal rate of return, and profitability index are equally effective in selecting economically sound, independent investment proposals. However, the payback method is inadequate since it does not consider the time value of money. For mutually exclusive projects, net present value, internal rate of return, and profitability index methods are not always able to rank projects in the same order; it is possible to come up with different rankings under each method. Almost all capital budgeting proposals can be viewed as real options. Risk should be taken into account in the capital budgeting process, such as by using probabilities, simulation, and decision trees.

CHAPTER 23

EVALUATION OF SEGMENTAL PERFORMANCE AND TRANSFER PRICING

CONTENTS

A segment is a part or activity of an organization from which a manager derives cost or revenue data. Examples of segments are divisions, sales territories, individual stores, service centers, manufacturing plants, sales departments, product lines, geographic areas, types of customers, types of employees, and states.

Analysis of segmental performance assists in determining the success or failure of the divisional manager as well as the division. Performance reports should include industry and competitor comparisons. Also, the performance reports should match cycles of major business lines, activities, and geographic areas.

Performance measures look to the contribution of the division to profit and quantity as well as whether the division meets the overall goals of the company. It is difficult to compare profit of different segments of a company, especially when segments are of different sizes or provide different kinds of products or services. Measures of divisional performance for a particular segment should be compared to previous periods, other segments, and predetermined standards.

Profit planning by segments applies to selecting among alternative uses of company resources to accomplish a target profit figure. Segmental profit planning necessitates that the profitability of each segment be measured to determine the overall profitability of all feasible combinations or alternatives.

APPRAISING MANAGER PERFORMANCE

In appraising manager performance, a determination must be made as to which factors were under the manager's control (e.g., advertising budget) and which factors were not (e.g., economic conditions). Comparison should be made of one division in the company to other divisions as well as of a division in the company to a similar division in a competing company. Appraisal should also be made of the risk and earning potential of a division. Graphic presentation shows comparisons, whether of an historical, current, or prognostic nature.

It is important to measure the performance of the divisional manager, because doing so:

- Assists in formulating management incentives and controlling operations to meet corporate goals.
- Directs upper management's attention to where it would be most productive.
- Determines whom to reward for good performance.
- Determines who is not doing well so corrective action may be taken.
- Provides job satisfaction, since the manager receives feedback.

In decentralization, profit responsibility is assigned among subunits of the company. The lower the level where decisions are made, the greater the decentralization. Decentralization is most effective in organizations where cost and profit measurements are necessary and is most successful in organizations where subunits are totally independent and autonomous. Decentralization is in different forms, including functional, geographical, and profit.

The advantages of decentralization are:

- Top management has more time for strategic planning.
- Decisions are made by managers with the most knowledge of local conditions.
- There is greater managerial input in decision making.
- Managers have more control over results, resulting in motivation.

The disadvantages of decentralization are:

- Managers become "narrow-sighted" and look solely at the division rather than at the company as a whole.
- Duplication of services can result.
- There is an increased cost in obtaining additional information.

For comparison purposes, replacement cost instead of historical cost should be employed. It furnishes a relative basis of comparison since it represents the comparable necessary investment at the end of a reporting period. Evaluating replacement cost assists in comparing asset valuation to current productivity. If replacement cost cannot be determined, valuation can be based on the present value of future net cash flows.

The major means of analyzing divisional performance is by responsibility center—revenue center, cost center, profit center, and investment center.

RESPONSIBILITY CENTERS

Responsibility accounting is the system for collecting and reporting revenue and cost information by areas of responsibility (responsibility centers). It operates on the premise that managers should be held responsible for their performance, the performance of their subordinates, and for all activities within their responsibility centers. It is both a planning and control technique. Responsibility accounting, also called profitability accounting and activity accounting, has the following advantages:

- It facilitates delegation of decision making.

- It helps management promote the concept of management by objective, in which managers agree on a set of goals. The manager's performance is then evaluated based on his or her attainment of these goals.

- It permits effective use of the concept of management by exception.

Exhibit 23-1 shows responsibility centers within a company; Exhibit 23-2 presents an organization chart of a company.

A well designed responsibility accounting system establishes responsibility centers within the organization. A responsibility center is defined as a unit in the organization that has control over costs, revenues, and investment funds. A responsibility center may be responsible for all three functions or for only one function. Responsibility centers can be found in both centralized and decentralized organizations. A profit center is often associated with a decentralized organization while a cost center is usually associated with a centralized one. However, this is not always the case.

There are lines of responsibility within the company. Shell, for example, is organized primarily by business functions: exploitation, refining, and marketing. General Mills, on the other hand, is organized by product lines.

Exhibit 23-1: Responsibility Centers within a Company

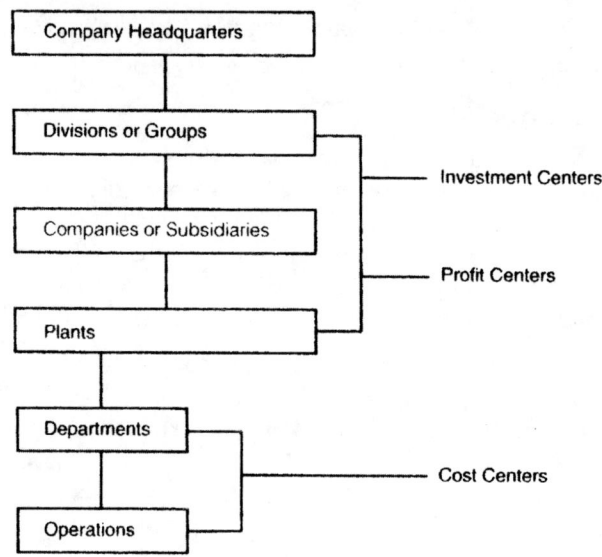

Revenue Center

A revenue center is responsible for obtaining a target level of sales revenue. An example is a district sales office. The performance report for a revenue center should contain the budgeted and actual sales for the center by product, including evaluation. Usually, the manager of the revenue center is responsible for marketing a product line. A revenue center typically has a few costs (e.g., salaries, rent). Hence, a revenue center is responsible mostly for revenues and only incidentally for some costs, typically not product costs.

Sales analysis may involve one or more of the following: prior sales performance, looking at sales trends over the years, and comparing actual sales to budgeted sales.

In a service business, some performance measures include billable time, average billing rate, and cost per hour of employee time.

Accountability for departmental sales revenue assumes the manager has authority to determine product sales prices.

Cost Center

A cost center is typically the smallest segment of activity or responsibility area for which costs are accumulated. This approach is usually employed by departments rather than divisions. A cost center has no control over sales or marketing activities. Departmental profit is difficult to derive because of problems in allocating revenue and costs.

A cost center is a department head having responsibility and accountability for costs incurred and for the quantity and quality of products or services. For example, the personnel manager is accountable for costs incurred and the quality of services rendered.

Examples of cost centers include a maintenance department and a fabricating department in a manufacturing company.

A cost center may be relatively small, such as a single department with a few people. It can also be very large, such as an administrative area of a large company or an entire factory. Some cost centers may consist of a number of smaller cost centers. An example is a factory that is segmented into numerous departments, each of which is a cost center.

A cost center is basically responsible for direct operational costs and in meeting production budgets and quotas. Authority and responsibility for cost centers must be under the control of the department head, usually a foreman.

In the cost center approach, compare budgeted cost to actual cost. Variances are investigated to determine the reasons for them, necessary corrective action is taken to correct problems, and efficiencies are accorded recognition.

Exhibit 23-2: Organization Chart of a Company

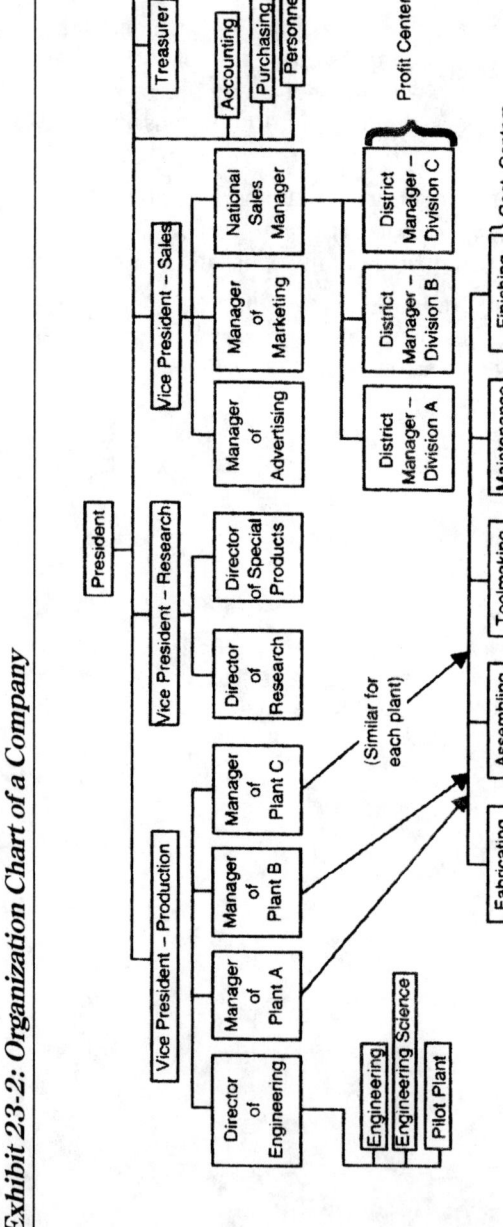

This topic is covered in detail in Chapter 17, "Cost-Volume-Profit Analysis and Leverage." The cost center approach is useful when a manager possesses control over his or her costs at a specified operating level.

Recommendation: Use this approach when problems arise in relating financial measures to output.

Suggestion: Cost center evaluation is most suitable for the following functions: accounting and financial reporting, legal, computer services, marketing, personnel, and public relations. In evaluating these functions, there is a problem in quantifying the output in financial terms.

Provision should exist for chargebacks, where appropriate. For example, if a quality control department made an error in its evaluation of product quality leading to acceptance by the purchasing department, the quality control department should be charged with the increased costs to improve the purchased goods to meet acceptable standards incurred by the purchasing department.

Note: The cost center approach may be appropriate for nonprofit and governmental units where budgetary appropriations are assigned. Actual expenditures are compared to budgetary amounts. A manager's performance depends on his or her ability to achieve output levels given budgetary constraints.

When looking at a manager's performance, say at bonus time, the relevant costs are those incremental costs over which he or she has control. Incremental costs are those expenditures that would not exist if the center were abandoned. Hence, allocated common costs (e.g., general administration) should not be included in appraising manager performance. Such costs should, however, be allocated in determining the profit figure for the entire division. Cost allocation must conform to goal congruence and autonomy and should be applied consistently among divisions.

Cost center evaluation will not be worthwhile unless reliable budget figures exist. If a division's situation significantly changes, an adjustment to the initial budget is necessary. In such a case, actual cost should be compared with the initial budget figure (original goal) and the revised budget. Flexible budgets should be prepared to enable the examination of costs incurred at different levels of capacity. For example, there can be figures budgeted for expected capacity, optimistic capacity, and pessimistic capacity. Better comparisons of budget to actual can thus be made given changing circumstances.

When a transfer occurs between cost centers, the transfer price should be based upon either actual cost, standard cost, or controllable cost. Transfer price is the price charged between divisions for a product or service.

Warning: Using actual cost has the problem of passing cost inefficiencies onto the next division. There is no incentive for the transferer to control costs.

Solution: Using standard cost corrects for the problem of transferring cost inefficiencies to the next division. However, standard cost includes allocated fixed cost, which might be subjective.

A good transfer price is a controllable cost.

What to Do: Charge the cost center with actual controllable cost and credit it with standard controllable cost for the assembled product or service to other divisions.

Rectifying the Problem: By solely including the controllable cost, the subjectivity of the allocation of fixed noncontrollable cost does not exist.

In evaluating administrative functions, prepare performance reports examining such dollar indicators as executive salaries and service department costs as well as nondollar measures such as number of files handled, phone calls taken, and invoices processed.

In appraising a cost center, look at the ratio of indirect to direct personnel. The ratio equals the number of indirect labor employees to the number of direct labor employees.

Note: Indirect manpower is not directly involved in production or performing customer services. The ratio of indirect to direct personnel reveals the division manpower planning and control. Manpower needs are based on the individual unit's variable activities and needs. In order to accomplish divisional goals, there should be a proper relationship between indirect labor and direct labor so that services are performed to generate maximum profitability. Indirect personnel should be closely monitored because of its effect on overhead costs.

Warning: A high ratio of indirect labor may mean the division is top heavy in administrative and clerical staff because of improper controls on the nature of the division's activities. Perhaps the support activities should be curtailed.

EXAMPLE 1: The indirect personnel to direct personnel ratio averaged about 45% each month over a six-month period. This is favorable because management has maintained a fairly consistent relationship between direct and indirect personnel.

In order to appraise the effectiveness of employee staff in generating divisional revenue, the following ratios may be computed:

- Sales to direct labor.
- Sales to total number of employees.
- Sales to total dollar salaries of employees.

Higher ratios are desirable because they indicate favorable employee performance in generating sales for the company. For example, an increasing trend in revenue per employee indicates greater productivity.

Caution: A decline in the ratios may be due to lower sales because of external factors beyond the control of the division manager,

Cost reduction measures may be implemented without having a negative long-term effect on the company. Such measures may improve short-term profitability. Short-term cost cutting measures may include:

- Marketing
    1. Paying salespeople on a commission basis instead of a fixed salary.
    2. Using distributors rather than direct selling.
- Manufacturing
    1. Hiring per diem laborers rather than subcontracting the work.
    2. Buying raw materials outside rather than producing them. When the quantity of the product required is relatively low, it is typically better to buy from the outside. Once production exceeds a specified level, the company can increase profitability by doing its own manufacturing.
    3. Using parts rather than subassemblies as the raw materials.

Profit Center

A profit center is a responsibility unit that measures the performance of a division, product line, geographic area, or other measurable unit. A profit center has revenue and expenses associated with it. Net income and contribution margin can be computed for a profit center. Profit centers typically do not have significant amounts of invested capital.

Benefits: The profit center approach enhances decentralization and provides units for decision making purposes.

When to Use: Use it when there is a self-contained division (with its own manufacturing and distribution facilities) and when there are a limited number of interdivision transfers. The reason for this is that the profit reported by the division is basically independent of other divisions' operating activities.

Each division's profit should be independent of performance efficiency and managerial decisions elsewhere in the company. Further, divisional earnings should not be increased by any action reducing overall corporate profitability. Also use a profit center when divisional managers have decision-making authority in terms of the quantity and mix of goods or services manufactured. Because with a profit center you determine net income as if the division were a separate economic entity, the manager is more cognizant of outside market considerations. There are different ways of expressing profit, such as net income, contribution margin, gross profit, controllable profit, and incremental profit. Examples of profit centers are an auto repair center in a department store and an appliance department in a retail store.

A profit center has the following characteristics: (1) defined profit objective, (2) managerial authority to make decisions impacting earnings, and (3) use of profit-oriented decision rules. A typical profit center is a division selling a limited number of products or serving a particular geographic area. It includes the means of providing goods and services and the means of marketing them.

In some instances, profit centers are formed when the company's product or service is used solely within the company. For example, the computer department of a company may bill each of the firm's administrative and operating units for computing services. It is not essential that fixed costs be allocated. Hence, contribution margin may be a good indicator of divisional performance. If each division meets its target contribution margin, excess contribution margin will be adequate to cover general corporate expenses. A contribution margin income statement can be prepared to evaluate divisional and managerial performance. It also aids in computing selling price, the price to accept an order given an idle capacity situation, output levels, maximization of resource uses, and break-even analysis. The contribution margin income statement is illustrated in Exhibit 23-3.

Note: Controllable costs are under the division manager's control. They are the incremental costs of operating a division, In effect, they are costs that could have been avoided by the company if the division were shut down. Non-controllable costs are common to a group of divisions that are rationally allocated to them.

A difficulty with the profit center idea is that profit is calculated after subtracting noncontrollable costs or costs that have been arbitrarily allocated and are not directly related to divisional activity. The ensuing profit figure may hence be erroneous. However, cost allocation is required since divisions must incorporate nondivisional costs that have to be met before the company will show a profit.

Special Note: Policies optimizing divisional earnings will likewise optimize corporate earnings even before the allocation of nondivisional expenses.

Exhibit 23-3: Contribution Margin Income Statement for Divisional Performance Evaluation

Sales

Less variable production cost of sales

Manufacturing contribution margin

Less variable selling and administrative expenses

Contribution margin

Less controllable fixed costs (i.e., salesperson salaries)

Controllable contribution margin by manager (measures performance of the segment manager)

Less uncontrollable fixed costs (i.e., depreciation, property taxes, insurance)

Segment contribution margin (measures performance of the division)

Less unallocated costs to divisions (excessively difficult to allocate objectively or illogical to allocate, such as the president's salary; corporate research)

Income before taxes (measures performance of the company in its entirety)

While an uncontrollable income statement item is included in appraising the performance of a profit center, it should not be used in evaluating the performance of the manager. An example is the effect of a casualty loss.

A profit center manager should be responsible not only for profit and loss items attributable directly in the division, but also for costs incurred outside the center (e.g., headquarters, other divisions) for which the center will be billed directly. The manager should also be responsible for an expense equal to the company's interest rate multiplied by controllable working capital. This charge will take into account tradeoffs between working capital levels and profits. For example, increased inventory balances will mean less loss from stock-outs. The profit center manager is the only person that comprehends these tradeoffs.

Advantages of the profit center approach are that it creates competition in a decentralized company, provides goal congruence between a division and the company, and aids performance evaluation. A drawback is that profits can be "massaged" since expenses may be shifted among periods. Examples of discretionary costs where management has wide latitude are research and repairs. Also, the total assets employed in the division to obtain the profit are not considered.

EXAMPLE 2: You can sell a product at its intermediate point in Division A for $170 or its final point in Division B at $260. The outlay cost in Division A is $120, while the outlay cost in Division B is $110. Unlimited product demand exists for both the intermediate product and the final product. Capacity is interchangeable. Division performance is:

	Division A	Division B
Selling price	$170	$260
Outlay cost—A	(120)	(120)
Outlay cost—B		(110)
Profit	$ 50	$ 30

Sell at the intermediate point because of the higher profit.

Other measures in appraising divisional performance that are not of a profit nature that must be considered are:

- Ratios between cost elements and assets to appraise effectiveness and efficiency.
- Productivity measures, including input-output relationships. An example is labor hours in a production run. Consider the input in terms of time and money, and the resulting output in terms of quantity and quality. Does the maintenance of equipment ensure future growth? Another example is the utilization rate of facilities.
- Personnel development (e.g., number of promotions, turnover).
- Market measures (e.g., market share, product leadership, growth rate, customer service).
- Product leadership indicators (e.g., patented products, innovative technology, product quality, safety record).
- Human resource relationships (e.g., employee turnover rate, customer relations, including on-time deliveries).
- Social responsibility measures (e.g., consumer medals).

A transfer price has to be formulated so that a realistic and meaningful profit figure can be determined for each division. It should be established only after proper planning. The transfer price is the one credited to the selling division and charged to the buying division for an internal transfer of an assembled product or service. It is the same for each as if an "arm's-length" transaction had taken place.

The choice of transfer prices not only affects divisional performance, but is also important in decisions involving make or buy, whether to sell or process further, and choosing between alternative production possibilities.

A transfer price should:

- Promote the goals of the company, and harmonize divisional goals with organizational goals.

- Be equitable to all parties involved.

- Preserve autonomy, so the selling and buying division managers operate their divisions as decentralized entities.

- Result in the minimization of duplication and paperwork.

- Provide flexibility.

- Be quick in responding to changing business conditions in various countries.

- Act as an incentive to keep costs under control.

- Be developed in such a way as to minimize the conflict between buying and selling divisions.

- Put profits where they are wanted. For example, put higher profits in low tax areas and lower profits in high tax areas. It should minimize tariffs in international dealings. Also, it should put profits where they can best be used such as constructing a new building.

- Satisfy legal requirements.

- Support cooperation across divisional and country lines.

- Support the existence of internal and external reliability.

Recommendation: The best transfer price is the negotiated market value of the assembled product or service, since it is a fair price and treats each profit center as a separate economic entity. It equals the outside service fee or selling price for the item (a quoted price for a product or service is only comparable if the credit terms, grade, quality, delivery, and auxiliary conditions are precisely the same) less internal cost savings that result from dealing internally within the organization (e.g., advertising sales commission, delivery charges, bookkeeping costs for customers' ledgers, credit and collection costs, and bad debts). Even though the selling center does not have a quantity discount policy, a discount may be factored into the transfer price. In many cases, if the buying center were an outside customer, the selling center would provide a volume discount, so a similar discount should be offered as an element of the transfer price. The market value of services performed is based on the going rate for a specific job (e.g., equipment tuneup) and/or the standard hourly rate (e.g., the hourly rate for a plumber). Market price may be determined from price catalogues, obtaining outside bids, and examining published data on completed market transactions.

Warning: An outside supplier may intentionally quote a low price to obtain the business with the thought of increasing the price at a later date. If two divisions cannot agree on the transfer price, it will be settled by arbitration at a higher level. A temporarily low transfer price (due to oversupply of the item, for example) or high transfer price (due to a strike situation causing a supply shortage, for example), should not be employed.

Solution: Use the average long-term market price.

A negotiated transfer price works best when outside markets for the intermediate product exist, all parties have access to market information, and one is permitted to deal externally if a negotiated settlement is impossible. If one of these conditions is violated, the negotiated price may break down and cause inefficiencies.

If the outside market price is not ascertainable (e.g., new product, absence of replacement market, or inappropriate or too costly to be used for transfer pricing), use budgeted cost plus profit markup, because this transfer price approximates market value and will spot divisional inefficiencies. Budgeted cost includes the factory cost and any administrative costs applicable to production, such as cost accounting, production planning, industrial engineering, and research and development. Direct material, direct labor, and variable factory overhead are based on standard rates for the budget period. Fixed factory overhead and administrative expenses are unitized at either forecast or normal volume. It is preferable to use normal volume because it levels out the intracompany prices over the years. Profit markup should take into account the particular characteristics of the division rather than the overall corporate profit margin. Profit is often calculated based on a percentage return on capital which is budgeted to be used at the budgeted or normal volume used for unitizing fixed costs. This percentage is established by company policy. It may be the average expected return for the manufacturing unit, purchasing unit, or company. When budgeted cost plus profit is used as the transfer price, a provision typically exists to adjust for changes in raw material prices and wage rates.

There is an incentive to the selling division to control its costs because it will not be credited for an amount in excess of budgeted cost plus a markup. Thus, if the selling division's inefficiencies resulted in actual costs being excessive, it would have to absorb the decline in profit to the extent that actual cost exceeded budgeted cost. Profit markup should be as realistic as possible given the nature of the division and its product.

Note: Even though actual cost plus profit markup may be used, it has the drawback of passing on cost inefficiencies. In fact, the selling division is encouraged to be cost inefficient, since the higher its actual cost, the higher its selling price will be (since it shows a greater profit). Some companies employ actual cost as the transfer price because of ease of use, but the problem is that no profit is shown by the selling division, and cost inefficiencies are passed on. Further, the cost-based method treats the divisions as cost centers rather than profit or investment centers. Therefore, measures such as return on investment and residual income cannot be used for evaluation purposes.

The variable-cost-based transfer price has an advantage over the full cost method because, in the short run, it may tend to ensure the best utilization of the overall company's resources. The reason is that, in the short run, fixed costs do not change. Any use of facilities, without incurrence of additional fixed costs, will increase the company's overall profits. In the case where division managers are responsible for costs in their divisions, the cost price approach to transfer pricing is often used.

A transfer price based on cost may be appropriate when there are minimal services provided by one department to another.

A company may have more than one department providing a product or service that is identical or very similar. It may be cost beneficial to centralize that product or service into one department. If more than one department provides an identical or very similar service, a cost basis transfer price may be used since the receiving department will select the services of the department providing the highest quality. Thus, the providing department has an incentive to do a good job.

A company may use a below-cost transfer price to favor a division newly spun off by the parent. This may provide the new firm with a better competitive position, allowing it to get started in an industry other than that of the parent, and compete effectively with established industry leaders.

Incremental cost is another transfer pricing possibility. Incremental costs are the variable costs of making and shipping goods and any costs directly and exclusively traceable to the product. This cost is quite good for use with the company as a whole, but does little for measuring divisional performance. The incremental cost approach assumes the selling division has sufficient capacity to satisfy internal company demands as well as demands of outside customers.

Another way of setting the transfer price is dual pricing. It occurs when the buying division is charged with variable cost ($1) and the selling division is credited with absorption cost and markup ($1.50 plus 60%). Under dual pricing, there is a motivational effect, since each division's performance is enhanced by the transfer. However, profit for the company as a whole will be less than the sum of the divisions' profits.

A last possibility is allocating profit among divisions, say, based on input by departments (e.g., time spent, costs incurred).

EXAMPLE 3: Division A manufactures an assembled product that can be sold to outsiders or transferred to Division B. Relevant information for the period is:

Division A	Units
Production	1,500
Transferred to Division B	1,200
Sold outside	300
Selling price	$25
Unit cost	$5

The units transferred to Division B were processed further at a cost of $7.

They were sold outside at $45. Transfers are at market value.

Division profit is:

	Division A	Division B	Company
Sales	$ 7,500	$54,000	$61,500
Transfer price	30,000		
	$37,500	$54,000	$61,500
Product cost	$ 7,500	$ 8,400	$15,900
Transfer price		30,000	
	$ 7,500	$38,400	$15,900
Profit	$30,000	$15,600	$45,600

EXAMPLE 4: Zeno Corporation manufactures radios. It has two production divisions (assembly and finishing) and one service division (maintenance). The assembly division both sells assembled radios to other companies and transfers them for further processing to the finishing division. The transfer price used is market value. Relevant data follow.

Assembly Division

Outside sales: 1,000 assembled radios at $30 (included in the price are selling commission fees of $1 per unit and freight costs of $2 per unit). Transferred to finishing division: 10,000 assembled radios.

Direct costs	$80,000
Indirect costs	$45,000

Finishing Division

Outside sales: 10,000 finished radios at	$55
Direct costs	$90,000
Indirect costs	$30,000

Maintenance Division

Direct costs (direct labor, parts)		$80,000
Indirect costs	$25,000	
9,000 hours rendered for servicing to assembly division		
12,000 hours rendered for servicing to finishing division		
Standard hourly rate: $8		

A schedule of the gross profit of the separate divisions and the gross profit of Zeno Corporation follows:

Gross Profit, Zeno Corporation

	Assembly	Finishing	Mainte-nance	Transfers	Zeno
Revenue					
Sales	$ 30,000	$550,000			$580,000
Transfers		270,000			$270,000
			$ 72,000	72,000	
			96,000	96,000	
Total	$300,000	$550,000	$168,000	$438,000	$580,000
Costs					
Direct	$ 80,000	$ 90,000	$ 80,000		$250,000
Indirect	45,000	30,000	25,000		100,000
Transfers:					
—Maintenance	72,000	96,000		$168,000	
—Assembly	270,000		270,000		
Total costs	$197,000	$486,000	$105,000	$438,000	$350,000
Gross profit	$103,000	$ 64,000	$63,000	–	$230,000

Assembly revenue
Sales $30 × 1,000
Transfer price $27 × 10,000

EXAMPLE 5: An assembly division wants to charge a finishing division $80 per unit for an internal transfer of 800 units. The variable cost per unit is $50. Total fixed cost in the assembly division is $200,000. Current production is 10,000 units. Idle capacity exists. The finishing division can purchase the item outside for $73 per unit.

The maximum transfer price should be $73, which is the cost to buy it from outside. The finishing division should not have to pay a price greater than the outside market price.

Whether the buying division should be permitted to buy the item outside or be forced to buy inside depends on what is best for overall corporate profitability. Typically, the buying division is required to purchase inside at the maximum transfer price ($73), as the selling division still has to meet its fixed cost when idle capacity exists. The impact on corporate profitability of having the buying division purchase outside of the company is determined as follows:

Savings to assembly division (units × variable cost per unit): $40,000
800 × $50

Cost to finishing division (units × outside selling price):

800 × $73	58,400
Stay inside	$18,400

The buying division will be asked to purchase inside the company, because if it went outside, corporate profitability would decline by $18,400.

Investment Center

An investment center is a responsibility center within an organization that has control over revenue, cost, and investment funds. It is a profit center whose performance is evaluated on the basis of the return earned on invested capital. Corporate headquarters and product line divisions in a large decentralized organization would be examples of investment centers. Investment centers are widely used in highly diversified companies.

A divisional investment is the amount placed in that division and placed under division management control. Two major divisional performance indicators are (1) return on investment and (2) residual income. Available total assets in these measures should be used to take into account all assets in the division, whether used or not. By including nonproductive assets in the base, the manager is motivated either to retain or sell them. Assets assigned to a division include direct assets in the division and allocated corporate assets. Assets are reflected at book value.

Suggestion: Include facilities being constructed in the investment base if the division is committing the funds for the new asset.

Distinguish between controllable and noncontrollable investment. While the former is helpful in appraising a manager's performance, the latter is used to evaluate the entire division. Controllable investment depends on the degree of a division's autonomy. Thus, an investment center manager accepts responsibility for both the center's assets and its controllable income.

In obtaining divisional investment, there has to be an allocation of general corporate assets to that division. These allocated assets are not considered part of controllable investment. Assets should be allocated to divisions on the basis of measures (e.g., area occupied).

What to Do: The allocated investment should be part of the division's investment base, but not as an element of controllable investment. Do not allocate general corporate assets attributable to the company as a whole (e.g., security investments).

Advice: Do not allocate an asset if it requires excessive subjectivity.

The optimal way to assign cash to a division is to agree upon a cash level that meets the minimum needs of the division. If cash is held in excess of this level, there should be an interest income credit using current interest rates. Because the division typically earns a higher return rate on investment than the prevailing interest rate, it will voluntarily return excess cash to the company. This policy maximizes the overall corporate return. Accounts receivable should be assigned to divisions based on sales. Finished goods should be included in the asset base. The division manager has control over it because that function determines the production level on the basis of expected sales. Excessive finished goods inventory is partly due to a division's inadequate planning.

Recommendation: Use the opportunity cost of funds tied up in inventory that could be invested elsewhere for a return in determining divisional profit. Plant and equipment should be allocated on the basis of square footage.

The valuation of assets can be based on book value, gross cost, consumer price index (CPI)-adjusted cost, replacement cost, or sales value. Typically, historical cost measures are employed in practice because of availability and consistency with balance sheet valuation.

Warning: Using book value for asset valuation will artificially increase divisional return on investment as assets become older, since the denominator using book value becomes lower over time. Gross cost corrects for this decline in value, but it still does not consider inflationary cost increases. However, an advantage of using gross book value to value assets is that it is not affected by changes in expansion rates.

Note: CPI-adjusted value takes into account changing price levels.

Recommendation: Replacement cost is ideal because it truly reflects the current prices of assets. Alternative ways exist to determine replacement cost (e.g., present value of future cash flows, specific price index of item, and current market value).

Tip: Inventory accounted for using LIFO should be adjusted to the FIFO basis or the replacement value, so that inventory is stated at current prices.

Current liabilities should be subtracted in determining the asset base because division financing policy depends on the decision of upper management.

Return on Investment. Net income determination for return on investment (ROI) purposes requires that divisional earnings measurements comply with the following guidelines:

- Divisional earnings should not be tied to operational efficiency and quality of managerial decisions of other segments.

- Divisional earnings should include all items the divisional manager has control over.

- Divisional earnings should not be increased because of any action that negatively affects current or future profits.

ROI is a superior indicator when the investment employed is outside of the manager's determination.

Caution: If a manager can significantly determine the capital employed, the return rate is a weakened tool.

$$\text{ROI} = \frac{\text{Net income}}{\text{Available total assets}}$$

Alternative measures are

$$\frac{\text{Operating profit}}{\text{Available total assets}}$$

$$\frac{\text{Controllable operating profit}}{\substack{\text{Controllable net investment} \\ \text{(Controllable assets—Controllable} \\ \text{liabilities)}}}$$

Note: With respect to the last measure, depreciation is a controllable cost since changes in the asset base are controllable by the division manager.

Interesting Point: Excluded from controllable investment is equipment the manager wants to sell but is unable to because the company is trying to get an alternative use by another division or central headquarters.

Recommendation: Transfer this asset from the division's controllable investment base. Also, controllable fixed assets allocated to divisions (e.g., research facilities, general administrative offices) should be excluded from controllable investment.

Assets have to be allocated to divisions on some rational basis. Actual cash at each location is known. Home-office cash is typically allocated to plants based on sales or cost of sales. Usually, accounts receivable are segregated by division or plant, but if not they may be allocated based on sales. Inventories and fixed assets are generally identified (e.g., account coding) to a specific plant or division. Other fixed assets (e.g., home-office building, equipment trucking, research facilities) may be allocated to plants and divisions based on services rendered. Building may be allocated based on physical space. Prepaid expenses, deferred charges, and other assets may be allocated based on sales or cost of sales.

Idle facilities should be included in the investment base when the inactivity of the assets is caused by a division not attaining the budgeted share of the actual market or results from insufficient maintenance.

ROI for each division enables management to appraise divisions from the view of efficient utilization of resources allocated to each division. Divisional management effectiveness is assessed and related to salary and/or bonuses. To work effectively, managers should have control over operations and resources.

Advantages of ROI. The advantages of determining for ROI are:

- It focuses on maximizing a ratio instead of improving absolute profits.
- It highlights unprofitable divisions. Perhaps some should be disposed of.

- It can be used as a base against which to evaluate divisions within the company and to compare the division to a comparable division in a competing company.
- It assigns profit responsibility.
- It aids in appraising divisional manager performance.
- When a division maximizes its ROI, the company similarly maximizes its ROI.
- It places emphasis on high-return items.
- It represents a cumulative audit or appraisal of all capital expenditures incurred during a division's existence.
- It serves as a guideline to the division manager in analyzing discounted cash flow internal rates of return for proposed capital expenditures.
- It is the broadest possible measure of financial performance. Because divisions are often geographically disbursed internationally, division managers are given broad authority in using division assets and acquiring and selling assets.
- It helps make the goals of the division manager coincide with those of corporate management.

Disadvantages of ROI. The disadvantages of determining for ROI are:
- It focuses on maximizing a ratio instead of improving absolute profits.
- Alternative profitability measures could be used in the numerator besides net income (e.g., gross profit, contribution margin, segment margin).
- Different assets in the division must earn the same return rate regardless of the assets' riskiness.
- Established rate of return may be too high and could discourage incentive.
- To boost profits, needed expenditures may not be incurred (e.g., repairs, research). Here, look at the ratio over time of discretionary costs to sales.
- A division may not want to acquire fixed assets because it will lower its ROI.
- A labor-intensive division generally has a higher ROI than a capital-intensive one.
- ROI is a static indicator; it does not show future flows.
- A lack of goal congruence may exist between the company and a division For instance, if a company's ROI is 12%, a division's ROI is 18%, and a project's ROI is 16%, the division manager will not accept the project because it will lower his or her ROI, even though the project is best for the entire company.
- It ignores risk.
- ROI emphasizes short-run performance instead of long-term profitability. To protect the current ROI, a manager is motivated to reject other profitable investment opportunities.

- ROI may not be completely controllable by the division manager because of the existence of committed costs. The inability to control ROI may be a problem in distinguishing between the manager's performance and the performance of the division as an investment.
- If the projected ROI at the beginning of the year is set unrealistically high, it could result in discouragement of investment center incentive.

A manager should not be criticized for a disappointing ROI if he or she does not have significant influence over the factors making up the ROI.

EXAMPLE 6: You are concerned about your company's current return on investment. Your company's income statement for year 2X14 follows.

Sales (100,000 units @ $10)	$1,000,000
Cost of sales	300,000
Gross margin	$ 700,000
Selling and general expenses	200,000
Income before taxes	$ 500,000
Taxes (40%)	200,000
Net income	$ 300,000

On December 31, total assets available consist of current assets of $300,000 and fixed assets of $500,000.

You forecast that sales for 2X15 will be 120,000 units at $11 per unit. The cost per unit is estimated at $5. Fixed selling and general expenses are forecasted at $60,000, and variable selling and general expenses are anticipated to be $1.50 per unit. Depreciation for the year is expected to be $30,000.

Forecasted earnings for 2X15 are calculated as follows:

Sales (120,000 @ $11)		$1,320,000
Cost of sales (120,000 @ $5)		600,000
Gross margin		$ 720,000
Selling and general expenses:		
Fixed	$ 60,000	
Variable (120,000 @ $1.50)	180,000	
Total		240,000
Income before tax		480,000
Tax (40%)		192,000
Net income		$ 288,000

The investment expected at December 31, 2X15 is:
Ratio of current assets to sales in 2X14:

$300,000/$1,000,000	30%

Expected current assets at December 31, 2X15:

30% × $1,320,000		$396,000
Expected fixed assets at December 31, 2X15:		
Book value on January 1	$500,000	
Less: depreciation for 2X15	30,000	470,000
Total investment		$866,000

$$\text{ROI} = \frac{\$2,888,000}{\$866,000} = 33.3\%$$

Residual Income. The optimal measure of divisional performance is residual income (RI), which equals divisional net income less minimum return times average available total assets.

EXAMPLE 7: Divisional earnings are $250,000, average available total assets are $2,000,000, and the cost of capital is 9%.

Residual income equals

Divisional net income	$250,000
Less minimum return × Average available total assets	
9% × $2,000,000	$180,000
Residual income	$ 70,000

The minimum rate of return is based upon the company's overall cost of capital adjusted for divisional risk. The cost of capital should be periodically calculated and used because of shifts in the money rate over time.

Residual income may be projected by division, center, or specific program to ensure that the company's rate of return on alternative investments is met or improved upon by each segment of the business.

By looking at residual income, there is assurance that segments are not employing corporate credit for less return than could be obtained by owning marketable securities or through investment in a different business segment.

A target residual income may be formulated to act as the division manager's objective. The trend in residual income to total available assets should be examined in appraising divisional performance. (See Exhibit 23-4.)

A division manager's performance should be appraised on the basis of controllable residual income. A manager should not be penalized for uncontrollable matters. To evaluate a division, net residual income after taxes is used. This is a key figure, because it aids in the decision to make new investments or withdrawals of funds in that division.

Exhibit 23-4: Residual Income Statement for Divisional Evaluation Purposes

Sales	$1,200,000	
Transfers at market value to other divisions	400,000	
Total		$1,600,000
Less		
Variable cost of goods sold and transferred	$800,000	
Variable divisional expenses	200,000	
Total		1,000,000
Variable income		$ 600,000
Less		
Controllable divisional overhead	$200,000	
Depreciation on controllable plant and equipment	110,000	
Property taxes and insurance on controllable fixed assets	40,000	
Total		$ 350,000
Controllable operating income		$ 250,000
Add		
Nonoperating gains	$300,000	
Nonoperating losses	20,000	
Net nonoperating gains		280,000
Total		$ 530,000
Less interest on controllable investment		30,000
Controllable residual income		$ 500,000
Less		
Uncontrollable divisional overhead (e.g., central advertising)	$40,000	
Incremental central expenses chargeable to the division	10,000	
Interest on noncontrollable investment	50,000	
Total		100,000
Residual income before taxes		$ 400,000
Less income taxes (40%)		160,000
Net residual income after taxes		$ 240,000

Advantages of Residual Income. These include:

- The same asset may be required to earn the same return rate throughout the company irrespective of the division the asset is in.

- Different return rates may be employed for different types of assets, depending on riskiness.

- Different return rates may be assigned to different divisions, depending on the risk associated with those divisions.

- Provides an economic income, taking into account the opportunity cost of tying up assets in the division.

- Identifies operating problem areas.

- Precludes the difficulty that a division with a high ROI would not engage in a project with a lower ROI even though it exceeds the overall corporate ROI rate. This is because residual income maximizes dollars instead of a percentage. It motivates divisional managers to take into account all profitable investments. Unprofitable investments are not included.

Disadvantages of Residual Income. These include:

- Assignment of a minimum return involves estimating a risk level that is subjective.

- It may be difficult to determine the valuation basis and means of allocating assets to divisions.

- If book value is used in valuing assets, residual income will artificially increase over time, since the minimum return times total assets becomes lower as the assets become older.

- It cannot be used to compare divisions of different sizes. Residual income tends to favor the larger divisions due to the large amount of dollars involved.

- It does not furnish a direct decision criterion for capital expenditures, which have to be based on incremental cash flows rather than incremental profits.

- As it is a mixture of controllable and uncontrollable elements, there is no segregation.

Computerized reports should be prepared at critical points for timely managerial action. Such instance may occur when a product's contribution margin percent is below target, or when a product is behind the scheduled days to produce it.

Reports showing excessive age of inventory should be prepared so needed action may be taken such as price reduction, package deals, or other promotions.

Accountants and financial managers aid management in making key decisions involving marketing and general business decisions. Examples are changes in sales mix, pricing, production, product expansion or contraction, territory evaluation, and customer analysis.

INVESTMENT DECISIONS UNDER ROI AND RI (EVA)

The decision whether to use return on investment or residual income as a measure of divisional performance affects financial managers' investment decisions. Under the ROI method, division managers tend to accept only the investments whose returns exceed the division's ROI; otherwise, the division's overall ROI would decrease. Under the RI method, on the other hand, division managers would accept an investment as long as it earned a rate in excess of the minimum required rate of return. The addition of such an investment would increase the division's overall RI.

EXAMPLE 8:

Divisional assets	$100,000
Divisional income	$18,000
Minimum required rate of return	13%
ROI = 18% and RI = $5,000	

A division is presented with a project that would yield 15% on a $10,000 investment. The division manager would not accept this project under the ROI approach, because the division is already earning 18%. Acquiring this project will bring down the present ROI to 17.73%, as shown below:

	Present	**New Project**	**Overall**
Divisional assets (a)	$100,000	$10,000	$110,000
Divisional income (b)	18,000	1,500*	19,500
ROI (b / a) 18%	15%	17.73%	

* $10,000 × 15% = $1,500

Under the RI approach, the manager would accept the new project because it provides a higher rate than the minimum required rate of return (15% versus 13%). Accepting the new project will increase the overall residual income to $5,200, as shown:

	Present	**New Project**	**Overall**
Divisional assets (a)	$100,000	$10,000	$110,000
Divisional income (b)	18,000	1,500	19,500
Minimum required income at 13%(c)	13,000	1,300*	14,300
RI (b–c)	$5,000	$200	$5,200

* $10,000 × 13% = $1,300

Special Note: Residual income is better known as economic value added (EVA). EVA is a registered trademark of Stern Stewart & Co. (www.sternstewart.com), which developed the concept.

Many firms are addressing the issue of aligning division managers' incentives with those of the firm by using EVA as a measure of performance. EVA encourages managers to focus on increasing the value of the company to shareholders, because EVA is the value created by a company in excess of the cost of capital for the investment base. A manager can improve the EVA of an investment center by increasing sales, decreasing costs, reducing assets, or lowering the cost of capital. This can be achieved in a variety of ways, including:

- Invest capital in high-performing projects.
- Use less capital.
- Increase profit without using more capital.

CONCLUSION

It is essential to evaluate a segment's performance to identify problem areas. Factors that are controllable or not controllable by the division manager must be considered. The various means of evaluating performance include cost center, profit center, revenue center, and investment center. The calculations for each method, along with proper analysis, are vital in appraising operating efficiency. The advantages and disadvantages of each method as well as when each is most appropriate should be understood.

The financial manager should be familiar with the profit and loss statements by territory, commodity, sale method, customer, and salesperson. The profit and loss figures will indicate areas of strength and weakness.

The establishment of a realistic transfer price is essential in order to evaluate divisional performance properly and to arrive at appropriate product costing and profitability.

CHAPTER 24

HOW TO ANALYZE AND IMPROVE MANAGEMENT PERFORMANCE AND THE BALANCED SCORECARD

CONTENTS

Exhibits

The ability to measure performance is essential in developing incentives and controlling operations toward the achievement of organizational goals. Perhaps the most widely used single measure of success of an organization and its subunits is the rate of return on investment (ROI). Related is the return to stockholders, known as the return on equity (ROE). This chapter discusses ROI, its components, how to increase it, and its relationship with ROE. Also presented is an alternative measure of stockholder wealth creation know as economic value added (EVA).

RETURN ON INVESTMENT

ROI relates net income to invested capital (total assets). It provides a standard for evaluating how efficiently management employs the average dollar invested in a firm's assets, whether that dollar came from owners or creditors. Furthermore, a better ROI can also translate directly into a higher return on the stockholders' equity.

ROI is calculated as:

$$\text{ROI} = \frac{\text{Net profit after taxes}}{\text{Total assets}}$$

EXAMPLE 1: Consider the following financial data:

Total Asset	$100,000
Net profit after taxes	18,000

$$\text{Then, ROI} = \frac{\text{Net profit after taxes}}{\text{Total assets}} = \frac{\$18,000}{\$100,000} = 18\%$$

The problem with this formula is that it reveals only how a company did and how well it fared in the industry. Other than that, it has very little value from the standpoint of profit planning.

COMPONENTS OF ROI—THE DUPONT FORMULA

In the past, managers tended to focus only on the margin earned and ignored the turnover of assets. Excessive funds tied up in assets can be just as much of a drag on profitability as excessive expenses. The DuPont Corporation was the first major company to recognize the importance of looking at both net profit margin and total asset turnover in assessing the performance of an organization. The ROI break-down, known as the DuPont formula, is expressed as a product of these two factors, as shown below.

$$\text{Then, ROI} = \frac{\text{Net profit after taxes}}{\text{Total assets}} = \frac{\text{Net profit after taxes}}{\text{Sales}} \times \frac{\text{Sales}}{\text{Total assets}}$$

$$= \text{Net profit margin} \times \text{Total assets turnover}$$

The DuPont formula combines the income statement and balance sheet into this otherwise static measure of performance. Net profit margin is a measure of profitability or operating efficiency. It is the percentage of profit earned on sales. This percentage shows how many cents attach to each dollar of sales. On the other hand, total asset turnover measures how well a company manages its assets. It is the number of times by which the investment in assets turns over each year to generate sales.

The breakdown of ROI is based on the thesis that the profitability of a firm is directly related to management's ability to manage assets efficiently and to control expenses effectively.

EXAMPLE 2: Assume the same data as in Example 1. Also assume sales of $200,000.

$$\text{Then, ROI} = \frac{\text{Net profit after taxes}}{\text{Total assets}} = \frac{\$18,000}{\$100,000} = 18\%$$

Alternatively,

$$\text{Net profit margin} = \frac{\text{Net profit after taxes}}{\text{Sales}} = \frac{\$18,000}{\$200,000} = 9\%$$

$$\text{Total asset turnover} = \frac{\text{Sales}}{\text{Total assets}} = \frac{\$200,000}{\$100,000} = 2 \text{ times}$$

Therefore,

$$\text{ROI} = \text{Net profit margin} \times \text{total asset turnover} = 9\% \times 2 \text{ times}$$

The breakdown provides a lot of insights to financial managers on how to improve profitability of the company and investment strategy. (Note that net profit margin and total asset turnover are called hereafter margin and turnover, respectively.) Specifically, this breakdown has several advantages over the original formula (i.e., net profit after taxes/total assets) for profit planning. They are:

- Focusing on the breakdown of ROI provides the basis for integrating many of the management concerns that influence a firm's overall performance. This will help managers gain an advantage in the competitive environment.

- The importance of turnover as a key to overall return on investment is emphasized in the breakdown. In fact, turnover is just as important as profit margin in enhancing overall return.

- The importance of sales is explicitly recognized, which does not occur in the original formula.

- The breakdown stresses the possibility of trading off one for the other in an attempt to improve the overall performance of a company. The margin and turnover complement each other. In other words, a low turnover can be made up for by a high margin and vice versa.

EXAMPLE 3: The breakdown of ROI into its two components shows that a number of combinations of margin and turnover can yield the same rate of return, as shown below:

	Margin	×	Turnover	=	ROI
(1)	9%	×	2 times	=	18%
(2)	6	×	3	=	18
(3)	3	×	6	=	18
(4)	2	×	9	=	18

The turnover-margin relationship and its resulting ROI is depicted in Exhibit 24-1.

ROI AND PROFIT OBJECTIVE

Exhibit 24-1 can also be looked at as showing six companies that performed equally well (in terms of ROI), but with varying income statements and balance sheets. There is no ROI that is satisfactory for all companies. Manufacturing firms in various industries will have low rates of return. Structure and size of the firm influence the rate considerably. A company with a diversified product line might have only a fair return rate when all products are pooled in the analysis. In such cases, it seems advisable to establish separate objectives for each line as well as for the total company.

Sound and successful operation must point toward the optimum combination of profits, sales, and capital employed. The combination will necessarily vary depending upon the nature of the business and the characteristics of the product. An industry with products tailor made to customers' specifications will have different margins and turnover ratios, compared with industries that mass produce highly competitive consumer goods. For example, in Exhibit 24-1, the combination (4) may describe a supermarket operation, which inherently works with low margin and high turnover, while the combination (1) may be a jewelry store, which typically has a low turnover and high margin.

Exhibit 24-1: The Margin-Turnover Relationship

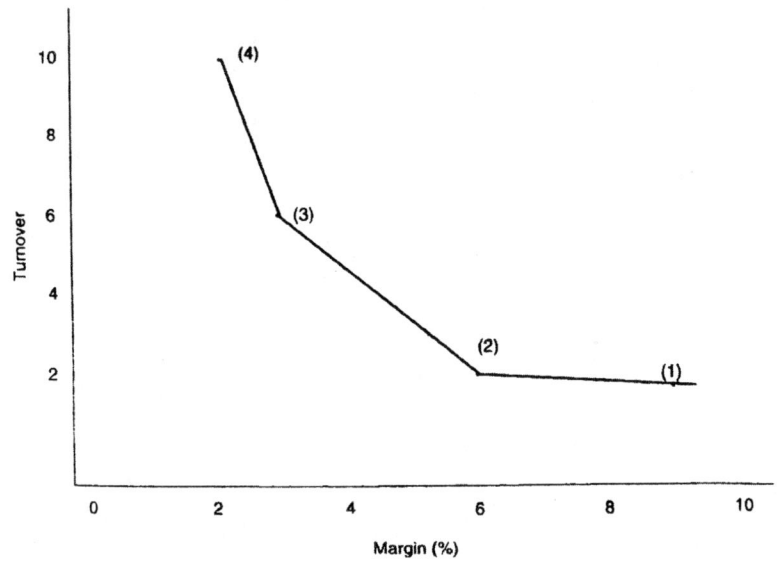

ROI AND PROFIT PLANNING

The breakdown of ROI into margin and turnover gives management insight into planning for profit improvement by revealing where weaknesses exist: margin or turnover or both. Various actions can be taken to enhance ROI. Generally, management can:

1. Improve margin.

2. Improve turnover.

3. Improve both margin and turnover.

Alternative 1 demonstrates a popular way of improving performance. Margins may be increased by reducing expenses, raising selling prices, or increasing sales faster than expenses. Some of the ways to reduce expenses are:

- Use less costly inputs of materials.

- Automate processes as much as possible to increase labor productivity.

- Bring the discretionary fixed costs under scrutiny, with various programs either curtailed or eliminated. Discretionary fixed costs arise from annual budgeting decisions by management. Examples include advertising, research and development, and management development programs. The cost-benefit analysis is called for in order to justify the budgeted amount of each discretionary program.

A company with pricing power can raise selling prices and retain profitability without losing business. Pricing power is the ability to raise prices even in poor economic times when unit sales volume may be flat and capacity may not be fully utilized. It is also the ability to pass on cost increases to consumers without attracting domestic and import competition, political opposition, regulation, new entrants, or threats of product substitution. The company with pricing power must have a unique economic position; companies that offer unique, high-quality goods and services (where the service is more important than the cost) have this economic position.

Alternative 2 may be achieved by increasing sales while holding the investment in assets relatively constant, or by reducing assets. Some of the strategies to reduce assets are:

- Use surplus cash to pare off debts, buy back own stocks, and/or pay cash dividends.

- Dispose of obsolete and redundant inventory. Enterprise Resource Planning (ERP) software can be extremely helpful in this regard, making perpetual inventory methods more feasible for inventory control and managing resource planning and supply-chain systems.

- Devise various methods of speeding up the collection of receivables and evaluate credit terms and policies.

- Determine if there are unused fixed assets.

- Use the converted assets obtained from the use of the previous methods to repay outstanding debts or repurchase outstanding issues of stock. They may be released elsewhere to get more profit, which will improve margin as well as turnover.

Alternative 3 may be achieved by increasing sales or by any combinations of alternatives 1 and 2.

Exhibit 24-2 shows complete details of the relationship of ROI to the underlying ratios—margin and turnover—and their components. This will help identify more detailed strategies to improve margin, turnover, or both.

Exhibit 24-2: Relationships of Factors Influencing ROI

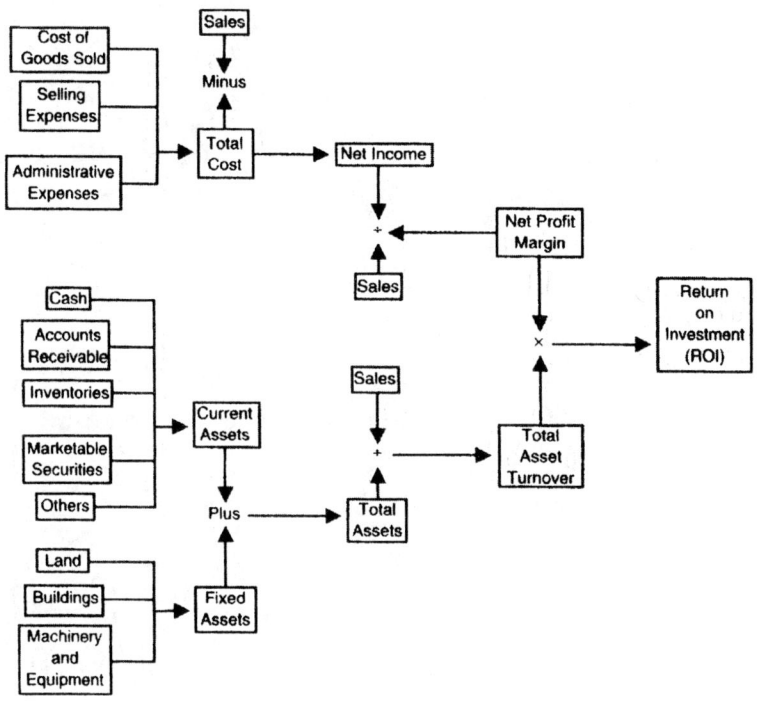

EXAMPLE 4: Assume that management sets a 20% ROI as a profit target. It is currently making an 18% return on its investment.

$$Ro = \frac{\text{Net profit after taxes}}{\text{Total assets}} = \frac{\text{Net profit after taxes}}{\text{Sales}} \times \frac{\text{Sales}}{\text{Total assets}}$$

Present situation:

$$18\% = \frac{18,000}{200,000} \times \frac{200,000}{100,000}$$

The following are illustrative of the strategies that might be used (each strategy is independent of the other).

Alternative 1: Increase the margin while holding turnover constant. Pursuing this strategy would involve leaving selling prices as they are and making every effort to increase efficiency so as to reduce expenses. By doing so, expenses might be reduced by $2,000 without affecting sales and investment to yield a 20% target ROI, as follows:

$$20\% = \frac{20,000}{200,000} \times \frac{200,000}{100,000}$$

Alternative 2: Increase turnover by reducing investment in assets while holding net profit and sales constant. Working capital might be reduced or some land might be sold, reducing investment in assets by $10,000 without affecting sales and net income to yield the 20% target ROI as follows:

$$20\% = \frac{18,000}{200,000} \times \frac{200,000}{90,000}$$

Alternative 3: Increase both margin and turnover by disposing of obsolete and redundant inventories or through an active advertising campaign. For example, trimming down $5,000 worth of investment in inventories would also reduce the inventory holding charge by $1,000. This strategy would increase ROI to 20%.

$$20\% = \frac{19,000}{200,000} \times \frac{200,000}{95,000}$$

Excessive investment in assets is just as much of a drag on profitability as excessive expenses. In this case, cutting unnecessary inventories also helps cut down expenses of carrying those inventories, so that both margin and turnover are improved at the same time. In practice, alternative 3 is much more common than alternative 1 or 2.

ROI AND RETURN ON EQUITY

Generally, better management performance (i.e., a high or above-average ROI) produces a higher return to equity holders. However, even a poorly managed company that suffers from a below average performance can generate an above-average return on the stockholders' equity, simply called the return on equity (ROE). This is because borrowed funds can magnify the returns a company's profits represent to its stockholders.

Another version of the DuPont formula, called the modified DuPont formula, reflects this effect. The formula ties together the ROI and the degree of financial leverage (use of borrowed funds). The financial leverage is measured by the equity multiplier, which is the ratio of a company's total asset base to its equity investment, or, stated another way, the ratio of how many dollars of assets held per dollar of stockholders' equity. It is calculated by dividing total assets by stockholders' equity. This measurement gives an indication of how much of a company's assets are financed by stockholders' equity and how much with borrowed funds.

The return on equity (ROE) is calculated as:

$$\text{ROE} = \frac{\text{Net profit after taxes}}{\text{Stockholders' equity}} = \frac{\text{Net profit after taxes}}{\text{Total assets}} \times \frac{\text{Total assets}}{\text{Stockholders' equity}}$$

ROE measures the returns earned on the owners' (both preferred and common stockholders') investment. The use of the equity multiplier to convert the ROI to the ROE reflects the impact of the leverage (use of debt) on stockholders' return.

$$\text{The equity multiplier} = \frac{\text{Total assets}}{\text{Stockholders' equity}}$$

$$= \frac{1}{(1\text{-debt ratio})}$$

Exhibit 24-3 shows the relationship among ROI, ROE, and financial leverage.

Exhibit 24-3: ROI, ROE, and Financial Leverage

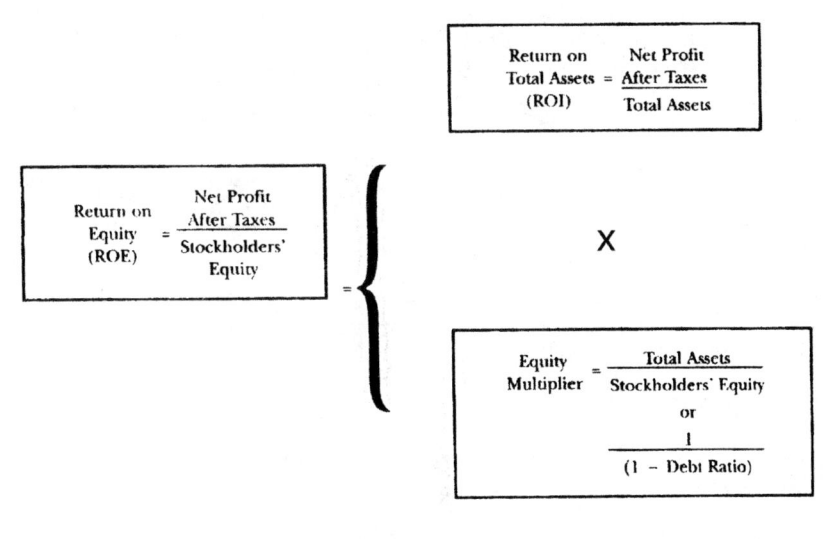

EXAMPLE 5: In Example 1, assume stockholders' equity of $45,000.

$$\text{Then, equity multiplier} = \frac{\text{Total assets}}{\text{Stockholders' equity}} = \frac{\$100,000}{45,000} = 2.22$$

$$= \frac{1}{(1 - \text{debt ratio})} = \frac{1}{(1 - .55)} = \frac{1}{.45} = 2.22$$

$$\text{ROE} = \frac{\text{Net profit after taxes}}{\text{Stockholders' equity}} = \frac{\$18,000}{\$45,000} = 40\%$$

$$\text{ROE} = \text{ROI} \times \text{Equity multiplier} = 18\% \times 2.22 = 40\%$$

If the company used only equity, the 18% ROI would equal ROE. However, 55% of the firm's capital is supplied by creditors ($45,000/$100,000 = 45% is the equity-to-asset ratio; $55,000/$100,000 = 55% is the debt ratio). Since the 18% ROI all goes to stockholders, who put up only 45% of the capital, the ROE is higher than 18%. This example indicates the company was using leverage (debt) favorably.

EXAMPLE 6: To further demonstrate the interrelationship between a firm's financial structure and the return it generates on the stockholders' investments, it is useful to compare two firms that generate, say, $300,000 in operating income. Both firms employ $800,000 in total assets, but have different capital structures. One firm employs no debt, whereas the other uses $400,000 in borrowed funds. The comparative capital structures are shown as:

	A	B
Total assets	$800,000	$800,000
Total liabilities	–	400,000
Stockholders' equity (a)	800,000	400,000
Total liabilities and stockholders' equity	$800,000	$800,000

Firm B pays 10% interest for borrowed funds. The comparative income statements and ROEs for firms A and B would look as follows:

	A	B
Operating income	$300,000	$300,000
Interest expense	–	(40,000)
Profit before taxes	$300,000	$260,000
Taxes (30% assumed)	(90,000)	(78,000)
Net profit after taxes (b)	$210,000	$182,000
ROE [(b)/(a)]	26.25%	45.5%

The absence of debt allows firm A to register higher profits after taxes. Yet the owners in firm B enjoy a significantly higher return on their investments. This provides an important view of the positive contribution debt can make to a business, but within a certain limit. Too much debt can increase the firm's financial risk and thus the cost of financing.

If the assets in which the funds are invested are able to earn a return greater than the fixed rate of return required by the creditors, the leverage is positive and the common stockholders benefit. The advantage of this formula is that it enables the company to break its ROE into a profit margin portion (net profit margin), an efficiency-of-asset-utilization portion (total asset turnover), and a use-of-leverage portion (equity multiplier). It shows that the company can raise shareholder return by employing leverage-taking on larger amounts of debt to help finance growth.

Since financial leverage affects net profit margin through the added interest costs, management must look at the various pieces of this ROE equation, within the context of the whole, to earn the highest return for stockholders. Financial managers have the task of determining just what combination of asset return and leverage will work best in its competitive environment. Most companies try to keep at least a level equal to what is considered to be normal within the industry.

ECONOMIC VALUE ADDED

EVA is a concept similar to residual income, but often applied at the overall firm level as well as at the departmental level. It is a registered trademark of Stern Stewart & Co. (www.sternstewart.com), which developed the concept.

EVA is a measure of economic profit, but not the accounting profit typically seen in a corporate profit and loss statement. It is a measure of an operation's true profitability. The cost of debt capital (interest expense) is deducted when calculating net income, but no cost is deducted to account for the cost of common equity. Hence, in an economic sense, net income overstates "true" income. EVA overcomes this flaw in conventional accounting.

EVA is found by taking the net operating profit after taxes (NOPAT) for a particular period (such as a year) and subtracting the annual cost of *all* the capital a firm uses. EVA recognizes all capital costs, including the opportunity cost of the shareholder funds. It is a business's true economic profit. Such economic profits are the basis of shareholder value creation. **Note:** The calculation of EVA can be complex because it makes various cost of capital and accounting principles adjustments.

The formula is:

$$
\begin{aligned}
\text{EVA} \; &= \; \text{NOPAT} - \text{After-tax cost of total capital} \\
&= \; \text{Earnings before interest and taxes (EBIT) } (1 - \text{tax rate}) \\
&\quad - \; (\text{Total capital}) (\text{After-tax cost of capital})
\end{aligned}
$$

Total capital used here is total assets *minus* current liabilities. Hence, it is long-term liabilities *plus* equity (preferred stock and common equity). Thus, EVA is an estimate of a business's true economic profit for the year, and it differs sharply from accounting profit. EVA represents the residual income that remains after the cost of *all* capital, including equity capital, has been deducted. Accounting profit is determined without imposing a charge for equity capital. Equity capital has a cost, because funds provided by shareholders could have been invested elsewhere where they would have earned a return. In other words, shareholders give up the opportunity to invest funds elsewhere when they provide capital to the firm. The return they could earn elsewhere in investments of equal risk represents the cost of equity capital. This cost is an *opportunity cost* rather than an *accounting cost,* but it is quite real nevertheless.

The following example illustrates how an operation's economic profit differs from its accounting profit.

EXAMPLE 7: A company with $100,000 in equity capital (stated at fair value) and $100,000 in 8% debt (also at fair value) had $60,000 in earnings before interest and taxes (EBIT). Assume also that $200,000 equals capital employed. The corporate tax rate is 40%. If that company's weighted-average after-tax cost of capital is 14%, the EVA is $2,000, calculated as follows:

EBIT	$60,000
Minus taxes (40% × $60,000)	(24,000)
NOPAT	$36,000
Capital charge (14% × $200,000)	(28,000)
EVA	$8,000

The company's traditional income statement reports income of $31,200, calculated as follows:

EBIT	$60,000
Minus interest (8% × $100,000)	(8,000)
Income before taxes	52,000
Income taxes (40% × $52,000)	(20,800)
Net income after taxes	$31,000

Initially, a 31.2% return on equity ($31,200 of net income/$100,000 of equity capital) seems favorable, but what is the cost of that equity capital? Given equal amounts of debt and equity, the cost of the equity capital must be 23.2%, because the after-tax weighted-average cost of capital was 14%, and the after-tax cost of debt capital was 4.8% = 8% (1.0 – 40%). Note: Because 14% = (4.8%) (1/2½) + X(1/2½), X = 23.2%.

Thus, $23,200 of the $31,200 of net income is nothing more than the opportunity cost of equity capital. The $8,000 of EVA is the only portion of earnings that has created value for the shareholders. Accordingly, if income after taxes had been only $20,000 (a 20% return on equity), shareholder value would have been reduced because the cost of equity capital would have exceeded the return.

EVA and Value Creation

In Example 7, the $2,000 of EVA is the only portion of earnings that has created value for the shareholders. EVA provides a good measure of whether the firm has added to shareholder value. Therefore, if managers focus on EVA, this will help to ensure that they operate in a manner that is consistent with maximizing shareholder value. EVA can also be determined for divisions—it is more often called *residual income*—as well as for the company as a whole, so it provides a useful basis for determining managerial compensation at all levels.

Although most companies adopt EVA for purposes of internal reporting and for calculating bonuses, some are publishing the results in the corporate annual reports. For example, Eli Lilly reports EVA in the Financial Highlights section of its annual report. In its 2010 annual report, SPX made it clear that "EVA is the foundation of everything we do. . . . It is a common language, a mindset, and the way we do business."

More on NOPAT

Before computing NOPAT, analysts routinely adjust the company's reported earnings figures. These adjustments fall into three broad categories:

1. Isolate a company's sustainable operating profits by removing nonoperating or nonrecurring items from reported income.

2. Eliminate after-tax interest expense from the profit calculation so that profitability comparisons over time or across companies are not clouted by differences in financial structure.

3. Adjust for distortions related to as accounting quality concerns, which involve potential adjustments to both income and assets for items such as the off-balance-sheet operating leases.

NOPAT is used to improve the comparability of EVA calculations. Otherwise, firms with different debt structures could have the same operating performance but different net incomes.

$$\text{NOPAT} = \text{Net income after taxes} + \text{charges and gains} \times (1 - \text{tax rate})$$
$$+ \text{Interest} \times (1 - \text{tax rate})$$

The following example illustrates the NOPAT computation.

EXAMPLE 8: Given the following income statement for years 2X14 and 2X15:

Comparative Income Statement

	2X15	2X14
Sales	$5,199.0	$5,954.0
Cost of sales		(2,807.5)
(3,294.4)		
Gross margin	2,391.5	2,659.6
Selling, general and administrative expenses	(1,981.0)	(2,358.8)
Restructuring charges and gains	113.4	1,053.5

Comparative Income Statement

	2X15	2X14
Interest expense	(106.8)	(131.6)
Other revenue and expenses	(1.5)	(2.2)
Before-tax income	415.6	1,220.5
Income taxes (40%)	(166.2)	(488.2)
Net income	$249.4	$732.3

NOPAT Calculations

	2X15	2X14
Net income as reported	$249.4	$732.3
Restructuring charges and gains after tax	−68.04	−632.1
Interest expense after tax	64.08	79.0
Net operating profit after taxes (NOPAT)	$245.4	$179.2

For example, for year 2X15,

$$\text{NOPAT} = \text{Net income after taxes} + \text{Charges and gains} \times (1 - \text{tax rate})$$
$$+ \text{Interest} \times (1 - \text{tax rate})$$
$$= \$249.4 - \$113.4(1 - .4) + \$106.8(1 - .4)$$
$$= \$249.4 - \$68.04 + \$64.08 = \$245.4$$

Capital Charge

The capital charge is the most distinctive and important aspect of EVA. Under conventional accounting, most companies appear profitable but many in fact are not. The capital charge equals the after-tax weighted-average cost of capital (calculated based on fair values of debt and equity) times the investment base or total capital employed (total assets minus current liabilities or the sum of long-term debt, preferred stock, and common equity).

Key Features of EVA

The four main characteristics of EVA are:

1. For internal purposes, EVA is a better measure of profitability than ROI because a manager with a high ROI would be reluctant to invest in a new project with a lower ROI than is currently being earned, even though that return might be higher than the cost of capital. Thus, including a capital charge on departmental income statements helps managers to make decisions that will benefit the company.

2. There is an evidence of a direct correlation between EVA and increases in stock prices. For example, AT&T found an almost perfect correlation between its EVA and its stock price. In fact, many analysts have found that stock prices track EVA far more closely than other factors such as earn-

ings per share (EPS), operating margin, or ROE. The argument is that simply having a continuing stream of income is not enough—that income must exceed the cost of capital for a stock to rise significantly in the stock market.

3. EVA uses dollars instead of percentages to measure changes. For example, it is much more appealing to report that the company generated $1 million in shareholder value than to say that the ROI increased from 10% to 15%.

4. EVA is the only financial management system that provides a common language for employees across all operating and staff functions and allows all management decisions to be modeled, monitored, communicated, and compensated in a single and consistent way—always in terms of the value added to shareholder investment.

What Value-Driven Managers Can Do to Improve EVA

As a simplified form,

EVA = NOPAT – (After tax weighted-average cost of capital) (Net assets)

Another way to look at is:

$$EVA = \frac{NOPAT}{(Net\ assets)} \ (Net\ assets) - (After\ tax\ weighted\text{-}average\ cost\ of\ capital)$$

(net assets)

$$EVA = \left[\frac{NOPAT}{(Net\ assets)} - (After\ tax\ weighted\text{-}average\ cost\ of\ capital) \right] (Net\ assets)$$

= (Return of net assets – After tax weighted-average cost of capital) (Net assets)

= (RONA – WACC) (Net assets)

Assuming other variables stay constant, EVA increases when RONA increase, or WACC decreases, or net assets increase (assuming profitable growth) or decrease (in the case of money-losing assets).

Evidence from EVA adopters shows several ways to achieve improvements:

- Increase asset turnover.
- Dispose of unprofitable businesses.
- Refurbish assets.
- Structure deals that require less capital.
- Increase leverage and use less equity finance.
- Invest in profitable growth.

The preceding actions (increasing asset turnover, repairing assets, and structuring deals with less capital) increase EVA through improvement in RONA. Disposing of unprofitable businesses increases EVA, providing improvements in the spread between RONA and WACC are greater than the reduction in net assets. Increasing leverage increases EVA by reducing WACC, assuming that the company is underlevered when it begins taking on more debt. Investing is profitable, and increases EVA, as long as the RONA on the investment exceeds the WACC.

EVA Compensation

EVA bonus plans do not motivate managers to think only about current EVA. If they did, managers would focus entirely on short-term performance at the expense of the future. Value-creating investments might be avoided because their immediate effects on EVA are negative. The solution is to give managers a direct economic state in future EVA, not just the current period. The performance evaluation will be more meaningful if the current EVA is compared to EVAs from other periods, target EVAs, and EVAs from other operating units or companies.

A Caveat

EVA is neither a panacea nor a substitute for sound corporate strategies. However, linked to EVA is at the center of a company's performance measurement system and linked to management bonus systems, and when bonus systems are linked, alignment between the interests of managers and shareholders improves. The effect is that, when managers make important decisions, they are more likely to do so in ways that deliver superior returns for shareholders.

Corporate Balanced Scorecard

A problem with just assessing performance with financial measures like profit, ROI and EVA is that the financial measures are "backward looking." In other words, today's financial measures tell about the accomplishments and failures of the past. An approach to performance measurement that also focuses on what managers are doing today to create future shareholder value is the corporate balanced scorecard.

Essentially, a balanced scorecard is a set of performance measures constructed for four dimensions of performance: financial, customer, internal processes, and learning and growth. Financial measures, even if backward looking, greatly affect the evaluation of the company by shareholders and creditors. Customer measures examine the company's success in meeting customer expectations; internal process measures examine the company's success in improving critical business processes; and learning and growth measures examine the company's success in improving its ability to adapt, innovate, and grow. The customer, internal processes, and learning and growth measures are generally thought to be predictive of *future* success (i.e., they are not backward looking).

A variety of potential measures for each dimension of a balanced scorecard are indicated in Exhibit 24-4. Balance is achieved in several ways:

- Performance is assessed across a *balanced set of dimensions* (i.e., financial, customer, internal processes, and innovation).

- *Quantitative* measures (e.g., number of defects) are balanced with *qualitative* measures (e.g., ratings of customer satisfaction).

- *Backward-looking* measures (e.g., financial measures like growth in sales) are balanced with *forward-looking* measures (e.g., number of new patents as an innovation measure).

Note: The balanced scorecard measures vary with a company's strategy and industry. Exhibit 24-5 lists examples of performance indicators for each balanced scorecard dimension across a wide rage of industries.

Exhibit 24-4: The Corporate Balanced Scorecard

Dimension	Description	Measures
Financial	Is the company achieving its financial goals?	Operating income Return on assets Return on equity Profit margin Cost variances Sales growth Cash flow from operations Reduction of administrative expense
Customer	Is the company meeting customer expectations?	Customer satisfaction scores Customer retention rates New customer acquisition Market share On-time delivery Time to fill orders
Internal Business Processes	Is the company improving critical internal processes?	Defect rate Lead time Number of suppliers Material turnover Percent of practical capacity Percentage of jobs completed on time Number of new contacts from advertising Fuel usage efficiency Number of "re-servicings"
Learning and Growth	Is the company improving its ability to innovate?	Amount spent on employee training Employee satisfaction Employee retention or turnover Hours of training Number of new products New product sales as a percent of total sales Number of patents

Exhibit 24-5: Balanced Scorecard Measures by Industry

Industry	Financial Dimension	Customer Dimension	Internal Business Process Dimension	Learning and Growth Dimension
Airlines	Return on assets	Frequent flier program participation rates	Percentage of on-time takeoffs and arrivals	Labor contract length
Consumer retail banks	Ratio of assets to debt	Number of new accounts opened	Number of new branches	Hours of employee training completed
Accounting, consulting, and law firms	Profit margin	Client retention rate	Percentage of projects completed on time	Certification and education levels of professionals
Computer manufacturers	Sales growth from new products	Number of corporate customers	Number of product defects	Percentage of factory employees who completed quality control training
Supermarkets	Inventory turnover	Customer satisfaction	Product spoilage rates	Employee turnover rates

The following list provides valuable resources for evaluating performance and business decision making across a wide range of industries:

- *The Balanced Scorecard Institute (balancedscorecard.org)*. This independent educational institute provides training and guidance to assist government agencies and companies in applying best practices in balanced scorecard and performance measurement for strategic management and transformation. Its Web site provides background information about implementing the balanced scorecard and the proper selection of nonfinancial measures, along with several examples of past successes.

- *American Productivity and Quality Center (apqc.org)*. An internationally recognized nonprofit organization with more than 450 prestigious global firms (e.g., 3M, AT&T, Cisco Systems, and Ernst & Young), APQC provides expertise in benchmarking and best practices research. It helps organizations adapt to rapidly changing environments, build new and better ways to work, and succeed in a competitive marketplace. The objective of this collaborative center is to "Understand how innovative organizations create succession management programs to identify and cultivate potential leaders who will provide a sustainable business advantage." The Best Practices and Free Resources links lead to many useful resources.

- *Free Management Library (managementhelp.org).* This Web site offers a robust "library" of decision-making tools and library resources. The site offers many resources on such topics as strategic planning, performance measurement, employee development, and make-or-outsource decisions. It also includes online discussion groups, decision-making guidance, and free reference material.

- *Performance Measurement Association (performanceportal.org).* This Web site, a home to the United Kingdom's Performance Measurement Association, covers references to valuable articles, a free newsletter, and insight into current trends in performance measurement. It offers a forum for exchanging ideas and developing personal and managerial skills.

Exhibits 24-6 through 24-9 present balanced scorecards for selected organizations.

Exhibit 24-6: Balanced Scorecard for a Biotechnology Firm

Strategic Objectives	Performance Measures
Financial Perspective:	
Growth	Percent increase in revenue of top line
Profitability	products
Industry leadership	Return on equity; earnings per share
	Market share
Customer Perspective	
Outcome:	
New products	Percent of sales from new products
Early purchase of seasonal	Percent of sales recorded by early
products	purchase date
Leading:	
Early payment	Percent of customers who pay early
Product quality	Product performance vs. industry quality
Customer satisfaction	standards
	Customer satisfaction surveys
Internal Processes Perspective	
Service-after-Sale:	
Accurate invoices	Percent of error-free invoices
Operations:	
Low-cost producer	Unit cost vs. competitors
Reduce inventory	Inventory as percent of sales

Strategic Objectives	Performance Measures
Innovation:	
New products	Number of actual introduction vs. target
New active ingredients	Number of new ingredients identified by
Proprietary positions	research program
	Number of patents that create exclusive
	marketing rights
Learning and Growth Perspective Outcome:	
Employee retention	Average employee years with company
Employee satisfaction	Employee satisfaction surveys
Leading:	
Employee capabilities	Training costs invested per employee;
Organizational structure	percent of employees participating
capabilities	annually in training
	Average weekly hours in teamwork
	settings; survey of effective teamwork

Exhibit 24-7: Balanced Scorecard for a Consumer Products Firm (A Maker of Small Home Appliances)

Strategic Objectives	Performance Measures
Financial Perspective:	
Increase profitability	ROI
Increase new customers and	Percentage of revenue from new
markets	sources
Reduce unit cost	Unit cost
Customer Perspective:	
Increase customer acquisition	New customers
Increase customer satisfaction	Survey ratings
Increase market share	Market share
Increase product quality	Returns
Improve product image and	Survey ratings
reputation	
Internal Processes Perspective:	
Improve process quality	Quality costs
Increase quality of purchased	Percentage of defective units
components	Redesign time
	Percentage of defective units
	Engineering hours

Strategic Objectives	Performance Measures
Learning and Growth Perspective Outcome:	
Increase employee capabilities	Training hours
Increase motivation and alignment	Job coverage ratio
Increase information system capabilities	Suggestions implemented
	Suggestions per employee
	On-time report percentage

Exhibit 24-8: Balanced Scorecard for a Gasoline Firm

	Strategic Themes	Strategic Objectives	Performance Measures
FINANCIAL	*Financial Growth*	Return on capital employed (ROCE) Existing asset utilization Profitability Industry cost leader Profitable growth	ROCE Cash flow Net margin rank Full cost per gallon Volume growth rate Premium ratio Nongasoline revenue
CUSTOMER	*Delight the Consumer*	Continually delight the targeted consumer	Share of segment in selected key markets Mystery shopper rating
	Win-Win Dealer Relations	Build win-win relations with the dealer	Dealer gross profit growth Dealer survey
INTERNAL	*Build the Franchise*	Innovative products and services Best in class franchise teams	New product ROI New product acceptance rate Dealer quality
	Safe and Reliable	Refinery performance	Yield gap Unplanned downtime
	Competitive Supplier	Inventory management Cost leader	Inventory levels Run-out rate Activity cost vs. competition
	Quality	On spec, on time	Perfect orders Number of environmental incidents
	Good Neighbor	Improve EHS	Days away from work rate

	Strategic Themes	Strategic Objectives	Performance Measures
LEARNING/ GROWTH	*Motivated Workforce*	Climate for action Core competencies and skills Access to strategic information	Employee survey Personal balanced scorecard Strategic competency availability Strategic information availability

For a school district, the following objectives are created for each of the following five categories. **Note:** The balanced scorecard categories should be adjusted to suit the specific needs of the organization.

1. *Financial Performance Objective:*

   a. Sound fiscal management

2. *Customer Satisfaction Objectives:*

   a. Safe and enriching school environment

   b. Parent satisfaction

   c. Community involvement

3. *Instructional and Administrative Processes Objectives:*

   a. Effective instruction

   b. Safe and efficient transportation

   c. Well-maintained facilities

4. *Staff Learning and Growth Objectives:*

   a. Competent staff

   b. Staff satisfaction

5. *Student Achievement Objectives:*

   a. Student mastery of curriculum

   b. Nationally competitive students

There are many different measures that can be used. Exhibit 24-9 illustrates some possible measures.

Exhibit 24-9: Balanced Scorecard for a School District

Goal Area	Strategic Objectives	Performance Measures
Financial Performance	Sound fiscal management	Revenue variances of actual to budget Expense variances of actual to budget Fund balances
Customer Satisfaction	Safe and enriching school environment Parent satisfaction Community involvement	Absenteeism and tardy rates Participation in extracurricular activities Perception of safety (student surveys) Scores on parent surveys Number of parent complaints Total volunteer hours Dollars donated Number of business partners
Instructional and Administrative Processes	Effective instruction Safe and efficient transportation Well-maintained facilities	Percent of students in summer school Percent of teachers certified in special programs Percent of teachers using technology Accidents per million miles On-time bus delivery Accidents per student days Scores on inspection reports Level of backlogged maintenance reports
Staff Learning and Growth	Competent staff Staff satisfaction	Percentage of teachers with 7+ years of experience Percentage of teachers with advanced degrees Percentage of board-certified teachers Absenteeism rates Percentage of teachers retiring early Scores on teacher surveys
Student Achievement	Student mastery of curriculum Nationally competitive students	Proficiency tests in various subjects Retention rates Drop-out rates SAT scores AP exam scores Enrollment in college credit courses

CHAPTER 25

ACTIVITY-BASED COSTING AND JUST-IN-TIME MANUFACTURING

CONTENTS

Many companies are using a traditional cost system such as job order costing or process costing, or some hybrid of the two. This system would tend to provide distorted product cost information. In fact, companies selling multiple products are making critical decisions about product pricing, making bids, or product mix, based on these inaccurate cost data. In all likelihood the problem is not with assigning the costs of direct labor or direct materials. These prime costs are traceable to individual products, and most conventional cost systems are designed to ensure that this tracing takes place. The assignment of overhead costs to individual products, however, is another matter. Using the traditional methods of assigning overhead costs to products—using a single predetermined overhead rate based on any single activity measure—can produce distorted product costs.

OVERHEAD COSTING: A SINGLE-PRODUCT SITUATION

The accuracy of overhead cost assignment becomes an issue only when multiple products are manufactured in a single facility. If only a single product is produced, all overhead costs are caused by it and traceable to it. The overhead cost per unit is simply total overhead for the year divided by the number of units produced. Accuracy is not an issue. The timing of the computation may be an issue, however; because of this, a predetermined overhead rate is usually required. The cost calculation for a single product is illustrated in Exhibit 25-1.

There is no question that the cost of manufacturing the product illustrated in Exhibit 25-1 is $28.00 per unit. All manufacturing costs were incurred specifically to make this product. Thus, one way to ensure product costing accuracy is to focus on producing one product. For this reason, some multiple product firms choose to dedicate plants to the manufacture of a single product.

By focusing on only one or two products, small manufacturers were able to calculate the cost of manufacturing the high-volume products more accurately and price them more effectively.

OVERHEAD COSTING: A MULTIPLE-PRODUCT SITUATION

In a multiple-product situation, manufacturing overhead costs are caused jointly by all products. The problem now becomes one of trying to identify the amount of overhead caused or consumed by each. This is accomplished by searching for cost drivers, or activity measures that cause costs to be incurred.

In a traditional setting, it is normally assumed that overhead consumption is highly correlated with the volume of production activity, measured in terms of direct labor hours, machine hours, or direct labor dollars. These volume-related cost drivers are used to assign overhead to products. Volume-related cost drivers use either plant-wide or departmental rates.

Case 1

To illustrate the limitation of this traditional approach, assume that ABC has a plant that produces two products: Thingone and Thingtwo. Product costing data are given in Exhibit 25-2. Because the quantity of Thingtwo produced is five times greater than that of Thingone, Thingone can be labeled a low-volume product and Thingtwo a high-volume product.

Exhibit 25-1: Unit Cost Computation: Single Product

	Manufacturing Costs	Units Produced	Unit Cost
Direct materials	$ 800,000	50,000	$16.00
Direct labor	200,000	50,000	4.00
Factory overhead	400,000	50,000	8.00
Total	$1,400,000	50,000	$28.00

Exhibit 25-2: Product Costing Data

	Thingone	Thingtwo	Total
Units produced per year	10,000	50,000	60,000
Production runs	20	30	50
Inspection hours	800	1,200	2,000
Kilowatt hours	5,000	25,000	30,000
Primecosts (direct materials and direct labor)	$50,000	$250,000	$300,000

Departmental Data

	Department 1	Department 2	Total
Direct labor hours:			
Thingone	4,000	16,000	20,000
Thingtwo	76,000	24,000	100,000
Total	80,000	40,000	120,000
Machine hours:			
Thingone	4,000	6,000	10,000
Thingtwo	16,000	34,000	50,000
Total	20,000	40,000	60,000
Overhead costs:			
Setup costs	$48,000	$48,000	$96,000
Quality control	37,000	37,000	74,000
Power	14,000	70,000	84,000
Maintenance	13,000	65,000	78,000
Total	$112,000	$220,000	$332,000

For simplicity, only four types of factory overhead costs are assumed: (1) setup, (2) quality control, (3) power, and (4) maintenance. These overhead costs are allocated to the two production departments using the direct method.

Assume that the four service centers do not interact. Setup costs are allocated based on the number of production runs handled by each department. Since the number is identical, each department receives 50% of the total setup costs. Quality control costs are allocated by the number of inspection hours used by each department. Power costs are allocated in proportion to the kilowatt hours used. Maintenance costs are allocated in proportion to the machine hours used.

Plant-Wide Overhead Rate

A common method of assigning overhead to products is to compute a plantwide rate, using a volume-related cost driver. This approach assumes that all overhead cost variation can be explained by one cost driver. Assume that machine hours is chosen.

Dividing the total overhead by the total machine hours yields the following overhead rate:

$$\text{Plant-wide rate} \quad = \quad \$332,000/60,000$$
$$= \quad \$5.53/\text{machine hour}$$

Using this rate and other information from Exhibit 25-2, the unit cost for each product can be calculated, as given in Exhibit 25-3.

Departmental Rates

Based on the distribution of labor hours and machine hours in Exhibit 25-2, Department 1 is labor intensive and Department 2 machine oriented. Further more, the overhead costs of Department 1 are about half those of Department 2. Based on these observations, it is apparent that departmental overhead rates would reflect the consumption of overhead better than a plant-wide rate.

Product costs would be more accurate using departmental rates. This approach would yield the following departmental rates, using direct labor hours for Department 1 and machine hours for Department 2:

$$\text{Department 1 rate} \quad = \quad \$112,000/80,000$$
$$= \quad \$1.40/\text{labor hour}$$
$$\text{Department 2 rate} \quad = \quad \$200,000/40,000$$
$$= \quad 5.50/\text{machine hour}$$

Using these rates and the data from Exhibit 25-2, the computation of the unit costs for each product is shown in Exhibit 25-4.

Problems with Costing Accuracy

The accuracy of the overhead cost assignment can be challenged regardless of whether the plant-wide or departmental rates are used. The main problem with either procedure is the assumption that machine hours or direct labor hours drive or cause all overhead costs.

Exhibit 25-3: Unit Cost Computation: Plant-Wide Rate

	Thingone
Prime costs ($50,000/10,000)	$5.00
Overhead costs ($5.53 × 10,000/10,000)	5.53
Unit cost	$10.53

Thingtwo	
Prime costs ($250,000/50,000)	$5.00
Overhead costs ($5.53 × 50,000/50,000)	5.53
Unit cost	$10.53

Exhibit 25-4: Unit Cost Computation: Department Rates

Thingone	
Prime costs ($50,000/10,000)	$5.00
Overhead costs [($1.40 × 4,000) + ($5.50 × 6,000)]/10,000	3.86
Unit cost	$8.86

Thingtwo	
Prime costs ($250,000/50,000)	$5.00
Overhead costs [($1.40 × 76,000) + ($5.50 × 34,000)]/50,000	5.87
Unit cost	$10.87

From Exhibit 25-2, we know that Thingtwo—with five times the volume of Thingone—uses 5 times the machine hours and direct labor hours. Thus, if a plant-wide rate is used, Thingtwo will receive 5 times more overhead cost. But does it make sense? Is all overhead driven by volume? Use of a single driver—especially volume-related—is not proper.

Examination of the data in Exhibit 25-2 suggests that a significant portion of overhead costs is not driven or caused by volume. For example, setup costs are probably related to the number of setups and quality control costs to the number of hours of inspection. Notice that Thingtwo has only 1.5 times as many setups as the Thingone (30/20) and only 1.5 times as many inspection hours (1,200/800). Use of a volume-related cost driver (machine hours or labor hours) and a plantwide rate assigns 5 times more overhead to the Thingtwo than to Thingone. For quality control and setup costs, then, Thingtwo is overcosted, and Thingone is undercosted.

The problems only worsened when departmental rates were used. Thingtwo consumes 19 times as many direct labor hours (76,000/4,000) as Thingone and 5.7 times as many machine hours (34,000/6,000). Thus, Thingtwo receives 19 times more overhead from Department 1 and 5.7 times more overhead from Department 2. As Exhibit 25-4 shows, with departmental rates, the unit cost of Thingone decreases to $8.86, and the unit cost of Thingtwo increases to $10.87. This change is in the wrong direction, which emphasizes the failure of volume-based cost drivers to accurately reflect each product's consumption of setup and quality control costs.

Why Volume-Related Cost Drivers Fail

At least two major factors impair the ability of a volume-related cost driver to assign overhead costs accurately: (1) the proportion of non-volume-related overhead costs to total overhead costs and (2) the degree of product diversity.

Non-Volume-Related Overhead Costs. In our example, there are four overhead activities: quality control, setup, maintenance, and power.

Two activities—maintenance and power—are volume related. Quality control and setup are less dependent on volume. As a result, volume-based cost drivers cannot assign these costs accurately to products.

Using volume-based cost drivers to assign non-volume-related overhead costs creates distorted product costs. The severity of this distortion depends on what proportion of total overhead costs these non-volume-related costs represent. For our example, setup costs and quality control costs represent a substantial share—50%—of total overhead ($170,000/$332,000). This suggests that some care should be exercised in assigning these costs. If non-volume-related overhead costs are only a small percentage of total overhead costs, the distortion of product costs would be quite small. In such a case, the use of volume-based cost drivers may be acceptable.

Product Diversity. When products consume overhead activities in different proportions, a firm has product diversity.

To illustrate, the proportion of all overhead activities consumed by both Thingone and Thingtwo is computed and displayed in Exhibit 25-5. The proportion of each activity consumed by a product is defined as the consumption ratio. As can be seen from the table, the consumption ratios for these two products differ from the non-volume-related categories to the volume-related costs.

Since the non-volume-related overhead costs are a significant proportion of total overhead and their consumption ratio differs from that of the volume-based cost driver, product costs can be distorted if a volume-based cost driver is used. The solution to this costing problem is to use an activity-based costing approach.

Exhibit 25-5: Product Diversity: Proportion of Consumption

Overhead Activity	Thingone	Thingtwo	Consumption Measure
Setups	.40[1]	.60[1]	Production runs
Quality control	.40[2]	.60[2]	Inspection hours
Power	.17[3]	.83[3]	Kilowatt hours
Maintenance	.17[4]	.83[4]	Machine hours

[1] 20/50 (Thingone) and 30/50 (Thingtwo)
[2] 800/2,000 (Thingone) and 1,200/2,000 (Thingtwo)
[3] 5,000/30,000 (Thingone) and 25,000/30,000 (Thingtwo)
[4] 10,000/60,000 (Thingone) and 50,000/60,000 (Thingtwo)

ACTIVITY-BASED PRODUCT COSTING

An activity-based cost system is one that first traces costs to activities and then to products. Traditional product costing also involves two stages, but in the first stage costs are traced to departments, not to activities. In both traditional and activity-based costing, the second stage consists of tracing costs to the product. The principal difference between the two methods is the number of cost drivers used. Activity-based costing uses a much larger number of cost drivers than the one or two volume-based cost drivers typical in a conventional system. In fact, the approach separates overhead costs into overhead cost pools, where each cost pool is associated with a different cost driver. Then a predetermined overhead rate is computed for each cost pool and each cost driver. In consequence, this method has enhanced accuracy.

First-Stage Procedure

In the first stage of activity-based costing, overhead costs are divided into homogeneous cost pools. A homogeneous cost pool is a collection of overhead costs for which cost variations can be explained by a single cost driver. Overhead activities are homogeneous whenever they have the same consumption ratios for all products. Once a cost pool is defined, the cost per unit of the cost driver is computed for that pool. This is referred to as the pool rate. Computation of the pool rate completes the first stage. Thus, the first stage produces two outcomes: (1) a set of homogeneous cost pools, and (2) a pool rate.

Exhibit 25-6: Activity-Based Costing: First-Stage Procedure

Pool 1:	
Setup costs	$ 96,000
Quality control costs	74,000
Total costs	$170,000
Production runs	50
Pool rate (Cost per run)	$ 3,400
Pool 2:	
Power costs	$ 84,000
Maintenance	78,000
Total costs	$162,000
Machine hours	60,000
Pool rate (Cost per machine hour)	$ 2.70

For example, in Exhibit 25-5, quality control costs and setup costs can be combined into one homogeneous cost pool and maintenance and power costs into a second. For the first cost pool, the number of production runs or inspection hours could be the cost driver. Since the two cost drivers are perfectly correlated, they will assign the same amount of overhead to both products. For the second pool, machine hours or kilowatt hours could be selected as the cost driver.

Assume for purpose of illustration that the number of production runs and machine hours are the cost drivers chosen. Using data from Exhibit 25-2, the first-stage outcomes are illustrated in Exhibit 25-6.

Second-Stage Procedure

In the second stage, the costs of each overhead pool are traced to products. This is done using the pool rate computed in the first stage and the measure of the amount of resources consumed by each product. This measure is simply the quantity of the cost driver used by each product. In the example, that would be the number of production runs and machine hours used by each product. Thus, the overhead assigned from each cost pool to each product is computed as follows:

Applied overhead = Pool rate × Cost driver units used

To illustrate, consider the assignment of costs from the first overhead pool to Thingone. From Exhibit 25-6, the rate for this pool is $3,400 per production run. From Exhibit 25-2, Thingone uses 20 production runs. Thus, the overhead assigned from the first cost pool is $68,000 ($3,400 × 20 runs). Similar assignments would be made for the other cost pool and for the other product (for both cost pools).

The total overhead cost per unit of product is obtained by first tracing the overhead costs from the pools to the individual products. This total is then divided by the number of units produced. The result is the unit overhead cost. Adding the per-unit overhead cost to the per-unit prime cost yields the manufacturing cost per unit. In Exhibit 25-7, the manufacturing cost per unit is computed using activity-based costing.

Comparison of Product Costs

In Exhibit 25-8, the unit cost from activity-based costing is compared with the unit costs produced by conventional costing using either a plant-wide or departmental rate. This comparison clearly illustrates the effects of using only volume-based cost drivers to assign overhead costs. The activity-based cost reflects the correct pattern of overhead consumption and is, therefore, the most accurate of the three costs shown in Exhibit 25-8. Activity-based product costing reveals that the conventional method undercosts Thingone significantly by at least 37.7% = ($14.50 – 10.53)/ $10.53 and overcosts Thingtwo by at least 8.1% = ($10.53 – $9.74)/$9.74).

Using only volume-based cost drivers can lead to one product subsidizing another. This subsidy could create the appearance that one group of products is highly profitable and adversely impact the pricing and competitiveness of another group of products. This seems to be one of the problems facing Sharp Paper. In a highly competitive environment, accurate cost information is critical for sound planning and decision making.

Selecting Cost Drivers

At least two major factors should be considered in selecting cost drivers: (1) the cost of measurement, and (2) the degree of correlation between the cost driver and the actual consumption of overhead.

Exhibit 25-7: Activity-Based Costing: Second-Stage Procedure Unit Costs

Thingone		
Overhead:		
Pool 1: $3,400 × 20	$68,000	
Pool 2: $2.70 × 10,000	27,000	
Total overhead costs		$ 95,000
Prime costs		50,000
Total manufacturing costs		$145,000
Units produced		10,000
Unit cost		$14.50

Thingtwo		
Overhead:		
Pool 1: $3,400 × 30	$102,000	
Pool 2: $2.70 × 50,000	135,000	
Total overhead costs		$237,000
Prime costs		250,000
Total manufacturing costs		$487,000
Units produced		50,000
Unit cost		$9.74

The Cost of Measurement. In an activity-based cost system, a large number of cost drivers can be selected and used. However, it is preferable to select cost drivers that use information that is readily available. Information that is not available in the existing system must be produced, which will increase the cost of the firm's information system. A homogeneous cost pool could offer a number of possible cost drivers. For this situation, any cost driver that can be used with existing information should be chosen. This choice minimizes the costs of measurement.

In our example, for instance, quality control costs and setup costs were placed in the same cost pool, giving the choice of using either inspection hours or number of production runs as the cost driver. If the quantities of both cost drivers used by the two products are already being produced by the company's information system, then which is chosen is unimportant. Assume, however, that inspection hours by product are not tracked, but data for production runs are available. In this case, production runs should be chosen as the cost driver, avoiding the need to produce any additional information.

Exhibit 25-8: Comparison of Unit Costs

	Thingone	*Thingtwo*	*Source*
Conventional:			
Plant-wide rate	10.53	10.53	Exhibit 25-3
Department rates	8.86	10.87	Exhibit 25-4
Activity-based cost	$14.50	$ 9.74	Exhibit 25-7

Indirect Measures and the Degree of Correlation. The existing information structure can be exploited in another way to minimize the costs of obtaining cost driver quantities. It is sometimes possible to replace a cost driver that directly measures the consumption of an activity with a cost driver that indirectly measures that consumption. For example, inspection hours could be replaced by the actual number of inspections associated with each product; this number is more likely to be known. This replacement works only if hours used per inspection are reasonably stable for each product. Linear regressions can be utilized to determine the degree of correlation.

A list of potential cost drivers is given in Exhibit 25-9. Cost drivers that indirectly measure the consumption of an activity usually measure the number of transactions associated with that activity. It is possible to replace a cost driver that directly measures consumption with one that only indirectly measures it without loss of accuracy provided that the quantities of activity consumed per transaction are stable for each product. In such a case, the indirect cost driver has a high correlation and can be used.

Hewlett-Packard Illustration of Multiple Cost Pools

Hewlett-Packard Company's Personal Office Computer Division uses two overhead application rates. One rate is based on direct labor and assigns overhead costs associated with production. The second rate is based on material cost and assigns overhead cost associated with procurement. Exhibit 25-10 illustrates these systems. Overhead costs are initially categorized into three cost pools. Then the overhead costs associated with overall manufacturing support functions are allocated between the production cost pool and the procurement cost pool. This allocation is based on the number of employees and the estimated percentage of time spent on these two types of activities.

Exhibit 25-9: Cost Drivers

Manufacturing:

Space occupied

Number of setups	Direct labor hours
Weight of material	Number of vendors
Number of units reworked	Machine hours
Number of orders placed	Number of labor transactions
Number of orders received	Number of units scrapped
Number of inspections	Number of parts
Number of material handling operations	

Nonmanufacturing:

Number of hospital beds occupied

Number of takeoffs and landings for an airline

Number of rooms occupied in a hotel

Case 2

Overhead Cost Pool	Budgeted Overhead Cost	Cost Driver	Predicted Level for Cost Driver	Predetermined Overhead Rate
Machine setups	$100,000	Number of setups	100	$1,000 per setup
Material handling	100,000	Weight of raw material	50,000 pounds	$2 per pound
Waste control	50,000	Weight of hazardous chemicals used	10,000 pounds	$5 per pound
Inspection	75,000	Number of inspections	1,000	$75 per inspection
Other overhead costs	$200,000	Machine hours	20,000	$10 per machine hour
	$525,000			

Exhibit 25-10: Multiple Overhead Cost Pools—Hewlett-Packard Company: Personal Office Computer Division

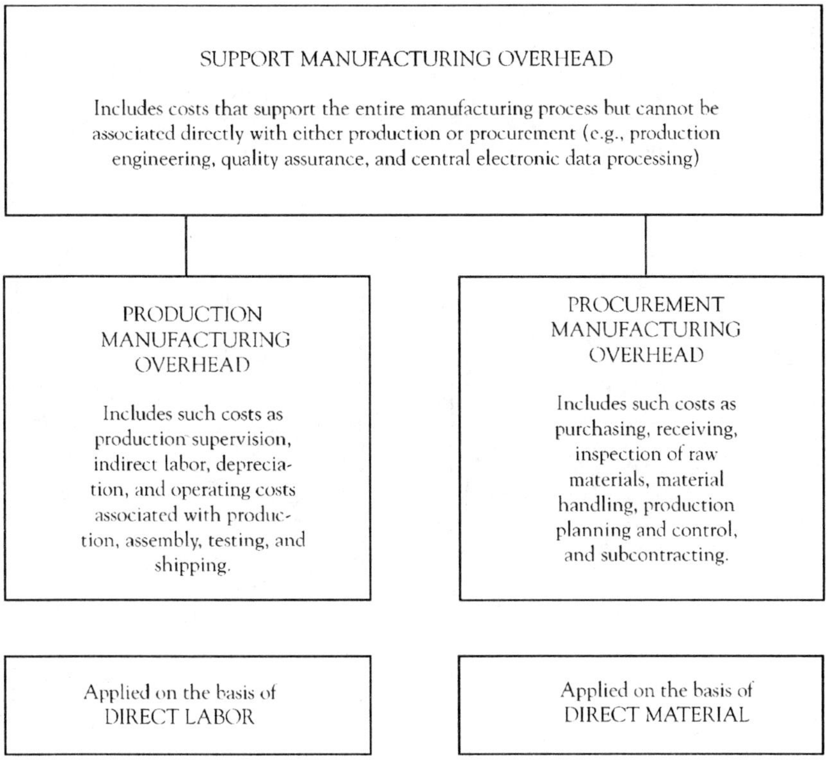

Source: Patell, J. "Cost Accounting, Process Control, and Product Design: A Case Study of the Hewlett-Packard Personal Office Computer Division," *Accounting Review*, October, 1987.

Job Number 3941 consists of 2,000 special-purpose machine tools with the following requirements:

Machine setups	2 setups
Raw material required	10,000 pounds
Waste materials required	2,000 pounds
Inspections	10 inspections
Machine hours	500 machine hours

The overhead assigned to Job Number 3941 is computed below.

Overhead Cost Pool	Predetermined Overhead Rate	Level of Cost Driver	Assigned Overhead Cost
Machine setups	$1,000 per setup	2 setups	$2,000
Material handling	$2 per pound	10,000 pounds	20,000
Waste control	$5 per pound	2,000 pounds	10,000
Inspection	$75 per inspection	10 inspections	750
Other overhead costs	$10 per machine hour	500 machine hours	5,000
Total			$37,750

The total overhead cost assigned to job Number 3941 is $37,750, or $18.88 per tool. Compare this with the overhead cost that is assigned to the job if the firm uses a single predetermined overhead rate based on machine hours:

$$\frac{\text{Total budgeted overhead cost}}{\text{Total predicated machine hour}} = \frac{\$525,000}{20,000}$$

$$= \$26.25 \text{ per machine hour}$$

Under this approach, the total overhead cost assigned to job Number 3941 is $13,125 ($26.25 per machine hour × 500 machine hours). This is only $6.56 per tool, which is about one third of the overhead cost per tool computed when multiple cost drivers are used.

The reason for this wide discrepancy is that these special-purpose tools require a relatively large number of machine setups, a sizable amount of waste materials, and several inspections. Thus, they are relatively costly in terms of driving overhead costs. Use of a single predetermined overhead rate obscures that fact.

Misestimating the overhead cost per drum to the extent illustrated in the foregoing can have serious adverse consequences for the firm. For example, it can lead to poor decisions about pricing, product mix, or contract bidding. The managerial accountant needs to weigh such considerations carefully in designing a product costing system. A costing system using multiple cost drivers is more costly to implement and use, but it may save millions through improved decisions.

Activity-based costing is a useful profit analysis tool that can reveal hidden profitability sources and embedded costs. It assists in cost-to-serve activities, customer profitability, channel income, capacity planning and drive predictive modeling, and is also a good source of performance measures.

ACTIVITY-BASED MANAGEMENT

Activity-based management (ABM) is one of the most important ways to be competitive. It is a system-wide, integrated approach that focuses management's attention on activities with the goal of improving customer value, reducing costs, and improving the resulting profit. The basic premise of ABM is: *Products consume activities; activities consume resources.* To be competitive, both (1) the activities that go into manufacturing the products or providing the services and (2) the cost of those activities must be known. To cut down a product's costs, the activities the product consumes will likely have to be changed. Ordering across-the-board cuts to reduce cost by 10%, for example, rarely obtains the desired results.

In order to achieve desired cost reductions, first identify the activities that a product or service consumes. Then figure out how to rework those activities to improve productivity and efficiency. Process value analysis is used to try to determine why activities are performed and how well they are performed. Activity-based costing, discussed in this chapter, is a tool used in activity-based management.

Process Value Analysis

Process value analysis is the process of identifying, describing, and evaluating the activities a company performs. It produces the following four outcomes:

1. What activities are performed.
2. How many people perform the activities.
3. The time and resources required to perform the activities.
4. An assessment of the value of the activities to the company, including a recommendation to select and keep only those that add value.

Understanding What Causes Costs

Effective cost control requires managers to understand how producing a product requires activities and how activities in turn generate costs. Consider the activities of a manufacturer facing a financial crisis. In a system of managing by the members, each department is told to reduce costs in an amount equal to its share of the budget cut. The usual response by department heads is to reduce the number of people and supplies, as these are the only cost items that they can control in the short run. Asking everyone to work harder produces only temporary gains, however, as the pace cannot be sustained in the long run.

Under ABM, the manufacturer reduces costs by studying what activities it conducts and develops plans to eliminate non-value-added activities and to improve the efficiency of value-added activities. Eliminating activities that do not create customer value is a very effective way to cut costs. For example, spending $100 to train all employees to avoid common mistakes will repay itself many times over by reducing customer ill will caused by those mistakes.

Value-Added and Non-Value-Added Activities

A *value-added activity* is an activity that increases the product's service to the customer. For instance, purchasing the raw materials to make a product is a value-added activity. Without the purchase of raw materials, the organization would be unable to make the product. Sanding and varnishing a wooden chair are value-added activities because customers do not want splinters. Value-added activities are evaluated by how they contribute to the final product's service, quality, and cost.

Good management involves finding and, if possible, eliminating non-value-added activities. *Non-value-added activities* are activities that, when eliminated reduce costs without reducing the product's potential to the customer. In many organizations, poor facility layout may require the work in process to be moved around or temporarily stored during production. For example, a Midwest steel company that was studied had more than 100 miles of railroad track to move things back and forth in a poorly designed facility. Moving work around a factory, an office, or a store is unlikely to add value for the customer. Waiting, inspecting, and storing are other examples of non-value-added activities.

Organizations must change the process that makes non-value-added activities necessary. Elimination of non-value-added activities requires organizations to improve the process so that the activities are no longer required. Organizations strive to reduce or eliminate non-value-added activities because, by doing so, they permanently reduce the costs they must incur to produce goods or services without affecting the value to the customer.

Although managers should pay particular attention to non-value-added activities, they should also carefully evaluate the need for value-added activities. For example, in wine production, classifying storage as a value-added activity assumes that the only way to make good-tasting wine is to allow it to age in storage. Think of the advantage that someone could have if he or she discovered a way to produce wine that tastes as good as *conventionally* aged wine but does not *require* long storage periods.

Activity Drivers and Categories

Activity output is measured by activity drivers. An activity driver is a factor (activity) that causes (drives) costs. Activity output measures can be identified by classifying activities into four general categories: (1) unit level, (2) batch level, (3) product level, and (4) facility level. Classifying activities into these general categories is useful because the costs of activities associated with the different levels respond to different types of activity drivers. Exhibit 25-11 describes how they are performed at each level, their output measures, and possible cost drivers.

The Value Chain of the Business Functions

The value chain concept of the business functions is used throughout the book to demonstrate how to use cost/managerial accounting to add value to organizations (see Exhibit 25-12). The *value chain* describes the linked set of activities that increase the usefulness (or value) of the products or services of an organization (value-added activities). Activities are evaluated by how they contribute to the final product's service, quality, and cost. In general, the business functions include:

- *Research and development*—the generation and development of ideas related to new products, services, or processes.
- *Design*—the detailed planning and engineering of products, services, or processes.
- *Production*—the aggregation and assembly of resources to produce a product or deliver a service.
- *Marketing*—the process that (a) informs potential customers about the attributes of products or services and (b) leads to the purchase of those products or services.

- *Distribution*—the mechanism established to deliver products or services to customers.

- *Customer service*—the product or service support activities provided to customers.

A *strategy and administration* function spans all the business activities described. Human resource management, tax planning, legal matters, for example, potentially affect every step of the value chain. Cost and managerial accounting is a major means of helping managers (a) run each of the business functions and (b) coordinate their activities within the framework of the entire organization.

Strategic Cost Analysis

Companies can identify strategic advantages in the marketplace by analyzing the value chain and the information about the costs of activities. A company that eliminates non-value-added activities reduces costs without reducing the value of the product to customers. With reduced costs, the company can reduce the price it charges customers, thus giving the company a cost advantage over its competitors. Or the company can use the resources saved from eliminating non-value-added activities to provide greater service to customers. *Strategic cost analysis* is the use of cost data to develop and identify superior strategies that will produce a sustainable competitive advantage. The idea here is simple. Look for activities that are not on the value chain. If the company can safely eliminate non-value-added activities, then it should do so. By identifying and cutting such activities, the company will save money and will be more competitive.

Global Strategies

Another approach to gaining a cost advantage is to identify where on the value chain the company has a strategic advantage. Many computer software companies, for example, are looking at foreign markets as a way to capitalize on their investment in research and development. The reservoir of intellectual capital gives these firms an advantage over local competitors who have not yet developed this expertise. These competitors would face research and development costs already incurred by established companies, making it difficult for the newcomers to charge competitive prices and still make a profit.

Exhibit 25-11: Activity Categories and Drivers

	Unit-Level Activities	Batch-Level Activities	Product-Level (Product and Customer-Sustaining) Activities	Facility-Level (Capacity-Sustaining) Activities
Types of activities:	Performed each time a unit is produced	Performed each time a batch is produced	Performed as needed to support a product	Sustain a factory's general manufacturing process
Examples:	Direct materials, direct labor, assembly, energy to run machines	Quality inspections, machine setups, production scheduling, material handling	Engineering changes, maintenance of equipment, customer records and files, marketing the product	Plant management, plant security, landscaping, maintaining grounds, heating and lighting, property taxes, rent, plant depreciation
Output measures:	Unit-level drivers	Batch-level drivers	Product-level drivers	Difficult to define
Examples:	Units of product, direct labor hours, machine hours	Number of batches, number of production orders, inspection hours	Number of products, number of changing orders	Plant size (square feet), number of security personnel

Exhibit 25-12: The Value Chain and Cost/Management Accounting

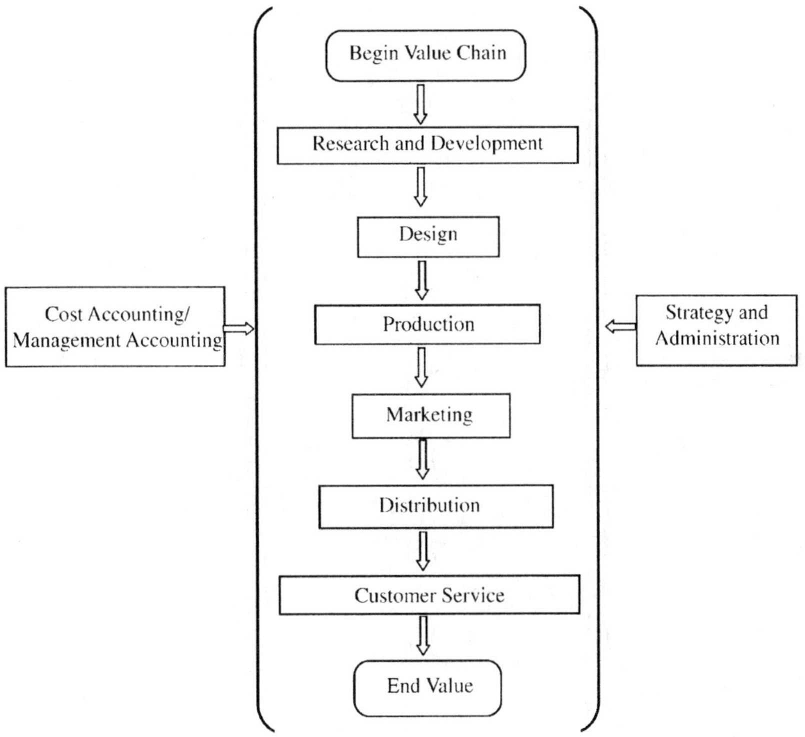

Throughput

One nonfinancial performance indicator that is becoming widely accepted is throughput or the number of good units or quantity of services produced and sold or provided by an organization within a specified time. Because its primary goal is to earn income, a for-profit organization must sell inventory (not simply produced) for throughput to be achieved. Throughput can be analyzed as a set of component elements similar to the way the Du Pont model includes components of return on assets (ROA). Throughput can be measured in either financial or nonfinancial terms (e.g., cash flows generated from selling products or services to customers, units of products, batches produced, dollar turnover, or other meaningful measurements). Components of throughput include manufacturing cycle efficiency, process productivity, and process quality yield.

Throughput can be calculated as follows:

$$\text{Throughput} = \begin{matrix}\text{Manufacturing}\\ \text{Cycle Efficiency}\end{matrix} \times \begin{matrix}\text{Process}\\ \text{Productivity}\end{matrix} \times \begin{matrix}\text{Process}\\ \text{Quality Yield}\end{matrix}$$

$$\text{Throughput} = \frac{\text{Value-Added Processing Time}}{\text{Total Time}} \times \frac{\text{Total Time}}{\text{Value-Added Processing Time}}$$

$$\times \frac{\text{Good Units}}{\text{Total Units}}$$

Manufacturing cycle efficiency is the proportion of value-added processing time to total processing time. Value-added processing time reflects activities that increase the product's worth to the customer. Total units produced during the period divided by the value-added processing time determines process productivity. Production activities can produce both good and defective units. The proportion of good units resulting from activities is the process quality yield. These calculations are presented in the following example.

Management should strive to increase throughput by decreasing non-value-added, increasing total unit production and sales, decreasing the per-unit processing time, increasing process quality yield, or a combination of these. Some companies have increased throughput significantly by the use of flexible manufacturing systems (FMS) and, in some cases, by reorganizing production operations. For example, at Intel Corporation throughput is enhanced by the technicians' ability to monitor automated operations from centralized locations, which allows for faster reaction time to production circumstances that might create downtime. Computer technologies such as bar coding, computer-integrated manufacturing (CIM), and electronic data interchange (EDI) have also enhanced throughput at many firms. Improved throughput means a greater ability to respond to customer needs and demands, reduce production costs, and reduce inventory levels and, therefore, the non-value-added costs of moving and storing goods.

EXAMPLE 1:

Given:

Total processing time	40,000 hours
Total value-added processing time	10,000 hours
Total quantity of product JKS #610 manufactured	50,000 tons
Total quantity of good production manufactured and sold	44,000 tons

Manufacturing Cycle Efficiency = Value-Added Processing Time/Total Processing Time = 10,000/40,000 = 25% (means that 75% of processing time is non-value-added)

Process Productivity = Total Units/Value-Added Processing Time = 50,000/10,000 = 5 (means that 5 units can be produced per hour)

Process Quality Yield = Good Units/Total Units = 44.000/50,000 = 88% (means that 12% of the yield was defective)

$$\text{Throughput} = \frac{\text{Manufacturing}}{\text{Cycle Efficiency}} \times \frac{\text{Process}}{\text{Productivity}} \times \frac{\text{Process}}{\text{Quality Yield}}$$

$= 0.25 \times 5 \times 0.88 = 1.1$ (means that 1.1 good units are produced per hour of total processing time, compared with the 5 units actually produced per value-added hour)

or

Throughput = Good Units/Total Processing Time

$= 44{,}000 \text{ units}/40{,}000 \text{ hours} = 1.1$

SOFTWARE AFFECTING VALUE CHAIN MANAGEMENT

Companies use a variety of software systems to process information and improve the operation of the value chain, the most common being enterprise resource planning (ERP) systems, supply chain management (SCM) systems, and customer relationship management systems (CRM).

Enterprise Resource Planning Systems

ERP systems grew out of material requirements planning (MRP) systems, which have been used for more than 20 years. MRP systems computerized inventory control and production planning. Key features included an ability to prepare a master production schedule and bill of materials and to generate purchase orders. ERP systems update MRP systems with better integration, relational databases, and graphical user interfaces. Features now encompass supporting accounting and finance, human resources, and various e-commerce applications, including SCM and CRM systems.

Selecting an ERP application is challenging. It is a time-consuming process for IT/IS managers as application vendors must be assessed and a comparison between what the vendors are offering and what the organization needs must be made. The following checklist was designed to expedite the selection process and to help ensure that all areas regarding the investigation of each vendor are covered.

Database and network

- How many user licenses are required?
- Is the ERP designed to work with RDBMS (relational database management systems) such as Oracle, Sybase, and Informix?
- Does the vendor have any built-in programs to handle integration?
- How will the data warehousing aspects be addressed?
- What is the maximum time it takes for uploading the remote data?
- What is the minimum time it takes for uploading the remote data?
- Does the software support distributed data processing?
- Does the software support a parallel processing option?
- Has the vendor had any previous problems regarding concurrency?
- Does the software have an audit trail on key transactions?

- How many security layers have been incorporated into the software?
- What kind of networking protocols does the software support?
- Does the software support data types such as LONG and BLOB?
- What is the largest database the vendor has handled so far for the modules of interest?
- What is the smallest database size handled by the vendor so far for the modules of interest?

Implementation

- Has the vendor implemented sites in the region?
- Has the vendor implemented ERP in the industry segment?
- Has the vendor implemented the same modules needed by the organization?
- Will there be immediate delivery of the product?
- Does the vendor have a specific implementation plan?
- How long did it take for the vendor to implement the same modules elsewhere?
- How many years of experience does the vendor have with implementation?
- Does the vendor have good project plan initiatives?
- Does the vendor have a good implementation team with the required skills?
- Does the vendor have the Certification of Excellence given by customers?
- What is the minimum implementation time for the modules chosen?
- What is the maximum implementation time for the modules chosen?

Business processes

- Does the vendor promise any reduction in lead times of those business processes of interest?
- What is the minimum processing time for MRP (material requirement planning)?
- What is the maximum processing time for MRP?
- What is the minimum processing time for MPS (master production schedule)?
- What is the maximum processing time for MPS?
- Does the software optimize the business processes after implementation?
- Does the software use a built-in business process modeler?

Hardware and software

- What kind of hardware support does the vendor offer?
- How many years of experience does the vendor have with the hardware/software that will be used for the project?
- Who are the alliance partners for the hardware support?

- What is the upgrade support for the software?
- Does the software have any interface to support the latest technology?
- How is the vendor maintaining the documentation for the software?
- Is the software Web-enabled?
- Will the software be implemented in modules?
- Will the software be purchased in modules?
- Will the software accounting adhere to international standards and adhere to each country's standards?
- How many operating systems does the software support?
- Does the software allow posting of transaction both in batch mode and online?
- Does the software support multilingual operation?

Support

- What support will the vendor provide after implementation?
- If the vendor is out-of-country, how is support provided?
- How much time will the vendor devote to ERP training for end users?
- Describe the UI (user interface)/GUI (graphical user interface) package support and how each will give end users ease of operation.
- Did the vendor complete any customization at any previously implemented sites? (Describe by percentage and the modules.)
- How will the vendor complete the reports' customization?
- Does the software have any built-in programs to handle data conversions?
- Is the front-end application developed using proprietary software?
- Is the customization cost included in the ERP cost?
- Can the vendor give approval for accessing other customers' data?
- Does the vendor have any test data built into the software for proper training?
- If any bugs are found in the software during or after implementation, what is the replacement support?
- Is the vendor ready to work with third-party tools and software?

Supply Chain Management Systems

SCM is the organization of activities between a company and its suppliers in an effort to provide for the profitable development, production, and delivery of goods to customers. By sharing information, production lead times and inventory holding costs have been reduced while on-time deliveries to customers have been improved. SCM software systems support the most efficient way to fill orders and help track products and components among companies in the supply chain. Wal-Mart and Procter & Gamble (P&G) are two companies that have become well known for their cooperation in the use of SCM. When P&G products are scanned at a Wal-Mart store, P&G receives information on the sale via satellite and thus knows when to make more product and to which specific Wal-Mart stores to ship it. Related cost savings are passed on, at least in part, to Wal-Mart customers.

Customer Relationship Management Systems

CRM systems automate customer service and support. They also provide for customer data analysis and support e-commerce storefronts. Although CRM is evolving, it has already led to some remarkable changes in the way companies interact with customers. For example, Federal Express allows customers to track their packages on the Web. This service is becoming commonplace, but it did not exist 10 years ago. Amazon.com uses CRM technology to make suggestions to customers based on their personal purchase histories. The ultimate development of CRM remains to be seen, but undoubtedly mobile communication will play a significant role. Many companies are already experimenting with systems to send messages to cell phone users offering them special discounts and buying "opportunities."

JUST-IN-TIME MANUFACTURING AND COST MANAGEMENT

The inventory control problem occurs in almost every type of organization. It exists whenever products are held to meet some expected future demand. In most industries, cost of inventory represents the largest liquid asset under the control of management. Therefore, it is very important to develop a production and inventory planning system that will minimize both purchasing and carrying costs.

During the 1960s and 1970s, material requirements planning (MRP) was adopted by many U.S. manufacturing companies as the key component of their production and inventory planning systems. While success has not been universal, users typically agreed that the inventory approach inherent in an MRP system generally is more effective than the classical approach to inventory planning. Aside from the manufacturing aspects, the purchasing function also is of major importance to the overall success of the system.

Even though MRP has received a great deal of attention, effective purchasing and management of materials is still a high-priority activity in most manufacturing firms. Material cost, as a proportion of total product cost, has continued to rise significantly during the last few years and hence is a primary concern of top management.

Competing on the basis of both price and quality, the Japanese have demonstrated the ability to manage their production systems effectively. Much of their success has been attributed to their just-in-time (JIT) approach to production and inventory control, which has generated a great deal of interest among practitioners. The Kanban system, as they call it, has been a focal point of interest, with its dramatic impact on the inventory performance and productivity of the Japanese auto industry.

This section provides an overview of the just-in-time approach and its impact on cost management as well as some examples of implementation of JIT by U.S. firms.

What Is Just-in-Time?

JIT is a demand-pull system. JIT production, in its purest sense, is buying and producing in very small quantities just in time for use. The basic idea has its roots in Japan's densely populated industrial areas and its lack of resources, both of which have produced frugal personal habits among the Japanese people. The idea was developed into a formal management system by Toyota in order to meet the precise demands of customers for various vehicle models and colors with minimum delivery delays. JIT is achieved by techniques such as smoothing production, designing flexible processes, standardizing jobs, and employing the Kanban system for conveying ordering and delivery information within the production system. Furthermore, the little inventory that exists in a JIT system must be of good quality. This requirement has led to JIT purchasing practices uniquely able to deliver high-quality materials. As a philosophy, JIT targets inventory as an evil presence that obscures problems that should be solved, and that, by contributing significantly to costs, keeps a company from being as competitive or profitable as it otherwise might be. Practically speaking, JIT has as its principal goal the elimination of waste, and the principal measure of success is how much or how little inventory there is. Virtually anything that achieves this end can be considered a JIT innovation.

JIT systems integrate five functions of the production process—sourcing, storage, transportation, operations, and quality control—into one controlled manufacturing process. In manufacturing, JIT means that a company produces only the quantity needed for delivery to dealers or customers. In purchasing, it means suppliers deliver subassemblies just in time to be assembled into finished goods. In delivery, it requires selecting a transportation mode that will deliver purchased components and materials in small lot sizes at the loading dock of the manufacturing facilities just in time to support the manufacturing process.

JIT versus Traditional Manufacturing

JIT manufacturing is a demand-pull, or Kanban system, rather than the traditional "push" approach. The philosophy underlying JIT manufacturing is to produce a product when it is needed and only in the quantities demanded by customers. Demand pulls products through the manufacturing process. Each operation produces only what is necessary to satisfy the demand of the succeeding operation. No production takes place until a signal from a succeeding process indicates a need to produce. Parts and materials arrive just in time to be used in production. To illustrate the differences between pull and push systems of material control, the example of a fast food restaurant is used:

> At McDonald's the customer orders a hamburger, the server gets one from the rack, the hamburger maker keeps an eye on the rack and makes new burgers when the number gets too low. The manager orders more ground beef when the maker's inventory gets too low. In effect, the customer purchase triggers the pull of materials through the system. . . . In a push system, the caterer estimates how many steaks are likely to be ordered in any given week. He/she reckons

how long it takes to broil a steak: he/she can figure out roughly how many meals are needed in a certain week. . . . [1]

Reduced Inventories. The primary goal of JIT is to reduce inventories to insignificant or zero levels. In traditional manufacturing, inventories result whenever production exceeds demand. Inventories are needed as a buffer when production does not meet expected demand.

Manufacturing Cells and Multifunction Labor. In traditional manufacturing, products are moved from one group of identical machines to another. Typically, machines with identical functions are located together in an area referred to as a department or process. Workers who specialize in the operation of a specific machine are located in each department. JIT replaces this traditional pattern with a pattern of manufacturing cells or work centers. Robots supplement people for many routine operations.

Manufacturing cells contain machines that are grouped in families, usually in a semicircle. The machines are arranged so that they can be used to perform a variety of operations in sequence. Each cell is set up to produce a particular product or product family. Products move from one machine to another from start to finish. Workers are assigned to cells and are trained to operate all machines within the cell. Thus, labor in a JIT environment is multifunction labor, not specialized labor. Each manufacturing cell is basically a minifactory or a factory within a factory. A comparison of the physical layout of JIT with the traditional system is shown in Exhibit 25-13.

Total Quality Control. JIT necessarily carries with it a stronger emphasis on quality control. A defective part brings production to a grinding halt. Poor quality simply cannot be tolerated in a stockless manufacturing environment. In other words, JIT cannot be implemented without a commitment to *total quality control (TQC)*. TQC is essentially an endless guest for perfect quality. This approach to quality is opposed to the traditional belief, called *acceptable quality level (AQL)*. AQL allows defects to occur provided they are within a predetermined level.

Exhibit 25-13: Physical Layout: Traditional versus JIT Manufacturing

Traditional Manufacturing		
Department A	*Department B*	*Department C*
<P1>X X	<P1>Y Y	<P1>Z Z
<P2>	<P2>	<P2>

Each product passes through departments that specialize in one process. Departments process multiple products.

---

[1] Karmarkar, Uday, "Getting Control of Just-In-Time," *Harvard Business Review*, September–October 1998, pp. 122–131.

		JIT Manufacturing				
	Product 1 (P1)				*Product 2 (P2)*	
	Manufacturing Cell 1				*Manufacturing Cell 2*	
	Y				Y	
P1>	X		Z	P2>	X	Z

Each product passes through its own cell. All machines necessary to process each product are placed within the cell. Each cell is dedicated to the production of one product or one subassembly.

Symbols:

X = Machine A

Y = Machine B

Z = Machine C

$P1$ = Product 1

$P2$ = Product 2

Decentralization of Services. JIT requires easy and quick access to support services, which means that centralized service departments must be scaled down and their personnel assigned to work directly to support production. For example, with respect to raw materials, JIT calls for multiple stock points, each one near where the material will be used. There is no need for a central warehouse location.

Better Cost Management. Cost management differs from cost accounting in that it refers to the management of cost, whether or not the cost has direct impact on inventory or the financial statements. The JIT philosophy simplifies the cost accounting procedure and helps managers manage their costs. JIT recognizes that with simplification comes better management, better quality, better service, and better cost. Traditional cost accounting systems have a tendency to be very complex, with many transactions and reporting of data. Simplification of this process will transform a cost "accounting" system into a cost "management" system that can be used to support management's needs for better decisions about product design, pricing, marketing, and mix, and to encourage continual operating movements.

The major differences between JIT manufacturing and traditional manufacturing are summarized in Exhibit 25-14.

Benefits of JIT

Potential benefits of JIT are numerous. First, JIT practice reduces inventory levels, which means lower investments in inventories. Since the system requires only the small quantity of materials that are needed immediately, it reduces the overall inventory level substantially. In many Japanese companies that use the JIT concept, inventory levels have been reduced to the point that makes the annual working capital turnover ratio much higher than that experienced by U.S. counterparts. For instance, Toyota once reported inventory turnover ratios of 41 to 63, while comparable U.S. companies reported inventory turnover ratios of 5 to 8.

Exhibit 25-14: Comparison of JIT and Traditional Manufacturing

JIT	Traditional
1. Pull, or Kanban system	1. Push system
2. Insignificant or zero inventories	2. Significant inventories
3. Manufacturing cells	3. "Process" structure
4. Multifunction labor	4. Specialized labor
5. Total quality control (TQC)	5. Acceptable quality level
6. Decentralized services	6. Centralized services
7. Simple cost accounting	7. Complex cost accounting

Second, since purchasing under JIT requires a significantly shorter delivery lead time, lead time reliability is greatly improved. Reduced lead time and increased reliability also contribute to a significant reduction in the safety stock requirements.

Third, reduced lead times and setup times increase scheduling flexibility. The cumulative lead time, which includes both purchasing and production lead times, is reduced. Thus, the firm schedule within the production planning horizon is reduced. This results in a longer "look-ahead" time that can be used to meet shifts in market demand. The smaller lot size production made possible by reduced setup time also adds flexibility.

Fourth, improved quality levels have been reported by many companies. When the order quantity is small, sources of quality problems are quickly identifiable, and can be corrected immediately. In many cases employee quality consciousness also tends to improve, producing an improvement in quality at the production source.

Fifth, the costs of purchased materials may be reduced through more extensive value analysis and cooperative supplier development activities.

Sixth, other financial benefits reported include:

1. Lower investments in factory space for inventories and production.
2. Less obsolescence risk in inventories.
3. Reduction in scrap and rework.
4. Decline in paperwork.
5. Reduction in direct material costs through quantity purchases.

Examples of JIT Implementation in the U.S.

The following are some of the many implementation experiences of JIT in the U.S.:

1. Ford introduced JIT production at its heavy-duty truck plant in Kentucky, which forced Firestone to switch the tire searching point from Mansfield to Dayton, Ohio. By combining computerized ordering and halving inventory, Firestone has been able to reduce its own finished goods inventory. In addition, its production planning is no longer guesswork.

2. Each day a truck from Harley-Davidson Motor Co. transports 160 motorcycle seats and assorted accessories 800 miles overnight to Harley's assembly plant in York, PA, as part of its advanced "Materials as Needed" (MAN) program—its version of JIT.

3. The Hoover Company has used JIT techniques in its two plants at North Canton, Ohio, for a number of years for production scheduling and material flow control of 360 different models and 29,000 part numbers.

4. Some plants of DuPont used JIT and had an inventory savings of 30 cents on the dollar for the first year.

5. The Vancouver division of Hewlett-Packard reported the following benefits two years after the adoption of the JIT method:

Work-in-process inventory dollars	down 82%
Space used	down 40%
Scrap/rework	down 30%
Production time:	
Impact printers	down 7 days to 2 days
Thermal printers	down 7 days to 3 hours
Labor efficiency	up 50%
Shipments	up 20%

JIT Costing and Cost Management

The cost accounting system of a company adopting JIT will be simple compared to job order or processing costing. Under JIT, raw materials and work-in-process (WIP) accounts are typically combined into one account called "resources in process" (RIP) or "raw and in-process." Under JIT, the materials arrive at the receiving area and are whisked immediately to the factory area. Thus, the Stores Control account vanishes. The journal entries that accompany JIT costing are remarkably simple as follows:

Raw and in-process (RIT) inventory	$45,000	
Accounts payable or cash		$45,000
To record purchases		
Finished goods	40,000	
RIP inventory		40,000
To record raw materials in completed units		

As can be seen, there are no Stores Control and WIP accounts under JIT. In summary, JIT costing can be characterized as follows:

1. There are fewer inventory accounts.

2. There are no work orders. Thus, there is no need for detailed tracking of actual raw materials.

3. With JIT, activities can be eliminated on the premise that they do not add value. Prime target for elimination are storage areas for WIP inventory and material-handling facilities.

4. The costs of many activities previously classified as indirect costs have been transferred to the direct cost in the JIT environment. For example, under the JIT system, workers on the production line will do plant maintenance and setups, while under traditional systems these activities were done by other workers classified as indirect labor. Exhibit 25-15 compares the traceability of some manufacturing costs under the traditional system with their traceability in the JIT environment.

   JIT manufacturing increases direct traceability of many manufacturing costs, which enhances the accuracy of product costing. However, JIT does not convert all indirect costs into direct costs. Even with JIT installed, a significant number of overhead activities remain common to the work centers. Nonetheless, JIT, coupled with activity-based accounting, gives rise to a tremendous improvement in product costing accuracy over the traditional approach.

5. Direct labor costs and factory overhead costs are not tracked to specific orders. Direct labor is now regarded as just another part of factory overhead. Furthermore, factory overhead is accounted for as follows. Virtually all of the manufacturing overhead incurred each month, now including direct labor, flows through to cost of goods sold in the same month. Tracking overhead through WIP and finished goods inventory provides no useful information. Therefore, it makes sense to treat manufacturing overhead as an expense charged directly to cost of goods sold. Overhead remaining in work-in-process and finished goods is maintained with end-of-month adjusting entries.

6. Many firms place great emphasis on purchase price variances in traditional purchasing environments. Favorable purchasing price variances can sometimes be achieved by buying larger quantities to take advantage of price discounts or by buying lower-quality materials. In JIT, the emphasis is on the total cost of operations and not just the purchase price. Factors such as quality and availability are given priority, even if they are accompanied by higher purchase prices.

Exhibit 25-15: Traceability of Product Cost: Traditional versus JIT Manufacturing

	Traditional	JIT
Direct labor	Direct	Direct
Direct materials	Direct	Direct
Material handling	Indirect	Direct
Repairs and maintenance	Indirect	Direct
Energy	Indirect	Direct
Operating supplies	Indirect	Direct
Supervision	Indirect	Direct
Insurance and taxes	Indirect	Indirect
Building depreciation	Indirect	Indirect
Equipment depreciation	Indirect	Direct
Building occupancy	Indirect	Indirect
Product support services	Indirect	Indirect
Cafeteria services	Indirect	Indirect

7. In many traditional plants, much of the internal accounting effort is devoted to setting labor and overhead standards and in calculating and reporting variances from these standards. Firms using JIT report reduced emphasis on the use of labor and overhead variances. Firms retaining variance analysis stress that a change in focus is appropriate in a JIT plant. The emphasis is on the analysis at the plant level with focus on trends that may be occurring in the manufacturing process rather than the absolute magnitude of individual variances.

8. Traditional performance measures (such as labor efficiency and machine utilization) that are commonplace in many cost accounting systems are not appropriate within the JIT philosophy of cost management. They are all inappropriate for the following reasons:

   a. They all promote building inventory beyond what is needed in the immediate time frame.

   b. Emphasizing performance to standard gives priority to output, at the expense of quality.

   c. Direct labor in the majority of manufacturers accounts for only 5 to 15% of total product cost.

   d. Using machine utilization is inappropriate because it encourages results in building inventory ahead of needs. Exhibit 25-16 lists typical performance measures under the traditional and JIT systems.

Exhibit 25-16: Performance Measures—Traditional versus JIT

Traditional	JIT
Direct labor efficiency	Total head count productivity
Direct labor utilization	Return on assets
Direct labor productivity	Days of inventory
Machine utilization	Group incentives
	Lead time by product
	Response time to customer feedback
	Number of customer complaints
	Cost of quality
	Setup reduction

Accounting in the JIT System

Accounting in a JIT system focuses on a plant's overall output to the customer. Although a company may wish to measure the output of each manufacturing cell or work center rather than total output, which can reveal problems in a given area, the practice does not correlate with the JIT philosophy, which emphasizes a team approach, plantwide attitude, and total cost picture. With the JIT system, all areas of a company are interlinked and dependent on each other, thus problems in one area will become apparent, as they will likely halt production. Moreover, daily accounting for the individual costs of production is no longer necessary; all costs should be at standard, since variations are observed and corrected almost immediately.

In a JIT system, since costs are more easily traced to their related output, fewer costs are arbitrarily allocated to products. Costs are incurred in specified cells on a per-hour or per-unit basis. Energy costs are directed to production in a comprehensive JIT system, as there should be a minimum of downtime by machines or unplanned idle time for workers. Virtually the only costs still being allocated are costs associated with the structure (i.e., building depreciation, rent, taxes, and insurance) and machinery depreciation. By comparison, activity-based costing attempts to allocate manufacturing overhead costs to products more accurately than under traditional cost accounting systems by using multiple cost drivers rather than by using departmental overhead application rates.

Backflush Costing

Backflush costing is a streamlined cost accounting method that is used in a JIT operating environment, where costing is delayed until goods are finished. It speeds up, simplifies, and reduces accounting effort in an environment that minimizes inventory balances, requires few allocations, uses standard costs, and has minimal variances from standard.

Standard costs are flushed backward through the system to assign costs to products, thus eliminating the detailed tracking of costs. The method then records purchases of raw material and accumulates actual conversion costs. Upon completion of production or the sale of goods, an entry is made to allocate the total costs incurred to cost of goods sold and to finished goods inventory, using standard production costs.

Implementation of a JIT system can result in significant cost reductions and productivity improvements. But even within a single company, not all inventories need to be managed according to a JIT philosophy. The costs and benefits of any inventory control system must be evaluated before management installs the system.

The following example provides information on a product of the Ivy Company. This information is used to illustrate the journal entries for backflush costing. The company has a long-term contract with its supplier for raw material at $75 per unit, so there is no material price variance. Ivy's JIT inventory system has minimum inventories that remain constant from period to period. Beginning inventories for June are assumed to be zero.

Example 2:

Ivy Company's standard production cost per unit:

Raw material	$ 75
Conversion	184
Total cost	$259

No beginning inventories exist.

(1) Purchased $1,530,000 of raw material in June:

Raw and in process inventory	1,530,000	
Accounts payable		1,530,000

Purchased material at standard cost under a long-term agreement with the supplier.

(2) Incurred $3,687,000 of conversion costs in June:

Conversion costs	3,687,000	
Various accounts		3,687,000

Record conversion costs. Various accounts include wages payable for direct and indirect labor, accumulated depreciation, supplies, etc.

(3) Completed 20,000 units of production in June:

Finished goods (20,000 × $259)	5,180,000	
Raw and in process inventory (20,000 × $75)		1,500,000
Conversion costs (20,000 × $184)		3,680,000

(4) Sold 19,800 units on account in June for $420:

(a) Cost of goods sold (19,800 × $259)	5,128,200	
Finished goods		5,128,200
(b) Accounts receivable (19,800 × $420)	8,316,000	
Sales		8,316,000

Ending inventories:

Raw and in process	$30,000
($1,530,000 − $1,500,000)	
Finished goods ($5,180,000 − $5,128,200)	51,800

In addition, there are underapplied conversion costs of $7,000 ($3,687,000 − $3,680,000).

Three alternatives are possible to the entries in the example. First, if Ivy's production time were extremely short, the company might not journalize raw material purchases until completion of production. In that case, entries (1) and (3) could be combined as follows:

Raw and in process inventory	30,000	
Finished goods	5,180,000	
Accounts payable		1,530,000
Conversion costs		3,680,000

If goods were immediately shipped to customers on completion, Ivy could use a second alternative, in which entries (3) and (4)(a) could be combined in the following manner to complete and sell the goods:

Finished goods	51,800	
Cost of goods sold	5,128,200	
Raw and in process inventory		1,500,000
Conversion costs		3,680,000

The third alternative reflects the ultimate JIT system, in which only one entry is made to replace entries (1), (3), and (4)(a). For Ivy, this entry would be:

Raw and in process inventory (minimal overpurchases)	30,000	
Finished goods (minimal overproduction)	51,800	
Cost of goods sold	5,128,200	
Accounts payable		1,530,000
Conversion costs		3,680,000

Note that in all cases, entry (2) is not affected. All conversion costs must be recorded as incurred, or accrued at the end of a period, because of their effect on a variety of accounts.

CONCLUSION

Activity costing provides more accurate product cost figures for product costing and pricing, using multiple overhead cost pools and cost drivers. Conventional cost systems are not able to assign the costs of non-volume-related overhead activities accurately. For this reason, assigning overhead using only volume-based drivers or a single driver can distort product costs. Activity-based costing may provide more accurate information about product costs than does traditional costing. It helps managers make better decisions about product design, pricing, marketing, and mix, and encourages continual operating improvements.

A quick or across-the-board adoption of the just-in-time concept is not recommended. In many companies (particularly U.S. firms), the JIT purchasing concept simply may not be practical or feasible. In others, it may not be applicable to all product lines. However, many progressive companies currently are either investigating or implementing some form of the system. The most important aspects of the JIT purchasing concept focus on: (1) new ways of dealing with suppliers, and (2) a clear-cut recognition of the appropriate purchasing role in the development corporate strategy. Suppliers should be viewed as "outside partners" that can contribute to the long-run welfare of the buying firm rather than as outside adversaries. JIT also affects product costing. Under JIT manufacturing, many indirect costs are converted to direct costs. This conversion reduces the need to use multiple cost drivers to assign overhead costs to products, thus enhancing product costing accuracy.

CHAPTER 26

TOTAL QUALITY MANAGEMENT, QUALITY COSTS, AND ENVIRONMENT COSTS

CONTENTS

TOTAL QUALITY MANAGEMENT

In order to be globally competitive in today's world-class manufacturing environment, firms place an increased emphasis on quality and productivity. Total quality management (TQM) is an effort in this direction. Simply put, it is a system for creating competitive advantage by focusing the organization on what is important to the customer. Total quality management can be broken down into: "Total": the whole organization is involved and understands that customer satisfaction is everyone's job. "Quality": the extent to which products and services satisfy the requirements of internal and external customers. "Management": the leadership, infrastructure, and resources that support employees as they meet the needs of those customers.

TQM is essentially an endless quest for perfect quality. It is a zero-defects approach. It views the optimal level of quality costs as the level where zero defects are produced. This approach to quality is opposed to the traditional belief, called acceptable quality level (AQL), which allows a predetermined level of defective units to be produced and sold. AQL is the level where the number of defects allowed minimizes total quality costs. The rationale behind the traditional view is that there is a tradeoff between prevention and appraisal costs and failure costs. Quality experts maintain that the optimal quality level should be about 2.5% of sales.

Principles of TQM

Making a product right the first time is one of the principal objectives of TQM. Implementing a successful TQM program will in fact reduce costs rather than increase them. There is no question that better quality will result in better productivity. This is based on the principle that when less time is spent on rework or repair, more time is available for manufacturing, which will increase productivity.

When an organization maintains accurate records of its cost of quality, TQM will demonstrate that effective quality assurance geared towards prevention versus correction will pay for itself. A good example of this is the situation where it is possible to eliminate 100% inspection with a good statistical process control (SPC) program. Elimination of high reject rates results in fewer products being repaired, reworked, or scrapped, with the obvious reductions in cost.

Tying the cost of quality to TQM is necessary in order to motivate management, who are cost-motivated in both industry and government. In a TQM environment, management will start utilizing the cost data to measure the success of the program. The corporate financial planner can determine that overall product costs are being reduced by the TQM program. Given this success in the prevention of defects, the following failure costs will be reduced or eliminated:

1. Rework or repair.
2. Inspection of rework.
3. Testing of rework.
4. Warranty costs.
5. Returned material.
6. Discounts, adjustments, and allowances.

The cost of prevention in TQM is minor when taken against the above-listed failure costs.

TQM features are as follows:

- A systematic way to improve products and services.
- A structured approach in identifying and solving problems.
- Long term.

- Conveyed by management's actions.
- Supported by statistical quality control.
- Practiced by everyone.

Elements of TQM

The principal elements of TQM are straightforward and embrace a commonsense approach to management. However, each of the individual elements must be integrated into a structured whole to succeed. The elements are as follows:

- *A focus on the customer.* Every functional unit has a customer, whether it be an external consumer or an internal unit. TQM advocates that managers and employees become so customer-focused that they continually find new ways to meet or exceed customers' expectations. Financial planners must accept the concept that quality is defined by the customer and meeting the customer's needs and expectations is the strategic goal of TQM.

- *A long-term commitment.* Experience in the U.S. and abroad shows that substantial gains come only after management makes a long-term commitment, usually five years or more, in improving quality. Customer focus must be constantly renewed to keep that goal foremost.

- *Top management support and direction.* Top management must be the driving force behind TQM. Senior managers must exhibit personal support by using quality improvement concepts in their management style, incorporating quality in their strategic planning process, and providing financial and staff support.

- *Employee involvement.* Full employee participation is also an integral part of the process. Each employee must be a partner in achieving quality goals. Teamwork involves managers, supervisors, and employees in improving service delivery, solving systemic problems, and correcting errors in all parts of work processes.

- *Effective and renewed communications.* The power of internal communication, both vertical and horizontal, is central to employee involvement. Regular and meaningful communication from all levels must occur. This will allow an agency to simultaneously adjust its ways of operating and reinforce the commitment of TQM.

- *Reliance on standards and measures.* Measurement is the springboard to involvement, allowing the organization to initiate corrective action, set priorities, and evaluate progress. Standards and measures should reflect customer requirements and changes that need to be introduced in the internal business of providing those requirements. The emphasis is on "doing the right thing right the first time."

- *Commitment to training.* Training is absolutely vital to the success of TQM. The process usually begins with awareness training for teams of top-level managers. This is followed by courses for teams of mid-level managers, and finally by courses for non-managers. Awareness training is followed by an identification of areas of concentration, or of functional areas where TQM will first be introduced. Implementing TQM requires additional skills training, which is also conducted in teams.

- *Importance of rewards and recognition.* Most companies practicing TQM have given wide latitude to managers in issuing rewards and recognition. Here, a common theme is that individual financial rewards are not as appropriate as awards to groups or team members, since most successes are group achievements.

In conclusion, quality management companies must understand customer needs and should aim to exceed customer expectations. Identifying, understanding, and managing interrelated procedures contributes to a company's efficiency and effectiveness in accomplishing its goals.

QUALITY COSTS

Costs of quality are costs that occur because poor quality may exist or actually does exist. More specifically, quality costs are the total of the costs incurred by (1) investing in the prevention of nonconformances to requirements; (2) appraising a product or service for conformance to requirements; and (3) failure to meet requirements.

Quality costs are classified into three broad categories: (1) prevention, (2) appraisal, (3) and failure costs. Prevention costs are those incurred to prevent defects. Amounts spent on quality training programs, researching customer needs, quality circles, and improved production equipment are considered in prevention costs. Expenditures made for prevention will minimize the costs that will be incurred for appraisal and failure. Appraisal costs are costs incurred for monitoring or inspection; these costs compensate for mistakes not eliminated through prevention. Failure costs may be internal (such as scrap and rework costs and reinspection) or external (such as product returns due to quality problems, warranty costs, lost sales due to poor product performance, and complaint department costs). Market shares of many U.S. firms have eroded because foreign firms have been able to sell higher-quality products at lower prices. Exhibit 26-1 provides a listing of quality costs and a general description of each type.

Studies indicate that costs of quality for American companies are typically 20% to 30% of sales. Quality experts maintain that the optimal quality level should be about 2.5% of sales.

Exhibit 26-1: Quality Costs—General Description

Prevention Costs

The costs of all activities specifically designed to prevent poor quality in products or services. Examples are the costs of new product review, quality planning, supplier capability surveys, process capability evaluations, quality improvement team meetings, quality improvement projects, quality education and training.

Appraisal Costs

The costs associated with measuring, evaluating, or auditing products or services to assure conformance to quality standards and performance requirements. These include the costs of incoming and source inspection/test of purchased material, in-process and final inspection/test, product, process, or service audits, calibration of measuring and test equipment, and the costs of associated supplies and materials.

Failure Costs

The costs resulting from products or services not conforming to requirements or customer/user needs. Failure costs are divided into internal and external failure cost categories.

Internal Failure Costs

Failure costs occurring prior to delivery or shipment of the product, or the furnishing of a service, to the customer. Examples are the costs of scrap, rework, reinspection, retesting, material review, and downgrading.

External Failure Costs

Failure costs occurring after delivery or shipment of the product, and during or after furnishing of a service, to the customer. Examples are the costs of processing customer complaints, customer returns, warranty claims, and product recalls.

Total Quality Costs

The sum of the above costs. It represents the difference between the actual cost of a product or service, and what the reduced cost would be if there were no possibility of substandard service, failure of products, or defects in their manufacture.

TWO VIEWS CONCERNING OPTIMAL QUALITY COSTS

The two views concerning optimal quality costs are:

1. **Traditional View.** The traditional approach uses an acceptable quality level (AQL) that permits a predetermined level of defective units to be produced and sold. AQL is the level where the number of defects allowed minimizes total quality costs. The reasoning of the traditional approach is that there is a trade-off between failure costs and prevention and appraisal costs. As prevention and appraisal costs increase, internal and external failure costs are expected to decrease. As long as the decrease in failure costs is greater than the corresponding increase in prevention and failure costs, a company should continue increasing its efforts to prevent or detect defective units.

2. **World-Class View.** The world-class view uses total quality control and views the optimal level of quality costs as the level where zero defects are produced. The zero-defects approach uses a quality performance standard that requires:

a. All products to be produced according to specifications.

b. All services to be provided according to requirements.

Zero defects reflect a total quality control philosophy used in just-in-time (JIT) manufacturing. Exhibit 26-2 illustrates the relationship between these two cost components under the two views.

Exhibit 26-2: Optimal Quality Costs: Traditional and World-Class Views

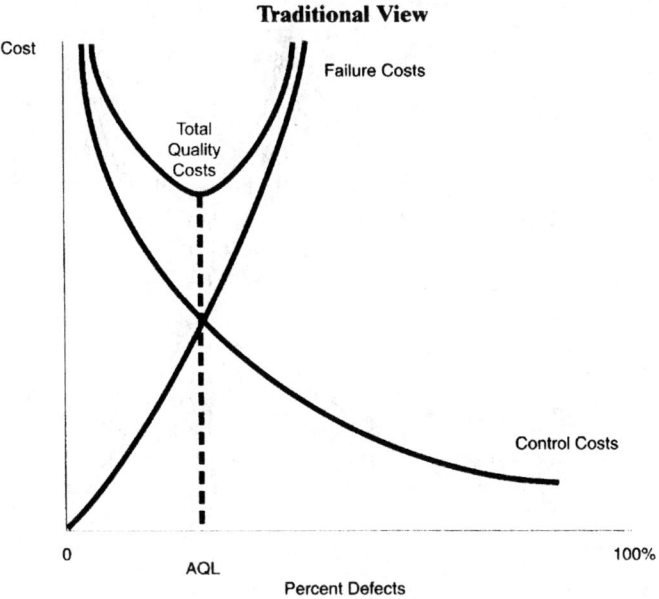

Traditional View

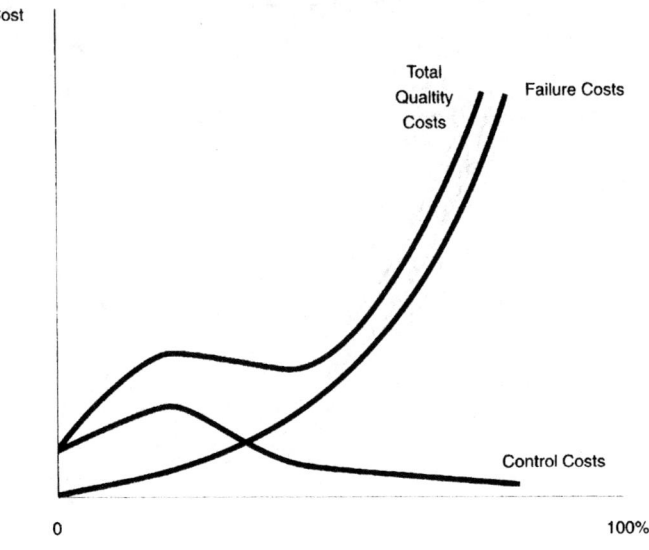

World-Class View

QUALITY COST AND PERFORMANCE REPORTS

The principal objective of reporting quality costs is to improve and facilitate managerial planning, control, and decision making. Potential uses of quality cost information include:

- Quality program implementation decisions.
- Evaluation of the effectiveness of quality programs.
- Strategic pricing decisions. For example, improved reporting of quality costs might be used by managers to target specific quality costs for reductions. A reduction in quality costs might enable a firm to reduce its selling price, improve its competitive position, and increase market share.
- Inclusion of quality costs in cost-volume-profit analysis. For example, over-looking quality cost savings results in a higher break-even and possible rejection of a profitable project.

The control process involves comparing actual performance with quality standards. This comparison provides feedback that can be used to take corrective action if necessary. The first step in a quality cost reporting system is to prepare a detailed listing of actual quality costs by category. Each category of quality costs is then expressed as a percentage of sales. This serves two purposes: (1) it permits managers to assess the financial impact of quality costs, and (2) it reveals the relative emphasis currently placed on each category.

Quality cost reports (as illustrated in Exhibit 26-3) can be used to point out the strengths and weaknesses of a quality system. Improvement teams can use them to describe the monetary benefits and ramifications of proposed changes. Return-on-investment (ROI) models and other financial analyses can be constructed directly from quality cost data to justify proposals to management. In practice, quality costs can define activities of quality program and quality improvement efforts in a language that management can understand and act on—dollars.

The negative effect on profits resulting from product or service of less than acceptable quality or from ineffective quality management is almost always dynamic. Once started, it continues to mushroom until ultimately the company finds itself in serious financial difficulties due to the two-pronged impact of an unheeded increase in quality costs coupled with a declining performance image. Management that clearly understands this understands the economics of quality.

Exhibit 26-3: Quality Cost Report

Allison Products
Quality Cost Report
for the Year Ended March 31, 2X15

	Quality Costs		Percentage of Sale[a]
Prevention costs:			
Quality training	$30,000		
Reliability engineering	79,000	$109,000	3.73%
Appraisal costs:			
Materials inspection	$19,000		
Product acceptance	10,000		
Process acceptance	35,000	$64,000	2.19%
Internal failure costs:			
Scrap		$40,000	
Rework	34,000	$74,000	2.53%
External failure costs:			
Customer complaints	$24,000		
Warranty		24,000	
Repair	15,000	$63,000	2.16%
Total quality costs		$310,000	10.62%[b]

[a] Actual sales of $2,920,000
[b] $310,000/2,920,000 = 10.62%. Difference is rounding error.

In the quality cost report, quality costs are grouped into one of four categories:

1. Prevention costs.

2. Appraisal costs.

3. Internal failure costs.

4. External failure costs.

In addition, each category of quality costs is expressed as a percentage of sales. The three types of performance reports to measure a company's quality improvement are as follows:

1. *Interim quality performance report.* It measures the progress achieved within the period relative to the planned level of progress for the period (as illustrated in Exhibit 26-4).

Exhibit 26-4: Interim Quality Performance Report

Allison Products
Interim Standard Performance Report
for the Year Ended March 31, 2X15

	Actual Costs	Budgeted Costs[a]	Variance
Prevention costs:			
Quality training	$30,000	$30,000	$0
Reliability engineering	79,000	80,000	1,000 F
Total prevention	$109,000	$110,000	$1,000 F
Appraisal costs:			
Materials inspection	$19,000	$28,000	$9,000 F
Product acceptance	10,000	15,000	5,000 F
Process acceptance	35,000	35,000	0
Total appraisal	$64,000	$78,000	$14,000 F
Internal failure costs:			
Scrap	$40,000	$44,000	$4,000 F
Rework	34,000	36,500	2,500 F
Total internal failure	$74,000	$80,500	$6,500 F
External failure costs:			
Fixed:			
Customer complaints	$24,000	$25,000	$1,000 F
Variable:			
Warranty	24,000	20,000	(4,000) U
Repair	15,000	17,500	2,500 F
Total external failure	$63,000	$62,500	($500) U
Total quality costs	$310,000	$331,000	$21,000 F
Percentage of actual sales[b]	10.62%	11.34%	0.72% F

[a] Based on actual sales
[b] Actual sales of $2,920,000

2. *One-year quality trend report.* It compares the current year's quality cost ratio with the previous year's ratio. More specifically, it compares the current year's variable quality cost ratio with the previous year's variable quality cost ratio, and the current year's actual fixed quality costs with the previous year's actual fixed quality costs (as illustrated in Exhibit 26-5).

Exhibit 26-5: One-Year Quality Trend Report

Allison Products
Quality Cost, One-Year Trend
for the Year Ended March 31, 2X15

	Actual Costs [a]	Budgeted Costs	Variance
Prevention costs:			
Quality training	$30,000	$36,000	$6,000 F
Reliability engineering	79,000	120,000	41,000 F
Total prevention	$109,000	$156,000	$47,000 F
Appraisal costs:			
Materials inspection	$19,000	$33,600	$14,600 F
Product acceptance	10,000	16,800	6,800 F
Process acceptance	35,000	39,200	4,200 F
Total appraisal	$64,000	$89,600	$25,600 F
Internal failure costs:			
Scrap	$40,000	$48,000	$8,000 F
Rework	34,000	40,000	6,000 F
Total internal failure	$74,000	$88,000	$14,000 F
External failure costs:			
Fixed:			
Customer complaints	$24,000	$33,000	$9,000 F
Variable:			
Warranty	24,000	23,000	(1,000) U
Repair	15,000	16,400	1,400 F
Total external failure	$63,000	$72,400	$9,400 F
Total quality costs	$310,000	$406,000	$96,000 F
Percentage of actual sales	10.62%	13.90%	3.29% F

[a] Based on actual sales = $2,920,000

3. *Long-range quality performance report.* It compares the current year actual quality costs with the firm's intended long-range quality goal (as illustrated in Exhibit 26-6).

Exhibit 26-6: Long-Range Quality Performance Report

Allison Products
Long-Range Performance Report
for the Year Ended March 31, 2X15

	Actual Costs	Target Costs[a]	Variance
Prevention costs:			
Quality training	$30,000	$14,000	($16,000) U
Reliability engineering	79,000	39,000	(40,000) U
Total prevention	$109,000	$53,000	($56,000) U
Appraisal costs:			
Materials inspection	$19,000	$7,900	($11,100) U
Product acceptance	10,000	0	(10,000) U
Process acceptance	35,000	12,000	(23,000) U
Total appraisal	$64,000	$19,900	($44,100) U
Internal failure costs:			
Scrap	$40,000	$0	($40,000) U
Rework	34,000	0	(34,000) U
Total internal failure	$74,000	$0	($74,000) U
External failure costs:			
Fixed:			
Customer complaints	$24,000	$0	($24,000) U
Variable:			
Warranty	24,000	0	(24,000) U
Repair	15,000	0	(15,000) U
Total external failure	$63,000	$0	($63,000) U
Total quality costs	$310,000	$72,900	($237,100) U
Percentage of actual sales	10.62%	2.50%	8.126% U

[a] Based on actual sales of $2,920,000. These costs are value-added costs.

ACTIVITY-BASED MANAGEMENT AND OPTIMAL QUALITY COSTS

Activity-based management supports the zero-defect view of quality costs.

Activity-based management classifies activities as: (1) value-added activities and (2) non-value-added activities.

Quality-related activities (internal and external failure activities, prevention activities, and appraisal activities) can be classified as value-added and non-value-added.

Internal and external failure activities and their associated costs are non-value-added and should be eliminated.

Prevention activities that are performed efficiently are value-added. (Costs caused by inefficiency in prevention activities are non-value-added costs.)

Appraisal activities may be value-added or non-value-added depending upon the activity. For example, quality audits may serve a value-added objective.

Once the quality-related activities are identified for each category, resource drivers can be used to improve cost assignments to individual activities. Root or process drivers can also be identified and used to help managers understand what is causing the cost of the activities.

MEASURING QUALITY COSTS

Quality costs can also be classified as observable or hidden. Observable quality costs are those that are available from an organization's accounting records, whereas hidden quality costs are opportunity costs resulting from poor quality. Opportunity costs usually are not recognized in accounting records. Yet, in all of the quality cost examples listed in the prior section, with the exception of lost sales, customer dissatisfaction, and lost market share, all of the quality costs are observable and available from the accounting records. Hidden quality costs, which reside in the external failure category, can be significant. Although they are difficult to estimate, the following three suggested methods for calculating them are: (1) the multiplier method, (2) the market research method, and (3) the Taguchi quality loss function.

The multiplier method assumes that the total failure cost is simply some multiple of measured failure costs. For example:

Total external failure cost = k (Measured external failure costs)

where k is the multiplier effect. The value of k is based on experience. For example, Westinghouse Electric Corporation reports a value of k between 3 and 4. Thus, if the measured external failure costs are $2 million, the actual external failure costs are between $6 million and $8 million. Including hidden costs in assessing the amount of external failure costs allows management to more accurately determine the level of resource spending for prevention and appraisal activities. Specifically, with an increase in failure costs, it is expected that management would increase its investment in control costs.

The market research method is used to assess the effect of poor quality on sales and market share. Customer surveys and interviews with members of a company's sales force can provide significant insights into the magnitude of a company's hidden costs. Market research results can be used to project future profit losses attributable to poor quality.

The traditional zero defects definition assumes that hidden quality costs exist only for units that fall outside the upper and lower specification limits. The *Taguchi loss function* assumes that any variation from the target value of a quality characteristic causes hidden quality costs. Furthermore, these hidden costs increase quadratically as the actual value deviates from the target value. The Taguchi quality loss function can be described by the following equation:

$$L(y) = k(y - T)^2$$

where

k = A proportionality constant dependent upon the organization's external failure cost structure

y = Actual value of quality characteristic

T = Target value of quality characteristic

L = Quality loss

The quality cost is zero at the target value and increases symmetrically, at an increasing rate, as the actual value varies from the target value. For example, taking into account that k = \$400 and T = 10 inches in diameter, Exhibit 26-7 illustrates the computation of the quality loss for four units. The cost quadruples when the deviation from the target doubles (from units 2 to 3). In addition, the average deviation is squared so the average loss per unit can be computed. These averages can be used to compute the total expected hidden quality costs for a product. For example, if the total units produced is 2,000 and the average squared deviation is 0.025, then the expected cost per unit is \$10 (0.025 × \$400) and the total expected loss of the 2,000 units is \$20,000 (\$10 × 2,000).

To apply the Taguchi loss function, k must be estimated. The value of k is computed by dividing the estimated cost at one of the specification limits by the squared deviation of the limit from the target value:

$$k = c/d^2$$

where

c = *Loss at the lower or upper specification limit*

d = *Distance of limit from target value*

Therefore, the loss for a given deviation from the target value must still be estimated. The first two methods, the multiplier method or the market research method, may be used to assist in this estimation (a one-time assessment need). Once k is known, the hidden quality costs can be estimated for any level of variation from the target value.

Exhibit 26-7: Quality-Loss Computation Illustrated

Unit	Actual Diameter (y)	y – T	(y – T)²	K(y – T)²
1	9.9	–0.10	0.010	\$ 4.00
2	10.1	0.10	0.010	4.00

Unit	Actual Diameter (y)	y – T	(y – T)²	K(y – T)²
3	10.2	0.20	0.040	16.00
4	9.8	–0.20	0.040	16.00
Total			0.100	$ 40.00
Average			0.025	$ 10.00

SIX-SIGMA

Six Sigma is a structured and disciplined, data-driven process for improving business performance. The Six Sigma methodology concentrates on reducing variability in processes. Sigma is a statistical term that measures how far a given process deviates from customer requirements and a measure of process capability. The term "Six Sigma" refers to the ability of highly capable processes to produce output within specification. In particular, processes that operate with six sigma quality produce at defect levels below 3.4 defects per (one) million opportunities. Six Sigma's implicit goal is to improve all processes to that level of quality or better. This is accomplished through the use of two Six Sigma methodologies: Define, Measure, Analyze, Improve, Control (DMAIC) and the Design for Six Sigma (DFSS). The Six Sigma DMAIC process is an improvement system for existing processes that fail to meet customer requirements, focusing on the elimination of errors and defects. The DFSS process is used to develop new products or processes at Six Sigma quality levels. It can also be employed if a current process requires more than just incremental improvement. Whereas DMAIC is focused on eliminating defects, DFSS is about preventing defects and errors by designing new products, services, and processes to meet customer needs. In summary, cost reduction is an integral process within overall cost management strategy, which is strategic journey, not a tactical exercise. Cost reduction opportunities exist not only in the general ledger accounts, but also in the business processes that transcend organizational boundaries.

ENVIRONMENT COSTS AND ECOEFFICIENCY

Measuring environmental costs has become an important issue for many companies. Increased interest in this issue is mainly because:

1. Many countries have increased their regulations and added enormous fines and penalties.

2. Successful treatment of environmental concerns is becoming a significant competitive issue.

An important concept in dealing with (2) above is called *ecoefficiency*, which essentially maintains that organizations can produce more useful goods and services while simultaneously reducing negative environmental impacts, resource consumption, and costs. Therefore, more goods and services are produced using less materials, energy, water and land, while minimizing air emissions, water discharges, waste disposal, and the dispersion of toxic substances. Ecoefficiency thus implies a positive relationship between environmental and economic performance.

Ecoefficiency is not the only environmental cost paradigm. Two competing paradigms are *compliance management* and *guided ecoefficiency*. Compliance management is the practice of achieving the minimal amount of environmental performance required by regulations with the least amount of cost. Guided ecoefficiency maintains that pollution is a form of economic inefficiency and that properly designed environmental regulations will stimulate innovation such that environmental performance and economic efficiency simultaneously improve.

There are at least five core objectives for the environmental perspective, including minimizing the use of raw or virgin materials; minimizing the use of hazardous materials; minimizing energy requirements for production and use of the product; minimizing the release of solid, liquid, and gaseous residues; and maximizing opportunities to recycle.

Exhibit 26-8 summarizes the objectives and measures for the environmental perspective.

Exhibit 26-8: Objectives and Measures for the Environmental Perspective

Objectives	*Measures*
Minimize hazardous materials	Types and quantities (total and per unit)
	Percent of total materials cost
	Productivity measures (output/input)
Minimize raw or virgin materials	Types and quantities (total and per unit)
	Productivity measures (output/input)
Minimize energy requirements	Types and quantities (total and per unit)
	Productivity measures (output/input)
Minimize release of residues	Pounds of toxic waste produced
	Cubic meters of effluents
	Tons of greenhouse gases produced
	Percent of reduction of packaging materials
Maximize opportunities to recycle	Pounds of materials recycled
	Number of different components
	Percent of units remanufactured
	Energy produced from incineration

Environmental costs are those that are incurred because poor environmental quality exists or may exist. Environmental costs can be classified into four categories: (1) prevention costs, (2) detection costs, (3) internal failure costs, and (4) external failure costs.

Environmental prevention costs are the costs of activities carried out to prevent the production of contaminants or waste that could cause damage to the environment. Pollution prevention activities, often called "P2" activities, include:

- Evaluating and selecting suppliers
- Evaluating and selecting pollution control equipment
- Designing processes
- Designing products
- Carrying out environmental studies
- Auditing environmental risks
- Developing environmental management systems
- Recycling products
- Obtaining ISO 14001 certification

Environmental detection costs are the costs of activities executed to determine if products, processes, and other activities within the firm are in compliance with appropriate environmental standards. Environmental detection costs include:

- Auditing environmental activities
- Inspecting products and processes
- Developing environmental performance measures
- Testing for contamination
- Verifying supplier environmental performance
- Measuring contamination levels

Environmental internal failure costs are costs of activities performed because contaminants and waste have been produced but not discharged into the environment. They are incurred to eliminate and manage contaminants or waste once produced.

Examples of environmental internal failure costs include:

- Operating pollution control equipment
- Treating and disposing of toxic waste
- Maintaining pollution equipment
- Licensing facilities for producing contaminants
- Recycling scrap

Environmental external failure costs are the costs of activities performed after discharging contaminants and waste into the environment. These costs are realized if incurred and paid for by the firm. They are unrealized or societal if they are caused by the firm but incurred and paid for by parties outside the firm. Examples of environmental external failure costs include:

- Cleaning up a polluted lake
- Cleaning up oil spills
- Cleaning up contaminated soil

- Settling personal injury claims (environmentally related)
- Restoring land to its natural state
- Losing sales due to a poor environmental reputation
- Using materials and energy inefficiently
- Receiving medical care due to polluted air
- Losing employment because of contamination
- Losing a lake for recreational use
- Damaging ecosystems from solid waste disposal

An *environmental cost report* may be prepared to report the details of environmental costs. It is a good idea to report the costs by category. Exhibit 26-9 presents an example of an environmental cost report.

Exhibit 26-9: A Sample Environmental Cost Report

XYZ Chemicals
Environmental Cost Report
For the Year Ended December 31, 2X15

	Environmental Costs		
Percent*			
Prevention costs:			
Evaluating suppliers	$ 120,000		
Recycling products	75,000	$ 195,000	0.33%
Detection costs:			
Inspecting products/processes	$ 600,000		
Developing performance measures	60,000	660,000	1.10
Internal failure costs:			
Treating toxic waste	$4,800,000		
Operating equipment	840,000		
Licensing facilities	360,000	6,000,000	10.00
External failure costs:			
Settling claims	$1,200,000		
Cleanup of soil	1,800,000	3,000,000	5.00
Totals		$9,855,000	16.43%

* Of operating costs: $60,000,000.

Relative Distribution: Environmental Costs

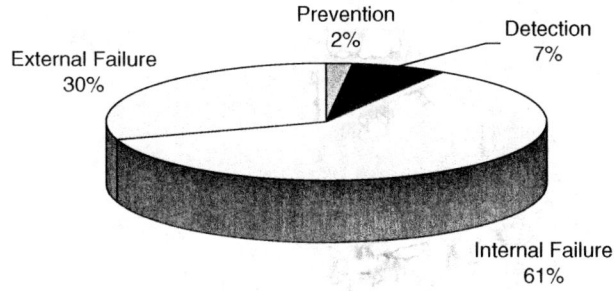

This distribution reveals that the company is paying little attention to preventing and detecting environmental costs. To improve environmental performance, much more needs to be invested in the prevention and detection categories.

CHAPTER 27

DECISION MODELING IN CORPORATE FINANCIAL MANAGEMENT

CONTENTS

The use of quantitative tools is commonplace in financial management. Also, in recent years, much attention has been given to using a variety of quantitative models in financial decision making. With the rapid development of microcomputers, financial officers find it increasingly easy to use quantitative techniques. Knowledge of mathematical and statistical methods will greatly aid financial managers and accountants in performing their functions. The so-called Decision Support System (DSS) is, in effect, the embodiment of this trend.

The term *quantitative models,* also known as operations research (OR) and management science, describes sophisticated mathematical and statistical techniques in the solution of planning and decision-making problems. There are numerous tools available under these subject headings. Nine of the most important of these techniques that have been widely applied in finance and accounting will be explored:

1. Statistical analysis and evaluation.

2. Decision N making.

3. Optimal budget and linear programming.

4. Multiple conflicting goals and goal programming.

5. Zero-one programming and capital rationing.

6. Beta and linear regression.

7. Learning curve.

8. Inventory planning.

9. Program Evaluation and Review Technique (PERT).

STATISTICAL ANALYSIS AND EVALUATION

In many situations, financial managers have a large volume of data that need to be analyzed. These data could be such things as earnings, cash flows, accounts receivable balances, and weights of an incoming shipment. The most commonly used statistics to describe the characteristics of the data are the mean and the standard deviation. These statistics are also used to measure the return and risk in investment and financial decision making in which the financial managers may be asked by the business entity to participate.

Standard Deviation

The standard deviation measures the tendency of data to be spread out. Accountants can make important inferences from past data with this measure. The standard deviation, denoted with and read as sigma, is defined as follows:

$$\sigma = \sqrt{\frac{\Sigma(x - \bar{x})^2}{n - 1}}$$

where $\bar{x}$ is the mean.

More specifically, the standard deviation can be calculated, step by step, as follows:

1. Subtract the mean from each value of the data.
2. Square each of the differences obtained in step 1.
3. Add together all the squared differences.
4. Divide the sum of all the squared differences by the number of values minus one.
5. Take the square root of the quotient obtained in step 4.

The standard deviation can be used to measure the variation of such items as the expected contribution margin (CM) or expected variable manufacturing costs. It can also be used to assess the risk associated with investment decisions.

EXAMPLE 1: One and one-half years of quarterly returns for United Motors stock are listed as follows:

Time Period	x	$(x - \bar{x})$	$(x - \bar{x})^2$
1	10%	0	0
2	15	5	25
3	20	10	100
4	5	−5	25
5	−10	−20	400
6	20	10	100
	60		650

From the above table, note that

$$\bar{x} = 60/6 = 10\%$$

$$\sigma = \sqrt{(x - \bar{x})^2/n - 1} = \sqrt{650/(6 - 1)} = \sqrt{130} = 11.40\%$$

The United Motors stock has returned on the average 10% over the last six quarters and the variability about its average return was 11.40%. The high standard deviation (11.40%) relative to the average return of 10% indicates that the stock is very risky.

DECISION MAKING

Decisions are made under certainty or under uncertainty. Decision making under certainty means that for each decision there is only one event and therefore only one outcome for each action. Decision making under uncertainty, which is more common in reality, involves several events for each action with its probability of occurrence.

Decision Making under Uncertainty

When decisions are made in a world of uncertainty, it is often helpful to make the computations of (1) expected value, (2) standard deviation, and (3) coefficient of variation.

Decision Matrix

Although statistics such as expected value and standard deviation are essential for choosing the best course of action under uncertainty, the decision problem can best be approached using what is called decision theory. Decision theory is a systematic approach to making decisions especially under uncertainty. Decision theory utilizes an organized approach such as a payoff table (or decision matrix), which is characterized by:

- The row representing a set of alternative courses of action available to the decision maker.

- The column representing the state of nature or conditions that are likely to occur over which the decision maker has no control.

- The entries in the body of the table representing the outcome of the decision, known as payoffs, which may be in the form of costs, revenues, profits, or cash flows. Computing expected value of each action enables the selection of the best one.

   EXAMPLE 2: Assume the following probability distribution of daily demand for a product:

Daily demand	0	1	2	3
Probability	.2	.3	.3	.2

Also assume that unit cost = $3, selling price = $5 (i.e., profit on sold unit = $2), and salvage value on unsold units = $2 (i.e., loss on unsold unit = $1). One can stock 0, 1, 2, or 3 units. The question is: How many units should be stocked each day? Assume that units from one day cannot be sold the next day. Then the payoff table can be constructed as follows:

		State of Nature				
	Demand **Stock (Probability)**	**0** **(2)**	**1** **(.3)**	**2** **(.3)**	**3** **(.2)**	**Expected** **Value**
	0	$0	0	0	0	$0
Actions	1	–1	2	2	2	1.40
	2	–2	1*	4	4	1.90**
	3	–3	0	3	6	1.50

* Profit for (stock 2, demand 1) equals (no. of units sold) (profit per unit) – (no. of units unsold) (loss per unit) = (1) ($5 – 3) – (1) ($3 – 2) = $1
** Expected value for (stock 2) is: – 2(.2) + 1(.3) + 4(.3) + 4(.2) = $1.90

The optimal stock action is the one with the highest expected monetary value (i.e., stock 2 units).

Expected Value of Perfect Information

Suppose the decision maker can obtain a perfect prediction of which event (state of nature) will occur. The expected value with perfect information would be the total expected value of actions selected on the assumption of a perfect forecast. The expected value of perfect information can then be computed as: Expected value with perfect information minus the expected value with existing information.

EXAMPLE 3: From the payoff table in Example 2, the following analysis yields the expected value with perfect information:

			State of Nature				
	Stock	**Demand**	**0** **(2)**	**1** **(.3)**	**2** **(.3)**	**3** **(.2)**	**Expected** **Value**
	0		$0				$0
Actions	1			2			.6
	2				4		1.2
	3					6	1.2
							$3.00

Alternatively,

$$\$0(.2) + 2(.3) + 4(.3) + 6(.2) = \$3.00$$

With existing information, the best that the decision maker could obtain was select (stock 2) and obtain $1.90. With perfect information (forecast), the decision maker could make as much as $3. Therefore, the expected value of perfect information is $3.00 – $1.90 = $1.10. This is the maximum price the decision maker is willing to pay for additional information.

Decision Tree

Decision tree is another approach used in discussions of decision making under uncertainty. It is a pictorial representation of a decision situation. As in the case of the decision matrix approach discussed earlier, it shows decision alternatives, states of nature, probabilities attached to the state of nature, and conditional benefits and losses. The decision tree approach is most useful in a sequential decision situation.

EXAMPLE 4: Assume XYZ Corporation wishes to introduce one of two products to the market this year. The probabilities and present values (PV) of projected cash inflows are given below:

Products Probabilities	Initial Investment	PV of Cash Inflows	
A	$225,000		1.00
		$450,000	0.40
		200,000	0.50
		– 100,000	0.10
B	80,000		1.00
		320,000	0.20
		100,000	0.60
		–150,000	0.20

A decision tree analyzing the two products is given below.

	Initial Investment (1)	Probability (2)	PV of Cash Inflow (3)	PV of Cash Inflow (2 × 3) (4)
		0.40	$450,000	$180,000
	$225,000	0.50	$200,000	100,000
Product A		0.10	–$100,000	10,000
		Expected PV of Cash Inflows		$270,000
Choice A or B				
Product B				
		0.20	$320,000	$ 64,000
	$ 80,000	0.60	$100,000	$ 60,000
		0.20	–$150,000	$ 30,000
		Expected PV of Cash Inflows		$ 94,000

For Product A:

Expected NPV = Expected PV – I = $270,000 – $225,000 = $45,000

For Product B:

Expected NPV = $94,000 – $80,000 = $14,000

Based on the expected net present value, the company should choose product A over product B.

OPTIMAL BUDGET AND LINEAR PROGRAMMING

Linear programming (LP) is a mathematical technique designed to determine an optimal decision (or an optimal plan) chosen from a large number of possible decisions. The optimal decision is the one that meets the specified objective of the company, subject to various restrictions or constraints. It concerns itself with the problem of allocating scarce resources among competing activities in an optimal manner. The optimal decision yields the highest profit, contribution margin (CM), or revenue, or the lowest cost. A linear programming model consists of the following two important components:

1. *Objective function.* The company must define the specific objective to be achieved.

2. *Constraints.* Constraints are in the form of restrictions on availability of resources or meeting minimum requirements. As the name linear programming indicates, both the objective function and constraints must be in linear form.

EXAMPLE 5: A firm wishes to find an optimal product mix. The optimal mix would be the one that maximizes its total CM within the allowed budget and production capacity. Or the firm may want to determine a least-cost combination of input materials while meeting production requirements, employing production capacities, and using available employees.

Applications of LP. Applications of LP are numerous. They include:

1. Developing an optimal budget.

2. Determining an optimal investment portfolio.

3. Scheduling jobs to machines.

4. Determining a least-cost shipping pattern.

5. Scheduling flights.

6. Gasoline blending.

Formulation of LP. To formulate an LP problem, certain steps are followed. They are:

1. Define decision variables that you are trying to solve for.

2. Express the objective function and constraints in terms of these decision variables. All the expressions must be in linear form. This section shows how optimization techniques such as linear programming or goal programming can help develop an optimal budget. For this purpose, we will illustrate with a simple example.

We will use this technique first to find the optimal product mix and then to develop the budget for the optimal program.

EXAMPLE 6: The Sigma Company produces and sells two products: snowmobiles (A) and outboard motors (B). The sales price of A is $900 per unit and that of B $800 per unit. Production department estimates on the basis of standard cost data are that the capacity required for manufacturing one unit of A is 10 hours while one unit of product B requires 20 hours. The total available capacity for the company is 160 hours. The variable manufacturing costs of A are $300 per unit and they are all paid in cash at the same rate at which the production proceeds. The variable manufacturing costs of B are $600 per unit. These costs are also paid in cash. For simplicity we assume no variable selling costs. Demand forecasts have been developed: the maximum amount of product A that can be sold is 8 units whereas that of B is 12 units. Product A is sold with one period credit while one half of the sales of product B is received in the same period in which the sales are realized.

Additional information:

• The company has existing loans which require $2,100 in payment.

• The company plans to maintain a minimum balance of $500.

- The accounts payable balance of $900 must be paid in cash in this period.
- The balance sheet and the fixed overhead budget are given below:

Balance Sheet

Assets			Liabilities		
Current assets			Current liabilities		
Cash	$1,000		Accounts payable	900	
Accounts Receivable		6,800	Short-term loan	10,000	10,900
Inventory	6,000	13,800			
Fixed assets		4,500	Equity		7,400
Total assets		$18,300	Total liabilities & equity		$18,300

Fixed Overhead Budget

Expenses involving cash	$1,900
Accruals	800
Depreciation	500
	$3,200

Formulation of the LP Model. We begin the formulation of the model by setting up the objective function which is to maximize the company's total contribution margin (CM). By definition, CM per unit is the difference between the unit sales price and the variable cost per unit:

	Product	
	A	**B**
Sales price	$900	$800
Variable cost	300	600
CM per unit	$600	$200

Let us define A = the number of units of product A to be produced
B = the number of units of product B to be produced

Then the total CM is:

$$TCM = 600A + 200B$$

Remember that demand forecasts show that there were upper limits of the demand of each product as follows:

$$A \leq 6, B \leq 10$$

The planned use of capacity must not exceed the available capacity. Specifically, we need the restriction:

$$10A + 20B \leq 160$$

We also need the cash constraint. It is required that the funds tied up in the planned operations will not exceed the available funds. The initial cash balance plus the cash collections of accounts receivable are available for the financing of operations. On the other hand, we need some cash to pay for expenses and maintain a minimum balance. The cash constraint we are developing involves two stages. In the first stage, we observe the cash receipts and disbursements that can be considered fixed regardless of the planned production and sales:

Funds initially available		
Beginning cash balance	$1,000	
Accounts receivable	6,800	7,800
Funds to be disbursed		
Accounts payable	$ 900	
Repayment of loans	2,100	
Fixed cash expenses	1,900	4,900
Difference	2,900	
Minus: Minimum cash balance required		500
Funds available for the financing of operations		$2,400

In the second stage, we observe the cash receipts and disbursements caused by the planned operations.

First, the total sales revenues:

Product	A	$900A$
	B	$800B$

The cash collections from:

Product	A	(0) $900A = 0$
	B	(.5) $800B = 400B$

Second, the variable manufacturing costs are:

Product	A	$300A$
	B	$600B$

Therefore, the cash disbursements for:

Product	A	(1) $300A = 300A$
	B	(1) $600B = 600B$

Then, the cash constraint is formulated by requiring that the cash disbursements for planned operations must not exceed the cash available plus the cash collections resulting from the operations:

$$300A + 600B \leq 2400 + 0 + 400B$$

This can be simplified to form the following:

$$300A + 200B \leq 2400$$

Using a widely used LP program known as LINDO (Linear Interactive Discrete Optimization) shown in Exhibit 27-1, we obtain the following optimal solution:

$$A = 6, B = 3, \text{ and } CM = \$4,200$$

Generation of Budgets on the Basis of Optimal Mix

The sales budget would look like:

Product	Price	Quantity	Revenues
A	$900	6	$5,400
B	800	3	2,400
			$7,800

Similarly, production and cost budgets can be easily developed. We will skip directly to show the cash budget, budgeted balance sheet, and budgeted income statement.

Cash Budget

Beginning cash balance			$1,000
Accounts receivable		6,800	
Cash collections from credit sales			
A: $(0)900A = (0)(900)(6)$	0		
B: $(.5)800B = 400B = 400(3)$	1,200	1,200	8,000
Total cash available			9,000
Cash disbursements:			
Production:			
A: $300A = 300(6)$	1,800		
B: $600B = 600(3)$	1,800	3,600	
Fixed cash expenses:			
Accounts payable balance	900		
Repayment of loan	2,100		
Fixed expenses	1,900	4,900	8,500
Ending cash balance			$ 500

Budgeted Income Statement

Sales		$7,800 (1)
Less: variable costs		3,600 (2)
Contribution margin (CM)		4,200
Less: fixed expenses		
Depreciation	500	
Payables in cash	1,900	

Budgeted Income Statement

Accruals	<u>800</u>	3,200
Operating income		<u>$1,000</u>

Supporting calculations:

A	B	Total
(1) 900(6) = 5,400	800(3) = 2,400	7,800
(2) 300(6) = 1,800	600(3) = 1,800	3,600

Budgeted Balance Sheet

Assets:		
Current assets:		
Cash	$ 500 (1)	
Accounts receivable	6,600 (2)	
Inventories	<u>6,000</u> (3)	
Total current assets		13,100
Fixed assets:		
Beginning balance	4,500	
Less: accumulated depreciation	<u>(500)</u>	<u>4,000</u>
Total assets		<u>$17,100</u>
Liabilities:		
Current liabilities:		
Accounts payable	800 (4)	
Short-term debt	<u>7,900</u> (5)	8,700
Equity		8,400 (6)
Total liabilities and equity		<u>$17,100</u>

Supporting calculations:

1. From the cash budget
2. A: 900(6) = 5,400

         B: 400(3) = <u>1,200</u>

                    6,600
3. Production and sales were assumed to be equal. This implies there is no change in inventories.
4. Accrual of fixed costs
5. Beginning balance – Repayment = $10,000 – 2,100 = 7,900
6. Beginning balance + Net income = $7,400 + 1,000 = 8,400

Exhibit 27-1: LINDO Output for Example 6

: MAX 600A + 200B

>ST

> A<6

> B<10

> 10A+20B<160

> 300A+200B<2400

> END

: LOOK ALL

MAX 600 A + 200 B

SUBJECT TO

    2) A £ 6

    3) B £ 10

    4) 10 A + 20 £160

    5) 300 A + 200 B £2400

:GO

    LP OPTIMUM FOUND AT STEP 2
                    OBJECTIVE FUNCTION VALUE

			Note:
1)		4200.00000	CM = $4,200

VARIABLE	VALUE	REDUCED COST	*Note:*
A	6.000000	.000000	A = 6
B	3.000000	.000000	B = 3

ROW	SLACK OR SURPLUS	DUAL PRICES
2)	.000000	300.000000
3)	7.000000	.000000
4)	40.000000	.000000
5)	.000000	1.000000

NO. ITERATIONS   2

DO RANGE (SENSITIVITY) ANALYSIS?>

4)	40.000000	.000000
5)	.000000	1.000000

NO. ITERATIONS   2
DO RANGE (SENSITIVITY) ANALYSIS? > YES

RANGES IN WHICH THE BASIS IS UNCHANGED
OBJ COEFFICIENT RANGES

VARIABLE	CURRENT COEF	ALLOWABLE INCREASE	ALLOWABLE DECREASE
A	600.000000	INFINITY	300.000000
B	200.000000	200.000000	200.000000

RIGHTHAND SIDE RANGES

ROW	CURRENT RHS	ALLOWABLE INCREASE	ALLOWABLE DECREASE
2	6.000000	2.000000	2.000000
3	10.000000	INFINITY	7.000000
4	160.000000	INFINITY	40.000000
5	2400.000000	400.000000	600.000000

GOAL PROGRAMMING AND MULTIPLE CONFLICTING GOALS

The previous section showed how an optimal program (or product mix) can be developed using LP. LP, however, has one important drawback in that it is limited primarily to solving problems where the objectives of management can be stated in a single goal, such as profit maximization or cost minimization. But management must now deal with multiple goals, which are often incompatible and conflicting with each other. Goal programming (GP) gets around this difficulty. In GP, unlike LP, the objective function may consist of multiple, incommensurable, and conflicting goals. Rather than maximizing or minimizing the objective criterion, the deviations from these set goals are minimized, often based on the priority factors assigned to each goal. The fact that management will have multiple goals that are in conflict with each other means that instead of maximizing or minimizing, management attempts to *satisfice*—that is, look for a satisfactory solution rather than an optimal solution.

Examples of Multiple Conflicting Goals

For example, consider a corporate investor who desires investments that will have a maximum return and minimum risk. These goals are generally both incompatible and unachievable. Other examples of multiple conflicting goals can be found in businesses that want to:

1. Maximize profits and increase wages paid to employees.
2. Upgrade product quality and reduce product costs.
3. Pay larger dividends to shareholders and retain earnings for growth.
4. Increase control of channels of distribution and reduce working capital requirements.
5. Reduce credit losses and increase sales.

To illustrate how a GP model can be used to develop an optimal—more exactly satisfactory—budget, the data used in Example 6 will be used in Example 7.

EXAMPLE 7: Referencing the information given in Example 6, we will further assume that:

- Fixed cash receipts include: (a) new short-term loan amount of $1,200, (b) a dividend payment of $700, and (c) a capital expenditure of $500.

Now the company has two goals, income and working capital. In other words, instead of maximizing net income or contribution margin, the company has a realistic, satisfactory level of income to achieve. On the other hand, the company wants to have a healthy balance sheet with working capital at least at a given level. (For example, a lending institution might want to see that before approving any kind of line of credit).

For illustrative purposes, we will make the following specific assumptions:

- The company wants to achieve a return of 20% on equity. That means 15% of $7,400 $1,110, which translates into a CM of $1,110 + 3,200 (fixed expenses) = $4,310.
- The company wants a working capital balance to be at least $3,000. Currently, it is $2,900 (Current assets of $13,800 – Current liabilities of $10,900 = $2,900).

These two goals are clearly in conflict. The reason is: we can increase the working capital by increasing cash funds or the inventory. However, the funds in the form of idle cash and the goods in the form of unsold inventories will not increase profits. The first goal can be set up as follows:

$$600A + 200B + d^- - d^+ = \$4,310$$

Note that working capital balance = beginning balance + net income + depreciation – dividends – capital expenditures = beginning balance + (sales – variable costs – fixed costs) – dividend capital expenditure. Using this definition, the second goal can be set up as follows:

←—— Sales ——→	←—Variable costs—→	←—Fixed expenses—→
$2,900 + \$900A + 800B$	$-300A - 600B$	$-2,700 - 700 - 500 \geq 3,000$

This can be simplified to form an inequality:

$$600A + 200B \geq 4,000$$

Then our GP model is as follows:

$$\text{Min D} = d^- = d^+$$

subject to

A			≤6
	B		≤10
10A +	20B		≤160
300A +	200B		≤2,400
600A +	200B		≤4,000
600A +	200B + d⁻ − d⁺		=4,310

all variables ≤ 0

This particular problem can be easily solved by LINDO. See Exhibit 27-2.

The GP solution is:

$$A = 6, B = 2, d^- = 310, d^+ = 0,$$

which means that the income target was underachieved by $310. Just in the case of LIP, financial executives will be able to develop the budget using this optimal solution in exactly the same manner as presented in the previous section. More sophisticated GP models can be developed with "preemptive" priority factors assigned to multiple goals. For example, the goal can be ranked according to "preemptive" priority factors. Also, the deviational variables at the same priority level may be given different weights in the objective function so that the deviational variables within the same priority have the different cardinal weights. (This topic is not treated here and should be referred to in an advanced operations research text).

Summary

It is not easy, however, to develop an optimization model that incorporates performance variables such as ROI, profits, market share, and cash flow as well as the line items of the income statement, balance sheet, and cash flow statement. Despite the availability of goal programming that handles multiple objectives, the possibility of achieving global optimization is very rare at the corporate level. The usage tends to be limited to submodels and suboptimization within the overall corporate level. Thus, the use of these models in corporate modeling will probably continue to be focused at the operational level. Production planning and scheduling, advertising, resource allocation, and many other problem areas will continue to be solved with huge success by these techniques.

Exhibit 27-2: LINDO Output for Example 7

MAX Dl + D2   *Note:* D1 = D⁻

                                                                         D2 = D⁺

SUBJECT TO

      2)   A £ 6

      3)   B £ 10

      4)   10 A + 20 B £ 160

      5)   300 A + 200 B £ 2400

6)   600 A + 200 B £ 4000
7)   D1 – D2 + 600 A + 200 B = 4310

END
: GO

OBJECTIVE FUNCTION VALUE

1)   310.000000

VARIABLE	VALUE	REDUCED COST	*Note:*
D1	310.000000	.000000	$D^- = 310$
D2	.000000	– 2.000000	$D^+ = 0$
A	6.000000	.000000	A = 6
B	2.000000	.000000	B = 2

ROW	SLACK OR SURPLUS	DUAL PRICES
2)	.000000	.000000
3)	8.000000	.000000
4)	60.000000	.000000
5)	200.000000	.000000
6)	.000000	– 1.000000
7)	.000000	1.000000

NO. ITERATIONS = 3

CAPITAL RATIONING AND ZERO-ONE PROGRAMMING

Many firms specify a limit on the overall budget for capital spending. Capital rationing is concerned with the problem of selecting the mix of acceptable projects that provides the highest overall net present value (NPV). The profitability index is used widely in ranking projects competing for limited funds.

EXAMPLE 8: A company with a fixed budget of $250,000 needs to select a mix of acceptable projects from the following:

Projects	I($)	PV($)	NPV($)	Profitability Index	Ranking
A	70,000	112,000	42,000	1.6	1
B	100,000	145,000	45,000	1.45	2
C	110,000	126,500	16,500	1.15	5
D	60,000	79,000	19,000	1.32	3
E	40,000	38,000	– 2,000	0.95	6
F	80,000	95,000	15,000	1.19	4

The ranking resulting from the profitability index shows that the company should select projects A, B, and D.

I		PV
A	$ 70,000	$112,000
B	100,000	145,000
D	60,000	79,000
	$230,000	$336,000

The overall profitability index for the best combination is:

$$\$336,000/\$230,000 = 1.46$$

Therefore,

NPV = $336,000 – $230,000 = $106,000

Unfortunately, the profitability index method has some limitations. One of the more serious is that it breaks down whenever more than one resource is rationed. In this case, the use of zero-one programming is suggested.

A more general approach to solving capital rationing problems is the use of *zero-one* integer programming. Here the objective is to select the mix of projects that maximizes the net present value (NPV) subject to a budget constraint.

EXAMPLE 9: A company with a fixed budget of $250,000 needs to select a mix of acceptable projects from the following:

Projects	I($)	PV($)	NPV($)
1	70,000	112,000	42,000
2	100,000	145,000	45,000
3	110,000	126,500	16,500
4	60,000	79,000	19,000
5	40,000	38,000	– 2,000
6	80,000	95,000	15,000

Using the data given above, we can set up the problem as a zero-one integer programming problem such that

$$x_j = \begin{cases} 1 \text{ if project } j \text{ is selected} \\ 0 \text{ if project } j \text{ is not selected } (j = 1,2,3,4,5,6) \end{cases}$$

The problem can then be formulated as follows:

Maximize:

NPV = $42,000x_1 + $45,000x_2 + $16,500x_3 + $19,000x_4 – $2,000x_5 + $15,000x_6 subject to

$$\$70,000x_1 + \$100,000x_2 + \$110,000x_3 + \$60,000x_4 - \$40,0300x_5$$
$$+ \$80,000x_6 \leq \$250,000$$

$$x_j = 0, 1 \ (j = 1, 2, \ldots, 6)$$

Using the zero-one programming solution routine, the solution to the problem is:

$$x_1 = 1, x_2 = 1, x_4 = 1$$

and the NPV is $106,000. Thus, projects 1, 2, and 4 should be accepted.

The strength of the use of zero-one programming is its ability to handle mutually exclusive and interdependent projects.

EXAMPLE 10: Suppose that exactly one project can be selected from the set of projects 1, 3, and 5. Because 1, 3, or 5 must be selected and only one can be selected, exactly one of the three variables x_1, x_3, or x_5, must be equal to 1 and the rest must be equal to 0. The constraint to be added is:

$$x_1 + x_3 + x_5 = 1$$

Note that, for example, if $x_3 = 1$, then $x_1 = 0$ and $x_5 = 0$ in order for the constraint to hold.

EXAMPLE 11: Suppose that projects 2 and 4 are mutually exclusive—that is, the company can select either project 2 or project 4 and can reject project 2 and project 4. Therefore, the constraint to be added is:

$$x_2 + x_4 \leq 1$$

Note that the following three pairs satisfy this constraint:

$$x_2 = 0 \text{ and } x_4 = 0$$
$$x_2 = 1 \text{ and } x_4 = 0$$
$$x_2 = 0 \text{ and } x_4 = 1$$

But $x_2 = 1$ and $x_4 = 1$ violates this constraint, since $1 + 1 = 2 > 1$

EXAMPLE 12: Suppose if project 3 is selected, then project 4 must be selected. In other words, a mutual dependence exists between projects 3 and 4. An example might be a project such as building a second floor that requires the first floor to precede it. Then the constraint to be added is:

$$x_3 \leq x_4$$

Note that if $x_3 = 1$, then x_4 must be equal to 1. However, x_4 can be equal to 1 and x_3 can be equal to either 1 or 0. That is, the selection of project 4 does not imply that project 3 must be selected.

EXAMPLE 13: Maximize:

$$NPV = \$42,000x_1 + \$45,000x_2 + \$16,500x_3 + \$19,000x_4 - \$2,000x_5 + \$15,000x_6$$

subject to

$$\$70,000x_1 + \$100,000x_2 + \$110,000x_3 + \$60,000x_4 - \$40,000x_5$$
$$+ \$80,000x_6 \leq \$250,000$$

$$x_1 + x_4 = 1 \text{ (Projects 1 and 4 are mutually exclusive)}$$

$$x_j = 0, 1 \; (j = 1, 2, \ldots 6)$$

Using the zero-one programming solution routine, the solution to the problem as shown in the LINDO output (see Exhibit 27-3) is:

$$x_1 = 1, x_2 = 1, x_6 = 1$$

and the NPV is $102,000. Thus, projects 1, 2, and 6 should be accepted.

Exhibit 27-3: LINDO's Zero-One Programming Output

: max 42000 × 1 + 45000 × 2 + 16500 × 3 + 19000 × 4 – 2000 × 5 + 1500 × 6

?st

? 70000 × 1 + 100000 × 2 + 110000 × 3 + 60000 × 4 + 40000 × 5 + 80000 × 6<250000

? × 1 + × 4 = 1

?end

: integer 6

: integer 1 1

: integer 1 2

: integer 1 3

: integer 1 4

: integer 1 5

: integer 1 6

: GO

OBJECTIVE FUNCTION VALUE

1)	102000.000	NPV = $102,000	

VARIABLE	VALUE	REDUCED COST	
X1	1.000000	–21500.000000	
X2	1.000000	–30000.000000	$X_1 = 1$
X3	.000000	.000000	$X_2 = 1$
X4	.000000	.000000	$X_6 = 1$
X5	.000000	8000.000000	
X6	1.000000	–3000.000000	

ROW	SLACK OR SURPLUS	DUAL PRICES
2)	.000000	.150000
3)	.000000	10000.000000

NO. ITERATIONS = 2
BRANCHES = 0 DETERM = ll.000E4
BOUND ON OPTIMUM: 102000.0
ENUMERATION COMPLETE. BRANCHES = 0 PIVOTS = 2
LAST INTEGER SOLUTION IS THE BEST FOUND
RE-INSTALLING BEST SOLUTION ...

HOW TO ESTIMATE BETA USING LINEAR REGRESSION

In measuring an asset's systematic risk, beta, an indication is needed of the relationship between the asset's returns and the market returns (such as returns on the Standard & Poor's 500 Stock Composite Index or Dow Jones 30 Industrials). This relationship can be statistically computed by determining the regression coefficient between asset and market returns. The formula is:

$$b = \frac{\text{Cov}(r_j, r_m)}{\sigma^2_m}$$

where $\text{Cov}(r_j,r_m)$ is the covariance of the returns of the assets with the market returns, and σ^2_m is the variance (standard deviation squared) of the market returns.

An easier way to compute beta is to determine the slope of the least-squares regression line

$$r_j = a + b\, r_m$$

where r_j = the return on a stock and r_m = return in the market. The formula for b is:

$$b = \frac{n\Sigma r_j r_m - (\Sigma r_j)(\Sigma r_m)}{n\Sigma r_m^2 - (\Sigma r_m)^2}$$

where n = number of years

EXAMPLE 14: Data for stock x and the market portfolio are:

Historic Rates of Return

Year	r_j (%)	r_m (%)
2X11	− 5	10
2X12	4	8
2X13	7	12
2X14	10	20
2X15	12	15

To compute the beta coefficient b, we used Excel's Regression command, as was discussed in detail in Chapter 16, "Analysis of Cost Behavior."

SUMMARY OUTPUT

Regression Statistics

Multiple R	0.65666
R Square	0.431203
Adjusted R Square	0.241603
Standard Error	5.796289
Observations	5

	Coefficients	Standard Error
Intercept	– 6.513636364	8.44042932
X Variable 1	0.931818182	0.617886516

The equation is: $r_j = -\,6.51 + .93\,r_m$,

Therefore, the beta is 0.93

LEARNING CURVE

The learning curve is based on the proposition that labor hours decrease in a definite pattern as labor operations are repeated. More specifically, it is based on the statistical findings that, as the cumulative production doubles, the cumulative average time required per unit will be reduced by some constant percentage, ranging typically from 10% to 20%. By convention, learning curves are referred to in terms of the complements of their improvement rates. For example, an 80% learning curve denotes a 20% decrease in unit time with each doubling of repetitions. As an illustration, a project is known to have an 80% learning curve. It has just taken a laborer 10 hours to produce the first unit. Then each time the cumulative output doubles, the time per unit for that amount should be equal to the previous time multiplied by the learning percentage. Thus:

Unit	Unit time (hours)
1	10
2 .8(10)	= 8
4 .8(8)	= 6.4
8 .8(6.4)	= 5.12
16 .8(5.12)	= 4.096

An 80% learning curve is shown in Exhibit 27-4.

Exhibit 27-4: An 80% Learning Curve

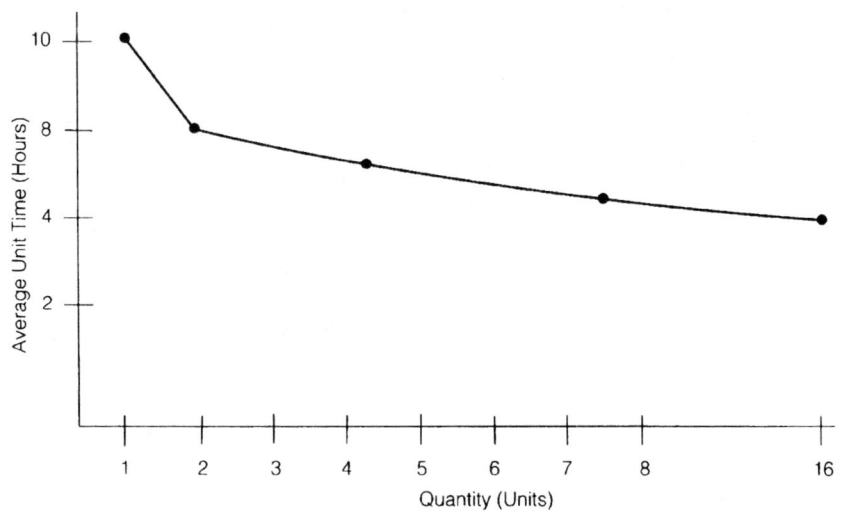

This example, however, raises an interesting question: How are time values for three, five, six, seven, and other units that do not fall into this pattern computed?

The unit time (i.e., the number of labor hours required) for the nth unit can be computed using the model:

$$y_n = a\ n^{-b}$$

where

y_n = Time for the nth unit

a = Time for the first unit (in this example, 10 hours)

b = The index of the rate of increase in productivity during learning (Log learning rate/log 2)

EXAMPLE 15: For an 80% curve with a = 10 hours, the time for the third unit would be computed as:

$$y_3 = 10(3^{-\log.8/\log2}) = 10(3^{(.3219)}) = 7.02$$

Fortunately, it is not necessary to grid through this model each time a learning calculation is made; values (n_{-b}) can be found using Exhibit 27-5 (Learning Curve Coefficients). The time for the nth unit can be quickly determined by multiplying the table value by the time required for the first unit.

EXAMPLE 16: NBRF Contractors, Inc. is negotiating a contract involving production of 20 jets. The initial jet required 200 labor-days of direct labor. Assuming an 80% learning curve, we will determine the expected number of labor-days for (1) the 20th jet, and (2) all 20 jets as follows:

Using table in Exhibit 27-5 with $n = 20$ and an 80% learning rate, we find: Unit = .381 and Total = 10,485. Therefore,

1. Expected time for the 20th jet = 200 (.381) = 76.2 labor-days.
2. Expected total time for all 20 jets = 200 (10.485) = 2,097 labor-days.

The learning curve theory has found useful applications in many areas including:

1. Scheduling labor requirements.
2. Setting incentive wage rates.
3. Pricing new products.
4. Negotiated purchasing.
5. Budgeting, purchasing, and inventory planning.

Exhibit 27-5: Learning Curve Coefficients

	70%		75%		80%		85%		90%	
Unit Number	Unit Time	Total Time	Unit Time	Total Time	Unit Time	Total Time	Unit Time	Total Time	Unit Time	Total Time
1	1.000	1.000	1.000	1.000	1.000	1.000	1.000	1.000	1.000	1.000
2	.700	1.700	.750	1.750	.800	1.800	.850	1.850	.900	1.900
3	.568	2.268	.634	2.384	.702	2.502	.773	2.623	.846	2.746
4	.490	2.758	.562	2.946	.640	3.142	.723	3.345	.810	3.556
5	.437	3.195	.513	3.459	.596	3.738	.686	4.031	.783	4.339
6	.398	3.593	.475	3.934	.562	4.299	.657	4.688	.762	5.101
7	.367	3.960	.446	4.380	.534	4.834	.634	5.322	.744	5.845
8	.343	4.303	.422	4.802	.512	5.346	.614	5.936	.729	6.574
9	.323	4.626	.402	5.204	.493	5.839	.597	6.533	.716	7.290
10	.306	4.932	.385	5.589	.477	6.315	.583	7.116	.705	7.994
11	.291	5.223	.370	5.958	.462	6.777	.570	7.686	.695	8.689
12	.278	5.501	.357	6.315	.449	7.227	.558	8.244	.685	9.374
13	.267	5.769	.345	6.660	.438	7.665	.548	8.792	.677	10.052
14	.257	6.026	.334	6.994	.428	8.092	.539	9.331	.670	10.721
15	.248	6.274	.325	7.319	.418	8.511	.530	9.861	.663	11.384
16	.240	6.514	.316	7.635	.410	8.920	.522	10.383	.656	12.040
17	.233	6.747	.309	7.944	.402	9.322	.515	10.898	.650	12.690
18	.226	6.973	.301	8.245	.394	9.716	.508	11.405	.644	13.334
19	.220	7.192	.295	8.540	.338	10.104	.501	11.907	.639	13.974
20	.214	7.407	.288	8.828	.381	10.485	.495	12.402	.634	14.608
21	.209	7.615	.283	9.111	.375	10.860	.490	12.892	.630	15.237
22	.204	7.819	.277	9.388	.370	11.230	.484	13.376	.625	15.862
23	.199	8.018	.272	9.660	.364	11.594	.479	13.856	.621	16.483
24	.195	8.213	.267	9.928	.359	11.954	.475	14.331	.617	17.100

	70%		75%		80%		85%		90%	
Unit Number	Unit Time	Total Time	Unit Time	Total Time	Unit Time	Total Time	Unit Time	Total Time	Unit Time	Total Time
25	.191	8.404	.263	10.191	.355	12.309	.470	14.801	.613	17.713
26	.187	8.591	.259	10.449	.350	12.659	.466	15.267	.609	18.323
27	.183	8.774	.255	10.704	.346	13.005	.462	15.728	.606	18.929
28	.180	8.954	.251	10.955	.342	13.347	.458	16.186	.603	19.531
29	.177	9.131	.247	11.202	.338	13.685	.454	16.640	.599	20.131
30	.174	9.305	.244	11.446	.335	14.020	.450	17.091	.596	20.727
31	.171	9.476	.240	11.686	.331	14.351	.447	17.538	.593	21.320
32	.168	9.644	.237	11.924	.328	14.679	.444	17.981	.590	21.911
33	.165	9.809	.234	12.158	.324	15.003	.441	18.422	.588	22.498
34	.163	9.972	.231	12.389	.321	15.324	.437	18.859	.585	23.084
35	.160	10.133	.229	12.618	.318	15.643	.434	19.294	.583	23.666
36	.158	10.291	.226	12.844	.315	15.958	.432	19.726	.580	24.246
37	.156	10.447	.223	13.067	.313	16.271	.429	20.154	.578	24.824
38	.154	10.601	.221	13.288	.310	16.581	.426	20.580	.575	25.399
39	.152	10.763	.219	13.507	.307	16.888	.424	21.004	.573	25.972
40	.150	10.902	.216	13.723	.305	17.193	.421	21.425	.571	26.543

Example 17 illustrates the use of the learning curve theory for the pricing of a contract.

EXAMPLE 17: Big Mac Electronics Products, Inc. finds that new product production is affected by an 80% learning effect. The company has just produced 50 units of output at 100 hours per unit. Costs were as follows:

Materials 50 units @ $20	$1,000
Labor and labor-related costs:	
Direct labor—100 hours @ $8	800
Variable overhead—100 hours @ $2	200
	$2,000

The company has just received a contract calling for another 50 units of production. It wants to add a 50% markup to the cost of materials and labor and labor-related costs. To determine the price for this job, the first step is to build up the learning curve table.

Quantity	Total Time (hours)	Average Time (per unit)
50	100	2 hours
100	160	1.6 (.8 × 2 hours)

Thus, for the new 50-unit job, it takes 60 hours total. The contract price is:

Materials 50 units @ $20	$1,000
Labor and labor-related costs:	
Direct labor—60 hours @ $8	480
Variable overhead—60 hours @ $2	120
	$1,600
50% markup	800
Contract price	$2,400

INVENTORY PLANNING

One of the most common problems financial managers face is inventory planning. This is understandable since inventory usually represents a sizable portion of a firm's total assets and, more specifically, on the average, more than 30% of total current assets in U.S. industry. Excessive money tied up in inventory is a drag on profitability. The purpose of inventory planning is to develop policies that will achieve an optimal investment in inventory. This objective is achieved by determining the optimal level of inventory necessary to minimize inventory related costs.

Inventory related costs fall into three categories:

1. Ordering costs, which includes all costs associated with preparing a purchase order.

2. Carrying (holding) costs, which include storage costs for inventory items plus the cost of money tied up in inventory.

3. Shortage (stockout) costs, which include those costs incurred when an item is out of stock. These include the lost contribution margin on sales plus lost customer goodwill.

Many available inventory planning models try to address basically the following two issues:

1. How much to order.

2. When to order.

These models include the so-called economic order quantity (EOQ) model, the reorder point, and the determination of safety stock.

Economic Order Quantity

The economic order quantity (EOQ) determines the order quantity that results in the lowest sum of carrying and ordering costs. The EOQ is computed as:

$$EOQ = \sqrt{\frac{2OD}{C}}$$

where C = carrying cost per unit, O = ordering cost per order, D = annual demand (requirements) in units.

If the carrying cost is expressed as a percentage of average inventory value (say, 12% per year to hold inventory), then the denominator value in the EOQ formula would be 12% times the price of an item.

EXAMPLE 18: Assume ABC Store buys sets of steel at $40 per set from an outside vendor. ABC will sell 6,400 sets evenly throughout the year. ABC desires a 16% return on investment (cost of borrowed money) on its inventory investment. In addition, rent, taxes, and so on for each set in inventory is $1.60. The ordering cost is $100 per order. Then the carrying cost per dozen is 16% ($40) + $1.60 = $8.00. Therefore,

$$EOQ = \sqrt{\frac{2(6,400)(\$100)}{8.00}} = 160,000 = 400 \text{ sets}$$

Total inventory costs = Carrying cost + Ordering cost
$$= C \times (EOQ/2) + O(D/EOQ)$$
$$= (\$8.00)(400/2) + (\$100)(6,400/400)$$
$$= \$1,600 + \$1,600 = \$3,200$$

Total number of orders per year = D/EOQ = 6,400/400 = 16 orders

Reorder Point

Reorder point (ROP), which answers when to place a new order, requires knowledge about the lead time, which is the time interval between placing an order and receiving delivery. Reorder point (ROP) can be calculated as follows:

Reorder point = (Average usage per unit of lead time × lead time) + safety stock

First, multiply average daily (or weekly) usage by the lead time in days (or weeks) yielding the lead time demand. Then add safety stock to this to provide for the variation in lead time demand to determine the reorder point. If average usage and lead time are both certain, no safety stock is necessary, and safety stock should be dropped from the formula.

EXAMPLE 19: Assume in Example 18 that lead time is constant at one week and that there are 50 working weeks in a year.

Then the reorder point is 128 sets = (6,400 sets/50 weeks) × 1 week. Therefore, when the inventory level drops to 128 sets, the new order should be placed. Suppose, however, that the store is faced with variable usage for its steel and requires a safety stock of 150 additional sets. Then the reorder point will be 128 sets plus 150 sets, or 278 sets.

Exhibit 27-6 shows this inventory system when the order quantity is 400 sets and the reorder point is 128 sets.

Assumptions and Applications

The EOQ model makes some strong assumptions. They are:

- Demand is fixed and constant throughout the year.

- Lead time is known with certainty.

- No quantity discounts are allowed.

- No shortages are permitted.

Exhibit 27-6: Basic Inventory System with EOQ and Reorder Point

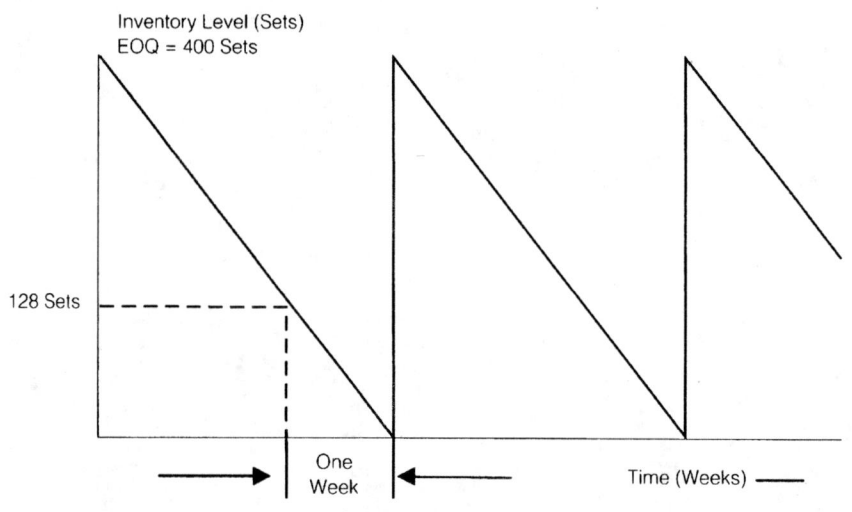

The assumptions may be unrealistic. However, the model still proves useful in inventory planning for many firms. In fact, many situations exist where a certain assumption holds or nearly holds. For example, subcontractors who must supply parts on a regular basis to a primary contractor face a constant demand. Even where demand varies, the assumption of uniform usage is not unrealistic. Demand for automobiles, for example, varies from week to week over a season, but the weekly fluctuations tend to cancel out each other so that seasonal demand can be assumed constant.

EOQ with Quantity Discounts

The economic order quantity (EOQ) model does not take into account quantity discounts, which is not realistic in many real-world cases. Usually, the more that is ordered, the lower the unit price paid. Quantity discounts are price reductions for large orders offered to buyers to induce them to buy in large quantities. If quantity discounts are offered, the buyer must weigh the potential benefits of reduced purchase price and fewer orders that will result from buying in large quantities against the increase in carrying costs caused by higher average inventories. Hence, the buyer's goal in this case is to select the order quantity that will minimize total costs, where total cost is:

$$\text{Total} = \text{Carrying cost} + \text{Ordering cost} + \text{Product cost}$$
$$= C \times (Q/2) + O(D/Q) + PD$$

where P = unit price, and Q = order quantity.

A step-by-step approach in computing economic order quantity with quantity discounts is as follows:

1. Compute the economic order quantity (EOQ) when price discounts are ignored and the corresponding costs using the new cost formula given above. Note EOQ = $\sqrt{2OD/C}$.

2. Compute the costs for those quantities greater than the EOQ at which price reductions occur.

3. Select the value of Q which will result in the lowest total cost.

EXAMPLE 20: In Example 18, assume that ABC store was offered the following price discount schedule:

Order Quantity (0)	Unit Price (P)
1 to 499	$40.00
500 to 999	39.90
1,000 or more	39.80

First, the EOQ with no discounts is computed as follows:

$$\text{EOQ} = \sqrt{2(6,400)(100)/8.00} = \sqrt{160,000} = 400 \text{ sets}$$

$$\text{Total cost} = \$8.000(400/2) + \$100(6,400/400) + \$40.00(6,400)$$

$$= \$1,600 + 1,600 + 256,000 = \$259,200$$

Exhibit 27-7: Inventory Cost and Quantity

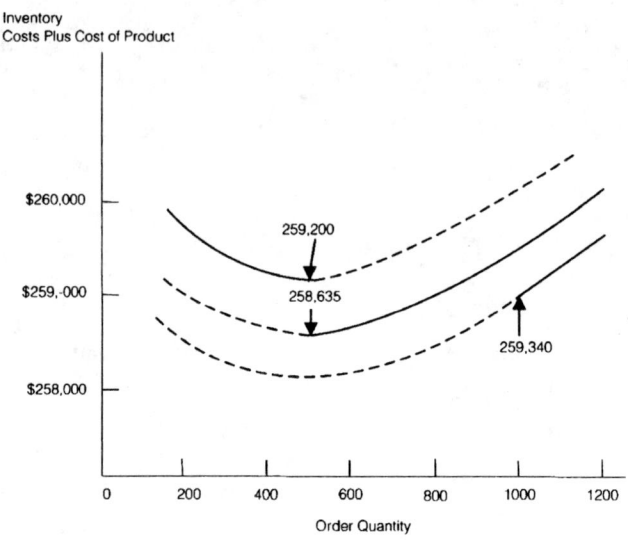

The value that minimized the sum of the carrying cost and the ordering cost but not the purchase cost was EOQ = 400 sets. As can be seen in Exhibit 27-7, the further the move from the point 400, the greater will be the sum of the carrying and ordering costs. Thus, 400 is obviously the only candidate for the minimum total cost value within the first price range. Q = 500 is the only candidate within the $39.90 price range and Q = 1,000 is the only candidate within the $39.80 price bracket. These three quantities are evaluated in Exhibit 27-8 and illustrated in Exhibit 27-7. The EOQ with price discounts is 500 sets. Hence, ABC store is justified in going to the first price break, but the extra carrying cost of going to the second price break more than outweighs the savings in ordering and in the cost of the product itself.

Exhibit 27-8: Annual Costs with Varying Order Quantities

Order Quantity	400	500	1,000
Ordering cost			
$100 × (6,400/order quantity)	$1,600	$1,280	$640
Carrying cost			
$8 × (order quantity/2)	1,600	2,000	4,000
Product cost			
Unit price × 6,400	256,000	255,360	254,720
Total cost	$259,200	$258,640	$259,360

Advantages and Disadvantages of Quantity Discounts

Buying in large quantities has some favorable and some unfavorable features. The advantages are lower unit costs, lower ordering costs, fewer stockouts, and lower transportation costs. On the other hand, there are disadvantages such as higher inventory carrying costs, greater capital requirement, and higher probability of obsolescence and deterioration.

Determination of Safety Stock

When lead time and demand are not certain, the firm must carry extra units of inventory, called safety stock, as protection against possible stockouts. Stockouts can be quite expensive. Lost sales and disgruntled customers are examples of external costs. Idle machines and disrupted production scheduling are examples of internal costs. An illustration of the probability approach will show how the optimal stock size can be determined in the presence of stockout costs.

EXAMPLE 21: In Examples 18 and 19, suppose that the total usage over a one-week period is expected to be:

Total Usage	Probability
78	.2
128	.4
178	.2
228	.1
278	.1
	1.00

Suppose further that a stockout cost is estimated at $12.00 per set. Recall that the carrying cost is $8.00 per set.

Exhibit 27-9 shows the computation of safety stock.

The computation shows that the total costs are minimized at $1,200, when a safety stock of 150 sets is maintained. Therefore, the reorder point is: 128 sets + 150 sets = 278 sets.

PROGRAM EVALUATION AND REVIEW TECHNIQUE

Program Evaluation and Review Technique (PERT) is a useful management tool for planning, scheduling, costing, coordinating, and controlling complex projects such as:

- Formulation of a master budget.
- Construction of buildings.
- Installation of computers.
- Scheduling the closing of books.
- Assembly of a machine.
- Research and development activities.

Questions to be answered by PERT include:

- When will the project be finished?
- What is the probability that the project will be completed by any given time?

The PERT technique involves the diagrammatic representation of the sequence of activities comprising a project by means of a network. The network: (1) visualizes all of the individual tasks (activities) to complete a given job or program; (2) points out interrelationships; and (3) consists of activities (represented by arrows) and events (represented by circles), as shown in Exhibit 27-10. *Arrows* represent "tasks" or "activities," which are distinct segments of the project requiring time and resources. *Nodes (circles)* symbolize "events," or milestone points in the project representing the completion of one or more activities and/or the initiation of one or more subsequent activities. An event is a point in time and does not consume any time in itself as does an activity.

Exhibit 27-9: Computation of Safety Stock

Safety stock levels in units	Stockout and probability	Average stockout in units	Average stockout costs	No. of orders	Total annual stockout costs	Carrying costs	Total
0	50 with .2 100 with .1 150 with .1	35*	$420**	16	$6,720***	0	$7,140
50	50 with .1 100 with .1	15	180	16	2,880	400****	3,280
100	50 with .1	5	60	16	960	800	1,760
150	0	0	0	16	0	1,200	1,200

*50(.2) + 100(.1) + 150(.1) = 10 + 10 + 15 = 35 units

**35 units × $12.00 = $420

***$420 × 16 times = $6,720

****50 units × $8.00 = $400

In a real world situation, the estimates of completion times of activities will seldom be certain. To cope with the uncertainty in activity time estimates, the PERT proceeds by estimating three possible duration times for each activity. As shown in Exhibit 27-10, the numbers appearing on the arrows represent these three time estimates for activities needed to complete the various events. These time estimates are:

- The most optimistic time (labeled *a*).

- The most likely time (labeled *m*).

- The most pessimistic time (labeled *b*).

For example, the optimistic time for completing activity B is one day, the most likely time is two days, but the pessimistic time is three days. The next step is to calculate an expected time, which is determined as follows:

Exhibit 27-10: Network Diagram

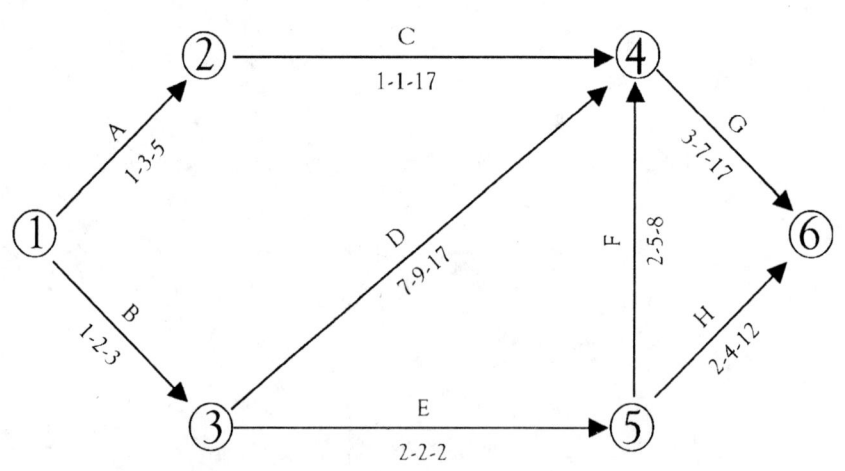

t_e (expected time) = $(a + 4m + b)/6$

For example, for activity B, the expected time is:

$$t_e = (1 + 4(2) + 3)/6 = 12/6 = 2 \text{ days}$$

As a measure of variation (uncertainty) about the expected time, the standard deviation is calculated as follows:

$$\sigma = (b - a)/6$$

For example, the standard deviation of completion time for activity B is:

$$\sigma = (3 - 1)/6 = 2/6 = .33 \text{ days}$$

Expected activity times and their standard deviations are computed in this manner for all the activities of the network and arranged in the tabular format as shown below.

Activity	Predecessors	*a*	*m*	*b*	t_e	*s*
A	None	1	3	5	3.0	.67
B	None	1	2	3	2.0	.33
C	A	1	1	7	2.0	1.00
D	B	7	9	17	10.0	1.67
E	B	2	2	2	2.0	0.00
F	E	2	5	8	5.0	.67
G	C,D,F	3	7	17	8.0	2.33
H	E	2	4	12	5.0	1.67

To answer the first question, the network's critical path must be determined. A path is a sequence of connected activities. In Exhibit 27-10, 1-2-4-6 would be an example of a path. The critical path for a project is the path that takes the longest amount of time. The sum of the estimated times for all activities on the critical path is the total time required to complete the project. These activities are "critical" because any delay in their completion will cause a delay in the project. The critical path is the minimum amount of time needed for the completion of the project. Thus, the activities along this path must be shortened to speed up the project. Activities not on the critical path are not critical, since they will be worked on simultaneously with critical path activities and their completion could be delayed up to a point without delaying the project as a whole.

An easy way to find the critical path involves the following two steps:

1. Identify all possible paths of a project and calculate their completion times.

2. Pick the path with the longest amount of completion time, which is the critical path.

(When the network is large and complex, a more systematic and efficient approach is needed, which is reserved for an advanced management science text.)

In the example:

Path	Completion time
A-C-G	13 days (3 + 2 + 8)
B-D-G	20 days (2 + 10 + 8)
B-E-F-G	17 days (2 + 2 + 5 + 8)
B-E-H	9 days (2 + 2 + 5)

The critical path is B-D-G, which means it takes 20 days to complete the project.

The next important information to obtain is "What is the chance that the project will be completed within a contract time, say, 21 days?" To answer the question, the standard deviation of total project time around the expected time is introduced, which is determined as follows:

$$\text{Standard deviation (project)} = \sqrt{\begin{array}{l}\text{the sum of the squares of the standard}\\\text{deviation of all critical path activities}\end{array}}$$

Using the standard deviation and table of areas under the normal distribution curve (Exhibit 17-4 of Chapter 17, "Cost-Volume-Profit Analysis and Leverage"), the probability of completing the project within any given time period can be determined.

Using the formula above, the standard deviation of completion time (the path B-D-G) for the project is as follows:

$$\sqrt{(.33)^2 + (1.67)^2 + (2.33)^2} = \sqrt{1089 + 2.7889 + 5.4289}$$
$$= \sqrt{8.3287} = 2.885 \, \text{days}$$

Assume the expected delivery time is, say, 21 days. The first step is to compute z, which is the number of standard deviations from the mean represented by the given time of 21 days. The formula for z is:

$$z = (\text{delivery time} - \text{expected time})/\text{standard deviation}$$

Therefore, z = (21 days – 20 days)/2.885 days = .35

The next step is to find the probability associated with the calculated value of z by referring to a table of areas under a normal curve.

From the table in Exhibit 17-4 in Chapter 17, the probability is .63683, which means there is close to a 64% chance that the project will be completed in less than 21 days.

To summarize, the following has been ascertained:

- The expected completion time of the project is 20 days.
- There is a better than 60% chance of finishing before 21 days. The chances of meeting any other deadline can also be ascertained.
- Activities B-D-G are on the critical path; they must be watched more closely than the others, for if they fall behind, the whole project falls behind.
- If extra effort is needed to finish the project on time or before the deadline, resources (such as money and labor) will need to be borrowed from any activity not on the critical path.
- It is possible to reduce the completion time of one or more activities, which will require an extra expenditure of cost. The benefit from reducing the total completion time of a project by accelerated efforts on certain activities must be balanced against the extra cost of doing so. A related problem is to determine which activities must be accelerated to reduce the total project

completion time. The Critical Path Method (CPM), also known as PERT/COST, is widely used to deal with this subject.

PERT is a technique for project management and control. It is not an optimizing decision model, since the decision to undertake a project is initially assumed. It will not evaluate an investment project according to its attractiveness or time specifications.

PROJECT BUDGETING AND CONTROL USING EARNED VALUE ANALYSIS

There are several alternatives for assessing project budgets over time. Fixed costs may be expensed at the start of an activity (e.g., equipment purchases) or at the end of an activity (e.g., paying a consultant), whereas variable costs may be expensed based on a project schedule or an employee's calendar (e.g., payroll).

EXAMPLE 22: The project below shows the budgeted costs associated with five activities. Variable costs are incurred in proportion to the activity duration; thus, for instance, the cost for task B is spread out over the two weeks the task is scheduled. The resulting cost schedule is referred to as the budgeted cost of work scheduled (BCWS) and is calculated by adding all of the costs on each week of the project, as shown in the last two lines of the table.

Task	Predecessor	Duration	Cost			by week		
A	—	1	$ 1,500	$ 1,500				
B	A	2	$ 3,510		$ 1,755	$ 1,755		
C	A	2	$ 5,000		$ 2,500	$ 2,500		
D	B	2	$ 2,000				$ 1,000	$ 1,000
E	B	2	$ 3,000				$ 1,500	$ 1,500
Total project budget			$ 15,010	$ 1,500	$ 4,255	$ 4,255	$ 2,500	$ 2,500
Cumulative project budget = budgeted cost of work scheduled (BCWS)				$ 1,500	$ 5,755	$ 10,010	$ 12,510	$ 15,010

By accurately tracking actual costs versus budgeted costs, the project manager can determine the degree of available managerial flexibility. Thus, BCWS information is very useful for controlling a project. For example, if by week 4 project costs have exceeded $12,510, then the project manager might wish to control future expenses more carefully, renegotiate the contract with the customer, and attempt to obtain additional funds in order to complete the project. Similarly, if the project incurs less cost by week 4, the project may be behind schedule and require a faster pace.

Concept of Earned Value Analysis

The project manager can also maintain control of a project through the use of earned value analysis, which is a uniform unit of measure that integrates project scheduling and costs to determine a project's progress and performance. For example, this analysis can determine whether a cost overrun is due to an unanticipated expense or to an increased rate of completion. Performing a separate analysis of a project's schedule and cost does not provide an entirely accurate or comprehensive picture of overall project status. Evaluating the amount of work being completed without considering the cost provides a distorted picture of the cost position. Similarly, using the rate of expenditure as a measure of project status leads to a distorted picture of the schedule position. For example, a project is under budget by approximately 10% with only 75% of the money spent. Based on this information, there is a very positive outcome if the project is near completion versus a very negative outcome if the work has barely started.

There are a number of formulas associated with the earned value technique. At the core of this technique are three basic components of measurement:

1. *Budgeted cost of work scheduled (BCWS)*—a measure of *what* is *expected to be accomplished.* Specifically, it uses the original cost estimates for activities to chart the cost (or value) of the work that is planned over time. It is equivalent to the conventional concept of the planned budget.

2. *Budgeted cost of work performed (BCWP)*—a measure of *the value of what has been accomplished.* It charts the cost (or value) of the work completed at any point in time. The original activity-based cost estimates are used to perform these calculations. This is considered to be the earned value.

3. *Actual cost of work performed (ACWP)*—refers to *the cost for what has been accomplished.* This is considered to be the actual cost expenditure at any point in time.

Conceptually, the schedule position is a comparison of BCWP and BCWS. In other words (using the terminology above), it compares *what is expected* to be *accomplished* and *what has actually been accomplished,* in terms of originally estimated dollar amounts.

The cost position can be evaluated by comparing BCWP and ACWP, in other words, *the anticipated cost* and *the actual cost—for a given amount of accomplishment.*

Earned value analysis is an approach for monitoring project costs and expenses. It involves specifying, on a periodic basis, how far each activity has progressed (% complete) and deriving the value of work completed from this information. Value is earned as activities are completed. The cumulative value of work completed on any week is then compared to actual costs incurred in completing that work and the amount of work budgeted for completion. Earned value is a uniform unit of measure and thus provides a consistent method for analyzing a project's progress and performance.

Establishing an earned value analysis system involves the following steps:

1. Establish the work breakdown structure (WBS) to divide the project into manageable portions.

2. Identify the activities to be scheduled.

3. Allocate the costs to be expended on each activity.

4. Schedule the activities over time and assess percent completion.

5. Tabulate, plot, and analyze the data to confirm that the plan is acceptable.

EXAMPLE 23: In Example 22, assume that on week 4, a manager assesses the actual costs and % complete for each activity, as shown in Exhibit 27-11.

Exhibit 27-11: Earned Value Data

Task	Predecessor	Duration	Budgeted Cost	Actual Cost	% Complete	Earned Value = Budgeted Cost × % Complete	By week Allocated Cost Week 1	Week 2	Week 3	Week 4	Week 5
A	—	1	$1,500	$1,600	100	$1,500	$1,500				
B	A	2	$3,510	$3,700	100	$3,510		$1,755	$1,755		
C	A	2	$5,000	$4,600	80	$4,000		$2,500	$2,500		
D	B	2	$2,000	$1,000	60	$1,200				$1,000	$1,000
E	B	2	$3,000	$500	10	$300				$1,500	$1,500
Total costs			$15,010	$11,400		$10,510	$1,500	$4,255	$4,255	$2,500	$2,500
Cumulative costs by period							$1,500	$5,755	$10,010	$12,510	$15,010

The earned value is calculated by multiplying the budgeted cost of the activity by the % complete and then adding the result over all activities. For example, on week 4, the status of the project is:

- Budgeted Cost of Work Scheduled (BCWS) = $12,510
- Actual Cost of Work Performed (ACWP) = $11,400
- Budgeted Cost of Work Performed (BCWP) = $10,510 (earned value by week 4)

The distinction between the BCWS and the BCWP is that the former represents the budget of the activities that were planned to be completed, and the latter represents the budget of the activities that actually were completed. BCWP is often referred to as *earned value.* In this case, the good news is that actual costs are less then planned costs (see Exhibit 8-17); however, the bad news is that work accomplished on the project is less than anticipated. For example, activity C should have been finished but is only 80% complete.

Forecasting Project Parameters Using Earned Value Methodology

Earned value methodology can be used to forecast the estimated completion time and costs of a project given the current status of the project. To distinguish between cost slippage and schedule slippage on the project, the following is defined:

$$\text{Schedule variance (SV)} = \text{BCWP} - \text{BCWS}$$

$$\text{Cost variance (CV)} = \text{BCWP} - \text{ACWP}$$

Schedule variance (SV) is the budgeted cost of work performed minus the budgeted cost of work scheduled = BCWP – BCWS. Schedule variance shows the difference between the scheduled completion of an activity and the actual completion of that activity. A negative schedule variance means it took longer than planned to perform the work, and a positive schedule variance means it took less time than planned to perform the work.

Cost variance (CV) is the budgeted cost of work performed minus the actual cost of work performed = BCWP – ACWP. In other words, cost variance shows the difference between the estimated cost of an activity and the actual cost of that activity. If cost variance is a negative number, it means performing the work cost more than planned. If cost variance is a positive number, it means performing the work cost less than planned.

In the example project at week 4, we compute SV = $10,510 – $12,510 = ($2,000) and CV = $10,510 – $11,400 = ($890). The value of SV indicates that the project is severely behind schedule, and CV indicates that we are also overspending on the project because work with a value of $10,510 was done by actually spending $11,400.

It is anticipated that, given the pace of work, the project is going to take longer than five weeks, and with the unfavorable cost variance, it is going to cost more than $15,010.

Forecasts can be made by calculating the following performance indices.

The schedule performance index (SP1) is the ratio of work performed to work scheduled (BCWP/BCWS) and can be used to estimate the projected time to complete the project. A schedule performance index of one or 100% means the project is on schedule. If the schedule performance index is greater than one or 100%, then the project is ahead of schedule. If the schedule performance index is less than one or 100%, the project is behind schedule.

The cost performance index (CPI) is the ratio of work performed to actual costs (BCWP/ACWP) and can be used to estimate the projected cost of completing the project. If the cost performance index is equal to one, then the budged and actual costs are equal, or the costs are exactly as planned. If the cost performance index is less than one or less than 100%, the project is over budget. If the cost performance index is greater than one or more than 100%, the project is under budget.

Note: In general, negative numbers for cost and schedule variance indicate problems in those areas. The project is costing more than planned or taking longer than planned. Likewise, CPI and SPI less than 100% also indicate problems. Earned value calculations for all project activities (or summary level activities) are required to estimate the earned value for the entire project. Some activities may be over budget or behind schedule, but others may be under budget and ahead of schedule. By adding all of the earned values for all project activities, one can determine how the project as a whole is performing.

The estimate at completion (EAC) is an estimate of the cost to complete the project based on performance to date. It indicates where the project cost is heading. One simple way to calculate this is

$$EAC = (BAG - BCWP)/CPI + ACWP$$

where BAG = budget at completion, the initial budget for the project.

This formula determines the unfinished or unearned work (BAC − BCWP) and divides it by the CPI. To that is added the sunk cost, or the cost of the completed work (ACWP). From this it is evident that poor cost performance, a CPI less than 1, would result in an EAC that is greater than the BAC.

EXAMPLE 24: For the example project, these calculations are

$$SPI = \$10,510/\$ 12,510 = 0.84$$

$$CPI = \$10,510/\$11,400 = 0.92$$

$$EAC = (\$15,010 - \$10,510)/0.92 + \$11,400 = \$4,891.07 + \$11,400 = \$16,291.07$$

A similar forecast can be made for the project duration using the SPI; if work progresses at the current pace (84% schedule efficiency), then the time to complete the project would be:

Time to complete the project (TT) = original project duration/ SPI = 5/0.84 = 5.95 weeks

Exhibit 27-12: Cumulative Budgeted, Actual, and Earned Value: BCWS, ACWP, and CCWP

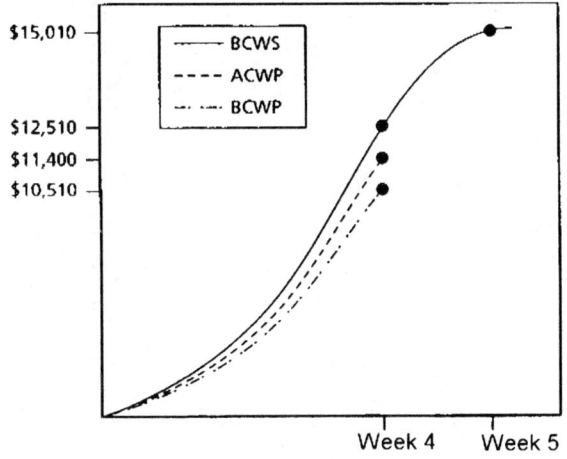

PART V

INTERNAL AUDITING AND CONTROL

CHAPTER 28

THE INTERNAL AUDIT FUNCTION AND INTERNAL CONTROL

CONTENTS

Internal auditing serves as an independent appraisal activity within an entity for the review of accounting, financial, and other operations as a basis of service to management.

Internal auditing can help improve the efficiency and profitability of the business. Proper review and appraisal of policies is essential. Audit procedures should be periodically performed on a cycle basis so that all individuals will know that the activity may be subject to audit. Where necessary, management may also request special audit reviews.

The purposes of internal auditing are to:

- Understand the nature and scope of the activity/function.
- Check on the administrative efficiency in terms of current policies and procedures while determining the extent of actual compliance with those policies and procedures.
- Appraise policies and procedures in terms of possible improvement.
- Increase efficiency (i.e., corporate welfare) by identifying any other means by which the activity/function can be made more effective.
- Ascertain the extent to which company assets are accounted for and safeguarded from losses of all kinds.
- Determine the reliability of management data developed within the organization.

Also relevant is the efficiency with which the various units of the organization are conducting their assigned tasks. Specific audit tasks should be properly communicated to staff by means of formal written documents.

Problem areas have to be uncovered, especially vulnerable ones. For example, the internal auditor's examination of sales, receivables, and credit activities may point to poor credit policies having a negative affect on profitability.

A vital aspect of internal auditing is the appraisal of internal control. Emphasis should be placed on the prevention rather than on the detection of fraud. The internal auditor should preferably be a planner, eliminating the conditions under which fraudulent activity may cultivate. If there is strong internal control, fraud has a higher probability of being detected.

This chapter considers the internal control of the company, internal audit techniques and approaches, audit programs, and internal audit reports.

A company's internal control structure consists of management's policies and procedures that are designed to provide reasonable, but not absolute, assurance that specific entity objectives will be achieved.

INTERNAL AUDITING ASPECTS

Internal auditing deals with those procedures and techniques emphasizing adherence to management policies, existence of internal controls, uncovering fraud, existence of proper record keeping, and effective operations of the business. The major elements of the internal auditor's task are to determine the reliability and accuracy of accounting information, determine whether corporate data have been determined in accordance with corporate policies and rules (e.g., manuals), and ascertain the adequacy of the internal control function. Internal auditing is the "eyes and ears of management." It deals not only with financial auditing but also operational auditing. Internal auditing should be carried out in conformity with the *Standards for the Professional Practice of Internal Auditing* and with the *Code of Ethics of The Institute of Internal Auditors.*

Besides looking at the safeguarding and existence of assets, the internal auditor must be assured that resources are used economically and efficiently. Are actual results in conformity with objectives?

The internal auditor plans the audit scope, conducts the audit, appraises the operation, communicates results to the audit manager and auditee, and follows up to ensure that deficiencies have been recognized and steps taken to address them.

The purpose of internal auditing is to ensure that there is proper discharge of responsibilities. The internal auditor provides analyses, appraisals, recommendations, and relevant comments regarding the activities.

Internal auditing involves many activities including:

- Reviewing and evaluating the reasonableness, adequacy, and application of accounting, financial, and other operating information and controls. Effective controls should be implemented at reasonable cost. For example, the telephone system should give a reading of numbers called and should block out exchange calls (i.e., 900 calls).

- Determining the degree of compliance with policies.

- Ascertaining the degree to which corporate assets are accounted for and safeguarded.

- Evaluating the quality of performance in conducting responsibilities.

- Determining the reliability of management data.

- Recommending improvements in performance.

- Assisting in ways to improve profit performance.

- Conducting special audits such as developing new procedures as well as the acquisition of subsidiaries and divisions.

In the audit process:

- Determine the audit scope during preaudit through the review of management reports and risk analysis. For example, the audit objective might be to determine if purchase orders are authorized and processed in accordance with policy.

- Identify applicable criteria for evaluation to determine acceptance or nonacceptance. An appropriate standard will have to be developed, such as anything over 10% is considered excessive (depends on materiality and exposure).

- Collect and evaluate information. An example is computing the actual turnover rate.

- Compare information against evaluative criteria. An example is comparing the actual turnover rate of 25% to a standard turnover rate of 10%.

- Form a conclusion, such as the turnover rate is excessive.

- Formulate and provide recommendations to solve the problem at hand.

An audit tool is a means by which the internal auditor achieves his or her objective. It may be either manual or automated. An example of an audit tool is the use of questionnaires in assessing internal control. Common tools in internal auditing include internal control questionnaires, narratives, flowcharts, and audit software. These tools serve to develop an understanding of the area being audited.

The amount of audit evidence required depends on the conclusions to be reached from the preliminary survey and the sufficiency of internal control. The audit evidence typically relates to random pieces of information that apply to particular events or transactions. Flowcharting is helpful in presenting a pictorial format.

The work papers should detail the transactions or accounts examined, the degree of testing, exceptions, and conclusions. The scope of the tests performed should be described along with the details of any errors or deficiencies. A record of internal audit operations is especially important when the company does not have standardized procedures.

In a new assignment, the internal auditor will initially examine the organization chart to determine the "key" people involved. For example, in examining procurement, those responsible for purchasing, accounts payable, and treasury functions will be identified. Interviews with these individuals will be held to develop an understanding of the system.

The purpose of testing data for a specific application is to evaluate the appropriateness of current controls, determine compliance with present policies and procedures regarding data reliability, and substantiate processed transactions.

The extent of audit testing necessary depends upon the quality of internal control, the areas tested, and the particular circumstances. If controls seem appropriate, the internal auditor will substantiate whether those controls are indeed operating effectively. If no reliance on the controls exists, the usual substantive testing must be carried out.

In poor internal control situations, detailed verification is required. Here, a large sample is needed. Less field work is necessary when the company has significant self-checking devices to highlight defects and alert management to control breakdowns. Of course, the self-checking devices will still have to be scrutinized by the internal auditor.

In audit testing, the actual results of examining selected transactions or processes are compared to prescribed standards. In so doing, the internal auditor will be able to form an audit opinion. Some or all of the transactions, functions, activities, records, and statements are examined.

The following steps are usually involved in audit testing: (1) determining standards, (2) defining the population, (3) selecting a sample, and (4) examining the sampled items.

Standards may be explicit or implicit. Explicit standards are clearly stated in job instructions, directives, laws, and specifications. An example of an explicit standard is that competitive bids must be received on contracts in excess of $500,000. However, competitive bids may be "rigged" by specification requirements so that only certain suppliers can compete. Implicit standards exist when management formulates objectives and goals but does not establish in particular how they are to be accomplished. In this case, the internal auditor, upon completing a review of the objectives considering the controls in place, will consult with management regarding what is satisfactory performance.

In travel, the policy of upgrading from coach class should be spelled out. Is there a separate travel department? Are employees abusing the frequent flier privilege? There should be a written policy of who may be entertained and how much cost may be incurred. What is the policy regarding company vehicles? The personal use of office supplies, copiers, and fax machines must also be controlled.

In proportional analysis, the auditor evaluates certain revenue and expense items by relating them to other revenue and expenses. For instance, the cost of shipping cartons should have a proportional relationship to the number of units sold and shipped.

The population to be tested takes into account audit objectives. If the purpose is to derive an opinion on transactions occurring after last year, all transactions constitute the population. If the objective is to formulate an opinion regarding current controls, the population becomes more restricted. Management wants to know if the system is working properly. If not, ways to improve it must be formulated.

In deriving the population to be tested, a determination must be made of the total transactions (e.g., purchase orders, invoices, billings). These should be serially numbered. If documents are missing, the reasons must be uncovered. The character and location of the inventory must be determined. Are transactions stratified by value or other characteristic?

Whether verifications and analyses are carried out in detail or on a test check basis depends on the importance of the item and the likelihood of material misstatement. In test-checking, a statistical sample is selected.

The sample should be selected according to the audit objective, whether it is judgmental or statistical. Reliable selection is from lists that are separate from the records themselves. This assures that items that may have been removed from the physical units have not been overlooked.

Statistical sampling used in the internal auditing process includes random, discovery, and multistage. Sampling techniques are used to verify such things as recorded amounts in the financial statements and product quality control.

The internal auditor should be assured that there is proper communication within the organization. Needed information should be available when a decision must be made and it must go to the appropriate party. The information must be clearly understood.

To develop an understanding of internal control, the internal auditor must become familiar with the operating unit or area being audited. The stages in this process are as follows:

- *Preaudit.* Information is gathered and the internal auditor becomes thoroughly familiar with the factual content. Departments or operational sections should be separated in the work papers and cross-referenced where there are overlapping data.

- *Scope.* The internal auditor meets with the unit or department manager to start the operational review in his or her area. The scope and objectives should be explained. The information should be filtered down through the organization. The internal auditor should stress that the purpose of an audit is to review internal controls and assess current operations to provide recommendations to improve controls and maximize efficiency to attain the company goal of maximizing profits. A meeting with the manager and supervisory personnel may be in order, depending on such factors as size. The following should be reviewed with the manager: organization charts, departmental budgets, policy manuals, procedure manuals, flowcharts, activities listings, forms and reports, records, and questions developed in the preaudit.

- *Comprehending Internal Control.* Based upon the information furnished by the department manager and other key employees, the internal auditor completes the applicable departmental internal control questionnaire (e.g., purchasing questionnaire). A general summary of the internal auditor's view of the existing situation and activities should be prepared for the functional unit under review. Questionnaires are reviewed and a determination is made of who is to be interviewed. (Sample internal control questionnaires are provided later in the chapter.) Questions should be summarized before interviewing to assure a planned approach and to minimize interview time and maximize efficiency of the audit. Show a desire to understand the person's job, its importance, and difficult tasks. Review in detail the position analysis questionnaires and discuss matters requiring clarification. In the course of interviewing, a definite effort should be made to put the employee at ease and draw out his or her complaints, criticisms, and improvement suggestions relative to the employee's individual job, the department's operations, and divisional operations. Summarize the results of the interview, paying particular attention to criticisms, complaints, and constructive suggestions to improve operations.

  It is then appropriate to determine specific areas to carry over into the evaluation phase, which may require the preparation of specific worksheets for further clarification. Some worksheets that may be required are: departmental functional activity analysis, forms involved in job function, reports generated or received by department, process worksheets, and paperwork flow analysis.

- *Verification.* During each segment of the verification phase, every situation uncovered and summarized in the scope and understanding phases of this review must be kept in mind. Refer to the summaries throughout this phase, testing each situation until satisfied. Challenge every aspect of significant situations to reveal every opportunity for possible improvement.

  Each area requires different techniques and amounts of verification. These will be dictated by the outcome of the scope and understanding phases. Based on departmental files and volume or population information, determine specific documents to be selected for sampling and prepare a listing of such documents to be accumulated by divisional personnel, if possible (selection of sample items), since the audit is limited to a specified time frame. Upon receipt of documents requested for sampling, enter required information and any other pertinent remarks on the sampling worksheet. While performing this step, determine compliance with policies and procedures, effectiveness of internal control, and possible areas for improvement. Before proceeding with this step, reference should be made to specific program segments for the department involved. Where specific report points for improvement in, for example, internal control and operation efficiency affect the operations of other departments or functions, the points in question should be checked and followed up on with the responsible operating personnel of such other departments. Notes should be prepared, summarizing the results of the follow-up with each employee contacted. Time devoted to this effort should be charged to this audit segment regardless of the specific segment in which the point in question arose.

- *Evaluation.* When the first four phases have been completed in each area, final evaluation should be initiated. Because of the understanding gained during the course of the review, it is extremely difficult not to form hasty opinions and initiate some preliminary evaluation throughout the review. This should be avoided. The final evaluation is the basis upon which recommendations will be determined and the report prepared, with all the facts being considered in their proper perspective. From the various data, interview notes, and verification summaries, prepare a summary of the major areas of improvement opportunity.

Work out details of report points and recommendations. Review these with other members of the audit team and appropriate divisional personnel. Restudy and verify apparent conflicts of facts or uncertain points. After this review and verification, finalize the report points and review again with other members of the audit team. When report points are finalized and there is agreement on the recommendations, set up a closing meeting with supervisors to coincide with reviews in other areas. Review report points and recommendations with local management.

Internal Audit Reports

The internal audit report should explain the scope of the review and detailed audit findings. The report should include a statement of the general scope of the examination. Further, background information should be given. If limiting factors exist, they should be stated. The body of the audit report contains details of the examination, which is cross-referenced to the summary. Written reports may emphasize:

- Details of verification including reasons for and disposition of exceptions.

- Financial accounting data.

- Information of special executive interest, such as highlighting unusual or defective situations along with corrective action, which will be taken by the auditee.

The internal audit report should include a summary of major findings and recommendations. A conclusion about what was uncovered by the audit will be provided. The internal audit report must be factual, based on hard evidence.

In forming the internal audit opinion, the auditor will typically express opinions on the findings. Contrary opinions by operating management should be noted. Even though opinions may differ, a disagreement as to facts should not exist. The internal auditor's conclusion should be stated clearly with objective support.

To nonaccountants, narrative reports are more meaningful than numerical tabulations. If there is significant numerical information, this should be contained in an exhibit supplementing the report. The body of the report should have a summary of the relevant reference to the exhibit and its importance.

All internal audit reports should contain the same basic structure, including:

- *Identification.* The name of the report should identify the unit or operational area reviewed. The auditors involved in the examination should be named. Give the date of the report along with the test period. Determine if the report is a regular one or a follow-up. Indicate the name of the auditor issuing the report.

- *Summary.* Highlight the major points for management so that it is easier to identify areas requiring action.

- *Scope.* Describe the objectives of the audit work performed.

- *Background.* Provide relevant background information to understand the findings and recommendations of the audit report. Examples are sales volume and number of employees.

- *Findings.* Present findings relating to the factual information uncovered in the review. The audit findings should be given in logical order of importance, or in terms of functions, phases, or account classifications. Prior to report issuance, findings should be discussed with local (auditee) management in a closing meeting to minimize disputes. If the dispute is unresolved, the positions of the auditor and management should be given. Where corrective action has been implemented by management, it should be referred to in the report.

- *Opinion and recommendations.* Present conclusions regarding the findings. Propose suggestions to solve the problems.

- *Signature.* Have the auditor-in-charge sign the report.

- *Acknowledgement.* Provide a statement recognizing help given the auditor by the manager along with a request for a reply to the report.

- *Appendices* (optional). Appendices should contain information not needed to comprehend the report but valuable if detailed information is desired. Examples are a listing of standards violated, explanations, and statistical information. These data should appear after the body of the report.

- *Graphics* (optional). Graphics help explain material in the report including graphs, charts, pictorial representations, and photographs. For instance, a flowchart can explain how a recommendation may be implemented.

The format of the internal audit report depends on the kind of report being issued (e.g., formal versus informal), the readers being addressed, and the nature and reasoning of the auditing activity. Different auditing organizations will use different report formats and divide their reports into different subsections. The format should be consistently used. The internal audit report must be accurate, concise, clear, and timely. The internal audit report should be distributed to those who have authority to take corrective action.

Audit Program

The audit program should be tailored to the specific internal audit assignment. Each work step should indicate why the procedure is being performed, the objective, and controls being tested. In-depth analysis and evaluations are required. There should be flexibility in the audit program so that a prescribed procedure may be altered or work extended depending on particular circumstances. Unusual risks should be identified and controls needed to eliminate that risk should be recommended. Audit findings should be stated along with recommended corrective action.

Compliance Auditing

An essential part of internal auditing is substantiating compliance with company and regulatory policies, procedures, and laws. It is essential to review whether employees are conducting their tasks as desired by management. Assurance must be obtained that controls are functioning and responsible parties have been assigned. There should be written compliance directives in such sources as manuals, bulletins, and letters.

In compliance testing, the internal auditor examines evidence to substantiate that the firm's internal control structure elements are performing as intended.

Tip: It is best to verify that internal controls are working through testing practices of the operations of the control techniques themselves instead of verifying the results of processing.

A key aspect of internal auditing deals with compliance as to accounting procedures. The accounting system must be operating as designed if reliable and consistent accounting data are to be provided. The appropriate forms have to be used in the prescribed manner.

Examples of areas subject to compliance testing are standards for data processing, controller's procedures, procurement, data retention requirements of the company and governmental agencies, security policies, personnel administration, planning, budgeting, payroll, and expense accounts.

Operational Auditing

Operational auditing examines the effectiveness, efficiency, and economy of operational performance in the business. It examines the reasonableness of recorded financial information. The performance of managers and staff are scrutinized. For example, there should be an examination of operational performance related to payroll, receiving, purchasing, and cost control. Generally, operations should be conducted in such a way that results in profitability.

A determination must be made as to whether corporate policies are being adhered to as well as whether such policies are reasonable in the current environment or if changes are necessary. Areas of inefficiency and uneconomical practice are identified.

Some internal audit departments have engineers to appraise productivity and assist in formulating work standards. Operational performance criteria include the sufficiency of resources acquired, response time to requests, efficient utilization of personnel, proper supervision, up-to-date equipment and technology, and adequacy of storage.

Management Auditing

The management audit is a special type of operational audit. Its ultimate outcome is to achieve operating effectiveness and efficiency. But the more immediate concern of the management auditor is more on the effectiveness of the management function than on efficiency. Management audits involve and affect management, typically all the way up to the senior level.

Functional Auditing

A functional audit looks at a process from beginning to end, crossing organizational lines. Functional auditing emphasizes operations and processes rather than administration and people. It looks at how well each department handles the function involved. Are departments cooperating in carrying out the task effectively and efficiently? Examples of functional audits relate to safety practices, uncovering conflicts of interest, changing products, ordering and paying for materials, and deliveries of supplies to user departments.

In performing a functional audit, auditors have to define job parameters, keep the parameters within reasonable range, and cover all major aspects of the function. Functional audits deal with several organizations, some where conflicts of interest exist. The advantages of functional audits are obtaining diverse viewpoints, identifying problem areas, reconciling different objectives, and highlighting duplications.

The internal auditor may be asked to engage in a special review of ongoing programs. A program relates to any funded effort for typical ongoing activities of the company. Examples include an employee benefit program, a new contract, an expansion program, a new computerized application, and a training program. The internal auditor provides management with cost data and the results of the program. Possible alternative ways of carrying out the function at less cost are examined.

Financial Auditing

In financial auditing, there is a determination of whether the financial statements present fairly the financial position and operating results of a company in accordance with generally accepted accounting principles. The company must comply with the relevant organizational policies and procedures as well as the laws and regulations governing the business. Work performed in an internal financial audit can be used to reduce fees of the external auditor.

Appraising Internal Control

An entity's internal control consists of five interrelated components:

1. Control environment.
2. Risk assessment.
3. Control activities.
4. Information and communication systems support.
5. Monitoring.

The Control Environment. The control environment, which is the foundation for the other components of internal control, provides discipline and structure by setting the tone of an organization and influencing control consciousness.

The factors to consider in assessing the control environment include:

- Integrity and ethical values, including:
  - management's actions to eliminate or mitigate incentives and temptations on the part of personnel to commit dishonest, illegal, or unethical acts
  - policy statements
  - codes of conduct.
- Commitment to competence, including management's consideration of competence levels for specific tasks and how those levels translate into necessary skills and knowledge.
- Board of directors or audit committee participation, including interaction with internal and external (independent) auditors.
- Management's philosophy and operating style, such as management's attitude and actions regarding financial reporting, as well as management's approach to taking and monitoring risks.
- The entity's organizational structure (i.e., the form and nature of organizational units).
- Assignment of authority and responsibility, including fulfilling job responsibilities.
- Human resource policies and practices, including those relating to hiring, orientation, training, evaluating, counseling, promoting, and compensating employees.

Risk Assessment. An entity's risk assessment for financial reporting purposes is its identification, analysis, and management of risks pertaining to financial statement preparation. Accordingly, risk assessment may consider the possibility of executed transactions that remain unrecorded.

The following internal and external events and circumstances may be relevant to the risk of preparing financial statements that are not in conformity with generally accepted accounting principles (or other comprehensive basis of accounting):

- Changes in operating and regulatory environment, including competitive pressures.
- New personnel that have a different perspective on internal control.
- Rapid growth that can result in a breakdown in controls.
- New technology in information systems and production processes.
- New lines, products, or activities.
- Corporate restructuring that might result in changes in supervision and segregation of job functions.
- Expanded foreign operations.
- Accounting pronouncements requiring adoption of new accounting principles.

Control Activities. Control activities are the policies and procedures management has implemented in order to ensure that directives are carried out.

Control activities may be classified into the following categories:

- Performance reviews, including comparisons of actual performance with budgets, forecasts, and prior-period results.
- Information processing. Controls relating to information processing are generally designed to verify accuracy, completeness, and authorization of transactions. Specifically, controls may be classified as general controls or application controls. The former might include controls over data center operations, systems software acquisition and maintenance, and access security; the latter apply to the processing of individual applications and are designed to ensure that transactions that are recorded are valid, authorized, and complete.
- Physical controls, which involve adequate safeguards over the access to assets and records, include authorization for access to computer programs and files and periodic counting and comparison with amounts shown on control records.
- Segregation of duties, which is designed to reduce the opportunities to allow any person to be in a position both to perpetrate and to conceal errors or irregularities (fraud) in the normal course of his or her duties, involves assigning different people the responsibilities of authorizing transactions, recording transactions, and maintaining custody of assets.

Information and Communication Systems Support. The information system generally consists of the methods and records established to record, process, summarize, and report entity transactions and to maintain accountability of related assets, liabilities, and equity.

Communication involves providing an understanding of individual roles and responsibilities pertaining to internal control.

Monitoring. Monitoring is management's process of assessing the quality of internal control performance over time. Accordingly, management must assess the design and operation of controls on a timely basis and take necessary corrective actions.

Monitoring may involve: (1) separate evaluations, (2) the use of internal auditors, and (3) the use of communications from outside parties (e.g., complaints from customers and regulator comments).

The Role of the Internal Audit Function

The internal audit function should play an important role in the monitoring of internal control. The internal auditor must obtain a sufficient knowledge of the five interrelated components in order to: (1) identify the types of misstatements that could occur in the financial records, and (2) ensure that the entity operates in such a way that goals are efficiently and effectively met. Since the entity's external auditors will most likely attempt to utilize internal control to restrict their testing of financial statement assertions, it is important that internal control be properly established and maintained.

The Cycle Approach

In setting up effective internal control, management should utilize the cycle approach, which first stratifies internal control into broad areas of activity and then identifies specific classes of transactions. Accordingly, the following cycles should be considered:

- Revenue cycle: revenue and accounts receivable (order processing, credit approval, shipping, invoicing, and recording) and cash receipts.

- Expenditure cycle: purchasing, receiving, accounts payable, payroll, and cash disbursements.

- Production or conversion cycle: inventories, cost of sales, and property, plant, and equipment.

- Financing cycle: notes receivable and investments, notes payable, debt, leases, other obligations, and equity accounts.

- External reporting cycle: accounting principles and preparation of financial statements.

Identifying Deficiencies in Internal Control

Internal control should be monitored in order to identify deficiencies that could adversely affect (1) the operation of the entity, and (2) the financial statement presentation.

The internal audit function has the responsibility of testing compliance with the policies and procedures (i.e., controls) embodied in internal control.

The illustrative internal control forms presented in Exhibits 28-1, 28-2, and 28-3 should prove useful in monitoring internal control. The forms are reprinted from the AICPA Audit and Accounting Manual (with permission). Although normally utilized by an outside independent auditor, the forms are also appropriate for internal use, since management objectives are clearly addressed.

The internal auditor must always be aware of the possibility of fraud. Fraud involves the taking of something of value from someone else through deceit. Fraud may involve the following:

- Failing to record sales while simultaneously stealing cash receipts
- Creating overages in cash funds and cash registers by intentionally under-recording cash receipts.
- The issuance of credit for counterfeit customer claims and returns
- Recording unwarranted cash discounts.
- Increasing amounts of suppliers' invoices by means of collusion.
- Overstating sales to obtain bonuses.

Possible indicators of management fraud include:

- Lack of compliance with company directives and procedures.
- Payments made to trade creditors that are supported by copies instead of original invoices.
- Consistently late reports.
- Higher commissions that are not based on increased sales.
- Managers who habitually assume the duties of their subordinates.
- Managers who handle matters beyond the scope of their authority.

The internal auditor must also be cognizant of embezzlement schemes. Possible indicators of embezzlement include:

- The tendency to cover up inefficiencies or "plug" figures.
- Excessive criticism of others in order to divert suspicion.
- Displaying annoyance with reasonable questioning.
- The continued willingness to work overtime.
- Reluctance to give custody of assets to others.
- The providing of misinformation or vague answers.

Internal control taken as a whole should therefore provide a system of checks and balances. As a result, no one individual should have complete control over a transaction from beginning to end. Furthermore, periodic rotation of job functions is essential. A proper system of internal checks and balances makes it difficult for an employee to steal cash or other assets and concurrently cover up the misappropriation by entering corresponding amounts in the accounts.

Key documents (for example, sales invoices) should be prenumbered and used in sequential order. Additionally, custody of and access to these documents should be controlled.

All parties involved in a particular transaction or activity should receive copies of the documents involved (e.g., invoice, order, correspondence). This provides an audit trail and aids in coordination among interested parties and assists in detecting errors and irregularities. Accordingly, good internal control requires standard policies regarding the distribution of materials throughout the organization. Access to inventory should be restricted.

Employee responsibilities should be monitored as far down in the company as practical. Employees will act more responsibly if they know that they are accountable and will have to justify deviations from prescribed procedures.

Transactions should be executed only after appropriate authorization is obtained. There are two types of authorization to be considered. General authorization specifies definite limits on what an employee can do without intervention of management (e.g., prices to charge, discounts that may be offered, and what costs are reimbursable). Specific authorization typically means that supervisory personnel must approve in writing a specific deviation from a company policy. For example, written authorization may be required for corporate expense reimbursement above a prescribed limit.

The Foreign Corrupt Practices Act

According to the Foreign Corrupt Practices Act of 1977 (FCPA), SEC-reporting companies must maintain books, records, and accounts that accurately reflect transactions. In this regard, the company must establish and maintain effective internal control that provides reasonable assurance that:

- Recorded transactions permit the preparation of financial statements in conformity with generally accepted accounting principles.
- Accountability over assets exist.
- Transactions are entered into in conformity with management's general or specific authorization.
- Access to assets is in accordance with corporate policies.

In addition, there should be periodic reconciliation of assets per books and the physical existence of such assets.

Internal auditors typically have the responsibility that the company's internal control is in conformity with the FCPA.

The FCPA also contains prohibitions against bribery and other corrupt practices.

Fraudulent Financial Reporting

The National Commission on Fraudulent Financial Reporting's Exposure Draft issued in 1987 may well have led to the largest growth in internal auditing. The report, known as the Treadway Commission Report, defined fraudulent financial reporting as "intentional or reckless conduct, whether act or omission, that results in materially misleading financial statements."

The report identifies opportunities for fraudulent financial reporting arising when there are:

- Weak or nonexistent internal controls that arise from:
  - Significant expansion in sales, overloading the revenue system.
  - Acquisition of new divisions or product lines.
  - New business.

- Unusual or complex transactions (e.g., closing an operation).

- Significant accounting estimates (e.g., reserve for loan losses).

- Ineffective internal audit staff resulting from inadequate staff size and severely limited audit scope.

A weak corporate ethical climate fosters these situations. Opportunities for fraudulent financial reporting also increase when accounting principles and guidelines for transactions are nonexistent, evolving, or subject to varying interpretations.

The internal auditor will be required to attest to the adequacy of financial reporting and also for the detection and prevention of fraudulent financial reporting.

Sarbanes-Oxley Act of 2002

Pursuant to the Sarbanes-Oxley Act of 2002, a publicly traded company is required to include in its annual report an assessment by management of the effectiveness of its internal controls over financial reporting. To date, no standard or illustrative report has been prescribed by the Securities and Exchange Commission or the Public Company Accounting Oversight Board. However, the Act does require management's report on its internal controls to include, at a minimum:

- A statement that management is responsible for establishing and maintaining adequate internal control over financial reporting.

- A statement that identifies the framework used by management to evaluate the effectiveness of its internal control over financial reporting.

- Management's assessment of the effectiveness of the entity's internal control over financial reporting as of the end of the most recent fiscal year. Management's assessment must include an explicit statement as to whether or not internal control over financial reporting is effective. Management must also disclose any material weaknesses in internal control identified by management.

- A statement that the entity's auditor has issued an attestation report on management's assessment. The auditor's attestation report must be included in the entity's annual report.

Exhibit 28-1: Internal Control Assessment Form

I. Document Your Understanding of the Control Environment

In the space provided below, indicate whether you strongly agree, somewhat agree, somewhat disagree, or strongly disagree with the following statements. Your answers should be based on

- Your previous experience with the entity
- Inquiries of appropriate management, supervisory, and staff personnel
- Inspection of documents and records
- Observation of the entity's activities and operations

	No Opinion	Strongly Disagree	Some-what Disagree	Some-what Agree	Strongly Agree

A. Control Environment Factors

Integrity and Ethical Values

1. Management has high ethical and behavioral standards.

2. The company has a written code of ethical and behavioral standards that is comprehensive and periodically acknowledged by all employees.

3. If a written code of conduct does not exist, the management culture emphasizes the importance of integrity and ethical values.

4. Management reinforces its ethical and behavioral standards.

5. Management appropriately deals with signs that problems exist (e.g., defective products or hazardous waste) even when the cost of identifying and solving the problem could be high.

6. Management has removed or reduced incentives and temptations that might prompt personnel to engage in dishonest, illegal, or unethical acts.

    For example, there is generally no

    • Pressure to meet unrealistic performance targets

    • High-performance dependent rewards.

    • Upper and lower cutoffs on bonus plans.

	No Opinion	Strongly Disagree	Some-what Disagree	Some-what Agree	Strongly Agree
7. Management has provided guidance on the situations and frequency with which intervention of established controls is appropriate.	_____	_____	_____	_____	_____
8. Management intervention is documented and explained appropriately.	_____	_____	_____	_____	_____

Commitment to Competence

9. Management has appropriately considered the knowledge and skill levels necessary to accomplish financial reporting tasks.	_____	_____	_____	_____	_____
10. Employees with financial reporting tasks generally have the knowledge and skills necessary to accomplish those tasks.	_____	_____	_____	_____	_____

Board of Directors and Audit Committee

11. The board of directors is independent from management.	_____	_____	_____	_____	_____
12. The board constructively challenges management's planned decisions.	_____	_____	_____	_____	_____
13. Directors have sufficient knowledge and industry experience and time to serve effectively.	_____	_____	_____	_____	_____
14. The board regularly receives the information they need to monitor management's objectives and strategies.	_____	_____	_____	_____	_____
15. The audit committee reviews the scope of activities of the internal and external auditors annually.	_____	_____	_____	_____	_____

	No Opinion	Strongly Disagree	Some-what Disagree	Some-what Agree	Strongly Agree
16. The audit committee meets privately with the chief financial and/or accounting officers, internal auditors and external auditors to discuss the	_____	_____	_____	_____	_____
• Reasonableness of the financial reporting process	_____	_____	_____	_____	_____
• System of internal control	_____	_____	_____	_____	_____
• Significant comments and recommendations	_____	_____	_____	_____	_____
• Management's performance	_____	_____	_____	_____	_____
17. The board takes steps to ensure an appropriate "tone at the top."	_____	_____	_____	_____	_____
18. The board or committee takes action as a result of its findings.	_____	_____	_____	_____	_____

Management's Philosophy and Operating Style

	No Opinion	Strongly Disagree	Some-what Disagree	Some-what Agree	Strongly Agree
19. Management moves carefully, proceeding only after carefully analyzing the risks and potential benefits of accepting business risks.	_____	_____	_____	_____	_____
20. Management is generally cautious or conservative in financial reporting and tax matters.	_____	_____	_____	_____	_____
21. There is relatively low turnover of key personnel (e.g., operating, accounting, data processing, internal audit).	_____	_____	_____	_____	_____
22. There is no undue pressure to meet budget, profit, or other financial and operating goals.	_____	_____	_____	_____	_____

	No Opinion	Strongly Disagree	Some-what Disagree	Some-what Agree	Strongly Agree
23. Management views the accounting and internal audit function as a vehicle for exercising control over the entity's activities.	____	____	____	____	____
24. Operating personnel review and "sign off" on reported results.	____	____	____	____	____
25. Senior managers frequently visit subsidiary or divisional operations.	____	____	____	____	____
26. Group or divisional management meetings are held frequently.	____	____	____	____	____

Organizational Structure

	No Opinion	Strongly Disagree	Some-what Disagree	Some-what Agree	Strongly Agree
27. The entity's organizational structure facilitates the flow of information upstream, downstream, and across all business activities.	____	____	____	____	____
28. Responsibilities and expectations for the entity's business activities are communicated clearly to the executives in charge of those activities.	____	____	____	____	____
29. The executives in charge have the required knowledge, experience, and training to perform their duties.	____	____	____	____	____
30. Those in charge of business activities have access to senior operating management.	____	____	____	____	____

Assignment of Authority and Responsibility

	No Opinion	Strongly Disagree	Some-what Disagree	Some-what Agree	Strongly Agree
31. Authority and responsibility are delegated only to the degree necessary to achieve the company's objectives.	____	____	____	____	____

	No Opinion	Strongly Disagree	Somewhat Disagree	Somewhat Agree	Strongly Agree
32. Job descriptions, for at least management and supervisory personnel, exist.					
33. Job descriptions contain specific references to control related responsibilities.					
34. Proper resources are provided for personnel to carry out their duties.					
35. Personnel understand the entity's objectives and know how their individual actions interrelate and contribute to those objectives.					
36. Personnel recognize how and for what they will be held accountable.					

Human Resource Policies and Practices

	No Opinion	Strongly Disagree	Somewhat Disagree	Somewhat Agree	Strongly Agree
37. The entity generally hires the most qualified people for the job.					
38. Hiring and recruiting practices emphasize educational background, prior work experience, past accomplishments, and evidence of integrity and ethical behavior.					
39. Recruiting practices include formal, in-depth employment interviews.					
40. Prospective employees are told of the entity's history, culture and operating style.					
41. The entity provides training opportunities, and employees are well-trained.					

	No Opinion	Strongly Disagree	Some-what Disagree	Some-what Agree	Strongly Agree
42. Promotions and rotation of personnel are based on periodic performance appraisals.	___	___	___	___	___
43. Methods of compensation, including bonuses, are designed to motivate personnel and reinforce outstanding performance.	___	___	___	___	___
44. Management does not hesitate to take disciplinary action when violations of expected behavior occur.	___	___	___	___	___

B. Other Internal Control Components with a Pervasive Effect on the Organization

Risk Assessment

	No Opinion	Strongly Disagree	Some-what Disagree	Some-what Agree	Strongly Agree
1. Special action is taken to ensure new personnel understand their tasks.	___	___	___	___	___
2. Management appropriately considers the control activities performed by personnel who change jobs or leave the company.	___	___	___	___	___
3. Management assesses how new accounting and information systems will impact internal control.	___	___	___	___	___
4. Management reconsiders the appropriateness of existing control activities when new accounting and information systems are developed and implemented.	___	___	___	___	___
5. Employees are adequately trained when accounting and information systems are changed or replaced.	___	___	___	___	___

	No Opinion	Strongly Disagree	Some-what Disagree	Some-what Agree	Strongly Agree
6. Accounting and information system capabilities are upgraded when the volume of information increases significantly.	_____	_____	_____	_____	_____
7. Accounting and data processing personnel are expanded as needed when the volume of information increases significantly.	_____	_____	_____	_____	_____
8. The entity has the ability to forecast reasonably operating and financial results.	_____	_____	_____	_____	_____
9. Management keeps abreast of the political, regulatory, business, and social culture of areas in which foreign operations exist.	_____	_____	_____	_____	_____

General Control Activities

	No Opinion	Strongly Disagree	Some-what Disagree	Some-what Agree	Strongly Agree
10. The entity prepares operating budgets and cash flow projections.	_____	_____	_____	_____	_____
11. Operating budgets and projections lend themselves to effective comparison with actual results.	_____	_____	_____	_____	_____
12. Significant variances between budgeted or projected amounts and actual results are reviewed and explained.	_____	_____	_____	_____	_____
13. The company has adequate safekeeping facilities for custody of the accounting records such as fireproof storage areas and restricted access cabinets.	_____	_____	_____	_____	_____
14. The entity has a suitable record retention plan.	_____	_____	_____	_____	_____

	No Opinion	Strongly Disagree	Some-what Disagree	Some-what Agree	Strongly Agree
15. The entity has adequate controls to limit access to computer programs and data files.	_____	_____	_____	_____	_____
16. Periodically, personnel compare counts of assets to amounts shown on control records.	_____	_____	_____	_____	_____
17. There is adequate segregation of duties among those responsible for authorizing transactions, recording transactions, and maintaining custody of assets.	_____	_____	_____	_____	_____

Information and Communication Systems Support

	No Opinion	Strongly Disagree	Some-what Disagree	Some-what Agree	Strongly Agree
18. Management receives the information they need to carry out their responsibilities.	_____	_____	_____	_____	_____
19. Information is provided at the right level of detail for different levels of management.	_____	_____	_____	_____	_____
20. Information is available on a timely basis.	_____	_____	_____	_____	_____
21. Information with accounting significance (for example, slow-paying customers) is transmitted across functional lines in a timely manner.	_____	_____	_____	_____	_____

Monitoring

	No Opinion	Strongly Disagree	Some-what Disagree	Some-what Agree	Strongly Agree
22. Customer complaints about billings are investigated for their underlying causes.	_____	_____	_____	_____	_____

	No Opinion	Strongly Disagree	Some-what Disagree	Some-what Agree	Strongly Agree
23. Communications from bankers, regulators, or other outside parties are monitored for items of accounting significance.	_____	_____	_____	_____	_____
24. Management responds appropriately to auditor recommendations on ways to strengthen internal controls.	_____	_____	_____	_____	_____
25. Employees are required to "sign off" to evidence the performance of critical control functions.	_____	_____	_____	_____	_____
26. The internal auditors are independent of the activities they audit.	_____	_____	_____	_____	_____
27. Internal auditors have adequate training and experience.	_____	_____	_____	_____	_____
28. Internal auditors document the planning and execution of their work by such means as audit programs and Working papers.	_____	_____	_____	_____	_____
29. Internal audit reports are submitted to the board of directors or audit committee.	_____	_____	_____	_____	_____

II. Determine Other Areas for Evaluation

The completion of section I of this form is the first of several forms that may be used to document your understanding of internal controls sufficiently to plan a primarily substantive audit. In the space provided below, determine which of the following areas apply. A "Yes" answer generally indicates you should complete the related form.

	No	Yes	W/P Ref.

Significant Account Balances and Transaction Cycles

	No	Yes	W/P Ref.
1. The following account balances or transaction cycles are significant to the company's financial statements.	_____	_____	_____

	No	Yes	W/P Ref.

a. Revenue Cycle, including sales, accounts receivable, or cash receipts. (Normally considered significant for most businesses.)   _____ _____ _____

If yes, the related Financial Reporting Information Systems and Controls Checklist can be found at   _____

b. Purchasing Cycle, including purchasing, accounts payable, or cash disbursements. (Normally considered significant for most businesses.)   _____ _____ _____

If yes, the related Financial Reporting Information Systems and Controls Checklist can be found at   _____

c. Inventory, including inventory and cost sales.   _____ _____ _____

If yes, the related Financial Reporting Information Systems and Controls Checklist can be found at   _____

d. Financing, including investments and debt.   _____ _____ _____

If yes, the related Financial Reporting Information Systems and Controls Checklist can be found at   _____

e. Property, Plant, and Equipment, including fixed assets and depreciation.   _____ _____ _____

If yes, the related Financial Reporting Information Systems and Controls Checklist can be found at   _____

f. Payroll.   _____ _____ _____

If yes, the related Financial Reporting Information Systems and Controls Checklist can be found at   _____

III. Assess Lack of Segregation of Duties

In the space provided below, assess risk due to a lack of segregation of duties for the company, based on the completion of sections I and II of this form. Your comments should address:

- The person with incompatible responsibilities and the nature of those responsibilities.

- Any mitigating factors or controls, such as direct management oversight.

- The risk that material misstatements might occur as a result of a lack of segregation of duties, and the type of those misstatements.

- How substantive procedures will be designed to limit the risk of those misstatements to an acceptable level.

_____

_____

_____

_____

_____

_____

_____

IV. Assess the Risk of Management Override

Even in effectively controlled entities—those with generally high levels of integrity and control consciousness—a manager might be able to override controls. The term management override means—

> Overruling prescribed policies or procedures for illegitimate purposes with the intent of personal gain or enhanced presentation of an entity's financial condition or compliance status.

Management might override the control system for many reasons: to increase reported revenue, to boost market value of the entity prior to sale, to meet sales or earnings projections, to bolster bonus pay-outs tied to performance, to appear to cover violations of debt covenant agreements, or to hide lack of compliance with legal requirements. Override practices include deliberate misrepresentations to bankers, lawyers, accountants, and vendors, and intentionally issuing false documents such as sales invoices.

An active, involved board of directors can significantly reduce the risk of management override.

Management override is different from management intervention, which is the overrule of prescribed policies or procedures for legitimate purposes. For example, management intervention is usually necessary to deal with nonrecurring and nonstandard transactions or events that otherwise might be handled by the system.

In the space below, assess the risk of management override for this company. You should consider the risk that management override possibilities exist, the risk that management will take advantage of those possibilities, and any evidence that management has engaged in override practices. If the risk of management override is greater than low, indicate how planned audit procedures will reduce this risk to an acceptable level.

_____

_____

_____

_____

_____

_____

V. Interpret Results

You should consider the collective effect of the strengths and weaknesses in various control components. Management's strengths and weaknesses may have a pervasive effect on internal control. For example, management controls may mitigate a lack of segregation of duties. However, human resource policies and practices directed toward hiring competent financial and accounting personnel may not mitigate a strong bias by management to overstate earnings.

A. Areas That May Allow for Control Risk to Be Assessed Below the Maximum

Based on the completion of sections I through IV of this form you may have become aware of certain accounts, transactions, and assertions where it may be possible and efficient to plan a control risk assessment below the maximum. In the area below, document those accounts, transactions, and assertions and the related tests of controls.

Accounts, Transactions, and Assertions	*Test of Controls Working Paper Reference*
_____	_____
_____	_____
_____	_____
_____	_____

B. Areas of Possible Control Weakness

Based on the completion of sections I through IV of this form, you may have become aware of certain areas that may indicate possible control weaknesses, not including those areas relating to segregation of duties and management override which were assessed and documented in sections III and IV.

In the space provided below, document those areas of possible weakness and the impact the identified weakness will have on the audit. Discuss—

- The nature of the identified possible weakness
- Any mitigating factors or controls, such as direct management oversight

- The risk that material misstatements might occur as a result of the weakness and the type of those misstatements
- How substantive procedures will be designed to reduce the risk of those misstatements to an acceptable level.

_____

_____

_____

_____

_____

_____

_____

_____

VI. Document Your Conclusion with Respect to Internal Controls

	20_	20_	20_	20_
Prepared or updated by: In-Charge				
Reviewed by:				

Exhibit 28-2: Computer Applications Checklist—Medium to Large Business

.01 This questionnaire may be used to document your understanding of the way computers are used in the information and communication systems of a medium to large business.

.02

I. Computer Hardware

Describe the computer hardware for the entity, and its configuration. Consider—

- The make and model of company's main processing computers
- Input and output devices
- Storage means and capabilities
- Local area networks
- Stand-alone microcomputers

You may wish to attach a separate page to this checklist to document the entity's computer hardware.

_____
_____
_____
_____
_____
_____
_____
_____
_____
_____
_____
_____
_____
_____
_____
_____

II. Computer Software

Describe the entity's main software packages and whether they are unmodified, commercially available packages, or were developed or modified in-house. (End-user computing applications will be considered only for significant account balances and transaction cycles. See the Financial Reporting Information Systems and Control Checklist—Medium to Large Business.)

	Unmodified Commercial	In-House	N/A
Operating system	_____	_____	_____
Access control	_____	_____	_____
General accounting	_____	_____	_____
Network	_____	_____	_____
Database management	_____	_____	_____
Communications	_____	_____	_____
Utilities	_____	_____	_____
Other:	_____	_____	_____

_____
_____
_____
_____

III. Computer Control Environment

In the space provided below, indicate whether you strongly agree, somewhat agree, somewhat disagree, or strongly disagree with the following statements. Your answers should be based on—

- Your previous experience with the entity
- Inquiries of appropriate management, supervisory, and staff personnel
- Inspection of documents and records
- Observation of the entity's activities and operations

	No Opinion	*Strongly Disagree*	*Some-what Disagree*	*Some-what Agree*	*Strongly Agree*
Acquisition of Hardware					
1. The company has a coherent management plan for the purchase and continued investment in computer hardware.					
2. The computer hardware is sufficient to meet the company's needs.					
3. The company's computer hardware is safely and properly installed.					
4. The company has standard, regular hardware maintenance procedures.					
Acquisition of Software					
5. The company has a coherent management plan for the purchase of and continued investment in computer software.					
6. The company researches software products to determine whether they meet the needs of the intended users.					
7. The company's application programs are compatible with each other.					
8. The company obtains recognized software from reputable sources.					

	No Opinion	Strongly Disagree	Some-what Disagree	Some-what Agree	Strongly Agree
9. Company policy prohibits the use of unauthorized programs introduced by employees.	_____	_____	_____	_____	_____
10. Company policy prohibits the downloading of untested software from sources such as dial-up bulletin boards.	_____	_____	_____	_____	_____
11. The company uses virus protection software to screen for virus infections.	_____	_____	_____	_____	_____

Program Development

12. Users are involved in the design and approval of systems.	_____	_____	_____	_____	_____
13. Users review the completion of various phases of the application.	_____	_____	_____	_____	_____
14. New programs are thoroughly tested.	_____	_____	_____	_____	_____
15. Users are involved in the review of tests of the program.	_____	_____	_____	_____	_____
16. Adequate procedures exist to transfer programs from development to production libraries.	_____	_____	_____	_____	_____

Program Changes

17. Users are involved in the design and approval of program changes.	_____	_____	_____	_____	_____
18. Program changes are thoroughly tested.	_____	_____	_____	_____	_____
19. Users are involved in the review of tests of the program changes.	_____	_____	_____	_____	_____
20. Adequate procedures exit to transfer changed programs from development to production libraries.	_____	_____	_____	_____	_____

	No Opinion	Strongly Disagree	Some-what Disagree	Some-what Agree	Strongly Agree

Logical Access

21. Management has identified confidential and sensitive data for which access should be restricted.

22. Procedures are in place to restrict access to confidential and sensitive data.

23. Procedures are in place to reduce the risk of unauthorized transactions being entered into processing.

24. The use of utility programs is controlled or monitored carefully.

25. Procedures are in place to detect unauthorized changes to programs supporting the financial statements.

26. Programmer access to production programs, live data files, and job control language is controlled.

27. Operator access to source code and individual elements of data files is controlled.

28. Users have access only to defined programs and data files.

Physical Security

29. The company has established procedures for the periodic back-up of files.

30. Back-up procedures include multiple generations.

31. Back-up files are stored in a secure, off-site location.

Computer Operations

32. Operations management reviews lists of regular and unscheduled batch jobs.

	No Opinion	Strongly Disagree	Some-what Disagree	Some-what Agree	Strongly Agree
33. Job control instruction sets are menu-driven.	____	____	____	____	____
34. Jobs are executed only from the operator's terminal.	____	____	____	____	____

IV. Outside Computer Service Organizations

This section should be used to document your understanding of how the company uses an outside computer service organization to process significant accounting information. Guidance on auditing entities that use computer service organizations is contained in SAS No. 70, *Reports on the Processing of Transactions by Service Organizations* (AU section 324).

1. List the name of the service organization and the general types of services it provides.

_____

_____

2. Are the general ledger and other primary accounting records processed by an outside service organization? _____ Yes _____ No

If yes, describe the source documents provided to the service organization, the reports and other documentation received from the organization, and the controls maintained by the user over input and output to prevent or detect material misstatement.

_____

_____

_____

3. List the type and date of the most recent service auditor report.

_____

_____

Exhibit 28-3: Financial Reporting Information Systems and Controls Checklist—Medium to Large Business

Revenue Cycle

Revenue, Accounts Receivable, and Cash Receipts

   .01 This checklist may be used on any audit engagement of a medium to large company when the revenue cycle is significant. Normally, the revenue cycle is significant in most audit engagements.

.02 The purpose of this checklist is to document your understanding of controls for significant classes of transactions. Your knowledge of the revenue cycle should be sufficient for you to understand—

- How cash and credit sales are initiated

- How credit limits are established and maintained

- How cash receipts are recorded

- How sales and cash receipts are processed by the accounting system

- The accounting records and supporting documents involved in the processing and reporting of sales, accounts receivable, and cash receipts

- The processes used to prepare significant accounting estimates and disclosures

Interpreting Results

.03 This checklist documents your understanding of how internal control over the revenue cycle is designed and whether it has been placed in operation. It should help you in planning a primarily substantive approach. To assess control risk below the maximum, you will need to design tests of controls and then test specific controls to determine the effectiveness of their design and operation.

.04 The processes, documents, and controls listed on this questionnaire are typical for medium to large business entities but are by no means all-inclusive. The preponderance of "No" or "N/A" responses may indicate that the entity uses other processes, documents, or controls in their information and communication systems. You should consider supplementing this questionnaire with a memo or flowchart to document significant features of the client's system that are not covered by this questionnaire. (See AAM section 4500 for example flowcharting techniques.)

.05

	Personnel	N/A	No	Yes
1. Revenue and Accounts Receivable				
A. Initiating Sales Transactions				
1. Credit limits are clearly defined.	___	___	___	___
2. Credit limits are clearly communicated.	___	___	___	___
3. The credit of prospective customers is investigated before it is extended to them.	___	___	___	___
4. Credit limits are periodically reviewed.	___	___	___	___

	Personnel	N/A	No	Yes
5. The people who perform the credit function are independent of—				
• Sales	___	___	___	___
• Billing	___	___	___	___
• Collection	___	___	___	___
• Accounting	___	___	___	___
6. Credit limits and changes in credit limits are communicated to persons responsible for approving sales orders on a timely basis.	___	___	___	___
7. The company has clearly defined policies and procedures for acceptance and approval of sales orders.	___	___	___	___
8. Prenumbered sales orders are used and accounted for.	___	___	___	___
9. Prenumbered shipping documents are used to record shipments.	___	___	___	___
10. Shipping document information is verified prior to shipment.	___	___	___	___
11. The people who perform the shipping function are independent of—				
• Sales	___	___	___	___
• Billing	___	___	___	___
• Collection	___	___	___	___
• Accounting	___	___	___	___
12. All shipping documents are accounted for.	___	___	___	___
13. Prenumbered credit memos are used to document sales returns.	___	___	___	___
14. All credit memos are approved and accounted for.	___	___	___	___
15. Credit memos are matched with receiving reports for returned goods.	___	___	___	___
16. Cash sales are controlled by cash registers or prenumbered cash receipts forms.	___	___	___	___

	Personnel	N/A	No	Yes
17. Someone other than the cashier has custody of the cash register tape compartment.				
18. Someone other than the cashier takes periodic readings of the cash register and balances the cash on hand.				

B. Processing Sales Transactions

	Personnel	N/A	No	Yes
19. Information necessary to prepare invoices (e.g., prices, discount policies) is clearly communicated to billing personnel on a timely basis.				
20. Prenumbered invoices are prepared promptly after goods are shipped.				
21. Quantities on the invoices are compared to shipping documents.				
22. The prices on the invoices are current.				
23. The people who perform the billing function are independent of—				
• Sales				
• Credit				
• Collection				
24. Invoices are mailed to customers on a timely basis.				
25. Invoices are posted to the general ledger on a timely basis.				
26. Standard journal entries are used to record sales.				
27. Invoices are posted to the sales and accounts receivable subsidiary ledgers or journals on a timely basis.				
28. Credit memos are posted to the general ledger on a timely basis.				

	Personnel	N/A	No	Yes

29. Credit memos are posted to the sales and accounts receivable subsidiary ledgers or journals on a timely basis. _____ _____ _____ _____

30. Procedures exist for determining proper cut-off of sales at month-end. _____ _____ _____ _____

31. The sales and accounts receivable balances shown in the general ledger are reconciled to the sales and accounts receivable subsidiary ledgers on a regular basis. _____ _____ _____ _____

C. Estimates and Disclosures for Sales Transactions

32. The accounting system generates a monthly aging of accounts receivable. _____ _____ _____ _____

33. The people who prepare the aging are independent of— _____ _____ _____ _____
   - Billing _____ _____ _____ _____
   - Collection _____ _____ _____ _____

34. Management uses the accounts receivable aging to investigate, write off, or adjust delinquent accounts receivable. _____ _____ _____ _____

35. Management uses the accounts receivable aging and other information to estimate an allowance for doubtful accounts. _____ _____ _____ _____

36. The person responsible for financial reporting identifies significant concentrations of credit risk. _____ _____ _____ _____

II. Cash Receipts

A. Initiating Cash Receipts Transactions

1. The entity maintains records of payments on accounts by customer. _____ _____ _____ _____

	Personnel	N/A	No	Yes
2. Someone other than the person responsible for maintaining accounts receivable opens the mail and lists the cash receipts.	____	____	____	____
3. Cash receipts are deposited intact.	____	____	____	____
4. Cash receipts are deposited in separate bank accounts when required.	____	____	____	____
5. People who handle cash receipts are adequately bonded.	____	____	____	____
6. Local bank accounts used for branch office collections are subject to withdrawal only by the home office.	____	____	____	____

B. Processing Cash Received on Account

	Personnel	N/A	No	Yes
7. Cash receipts are posted to the general ledger on a timely basis.	____	____	____	____
8. Cash receipts are posted to the accounts receivable subsidiary ledger on a timely basis.	____	____	____	____
9. Standard journal entries are used to post cash receipts.	____	____	____	____
10. The people who enter cash receipts to the accounting system are independent of the physical handling of collections.	____	____	____	____
11. Timely bank reconciliations are prepared or reviewed by someone independent of the cash receipts function.	____	____	____	____

End-User Computing in the Revenue Cycle

.06 End-user computing occurs when the user is responsible for the development and execution of the computer application that generates the information used by that same person. For example, an accounting clerk prepares a spreadsheet which shows amortization of premiums or discounts, and the information from the spreadsheet is the source of a journal entry.

.07 The Computer Applications Checklist—Medium to Large Business was used to document your understanding of computer applications operated by the company's MIS department. In this section of the Financial Reporting Information Systems and Controls Checklist, you may document your understanding of how end-user computing is used in the revenue cycle to process significant accounting information outside of the MIS department.

.08 You should obtain an understanding of any spreadsheet application, database, or separate computer system that has been developed by end-users to—

- Process significant accounting information outside of the MIS-operated accounting application. For example, a spreadsheet accumulates invoices for batch processing.

- Make significant accounting decisions. For example, a spreadsheet application that ages accounts receivable and helps in determining writeoffs.

- Accumulate footnote information. For example, a database of customers provides information about the location of customers for possible concentration of credit risk disclosures.

.09 In the space provided below, describe how end-user computing is used in the revenue cycle. Describe—

- The person or department who performs the computing

- A general description of the application and its type (e.g., spreadsheet)

- The source of the information used in the application

- How the results of the application are used in further processing or decision making

_____

_____

_____

_____

_____

_____

_____

_____

_____

_____

_____

Procedures and Controls over End-User Computing

.10 Answer the following questions relating to procedures and controls over end-user computing related to the revenue cycle.

	Personnel	N/A	No	Yes

Revenue Cycle

1. End-user applications listed in paragraph .09 of this form have been adequately tested before use.

2. The application has an appropriate level of built-in controls, such as edit checks, range tests, or reasonableness checks.

3. Access controls limit access to the end-user application.

4. A mechanism exists to prevent or detect the use of incorrect versions of data files.

5. The output of the end-user applications is reviewed for accuracy or reconciled to the source information.

Information Processed by Outside Computer Service Organizations

.11 The Computer Applications Checklist—Medium to Large Business Computer Applications was used to document your understanding of the client's use of an outside computer service organization to process entity-wide accounting information such as the general ledger. In this section you will document your understanding of how the entity uses an outside computer service organization to process information relating specifically to the revenue cycle.

.12 In the space below, describe the revenue cycle information processed by the outside computer service bureau. Discuss—

* The general nature of the application

* The source documents used by the service organization

* The reports or other accounting documents produced by the service organization

* The nature of the service organization's responsibilities. Do they merely record entity transactions and process related data, or do they have the ability to initiate transactions on their own?

* Controls maintained by the entity to prevent or detect material misstatement in the input or output.

_____

_____

_____

Purchasing Cycle
_____

Purchasing, Accounts Payable, and Cash Disbursements

.13 This checklist may be used on any audit engagement of a medium to large business where the purchasing cycle is significant. Normally, the purchasing cycle is significant for most businesses.

.14 The purpose of this checklist is to document your understanding of controls for significant classes of transactions. Your knowledge of the purchasing cycle should be sufficient for you to understand—

- How purchases are initiated and goods received
- How cash disbursements are recorded
- How purchases and cash disbursements are processed by the financial reporting information system
- The accounting records and supporting documents involved in the processing and reporting of purchases, accounts payable, and cash disbursements
- The processes used to prepare significant accounting estimates and disclosures

Interpreting Results

.15 This checklist documents your understanding of how internal control over the purchasing cycle is designed and whether it has been placed in operation. It should help you in planning a primarily substantive approach. To assess control risk below the maximum, you will need to design tests of controls and then test specific controls to determine the effectiveness of their design and operation.

.16 The processes, documents, and controls listed on this questionnaire are typical for medium to large business entities but are by no means all-inclusive. The preponderance of "No" or "N/A" responses may indicate that the entity uses other processes, documents, or controls in their information and communication systems. You should consider supplementing this questionnaire with a memo or flowchart to document significant features of the client's system that are not covered by this questionnaire. (See AAM section 4500 for example flowcharting techniques.)

.17

	Personnel	N/A	No	Yes

1. Purchases and Accounts Payable

A. Initiating Purchases and Receipt of Goods

1. All purchases over a predetermined amount are approved by management.

2. Nonroutine purchases (for example, services, fixed assets, or investments) are approved by management.

3. A purchase order system is used, prenumbered purchase orders are accounted for, and physical access to purchase orders is controlled.

4. Open purchase orders are periodically reviewed.

5. The purchasing function is independent of—
   - Receiving
   - Invoice processing
   - Cash disbursements

6. All goods are inspected and counted when received.

7. Prenumbered receiving reports, or a log, are used to record the receipt of goods.

8. The receiving reports or log indicate the date the items were received.

9. The receiving function is independent of—
   - Purchasing
   - Invoice processing
   - Cash disbursements

B. Processing Purchases

10. Invoices from vendors are matched with applicable receiving reports.

11. Invoices are reviewed for proper quantity and prices, and mathematical accuracy.

	Personnel	N/A	No	Yes
12. Invoices from vendors are posted to the general ledger on a timely basis.	_____	_____	_____	_____
13. Invoices from vendors are posted to the accounts payable subsidiary ledger on a timely basis.	_____	_____	_____	_____
14. The invoice processing function is independent of—	_____	_____	_____	_____
• Purchasing	_____	_____	_____	_____
• Receiving	_____	_____	_____	_____
• Cash disbursements	_____	_____	_____	_____
15. Standard journal entries are used to post accounts payable.	_____	_____	_____	_____
16. Accounts payable account per the general ledger is reconciled periodically to the accounts payable subsidiary ledger.	_____	_____	_____	_____
17. Statements from vendors are reconciled to the accounts payable subsidiary ledger.	_____	_____	_____	_____

C. Disclosures

	Personnel	N/A	No	Yes
18. Management has the information to identify vulnerability due to concentrations of suppliers (ASC 275).	_____	_____	_____	_____

II. Cash Disbursements

A. Initiating Cash Disbursements

	Personnel	N/A	No	Yes
1. All disbursements except those from petty cash are made by check.	_____	_____	_____	_____
2. All checks are recorded.	_____	_____	_____	_____
3. Supporting documentation such as invoices and receiving reports are reviewed before the checks are signed.	_____	_____	_____	_____
4. Supporting documents are canceled to avoid duplicate payment.	_____	_____	_____	_____

	Personnel	N/A	No	Yes

B. Processing Cash Disbursements

5. Cash disbursements are posted to the general ledger on a timely basis. _____ _____ _____ _____

6. Cash disbursements are posted to the accounts payable subsidiary ledger on a timely basis. _____ _____ _____ _____

7. Standard journal entries are used to post cash disbursements. _____ _____ _____ _____

8. Timely bank reconciliations are prepared or reviewed by the owner or manager or someone independent of the cash receipts function. _____ _____ _____ _____

End-User Computing in the Purchasing Cycle

.18 End-user computing occurs when the user is responsible for the development and execution of the computer application that generates the information used by that same person. For example, an accounting clerk prepares a spreadsheet that amortizes premiums or discounts, and the information from the spreadsheet is the source of a journal entry.

.19 The Computer Applications Checklist—Medium to Large Business was used to document your understanding of computer applications operated by the company's MIS department. In this section of the Financial Reporting Information Systems and Controls Checklist, you may document your understanding of how end-user computing is used in the purchasing cycle to process significant accounting information outside of the MIS department.

.20 You should obtain an understanding of any spreadsheet application, database, or separate computer system that has been developed by end-users to—

- Process significant accounting information outside of the MIS-operated accounting application. For example, a spreadsheet accumulates nonroutine purchases for batch processing

- Make significant accounting decisions

- Accumulate footnote information. For example, a database of vendors provides information for possible concentration of risk disclosures

.21 In the space provided below, describe how end-user computing is used in the purchasing cycle. Describe—

- The person or department who performs the computing

- A general description of the application and its type (e.g., spreadsheet)

- The source of the information used in the application
- How the results of the application are used in further processing or decision making

_____

_____

_____

_____

_____

_____

_____

_____

_____

_____

_____

Procedures and Controls Over End-User Computing

.22 Answer the following questions relating to procedures and controls over end user computing related to the purchasing cycle.

	Personnel	*N/A*	*No*	*Yes*

Purchasing Cycle

1. End user applications listed in paragraph .21 of this form have been adequately tested before use.

2. The application has an appropriate level of built-in controls, such as edit checks, range tests, or reasonableness checks.

3. Access controls limit access to the end user application.

4. A mechanism exists to prevent or detect the use of incorrect versions of data files.

5. The output of the end-user applications is reviewed for accuracy or reconciled to the source information.

Information Processed by Outside Computer Service Organizations

.23 The Computer Applications Checklist—Medium to Large Business was used to document your understanding of the client's use of an outside computer service organization to process entity-wide accounting information such as the general ledger. In this section you will document your understanding of how the entity uses an outside computer service organization to process information relating specifically to the purchasing cycle.

.24 In the space below, describe the purchasing cycle information processed by the outside computer service bureau. Discuss—

- The general nature of the application
- The source documents used by the service organization
- The reports or other accounting documents produced by the service organization.
- The nature of the service organization's responsibilities. Do they merely record entity transactions and process related data, or do they have the ability to initiate transactions on their own?
- Controls maintained by the entity to prevent or detect material misstatement in the input or output.

_____

_____

_____

_____

_____

Inventory

Inventory and Cost of Sales

.25 This checklist may be used on any audit engagement of a medium to large business where inventory is a significant transaction cycle.

.26 The purpose of this checklist is to document your understanding of controls for significant classes of transactions. Your knowledge of the inventory cycle should be sufficient for you to understand—

- How costs are capitalized to inventory
- How cost is relieved from inventory
- How inventory costs and cost of sales are processed by the accounting system
- The procedures used to take the physical inventory count
- The accounting records and supporting documents involved in the processing and reporting of inventory and cost of sales
- The processes used to prepare significant accounting estimates and disclosures

Interpreting Results

.27 This checklist documents your understanding of how internal control over the inventory cycle is designed and whether it has been placed in operation. It should help you in planning a primarily substantive approach. To assess control risk below the maximum, you will need to design tests of controls and then test specific controls to determine the effectiveness of their design and operation.

.28 The processes, documents, and controls listed on this questionnaire are typical for medium to large business entities but are by no means all-inclusive. The preponderance of "No" or "N/A" responses may indicate that the entity uses other processes, documents, or controls in their information and communication systems. You should consider supplementing this questionnaire with a memo or flowchart to document significant features of the client's system that are not covered by this questionnaire. (See AAM section 4500 for example flowcharting techniques.)

.29

	Personnel	*N/A*	*No*	*Yes*

1. Inventory and Cost of Sales

   A. Capturing Capitalizable Costs[1]

   1. Management prepares production goals and schedules based on sales forecasts.

   2. The company budgets its planned inventory levels.

   3. All releases from storage of raw materials, supplies, and purchased parts inventory are based on approved requisition documents.

   4. Labor costs are reported promptly and in sufficient detail to allow for the proper allocation to inventory.

   5. The entity uses a cost accounting system to accumulate capitalizable costs.

   6. The cost accounting system distinguishes between costs that should be capitalized for GAAP purposes and those that should be capitalizable for tax purposes.

   7. For standard cost systems:
       • Standard rates and volume are periodically compared to actual and revised accordingly.
       • Significant variances are investigated.

---

[1] You should also consider completing the Financial Reporting Information Systems and Controls Checklist for the purchasing cycle to document your understanding of how the purchase of inventory is initiated.

	Personnel	N/A	No	Yes
8. The cost accounting system interfaces with the general ledger.	___	___	___	___
9. Transfers of completed units from production to custody of finished goods inventory are based on approved completion reports that authorize the transfer.	___	___	___	___
10. The people responsible for maintaining detailed inventory records are independent from the physical custody and handling of inventories.	___	___	___	___
11. Production cost budgets are periodically compared to actual costs, and significant differences are explained.	___	___	___	___

B. Inventory Records

	Personnel	N/A	No	Yes
12. The entity maintains adequate inventory records of prices and amounts on hand.	___	___	___	___
13. Withdrawals from inventory are based on prenumbered finished inventory requisitions, shipping reports, or both.	___	___	___	___
14. Additions to and withdrawals from inventory are posted to the inventory records and the general ledger.	___	___	___	___
15. Standard journal entries are used to post inventory transactions to the inventory records and the general ledger.	___	___	___	___
16. Inventory records are periodically reconciled to the general ledger.	___	___	___	___
17. Inventory records are reconciled to a physical inventory count.	___	___	___	___

C. Physical Inventory Counts

	Personnel	N/A	No	Yes
18. Inventory is counted at least once a year.	___	___	___	___

	Personnel	N/A	No	Yes
19. Physical inventory counters are given adequate instructions.	_____	_____	_____	_____
20. Inventory count procedures are sufficient to provide an accurate count, including steps to ensure—	_____	_____	_____	_____
• Proper cut-off	_____	_____	_____	_____
• Identification of obsolete items	_____	_____	_____	_____
• All items are counted once and only once	_____	_____	_____	_____

D. Estimates and Disclosures

21. Management is able to identify excess, slow-moving, or obsolete inventory.	_____	_____	_____	_____
22. Excess, slow-moving, or obsolete inventory is periodically written off.	_____	_____	_____	_____
23. Management can identify inventory subject to rapid technological obsolescence that may need to be disclosed under ASC 275.	_____	_____	_____	_____

End-User Computing in the Inventory Cycle

.30 End-user computing occurs when the user is responsible for the development and execution of the computer application that generates the information used by that same person. For example, an accounting clerk prepares a spreadsheet that amortizes premiums or discounts, and the information from the spreadsheet is the source of a journal entry.

.31 The Computer Applications Checklist—Medium to Large Business was used to document your understanding of computer applications operated by the company's MIS department. In this section of the Financial Reporting Information Systems and Controls Checklist, you may document your understanding of how end-user computing is used in the inventory cycle to process significant accounting information outside of the MIS department.

.32 You should obtain an understanding of any spreadsheet application, database, or separate computer system that has been developed by end-users to—

- Process significant accounting information outside the MIS-operated accounting application. For example, a spreadsheet calculates overhead cost allocations.

- Make significant accounting decisions. A spreadsheet application tracks slow-moving items for possible write-off.

- Accumulate footnote information.

.33 In the space provided below, describe how end user computing is used in the inventory cycle. Describe—

- The person or department who performs the computing.

- A general description of the application and its type (e.g., spreadsheet).

- The source of the information used in the application.

- How the results of the application are used in further processing or decision making.

_____

_____

_____

_____

_____

_____

_____

_____

_____

_____

_____

_____

_____

_____

Procedures and Controls Over End-User Computing

.34 Answer the following questions relating to procedures and controls over end user computing related to the inventory cycle.

	Personnel	*N/A*	*No*	*Yes*
Inventory Cycle				
1. End-user applications listed in paragraph .33 of this form have been adequately tested before use.	_____	_____	_____	_____
2. The application has an appropriate level of built-in controls, such as edit checks, range rests, or reasonableness checks.	_____	_____	_____	_____

	Personnel	*N/A*	*No*	*Yes*
3. Access controls limit access to the end user application.	_____	_____	_____	_____
4. A mechanism exists to prevent or detect the use of incorrect versions of data files.	_____	_____	_____	_____
5. The output of the end-user applications is reviewed for accuracy or reconciled to the source information.	_____	_____	_____	_____

Information Processed by Outside Computer Service Organizations

    .35 The Computer Applications Checklist—Medium to Large Business was used to document your understanding of the client's use of an outside computer service organization to process entity-wide accounting information such as the general ledger. In this section you will document your understanding of how the entity uses an outside computer service organization to process information relating specifically to the inventory cycle.

    .36 In the space below, describe the inventory cycle information processed by the outside computer service bureau. Discuss—

- The general nature of the application.
- The source documents used by the service organization.
- The reports or other accounting documents produced by the service organization.
- The nature of the service organization's responsibilities. Do they merely record entity transactions and process related data, or do they have the ability to initiate transactions on their own?
- Controls maintained by the entity to prevent or detect material misstatement in the input or output.

Financing

Investments and Debt

    .37 This checklist may be used on any audit engagement of a medium to large business where investments or debt are a significant transaction cycle.

    .38 The purpose of this checklist is to document your understanding of controls for significant classes of transactions. Your knowledge of the financing cycle should be sufficient for you to understand

- How investment decisions are authorized and initiated
- How financing is authorized and captured by the accounting system
- How management classifies investments as either trading, available-for-sale, or held to maturity

- How investment and debt transactions are processed by the accounting system
- The accounting records and supporting documents involved in the processing and reporting of investments and debt
- The processes used to prepare significant accounting estimates, disclosures, and presentation

Interpreting Results

.39 This checklist documents your understanding of how internal control is designed and whether it has been placed in operation. It should help you in planning a primarily substantive approach. To assess control risk below the maximum, you will need to design tests of controls and then test specific controls to determine the effectiveness of their design and operation.

.40 The processes, documents, and controls listed on this questionnaire are typical for medium to large business entities but are by no means all-inclusive. The preponderance of "No" or "N/A" responses may indicate that the entity uses other processes, documents, or controls in their information and communication systems. You should consider supplementing this questionnaire with a memo or flowchart to document significant features of the client's system that are not covered by this questionnaire. (See AAM section 4500 for example flowcharting techniques.)

.41

	Personnel	N/A	No	Yes

I. Investments

A. Authorization and Initiation

1. Investment transactions are authorized by management.
2. The company has established policies and procedures for determining when board of director approval is required for investment transactions.
3. Management and the board assess and understand the risks associated with the entity's investment strategies.
4. Investments are registered in the name of the company.
5. At acquisition, investments are classified as trading, available-for-sale, or held-to-maturity.

	Personnel	N/A	No	Yes

B. Processing

6. Investment transactions are posted to the general ledger on a timely basis.

7. Account statements received from brokers are reviewed for accuracy.

8. Discounts and premiums are amortized regularly using the interest method.

9. Procedures exist to determine the fair value of trading and available-for-sale securities.

10. The general ledger is periodically reconciled to account statements from brokers or physical counts of securities on hand.

C. Disclosures

11. Management identifies investments with off-balance-sheet credit risk for proper disclosure.

12. Management distinguishes between derivatives held or issued for trading purposes and those held or issued for purposes other than trading.

13. The entity accumulates the information necessary to make disclosures about derivatives.

II. Debt

A. Authorization and Initiation

1. Financing transactions are authorized by management.

2. The company has established policies and procedures for determining when board of director approval is required for financing transactions.

3. Management and the board assess and understand all terms, covenants, and restrictions of debt transactions.

	Personnel	N/A	No	Yes

B. Processing and Documentation

4. Debt transactions are posted to the general ledger on a timely basis.

5. Any premiums or discount are amortized using the interest method.

6. The company maintains up-to-date files of all notes payable.

C. Disclosure

7. Procedures exist to determine the fair value of notes payable for proper disclosure.

8. Management reviews their compliance with debt covenants on a timely basis.

End-User Computing in the Financing Cycle

.42 End-user computing occurs when the user is responsible for the development and execution of the computer application that generates the information used by that same person. For example, an accounting clerk prepares a spreadsheet that amortizes premiums or discounts, and the information from the spreadsheet is the source of a journal entry.

.43 The Computer Applications Checklist—Medium to Large Business was used to document your understanding of computer applications operated by the company's MIS department. In this section of the Financial Reporting Information Systems and Controls Checklist, you may document your understanding of how end-user computing is used in the financing cycle to process significant accounting information outside of the MIS department.

.44 You should obtain an understanding of any spreadsheet application, database, or separate computer system that has been developed by end-users to—

- Process significant accounting information outside of the MIS-operated accounting application. For example, a spreadsheet application calculates the amortization of premiums and discounts on investments.
- Make significant accounting decisions.
- Accumulate footnote information. For example, a spreadsheet application calculates five-year debt maturities for footnote disclosure.

.45 In the space provided below, describe how end-user computing is used in the financing cycle. Describe—

- The person or department who performs the computing.
- A general description of the application and its type (e.g., spreadsheet).

- The source of the information used in the application.
- How the results of the application are used in further processing or decision making.

_____

_____

_____

_____

_____

_____

_____

_____

_____

_____

_____

_____

_____

_____

Procedures and Controls over End-User Computing

.46 Answer the following questions relating to procedures and controls over end user computing related to the financing cycle.

	Personnel	N/A	No	Yes

Financing Cycle

1. End-user applications listed in paragraph .45 of this form have been adequately tested before use.

2. The application has an appropriate level of built-in controls, such as edit checks, range tests, or reasonableness checks.

3. Access controls limit access to the end user application.

4. A mechanism exists to prevent or detect the use of incorrect versions of data files.

5. The output of the end-user applications is reviewed for accuracy or reconciled to the source information.

Information Processed by Outside Computer Service Organizations

.47 The Computer Applications Checklist—Medium to Large Business was used to document your understanding of the client's use of an outside computer service organization to process entity-wide accounting information such as the general ledger. In this section you will document your understanding of how the entity uses an outside computer service organization to process information relating specifically to the financing cycle.

.48 In the space below, describe the financing cycle information processed by the outside computer service bureau. Discuss

- The general nature of the application.

- The source documents used by the service organization.

- The reports or other accounting documents produced by the service organization.

- The nature of the service organization's responsibilities. Do they merely record entity transactions and process related data, or do they have the ability to initiate transactions on their own?

- Controls maintained by the entity to prevent or detect material misstatement in the input or output.

Property, Plant, and Equipment

Fixed Assets and Depreciation

.49 This checklist may be used on any audit engagement where fixed assets are a significant transaction cycle.

.50 The purpose of this checklist is to document your understanding of controls for significant classes of transactions. Your knowledge of the property, plant, and equipment cycle should be sufficient for you to understand—

- How fixed asset transactions are authorized and initiated. (Additional information on the acquisition of fixed assets is documented on the Accounting Systems and Control Checklist for the Purchasing Cycle.)

- How fixed assets transactions and depreciation are processed by the accounting system.

- The accounting records and supporting documents involved in the processing and reporting of fixed assets and depreciation.

- The processes used to prepare significant accounting estimates and disclosures.

Interpreting Results

.51 This checklist documents your understanding of how internal control over property, plant, and equipment is designed and whether it has been placed in operation. It should help you in planning a primarily substantive approach. To assess control risk below the maximum, you will need to design tests of controls and then test specific controls to determine the effectiveness of their design and operation.

.52 The processes, documents, and controls listed on this questionnaire are typical for medium to large business entities but are by no means all-inclusive. The preponderance of "No" or "N/A" responses may indicate that the entity uses other processes, documents, or controls in their information and communication systems. You should consider supplementing this questionnaire with a memo or flowchart to document significant features of the client's system that are not covered by this questionnaire. (See AAM section 4500 for example flowcharting techniques.)

.53

	Personnel	*N/A*	*No*	*Yes*
1. Fixed Assets and Depreciation				
A. Authorization and Initiation				
1. Fixed asset acquisitions and retirements are authorized by management.	_____	_____	_____	_____
B. Processing and Documentation				
2. The company maintains detailed records of fixed assets and the related accumulated depreciation.	_____	_____	_____	_____
3. Responsibilities for maintaining the fixed asset records are segregated from the custody of the assets.	_____	_____	_____	_____
4. The general ledger and detailed fixed asset records are updated for fixed asset transactions on a timely basis.	_____	_____	_____	_____
5. A process exists for the timely calculation of depreciation expense for both book and tax purposes.	_____	_____	_____	_____

	Personnel	*N/A*	*No*	*Yes*
6. The general ledger and detailed fixed asset records are updated for depreciation expense on a timely basis.	_____	_____	_____	_____
7. The general ledger is periodically reconciled to the detailed fixed asset records.	_____	_____	_____	_____

C. Disclosure and Estimation

8. Management identifies events or changes in circumstances that may indicate fixed assets have been impaired (FAS 121).	_____	_____	_____	_____
9. Management assesses and understands the risk of specialized equipment becoming subject to technological obsolescence (ASC 275).	_____	_____	_____	_____

End-User Computing in the Property, Plant, and Equipment Cycle

.54 End-user computing occurs when the user is responsible for the development and execution of the computer application that generates the information used by that same person. For example, an accounting clerk prepares a spreadsheet that amortizes premiums or discounts, and the information from the spreadsheet is the source of a journal entry.

.55 The Computer Applications Checklist—Medium or Large Business was used to document your understanding of computer applications operated by the company's MIS department. In this section of the Financial Reporting Information Systems and Controls Checklist, you may document your understanding of how end-user computing is used in the revenue cycle to process significant accounting information outside of the MIS department.

.56 You should obtain an understanding of any spreadsheet application, database, or separate computer system that has been developed by end-users to—

- Process significant accounting information outside of the MIS-operated accounting application. For example, a spreadsheet application calculates the depreciation expense.

- Make significant accounting decisions. For example, a spreadsheet application is used to analyze lease or buy decisions.

- Accumulate footnote information.

.57 In the space provided below, describe how end-user computing is used in the property, plant, and equipment cycle. Describe—

- The person or department who performs the computing.

- A general description of the application and its type (e.g., spreadsheet).

- The source of the information used in the application.

- How the results of the application are used in further processing or decision making.

_____

_____

_____

_____

_____

_____

_____

_____

_____

_____

Procedures and Controls Over End-User Computing

.58 Answer the following questions relating to procedures and controls over end user computing related to the property, plant, and equipment cycle.

	Personnel	*N/A*	*No*	*Yes*

Property, Plant, and Equipment Cycle

1. End user applications listed in paragraph .57 of this form have been adequately tested before use.

2. The application has an appropriate level of built-in controls, such as edit checks, range tests, or reasonableness checks.

3. Access controls limit access to the end-user application.

4. A mechanism exists to prevent or detect the use of incorrect versions of data files.

5. The output of the end-user applications is reviewed for accuracy or reconciled to the source information.

Information Processed by Outside Computer Service Organizations

.59 The Computer Applications Checklist—Medium to Large Business was used to document your understanding of the client's use of an outside computer service organization to process entity-wide accounting information such as the general ledger. In this section you will document your understanding of how the entity uses an outside computer service organization to process information relating specifically to the property, plant, and equipment cycle.

.60 In the space below, describe the property, plant, and equipment cycle information processed by the outside computer service bureau. Discuss

- The general nature of the application.
- The source documents used by the service organization.
- The reports or other accounting documents produced by the service organization.
- The nature of the service organization's responsibilities. Do they merely record entity transactions and process related data, or do they have the ability to initiate transactions on their own?
- Controls maintained by the entity to prevent or detect material misstatement in the input or output.

_____

_____

_____

_____

_____

Payroll Cycle

I. Payroll Expense

.61 This checklist may be used on any audit engagement of a medium to large business where the payroll cycle is significant.

.62 The purpose of this checklist is to document your understanding of controls for significant classes of transactions. Your knowledge of the payroll cycle should be sufficient for you to understand—

- How the time worked by employees is captured by the accounting system.
- How salaries and hourly rates are established.
- How payroll and the related withholdings; are calculated.
- The accounting records and supporting documents involved in the processing and reporting of payroll.

Interpreting Results

.63 This checklist documents your understanding of how internal control over the payroll cycle is designed and whether it has been placed in operation. It should help you in planning a primarily substantive approach. To assess control risk below the maximum, you will need to design tests of controls and then test specific controls to determine the effectiveness of their design and operation.

.64 The processes, documents, and controls listed on this questionnaire are typical for medium to large business entities but are by no means all-inclusive. The preponderance of "No" or "N/A" responses may indicate that the entity uses other processes, documents, or controls in their information and communication systems. You should consider supplementing this questionnaire with a memo or flowchart to document significant features of the client's system that are not covered by this questionnaire. (See AAM section 4500 for example flowcharting techniques.)

.65

	Personnel	N/A	No	Yes

I. Payroll

A. Initiating Payroll Transactions

		Personnel	N/A	No	Yes
1.	Wages and salaries are approved by management.	_____	_____	_____	_____
2.	Salaries of senior management are based on written authorization of the board of directors.	_____	_____	_____	_____
3.	Bonuses are authorized by the board of directors.	_____	_____	_____	_____
4.	Employee benefits and perks are granted in accordance with management's authorization.	_____	_____	_____	_____
5.	Senior management benefits and perks are authorized by the board of directors.	_____	_____	_____	_____
6.	Proper authorization is obtained for all payroll deductions.	_____	_____	_____	_____
7.	Access to personnel files is limited to those who are independent of the payroll or cash functions.	_____	_____	_____	_____
8.	Wage and salary rates and payroll deductions are reported promptly to employees who perform the payroll processing function.	_____	_____	_____	_____
9.	Changes in wage and salary rates and payroll deductions are reported promptly to employees who perform the payroll processing function.	_____	_____	_____	_____

	Personnel	N/A	No	Yes
10. Adequate time records are maintained for employees paid by the hour.	_____	_____	_____	_____
11. Time records for hourly employees are approved by a supervisor.	_____	_____	_____	_____

B. Processing Payroll

	Personnel	N/A	No	Yes
12. Payroll is calculated using authorized pay rates, payroll deductions, and time records.	_____	_____	_____	_____
13. Payroll registers are reviewed for accuracy.	_____	_____	_____	_____
14. Standard journal entries are used to post payroll transactions to the general ledger.	_____	_____	_____	_____
15. Payroll cost distributions are reconciled to gross pay.	_____	_____	_____	_____
16. Payroll information such as hours worked is periodically compared to production records.	_____	_____	_____	_____
17. Net pay is distributed by persons who are independent of personnel, payroll preparation, time-keeping, and check preparation functions.	_____	_____	_____	_____
18. The responsibility for custody and follow-up of unclaimed wages is assigned to someone who is independent of personnel, payroll processing, and cash disbursement functions.	_____	_____	_____	_____
19. Procedures are in place to estimate the fair value of stock-based compensation plans.	_____	_____	_____	_____

End-User Computing in the Payroll Cycle

.66 End-user computing occurs when the user is responsible for the development and execution of the computer application that generates the information used by that same person. For example, an accounting clerk prepares a spreadsheet that amortizes premiums or discounts, and the information from the spreadsheet is the source of a journal entry.

.67 The Computer Applications Checklist—Medium to Large Business was used to document your understanding of off-the-shelf computer software accounting applications such as the general ledger. In this section of the Financial Reporting Information Systems and Controls Checklist, you may document your understanding of how end-user computing is used in the payroll cycle to process significant accounting information outside of the general accounting software.

.68 You should obtain an understanding of any spreadsheet application, database, or separate computer system that has been developed by end-users to—

- Process significant accounting information outside of the MIS-operated accounting application, for example, a spreadsheet accumulates time card information for batch processing
- Make significant accounting decisions, for example, a spreadsheet application is used to accumulate payroll information by job for further analysis
- Accumulate footnote information

.69 In the space provided below, describe how end-user computing is used in the payroll cycle. Describe—

- The person or department who performs the computing
- A general description of the application and its type (e.g., spreadsheet)
- The source of the information used in the application
- How the results of the application are used in further processing or decision making

_____

_____

_____

_____

_____

_____

_____

_____

_____

_____

_____

_____

_____

_____

_____

Procedures and Controls Over End-User Computing

.70 Answer the following questions relating to procedures and controls over end-user computing related to the payroll cycle.

	Personnel	*N/A*	*No*	*Yes*

Payroll Cycle

1. End-user applications listed in paragraph .69 of this form have been adequately tested before use. _____ _____ _____ _____

2. The application has an appropriate level of built-in controls, such as edit checks, range rests, or reasonableness checks. _____ _____ _____ _____

3. Access controls limit access to the end-user application. _____ _____ _____ _____

4. A mechanism exists to prevent or detect the use of incorrect versions of data files. _____ _____ _____ _____

5. The output of the end-user applications is reviewed for accuracy or reconciled to the source information. _____ _____ _____ _____

Information Processed by Outside Computer Service Organizations

.71 The Computer Applications Checklist—Medium to Large Business was used to document your understanding of the client's use of an outside computer service organization to process entity-wide accounting information such as the general ledger. In this section you will document your understanding of how the entity uses an outside computer service organization to process information relating specifically to the payroll cycle.

.72 In the space below, describe the inventory cycle information processed by the outside computer service bureau. Discuss—

- The general nature of the application.
- The source documents used by the service organization.
- The reports or other accounting documents produced by the service organization.
- The nature of the service organization's responsibilities. Do they merely record entity transactions and process related data, or do they have the ability to initiate transactions on their own?
- Controls maintained by the entity to prevent or detect material misstatement in the input or output.

_____

_____

_____

_____

_____

_____

_____

CHAPTER 29

INTERNAL AUDIT OF FINANCIAL STATEMENT ACCOUNTS

CONTENTS

An important function of the internal audit staff is to ensure that the financial statements prepared by management are presented fairly, in all material respects, in conformity with generally accepted accounting principles. This will facilitate the annual audit performed by the independent certified public accountant.

This chapter addresses the objectives and procedures to consider in auditing major financial statement accounts. The results of audit testing should be clearly documented. Discrepancies between the audit results and the books and records should be investigated. The exceptions could be indicative of widespread problems that could have an overall adverse effect on the entity.

FINANCIAL STATEMENT ASSERTIONS

Financial statements, in general, consist of assertions that are representations of the management of the company.

Specific financial statement assertions include:

- *Existence or occurrence.* Assertions about existence or occurrence are concerned with whether assets or liabilities of the entity exist at a particular date and whether recorded transactions have truly occurred during a specified time period.

- *Completeness.* Assertions pertaining to completeness apply to whether all transactions and accounts that should be included in the financial statements are actually included.

- *Rights and obligations.* Assertions relating to rights and obligations deal with whether the entity has legal title to assets and whether the recorded liabilities are in fact obligations of the entity.

- *Valuation or allocation.* Assertions about valuation or allocation are concerned with whether asset, liability, revenue, and expense components have been included in the financial statements at appropriate amounts.

- *Presentation and disclosure.* Assertions about presentation and disclosure deal with whether particular components of the financial statements are properly described, disclosed, and classified.

AUDITING OBJECTIVES AND PROCEDURES

After financial statement assertions are identified, the internal auditor should then develop audit objectives, which are often restatements of the broad assertions but fine tuned for the specific accounts being examined.

In developing an internal audit work program, the auditor must also establish the procedures to be used.

Some of the more common auditing procedures include:

- *Inquiry.* Often defined as the seeking of information, inquiry is based on interviewing appropriate personnel at all organizational levels. The responses derived from inquiry may be written or oral but should be corroborated by more additional evidence.

- *Observation.* Involves watching employees perform their assigned functions.

- *Inspection.* Entails careful examination of pertinent documents and records as well as the physical examination of assets.

- *Tracing.* Involves tracking source documents from their creation to the recorded amounts in the books of original entry.

- *Reperformance.* Repeating an activity.

- *Vouching.* Involves selecting amounts recorded in the books and examining documents that support those recorded amounts.

- *Scrutinizing.* A careful visual review of records, reports, and schedules in order to identify unusual items.

- *Confirmation.* A process whereby the auditor can obtain corroborating evidential matter from an independent party outside the organization.

- *Analytical procedures.* Involve the study and comparison of the plausible relationships that exist among financial and nonfinancial data. Analytical procedures include ratio analysis and comparisons of current-period financial information to: (1) prior-period financial information, (2) anticipated results, (3) predictable patterns, (4) similar information within the same industry, and (5) nonfinancial data.

In addition to the procedures reviewed above, other basic procedures may be used. Accordingly, the following should also be considered:

- Reading and reviewing pertinent documents.
- Analyzing details of account balances.
- Verifying the validity of statements or representations.

Since an audit procedure may enable satisfaction of more than one audit objective, it is practical to establish the audit objectives and then select audit procedures that avoid duplication of work.

SAMPLE AUDIT PROGRAMS

Presented in Exhibit 29-1 are sample audit programs for: cash in bank, trade accounts and notes receivable, inventory, fixed assets, prepaid expenses and deferred charges, accounts payable, stockholders' equity, sales and other types of income, and expense items.

Exhibit 29-1: Sample Audit Programs

	Date Completed	*Performed By (N/A)*	*Workpaper Reference*
Cash in Bank			
I. Audit Objectives			
1. Determine that cash recorded in books exists and is owned by the company (Existence).	_____	_____	_____
2. Determine that cash transactions are recorded in the correct accounting period (i.e., that there is a proper cut-off of cash receipts and disbursements) (Completeness).	_____	_____	_____
3. Determine that balance sheet amounts include items in transit as well as cash on deposit with third parties (Completeness).	_____	_____	_____
4. Determine that cash is properly classified in the balance sheet and that relevant disclosures are presented in the financial statement notes (Presentation and Disclosure).	_____	_____	_____

	Date Completed	Performed By (N/A)	Workpaper Reference

II.   Audit Procedures

1.   With respect to the bank reconciliations prepared by accounting personnel:

a.   Trace book balances to general ledger control totals.

b.   Compare ending balances per the bank statements to the ending balances on the bank reconciliation.

c.   Verify the mathematical and clerical accuracy, including checking extensions.

d.   Identify unusual reconciling items and obtain documentation to corroborate the validity of such items.

e.   Trace deposits in transit and outstanding checks to subsequent months' bank statements intercepted before accounting personnel have access to them.

f.   Inspect canceled checks for dates of cancellation in order to identify checks not recorded in the proper accounting period.

g.   Ascertain that checks listed as outstanding are in fact: (1) recorded in the proper time period, and (2) checks that have not cleared. Scrutinize data when outstanding checks have cleared to determine if the books have been held open to improve ratios.

h.   Identify and investigate checks that are: (1) above limits prescribed by management, (2) drawn to "bearer," and (3) drawn payable to cash.

i.   Inquire about checks that have been outstanding for a more than reasonable time period.

j.   If balances have been confirmed with banks, compare confirmed balances with bank balances per the year-end bank statements.

2.   With respect to listings of cash investments:

a.   Trace book balances to general ledger control accounts.

	Date Completed	Performed By (N/A)	Workpaper Reference
b. Verify the accuracy of all extensions and footings.	_____	_____	_____
c. Consider confirming balances directly with bank personnel.	_____	_____	_____
d. Obtain and inspect passbooks and certificates of deposit.	_____	_____	_____
e. Recalculate income derived from cash investments and trace the income amounts to the books of original entry. Also, reconcile for reasonableness interest revenue amounts to the amount of cash investments.	_____	_____	_____
f. Consider using a custodian to maintain physical custody for safekeeping and to guard against forgeries.	_____	_____	_____
3. Prepare a bank transfer schedule that identifies:			
a. Name of disbursing bank.	_____	_____	_____
b. Check number.	_____	_____	_____
c. Dollar amount.	_____	_____	_____
d. Date disbursement is recorded in books.	_____	_____	_____
e. Name of receiving bank.	_____	_____	_____
f. Date receipt is recorded in books.	_____	_____	_____
g. Date receipt is recorded by bank.	_____	_____	_____
4. Perform cut-off test wherein transactions for the last few days of the year and the first few days of the next year are scrutinized.	_____	_____	_____
5. Inspect bank statements in order to identify obvious erasures or alterations.	_____	_____	_____
6. Inspect debit and credit memos and trace them to the bank statements.	_____	_____	_____
7. Read financial statements and investment certificates for appropriate classification of cash balances.	_____	_____	_____
8. With respect to cash on hand (i.e., petty cash funds):			
a. Determine the identity of all funds.	_____	_____	_____

	Date Completed	Performed By (N/A)	Workpaper Reference

b.   Select funds to be counted and list currency and coins by denomination; account for vouchers, stamps, and checks; trace fund balances to general ledger control accounts.

9.   Investigate the reasons for delays in deposits.

10. Note unusual activity in inactive accounts since it may be indicative of cash being hidden.

11. In a cash-basis entity, reconcile sales with cash receipts.

12. List unusual cash receipts (e.g., currency receipts).

13. Examine third-party endorsements by reviewing canceled checks.

Trade Accounts and Notes Receivable

I.   Audit Objectives

1.   Determine that the trade accounts and notes receivable represent bonafide receivables and are valued properly (Existence and Valuation).

2.   Determine that the allowances for doubtful accounts are adequate and reasonable (Valuation).

3.   Determine the propriety of disclosures pertaining to pledging, assigning, and discounting of receivables (Presentation and Disclosure).

4.   Determine the correctness of the recorded interest income that is attributable to accounts and notes receivable (Completeness).

5.   Determine that receivables are properly classified in the balance sheet (Presentation and Disclosure).

II. Audit Procedures

1.   Scan general ledger accounts in order to identify significant and unusual transactions.

2.   Compare opening general ledger balances with closing general ledger balances of the prior period.

	Date Completed	*Performed By (N/A)*	*Workpaper Reference*

3. Perform analytical procedures by evaluating the relationships between: (1) receivables and sales, and (2) notes receivable and interest income attributable thereon.

4. With respect to the aged trial balance prepared by accounting personnel:

    a. Verify extensions and footings.

    b. Trace the total of the aged trial balance to the general ledger control total.

    c. Trace selected entries on the aging schedule to respective accounts in the subsidiary ledger.

    d. Trace selected subsidiary ledger balances to the aging schedule.

    e. Verify extensions and footings in subsidiary ledger accounts.

    f. Investigate negative (i.e., credit) balances.

5. Consider confirmation of account balances with customers:

    a. Select accounts for positive confirmation.

    b. Select accounts for negative confirmation.

    c. Control confirmation requests by mailing in internal audit department envelopes and with the return address of the internal audit department. Consider using a post office box to ensure that unauthorized individuals cannot tamper with responses.

    d. After 14 days, mail second requests to all those not replying to a positive request.

    e. Investigate all accounts for which envelopes are returned as undeliverable.

    f. Reconcile differences reported by customers.

	Date Completed	Performed By (N/A)	Workpaper Reference

g. Review accounts of significant customers not replying to a second request by examining subsequent receipts and supporting documentation (i.e., remittance advices, invoices, and/or shipping documents) in order to corroborate that the amounts represent bonafide receivables for goods or services.

h. Prepare a schedule summarizing the receivable confirmations as follows:

	No.	%	**Dollar Amount**	%
Total at Confirm Date Requested				
Total Positive Type				
Total at Confirm Date Requested				
Total Negative Type				
Total Requested				
Results				
Positive Exceptions				
Positive Clean				
Positive Nonreplies				
Total Positive Type Exceptions				
Total Negative Type Exceptions				

6. Examine cash receipts in subsequent periods in order to identify receivables which have not been recorded previously.

7. With respect to trade notes receivable, prepare or verify schedules and analyses that detail the following:

   a. Makers of the notes.

   b. Dates the notes were made.

   c. Due dates of the notes.

   d. Original terms of repayment.

e.   Any collateral.

f.   Applicable interest rates.

g.   Balances at the end of the prior accounting period.

h.   Additions and repayments of principal.

8.   Inspect notes and confirm notes receivable discounted with banks.

9.   Identify collateral and verify that such amounts are not recorded as assets.

10. Verify the accuracy of interest income, accrued interest, and unearned discount by recalculating such amounts.

11. Read pertinent documents, including the minutes of board meetings, in order to identify situations in which receivables have been pledged as collateral, assigned, or discounted. Verify that such situations are disclosed in the financial statements.

12. Obtain evidence pertaining to related-party transactions that need to be disclosed in the financial statements.

13. With respect to the analysis of the allowance for doubtful accounts prepared by accounting personnel:

a.   Ascertain that write-offs have in fact been authorized.

b.   Ascertain the reasonableness of the allowance.

c.   Perform analytical procedures by comparing:

i.   Accounts receivable to credit sales.

ii.   Allowance for doubtful accounts to accounts receivable totals.

iii. Sales to sales returns and allowances.

iv.   Doubtful accounts expense to net credit sales.

v.   Accounts receivable to total assets.

vi.   Notes receivable totals to accounts receivable totals.

   d.   Consider differences between the book and tax basis for doubtful accounts expense.

Inventory

I. Audit Objectives

1.   Determine that inventory quantities properly include products, materials, and supplies on hand, in transit, in storage, and out on consignment to others (Existence, Completeness, and Valuation or Allocation).

2.   Determine that inventory items are priced consistently in accordance with GAAP (Valuation or Allocation).

3.   Determine that inventory listings are accurately compiled, extended, footed, and summarized and determine that the totals are properly reflected in the accounts (Existence, Completeness, and Valuation or Allocation).

4.   Determine that excess, slow-moving, obsolete, and defective items are reduced to their net realizable value (Valuation or Allocation).

5.   Determine that the financial statements include disclosure of any liens resulting from the pledging or assignment of inventories (Presentation and Disclosure).

II. Audit Procedures

1.   Review management's instructions pertaining to inventory counts and arrange to have sufficient internal audit personnel present to observe the physical count at major corporate locations. Keep in mind that all locations should be counted simultaneously in order to prevent substitution of items.

2.   At each location where inventory is counted:

   a.   Observe the physical inventory count, record test counts, and write an overall observation memo.

   b.   Determine that prenumbered inventory tags are utilized.

   c.   Test the control of inventory tags.

    d. Test shipping and receiving cut-offs.

    e. Discuss obsolescence and overstock with operating personnel.

    f. Verify that employees are indicating on inventory tags obsolete items.

    g. Note the condition of inventory.

    h. Note pledged or consigned inventory.

    i. Determine if any inventory is at other locations and consider confirmation or observation, if material.

    j. Determine that inventory marked for destruction is actually destroyed and is destroyed by authorized personnel.

3. Follow up all points that might result in a material adjustment.

4. Trace recorded test counts to the listings obtained from management, list all exceptions, and value the total effect.

5. Trace the receiving and shipping cut-offs obtained during the observation to the inventory records, accounts receivable records, and accounts payable records. Also trace inventory to production and sales.

6. Obtain a cut-off of purchases and sales subsequent to the audit date and trace to accounts receivable, accounts payable, and inventory records.

7. Note any sharp drop in market value relative to book value.

8. "Red flag" excessive product returns that might be indicative of quality problems. Returned merchandise should be warehoused apart from finished goods until quality control has tested the items. Are returns due to the salesperson overstocking the customer? Returns should be controlled as to actual physical receipt, and the reasons for the returns should be noted for analytical purposes.

9. Trace for possible obsolete merchandise that is continually carried on the books. For example, a situation arose in which a company continued to carry obsolete goods on the books even though it wrote off only a small portion. _____ _____ _____

10. With respect to price tests of raw materials:

  a. Ascertain management's inventory pricing procedures. _____ _____ _____

  b. Schedule, for a test of pricing, all inventory items in excess of a prescribed limit and sample additional items. _____ _____ _____

  c. Inspect purchase invoices and trace to journal entries. _____ _____ _____

  d. Inquire and investigate whether trade discounts, special rebates, and similar price reductions have been reflected in inventory prices. _____ _____ _____

  e. Determine and test treatment of freight and duty costs. _____ _____ _____

  f. If standard costs are utilized:

    i. Determine whether such costs differ materially from actual costs on a first-in, first-out basis. _____ _____ _____

    ii. Investigate variance accounts and compute the effect of the balances in such accounts on inventory prices. _____ _____ _____

    iii. Ascertain the policy and practice as to changes in standards. _____ _____ _____

    iv. With respect to changes during the period, investigate the effect on inventory pricing. _____ _____ _____

    v. If process costs are used, trace selected quantities per the physical inventory to the departmental cost of production reports and determine that quantities have been adjusted to the physical inventory as of the date of the physical counts. _____ _____ _____

11. With respect to work-in-process and finished goods:

  a. Ascertain the procedures used in pricing inventory and determine the basis of pricing. _____ _____ _____

b.   Review tax returns to determine that the valuation methods conform to those methods used for financial statement purposes.

c.   On a test basis, trace unit costs per the physical inventory to the cost accounting records and:

i.   Obtain, review, and compare the current-period and prior period's trial balances or tabulations of detailed components of production costs for the year; note explanations for apparent inconsistencies in classifications and significant fluctuations in amounts; ascertain that the cost classifications accumulated as production costs and absorbed in inventory are in conformity with GAAP.

ii.   Review computations of unit costs and costs credited against inventory and charged to cost of sales.

iii.   Review activity in the general ledger control accounts for raw materials, supplies, and work-in-process and finished goods inventories and investigate any significant and unusual entries or fluctuations.

iv.   Review labor and overhead allocations to inventory and cost of sales, compare to actual labor and overhead costs incurred, and ascertain that variances appear reasonable in amount and have been properly accounted for.

v.   Trace who obtains the funds received from the sale of scrap.

Fixed Assets

I.   Audit Objectives

1.   Determine that fixed assets exist (Existence or Occurrence).

2.   Determine that fixed assets are owned by the entity (Rights and Obligations).

3.   Determine that fixed asset accounts are recorded at historical cost (Valuation or Allocation).

4. Determine that depreciation is calculated and recorded in conformity with generally accepted accounting principles (Valuation or Allocation).   _____ _____ _____

5. Determine that relevant disclosures are made in the financial statements (Presentation and Disclosure).   _____ _____ _____

II. Audit Procedures

1. With respect to the schedule of fixed assets prepared by accounting personnel:

   a. Trace beginning balances to prior-year schedules.   _____ _____ _____

   b. Trace ending balances to general ledger control accounts.   _____ _____ _____

   c. Verify that additions are recorded at historical cost.   _____ _____ _____

   d. Examine supporting documentation—purchase contracts, canceled checks, invoices, purchase orders, receiving reports, retirement work orders, sale contracts, bills of sale, bills of lading, trade-in agreements—for asset additions, retirements, and dispositions.   _____ _____ _____

   e. Verify that depreciation methods, estimated useful lives, and estimated salvage values are in accordance with generally accepted accounting principles (GAAP).   _____ _____ _____

   f. Recalculate gains and losses on dispositions of fixed assets in accordance with methods that are in conformity with GAAP.   _____ _____ _____

2. Determine that additions, retirements, and dispositions have been authorized by management.   _____ _____ _____

3. Analyze repairs and maintenance accounts to ascertain the propriety of classification of transactions.   _____ _____ _____

4. Tour facilities in order to physically inspect fixed assets. A lack of cleanliness and orderliness infer the possible existence of internal control problems.   _____ _____ _____

5. To verify ownership, examine:

   a. Personal property tax returns.   _____ _____ _____

   b. Tide certificates.   _____ _____ _____

   c. Insurance policies.   _____ _____ _____

   d. Invoices. _____ _____ _____

   e. Purchase contracts. _____ _____ _____

6. Read lease agreements and ascertain that the accounting treatment is in conformity with GAAP. _____ _____ _____

7. Ascertain that obsolete assets are given proper accounting recognition. Trace salvage receipts to source. _____ _____ _____

8. Perform analytical procedures by comparing:

   a. Dispositions of fixed assets to replacements. _____ _____ _____

   b. Depreciation and amortization expenses to the cost of fixed assets. _____ _____ _____

   c. Accumulated depreciation to the cost of fixed assets. _____ _____ _____

9. Read: (1) minutes of board meetings, (2) note agreements, and (3) purchase contracts to identify situations in which assets have been pledged as collateral. _____ _____ _____

Prepaid Expenses and Deferred Charges

I. Audit Objectives

1. Determine that balances represent proper charges against future operations and can reasonably be realized through future operations or are otherwise in conformity with GAAP (Valuation or Allocation). _____ _____ _____

2. Determine that additions during the audit period are proper charges to these accounts and represent actual cost (Existence or Occurrence and Valuation or Allocation). _____ _____ _____

3. Determine that amortization or write-offs against revenues in the current period and to date have been determined in a rational and consistent manner (Valuation or Allocation). _____ _____ _____

4. Determine that material items have been properly classified and disclosed in the financial statements (Presentation and Disclosure). _____ _____ _____

II. Audit Procedures

1. Obtain or prepare a schedule of the prepaid and deferred items. _____ _____ _____

2.   Perform analytical procedures by comparing current-period amounts to those of the prior period; investigate significant fluctuations.   _____ _____ _____

3.   With respect to prepaid insurance:

a.   Obtain a schedule of insurance policies, coverage, total premiums, prepaid premiums, and expense as of the audit date; note that some companies maintain an insurance register.   _____ _____ _____

b.   Verify the clerical and mathematical accuracy of schedules or insurance registers.   _____ _____ _____

c.   Trace schedule or register totals to trial balances and general ledger control accounts.   _____ _____ _____

d.   Inspect policies on hand and check details of schedules or registers.   _____ _____ _____

e.   Vouch significant premiums paid during the audit period.   _____ _____ _____

f.   Obtain confirmation directly from insurance brokers of premiums and other significant and relevant data.   _____ _____ _____

g.   Verify that proper accounting treatment is applied to advance or deposit premiums, as well as dividend or premium credits.   _____ _____ _____

h.   Test check calculations of prepaid premiums and investigate and determine the disposition of major differences.   _____ _____ _____

4.   With respect to prepaid taxes:

a.   Obtain or prepare an analysis of prepaid taxes, including taxes charged directly to expense accounts.   _____ _____ _____

b.   Verify the mathematical and clerical accuracy of the analysis.   _____ _____ _____

c.   Trace amounts on the analysis to the trial balance and pertinent general ledger control accounts.   _____ _____ _____

d.   Examine tax bills and receipts or other data that corroborate prepaid taxes.   _____ _____ _____

e.   Ascertain that prepaid tax accounts have been accounted for consistently in conformity with GAAP.   _____ _____ _____

5. With respect to other major items:

   a. Review deferred expenses such as moving costs and determine:

      i. What procedures are used to evaluate the future usefulness of the asset. _____ _____ _____

      ii. How these assets will benefit the future. _____ _____ _____

   b. Test the amortization of material prepaid or deferred items and trace to the income statement and general ledger accounts. _____ _____ _____

   c. Inspect relevant documents. _____ _____ _____

Accounts Payable

I. Audit Objectives

1. Determine that accounts payable in fact exist (Existence or Occurrence). _____ _____ _____

2. Determine that accounts payable represent authorized obligations of the entity (Existence or Occurrence). _____ _____ _____

3. Determine that accounts payable are properly classified in the financial statements (Presentation and Disclosure). _____ _____ _____

4. Determine that recorded accounts payable are complete (Completeness). _____ _____ _____

5. Determine that appropriate disclosures are included in the financial statements (Presentation and Disclosure). _____ _____ _____

II. Audit Procedures

1. With respect to the schedule of accounts payable prepared by accounting personnel:

   a. Verify mathematical accuracy of extensions and footings. _____ _____ _____

   b. Trace totals to general ledger control accounts. _____ _____ _____

   c. Trace selected individual accounts to the accounts payable subsidiary ledger. _____ _____ _____

   d. Trace individual account balances in the subsidiary ledger to the accounts payable schedule. _____ _____ _____

   e. Investigate accounts payable that are in dispute. _____ _____ _____

   f. Investigate any debit balances. _____ _____ _____

g.   Read minutes of board meetings to ascertain the existence of pledging agreements.

2.   Consider confirming accounts payable if there is (1) poor internal control structure, or (2) suspicion of misstatement.

3.   Search for unrecorded liabilities by:

a.   Examining receiving reports and matching them with invoices.

b.   Inspecting unprocessed invoices.

c.   Inspecting vendor's statements for unrecorded invoiced amounts.

d.   Examining cash disbursements made in the period subsequent to year-end and examining supporting documentation in order to ascertain the appropriate cut-off for recording purposes.

4.   With respect to obligations for payroll tax liabilities:

a.   Examine payroll tax deposit receipts.

b.   Examine cash disbursements in the period subsequent to year-end to identify deposits that relate to prior period.

c.   Reconcile general ledger control totals to payroll tax forms.

d.   Trace liabilities for amounts withheld from employee checks to payroll registers, journals, and summaries.

e.   Perform analytical procedures by comparing: Payroll tax expense to liabilities for payroll taxes, liability to accrued payroll taxes.

f.   Reconcile calendar year payroll returns to fiscal year financial statements for payroll amounts.

5.   Reconcile vendor statements with accounts payable accounts.

6.   Compare vendor invoices with purchase requisitions, purchase orders, and receiving reports for price and quantity.

7.   Investigate unusually large purchases.

8.   With respect to accrued expenses:

a.   Consider the existence of unasserted claims.   _____   _____   _____

b.   Obtain schedule of accrued expenses from accounting personnel.   _____   _____   _____

c.   Recalculate accruals after verifying the validity of assumptions utilized.   _____   _____   _____

d.   Perform analytical procedures by comparing current-and prior-period accrued expenses.   _____   _____   _____

e.   Ascertain that accrued expenses are paid within a reasonable time after year-end.   _____   _____   _____

f.   Inquire of management and indicate all details of contingent or known liabilities arising from product warranties, guarantees, contests, advertising promotions, and dealer "arrangements or promises."   _____   _____   _____

g.   Determine liability for expenses in connection with pending litigation:

i.   Inquire of management.   _____   _____   _____

ii.   Confirm in writing with outside legal counsel.   _____   _____   _____

Stockholders' Equity

I.   Audit Objectives

1.   Determine that all stock transactions (including transactions involving warrants, options, and rights) have been authorized in accordance with management's plans (All Assertions Are Addressed).   _____   _____   _____

2.   Determine that equity transactions are properly classified in the financial statements (Presentation and Disclosure).   _____   _____   _____

3.   Determine that equity transactions have been recorded in the proper time period at the correct amounts (Existence or Occurrence, Completeness, and Presentation and Disclosure).   _____   _____   _____

4.   Determine that equity transactions are reflected in the financial statements in accordance with generally accepted accounting principles (Presentation and Disclosure).   _____   _____   _____

II. Audit Procedures

1. With respect to each class of stock, identify:

    a. Number of shares authorized. _____ _____ _____

    b. Number of shares issued. _____ _____ _____

    c. Number of shares outstanding. _____ _____ _____

    d. Par or stated value. _____ _____ _____

    e. Privileges. _____ _____ _____

    f. Restrictions. _____ _____ _____

2. With respect to the schedule of equity transactions prepared by accounting personnel:

    a. Trace opening balances of the current year to the balance sheet and ledger accounts as of the prior year's balance sheet date. _____ _____ _____

    b. Account for all proceeds from stock issues by recomputing sales prices and relevant proceeds. _____ _____ _____

    c. Verify the validity of the classification of proceeds between capital stock and additional paid-in capital. _____ _____ _____

    d. Reconcile ending schedule balances with general ledger control totals. _____ _____ _____

    e. Verify that equity transactions are not in conflict with the requirements of the corporate charter (or articles of incorporation), or with the applicable statutes of the state of incorporation. _____ _____ _____

3. Account for all stock certificates that remain unissued at the end of the accounting period. _____ _____ _____

4. Examine stock certificate books or confirm stock register. _____ _____ _____

5. With respect to schedules of stock options and related stock option plans prepared by accounting personnel, verify:

    a. The date of the plan. _____ _____ _____

    b. Class and number of shares reserved for the plan. _____ _____ _____

    c. The accounting method used for determining option prices. _____ _____ _____

    d. The names of individuals entitled to receive stock options. _____ _____ _____

e. The names of individuals to whom options have been granted. _____ _____ _____

f. The terms relevant to options that have been granted. _____ _____ _____

g. That measurement of stock options granted is in accordance with generally accepted accounting principles. _____ _____ _____

6. With respect to stock subscriptions receivable:

a. Ascertain that execution of such transactions is approved by appropriate personnel. _____ _____ _____

b. Verify that stock subscriptions receivable are properly classified in the financial statements. _____ _____ _____

7. With respect to treasury stock:

a. Verify the validity of treasury stock acquisitions by examining canceled checks and other corroborating documentation. _____ _____ _____

b. Inspect treasury stock certificates in order to ascertain their existence. _____ _____ _____

c. Obtain assurance that treasury stock certificates have been endorsed to the company or are in the company's name by physically inspecting the certificates. _____ _____ _____

d. Reconcile treasury stock totals to general ledger control accounts. _____ _____ _____

8. With respect to retained earnings:

a. Trace the opening balance in the general ledger to the ending balance in the general ledger of the prior period. _____ _____ _____

b. Analyze current-year transactions and obtain corroborating documentation for all or selected transactions. _____ _____ _____

c. Verify that current-year net income or loss has been reflected as a current-year transaction. _____ _____ _____

d. With respect to dividends declared and or paid: _____ _____ _____

i. Ascertain the authorization of such dividends by reading the minutes of board meetings. _____ _____ _____

ii. Examine canceled checks in support of dividend payments. _____ _____ _____

iii. Verify the accuracy of dividend declarations and payments by recalculating such dividends.   _____ _____ _____

iv. Ascertain that prior-period adjustments have been given proper accounting recognition in accordance with generally accepted accounting principles.   _____ _____ _____

v. Apply other appropriate procedures to determine the existence of restrictions on or appropriations of retained earnings.   _____ _____ _____

9.   Ascertain that the financial statements include adequate disclosure of:

   a.   Restrictions on stock.   _____ _____ _____

   b.   Stock subscription rights.   _____ _____ _____

   c.   Stock reservations.   _____ _____ _____

   d.   Stock options and warrants.   _____ _____ _____

   e.   Stock repurchase plans or obligations.   _____ _____ _____

   f.   Preferred dividends in arrears.   _____ _____ _____

   g.   Voting rights in the event of preferred dividend arrearages.   _____ _____ _____

   h.   Liquidation preferences.   _____ _____ _____

   i.   Other relevant items.   _____ _____ _____

Sales and Other Types of Income

I.   Audit Objectives

1.   Determine that proper income recognition is afforded ordinary sales transactions (Existence or Occurrence, Rights and Obligations, Valuation or Allocation, and Presentation and Disclosure).   _____ _____ _____

2.   Determine that sales transactions have been recorded in the proper time period (Existence or Occurrence, Completeness, and Presentation and Disclosure).   _____ _____ _____

3.   Determine that all types of revenues are properly classified and disclosed in the financial statements (Valuation or Allocation and Presentation and Disclosure).   _____ _____ _____

II.   Audit Procedure

1.   Trace sales and cash receipts journal totals to relevant general ledger control accounts.   _____ _____ _____

2.   Trace sales and cash receipts journal entries to applicable subsidiary ledger accounts.   _____ _____ _____

3.   Verify the mathematical accuracy of footings and extensions in sales and cash receipts journals.   _____ _____ _____

4.   Perform analytical procedures by:

a.   Comparing current- and prior-period sales, returns and allowances, discounts, and gross profit percentages.   _____ _____ _____

b.   Comparing the current-period items—sales, returns and allowances, discounts, and gross profit percentages—to anticipated results (i.e., budgeted amounts).   _____ _____ _____

c.   Comparing company statistics (e.g., gross profit percentage) to industry standards.   _____ _____ _____

d.   Investigating any significant or unexplained fluctuations.   _____ _____ _____

5.   With respect to consignment shipments to others:

a.   Examine applicable consignment agreements.   _____ _____ _____

b.   Verify that consignment transactions are afforded proper accounting treatment in accordance with generally accepted accounting principles.   _____ _____ _____

6.   Ascertain that sales to related parties are accounted for at arm's length terms.   _____ _____ _____

7.   Perform sales and inventory cut-off tests at the end of the fiscal year.   _____ _____ _____

8.   Verify by recalculation that the following have been properly recorded and disclosed:

a.   Dividend income.   _____ _____ _____

b.   Interest income.   _____ _____ _____

c.   Gains on dispositions of marketable securities.   _____ _____ _____

d.   Gains on dispositions of fixed assets.   _____ _____ _____

e.   Increases in investment accounts reflecting the equity method of accounting.   _____ _____ _____

f.   Other or miscellaneous income accounts.   _____ _____ _____

Expense Items

I.   Audit Objectives   _____ _____ _____

1.   Determine that expenses are recorded in the proper time period (Existence or Occurrence and Completeness).   _____ _____ _____

2.   Determine that expenses have been properly classified and disclosed in the financial statements (Presentation and Disclosure).   _____ _____ _____

3.   Determine that expense items are recognized in accordance with generally accepted accounting principles (Valuation or Allocation).   _____ _____ _____

II.   Audit Procedures   _____ _____ _____

1.   Trace cash disbursements journal totals to relevant general ledger control accounts.   _____ _____ _____

2.   Trace cash disbursements journal items to relevant subsidiary ledgers (e.g., payroll subledger).   _____ _____ _____

3.   Verify the mathematical accuracy of footings and extensions of relevant journals.   _____ _____ _____

4.   Perform analytical procedures by:

a.   Comparing current- and prior-period expense items.   _____ _____ _____

b.   Comparing the current-period expense items to anticipated results (i.e., budgeted amounts).   _____ _____ _____

c.   Comparing the current-period expense items to industry standards.   _____ _____ _____

d.   Relating various expense items to gross sales or revenue by means of percentages.   _____ _____ _____

e.   Investigating any significant or unexplained fluctuations.   _____ _____ _____

f.   Vouching bills on a sampling basis.   _____ _____ _____

5. Consider analyzing the following accounts, which are often subject to intentional or unintentional misstatement:

   a. Depreciation and amortization. _____ _____ _____

   b. Taxes:

      i. Real estate. _____ _____ _____

      ii. Personal property. _____ _____ _____

      iii. Income. _____ _____ _____

      iv. Payroll. _____ _____ _____

      v. Rent. _____ _____ _____

   c. Insurance. _____ _____ _____

   d. Bad debts. _____ _____ _____

   e. Interest. _____ _____ _____

   f. Professional fees. _____ _____ _____

   g. Officers' salaries. _____ _____ _____

   h. Directors' fees. _____ _____ _____

   i. Travel and entertainment. _____ _____ _____

   j. Research and development. _____ _____ _____

   k. Charitable contributions. _____ _____ _____

   l. Repairs and maintenance. _____ _____ _____

6. With respect to payroll:

   a. Search for fictitious employees. _____ _____ _____

   b. Determine improper alterations of amounts. _____ _____ _____

   c. Verify that proper tax deductions are taken. _____ _____ _____

   d. Examine time cards and trace to payroll records in order to verify the proper recording of employee hours. _____ _____ _____

   e. Verify the accuracy of pay rates by obtaining a list of authorized pay rates from the personnel department. _____ _____ _____

   f. Review the adequacy of internal controls relating to hiring, overtime, and retirement. _____ _____ _____

   g. Determine if proper payroll forms exist, such as W-4s and I-9s. _____ _____ _____

CHAPTER 30

FORENSIC ACCOUNTING

CONTENTS

Forensic accounting is a science (i.e., a department of systemized knowledge) dealing with the application of accounting facts gathered through auditing methods and procedures to resolve legal problems. Forensic accounting is much different from traditional auditing. The main purpose of a traditional audit is to examine the financial statements of an organization and express an opinion on the fairness of the financial statements. In other words, auditors give an opinion as to whether the financial statements have been prepared in accordance with generally accepted accounting principles. Auditors employ limited procedures and use extensive testing and sampling techniques. Audits are performed by independent accountants and are not conducted with a view to presenting the evidence in a judicial forum. An audit is not an investigation; its main objective is not to uncover fraud.

Forensic accounting, on the other hand, is for investigation of an allegation with the assumption that the forensic accountant will have to present the evidence in a judicial forum. A forensic accountant often employs specialists in other areas as part of a team to gather evidence. In order to present the evidence in court, there must be absolute assurance; thus testing and sampling methods are usually not employed as part of the evidence-gathering procedures. The scope of the investigation is limited because it is determined by the client.

Forensic accounting, therefore, is a specialty requiring the integration of investigative, accounting, and auditing skills. The forensic accountant looks at documents and financial and other data in a critical manner in order to draw conclusions and to calculate values, and to identify irregular patterns and/or suspicious transactions. A forensic accountant understands the fraud risk areas and

This chapter is contributed by Frank Grippo, Dean, School of Business, William Paterson University.

has extensive fraud knowledge. A forensic accountant does not merely look at the numbers but rather, looks behind the numbers.

One can extend this definition to say that forensic accounting is a discipline consisting of two areas of specialization: litigation support specialists and investigation or fraud accountants. Litigation support specialists concern themselves with business valuation, testimony as expert witnesses, future earnings evaluation, and income and expense analysis. On the other hand, fraud accountants apply their skills to investigate areas of alleged criminal misconduct in order to support or dispel damages. These fields overlap: A forensic accountant may do litigation support work on one engagement and act as a fraud accountant on another. Both of these engagements could result in expert testimony by the forensic accountant. Thus, forensic accounting can be defined in generic terms as a discipline whereby auditing, accounting, and investigative skills are used to assist in disputes involving financial issues and data, and where there is suspicion or allegation of fraud. The expertise of the forensic accountant may be used to support a plaintiff who is trying to establish a claim, or to support a defendant in order to minimize the impact of a claim against him or her. Usually such investigations involve litigation; sometimes, however, such disputes are settled by negotiation. In either case, persuasive and authoritative evidence resulting from the financial and investigative skills of the forensic accountant is imperative. Therefore, the forensic accountant must be a good businessperson and be aware of statutory law, common law, and the laws of evidence and procedure.

Usually the forensic accountant's findings are based on facts, not opinions. Facts can be investigated, and the forensic accountant can prepare a definitive report on these facts. Nevertheless, there are situations in which the forensic accountant may rely on professional judgment and present findings using an opinion-type report. Needless to say, the reports based on facts usually do not present problems in court cases because they are supported by underlying documentation. Opinion reports, on the other hand, are subjective and require the forensic accountant to demonstrate competency and to provide adequate logic for the stated opinion.

Two points often overlooked when one is involved in a case as a forensic accountant are (1) the other side usually employs a forensic accountant as well and (2) the credibility of a forensic accountant is extremely important. Thus the forensic accountant must have high professional standards and ethics.

WHY FORENSIC ACCOUNTING IS NECESSARY

Business and criminal activities have become so complex that lawyers and criminal investigators often do not have the expertise necessary to discharge their responsibilities. This fact plus the marked increase in white collar crime, marital and business disputes, and other claims have created the need for the new industry of forensic accounting. Although this specialty is not limited to fraud issues, nevertheless, the reality of forensic accounting is that most of the work does involve fraud investigations. In the case of fraud, the work of a forensic accounting team is crucial, as the survival of the business may rest on the outcome. Good businesspeople must realize that fraud is a permanent risk in any and all businesses. Thus company leaders must devise ways to prevent fraud rather than trying to manage the consequences of fraud. The instances of fraud have increased because of lack of government commitment, more sophisticated criminals, inefficiency of the judicial system, more complex technology, lack of adequate penalties and deterrents, and old-fashioned greed and arrogance. Studies have shown that fraud will continue to increase. Currently, about 75% of fraud results from employees; other sources of fraud include customers, management, suppliers, and service providers. In addition, about 55% of fraud is discovered as a result of strong internal controls. Other methods of discovery include whistle-blowers, customers, internal auditors, and accidental or formal investigation.

WHEN TO EMPLOY A FORENSIC ACCOUNTANT

Clients retain forensic accountants when they are interested in either litigation support or investigations.

Litigation Support

This is a situation in which the forensic accountant is asked to give an opinion either on known facts or facts yet uncovered. The forensic accountant is an integral part of the legal team, helping to substantiate allegations, analyze facts, dispute claims, and develop motives. The amount of involvement and the point at which the forensic accountant gets involved vary from case to case. Sometimes the forensic accountant is called upon from the beginning of the case; at other times the forensic accountant is summoned before the case is scheduled to go to court and after out-of-court settlements have failed. Thus, in litigation support, the forensic accountant assists in obtaining documentation to support or dispel a claim, reviewing documentation to give an assessment of the case to the legal team, and/or identifying areas where loss occurred. Moreover, the forensic accountant may be asked to get involved during the discovery stage to help formulate questions, and may be asked to review the opposing expert's witness report to give an evaluation of its strengths and weaknesses. During trial, the forensic accountant may serve as an expert witness, help to provide questions for cross-examination, and assist with settlement discussions after the trial.

Investigations

Investigations most often involve fraud and are associated with criminal matters. Typically, an investigative accounting assignment would result from a client's suspicion that there is employee fraud. Other parties, such as regulatory agencies, police forces, and attorneys, may retain a forensic accountant to investigate securities fraud, kickbacks, insurance fraud, money laundering schemes, and asset search and analysis.

WHERE FORENSIC ACCOUNTANTS ARE USED

A forensic accountant is used in a number of situations, including, but not limited to the following:

- *Business valuations.* A forensic accountant evaluates the current value of a business for various personal or legal matters.
- *Personal injury and fatal accident claims.* A forensic accountant may help to establish lost earnings (i.e., those earnings that the plaintiff would have

accrued except for the actions of the defendant) by gathering and analyzing a variety of information and then issuing a report based on the outcome of the analyses.

- *Professional negligence.* A forensic accountant helps to determine if a breach of professional ethics or other standards of professional practice has occurred (e.g., failure to apply generally accepted auditing standards by a CPA when performing an audit). In addition, the forensic accountant may help to quantify the loss.

- *Insurance claims evaluations.* A forensic accountant may prepare financial analyses for an insurance company of claims, business income and losses, expenses, and disability, liability, or workers' compensation insurance losses.

- *Arbitration.* A forensic accountant is sometimes retained to assist with alternative dispute resolution (ADR) by acting as a mediator to allow individuals and businesses to resolve disputes in a timely manner with a minimum of disruption.

- *Partnership and corporation disputes.* A forensic accountant may be asked to help settle disputes between partners or shareholders. Detailed analyses are often necessary of many records spanning a number of years. Most of these disputes relate to compensation and benefit issues.

- *Civil and criminal actions concerning fraud and financial irregularities.* These investigations are usually performed by the forensic accountant for police forces. A report is prepared to assist the prosecutor's office.

- *Fraud and white collar crime investigations.* These types of investigations can be prepared on behalf of police forces as well as for private businesses. They usually result from such activities as purchasing/kickback schemes, computer fraud, labor fraud, and falsification of inventory. The investigation by the forensic accountant often involves fund tracing, asset identification, and recovery.

HOW FORENSIC ACCOUNTANTS WORK

Although each case is distinct and requires accounting and auditing procedures unique to the assignment, many forensic accounting assignments would include the following steps:

1. *Meet with the client.* The forensic accountant should meet with the client to determine the scope of the engagement. In addition, it is advisable to obtain an engagement letter specifying the terms of the engagement.

2. *Determine independence.* It is understood that a CPA should be independent when performing an audit or other attest services for clients. It is mandatory as well that the forensic accountant be independent, otherwise the credibility of the forensic accountant will be questioned if the engagement results in a legal case.

3. *Plan the engagement.* Proper advance planning is essential to any type of engagement. The plan should be similar to an audit program, detailing objectives and procedures in a form that addresses the scope of the engagement so that some type of conclusion can be reached.

4. *Gather evidence and perform analyses.* The forensic accountant should match the auditing, accounting, or investigative technique employed with the type of evidence to be obtained. A specific technique may satisfy more than one objective. When the forensic accountant, for example, performs an audit technique for a particular account, evidence for other accounts may be discovered based on the double-entry system of accounting. Forensic accountants use a variety of techniques including inquiry, confirmation, physical examination, observation, inspection, reconciliation, tracing, vouching, reperformance, and analytical procedures.

5. *Arrive at a conclusion and prepare the report.* The forensic accountant should write the final report in a manner that clearly explains the nature of the assignment and the scope of the work. It should indicate the approach used for discovery of information, and detail findings and/or opinions.

A CASE IN FORENSIC ACCOUNTING

The following is an actual case involving the purchase of a business. The plaintiff alleges that the records shown to him were not accurate and that the lawyer who handled the closing for him was negligent.

MAGYAR, INC.

A Case Study in Fraud

"Since I was a little boy, I wanted to own a business. I never wanted to work for anyone else," Omar Saleem said to his wife, Sylvia.

Omar Saleem was 50 years old, came to the United States 30 years ago, and has worked for a large furniture manufacturer for 28 years. One day, he was reading the classified advertisements of the newspaper and noticed an office business for sale in the next town. He discussed the idea with his wife and she approved. So he contacted the seller and made an appointment.

Three days later Omar met with Rahman Magyar, the sole owner of Magyar, Inc. Rahman was an engaging individual, very smooth and personable. Omar was very impressed with Rahman's knowledge of the business and with his self-confidence. Rahman told Omar that he was selling the business because he was bored with it. He had built the company from nothing into a very successful business and now wanted to try something else. Omar believed everything that Rahman said. Rahman said he would be glad to open his books to Omar, but would require a goodfaith, refundable deposit of $1,000. Omar agreed and made another appointment for the following week.

Omar met with Rahman and gave the $1,000 good-faith deposit. Rahman in turn showed Omar his equipment and inventory and explained more about the business. Specifically he told him that he averages about $120,000 per year in office supplies and equipment sales, and about $30,000 in services. The latter is a mail service whereby he prepares and mails packages for customers. Rahman produced a fee schedule and claimed that this end of the business had been very lucrative. After showing Omar the inventory, Rahman flashed some papers and tax returns in front of Omar to show him the growth since he opened the business in February 2005. Rahman said that the business had averaged about 20% growth each year. Omar looked at the papers, but actually didn't know what he was looking at. Furthermore, Rahman assured him that the paperwork was in order since his brother-in-law prepared it. He said his brother-in-law, Raj Kupar, was a CPA and that everything was in order. Rahman said that he would sell the business for $160,000, which is less than the normal selling price for this type of business. He said that the selling price is usually one times annual sales. He further said that "since you and I are from the same country, I will help you out. I prefer to sell to you over someone else."

He convinced Omar that he could easily make $75,000 from the business. Furthermore, he suggested that Omar move fast as there were a number of people interested in the business. Omar said that he would have to get an attorney. He promised to get back to Rahman in a week or so. Rahman even suggested an attorney.

Omar was quite excited and couldn't wait to get home to tell his wife. His wife was very supportive. Therefore, Omar asked his good friend, Stanley, if he knew an attorney. Stanley referred him to Neil Klavin, an attorney in town. On the following Monday, Omar called the attorney and made an appointment for Friday of that week. Before the meeting, Omar called Rahman and asked if he would accept $150,000 for the business. Rahman said that he would, but he wanted cash and that he would not want to finance the business. Omar said that he had $110,000 in cash, but would require a loan of $40,000. Rahman surprisingly agreed to finance $40,000, but wanted 8% interest. They verbally agreed. Omar said that he was going to see an attorney on Friday to explain the deal. Rahman said that was great.

On Friday, Omar went to the attorney, Neil Klavin, with his wife. Omar and the attorney discussed the business deal at length. Klavin said that he would be happy to represent Omar and would gladly review the contract drawn up by Rahman's attorney. Omar told the attorney that he had seen some documentation regarding income and expenses including the tax returns. Omar told Klavin that he would like him to review the documentation as well. The attorney said fine. Omar left the office and then contacted Rahman. He gave Rahman his attorney's name and told him to have his lawyers draw up the paperwork. Omar's wife asked if he was moving a little too fast. Omar said that he had to move fast as it was a good deal and Rahman had other interested buyers. He felt comfortable that his attorney would say it was a good deal after the attorney reviewed the numbers.

About two weeks later, Neil Klavin received the financial information from Rahman's attorney along with a contract of sale and promissory note for $40,000 at 8% interest. Neil reviewed the information and appeared to find everything in order. Although he did not understand the financials and tax returns that well, he did not suggest to Omar that anything was improper. Nor did he suggest soliciting the help of an expert. For example, he did not suggest contacting a CPA to review the books, financials, and tax returns. The closing was scheduled for December 27, 2007. Rahman and Omar appeared at the closing with their wives. The contract and promissory note were signed. Omar was to start on the following Monday. Rahman agreed to stay around for a month to train both Omar and his wife. Since this was a family business (husband and wife), they only had the need for occasional casual labor. Rahman never had a payroll.

Omar showed up on January 2, 2008 eager to learn all about the business. He met Rahman, who turned over the keys to the store. Rahman was very gracious and patient as he explained things to Omar and his wife. This went on for the whole month as agreed upon at closing. During the month, Omar and his wife discussed the relative inactivity. They even mentioned this to Rahman, who replied that January is always slow because it is after the holidays. Rahman said don't worry as December more than makes up for January. Omar and his wife didn't think too much about it.

Omar was now on his own. He and his wife worked diligently at the business each day. His wife prepared advertisements for the newspaper and ran a number of specials. They methodically kept track of daily revenues and expenses. It became apparent after seven months that the volume was nothing like Rahman had said. They both wondered what they were doing wrong. They were somewhat in denial and did not want to think that they may have been misled and/or tricked. They talked between themselves and decided to talk to an attorney, but not Neil Klavin. Instead they discussed the matter with one of their customers, an attorney named Ted Rich. Ted often came into the store to buy supplies and do special mailings of packages. He took a personal interest in both Omar and his wife, Sylvia. Therefore, he suggested that they make an appointment and discuss the matter further.

Omar and Sylvia talked more about the problem. Another two months went by without any appreciable increase in sales numbers. Finally they made an appointment with Ted Rich. Omar did most of the talking. He also brought copies of all the paperwork that he had, including any financial information that he received from Rahman. He also included summaries of his revenues and expenses for the last nine months. They discussed alternatives. Ted asked a number of pertinent questions including whether Omar had an accountant, preferably a CPA, to review the financial information that he received from Rahman. Omar said that he hadn't. He said that he gave all the information to his attorney to review. Omar made it clear to Ted that he depended on his attorney, Neil Klavin, for advice. Ted was not in the business of suing other attorneys, however, he was upset that Klavin was so sloppy with the closing. He knew that Omar and his wife were naive. Nevertheless, that was no excuse for not following due diligence procedures. He believed that Klavin should have realized this and looked out for the welfare of his client. Not wanting to make an immediate decision, Ted told Omar that he would review the information and get back to him in a couple of weeks.

A few days later, Ted reviewed the file and decided that the best way to handle the case was to get an accountant to review the financial information, including the tax returns for 2005, 2006, and 2007. Ted called Omar to ask for approval to retain an accountant. Omar agreed.

The next day Ted called George Spyros, a CPA and CFE (certified fraud examiner). George had a small forensic practice and had done work for Ted in the past. Ted and George met for about an hour the following day.

George looked at the financial statements and tax returns. The first thing George did was check to see if Rahman's brother-in-law was indeed a CPA. He was not. The reason he did that first was because his cursory review of the tax returns revealed gross preparation errors. It took George only about eight hours to do a detailed review of the paperwork. George then prepared a report for Ted (Exhibit A).

Ted reviewed the report prepared by Spyros and Company. Based on the report and his discussions with George Spyros, he decided to take the case and pursue suing Neil Klavin. Over the next few months, Ted diligently worked on the case, including obtaining interrogatories from a number of individuals including Omar and his wife, Rahman Magyar, and Neil Klavin.

Ted knew that the case was not solid. Therefore, he asked for the opinion of another attorney, Richard Darius of Darius and Spivack. He also asked for a second opinion from Edward Caruso. Both of these attorneys had experience suing other attorneys. Their opinions can be found in Exhibit B and Exhibit C, respectively.

Since the two attorneys had different opinions, Ted thought that it would be in the best interest of his client to try to settle out of court.

Exhibit A: SPYROS AND COMPANY

CERTIFIED PUBLIC ACCOUNTANTS
447 PEARL STREET
WOODBRIDGE, NEW JERSEY 07095

Mr. Theodore R. Rich

400 Pearl Street

Woodbridge, New Jersey 07095

Dear Mr. Rich,

In accordance with your request, we have reviewed the Federal income tax returns (Form 1120) of Magyar, Inc. for the eleven months ended December 31, 2005, and the years ended December 31, 2006 and 2007. The purpose of our review was to obtain reasonable assurance about whether the tax returns are free of material misstatement. Our review included examining the propriety of the amounts presented on the returns based on analytical procedures. Specifically, we have determined that:

(1) The company employed the accrual basis of accounting (see box checked on page 2 of the 2005 return). Since the balance sheets each year do not show any accounts receivable or accounts payable, one can logically conclude that all revenues and expenses were for cash.

(2) Based on the conclusion reached in (1) above, the cash balances reflected on the balance sheets on page 4 of the 2006 and 2007 tax returns are not reasonable. This fact can be supported by the following reconciliation:

Increase (decrease) in cash—

Cash balance at inception	$_____
Issuance of stock in 2005	7,536
Loans in 2005	29,438
Equipment	(16,251)
Sales	101,792
Cost of sales	(118,326)
Expenses (excluding depreciation of $638)	(25,812)
Cash balance on December 31, 2005 should be	$(21,623)
Cash balance on December 31, 2005 per tax return	$250

Comments: It is unreasonable for cost of sales to be more than sales. Cash is misstated by $21,873.

Recalculated cash balance on January 1, 2006	$(21,623)
Additional issuance of stock in 2006	23,960
Payoff of loans	(29,438)
Sales	141,158
Cost of sales	(139,617)
Expenses (excluding depreciation of $638)	(38,102)
Cash balance on December 31, 2006 should be	$(63,662)
Cash balance on December 31, 2006 per tax return	$250

Comments: It is unreasonable for cost of sales to be 99% of sales. Cash is misstated cumulatively by $63,912.

Recalculated cash balance on January 1, 2007	$(63,662)
Sales	157,572
Cost of sales	(145,710)
Expenses (excluding depreciation of $638)	(24,417)
Cash balance on December 31, 2007 should be	$(76,217)
Cash balance on December 31, 2007 per tax return	$295

Comments: It is unreasonable for cost of sales to be 93% of sales. Cash is misstated cumulatively by $76,512.

We also compared the tax returns to the internal financial statements prepared by Raj Kupar, who we understand is a CPA and brother-in-law of the prior owner of the business, Rahman Magyar. Please be advised that we could not find a relationship between the financial statements and the tax returns. The tax returns were materially different from the internal financial statements.

Revenues on the internal financials were approximately $15,000 higher in 2005, $18,000 lower in 2006 and $30,000 higher in 2007. There appeared to be only a partial listing of expenses, such that 2005 showed a profit of $70,000, 2006 a profit of $65,000 and 2007 a profit of $74,000. The costs and expenses were substantially less than those shown on the tax returns. In addition, the tax returns reflected substantial losses each year. Finally, the internal financial statements were not prepared in accordance with generally accepted accounting principles.

You also asked us to check whether or not Mr. Kupar is a practicing CPA in New Jersey. We did check with the New Jersey State Board of Public Accountants. He is neither a licensed CPA nor a licensed public accountant.

Thank you for the opportunity of serving you. If you have any questions about this report, please contact us directly.

Woodbridge, New Jersey

July 24, 2009

Exhibit B: DARIUS AND SPIVACK

One Main Street
Hackensack, NJ 07601

March 25, 2010

Theodore R. Rich, Esq.

100 Pearl Street

Woodbridge, New Jersey 07095

Re: Saleem v. Klavin

Dear Mr. Rich:

This report relates to an action for legal malpractice brought by your clients, **Omar and Sylvia Saleem**, against **Neil Klavin**, a member of the New Jersey Bar. It derives from your request for my opinion as to whether third-party defendant Klavin breached any duty to his former clients, the third-party plaintiffs herein, when he undertook to represent them in July 2007, with respect to the purchase of a certain office supply and mail box business, known as Magyar, Inc., located at 189 Princeton Road, Woodbridge, New Jersey.

For purposes of this report, I have read, analyzed and relied upon multiple documents contained in all your litigation files, including the February 9, 2009 depositions of Omar Saleem, Sylvia Saleem and Rahman Magyar; the December 27, 2007 Contract of Sale between Magyar, Inc., and Omar and Sylvia Saleem; the January 4, 2008 addendum to closing statement; the January 2, 2008 Lease between Magyar, Inc. and Marjama Company; Rahman Magyar's answers to interrogatories; the December 27, 2007 note from Omar and Sylvia Saleem to Rahman Magyar; correspondence between attorneys D'Orio (for seller) and Klavin (for buyer) dated respectively October 14, 2007 and November 2, 2007 and December 3, 2007. Kindly note that the documents listed above do not include all the materials examined by me, such as all correspondence between and among the parties, all pleadings, all discovery, and the like. Most especially did I review and analyze the July 24, 2009 expert report of Spyros and Company, Certified Public Accountants, rendered on behalf of Omar and Sylvia Saleem.

STATEMENT OF FACTS

In early 2007, Omar Saleem, a native of Syria, but living and working in the United States since 1966, expressed interest in buying a small business. He read about a business for sale in the local newspaper. He answered the advertisement and soon met one Rahman Magyar, the owner of Magyar, Inc., a company engaged in the office supply and mail service business. Later, at a meeting held in the Rahman Magyar's office, Omar verbally said that he was interested in purchasing the business. About a week later Saleem called Magyar. The two agreed on a price of $150,000 including a $40,000 promissory note to Magyar. During the course of the preliminary negotiations, Magyar had assured the Saleems that the business was a very simple operation which they would have no problem understanding and that he would agree to work a month in the business free of charge to train both Omar and his wife. For whatever reason, Magyar never offered the Saleems an opportunity to examine the books and records of the Company, or to have them examined by an outside accountant. However, he did show them some tax returns and financial statements prepared by his brother-in-law, whom he alleged was a CPA. After the closing, Magyar did provide on-the-job training, but it was hurried and hardly afforded the Saleems an opportunity to understand the economics of the business.

The essential complaint of the Saleems is that their attorney Klavin failed to provide them with appropriate legal advice and counsel in connection with the actual purchase of the business. In this regard the Saleems contend that Klavin failed to incorporate certain conditions and contingencies in the December 27, 2008 contract, which would have made the sale subject to a review of all books, records, income tax returns by a certified public accountant acting on behalf of the buyers. Thus, instead of advising the Saleems not to sign the contract and make any substantial deposit until the Saleems had all the books and records examined by their accountant, and having, alternatively, failed to incorporate such protective contingencies and conditions in the contract, Klavin put his clients on the horns of a dilemma faced, as they unfortunately were, with either losing their $1,000 deposit or purchasing the business in total ignorance of its monthly income and expenses.

CONCLUSIONS OF LAW

The matter of attorney negligence arising out of this matter must, of course, be evaluated and judged in accordance with the standard of care applicable in legal malpractice actions. In this regard, it is settled that an attorney is obligated to exercise on behalf of his client the knowledge, skill, and ability ordinarily possessed and exercised by members of the legal profession similarly situated, and to employ reasonable care and prudence in connection therewith. *(McCullough v. Sullivan,* 102 N.J.L. 381, 384 (E. & A. 1926); *Sullivan v. Stoudt,* 120 N.J.L. 304, 308 (E. & A. 1938; *Taylor v. Shepard,* 136 NJ Super. 85, 90 (App. Div. 1982); *Saint Pius X House of Retreats v. Camden Diocese,* 88 N.J. 571, 588 (1982). Perhaps the most quoted statement of the rule of care applicable to attorney negligence suits is found in *Hodges v. Carter,* 239 N.C. 517, 80 S.E. 2d 144 (1954):

Ordinarily when an attorney engages in the practice of the law and contracts to prosecute an action in behalf of his client, he impliedly represents that (1) he possesses the requisite degree of learning, skill and ability necessary to the practice of his profession and which others similarly situated ordinarily possess; (2) he will exercise his best judgment in the prosecution of the litigation entrusted to him; and (3) he will exercise reasonable and ordinary care and diligence in the use of his skill and in the application of his knowledge to his client's cause (Id. at 519, 80 S.E. 2d at 145–146).

What constitutes a reasonable degree of care is not to be considered in a vacuum. On the contrary, it must be the facts and circumstances of each specific case, and the type of service the attorney undertakes therein. With this in mind, I now proceed to examine the conduct of the subject defendant attorney in connection with his professional duties and conduct in the management of the above matter. The record shows an egregious failure on the part of attorney Klavin to safeguard and protect the interests of his clients when he undertook to represent them in the purchase of Magyar, Inc. This conclusion is based upon the fact that defendant Klavin made no attempt to follow the standard and elementary procedures mandated for any attorney representing a buyer in the acquisition of a corporation. Thus, if Klavin had truly represented the interests of the Saleems, he would not only have examined all Magyar Inc.'s Federal and State tax returns, he would also, as a part of that investigation, have conducted a lien search in every place that Magyar conducted its business; would have obtained from Magyar an up-to-date financial statement in order to understand the economic aspects of the deal; would have obtained an independent audit of that financial statement; would have checked the terms, acceleration clauses, and restrictions on any notes or mortgages or other indebtedness of the corporation; would have examined all insurance policies to discover what unknown liabilities existed; would have examined the viability and collectability of all accounts receivable; would have made a complete physical inventory of all corporate assets, together with a current market evaluation of same; would have examined the important contracts of Magyar and its customers, which constituted the lifeblood of that corporation; and would have performed other common-sense duties, such as talking to the main customers of Magyar, all for the overall purpose of insuring that the interests of his clients, the Saleems, were fully protected and safeguarded.

It is my opinion that if Klavin had conducted this type of basic and common-sense investigation, as he was bound to do in accordance with his duties as an attorney of this state, the Saleems would not have undertaken to purchase

Magyar, and would thereby have escaped all the financial damage, loss of time, mental stress and anguish that they unfortunately suffered as a result of this purchase. Indeed, we now know that as a direct result of his negligence, Klavin caused his clients to lose at least $110,000 due to the misrepresentations made by the seller. In short, I find on the facts and the law that defendant Klavin, in his attorney-client relationship with the Saleems, fell below the standard of care and prudence exercised by ordinary members of the New Jersey Bar. Otherwise put, attorney Klavin, in his relationship with the Saleems, deviated substantially from the standard of care expected of New Jersey attorneys.

But it remains basic to the Saleems' cause of action for legal malpractice that the wrongful conduct or failures of attorney Klavin are a proximate cause of their injuries. In order to establish causation, the burden is clearly upon the Saleems to prove that the negligence of Klavin was more likely than not a substantial factor in causing the unfavorable result. (Lecral Malpractice, Mallen & Levit, at pg. 502; and also see Lieberman v. Employers Ins. of Wassau, 85 N.J. 325, 341 (1980); Hoppe v. Ranzini, 58 N.J. Super. 233, 238-239 (App. Div. 1975), certif. den. 70 N.J. 144 (1976); Lamb v. Barbour, 188 N.J. Super. 6, 12 (App. Div. 1982); and as to the test of proximate cause see State v. Jersey Central Power & Light Co., 69 N.J. 102, 100 (1976); Ettin v. Ava Truck Leasing Inc., 153 N.J. 463, 483 (1969).) And plaintiff is obliged to carry this burden of proof by the presentation of competent, credible evidence, which proves material facts; and not conjecture, surmise or suspicion. (Lang v. Landy, 35 N.J. 44, 54 (1961); Modla v. United States, 15 F Supp. 198, 201, (D.N.J. 1957).) Otherwise stated, third-party plaintiffs herein must establish a chain of causation between their damages and the negligence or other wrongful conduct on the part of defendant Klavin. (Catto v. Schnepp, 21 N.J. supra. 506, 511 (App. Div.) affld o.b. 62 N.J. 20 (1972).)

Based upon the facts presented to me, and the applicable law, it is my view that the inexplicable failure of defendant Klavin to inspect or provide for the inspection of all Magyar, Inc. tax returns and corporate books and records, were the immediate factors that caused the Saleems to sustain heavy losses. It follows, therefore, that third-party defendant Klavin is liable to the third-party plaintiffs Saleems for legal malpractice and all causally related damages.

Very truly yours,

Richard M. Darius

Exhibit C: EDWARD J. CARUSO

Counselor at Law
300 Broad Street
Newark, New Jersey 07104

June 8, 2010

Theodore R. Rich, Esq.

100 Pearl Street

Woodbridge, New Jersey 07095

Re: Saleem v. Klavin

Dear Mr. Rich:

Please be advised that this opinion relates to an action for legal malpractice brought by your clients, **Omar and Sylvia Saleem**, against **Neil Klavin**, a member of the New Jersey Bar. It derives from your request for my opinion as to whether third-party defendant Klavin breached any duty to his former clients, the third-party plaintiffs herein, when he undertook to represent them in July 2007, with respect to the purchase of a certain office supply and mail box business, known as Magyar, Inc., located at 189 Princeton Road, Woodbridge, New Jersey.

For purposes of this report, I have read, analyzed and relied upon the following documents contained in all your litigation files:

- February, 9, 2009 depositions of Omar Saleem, Sylvia Saleem and Rahman Magyar;

- December 27, 2007 Contract of Sale between Magyar, Inc., and Omar and Sylvia Saleem;

- January 4, 2008 addendum to closing statement;

- January 2, 2008 Lease between Magyar, Inc. and Marjama Company;

- Rahman Magyar answers to interrogatories;

- December 27, 2007 note from Omar and Sylvia to Rahman Magyar;

- Correspondence between attorneys D'Orio (for seller) and Klavin (for buyer) dated respectively October 14, 2007 and November 2, 2007 and December 3, 2007.

- July 24, 2009 expert report prepared by the CPA firm of Spyros and Company; and

- March 25, 2010 expert opinion of Darius and Spivack

Also please note that the documents listed above do not include all the materials examined by me, such as all correspondence between and among the parties, all pleadings, all discovery, and the like.

I have reviewed the documents referred to above in order to provide you with my opinion as to whether Neil Klavin deviated from the standard of care, which would be applicable in this transaction. Based on my review of all the documents set forth above, I am of the opinion that Mr. Klavin did not deviate from the standard of care for the reasons set forth below.

The transaction that is the subject of the litigation and this report involved the purchase of a business known as Magyar, Inc. The plaintiffs, Omar and Sylvia Saleem, executed a contract to purchase the aforesaid business from Magyar, Inc. In connection with the original negotiations relative to the business, the plaintiffs received a document showing projection of income and return on equity in connection with the business. This document was reviewed by the plaintiffs prior to the execution of the contract. The document was, in fact, executed by both of the plaintiffs, namely Omar and Sylvia Saleem.

After the parties agreed on all relevant terms for the transaction, the seller's attorney, Louis D'Orio, prepared a contract of sale. Ultimately, the contract was taken to Mr. Klavin by Omar Saleem. After reviewing the contract, Klavin prepared a review letter dated November 2, 2007. The review letter set forth a number of contingencies including, but not limited to, the following:

1. Review and approval of the existing lease . . .

2. A requirement that the buyer be permitted to review the books of the seller . . . and

3. Inclusion in the contract of a more detailed listing of scheduled assets.

The response to Mr. Klavin's letter was Mr. D'Orio's letter dated December 3, 2007. In that letter Mr. D'Orio advised Mr. Klavin that a lease contingency was not necessary since the lease had already been reviewed and approved by Mr. Klavin's clients. Mr. Klavin did question his clients in connection with the aforesaid lease and ultimately was satisfied that his clients read, understood, and were willing to accept same.

The next item discussed in Mr. D'Orio's letter was Mr. Klavin's request that his clients be permitted access to the books and records of the selling corporation. Mr. D'Orio requested that the review period be limited to five days and that there be some ascertainable standard as to whether or not the review was acceptable or unacceptable. In the last section of his letter, Mr. D'Orio provides Mr. Klavin with a more detailed schedule of assets.

It is obvious that the contents of Mr. D'Orio's letter were reviewed by Mr. Klavin and further reviewed by Mr. Klavin with his clients. I note that Mr. D'Orio requested that Mr. Klavin and/or his clients execute the letter so same could be incorporated as a part of the contract. I further note that Mr. Klavin, in fact, had his clients execute the letter after he reviewed same with him.

It is interesting that when Mr. Klavin forwarded the December 3, 2007 letter, which was executed by his clients, he included a cover letter in an effort to resolve the issue relative to a satisfactory review of the books and records. In that letter, Mr. Klavin indicates that his clients review of the books would be acceptable provided the books and records indicate gross receipts in excess of $175,000. I believe it is unequivocally clear that Mr. Klavin was sensitive to his clients' needs to review the books and records and furthermore had a discussion with his clients in connection with same. Stated another way, Mr. Klavin had placed his clients in a position where they were able to have access to the books and records before performing the contract.

In addition, the other elements of the transaction, including lease review, etc., were all properly handled by Mr. Klavin. All of the critical issues in connection with the purchase of a business were considered and reviewed with the client and were also the subject of informed consent.

In the opinion letter of Darius and Spivak. Mr. Darius suggests that "Klavin failed to incorporate certain conditions and contingencies in the December 27, 2007 contract, which would have made the sale subject to a review of all books . . ." This obviously is in opposite to the existing fact pattern, since the letter of December 3, 2007 clearly incorporates that contingency. Mr. Darius goes on to indicate that Mr. Klavin should have advised the Saleems not to sign the contract and make a deposit until the Saleems had all the books and records examined by their accountant. This simply flies in the face of the normal business practice in connection with the sale of a business. Having conducted numerous business closings over my 31 years of practice, it is my opinion that it would be extremely unusual to be involved in a transaction where a seller would let a buyer review books on any basis unless a substantial good faith deposit was made and a contract was executed by the parties.

Finally, Mr. Darius suggests that Mr. Klavin put his clients on the horns of a dilemma, which resulted in their being faced with either losing a deposit or purchasing a business in total ignorance of the monthly income. This dilemma was not created by Klavin. Mr. Klavin clearly gave his clients the opportunity to have the books and records reviewed. He received representations from his clients that they were reviewed and understood. If Mr. Klavin's clients had, in fact, performed their due diligence and reviewed the books and were unsatisfied with the result of their review, the contract could have been voided provided the review occurred within the contractual period. It was only at the day of the closing that the plaintiffs first indicated that they had not an opportunity to review the books and records of the corporation.

At that point, Mr. Klavin properly advised his clients that in the event they refused to consummate the transaction, they faced a possible loss of their deposit, and possibly other damages for breach of contract, since they did not avail themselves of the accounting contingency within the time period set forth in the contract.

I note that Mr. Darius states in his report that if Klavin had truly represented the interest of the Saleems, he would not only have examined all Magyar's Federal and State tax returns; he would also, as part of the investigation, have conducted a lien search. It appears that Mr. Darius is suggesting that Mr. Klavin should fulfill the role of an accountant and examine the books and records of the corporation. This is simply not an accurate statement, nor an accurate reflection of the duty of a closing attorney. Insofar as the lien search is concerned, same was, in fact, conducted by Mr. Klavin who ordered what is the normal and customary business search in connection with the proposed closing.

Mr. Darius goes on to indicate in his letter various undertakings that should have been performed by Mr. Klavin. Many of the undertakings set forth in Mr. Darius' letter do not fall in the ambit of a lawyer's duty to his client. Many of the functions would be performed by an accountant or other professional and are not within the scope of a duty owed by an attorney to his client.

In the case at bar, I believe it is clear from the deposition transcript and the correspondence referred to above, that Mr. Klavin adequately performed these duties.

Very truly yours,

Edward J. Caruso

PART VI

FINANCIAL AND RISK ANALYSIS AND FINANCIAL FORECASTING

CHAPTER 31

FINANCIAL STATEMENT ANALYSIS

CONTENTS

Under the Sarbanes-Oxley Act, annual reports are due within 60 days of year-end. Quarterly reports are due within 35 days. The rules apply to public companies having a market value capitalization of $75 million or more.

Financial statement analysis is an appraisal of a company's previous financial performance and its future potential. It looks at the overall health and operating performance of the business. This chapter covers analytical tools to be followed in appraising the balance sheet, analyzing the income statement, and evaluating financial structure. Financial management analyzes the financial statements to see how the company looks to the financial community and what corrective steps and policies can be initiated to minimize and solve financial problems. Areas of risk are identified. Means to efficiently utilize assets and earn greater returns are concentrated on. Financial statement analysis aids in determining the appropriateness of mergers and acquisitions.

We express our appreciation to Stan Chu, MS, CPA, of the City University of New York, for his coauthoring of this chapter, and to Hilmi Elifoglu, Ph.D., CISA, Profes- sor of Accounting and Information Systems, for his coauthoring of the material on XBRL at the end of the chapter.

A company's financial health has a bearing upon its price-earnings ratio, bond rating, cost of financing, and availability of financing. The importance of a sound financial statement analysis is evidenced by Enron.

To obtain worthwhile conclusions from financial ratios, the financial manager has to make two comparisons:

1. *Industry Comparison.* The financial executive should compare the company's ratios with those of competing companies in the industry or with industry standards. Industry norms can be obtained from such services as Dun and Bradstreet, Robert Morris Associates, Standard and Poor's, and Value Line.

   EXAMPLE 1: Dun and Bradstreet computes 14 ratios for each of 125 lines of business. They are published annually in Dun's Review and Key Business Ratios, Robert Morris Associates publishes Annual Statement Studies. Sixteen ratios are computed for more than 300 lines of business, as is a percentage distribution of items on the balance sheet and income statement (common size financial statements).

   In analyzing a company, you should appraise the trends in its industry. What is the pattern of growth or decline in the industry? The profit dollar is worth more if earned in a healthy, expanding industry than in a declining one.

   You have to make certain that the financial data of competitors are comparable to yours. For example, you cannot compare profitability when your company uses FIFO while a competitor uses LIFO for inventory valuation. In this case, you must restate the earnings of both companies on a comparative basis.

2. *Trend Analysis.* A company's ratio may be compared over several years to identify direction of financial health or operational performance. An attempt should be made to uncover the reasons for the change.

   The optimum value for any given ratio usually varies across industry lines, through time, and within different companies in the same industry. In other words, a ratio deemed optimum for one company may be inadequate for another. A particular ratio is typically deemed optimum within a given range of values. An increase or decrease beyond this range points to weakness or inefficiency.

   EXAMPLE 2: Whereas a low current ratio may indicate poor liquidity, a very high current ratio may reflect inefficient utilization of assets (e.g., excessive inventory) or inability to use short-term credit to the firm's advantage.

   For a seasonal business, you may find that year-end financial data are not representative. Thus, averages based on quarterly or monthly information may be used to level out seasonality effects.

   When computing ratios for analytical purposes, you may also want to use the realistic values for balance sheet accounts rather than reported amounts.

For example, in ratios, including the asset and its market value is more relevant than its historical cost.

A distorted trend signals a possible problem requiring management attention. However, a lack of change does not always mean normalcy. For example, labor growth may be up but production/sales may be static or down. Hence, labor costs may be disproportionate to operational activity.

AUDIT ATTENTION

Financial statement analysis indicates areas requiring audit attention. You should look at the percentage change in an account over the years or relative to some base year to identify inconsistencies.

EXAMPLE 3: If promotion and entertainment expense to sales was 3% last year and shot up to 15% this year, the internal auditor would want to know the reasons. This would be particularly disturbing if other competing companies still had a percentage relationship of 3%. The internal auditor might suspect that the promotion and entertainment expense account contained some personal rather than business charges. Supporting documentation for the charges would be requested and carefully reviewed by the internal auditor.

HORIZONTAL AND VERTICAL ANALYSIS

Horizontal analysis looks at the trend in accounts over the years and aids in identifying areas of wide divergence mandating further attention. Horizontal analysis may also be presented by showing trends relative to a base year.

EXAMPLE 4: X Company's revenue in 2X11 was $200,000 and in 2X12 was $250,000.

The percentage increase equals:

$$\frac{\text{Change}}{\text{Prior Year}} = \frac{\$50,000}{\$200,000} = 25\%$$

In vertical analysis, a significant item on a financial statement is used as a base value, and all other items on the financial statement are compared to it. In performing vertical analysis for the balance sheet, total assets is assigned 100%. Each asset is expressed as a percentage of total assets. Total liabilities and stockholders' equity is also assigned 100%. Each liability and stockholders' equity account is then expressed as a percentage of total liabilities and stockholders' equity. In the income statement, net sales are given the value of 100% and all other accounts are appraised in comparison to net sales. The resulting figures are then given in a common size statement.

Vertical analysis is helpful in disclosing the internal structure of the business and possible problem areas. It shows the relationship between each income statement account and revenue. It indicates the mix of assets that produces the income and the mix of the sources of capital, whether by current or long-term liabilities or by equity funding. Besides making internal evaluation possible, the results of vertical analysis are also employed to appraise the company's relative position in the industry. Horizontal and vertical analysis point to possible problem areas to be evaluated by the financial manager.

EXAMPLE 5:

	X Company Common-Size Income Statement for the Year Ended 12/31/2X12	
Sales	$40,000	100%
Less: Cost of Sales	10,000	25%
Gross Profit	$30,000	75%
Less: Expenses	4,000	10%
Net Income	$26,000	65%

BALANCE SHEET ANALYSIS

As a financial manager, you have to be able to analyze asset and liability accounts, evaluate corporate liquidity, appraise business solvency, and look to signs of possible business failure. You are concerned with the realizability of assets, turnover, and earning potential. Besides analyzing your company's financial health, you will want to make recommendations for improvement so that financial problems are rectified. Also, you can identify corporate strength which may further be taken advantage of. The evaluation of liabilities considers their possible overstatement or understatement.

Appraising Asset Quality

Asset quality applies to the certainty associated with the amount and timing of the realization of the assets in cash. Therefore, assets should be categorized by risk category.

What to Do: Calculate the following ratios: (1) high-risk assets to total assets, and (2) high-risk assets to sales. If high risk exists in assets, future write-offs may occur. For instance, the realization of goodwill is more doubtful than machinery. Also evaluate the risk of each major asset category. For example, receivables from an economically unstable government (e.g., Mexico) have greater risk than a receivable from ITT.

Special Note: Single-purpose assets have greater risk than multipurpose ones.

What to Watch Out for: Assets with no separable value that cannot be sold easily, such as intangibles and work-in-process. On the contrary, marketable securities are readily salable.

In appraising realization risk in assets, the effect of changing government policies on the entity has to be taken into account. Risk may exist with chemicals and other products deemed hazardous to health. Huge inventory losses may have to be taken.

EXAMPLE 6: Company A presents total assets of $6 million and sales of $10 million. Included in total assets are the following high risk assets:

Deferred moving costs	$300,000
Deferred plant rearrangement costs	100,000
Receivables for claims under a government contract	200,000
Goodwill	150,000

Applicable ratios are:

$$\frac{\text{High-risk assets}}{\text{Total assets}} = \frac{\$750,000}{\$6,000,000} = 12.5\%$$

$$\frac{\text{High-risk assets}}{\text{Sales}} = \frac{\$750,000}{\$10,000,000} = 7.5\%$$

Cash

How much of the cash balance is unavailable for use or restricted? Examples are a compensating balance and cash held in a foreign country where remission restrictions exist. Note that foreign currency holdings are generally stated at year-end exchange rates but may change rapidly.

You should determine the ratio of sales to cash. A high turnover rate may indicate a deficient cash position. This may lead to financial problems if additional financing is not available at reasonable interest rates. A low turnover ratio indicates excessive cash being held.

EXAMPLE 7:

	2X12	2X13
Cash	$500,000	$400,000
Sales	8,000,000	9,000,000
Industry norm for cash turnover rate	15.8 times	16.2 times

The turnover of cash is 16 ($8,000,000/$500,000) in 2X12 and 22.5 ($9,000,000/$400,000) in 2X13. It is clear that the company has a cash deficiency in 2X13, which implies a possible liquidity problem.

Distinguish between two types of cash: (1) cash needed for operating purposes and (2) cash required for capital expenditures. While the former must be paid, the latter is postponable.

Accounts Receivable

Realization risk in receivables can be appraised by studying the nature of the receivable balance. Examples of high risk receivables include amounts from economically unstable foreign countries, receivables subject to offset provisions, and receivables due from a company experiencing severe financial problems. Further, companies dependent on a few customers have greater risk than those with a large number of important accounts. Receivables due from industry are typically safer than receivables arising from consumers. Fair trade laws are more protective of consumers.

Accounts receivable ratios include the accounts receivable turnover and the average collection period. The accounts receivable turnover ratio reveals the number of times accounts receivable is collected during the period. It equals net sales divided by average accounts receivable. Average accounts receivable for the period is the beginning accounts receivable balance plus the ending accounts receivable balance divided by 2. (However, in a seasonal business where sales vary greatly during the year, this ratio can become distorted unless proper averaging takes place. In such a case, monthly or quarterly sales figures should be used). A higher turnover rate is generally desirable because it indicates faster collections. However, an excessively high ratio may point to too tight a credit policy, with the company not tapping the potential for profit through sales to customers in higher risk classes. But in changing its credit policy, the company must weigh the profit potential against the risk inherent in selling to more marginal customers.

The average collection period (days sales in receivables) is the number of days it takes to collect receivables.

$$\text{Average collection period} = \frac{365}{\text{Account receivable turnover}}$$

Separate collection periods may be calculated by type of customer, major product line, and market territory.

A significant increase in collection days may indicate a danger that customer balances may become uncollectible. However, reference should be made to the collection period common in the industry. One reason for an increase may be that the company is now selling to highly marginal customers. The financial manager should compare the company's credit terms with the degree to which customer accounts are delinquent. An aging schedule is helpful.

The quality of receivables may also be appraised by referring to customer ratings given by credit agencies.

Also look for a buildup over time in the ratios of (1) accounts receivable to total assets, and (2) accounts receivable to sales as indicative of a receivable collection problem. Receivables outstanding in excess of the expected payment date and relative to industry norm implies a higher probability of uncollectibility.

The financial manager should appraise the trends in bad debts to accounts receivable and bad debts to sales. An unwarranted decrease in bad debts lowers the quality of earnings. This may happen when there is a decline in bad debts even though the company is selling to less creditworthy customers and/or actual bad debt losses are increasing.

EXAMPLE 8: A company reports the following information:

	2X12	2X13
Sales	$100,000	$130,000
Accounts receivable	30,000	40,000
Bad debts	2,000	2,200

You conclude that the company is selling to more risky customers in 2X13 relative to 2X12.

Relevant ratios follow:

	2X12	2X13
Bad debts to sales	2.0%	1.7%
Bad debts to accounts receivable	6.7%	5.5%

Because the company is selling to more marginal customers, its bad debt provision should increase in 2X13. However, the ratios of bad debts to sales and bad debts to accounts receivable actually decreased. The impact of understating bad debts is to overstate net income and accounts receivable. Thus, net income should be lowered for the incremental profit arising from the unwarranted lowering of bad debts. If you decide that a realistic bad debt percentage to accounts receivable is 6.5%, then the bad debt expense should be $2,600 ($40,000 × 6.5%). Net income should thus be reduced by $400 ($2,600 – $2,200).

Receivables are of low quality if they arose from loading customers up with unneeded merchandise by giving generous credit terms. "Red flags" as to this happening include:

- A significant increase in sales in the final quarter of the year.
- A substantial amount of sales returns in the first quarter of the next year.
- A material decrease in sales for the first quarter of the next year.

The trend in sales returns and allowances is often a good reflection of the quality of merchandise sold to customers. A significant decrease in a firm's sales allowance account as a percentage of sales is not in conformity with reality when a greater liability for dealer returns exist. This will result in lower earnings quality.

EXAMPLE 9: Company X's sales and sales returns for the period 2X11 to 2X13 follow:

	2X13	2X12	2X11
Balance in sales returns account at year-end	$2,000	$3,800	$1,550
Sales	$240,000	$215,000	$100,000
Percentage of sales returns to sales	.0083	.0177	.0155

The reduction in the ratio of sales returns to sales from 2X12 to 2X13 indicates that less of a provision for returns is being made by the company. This would appear unrealistic if there is a greater liability for dealer returns and credits on an expanded sales base.

Inventory

An inventory buildup may mean realization problems. The buildup may be at the plant, wholesaler, or retailer. A sign of a buildup is when inventory increases at a much faster rate than the increase in sales.

What to Watch Out For: A decline in raw materials coupled with a rise in work-in-process and finished goods pointing to a future production slowdown.

If the company is holding excess inventory, there is an opportunity cost of tying up money in inventory. Further, there is a high carrying cost for storing merchandise. Why aren't certain types of merchandise selling well? Calculate turnover rates for each inventory category and by department.

Possible reasons for a low turnover rate are overstocking, obsolescence, product line deficiencies, or poor marketing efforts. There are cases where a low inventory rate is appropriate.

EXAMPLE 10: A higher inventory level may arise because of expected future increases in price or when a new product has been introduced for which the advertising efforts have not yet been felt.

Note: The turnover rate may be unrepresentatively high when the business uses a "natural year-end" because at that time the inventory balance will be exceptionally low.

What to Do: Compute the number of days inventory is held and compare it to the industry norm and previous years.

$$\text{Inventory turnover} = \frac{\text{Cost of Goods Sold}}{\text{Average Inventory}}$$

$$\text{Age of inventory} = \frac{365}{\text{Turnover}}$$

Also look at the trend in inventory to sales.

The effect of changing government policies on the entity has to be taken into account. Risk may exist, for example, with chemicals and other products deemed hazardous to health. Huge inventory losses may have to be taken.

A high turnover rate may point to inadequate inventory, possibly leading to a loss in business.

What to Watch Out For: Merchandise that is susceptible to price variability: "fad," specialized, perishable, technological, and luxurious goods. Standardized, staple, and necessity items have a low realization risk.

Note: Raw material inventory is safer than finished goods or work-in-process since raw material has more universal and varied uses.

Questions to be asked:

• Is inventory collateralized against a loan? If so, creditors can retain it in the event of nonpayment of the obligation.

• Is there adequate insurance in case of loss? There is a particular problem when insurance cannot be obtained for the item because of high risk (e.g., geographic location of inventory is in a high crime area or there is susceptibility to floods).

• Is it subject to political risk (e.g., big cars and an oil crisis)?

Look for inventory that is overstated due to mistakes in quantities, costing, pricing, and valuation.

Warning: The more technical a product is and the more dependent the valuation is on internally developed cost records, the more susceptible are cost estimates to misstatement. Also, sudden inventory write-offs raise questions about the overall salability of inventory.

Is the change in inventory method appropriate (e.g., new FASB pronouncement, SEC release, or IRS ruling)?

In gauging manufacturing efficiency, you should look at the relationship between indirect labor and direct labor, as a constant level of both are needed to run the organization efficiently.

EXAMPLE 11: A company presents the following makeup of inventory:

	2X11	2X12
Raw materials	$89,000	$78,000
Work-in-process	67,000	120,000
Finished goods	16,000	31,000

Your analysis of the inventory shows there was a material divergence in the inventory components between 2X11 and 2X12. There was a reduction in raw material by 12.4% ($11,000/$89,000), while work-in-process rose by 79.1% ($53,000/$67,000) and finished goods rose by 93.8% ($15,000/$16,000). The lack of consistency in the trend between raw materials relative to work-in-process and finished goods may imply a forthcoming cutback in production. An obsolescence problem may also exist applicable to work-in-process and finished goods due to the sizable buildup.

The company's operating cycle, which equals the average collection period plus the average age of inventory, should be determined. A short operating cycle is desired so that cash flow is expedited.

Investments

An indication of the fair value of investments may be the revenue (dividend income, interest income) obtained from them. Have decreases in portfolio market values been recognized in the accounts? Higher realization risk exists where there is a declining trend in the percentage of earnings derived from investments to their carrying value. Also check for unrealized losses in the portfolio occurring after year-end.

EXAMPLE 12: Company X presents the following information:

	2X11	2X12
Investments	$50,000	$60,000
Investment income	$7,000	$5,000

The percent of investment income to total investments decreased from 14% in 2X11 to 8.3% in 2X12, pointing to higher realization risk in the portfolio.

If a company is buying securities in other companies for diversification purposes, this will reduce overall risk. Risk in an investment portfolio can be ascertained by computing the standard deviation of its rate of return.

An investment portfolio of securities fluctuating widely in price is of higher realization risk than a portfolio that is diversified by industry and economic sector. However, the former portfolio will show greater profitability in a bull market.

Recommendations: Appraise the extent of diversification and stability of the investment portfolio. There is less risk when securities are negatively correlated (price goes in opposite directions) or not correlated compared to a portfolio of positively correlated securities (price goes in same direction). Is the portfolio of poor quality securities, such as "junk" bonds?

Note cases where held-to-maturity securities have an amortized cost different from market value.

Fixed Assets

Is there sufficient maintenance of productive assets to ensure current and future earning power? Lessened operational efficiency and breakdowns occur when obsolete assets have not been replaced and/or required repairs made.

What to Do: Determine the age and condition of each major asset category, as well as the cost to replace old assets. Determine output levels, downtime, and temporary discontinuances. Inactive and unproductive assets are a drain on the firm. Are the fixed assets specialized or risky, making them susceptible to obsolescence?

Note: Pollution-causing equipment may necessitate replacement or modification to meet governmental ecology requirements.

Ratio trends to be calculated are:

- Fixed asset acquisitions to total assets. The trend is particularly revealing for a technological company that has to keep up to date. A decrease in the trend points to the failure to replace older assets on a timely basis.
- Repairs and maintenance to fixed assets.
- Repairs and maintenance to sales.

- Sales to fixed assets.
- Net income to fixed assets.

The fixed asset turnover ratio (net sales to average fixed assets) aids in appraising a company's ability to use its asset base efficiently to obtain revenue. A low ratio may mean that investment in fixed assets is excessive relative to the output generated.

A high ratio of sales to floor space indicates the efficient utilization of space.

A company having specialized or risky fixed assets has greater vulnerability to asset obsolescence. Examples include machinery used to manufacture specialized products and "fad" items.

When a company's rate of return on assets (e.g., net income to fixed assets) is poor, the firm may be justified in not maintaining fixed assets. If the industry is declining, fixed asset replacement and repairs may have been restricted. It is better for a company when assets are mobile and/or can easily be modified since it affords the firm greater flexibility. If the assets are easily accessible, it will also be easier to repair them. The location of the assets is also important since that may affect their condition and security. The location will also affect property taxes, so a company may be able to save on taxes by having the plant located in a low-tax area.

EXAMPLE 13: The following information applies to X Company:

	2X11	2X12
Depreciation expense to fixed assets	5.3%	4.4%
Depreciation expense to sales	4.0%	3.3%

The above declining ratios indicate improper provision for the deterioration of assets.

Recommendation: Use a depreciation method that best approximates the decline in usefulness of the fixed asset. Compare the depreciation rate to the industry norm.

What to Do: Calculate the trend in depreciation expense to fixed assets and depreciation expense to sales. If there are decreasing trends, inadequate depreciation charges may exist. Compare the book depreciation rate to the tax depreciation rate.

A vacillating depreciation policy will distort continuity in earnings.

What to Watch Out For: A material decline in sales coupled with a significant increase in capital expenditures may be inconsistent. It could point to over-expansion and later write-offs.

EXAMPLE 14: Company T presents the following information regarding its fixed assets:

	2X11	2X12
Fixed assets	$120,000	$105,000
Repairs and maintenance	6,000	4,500
Replacement cost	205,000	250,000

The company has inadequately maintained its assets as indicated by:

- The reduction in the ratio of repairs and maintenance to fixed assets from 5% in 2X11 to 4.3% in 2X12.
- The material variation between replacement cost and historical cost.
- The reduction in fixed assets over the year.

Management of Fixed Assets

Fixed assets should meet the operational needs of the business with maximum productivity at minimum cost. These long-term expenditures are significant in amount, and can result in great loss to the company if fixed assets are improperly managed. Capital investments result in a higher breakeven point due to the resulting costs associated with them including depreciation, insurance, and property taxes.

A new company requires greater capital expansion for growth. There is less of a need for additional capital facilities by an established, mature company with strong market share.

For control purposes, unique control numbers should be securely affixed to fixed assets. There should be periodic appraisals to assess the adequacy of insurance coverage.

You should not buy elaborate manufacturing facilities for a new product until it has shown success. In the initial stages, it is recommended that production be subcontracted. With an established product, productivity is achieved through internal capital expansion. In evaluating production facilities, consideration should be given to scrap, rejects, cost per unit, and malfunctioning time.

The financial manager is concerned with the following in managing fixed assets:

- Purchasing the "right" equipment for the firm's needs.
- Proper timing of capital expenditures.
- Keeping capital expenditures within the financial capabilities of the firm.
- Optimally financing capital expenditures.
- Physical care and security of property.
- Correlating capital expenditures to use tax breaks fully.

Intangible Assets

Realization risk is indicated when there is a high ratio of intangible assets to total assets. The amounts recorded for intangibles may be overstated relative to their market value or to their future income-generating capacity. For instance, in a recessionary environment, goodwill on the books may be worthless.

What to Do: Calculate trends in the following ratios:

- Intangible assets to total assets.
- Intangible assets to stockholders' equity.
- Intangible assets to sales.

- Intangible assets to net income.

- Specific, questionable intangible assets (e.g., goodwill) to total assets.

- Change in intangible assets to change in net income.

EXAMPLE 15: A company shows the following data:

	2X12	2X13
Intangible assets	$ 58,000	$187,000
Total assets	512,000	530,000
Sales	640,000	655,000
Net income	120,000	140,000

Relevant ratios can now be computed as follows:

	2X12	2X13
Intangible assets to total assets	11.3%	35.3%
Intangible assets to sales	9.1%	28.5%

Higher realization risk in intangibles is indicated by the higher ratios of intangible assets to total assets and intangible assets to sales. Also, the 222.4% increase in intangibles along with the 16.7% increase in net income imply that earnings have been overstated as a result of the failure to incorporate items that have been expensed rather than capitalized.

What to Watch Out For: Leasehold improvements, because they have no cash realizability.

Note: In some instances, intangible assets may be undervalued, such as a highly successful patented product. However, can the patent be infringed upon by minor alteration? Is it a high-technological item? What is the financial strength of the company to defend itself against those infringing upon its patent? What are the expiration dates of patents, and are new ones coming on stream?

A company's goodwill account should be appraised to ascertain whether a firm acquired has superior earning potential to justify the excess of cost over fair market value of net assets paid for it. If the acquired company does not have superior profit potential, the goodwill has no value because excess earnings do not exist relative to other companies in the industry. However, internally developed goodwill is expensed and not capitalized. It represents an undervalued asset, such as the good reputation of McDonald's.

Deferred Charges

Deferred charges depend on estimates of future probabilities and developments to a greater extent than do other assets. These estimates are often overly optimistic. Is the business deferring an item that has no future economic benefit only to defer costs so as not to burden reported results? Further, deferred charges do not constitute cash-realizable assets, and thus cannot meet creditor claims. Examples of questionable deferred costs are startup costs, rearrangement costs, and promotional costs.

What to Do: Calculate trends in the ratios of (1) deferred charges to sales, (2) deferred charges to net income, and (3) deferred charges (e.g., advertising) to total expenditures (e.g., total advertising). Watch out for increasing trends.

A high ratio of intangible assets and deferred charges to total assets points to an asset structure of greater realization risk. Overstated assets in terms of realizability may necessitate later write-offs.

EXAMPLE 16: A company presents the following information:

	2X13	2X14
Deferred charges	$ 47,000	$121,000
Total assets	580,000	650,000
Sales	680,000	720,000
Net income	190,000	205,000

Relevant ratios are now calculated as follows:

	2X13	2X14
Deferred charges to total assets	8.1%	18.6%
Deferred charges to sales	6.9%	16.8%
Deferred charges to net income	24.7%	59.0%

Greater realization risk is indicated from the higher ratios. The net income for 2X14 is most likely overstated, since items that should have been expensed are probably included in the deferred charge balance.

Asset Utilization

Asset utilization may be measured by the total asset turnover. It is useful in appraising an entity's ability to use its asset base efficiently to obtain revenue. A low ratio may be caused from numerous factors, and it is essential to identify the causes. For instance, it must be determined if the investment in assets is excessive relative to the value of the output being produced. If so, the business may wish to consolidate its present operation, perhaps by selling some of its assets and investing the funds for a higher return or using them to expand into a more profitable area.

$$\text{Total asset turnover} = \frac{\text{Net sales}}{\text{Average total assets}}$$

The operating assets ratio (total operating assets to total assets) concentrates on those assets actively employed in current operations. Such assets exclude (1) past-oriented assets and (2) future-oriented assets. Past-oriented assets arise from prior errors, inefficiencies, or losses because of competitive factors or changes in business plans. These assets have not yet been formally recognized in the accounts. Examples are obsolete goods, idle plants, receivables under litigation, delinquent receivables, and nonperforming loans (no interest being recognized). Future-oriented assets are acquired for corporate growth or generating future sales. Examples are land held for speculation and factories under construction. Nonoperating assets reduce profits and return on investment because no benefit to current operations occurs. They neither generate sales nor reduce costs. Rather, they are a drain on the company and may require financing.

Asset Profile

Are any of the current assets used to secure long-term debt or contingent liabilities as pledges or guarantees?

Even though current assets are about the same or slightly above current liabilities, the company may still experience liquidity difficulties if the maturity schedule of the liabilities is ahead of the expected cash realization of the assets. For example, the payment schedule of the debts may be concentrated toward the beginning of the year, but the cash realization of the assets may be evenly disbursed throughout the year. If this occurs, the company may be forced to discount its receivables or quickly liquidate inventory at lower prices. Although this will generate immediate cash, it dilutes the realizable value of the current assets. In effect, the actual value of the assets becomes less than the fair value of the liabilities.

Assets that are interdependent create a financial disadvantage for the company. For example, the sale of equipment on the assembly line may adversely affect the remaining equipment. On the other hand, you can sell one marketable security without affecting another.

Sharp vacillation in the price of assets is a negative sign, because the company may be forced to sell an asset at a time of financial need at great loss (i.e., market value is significantly less than book value). Greater liquidity risk exists with non-current assets than with current assets because of the greater disposition difficulty.

Also, a determination as to whether off-balance-sheet assets (unrecorded resources) exist must be made. Examples are a tax loss carryforward benefit, expected rebates, and a purchase commitment to acquire an item at a price lower than the prevailing price. You should also review for assets that are reflected on the balance sheet at an amount substantially less than their real value. Examples are patents recorded at cost, even though the present value of future benefits substantially exceeds it, and land that does not reflect its appreciated value.

ASC 715, *Defined Benefit Plans—Pensions* (ASC 715-30), does not allow the recognition of a minimum asset for the excess of the fair value of pension plan assets less the accumulated benefit obligation. For analytical purposes, such minimum asset should be considered as an unrecorded asset for the excess of fair value of plan assets over the projected benefit obligation.

Recommendation: Note the existence of unrecorded assets representing resources of the business or items expected to have future economic benefit.

Liabilities

If liabilities are understated, net income is overstated because it does not include necessary charges to reflect the proper valuation of liabilities.

The provision for estimated liabilities for future costs and losses (e.g., lawsuits, warranties) may impair the significance of net income. In evaluating the adequacy of estimated liability accounts, you should carefully examine footnote disclosures and familiarize yourself with the financial and accounting characteristics of the industry.

What to Do: Eliminate arbitrary adjustments of estimated liabilities in arriving at corporate earning power. Estimated liability provisions should be realistic given the nature of the circumstances.

Example: Profits derived from a recoupment of prior-year reserves may necessitate elimination.

What to Watch Out For: An unrealistically low provision for future costs. For example, it is inconsistent for a firm to decrease its warranty provision when previous experience indicates a poor-quality product.

An overprovision in estimated liabilities is sometimes made. In effect, the company is providing a reserve for a "rainy day."

Example: Profits are too high and management wants to bring them down.

Note: Poor earnings quality is indicated when more operating expenses and losses are being charged to reserve accounts compared to prior years.

EXAMPLE 17: A company reports the following data:

	2X12	**2X13**	**2X14**
Estimated liability for warranties	$ 30,000	$ 33,000	$ 40,000
Sales	100,000	130,000	190,000

From 2X12 to 2X14, the company reports that there has been a higher rate of defective merchandise that has to be repaired.

Relevant ratios follow:

	2X12–2X13	**2X13–2X14**
Percentage increase in the estimated liability account	10.0%	21.2%
Percentage increase in sales	30.0%	46.2%

The percentage increase in the estimated liability account is materially less than the percentage increase in sales. Since the firm is experiencing quality problems, it is clear that the estimated liability account is understated.

Calculate the trends in the ratios of:

- Current liabilities to total liabilities.
- Current liabilities to stockholders' equity.
- Current liabilities to sales.

Increasing trends point to liquidity difficulty.

Caution: Stretching short-term payables is not a good sign.

Determine the trend in "patient" (e.g., supplier) to "pressing" (e.g., bank, IRS) liabilities. When liquidity problems exist, you are better off with patient creditors who will work with you. Thus, a high ratio of pressing liabilities to total liabilities is disadvantageous.

Useful disclosures of long-term obligations are mandated by ASC 440, *Commitments* (ASC 440-10). The financial manager may want to review commitments applicable to unconditional purchase obligations and future payments on long-term debt and redeemable stock.

ASC 835, *Interest* (ASC 835-20), requires disclosure of indirect guarantees of indebtedness. Included are contracts in which a company promises to advance funds to another if financial problems occur, as when sales drop below a stipulated level.

EXAMPLE 18: A company presents the following information:

	2X11	2X12
Current liabilities		
Trade payables	$ 33,000	$ 28,000
Bank loans	51,000	78,000
Commercial paper	35,000	62,000
Taxes payable	8,000	12,000
Total current liabilities	$127,000	$180,000
Total noncurrent liabilities	$310,000	$315,000
Total liabilities	$437,000	$495,000
Total revenue	$1,100,000	$1,150,000

Relevant ratios are:

Current liabilities to total revenue	11.5%	15.7%
Current liabilities to total liabilities	29.1%	36.4%
Pressing current liabilities to patient current liabilities	2.85	5.43

There is more liquidity risk in 2X12, as reflected by the higher ratios. In fact, pressing liabilities have significantly risen in terms of percentage.

Overstated Liabilities

Certain liabilities shown in the balance sheet should not be considered obligations for analytical purposes because they may not require future payment. Examples are:

- The deferred tax credit account if it applies to a temporary difference that will keep recurring (e.g., depreciation as long as capital expansion occurs).
- Unearned revenue related to passive income sources, such as rents.
- Convertible bonds with an attractive conversion feature.

Undervalued or Unrecorded Liabilities

Corporate obligations that are not recorded in the balance sheet must be considered when evaluating the entity's going-concern potential. Examples are lawsuits, dispute under a government contract, operating leases, commitments for future loans to a troubled company, guarantees of future performance, and bonus payment obligations.

The minimum liability for the pension plan equals the accumulated benefit obligation less the fair value of pension plan assets. However, the projected benefit obligation (based on anticipated future salaries) is a better measure of the plan's obligation than the accumulated benefit obligation (based on current salaries). Therefore, we should consider as an unrecorded liability the excess of the projected benefit obligation over the accumulated benefit obligation.

EXAMPLE 19:

Accumulated benefit obligation	$50,000,000
Less: fair value of plan assets	40,000,000
Minimum (booked) liability	$10,000,000

If the projected benefit obligation is $58 million, the unrecorded liability is $8 million ($58 million less $50 million).

An equity account may be in essence a liability, such as preferred stock with a maturity date or subject to sinking fund requirements.

Avenues of Financing

The company's ability to obtain financing at reasonable rates is affected by external considerations (e.g., Federal Reserve policy) and internal considerations (e.g., degree of existing debt).

The extent of loan restrictions on the company should be examined. How close is the company to violating a given restriction, which may in turn call the loan?

Can the company issue commercial paper and short-term bank debt? If there is a loan, has the collateral value of the loan diminished relative to the balance of the loan? If so, additional security may be required. Also examine the trend in the effective interest rate and compensating balance requirement relative to competition. Does the weighted-average debt significantly exceed the year-end debt balance?

Management of Liabilities

In managing liabilities, a prime purpose is to assure that the business has sufficient funds to meet maturing debt. Otherwise, the company will be in financial difficulty. The debt structure affects both the short-term and long-term financial position of the company.

The financial manager must be assured that all financial obligations are properly presented and disclosed in the financial statements. Also, the liability position and related financial ratios must satisfy any restrictions in loan agreements. The financial manager must borrow money when needed on a timely basis and at a reasonable interest rate.

Liability management involves the proper planning of all types of obligations. The financial manager must know current balances of accounts payable and accrued expenses and how far they may be stretched. Are liabilities within acceptable industry norms? Can the firm withstand periods of adversity? How does the overall economic picture look, and what effect does it have on the company?

The controller should prepare a number of reports to analyze the actual status of liabilities and to properly plan the debt structure. Some useful reports include:

- Periodic reports (e.g., quarterly, monthly) on the status of material liabilities, such as pensions, leases, and health care.
- Periodic reports comparing actual liabilities with amounts by category to allowable amounts in credit agreements.
- Comparisons of budgeted liabilities to actual liabilities.
- Listing and status of contingent liabilities and their values.
- Aging of accounts payable.

Stockholders' Equity

If a company cuts back on its dividends or omits them, it may mean it is having financial problems. It is better when a company varies its dividends rather than pays constant dividends so it can more easily reduce them in troubled times. If stockholders are used to receiving constant dividends each time, it will be more difficult for the company to adjust such dividends without materially upsetting stockholders.

If a loan agreement places restrictions on the company, such as its ability to pay dividends, this inhibits management's freedom of action and is a negative sign.

If treasury stock is acquired, the market price of the company's stock will rise because less shares will be on the market. If a company had previously purchased treasury stock at a cost significantly below the current market price, it is "sitting on" a significant potential increase in cash flow and paid-in capital.

If a company issues preferred stock for the first time or if it substantially issues preferred stock in the current year, it may mean the company had problems with issuing its common stock. This is a negative sign since the investing public may be viewing its common stock as too risky.

If convertible bonds or convertible preferred stock are converted to common stock, the bondholders or preferred stockholders are optimistic about the company. However, this will result in a drop in the market price of common stock as more shares are issued. On the plus side, the company will be able to omit the interest payment on bonds and the dividend payment on preferred stock.

A high ratio of retained earnings to stockholders' equity is a good sign because it indicates that capital financing is being achieved internally.

Stockholders are interested in dividends and prefer high ratios for dividend yield (dividends per share/market price per share) and dividend payout (dividends per share/earnings per share). A decline in these ratios may cause concern among stockholders.

Liquidity Analysis

Liquidity is the company's ability to convert noncash assets into cash or to obtain cash to meet impending obligations. You have to look at the stock and flow of liquid resources. Also, what is the timing of the cash inflows and outflows?

Liquidity is important in carrying out business activity, especially in times of adversity, such as when a business is shut down by a strike or when operating losses result from a recession or a significant rise in the price of a raw material. If liquidity is inadequate to cushion such losses, serious financial problems may ensue. Poor liquidity is analogous to a person having a fever-it is a symptom of a fundamental problem.

Liquidity is affected by the company's ability to obtain financing (e.g., lines of credit) and to postpone cash payments. Also considered is the mixture of current assets and current liabilities. How "close to cash" are the assets and liabilities? If a company's liquidity position is poor, it may be unable to make timely interest and principal payments on debt.

Liquidity ratios are static in nature as of year-end. Thus, it is essential for the financial manager to examine expected future cash flows. If future cash outflows are significantly more than inflows, a deteriorating liquidity position will occur.

What to Watch Out For: If you are a seasonal business, year-end financial data are not representative. Instead, use averages based on quarterly or monthly information to level out seasonal effects.

A seasonal business that is a net borrower should use more long-term financing as a precautionary measure. Also, a company with financial troubles should have debts mature during the peak rather than the trough.

Can you adjust to unexpected difficulties by changing the amount and timing of future cash flows? Consideration should be given to the closeness to cash of assets, ability to obtain further financing, degree of nonoperating assets that can be sold, ability to change operating and investing activities, and short payback periods on projects.

Funds Flow Ratios

- $$\text{Current ratio} \; = \; \frac{\text{Current assets}}{\text{Current liabilities}}$$

  Seasonal fluctuations will have an impact on this ratio. The current ratio is used to appraise the ability of the company to satisfy its current debt out of current assets. A high ratio is required if the company has a problem borrowing quickly, and if there are turbulent business conditions, among other reasons. A limitation of this ratio is that it may increase just prior to financial distress because of a company's attempt to improve its cash position by selling property and equipment. Such dispositions have a negative effect upon productive capacity. Another limitation of the ratio is that it will be higher when inventory is carried on a LIFO basis.

  Note: Current assets that are pledged to secure long-term liabilities are not available to meet current debt. If these current assets are included in the calculation of the ratio, a distortion results.

- $$\text{Quick ratio} \; = \; \frac{\text{Cash} + \text{Trading securities} + \text{Accounts receivable}}{\text{Current liabilities}}$$

  This is a more stringent test of liquidity than the current ratio because it excludes inventories and prepaid expenses.

- Working capital = Current assets – Current liabilities

  A high working capital is needed when the company may have difficulty borrowing on short notice. However, an excess working capital may be bad because funds could be invested in noncurrent assets for a greater return. Working capital should be compared to other financial statement items such as sales and total assets. For example, working capital to sales indicates if the company is optimally employing its liquid balance. To identify changes in the composition of working capital, the financial manager should ascertain the trend in the percentage of each current asset to total current assets. A movement from cash to inventory, for instance, points to less liquidity.

- $$\frac{\text{Working capital}}{\text{Long-term debt}}$$

  This ratio reveals whether sufficient working capital exists to satisfy long-term debt obligations.

- $$\frac{\text{Working capital}}{\text{Current liabilities}}$$

  A low ratio indicates poor liquidity because liquid funds are insufficient to meet current debt.

- $$\frac{\text{A specific current asset}}{\text{Total current assets}}$$

  For example, a shift of cash to inventory indicates less liquidity.

- $$\frac{\text{Sales}}{\text{Current assets}}$$

  A high ratio infers deficient working capital. Current liabilities may be due prior to inventories and receivables turning over to cash.

- $$\frac{\text{Working capital provided from operations}}{\text{Net income}}$$

  A high ratio is desirable because it indicates the profits are backed up by liquid funds.

- $$\frac{\text{Working capital provided from operations}}{\text{Total liabilities}}$$

  This shows the extent to which internally generated working capital can meet obligations.

- $$\frac{\text{Cash + Trading securities}}{\text{Current liabilities}}$$

  This reflects the cash available to meet short-term debt.

- $$\frac{\text{Cost of sales, operating expenses, and taxes}}{\text{Average total current assets}}$$

  This ratio indicates the adequacy of current assets in meeting ongoing business-related expenses.

- $$\frac{\text{Quick assets}}{\text{Year's cash expenses}}$$

  This tells how many days of expenses the highly liquid assets could meet.

- $$\frac{\text{Sales}}{\text{Short-term trade liabilities}}$$

  This indicates whether the business could partly finance its operations with cost-free funds. If the firm can readily get trade credit, this is a positive sign. A decline in trade credit means creditors have less faith in the financial strength of the business.

- $$\frac{\text{Net income}}{\text{Sales}}$$

  This indicates the profitability generated from revenue and hence is an important measure of operating performance. It also provides clues to a company's pricing, cost structure, and production efficiency. If the ratio drops, loan repayment difficulty may be indicated because a lack in profitability spells financial distress.

- $$\frac{\text{Fixed assets}}{\text{Short-term debt}}$$

  If you finance long-term assets with current debt, there may be a problem in meeting the debt when due because the return and proceeds from the fixed asset will not be realized before the maturity dates of the current debt.

- $$\frac{\text{Short-term debt}}{\text{Long-term debt}}$$

  A high ratio indicates greater liquidity risk. The entity has vulnerability in a money-market squeeze.

- $$\frac{\text{Accounts payable}}{\text{Average daily purchases}}$$

  This indicates the number of days required for the firm to pay creditors. Is the company meeting its payables commitment?

Accounts payable payment period (in days) equal to:

•

$$\frac{365}{\text{Accounts payable turnover}}$$

(The accounts payable turnover equals purchases divided by accounts payable).

A decline in the payment period may indicate the company is taking advantage of prompt payment discounts, or has used the shorter purchase terms as leverage in negotiating with suppliers in order to lower the purchase price. However, an extension of the payment terms may infer the company is having financial problems. Perhaps that is why the firm is stretching its payables. Alternatively, the lengthening of the payment terms may mean the business is properly managing its payables. By delaying payments to creditors, it is taking greater advantage of interest-free financing.

•

$$\frac{\text{Current liabilities}}{\text{Total liabilities}}$$

A high ratio means less corporate liquidity since there is a greater proportion of current debt.

(Accounts receivable + Inventory) – (Accounts payable + Accrued expenses payable)

Some banks look at this figure as a major indicator of a company's liquid position since it deals with major current accounts.

• Liquidity Index. This applies to the number of days current assets are removed from cash. A shorter period is preferred.

EXAMPLE 20:

	Amount	Days Removed from Cash	Total
Cash	$ 10,000 ×	—	—
Accounts receivable	40,000 ×	25	$1,000,000
Inventory	60,000 ×	40	2,400,000
	$110,000		$3,400,000

$$\text{Index} = \frac{\$3,400,000}{\$110,000} = \underline{30.9} \text{ days}$$

EXAMPLE 21:

Company B provides the following financial information:

Current assets	$ 400,000
Fixed assets	800,000
Current liabilities	500,000
Noncurrent liabilities	600,000
Sales	5,000,000
Working capital provided from operations	100,000
Industry norms are:	
Fixed assets to current liabilities	4.0 times
Current liabilities to noncurrent liabilities	45.0%
Sales to current assets	8.3 times
Working capital provided from operations to total liabilities	30.5%
Company B's ratios are:	
Fixed assets to current liabilities	1.6 times
Current liabilities to noncurrent liabilities	83.3%
Sales to current assets	12.5 times
Working capital provided from operations to total liabilities	9.1%

Company B's liquidity ratios are all unfavorable compared to industry standards. There is a high level of short-term debt as well as deficiency in current assets. Also, working capital provided from operations to satisfy total debt is inadequate.

A company's failure to take cash discounts raises a question as to management's financial astuteness because a high opportunity cost is involved.

EXAMPLE 22: Company C bought goods for $300,000 on terms of 2110, net/60. It failed to take advantage of the discount. The opportunity cost is:

$$\frac{\text{Discount foregone}}{\text{Proceeds use of}} \times \frac{360}{\text{Days delayed}}$$

$$\frac{\$6,000}{\$294,000} \times \frac{360}{50} = 14.7\%$$

The firm would have been better off financially paying within the discount period by taking out a loan since the prime interest rate is below 14.7%.

There is a tradeoff between liquidity risk and return. Liquidity risk is minimized by holding greater current assets than noncurrent assets. However, the return rate will drop because the return on current assets (e.g., marketable securities) is usually less than the rate earned on productive fixed assets. Further, excessively high liquidity may mean that management has not aggressively searched for desirable capital investment opportunities. Having a proper balance between liquidity and return is essential to the overall financial health of the business.

Appraisal of Solvency

Solvency is the ability of a company to meet its long-term debt payments (principal and interest). Long-term creditors (e.g., suppliers, loan officers) are interested in whether the company will have adequate funds to satisfy obligations when they mature. Consideration is given to the long-term financial and operating structure of the business. An analysis is made of the magnitude of non-current liabilities and the realization risk in noncurrent assets. There should be a high ratio of long-term assets to long-term liabilities. Corporate solvency also depends on earning power since a company will not be able to satisfy its obligations unless it is profitable.

When it is practical to do so, the financial manager should use market value of assets instead of book value in ratio computations since it is more representative of current value.

Stability in earnings and cash flow from operations enhances confidence in the firm's ability to meet debt. Long-term debt-related ratios to be examined include:

- *Total liabilities to total assets.* This ratio reveals the percentage of total funds obtained from creditors. Creditors would prefer to see a low ratio since there is a better cushion for creditor losses if the company goes bankrupt. At the optimum debt/assets ratio, the weighted-average cost of capital is less than at any other debt-to-asset level.

- *Long-term debt to stockholders' equity.* High leverage indicates risk because it may be difficult for the company to meet interest and principal payments as well as obtain further reasonable financing. The problem is particularly acute when a company has cash problems. Excessive debt means less financial flexibility because the entity will have more of a problem obtaining funds during a tight money market. A desirable debt-equity ratio depends on numerous factors, including the rates of other firms in the industry, the access to debt financing, and earnings stability.

- *Cash flow from operations to long-term debt.* This ratio shows whether internally generated cash funds are adequate to meet noncurrent liabilities.

- *Interest coverage (net income + interest + taxes/interest).* This reveals the adequacy of earnings to meet interest charges. A high ratio is desired. It is a safety margin indicator that shows the degree of decline in income the company can tolerate.

- *Cash flow generated from operations plus interest to interest.* This ratio indicates available cash to meet interest charges. Cash, not profit, pays interest. A higher ratio is needed for a cyclical business.

- *Net income before taxes and fixed charges to fixed charges.* This ratio helps in appraising a firm's ability to meet fixed costs. A low ratio points to risk since, when corporate activity falls, the company is unable to meet its fixed charges.

- *Cash flow from operations plus fixed charges to fixed charges.* A high ratio indicates the ability of the company to meet its fixed charges. Further, a company with stability in operations is better able to meet fixed costs.

- *Noncurrent assets to noncurrent liabilities.* Long-term debt is ultimately paid from long-term assets. Thus, a high ratio affords more protection for long-term creditors.

- *Retained earnings to total assets.* The trend in this ratio reflects the firm's profitability over the years.

- *Total liabilities to sales.* This ratio reflects the amount of sales financed by creditors.

- *Stockholders' equity to sales.* This ratio indicates the proportion of sales financed by stockholders' equity. It is generally safer for sales to be financed through equity capital than debt funds. An examination of the ratio will reveal if the owners are investing too much or too little for the sales volume involved. Is owners' equity being employed effectively?

EXAMPLE 23: The following partial balance sheet and income statement data are provided for Company D:

Long-term assets	$700,000
Long-term liabilities	500,000
Stockholders' equity	300,000
Net income before tax	80,000
Cash flow provided from operations	100,000
Interest expense	20,000
Average norms taken from competitors:	
Long-term assets to long-term liabilities	2.0
Long-term debt to stockholders' equity	.8
Cash flow to long-term liabilities	.3
Net income before tax plus interest to interest	7.0
Company D's ratios are:	
Long-term assets to long-term liabilities	1.4
Long-term debt to stockholders' equity	1.67
Cash flow to long-term liabilities	.2
Net income before tax plus interest to interest	5.0

After comparing the company's ratios with the industry norms, it is evident that the firm's solvency is worse than its competitor's due to the greater degree of long-term liabilities in the capital structure and lower interest coverage.

POTENTIAL FOR BUSINESS FAILURE

Will your company go bankrupt? Will your major customers or suppliers go bankrupt? What warning signs exist and what can be done to avoid failure?

Bankruptcy occurs when the company is unable to meet maturing financial obligations. We are thus particularly interested in predicting cash flow. Financial difficulties affect the P/E ratio, bond ratings, and the effective interest rate.

A comprehensive quantitative indicator used to predict failure is Altman's Z-score. The Z-score is known to be about 90% accurate in forecasting business failure one year in the future and about 80% accurate in forecasting it two years in the future.

The Z-Score equals:

$$\frac{\text{Working Capital}}{\text{Total Assets}} \times 1.2 + \frac{\text{Retained Earnings}}{\text{Total Assets}} \times 1.4$$

$$+ \frac{\text{Operating Income}}{\text{Total Assets}} \times 3.3 + \frac{\text{Market Value of Common and Preferred Stocks} \times 0.6}{\text{Total Liabilities}} + \frac{\text{Sales}}{\text{Total Assets}} \times 1$$

The scores and the probability of short-term illiquidity follow:

Score	Probability of Illiquidity
1.80 or less	Very high
1.81–2.7	High
2.8–2.9	Possible
3.0 or greater	Not likely

EXAMPLE 24:

A company presents the following information:

Working capital	$280,000
Total assets	875,000
Total liabilities	320,000
Retained earnings	215,000
Sales	950,000
Operating income	130,000
Common stock	
Book value	220,000
Market value	310,000
Preferred stock	
Book value	115,000
Market value	170,000

$$\frac{\$280,000}{\$875,000} \times 1.2 + \frac{\$215,000}{\$875,000} \times 1.4 + \frac{\$130,000}{\$875,000} \times 3.3$$

$$+ \frac{\$480,000}{\$320,000} \times 0.6 + \frac{\$950,000}{\$875,000} \times 1$$

$$= 0.384 + 0.344 + 0.490 + 0.9 + 1.0857 = \underline{3.2037}$$

The probability of failure for the company in Example 24 is not likely.

The liquidation value of a company may be estimated by using J. Wilcox's gambler's ruin prediction formula:

> Cash + (Marketable securities at market value) + (70% of inventory, accounts receivable, and prepaid expenses) + (50% of other assets) – (Current liabilities + Long-term liabilities).

Quantitative Factors in Predicting Corporate Failure

- Low cash flow to total liabilities.
- High debt-to-equity ratio and high debt to total assets.
- Low return on investment.
- Low profit margin.
- Low retained earnings to total assets.
- Low working capital to total assets and low working capital to sales.
- Low fixed assets to noncurrent liabilities.
- Inadequate interest-coverage ratio.
- Instability in earnings.
- Small-size company measured in sales and/or total assets.
- Sharp decline in price of stock, bond price, and earnings.
- A significant increase in Beta. Beta is the variability in the price of the company's stock relative to a market index.
- Market price per share is significantly less than book value per share.
- Reduction in dividend payments.
- A significant rise in the company's weighted-average cost of capital.
- High fixed cost to total cost structure (high operating leverage).
- Failure to maintain capital assets. An example is a decline in the ratio of repairs to fixed assets.

Qualitative Factors in Predicting Failure

- Poor financial reporting system and inability to control costs.
- New company.
- Declining industry.
- High degree of competition.
- Inability to obtain adequate financing, and when obtained entails significant loan restrictions.
- Inability to meet past-due obligations.
- A lack in management quality.
- Moving into new areas in which management lacks expertise.
- Failure of the company to keep up to date, especially in a technologically oriented business.

- High business risk (e.g., positive correlation in the product line; susceptibility to strikes).
- Inadequate insurance coverage.
- Fraudulent actions (e.g., misstating inventories to stave off impending bankruptcy).
- Cyclicality in business operations.
- Inability to adjust production to meet consumption needs.
- Susceptibility of the business to stringent governmental regulation (e.g., companies in the real estate industry).
- Susceptibility to energy shortages.
- Susceptibility to unreliable suppliers.
- Renegotiation of debt and/or lease agreements.
- Deficient accounting and financial reporting systems.

If you can predict with reasonable accuracy that the company is developing financial distress, you can better protect yourself and recommend means for corrective action.

Financial/Quantitative Factors That Minimize the Potential for Failure

- Avoid heavy debt. If liabilities are excessive, finance with equity.
- Dispose of losing divisions and product lines.
- Manage assets for maximum return and minimum risk.
- Stagger and extend the maturity dates of debt.
- Use quantitative techniques such as multiple regression analysis to compute the correlation between given variables and the likelihood of business failure.
- Assure that there is a "safety buffer" between actual status and compliance requirements (e.g., working capital) in connection with loan agreements.
- Have a negative correlation in product line and in investments held.
- Lower dividend payouts.

Nonfinancial Factors That Minimize the Potential for Failure

- Vertically and horizontally diversify the product line and operations.
- Finance assets with liabilities of similar maturity (hedging).
- Diversify geographically.
- Have adequate insurance.
- Enhance the marketing effort (e.g., advertise in the right place).
- Engage in cost reduction programs.
- Improve productivity (e.g., use timely and detailed variance analysis).
- Implement computer technology (e.g., microcomputers).
- Minimize the adverse effect of inflation and recession on the entity (e.g., price on a next-in, first-out basis).

- Invest in multipurpose, rather than single-purpose, assets because of their lower risks.
- Reconsider entering new industries that have a predicted high rate of past failure.
- Have many projects, rather than only a few, that significantly affect operations.
- Consider introducing product lines that are the least affected by the business cycle and that possess stable demand.
- Avoid going from a labor-intensive to a capital-intensive business, as the latter has a high degree of operating leverage.
- Avoid long-term fixed-fee contracts to customers. Rather, incorporate inflation adjustment and energy-cost indices in contracts.
- Avoid entering markets that are on the downturn or that are already highly competitive.
- Adjust to changes in technology.

INCOME STATEMENT ANALYSIS

The analysis of the income statement indicates a company's earning power, quality of earnings, and operating performance. The financial manager should be familiar with the important factors in appraising the income statement. Net income backed up by cash is essential for corporate liquidity. The accounting policies should be realistic in reflecting the substance of the transactions. Accounting changes should be made only for proper reasons. Further, a high degree of estimation in the income measurement process results in uncertainty in reported figures. Earnings stability enhances the predictability of future results based on currently reported profits.

In analyzing the income statement, you should look at quantitative (e.g., ratio analysis) and qualitative factors (e.g., pending litigation). Reported earnings can be adjusted to make them relevant to suit your needs for analytical purposes. Data in the footnotes will assist in the restatement process.

Your company's earnings quality relates to the degree net income is overstated or understated, as well as to the stability of income statement elements. Earnings quality affects the price-earnings, ratio, bond rating, effective interest rate, compensating balance requirement, availability of financing, and desirability of the firm as either an acquirer or acquiree. Earnings quality attributes exist in different proportions and intensities in the earnings profiles of different companies. The favorable and unfavorable characteristics of your company's earnings are carefully examined by investors, creditors, and suppliers.

Analyzing Discretionary Costs

Discretionary costs can be changed at management's will. They may be decreased when a company is having problems or wants to show a stable earnings trend.

What to Do: Examine current discretionary costs relative to previous years and to future requirements. An index number may be used to compare the current-year discretionary cost to the base amount. A reduction in discretionary costs is undesirable if their absence will have a detrimental effect on the future (e.g., advertising, research, repairs) by starving the company of needed expenses.

Recommendation: Analyze the trend in the following ratios: (1) discretionary costs to sales, and (2) discretionary costs to assets. If, in connection with a cost reduction program, material cuts are made in discretionary costs, future profitability will suffer. However, cost control is warranted when: (1) in prior years discretionary expenditures were excessive because of deficient and ill-conceived corporate strategy, or (2) competition has decreased. A material increase in discretionary costs in a given year may have a significant positive impact on corporate earning power and future growth.

EXAMPLE 25: The following data are supplied:

	2X12	2X13	2X14
Sales	$95,000	$125,000	$84,000
Research	9,000	14,000	3,000

The most representative year (base year) is 2X12. After 2X15, you believe that research is essential for the company's success because of technological factors in the industry.

	2X12	2X13	2X14
Research to sales	9.5%	11.2%	3.6%

Looking in base dollars, 2X12 represents 100. 2X13 is 156 ($14,000/$9,000). 2X14 has an index of 33 ($3,000/$9,000).

A red flag is posted for 2X14. Research is lower than in previous periods. There should have been a boost in research in light of the technological updating needed for 2X15.

EXAMPLE 26: The following information applies for a company with respect to its plant assets:

	2X13	2X14
Equipment	$ 4,500	$ 4,800
Less: accumulated depreciation	3,000	3,200
Book value	$ 1,500	$ 1,600
Repairs	400	320
Replacement cost of equipment	6,800	7,700
CPI value of equipment	7,400	8,500
Revenue	48,000	53,000
Working capital	2,900	2,600
Cash	1,100	970
Debt-to-equity ratio	42%	71%
Downtime of equipment	2%	5%

Finance company loans have increased relative to bank loans over the year.

You want to analyze equipment and repairs.

Repairs to gross equipment decreased from 8.9% in 2X13 ($400/$4,500) to 6.7% in 2X14 ($320/$4,800). In a similar vein, repairs to revenue went from 0.83% in 2X13 ($400/$48,000) to 0.6% in 2X14 ($320/$53,000).

Over the year there was a greater variation between replacement cost and book value and CPI value and book value, indicating equipment is aging.

As indicated by the greater amount of downtime, more equipment malfunction is taking place.

Equipment purchased over the year was minimal, 6.7% ($300/$4,500). The company's capital maintenance is deficient. Repairs to fixed assets and repairs to revenue are down, and insufficient replacements are being made. Perhaps these are the causes for the greater downtime.

It may be a problem for the company to purchase fixed assets when required because of the deterioration in its liquidity position. Financial leverage has significantly increased over the year. It is more difficult for the company to obtain adequate financing at reasonable interest rates, as evidenced by the need to borrow to a greater extent from finance companies than from banks.

Cash Flow from Operations

Cash flow from operations equals net income plus noncash expenses less noncash revenue. You should evaluate the trend in the ratio of cash flow from operations to net income. A higher ratio is desirable because it means that earnings are backed up by cash.

The closer a transaction is to cash, the more objective is the evidence supporting revenue and expense recognition. As the proximity to cash becomes less, the less objective is the transaction and the more subjective are the interpretations. Higher earnings quality relates to recording transactions close to cash realization.

In appraising the cash adequacy of a company, compute the following:

- Cash flow generated from operations before interest expense.
- Cash flow generated from operations less cash payments to meet debt principal, dividends, and capital expenditures.

EXAMPLE 27: The following condensed income statement appears for a company:

Sales	$1,300,000
Less: cost of sales	400,000
	$ 900,000

Gross margin		
Less: operating expenses		
Wages	$150,000	
Rent	80,000	
Electricity	50,000	
Depreciation expense	90,000	
Amortization expense	70,000	
Total operating expenses		440,000
Income before other items		$460,000
Other revenue and expenses:		
Interest	$ 60,000	
Amortization of deferred revenue	20,000	
Total other items		40,000
Net income		$ 420,000
The ratio of cash flow from operations to net income is:		
Net income		$ 420,000
Add: noncash expenses		
Depreciation expense	$ 90,000	
Amortization expense	70,000	160,000
Less: noncash revenue		
Amortization of deferred revenue		(20,000)
Cash flow from operations		$ 560,000

$$\frac{\text{Cash flow from operations}}{\text{Net income}} = \frac{\$560,000}{\$420,000} = 1.33$$

The Role of Taxable Income

If a company reports significant stockholder earnings and a substantial tax loss, evaluate the quality of reported results.

A company having a significant deferred income tax credit account will have book profits in excess of taxable earnings. An increase in the deferred tax credit account may indicate the company is moving toward more liberal accounting policies. This is because a widening gap in the deferred tax credit account indicates a greater disparity between book earnings and taxable earnings.

You should determine the effective tax rate, which equals tax expense divided by income before tax. A low effective tax rate for the current year due to a one-time source (e.g., tax credit for a one-time major item, a loss carryforward that will shortly expire) will not repeat to benefit later years. However, the effective tax rate may be stable when it results from a recurring source (e.g., foreign tax credit, interest on municipal bonds).

Earnings are not really available if there is a high percentage of foreign profits that will not be repatriated to the U.S. for a long time.

It is better if your company's earnings and growth do not rely on a lowered tax rate that is vulnerable to a future change in the tax law or that places material restrictions on the firm.

Residual Income

Residual income represents an economic income, taking into account the opportunity cost of putting money in the business. An increasing trend in residual income to net income points to a strong degree of corporate profitability because the company is earning enough to meet its imputed cost of capital.

Residual income equals:

Net income

Less: minimum return (cost of capital) × Total assets

Residual income

EXAMPLE 28: A company's net income is $800,000, total assets are $4,600,000, and cost of capital is 13.40%.

Residual income equals:

Net income	$800,000
Less: minimum return total assets	616,400
13.40% × $4,600,000	
Residual income	$183,600

The ratio of residual income to net income is 23% ($183,600/$800,000).

Accounting Policies

Conservatively determined net income is of higher quality than liberally determined net income. Conservatism relates to the accounting methods and estimates employed. A comparison should be made between the company's accounting policies and the prevailing accounting policies in the industry. If the firm's policies are more liberal, earnings quality may be lower. The financial manager should consider the firm's timing of revenue recognition and the deferral of costs compared to usual industry practices.

The accounting policies should be realistic in reflecting the economic substance of the company's transactions. The underlying business and financial realities of the company and industry have to be taken into account. For example, the depreciation method should approximately measure the decline in usefulness of the asset. Examples of realistic accounting policies are cited in AICPA Industry Audit Guides and in accounting policy guides published by various CPA firms. If the use of realistic policies would have resulted in substantially lower earnings than the policies used, earnings quality is lower.

Accounting changes made to conform with new FASB statements, AICPA Industry Audit Guides, and IRS regulations are justifiable. However, an unjustified accounting change causes an earnings increment of low quality. Unwarranted changes may be made in accounting principles and estimates. If there are numerous accounting changes, it will be more difficult to use current profits as a predictor of future earnings.

Accounting Estimates

The greater the degree of subjective accounting estimates in the income measurement process, the more uncertainty is associated with net income.

What to Do: Examine the difference between actual experience and the estimates employed. The wider the difference, the more uncertain is profitability. Look at the variation over time between a loss provision and the actual loss. A continually understated loss provision means inaccurate estimates. Sizable gains and losses on the sale of assets may infer inaccurate depreciation estimates.

Examine the trend in the following ratios:

- High estimation assets (e.g., fixed assets) to total assets.
- Cash expenses to revenue.
- Estimated expenses to revenue.
- Cash revenue to revenue.
- Estimated revenue to revenue.
- Estimated expenses to net income.
- Estimated revenue to net income.

Higher estimation is indicated by long-term construction work using the percentage-of-completion contract method, and a material amount of estimated liability provisions. Also, a higher percentage of assets subject to accounting estimates (e.g., intangibles) to total assets means uncertain earnings.

EXAMPLE 29: The following information applies to a company:

	2X14	2X15
Cash and near-cash revenue	$ 98,000	$107,000
Noncash revenue items	143,000	195,000
Total revenue	$241,000	$302,000
Cash and near-cash expenses	$ 37,000	$ 58,000
Noncash expenses	67,000	112,000
Total expenses	$104,000	$170,000
Net income	$137,000	$132,000

Estimation-related ratios can now be calculated.

	2X14	2X15
Estimated revenue to total revenue	59%	65%
Estimated revenue to net income	104%	148%
Estimated expenses to total expenses	64%	66%
Estimated expenses to total revenue	28%	37%
Estimated expenses to net income	49%	85%

In every case, there was greater estimation involved in the income measurement process in 2X15 relative to 2X14. The higher degree of estimation resulted in uncertain earnings.

Discontinued Operations

Income from discontinued operations is usually of a one-time nature and should be ignored when forecasting future earnings. Further, a discontinued operation implies a company is in a state of decline or that a poor management decision is the cause for the firm's entering the discontinued line of business in the first place.

Profitability Measures

A sign of good financial health and how effectively the firm is managed is its ability to generate a satisfactory profit and return on investment. Investors will refrain from investing in the business if it has poor earning potential because of the adverse effect on market price of stock and dividends. Creditors will be reluctant to get involved with a company having poor profitability because of collection risk. Absolute dollar profit by itself has minimal significance unless it is compared to its source.

A company's profit margin (net income to sales) indicates how well it is being managed and provides clues to a company's pricing, cost structure, and production efficiency. A high gross profit percent (gross profit to sales) is favorable since it indicates the company is able to control its manufacturing costs.

Return on investment points to the degree to which profit is achieved on the investment. Two key ratios of return on investment are (1) *return on total assets* and (2) *return on owners' equity.*

The return on total assets (net income/average total assets) points to the efficiency with which management has employed its resources to obtain income. Further, a decline in the ratio may result from a productivity problem.

The return on common equity (earnings available to common stock/average stockholders' equity) measures the rate of return on the common stockholders' investment.

An increase in the gross profit margin (gross profit to sales) may mean the company was able to increase its sales volume or selling price, or to reduce its cost of sales. In general, manufacturers have higher gross profit rates than merchandisers.

The net operating profit ratio (net operating profit to sales) reveals what is left over for interest, nonrecurring charges, taxes and profit for the stockholders. It may be used as a basis to evaluate operating managers. The analysis is before considering interest expense since financing is typically arranged by the finance managers.

A high ratio of sales to working capital indicates efficient utilization of liquid funds. The sales backlog should be used to monitor sales status and planning. Compute the days of sales in backlog equal to:

$$\frac{\text{Backlog balance}}{\text{Sales volume divided by days in period}}$$

Is the backlog for long-range delivery (e.g., five years from now) or on a recurring basis to maintain continuing stability?

Some other ratios reflective of operations are:

- Revenue to number of employees as well as revenue to employee salaries. Higher ratios are reflective of better employee productivity.

- Average yearly wage per employee and average hourly wage rate. These ratios examine the ability to control labor costs.

- Average fixed assets per employee. This shows the productivity of using fixed assets by employees.

- Indirect labor to direct labor. A low ratio is reflective of controlling the labor component of overhead.

- Purchase discounts to purchases. A high ratio indicates effective management of purchases.

- General and administrative expenses to selling expense. This ratio indicates the degree of control and surveillance over G&A expense relative to sales activities. G&A expenses relative to selling expenses should decline with increased sales volume. If the ratio is increasing, inadequate controls over administrative activities may exist.

Growth Rate

A company's growth rate should be compared to that of competitors and industry norms.

Measures of growth rate =

$$\frac{\text{Change in retained earnings}}{\text{Stockholders' equity at beginning of year}}$$

$$\frac{\text{EPS (end of year)} - \text{EPS (beginning of year)}}{\text{EPS (beginning of year)}}$$

The growth rate in sales, dividends, total assets, and the like may be computed in a similar fashion.

Internal Control and Management Honesty

Deficient internal control casts doubt upon the integrity of the earnings stream. Look at the trend in audit fees and in audit time over the years. Increasing trends may point to internal control and audit problems. Examine disclosure of previous accounting errors. Are there any indicators of a dishonest management, such as corporate bribes, payoffs, or hiding of defective merchandise?

Market Value Measures

Market value ratios apply to a comparison of the company's stock price to its earnings (or book value) per share. Also involved are dividend-related ratios. Included are:

- Earnings per share
- Price-earnings ratio
- Book value per share. This equals:

$$\frac{\text{Total stockholder's equity} - (\text{Liquidation value of preferred stock} + \text{Preferred dividends in arrears})}{\text{Common stock outstanding}}$$

  By comparing book value per share to market price per share, the financial manager can see how investors feel about the business.
- Dividend yield. This equals dividends per share divided by market price per share.
- Dividend payout. This equals dividends per share divided by earnings per share. The investing public looks unfavorably upon lower dividends since dividend payout is a sign of the financial health of the entity.

HOW TO ANALYZE THE FINANCIAL STRUCTURE OF THE FIRM

Various quantitative measurements can be used to analyze a firm's stability over time. Comparisons can then be made to prior years of the firm, competing companies, and industry norms.

Types of Stability Measurements

- *Trend in average reported earnings.* Average earnings over a relatively long period (such as five years) will level out abnormal and erratic income statement components as well as cyclical effects upon the business.
- *Average pessimistic earnings.* This represents the average earnings based on the worst possible scenario for the company's operational activities. The average minimum earnings is useful in appraising a risky company.
- *One-time gains or losses to net income and/or sales.* A high percentage of nonrecurring items to reported earnings indicates instability in income statement components, pointing to uncertainty and unrepresentativeness of what is typical. An example is the gain on the sale of low-cost basis land.

- *Standard Deviation.*

$$S.D. = \sqrt{\frac{\Sigma(y - \bar{y})^2}{n}}$$

where

y = net income for period t

$\bar{y}$ = average net income

n = number of periods

The higher the standard deviation, the greater is the instability.

- *Coefficient of Variation.*

$$C.V. = \frac{S.D.}{\bar{y}}$$

The coefficient of variation is a relative measure of instability to facilitate a comparison between competing companies. The higher the coefficient, the greater is the risk.

- *Instability Index of Earnings.*

$$I = \sqrt{\frac{\Sigma(y - y^T)^2}{n}}$$

where

y^T = trend earnings for period t, and is determined as follows:

$y^T = a + bt$

where

a = dollar intercept

b = slope of trend line

t = time period

Trend income is computed using a simple trend equation solved by computer. The index reflects the deviation between actual income and trend income. A higher index is reflective of greater instability.

- *Beta.* Beta is calculated by a computer run based on the following equation:

$$r_{jt} = a_j + B_j r_{Mt} + E_{jt}$$

where

r_{jt} = return of security j for period t

a_j = constant

B_j = Beta for security j

r_{Mt} = return on a market index such as the New York Stock Exchange Index

E_{jt} = error term

Beta measures the systematic risk of a stock. A Beta greater than one indicates the company's market price of stock vacillates more than the change in the market index, pointing to a risky security. Fluctuation in stock price implies greater business risk and instability with the firm. For example, a Beta of 1.3 means the company's stock price rises or falls 30% faster than the market. A Beta of 1 means the company's stock price moves the same as the market index. A Beta of less than 1 indicates the company's stock price vacillates less than the stock market index, pointing to lower corporate risk. Of course, a company's Beta may change over time. Betas for individual companies may be gotten from various sources, such as Standard and Poor's.

EXAMPLE 30: A company shows the following trend in reported earnings:

2X11	$100,000
2X12	110,000
2X13	80,000
2X14	120,000
2X15	140,000

$$\text{Standard Deviation} = \sqrt{\frac{\Sigma(y - \bar{y})^2}{n}}$$

$$y = \Sigma \frac{\bar{y}}{n} = \frac{\begin{array}{c}100,000 + 110,000 + 80,000 \\ 120,000 + 140,000\end{array}}{5} = \frac{550,000}{5} = 110,000$$

Year	$(y - \bar{y})$	$(y - \bar{y})^2$
2X11	– 10,000	100,000,000
2X12	0	0
2X13	– 30,000	900,000,000

Year	$(y - \bar{y})$	$(y - \bar{y})^2$
2X14	+ 10,000	100,000,000
2X15	+ 30,000	900,000,000
		2,000,000,000

$$\text{Standard Deviation} = \sqrt{\frac{2,000,000,000}{5}} = \sqrt{400,000,000} = 20,000$$

$$\text{Coefficient of Variation} = \frac{\text{Standard Deviation}}{\bar{y}}$$

$$= \frac{20,000}{110,000} = 18.2\%$$

Operating Leverage

Operating leverage is the degree to which fixed charges exist in a company's cost structure. Measures of operating leverage are:

- Fixed costs to total costs.
- Percentage change in operating income to the percentage change in sales volume.
- Net income to fixed costs.

Note: An increase in (1) and (2) or decrease in (3) may point to lower earnings quality because higher fixed charges may result in greater earnings instability.

Note: A high percentage of variable costs to total costs indicates greater earnings stability. Variable costs can be adjusted more easily than fixed costs in meeting a decline in product demand.

Note: A high break-even company is very susceptible to economic declines.

Stability Elements

In looking at earnings stability, it should be noted that the trend in income is more important than its absolute size. Stable revenue sources include the following:

- Nonoperating income that is recurring and serves as a cushion to total income. Examples are royalty income under long-term contracts with financially secure parties and rental income under long-term leases. Increased trends in the percentage of stable revenue sources to gross income and to net income are positive indicators.
- Obtaining further revenue from original sales. An example is maintenance services and replacement parts derived from selling an item. You should calculate the trend in replacement and maintenance revenue as a percentage of (1) new sales, (2) total revenue, and (3) net income.
- Sales to diversified industries (industries affected in different ways by cyclical factors).

  Abnormal and erratic income statement items (e.g., gain on the sale of land) distort the current year's net income as a predictor of future earnings.

Warning: Watch out for a company that starts selling off part of its fixed assets, since it may be in a state of contraction.

Examples of unstable revenue sources are listed below.

• Export sales to a major foreign market that will disappear as that country develops a domestic capacity to manufacture the item. An opportunist market (e.g., electronic calculators) is a nonrepetitive source of earnings, since the saturation of a company's market will reduce its potential to derive continued earnings.

• Short-term schemes (e.g., a single government contract) increase earnings temporarily. You should determine the percentage of short-lived income to total revenue and to net income.

• The loss of a unique advantage in the near future that will hurt future years' revenues, such as the exhaustion of mineral rights.

Product Line Characteristics

A company's product line deeply affects its overall business stability and profitability. Where possible, product risk should be minimized, such as by moving toward negative correlation among products.

Product Line Measures

• The degree of correlation between products is evident from a correlation matrix determined by a computer run.

• Product demand elasticity is determined as follows:

$$\frac{\text{Percentage change in quantity}}{\text{Percentage change in price}}$$

If > 1 Elastic demand

If = 1 Unitary demand

If < 1 Inelastic demand

Red Flag: Products that are positively correlated and have elastic demands are of high risk. On the other hand, companies with product lines having negative correlations and inelastic demand (e.g., health care products) are stable. Further, products with different seasonal peaks should be added to stabilize production and marketing operations.

EXAMPLE 31: The correlation matrix of a product line follows:

Product	A	B	C	D	E	F
A	1.0	.13	−.02	−.01	−.07	.22
B	.13	1.0	−.02	−.07	.00	.00
C	−.02	−.02	1.0	.01	.48	.13
D	−.01	−.07	.01	1.0	.01	−.02
E	−.07	.00	.48	.01	1.0	.45
F	.22	.00	.13	−.02	.45	1.0

Obviously, perfect correlation exists with the same product. For instance, the correlation between product F and product F is 1.0.

High positive correlation exists between products E and C (.48) and products E and F (.45). Because these products are tightly interwoven, risk exists.

Low negative correlation exists between products A and D (– .01) and products A and C (– .02).

No correlation is present between products B and E (.00) and products B and F (.00).

It would be better if some products had significant negative correlations (e.g., – .7), but such is not the case.

EXAMPLE 32: Data for products X and Y follow:

	X	Y
Selling price	$10	$8
Unit sales	10,000	13,000

If the selling price of product X is increased to $11, it is predicted that sales volume will decrease by 500 units. If the selling price of product Y is raised to $9.50, sales volume is anticipated to fall by 4,000 units.

Product demand elasticity equals:

$$\frac{\text{Percentage change in quantity}}{\text{Percentage change in price}}$$

Inelastic demand exists with product X:

$$\frac{\dfrac{500}{10,000}}{\dfrac{\$1}{\$10}} = \frac{.05}{.10} = .5$$

Elastic demand occurs with product Y:

$$\frac{\dfrac{4,000}{13,000}}{\dfrac{\$1.50}{\$8.00}} = \frac{.307}{.188} = 1.63$$

Variances in the product line may exist for volume, price, and cost. The greater the fluctuation in each, the wider is the variability in earnings. You should examine variability for each major product by:

- Charting via graphs to uncover trends.
- Determining the standard deviation.
- Computing variances.

Product Lines Promoting Stability

- Necessity items.
- Retail trade (mostly low-priced items appealing to a wide market).
- Growth and mature products.
- Low unit-cost items. These have a greater chance of succeeding in periods of economic health and also have greater resistance to declining demand in recessionary periods. If a firm with low-priced goods also provides a substitute for more expensive items (e.g., cereal for meat), it has a built-in hedge in inflationary and recessionary periods.
- "Piggy-back" product base where similar products are associated with the company's basic business.
- Ability to introduce new products. What is the number of patented products that come on stream annually?

Product Lines Causing Instability

- Novelty and nonessential goods
- High-priced items (e.g., expensive jewelry) that add to variable demand during recessionary times. An exception is high-priced quality goods serving a select market, such as Mercedes-Benz, because the wealthy are not materially impacted by a temporary decline in economic conditions.
- Heavy goods and raw materials, because reduction in buying is magnified as it goes from the consumer to the source of production. For raw materials, there is price fluctuation in commodity markets as well as instability in demand for end products. With capital goods sales, industry can postpone purchases of durable equipment.
- A single-product company since it has less stability and more obsolescence risk than a multiproduct one.

Recommendation: Have a diversified product line to guard against adverse effects resulting from differing economic conditions. It is best to have negatively correlated items (e.g., winter clothing and summer clothing) to promote stability, as revenue obtained from one product increases while revenue obtained from the other decreases. At a minimum, there should be no correlation (e.g., food and office furniture).

Danger: If a positive correlation exists between products (e.g., autos and steel) there is significant risk, since product demand moves in the same direction for both.

- Products that are susceptible to rapid changes in consumer tastes, such as novelty goods that depend on fads.
- Products closely tied to changes in real gross national product. You should try to move toward stable demand items.

- Products for which demand is obtained from a very few large industrial users. The loss of one customer can have a significant negative effect.
- Products with unusual demand coupled with skyrocketing prices (e.g., copper).
- High percentage of developmental products.
- Low-profit-margin products.

Ways to Measure Marketing Effectiveness

- Evaluate product warranty complaints and their dispositions.
- Calculate revenue, cost, and profit by product line, customer, industry segment, geographic area, distribution channel, type of marketing effort, and average order size.
- Evaluate new products in terms of risk and profitability.
- Appraise strengths and weaknesses of competition as well as their reactions to your promotion efforts.
- Determine revenue, marketing costs, and profits prior to, during, and subsequent to promotion programs.
- Appraise sales generated by different types of selling efforts (e.g., direct mail, television, newspaper).
- Analyze sales force effectiveness by determining the profit generated by salespeople, call frequency, sales incentives, sales personnel costs (e.g., auto), and dollar value of orders obtained per hour spent.
- Determine revenue and/or net income per employee.
- Examine the trend in the ratio of marketing costs to sales.
- Determine marketing share.
- Evaluate the trend in inventory at wholesalers and retailers, including order processing, packaging, warehousing, carrier, and customer services.

Consider Raw Materials

In analyzing raw materials, we should determine variability in cost.

Recommendation: Review trade publications for price instability. A problem exists if there is a lack of alternative raw material sources, especially if the current source of supply is unreliable.

Special Note: Vertical integration reduces price and supply risk.

Management Quality

The success of a business depends greatly on the quality of executive decisions. Deficient competence in management holds in question the viability of the enterprise.

Signs of Poor Management Quality

- Instability and lack of experience of leadership.
- Previous incidents of mismanagement.
- Past occurrence of corporate bankruptcy.

- Prior inaccurate management projections (e.g., overexaggerated predictions in the president's letter in the annual report).

- Inability to adjust to changing times (e.g., nature of the business).

Employees

Labor tranquility can be appraised by determining the number and duration of prior strikes, degree of union militancy, and employee turnover. However, consideration should be given to the ratio of fringe benefits to total labor dollars. Fringe benefits include retirement, insurance, sick leave, vacation, and so on. The trend in this ratio with comparisons to other companies will reveal whether fringe benefits are proportionately higher than they should be.

A constant relationship should typically exist between indirect labor and direct labor since both are needed to run the organization efficiently.

Risk

In evaluating risk, you should compare the company's risk exposure to the competition and to past trends of the firm. Uncertainty about the business makes it difficult to predict future performance reliably.

The following are some of the main risks you should consider:

- *Corporate risk, such as overdependence on a few key executives or the underinsurance of assets (e.g., declining trend in insurance expense to fixed assets, unusual casualty losses).* One means of minimizing corporate risk is to diversify operations.

- *Social risk, such as a company experiencing customer boycotts or bias suits.* One way of reducing social risk is to have some degree of community involvement with the firm.

- *Environmental risk, such as a product line or service susceptible to changes in the weather.* A way to lower this risk is to have counterseasonal products.

- *Industry risk, such as an industry under public and governmental scrutiny (e.g., real estate tax shelters).* An approach to diminish industry risk is to move toward a variable-cost-oriented business.

- *Economic risk, such as the effect of a depression on product demand.* Curtail this risk by having a low-priced product substitute for a high-priced item (i.e., cereal for meat).

- *Political risk, such as the need for lobbying efforts.* Avoid operations in strictly regulated areas.

Risks associated with the company must be measured, evaluated, controlled, reduced, and even, where appropriate, taken advantage of. In risk management, the corporate controller should identify possible risks, formulate risk management policies, assess profitability, appraise risk level, ascertain the business environment, monitor efficiency, integrate processes, establish risk tolerance, assess vulnerability, set corporate values, and assign responsibilities and authority. The controller should rank risks in priority order to make informed decisions.

To be successful, risk management must be in conformity with the organizational goals, purposes, policies, and operating environment. The degree of the company's acceptable risk tolerance must also be factored in.

Types of risk that the corporate controller must address include customer satisfaction, competitor actions (e.g., price wars), cultural implications especially in foreign markets, catastrophic events, and quality of goods and services.

Risks should be evaluated relative to potential returns. For example, profit potential may outweigh the risk. As a case in point, in giving a training program to Citicorp executives, one of the authors pointed out the excessive risk on loans to Argentina even though the interest rate was very high. Excessive risks should be avoided. Can risks be transferred to third parties, such as through insurance, outsourcing, or futures contracts?

The controller must monitor success factors and performance indicators of whether a corporate risk management strategy was succeeding or failing. Employees should be encouraged to identify and manage risk. The controller should ask and answer the following questions:

- Are risk control objectives being satisfied?
- Are we learning from our experiences?

In tracking risk the controller should look at the probability of events happening and their impact on the company. Is the chance of the event happening remote, possible, or probable? Is the risk considered to be low, moderate, or high?

Industry Characteristics

Corporate earnings are worth more if earned in a healthy, expanding industry than in an unhealthy, declining one. For example, an expanding and mature industry in which a restricted number of companies control a high percentage of the market and whose selling prices can be upwardly adjusted for rising costs, is in a strong position.

Labor-intensive businesses typically have greater stability than capital-intensive ones, since the former have a higher percentage of variable costs whereas the latter have a higher percentage of fixed costs. Capital-intensive industries have a higher susceptibility to cyclical performance. Companies in a staple industry have greater stability because of inelastic product demand.

A company may have variability because of an industry cycle. An example is the steel industry, which has a five- to ten-year cycle because of the refurbishing of steel furnaces.

Industry Characteristics Indicative of Greater Risk

- High degree of competition. What is the ease of entry, frequency of price wars, and impact of cheaper imports?
- Highly technological (e.g., computers), causing obsolescence risk and difficulty in keeping up to date.

- Overly dependent on energy, making it prone to energy shortages and price rises.

- Subject to tight governmental regulation, such as by a utility regulatory commission.

- Susceptibility to cyclical effects.

High-risk product line without sufficient insurance coverage. If you have difficulty obtaining insurance in your industry, try to pool risks by setting up mutual insurance companies.

Political Factors

Political risk refers to foreign operations and governmental regulation. Multinational companies with significant foreign activities have uncertainties with respect to repatriation of funds, currency fluctuations, and local customs regulations. Operations in politically and economically unstable foreign regions means instability.

Ratios to Be Examined

- Questionable foreign revenue to total revenue.

- Questionable foreign earnings to net income.

- Total export revenue to total revenue.

- Total export earnings to net income.

- Total assets in "questionable" foreign countries to total assets.

- Total assets in foreign countries to total assets.

Considerations in Foreign Operations

- Foreign exchange rates.

Red Flag: Vacillating foreign exchange rates, which can be measured by the percentage change over time and/or its standard deviation. Also look at the trend in the ratio of foreign translation gains and losses (reported in the stockholders' equity section). When foreign assets are appropriately balanced against foreign liabilities, you are better insulated from changes in exchange rates, thus stabilizing earnings. Evaluate your exposed position for each foreign country in which there is a major operation. When the dollar is devalued, net foreign assets and income in countries with strong currencies are worth more dollars. Forward exchange contracts should be viewed positively, since the company is trying to minimize its foreign currency exposure by hedging against exchange risks emanating from foreign currency transactions.

- Foreign country's tax rate and duties.

- Varying year-ends of foreign subsidiaries.

- Degree of intercountry transactions.

Companies dependent on government contracts and subsidies have more instability, since government spending is vulnerable to changing political whims of legislators and war-threatening situations.

Suggestion: Determine the percentage of earnings obtained from government contract work and subsidies, and the extent to which such work and subsidies are recurring.

Look at the degree of government regulation over the company since it affects the bottom line (e.g., utility rate increases are less than what have been asked for).

Recommendation: Examine present and prospective effects of governmental interference on the company by reviewing current and proposed laws and regulations of governmental bodies. Possible sources of such information are legislative hearings, trade journals, and newspapers. Stringent environmental and safety regulations may eat into profits.

Analyze the effect on the company of present and proposed tax legislation. What are the areas of IRS scrutiny?

EXTENSIBLE BUSINESS REPORTING LANGUAGE (XBRL): FINANCIAL REPORTING ON THE INTERNET

XBRL, an accounting and financial language for the Internet, is a major step forward in the preparation, publication, exchange, and analysis of financial data. It is a simpler process for issuing financial reports and presents financial data using common terms and definitions.

As a standard specifically designed for reporting accounting and finance information on the Internet, XBRL specifies a set of vocabulary for the electronic interchange of financial information and "tags" specific information with a precise contextual description. It shows relationships, such as associating the cash position and cash flow of a company in related financial statements (e.g., the balance sheet and statement of cash flows). An example is associating a number with variables. XBRL is a freely licensed standard that can be used across any platform, software format, or technology. It is an *intelligent* Internet language that can be used in business by preparers and users of financial statements.

The major problems solved by XBRL are seen in the preparation and use of business reports:

- *Budget preparation.* The same report, if prepared in XBRL format, will be used for printing (word processing), filing (EDGAR), or posting to a Web site (HTML). That is, the information is entered once and used many times. For example, a report originally prepared for EDGAR may be used for banking and other regulatory reports.

- *Data extraction.* Today, extracting specified detailed information from a financial statement published on the Internet, even an electronic financial statement like an EDGAR filing, is a difficult and time-consuming task. A user cannot, for example, obtain inventory turnover ratios of one or more companies from the EDGAR Web site. If, however, a financial statement is prepared with XBRL standards, numerous computer programs can easily extract every piece of information to that statement.

Corporate accountants devote a significant amount of time to creating and formatting reports. The XBRL framework will help hasten financial reporting and user access to that information, reduce financial reporting costs by eliminating redundancies in financial report production, reduce the chance of manual reentry error, streamline the process of publishing the financial data to the external or internal users, and provide greater flexibility to investment and credit professionals. With XBRL, corporate accountants will be able to render the basic financial information once and deliver it in whatever format is needed, whether the company's Web site, regulatory reporting and disclosure, or internal management use.

There are several useful XBRL products for corporate accountants, such as PricewaterhouseCoopers' *Edgar Scan*, which is an interface to SEC EDGAR filings. Edgar Scan takes filings from the SEC's servers and breaks them down automatically to find key financial tables and standardizes financials to a common format for all companies. Using hyperlinks, users of financial reports can access specific sections of the filing, including the financial statements, footnotes, extracted financial information, and relevant financial ratios. Tables of financial data and comparisons can be downloaded as Excel charts. Edgar Scan's XBRL Query Service converts extracted SEC filing information into XBRL instances. This HTTP service makes available XBRL data for in excess of 500 of the largest U.S. businesses. Corporate accountants can request the XBRL data on these companies or other information about this product from PricewaterhouseCoopers at http:/ /edgar-scan.pwcglobal.com/XBRL or by e-mailing edgar@uspwcglobal.com.

KPMG's *Columbus* is an application service provider (ASP) that is XBRL-enabled. Columbus provides interactive Internet applications, including corporate performance indicators, analysis and benchmarking of reported financial information, a "traffic-light signal" system to summarize earnings and liquidity, and forecasted financial figures. For information, visit www.kpmg.nl/columbus.

CONCLUSION

An analysis of a company's financial position and funds flow is essential in ascertaining its ability to continue and prosper. Areas of deficiency and potential ramifications can be highlighted so that corrective action may be taken. Managers closely scrutinize segmental operations to identify areas of risk and poor profit potential.

Quality of earnings involves those factors that would influence investors or creditors considering investing or giving credit to your company. The key in evaluating a company's earnings quality is to compare its earnings profile (the mixture and degree of favorable and unfavorable characteristics associated with reported results) with the earnings profile of other companies in the same industry. You assess earnings quality in order to render earnings comparable among competing companies, and to determine what valuation should be placed upon them.

Quality of earnings can be looked at only in terms of accounting and financial characteristics that have an effect on the earning power of a firm, as shown in its net income figure. These characteristics are complex and interrelated, and are subject to wide varieties of interpretation depending upon your own analytical objective. Further, measurements of some of the characteristics may be very difficult. Nevertheless, you cannot avoid sorting through the characteristics to determine which of them are favorable in terms of earnings quality and which are unfavorable, and to determine the degree to which they exist. Then it is possible to rank the relative quality of earnings of the company to those of others.

An analysis and evaluation of the company's financial structure and stability is needed to ascertain profit potential, degree of risk, and viability.

Areas of analysis include sources of earnings, economic and inflationary effects, political aspects, industry characteristics, and marketing effectiveness. Quantitative measurements can be looked at over time to gauge performance.

After completing his or her financial statement analysis, the financial manager will consult with top management to discuss plans and prospects, any problem areas that surfaced in the analysis, and possible solutions.

CHAPTER 32

MANAGEMENT ANALYSIS OF OPERATIONS

CONTENTS

This chapter discusses the analysis of a company's profit, including the revenue and cost components. Means to control costs are included. There is a discussion of the cost of quality and the cost of prediction errors. The chapter presents performance measures, productivity concerns, monitoring of sales efforts, appraising personnel, evaluating the efficiency of space utilization, and analysis of business processes. The corporate controller must also take into account life cycles and time considerations. Divestitures may be necessary to get rid of operations draining the firm, such as those losing money or generating excessive risk levels.

ANALYSIS OF PROFIT

Profit margin (net income/net sales) measures the profitability of each sales dollar. Profitability should be determined by source (product, service, customer, including customer profiles), age group, industry segment, geographic area, channel of distribution, type of marketing effort, market segment, and responsibility center (division, plant, department, and units within the department). Profit variance analysis should be performed to identify causes for actual profit being less than expected. Problems should be immediately identified and corrected. Profit maximization strategies should be formulated. Reports should be prepared by profit-generating source (e.g., market, client). Profit planning including strategic pricing and volume plans should be undertaken.

ANALYSIS OF REVENUE

An analysis should be made of sales mix, product demand, order quantities, product obsolescence, manufacturing schedules, storage space, and competition. Appraise sales generated by different types of selling efforts (direct mail, television, newspaper). Also, compare sales and profit before and after product refinement. The amount of sales returns and allowances is a good indicator of the quality of merchandise. If returns and allowances are high relative to sales, buyer dissatisfaction exists and is having a negative effect on the company's reputation. Further, the company may have to pay the freight for returned goods.

Sales ratios include:

- Quality of sales = cash sales/total sales.
- Days of sales backlog = backlog balance/sales volume divided by sales in period. This ratio helps to monitor sales status and planning.
- Sales per customer = net sales/average number of customers.
- Order response rate average number of transactions/average number of solicitations.
- Sales response rate average dollar sales/average solicitations.
- Customer contact ratio = calls to customers/total calls.

The ratio of sales to current debt looks at the degree to which short-term liabilities finance sales growth.

Determine the variability in volume, price, and cost of each major product or service.

Questions to be asked and answered are:

- Should products or services be more personalized?
- Which services or products are ineffective and/or excessively costly?
- How can products, services, manufacturing, or distribution be redesigned to make them more profitable?

A "close to the customer" strategy assures more useful customer information, improved sales, and lower distribution costs.

COST ANALYSIS AND CONTROL

Cost Analysis

A company's costs should be compared over the years to determine if there is a problem in cost incurrence. The reasons for unusual changes in costs should be noted and corrective steps taken when warranted.

Direct cost ratios may be used in analyzing operating costs, such as (1) direct labor/sales, (2) direct travel/sales, and (3) computer usage/sales.

Determine if costs are excessive relative to production volume. The ratio of selling expenses to net sales reflects the cost of selling the product. Is such cost excessive?

Locked-in (designed) costs will be incurred in the "future" based on decisions already made. It is difficult to reduce locked-in costs. "Cost down" is reducing product costs but still fulfilling customer expectations. Also, compare the number of project rejections due to high initial costs to total projects available.

Proper cost allocation should be made to responsibility centers, geographic areas, products, services, and customers.

Cost Control

Recommendations should be made for improving quality control. Expenses are often related to sales to determine if proper controls exist and if the expenditures are resulting in improved revenue and/or profitability. Examine the following ratios:

- Total operating expenses/net sales.
- Specific expense/net sales.
- Utilities expense/net sales.
- Selling expenses/net sales.

A cost/benefit analysis is crucial. Costs should be controlled by major type (e.g., manufacturing, selling, administrative, legal, insurance). Cost control reports should be prepared. Cost control may be evaluated by doing the following:

- Undertake a cost reduction program for projects, products, and services. Such a program may eliminate waste and inefficiency, resulting in improved profitability. However, cost reductions must make sense.
- Evaluate leased premises to reduce rental charges.
- Consider joint ventures to reduce costs.
- Eliminate duplicate facilities and activities by streamlining operations.
- Implement an energy conservation program.
- Place "caps" on expense categories (e.g., telephone, travel, and entertainment). Pinpoint those responsible for excessive costs (e.g., excessive telephone calls). Authorization will be needed on a per-employee basis for amounts exceeding ceiling levels.
- Assign each employee an identification number for Xerox, fax, and computer use.
- Substitute cheaper sources of supply or self-manufacture the part.
- Undertake an engineering study to see if manufactured goods can be redesigned to save costs.
- Perform inspections at key points in the manufacturing cycle to correct problems early.
- Adjust output levels as needed.

- Contract for long-term purchase agreements.
- Obtain competitive bids and change suppliers, insurance companies, consultants, etc. when lower fees are obtained, assuming similar levels of quality.
- Redesign the delivery system to reduce fuel costs.
- Tie salary increments to increased productivity.
- Subcontract work if lower costs result.

COST OF QUALITY

The cost of quality (COQ) is defined as any costs to correct poor quality or to enhance good quality. It takes into account the costs to "prevent" product defects (e.g., employee training, machine maintenance), appraisal costs (e.g., testing, inspecting), and the cost of the failure to control (e.g., scrap, rework, warranties). Problems must be detected and corrected in a timely fashion. There is also an opportunity cost of foregone earnings arising from customers switching to other suppliers because of the company's poor quality products or services. The following ratios may be enlightening: (1) cost of quality/total operating costs and (2) cost of quality/sales. The manager's objective is to minimize COQ subject to the constraints of corporate policy, customer requirements, and manufacturing limitations. Ultimately, the overall quality of the company's goods benefits.

COST OF PREDICTION ERRORS

The failure to accurately project sales could result in poor production planning, improper labor levels, etc., causing potentially huge financial losses. The cost of the prediction error is the profit lost because of the inaccurate prediction. It can be measured in lost sales, disgruntled customers, and idle machinery. It is important to determine the cost of the prediction error so as to minimize the potential negative effect on the business. Prediction relates to sales, expenses, and purchases.

PERFORMANCE MEASURES

Performance evaluation must consider the trend in a measure over time within the company, compared to competing companies, and compared to industry norms. Index numbers may be used to compare current-year figures to base-year (representative, typical year) figures. Revenue, cost, and profit may be tracked by division, department, product, service, process, contract, job, sales territory, and customer. Measures of performance include:

- Repeat sales to customers.
- Backup of orders.
- Number of skills per worker.
- Number of complaints and warranty required services.
- Rework costs relative to cost of goods manufactured.
- Setup time relative to total manufacturing time.
- Number and length of equipment breakdowns.

- Number and duration of manufacturing delays.
- Output per manhour.
- Manufacturing costs to total costs.
- Manufacturing costs to revenue.
- Lead time.
- Time per business process.
- Time between receipt of an order and delivery.
- Time between order placement and receipt.
- Non-value-added cost to total cost.
- Percentage of declining and developmental products to total products.

"Production run size" is an optimum production run quantity which minimizes the sum of carrying and setup costs.

STUDYING PRODUCTIVITY

Productivity is enhanced by minimizing direct labor cost. Also, an attempt should be made to reduce indirect costs relative to direct labor costs. Management might consolidate facilities and equipment to achieve a more efficient productivity level. A measure of productivity is the relationship of the cost, time, and quality of an "input" to the quality and units generated for the "output." A proper input-output balance is needed. Resources should be utilized in optimum fashion.

SALES EFFORTS

An appraisal should be made of salesperson effectiveness (e.g., income generated by salesperson, cost per salesperson, salesperson incentives, call frequency, dollar value of orders obtained per hour spent), promotional and advertising effectiveness (marketing costs to sales, dollar expenditure by media compared to sales generated, media measures, comparison of profit before and after promotion), test market analysis (consumer vs. industry), and activity analysis (sales and marketing, customer support, order management). An analysis should also be made of product/service warranties and complaints.

LOOKING AT PERSONNEL

The ratio of sales to personnel represents a comparison of sales dollars and/or sales volume generated relative to the number of employees. It provides insight into levels of employee productivity. The following ratios should be computed: (1) sales/number of employees, (2) sales volume/number of employees, (3) sales/ salaries expense. Other useful ratios are: (1) net income/manpower, (2) number of transactions/average number of employees, (3) total tangible assets/number of workers, (4) labor costs/total costs, (5) labor costs/sales, and (6) labor costs/net income. Another consideration as to employee efficiency and morale is employee turnover (number of employees leaving/average number of employees).

The ratio of indirect labor to direct labor monitors indirect labor planning and control. Labor planning and control are crucial at all supervisory levels to produce competitive products and/or to perform profitable services. Management uses this ratio to appraise indirect personnel requirements through the impact of these requirements on operations, earnings, and overhead costs. A declining ratio is unfavorable because it shows management has not maintained a desirable relationship.

Consider automation and up-to-date technology to decrease labor costs.

EFFICIENCY OF SPACE USE

The usefulness of space may be computed as follows:

- Revenue per square foot = net sales/square feet of space.
- Sales per square foot of machinery = net sales/square feet of space for machinery.
- Production per square foot = total units produced/square feet of space for machinery.
- Profit per square foot = net income/square feet of space.
- Customer space = number of customers/square feet of space.
- Employee space = square feet of space/number of employees.
- Parking lot space = square feet of parking lot space/number of customers.
- Rent per square foot = rent expense/square feet of space.
- Expenses per square foot for owned property = expenses of owning property/square feet of space.

BUSINESS PROCESSES

A business process is an operation, function, or activity that crosses among divisions or departments of a company to manufacture the product or render the service. By concentrating on the process itself (rather than each department separately), operations and product/service quality may be improved, costs slashed, and processing time reduced.

By analyzing a process itself, it is easier to understand the complexities and interrelationships among units of the organization, and aid in better communication as to where each responsibility unit fits in. Concentrating on and improving the business process (as distinct from individual departments) results in greater efficiency and effectiveness. In appraising business processes, consider:

- What the process costs and how long it takes.
- Whether the process involves irrelevant and unneeded steps that can be cut.
- The quality associated with the process.
- What problems or bottlenecks exist.
- The work flow.

The financial manager should identify cases in which work performed by the client is redundant or unnecessary, or in which such work is too costly or time-consuming. Further, procedures, activities, or policies may be unjustifiably complex and can be simplified. A process needs to be revamped when its cost or time does not add value for the customer. Therefore, a customer survey may be warranted. The CPA may decide to recommend modifying, adding, or dropping a process.

The business process might be improved by doing the following: Reduce the number of employees involved or functions required, reduce cycle time, reduce the number of individuals required to approve the process or modification thereto, reorganize the procedures, eliminate illogical administrative steps, improve the sequence of the operation, prioritize strategies, cut out excessive paperwork, improve training, clarify job descriptions and instructions, upgrade equipment, and use up-to-date technology.

Cycle time should be expressed as average and maximum. An example of cycle time is how long it takes to process a bill to a customer. The efficiency with which a cycle is performed may be expressed by the ratio of total processing time divided by total processing plus non-processing time. A lower ratio is unfavorable and requires corrective action.

"A value-added evaluation" should be conducted for each operation, function, or responsibility unit. How much is the value-added? Is it sufficient to justify that activity or business segment? If not, what should be done (e.g., improvements made, disbandonment)? Work improvement teams can be used in production, material handling, shipping, and accounting. Such teams should document the process flows, layouts, etc. and find ways to reorganize the process to make it better.

A business process analysis may be undertaken as a preemptive trouble-shooter and should be conducted on an ongoing basis. Examples of situations in which a business process analysis is crucial are when profit margins for a product line are shrinking, market share is dramatically declining, service quality is deteriorating, and customer response time is becoming prohibitive.

Operational audits should be performed to examine corporate policies and procedures and assure that they are functioning properly.

LIFE CYCLES

There are different types of life cycles affecting a business. "Product life cycle" is the time from the start of the R&D effort to the ending of customer support for the product. A "life-cycle budget" of costs for this time period aids in formulating selling prices. Many costs occur even before production starts. The development product period may range from short to long. "Product life-cycle reporting" is not on a calendar year basis but rather tracks the revenue and costs for each product over several calendar years. Product cost analysis is done by product over each major stage in the product's life cycle (early, middle, late). There is a highlighting of cost interrelationships among major business functions. "Life-cycle costing" organizes costs based on the product or service life cycle. It monitors and computes the actual total costs of the product or service from beginning to end. Decisions are then made about the good or service based on its profile. "Customer life-cycle costs" concentrate on the total costs to a customer of buying and using a product over its life.

TIME CONSIDERATIONS

Time-based competition stresses the customer and considers product quality, timing, and cost/pricing. An example is how long it takes to design a new product model to meet customer demand. Another example is how long it takes to fill a customer's order. Such analysis strives to enhance productivity, improve market position, raise selling prices, and reduce risk. Efforts should be made to streamline operations.

The time between developing and marketing a product or service should be minimized to lower up-front costs (e.g., design, process, and promotion). Revenue must be generated as quickly as possible to recoup such costs.

DIVESTITURES

Divestitures may be made of unprofitable and/or risky business segments. Divestiture involves the complete or partial conversion, sale, or reallocation of capital or human resources as well as product/service lines. Freed resources may be used for some more productive business purpose. A business segment may qualify for divestiture if it is providing a poor rate of return, does not generate adequate cash flow, does not mesh with overall company strategy, has excessive risk (e.g., vulnerable to lawsuits), is in a state of decline, or when the pieces are worth more than the whole. The objectives of divestiture include repositioning the company in the industry, getting out of an industry, meeting market changes, obtaining needed funds, and cutting losses. Before a divestiture is made, a joint venture may be considered with another company.

CHAPTER 33

ANALYSIS, EVALUATION, AND CONTROL OF REVENUE AND COSTS

CONTENTS

A company can improve its bottom line and overall operations by analyzing, planning, monitoring, and controlling revenue and costs. Control reports will help in this process. This chapter provides some benchmarks in this evaluation and control process.

CONTROL REPORTS

Control reports are issued in order to highlight poor performance so that timely corrective action may be taken. The reports should be frequent, detailed, and look at each important operational level.

Summary reports should also be prepared presenting performance over a long time period (e.g., monthly) and providing an overview of performance.

The form and content of the control report should vary depending upon the functions and responsibilities of the executives receiving it. The reports may take the form of narrative, tabular, or graphic. A lower level manager is more concerned with details. A higher level manager is more interested with departmental summaries, trends, and relationships. The reports may be in both financial and nonfinancial terms.

CONTROL OF REVENUE

Important questions needing answering in sales analysis are: What was sold? Where was it sold? Who sold it? What was the profit?

Sales and profitability analysis involves the following:

- *Customer*—industry or retail, corporate or governmental, domestic or foreign.
- *Product*—type of commodity, size, price, quality, and color.

- *Distribution channel*—wholesaler, retailer, agent, broker.
- *Sales effort*—personal visit, direct mail, coupon, ad (e.g., newspaper, magazine), media (television, radio).
- *Territory*—country, state, city, suburb.
- *Order size*—individual purchase.
- *Organization*—department, branch.
- *Salesperson*—group, individual.
- *Terms of sale*—cash purchase, cash on delivery, charge account, installment purchase.

Profitability may be determined by territory, product, customer, channel of distribution, salesperson, method of sale, organization, and operating division. In deciding upon a product line, economies of production have to be taken into account.

The financial manager should watch out for significant changes in sales trends in terms of profit margin and distribution channels. How do actual sales conform to sales goals and budgets? In analyzing the trend in sales, the financial manager may see the need to redirect sales effort and/or change the product. The types and sizes of desirable accounts and orders should be determined. Volume selling price breaks may be given for different order sizes.

In appraising sales volume and prices, the manager should not ignore the possibility that unfavorable variances have arisen from salespeople having excessive authority in establishing selling prices.

Pricing should be periodically reviewed after considering relevant factors such as increasing costs. All types of cost must be considered including total cost, marginal cost, and out-of-pocket costs.

The financial manager should compare the profit margins on alternative products in deciding which ones to emphasize. He or she should also consider the probable effect of volume on the profit margin. Consideration should also be given to the importance of changes in composition, manufacturing processes, and quality on the costs to produce and distribute the product.

The financial manager should determine the following:

- The least-cost geographic location for warehouses.
- The minimum acceptable order.
- How best to serve particular accounts, such as by mail order, telephone, jobber, and so on.

The financial manager may find that most sales are concentrated in a few products. In fact, a few customers may represent a significant portion of company sales. This involves a small amount of the sales effort. The financial manager may be able to reduce selling costs by concentrating sales effort on the major customers and products. Perhaps salesperson assignments should be modified, such as concentrating on only a few territories. Perhaps a simplification of the product line is needed.

The controller should provide the alternative costs for the varying methods of sale. For example, how should samples be distributed to result in the best effect on sales at minimum cost.

In evaluating sales effort, we should consider the success of business development expense (e.g., promotion and entertainment) by customer, territory, or salesperson.

Customer analysis should indicate the number of accounts and dollar sales by customer volume bracket and average order size. A small order size may result in unprofitable sales because of such factors as high distribution costs and high order costs. In this case, the controller should analyze distribution costs by size of order in order to bring the problem under control and take appropriate corrective action.

It may cost more to sell to certain types of customers than others among different classes as well as within a particular class. For example, a particular customer may require greater services than typical, such as delivery and warehousing. A particular customer may demand a different price, such as for volume purchases. Profitability analysis by customer should be made so as to see where to place salesperson time, what selling price to establish, where to control distribution costs, and what customer classes to discontinue. A determination should also be made as to which customers have increasing or decreasing sales volume. Sales effort may be curtailed on: (1) large volume accounts that buy only low-profit-margin items, and (2) low volume accounts that are at best marginally profitable.

It may not pay to carry all varieties, sizes, and colors from a sales and profitability perspective. The company should emphasize the profitable products which may not be the odd items (e.g., unusual colors, odd sizes). Sales which have not been realized should be listed and analyzed, particularly with regard to any problems that may have been experienced. Such analysis involves the following:

- Orders received.
- Unfilled orders.
- Lost sales.
- Cancellations.

Note: The analysis of orders is particularly crucial when goods are made to order.

Sales deductions should be analyzed to indicate problems possibly leading to deficient profits. Problems may be indicated when excessive discounts, allowances, and freight costs exist. What is the extent and reasons for returns, price adjustments, freight allowances, and so on. A determination should be made of whom is responsible. A defective product is the responsibility of manufacturing. An excessive freight cost or wrong delay is the responsibility of traffic.

In conclusion, sales should be analyzed in terms of both price and volume to identify unfavorable trends, weaknesses, and positive directions.

CONTROL OF COSTS

Cost control must be exercised over manufacturing and nonmanufacturing costs. Costs should be incurred only for necessary business expenditures that will provide revenue benefit to the firm.

Manufacturing Costs

The purpose of cost control is to obtain an optimum product consistent with quality standards from the various input factors including material, labor, and facilities. The input-output relationship is crucial. In other words, the best result should be forthcoming at the least cost. The office should be shut down when the factory is not in operation. Because most costs are controllable by someone within the organization, responsibility should be assigned.

Changes in standard prices for material, labor, and overhead should be noted along with their effects upon the unit standard cost of the product. Perhaps there is a need for material substitutions or modifications in specifications or processes.

Labor control should be jointly developed between staff and management. Line supervisors have prime responsibility to control labor costs. Actual performance of labor should be compared against a realistic yardstick. Unfavorable discrepancies should be followed up.

The controller may assist in controlling labor costs in the following ways:

- Prepare an analysis of overtime hours and cost. Make sure overtime is approved in advance.
- Prepare a report on labor turnover, training cost, and years of service.
- Determine the standard labor-hours for the production program.
- Establish procedures to limit the number of employees placed on the payroll to that called for by the production plan.
- Make sure that an employee is performing services per his or her job description. Are high-paid employees doing menial work?
- Consider overtime hours and cost, turnover rate, output per worker, and relationship between indirect labor and direct labor.
- Working conditions should be improved to enhance productivity.
- Analyze machinery to assure it is up to date.

Because most overhead items are small in amount, proper control may be neglected. Of course, in the aggregate, overhead may be substantial. Areas to look at include the personal use of supplies and xeroxing, and use of customized forms when standardized ones would suffice.

In order to control overhead, standards must be established and compared against actual performance. Periodic reports of budget and actual overhead costs should be prepared to identify problem areas. Preplanning of overhead costs may be done such as planning indirect labor staff (e.g., maintenance) to avoid excessive hours. The preplanning approach may be beneficial when significant dollar cost is involved, such as in the purchase of repair material and supplies. A record of purchases by responsibility unit may be helpful. Purchase requirements should be properly approved.

The cost of idle equipment should be determined to gauge whether facilities are being utilized properly. What is the degree of plant utilization relative to what is normal?

Nonmanufacturing Costs

The control of distribution costs is a much more difficult problem than the control of manufacturing costs. In distribution, we have to consider the varying nature of the personality of seller and buyer. Competitive factors must be taken into account. On the contrary, in production the worker is the only human element. In marketing, there are more methods and greater flexibility relative to production. Several distribution channels may be used. Because of the greater possibility for variability, distribution processes are more difficult to standardize than production activities. If distribution costs are excessive, with whom and where does the responsibility lie? Is it a problem territory? Is the salesperson doing a poor job?

Distribution costs and effort must be planned, controlled, and monitored. Distribution costs may be analyzed by functional operation, nature of expense, and application of distribution effort.

In functional operation, distribution costs are analyzed in terms of individual responsibility. This is a particularly useful approach in large companies. Functional operations requiring measurement are identified. Examples of such operations might be circular mailing, warehouse shipments, and salesperson calls on customers.

In looking at the nature of the expense, costs are segregated by month and trends in distribution costs are examined. The ratio of distribution costs to sales over time should be enlightening. A comparison to industry norms is recommended.

In looking at the manner of application, distribution costs must be segregated into direct costs, indirect costs, and semidirect costs.

Direct costs are specifically identifiable to a particular segment. Examples of direct costs assignable to a salesperson are salary, commission, and travel and entertainment expense. But these same costs may be indirect or semidirect if attributable to product analysis. An expense that is direct in one application may not be in another.

Indirect costs are general corporate costs and must be allocated to segments (e.g., territory, product) on a rational basis. Examples are corporate advertising and salaries of general sales executives. Advertising may be allocated based on sales. General sales executives' salaries may be allocated based on time spent by territory or product. Here, a time log may be kept.

Semidirect costs are related in some measurable way to particular segments. Such costs may be distributed in accordance with the services required. For example, the variable factor for warehousing may be weight handled. Order handling costs may be in terms of the number of orders. The allocation base is considerably less arbitrary than with indirect costs.

A comparison should be made between actual and budgeted figures for salesperson salaries, bonuses, and expenses. The salary structure in the industry may serve as a good reference point.

An examination should be made as to the effect of advertising on sales. Perhaps a change in media is needed.

Telephone expense may be controlled in the following ways:

- Prior approval for long-distance calls.
- Controls to restrict personal use of the telephone, such as a key lock.
- Discarding or returning unnecessary equipment.

The trend in warehouse expense to sales should be analyzed. Increasing trends may have to be investigated.

To control dues and subscription expenses, a control is necessary such as having a card record of each publication by subscribed to, by whom, and why. If another employee must use that publication, he or she knows where to go.

There should be centralized control over contributions such as in the hands of a committee of senior management. A general policy must be established as to amount and for what purposes.

CHAPTER 34

RISK MANAGEMENT AND ANALYSIS

CONTENTS

The news dominating the world's attention in recent years—terrorist attacks; corporate scandals; the SARS or E-coli outbreak; natural disasters such as hurricanes, earthquakes, and tsunamis; and turbulent financial markets—has triggered a shift in corporate risk management practices. The calculation of risk has always been central to managerial decision making, but CEOs and CFOs are acutely aware of the need to deal proactively with uncertainties that can threaten their business.

With this in mind, larger firms have designated a chief risk officer (CRO), whose prime function is to make risk management a central part of the business. The CRO reports to the CFO, whereas the CFO of a smaller firm personally assumes risk management responsibilities, known as enterprise risk management (ERM). Risks are often closely connected. For example, operational risks can quickly evolve into market risks if word gets out and the share price falls.

Risk management involves identifying risk exposure, analyzing risk, measuring potential loss, determining the best insurance strategy (or whether to self-insure), cost projections and control, volatility of operations, timing of adverse events, claims adjustment, proper cost allocation, and the use of risk management software.

Risks facing a business may negatively affect its reputation, bottom line, cost and availability of financing, credit rating, market price of stock, regulatory or legislative changes, and elimination of barriers to entry.

An evaluation must be made of the trade-off between risk and return. A higher risk mandates a higher rate of return to justify taking the extra risk.

A risk program must be in place. The program must have built-in flexibility to adjust, as conditions require. The program must conform to the goals, objectives, and policies of the business.

The company must have a workable contingency plan such as a recovery plan. Employees must be instructed what to do in such eventualities. Test runs should be practiced. Contingency plans must be updated periodically to incorporate new technologies, changing staff, and new areas of business activity.

Areas of risk must be identified and corrective action taken to reduce those risks. Unusually high risk will not only have negative effects on earnings but might also place in question the continuity of the operation.

Models and quantitative approaches including actuarial techniques may be used to appraise potential catastrophic losses, product/service liability, intellectual property losses, and business interruption. Probability distributions should be arrived at of expected losses based on the model or quantitative technique used.

APPRAISAL OF RISK

The "red flags" of undue risk must be identified and controlled. "Red flags" include poor employee training and performance, inadequate planning, fragmentation, poor communication, lateness, improper focus, failure to observe government regulations or laws (e.g., the federal Comprehensive Environmental Response, Compensation and Liability Act covering the release and disposal of hazardous substances and wastes), overconfidence, and "hostile" attitudes.

When appraising a particular situation, evaluate the risk profile, financial status, and acceptable risk exposure. What is the entity's risk tolerance level? To what extent does the risk of a situation exceed predetermined maximum risk levels? Has management received proper approval to undertake the high-risk level? Has proper planning been performed to take into account the adverse effects on the business if things do not work out? For example, if losses are incurred that significantly exceed the entity's traditional insurance program, the company might be permanently crippled. Examples include a business interruption resulting from a terrorist bombing, loss of a major vendor, misinterpretation of law, or a product recall.

In appraising risk, consideration must be given to the company's liquidity and solvency position to withstand loss. A determination must be made of the costs associated with various risks.

Risk should be evaluated and minimized. Risk may be reduced through the following means:

- Vertically integrate to reduce the price and supply risk of raw materials.

- Take out sufficient insurance coverage for possible asset and operating losses (including foreign risk protection). A lower trend in insurance expense to the asset insured may indicate inadequate coverage.

- Diversify activities, product/service line, market segments, customer bases, geographic areas, and investments.

- Sell to diversified industries to protect against cyclical turns in the economy.

- Sign a forward contract to take delivery of raw materials at fixed prices at a specified future date so the entity insulates itself from price increases.

- Enter into foreign currency futures contracts to lock in a fixed rate.

- Participate in joint ventures and partnerships with other companies. In so doing, obligations of the parties must be taken into account. For example, questions to be asked are: Which company is to absorb most of the losses? What are our company's duties and exposure under the agreement?

- Sell low-priced products as well as more expensive ones to protect against inflationary and recessionary periods.

- Change suppliers who provide unreliable products or services.

- Take steps so the company is less susceptible to business cycles (e.g., inelastic demand products, negatively correlated products/services).

- Add products or services having different seasonal attractiveness and demand.

- Emphasize a piggyback product base (similar merchandise associated with the basic business).

- Balance the company's financing mix.

In analyzing the company's product/service line, determine:

- Extent of correlation between products. Positive correlation means high risk because the demand for all the products goes in the same direction. Negative correlation minimizes the risk. No correlation means indifference between products.

- Product demand elasticity equal to the percentage change in quantity relative to the percentage change in price. Elastic demand means that a minor change in price has a significant impact on quantity demanded. This indicates higher risk. Inelastic product demand minimizes risk because a change in price will have little effect on quantity demanded.

In analyzing the risk associated with multinational companies, compute:

- Total assets in high-risk foreign countries to total assets.
- High-risk foreign revenue to total revenue. High-risk revenue is based on risk ratings of companies in published sources (e.g., International Country Risk Guide).
- High-risk foreign revenue to net income.
- Percentage of earnings associated with foreign government contracts.
- Fluctuation in foreign exchange rates.

When evaluating risk, a number of questions must be answered:

- What is the internal process in place to reduce risk?
- What appraisal is being made of control aspects?
- Are controls effective?
- Do controls function as planned?
- Who is responsible for risk management?
- Is risk being managed properly to prevent fraud?
- What are the specific areas of risk vulnerability?
- Is financial and operational information being reported correctly?

TYPES OF RISK

Senior management needs to take into account the various types of risk the entity faces. For example, corporate risk may be in the form of overrelying on a few key executives or the underinsurance of assets. Industry risk may be the high technological environment, or an industry scrutinized under the "public eye," or a capital-intensive business. Moving toward a variable cost-oriented business may minimize industry risk. Economic risk includes susceptibility to the business cycle. This risk may be reduced by having a low-priced substitute for a high-priced one.

Social risk occurs when a company experiences customer boycott or discrimination cases. A way to reduce this risk is to be engaged in community involvement and sensitivity training.

A company must properly instruct its personnel not to intrude with electronic mail, slander others, or commit libel. The company must carefully train and monitor staff to guard against possible infractions causing employee lawsuits or federal/local government investigation.

Political risk applies to relations with U.S. and local government agencies, and with foreign governments when operations are carried out overseas. This risk may be reduced through lobbying efforts and by avoiding activities or placing assets in high-risk foreign areas.

Environmental risk includes product lines and services susceptible to changes in the weather. Having counterseasonal goods and services or moving to another geographic location may reduce this risk. Multinational entities are susceptible to environmental risk, particularly in the former Iron Curtain countries. There are often problems with land and resource use, including pollution and hazardous waste. The acquiring company must be cautious of not only the cleanup costs, but also associated penalties and fines. Prior to acquisition, the acquirer must be assured that there is a contract under which the seller will be responsible for all or part of the environmental obligations. A high-risk premium applies to corporate investments in countries with environmental problems. For example, insurance companies should reject potential clients that are not environmentally certified or fail to meet particular environmental norms. Banks need to be concerned with the collectibility of loans to companies with major environmental exposure. If a company is "dirty," it may have difficulty obtaining adequate insurance or loans. Further, the effect of impending government environmental laws on the business must be considered. Environmental problems and disasters may significantly hurt earnings.

Terrorism is also of concern to certain types of businesses. Security measures must be in place to guard against bombing.

A determination must be made as to how the risks facing a business interact. A model must consider alternative scenarios. There are some commonly used terms that describe different risks. Some of these risks can be mitigated, or managed, which is the job of risk management:

1. *Pure risks* are risks that offer only the prospect of a loss. Examples include the risk that a plant will be destroyed by fire or that a product liability suit will result in a large judgment against the firm.

2. *Speculative risks* are situations that offer the chance of a gain but might result in a loss. Thus, investments in new projects and marketable securities involve speculative risks.

3. *Demand risks* are associated with the demand for a firm's products or services. Because sales are essential to all businesses, demand risk is one of the most significant risks that firms face.

4. *Input risks* are risks associated with input costs, including both labor and materials. Thus, a company that uses copper as a raw material in its manufacturing process faces the risk that the cost of copper will increase and that it will not be able to pass this increase on to its customers.

5. *Financial risks* are risks that result from financial transactions. As seen, if a firm plans to issue new bonds, it faces the risk that interest rates will rise before the bonds can be brought to market. Similarly, if the firm enters into contracts with foreign customers or suppliers, it faces the risk that fluctuations in exchange rates will result in unanticipated losses.

6. *Property risks* are associated with destruction of productive assets. Thus, the threat of fire, floods, and riots imposes property risks on a firm.

7. *Personnel risks* are risks that result from employees' actions. Examples include the risks associated with employee fraud or embezzlement, or suits based on charges of age or sex discrimination.

8. *Environmental risks* include risks associated with polluting the environment. Public awareness in recent years, coupled with the huge costs of environmental cleanup, has increased the importance of this risk.

9. *Liability risks* are associated with product, service, or employee actions. Examples include the very large judgments assessed against asbestos manufacturers and some health care providers, as well as costs incurred as a result of improper actions of employees, such as driving corporate vehicles in a reckless manner.

10. *Insurable risks* are risks that can be covered by insurance. In general, property, personnel, environmental, and liability risks can be transferred to insurance companies. Note, though, that the *ability* to insure a risk does not necessarily mean that the risk *should be* insured. Indeed, a major function of risk management involves evaluating all alternatives for managing a particular risk, including self-insurance, and then choosing the optimal alternative.

11. *Foreign exchange rate risks* (or currency risks) exist when a contract is written in terms of the foreign currency or denominated in foreign currency. Exchange rate fluctuations increase the riskiness of the investment and incur cash losses. A controller must not only seek the highest return on temporary investments but must also be concerned about changing values of the currencies invested. You do not necessarily eliminate foreign exchange risk. You may only try to contain it.

12. *Political risks* result from potential changes in a nation's laws and regulations. These changes can affect the value of foreign operations. International financial management includes measuring and controlling the effect of political changes on the business.

13. *Reputational risks* are a potential loss in reputation that could lead to negative publicity, loss of revenue, costly litigation, a decline in the customer base or the exit of key employees. A comprehensive reputational risk assessment is an estimate of the organization's current standing across all its constituencies and its ability to operate successfully in the current environment.

14. *Technical risks* (or innovation risks) are risks that apply to all types of projects and refer to whether the proposed work can be done within the required time frame and within budget. Many products fail because they do not solve the technical issues—for example, consider the washing powder PersilPower, which removed stains but in the process damaged fabrics, or the Apple Newton, the palm top computer that promised but failed to recognize users' handwriting.

15. *Information risks* arise as companies across the world become increasingly dependent on information technology (IT). Mission critical systems processing information over rapidly expanding networks can affect the integrity, availability, and confidentiality of information resources. Electronic commerce and more recently mobile commerce across wireless networks have created additional layers of complexity.

16. *Compliance risks* exist when companies are not in compliance with rules and regulations. At present, risk management is largely being driven by a

number of recent high-profile regulations and reports, including: the Sarbanes-Oxley Act, which is designed to address fraudulent financial statements; the Basel II Accord, which addresses financial and operational risk in the financial services industry; Cobit, a framework for IT risks developed by The Information Systems Audit and Control Association; and the Combined Code, which consolidates previous corporate governance reports by the Cadbury, Greenbury, and Hampel committees. These regulations and proposals encourage better risk management procedures beyond the financial controls that companies have historically had in place.

Note that the risk classifications used here are somewhat arbitrary, and different classifications are commonly used in different industries. However, the list does give an idea of the wide variety of risks to which a firm can be exposed.

AN APPROACH TO RISK MANAGEMENT

Firms often use the following process for managing risks:

1. Identify the risks faced by the firm. Here the risk manager identifies the potential risks faced by his or her firm.

2. Measure the potential impact of each risk. Some risks are so small as to be immaterial, whereas others have the potential for dooming the company. It is useful to segregate risks by potential impact and then to focus on the most serious threats.

3. Decide how each relevant risk should be handled. In most situations, risk exposure can be reduced through one of the following techniques:

    a. Transfer the risk to an insurance company. Often, it is advantageous to insure against, hence transfer, a risk. However, insurability does not necessarily mean that a risk should be covered by insurance. In many instances, it might be better for the company to *self-insure,* which means bearing the risk directly rather than paying another party to bear it.

    b. Transfer the function that produces the risk to a third party. For example, suppose a furniture manufacturer is concerned about potential liabilities arising from its ownership of a fleet of trucks used to transfer products from its manufacturing plant to various points across the country. One way to eliminate this risk would be to contract with a trucking company to do the shipping, thus passing the risks to a third party.

    c. Purchase derivative contracts to reduce risk. As indicated earlier, firms use derivatives to hedge risks. Commodity derivatives can be used to reduce input risks. For example, a cereal company may use corn or wheat futures to hedge against increases in grain prices. Similarly, financial derivatives can be used to reduce risks that arise from changes in interest rates and exchange rates.

    d. Reduce the probability of occurrence of an adverse event. The expected loss arising from any risk is a function of both the probability of occurrence and the dollar loss if the adverse event occurs. In some instances, it is possible to reduce the probability that an adverse event will occur. For example, the probability that a fire will occur can be reduced by instituting a fire prevention program, by replacing old electrical wiring, and by using fire-resistant materials in areas with the greatest fire potential.

e. Reduce the magnitude of the loss associated with an adverse event. Continuing with the fire risk example, the dollar cost associated with a fire can be reduced by actions such as installing sprinkler systems, designing facilities with self-contained fire zones, and locating facilities close to a fire station.

f. Totally avoid the activity that gives rise to the risk. For example, a company might discontinue a product or service line because the risks outweigh the rewards, as with the recent decision by Dow-Corning to discontinue its manufacture of silicon breast implants.

Note that risk management decisions, like all corporate decisions, should be based on a cost/benefit analysis for each feasible alternative. For example, suppose it would cost $50,000 per year to conduct a comprehensive fire safety-training program for all personnel in a high-risk plant. Presumably, this program would reduce the expected value of future fire losses. An alternative to the training program would be to place $50,000 annually in a reserve fund set aside to cover future fire losses. Both alternatives involve expected cash flows, and from an economic standpoint the choice should be made on the basis of the lowest present value of future costs.

Thus, the same financial management techniques applied to other corporate decisions can also be applied to risk management decisions. Note, though, that if a fire occurs and a life is lost, the trade-off between fire prevention and expected losses may not sit well with a jury. The same holds true for product liability, as Toyota, GM, and others have learned.

RISK MODELING SOFTWARE APPLICATIONS

Risk modeling is a decision-making aid to the financial manager. Models may be used in analyzing risks, while financial models can evaluate the financial consequences arising from accidents or other adverse developments. Risk models may be developed for measuring the financial impact due to catastrophes (fire, flood, earthquake, nuclear). The probable loss arising from the accident, disaster, or other event may be estimated. The model may also determine the probable effects on business activities as well as possible competitive reactions. A contingency model may help in planning an appropriate strategy and response. Risk modeling may be used to identify and define the type and amount of risks related to various exposures. A priority ranking based on risk and uncertainty may also be prepared and studied. Risk problem areas may be analyzed along with a set of appropriate alternative responses.

A "what-if" scenario analysis may be formulated to see the end-result effects of changing input variables and factors. An example of a scenario modeling analysis is to simulate the possible operating and financial consequences to the company from various possibilities arising from a hurricane. The company's risk vulnerability from such an event may be "mapped" and appraised. The "best-case," "worst-case," and "likely" scenarios may be depicted and reviewed. The model simulation has the benefit of aiding the company in determining beforehand how to best minimize the damage operationally and financially and how to provide proper protective measures.

The software enables the company to determine the areas, types, and degrees of risk facing the business. A minimum-maximum range of loss figures may be derived. Software is available to assess, evaluate, and control the risks facing a company. A risk management information system (RMIS) includes hardware and software components. However, we consider here software availability, implications, benefits, and applications. The software selected should be that which offers a proper "fit" with the environment and circumstances of the company.

In deciding on the "right" the CFO or CRO should consider the company's requirements and expectations, corporate culture, report preparation needs, regulatory reporting mandates, product/service line, nature of operations, claims processing and administration, government compliance laws, business policies and procedures, insurance coverage, technological resources, employee background and experience, levels of communication, legal liability aspects, organizational structure, and work flow. The risk management and analysis software should include the ability to manipulate data into risk patterns.

Are the "right" managers being provided with the appropriate information on a timely basis? A determination must also be made of the communication and distribution features of the software. The software should be flexible so that reports may be customized depending on the data needed and for whom. For example, a factory supervisor or manager wants to know how many employee injuries occurred and of what nature. On the other hand, the accounting department manager wants to know the negative financial effects the accidents have on the company's financial position and operating performance.

Software may be used to evaluate safety statistical data by division, department, responsibility unit, geographic location, and manager. Potential difficulties may be highlighted. An example of a risk management software application is providing a report on how many employee injuries took place by department, operation, and activity. Is the client's incidence rate above or below expected ranges? How does the client injury rate compare to competitors and industry averages? There should be a software feature, such as an expert system, on how to correct the problem of a high rate of employee accidents and offer other relevant recommendations.

If a company is exchanging risk information with others (e.g., insurance company, investment banker, and government agencies), then software compatibility is needed. Further, there should exist appropriate operating systems and network support. A company may use its intranet to expand risk management throughout the company. It is important that there be proper user interfaces.

RISK CONTROL

Risk control includes environmental compliance, periodic inspections, and alarm systems. Loss prevention and control must consider physical and human aspects. For example, "safer" machines may be used to prevent worker injury. Appropriate sprinklers may be installed to prevent fires. Consultants may be retained in specialized areas such as industrial hygiene. Product labeling should be appraised as to appropriateness and representation. Any consumer complaints should be immediately investigated to avoid possible government action or litigation.

The CFO or CRO must determine the best kind, term, and amount of insurance to carry to guard against losses. Insurance coverage may be taken out for losses to plant, property, and equipment, product/service deficiencies, and employee conduct. The financial manager should consider insuring areas not typically insured against, such as industrial espionage, loss of intellectual property, or employee theft. An example of the latter is employment practice liability insurance (EPLI). This policy is available from many insurance companies, such as Chubb and Lexington. Unfortunately even this type of policy often excludes coverage for bodily injury, workers' compensation, and infractions under ERISA. It is not unusual for an employee to sue because of an employer's promotion and hiring policies. The insurance premium may be lowered by increasing the deductible or changing to less expensive insurance carriers.

The financial manager must carefully monitor the entity's fiduciary responsibilities, working conditions, contractual commitments, and employment practices. Systems such as fire alarm devices must be checked on an ongoing basis for defects in functioning. The company must be certain that its employee policies are fair and in conformity with federal and local laws.

Risk control includes provisions against terrorist acts related to loss of life, product losses, and property damage. Security procedures including access controls must be strong in high-risk areas, such as in a foreign country with extremist groups. Employees must be instructed to use safety precautions.

ONLINE RISK MANAGEMENT DATABASE SERVICES

There are many online services available providing important risk management information. For example, the National Council on Compensation Insurance (NCCI) Inc. (https://www.ncci.com/nccimain/pages/default.aspx) provides an online InsNet Workers' Compensation Characteristic Series containing claims data useful in having a cost-effective workers' compensation system. The service aids in evaluating risks, determining and appraising workers' compensation costs including frequency data, specifying injury claim characteristics, providing demographic and body claim characteristics, and specifying benefit type information.

MANAGING FRAUD RISK

In 2008, the American Institute of CPAs (www.aicpa.org), The Institute of Internal Auditors (www.theiia.org), and the Association of Certified Fraud Examiners (www.acfe.com) jointly created *Managing the Business Risk of Fraud: A Practical Guide*, to assist boards, senior management, and internal auditors in their management of fraud risk within organizations. The guide defines the following five principles for fraud risk management:

1. *Principle 1:* As part of an organization's governance structure, a fraud risk management program should be in place, including a written policy (or policies) to convey the expectations of the board of directors and senior management regarding managing fraud risk.

2. *Principle 2:* Fraud risk exposure should be assessed periodically by the organization to identify specific potential schemes and events that the organization needs to mitigate.

3. *Principle 3:* Prevention techniques to avoid potential key fraud risk events should be established, where feasible, to mitigate possible impacts on the organization.

4. *Principle 4:* Detection techniques should be established to uncover fraud events when preventive measures fail or unmitigated risks are realized.

5. *Principle 5:* A reporting process should be in place to solicit input on potential fraud, and a coordinated approach to investigation and corrective action should be used to help ensure potential fraud is addressed appropriately and timely.

The guide describes how organizations of all sizes can establish their own fraud risk management programs and includes examples of key program components and resources that organizations can use as a starting point to develop an effective and efficient fraud risk management program.

ENTERPRISE RISK MANAGEMENT

Enterprise risk management (ERM) is a process, effected by an entity's board of directors, management, and other personnel, applied strategically across the enterprise, designed to identify potential events that may affect the entity, and manage risks, to provide reasonable assurance regarding the achievement of entity objectives.

ERM is widely used as a way to effectively manage the complex portfolio of risks that exist across an organization. Instead of relying on a traditional, "silo-based" strategy, where each area of the organization manages its own risk, ERM adopts a broader top-down view of risks that integrates and coordinates risk oversight across the entire enterprise. An effectively implemented ERM process should provide auditors important information about the client's most significant business risk exposures.

ERM is a systematic way of understanding and managing the various risks companies face. It involves identifying risk exposure; analyzing risk; measuring potential loss; determining the best insurance strategy (or whether to self-insure); making cost projections and control; and considering volatility of operations, timing of adverse events, claims adjustment, proper cost allocation, and the use of risk management software.

The risks that a business faces may negatively affect its reputation, bottom line, cost and availability of financing, credit rating, market price of stock, regulatory or legislative changes, and elimination of barriers to entry. The firm must make an evaluation of the trade-off between risk and return. A higher risk mandates a higher rate of return to justify taking the extra risk. A risk program must be in place and must have built-in flexibility for adjustment, as conditions require. The program must conform to the goals, objectives, and policies of the business. A well-managed ERM policy encourages a common language of risk among board members, managers, suppliers, customers, and investors. It helps people at the front line—who spot warning signals of potential problems—to communicate them more quickly to those who can take evasive action.

ENTERPRISE RISK OVERSIGHT

Expectations that boards and audit committees are effectively overseeing an organization's risk management processes are at all-time highs. As the volume and complexity of risks increase due to highly volatile economic conditions, globalization, emerging technologies and complex business transactions, key stakeholders are putting pressure on boards and senior executives to strengthen their approach to risk management. For example, the New York Stock Exchange Final Governance Rules require the audit committee to discuss management's guidelines and policies for risk oversight. Standard & Poor's evaluates an entity's enterprise-wide risk management as part of its credit rating analysis procedures. Effective March 1, 2010, the SEC requires the board of directors to provide disclosures in proxy statements to stockholders that describe the board's involvement in risk oversight.

Especially, the recent financial crisis and natural disasters in Japan that crippled global production is leading to a renewed focus on how senior executives approach risk management, including the board's role in risk oversight. Companies exist to provide value for stakeholders, but face uncertainty in their attempts to grow stakeholder value. A challenge for management is to determine how much uncertainty to accept, and how to effectively deal with uncertainty and associated risks. Senior executives are working to strengthen risk oversight so that both management and the board are better informed about emerging risk exposures, particularly those impacting strategy.

THE UPDATED COSO MODEL FOR ENTERPRISE RISK MANAGEMENT – INTEGRATING WITH STRATEGY AND PERFORMANCE (2017)[1]

In 2004, the Committee of Sponsoring Organizations of the Treadway Commission (COSO) published a document entitled *Enterprise Risk Management (ERM)-Integrated Framework,* which gained general acceptance over the years as the gold standard organizations followed in the pursuance of managing risk. More recently, it became evident that not only have unexpected new risks emerged but their complexity has significantly increased. This change signaled a need on the part of

---

[1] The following discussion is a comprehensive overview and summary of the Committee of Sponsoring Organizations of the Treadway Committee's 2017 update of the COSO Model for Enterprise Risk Management of 2004: Association of International Certified Professional Accountants, *Enterprise Risk Management—Integrating with Strategy and Performance,* Committee of Sponsoring Organizations of the Treadway Committee, Executive Summary, pp.1-8, and Volume 1-110, June 2017.

boards of directors and managerial executives for an improved approach to managing risk in order to stay competitive and satisfy the increased demand for stakeholder confidence in the organization. In response to these considerations, COSO issued, what is termed an update to the 2004 integrated model, entitled *Enterprise Risk Management—Integrating with Strategy and Performance,* which was published in June 2017. A key improvement of the update over its predecessor document is the emphasis of integrating risk management practices with strategy setting and performance considerations in management practices. The update is essentially divided into two parts. The first part involves ERM concepts and ERM applications. The second part consists of the newly created five-part ERM framework (comprising five components and 20 underlying supporting principles) which emphasizes the importance of ERM in establishing an entity's strategy and provides the overriding guidance to be used throughout the organization. The improvements made by this update are summarized below:

- Emphasizes and clarifies the importance of using ERM when creating and deploying an entity's strategy.
- Emphasizes the function of governance and oversight in the ERM function.
- Emphasizes the importance of performance and ERM in setting performance targets. Underlying this emphasis is the user's understanding of the effect of risk on performance.
- Newly designed to accommodate current business entities by recognizing the existence of global operations and markets and by emphasizing the need to create tailored uniform approaches that can be utilized across different countries.
- Establishes new ways to achieve business objectives using risk to set those objectives.
- Establishes greater stakeholder transparency in the area of ERM reporting.
- Simplifies the design and implementation of ERM practices by all levels of management by clearly explaining ERM core definitions, framework components, and principles.
- Is sufficiently elastic to accommodate newly created technologies that may surface in the future as well as newly designed data metrics that are used in the decision-making process.

The emphasis of the 2017 update is the newly created five-part ERM framework. Therefore, this discussion will emphasize that framework and will incorporate the discussion of relevant ERM concepts and applications as part of this.

Components of the New ERM Framework

The following is an overview and summary of each of the components of the new ERM framework. Following each component is an enumeration of the principles underlying the essential concepts associated with each component. A detailed discussion of the supporting principles will follow this section:

1. Governance and Culture—The basis for all the other four components of the ERM framework is governance and culture. Governance has the responsibility of ensuring all members of the entity fully understand the importance of and are committed to the concepts and procedures of ERM. In addition, governance is responsible for establishing the ERM oversight responsibilities. The entity's culture is embodied and reflected in the organization's decision making process. Governance and Culture encompasses:

    a. Exercising Board Risk Oversight (Principle 1)

    b. Establishing Operating Structures (Principle 2)

    c. Defining the Desired Entity Culture (Principle 3)

    d. Demonstrating Commitment to Core Values (Principle 4)

    e. Attracting, Developing, and Retaining Capable Individuals (Principle 5)

2. Strategy and Objective-Setting—The process of setting strategy and business objectives for the entity is based on the integration of ERM into the entity's strategic plan. An entity establishes its risk tolerance in conjunction with strategy setting. The entity's predetermined objectives permit its strategy to be put into operation and guide the entity's day-to-day activities, practices, and actions. Strategy and Objective-Setting encompasses:

    a. Analyzing Business Context (Principle 6)

    b. Defining Risk Appetite (Principle 7)

    c. Evaluating Alternative Strategies (Principle 8)

    d. Formulating Business Objectives (Principle 9)

3. Performance—As part of its pursuit of achieving its strategy and accomplishing its business objectives, it will be necessary for the entity to identify and assess the risks that influence these goals. It also ranks its risks in accordance with their severity and the entity's risk tolerance. The organization then chooses the risk response that is needed and monitors the effect. This way the entity develops a portfolio of the amount of risk it is tolerating in pursuing its strategy and business objectives. Performance encompasses:

    a. Identifying the Entity's Risk (Principle 10)

    b. Assessing the Severity of the Risk (Principle 11)

    c. Prioritizing the Risks (Principle 12)

    d. Implementing Risk Responses (Principle 13)

    e. Developing a Portfolio View of Risk (Principle 14)

4. Review and Revision—An assessment is made of how well the entity's ERM practices and procedures have increased the value of the entity and will continue to do so as warranted changes are made to continue to augment value. Review and Revision encompasses:

    a. Assessing Substantial Change (Principle 15)

    b. Reviewing Risk and Performance (Principle 16)

    c. Pursuing Improvement in ERM (Principle 17)

5. Information, Communication, and Reporting—The entity ongoingly aggregates, processes, and analyzes information throughout the period from both internal and external sources and then distributes this information throughout the organization. This continual information update is then applied to all components of the ERM framework so that the entity can report on its risk, culture, and performance. Information, Communication, and Reporting encompasses:

   a. Leveraging Information and Technology (Principle 18)

   b. Communicating Risk Information (Principle 19)

   c. Reporting on Risk, Culture, and Performance (Principle 20)

It is the responsibility of the organization to provide its stakeholders with the assurance that it is able to manage risk at a desired tolerable amount. In order to do this, it is necessary to assess the entity's ERM practices that are in place and report their status to the stakeholders. During an assessment, the entity determines if:

- The components and their principles are present and functioning properly.

- The components of the ERM framework are working together in a cohesive integrated manner.

- The controls needed to put into effect the appropriate components and principles are present and functioning. (For a more comprehensive discussion of these controls *see* the Internal Control-Integrated framework following this discussion on the ERM framework.)

Principles of the ERM Framework Classified by Component

Principles Relating to Governance and Culture

Principle 1: The board of directors (BD) provides the oversight of the entity's strategy and executes its governance responsibilities to support management in achieving the entity's strategy and business objectives.

- Accountability and Responsibility—The BD is primarily responsible for the oversight of risk in the organization, including conducting reviews of the entity's ERM procedures. Although the BD has full responsibility for risk oversight, management is responsible for the organization functioning and day-to-day management. The BD generally also has a fiduciary responsibility to the organization's stakeholders.

- Skills, Experience, and Business Knowledge—As oversight in the area of risk is the primary responsibility of the BD, it is imperative that board members fully understand the entity's strategy, industry, and the pertinent issues and problems challenging it. The board must set standards for itself and periodically assess that it has the collective knowledge, experience, and skills to provide qualitative risk oversight.

- Independence—A board that is independent can successfully insure that the entity is functioning in the best interest of stakeholders. Independence insures that the directors are acting objectively without any conflict of interest or outside influences. Independence is assessed by evaluating the ability of each board member to act objectively.

- Suitability of ERM—It is imperative that board members fully understand how the ERM system works including how ERM management capabilities and procedures increase the entity's value. In order to do this, the BD must frequently communicate with management to ascertain that the ERM system is continually functioning and successfully creating value for the entity.

- Organizational Bias—Bias in decision making is a board reality. It may be due to dominant members of the board, a tendency of board members for risk taking or avoidance of risk, denial of contrary information, and other factors. The board must be cognizant of the existence of organizational bias and insure that it is being properly managed with respect to its ERM decisions.

Principle 2: The organization establishes operating structures in the pursuit of strategy and business objectives.

By definition, an operating structure is a description of the way an entity carries out its normal regular recurring operations. It is through the entity's operating structures that management incorporates and implements its risk management procedures and attempts to manage in conjunction with the entity's values.

- Operating Structure and Reporting Lines—In creating an operating structure, the entity must also design reporting lines to set up accountabilities for getting the job done. In creating an operating structure, the following should be considered:

  — The strategy and objectives of the business.

  — Risks associated with the entity's strategy and objectives—that is, tax exposure, concentration of entity's revenue in a few large customers, foreign exchanges issues, etc.

  — The type, size, and distribution of the entity's products.

  — The delegation of accountability and responsibility to various levels of the entity.

  — Any regulatory, financial, tax, and other reporting requirements.

  — The nature of reporting lines—that is, direct or indirect and communication flow.

- ERM Structures—In creating the operating structures of the entity, management must incorporate and implement ERM designs and procedures. Accordingly, information on risk associated with the entity's strategy must be gathered so that appropriate management can be executed. One way of gathering this information is to delegate the risk data aggregation of the entity to a committee whose members consist of executives of the company appointed by management who have the skill, experience, and knowledge in order to fully understand risk oversight responsibilities. In large organizations, with complex structures, there may be several committees performing this job with overlapping committee membership.

- Authority and Responsibilities—Generally, the BD requests management to design and implement practices that will result in the achievement of the entity's business strategy and objectives. In addition, as part of this process, management establishes the necessary authority accountabilities in the form of individuals, teams, divisions, and functions needed to support these strategies and business objectives. In establishing the key roles:

  — In general, those chosen for managerial roles are the ones who have the authority and responsibility to oversee and make the decisions needed to achieve the entity's strategies and objectives. The chief risk officer is the individual who is accountable for providing expertise and oversight for all ERM considerations.

  — Other individuals involved in ERM activities at various levels of the company should be those who clearly understand their own responsibilities as well as the entity's standards of conduct and objectives in relation to the entity's ERM practices.

- ERM and the Evolving Entity—As companies compete in the market place, they are constantly changing and evolving to improve and outperform their competition. Management expects the ERM system to be sufficiently elastic to accommodate these changes and successfully manage new risks that surface. For example, as more business is conducted on the internet, the business must adjust, new strategies must evolve, and new operating structures must be created. These changes create new risks that must be considered and accommodated commensurate to the changes, as technology becomes dominant for the institution. Management and its management of enterprise risk must be sufficiently innovative and flexible (evolving) to absorb these modifications.

Principle 3: The organization defines the desired behaviors that characterize the entity's desired culture.

- Culture and Desired Behaviors—The BD and management of an entity have the responsibility for defining and creating the entity's culture. They are also responsible for establishing the entity's core values, which guide the decisions being made and ensure that they are in accordance with stakeholder expectations. In order for the organization to appropriately manage risk in the course of achieving its strategy and objectives, it is imperative that company personnel accept and adhere to the company's culture. The factors responsible for determining an entity's culture include decision-making autonomy on the part of the entity's employees; the quality of interaction among employees and their managers, and among themselves; the hierarchical reward system in the company; and customer expectations. All these factors influence where the company lies on the culture/risk spectrum, ranging from being risk averse to risk aggressive. This spectrum is shown below:[2]

---

[2] COSO, *Enterprise Risk Management—Integrating with Strategy and Performance*, p. 33, June 2017.

Culture/Risk Spectrum

Risk Averse	Risk Neutral	Risk Aggressive

Under the general culture/risk umbrella of the entity, each operating unit and manager establishes its level of acceptable risk. The goal is that a shared understanding of the acceptable risk decision will ensure a successfully integrated acceptance of risk tolerance needed to achieve the overall entity's business strategy and objectives.

- Applying Judgment—Judgment significantly influences the culture of the entity and its management of risk. Judgment is needed to help consummate decisions especially when there is limited data or information available, when there are unexpected changes in the strategy and objectives of the organization, and during periods of disruptions and confusion when successful navigation through them is needed. In addition, judgment influences the extent of nurturing innovation and identifying opportunities for the entity. For example, culture fostering strict adherence to the entity's strategy with limited room for creative judgment will not be successful in establishing innovations. On the other hand, a culture that relies heavily on judgment in making decisions will seek new opportunities in line with its risk appetite and will be much more open in seeking new advances.

- Effect of Culture—The effect of organizational culture on risk is significant. It influences how risk is identified, assessed, and responded to. In addition,

  - The culture of an organization may influence strategy alternatives considered by the entity.

  - The nature and type of risks and opportunities are a function where the firm is situated on the culture/risk spectrum. Some firms are risk-averse while others thrive on the opportunities that risk-oriented strategies provide them.

  - An entity's position on risk will determine how resources should be utilized. A risk-averse company may choose to pay a high rent in a high traffic area of a city, while a more risk-aggressive entity may believe it is in the company's best interest to base itself in a less expensive area and hope that their superior product will generate a high sales volume.

  - Risk may determine the speed with which an entity reacts to strategy changes. A risk-aggressive firm may be more willing to sustain a strategy that has resulted in a prolonged downturn in business, while a risk averse entity would be much more willing to quickly abort that strategy and move on to something else.

- Aligning Core Value, Decision Making, and Behaviors—Strategies and business objectives frequently fail when an entity's behaviors and decisions do not align with its core values. The outcome of this is a loss of confidence from stakeholders. A lack of adherence to core values may also occur as a result of the following:

— The BD oversight of management is poor.

— The BD is poorly conveying expectations to the entity.

— Middle management is not on board with the entity's mission, vision, and strategy.

— Risk management is not being integrated into strategy-setting and planning.

— Incentives or pressures utilized in the company are not in alignment with the entity's core values.

— There is no escalation policy on important risk and performance matters.

— There are poor investigation and resolution responses to risk-taking.

— Management and other company personnel intentionally do not act in a way that is in conjunction with the company's values.

In a risk-aware culture, parameters of operations are openly known and risks that have been clearly established are followed by managers to achieve the entity's strategy and behaviors. The openness of this type of organization provides for a clear alignment of values, decision making, and behaviors.

• Shifting Culture—An entity's culture is not a stagnant concept. A cultural change might occur as a result of several factors such as new leadership, a change of ownership due to a merger, acquisition, or consolidation, and external and internal pressures.

Principle 4: The organization demonstrates a commitment to the entity's core values.

• Reflecting Core Values Throughout the Organization—Core values of an entity are its beliefs and ideals about what is acceptable or unacceptable. They may also be viewed as what is good or bad for the entity. A similar term "tone" refers to the manner in which these values are communicated across the company. Core values of an entity have a significant effect on all the actions and decisions made in the organization and accordingly play an important part in management of risk. In addition, the tone (i.e., communication of the values) should be communicated consistently from the top of the corporate hierarchy down so that the organization pursues its strategy and objectives in a strong, unified way.

• Embracing a Risk-Aware Culture—The entity can cultivate a culture that is risk-aware by pursuing the following activities:

— Encourage an active participative management style.

— Ensure there is full accountability for all actions taken.

— Maintain strong leadership—From the board down, make sure the entity's culture is risk-aware.

— Align risk-aware behaviors and decision making with performance. In addition, use incentives and compensation to ensure these are aligned and consistent with the core values of the entity.

— Embed risk in decision making—Whenever a decision is made, risk management should be considered.

— Encourage open discussions about the risks facing the organization and make sure management understands managing risk is imperative to the accomplishment of the entity's strategies and objectives.

— Make sure all personnel are risk aware. All personnel should be cognizant that managing risk an important part of their job.

• Enforcing Accountability—The BD relegates the responsibility for managing risk and establishing ERM practices and procedures to the chief executive officer (CEO). The CEO and management team are, in turn, responsible for all facets of accountability. Accountability is reinforced when:

— The BD and management communicate the enforcement of standards of conduct to all personnel.

— All employees fully understand that risk considerations should always be considered as part of the decisions they make.

— Employees align their individual performance targets with the entity's objectives.

— Management is highly responsive to deviations from company standards by taking corrective actions or even terminating the individual if the seriousness of the action merits it.

• Holding Itself Accountable—Generally, performance evaluations are hierarchical. That is, the BD does a self-evaluation to assess its own performance and identifies areas of improvement. It also evaluates the track record of the CEO who, in turn, evaluates the next level of management who, in turn, then evaluates the next lower level of management. At each personnel level, desired culture behaviors and values are evaluated and either appropriate rewards are applied or disciplinary action is taken.

• Keeping Communication Open and Free from Retribution—It is vital that management encourages a free and open discourse in the entity regarding risk and risk-taking expectations. Open discussion allows all personnel to work together to share risk information to ensure the current ERM practices and procedures are proper. Transparency should prevail. Information that is gathered is communicated to the relevant managerial level in the entity. Ultimately, this provides the BD with the data needed to gauge the efficacy of the current ERM program. Successful adjustments to excessive risk-taking or risk-aversion behavior or conduct are only possible in an entity that has an open and transparent work environment and channels of communication. Inherent in such an environment is the assumption that any form of retribution or retaliation against a company employee for being direct, honest, and truthful would be subject to harsh disciplinary action.

• Responding to Deviation in Core Values and Behaviors—Even in well-run companies that clearly demonstrate a commitment to their core values, crisis, failures, and scandals occur. The entity should make certain that personnel know that all unacceptable behavior will be appropriately and consistently addressed. An example from the updated COSO framework[3] clearly demonstrates this point. In the pharmaceutical industry, during the research and development (R&D) stage of bringing a drug to market, it is imperative that all side effects be identified so that an appropriate decision can be made regarding whether the drug being tested should be moved to production and released to the public. If the drug has not been thoroughly tested for dangerous side effects, individuals using the drug could die. Clearly, R&D failure would be a horrible violation of the desired conduct of the entity.

Principle 5: The organization is committed to building human capital in alignment with the strategy and business objectives of the entity.

- This is accomplished by:

  — Establishing and Evaluating Competence—Management must be cognizant of the competencies and skills needed to carry out the various business functions required by the business. These functions are hierarchically based. That is, the BD must be knowledgeable of the competencies required of the CEO, and the CEO must be familiar with the skills required of management and the heads of each division, operating unit, etc., who, in turn, must be familiar with all important functions in the company. Human resources assist in this function by aiding management in establishing job descriptions, roles and responsibilities; creating training programs; and creating evaluation standards of performance for managing risk.

  — Attracting, Developing, and Retaining Individuals—The attraction, development, and retention of employees are a function of several important considerations executed by human resources (HR). For example, HR should develop methods to seek out and attract individuals who have the talents and abilities commensurate to roles and functions established by the company. Training through classroom instruction, self-study, and on the job (training) should be established to enable hired individuals to develop and maintain the ERM competencies required for specific jobs and roles. In addition, mentorship responsibilities should be created in order to guide standards of competence, performance, skills, expertise, and parameters relating to personnel ERM functions. Performance evaluation standards developed by HR enables management to assess the achievement of the company's objectives and ERM competencies of employees. Finally, the creation of incentives by HR enables the company to encourage individuals to perform well and motivates them to seek advancement up the company hierarchy.

  — Rewarding Performance—Management and the BD have the responsibilities for creating incentives which reward performance. In order to establish a successful incentive program, it is necessary to enumerate

---

[3] COSO, *Enterprise Risk Management—Integrating with Strategy and Performance*, p.40, June 2017.

goals and standards of conduct upon which employees will be assessed for success. Promotions, salary increments, bonuses, and similar rewards should be based on the accomplishment and adherence by employees to these standards. Other more subtle non-monetary rewards which are equally effective include being given more responsibility, recognition, and visibility.

— Addressing Pressure—Pressure on employees is a natural outcome of individuals trying to satisfy strategy and business objectives. It either motivates employees or causes unwanted fears that goals will not be met. Excessive pressure frequently occurs when there are unrealistic performance goals and targets. It can also result from conflicting business objectives and changes in the entity's strategy, operating goals, etc. It is the job of the BD and management to ensure that in assigning responsibilities, the amount of associative pressure is realistic and does not cause counterproductive results.

— Preparing for Succession—To ensure the smooth ongoing transition of ERM practices and procedures, it is imperative that the BD and management have standing plans for succession of key executives. As part of this plan, all succession individuals should be appropriately coached, trained, and mentored so that they are able to step into their new roles if the circumstances require succession.

Principles Relating to Strategy and Objective-Setting

Principle 6: The organization must consider the potential effects of the business context on the entity's risk profile.

• Understanding the Entity's Business Context—Business context is defined as the trends and relationships that influence an entity's strategies and business objectives. Business contexts may be viewed as being:

— Dynamic—In this environment, the entity is faced with constant change resulting in the surfacing of new risks. For example, a company operating in a highly competitive technological environment where their products are constantly changing is facing constant obsolescence.

— Complex—This type of entity has many operating units around the world where each unit is faced with different governments, regulatory policies, taxation requirements, etc. (e.g., a multinational corporation).

— Unpredictable—In this environment, the entity is faced with unexpected, sudden change. For example, constant political upheaval or currency devaluation.

• External Environment and Stakeholders—The external environment and its stakeholders consist of anything outside the environment that has an effect on the entity's ability to achieve its strategy and objectives. For example, an external stakeholder may be a regulatory agency that has control over the entity or an investor who contributes capital to the company. An entity that clearly identifies and understands its external environment and stakeholders is in a good position to anticipate and adjust to any change that occurs.

The external environment influencing the entity generally consists of the following categories: political; economic; social; technological; legal; and environmental.

- Internal Environment and Stakeholders—The entity's internal environment relates to anything inside the business that influences the achievement of its strategy and goals. For example, internal stakeholders are the people and employees working inside the entity who directly influence it. The BD, management, and other employees are such individuals. The internal environment consists of the following categories: capital; people; process; and technology.

- The Business Context Affects the Entity's Risk Profile—In analyzing how the business context affects the company's risk profile, the company should review its past performance. That will enable the company to see what actions worked and which did not. In addition, current performance enables the entity to ascertain how current trends affect its risk profile. Also, by projecting the outcome of these considerations, the company can estimate where it believes it will be in the future.

Principle 7: The organization defines risk appetite in the context of creating, preserving, and realizing value.

- Determining Risk Appetite: The risk appetite of an entity is a function and reflection of the entity's culture. Some companies define their risk appetite in quantitative terms using metrics such as growth levels and returns while others define it in qualitative terms. Nonetheless, the main objective in seeking the optimum level of tolerable risk is to find the balance between risk and amount of opportunity to be gained. Unfortunately, the alignment of these two metrics is not always easy. An entity may use a variety of descriptors to define its risk appetite. These may include:

  — Strategic parameters, such as what products to pursue or avoid, the amount of capital expenditures to be made in a given year, merger and acquisition goals, etc.

  — Financial parameters, such as the expected return on assets or return on capital, target debt rating, target debt/equity ratio, target profit levels, etc.

  — Operating parameters, such as environmental requirements, safety targets, quality targets, etc. Other considerations in the determination of an entity's risk appetite is to analyze its (the entity's) risk profile, risk capacity, and ERM capability and maturity. A description of each of these concepts follows:

    - Risk profile indicates the amount of risk currently being sustained by the entity, as well as how it is distributed across the entity. This includes the different categories of risk currently facing the organization. New organizations clearly will not have an existing risk profile but may derive valuable information on risk from competitors in their industry.

- Risk capacity represents the maximum amount of risk that the entity can tolerate in pursuit of its business strategies and objectives. For example, if the entity's risk appetite exceeds its risk capacity, the entity could fail. If, on the other hand, risk capacity significantly exceeds its risk appetite, then opportunities which could add value for stakeholders that have not been undertaken would be lost.

- ERM capability and maturity conveys data on how well the entity is functioning. It is a measure of how well an entity is operating within its risk appetite. For example, a mature organization that has been in business for many years has better insights into what level of risk appetite it can successfully undertake without jeopardizing itself by taking on detrimental risk burdening projects. On the other hand, a less mature company does not have this experience and understanding and is lacking the capabilities needed to maximize its opportunities. Accordingly, it must be much more careful than the former in deciding whether to expand its risk appetite or contract from its current position.

- Communicating Risk Appetite—Risk appetite is articulated by management to all levels of the entity after being approved by the BD. This articulation is imperative because the decision makers of the entity must be fully cognizant of the range of risk that may be undertaken in order to achieve their goals and objectives.

The risk appetite of an entity may be conveyed in the context of:

— Specific objectives and strategies that align the entity's mission, vision, and core values.

— Business objective categories.

— Specific performance targets that must be met.

Risk appetite should naturally be integrated into how the organization operates and should guide the range of decisions that are made. In addition, management, with BD oversight, should constantly monitor operations and decisions being made at all levels to ensure that the entity's current level of risk appetite is in line with its mission, vision, and core values. These ongoing activities are all part of the entity's culture that supports and values enterprise risk management.

Principle 8: The organization evaluates alternative strategies and their potential impact on risk profile.

- Understanding the Implications of a Chosen Strategy—Clearly, the entity's chosen strategy must support its mission and vision, and must be in alignment with its core values and risk appetite. A strategy that is not so aligned may adversely affect the value of the entity and stakeholders. Therefore, it is imperative that in choosing a particular strategy, the company must carefully weigh its risks and opportunities so that maximum benefit is provided. To accomplish this, a risk profile is prepared for each strategy which in turn is used by management and the BD to help them decide which strategy is best. Because of the interdependency of two or more strategies, it might be necessary to analyze multiple strategies to choose the appropriate ones. In addition, management and the BD must be cognizant of the associated context, resources, and entity capabilities that will be required for each strategy. These items are sometimes called the supporting assumptions associated with the given strategy. These assumptions are an important part of the potential strategy and have a direct effect on its risk profile. Therefore, these assumptions must be thoroughly understood by the decision makers. In general, the greater the number of assumptions associated with a strategy, the greater the strategy's risk profile. Once management and the BD know the risk profile of each strategy, they can ascertain what resources of the entity will be required for execution. Resources that need to be used include working capital, technical expertise, and infrastructure utilization.

Popular techniques for analyzing and choosing alternative strategies include the following: modeling, valuation, revenue forecasting, scenario analysis, and SWOT analysis (SWOT is an acronym for strengths, weaknesses, opportunities, and threats). SWOT analysis evaluates each of these four elements of the strategy. (A description of each evaluative technique is not included in this writing).

- Aligning Strategy with Risk Appetite—A basic assumption in ERM is that the strategy selected by management and sanctioned by the BD is one that is aligned with the entity's risk appetite. In order to maximize value for the organization's stakeholders, there must be an equilibrium between the entity's strategy vehicle and the associative level of risk that can be sustained. If not, either a new strategy must be found or the level of risk appetite must be adjusted. For example, assume a retailer of mid-level-priced furniture aims to expand its business by opening new stores in neighborhoods whose demand for this product has potential but is not a certainty. If a market for its products in these neighborhoods can be established, it is believed that high returns might result. After further analysis, it is decided that some neighborhoods presented levels of risk that the BD was not willing to chance. To reduce the amount of risk to a sustainable level, it is decided that extensive marketing studies of the potential neighborhoods is be required to ensure that a high probability of success is likely.

Principle 9: The organization considers risk while establishing the business objectives at various levels that align and support strategy.

- Establishment of Business Objectives—To ensure attainable goals, it is required that an entity develop tangible business objectives that are well defined, measurable, and relevant to the company's mission. The following six illustrative objectives are listed in the updated ERM model[4]:

---

[4] COSO, *Enterprise Risk Management—Integrating with Strategy and Performance*, p.59, June 2017.

- Financial performance—Maintain profitable operations for all businesses.

- Customer satisfaction—Create customer service centers in convenient locations for the company's customers.

- Operational continuity—Successfully negotiate competitive labor contracts to sustain ongoing operations and retain employees.

- Compliance operations—Be in compliance with health and safety laws on the company's work locations.

- Energy efficiency—Perform business operations in an energy efficient environment.

- Become a leader in product innovation—Stay ongoingly competitive by frequently creating new innovative products and services.

Inherent in the establishment of the entity's objectives is that the objectives are aligned and support the entity's strategy so that the entity may successfully achieve its mission and vision. In addition, they must align with the entity's appetite for risk so that the creation of value for the organization's stakeholders is maximized.

- Tolerance—Tolerance is an operational concept linked to risk appetite. Tolerance is the range of acceptable outcomes for a given level of risk appetite for achieving a business objective. It focuses on objectives and performance. Tolerance conveys the variation in performance which is considered acceptable for the achievement of a business objective. In general, risk appetite is considered a broad-based concept while tolerance is precise and specific. It is usually expressed in measurable units and can be applied to all business objectives. Those objectives that are considered very important or necessary to satisfy an entity's strategy, mission or vision will frequently have a smaller range than objectives that are less important. Operating in a defined tolerance range enables management to know, with a high degree of confidence, that it is successfully achieving its business objective.

- Performance Measures and Established Tolerances—Performance measures are concrete measures that enable management to confirm that performance has fallen into an acceptable tolerance range. Performance measures may be either quantitative or qualitative. The following based on an example in the updated guide to ERM[5] illustrates these concepts.

---

[5] COSO, *Enterprise Risk Management—Integrating with Strategy and Performance*, p. 63, Example 7.11, June 2017.

Performance Measure	Business Objective	Target	Tolerance
Return on investment (ROI)	Maximize ROI for an asset manager	5% annual return on portfolio	3% to 7% annual return
On-line home delivery orders	Minimize time for on-line home	Delivery within 40 minutes	30 to 50 minute delivery time
Missed calls from a call center	Minimize missed call from a call center	2% of overall calls	1% to 5% of overall calls

Principles Relating to Performance

Principle 10: The organization must identify risk that impacts the performance of strategy and business objectives.

- It is imperative that the entity identify any new developing risks that challenge the achievement of its strategy and business objectives. The identification of new emerging risks generally occurs as a result of experiencing normal ongoing operations each day. In addition, the entity may participate in risk identification activities to confirm the completeness of the entity's risk inventory. A risk inventory is a listing of all the risks an entity faces. Management attempts to identify risks across all of the company's functions and levels as well as those associated with products, service offering, and functions to ensure that a comprehensive risk identification has been carried out.

- Approaches to Identifying Risk—The following is a brief enumeration of various approaches that may be used by an entity to identify risks. Some of these may already have been noted:

  — Through normal operating activities such as budgeting, business planning, performance reviews, discussions in the approval process for new products and designs, analysis of customer complaints, and related incidents.

  — Through the use of targeted questionnaires, facilitated workshops, and interviews.

  — Through the analysis of collected internal data on historical incidents and losses to analyze new, emerging, and changing risks.

  — Utilizing information from other organizations in the same industry (with their obvious permission) to ascertain potential risks.

  — Through cognitive computing, which enables entities to collect and analyze large volumes of data for the purpose of sensing and detecting future trends, and identifying new and emerging risks as well as changes to existing risks.

— Through data tracking of past risk-related events as a means of projecting future ones—Although data tracking is commonly used in risk assessments, it is also used to detect subtle interdependencies and predictive modeling. In addition, Third-party database service providers, which collect information in an industry or region on incidents and losses that have occurred (subscription based), may detect potential risk for an entity.

— Interview and survey solicitation—By canvassing large groups of people regarding past and potential adverse events through interviews and surveys, unexpected and unpredicted risks may be detected.

— Key indicators—These are quantitative or qualitative metrics that help identify any change to existing risk. For example, a significant and unexpected drop in the entity's current ratio clearly is indicative of an increased liquidity risk facing the company.

— Process analysis—This involves the preparation of a diagram of an entity's processes so that the interrelationship of its inputs, tasks, outputs, and responsibilities becomes evident. When the diagram is analyzed, risks can be identified and considered against business objectives.

— Workshops—This provides for an aggregation of individuals from different functions and levels of the entity Their collective knowledge can be analyzed for the purpose of developing an enumeration of risks relating to the entity's strategy or business objectives.

Principle 11: The organization must assess the severity of risk.

• Selecting Severity Measures—Risks are identified and aggregated in an inventory in order to better understand the relationship of each risk to the achievement of the entity's strategy and objectives. Risk assessment guides the determination of risk responses by the entity. The determination of the severity of the risks identified by the entity enables it to determine the amount of resources and organizational capabilities that will be needed to stabilize the entity's risk.

Management must determine the measures needed to assess the severity of risk. These measures may include:

— —The impact or effect of the risk—There may be a range of impacts, both positive or negative, relative to the entity's strategy or business objective.

— —Likelihood—This relates to the prospect of a risk occurring. Likelihood may be articulated in the following ways:

  • Qualitatively—that is, we believe the risk of a downturn in yearly revenue due to a competitor opening its doors only a half a mile away is not significant.

  • Quantitatively—that is, we believe the risk of a downturn in yearly revenue due to a competitor opening its doors only a half a mile away is less than 20%.

- Frequency—that is, we believe the risk of a downturn in yearly revenue due to a competitor opening its doors only a half a mile away is limited. As a result, we think our business volume will only insignificantly dip in two or three months in the next fiscal year compared to last year.

Management should consider the combination of both likelihood and impact when assessing a risk. In addition, it should be cognizant that risk may originate from multiple sources and result in diverse impacts. When this occurs, the root causes should be determined and evaluated.

- Assessment Approaches—Risk assessment approaches may be either quantitative, qualitative, or a combination of both.

  — Qualitative assessments—These techniques are used when it is not possible or cost effective to obtain needed data for quantification. Although they are effective, they are limited in being able to determine possible correlations or to derive cost-benefit analysis. They include, for example, surveys, workshops, and interviews.

  — Quantitative assessments—These methodologies are generally used in assessing complex activities that allow for mathematical precision. They include probabilistic and non-probabilistic models. Probabilistic models generate a range of risk-producing events and associative impacts with a likelihood of occurrence. This enables management to understand the effect of each risk factor and its impact and allows for the improved management of risk. Examples of probabilistic models include value at risk, cash flow at risk, and operational loss distributions. Non-probabilistic models use subjective assumptions, without quantification of likelihood, to appraise the impact of events on a business objective. Examples of this methodology include sensitivity analysis and scenario analysis.

- Inherent, Target, and Residual Risk Definitions—Risk assessment requires management to consider and evaluate inherent, target, and residual risk. These concepts are defined as follows:

  — *Inherent risk* is the risk to the entity without any actions being undertaken by management to modify its severity.

  — *Target residual risk* is the amount of risk that the organization is willing to undertake in achieving its strategy and objectives assuming that management will take or has taken necessary actions to modify the severity of the risk when necessary.

  — *Actual residual risk* is the risk that is left after management has taken actions to modify the risk. After management has taken appropriate actions to control the severity of the risk, actual residual risk should be less than or equal to the target residual risk. However, if it turns out that the actual risk is greater than the target risk, then management must undertake additional actions to further modify it to acceptable levels.

  — In evaluating current responses to risks, management may determine that certain actions are either unnecessary or redundant. The latter are those responses that had no measurable effect on the severity of risk and therefore should be removed so that the entity's resources may be better put to use.

- Triggers for Reassessment—Triggers that prompt a reassessment of the severity of a risk should be identified. Triggers may be precipitated by changes in risk appetite or changes in the business context such as an increase in customer complaints, a downturn in sales, or increased competition. The speed and/or frequency of the reassessment is a function of the severity of the risk and the frequency at which severity may change. For example, a risk reassessment relating to a threat to an entity's primary projected revenue flow due to new and unexpected competition would necessitate an immediate risk response. On the other hand, the response to customers' changing color tastes relating to one of the entity's products would be much slower and infrequent.

Principle 12: The organization prioritizes risks as a basis for selecting responses to risks.

- In order to maximize the benefits of resource allocation, management must prioritize their response to risks. That is, they must carefully evaluate the benefit of controlling one risk compared to another.

The prioritization process is a function of the application of the following criteria:

— Adaptability—This refers to the ability of the organization to adapt and appropriately respond to risks. For example, adapting to a change in risk severity due to a change in the entity's competitors' product line.

— Complexity—This refers to fully understanding the scope and nature of the interdependency of risks facing the entity in its quest to achieving success. If a company's objective is to be a technology leader and have outstanding customer service, the risks of product obsolescence and a resulting drop in sales are paramount.

— Velocity—This refers to the speed at which a risk affects an organization. For example, unexpected snow storms affecting the ability of the firm to satisfy its orders during the holiday season have high velocity.

— Persistence—This refers to how long a risk will have an impact on an organization. If a company's products cause the death of several customers, how long will it take for people, who abandoned the company after reading about this occurrence in the newspapers, to return to the company's customer base.

— Recovery—This refers to the ability of the firm to return to its functioning level after a disruption.

Prioritizing considers the severity of the risk relative to the entity's risk appetite. In addition, a company generally gives greater priority to those risks facing the company that equate to or exceed the company's risk appetite. Clearly, risk responses are a function of both its severity (i.e., likelihood and impact) and prioritization (e.g., adaptability, complexity, velocity, persistence, recovery).

Principle 13: The organization identifies and selects risk responses.

- When risks are identified, management must react by deciding and deploying an appropriate response. This determination is a function of the severity, prioritization, and business context associated with the risks. Responses to risks are categorized as follows:

  — Accept—In this scenario, no action is taken to modify the severity of the risk. The lack of action in this case is deemed acceptable because it is assumed in this context that the risk associated with achieving the entity's strategy and objectives are within the entity's risk appetite.

  — Avoid—In this case, management decides that there is no reasonable response that could be executed that would mitigate the risk to an acceptable level. Accordingly, action must be taken to eliminate the cause of the risk. For example, a company might decide not to divest itself of a division that initially was viewed as a good idea or not moving forward with a new product line that would result in head-to-head competition with an opponent.

  — Pursue—Here, management is aware of the increased risk that might occur by pursuing a given activity but decides that it is in its best interests to accept and absorb this risk so that the outcome may be achieved. For example, management may decide to move forward and expand into a new geographical area although it is aware that competition in this new geographical area may be fierce. In this case, management believes that the new risks the company may be facing in pursuing this performance activity will not exceed the company's tolerable risk level.

  — Reduce—In this scenario, management decides that it is necessary to take appropriate action to reduce the severity of the risk until it is brought into line with the company's risk appetite. For example, after the decision to introduce a new product into a new geographical area was made last year to stay competitive, it is apparent that the number of new products that were introduced must now be reduced because the market has become saturated and sales are slumping.

  — Share—In this response, action is taken to reduce the severity of the risk faced by the company as in the prior category (Reduce). However, it is done not by reduction but by shifting a portion of the risk to an outside entity. For example, shifting risk by purchasing insurance or undertaking outsourcing activities to reduce its own performance activity.

  — Revise the entity's business objective and/or strategy—If the prior risk responses are viewed as not being effective in managing a given risk, the entity may choose to revise its business objective and/or strategy given the level of risk that has been identified and the risk appetite of the entity.

- Selecting and Deploying Risk Responses—When deciding upon the risk response it will use, the following factors should be considered:

  — Business context—In deploying the appropriate risk response strategy, management should always consider the environment in which the company operates. This includes the industry, geography, regulatory environment, and the operating structure (i.e., component, operating segment, department, division, subsidiary, etc.).

  — Costs versus benefits—Costs and benefits must always be considered in selecting and deploying a risk response. In addition, they should be reasonable and appropriate to the severity and prioritization of the risk.

  — Obligations and expectations—The risk response should be acceptable to and not conflict with the vision and mission of the organization, the standards of the industry, and the stakeholders' expectations.

  — Risk Prioritization—The selection of a response should be based on its risk prioritization and the amount of resources that it requires.

  — Risk Appetite—Any choice of a risk response should always be consistent with the risk appetite of the organization.

  — Risk Severity—The choice of a risk response should reflect the nature of the risk as well as its size and scope.

  Once management executes a risk response, the internal controls (discussed in the following section of this book) of the organization ensure that it is carried out as intended.

Principle 14: The organization develops and evaluates a portfolio of risk.

- Understanding a Portfolio View of Risk—ERM allows an entity to evaluate its risk profile from an entity-wide perspective or portfolio perspective. In this perspective, management considers risk relating to each division, operating unit, or function. Each unit manager develops a composite assessment of risks that reflect the unit's risk profile relating to its business objective and tolerance. The portfolio perspective enables the BD and management to consider the type, severity, and interdependence of risks and determine how they may affect performance. The entity identifies the risks that are considered severe at the entity level. Management then evaluates whether the entity's risk profile is in alignment with its risk appetite.

- Developing a Portfolio View—In general, there are several ways that a portfolio view of risk may be developed. For example, in developing a view of risk, there are four levels in order of ascending integration, from minimal to maximum, that may be used. A brief description of these follow:

  — Minimal Integration – Risk View—This is sometimes called a risk-centric view. In this view, discreet risks are identified. The main focus in the category is the identification of the underlying risk, rather the entity's objective. For example, the entity might focus on and assess its risk of: low sales, poor customer experiences, product obsolescence, product recall, etc.

— Limited Integration – Risk Category View—This category organizes risks using categories of risks or related classification schemes. Risk categories may reflect the entity's operating structure, roles, or responsibilities. For example, operating departments will have the organizational responsibility for managing the risk of their respective responsibilities such as customer risk, compliance risk, operational risk, financial risk, etc.

— Partial Integration – Risk Profile View—This view applies a more integrated view relative to the prior classifications. For example, it might focus on business objectives and the risks related to achievement of those objectives. In addition, any dependencies that exist between business objectives are identified and analyzed. Examples of business objectives in this category include: minimizing losses and production inefficiencies, maintaining customer satisfaction, optimizing working capital, maintaining a leadership role in the innovation of new products, investing in quality technology, and improving the quality of the entity's credit portfolio.

— Full Integration – Portfolio View—This view focuses on the entity's strategy and entity objectives. In this category, the BD and management primarily focus on the achievement of the entity's strategy. Examples of the entity objectives view include: strengthening the balance sheet, enhancing operational excellence, and increasing market share. An example of a strategic view is to become an industry leader by augmenting qualitative customer service and product design.

Principles Relating to Review and Revision

Principle 15: The organization identifies and assesses changes that may substantially affect its strategy and business objectives.

Companies, during the course of their operations, may be faced with substantial changes beyond what was anticipated in the setting of their strategy and business objectives. These changes may result in new, unanticipated risks as well as having to change the basic strategy and assumptions which underpin the organization. Management must be aware of the occurrence of these changes and establish procedures for identifying them and establishing plans for adapting to the change. For example, a merger that requires the integration of the new company into the existing company could result in significant risks to ownership, changes to the entity's culture, and the way business is done day to day. Organizations must consider how these substantial changes will affect their ERM, strategy, and business objectives. In addition, companies must identify and be vigilant to substantial changes that may occur in the entity's internal environment and external environment. A short discussion of these considerations follows. It consists of examples of internal and external substantial changes that a company may face.

- Substantial Changes in Internal Environment:

   — Rapid growth—When there is rapid internal growth, many facets of the business are affected.

- Supervisors may not be able to acclimate to the higher levels of activity required such as increased personnel shifts, additional shifts that are now required, etc.

- A significant increase in the execution of transactions puts a strain on the entity's accounting and information system which may now face obsolescence risk and may need a major overhaul to accommodate the increased volume of activity.

- Risk oversight roles and responsibilities need to be modified and redefined due to organizational changes that are necessary.

- Resources may now be strained affecting current risk responses.

— Innovation—Whenever innovation is introduced into an entity, risk responses must be modified to accommodate the entity's new way of doing things.

- Training programs will be required to help employees accommodate the change.

- Access controls relating to the technology must be developed.

- ERM of the entity must be enhanced due to the innovation. Accordingly, risks, as well as risk responses, must now be adjusted.

— Substantial Changes to Leadership and Personnel—The introduction of new members to the management team will have a significant effect on the entity's ERM. New managers must acclimate to the entity's culture, philosophy, required performance, etc.

- Substantial Changes in External Environment—Changes in the regulatory and the economic environment can result in:

— Increased competition.

— Changes in operating requirements.

— Changes in the entity's risks.

— Decisions being made that are not aligned with the entity's risk appetite, thereby exposing it to new increased risk.

The entity must be able to identify substantial changes such as those described above and respond in a systematic and suitable way. Companies sometimes perform a "post mortem" review after the occurrence of substantial changes to ensure that the company responded appropriately to the change.

Principle 16: The organization reviews entity performance and considers risk.

- Over time, an entity may ascertain that it is not performing as efficiently as possible causing an unexpected level of increased risk. In addition, entity performance may be affected by risk which cannot be predicted or controlled completely. ERM practices attempt to control this risk as much as possible. Therefore, entities may want to periodically evaluate their ERM capabilities and practices. The purpose of performing this evaluation is to both ensure that the amount of risk facing the entity is at acceptable levels as well as determine the existence of incorrect assumptions, practices, and cultural considerations that may be causing an imbalance. As part of this investigation, the entity seeks answers to the following queries:

— Are we performing as efficiently as we should be and are we achieving our expected target levels?—Using accounting and financial metrics, variations from expected target levels are computed and their causes are investigated. The outcome may result in the modification of strategy, business objectives, and performance targets.

— What risks are influencing performance?—The evaluation allows the entity to confirm that the risks thought to exist are still present or ascertain whether new risks have emerged. In addition, a determination can be made whether risk levels fall within the entity's parameters for risk tolerance.

— Is the entity absorbing sufficient risk to ensure that targets are being met?—The evaluation may indicate that the cause of the failure to meet target levels is due to the entity not taking on sufficient risk to support the achievement of projected performance levels. In this case, the entity is operating below its capacity and resources are being wasted.

— Was the risk level estimated accurately?—The entity should make sure that risk was accurately estimated and if not, a reevaluation of the business context and assumptions underlying the risk determination must be undertaken. In addition, the entity should determine that any new information that has become available is being used to ensure accuracy.

• If the entity determines that its performance does not fall into a tolerable range, it may need to perform one or more of the following actions. The extent of corrective actions is a function of the magnitude of the performance deviation that has occurred, the importance of the business objective affected, and consideration of the cost/benefits associated with any modifications that may be made.

— Reevaluate the entity's business objectives.

— Review and consider revising its strategy.

— Review the entity's culture—Analyze the culture to ascertain whether the entity is tolerating enough risk to succeed or taking on too much risk with adverse outcomes.

— Revise target performance.

— Reassess risk severity.

— Review and revise how risks are prioritized in support of resource allocation.

— Revise risk responses to bring risk in line with target performance and risk profile.

— Consider revising the entity's risk appetite to ensure performance goals are satisfied. This may require review and approval of the BD.

Principle 17: The organization pursues improvement of enterprise risk management.

- Pursuing Improvement—Management should support a policy of ongoing improvement relating to ERM efficiency and usefulness at all levels of organization. Constantly changing environmental considerations and competition virtually ensure that ongoing evaluation of an entity's business practices will yield improvement. Improvements of efficiencies and usefulness may occur in any of the following areas:

  — New technology—Efficiency is clearly improved by new technology. For example, using new data mining technology would enable a company to accurately and quickly ascertain where efficiencies could be improved.

  — Historical Deficiencies—Reviewing and analyzing past performances helps an entity ascertain the cause of past failures in its ERM system enabling it to achieve improvement solutions.

  — Organizational change—The need for organizational change to an entity's ERM system frequently surfaces when the company seeks and pursues continual improvement on a regular and ongoing basis. For example, a company may decide to make a change in its ERM governance structure because of the determination of lackluster performance of new products introduced in prior periods.

  — Risk appetite—Reviewing entity performance enables an entity to discover the factors influencing its risk appetite and provides insight on how that appetite may be refined.

  — Risk categories—Through the pursuit of continual review and evaluation of its ERM system, an entity is ongoingly updated on new risk considerations because of changes in its business context. For example, assume the introduction into the food production business due to a recent acquisition creates a food toxication risk that a firm never had before. By putting this risk on the radar, the firm's risk categories are augmented to accommodate this new risk so that an appropriate response can be prepared.

  — Peer comparisons—Constant monitoring of an entity's competitors' operating results enables it to gain assurances that it is operating within acceptable industry parameters. For example, ongoing peer comparisons ensures that an organization is maintaining its market share, reputation, and status as one of the leaders in its industry.

  — Rate of change—An entity's ERM system should consider the frequency of change in the environment in which the company operates (i.e., in a high-tech environment, an entity must be more sensitive to new evolving risks, opportunities, and need for increased efficiencies, etc, as opposed to one where infrequent change occurs).

— Communications—Ongoing performance assessments revealing less-than-excellent results may signal, among other considerations, that the firm's communication system has broken down requiring a speedy and immediate response. For example, a firm may discover that its e-mails, messages, and blogs are not being read requiring it to create new ways of getting its directives and initiatives through to employees.

Principles Relating to Information, Communication, and Reporting

Principle 18: The organization leverages its information and technology systems to support enterprise risk management.

- Putting Relevant Information to Use—Relevant information is information that assists the organization in maintaining a competitive position by anticipating circumstances that may hinder it from achieving its strategy and business objectives. Risk information enables the entity to prepare a current and sensitive, ever-evolving, risk profile. Information supports ERM practices in any of the following ways:

  — Governance and culture-related practices—The organization may need information on the standards of conduct and professionalism that its clients and the public expect of it. For example, the industry in which the entity operates may have a code of behavior or ethics that must be adhered to in order for business to take place. It is imperative that the employees of the company clearly understand what is expected of them. Employee meetings and training programs can be used to reinforce this information.

  — Strategy- and objectives-related practices—The organization needs information regarding stakeholders' expectation of risk management. For example, an entity's investors and customers may articulate these expectations through analyst calls, blog postings, contracts, etc., which provide the entity with information regarding the type and amount of risk it is willing to accept.

  — Performance-related practices—An entity needs current and up-to-date information on its competitors so that it may appropriately adjust the amount of risk it must absorb to sustain or increase its market share of business. For example, relevant information in this area consists of knowing about competitors' new marketing or new pricing programs that have been or will soon be introduced by them.

  — Review and revision-related practices—New trends in ERM are constantly surfacing. Companies need information related to these changes in order to make the appropriate changes in their ERM programs to maintain their competitive edge. Information such as this may be obtained by having representation at ERM conferences and following industry blogs relating to such information.

- Managing Data—In order to support risk-oriented decisions, it is important that data be well managed. This requires that the data quality be preserved while allowing different technologies to exchange and use it. Effective data management considers the following three factors:

— Data and information governance—This refers to delivering high quality, standardized, timely, verifiable, and secure data to end users. It is also concerned with the standardization of data architecture (see below), authorized standards, assigned accountability, and the maintenance of data quality. In addition, it is concerned with defining clear roles and responsibilities for employees in the data and information risk area.

— Processes and controls—Refers to reinforcing the reliability of data and the execution of needed corrections. It is also concerned with the identification of data consistency, redundancy, availability, and accuracy in addition to preventing damaging and detrimental effects from occurring.

— Data management architecture—Refers to the design of technology concerned with how data is stored, arranged, integrated, put to use in information systems, and used in an entity. Businesses establish standards and provide rules dictating the structuring of information so that it may be reliably read, sorted, indexed, retrieved, and utilized by internal and external stakeholders.

Principle 19: The organization uses communication channels to support enterprise risk management.

- Communicating with Stakeholders
  — There are several channels available to the entity which may be used for communicating risk data and information to stakeholders. Stakeholders may be internal and external.
  — With respect to internal stakeholders, management must use communication channels to articulate the entity's strategy and business objectives to its employees at all levels of the entity so that everyone understands their individual roles. These channels enable management to communicate the:
    - Relevance, importance, and value of enterprise risk management.
    - Desired behaviors, characteristics and core values that define the culture of the entity.
    - Strategy and business objectives of the entity.
    - Entity's risk appetite and risk tolerance.
    - Expectations of management and personnel in relation to enterprise risk and performance management.
    - Expectations of the entity on important matters relating to ERM, including the existence of weaknesses, deterioration, and non-compliance.
  — With respect to external stakeholders and other external parties, management uses communication channels to communicate information relating to the entity's strategy, business objectives, and performance. In addition, the entity's ERM strategy and steps taken by management to

achieve it should be vigorously communicated. This external communication frequently takes the form of quarterly analyst meetings.

— An entity with fluid communication channels may also be on the receiving side of important information from external stakeholders. For example, information may come from e-mail, hotlines to the entity, public forums, blogs, and similar channels.

- Communicating with the Board

  — Clear and direct communication with the BD and management is imperative if the entity is to achieve its strategy and business objectives. Entities should scrutinize their governance structure to make sure that responsibilities are clearly defined at the BD and managerial levels and that there are well-defined lines of communication that promote discussion.

  — To maximize communication, it is important that the BD and management both fully understand risk and its relationship to the achievement of the entity's strategy and business objectives. Frequently, BD members will use on-site visits as a communication channel with management and other members of the entity to pursue this goal.

  — Risk appetite is a topic of frequent discussion between the BD members and management. Related matters of discussion include the risks affecting the entity's strategy, risk appetite and profile, and the overall effectiveness of the entity's ERM program.

  — It is the responsibility of management to provide all information to the BD that will enable the latter to satisfy its oversight responsibilities. The following are some useful approaches for accomplishing this objective:

    • Provide information on risks determined by the entity's strategy and business objectives.

    • Aggregate and align information at the level that is consistent with the BD oversight responsibilities and that which the BD has defined or signaled as being important and necessary.

    • Make sure that reports filed with the BD on risk have the entity's risk profile aligned with its risk appetite statement. In addition, reported risk information should be in line with the entity's risk tolerances.

    • Provide the BD with data where the entity's current performance levels are approaching tolerance levels of performance variation and indicate to the BD what steps management plans to take to control performance.

    • Provide the BD with a longitudinal analysis of risk exposure, including historical data, trends, and projections into the future based on the entity's current position.

    • Provide the BD with appropriate risk information at a frequency that is consistent with its projected risk evolution and severity.

    • To maintain consistent and structured risk presentations, use standardized templates.

— The BD should nurture a climate of openness and comfortability such that management feels sufficiently at ease to communicate emerging risks with the BD even though no risk response has yet been prepared. This ensures that the BD will obtain timely information about emerging risk so that a response may be prepared before the risk has evolved into a force that could present problems for the entity.

- Methods of Communication—There are a wide range of approaches that can be used to communicate information throughout all levels of the entity. Communication vehicles should be periodically evaluated and updated to ensure they are working. The following is an enumeration of some commonly used forms:

  — Electronic messages: e-mails, text messages, instant messaging, and social media.

  — External/third party materials: industry, trade, and professional journals, internal and external indexes, peer company websites, media reports, etc.

  — Public events: industry and technical conferences, town hall meetings, and roadshows.

  — Training programs and seminars: online and live training, webcasts, workshops, and other video forms.

  — Written internal documents: questionnaires, surveys, FAQs, policies and procedures, briefing documents, and dashboards.

  — Informal/verbal communications: meetings and one-on-one discussions.

  — Whistle-blower hotlines and related direct communication devices.

Principle 20: The organization reports on risk, culture, and performance at multiple levels and across the entity.

- Identify Report Users and Their Roles—Reporting to entity personnel occurs at all managerial levels of the enterprise. Although reports support the BD and management in their decision-making process, common sense and good judgment should always prevail as well in the pursuit and achievement of the entity's business objectives. Clearly, reporting requirements are a function of the needs of the user of the report. Report users may include the following:

  — The BD and management who have entity governance and oversight responsibilities.

  — Risk owners who are responsible and accountable for the management of identified risks.

  — Assurance providers who require insight into the entity's performance and the effectiveness of its risk responses.

— External stakeholders (e.g., rating agencies, regulators, community groups, and others).

— Other parties that require a report relating to the entity's risk so that they may satisfy their role.

- Clearly, each report user will require different levels of risk detail and performance information in order to satisfy his or her responsibilities to the entity.

- Reporting Attribute—Reporting information may consist of the following attributes. Reports may be:

— Quantitative.

— Qualitative.

— A combination of both of the above.

— Presented in a simple or complex way, or may be anywhere in between.

- Types of Reports—Risk reporting may include any of the following forms:

— Portfolio view of risk—This is an outline of the severity of risks that affects the entity's ability to achieve its strategy and business objectives (entity level). It emphasizes the greatest risks facing the entity, interdependencies between specific risks, and opportunities. This type of report generally is submitted to the BD and upper management levels.

— Profile view of risk—This report also outlines the severity of risks and in this sense is similar to the portfolio view. However, this report focuses on specific levels within the entity. For example, it is concerned with the risk profile of a division, department, or operating unit of the entity and is specifically designed for the management of those areas.

— Analysis of root causes—This report enables users to understand the underlying assumptions and changes underpinning the portfolio and profile views of risk.

— Sensitivity analysis—This report measures the sensitivity of changes in key assumptions supporting the entity's strategy and the potential effect on its strategy and business objectives.

— Analysis of new, emerging, and changing risks—This report anticipates and provides a forward-looking view regarding changes to the entity's risk inventory, its effect on resource requirements and their allocation, and expected future performance levels of the entity.

— Key performance indicators and measures—This report summarizes the risk tolerance of the entity and indicates the potential risk to a strategy or to a business objective.

— Trend analysis—This report indicates movements and changes in the portfolio view risk, risk profile, and performance of the entity.

— Disclosure of incidents, breaches, and losses—This report summarizes and provides insight into the effectiveness of the entity's responses to the aforementioned risks.

— Tracking ERM plans and initiatives—This report summarizes the plan and initiatives in establishing and maintaining ERM practices.

In addition, it is important to note that analysis, comments, and observations made by specialists such as compliance, legal, and technology experts of the firm commonly supplement risk reports.

- Reporting Risk to the Board—Reporting to the BD consists of the following considerations:

  — Reports to the BD include both formal and informal information sharing.

    - Formal reporting when the BD considers, for example, risks to executing strategy, reviewing risk appetite, or overseeing ERM practices that are being used by the entity, and

    - Informal discussions with management about the possibility of a given strategy and the implications of alternatives using risk profiles and other analyses as support.

  — Reports to the BD are considered the highest level of reporting and include the entity's portfolio view of risk.

  — All reports to the BD should focus on the link between the entity's strategy, business objectives, risk, and performance.

- Reporting on Culture—An entity's culture derives from the behavior and attitudes of its employees. Reporting on culture may be found in:

  — Analytics of cultural trends.

  — Benchmarking to other entities and standards.

  — Compensation schemes and its potential influence on decision making.

  — "Lessons learned" analysis.

  — Surveys of risk attitudes and risk awareness.

- Key Indicators—Key indicators are used to predict the emergence of a risk. They have the following characteristics:

  — They can be qualitative but are usually quantitative.

  — They are reported to the levels of the organization that are in the best position to manage the onset of a risk.

  — They should be reported together with key performance indicators to show and support the interrelationship between performance and risk.

  — They demonstrate a proactive approach to performance management.

  — Key indicators and key performance indicators can be expressed in a single measure.

  — Key indicators are reported along with corresponding targets and acceptable variations so decisions relating to performance may be made.

THE COSO MODEL FOR INTERNAL CONTROL[6]

Enterprise risk management is a much broader concept than internal control. ERM is concerned with issues such as strategic planning, objective setting, and the articulation and monitoring of the entity's risk appetite. Internal control is concerned with providing assurance that established objectives are, in fact, being achieved. Thus, internal control is an integral part of ERM.

Internal control is defined by COSO as a process effected by the board, management, and other personnel that is designed to provide reasonable assurance regarding the achievement of objectives relating to operations, reporting, and compliance. Internal control supports the organization in achieving these objectives through the following five components:

1. *Control environment.* The standards, processes, and structures that enable the entity to achieve internal control throughout the organization. The board of directors and senior management set the tone and importance of internal control including expected standards of conduct.

2. *Risk assessment.* The processes of identifying and analyzing risks that are associated with the entity's objectives (including their evaluation) so that they may be managed to ensure they fall within the parameters of acceptability (relative to established risk tolerances).

3. *Control activities.* The policies and procedures established by management to reduce the risks associated with the achievement of the entity's objectives. These policies and procedures are carried out throughout the entity and in all of its activities.

4. *Information and communication.* All of the information and communication data that flows throughout all levels of the company to support its internal control. This flow occurs among employees inside the company (flowing up, down, and across the entity) as well as to outside groups such as investors, customers, creditors, and governmental agencies.

5. *Monitoring activities.* Those evaluative procedures that the entity does to ensure that the entity's internal control system is operating in accordance with its design. The findings of the monitoring process are then compared to criteria established by management, the board of directors, regulatory bodies, and standard-setting bodies with all resulting deficiencies communicated to management and the board.

The relationship between the aforementioned components of internal control, the entity's objectives (including operations, reporting, and compliance) and its structure (entity level, division, operating units, and function) are shown as a matrix in the form of a cube in Exhibit 34-1, "COSO Internal Control Framework." The five components of internal control are enumerated as rows, the three categories of objectives appear as columns, and the structure of the entity is depicted by the side dimension of the cube. Thus, a comprehensive integrative relationship exists

---

[6] Committee of Sponsoring Organizations of the Treadway Commission, COSO Internal Control Framework, May 2013.

between what an entity is striving to achieve (its objectives), the five internal control components (what must be done to achieve these objectives) and the various parts and activities of the entity.

Exhibit 34-1: COSO Internal Control Framework

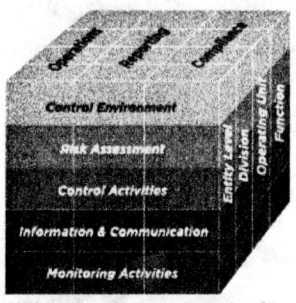

©2013, Committee of Sponsoring Organizations of the
Treadway Commission (COSO). Used by permission.

COSO INTERNAL CONTROL PRINCIPLES

The Sarbanes-Oxley Act Rule 404 requires public companies to publish information in their annual reports concerning the scope and adequacy of the internal control structure, the procedures for financial reporting, and an assessment of the effectiveness of such internal controls and procedures. In addition, the company's external auditors are required, in the same report, to attest to and report on the assessment and effectiveness of the internal control structure and procedures for financial reporting. In the past, most companies used COSO's original 1992 model in evaluating and determining the efficacy of their internal control. However, in May 2013, this framework was updated. Although the new framework maintained the original components of internal control, the new 2013 framework adopts an explicitly stated principles-based approach to internal control.

An enumeration of the 17 newly adopted COSO internal control principles categorized by the five internal control components from which they are derived are shown below.[7] Because the principles were developed directly from the five components, effective internal control can be obtained by applying all of the principles:

1. *Control Environment*

    a. The organization, including the board, management, and other personnel demonstrates a commitment to ethics and integrity.

    b. The board of directors is independent from management and, therefore, is able to exercise oversight in the development and performance of internal control.

---

[7] Internal Control—Integrated Framework—Executive Summary, The Committee of Sponsoring Organizations of the Treadway Commission, May 2013, pp.6-7.

    c. In pursuit of the entity's objectives, management with the oversight of the board, establishes structures, reporting lines, and appropriate authorities.

    d. The organization is committed to attract, develop, and retain competent individuals in pursuit of their objectives.

    e. In pursuit of the entity's objectives, the organization holds individuals accountable for their internal control responsibilities.

2. *Risk Assessment*

    a. Objectives of the entity are articulated with sufficient clarity to enable the identification and assessment of related risks.

    b. The identification of risks and their analysis related to the achievement of the entity's objectives enables the entity to determine how to manage those risks.

    c. In assessing risk in the achievement of its objectives, the organization considers the potential for fraud.

    d. The organization continually identifies and assesses all changes that might have a significant impact on its internal control.

3. *Control Activities*

    a. Control activities are chosen and developed that contribute to the mitigation of risks to acceptable levels.

    b. General control activities are chosen and developed over technology to support the achievement of the entity's objectives.

    c. Control activities are utilized through policies that establish what is expected as well as procedures that put policies into action.

4. *Information and Communication*

    a. The organization obtains, generates, and uses relevant, quality information to support its internal control.

    b. The entity internally communicates information, including objectives and responsibilities for internal control, that supports the internal control function.

    c. External parties are communicated with regarding the functioning of internal control.

5. *Monitoring Activities*

    a. The organization chooses, develops, and performs ongoing and/or separate evaluations to determine whether all the components of its internal control are functioning.

    b. If deficiencies are found, the organization evaluates and communicates them in a timely manner to senior management, the board of directors, and other parties who are responsible for taking corrective action as deemed appropriate.

CONTINGENCY PLANNING

An understanding of risk is essential in crisis management. Once a range of possible future crises has been established, *contingency plans* such as *continuity* or *recovery plans* can be put in place. Employees must be instructed on what to do in such cases. Test runs should be practiced, and contingency plans must be updated periodically to incorporate new technologies, changing staff, and new areas of business activity. Areas of risk must be identified, and corrective action must be taken to reduce those risks. Unusually high risk will not only have negative effects on earnings but may also place in question the continuity of the operation.

Models and quantitative approaches including actuarial techniques may be used to appraise potential catastrophic losses, product/service liability, intellectual property losses, and business interruption. Probability distributions of expected losses should be arrived at based on the model or quantitative technique used.

CHAPTER 35

REENGINEERING AND OUTSOURCING THE BUSINESS

CONTENTS

Reengineering includes downsizing and restructuring. It should be properly balanced. Outsourcing is contracting out production or service functions performed by the company to save on costs or to establish efficiencies. The financial manager must identify problems within the organization and recommend solutions. The financial manager must therefore understand what reengineering and outsourcing are about, how they affect the business, and how they may be implemented correctly. The financial manager needs to analyze, evaluate, offer suggestions, and comment on the company's existing or possible efforts to reengineer, downsize, restructure, and outsource the business.

REENGINEERING

A strategy is the implementation of a company's plans and tactics. A company may downsize or right-size to its "core" to create value. Reengineering is defined as a multidisciplinary approach to making fundamental changes in how operations, activities, functions, and procedures are conducted within a business. The objective of such change is to improve performance, productivity, and profitability. Reengineering should be undertaken if the benefit exceeds the cost of doing so, considering money and time. There should be a "road map" of the steps in the reengineering process. Reengineering may be done for the company as a whole, for one or more business units, or for particular geographic locations. There is a risk in reengineering of making not enough or too much change. For reengineering to succeed, the following should be present: employee understanding and cooperation, good project planning and management, timely assessment, benchmarks, and realistic expectations. Reengineering may take different forms of approach, including business process redesign (redesigning processes to achieve efficiencies and enhance service quality) and process innovation (making fundamental changes to improve the importance of processes). Reengineering attempts to effect continual improvement in business procedures.

In reengineering, the focus should be on the current and potential customer and then on corporate structure and processes designed accordingly—in other words, reengineering from the outside in. Managers must monitor and track the current and emerging satisfaction needs of customers and formulate the products and services they demand. New product innovation and creativity may be required. Reengineering must create "real value" for the customer. In so doing, consider whether the current product/service line helps in keeping present customers and expanding the customer base.

Objectives for cost reduction should be established, such as time for each job (task, operation, or activity), expected maintenance, and compatibility.

Employees must understand the why of reengineering so their support, contribution, and continued morale may be obtained. Cultural differences have to be taken into account. Disproportionate downsizing is a mistake. The company must be restructured logically and practically. Proper planning is required to avoid any surprises.

Reengineering may aid in developing new products and/or services, improving product distribution, and achieving growth. A successful strategy can include joint ventures and franchising. The purposes of reengineering include:

- Cost control and reduction (e.g., employee costs).
- Revenue, profit, and rate of return maximization.
- Growth and capacity.
- Reduction in risk.
- Appreciation in stock and bond price.
- Improvement in bond rating.
- Lowering the cost of financing.
- Inventory reduction.
- Improved market share.
- Remaining competitive.
- Reduction in headcount.
- Change in corporate culture.
- Additional flexibility.
- Spinoff of a segment or operation.
- Improved quality.
- Improved integration.
- Streamlining production and distribution.
- Staying current with the latest technology.
- Improved productivity.
- Improved interaction and communication.
- Improved product delivery and service.
- Change in the product/service mix.

In reengineering, consideration should be given to the cost and time of doing so, new ideas, developing products and services, managing operations and projects, portfolio management, retraining, acquisitions and mergers, joint ventures, automation, amount of restructuring needed, change to equipment, employee training, inspection requirements, infrastructure, risk profile, whether fundamental or incremental change is needed, reassignment (if any) of displaced employees, and legal and contractual provisions and limitations.

The right resources must be at the right places at the right time. Processes may be redesigned to improve service quality and promote efficiencies. Continuous improvement in processes and procedures, job descriptions, and workflow mandate commitment and follow through. However, be careful not to make inappropriate or incorrect changes to the system or process. The effect of current changes on the future must be taken into account. A manager does not want to make a change that will have an immediate benefit but will have a long-term negative effect. An example is laying off experienced supervisors who will be needed to train employees when business picks up in the future. Questions to be answered in reengineering follow:

- Should the reengineering effort be centralized or decentralized? If decentralized, how will integration be accomplished?

- Where does reengineering begin and end?

- What expectations are there to be achieved?

- What is the role of technology in the reengineering effort?

- What are the logistics throughout the project's life?

- What effect do reengineering efforts have on the environmental program of the business?

- How much value does the reengineering plan achieve?

- What uncertainties and risks does reengineering have and what steps have been undertaken to reduce such risks? The risks associated with reengineering include financial, technological, operational, and political.

- What legal issues and contract commitments are raised because of the reengineering program?

- Will outside consultants be involved? If so, to what extent?

- When and how will periodic reviews (reports) take place?

- Is reengineering proceeding as scheduled? If not, what is the problem and how may it be rectified?

- Who will be assigned to the reengineering effort, and why? What are their qualifications and time commitment?

Before full-scale reengineering takes place at the entire company, a pilot program and prototyping should be conducted to identify problems, learn from mistakes, and formulate sound strategies and approaches based on experience. By developing solutions to expected problems before full-scale implementation, the company may save in cost and time as well as reduce risks. It is best to complete one reengineering project before proceeding to the next, because the manager becomes more focused and learns from experience.

Scenario analysis should be undertaken, looking at high, low, and average situations. Probabilities, weights, and rankings may be assigned to alternative scenario situations as part of the evaluative process. There is a link between scenario planning and business reengineering. Scenario analysis considers uncertainties, range of possibilities (outcomes), what is critical and what is not, controllable and uncontrollable factors, the effect on other areas of implementing a strategy in one area, contingent possibilities (a course of action is valuable only in particular scenario settings). Scenario analysis considers advisable steps to take now or in the future, or if a particular change in circumstance occurs. It is similar to a simulation to determine what will happen in the "real world." "Red flags" should be recognized and corrective action taken. What are the positive and negative outcomes from implementing a particular procedure or strategy? Scenario analysis assists in reducing risk and focusing on reengineering efforts. The scenario program provides "visions" as to the future. Its results suggest what activities should be emphasized or deemphasized, and what actions should be eliminated. Scenario analysis looks at the alternative possibilities available and aids in timely implementation. A priority ranking of alternatives may be established.

Reengineering in the plant may take the form of automating operations, updating manufacturing approaches, and accomplishing greater flexibility. It may involve reorganizing the human resource function to achieve economies and eliminate duplication. Internal organizational processes and product/service deliveries may be redesigned.

One must be careful that reengineering does not result in "dumb-sizing," whereby the entity's long-term financial position and operating results are adversely impacted. Does the reengineering program lay off experienced personnel, cut vital services, increase risk, result in legal liability, cause conflicts with vendors or customers, result in worker mistrust, cause injuries or malfunctioning of equipment, or cause other negative aspects that outweigh any benefits achieved? The authors are aware of instances when in fact a reengineering program that was improperly administered was counterproductive.

The reengineering team should consist of those who are representative of those to be affected within the department by the ultimate outcome of the proposed reengineering. The group should be a cross section of individuals within the company. In other words, there should be organizational diversity. Determine who is responsible for what and how, and how often performance will be measured. If individuals are trying to sabotage the reengineering effort, take necessary steps to remove the roadblock, such as dismissing uncooperative employees.

OUTSOURCING

A corporate policy must be established regarding outsourcing. Outsourcing is contracting to others work that was formerly done within the company. It includes buying goods and services from vendors. As a general rule, outsourcing is more appropriate for "core" activities than "noncore" operations. Companies more suitable for outsourcing are those that are decentralized, are engaged in restructuring (e.g., downsizing), and are out-of-date.

There are many outsourcing service providers in areas such as finance, administration, engineering, manufacturing, buying, human resources, customer service, real estate management, computer systems, marketing and sales, investment management, maintenance, product procurement, distribution (e.g., shipping) and logistics, technology, and transportation. For example, information technology services are provided by Integrated Systems Solutions of White Plains, NY. Xerox Corporation offers many business services related to office work and duplication functions.

Before outsourcing, consideration should be given to whether it makes sense in light of expectations, company objectives and needs, business plans, major sources of revenue, cost (including conversion costs), risk (including business uncertainties), contract period, legal liability, availability, security, confidentiality, time constraints (including time to implement and schedule), capacity limitations, employee expertise and proficiency, employee morale, time concerns, nature of item (e.g., critical importance), compatibility, corporate culture, degree of control sought, innovation and creativity, logistics, and cost of redeployment and relocation. A company may be able to outsource an aspect of its operations for less than it costs to train and manage employees to conduct the same function within the business. If a function is "mission critical," it probably should not be outsourced because management would want to retain control over it. An activity that gives the company a significant competitive advantage (differentiation) should most likely stay within the company.

Outsourcing allows a business to be more efficient and effective, engage in subcontracting legacy systems, reduce costs (e.g., staff), reduce risk, streamline and simplify operations, improve quality, focus on core activities and competencies, free up capital and human resources, improve existing processes, improve delivery of activities, generate efficiencies and effectiveness, enhance flexibility, obtain a competitive advantage, redeploy staff and assets, achieve economies, enhance productivity, convert fixed costs to variable costs, and obtain improved up-to-date technology.

In selecting an outsourcing vendor, consider reputation, contacts, references, reliability, experience, specialty and focus, fees, flexibility, stability, expertise (specialized skills), cost, quality of service, creativity and innovation, upgrade potential, communications, commitment, contract provisions and restrictions (e.g., penalty and cancellation clauses), and "fit."

Ask the outsource vendor for a "trial period" to see how things are going before entering into a regular contract. However, avoid long-term contracts, especially those that are rigid in their terms. You want flexibility and do not want to be locked in for the long term. We recommend renewable, short-term contracts. The contract should be updated as the environment and circumstances change.

Insist that outsourcing contracts contain provisions regarding performance expectations (e.g., service-level goals) and measurement guidelines. Undertake periodic performance appraisals. Customer satisfaction with the outsourcer's services is crucial, so surveys should be conducted periodically.

INSOURCING

Insourcing is the self-manufacture of goods or services. Instead of buying the items from outside, the company produces the product or renders the service in an attempt to lower costs, improve quality, hasten availability, and be less reliant on outsiders. The costs and benefits of insourcing must be carefully evaluated.

CHAPTER 36

INSURANCE AND LEGAL CONSIDERATIONS

CONTENTS

The financial manager should have some familiarity with insurance and law in performing his or her functions. Governmental and private insurance coverage can be used to protect against such things as inconvertibility of assets and contract repudiation. Federal and state laws affect the relationship between employer and employee.

INSURANCE COVERAGE

In a large company, a risk manager may be held responsible for insurance matters. He or she will report directly to the treasurer or controller. In a smaller company, this function may be one of the duties of the controller, treasurer, or other corporate officer.

One of the functions of the financial manager's job may be to provide insurance coverage for the company so as to control the risks the firm is susceptible to. Some insurance coverage is required by law such as worker's compensation. Some coverage is required by contract such as fire insurance in order to abide by the terms of a loan agreement. Other coverage is to protect against the general risk inherent in the business. The financial manager must comprehend insurance requirements and procedures and furnish needed information and advice. The financial manager should attempt to find ways to monitor and control costs while maintaining adequate insurance protection. Consideration has to be given to the limits for risk assumption or retention, self-insurance, and uninsurable risks. Further, there should be proper documentation of insurance procedures.

The financial manager has many duties in insurance protection including identifying and evaluating risks, maintaining records of insurance administration, keeping up to date with new developments in insurance, monitoring changes in the corporate environment as they affect insurance, estimating the probability of loss, and assuring compliance with federal and local regulatory requirements.

The financial manager in appraising insurable hazards should analyze in detail properties and locations along with related contractual obligations (e.g., mortgages, leases). Each structure should be listed along with its location, condition, safety, and replacement cost.

In the case of insignificant risk areas, deductibles should be established to meet company needs and result in premium savings.

Tip: A new business should have higher deductibles until experience can be gotten of the number of incidences of losses and their magnitude.

At periodic times, insurance coverage should be reviewed to avoid uninsured losses. As the company changes in size, products, geographic areas, and so on, it may have to alter the type and amount of insurance coverage. Policy limits and deductibles may have to be revised given the company's current setting. The higher the deductible of a policy, the lower is the premium. Some considerations in the insurance review process are new risks (e.g., AIDS), trends in legal cases, sale or purchase of fixed assets, changes in inventory policy, switch in distribution channels, and fair market value of property.

Note: Not everything needs to be insured. In some nonessential areas, self insurance may be sufficient. In deciding whether to insure against a risk, the financial manager must weigh the probability of loss and amount against the insurance premium cost. If the difference is marginal, it may not be financially advantageous to insure.

General Rule: Insure potential catastrophes that would significantly impair the ongoing operations of the business and result in financial hardship.

Insurance Records

There are many insurance records that should be kept, including:

- Expense distribution records including information about payments, refunds, accruals, write-offs, and allocation amounts and bases to segments.
- Records of premiums, losses, and settlements. A ratio of premiums to losses should be determined.
- Records of the approved values of insured items.

- Claim records including the names of claim representatives, claim procedures, documentation, claim information (e.g., date), and status of the claim.
- Location records describing the physical location of the insured items among the various plant facilities.
- Transportation logs for corporate vehicles including delivery trucks and automobiles. Information includes miles driven and to be driven, condition, and location.
- Binder records of pending insurance coverage.
- Other files including dates premiums are due, notice of hearings, and inspections.

An insurance manual should be kept detailing the procedures to be followed on all aspects of insurance coverage by type including obtaining insurance, filing claims, financial reporting and presentation, allocation bases to allocate premiums to reporting units, and settlement issues.

All insurable losses must be immediately reported and documented. The financial manager must know what types of losses have occurred, where, and their magnitude. Damaged items must be segregated until the adjuster has made a review. The appropriate claims representative should be contacted. The financial manager should evaluate the cause of the loss and suggest necessary remedial measures.

An insurance report should be prepared at the end of the year. Information contained therein should include a description of the types of insurance and related coverage, premiums paid, self-insured items, and the adequacy of established reserves.

An illustrative insurance record appears in Exhibit 36-1. The insurance record lists all insurance policies, policy dates, annual premium, and what is covered under the policies.

The controller keeps records related to the history of acquisition, use, and sale of fixed assets. Information about insurance claims for cash, securities, and inventory are also kept. Internal auditors should check the track record, support, and documentation for all claims.

Deciding on an Insurance Broker

In selecting an insurance broker, the following should be taken into account:

- Financial strength of the insurer.
- Types of coverage.
- Insurance rates.
- Services provided and expertise of staff.
- Timely resolution of insurance claims.
- Latest insurance products.

Exhibit 36-1: Insurance Record

Insurance Company	Name of Broker	Identifying Number of Policy	Amount of Policy	Term	Expiration Date	Annual Premium	Coverage	Exclusions

The types of business insurance include product liability, commercial property, umbrella excess liability, marine, contingent business interruption, automobile, and aircraft.

Product Liability

Insurance protection is needed for loss arising from damages suffered by other parties due to defects in the company's products, services, operations, or acts of employees. Here, an analysis should be made of contracts, leases, and sales orders. It is essential to consider federal and state statutes applying to the company's product liability requirements. What is the probability of loss, the degree, and the frequency?

Commercial Property Policy

The commercial property policy is an "all-risk" policy in insuring inventory on the premises, in warehouses, and in transit. It also covers personal injuries, property damage, product liability, advertising liability, fire damage on rental premises, loss of valuable records, and flood and earthquake losses. Excluded are coverage for cash and securities, property sold under installments, imports or exports, precious metals, and aircraft. These are covered under other policies mentioned herein. Everything is covered except the specific excluded items.

The commercial property policy is the prime "all-risk" policy of the company. Losses exceeding the policy limits may be recovered under the umbrella policy.

Casualty Insurance Computations

Casualty insurance covers such items as fire loss and water damage. The premiums are usually paid in advance and debited to Prepaid Insurance which is then amortized over the policy period. Casualty insurance reimburses the holder for the fair market value of property lost. Insurance companies typically have a coinsurance clause so that the insured bears part of the loss. The insurance reimbursement formula follows (assumes an 80% coinsurance clause):

$$\frac{\text{Face of policy}}{.8 \times \text{Fair market value of insured property}} \times \text{Fair market value of loss} = \text{Possible reimbursement}$$

Insurance reimbursement is based on the lower of the face of the policy, fair market value of loss, or possible reimbursement.

EXAMPLE 1:

Case	Face of Policy	Fair Market Value of Property	Fair Market Value of Loss
A	$ 4,000	$10,000	$ 6,000
B	6,000	10,000	10,000
C	10,000	10,000	4,000

Insurance reimbursement follows:

Case A:

$$\frac{\$4,000}{.8 \times \$10,000} \times \ \$6,000 = \$3,000$$

Case B:

$$\frac{\$6,000}{.8 \times \$10,000} \times \ \$10,000 = \$7,500$$

Case C:

$$\frac{\$10,000}{.8 \times \$10,000} \times \ \$4,000 = \$5,000$$

A blanket policy covers several items of property. The face of the policy is allocated based upon the fair market values of the insured assets.

EXAMPLE 2: A blanket policy of $15,000 applies to equipment I and equipment II. The fair value of equipment I and II are $30,000 and $15,000, respectively. Equipment II is partially destroyed resulting in a fire loss of $3,000.

The policy allocation to equipment II is computed below:

		Fair Market Value	Policy
Equipment I	$30,000	$10,000	
Equipment II		15,000	5,000
		$45,000	$15,000

The insurance reimbursement is:

$$\frac{\$5,000}{.8 \times \$15,000} \times \ \$3,000 = \$1,500$$

When a fire loss occurs, the asset destroyed has to be removed from the accounts with the resulting fire loss recorded based on book value. The insurance reimbursement reduces the fire loss. The fire loss is an extraordinary item (net of tax).

EXAMPLE 3: The following fire loss information exists for ABC Company. Merchandise costing $5,000 is fully destroyed. There is no insurance for it. Furniture costing $10,000 with accumulated depreciation of $1,000 and having a fair market value of $7,000 is entirely destroyed. The policy is for

$10,000. Building costing $30,000 with accumulated depreciation of $3,000 and having a fair market value of $20,000 is 50% destroyed. The face of the policy is $15,000. The journal entries to record the book loss follow:

Fire loss	5,000	
Inventory		5,000
Fire loss	9,000	
Accumulated depreciation	1,000	
Furniture		10,000
Fire loss	13,500	
Accumulated depreciation	1,500	
Building		15,000

Insurance reimbursement totals $16,375 computed as follows:

Furniture:

$$\frac{\$10,000}{.8 \times \$7,000} \times \$7,000 = \$12,500$$

Building:

$$\frac{\$15,000}{.8 \times \$20,000} \times \$10,000 = \$9,375$$

The journal entry for the insurance reimbursement is:

Cash	16,375	
Fire loss		16,375

The net fire loss is $11,125 ($27,500 – $16,375), which will typically be shown as an extraordinary item.

Boiler Explosion Insurance

This insurance covers losses to the property insured and to others caused from the explosion.

Umbrella Excess Liability Policy (Blanket Policy)

The umbrella policy insures against all risk not covered under another policy. For example, if the commercial property policy covers up to $10 million, the umbrella policy would provide coverage in excess of $10 million but not to exceed $25 million. It is an "excess coverage" policy coming into being only after another policy has reached its limit. The umbrella policy is a must in a complete insurance program.

Marine Open Cargo Policy

This policy is suggested when the company imports goods on terms of FOB shipping point. The policy covers goods in transit. Because the company obtains title when the goods are shipped, insurance coverage is needed. Each shipment is covered separately and the premium is directly tied to the value of that shipment. Coverage should be to the receiving warehouse dock, where the commercial property policy will pick up the coverage.

Note: Also take out a General Term Bond for Entry of Merchandise which covers landed merchandise while it passes through customs and brokers' hands.

Contingent Business Interruption Coverage

This provides insurance coverage if business operations are interrupted or ceased because of an unpredictable or infrequent event, such as fire, earthquake, flood, tornado, and vandalism. This policy reimburses for the loss of net income during the shutdown, continuing fixed costs, incremental costs to replace equipment, overtime, or cost of having the goods manufactured elsewhere. The policy may also cover losses because of a supplier's inability to deliver because of an unexpected, unusual, and infrequent event.

Automobile and Aircraft Insurance

Adequate insurance is needed for company-owned vehicles. Insurance for corporate planes includes normal property damage and liability insurance to insured parties.

Insurance Bonds

There are several types of insurance bonds that may be needed including comprehensive bond and miscellaneous bid and performance bond. A comprehensive bond is fidelity coverage for employees due to theft of cash or property. If the company sells to a municipality, it may be required to have miscellaneous bid and performance bonds. The bid bond is typically in lieu of a certified check which has to accompany government bonds. The performance bond insures against the company's inability to perform under the government contract.

Medical and Catastrophe Coverage

Many employers provide medical and catastrophe insurance for current and retired employees.

Workers' Compensation

This policy covers the employer for liability due to occupational health hazards which fall under state law. It typically also covers the employer's liability for employee suits charging personal injuries. The premium is based on the total dollar payroll.

Disability Coverage

Some states require the employee to take out coverage for accidents and disabilities occurring off the job. The premium is set by state statute and paid for by the employee. Sometimes, the employer elects to pay the entire premium as a fringe benefit. If a state does not have a disability law, private insurance may be taken out.

Life Insurance

Life insurance may be taken out on "key" executives. The insurance may also provide cash to buy the deceased's shares.

Note: If the company is the beneficiary, the premiums are not deductible for tax purposes although they are an expense for financial reporting purposes. The proceeds received upon death are not taxable income.

Cash surrender value of life insurance is the sum payable upon cancellation of the policy by the insured; the insured will of course receive less than the premiums paid in. Cash surrender value is classified under long-term investments. It applies to ordinary life and limited payment policies. It is not usually applicable to term insurance. The insurance premium payment consists of two elements: expense and cash surrender value.

> **EXAMPLE 4:** A premium of $6,000 is paid that increases the cash surrender value by $2,000. The appropriate entry is

Life insurance expense	4,000	
Cash surrender value of life insurance	2,000	
Cash		6,000

The gain on a life insurance policy is not typically considered an extraordinary item since it is in the ordinary course of business.

CONTRACTS

While the corporate controller is not ordinarily trained in legal matters, he or she is often relied upon to recognize situations requiring the need for legal counsel. When contracts are drawn, the controller is often consulted on accounting and other business matters. The area of contracts therefore represents an area with which the controller needs some basic familiarity.

By definition, a contract is a legally enforceable agreement, and is governed by (1) Article 2 of the Uniform Commercial Code (UCC) if the contract pertains to the sale of tangible personal property (i.e., goods), and (2) common law if the subject matter covered by the contract is real estate, services, or intangibles.

The controller should be able to recognize when a contract exists. Accordingly, he or she must understand the basic elements of a contract. Further, the controller needs to be cognizant of the statute of frauds and the parol evidence rule. Not being a legal expert, the controller should contact the appropriate legal counsel if he or she perceives that (1) a contract has been breached, (2) a contract is not valid, or (3) a modification to a contract is being attempted.

Types of Contracts

Essentially, there are nine types of contracts:

1. An *executory* contract is based on conditions that have not yet been fully performed by both parties to the contract.

2. An *executed* contract is created when both parties have fully performed the conditions required by the contract.

3. An *express* contract involves an agreement expressed in words, whether spoken or written.

4. An *implied* contract is a contract that is inferred as a result of the acts or conduct of the parties involved.

5. A *bilateral* contract arises when one promise is given in exchange for another.

6. A *unilateral* contract involves an offer of a promise and an act that is committed as a result of reliance on the promise.

7. A *quasi*-contract represents an obligation created by law in order to prevent unjust enrichment.

8. A *void* contract is a contract without any legal obligations on the part of each party.

9. A *voidable* contact is a contract that may be avoided or ratified by one or more of the parties.

Contract Elements

The four elements required for a contract are: (1) agreement; (2) consideration; (3) legality; and (4) capacity of the parties.

Agreement. Agreement involves an offer and acceptance. The terms of an offer must be definite and must demonstrate an intent to incur a legal obligation. To be valid, an offer must be communicated to the offeree by the offeror (or his or her agent) and is deemed to be effective when the offeree receives it. The offeree may accept an offer until it is terminated. In general, an offer will terminate if (1) the offer has expired (i.e., it is not accepted within the time specified or within a reasonable period of time, if no time is stipulated), (2) the offer is revoked at any time prior to acceptance, (3) the offer is rejected, (4) a counteroffer is made, (5) either party dies or becomes disabled, (6) the subject matter of the offer is destroyed, or (7) the subject matter of the offer subsequently becomes illegal. In connection with point 2, it should be noted that certain offers are irrevocable. An option contract, which is irrevocable, involves an offer supported by consideration; therefore, it cannot be withdrawn prior to the expiration of the stated period of time, or a reasonable period of time if no time is specified. A firm offer, which is also irrevocable, involves a merchant who makes a written offer to buy or sell goods and specifies that the offer will remain open for a specified period. Finally, in a unilateral contract, even though the act necessary to accept the offer has not been completed, performance has begun, and the offer becomes irrevocable.

Acceptance of the offer must be unequivocal. Accordingly, the offeree cannot alter or qualify the provisions of the offer. Acceptance may be effected by any reasonable means of communication, unless a specific means of acceptance is stipulated by the offeror. Acceptance is generally effective upon dispatch (e.g., when mailed).

Consideration. Consideration is a necessary element of a contract. As such, both parties to the contract must give consideration. For consideration to exist, there must be legal sufficiency (i.e., something of value) and a bargained-for exchange. It should be noted, however, that some types of transactions do not require consideration for enforcement. For example, promissory estoppel, also known as the doctrine of detrimental reliance, prevents the promisor from pleading lack of consideration for his or her promise where he or she has induced the promisee to make a substantial change of position in reliance thereon. In addition, no consideration is necessary in order to modify contracts for the sale of goods.

Legality. The subject matter of a contract must be legal. An agreement will be illegal and unenforceable when formation or performance of an agreement is criminal, tortious, or otherwise opposed to public policy. In these circumstances, the contract is void.

Capacity of the Parties. Capacity of the parties is also necessary for a contract to be valid. While a contract made by a minor is voidable at his or her election, it may be ratified upon reaching majority. Further, a contract made by a legally insane person is generally voidable. Where one has been legally declared insane, attempted contracts are void. Last, with respect to an intoxicated individual, a contract is voidable if the degree of intoxication was such that the individual did not realize he or she was entering into a contract.

The Statute of Frauds

Pursuant to the statute of frauds, to be enforceable, certain executory contracts must be in writing and signed by the party to be charged with performance. The written contract may be formal or informal and may be set forth in one or more documents, but must clearly indicate the parties, specify the subject matter and essential terms, and include the signature of the party against whom enforcement is sought. The contracts covered by the statute of frauds include, but are not limited to:

- Contracts involving the sale of goods with a price of at least $500.
- Contracts involving the sale of investment securities.
- Contracts conveying an interest in real property.
- Contracts that cannot be performed within one year after the contract is made.
- Contracts of guaranty.

There are exceptions to the statute of frauds. For example, with respect to sales of real property, under the doctrine of part performance, an oral contract is enforceable if the buyer makes full or partial payment, and either (1) the buyer takes possession of the property (with the seller's approval), or (2) valuable and permanent improvements have been made to the property by the buyer. With respect to the sale of goods, an oral contract will fall outside the statute of frauds if the contract covers specially manufactured goods. A written contract is also unnecessary with respect to goods that have been accepted or for which payment has been made. Finally, it should be obvious that the statute of frauds is not applicable when a party admits in court that a contract was in fact made.

The Parol Evidence Rule

Any written or oral evidence that is not contained in the written contract is known as parol evidence. The parol evidence rule stipulates that no parol evidence of any prior or contemporaneous agreement will be allowed to change or otherwise modify any of the terms or provisions of an existing written agreement. The parol evidence rule, however, is sometimes inapplicable. For example, the rule does not apply (1) to contracts that are partly written and partly verbal, (2) to an obvious clerical or typographical error, or (3) when it is necessary to explain terms that are ambiguous.

SALES

Generally accepted accounting principles require that a sale be afforded accounting recognition upon its execution.

In general, the concepts of contract law are applicable to sales. It should be obvious that the seller is required to deliver the full agreed-upon quantity to the buyer. Unless otherwise stipulated, if a carrier is involved, the seller's delivery obligation depends on the pertinent shipment terms (i.e., F.O.B. shipping point or F.O.B. destination point). The place of delivery is deemed to be the seller's place of business, however, if no carrier is involved. The buyer is of course entitled to full delivery and has the right to reject delivery of a partial or excess quantity. Upon acceptance, however, the buyer will be responsible for those items accepted. In general, the buyer has the right to examine goods prior to accepting them or paying for them. However, with respect to Collect on Delivery (C.O.D.) sales, payment by the buyer is necessary before inspection. Said payment does not constitute acceptance and any nonconforming goods may be rejected.

Remedies for Breach

The various remedies for breach of a sales contract are dependent upon which party caused the breach.

Seller. If the buyer causes the breach, the seller may generally withhold delivery. If a down payment was received by the seller, and a liquidating damages clause is not included in the contract, then the seller is entitled to keep the smaller of 20% of the purchase price or $500. The excess down payment must therefore be returned to the buyer.

A breach on the part of the buyer also entitles the seller to stop delivery of goods in transit or in possession of a third party.

Further, the seller may reclaim goods if demand is made within ten days of receipt by an insolvent buyer.

In situations where the seller has attempted to deliver nonconforming goods, the seller has the right to notify the buyer of an intent to cure and deliver conforming goods within the time limits specified in the original contract.

With respect to manufactured goods, the seller is permitted to complete manufacture of unfinished goods, identify them to the contract, and sell them, or cease their manufacture and sell the remainder for scrap. In any event the seller is entitled to recover the difference between the contract and selling prices.

Finally, in certain instances, the seller may either cancel the contract or sue for the contract price and/or damages. Legal counsel should of course be consulted if a lawsuit is contemplated.

Buyer. If the seller effectuates the breach, the buyer may reject the goods if they are nonconforming. The seller must be given notice, and if the buyer is a merchant, the buyer is required to follow the seller's reasonable instructions pertaining to the rejected goods.

When goods are not in conformity with the contract, and the nonconformity decreases the value of the goods, the buyer may generally revoke acceptance.

Alternatively, the remedy of "cover" may be available. In situations where the buyer procures the same or similar goods from another vendor, the buyer may be entitled to recover the difference between the cost of cover and the contract price, increased by any incidental damages, but reduced by any expenses saved as a result of the seller's breach.

In lieu of suing for cover, the buyer may be entitled to sue for damages. In these instances, the measure of damages is the difference between the market price at the time the buyer learned of the breach and the contract price, increased by any incidental damages, but reduced by any expenses saved as a result of the seller's breach.

INVESTMENT SECURITIES

There are two types of investment securities: (1) those that are "certificated," and (2) those that are "uncertificated." Only certificated securities are negotiable.

To be certificated, an investment security must be registered to a specific party or be in bearer form. A registered security states the name of the party entitled to the security or the rights it represents. Accordingly, the issuer must maintain books to record its transfer.

To be a bona fide purchase of an investment security, the purchase must be made (1) for value, (2) in good faith, and (3) without notice of any adverse claim. Investment securities should be carefully safeguarded because stolen securities that are properly endorsed may actually be transferred to a bona fide purchaser who takes them free of the prior party's title claim.

The transfer of a certificated security to a purchaser for value carries with it the implied warranties that the transfer is effective and rightful, the security is genuine and has not been materially altered, and the transferor is unaware of any facts that might impair the security's validity.

Endorsement of a security, by itself, does not constitute a transfer; delivery of the security on which the endorsement appears must take place for a transfer to be consummated.

The controller should also be aware that the statute of frauds is applicable to contracts involving the sale of securities; accordingly, the contract must generally be in writing.

Sometimes, no matter how tight controls are, investment securities may be lost, stolen, or accidentally destroyed. In these instances, the owner is entitled to a replacement certificate provided that (1) a request for a replacement is made before the issuer becomes aware that the security has been transferred to a bona fide purchaser, (2) a sufficient indemnity bond is filed with the issuer, and (3) all reasonable requirements of the issuer are met.

EMPLOYMENT REGULATIONS

An awareness of the provisions contained in this section will enable the controller to interface with responsible individuals in the personnel department.

The Federal Occupational and Safety Health Act

The Occupational Safety and Health Administration (OSHA) of the Department of Labor is authorized to administer and enforce the Act. Its objective is to promote safety in the work environment.

The Act, while not applicable to federal, state, and local governments, applies to virtually all private employers.

Under the Act, a general duty is imposed on employers to furnish a work environment that is "free from recognized hazards that are causing or are likely to cause death or serious physical harm" to employees. An employer's liability under the Act arises only where the employer actually knew or should have known of danger. In addition to complying with the general standards of the Act, employers must also comply with certain industry-specific OSHA standards.

Workplace inspections, which are conducted without prior notification, represent the Act's simple means of enforcing compliance. To be legal, however, inspections are generally subject to employer permission. Alternatively, where the government has probable cause, a search warrant may be secured.

Employers are subject to both civil and criminal penalties for violations of the Act's provisions. Civil penalties as high as $1,000 per violation may be imposed; a $10,000 penalty may be imposed for repeated violations. An employer deemed to be a willful violator may be fined up to $10,000 and/or imprisoned for up to six months.

Finally, it is illegal to fire an employee who reveals an OSHA violation.

The Federal Fair Labor Standards Act

The Federal Fair Labor Standards Act (FLSA) requires that employers pay a minimum hourly wage; further, employers must generally pay an overtime rate equal to time-and-a-half for work in excess of 40 hours per week. The Act, however, exempts professionals, administrative employees, executives, and outside sales workers from the minimum wage and overtime provisions.

In addition, the Act regulates the employment of children in nonagricultural positions. Under the Act, children under the age of 14 may generally not be employed. However, they may be employed for newspaper delivery, acting, and working for their parents. Children between the ages of 14 and 15 may be employed to a limited extent outside of school hours in nonhazardous work. Finally, a child who is either 16 or 17 years old may be employed to perform nonhazardous tasks.

The Equal Pay Act

The Equal Pay Act makes it illegal for an employer to discriminate on the basis of gender by paying different wages for substantially equal work. The Act does, however, permit payment of different wages based on seniority, merit, quantity or quality of work, or any other factor not relating to gender. Should an employer violate the Act, it may be directed to discontinue its illegal pay structure and it may be required to provide back pay to any injured employees.

The Civil Rights Act of 1964

The Civil Rights Act makes it illegal for an employer to discriminate on the basis of race, color, religion, gender, or national origin. The Act also prohibits sexual harassment but not discrimination based on sexual preference. The Act is applicable to entities that employ 15 or more employees for 20 weeks in the current or preceding year. After enactment, the Act was modified to include The Pregnancy Discrimination Act Amendment, which forbids employment discrimination based on pregnancy, childbirth, or related medical conditions. It should be noted that employment discrimination based on gender, religion, and national origin (but not race) is allowable if the employer can show it to be a bona fide occupational qualification. Employment practices dependent on seniority systems and work-related merit are also permitted. Violations of the Civil Rights Act may entitle victims to up to two years' back pay in addition to recovery of reasonable legal fees. Reinstatement, injunctive relief, and affirmative action represent possible equitable remedies.

Age Discrimination in Employment Act

The Act, which is applicable to nonfederal employers with 20 or more employees, forbids employment discrimination based solely on age. ADEA is applicable to all employees at least 40 years old; the Act also contains a prohibition against mandatory retirement of nonmanagerial employees based on age. Subsequent to enactment, the ADEA was amended to ban age discrimination with respect to employee benefits. The Act does, however, allow age discrimination where justified by a bona fide seniority system, a bona fide occupational qualification, or a bona fide employee benefit plan. Injured individuals may seek injunctive relief, affirmative action, and back pay.

Rehabilitation Act of 1973

The Rehabilitation Act of 1973 was enacted to prevent discrimination on the basis of handicap by any employer that is the recipient of federal assistance or contracts. While employers subject to the Act are required to make reasonable efforts to accommodate the handicapped, they are not required to hire or promote handicapped persons who are unable to perform the job after reasonable accommodations are made. Persons with physical and mental handicaps are covered by the Act, while persons with alcohol or drug abuse problems are not.

Americans with Disabilities Act

Americans with Disabilities Act (ADA), which is applicable to entities employing 15 or more individuals, prevents an employer from employment discrimination against qualified individuals with disabilities. A qualified individual with a disability is an individual who is able to perform the essential job function, with or without reasonable accommodation. A disabled person is an individual with or without a history of a physical or mental impairment that substantially limits one or more major life activities. In this connection, ADA affords protection to persons afflicted with cancer and HIV infections; recovering alcoholics and drug addicts are also protected. The Act bars employers from asking job applicants about disabilities but does allow inquiry about the applicant's ability to perform job-related tasks. Prospective employees are also protected by the Act's prohibition of pre-employment medical exams. However, if such exams are required of all other job applicants, the employer is not barred. The Act does afford protection to an employer as well. Accordingly, an employer may refuse to hire or promote a disabled person in situations where (1) accommodation would present an undue hardship, (2) the disabled person cannot fulfill job-related criteria that cannot be reasonably accommodated, and (3) the disabled person would represent a direct threat to the health of other individuals.

Consolidated Omnibus Budget Reconciliation Act of 1985

The Consolidated Omnibus Budget Reconciliation Act of 1985 (COBRA) mandates that employers allow voluntarily or involuntarily terminated (and certain disabled) employees to continue their group health insurance coverage for a period not to exceed to 18 (if disabled, up to 29) months following termination. The terminated employee must, however, bear the expense of the premiums. COBRA applies to nongovernmental entities (1) employing at least 20 individuals and (2) offering an employer sponsored health plan to employees. An employee's spouse and minor children must also be given the right to continue their group health coverage.

Worker Adjustment and Retraining Notification Act

The Worker Adjustment and Retraining Notification (WARN) Act, which is applicable to employers of more than 100 employees, requires that employees be given 60 days notice of plant closures or mass layoffs. A plant closing is defined as the permanent or temporary closing of a single plant or parts of a plant but only if at least 50 employees will lose their jobs within a specified 30-day period. A mass layoff arises when the jobs of at least 500 employees are terminated during a 30-day period, or the jobs of at least one-third of the employees are terminated at a given site, if that one-third equals at least 50 employees.

The Family and Medical Leave Act

The Family and Medical Leave Act (FMLA), which is applicable to entities with at least 50 employees, requires an employer to provide 12 weeks unpaid leave each year for medical or family reasons. While on leave, an employee is entitled to continued medical benefits, and upon return, an employee is entitled to the same or an equivalent job.

SECURED TRANSACTIONS

A secured transaction is defined as any transaction that is aimed at creating a security interest in personal property or fixtures. When an agreement between a debtor and creditor has been reached, whereby the creditor shall have a security interest, a security agreement results. The security agreement must be in writing, must be signed by the debtor, and must delineate any collateral, if the agreement pertains to a nonpossessory interest.

When an interest in personal property or fixtures that secures payment or performance of an obligation exists, by definition, a security interest is created. Security interests may be either possessory or nonpossessory. Attachment must occur in order for rights of a secured party to be enforceable against the debtor. Perfection is necessary in order to make the security interest effective against most third parties.

In order for attachment to occur, (1) the secured party must have collateral pursuant to an agreement with the debtor (or the debtor must have signed a security agreement delineating collateral), (2) the creditor gives value, which may be any consideration that would support a simple contract, and (3) the debtor is afforded property rights in collateral.

Once the security interest has attached, perfection is said to have occurred. In general, the filing of a financing statement with the appropriate public official accomplishes perfection. The content of the financing statement is usually governed by state law, but generally includes, at a minimum, the names and addresses of the secured party and debtor, specification of the collateral, and the signature of the debtor.

Perfection may also be accomplished by attachment alone, without filing, through the use of a purchase money security interest (PMSI) in consumer goods. This form of perfection provides protection against a debtor's other creditors and a debtor's trustee in bankruptcy.

Finally, perfection is achieved when the creditor is in possession of the collateral. This means of perfection is useful for a security interest in goods, instruments, negotiable documents, and letters of credit. In the case of negotiable instruments, this is the only acceptable means of perfection.

It should be understood that there are two types of secured transactions; namely, a secured credit sale and a secured loan transaction. The former concerns a sales transaction in which the creditor is involved either as a seller or a money lender. The creditor takes a purchase money security interest (PMSI). Possession and risk of loss pass to the buyer, but the creditor retains a security interest in the goods until he or she has been paid in full. In the case of the latter, there is no sale of goods. Rather, the creditor lends money while simultaneously accepting a debtor-pledged security interest in collateral.

Essentially, there are four types of collateral; i.e., goods, negotiable instruments, intangibles, and fixtures.

Goods include consumer goods, inventory and equipment. Consumer goods consist of items that are used or purchased for use primarily for personal, family, or household purposes. Inventory, on the other hand, includes goods held for sale or lease, including unfinished goods. A security interest in inventory may result in a "floating lien," whereby the lien attaches to inventory in the hands of the dealer as it is received by the dealer. Equipment, it should noted, may also be subject to a "floating lien."

Negotiable instruments include commercial paper, documents of title, and investment securities.

Intangibles include both accounts receivable and contract rights.

Perfecting a Security Interest

As previously noted, to accomplish perfection, a financing statement must be filed with an appropriate public official. In instances where conflicting interests exist, the order of perfection is crucial and will decide priority, regardless of attachment. The first security interest to attach is afforded priority in cases where none of the conflicting security interests have been perfected.

If, within a ten-day period before or after the debtor takes possession of the collateral, a purchase money security interest in noninventory collateral is filed, the creditor will be protected as of the day on which the security interest was created (i.e., the day on which the debtor takes possession of the collateral) against any nonpurchase money security interest previously filed during the ten-day period. Creditor protection also applies to previously filed floating liens. In the event that the security interest is perfected after the ten-day period, the secured party will be afforded protection as of the date of filing but will not be able to secure protection against previously perfected non-PMSI.

A PMSI in inventory takes priority over conflicting security interests (i.e., previously perfected non-PMSI) but only if both (1) the PMSI-holder perfected the interest in the inventory on or before the date the inventory was received by the debtor and (2) the PMSI-holder furnished written notice (before the debtor takes possession of the inventory) indicating the acquisition of the interest and describing the secured inventory to all holders of conflicting security interests that previously filed a financing statement pertaining to the same type of inventory.

A filing will be necessary to protect against an innocent, nonmerchant purchaser from the consumer/debtor, even though no filing is required in order to perfect a purchase money security interest in consumer goods.

The written financing statement needed to perfect a security interest must generally include the names and addresses of both the debtor and the creditor. Only the debtor must sign the statement. The financing statement must also describe the collateral covered, and is effective for a five-year period commencing on the date filed. In order to extend the original five-year period for another five years, a continuation statement, signed by the secured party, is necessary and must be filed by the secured party within the six-month period prior to the original statement's expiration date.

Rights of Parties upon Default

The secured party may, upon default by the buyer/debtor, have the right to repossess the goods without going through legal channels. Alternatively, the secured party may sell the goods and apply the proceeds to any outstanding debt.

The secured party generally will be protected against subsequent creditors and most other third parties if a security interest has been perfected. However, holders in due course will defeat the claims of any and all secured parties. Furthermore, a buyer in the ordinary course of business is not controlled by a seller-created security interest, even in instances where the security interest was perfected and the buyer was conscious of it. This is quite prevalent where inventory has been pledged as collateral.

Upon default, the secured party may exercise a privilege to notify the obligor on accounts receivable, contract rights, instruments, etc., to directly remit remuneration.

While the debtor has the right to redeem collateral prior to disposition, the creditor has the right to retain goods. However, unless the debtor had relinquished rights after default, the creditor must give the debtor written notice about his or her intention(s). Furthermore, except in cases involving consumer goods, the creditor must send this notice to all other interested secured parties. If the creditor receives an objection to his or her retention within a 21-day period following the sending of this notice, then the creditor is required to dispose of the property.

If the debtor has satisfied at least 60% of the obligation, and the collateral consists of consumer goods with a PMSI, then the creditor is forced to sell the collateral within 90 days of the collateral's repossession, unless the debtor has relinquished his or her rights after default. Any excess debt owed, plus repossession costs, must be returned by the secured party to the debtor.

When, for value and without knowledge of any defects in the sale, a good-faith purchaser acquires collateral that was disposed of after default, the acquisition is free of any subordinate (but not superior) security interests. Finally, the debtor has no right to redeem collateral sold to a good-faith purchaser.

SURETYSHIP AND CREDITOR'S RIGHTS

Suretyship involves situations where one party agrees to be unconditionally liable for the debt or default of another party.

The parties involved in suretyship include the surety or guarantor (i.e., the party, whether compensated or not, who is responsible for the debt or obligation of another), the creditor (i.e., the party who is owed the debt or obligation), and the debtor or principal debtor (i.e., the party whose obligation it is). It should be noted that cosureties may exist. If this is the case, more than one surety is obligated for the same debt, although each co-surety may not be liable for the same amount nor may they be aware of each other's existence.

Since guaranty of collection imposes only a secondary liability upon the guarantor, the creditor must initially attempt collection from the debtor before attempting collection from the guarantor. Except in instances where collection is subject to some condition, guaranty and suretyship are synonymous terms.

Under the statute of frauds discussed earlier, a promise of guaranty must be set forth in writing and signed by the guarantor in order to be enforceable. On the other hand, a surety agreement does not have to be set forth in writing.

While the surety/guarantor need not receive consideration, consideration is needed to support the surety/guarantor's promise, and is usually represented by the creditor's granting of the loan.

Surety's Rights Against Debtor or Co-Sureties

Once payment is made by the surety to the creditor, the surety is entitled to seek indemnification or reimbursement from the debtor.

In situations involving co-sureties, once the surety has made payment to the creditor, one co-surety may seek a proportionate share from any other co-sureties.

A co-surety's share of the principal debt is calculated by multiplying the amount of principal debt by a fraction, the numerator of which is the amount for which the co-surety is liable and the denominator of which is the total amount of liabilities for all co-sureties.

In the event that a co-surety is released by a creditor, any remaining cosureties will be liable, but only to the extent of their proportionate shares.

After the creditor is paid by the surety, the surety stands in the shoes of the creditor; this is known as subrogation.

If the debtor defaults, the surety may seek relief from the courts. The courts may order the debtor to pay the creditor. A surety may seek similar relief against co-sureties. This equitable right of the surety against the debtor is known as exoneration.

Defenses of a Surety

In general, a surety may raise any defense that may be raised by a party to an ordinary contract. As such, a surety may claim mutual mistake, lack of consideration, undue influence, and creditor fraud.

On the other hand, a surety may not claim such defenses as death, insolvency, or bankruptcy of the debtor. The statute of limitations is similarly barred as a defense.

Another possible defense arises when the surety is not advised by the creditor about matters material to the risk when the creditor reasonably believes that the surety does not possess knowledge of such matters.

A defense also arises if the surety does not consent to material modification of the original contract. There is, however, a difference between a noncompensated surety and a compensated surety. The former is completely discharged automatically. The latter is discharged only to the extent that the material modification results in the surety sustaining a loss.

The release of the debtor by the creditor without the surety's consent may also be claimed as a defense. However, if the creditor specifically reserves his or her rights as against the surety, the reservation of rights will be effective and the surety shall remain liable pursuant to the original promise.

When the security is released or its value is impaired by the creditor, the surety is discharged but only to the extent of the security released or impaired.

Finally, the debtor's tender of payment to the creditor may be used as a defense.

Rights of the Creditor

The rights of the creditor, like the defenses of the surety, depend on the facts and circumstances of the events giving rise to the suretyship.

When improvements are made to real property and the provider is not paid for labor or materials, the creditor has the right to place a mechanic's lien on the property.

Pursuant to writ of execution, which is a postjudgment remedy, a court directs the sheriff to (1) seize and sell a debtor's nonexempt property and (2) apply the proceeds to the costs of execution and the creditor's judgment.

A writ of attachment, on the other hand, is a prejudgment remedy whereby the sheriff is directed to seize the debtor's nonexempt property. The seized property is then sold to pay the judgment, but only if a judgment against the debtor is secured. This remedy is not obtained easily and requires the creditor to post a bond sufficient to cover court costs and damages for a possible wrongful attachment action by the debtor.

Alternatively, a creditor may wish to secure a writ of garnishment. This course of action may be a prejudgment or postjudgment remedy. The writ of garnishment is aimed at a third party, such as a bank or employer, holding debtor-owned funds. The third party is directed to pay a regular portion of those funds to the creditor. The federal government's desire to prevent abusive and excessive garnishment resulted in enactment of the Consumer Credit Protection Act. Under the Act, a debtor may retain the larger of 75% of the weekly disposable earnings, or an amount equal to 30 hours of work at the federal minimum wage rate.

An assignment for the benefit of creditors is also a viable option. Under this option, a debtor voluntarily transfers property to a trustee, who then sells the property and applies the sale proceeds on a pro rata basis to the creditors of the debtor.

It should be noted that a homestead exemption is afforded to a debtor in bankruptcy. Accordingly, the debtor is permitted to retain a family home, or a portion of the proceeds from the sale of a family home, free from the claims of unsecured creditors and trustees. However, the protection of the homestead exemption is not available to tax liens, liens for labor or materials pertinent to real property improvements, and contract obligations for the purchase of real property.

Finally, if a debtor transfers property to a third party with the intent of defrauding the debtor's creditors, and the property becomes unavailable to the debtor's creditors, a fraudulent conveyance has taken place, and is voidable at the option of the debtor's creditors.

Federally Enacted Statutes

The federal government passed the Truth-in-Lending Act (TLA) to require that creditors disclose finance charges and credit extension charges. TLA also sets limit on garnishment proceedings. Further, a consumer who uses his or her principal residence as security for credit purposes is given the right to cancel the transaction within three business days of the credit transaction date, or the date the creditor provided the debtor with a required notice of the right to cancel, whichever is later. In general, TLA applies to consumer credit purchases up to $25,000. The $25,000 limit is not applicable, however, where the creditor maintains a security interest in the principal dwelling of the debtor.

TLA was later amended to include the Consumer Leasing Act (CLA) to expand its disclosure requirements to leases of consumer goods of up to $25,000. The provisions of CLA, however, are not applicable to real estate leases or leases between consumers.

Another amendment to TLA is the Fair Credit and Charge Card Disclosure Act, which requires disclosure of credit terms on credit and charge card solicitations and applications.

In an effort to ensure that there is no discrimination in the extension of credit, the Equal Credit Opportunity Act was enacted. Under the Act, it is illegal to discriminate on the basis of race, color, national origin, religion, age, gender, marital status, or receipt of income from public assistance programs.

By virtue of the Fair Credit Billing Act (FCBA), payment may be withheld by a credit card customer for supposedly defective products. FCBA regulates credit billing and establishes a mechanism enabling consumers to challenge and correct billing errors.

Finally, the Fair Debt Collection Practices Act may be useful as it affords protection to consumer-debtors from abusive, deceptive, and unfair practices by debt collectors.

DOCUMENTS OF TITLE

The controller should have a basic knowledge of documents of title because they indicate ownership of goods and emanate from shipment or storage of goods. Documents of title may be sold, transferred, or even pledged as collateral, and include bills of lading issued by a carrier to evidence the receipt of shipment and warehouse receipts used to evidence receipt of goods by persons hired to store goods.

There is a difference between a negotiable document and a nonnegotiable document. In the case of the former, the document states that goods are to be delivered to "bearer" or to the "order of" a named person. Accordingly, the goods are required to be delivered to the holder of the document. A negotiable document of title is not, however, payable in money, as commercial paper is. In the case of the latter, goods are consigned to a specified person, and therefore delivery must be made to the specified person. A nonnegotiable document, also known as a straight bill of lading, represents a receipt for the goods rather than a document of title.

Transfer or Negotiation

Transfer of nonnegotiable documents is in essence an assignment, whereby the assignee is effectively subject to all defenses that are available against the assignor.

The rules applicable to negotiable documents are much more complex and depend on whether the document is order paper or bearer paper.

With respect to order paper, which is negotiable by endorsement and delivery, a transferee of an order document which was not endorsed has a right to obtain such endorsement. It should be noted that the endorsement of a document of title does not render the endorser liable for any default by the bailee or by previous endorsers.

An endorser does, however, warrant to the immediate purchaser (1) the genuineness of the document, (2) that the transferor has no knowledge of any fact that would impair the validity of the document, and (3) that the transferor's negotiation is rightful and fully effective with respect to the document's title and the goods represented by the document.

Bearer paper, on the other hand, is negotiable by delivery alone.

To be "duly negotiated," a document must be properly negotiated to a holder who, in the regular course of business or financing and not in settlement or payment of a money obligation, has purchased the document in good faith, for value, and without notice of defenses.

To secure proper negotiation of order paper, the transferor must obtain a document with proper consent of the owner, and with the owner's endorsement.

Warehouse Obligations

Goods should only be delivered to the person possessing the negotiable document, which is required to be surrendered for cancellation.

Further, a warehouse has the right to refuse delivery of the goods until payment for the goods has been made.

Finally, a completed warehouse receipt, issued with blanks and purchased in good faith, entitles the purchaser to recover from the warehouse that issued the incomplete document.

CORPORATIONS

By definition, a corporation is a separate legal entity that possesses certain powers stipulated in its charter or by governing statutes.

Classification of Corporations

The eight classifications of corporations are as follows:

1. *A public corporation.* A corporation that is formed for governmental purposes.

2. *A private corporation.* Essentially includes all other corporations, whether publicly held or not.

3. *A domestic corporation.* A corporation organized under the laws of a particular state.

4. *A foreign corporation.* A corporation deemed to be "foreign" with respect to every state other than the state of incorporation.

5. *A closely held corporation.* A corporation, the stock of which is owned by a small number of persons, who are quite commonly related to each other.

6. *A publicly held corporation.* A corporation, the stock of which (1) is owned by a large number of persons, and (2) is widely traded through one of the stock exchanges.

7. *A professional corporation.* A corporation enabling professionals, including certified public accountants, to operate utilizing the corporate form.

8. *An S corporation.* As discussed in Chapter 49, "Inventory Management," is a corporation that (1) has satisfied certain IRS requirements, and (2) is electing to be taxed essentially like a partnership.

Parties to a Corporation

If the decision is made to form a publicly held corporation, the services of a promoter are usually necessary. The promoter is responsible for developing ideas pertinent to the corporation, securing stock subscribers, and entering into contracts on behalf of the corporation to be established. While corporations are generally not legally bound by contracts until a preincorporation contract is assumed by the formed corporation, promoters are generally deemed to be personally liable on contracts.

An incorporator is an important party as well, since he or she is the individual charged with devising the formal application needed to create the corporation. Corporate existence only begins upon the state's issuance of the certificate of incorporation.

The stockholders are the owners of the corporation's stock. They are empowered to elect directors who will manage the entity, vote on important issues, inspect books and records, and receive financial statements. Since stockholders, as owners, share in the corporation's profits, they are entitled to receive dividends declared at the discretion of the board of directors. Stockholders may force the board to make dividend payments only when directors are found to have abused their judgment regarding dividend declaration. It should be noted that a dividend received by a stockholder during the period of a company's insolvency must be returned to the corporation.

One of the greatest advantages of the corporate form, from the stockholders' point of view, is that stockholders are generally not liable beyond their investment. The courts may, however, "pierce the corporate veil," and hold the stockholders liable if, among other circumstances, the courts determine that the corporation (1) was established in order to perpetrate a fraud, or (2) is under-capitalized.

Directors, elected by the stockholders, are charged with establishing the corporation's essential policies and electing corporate officers. Since directors are employed in a fiduciary capacity, they are liable for negligence but not errors in judgment. Stockholders may commence a derivative action to cure any damage done by the directors. Directors acting in a representative capacity, however, are entitled to corporate indemnification with respect to acts performed on behalf of the corporation. While directors have the discretion to declare dividends, they will be held to be personally liable for illegal dividends; i.e., dividend payments made during the corporation's period of insolvency, or dividend payments that force the corporation into insolvency, or dividend payments made from an unauthorized account.

The corporate officers are responsible for managing the daily operations of the corporation, and their rights and powers are governed by agency law and are limited by the corporation's charter and bylaws. Corporate officers, appointed by the board of directors, while liable for negligent acts, are entitled to indemnification for acts performed within the scope of their authority, so long as they acted in good faith.

Powers and Rights of a Corporation

A corporation's sources of power include the corporation's charter and bylaws as well as relevant statutes. A corporation is normally empowered to borrow and lend money, enter into contracts, acquire and dispose of property, have perpetual existence, and have exclusive use of its legal corporate name.

Dissolution or Termination of Corporations

While a corporation normally is afforded perpetual existence, there are circumstances that enable a corporation to terminate its existence. Termination may be accomplished by voluntary or involuntary dissolution.

In order to dissolve voluntarily, the board of directors must approve a corporate resolution. Approval generally requires a majority vote on the part of stockholders possessing stock with voting rights. A special shareholders' meeting is needed and all shareholders must be provided written notice of the purpose, time, date, and location of the special meeting.

Involuntary dissolution, on the other hand, may result from an administrative hearing on the part of the secretary of state, or from a judicial proceeding prompted by either a shareholder or corporate creditor.

To force an involuntary dissolution based on an administrative hearing, the secretary of state must prove that the corporation has failed to comply with state laws. Accordingly, the corporation's failure to file required annual reports or pay taxes may result in an involuntary dissolution.

A court may also force a corporation to dissolve. To do so, it must prove that the corporation fraudulently obtained its charter, the corporation was involved in ultra vires acts (i.e., those abusing or in excess of its authority), the board of directors was involved in an illegal or fraudulent act, or the assets of the corporation are being wasted or misapplied. A court-forced dissolution may also result when either (1) the shareholders are deadlocked and have failed to elect directors for at least two consecutive annual meetings, or (2) the directors are deadlocked, the shareholders cannot break the deadlock, and irreparable damage is threatened or being suffered by the corporation.

Consolidation or Merger

From a legal standpoint, a consolidation involves joining two or more corporations in order to form a new entity with the assets and liabilities of the old corporations. A merger, on the other hand, occurs when one corporation absorbs another. The corporation absorbed is accordingly terminated, while the other corporation (i.e., the survivor) continues its existence. The survivor logically assumes the liabilities of the corporation absorbed in the merger.

In order to effectuate a consolidation or merger, the board of directors of each corporation must ratify a formal plan, which must then be submitted to the stockholders of each corporation for their approval. Approval constitutes the consent of a majority of each corporation's voting shareholders, following due notice of a special shareholders' meeting. Furthermore, each voting shareholder must be given a copy of the merger or consolidation plan.

Any dissenting shareholders must be provided an appraisal remedy; i.e., they must be given the value of the shares immediately prior to the action to which the dissenter objects plus accrued interest, if any. In order to obtain an appraisal remedy, a dissenting shareholder must (1) file a written notice of dissent with the corporation prior to the vote of the shareholders, (2) vote against the proposed transaction, and (3) demand in writing that an appraisal remedy be made after the shareholders' vote of approval.

Finally, articles of consolidation or merger must be filed with the absorbing corporation's state of incorporation. The merger or consolidation is effective only when this document is filed.

It should be noted that a short-form merger is often permitted when a merger of a subsidiary into a parent corporation is desired. To qualify, a parent corporation must own at least 90% of the outstanding shares of each class of stock in a subsidiary. It is interesting to note that only the approval of the parent corporation's board of directors is necessary. It is not necessary to secure the approval of either the shareholders of each corporation or the board of directors of the subsidiary corporation. Additionally, only the shareholders of the subsidiary corporation need be given an appraisal remedy.

BANKRUPTCY

Knowledge of bankruptcy law is essential, given today's economic conditions and competitive markets. From a legal standpoint, the primary basis for bankruptcy is insolvency in the equity sense as opposed to balance sheet insolvency. Accordingly, the entity must be unable to pay debts as they become due as opposed to merely having an excess of liabilities over assets. (See Chapter 41, "Failure and Reorganization," for a discussion of the Bankruptcy Abuse Prevention and Consumer Protection Act of 2005.)

Bankruptcy Reform Act of 1994

The Bankruptcy Reform Act of 1994 essentially contains two chapters applicable to corporations.

Chapter 7 permits the voluntary or involuntary liquidation of a debtor's nonexempt assets, the distribution of the proceeds to creditors, and the discharge of the remaining business and/or personal debt of the debtor. While Chapter 7 relief is available to corporations, a discharge of indebtedness is not available if the debtor is a corporation, since the limited liability of shareholders would preclude the need for a discharge. Under Chapter 7, it should be apparent that the business no longer continues to operate.

Chapter 11, on the other hand, is quite different. Chapter 11 relief, which is generally available if the entity is eligible for relief under Chapter 7, enables reorganization by the entity's business debtors, in order to keep the financially troubled business in operation. Fraud, incompetence, or gross mismanagement, however, will prevent the desired continuity.

A petition under Chapter 11 may be voluntary or involuntary, and insolvency in the balance sheet sense is not a condition precedent. The filing of a voluntary petition by an eligible debtor operates as an order for relief, effectively eliminating the need for a formal hearing.

Appointment of a committee of unsecured creditors follows an order of relief. The parties holding the seven largest unsecured claims against the debtor usually sit on the committee.

Under Chapter 11, the debtor usually remains in possession and control of the business. However, a trustee may be appointed by the court for cause, which includes, but is not limited to, fraud on the part of the debtor or incompetence of the debtor.

The right to file a reorganization plan during the first 120 days following the order for relief rests with the debtor, unless the court has appointed a trustee. If the creditors do not accept a timely filed plan, then no other party is permitted to file a plan for reorganization during the first 180 days after the order for relief, Thereafter, however, a plan for reorganization may be filed by one or more interested parties.

In order to be effective, each class of creditors must accept the proposed plan for reorganization. Confirmation by the Bankruptcy Court is then required. Acceptance by a class of creditors requires approval by creditors holding at least two-thirds of the debt owed to that class of creditors and holding more than one-half of the allowed claims for that class.

Upon confirmation by the court, a final decree is entered, resulting in the discharge of the debtor from most preconfirmation debts.

An expedited reorganization process is available to a qualified small business, which is defined as a business whose aggregate noncontingent liquidated secured and unsecured debts are less than $2 million. The expedited process enables elimination of creditor committees and affords the debtor the exclusive right to file a reorganization plan within 100 days.

Bankruptcy Petitions

A bankruptcy petition must be filed in order to begin bankruptcy proceedings. If the debtor files the petition, it is said to be a voluntary petition. A voluntary petition generally lists the entity's creditors, exempt property, and a description of financial condition. Upon filing a voluntary petition, an order for relief is entered.

If the creditors of the entity file the petition, it is referred to as an involuntary petition. The debtor, of course, has the right to contest the petition in court. An order for relief, however, is entered only after a court hearing.

Three petitioning creditors are required when the debtor has 12 or more creditors; only one creditor is required if the debtor has less than 12 creditors. In either situation, the petition must allege unsecured debts of at least $11,625 owed by the debtor to the petitioning creditors.

If the petition is opposed by the debtor, the court may enter an order of relief only if (1) the debtor is not paying debts as they mature, or (2) within 120 days before the petition is filed, to enforce a lien against the property, a receiver took possession of substantially all of the debtor's property.

A successful contest of an involuntary bankruptcy petition by the debtor may result in the court granting a judgment for (1) costs, (2) reasonable attorney's fees, and (3) compensatory damages. The debtor may also be awarded punitive damages should the court determine that the petition was filed in bad faith.

Priority of Claims

The priority of a claim depends on whether it is a secured claim or an unsecured claim. A creditor with a perfected secured claim against specific property of the debtor is afforded first priority to the proceeds from that property. To the extent that the proceeds of the sale of the secured asset are not sufficient to fully discharge the claim of the secured party, the creditor is considered to be an unsecured creditor.

After secured claims are satisfied, unsecured creditors are entitled to any remaining assets. Since some unsecured claims are given priority, they must be paid in full before payment is made to subordinate claims. In the event that a debtor's assets are not sufficient to fully pay unsecured creditors with the same priority, payments must be made on a pro rata basis.

The general order of priority applicable to nonsecured claims is (1) administrative expenses, (2) debt obligations incurred after commencement of an involuntary bankruptcy case, but before the order for relief or appointment of a trustee, (3) unsecured claims for wages earned within 90 days before the filing of a bankruptcy petition or cessation of business, whichever is first, limited to $4,650 for each employee, (4) contributions to employee benefit plans based on services rendered within 180 days before the filing of the bankruptcy petition, but limited to $4,650 per employee, (5) deposits with the debtor to the extent of $2,100 per individual for the purchase, rental, or lease of property or personal services, for family or household use, (6) taxes, and (7) general creditor claims.

Discharge of Debt

While a discharge in bankruptcy generally discharges debt, certain obligations are not discharged. Some of the more common debts that are not discharged include taxes in general; unlisted debts and debts where the creditor notice did not stipulate the debtor's name, address, and taxpayer identification number; debts for fraud, embezzlement, or larceny; liability for injury that was willful and malicious; fines and penalties; debts surviving an earlier bankruptcy proceeding; and loans used to pay federal taxes.

Discharge of debt will be denied if the debtor, within a one-year period before the petition is filed, or during the hearing of the case, (1) directly or indirectly transferred, destroyed, or concealed property, (2) concealed, destroyed, falsified, or failed to preserve any records necessary for determining financial condition, (3) committed fraud, refused to testify, or attempted bribery in connection with the bankruptcy, (4) failed to explain satisfactorily any loss or deficiency of assets, (5) refused to obey a lawful court order, (6) has been granted a discharge in a case commenced within six years before the date of the filing of the petition, or (7) executed a court-approved written waiver of discharge after the order for relief.

Under certain conditions, a debtor and a creditor may agree to honor a discharged debt. The agreement is known as a reaffirmation agreement.

ENVIRONMENTAL LAW

Violation of environmental law may subject the corporation to stiff criminal and civil fines and penalties. As a valued member of management, the controller should possess some basic knowledge of relevant federal statutes pertinent to environmental law.

Federal statutes have been enacted to extend common law liability for nuisance (i.e., unreasonable interference with use and enjoyment of another's land) and trespass (i.e., the intentional and unlawful entry upon another's land).

The Environmental Protection Agency (EPA) is a federal administrative agency that is charged with administering federal laws designed to protect the environment.

The National Environmental Policy Act (NEPA) requires the federal government to consider the "adverse impact" of proposed legislation, rulemaking, or other federal government action on the environment before the action is set in motion. Under the law, an environmental impact statement must be prepared in connection with all proposed federal legislation or major federal action that significantly impacts the quality of the human environment.

The Clean Air Act, which regulates air quality, specifically addresses (1) national ambient air quality standards, (2) stationary sources of air pollution, (3) mobile sources of air pollution, and (4) toxic air pollutants.

The Clean Water Act enables the EPA to establish water quality criteria in order to regulate the concentrations of permissible pollutants in a body of water and limit the amounts of pollutants that are discharged from a particular source. Enforcement of the Act is delegated to individual states.

The Noise Control Act enables the EPA to establish noise standards for new products. Under the Act, the EPA (with the Federal Aeronautics Administration) is empowered to establish noise limits for new aircraft and to regulate, with the assistance of the Department of Transportation, noise emissions from trucks.

The Resource Conservation and Recovery Act (RCRA) authorizes the EPA to identify hazardous wastes. Further, the Act authorizes the EPA to regulate entities that generate, treat, store, and dispose of wastes deemed to be hazardous.

Finally, the Comprehensive Environmental Response, Compensation, and Liability Act (CERCLA), often referred to as the "Superfund" law, mandates that the EPA identify hazardous waste sites. The EPA must rank the identified sites according to the severity of the environmental risk they pose.

Should the EPA have to clean up a hazardous site, it may recover the cost of the cleanup from one or more responsible parties.

CHAPTER 37

WHAT YOU SHOULD KNOW ABOUT ECONOMICS

CONTENTS

Exhibits

Financial management is a type of applied economics significantly based on economic theory. In effect, the parent discipline of finance is economics. Financial managers require familiarity with some selected concepts, terms, and tools utilized in economics to better understand the effect of the economy on the company as well as to comprehend the financial setting in order to make proper financial and investment decisions.

The two general divisions of economics are (1) microeconomics and (2) macroeconomics. The dividing line between them may sometimes overlap.

MICROECONOMICS

Microeconomics is the study of the individual units of the economy-individuals, households, firms, and industries. Microeconomics zeros in on such economic variables as the prices and outputs of specific firms and industries, the expenditures of consumers, wage rates, competition, and markets.

Microeconomics examines corporate policies and activities. Examples of relevant microeconomics as it affects the company are supply-demand relationships and profit maximization strategies. Microeconomics affects product pricing, productive inputs, and so on.

Questions answered by microeconomics include:

- What determines the price and output of individual goods and services in the department?

- What are the factors that determine supply and demand of a particular manufactured good?

- How do government policies such as price controls, subsidies, and excise taxes affect the price and output levels of the individual product markets?

Demand, Supply, and Market Equilibrium

There exists a relationship between the market price of a good (such as wheat) and the quantity demanded. This relationship between price and quantity is called the demand function. On the other hand, the relationship between the market price of the good and the amount of that good the producers are willing to supply is the supply function.

Market equilibrium can take place as shown in Exhibit 37-1 only at a price where the quantities supplied and demanded are equal. At any price higher than the equilibrium price, the quantity producers will want to go on supplying will exceed the quantity that consumers will want to go on demanding. Downward pressure on price will then result as some of the excess sellers undermine the going price. Similarly, a price that is lower than the equilibrium price will tend to generate shortages and to meet upward pressure from bids of excess buyers.

EXAMPLE 1: The interest rate, which is the price of money, is determined in the market based on the demand for a supply of capital, as shown in Exhibit 37-2.

Profit Maximization

Your company will find its maximum profit position where the last unit it sells brings in extra revenue just equal to its extra cost. That is, marginal revenue (MR) = marginal cost (MC). The reasoning is that as long as MR exceeds MC, the supplier expands output, adding more to total revenue than to total cost, and so total profits rise. On the other hand, it does not pay for the manufacturer to produce when MR is smaller than MC because it would be adding more to total costs than to total revenue, and the total profit could fall. This leaves the output at which MR = MC as the profit maximization or best level of output for the manufacturer. In summary, corporate actions should be taken as long as marginal profitability results (MR > MC).

Exhibit 37-1: Market Equilibrium

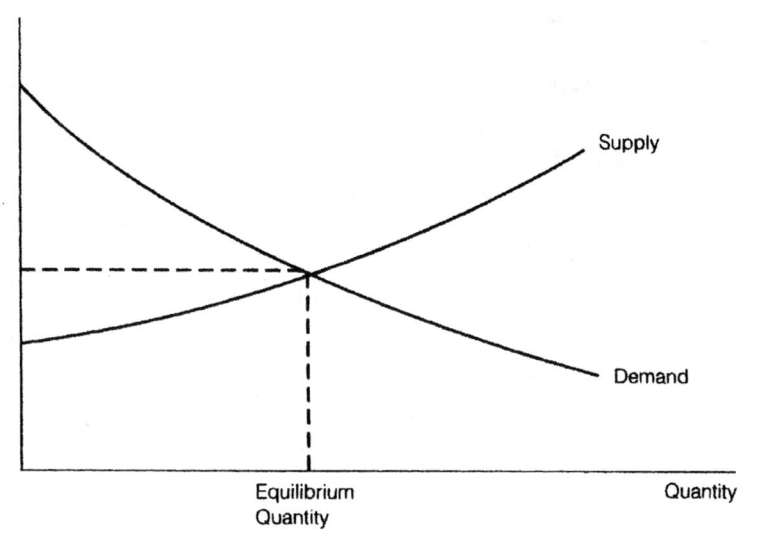

Exhibit 37-2: Interest Rate Determination

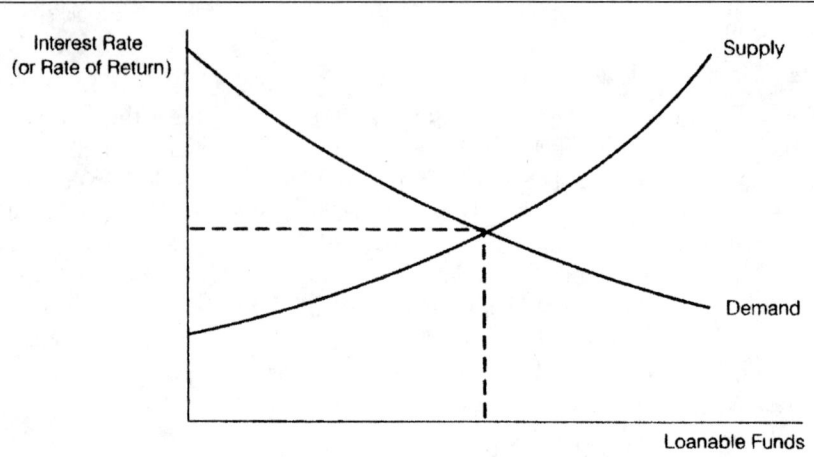

MACROECONOMICS

Macroeconomics is the study of the national economy as a whole, or of its major sectors. It looks at the general institutional and international environment the company operates in. It deals with national output, employment levels, inflation, budgetary condition, tax policies, and international trade. There is an intermingling between economics and politics.

Macroeconomics looks at governmental policies and regulations as well as those of private institutions that influence economic activities. Macroeconomics examines the structure of the federal treasury, financial intermediaries, banking system, and governmental economic policies. The objectives of macroeconomics are to have the free flow of funds, reduce unemployment, and generate a stable economic environment.

Typical macroeconomics questions include:

- What determines national income and employment levels and how does that affect your department's activities?

- What determines the general price level or rate of inflation and what impact does it have on your pricing of products?

- What are the fiscal and monetary policies that combat typical economic problems such as inflation, unemployment, and recession? How does the economic environment impact upon your department's operations?

You should be familiar with the macroeconomic setting since your company operates in this environment. The effect of a change in the economic situation (e.g., inflation, recession) on your company must be understood so needed adjustments to cope may be made. What would happen to the company's financial condition if credit is tightened or cased? For example, the tightening of credit may cause problems in obtaining funds. An understanding of financial institutions is needed so that a careful appraisal may be made of prospective financing and investment possibilities.

Let us now look at specific macroeconomic areas.

Monetary Policy. Monetary policy is the policy of the Federal Reserve System (FRS) in exercising its control over money supply, thereby affecting interest rates, price levels, and credit conditions. The "narrowly defined" money supply (MI) consists of coins, paper currency, plus all demand or checking deposits; this is narrow, or transactions, money. The "broadly defined" money supply (M2) includes all items in MI plus "time deposits"—savings deposits, money funds, and the like, against which checks may not be drawn. The instruments of monetary policy are primarily open-market operations involving sale and purchase of government securities, reserve requirements, and the discount rate.

When the money supply increases more than the normal increase in activity (usually about 4%), the economy is heating up and therefore inflationary. This is when FRS usually steps in and tries to reduce the money supply, for example, by raising the discount rate. The increased interest rates, however, tend to dampen the loan demand and bring recession.

Some economists believe that as money supply expands there will be greater economic activity resulting in more employment. They favor FRS to increase the money supply so that interest rates will drop causing an increase in corporate capital spending.

FRS may use the aforementioned tool to control money supply and affect interest rates. Tight-money policy restrains or reduces the money supply and raises interest rates. These steps are taken to hold down or reduce the level of real GDP, reduce inflation, or strengthen the balance of international payments by attracting capital inflows. Easy-money policy, on the other hand, is designed to increase the money supply to reduce interest rates. The intent of such a policy is to increase aggregate demand and thereby raise real GDP.

Fiscal Policy. Fiscal policy is governmental policies regarding tax law, federal budgets, and financing the deficit to increase aggregate demand. A lowering in taxes for a particular industry (e.g., oil and natural gas) stimulates more activity in it because the additional earnings can be reinvested. As an example, the job tax credit results in greater employment.

The federal budget significantly affects economic activity. Governmental expenditures positively affect economic activity and employment. But if governmental revenues are not obtained to offset increased expenditures, a budget deficit will result. However, additional revenues come from taxes, resulting in less consumer spending, thus slowing economic activity.

In the short run, a federal budget deficit generates demand. Some economists believe this action results in increased inflation having a long-term negative effect on the economy. Furthermore, the financing of the federal deficit by the issuance of debt will compete for funds to be raised by companies and will detract from economic expansion. This is called the "crowding-out effect." The payment of debt by the government has the effect of redistributing income from taxpayers to the holders of debt obligations.

Government Regulation. The government can regulate corporate policies, such as those related to products, services, output, and employment. Restrictive governmental actions can adversely affect economic activities and may raise company prices for goods and services.

Supply-Side Economics. In contrast with Keynesian economics, which focuses on increasing aggregate demand, supply-side economics concentrates on increasing supply. It is a view emphasizing policy measures to affect aggregate supply or potential output. In this approach, it is believed that high marginal tax rates on labor and capital incomes reduce work effort and saving; a cut in marginal tax rates will thereby increase factor supplies and total output. An extreme view, sometimes put forth by Professor Laffer, is that a tax cut will actually raise total tax revenues. The reasoning goes that the improved output through tax cuts lowers the inflation rate, increases employment, and enhances overall economic activity.

In addition to lower tax rates, in the view of supply-side economists, other governmental measures to achieve price stability and economic growth are increased depreciation allowances and reduction in regulatory requirements.

Budget Deficits. Economists generally believe that larger federal deficits result in higher interest rates. There are two reasons for this belief. First, increased budget deficits raise the demand for loanable funds, shifting the demand curve upward from D_1 to D_2 (see Exhibit 37-3) and raising interest rates (I_1 to I_2). Second, financial market participants may believe that larger deficits arc likely to lead to higher inflation. This may be true either because the sources of the increased deficits larger government spending and/or lower taxes-result directly in greater pressure for loan demand and hence inflation, or because the deficits will induce the FRS to expand the money supply to help finance the deficits, thus causing inflation. In any event, if the increased deficits elevate the public's expectation of inflation, it will tend to raise the level of interest rates.

The controller should have an understanding of economics and its effect on the company. The controller should know how to read and interpret various economic indices and statistics that are vital to the success of the business in a dynamic, ever-changing economic environment. This knowledge will enable better financial and investment decisions.

Exhibit 37-3: Demand for Loanable Funds and Interest Rates

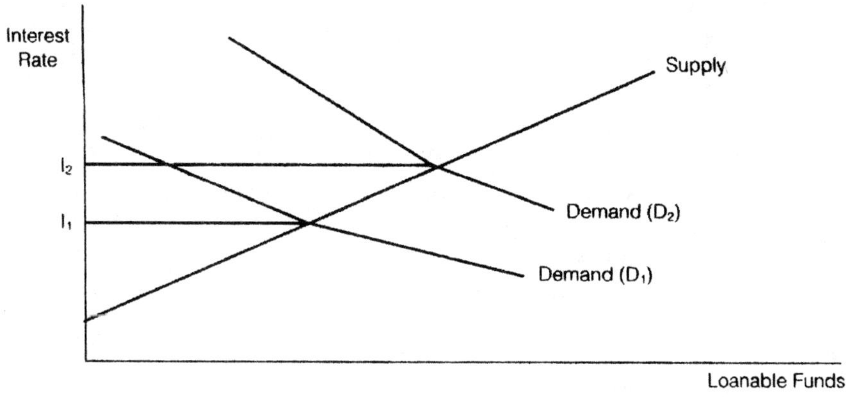

ECONOMIC AND MONETARY INDICATORS

To sort out the confusing mix of statistics that flow almost daily from the government and to help you keep track of what is going on in the economy, we examine various economic and monetary indicators. Economic and monetary indicators reflect where the economy seems to be headed and where it has been. Each month government agencies, including the Federal Reserve Board, and several economic institutions publish various indicators. These may be broken down into six broad categories.

Economic Indicators and Bond Yields

The bond investor makes an analysis of the economy primarily to determine his or her investment strategy. It is not necessary for the investor to formulate his or her own economic forecasts. The investor can rely on published forecasts in an effort to identify the trends in the economy and adjust his or her investment position accordingly.

The investor must keep abreast of the economic trend and direction and attempt to see how they affect bond yields and bond prices. Unfortunately, there are too many economic indicators and variables to be analyzed, each with its own significance. In many cases, these variables could give mixed signals about the future of the economy and therefore mislead the investor.

Various government agencies and private firms tabulate the appropriate economic data and calculate various indices. Sources for these indicators are easily subscribed at an affordable price or can be found in the local public and college libraries. They include daily local newspapers and national newspapers, such as *USA Today*, the *Wall Street Journal*, *Investor's Business Daily*, *Chicago Tribune*, and *New York Times*, or periodicals, such as *Business Week, Forbes, Fortune, Money, Kiplinger's Personal Finance Magazine, Worth, Barron's, Smart Money, Nation's Business*, and *U.S. News and World Report*.

Exhibit 37-4 provides a concise and brief list of the significant economic indicators and how they affect bond yields. This list, however, serves as a handy guide and should not be construed as an accurate predictor in all cases. Remember, bond yields and bond prices act conversely, so a rise in yields means a fall in prices and vice versa. Many times, the anticipation of good or bad news is built into the market and when the news comes out, the reverse move happens. That is because traders are unwinding the positions they took to profit from that news. Internet users can look at the White House Web site's Economic Statistics Briefing Room, which provides easy access to current federal economic indicators. The Briefing Room is at www.whitehouse.gov/fsbr/esbr.html. Haver Analytics (www.haver.com) provides database and software products for economic analysis and business decision-making and maintains more than 150 economic and financial databases from over 550 government and private sources. Databases cover the United States and its metro areas and counties, Canada, Europe, Japan, Australia, New Zealand, China, and other emerging markets. Haver Analytics also maintains key third-party data, including forecast and specialized databases covering the world economies.

Exhibit 37-4: Probable Effects of Economic Variables on Bond Yields

Indicators*	Effects on Bond Yields**	Reasons
Business Activity		
GDP and industrial production falls	Fall	As economy slows, Fed may ease credit by allowing rates to fall.
Unemployment rises	Fall	High unemployment indicates lack of economic expansion. Fed may loosen credit.
Inventories rise	Fall	Inventory levels are good indicators of duration of economic slowdown.
Trade deficit rises	Fall	Dollar weakens. That is inflationary.
Leading indicators	Rise	Advance signals about economic rise/health; Fed may tighten credit.
Housing starts rise	Rise	Growing economy due to increased new housing demand; Fed may tighten; mortgage rates rise.
Personal income rises	Rise	Higher income means higher consumer spending, thus inflationary; Fed may tighten.
Inflation		
Consumer Price Index	Rise	Inflationary rises.
Producer Price Index	Rise	Early signal for inflation increase.

Indicators*	Effects on Bond Yields**	Reasons
Monetary Policy		
Money supply rises	Rise	Excess growth in money supply is inflationary; Fed may tighten.
Fed funds rate rises	Rise	Increase in business and consumer loan rates; used by Fed to slow economic growth and inflation.
Fed buys (sells) bills	Rise (fall)	Adds (deducts) money to the economy; interest rates may go down (up).
Required reserve rises	Rise	Depresses bank's lending.

* This table merely serves as a handy guide and should not be construed as accurate at all times.

** A fall in any of these indications will have the opposite effect on bond yields.

Note: The effects are based on yield and are therefore opposite of how bond prices will be affected.

Economic Indicators and Stocks

Various government agencies and private firms tabulate the appropriate economic data and calculate various indices that the investor can use determine his or her investment strategy. Sources for these indicators are easily subscribed at an affordable price or can be found in your local public and college libraries. They include the same daily local newspapers, national newspapers, and periodicals as previously mentioned. In addition, the White House Web site's Economic Statistics Briefing Room (www.whitehouse.gov/fsbr/esbr.html) provides easy access to current federal economic indicators.

Exhibit 37-5 summarizes the types of economic variables and their probable effect on the security market and the economy in general.

Exhibit 37-5: Probable Effects of Economic Variables on Stocks

Economic Variables	Impact on Security Market and Business
Real growth in GDP	Positive (without inflation) for stocks and business.
Industrial Production	Consecutive drops are a sign of recession. Bad for stocks and business.
Inflation	Detrimental to stocks and business.
Capacity utilization	A high percentage is positive, but full capacity is inflationary.
Durable goods orders	Consecutive drops are a sign of recession. Very bad for stocks and business in cyclical industries

Economic Variables	Impact on Security Market and Business
Increase in business investment, consumer confidence, personal income	Positive for businesses, especially retailing. Worrisome for utility companies.
Leading indicators	Rise is bullish for the economy and businesses; drops are a sign of bad times ahead.
Housing starts	Rise is positive for housing business.
Corporate profits	Strong corporate earnings are positive for businesses; Corporate bonds also fare well.
Unemployment	Upward trend unfavorable for businesses and economy.
Increase in business inventories	Positive for those fearful of inflationary; negative for those looking for growing economy.
Lower federal deficit	Lowers interest rates, good for many businesses. Potential negative for depressed economy.
Deficit in trade and balance of payments	Negative for economy and businesses of companies facing stiff import competition.
Weak dollar	Negative for economy; good for companies with stiff foreign competition.
Interest rates	Rising rates can choke off investment in new plants and lure skittish investors from business.

It is intended only as a handy guide and should not be construed as an accurate predictor in all cases.

Factory Orders and Purchasing Manager's Index

The factory order series presents new orders received by manufacturers of durable goods other than military equipment. (Durable goods are those having a useful life of more than three years.) Non-defense equipment represents about one-fifth to one-third of all durable goods production. The series includes engines, construction, mining, and materials handling equipment; office and store machinery; electrical transmission and distribution equipment and other electrical machinery (excluding household appliances and electronic equipment); and railroad, ship, and aircraft transportation equipment. Military equipment is excluded because new orders for such items do not respond directly to the business cycle. The National Association of Purchasing Management releases its monthly *Purchasing Index*, which indicates the buying intentions of corporate purchasing agents.

The factory order series is released by the Department of Commerce. Each month, more than 2,000 companies are asked to file a report covering orders, inventories, and shipments. As for the *Purchasing Index*, the National Association of Purchasing Agents conducts a survey that polls purchasing managers from key industries. They are reported in daily newspapers and business dailies. Commerce Department statistics can be found at www.census.gov/econ/on the Internet.

Economists typically count on factory production, particularly of "big ticket" durable goods, ranging from airplanes to home appliances, to help lift the economy from downturn. A decline in this series suggests that factories are unlikely to hire new workers. A drop in the backlog of unfilled orders is also an indication of possible production cutbacks and layoffs. The wider dispersal of gains in many types of goods is looked upon as a favorable sign for the economic recovery. The broader the dispersal of order increases, the broader the rehiring.

The purchasing managers are responsible for buying the raw materials that feed the nation's factories. Their buying patterns are considered a good indication of the direction of the economy. A reading of 50% or more indicates that the manufacturing economy is generally expanding. A reading above 44.5% over a period of time indicates that the overall economy is augmenting.

A Word of Caution: Again, in order to make an overall assessment of the economy, the investor must look to other important economic indicators.

Gross Domestic Product

The Gross Domestic Product (GDP) measures the value of all goods and services produced by the economy within its boundaries and is the nation's broadest gauge of economic health. The GDP is normally stated in annual terms, though data are compiled and released quarterly. The Department of Commerce compiles the GDP. It is reported as a "real" figure, that is, economic growth minus the impact of inflation. The figure is tabulated on a quarterly basis, coming out in the month after a quarter has ended. It is then revised at least twice, with those revisions being reported once in each of the months following the original release.

The GDP reports appear in most daily newspapers and in online services, such as America Online, as well as the Federal Government Statistics Web site on the Internet at http://www.fedstats.gov/.

The GDP is often a measure of the state of the economy. For example, many economists speak of recession when there has been a decline in GDP for two consecutive quarters. The GDP in dollar and real terms is a useful economic indicator. An expected growth rate of 3% in real terms would be very attractive for long-term investment and would affect the stock market positively. Because inflation and price increases are detrimental to equity prices, a real growth of GDP without inflation is favorable and desirable.

It is generally thought that an increasing GDP leads to increased corporate profits, yielding and increase on dividends, which results in rising stock prices. Too much growth, however, is inflationary and thus negative for the stock and bond markets. When companies are producing "flat out," they need workers desperately and are willing to pay big wage increases to attract new workers and keep them. However, these wage increases raise business costs and lead firms to raise prices and must be avoided. Too little production is undesirable as well. Low levels of production mean layoffs, unemployment, low incomes for workers, and tend to depress the stock market.

Investors watching for signs of inflation should check the "deflator" portion of the GDP report, which contains what some experts feel is the most detailed tracking of price pressures from the government.

A Word of Caution: The GDP fails the timely release criterion for useful economic indicators. Unfortunately, there is no way of measuring whether the economy is in a recession or period of prosperity currently, based on the GDP measure. Only after the quarter is over can it be determined whether there was growth or decline. Experts look to other measures, such as unemployment rate, industrial production, durable orders, corporate profits, retail sales, and housing activity for signs of recession.

Housing Starts and Construction Spending

Housing starts is an important economic indicator that is followed by investors and economists. It offers an estimate of the number of dwelling units on which construction of new homes and apartments has begun during a stated period. When an economy is going to take a downturn, the housing sector is the first to decline. This measure indicates the future strength of the housing sector of the economy and is closely related to interest rates and other basic economic factors.

The statistics for construction spending covers homes, office buildings, and other construction projects. Both housing starts and construction spending figures are issued monthly by the Department of Commerce, and are available on the Federal Government Statistics Web site (http://www.fedstats.gov/). National business daily newspapers and many local newspapers report on these property-related figures as do any reliable Internet-based financial news service.

Housing is a key interest-sensitive sector that usually leads the rest of the economy out of the recession. Also, housing is vital to a broader economic revival, not only because of its benefits for other industries but also because it signals consumer confidence in making long-term financial commitments.

A Word of Caution: For the housing sector to be sustained, housing start figures need to be backed by building permits. Permits are considered a leading indicator of housing starts.

NAHB-Wells Fargo Housing Opportunity Index

The Housing Opportunity Index (HOI) for a given area (http://www.nahb.org/generic.aspx?sectionID=135&genericContentID=533) is defined as the share of homes sold in that area that would have been affordable to a family earning the local median income based on standard mortgage underwriting criteria. It is an index calculated quarterly by the National Association of Home Builders that compares the median income in a locality with the median home price. The index is stated as the percent of the population with the median income in the area that would be able to afford the median-priced house. For example, in 2000 81% of median-income households in Indianapolis (with a median income of $57,700) could afford a median-priced home (which cost $122,000). In comparison, San

Francisco, with a median income of $74,900 and a median house price of $464,000, had a return on investment (ROI) of 10.3%. Therefore, there are two major components of the index, income and housing cost. For income, NAHB uses the annual median family income estimates for metropolitan areas published by the Department of Housing and Urban Development. NAHB assumes that a family can afford to spend 28% of its gross income on housing; this is a conventional assumption in the lending industry. That share of median income is then divided by 12 to arrive at a monthly figure. Regarding cost, NAHB receives every month a CD of sales transaction records from First American Real Estate Solutions (formerly, TRW). The data include information on state, county, date of sale, and sales price of homes sold.

S&P/Case-Shiller Home Price Indices

This is a measure of the residential housing market, tracking changes in the value of the residential real estate market in 20 metropolitan regions across the United States. These indices use the repeat sales pricing technique to measure housing markets. First developed by Karl Case and Robert Shiller, this methodology collects data on single-family home re-sales, capturing re-sold sale prices to form sale pairs. This index family consists of 20 regional indices and two composite indices as aggregates of the regions. The S&P/Case-Shiller Home Price Indices are calculated monthly and published with a two-month lag. New index levels are released at 9:00 a.m. eastern standard time on the last Tuesday of every month. In addition, the S&P/Case-Shiller U.S. National Home Price Index is a broader composite of single-family home price indices for the nine U.S. Census divisions and is calculated quarterly.

Index of Leading Indicators

The Index of Leading Indicators is the economic series of indicators that tends to predict future changes in economic activity. This index was designed to reveal the direction of the economy in the next six to nine months. By melding ten economic yardsticks, an index is created that has shown a tendency to change before the economy makes a major turn. The index is designed to forecast economic activity six to nine months ahead.

This series, calculated and published monthly by the Conference Board, consists of the following indicators:

- *Average weekly hours for U.S. manufacturing workers.* Employers find it a lot easier to increase the number of hours worked in a week than to hire more employees.

- *Average weekly initial claims for unemployment insurance.* The number of people who sign up for unemployment benefits signals changes in present and future economic activity.

- *Manufacturers' new orders, consumer goods, and materials.* New orders mean more workers hired, more materials and supplies purchased, and increased output. Gains in this series usually lead recoveries by as much as four months.

- *Vendor performance, slower deliveries diffusion index.* This indicator represents the percentage of companies reporting slower deliveries. As the economy grows, firms have more trouble filling orders.

- *Manufacturers' new orders, non-defense capital goods.* Factories will employ more as demand for big-ticket items, especially those not bought by the government, stay strong.

- *Building permits, new private housing units.* Optimistic builders often a good sign for the economy.

- *Stock prices, 500 common stocks.* Stock market advances usually precede business upturns by three to eight months.

- *Money supply, M2.* A rising money supply means easy money that sparks brisk economic activity. This usually leads recoveries by as much as 14 months.

- *Interest rate spread, 10-year Treasury bonds minus federal funds rate.* A steep yield curve, when long rates are much higher than short ones, is sign of healthy economic outlook.

- *Consumer expectations index.* Consumer spending buys two-thirds of GDP (all goods and services produced in the economy), so any sharp change could be an important factor in an overall turnaround.

The monthly report is well covered by daily business publications, major newspapers, business TV shows, and the Internet. The Conference Board's Web site, www.conference-board.com, posts relevant information as well. If the index is consistently rising, even only slightly, the economy is chugging along and a setback is unlikely. If the indicator drops for three or more consecutive months, an economic slowdown and possibly a recession may be expected in the next year or so. However, the Conference Board points out that, although it is often stated in the press that three consecutive downward movements in the leading index signal a recession, the Conference Board does not endorse the use of such a simple, inflexible rule. Its studies show that a 1% decline (2% when annualized) in the leading index, coupled with declines in a majority of the ten components, provides a reliable, but not perfect, recession signal.

A rising (consecutive percentage increases in) indicator is bullish for the economy and the stock market, and vice versa. Falling index results could be good news for bondholders looking to make capital gains from falling interest rates.

A Word of Caution: The composite figure is designed to tell only in which direction business will go. It is not intended to forecast the magnitude of future ups and downs. The index has also given some false warning signals in recent years.

Industrial Production and Capacity Utilization

The Federal Reserve Board Index of Industrial Production, measures changes in the output of the mining, manufacturing, and gas and electric utilities sectors of the economy. Detailed breakdowns of the index provide a reading on how individual industries are faring. Industrial production is narrower than gross domestic product

(GDP) because it omits agriculture, construction, wholesale and retail trade, transportation, communications, services, finance, and government.

Another way to view the performance of the real economy is to look at industrial production relative to the production capacity of the industrial sector. The actual production level as a percentage of the full capacity level is called the rate of capacity utilization. This monthly rate is limited to manufacturing industries.

Data for the index is drawn from 250 data series obtained from private trade associations and internal estimates. This monthly Index of Industrial Production, released only two weeks into the next month, is published by the Federal Reserve Board. The rate of capacity utilization is announced every month by the Fed, one day after the Index of Industrial Production. Both are published in the Federal Reserve Bulletin and appear in major daily newspapers and in online computer news services, such as America Online.

As the index rises, this is a sign that the economy will strengthen and that the stock market should turn up. A falling industrial production should be a concern for the economy and the investor. Regardless of the state of the economy, however, detailed breakdowns of the index provide a reading on how individual industries are faring and on what industries should be attended by investors.

A rising rate of capacity utilization is positive for the economy and the stock market; a falling rate is an indication of a sinking economy and thus negative for the stock market.

A Word of Caution: Industrial production is more volatile that GDP, because GDP, unlike industrial production, includes activities that are largely spared cyclical fluctuations, such as services, finance, and government.

Inflation

Inflation is the general rise in prices of consumer goods and services. Various price indices are used to measure living costs, price level changes, and inflation. The four key indices used by the federal government follow:

1. *Consumer Price Index.* The CPI, is the most well known inflation gauge, is used as the cost-of-living index, which labor contracts and social security are tied to. The CPI measures the cost of buying a fixed basket of goods (some 400 consumer goods and services), representative of the purchase of the typical working-class urban family. The fixed basket is divided into the following categories: food and beverages, housing, apparel, transportation, medical care, entertainment, and other. This cost-of-living index is published by the Bureau of Labor Statistics of the U.S. Department of Labor. The CPI is widely used for escalation clauses.

   The base year for the CPI index was 1982–1984, at which time it was assigned 100.

2. *Producer Price Index.* Like the CPI, the PPI is a measure of the cost of a given basket of goods priced in wholesale markets, including raw materials, semifinished goods, and finished goods at the early stage of the distribution system. The PPI is published monthly by the Bureau of Labor

Statistics of the Department of Commerce. It signals changes in the general price level, or the CPI, some time before they actually materialize. (Because the PPI does not include services, caution should be exercised when the principal cause of inflation is service prices). For this reason, the PPI and especially some of its subindexes, such as the index of sensitive materials, serve as one of the leading indicators that are closely watched by policy makers.

3. *GDP Deflator.* This index of inflation is used to separate price changes in GDP calculations from real changes in economic activity. The Deflator is a weighted-average of the price indexes used to deflate GDP so that true economic growth can be separated from inflationary growth. Thus, it reflects price changes for goods and services bought by consumers, businesses, and governments. Because it covers a broader group of goods and services than the CPI and PPI, the GDP Deflator is a very widely used price index that is frequently used to measure inflation. The GDP deflator, unlike the CPI and PPI, is published only quarterly—not monthly—by the U.S. Department of Commerce.

4. *Employment Cost Index.* The ECI is most comprehensive and refined measure of underlying trends in employee compensation as a cost of production. It measures the cost of labor and includes changes in wages and salaries and employer costs for employee benefits. ECI tracks wages and bonuses, sick and vacation pay, plus such benefits as insurance, pension and Social Security and unemployment taxes from a survey of 18,300 occupations at 4,500 sample establishments in private industry and 4,200 occupations within about 800 state and local governments.

Price indices receive major coverage in daily newspapers and business dailies, on business TV programs, such as on *Bloomberg* and *CNBC*, and in Internet financial news services. The government Web sites www.stats.bls.gov and www.census.gov/econ/www/also provide this data.

Controllers should check to see whether the inflation rate has been rising—a negative, or bearish, sign for stock and bond investors—or falling, which is bullish.

Rising prices are public enemy no. 1 for stocks and bonds. Inflation usually hurts stock prices because higher consumer prices lessen the value of future corporate earnings, which makes shares of those companies less appealing to investors. By contrast, when prices rocket ahead, investors often flock to long-term inflation hedges, such as real estate.

Lower rates of inflation can lead to increased consumer spending and possibly, an up stock market. When inflation is down, real personal income increases causing consumer confidence to jump, which spurs consumer spending. Retail sales then surge as housing starts rise and auto sales rise, and the stock market goes up.

Note: Former Federal Reserve Chairman Alan Greenspan used the ECI to gauge whether wage pressures are sparking inflation.

A Word of Caution: Deflation—that is, sharp falling prices—is disastrous, as in the Texas real estate decline in the 1980s, California property woes of the early 1990s, or the Great Depression of the 1930s.

When demand for goods is so weak that merchants have to brutally slash prices just to stay in business, that is deflation. It leads to layoffs and recession. This is bad for stock investors as profits shrink, but good for bondholders, as long as they own a bond backed by an issuer who can pay it back.

Money Supply

This is the level of funds available at a given time for conducting transactions in an economy, as reported by the Federal Reserve. The Federal Reserve System can influence money supply through its monetary policy measures. There are several definitions of the money supply: M1 (which is currency in circulation, demand deposits, traveler's checks, and those in interest-bearing accounts), M2 (the most widely followed measure, equaling M1 plus savings deposits, money market deposit accounts, and money market funds), and M3 (which is M2 plus large certificates of deposit).

The Federal Reserve System computes these measures. The weekly money supply figures are released on Thursday afternoons by the Federal Reserve Board and reported in daily newspapers and the *Wall Street Journal* and *Barron's*.

Economists attempt to compare the money supply with targets proposed by the Fed. The Fed affects money supply through its monetary policy, such as its open market operations. The following scenarios summarize the Fed's possible impact on the economy and the stock market:

- *Easy money policy.* When the Fed buys securities, bank reserves rise causing bank lending and therefore the money supply to increase. Interest rates decrease as bond prices rise, loan demand goes up, and the stock market rises.

- *Tight money policy.* When the Fed sells securities, the bank reserves fall and bank lending decreases, lowering the money supply and increasing interest rates. Bond prices fall, and loan demand is down, so the stock market falls.

A Word of Caution: A rapid growth (excessively easy monetary policy) is viewed as inflationary and can affect the economy adversely. In contrast, a sharp drop in the money supply is considered to be recessionary and can hurt the economy and the stock market. Moderate growth is thought to have a positive impact on the economy.

Interest Rates

Broad trends are detected by focusing on two rates. One is the *prime rate,* which is what banks charge their best customers for short-term loans. When the prime rate is climbing, it indicates companies are borrowing heavily and the economy is still on an upward swing. The second rate that should be followed is the yield on *90-day Treasury bills.* When yields on 90-day bills rise sharply, this may signal a resurgence of inflation. Subsequently, the economy could slow down. Interest rates are controlled by the Fed's monetary policy. The Fed's monetary policy tools involve: (1)

changes in the required reserve ratio; (2) changes in the discount rate; and (3) open market operations; that is, purchase and sale of government securities. The *discount rate* is the interest rate the Fed charges its member banks to "cover their requirement." If the bank's reserves fall below the required level, the bank can borrow reserves from the Fed—for a price. Raise the discount rate, and banks will be loathed to loan up to their limit. More importantly, most institutional lenders index their loan rates to the Fed's discount rate. Therefore, an increase in the discount rate will send all interest rates up. Cuts in the discount rate are aimed at stimulating the economy—a positive development for stocks. The figure below summarizes the effect of cutting the discount rate on the economy.

THE EFFECTS OF LOWERING THE DISCOUNT RATE

- **The players:** The Federal Reserve is the nation's central bank. It regulates the flow of money through the economy.

- **The action:** The discount rate is what the Federal Reserve charges on short-term loans to member banks. When the Fed cuts the discount rate, it indicates that banks can obtain money cheaper and thus charge less on loans.

- **The first effect:** Within a few days, banks are likely to start passing on the discounts by cutting their prime rate, which is what banks charge on loans to their best corporate customers.

- **Impact:** Businesses are more likely to borrow. Second, adjustable consumer loans are tied to the prime, such as credit card rates. These become cheaper, stimulating spending.

- **The second effect:** Within a few weeks, rates on mortgage, auto, and construction loans decrease.

- **The third effect:** The lower rates drop, the more investors move their cash to stocks, creating new wealth.

- **The goal:** To stimulate the economy. Lowered interest rates encourage business growth. This results in more jobs, which decreases the unemployment rate. With additional salaries, there is more money to spend on products, thus increasing sales. Hence, the economy starts to rebound.

Some other important interest rates are briefly explained as follows:

1. **Federal funds rate.** The rate on short-term loans among commercial banks for overnight use. The Fed influences this rate by open market operations and by changing the bank's required reserve.

2. **Discount rate.** The charge on loans to depository institutions by the Fed. A change in the discount rate is considered a major economic event and is expected to have an impact on security prices, especially bonds. A change in the prime rate usually follows a change in the discount rate.

3. **5-year Treasury notes.** The yields on these notes give an idea of the prevailing interest rates for intermediate-term, fixed-income securities.

4. **10-year Treasury bonds.** This yield, also called the long bond yield, is a closely watched indicator of long-term interest rates, as the entire bond market (and sometimes the stock market) often moves in line with this rate.

Note: *The Wall Street Journal* carries key interest rates. The Federal Reserve Bank of St. Louis charts these key rates and others.

Exhibit 37-6 presents sample interest rates.

Exhibit 37-6: Key Interest Rates

(December 6, 2010)

All data are annualized to represent a one-year rate. A "real" return can be estimated by subtracting inflation.	
Consumer price index	**Treasury securities**
1-year inflation U.S. **1.2%**	13-week **0.13%**
1-year inflation SoCal **0.7**	26-week **0.18**
	2-year **0.46**
Benchmark rates	5-year **1.61**
Prime bank rate **3.25%**	10-year **3.01**
Federal discount rate **0.75**	30-year **4.31**
Federal funds rate **0-0.25**	
Series EE Savings Bonds **0.60**	**Mortgage guides**
Series I Savings Bonds **0.74**	LIBOR 6-month **0.47%**
Muni bond funds **5.32**	11th District cost of funds **1.654**
Corporate bond index **3.94**	Fannie Mae 30-year **4.14**
Junk bond funds **7.75**	1-year T-bill, wkly. avg. **0.27**

Personal Income and Confidence Indices

Personal income shows the before-tax income received by individuals and unincorporated businesses, such as wages and salaries, rents, and interest and dividends, and other payments (e.g., unemployment and Social Security).

Popular indices that track the level of consumer confidence are the Conference Board of New York, an industry-sponsored, nonprofit economic research institute, and the Index of Consumer Sentiment, compiled by the University of Michigan's Survey Research Center. The Index of Consumer Sentiment measures consumers' personal financial circumstances and their outlook for the future. Personal income data are released monthly by the Commerce Department. The Conference Board's index is derived from a survey of 5,000 households nationwide, covering questions that range from home-buying plans to the outlook for jobs, both presently and during the next six months. The University of Michigan's index is compiled through a telephone survey of 500 households. Daily newspapers, financial television and online business news services cover these releases.

Personal income represents consumers' spending power. When personal income rises, it usually means that consumers will increase their purchases, which will in turn favorably affect the investment climate. The Conference Board's index is considered a useful economic barometer because it provides insight into consumer spending and borrowing, which are critical to any sustainable economic upswing. Consumers account for two-thirds of the nation's economic activity (i.e., national gross domestic product) and thus drive recovery and expansion.

A low or decreased level of consumer confidence indicates concern about their employment prospects and their earnings in the months ahead. Uncertainty requires cautions in investing. On the other hand, an increased level of consumer confidence spells economic recovery and expansion, thus presenting an investment opportunity. In summary, an increase in personal income, coupled with substantial consumer confidence, is bullish for the economy and the stock market.

A Word of Caution: The controller must look carefully at how consumers are sustaining confidence. The personal income figures, when measured against spending and borrowing patterns, may show that consumers are dipping into savings or even running up big debt to pay for buying sprees. This is an expansion that is rarely sustainable. To formulate the future prospects about the economy, investors must weigh various economic indicators, such as inflation measures.

The IPA Small Business Confidence Index (IPASBCI), created by the Small Business Research Board (www.ipasbrb.com), management consulting firm, International Profit Associates (www.ipasbrb.com/sbci.htm), measures small business expectations about revenue growth, the general economy, and hiring. It provides an ongoing view of the business climate from a small business perspective each quarter and shows how small businesses are reacting and responding to swings in economic and business conditions over time.

The Institute for Supply Management's Index (www.ism.ws), based on a survey of 375 companies in 17 industries, measures new orders, inventories, exports, and employment in the service sector. Services account for five-sixths of the $10-trillion U.S. economy and include industries such as entertainment, utilities, health care, farming, insurance, retail, restaurants, and zoos.

Productivity

Productivity measures the relationship between real output and the labor time involved in its production, or output per hour of work. The Department of Labor compiles productivity figures from its own job surveys that produce unemployment reports and the Commerce Department's work that creates gross domestic product figures. Only business sector output—GDP minus government and not-for-profit organizations—is used in the productivity calculation.

Productivity measures reflect the joint effects of many influences, including changes in technology; capital investment; level of output; utilization of capacity, energy, and materials; the organization of production; managerial skill; and the characteristics and effort of the work force.

Daily newspapers, financial television and online business news services cover these releases. The ECI is provided quarterly by the Bureau of Labor Statistics (BLS) in the U.S. Department of Labor. The data are published in a press release, in BLS journals, and the BLS' Web site, www.stats.bls.gov.

Economists consider productivity the key to prosperity. Sizable gains mean companies can pay workers more, hold the line on prices and still earn the kind of profits that keep stock prices rising. Increased productivity, or getting more worker output per hour on the job, is considered vital to increasing the nation's standard of living without inflation.

A Word of Caution: The productivity statistic mainly covers the manufacturing sector of the economy and does not deal substantively with the large service sector.

Note: High productivity may be good for stocks, but low productivity is just a mixed bag. Consider that productivity grew at a brisk 2.9% annual rate in the 1960s and early 1970s, relatively good times for stock investors. Productivity then slowed to a paltry 1% from 1974 through 1995, both horribly weak and extremely strong stock periods. A new era of high productivity, driven by computers and other high-tech innovations, seems to bode well for stocks and inflation.

Recession

Recession is a sinking economy. Unfortunately, there is no consensus definition and measure of recession. In general, it occurs when the economy shrinks in size and more jobs are lost than are created. Here are three primary ways economists define a recession:

1. Three or more straight monthly drops in the Index of Leading Economic Indicators.

2. Two consecutive quarterly drops of Gross Domestic Product (GDP).

3. Consecutive monthly drops of durable goods orders, which most likely result in less production and increasing layoffs in the factory sector.

Recession dampens the spirits of consumers and investors and thus depresses prices of various investment vehicles including securities and real estate.

A Word of Caution: Not all industries in the economy during recession go bad. Some industrial sectors (e.g., the consumer products industry) are recession resistant or defensive. Investors must analyze industry by industry.

Recessions (or depressions) also have political impact for the nation. Political analysts say that then-President George H. W. Bush lost the 1992 presidential election—just a year after his leadership of victorious Allied forces in the Persian Gulf—because the U.S. economy grudgingly recovered from a recession throughout the campaign. In fact, there is so much political power in defining when the country is actually in recession, that a nonpartisan group of economists known as the National Bureau of Economic Research are the official arbiters of a recession's start and end.

Retail Sales

Retail sales is the estimate of total sales at the retail level. It includes everything from bags of groceries to durable goods, such as automobiles and is used as a measure of future economic conditions (a long slowdown in sales could spell cuts in production). Data is issued monthly by the Commerce Department, which conducts a mail survey of about 4,100 merchants. That previous month's sales figure is an estimate of sales activity based on percentage changes by industry aggregates from older, revised and more reliable data that is derived from larger samplings. The median revision is a change of two-tenths of a percentage point in sales.

Daily newspapers, financial television, and online business news services such as MSN cover these releases. Commerce Department statistics can be found at www.census.gov/econ/www/on the Internet.

Retail sales are a major concern of analysts because they represent about half of overall consumer spending. Consumer spending, in turn, accounts for about two-thirds of the nation's gross domestic product. The amount of retail sales depends heavily on consumer confidence about the economy.

A Word of Caution: This number is volatile and subject to occasionally steep revisions. Strong retail sales could spur fears of inflation, hurting stock and bond markets.

Same-store sales, also known as *comps, comp sales, or comparable-store sales,* is an indicator used in retail industry analysis. It compares sales of stores that have been open for a year or more. This yardstick allows us to determine what portion of new sales has come from sales growth and what portion has come from opening new stores. This type of analysis is useful. Yet, with new stores there is a saturation point where future sales growth is determined by same store sales growth. Same store sales are usually released by retail companies on a monthly basis.

Note: E-commerce retail sales measures sales of retail goods purchased through the Internet. E-commerce as a percentage of total retail sales excluding food service—mainly restaurant and bar sales—continues its steady climb.

Unemployment Rate, Initial Jobless Claims, Help-Wanted Index, and Establishment Payroll Survey

Unemployment is the unavailability of jobs for people able and willing to work at the prevailing wage rate. It is an important measure of economic health, because full employment is generally construed as a desired goal. When the various economic indicators are mixed, many analysts look to the unemployment rate as being the most important. Weekly initial claims for unemployment benefits are watched closely along with the unemployment rate to judge the jobless situation in the economy. The help-wanted advertising index tracks employers' advertisements for job openings in the classified section of newspapers in 50 or so labor market areas. The index represents job vacancies resulting from turnover in exiting positions, such as from workers changing jobs or retiring and from the creation of new jobs. The help-wanted figures are adjusted seasonally.

The unemployment rate is the number of unemployed workers divided by total employed and unemployed who constitute the labor force. Both statistics are released by the Department of Labor (DOL). The help-wanted advertising figures are obtained from classified advertisement in newspapers in major labor markets. They are frequently reported in daily newspapers, business dailies, business TV shows, and through online services. DOL releases can be found at www.stats.bls.gov on the Internet. The Establishment Payroll Survey, known as the Current Employment Statistics (CES) Survey, is based on a survey of approximately 140,000 businesses and government agencies representing approximately 410,000 worksites throughout the United States. The primary statistics derived from the survey are monthly estimates of employment, hours, and earnings for the nation, states, and major metropolitan areas. Another survey called the *Current Population Survey (CPS)* is the source of statistics on the activities of the labor force, including unemployment and the nation's unemployment rate.

An increase in employment, a decrease in initial jobless claims, and a decrease in unemployment are favorable for the economy and the stock market; the opposite situation is unfavorable. The help-wanted index is inversely related to unemployment: when help-wanted advertisements increase, unemployment declines; a decline in help-wanted advertisements is accompanied by a rise in unemployment.

The effects of unemployment on the economy are summarized as follows:

- *Less tax revenue.* Fewer jobs results in less income tax to the state and nation, which produces a bigger U.S. government deficit and forces states to make cuts in programs to balance their budgets.

- *Higher government costs.* When people lose jobs, they often must turn to the government for benefits.

- *Less consumer spending.* Without a job, individuals cannot afford to buy cars, computers, or houses, or to take vacations.

- *Empty stores.* Retailers and homebuilders cannot absorb lower sales for long. Soon they have to lay off workers and, in more serious shortfalls, file for bankruptcy.

- *Manufacturing cuts.* The companies that make consumer products or housing materials are forced to cut jobs, too, as sales of their goods fall.

- *Real estate pain.* As companies fail and as individuals struggle, mortgages and other bank loans go unpaid. That causes real estate values to go down and pummels lenders.

A Word of Caution: No one economic indicator can accurately predict the direction in which an economy is heading. Many indicators commonly give mixed signals regarding, for example, the possibility of a recession. Perhaps the best example of economic theory being turned on its head is the low unemployment figures in 1998 not creating inflationary pressures. Investors, and shoppers, can thank increased productivity and cheap foreign goods for that change.

U.S. Balance of Payments and the Value of the Dollar

A balance of payments is a systematic record of a country's receipts from, or payments to, other countries. In a way, it is like the balance sheets for businesses, only on a national level. References in the media to the "balance of trade" usually refer to goods within the goods-and-services category of the current account. It is also known as merchandise or "visible trade" because it consists of such tangibles as foodstuffs, manufactured goods, and raw materials. Services, the other part of the category, is known as "invisible trade" and consists of such intangibles as interest or dividends, technology transfers, services (e.g., insurance, transportation, financial).

When the net result of both the current account and the capital account yields more credits than debits, the country is said to have a surplus in its balance of payments. When there are more debits than credits, the country has a deficit in the balance of payments.

When deficits in the balance of payments persist, the value of the dollar generally becomes depressed and inflation is boosted. The reason is a weak dollar makes foreign goods relatively expensive, often allowing U.S. makers of similar products to raise prices as well.

Trade data is collected by the U.S. Customs Service. Figures are reported in seasonally adjusted volumes and dollar amounts. It is the only nonsurvey, non-judgmental report produced by the Department of Commerce. Foreign exchange rates are compiled from trading activity both in bulk transactions among dealers and in commodity markets trading forward contracts.

Trade figures and foreign exchange rates are quoted daily in business dailies as well as major newspapers, computer services, and on financial TV networks and specialty shows.

It is necessary for an investor to know the condition of a country's balance of payments, because resulting inflation will affect the market.

What is better, a strong dollar or a weak dollar? The answer is, unfortunately, it depends. A strong dollar makes Americans' cash go further overseas and reduces import prices—generally positive for U.S. consumers and for foreign manufacturers. If the dollar is overvalued, U.S. products are harder to sell abroad and at home, where they compete with low-cost imports. This helps give the U.S. its huge trade deficit.

A weak dollar can restore competitiveness to American products by making foreign goods comparatively more expensive. But too weak a dollar can spawn inflation, first through higher import prices and then through spiraling prices for all goods. Even worse, a falling dollar can drive foreign investors away from U.S. securities, which lose value along with the dollar. A strong dollar can be induced by interest rates. Relatively higher interest rates abroad will attract money, dollar-denominated investments, which will raise the value of the dollar.

Those Americans owning foreign investments must watch the dollar carefully. A weak dollar makes overseas investments more valuable because assets sold in the foreign currency will yield more dollars. Conversely, a strong dollar will hurt the value of an American's overseas holdings. Assets priced overseas in this scenario would yield less dollars than the depressed local currency. Exhibit 37-7 shows the possible impact of changes in foreign exchange rates.

Exhibit 37-7: The Impact of Changes in Foreign Exchange Rates

	Weak Currency (Depreciation/Devaluation)	*Strong Currency (Appreciation/Revaluation)*
Imports	More expensive.	Cheaper.
Exports	Cheaper.	More expensive.
Payables	More expensive.	Cheaper.
Receivables	Cheaper.	More expensive.
Inflation	Fuels inflation by making imports more costly.	Low inflation.
Foreign investment	Discourages foreign investment lower return on investments by international investors.	High interest rates could attract foreign investors.
The effect	Rising interests could slow down the economy.	Reduced exports could trigger a trade deficit.

A Word of Caution: Unfortunately, it is difficult to establish a dependable correlation between the dollar's value and the U.S. stock market's performance. Attention should be focused on the domestic scene as well as international economic developments.

CHAPTER 38

FINANCIAL DERIVATIVE PRODUCTS AND FINANCIAL ENGINEERING

CONTENTS

FINANCIAL DERIVATIVES

A derivative is simply a transaction, or contract, whose value depends on (or, as the name implies, derives from) the value of underlying assets such as stocks, bonds, mortgages, market indexes, or foreign currencies. One party with exposure to unwanted risk can pass some or all of that risk to a second party. The first party can assume a different risk from the second party, pay the second party to assume the risk, or, as is often the case, create a combination.

The participants in derivatives activity can be divided into two broad types-dealers and endusers. Dealers, few in numbers, include investment banks, commercial banks, merchant banks, and independent brokers. In contrast, the number of end-users is large and growing as more organizations are involved in international financial transactions. End-users include businesses, banks, securities firms, insurance companies, governmental units at the local, state, and federal levels, "supernational" organizations such as the World Bank, mutual funds, and both private and public pension funds.

The objectives of end-users may vary. A common reason to use derivatives is so that the risk of financial operations can be controlled. Derivatives can be used to manage foreign exchange exposure, especially unfavorable exchange rate movements. Speculators and arbitrageurs can seek profits from general price changes or simultaneous price differences in different markets, respectively Others use derivatives to hedge their position; that is, to set up two financial assets so that any unfavorable price movement in one asset is offset by favorable price movement in the other asset.

There are five common types of derivatives: options, futures, forward contracts, asset swaps, and hybrid. The general characteristics of each are summarized in Exhibit 38-1, although only two most common types—options and futures—are covered in detail in this chapter.

An important feature of derivatives is that the types of risk are not unique to derivatives and can be found in many other financial activities. The risks for derivatives are especially difficult to manage for two principal reasons: (1) The derivative products are complex, and (2) there are very real difficulties in measuring the risks associated with derivatives. It is imperative for financial officers of a firm to know how to manage the risks from the use of derivatives.

Exhibit 38-1: General Characteristics of Major Types of Financial Derivatives

Type	Market	Contract	Definition
Option	OTC or Organized Exchange	Custom* or Standard	Gives the buyer the right but *not* obligation to buy or sell a specific amount at a specified price within a specified period.
Futures	Organized Exchange	Standard	Obligates the holder to buy or sell at a specified price on a specified date.
Forward	OTC	Custom	Same as futures
Swap	OTC	Custom	Agreement between the parties to make periodic payments to each other during the swap period.
Hybrid	OTC	Custom	Incorporates various provisions of other types of derivatives.

* Custom contracts vary and are negotiated between the parties with respect to their value, period, and other terms.

According to Accounting Standards Update (ASU) No. 2013-10 (July 2013), *Derivatives and Hedging* (Topic 815), *Inclusion of the Fed Funds Effective Swap Rate as a Benchmark Interest Rate for Hedge Accounting Purposes*, the Fed Funds Effective Swap Rate may be used as a benchmark interest rate for hedge accounting purposes.

OPTIONS

An option is a contract to give the investor the right-but not an obligation to buy or sell something. It allows an investor to "lock in" a specified number of shares of stock at a fixed price per share (strike or exercise price) for a limited length of time.

For example, if you have purchased an option on a stock, you have the right to "exercise" the option at any time during the life of the option. This means that, regardless of the current market price of the stock, you have the right to buy or sell a specified number of shares of the stock at the strike price (rather than the current market price).

Options possess their own inherent value and are traded in secondary markets. You may want to acquire an option so that you can take advantage of an expected rise in the price of the underlying stock. Option prices are directly related to the prices of the common stock they apply to. Investing in options is very risky and requires specialized knowledge.

KINDS OF OPTIONS

All options are divided into two broad categories: calls and puts. A call option gives you the right (but not the obligation) to buy 100 shares of a specific stock at a fixed price per share (strike or exercise price) for up to nine months, depending on the expiration date of the option.

When you purchase a call, you are buying the right to purchase stock at a set price. You expect price appreciation to occur. You can make a sizable gain from a minimal investment, but you may lose all your money if stock price does not go up.

EXAMPLE 1: You purchase a 3-month call option on Dow Chemical stock for $4 1/2 at an exercise price of $50 when the stock price is $53.

On the other hand, a single put option gives you the right (but not the obligation) to sell 100 shares of a specific stock at a fixed price (strike price) for up to nine months, depending on the expiration date of the option.

Purchasing a put gives you the right to sell stock at a set price. You buy a put if you expect a stock price to fall. You have the chance to earn a considerable gain from a minimal investment, but you lose the whole investment if price depreciation does not materialize.

The buyer of the contract (the "holder") pays the seller (the "writer") a premium for the contract. In return for the premium, the buyer obtains the right to buy securities from the writer or sell securities to the writer at a fixed price over a stated period of time.

Option holder = Option buyer = Long position

Option writer = Option seller = Short position

	Call Option	*Put Option*
Buy (long)	The right to call (buy) from the writer	The right to put (sell) from the writer
Sell (short)	known as writing a call, being obligated to sell if called	known as writing a put, if the stock or contract is put

Calls and puts are typically for widely held and actively traded securities on organized exchanges. With calls there are no voting privileges, ownership interest, or dividend income. However, option contracts are adjusted for stock splits and stock dividends.

Calls and puts are not issued by the company with the common stock but rather by option makers or option writers. The maker of the option receives the price paid for the call or put minus commission costs. The option trades on the open market. Calls and puts are written and can be acquired through brokers and dealers. The writer is required to purchase or deliver the stock when requested.

Holders of calls and puts do not have to exercise them to earn a return. They can trade them in the secondary market for whatever their value is. The value of a call increases as the underlying common stock goes up in price. The call can be sold on the market before its expiration date.

WHY INVESTORS USE OPTIONS

Why use options? Reasons can vary from the conservative to the speculative. The most common reasons are:

- One can earn large profits with *leverage*, that is, without having to tie up a lot of one's own money. The leverage with options typically runs 20:1 (each investor dollar controls the profit on twenty dollars of stock) as contrasted with the 2:1 leverage with stocks bought on margin or the 1:1 leverage with stocks bought outright with cash. *Note*: Leverage is a two-edged sword. It works both ways—one can lose a lot, too. That is why using leverage is risky.

- Options may be purchased as "insurance or hedge" against large price drops in underlying stocks already held by the investor.

- If you are neutral or slightly bullish in the short term on stocks you own, you can sell (or write) options on those stocks and realize extra profit.

- Options offer a range of strategies that cannot be obtained with stocks. Thus, options are a flexible and complementary investment vehicle to stocks and bonds.

HOW OPTIONS ARE TRADED

Options are traded on listed option exchanges (secondary markets) such as the Chicago Board Options Exchange, American Stock Exchange, Philadelphia Stock Exchange, and Pacific Stock Exchange. They may also be exchanged in the over-the-counter (OTC) market. Option exchanges are only for buying and selling call and put options. Listed options are traded on organized exchanges. Conventional options are traded in the OTC market.

The Options Clearing Corporation (OCC) acts as principal in every options transaction for listed options contracts. As principal it issues all listed options, guarantees the contracts, and is the legal entity on the other side of every transaction. Orders are placed with this corporation, which then issues the calls or closes the positions. Since certificates are not issued for options, a brokerage account is required. An investor who exercises a call goes through the Clearing Corporation, which randomly selects a writer from a member list. A call writer is obligated to sell 100 shares at the exercise price.

Exchanges permit general orders (i.e., limit) and orders applicable only to the option (i.e., spread order).

TERMS OF AN OPTION

Three key terms in connection with options with which investors must be familiar are: (1) the exercise or strike price; (2) expiration date; and (3) option premium.

The *exercise price* is the price per share for 100 shares, which may be bought at (call). For a put, it is the price at which the stock may be sold. The purchase or sale of the stock is to the writer of the option. The *strike price* is set for the life of the option on the options exchange. When stock prices change, new exercise prices are introduced for trading purposes, reflecting the new value.

In case of conventional calls, restrictions do not exist on what the strike price should be. However, it is usually close to the market price of the stock it relates to. In the case of listed calls, stocks having a price lower than $50 a share must have strike prices in $5 increments. Stocks between $50 and $100 have striking prices in $20 increments. Strike prices are adjusted for material stock splits and stock dividends.

The *expiration date* of an option is the last day it can be exercised. For conventional options, the expiration date can be any business day; for a listed option there is a standardized expiration date.

The cost of an option is referred to as a *premium*. It is the price the buyer of the call or put has to pay the seller (writer). In other words, the option premium is what an option costs to the buyer. **Note:** With other securities, the premium is the excess of the purchase price over a determined theoretical value.

USING PROFIT DIAGRAMS

In order to understand the risks and rewards associated with various option strategies, it is very helpful to understand how the profit diagram works. In fact, it is essential to understanding how an option works. The profit diagram is a visual portrayal of profit in relation to the price of a stock at a single point in time.

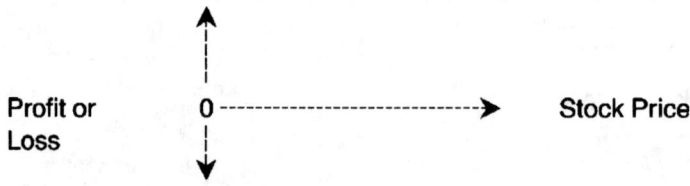

EXAMPLE 2:

ExxonMobil Stock Price in 3 months	Profit (Loss)
$ 60	-$ 2000
$ 70	-$ 1000
$ 80	$ 0
$ 90	$ 1000
$ 100	$ 2000

The following shows the profits diagram for 100 shares of ExxonMobil (XOM) stock if you bought them today at $80 per share and sold them in three months. (Commissions are ignored in this example.)

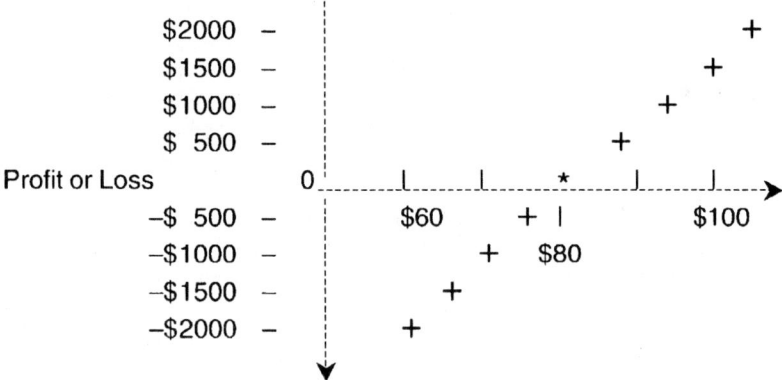

Note that all stocks have the same shape on the profit diagram at any point in the future. You will later see that this is not the case with options.

EXAMPLE 3: Assume that on April 7, an investor becomes convinced that ExxonMobil stock, which is trading at $80 a share, will move considerably higher in the next few months. So, he or she buys one call option on ExxonMobil stock with a premium of $2 a share. Since the call option involves a block of 100 shares of stock, it costs a total of $2 times 100 shares or $200. Assume further that this call option has a striking price of $85 and an expiration date near the end of September. What this means is that for $200 the investor has the right to buy:

1. 100 shares of ExxonMobil stock

2. At $85 a share

3. Until near the end of September.

This may not sound like much for $200, but if ExxonMobil stock goes up to $95 a share by the end of September, the investor has the right to purchase 100 shares of ExxonMobil stock for $8,500 ($85 times 100 shares) and to turn right around and sell them for $9,500, keeping the difference of $1,000, an $800 profit. That works out to 400% profit in less than five months.

However, if the ExxonMobil stock goes down in price, the most an investor could lose would be the price of the option, $200. The following displays the profit table for this example.

If the ExxonMobil stock price in September turns out to be:	The value of the call option would be:	And your profit would be:
$75	$ 0	$200
$80	$ 0	$200
$85	$ 0	$200
$87	$ 200	$ 0
$90	$ 500	$300
$95	$1000	$800

The profit diagram will look like this:

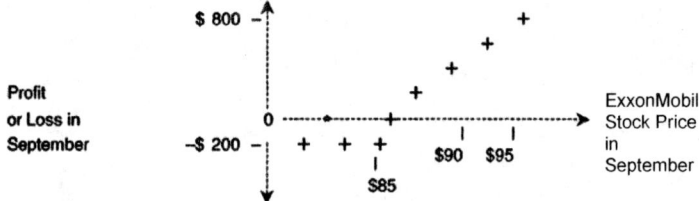

You are "long 1 ExxonMobil Sep 85 call" option.

Notice where the profit line bends—at $85, unlike stocks that have the same shape on the profit diagram at any point in the future. This is not the case with options. The investor starts making money after the price of ExxonMobil stock goes higher than the $85 striking price of the call option. When this happens, the option is called "in the money."

On the other hand, the profit diagram for a put option looks like this:

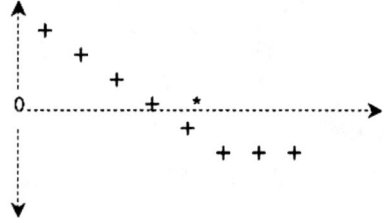

So, a put is typically used by an investor who is bearish on that particular stock. The put option can also be used as "insurance" against price drops for the investor with a long stock position.

OPTION COSTS

The premium for an option (or cost of an option) depends primarily on:

- Fluctuation in price of the underlying security. (A higher variability means a higher premium because of the greater speculative appeal of the option.)

- Time period remaining before the option's expiration. (The more time there is until the expiration, the greater the premium you must pay the seller.)
- Price spread between the stock price and the option's strike price. (A wider difference translates to a higher price.)

EXAMPLE 4: ABC stock is selling at $32 a share today. Consider two options:

1. Option X gives the right to buy the stock at $25 per share.
2. Option Y gives the right to buy the stock at $40 per share.

Since you would rather have an option to pay $25 for a $32 stock instead of $32, Option X is more valuable than Option Y. Thus, it will cost more to buy Option X than to buy Option Y.

Other factors that determine the cost of an option are:

- The dividend trend of the underlying security
- The volume of trading in the option
- The exchange the option is listed on
- "Going" interest rates
- The market price of the underlying stock

In-the-Money, At-the-Money, and Out-of-the-Money Call Options

Options may or may not be exercised, depending on the difference between the market price of the stock and the exercise price.

Let P = the price of the underlying stock

Let X = the exercise price

There are three possible situations:

1. If $P > X$ or $P - X > 0$, then the call option is said to be *in the money*. By exercising the call option, you, as a holder, realize a positive profit, $P - X$. The value of the call in this case is:

Value of call = (Market price of stock – Exercise price of call) × 100

EXAMPLE 5: Assume that the market price of a stock is $90, with a strike price of $80. The call has a value of $1,000.

2. If $P - X = 0$, then the option is said to be *at the money*.
3. If $P - X < 0$, then the option is said to be *out of the money*. It is unprofitable. The option holder can purchase the stock at the cheaper price in the market rather than exercising the option, and thus the option is thrown away. Out-of-the-money call options have no intrinsic value.

If the total premium (option price) of an option is $14 and the intrinsic value is $6, there is an additional premium of $8 arising from other factors.

Total premium comprises the intrinsic value and speculative premium (time value) based on variables like risk, expected future prices, maturity, leverage, dividend, and fluctuation in price.

Total premium = intrinsic value + speculative premium (time value)

1. Intrinsic value = In the money option

   i.e., P – X > 0 for a call and X – P > 0 for a put option.

2. Time value—For in-the-money options, time value is the difference between premium and intrinsic value. For other options, all value is time value.

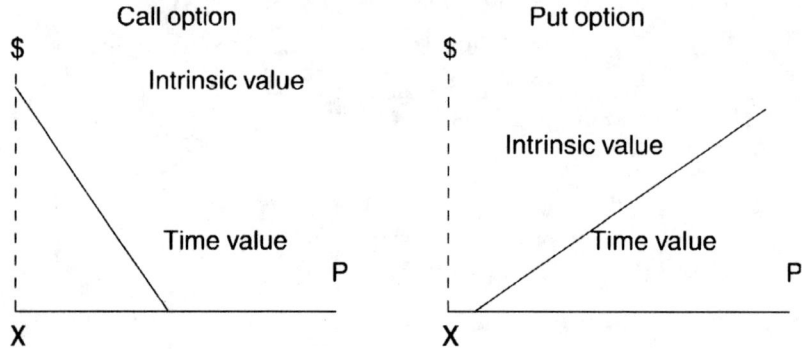

In-the-Money and Out-of-the-Money Put Options

A put option on a common stock allows the holder of the option to sell ("put") a share of the underlying stock at an exercise price until an expiration date. The definition of in-the-money and out-of-the-money are different for puts since the owner may sell stock at the strike price. For a put option, the option is in the money if P – X < 0.

Its value is determined as follows:

Value of put = (exercise price of put – market price of stock) × 100

The option is out of the money when P – X > 0 and has no value.

EXAMPLE 6: Assume a stock has a market price of $100 and a strike price of the put is $116. The value of the put is $1,600.

If market price of stock exceeds strike price, an out-of-the money put exists. Because a stock owner can sell it for a greater amount in the market relative to exercising the put, no intrinsic value exists for the out-of-money put.

	ABC Calls at 60 Strike Price Stock Price	ABC Puts at 60 Strike Price Stock Price
In-the-money	Over 60	Under 60
At-the-money	60	60
Out-of-money	Under 60	Over 60

The theoretical value for calls and puts reflects the price at which the options should be traded. But usually they are traded at prices exceeding true value when options have a long period to go. This difference is referred to as investment premium.

$$\text{Investment premium} \quad = \quad \frac{\text{Option premium} - \text{Option value}}{\text{Option value}}$$

EXAMPLE 7: Assume a put with a theoretical value of $2,500 and a price of $3,000. It is therefore traded at an investment premium of 20% [($3,000 – $2,500)/$2,500].

THE RISKS AND REWARDS OF OPTIONS

The risk in buying options is limited to the premium paid. That is the downside risk for option investing. For example, assume you own a two-month call option to acquire 500 shares of ABC Company at $20 per share. Within that time period, you exercise the option when the market price is $38. You make a gain of $9,000 ($18 × 500 shares) except for the brokerage commission. Of course, the higher the stock's price goes, the more you can profit. However, if the market price had declined from $20, you would not have exercised the call option, and you would have lost the cost of the option. *Note:* If you owned the stock whose price fell $10 per share, you would have lost $10 a share. But if you had an option to buy that stock, you could have lost only the cost (premium) of that option, no matter how far the stock price fell.

How Calls Work

By buying a call an investor can own common stock for a low percentage of the cost of buying regular shares. Leverage is obtained since a small change in common stock price can magnify a major move in the call option's price. An element of the percentage gain in the price of the call is the speculative premium related to the remaining time left on the call. Calls can also be viewed as a way of controlling 100 shares of stock without a large monetary commitment.

EXAMPLE 8: Assume that a security has a present market price of $70. A call can be bought for $600 permitting the purchase of 100 shares at $70 per share. If the stock price goes up, the call increases in value. Assume the stock goes to $95 at the call's expiration date. The profit is $25 per share in the call, or a total of $2,500 on an investment of $600. There is a return of Al 7%. When you exercise the call for 100 shares at $70 each, you can immediately sell them at $95 per share.

Note: You could have earned the same amount by investing directly in the common stock. However, you would have needed to invest $7,000, resulting in a much lower return rate.

How Puts Work

The put holder may sell 100 shares at the exercise price for a specified time period to a put writer. A put is bought when a price decline is expected. Like a call option, the entire premium cost (investment) would be lost if the price does not drop.

EXAMPLE 9: Assume that a stock has a market price of $80. You buy a put to sell 100 shares of stock at $80 per share. The put cost is $500. At the exercise date, the price of the stock goes to $70 a share. The profit is $10 per share, or $1,000. You just buy on the market 100 shares at $70 each and then sell them to the writer of the put for $80 each. The net gain is $500 ($1,000 – $500).

The following tables summarize payoffs, risks, and break-even stock prices for various option participants.

Option Payoffs and Risks

	Call Buyer	*Call Seller (Writer)*
Payoff	$-c + (P - X)$ where c = the call premium For a break-even, $-c + (P - X) = 0$ or $P = X + c.$	$+c - (P - X)$
Risk	Maximum risk is to lose the premium because investor throws away the out-of-the-money option	No risk limit as the stock price rises above the exercise price—uncovered (naked) option To be covered, investor should own the underlying stock or hold a long call on the same stock

	Put Buyer	*Put Seller (Writer)*
Payoff	$-c + (X - P)$ where c = the put premium For a break-even, $-c + (X - P) = 0$ or $P = X - c$	$+c - (X - P)$
Risk	Maximum risk is to lose the premium	Maximum risk is the strike price when the stock price is zero—uncovered (naked) option To be covered, investor should sell the underlying stock short or hold a long put on the same stock

Break-Even Points for Option Parties

Option Parties	*Break-Even Market Price*
A call holder	the strike price + the premium
A put holder	the strike price – the premium
A call writer	the strike price + the premium
A put writer	the strike price – the premium
A covered call writer	the original cost of the security – the premium
A covered put writer	the strike price + the premium (short the stock)

CALL AND PUT INVESTMENT STRATEGIES

Investment possibilities with calls and puts include (1) hedging, (2) speculation, (3) straddles, and (4) spreads. If one owns call and put options, one can hedge by holding two or more securities to reduce risk and earn a profit. An investor may purchase a stock and subsequently buy an option on it. For instance, he or she may buy a stock and write a call on it. Further, if an investor owns a stock that has appreciated, he or she may buy a put to insulate from downside risk.

> *EXAMPLE 10:* You bought 100 shares of XYZ at $52 per share and a put for $300 on the 100 shares at an exercise price of $52. If the stock does not move, you lose $300 on the put. If the price falls, your loss offsets your gain on the put. If stock price goes up, you have a capital gain on the stock but lose your investment in the put. To obtain the advantage of a hedge, you incur a loss on the put. Note that at the expiration date, you have a loss with no hedge any longer.

You may employ calls and puts to speculate. You may buy options when you believe you will make a higher return compared to investing in the underlying stock. You can earn a higher return at lower risk with out-of-the-money options. However, with such an option, the price is composed of just the investment premium, which may be lost if the stock does not increase in price. Here is an example of this kind of speculation.

> *EXAMPLE 11:* You speculate by buying an option contract to purchase 100 shares at $55 a share. The option costs $250. The stock price increases to $63 a share. You exercise the option and sell the shares in the market, recognizing a gain of $550 ($63 – $55 – $2.50 = $5.50 × 100 shares). You, as a speculator, can sell the option and earn a profit due to the appreciated value. But if the stock price drops, your loss is limited to $250 (the option's cost). Obviously, there will also be commissions. In sum, this call option allowed you to buy 100 shares worth $5,500 for $250 up to the option's expiration date.

Straddling combines a put and call on the identical security with the same strike price and expiration date. It allows you to trade on both sides of the market. You hope for a substantial change in stock price either way so as to earn a gain exceeding the cost of both options. If the price change does materialize, the loss is the cost of both options. You may increase risk and earning potential by closing one option prior to the other.

> *EXAMPLE 12:* You buy a call and a put for $8 each on October 31 when the stock price is $82. There is a three-month expiration date. Your investment is $16, or $1,600 in total. If the stock increases to $150 at expiration of the options, the call generates a profit of $60 ($68 – $8) and the loss on the put is $8. Your net gain is $52, or $5,200 in total.

In a *spread,* you buy a call option (long position) and write a call option (short position) in the identical stock. A sophisticated investor may write many spreads to profit from the spread in option premiums. There is substantial return potential but high risk. Different kinds of spreads exist, such as a *bull call spread* (two calls having the same expiration date) and a *horizontal spread* (initiated with either two call options or two put options on the identical underlying stock). These two options must be with the same strike price but different expiration dates.

You may purchase straddles and spreads to maximize return or reduce risk. You may buy them through dealers belonging to the Put and Call Brokers and Dealers Association.

HOW OPTION WRITING WORKS

The writer of a call contracts to sell shares at the strike price for the price incurred for the call option. Call option writers do the opposite of buyers. Investors write options expecting price appreciation in the stock to be less than what the call buyer anticipates. They may even anticipate the price of the stock to be stable or to decrease. Option writers receive the option premium less applied transaction costs. If the option is not exercised, the writer earns the price he paid for it. If the option is exercised, the writer incurs a loss, possibly significant.

If the writer of an option elects to sell, he must give the stock at the contracted price if the option is exercised. In either instance, the option writer receives income from the premium. (Shares are in denominations of 100.) An investor typically sells an option when he anticipates it not to be exercised. The risk of option writing is that the writer, if uncovered, must purchase stock or, if covered, loses the gain. The writer can purchase back an option to end exposure.

> *EXAMPLE 13:* Assume a strike price of $50 and a premium for the call option of $7. If the stock is below $50, the call would not be exercised, and you earn the $7 premium. If the stock is above $50, the call may be exercised, and you must furnish 100 shares at $50. But the call writer loses money if the stock price is above $57.

SELLING AN OPTION ON SOMETHING YOU DO NOT OWN

Naked (uncovered) and *covered* options exist. Naked options are on stock the writer does not own. There is much risk because you have to buy the stock and then immediately sell it to the option buyer on demand, irrespective of loss. The investor writes the call or put for the premium and will retain it if the price change is beneficial to him or insignificant. The writer has unlimited loss possibilities.

To eliminate this risk, the writer may write *covered options* (options written on stocks owned). For instance, a call can be written for stock the writer owns or a put can be written for stock sold short. This is a conservative strategy to generate positive returns. The objective is to write an out-of-the-money option, retain the premium paid, and have the stock price equal but not exceed the option exercise price. The writing of a covered call option is like hedging a position, because if the stock price drops, the writer's loss on the security is partly offset against the option premium.

OPTION STRATEGIES

Currently, about 90% of the option strategies implemented by investors are long calls and long puts only. These are the most basic strategies and are the easiest to implement. However, they are usually the riskiest in terms of a traditional measure of risk: variability (uncertainty) of outcomes. A variety of other strategies can offer better returns at less risk.

1. *Long Call*. This strategy is implemented simply by purchasing a call option on a stock. This strategy is good for a very bullish stock assessment.

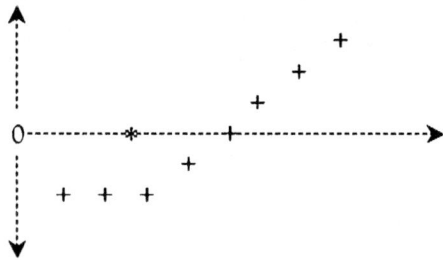

2. *Bull Call Spread*. This strategy requires two calls, both with the same expiration date. It is good for a mildly bullish assessment of the underlying stock.

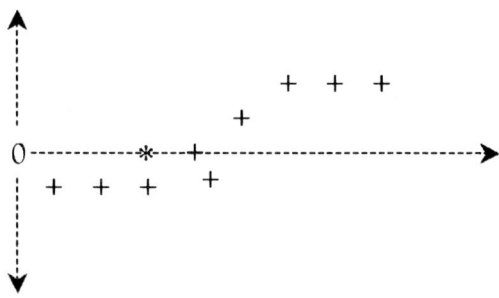

3. *Naked Put Write*. This strategy is implemented by writing a put and is appropriate for a neutral or mildly bullish projection on the underlying stock.

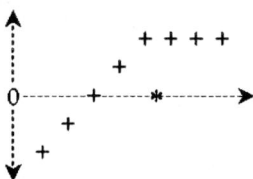

4. *Covered Call Write*. This strategy is equivalent to the naked put write. This strategy is good for a neutral or mildly bullish assessment of the underlying stock.

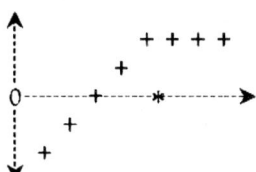

5. *Straddle.* This strategy is implemented by purchasing both a call and a put option on the same underlying stock. This strategy is good when the underlying stock is likely to make a big move but there is uncertainty as to its direction.

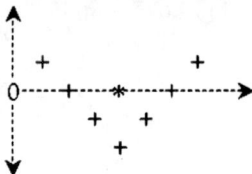

6. *Inverse Straddle.* This strategy is implemented by writing both a call and a put on the same underlying stock. This strategy is appropriate for a neutral assessment of the underlying stock. A substantial amount of collateral is required for this strategy due to the open-ended risk should the underlying stock make a big move.

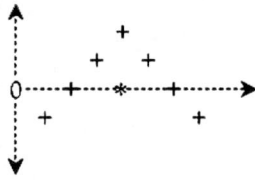

7. *Horizontal Spread.* This strategy is implemented with either two call options or two put options on the same underlying stock. These two options must have the same striking price but have different expiration dates.

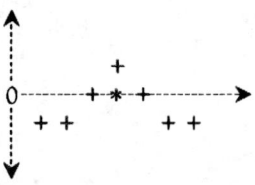

8. *Naked Call Write.* This strategy is implemented by writing a call and is appropriate for a neutral or mildly bearish assessment on the underlying stock. A substantial amount of collateral is required for this strategy due to the open-ended risk should the underlying stock rise in value.

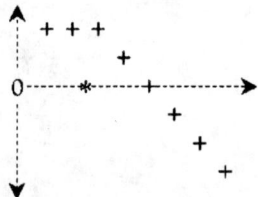

9. *Bear Put Spread.* This strategy is the opposite of the bull call spread. It is implemented with two puts, both with the same expiration date. This strategy is appropriate for a mildly bearish assessment of the underlying stock.

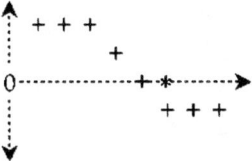

10. *Long Put.* This strategy is implemented simply by purchasing a put option on a stock. It is good for a very bearish stock assessment.

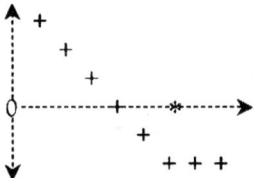

Note: Computer software such as OptionVue plots profit tables and diagrams and helps evaluate large numbers of options for minimum risk and maximum reward.

CHOOSING AN OPTION STRATEGY

The key questions remain: Which option strategy should you choose? What factors should be considered? What would be a typical decision process? There are three major steps in the decision process:

1. *Select the underlying stock.* First, you should decide which stock to consider and do a thorough analysis on the stock, including the effects of current market trends.

2. *Choose the strategy.* You then determine the risk involved in the stock based on its volatility. Computer software can be of great help. Based on the assessment on the stock (bullish or bearish) and its volatility, a strategy is chosen. For example, a strongly bullish, high volatility stock would indicate a long call strategy, as the underlying stock is likely to increase substantially.

The ranking of strategies so far discussed, from bullish to bearish, is as follows:

Bullish	• Long Call • Bull Call Spread • Naked Put Write (Covered Call Write)
Neutral	• Straddle • Inverse Straddle • Horizontal Spread

Bearish	• Naked Call Write
	• Bear Put Spread
	• Long Put

Note: The key to choosing the specific option contracts to implement a strategy is to accurately forecast both the price of the underlying stock and the amount of time it will take to get to that price. This will facilitate choosing the striking price and expiration date of the options to be used.

3. *Assess the risk.* Option strategies have some interesting risk/reward trade-offs. Some strategies have a small chance of a very large profit, while other strategies have a large chance of making a small profit. You have to decide exactly how much to risk for how much reward.

INDEX OPTIONS

Options on stock indexes rather than on individual stocks have been popular among investors. Index options include ones on S&P 100, S&P OTC 250, S&P 500, Gold/Silver Index, and Computer Technology Index.

Index options offer advantages over stock options in several ways:

1. There is greater stability in a stock index due to diversification. Because an index is a composite of stocks, the effects of mergers, announcements, and reports are much milder in an index than on an individual stock.

2. Index options provide a wider selection of striking prices and expiration dates than stock options.

3. It appears easier to predict the behavior of the market than an individual stock.

4. More liquidity exists with index options. Due to the high volume of activity, it is easier to buy and sell index options for the price you want. This is especially helpful for far out-of-the-money or deep in-the-money options.

5. Index options are always settled in cash, never in shares of the underlying stock. This settlement is automatic at expiration and the cash settlement prevents unintended stock assignment.

A disadvantage of index options is that no covered writing is possible on index options.

SOFTWARE FOR OPTIONS ANALYSIS

Value Line Daily Options Survey (www.valueline.com) provides daily evaluations and ranks of 200,000 stocks and stock index options. Also included is *The Option Strategist* (www.optionstrategist.com), an online publication offering advice about investing with options. The following is a list of popular options software.

• *Open Interest*

Rocky Point Software

www.rpsw.com

- *Visual Options Analyzer (VOptions)*
  Analyzer
  www.voptions.com
- *Optionetics Platinum*
  OptionsAnalysis
  www.optionetics.com
- *OptionsXpress*
  www.optionsXpress.com

THE BLACK-SCHOLES OPTION PRICING MODEL

The model provides the relationship between call option value and the five factors that determine the premium of an option's market value over its expiration value:

1. *Time to maturity.* The longer the option period, the greater the value of the option.
2. *Stock price volatility.* The greater the volatility of the underlying stock's price, the greater its value.
3. *Exercise price.* The lower the exercise price, the greater the value.
4. *Stock price.* The higher the price of the underlying stock, the greater the value.
5. *Risk-free rate.* The higher the risk-free rate, the higher the value.

The formula is:

$$V = P[N(d_1)] - Xe^{-rt}[N(d_2)]$$

where

V = current value of a call option

P = current price of the underlying stock

N(d) = cumulative normal probability density function = probability that a deviation less than d will occur in a standard normal distribution.

X = exercise or strike price of the option

t = time to exercise date (For example, 3 months means t = 3/12 = 1/4 = 0.25)

r = (continuously compounded) risk-free rate of interest

e = 2.71828

$$d_1 = \frac{\ln(P/X) + [r + s^2/2]t}{s\sqrt{t}}$$
$$d_2 = d_1 - s\sqrt{t}$$

s^2 = variance per period of (continuously compounded) rate of return on the stock

The formula, while somewhat imposing, actually requires readily available input data, with the exception of s², or volatility. P, X, r, and t are easily obtained. The implications of the option model are the following:

1. The value of the option increases with the level of stock price relative to the exercise price (P/X), the time to expiration times the interest rate (rt), and the time to expiration times the stock's variability (s²t).

2. Other properties:

   a. The option price is always less than the stock price.

   b. The optional price never falls below the payoff to immediate exercise (P – EX or zero, whichever is larger).

   c. If the stock is worthless, the option is worthless.

   d. As the stock price becomes very large, the option price approaches the stock price less the present value of the exercise price.

EXAMPLE 14: You are evaluating a call option that has a $20 exercise price and sells for $1.60. It has three months to expiration. The underlying stock price is also $20 and its variance is 0.16. The risk-free rate is 12%. The option's value is:

First, calculate d_1 and d_2:

$$d_1 = \frac{1n(P/X) + [r + s^2/2]t}{s\sqrt{t}}$$

$$= \frac{1n(\$20\$20) + [0.12 + (0.16/2)](0.25)}{(0.40)\sqrt{0.25}}$$

$$= \frac{0 + 0.05}{0.20} = 0.25$$

$$d_2 = d_1 - s\sqrt{t} = 0.25 - 0.20 = 0.05$$

Next, look up the values for $N(d_1)$ and $N(d_2)$:

$$N(d_1) = N(0.25) = 1 - 0.4013 = 0.5987$$

$$N(d_2) = N(0.05) = 1 - 0.4801 = 0.5199$$

Finally, use these values to find the option's value:

$$V = P[N(d_1)] - Xe^{-rt}[Nd_2)]$$

$$= \$20[0.5987] - \$20e^{(-0.12)(0.25)}[0.5199]$$

$$= \$11.97 - \$19.41(0.5199)$$

$$\$11.97 - \$10.09 = \$1.88$$

At $1.60, the option is undervalued according to the Black-Scholes model. The rational investor would buy one option and sell .5987 shares of stock short.

Many websites, such as www.money-zine.com/Calculators/Investment-Calculators/Black-Scholes-Calculator, provide a calculator for option calculations. One example is given in Exhibit 38-2.

EXHIBIT 38-2
BLACK-SCHOLES CALCULATOR

Black Scholes Calculator

This Black-Scholes calculator allows you to figure out the value of a European call or put option. The calculator uses the stock's current share price, the option strike price, time to expiration, risk-free interest rate, and volatility to derive the value of these options. The Black Scholes calculation used by this tool assumes no dividend is paid on the stock.

Black Scholes Calculator

Current Share Price ($)	55.00
Option Strike Price ($)	50.00
Time to expiration (Years)	0.3333
Risk-Free Interest Rate (%)	8.000%
Volatility	10.000%
Calculator Results	
European Call Value ($)	6.3342
European Put Value ($)	0.0186

Source: www.money-zine.com/Calculators/Investment-Calculators/Black-Scholes-Calculator.

Note: Under ASC 718, *Accounting for Stock-Based Compensation*, companies are required to provide new footnote disclosures about employee stock options based on their fair value at the date of the grant. Since options granted to employees generally are not traded on an organized exchange, ASC 718-10 requires companies to use recognized option pricing models such as the Black-Scholes model to estimate the fair values.

The Black-Scholes Problem and Other Option Models

The Black-Scholes model, however, is widely considered to overstate the value of employee stock options by an unacceptable margin because it does not take into account the essential differences between traditional exchange-traded stock options and those granted to employees.

Unlike conventional options, employee options are subject to vesting schedules and forfeiture conditions, and cannot be transferred. As a result, they are invariably exercised before their usual 10-year term expires. These characteristics reduce the value of an option. In its proposed rule for expensing stock options, the Financial Accounting Standards Board has acknowledged that the Black-Scholes model, though the most popular option-pricing model, may be less appropriate than a lattice-based method for valuing employee grants. This is simply because a lattice-based method can take into account assumptions that reflect the conditions under which employee options are typically granted. The binomial model is the most commonly used lattice-based method, but other Models that may be better suited to compensation programs that link vesting to specific performance objectives are as follows:

- *Binomial.* The most commonly used lattice-based model, the binomial model can calculate option values when the price of the underlying stock moves either up or down over a short interval. It is considered better than Black-Scholes at taking into account how factors such as forfeiture and exercise before expiration, as well as an employee's risk aversion and lack of diversification, affect an option's value at the time it is granted.

- *Trinomial.* The trinomial model goes a step further by allowing for the underlying stock price to either remain unchanged or move up or down. This is useful for valuing performance-based options that vest only if the stock price exceeds a certain level over time.

- *Multinomial.* This model can take many more factors into account than either the binomial or trinomial framework. Such additional flexibility may be required to value options that cannot be exercised unless the underlying stock price exceeds the performance of one or more indices. But when there are more than two such sources of uncertainty, however, a Monte Carlo simulation may be preferable, as it is easier to apply than lattice models.

FUTURES CONTRACTS

Futures are another form of derivative instrument. Futures are contracts to purchase or sell a given amount of an item for a given price by a certain date in the future (thus the name "futures market"). The seller of a futures contract agrees to deliver the item to the buyer of the contract, who agrees to purchase the item. The contract specifies the amount, valuation, method, quality, month, and means of delivery, and exchange to be traded in. The month of delivery is the expiration date; in other words, the date on which the commodity or financial instrument must be delivered.

Commodity contracts are guarantees by a seller to deliver a commodity (e.g., cocoa or cotton). Financial contracts are commitments by the seller to deliver a financial instrument (e.g., a Treasury bill) or a specific amount of foreign currency.

For embedded credit derivatives, Accounting Standards Update (ASU) No. 2010-11 (March 2010), *Derivatives and Hedging* (ASC Topic 815), *Scope Exception Related to Embedded Credit Derivatives,* states the following.

These two items do not meet the scope exception for embedded credit derivatives:

1. The possible future payments due to factors excluding subordination.

2. A derivative characteristic applied to a different risk included in a securitized security.

A company may select the fair value option for a securitized security. A change in fair value over an accounting period is recognized in the income statement.

A credit derivative is a bilateral financial contract that isolates specific aspects of credit risk from an underlying instrument and may be utilized to transfer default risk from the holder of the instrument to a counterparty that will be compensated for taking on that risk. The fair value of a credit derivative is based on the changing credit risk of the underlying financial instrument. Credit derivatives may be used to reduce the risk of holding a financial instrument or for speculative purposes. The holder (purchaser) of a credit derivative is exposed to the credit risk of the protection seller should that protection seller be unable to pay if there is a credit default by the obligor on the underlying financial instrument.

An embedded derivative applies to the terms impacting the cash flows required by a contract in a similar way as a derivative instrument.

The Difference between a Long and Short Position

A long position is the purchase of a contract expecting the price to increase. A short position is selling expecting the price to decrease. The position may be terminated by reversing the transaction. For example, the long buyer can subsequently engage in a short position of the commodity or financial instrument. Mostly all futures are offset (canceled out) prior to delivery. It is unusual for delivery to settle the futures contract.

How Futures Contracts Are Traded

A futures contract is traded in the futures market. Trading is performed by specialized brokers. Some commodity firms deal exclusively in futures. The fee for a futures contract is tied to the amount of the contract and the item's price. Commissions vary depending on the amount and nature of the contract. The trading in futures is basically the same as with stocks, except the investor needs a commodity trading account. However, the margin buying and the types of orders are the same. You buy or sell contracts with desired terms.

FUTURES TRADING AND RISK

Futures trading may assist an investor handling inflation, but is specialized and has much risk. Loss may be magnified due to leverage. Leverage (using of other people's money) means with a minimal down payment you control something of much greater value. For instance, you can put down $2,000 to control a futures contract valued at $40,000. Each time the price of a commodity increases $1, you could earn or lose $20. With an option, you lose just the money invested. With a futures contract, you lose a lot more. Further, futures contract prices may be very unstable. However, many exchanges place per-day price limits on each contract trading, to insulate traders from huge losses.

COMMODITIES FUTURES

A commodity contract involves a seller who contracts to deliver a commodity by a specified date at a set price. The contract stipulates the item, price, expiration date, and standardized unit to be traded (e.g., 100,000 pounds). Commodity contracts may last up to one year. The impact of market activity on the contract's value must always be appraised.

Assume that you purchase a futures contract for the delivery of 2,000 units of a commodity six months from now at $5.00 per unit. The seller of the contract does not have to have physical custody of the item, and the contract buyer does not have to take possession of the commodity at the "deliver" date. Commodity contracts are typically reversed, or terminated, before consummation. For example, as the initial buyer of 5,000 bushels of wheat, you may engage in a similar contract to sell the same amount, in effect closing your position.

You may enter into commodity trading to achieve high return rates and hedge inflation. In times of increasing prices, commodities react favorably because they are tied to economic trends. However, there is high risk and uncertainty since commodity prices fluctuate and there is a lot of low-margin investing. You need a lot of cash in case of a margin call to cover losses. To minimize risk, hold a diversified portfolio. Futures contracts are only for knowledgeable and experienced investors.

The buyer of a commodity can opt to terminate the contract or continue holding on expectation of higher profits. Conversely, the investor may use the earnings to furnish margin on another futures contract (called an inverse pyramid in a futures contract).

Commodity futures enable buyers and sellers to negotiate cash (spot) prices. Cash is paid to immediately obtain custody of a commodity. Prices in the cash market depend partly upon prices in the futures market. There may be higher prices for the commodity over time, taking into account carrying costs and expected inflation.

Commodity futures are traded in the Chicago Board of Trade (CBOT), the largest exchange. There are other exchanges specializing in particular commodities such as the New York Cotton Exchange (NCTN), Chicago Mercantile Exchange (CME), and Kansas City Board of Trade (KBOT). Because of the possibility of substantial gains and losses in commodities, exchanges have caps on the highest daily price changes for a commodity. The Federal Commodity Futures Trading Commission regulates commodities exchanges. Commodity futures trading is accomplished through open outcry auction.

RETURNS AND RISKS FOR FUTURES CONTRACTS

The return on a futures contract stems from capital appreciation (selling price less acquisition cost) because no current income is earned. Significant capital gain may arise from price fluctuation in the commodity and the impact of leverage due to low margin. If things go against you, much of your investment may be lost. The return on investment in commodities (a long or short position) equals:

$$\text{Return on investment} = \frac{\text{Selling price} - \text{Purchase price}}{\text{Margin deposit}}$$

EXAMPLE 15: Assume you buy a contract on a commodity for $80,000, with a deposit of $10,000. Subsequently, you sell the contract for $85,000. The return is:

$$\frac{\$85,000 - \$80,000}{\$10,000} = 50\%$$

The margin requirement for commodity contracts is small, typically from 3% to 6% of the contract's value. (For stocks, recall that the margin requirement is 50%.) Because in commodities trading there is no loan involved, there is no interest.

An *initial margin* deposit must be made on a futures contract so as to cover a drop in market price on the contract. Such deposit varies with the type of contract and the particular commodity exchange.

A *maintenance deposit*, which is lower than the initial deposit, may also be required. It furnishes the minimum margin that must be kept in the account. It is typically about 80% of the initial margin.

EXAMPLE 16: On September 1, you contract to purchase 50,000 pounds of sugar at $2 a pound to be delivered by December 31. The value of the total contract is $100,000. The initial margin requirement is 15%, or $15,000. The margin maintenance requirement is 80%, or $12,000. Assuming a contract loss of $2,500, you must pay $2,500 to cover the margin position. If not, the contract will be terminated with the ensuing loss.

WHO USES FUTURES

Trading in futures is performed by hedgers and speculators. Investors employ hedging to protect their positions in a commodity. For instance, a farmer (the seller) may hedge to obtain a higher price for goods while a processor (or buyer) of the product will hedge to get a lower price. By hedging you reduce the risk of loss but forego earning a sizable profit.

EXAMPLE 17: Commodities are currently selling at $160 a pound. The potential buyer (assume a manufacturer) anticipates the price to increase. To protect against higher prices, the purchaser buys a futures contract selling at $175 a pound. Five months later, the commodity price is $225. The futures contract price will similarly increase, say to $250. The buyer's profit is $75 a pound. If 10,000 pounds are involved, the total profit is $750,000. However, the cost on the market rose by only $65 pound, or $650,000. The producer has hedged the position, deriving a profit of $100,000, and has put a tip on the rising commodity costs.

Commodities may also be used for speculation in the market. Speculators engage in futures contracts to obtain capital gain on price increases of the commodity, currency, or financial instrument.

EXAMPLE 18: You buy a September futures contract for 20,000 pounds of wheat at $2 a pound. If the price rises to $2.20, you'll gain $.20 a pound for a total gain of $4,000. The percent gain, assuming an initial margin requirement of 5%, is 200% ($.2/$.1). Assuming transactions occur over a three-month period, the annual gain would be 800% (200% 12 months/3 months). This resulted from a mere 10% ($.2/$2.00) gain in the price of a pound of wheat.

HOW TO MINIMIZE RISKS

Spreading capitalizes on wide swings in price and at the same time limits loss exposure. Spreading is like stock option trading. You engage in at least two contracts to earn some profit while capping loss potential. You buy one contract and sell the other, expecting to achieve a reasonable profit. If the worst occurs, the spread aids in minimizing the investor's loss.

> **EXAMPLE 19:** You buy Contract A for 20,000 pounds of commodity T at $300 a pound. Simultaneously, you sell short Contract B for 20,000 pounds of the identical commodity at $325 per pound. Later, you sell Contract A for $325 a pound and buy Contract B for $345 a pound. Contract A earns a profit of $25 a pound while Contract B has a loss of $20 a pound. The net effect is a profit of $5 a pound, or a total gain of $100,000.

FINANCIAL FUTURES

Financial futures include (1) interest rate, (2) foreign currency, and (3) stock index. Financial futures trading is similar to commodity trading. It represents about 70 percent of all contracts. Due to fluctuation in interest and exchange rates, financial futures can be used as a hedge. They may also be used to speculate, having potential for wide price swings. Financial futures have a lower margin requirement than commodities do. For instance, the margin on a U.S. Treasury bill might be as low as 2%.

Financial futures are traded in the New York Futures Exchange, Amex Commodities Exchange, International Monetary Market (part of Chicago Mercantile Exchange), and the Chicago Board of Trade.

How Interest Rate Futures Work

An interest rate futures contract gives the holder the right to a specified amount of the underlying debt security at a later date (typically not exceeding three years). They may be in such forms as Treasury bills, notes, and bonds, paper, "Ginnie Mae (GNMA)" certificates, CRB Index, Eurodollars, and U.S. Dollar Index.

Interest rate futures are expressed as a percentage of the face value of the applicable debt security. The value of interest rate futures contracts is linked to interest rates. For instance, as interest rates drop, the contract's value rises. If the price or quote of the contract increases, the buyer gains but the seller loses. A change of one basis point in interest rates causes a price change. A basis point equals 1/100 of 1%.

Those trading in interest rate futures do not typically take custody of the financial instrument. The contract is employed either to hedge or to speculate on future interest rates and security prices.

How Currency Futures Work

A *currency futures contract* provides the right to a stipulated amount of foreign currency at a later date. The contracts are standardized, and secondary markets exist. Currency futures are stated in dollars per unit of the underlying foreign currency. They usually have a delivery date not exceeding one year.

Currency futures may be used either to hedge or speculate. Hedging in a currency may lock you into the best possible money exchange.

STOCK INDEX FUTURES CONTRACTS

A *stock index futures contract* is linked to a stock market index (e.g., the S&P 500 Stock Index, New York Stock Exchange Composite Stock Index). But smaller investors can use the S&P 100 futures contract, which has a lower margin deposit. Stock index futures allow you to participate in the overall stock market. You can buy and sell the "market as a whole" instead of one security. If you expect a bull market but are not certain which stock will increase, you should purchase (long position) a stock index future. Since there is a lot of risk, trade in stock index futures only to hedge.

TRANSACTING IN FUTURES

You may invest directly in a commodity or indirectly through a mutual fund. A third way is to buy a *limited partnership* involved with commodity investments. The mutual fund and partnership approaches are more conservative, because risk is spread and there is professional management.

Futures may be directly invested in as follows:

1. *Commodity pools.* Professional traders manage a pool. A filing is made with the Commodity Futures Trading Commission (CFTC).
2. *Full-service brokers.* They may recommend something, when attractive.
3. *Discount brokers.* Investors must decide when and if to trade.
4. *Managed futures.* Investors deposit funds in an individual managed account and choose a commodity trading advisor (CTA) to trade it.

To obtain information on managed futures, refer to:

1. *ATA Research Inc.* provides information on trading advisors and manages individuals' accounts via private pools and funds.
2. *Barclay Trading Group* publishes quarterly reports on trading advisers.
3. *CMA Reports* monitors the performance of trading advisers and private pools.
4. *Managed Account Reports*, monthly newsletters, track the funds and furnish information on their fees and track records.
5. *Trading Advisor* follows more than 100 trading advisers.

The drawbacks to managed futures include:

- High cost of a futures program, ranging from 15% to 20% of the funds invested.
- Substantial risk and inconsistent performance of fund advisors. *Note:* Despite its recent popularity, management futures are still a risky choice and should not be done apart from a well-diversified portfolio.

PRINTED CHART SERVICES AND SOFTWARE FOR FUTURES

Among the many printed chart services are companies such as Future Charts (http://futures.tradingcharts.com). Computer software programs for futures analysis and charting services include the following:

- Go Futures

  www.gofutures.com
- E-min: Quotes and Charts

  www.iqchart.com
- OptionsXpress

  www.optionsxpress.com

  For further chart directories on the web, visit www.giantexplorer.com.

FINANCIAL ENGINEERING

Closely related to the use of financial derivatives for risk management is *financial engineering*. Financial engineering, an obscure term in finance and investments, is based on financial economics, or the application of economic principles to the dynamics of securities markets, especially for the purpose of structuring, pricing, and managing the risk of financial contracts. In designing a risk-management strategy, the financial engineer, like the civil engineer designing a bridge, works within budgetary and physical restrictions. How much will it cost? How will it perform under present and future tax and accounting regulations and rules? Will it survive a financial earthquake, such as an opposite party's default? Will the strategy perform even if the market moves abruptly and severely? Basically, to be successful, the financial engineer must seek optimal solutions within many diverse and often conflicting constraints.

These varied restrictions lead to different solutions. Financial engineers can design different types of financial instruments or strategies to produce a desired outcome. Robert C. Merton has presented a concrete example of the financial engineer's ability to develop alternative routes to the same end, all basically similar but each with its pros and cons (*Journal of Banking and Finance*, June 1995). For instance, assume a corporate investor wishes to take a leveraged position in the S&P 500 basket of American stocks. Merton lists and dwells on eleven ways of accomplishing that goal. The first three are conventional ways:

1. Buying each stock individually on the margin.
2. Borrowing to buy shares in a S&P 500 index fund.
3. Borrowing to purchase a basket of stocks such as AMEX's SPDR product.

The next three are products in which traditional financial intermediaries act as principals and offer payoffs that closely emulate the leveraged stock position; the actual products are structured as bank CDs, indexed notes, or variable rate annuities. The last five deal with buying so-called financial derivatives, such as futures, forwards, swaps, or one of two options on the S&P index. They are so called in that their payoffs are a function (or are derived from) the value of an underlying index.

Each of the eleven instruments or strategies can give the investor exposure to the stock market, and each produces functionally similar payoffs. The multitude of solutions exists due to the differing constraints facing the financial engineer. It is important to realize that as bridges often collapse, financial engineered products can fail, and examining their wreckage to determine culpability is equally difficult.

Nevertheless, financial managers need to benchmark and keep abreast of their rivals' successful uses of financial engineering. CPAs need to be familiar with financial derivative products. The issuance of ASC 718 means CPAs who prepare and audit the financial statements of the companies that issue employee stock options will need to become familiar with option pricing models—including the Black-Scholes model.

ASC 718-10 requires a public entity to measure the cost of employee services received in exchange for an award of equity instruments based on the grant-date fair value of the award (with limited exceptions). That cost will be recognized over the period during which an employee is required to provide service in exchange for the award—the requisite service period (usually the vesting period). The grant-date fair value of employee share options and similar instruments will be estimated using option-pricing models (such as the Black-Scholes or the lattice method of valuation).

Option theory has many applications addressed to CFOs and other financial officers. Besides the Black-Scholes solution for a relatively simple option, many capital budgeting projects have option components: Corporate debt is callable or convertible, a decision may be made to prepay a mortgage, labor contracts may endow options on workers (e.g., the choice of early retirement), real estate leases can be renewed, a mine can be opened or closed, and bank lines of credit often contain contingent elements. The correct valuations of so many interest-rate-contingent securities depend on a satisfactory dynamic model of the interest rate process.

The Use and Misuse of Financial Engineering

Most of the news stories about derivatives are related to financial disasters. Much less is heard about the benefits of derivatives. Because of these benefits, more than 90% of large U.S. companies use derivatives on a regular basis. It will be necessary for all controllers and CFOs to understand derivatives to do their job well. Even now, sophisticated investors and analysts are demanding that firms use derivatives to hedge certain risks. For example, Compaq Computer was sued by a shareholder group for failing to properly hedge its foreign exchange exposure. The shareholders lost the suit, but Compaq got the message and now uses currency futures to hedge its international operations. In another example, Prudential Securities reduced its earnings estimate for Cone Mills, a North Carolina textile company, because Cone did not sufficiently hedge its exposure to changing cotton prices.

These examples show that if a company can safely and inexpensively hedge its risks, it should do so. It should not speculate with derivatives in an effort to increase profits. Hedging allows managers to concentrate on running their core businesses without having to worry about interest rate, currency, and commodity price variability. However, problems can arise quickly when hedges are improperly constructed or when a corporate treasurer, eager to report relatively high returns, uses derivatives for speculative purposes.

One interesting example of a derivatives debacle involved Kashima Oil, a Japanese firm that imports oil. It pays with U.S. dollars but then sells oil in the Japanese market for yen. Kashima began by using currency futures to hedge but then started to speculate on dollar–yen price movements, hoping to increase profits. When the currency markets moved against Kashima's speculative position, lax accounting rules permitted it to avoid reporting the losses by simply rolling over the contract. By the time Kashima bit the bullet and closed its position, it had lost $1.5 billion. Other companies have experienced similar problems.

Other financial engineering schemes were skillfully designed to achieve desired financial goals (such as to hide losses). Many dubious financial transactions created to conceal potential financial problems surfaced in year 2002. Enron, Global Crossing, and the Baptist Foundation of Arizona are cases in point. In order to "manage earnings," they all set up off-balance-sheet ventures and did not disclose much of their off-balance sheet debt. Enron engaged in complicated financial engineering to keep a strong investment credit and stock price. Enron chose to achieve this not through the old-fashioned means of issuing equity (which dilutes existing shares) or selling assets outright (cash does not earn much), but by shifting debt off the balance sheet through special-purpose entities and other unconsolidated affiliates. Enron also used another device called a "synthetic lease," which has been very popular among financial engineers. The goal of such a lease is to keep reported earnings high and balance sheet assets low because small boosts to earnings can have a significant impact on the stock price. In addition, for GAAP reporting, the financing is reported as an operating lease, yet the firm retains control and tax benefits of ownership. It is the financial equivalent of eating one's cake and having it, too. This kind of lease structure works well for technology firms, retailers, and others. The benefits range from helping to keep stock prices high, adding stores "off balance sheet" and polishing debt-to-equity ratios.

Enron also had been accused of using financial derivatives to manipulate company earnings figures, not just to hedge or protect itself from some sort of risk. For example, one use of the "mark-to-market accounting" rule is to estimate the value of a contract to deliver a product or service at a future time. This works where there are established futures markets but becomes difficult for assets that cannot be easily sold or in areas where there are uniform markets, such as in natural gas or electricity futures. Enron booked revenue and earnings that go out 20 years, which is like pricing by rumor.

Note that derivatives can be useful but deceptive tools. They should be used to hedge against certain risks, but the leverage inherent in derivatives contracts makes them potentially dangerous instruments. Also, CFOs, CEOs, and board members should be reasonably knowledgeable about the derivatives their firms use, should establish policies regarding when they can and cannot be used, and should establish audit procedures to ensure that the policies are actually carried out. Moreover, a firm's derivatives position should be reported to stockholders, because stockholders have a right to know when situations such as that involving P&G or Kashima might arise.

CHAPTER 39

MERGERS AND ACQUISITIONS[*]

CONTENTS

[*] Adrian P. Fitzsimons Ph.D., CPA (St. John's University, NY), and Biagio Pilato, LL.M., CPA (St. John's University, NY), contributed to the updates in this chapter.

Exhibits

Accounting Standards Update (ASU) No. 2017-01 (January 2017), *Business Combinations (Topic 805), Clarifying the Definition of a Business*, defines a business as an integrated set of activities (e.g., input, process) that must have a significant impact resulting in an output. If fair value of gross assets bought is concentrated in one identifiable asset or group of similar assets, the set is not deemed a business. An example of an identifiable asset is one that is connected to another identifiable asset and cannot be removed and used separately without substantial cost.

This chapter discusses all facets of mergers and acquisitions including deciding on terms, key factors to consider, pros and cons of mergers, types of arrangements, evaluative criteria, valuation methods, financial effects of the merger, holding companies, takeover bids, SEC filing requirements, accounting and reporting requirements for business combinations, and financial analysis of combinations. External growth occurs when a business purchases the existing assets of another entity through a merger. You are often required to appraise the suitability of a potential merger as well as participate in negotiations. Besides the growth aspect, a merger may reduce risk through diversification. The three common ways of joining two or more companies are a merger, consolidation, or a holding company.

In a merger, two or more companies are combined into one, where only the acquiring company retains its identity. Generally, the larger of the two companies is the acquirer.

With a consolidation, two or more companies combine to create a new company. None of the consolidation firms legally survive. For example, companies A and B give all their assets, liabilities, and stock to the new company, C, in return for C's stock, bonds, or cash.

A holding company possesses voting control of one or more other companies. The holding company comprises a group of businesses, each operating as a separate entity. By possessing more than 50% of the voting rights through common stock, the holding company has effective control of another company with a smaller percent of ownership.

Depending on the intent of the combination, three common ways in which businesses get together so as to obtain advantages in their markets are:

1. *Vertical merger.* This occurs when a company combines with a supplier or customer. An example is when a wholesaler combines with retailers.

2. *Horizontal merger.* This occurs when two companies in a similar business combine. An example is the combining of two airlines.

3. *Conglomerate merger.* This occurs when two companies in unrelated industries combine, such as where an electronics company joins with an insurance company.

MERGERS

A merger may be accomplished in one of two ways. The acquirer may negotiate with the management of the prospective acquired company, which is preferred. If negotiations fail, the acquirer may make a tender offer directly to the stockholders of the targeted company. A tender offer represents a cash offering (but can be a stock offering) for the common shares held by stockholders. A good takeover candidate includes a cash-rich business, a company with significant growth potential, and a company with a low debt-to-equity ratio.

In discussions with management, the acquirer typically makes a stock offer at a specified exchange ratio. The merger may take place if the acquired company receives an offer at an acceptable premium over the current market price of stock. Sometimes contingent payments are also given, such as stock warrants.

There are several financing packages that buyers may use for mergers, such as common stock, preferred stock, convertible bonds, debt, cash, and warrants. A key factor in selecting the final package is its impact on current earnings per share (EPS).

If common stock is exchanged, the seller's stock is given in exchange for the buyer's stock, resulting in a tax-free exchange. The drawback is that the stock issuance lowers earnings per share because the buyer's outstanding shares are increased. When there is an exchange of cash for common stock, the selling company's stockholders receive cash, resulting in a taxable transaction. This type of exchange may increase EPS since the buying company is obtaining new earnings without increasing outstanding shares.

There are many reasons why your company may prefer external growth through mergers instead of internal growth.

Advantages of a Merger

The advantages of a merger are as follows:

- Increases corporate power and improves market share and product lines
- Aids in diversification, such as reducing cyclical and operational effects
- Helps the company's ability to raise financing when it merges with another entity having significant liquid assets and low debt
- Provides a good return on investment when the market value of the acquired business is significantly less than its replacement cost
- Improves the market price of stock in some cases, resulting in a higher P/E ratio. For example, the stock of a larger company may be viewed as more marketable, secure, and stable.
- Provides a missed attribute; that is, a company gains something it lacked. For instance, superior management quality or research capability may be obtained.
- Aids the company in financing an acquisition that would not otherwise be possible to obtain, such as where acquiring a company by exchanging stock is less costly than building new capital facilities, which would require an enormous cash outlay. For instance' a company may be unable to finance significant internal expansion but can achieve it by purchasing a business already possessing such capital facilities.
- Achieves a synergistic effect, which means that the results of the combination are greater than the sum of the parts. For instance, greater profit may result from the combined entity than would occur from each individual company due to increased efficiency (e.g., economics of scale) and cost savings (e.g., eliminating overlapping administrative functions, volume discounts on purchases). There is better use of people and resources. A greater probability of synergy exists with a horizontal merger since duplicate facilities are eliminated.
- Obtains a tax loss carryforward benefit if the acquired company has been losing money. The acquirer may utilize the tax loss carryforward benefit to offset its own profitability, thus reducing its taxes. The tax loss may be carried forward 20 years to reduce the acquiring company's future earnings. In effect, the government is financing part of the acquisition.

EXAMPLE 1: H Company is deciding whether to buy S Company. S has a tax loss of $500,000. H Company anticipates pretax earnings of $400,000 and $300,000 for the next two years. The tax rate is 34%. The taxes to be paid by H Company follow:

Year 1: $400,000 – $400,000 = 0

Year 2: $300,000 – $100,000 = $200,000 × 34% = $68,000

Disadvantages of a Merger

- Reverse synergies which reduce the net value of the combined entity (e.g., adjustments of pay scales, costs of servicing acquisition debt, defections of key acquired company staff)
- Adverse financial effects because the anticipated benefits did not materialize; for example, expected cost reductions were not forthcoming
- Antitrust action delaying or preventing the proposed merger
- Problems caused by dissenting minority stockholders

In evaluating a potential merger, you have to consider its possible effect upon the financial performance of the company, including:

- *Earnings per share.* The merger should result in higher earnings or improved-stability.
- *Dividends per share.* The dividends before and after the merger should be maintained to stabilize the market price of stock.
- *Market price of stock.* The market price of the stock should be higher or at least the same after the merger.
- *Risk.* The merged business should have less financial and operating risk than before.

DECIDING ON ACQUISITION TERMS

In deciding on acquisition terms, consideration should be given to the following:

- Earnings in terms of absolute dollars and percentage change.
- Dividends.
- Market price of stock.
- Book value per share.
- Net working capital per share.

The weight assigned to each of the above varies with the circumstances involved.

Earnings

In determining the value of earnings in a merger, you should take into account anticipated future earnings and projected P/E ratio. A rapidly growing company is expected to have a higher P/E multiple.

Dividends

Dividends are attractive to stockholders. However, the more a company's growth rate and earnings, the less is the impact of dividends on market price of stock. On the other hand, if earnings are falling, the effect of dividends on per share price is greater.

Market Price of Stock

The price of a security considers projected earnings and dividends. The value assigned to the company in the acquisition will most likely be greater than the present market price in the following instances:

- The business is in a depressed industry.
- The acquired company is of greater value to the acquirer than to the stock market in general.
- A higher market price than the current one is offered to induce existing stockholders to give up their shares.

Book Value per Share

Since book value is based on historical cost rather than current value, it is not a key factor to consider. However, when book value exceeds market value, there may be an expectation that market price will increase subsequent to the merger due to improved circumstances (e.g., superior management).

Net Working Capital per Share

If the acquired company has very low debt or very liquid assets, the acquirer may borrow the funds for the acquisition by using the acquired company's strong liquidity position.

FACTORS IN DETERMINING A PRICE

There are many factors to be considered in determining the price to be paid for a business, including:

- Financial health of the acquired company (e.g., quality of earnings, growth rate, realizability of assets).
- Type and stability of operations.
- Maturity of business.
- Degree of competition.
- Tax consequences, such as unused tax credits.
- Expected return on assets and sales.
- Employee relations, such as the absence of unionization.
- Risk level, such as having adequate insurance.
- Corporate characteristics, including having negatively correlated product lines, and favorable lease terms.
- Management quality, such as experienced executives.
- Marketing position, such as quality product line, market share, distribution channels, and customer base.
- Economic environment, including recession-resistant business.
- Political environment, such as the absence of strict governmental regulation and operations in politically unstable areas.

- Structure of the arrangement, including debt or equity, cash or stock, costs of the transaction, and time period.

- Improvement in diversification and/or integration.

- Ease of transferability of ownership.

- Exchange rate fluctuations.

- Legal issues, such as the possibility of stockholder liability suits.

- Industry characteristics, such as being in a growing industry instead of a declining one.

- Impact of the acquisition on the acquiring company's financial strength and operating performance. For instance, Baldwin United's acquisition of Mortgage Guaranty Insurance ultimately forced both companies into bankruptcy. There was an evident failure to appraise appropriately the effect of the acquisition on financial posture.

- Possible violation of antitrust laws. These laws are administered by the Department of justice's Antitrust Division and the Federal Trade Commission.

When looking at the targeted company, see what the positive and negative effects of the acquisition would be on you. By examining what the overall picture after the merger would be, you can properly assess what to pay for the candidate. If your analysis includes many uncertain factors, sensitivity analysis may be used to look at the effect of changes in outcome.

Be Careful: Detailed financial planning and analysis are required in the acquisition process.

Warning: If an acquiring company overpays for a target company, this negatively affects its financial position. For example, was it worth it to J. Ray McDermott to fight off United Technologies to obtain control of Babcock and Wilcox, even though it pushed the stock price up from about $35 to $65?

GRADING CRITERIA

In acquisition strategy, you document what you want to accomplish by the acquisition and how the acquisition will complement your overall strategy. Industries and companies are then screened by employing various quantitative measures and considering qualitative factors. The broad industry sectors should be narrowed down by comparing each industry to your specified industry criteria. The industry best satisfying your goals is then selected. After you have identified the target industry, companies in that industry are then screened. Make sure to compare the target's trend to industry averages to determine the company's relative position.

In identifying an acquisition target, clearly defined criteria should be established for acceptable candidates, all companies within the category should be reviewed, suitable companies should be listed in priority order, and a short list of targets (generally no more than ten) coming closest to the ideal profile should be prepared. This short list can either consist of the highest-scoring companies regardless of score or all companies. The profile criteria include what is important to you, such as industry classification, size, profitability, leverage, market share, and geographic area. You may not be able to get your first choice, so flexibility is needed.

Different criteria should have different weights depending upon importance to you. For example, the weight may go from 1 (least important) to 10 (most important). For example, you may decide to assign a 1 to dividend history and a 10 to industry. Most criteria will fall between 1 and 10 (e.g., leverage may be assigned a weight of 2 because all candidates have already been screened to have a debt-to-equity ratio below 25%). Intermediate attributes within a range may also be scored. For example, revenues under $100 million or above $300 million may be given a score of 4. An illustrative grading guide follows.

Illustrative Grading Guide

Industry Classification

 1 = specify shops, diversified companies in which food products retailing is only minor

10 = convenience store chain

Size

 1 = revenues under $10 million or over $40 million

10 = revenues of $300 million

Fixed Assets (book value)

1 = $2 million 10 = over $5 million

Net Income

1 = Profit margin below 2%

5 = Profit margin above 10%

Leverage

 1 = Over 40% debt-to-equity ratio

10 = Below 5% debt-to-equity ratio

Geographies

 1 = West

 5 = South

10 = Northeast

You can save time by using a computer database to find possible target companies. The database enables you to select ranges for size, profitability, leverage, and so on and then screen out candidates fulfilling your requirements. Information on publicly held companies is much more available than for closely held businesses.

ACQUISITION STRATEGY AND PROCESS

A brochure should be prepared by the buyer of itself so the target company may be acquainted with the buyer's objectives, philosophy, and background. A proposal should also be prepared explaining to the target company the financial and operating benefits to it of a merger.

Planning to integrate the acquired company into the buyer should take place early in the acquisition process. Areas requiring planning include policies and procedures, data processing, organizational and management structure, personnel, operations, financial reporting, customer base, and supplier relationships.

After discussions become serious, the investigation of the target company should involve reviewing available financial information and audit work papers, tax returns, visiting the target's facilities, and interviewing management (e.g., research and development programs, manufacturing and distribution methods). There should be a purchase audit, particularly to "key" accounts and exposure areas to uncover problems and issues not fully disclosed in the financial statements. For example, inventory should be observed and counted and a determination made whether their valuation in the financial records is appropriate. The purchase audit must consider financial, accounting, and operating matters. Outside consultants may need to be retained in specialized areas (e.g., technology, product capability).

The areas of investigation include:

- Industry (e.g., competition, growth rate, governmental regulation, barriers to entry).

- Target company background and history (e.g., nature of business, locations and facilities, lawsuits, environmental considerations).

- Financial and accounting information (e.g., ratios by major business segment, effect of inflation or recession on company, current values). The financial statements for the last three years should be reviewed.

- Taxes (e.g., tax attributes of target, tax-planning strategies). Tax returns should be reviewed and analyzed for the last three years. Financial income and taxable income should be reconciled. Does the state penalize multistate enterprises? Will foreign countries impose significant tax burdens? What tax benefits will the purchase accomplish (e.g., available tax credits)? Are there any questionable items or limitations that may be challenged by the tax authorities?

- Management quality (particularly important when moving into an unrelated industry).

- Pension and health care obligations.

- Marketing (e.g., backlog, new product developments, obsolescence problems).

- Manufacturing (e.g., production facilities, manufacturing processes and efficiencies).

- Distribution network, facilities, and methods.

- R&D experience.

Watch out for litigation matters, tax contingencies, regulatory problems, reliance on a few contracts and/or customers, "window-dressing" management honesty, and poor financial and operating controls.

FINANCING OF THE MERGER

The range of possible transaction structures is infinite. Some of the basic alternatives are as follows:

- All cash transaction, financed from existing cash resources.
- All cash transaction, financed by issuing stock.
- Stock transaction, merger through exchange of stock.
- Mixed stock/cash.
- Leveraged cash transaction, financed through debt issue.
- Leveraged buyout, majority of equity replaced by debt.
- Debt transaction, debt offered to selling company shareholders.
- Mixed cash/debt.

Should stock or assets (generally cash) be given in the acquisition?

Giving Stock

The advantages of giving stock are:

- No cash or financing requirement for acquirer.
- Quick and simple in terms of document preparation. There is a transfer of stock certificates in exchange for immediate or deferred payment.
- In certain cases, stock transactions can be exempt from taxation to shareholders, thus potentially raising the value of the transaction.
- A stock acquisition can maintain the equity-to-assets ratio, and even provide additional capital for further growth strategies.
- Target shareholders share risk of acquisition.
- Minority stockholders may not have appraisal rights.
- Typically, stockholder votes authorizing the purchase or sale are not required.
- May take advantage of acquirer's high stock price.
- Target management has incentive to maintain commitment.

The disadvantages of giving stock are:

- Can be less attractive to target shareholders.
- The acquirer, in buying stock of the target company, assumes its liabilities, whether disclosed or not.
- Dilution of acquirer shareholder earnings.
- Dilution of ownership/control.
- Risk of conflict after merger.
- If the target is liquidated subsequent to acquisition, much work is needed in conveying the target company's assets as part of the liquidation.

Giving Assets

The advantages of giving assets are:

- Acquirer has complete control over the assets it buys and the liabilities it assumes.
- Attractive to shareholders because they receive value immediately and have no risk.
- Typically, no acquiring company stockholder vote is needed.
- Easier to understand.

The disadvantages of giving assets are:

- Dilution of earnings.
- Difficult to determine the fair value of each asset.
- Current target management may have little incentive to facilitate transaction or maintain commitment after transaction.
- Target company's stockholders must approve.
- State transfer taxes must be paid.
- A cash acquisition can materially lower the equity to assets ratio of the surviving company.
- Creation of goodwill which is amortized to expense but not tax deductible. Further, income depressed by significant amortization costs may result in a lower stock price, potentially making the buyer in turn vulnerable to takeover.
- Creditor agreement may be needed for certain transfers and assignments.
- Must conform to bulk sales laws.

If the decision is made to give cash to the targeted company shareholders, some form of equity and/or debt will have to be issued because it is unusual for the acquiring company to have sufficient cash or liquid assets to finance the entire transaction. Debt financing may range from an intermediate-term loan for part of the purchase price to structural debt financing of 90% or more of the price (leveraged buyout). There are many considerations in deciding whether to use leverage and in determining the appropriate amount of leverage.

Leverage

The advantages of leverage are:

- Interest expense is tax deductible.
- Increased return to shareholders.
- Since shareholders' ownership is maintained, there is a lack of dilution.

The disadvantages of leverage are:

- Creditors have priority claim on merged company.
- The greater financing risk may lower the company's stock and bond prices as well as result in increasing costs of financing.

- Possible lowering in credit standing and bond ratings.
- A cash problem may result in default.
- Interest payments lower earnings.
- Interest and principal payments reduce cash flow.

Leveraged buyouts are quite popular. A leveraged buyout occurs when an entity primarily borrows money (sometimes 90% or more) in order to buy another company. Typically, the acquiring company uses as collateral the assets of the acquired business. Generally, repayment of the debt will be made from the yearly operating funds flow of the acquired company. A leveraged buyout may also be made when the acquiring company uses its own assets as security for the loan. It may also be used if a firm wishes to go private. In most cases, the stockholders of the acquired company will receive an amount greater than the current price of the stock. A leveraged buyout involves more risk than an acquisition done through the issuance of equity securities.

The high debt service requirement drains cash flow during the period that the debt is outstanding. However, once debt is retired, shareholders enjoy ownership of the remaining enterprise. The debt may be reduced rapidly by selling off some assets or divisions of the acquired company, if warranted.

The characteristics conducive to a leveraged buyout are:

- The earnings and cash flow of the company must be predictable so they may cover interest and principal payments on the debt financing.
- The growth rate of the firm should exceed the inflation rate.
- There must be a good market share and product line otherwise the firm is vulnerable to an economic decline or competitive actions.
- There should be a good asset base to serve as collateral.
- The assets should not be presently encumbered and the debt-equity ratio should currently be low.
- There are minimal capital expenditure requirements.
- The company should be liquid so that it has enough cash to meet its debt obligations.
- There is future salability of the company, if desired.
- Technological change is not a problem.
- Management is highly qualified and is given a significant equity stake.
- The business is selling at a low P/E ratio.

USING CAPITAL BUDGETING TECHNIQUES IN APPRAISING THE ACQUISITION

In deciding whether to buy another business, capital budgeting may be used. Also, the effect of the new capital structure on the firm's overall cost of capital has to be projected.

> **EXAMPLE 2:** W Company is contemplating purchasing P Company for $95,000. W's current cost of capital is 12%. P's estimated overall cost of capital after the acquisition is 10%. Projected cash inflows from years one through eight are $13,000. (Assume no residual value.)

The net present value is:

Year	Present Value
0 (–$95,000 × 1)	–$95,000
1–8 (13,000 × 5.3349)	+ 69,354*
Net present value	–$25,646

* Using 10% as the discount rate.

The acquisition is not feasible since there is a negative net present value.

EXAMPLE 3: C Company wants to buy some fixed assets of B Company. However, the latter wants to sell out its business. The balance sheet of B Company follows:

Assets

Cash	$ 4,000
Accounts receivable	8,000
Inventory	10,000
Equipment 1	16,000
Equipment 2	28,000
Equipment 3	42,000
Building	110,000
Total assets	$218,000

Liabilities and Stockholders' Equity

Total liabilities	$ 80,000
Total equity	138,000
Total liabilities and equity	$218,000

C wants only equipment 1 and 2 and the building. The other assets, excluding cash, can be sold for $24,000. The total cash received is thus $28,000 ($24,000 + $4,000 initial cash balance). B desires $50,000 for the whole business. C will thus have to pay a total of $130,000, which is $80,000 in total liabilities and $50,000 for its owners. The actual net cash outlay is therefore $102,000 ($130,000 – $28,000). It is expected that the after-tax cash inflows from the new equipment will be $27,000 per year for the next five years. The cost of capital is 8%. (Assume no residual value.)

The net present value of the acquisition is:

Year	Present Value
0 (–$102,000 × 1)	–$ 102,000
1–5 (27,000 × 3.9927)	107,803
Net present value	$ 5,803

Since there is a positive net present value the acquisition should be made.

EXCHANGE RATIO

T Company buys B Company. T Company's stock sells for $75 per share while B's stock sells for $45. As per the merger terms, T offers $50 per share. The exchange ratio is 0.667 ($50/$75). Thus, T exchanges 0.667 shares of its stock for one share of B.

EFFECT OF MERGER ON EARNINGS PER SHARE AND MARKET PRICE PER SHARE

A merger can have a positive or negative impact on net income and market price per share of common stock.

   EXAMPLE 4: Relevant information follows:

	Company A	Company B
Net income	$50,000	$84,000
Outstanding shares	5,000	12,000
EPS	$ 10	$ 7
P/E ratio	7	10
Market price	$ 70	$ 70

   Company B acquires Company A and exchanges its shares for A's shares on a one-for-one basis. The effect on EPS follows:

	B Shares Owned after Merger	EPS before Merger	EPS after Merger
A stockholders	5,000	$10	$7.88*
B stockholders	12,000	7	7.88*
Total	17,000		

Total net income is determined as:

5,000 shares × $10	$ 50,000
12,000 shares × $7	84,000
	$134,000

$$\text{EPS} = \frac{\text{Net income}}{\text{Total shares}} = \frac{\$134,000}{17,000} = \$7.88$$

EPS decreases by $2.12 for A stockholders and increases by $0.88 for B stockholders.

The effect on market price is not clear. Assuming the combined entity has the same P/E ratio as Company B, the market price per share will be $78.80 (10 × $7.88). The stockholders experience a higher market value per share. The increased market value occurs because net income of the combined entity is valued at a P/E ratio of 10, the same as Company B, while before the merger Company A had a lower P/E multiplier of 7. However, if the combined entity is valued at Company As multiplier of 7, the market value would be $55.16 (7 × $7.88). In this case, the stockholders in each firm experience a reduction in market value of $14.84 ($70.00 – $55.16).

Since the effect of the merger on market value per share is not clear, the crucial consideration is EPS.

EXAMPLE 5: The following situation exists:

Market price per share of acquiring company = $100
Market price per share of acquired company = $20
Price per share offered = $24

The exchange ratio equals:

Shares $24/$100 = 0.24
Market price $24/$20 = 1.20

EXAMPLE 6: M Company wants to buy J Company by issuing its shares. Relevant information follows:

	M Company	J Company
Net income	$40,000	$26,000
Outstanding shares	20,000	8,000

The exchange ratio is 2 to 1. The EPS based on the original shares of each company follows:

$$\text{EPS of combined entity} = \frac{\text{Combined net income}}{\text{Total shares}}$$

$$\frac{\$66,000}{20,000 + (8,000 \times 2)} = \frac{\$66,000}{36,000 \text{ shares}} = \$1.83$$

EPS of M = $1.83
EPS of J = $1.83 × 2 = $3.66

EXAMPLE 7: O Company wants to buy P Company by exchanging 1.8 shares of its stock for each share of P. O expects to have the same P/E ratio after the merger as before. Applicable data follow:

	O Company	P Company
Net income	$500,000	$150,000
Shares	225,000	30,000
Market price per share	$ 50	$ 60

The exchange ratio of market price equals:

$$\frac{\text{Offer price}}{\text{Market price of P}} = \frac{\$50 \times 1.8}{\$60} = \frac{\$90}{\$60} = 1.5$$

EPS and P/E ratios for each company follow.

O Company	P Company
EPS $500,000/225,000 = $2.22	$150,000/30,000 = $5
P/E ratio $50/$2.22 = 22.5	$60/$5 = 12

The P/E ratio used in obtaining P is:

$$\frac{1.8 \times \$50}{\$5} = \frac{\$90}{\$5} = 18 \text{ times}$$

The EPS of O after the acquisition is:

$$\frac{\$650,000}{225,000 + (30,000 \times 1.8)} = \frac{\$650,000}{279,000 \text{ shares}} = \$2.33$$

The expected market price per share of the combined entity is:

$$\$2.33 \times 22.5 \text{ times} = \$52.43$$

RISK OF THE ACQUISITION

In appraising the risk associated with an acquisition, a scenario analysis may be used, looking at the best case, worst case, and most likely case. Operating scenarios consider assumptions as to variables, including sales, volume, cost, competitive reaction, governmental interference, and customer perception. You derive the probability for each scenario on the basis of experience. Sensitivity analysis may be used to indicate how sensitive the project's returns are to variances from expected values of essential variables. (Sensitivity analysis is discussed in Chapter 22, "The Use of Capital Budgeting in Decision Making"). For example, you may undertake a sensitivity analysis on selling prices assuming they are, for example, 10% to 15% higher or lower than expected. The theory behind sensitivity analysis is to adjust key variables from their expected values in the most likely case. The analysis can be performed assuming one purchase price or all possible purchase prices. What is the effect, for example, of a 4% change in the gross profit rate on projected returns?

Based on sensitivity analysis, you should pay an amount for a target company resulting in a cutoff return given the most likely operating scenario.

Warning: It is difficult to accomplish successful unrelated diversification. An example is General Electric's acquisition of Utah International. The firm eventually divested of its acquisition.

Recommendation: Acquisition of companies operating in related fields usually has a higher success rate.

HOLDING COMPANY

A holding company is one whose sole purpose is to own the stock of other companies. To obtain voting control of a business, the holding company may make a direct market purchase or tender offer. A company may elect to become a holding company if its basic business is declining and it decides to liquidate its assets and uses the funds to invest in growth companies.

Since the operating companies owned by the holding company are separate legal entities, the obligations of one are isolated from the others.

Recommendation: A loan officer lending to one company should attempt to obtain a guarantee by the other companies.

The advantages of a holding company include:

- Risk protection, in that the failure of one company does not cause the failure of another or of the holding company. If the owned company fails, the loss of the holding company is restricted to its investment in it.

- Ability to obtain a significant amount of assets with a small investment. The holding company can control more assets than it could acquire through a merger.

- Ease of obtaining control of another company; all that is needed is to purchase enough stock in the marketplace. Unlike a merger which requires stockholder or management approval, no approval is needed for a holding company.

The disadvantages of a holding company include:

- More costly to administer than a single company resulting from a merger because economies of scale are not achieved.

- The chance that the U.S. Department of Justice will deem the holding company a monopoly and force dissolution of some, of the owned companies.

- Multiple taxes because the income the holding company receives is in the form of cash. Before paying dividends, the subsidiary must pay taxes on the earnings. When profit is distributed to the holding company as dividends, it must pay tax on the dividends received less an 80% dividend exclusion. However, if the holding company owns 80% or more of the subsidiary's shares, a 100% dividend exemption exists. No multiple tax exists for a subsidiary that is part of a merged company.

EXAMPLE 8: A holding company owns 70% of another firm. Dividends received are $20,000. The tax rate is 34%. The tax paid on the dividends follows:

Dividend	$20,000
Dividend exclusion (80%)	16,000
Dividend subject to tax	$4,000
Tax rate	× 34%
Tax	$ 1,360

The effective tax rate is 6.8% ($1,360/$20,000).

HOSTILE TAKEOVER BIDS

If a negotiated takeover of another company is impossible, a hostile bid may be needed. In a hostile bid management of the targeted company is bypassed, and the stockholders are approached directly. The acquirer argues that management is not maximizing the potential of the company, and is not protecting the interests of shareholders.

In a tender offer, the buyer goes directly to the stockholders of the target business to tender (sell) their shares, typically for cash. The tender in some cases may be shares in the acquiring company rather than cash. If the buyer obtains enough stock, it can gain control of the target company and force the merger. Cash rather than securities is usually used because a stock offering requires a prospectus thereby losing the advantages of timeliness and surprise. Stockholders are induced to sell when the tender price substantially exceeds the current market price of the target company stock. Typically, there is an expiration date to the tender.

Hostile takeovers are typically quite costly because they usually involve a significant price incentive, and antitakeover measures. They can be disruptive to both buyer and seller because of "slur" campaigns. It is rare that smooth transitions of management take place.

The typical features of a hostile takeover candidate may include:

- A multidivisional organization has diverse business activities
- Asset values of component divisions are not reflected in the market price of the company's stock.
- Financial performance of the individual business lines could be better.
- Existing management are unable to realize the true value of the company.

The usual initial step in launching a hostile bid is to buy stock of the target company in the open market. The SEC requires that any investor who buys more than a 5% interest in a public company should register his or her holding and provide the intent (e.g., passive or to gain eventual control) through a Schedule 13-D filing. Beyond 5% ownership, it becomes difficult to make open-market purchases of stock without revealing the intention to acquire control—except that acquirers may accumulate a greater holding within the five days allowed for the

Chapter 39: Mergers and Acquisitions

13-D filing, or they may elect to make a passive investment for a limited period before reassessing the intention to acquire control. The acquiring business must furnish to the management of the potential acquired company and to the SEC, 30 days notice of its intent to acquire. Once the intention to acquire control is made public, the stock price of the target company generally rises in expectation of a tender offer at a higher price.

The direct appeal to shareholders which often follows is frequently made through a public tender offer. Management of the target company will typically recommend that shareholders reject the offer, and possibly propose an alternative restructuring arrangement.

The management of a targeted company can fight the takeover attempt in the following ways:

- Purchase treasury stock to make fewer shares available for tendering.

- Initiate legal action to prevent the takeover, such as by applying antitrust laws.

- Postpone the tender offer (some states have laws to delay the tender offer).

- Declare an attractive dividend to keep stockholders happy.

The advantages of a hostile bid are:

- Direct communication with stockholders to bypass management intransigency.

- Flexibility to alter terms.

- Increased value of existing stake.

- Improved profitability of the target.

The disadvantages of a hostile bid are:

- Price: hostile bidders may pay a high premium especially if competition arises in the takeover attempt.

- Cost: high transaction and advisory costs.

- Risk: hostile bids often fail.

- Creation of ill will and problems with integrating the target after merger.

- Possible adverse litigation or regulatory action.

- Possible retaliatory action by target (see Defensive Measures by Targeted Company).

SEC FILING REQUIREMENTS

When an acquisition of a significant business will occur, the buyer and, where appropriate, the target company must file a Form 8-K (filing for important events), a proxy or information statement (if shareholders must vote), and a registration statement (if securities are to be issued). Significant means the acquirer's investment in the target exceeds 10% of its consolidated assets. In addition, certain information on the acquisition must be presented in Form 10-Q (quarterly filing).

If a significant business has been acquired, a Form 8-K must be filed within 15 days containing information about the acquisition and including historical financial statements and pro forma data.

If the combination must be voted upon by shareholders of any of the companies, a Form S-4 must be filed. In other cases, one of the other S forms (e.g., S-1 or S-3) must be filed.

If Form S-4 is filed, there is a 20-business-day waiting period between the date the prospectus is sent to stockholders and the date of the stockholder meeting. Also, if the acquisition must be voted upon by shareholders of one or both of the companies, a proxy or information statement must be furnished to shareholders and filed with the SEC.

Regulation S-X requires audited historical financial statements of a business to be acquired. The financial statements must be for the last three years and any interim period. In a purchase combination, there must be a pro forma statement of income for the most recent year and interim period. In a pooling, the financial statements are typically restated.

TAX CONSIDERATIONS

The tax effect of a transaction may require an adjustment in selling price. It may be desirable to have an "open-end" arrangement, whereby with the attainment of a given sales volume or profit, additional stock will be issued by the purchaser to the selling company or its stockholders-so handled to be nontaxable.

The acquiring company should prefer a taxable transaction. In a taxable transaction, the acquiring company must allocate its purchase cost among the assets acquired based on the present values of those assets. Any residual balance is goodwill. The acquired company's net assets will typically have a book value far below their fair market value. A taxable transaction allows the acquiring company to step up the tax basis of these assets, sometimes to a level even higher than original cost, and to start the depreciation cycle all over again. When the acquired company's assets are sold, this stepped-up basis will reduce the taxable gain on the sale.

Also see Chapter 59 on taxation.

DEFENSIVE MEASURES BY TARGETED COMPANY

The targeted company may have in place preventive measures against being taken over, including the following seven:

1. *Golden parachute.* Management compensation arrangements that are triggered when there is a purchase of the business such as lump-sum benefits, employment agreements, and stock options. Examples are Greyhound and Hughes Tool.

2. *Poison pill.* When a hostile bid is eminent, the targeted company takes out significant debt (or issues preferred stock) hat makes the company unattractive to the hostile acquirer because of the high debt position. Examples are Union Carbide and CBS, Inc.

3. *Self-tender.* After a hostile bid, the target company itself makes a counter-offer for its own shares. An example is Newmont Mining.

4. *Greenmail.* The target company buys back the stock accumulated by the raider, at a premium. Examples are Texaco, Walt Disney, and Goodyear.

5. *PAC-MAN.* The defending company makes a counteroffer for the stock of the raiding company. Examples are American Brands and Bendix Corporation.

6. *White knight.* The defending company finds a third party who is willing to pay a higher premium, typically with "friendlier" intentions than the raider. Examples are Gulf Oil Corp. (Chevron) and Sterling Drugs (Eastman Kodak).

7. *Asset spinoff.* The defending party identifies the assets most desirable to the raider. It then spins off the assets to one of its separate companies or sells them to a third party. Examples are Union Carbide and Marathon Oil.

THE VALUATION OF A TARGETED COMPANY

In a merger, we have to value the targeted company. As a starting point in valuation, the key financial data must be accumulated and analyzed including historical financial statements, forecasted financial statements, and tax returns. The assumptions of the valuation must be clearly spelled out.

The valuation approaches may be profit-oriented or asset-oriented. Adjusted earnings may be capitalized at an appropriate multiple. Future adjusted cash earnings may be discounted by the rate of return that may be earned. Assets may be valued at fair market value, such as through appraisal. Comparative values of similar companies may serve as excellent benchmarks. Commercial software programs are available to do merger analysis.

Comparison with Industry Averages

Valid comparisons can be made between the entity being valued and others in the same industry. Industry norms should be noted. General sources of comparative industry data found in financial advisory services include Standard and Poor's, Moody's, Value Line, Dun and Bradstreet, and Robert Morris Associates. Trade publications may also be consulted. Reference may be made to the *Almanac of Business and Industrial Financial Ratios* (based on corporate tax returns to the Internal Revenue Service) written by Leo Troy and published by Prentice Hall. If a small company is being acquired, reference may be made to *Financial Studies of the Small Business* published annually by Financial Research Associates (Washington, D.C.: Financial Research Associates, 1984).

Publicly available information on the targeted company include the annual report; SEC Forms 10-K, 10-Q, and 8-K; interim shareholder reports; proxy statements; press releases; and offering prospectuses.

Discussed below are the various approaches to business valuation consisting of capitalization of earnings, capitalization of excess earnings, capitalization of cash flow, present value (discounted) of future cash flows, book value of net assets, tangible net worth economic net worth, fair market value of net assets, gross revenue multiplier, profit margin/capitalization rate, price earnings factor, comparative value of similar going concerns and recent sales of stock. A combination of approaches may be used to obtain a representative value.

Capitalization of Earnings

Primary consideration should be given to earnings when valuing a company. Historical earnings are typically the beginning point in applying a capitalization method to most business valuations. In general, historical earnings are a reliable predictor of future earnings. According to IRS Revenue Ruling 59-60 [1959-1, C.B. 237], the greatest emphasis should be placed on profitability when looking at a "going concern."

The value of the business may be based on its adjusted earnings times a multiplier for what the business sells for in the industry.

Net income should be adjusted for unusual and nonrecurring revenue and expense items. In adjusting net income of the business, we should add back the portion of the following items if personal rather than business-related: auto expense, travel expense, and promotion and entertainment expense. Interest expense should also be added back to net income because it is the cost to borrow funds to buy assets or obtain working capital and, as such, is not relevant in determining the operating profit of the business. In the event lease payments arise from a low-cost lease, earnings should be adjusted to arrive at a fair rental charge. Extraordinary items (e.g., gain on the sale of land) should be removed from earnings to obtain typical earnings. If business assets are being depreciated at an accelerated rate, you should adjust net income upward.[1] Therefore, the difference between the straight line method and an accelerated depreciation method should be added back.

We should add back expenses for a closely held business solely for fringe benefits, health plan, pension plan, and life insurance. In addition, we should add back excessive salary representing the difference between the owner's salary and what a reasonable salary would be if we hired someone to do the job. All compensation should be considered including perks.[2] Thus, if the owner gets a salary of $300,000 and a competent worker would get $80,000, the add-back to net income is $220,000.

A tax provision (if none exists) should be made in arriving at the adjusted net income. The tax provision should be based on the current rates for each of the years.

If the company has a significant amount of investment income (e.g., dividend income, interest income, rental income from nonoperating property), net income may be reduced for the investment income with taxes being adjusted accordingly. We are primarily concerned with the income from operations.

The adjusted (restated) earnings results in a quality of earnings figure. The restated earnings is then multiplied by a multiplier to determine the value of a business. The multiplier should be higher for a low risk business but generally not

---

[1] Irving Blackman, *The Valuation of Privately-Held Businesses* (Illinois: Probus Publishing, 1986), p. 23.

[2] Shannon Pratt, Valuing Small Businesses and Professional Practices (Illinois: Dow-Jones-Irwin, 1986), p. 59.

more than 10. The multiplier should be lower for a high risk business, often only 1 or 2. Of course, an average multiplier, such as 5, would be used when average risk exists. The P/E ratio for a comparable company would be a good benchmark.

Some investment bankers use in valuation a multiple of the latest year's earnings, or the annual rate of earnings of a current interim period (if representative). An example follows based on a multiplier of one-year profits.

EXAMPLE 9:

Adjusted net income for the current year	$400,000*
× Multiplier	× 4*
Valuation	$1,600,000
Reported net income	$325,000
Adjustments:	
Personal expenses (e.g., promotion and entertainment)	50,000
Extraordinary or nonrecurring gain	(60,000)
Owner's fringe benefits (e.g., pension plan)	40,000
Excessive owner's salary relative to a reasonable salary	30,000
Interest expense	20,000
Dividend revenue	(10,000)
Low-cost rental payments relative to a fair rental charge	(5,000)
Excess depreciation from using an accelerated method	10,000
Restated net income	$400,000

* The adjusted net income is computed below:

Typically, a five-year average adjusted historical earnings figure is used. The five years' earnings up to the valuation date demonstrate past earning power.

Note that for SEC registration and reporting purposes a five-year period is used. Assuming a simple average is used, the computation follows:

Simple average adjusted earnings over 5 years × Multiplier
(Capitalization factor, P/E ratio) of 5 (based on industry standard)

Value of business

EXAMPLE 10: Assume the following net incomes:

2X17	$120,000
2X16	$100,000
2X15	$110,000
2X14	$ 90,000
2X13	$115,000

The multiplier is 4.

$$\text{Simple average earnings} = . \quad \frac{\$120,000 + \$100,000 + \$110,000 + \$90,000 + \$115,000}{5}$$

$$= \frac{\$535,000}{5} = \$107,000$$

Simple average adjusted earnings over 5 years	$107,000
× Multiplier	× 4
Value of business	$428,000

Instead of a simple average, a weighted-average adjusted historical earnings figure is recommended. This gives more weight to the most recent years[3] which reflects higher current prices and recent business performance. If a five-year weighted average is used, the current year is given a weight of 5 while the first year is assigned a weight of 1. The multiplier is then applied to the weighted-average five-year adjusted earnings to get the value of the business.

EXAMPLE 11:

Year	Net Income	×	Weight	=	Total
2X17	$120,000	×	5	=	$600,000
2X16	100,000	×	4	=	400,000
2X15	110,000	×	3	=	330,000
2X14	90,000	×	2	=	180,000
2X13	115,000	×	1	=	115,000
			15		$1,625,000

Weighted-average five-year earning:

$$\$1,625,000/15 = \$108,333$$

Weighted-average 5-year earnings:	$108,333
× Capitalization factor	× 4*
Capitalization-of-earnings valuation	$433,332

* The capitalization factor should be based on such factors as risk, stability of earnings, expected future earnings, liquidity, etc.

If the company's financial statements are not audited, you should insist on an audit to assure accurate reporting.

Has the owner of a closely held company failed to record cash sales to hide income? One way of determining this is to take purchases and add a typical profit

---

[3] American Institute of CPAs, Valuation of a Closely-Held Business, Small Business Consulting Practice Aid   No. 8, Management Advisory Services Practice Aids, New York, 1987, p. 13.

markup in the industry. To verify reported profit, you can multiply the sales by the profit margin in the industry. If reported earnings are significantly below what the earnings should be based on the industry standard, there may be some hidden income.

Capitalization of Excess Earnings

The best method is to capitalize excess earnings. The normal rate of return on the weighted-average net tangible assets is subtracted from the weighted-average adjusted earnings to determine excess earnings. It is suggested that the weighting be based on a five-year period. The excess earnings are then capitalized to determine the value of the intangibles (primarily goodwill). The addition of the value of the intangibles and the fair market value of the net tangible assets equals the total valuation. As per IRS Revenue Ruling 68-609 [1968-2 C.B. 327], the IRS recommends this method to value a business for tax purposes. The Revenue Ruling states that the return on average net tangible assets should be the percentage prevailing in the industry. If an industry percentage is not available, an 8% to 10% rate may be used. An 8% return rate is used for a business with a small risk factor and stable earnings while a 10% rate of return is used for a business having a high risk factor and unstable earnings. The capitalization rate for excess earnings should be 15% (multiple of 6.67) for a business with a small risk factor and stable earnings and a 20% capitalization rate (multiple of 5) should be used for a business having a high risk factor and unstable earnings. Thus, the suggested return rate range is between 8% to 10%. The range for the capitalization rate may be between 15% to 20%.

> **EXAMPLE 12:** Weighted-average net tangible assets are computed below:

Year	Amount	×	Weight	=	Total
2X13	$ 950,000	×	1	=	$ 950,000
2X14	1,000,000	×	2	=	2,000,000
2X15	1,200,000	×	3	=	3,600,000
2X16	1,400,000	×	4	=	5,600,000
2X17	1,500,000	×	5	=	7,500,000
			15		$19,650,000

Weighted-average net tangible assets:

$19,650,000/15 = $1,310,000

Weighted-average adjusted net income (5 years)—assumed	$600,000
Tangle net assets ($1,310,000 × 10%)	131,000
Excess earnings	$469,000
Capitalization rate (20%)	× 5
Value of intangibles	$2,345,000

| Fair market value of net tangible assets | 3,000,000 |
| Capitalization-of-excess-earnings valuation | $5,345,000 |

Capitalization of Cash Flow

The adjusted cash earnings may be capitalized in arriving at a value for the firm. This method may be suitable for a service business.

EXAMPLE 13:

Adjusted cash earnings	$100,000
× Capitalization factor (25%)	× 4
Capitalization of cash flow	$400,000
Less liabilities assumed	50,000
Capitalization-of-cash-flow earnings	$350,000

Present Value (Discounting) of Future Cash Flows

A business is worth the discounted value of future cash earnings plus the discounted value of the expected selling price. Cash flow may be a more valid criterion of value than book profits because cash flow can be used for reinvestment. The growth rate in earnings may be based on past growth, future expectations, and the inflation rate. This approach is suggested in a third party sale situation. We also have more confidence in it when the company is strong in the industry and has solid earnings growth. The problem with the method is the many estimates required of future events. It probably should not be used when there has been an inconsistent trend in earnings.

> *Step 1:* Present Value of Cash Earnings. The earnings should be estimated over future years using an estimated growth rate. A common time frame for a cash flow valuation is ten years. Once the future earnings are determined, they should be discounted. Future earnings may be based on the prior years' earnings and the current profit margin applied to sales. Cash earnings equals net income plus noncash expense adjustments such as depreciation.

> *Step 2:* Present Value of Sales Price. The present value of the expected selling price of the business at the date of sale should be determined. This residual value may be based on a multiple of earnings or cash flow, expected market value, and so on.

You may use as the discount rate the minimum acceptable return to the buyer for investing in the target company. The discount rate may take into account the usual return rate for money, inflation rate, a risk premium (based on such factors as local market conditions, earnings instability, and level of debt), and maybe a premium for the illiquidity of the investment. If the risk-free interest rate is 7% (on government bonds), the risk premium is 8%, and the illiquidity premium is 7%, the capitalization (discount) rate will be 22%. The risk premium may range from 5% to 10% while the illiquidity premium may range from 5% to 15%.[4] Some evaluators

[4] Charles Hays and Lawrence Finley, "Valuation of the Closely Held Business," *National Public Accountant,* March 1989, p. 31.

simply use as the discount rate the market interest rate of a low-risk asset investment.

Assuming you expect to hold the business for 14 years, and anticipate a 12% rate of return and constant earnings each year, the value of the business is based on:

For cash earnings: present value of an ordinary annuity for $n = 14$, $i = 12\%$

For selling price: present value of $1 for $n = 14$, $i = 12\%$

Total present value

If earnings grow at an 8% rate, a Present Value of $1 table would be used to discount the annual earnings, which would change each year.

EXAMPLE 14: In 2X13, the net income is $200,000. Earnings are expected to grow at 8% per year. The discount rate is 10%. You estimate that the business is worth the discounted value of future earnings. The valuation equals:

Year	Net Income (based on an 80% growth rate)		PV of $1 Factor (at 10% interest)	Present Value
2X13	$200,000	×	.909	$181,800
2X14	208,000	×	.826	171,808
2X15	224,600	×	.751	168,675
2X16	242,568	×	.683	165,674
2X17	261,973	×	.621	162,685
Present value of future earnings				$850,642

If the expected selling price at the end of year 2X17 is $600,000, the valuation of the business equals:

Present value of earnings	$ 850,642
Selling price in 2X17 $600,000 × .621	372,600
Valuation	$1,223,242

EXAMPLE 15 (A Comprehensive Case): ACQ Home Repair Company, a regional hardware chain that specializes in "do-it-yourself" materials and equipment rentals, is cash rich because of several consecutive good years. One of the alternative uses for the excess funds is an acquisition. Julie Kerr, ACQ's CFO, has been asked to place a value on a potential target, TGT's Hardware, a small chain that operates in an adjacent state, and she has enlisted your help. The table below indicates Kerr's estimates of TGT's earnings potential if it came under ACQ's management.

		(In millions of dollars)		
	2X14	*2X15*	*2X16*	*2X17*
Net sales	$60.0	$90.0	$112.5	$127.5
Cost of good sold (60%)	$36.0	$54.0	$67.5	$76.5
Selling/Administrative expense	$4.5	$6.0	$7.5	$9.0
Interest expense	$3.0	$4.5	$4.5	$6.0
Necessary retained earnings	$0.0	$7.5	$6.0	$4.5

The interest expense listed above includes the interest (1) on TGT's existing debt, (2) on new debt that ACQ would issue to help finance the acquisition, and (3) on new debt expected to be issued over time to help finance expansion within the new "H Division," the code name given to the target firm. The retentions represent earnings that will be reinvested within the H Division to help finance its growth.

TGT's hardware currently uses 40% debt financing, and it pays federal-plus-state taxes at a 30% rate. Security analysts estimate TGT's beta to be 1.2. If the acquisition were to take place, ACQ would increase TGT's debt ratio to 50%, which would increase its beta to 1.3. Further, because ACQ is highly profitable, taxes on the consolidated firm would be 40%. Kerr realizes that TGT's Hardware also generates depreciation cash flows, but she believes that these funds would have to be reinvested within the division to replace worn-out equipment.

```
INPUT DATA
Current Company Information:
Debt ratio                          40%
Tax rate                            30%
Beta                                1.2

Post-Merger Company Information:
Debt ratio                          50%
Beta                                1.3
Tax rate                            40%

Stock and Market Information:
Risk-free rate                       9%
Market risk premium                  4%
Net cash flow growth rate            6%
```

Kerr estimates the risk-free rate to be 9% and the market risk premium to be 4%. She also estimates that net cash flows after 2X17 will grow at a constant rate of 6%. The following is the H Division's cash flow statements for 2X14 through 2X17, assuming the acquisition is made.

	(In millions of dollars)			
	2X14	*2X15*	*2X16*	*2X17*
Net sales	$60.0	$90.0	$112.5	$127.5
Cost of good sold (60%)	$36.0	$54.0	$67.5	$76.5
Selling/Administrative expense	$4.5	$6.0	$7.5	$9.0
Interest expense (a)	$3.0	$4.5	$4.5	$6.0
EBT	$16.5	$25.5	$33.0	$36.0
Taxes (40%) (b)	$6.6	$10.2	$13.2	$14.4
Net Income	$9.9	$15.3	$19.8	$21.6
Less: retentions needed for growth (c)	$0.0	$7.5	$6.0	$4.5
Cash Flow	$9.9	$7.8	$13.8	$17.1
Plus: terminal value (d)				$566.4
Net Cash Flow to ACQ (e)	$9.9	$7.8	$13.8	$583.5

NPV = $436.58

Note:

(a) Interest payments are estimates based on TGT's existing debt, plus additional debt required to finance growth.

(b) ACQ will file a consolidated tax return after the merger. Thus, the taxes shown here are the full corporate taxes attributable to TGT's operations: there will be no additional taxes on any cash flows passed from TGT to ACQ.

(c) Some of the cash flows generated by the TGT subsidiary after the merger must be retained to finance asset replacements and growth, while some will be transferred to ACQ to pay dividends on its stock or for redeployment within the corporation. These retentions are net of any additional debt used to help finance growth.

(d) TGT's available cash flows are expected to grow at a constant 6 percent rate after 2X17. The value of all post-2X17 cash flows as of December 31, 2X17, is estimated by use of the constant growth model to be $566.44 million:

$$P_0 = \frac{CF_{2X18}}{r - g} = \frac{(\$21.6 - \$4.5)(1.06)}{0.092 - 0.06} = \$566.44 \text{ million}$$

Where r = required rate of return.

Note: TGT estimated 9.2 percent cost of equity is computed, using the CAPM model. Required rate of return = risk free rate + beta x market risk premium = 4% + 1.3 (4%) = 9.2%.

(e) These are the net cash flows projected to be available to ACQ by virtue of the acquisition. The cash flows could be used, for example, as dividend payments to ACQ stockholders or to finance asset expansion in ACQ's other divisions and subsidiaries.

(f) The $436.58 million is the PV at the end of 2X17 of the stream of cash flows for Year 2X18 and thereafter.

Note that these statements are identical to standard capital budgeting cash flow statements except that both interest expense and retentions are included in merger analysis. In straight capital budgeting, all debt involved is new debt that is issued to fund the asset additions. Hence, the debt involved all costs the same and this cost is accounted for by discounting the cash flows at the firm's cost of capital. However, in a merger the acquiring firm usually both assumes the existing debt of the target and issues new debt to help finance the takeover. Thus, the debt involved has different costs, and hence cannot be accounted for as a single cost in the cost of capital. The easiest solution is to explicitly include interest expense in the cash flow statement.

With respect to retentions, all of the cash flows from an individual project are available for use throughout the firm, but some of the cash flows generated by an acquisition are generally retained with the new division to help finance its growth. Because such retentions are not available to the parent company for use elsewhere, they must be deducted in the cash flow statement.

With interest expense and retentions included in the cash flow statements, the cash flows are residuals that are available to the acquiring firm's equity holders. ACQ's management could pay these out as dividends or reinvest them in other divisions of the firm. **Note:** If another firm were valuing TGT, they would probably obtain an estimate different from $436.58 million. Most importantly, the synergies involved would likely be different, and hence, the cash flow estimates would differ. In addition, another potential acquirer might use different financing, or have a different tax rate, and hence, estimate a different discount rate.

EXAMPLE 16 : Assume in Example 15 that TGT has 10 million shares outstanding. These shares are traded relatively infrequently, but the last trade, made several weeks ago, was at a price of $35 per share. Should ACQ make an offer for TGT? If so, how much should it offer per share? With a current price of $35 per share and 10 million shares outstanding, TGT's current market value is $35(10) = $350 million. Because TGT's expected value to ACQ is $436.58 million, it appears that the merger would be beneficial to both sets of stockholders. The difference, $436.58 − $350 = $86.58 million, is the added value to be apportioned between the stockholders of both firms.

The offering range is from $9 per share to $436.58/10 = $43.66 per share. At $35, the benefit of the merger goes to ACQ shareholders while at $43.66, the value created goes to TGT shareholders. If ACQ offers more than $43.66 per share, then wealth would be transferred from ACQ stockholders to TGT stockholders.

As to the actual offering price, ACQ should make the offer as low as possible, yet acceptable to TGT shareholders. A low initial offer, say $35.50 per share, would probably be rejected and the effort wasted. Further, the offer may influence other potential suitors to consider TGT, and they could end up outbidding ACQ. Conversely, a high price, say $44, passes almost all of the gain to TGT stockholders, and ACQ managers should retain as much of the synergistic value as possible for their own shareholders.

Operating Cash Flow

Some businesses may be valued at a multiple of operating cash flow. For example, radio and TV stations often sell for between 8 to 12 times operating cash flow.

Book Value (Net Worth)

The business may be valued based on the book value of the net assets (assets less liabilities) at the most recent balance sheet date. This method is unrealistic because it does not take into account current values. It may be appropriate only when it is impossible to determine fair value of net assets and/or goodwill. However, book value may be adjusted for obvious understatements such as excess depreciation, LIFO reserve, favorable leases, and for low debt (e.g., low rental payments or unfunded pension and postretirement benefits). Unfortunately, it may be difficult for a buying company to have access to information regarding these adjustments.

Tangible Net Worth

The valuation of the company is its tangible net worth for the current year equal to:

Stockholders' equity

Less: intangible assets

Economic Net Worth (Adjusted Book Value)

Economic net worth equals:

Fair market value of net assets

Plus: goodwill (as per agreement)

Fair Market Value of Net Assets

The fair market value of the net tangible assets of the business may be determined through independent appraisal. To it, we add the value of the goodwill (if any). Note that goodwill applies to such aspects as reputation of the company, customer base, and high quality merchandise. IRS Appeals and Review Memorandums (ARM) 34 and 38 present formula methods to value goodwill. In the case of a small business, a business broker may be retained to do the appraisal of property, plant, and equipment. A business broker is experienced because he or she puts together the purchase of small businesses. According to Equitable Business Brokers, about 25% of businesses changing hands are sold through business brokers. Typically, the fair value of the net tangible assets (assets less liabilities) is higher than book value.

The general practice is to value inventory at a maximum value of cost.[5] IRS Revenue Procedure 77-12 [1977-1 C.B. 161] provides acceptable ways to allocate a lump-sum purchase price to inventories.

Unrecognized and unrecorded liabilities should be considered when determining the fair market value of net assets. For example, one company the author consulted had both an unrecorded liability for liquidated damages for nonunion contracts of $3,100,000 and an unrecorded liability for $4,900,000 related to the estimated employer final withdrawal liability. Obviously, as a result of unrecorded liabilities the value of a business will be reduced further.

A tax liability may also exist that has not been recognized in the accounts. For example, the company's tax position may be adjusted by the IRS which is currently auditing the tax return. This contingent liability should be considered in valuing the business.

In a similar vein, unrecorded and undervalued assets, such as customer lists, patents, and licensing agreements, should be considered because they increase the value of the business.

Note: IRS Revenue Ruling 65-193 [1965-2 C.B. 370] approves only those approaches where valuations can be determined separately for tangible and intangible assets.

Liquidation Value

Liquidation value is a conservative figure of value because it does not take into account the earning power of the business. Liquidation value is a "floor" price in negotiations. Liquidation value is the estimated value of the company's assets, assuming their conversion into cash in a short time period. All liabilities and the costs of liquidating the business (e.g., appraisal fees, real estate fees, legal and accounting fees, recapture taxes) are subtracted from the total cash to obtain net liquidation value.

Liquidation value may be computed based on an orderly liquidation or a forced (rapid) liquidation. In the case of the latter, there will obviously be a lower value.

Replacement Cost

Replacement cost ("new") is the cost of duplicating from scratch the business' assets on an "as-if-new" basis. It will typically result in a higher figure than book value or fair market value of existing assets. Replacement cost provides a meaningful basis of comparison with other methods but should not be used as the acquisition value. A more accurate indicator of value is when replacement cost is adjusted for relevant depreciation and obsolescence.

Secured-Loan Value

The secured-loan value reflects the borrowing power of the seller's assets. Typically, banks will lend up to 90% of accounts receivable and 10% to 60% of the value of inventory depending on how much represents finished goods, work-in-process, and

---

[5] Charles Hays and Lawrence Finley, *op. cit.,* p. 32.

raw materials. The least percentage amount will be work-in-process because of its greater realization risk and difficulty of sale. Also considered are turnover rates.

Gross Revenue Multiplier

The value of the business may be determined by multiplying the revenue by the gross revenue multiplier common in the industry. The industry standard gross revenue multiplier is based on the average ratio of market price to sales prevalent in the industry. This approach may be used when earnings are questionable.

EXAMPLE 17: If revenue is $14,000,000 and the multiplier is .2, the valuation is:

$14,000,000 × .2 = $2,800,000.

In a similar fashion, insurance agencies often sell for about 150% of annual commissions.

Profit Margin/Capitalization Rate

The profit margin divided by the capitalization rate provides a multiplier which is then applied to revenue. A multiplier of revenue that a company would sell at is the company's profit margin. The profit margin may be based on the industry average. The formula is:

$$\frac{\text{Profit margin}}{\text{Capitalization rate}} = \frac{\text{Net income/sales}}{\text{Capitalization rate}} = \text{Multiplier}$$

The capitalization rate in earnings is the return demanded by investors. In arriving at a capitalization rate, the prime interest rate may be taken into account. The multiplier is what the buyer is willing to pay.

EXAMPLE 18: Assume sales of $14,000,000, a profit margin of 5%, and a capitalization rate of 20%. The multiplier is 25% (5%/20%). The valuation is:

Sales × 25%

$14,000,000 × 25% = $3,500,000

The IRS and the courts have considered recent sales as an important factor.[6]

Price-Earnings Factor

The value of a business may be based on the price-earnings factor applied to current (or expected) earnings per share (EPS). For publicly traded companies, the P/E ratio is known. Valuation for a privately held company is more difficult. Historical earnings must be adjusted for a closely held company to be consistent with the reported earnings of a public company. After suitable adjustments have been made, the average P/E ratio for the industry or for several comparable public companies is used to arrive at a value. Typically, a premium is added to the value estimate to incorporate uncertainty and additional risk and lack of marketability

---

[6] American Institute of Certified Public Accountants, *op. cit.*, p. 16.

associated with private companies. A variation of the P/E method may also be used. Assuming an expected earnings growth rate of the seller and a desired ROI, the acquirer determines an earnings multiple he or she would pay to achieve the ROI goal. Under this approach, the buyer determines the price he or she would be willing to pay instead of using a stock-market-related price.

EXAMPLE 19:

Net income	$ 800,000
Outstanding shares	/100,000
EPS	$ 8
P/E multiple	× 10
Market price per share	$ 80
× Number of shares outstanding	× 100,000
Price-earnings valuation	$8,000,000

Comparative Values of Similar Going Concerns

What would someone pay for this business? Reference may be made to the market price of similar publicly traded companies. Under this approach, you obtain the market prices of companies in the industry similar in nature to the one being examined. Recent sales prices of similar businesses may be used and an average taken. Upward or downward adjustments to this average will be made depending on the particular circumstances of the company being valued. There are two ways of arriving at an adjusted average value for a company based on comparable transactions. Under the equivalency adjustment method, you make an adjustment to each transaction before averaging based on such factors as size, profitability, earnings stability, and transaction structure. Transactions are adjusted downward if you deem a higher price was paid than would be appropriate for the target company, and vice versa. The average of the adjusted comparables approximates the estimated value of the target company. With the simple averaging method, you determine a simple average of the comparable transactions, after excluding noncomparable cases, and adjust the target company's price insofar as it differs from the average features of the companies purchased in comparable transactions. The former approach is suggested where extensive data are available on the comparable transactions, and where they differ substantially in their features. The latter approach is preferable where the comparable transactions are broadly similar, or where many comparable transactions have occurred.

While a perfect match is not possible, the companies should be reasonably similar (e.g., size, product, structure, geographic locations, diversity). The comparable transactions value will often be higher than the market value of the target's stock price. Several sources of industry information are Standard & Poor's, Dow Jones-Irwin, online information services (e.g., Compustat, Media General), and trade association reports. Extensive databases exist to assist in the analysis of merger-market history.

EXAMPLE 20: A competing company has just been sold for $6,000,000. We believe the company is worth 90% of the competing business. Therefore, the valuation is $5,400,000.

Sales of Stock

The value of the business may be based on the outstanding shares times the market price of the stock. For an actively traded stock, the stock price provides an important benchmark. For a thinly traded stock, the stock price may not reflect an informed market consensus. Typically, the market price of the stock should be based on a discounted amount from the current market price since if all the shares are being sold the market price per share may drop somewhat based on the demand-supply relationship. Further, market value of stock is of use only in planning the actual strategy of acquiring a target company since the stock may be overvalued or undervalued relative to the worth of the target company to the acquirer.

Combination of Methods

The value of the business may be approximated by determining the average value of two or more methods.

EXAMPLE 21: Assume that the fair market value of net assets approach gives a value of $2,100,000 while the capitalization of excess earnings method provides a value of $2,500,000. The value of the business would then be the average of these two methods, or $2,300,000 ($2,100,000 + $2,500,000)/2.

Some courts have found a combination of methods supportable as long as greater weight is given to the earnings methods. S. Pratt writes that the most weight should be placed on the earnings approaches and less on the asset approaches.[7]

EXAMPLE 22: Using the same information as in the prior example, if a 2 weight were assigned to the earnings approach and a 1 weight were assigned to the fair market value of net assets method, the valuation would be:

Method	Amount	×	Weight	=	Total
Fair market value of net assets	$2,100,000	×	1		$2,100,000
Capitalization-of-excess earnings	2,500,000	×	2		5,000,000
			3		$7,100,000
					/3
Valuation					$2,366,667

---

[7] Shannon Pratt, *op. cit.*, p. 196.

Accounting Adjustments

Material accounting adjustments should be made to the acquired company's figures to place them on a comparable basis to those of the acquirer. Adjustments should be made, where practical, for savings in administrative, technical, sales, plant, and clerical personnel costs resulting from the combination. These savings arise from the elimination of duplicate personnel, plant, office, and warehouse facilities. Savings in freight may result from the combination by shifting production to plants closer to markets.

ACCOUNTING, REPORTING, AND DISCLOSURES FOR BUSINESS COMBINATIONS

Business combinations in the form of mergers and acquisitions occur when companies choose to combine (rather than grow internally) to take advantage of cost efficiencies or transform their businesses to the next level. The result of a business combination is that the combined company may have additional product offerings, greater geographic presence, increased market share, as well as control over all sources of production and product distribution (vertical integration). The accountant is frequently called upon to advise management of the impact of proposed combinations, as well as to prepare consolidated financial statements for completed transactions. Knowledge of the emerging accounting rules in this area is critical in supporting both functions.

With the exception of the elimination of pooling of interests for new acquisitions (in 2001) and the required consolidation of variable interest entities (revised in 2003), the accounting rules for business combinations and consolidations remained largely unchanged for over 50 years until December 2007, when the FASB, after many years of deliberation, simultaneously issued two new standards, FASB Statement No. 141R (FASB-141R), *Business Combinations* (ASC 805) (a revision of FASB Statement No. 141), and FASB Statement No.160 (FASB-160), *Noncontrolling Interests in Consolidated Financial Statements—An Amendment of ARB No. 51* (ASC 810-10-65-1). These statements, which require prospective treatment for new business combinations having fiscal years beginning after December 15, 2008, mandate what is referred to as the acquisition method. Moreover, the purchase method of accounting will no longer be permitted for acquisitions closed after the effective date of the new rules. (**Note:** ASC 805 completes a joint effort by the FASB and IASB to standardize reporting for business combinations as part of the international convergence project. IFRS 3, *Business Combinations*, was issued in 2007 and for the most part, mirrors the rules found in the newly issued ASC 805.)

A critical distinction is that the new rules abandon the historical cost-based structure of accounting for acquisitions at the price paid and require that consolidation of the acquiree is at "business fair value." As retroactive adoption of the new standards is not permitted, mergers completed before the effective date must continue to be treated in accordance with the accounting standards that were in effect at the date of the original business combination. Therefore, there will continue to be many mergers that will be "grandfathered" under the accounting rules in existence at the dates they were completed (i.e., purchase method and pooling of interests method).

Acquisition Method

Under the acquisition method, an acquirer in a business combination is required to measure the identifiable assets acquired, the liabilities assumed, and any non-controlling interest in the acquiree at the acquisition-date fair values. The acquisition date is usually the date that the acquirer legally transfers the consideration, acquires the assets, and assumes the liabilities of the acquiree (i.e., the closing date).

ASC 805 requires the calculation of the consideration transferred in a business combination to include the acquisition-date fair values of the assets (including cash) transferred by the acquirer, the liabilities incurred by the acquirer of the former owners of the acquiree, and the equity interests issued by the acquirer. Costs an acquirer incurs to effect a business combination (such as finder's fees; legal, accounting, and other professional fees; and general administrative costs) are reported as acquisition-related costs, and expensed in the periods in which the costs are incurred and the services received. The costs to register and issue debt or equity securities are not acquisition-related costs and thus, are recognized and amortized over the life of the debt or as a reduction of additional paid in capital.

ASC 805 clarifies that the acquirer may not recognize acquiree goodwill, if any, or the deferred income taxes recorded by an acquiree before the business combination; however, a deferred tax liability or asset must be recognized for differences between the carrying values assigned in the business combination and the tax bases of the recognized assets acquired and liabilities assumed.

Under ASC 805, an intangible asset can be recognized separately from goodwill if it arises from a contractual or other legal right, regardless of whether the right is transferable or separable. An intangible asset can only be recognized separately from goodwill if it is capable of being separated or divided from the acquired assets and can be sold, transferred, licensed, rented, or exchanged individually or together with a related contract, identifiable asset, or liability. ASC 805 provides examples of intangible assets that can be recognized separately from goodwill (i.e., a favorable leasehold right, trademark, trade name, Internet domain name, and non-competition agreements).

ASC 805 requires the acquirer to compute the amount recognized as goodwill in a business combination. Goodwill is calculated as the excess of the sum of the consideration transferred and the fair value of any non-controlling interest in the acquiree over the net of the acquisition-date amounts of the identifiable assets acquired and the liabilities assumed. An acquired intangible asset of the acquiree that is not capable of being separated or divided is treated as goodwill.

ASC 805 requires that if the total acquisition-date amount of the identifiable net assets acquired exceeds the consideration transferred plus the fair value of any non-controlling interest in the acquiree (i.e., a bargain purchase), the acquirer must reassess whether it has correctly identified all of the assets acquired and all the liabilities assumed and recognize any additional assets or liabilities that are identified in that review. If that excess remains after the review, the acquirer will recognize that excess as a gain attributable to the acquirer on the acquisition date.

According to ASC 805, the historical equity capital balances of the acquired business are carried forward on the acquirer's consolidated balance sheet under the acquisition method. The operating results of the acquiree are included in the income and expenses of the acquirer only from the acquisition date. If the ownership interest in the acquiree is obtained in a series of purchase transactions, the equity interest in the acquiree previously held by the acquirer is re-measured at its acquisition-date fair value and any resulting gain or loss is recognized in the acquirer's earnings.

Contrast between the Acquisition Method and the Purchase and Pooling of Interest Methods

Prior to the effective dates of ASC 805, *Business Combinations*, and ASC 810, *Consolidation*, previously completed business combinations were accounted for under the purchase method or the pooling of interests method. Because the new rules are grandfathered, those business combinations will continue to be accounted for under the rules that were in place at the time the transaction closed.

A listing of the main points of each method is as follows:

1. *Acquisition method* (effective for new acquisitions by acquirers having fiscal years beginning after December 15, 2008):

   a. Focus is on fair value of the acquired entity.

   b. Direct combination costs are expensed.

   c. Stock issuance costs are treated as a reduction of Additional Paid in Capital.

   d. Bargain purchase is treated as income to the acquirer.

   e. Fair value of contingent consideration at acquisition date is considered part of the fair value of the acquired entity.

   f. Subsequent resolution of contingent consideration at a value different from that recorded at the acquisition date is run through the income statement.

   g. Acquiree in process research and development costs and other purchased intangibles are recorded at fair value at the acquisition date.

   h. Preacquisition contingencies that are resolved after the acquisition closing date are expensed.

   i. Acquiree assets and liabilities are reported in the consolidated entity at fair value.

2. *Purchase method* (effective for acquisitions closed prior to December 15, 2008, that have been accounted for under the purchase method):

   a. Acquisitions continue to be accounted for under the purchase method.

   b. Focus is on historical cost of the acquisition (i.e., the price paid to acquire an entity).

    c. Direct combination costs are capitalized as part of the investment cost.

    d. Stock issuance costs are treated as a reduction of Additional Paid in Capital.

    e. Bargain purchase results in a proportional reduction of noncurrent assets of the acquiree with any excess treated as an extraordinary gain.

    f. Contingent consideration is not recorded as part of acquisition cost until it is subsequently resolved. (**Note:** If the resolution of the contingency requires an additional payment to be made by the acquirer, that payment will either increase goodwill or lessen the reduction to noncurrent assets in the case of a bargain purchase).

    g. Acquiree in process research and development costs is included in the acquisition cost only where considered either technologically feasible or subject to alternative future use.

    h. Assets and liabilities of the acquiree are reported at fair value, subject to any reduction in acquiree noncurrent assets due to a bargain purchase.

3. *Pooling of interest method* (effective for acquisitions completed prior to June 30, 2001, assuming they met all 12 of the specific criteria in existence at that time):

    a. Acquisitions will continue to be consolidated under this method, until the entities are sold, closed, or otherwise disposed of.

    b. Assets and liabilities are consolidated at their book values.

    c. There are no adjustments to either the balance sheet (fair value allocations) or the income statement (amortization of fair value adjustments).

    d. Income and expense of the acquiree are reported retrospectively; that is, they are retroactively restated for all periods presented.

Exhibit 39-1 presents the main differences between the acquisition and purchase methods of accounting:

EXHIBIT 39-1: Acquisition Method vs. Purchase Method

	New Rules (Acquisition Method) ASC 805 (FAS-141R); ASC 810 (FAS-160)	Old Rules (Purchase Method) ASC 805 (FAS-141); ASC 810 (ARB 51)
Focus	Fair value of entity acquired, referred to as "business fair value"	Historical cost; that is, price paid to acquire the entity
Direct combination costs	Expensed	Treated as part of cost of acquisition
Bargain purchase	Recognize as income on transaction closing date	Reduce noncurrent assets proportionately; any excess is extraordinary gain

	New Rules (Acquisition Method) ASC 805 (FAS-141R); ASC 810 (FAS-160)	Old Rules (Purchase Method) ASC 805 (FAS-141); ASC 810 (ARB 51)
Stock issuance costs	Decrease (debit) to Additional Paid In Capital	Same
Contingent consideration	Recorded at fair value at transaction closing date; subsequent changes in fair value recorded in income statement	Not recorded as part of acquisition cost until contingency is resolved. This will result in additional goodwill or less reduction to noncurrent assets (bargain purchase)
In process research and development costs	Capitalize at fair value as intangible assets, subject to impairment testing or amortization	Expensed
Preacquisition contingencies	Contractual contingencies recorded at fair value; noncontractual contingencies recorded at fair value if they meet "more likely than not" criteria for definition of an asset or liability	Not recorded unless FAS-5 (ASC 450) criteria are met (i.e., probable and reasonably estimable)
Valuation of equity issued	Fair value at transaction closing date	Fair value at the date the acquisition is announced
Other intangible assets	Recorded at fair value	Recorded as part of investment cost if meeting contractual criteria (e.g., patents) or separability (e.g., technology)

Pushdown Accounting

Pushdown accounting is defined as an acquiree's establishment of a new accounting basis in its separate financial statements when an acquirer obtains control of the acquired entity. Accounting Standards Update (ASU) No. 2015-08, *Business Combinations* (Topic 805): *Pushdown Accounting—Amendments to SEC Paragraphs Pursuant to Staff Accounting Bulletin No. 115*, amended various SEC paragraphs pursuant to the issuance of Staff Accounting Bulletin 115, to reflect the guidance in Accounting Standards Update (ASU) No. 2014-17, *Business Combinations* (Topic 805): *Pushdown Accounting (A Consensus of the FASB Emerging Issues Task Force)*. ASU 2014-17 allows an acquiree that retains its separate corporate existence to elect to apply pushdown accounting upon a change-in-control event. The pushdown accounting elective is available for all entities, public and nonpublic, with the election available at each change-in-control event. A change-in-control event occurs when an acquirer obtains a controlling financial interest in an acquiree. A controlling financial interest typically requires ownership of more than 50 percent of the voting rights in an acquired entity.

When an acquiree elects pushdown accounting, it reports in its separate financial statements the new basis of accounting established by the acquirer under which the acquiree's identifiable assets, liabilities, and non-controlling interests are restated to their acquisition-date fair values using the definition of fair value in ASC 820, *Fair Value Measurements and Disclosures.* The assets acquired, including goodwill, and liabilities assumed, measured at their acquisition-date fair values, are reported in the separate financial statements of the acquiree and the consolidated financial statements of the acquirer. However, any bargain purchase gain recognized by the acquirer when applying the acquisition method cannot be reported in the acquiree's income statement. The effect of any bargain purchase gain recognized by the acquirer is reflected in the acquisition-date measurement of the acquiree's additional paid-in capital account, not in the acquiree's income statement.

ASU No. 2015-08 provides an acquiree with the option to apply pushdown accounting each time there is a transaction or event in which the acquirer obtains control of the entity. An acquirer may obtain control of the entity either directly through purchase of the acquiree's equity interests (or equity interests of the acquiree's parent), or without transferring consideration, such as when certain rights in a contract lapse.

The election to apply pushdown accounting is made in the period in which the change-in-control event occurs. Once pushdown accounting is applied, it is irrevocable. If an acquiree did not apply pushdown accounting at the time of its most recent change-in-control event, it can elect to do so retrospectively as a change in accounting policy in a subsequent period. An acquiree that did not elect pushdown accounting for a change in control event that occurred prior to the effective date may do so as a change in accounting policy.

Disclosures

For each acquisition that occurs during the reporting period or after the reporting period but before financial statements are issued, the acquirer must disclose:

- Name and description of the acquiree.
- Acquisition date.
- Percentage of voting interest acquired.
- Rationale for the business combination and how the acquirer obtained control of the acquiree.
- Qualitative factors supporting any goodwill from the transaction (e.g., expected synergies from combined operations or description of intangible assets not qualifying for separate recognition).
- Fair value of total consideration transferred, as well as fair value of each component.
- Amount and description of any contingent consideration, as well as a discussion of the circumstances in which payment will be made; also

included should be a range of possible outcomes or, if a range cannot be estimated, the reasons why.

- Amounts recognized at the acquisition date for each major class of assets acquired and liabilities assumed.

- Nature of recognized and unrecognized contingencies along with a range of possible outcomes.

- Total goodwill expected to be deducted for tax purposes.

- If acquirer is required to disclose segment information, the amount of goodwill by reportable segment (this information will be used in the goodwill impairment test).

- Where acquirer and acquiree have previously had a business relationship, any amounts that are not part of the exchange in the business combination between the acquirer and acquiree should be identified.

- Any acquisition-related costs and, where reported in the financial statements, that is, expense, reduction of paid in capital, or other category.

- For any bargain purchase, the amount of the gain included in the consolidated income statement and the reason why the business combination resulted in a gain.

- Fair value of any noncontrolling interest and valuation techniques used to measure fair value.

- For step acquisitions, the fair value of any equity interest held immediately prior to the acquisition date and the amount of gain or loss recognized as a result of remeasuring to fair value.

- For public companies, the amount of revenue and earnings subsequent to the acquisition date, reported in the consolidated income statement.

- Supplemental pro forma information, showing revenue and earnings for any comparative period for which financial statements are presented, including the as of the beginning of the current reporting period.

Note: As clarified by Accounting Standards Update (ASU) No. 2010-29 in December 2010, supplemental pro forma information, showing revenue and earnings of the acquiree as though the business combination occurred as of the beginning of the comparable annual reporting period. For example, if a calendar year-end company completed a business combination in April 2011, disclosures would be provided as if the business combination occurred as of January 1, 2010. In addition, disclosure is required of any material nonrecurring transactions included in the pro forma adjustments.

FINANCIAL STATEMENT ANALYSIS OF BUSINESS COMBINATIONS

The analyst must carefully scrutinize disclosures relating to deriving fair market values of the assets and liabilities of the acquired company. He must ascertain the reasonableness of such valuations.

If equity securities are involved in the purchase transaction, the analyst should determine whether the market prices of the securities were unusually high at the transaction date. If so, net assets will be inflated due to the temporary ceiling market prices. In this case, the analyst may wish to use the average market price of the securities for his or her own valuation of the acquired assets.

The analyst must be alert to the possible overstatement of estimated liabilities for future costs and losses that may increase postacquisition earnings.

CONCLUSION

Generally, do not acquire another business unless you are a growth, successful company. Do not try to make a "bargain" purchase. You get what you pay for!

In analyzing a potential merger and acquisition, many considerations must be taken into account, such as the market price of stock, earnings per share, dividends, book value of assets, risk, and tax considerations. A detailed analysis of the target company is required to ensure that a realistic price is paid based on the particular circumstances.

The price to be paid for a business depends upon many factors including the seller's strengths, weaknesses, and prospects. The buyer's objectives and requirements are also relevant. A total cash transaction justifies a lower price than an installment sale because with an installment sale there are the uncertainties of cash collection and the time value of money.

When valuing a company, more weight should be placed on the earnings approaches and less on the asset approaches. Valuation may be based on a combined approach of methods including earnings and asset valuation. In deriving a value, industry standards may be quite helpful. Consideration should be given to adjusted cash earnings, gross revenue, fair value of net assets, and recent sales of similar businesses. A proper valuation is needed so as to come up with a realistic price that is fair to all concerned parties. IRS Revenue Procedure 66-49 [1966-2, C.B. 1257] discusses how the IRS comes up with its valuations. Some of the contents of what should be in a valuation report are mentioned.

CHAPTER 40

DIVESTITURE

CONTENTS

The divestiture of business segments by corporations has become an accepted strategy for growth rather than diversification. Divestiture involves the partial or complete conversion, disposition, and reallocation of people, money, inventories, plants, equipment, and products. It is the process of eliminating a portion of the enterprise for subsequent use of the freed resources for some other purpose. A divestment may involve a manufacturing, marketing, research, or other business function. A parent may sell a segment because it needs funds to pay off debt.

A business segment may be subject to divestiture if:

- It does not produce an acceptable return on invested capital.
- It does not generate sufficient cash flow.
- It does not fit in with the overall corporate strategy.
- The worth of the pieces is greater than that of the whole.

During the 1960s, many corporations were acquiring other firms, often in different industries, to form large conglomerates. In the 1970s a general economic downturn made many companies reduce the pace of the acquisition process. Divestiture first appeared in the early stages of the downturn as corporations needed cash. Many dynamic, fast-growing companies were combining with slower-growing, mature companies to produce a more diversified corporate portfolio. However, during this time many companies found that if you have too many businesses it spreads the cash too thin. Also, this random mixture of businesses under one corporate umbrella caused a great deal of concern within the financial industry. The mix made it difficult to measure actual segment performance.

In 1976, the Securities and Exchange Commission persuaded the Financial Accounting Standards Board (FASB) that publicly held companies should report the assets held and income generated by disaggregated corporate segments of similar products and services. Thus, for the first time, the public found out that many of a company's business segments were unprofitable! This disclosure forced management to explain to the shareholders why certain segments of the corporation were producing such low returns on the stockholders' invested capital. For the first time, corporate executives were forced into developing divestiture strategies to eliminate the unprofitable section of the business.

Resource allocation becomes an important consideration in a diversified business. These resources are not only capital, but also include management talent. If management finds itself spending an excessive amount of time and energy on one segment of the corporation, that segment may be a candidate for divestiture. Then those resources can be redirected to the growing segments of the business. However, this operation also requires the attention of management.

When developing the strategies involved with divestiture, management must consider the interrelationships between that division and the rest of the company and the costs of discontinuing that operation. The carrying out of a divestiture has an effect across the whole company, including the production, distribution, and marketing areas. Divestiture may also greatly affect the public's image of the company.

OBJECTIVES AND TYPES OF DIVESTITURES

Sooner or later a corporation will find itself in the position of needing to divest some of its assets. This may be for a variety of reasons. The usual objectives behind divestiture are to reposition the company in a market, raise cash, and reduce losses. The other alternatives to divestiture are liquidation and bankruptcy; however, in this time of acquisitions and buyouts a buyer can usually be found for the other company's dog. There are four primary types of divestitures:

1. Sale of an operating unit to another firm.

2. Sale of the managers of the unit being divested.

3. Setting up the business to be divested as a separate corporation and then giving (or "spinning off") its stock to the divesting firm's stockholders on a pro rata basis.

4. Outright liquidation of assets.

When the divestiture is in the form of a sale to another firm, it usually involves an entire division or unit and is generally for cash but sometimes for stock of the acquiring firm. In a managerial buyout, the division managers themselves purchase the division, often through a leveraged buyout (LBO), and reorganize it as a closely held firm. In a spinoff, the firm's existing stockholders are given new stock representing separate ownership in the company that was divested. The new company establishes its own board of directors and officers and operates as a separate entity. In a liquidation, the assets of the divested unit are sold off separately instead of as a whole.

REASONS FOR DIVESTITURE

Prior to formulating a divestiture strategy and determining which segments should be divested, the reasons for divestiture need to be listed. The reasons given by management for divesting segments of their business are:

- Poor performance.
- Changes in plans.
- Excessive resource needs.
- Constraints in operation.
- Source of funds.
- Antitrust.

As a result of ASC 410, *Asset Retirement and Environmental Obligations* (ASC 410-20-55) (see Chapter 13, "Interim and Segment Reporting"), regarding the reporting of each business segment's operating costs and whether a profit is made or not, corporate management has been more reluctant to hold on to poorly performing business segments. However, there may be a logical reason to keep a poorly performing segment, such as a turnaround is expected or the unit provides components or a service to another unit within the company.

A diversified decision may result after the corporation has reviewed its operational philosophy and overall business strategy (whether this reevaluation was voluntary or forced by environment changes), and found business segments that no longer fit into the corporate image or are a business the company does not want to be involved in any more. An example of this is Schering-Plough's attempt to sell its Maybelline Cosmetics Division so they can concentrate their resources and time on their more profitable prescription and consumer drug businesses. This restructuring will allow Schering-Plough to earn more on its invested capital. Operating margins for drugs are near 24%, which is more than twice that of the Maybelline Division.

The need to raise cash to pay off debt resulting from operations or acquisition/ diversification is another frequent reason for selling off a segment of the corporation. In this case, though, many times the segment being sold is a winner. By selling a winning segment the company may hope to put itself on firmer financial ground by reducing debt. In this case where the company is trying to raise cash, the best segment to sell is the one that would require the least work to sell and would bring in the greatest amount of cash over book value. For example, if a company had two divisions, a retail operation and the other which builds and leases railcars, and the sale of either would make a significant dent in the company's debt load, which division should be sold? In this case, the retail should be sold because the market for that type of operation is much better than for railcars.

There are other less common reasons such as personality conflicts among division management and that of the parent company, government decree or public outcry, as in the case of many companies that had dealings in South Africa. On a rare occasion, the company may actually be approached and asked if they would be willing to sell the business.

DETERMINING WHAT AREAS OR UNITS SHOULD BE SOLD

When trying to determine which areas or units of the company could be sold off, there are some simple guidelines that management should follow:

- The sum of a division's parts may be greater in value than the whole division.

- Simple components of a division may be sold more easily than the whole division itself.

- The disposal of a corporate division is a major marketing operation.

- Planning should include an evaluation from the viewpoint of the potential buyer.

- A spinoff should be considered if the division is large enough and may be potentially publicly traded.

In addition, management must review existing operations and identify those divisions that don't relate to the primary focus of the company or don't meet internal financial and performance standards. Special strength of each division must also be considered. Does a division provide a unique service, have a special marketing, distribution system or production facilities that may be of more value to another company? Also, the financial aspects must be considered. The historical and projected returns on investment need to be calculated and tabulated for each division.

Using these guidelines and the information determined in the foregoing, management can focus on three topics: first, the attractiveness and value to others versus the arguments for keeping the division; second, what corrective action would need to be taken to make the division a keeper; and third, the current value of the division to the company. Only after considering all of these factors can a divestiture decision be made for a division.

EMPLOYEE CONSIDERATIONS

Once the decision to divest a division has been made, there are two approaches to dealing with employees. The first, and least often done, is to be up front and tell them that the division is for sale. This can result in a variety of negative responses. The employees' morale may further deteriorate (usually the morale is already poor because the division is not doing well), or worse, the employees may engage in a job action. The employees can also be a potential source of a buyout of the company so unless upper management is very aware of the employees' attitude, the decision to tell or not is a difficult one. Another tactic is for management to tell the employees that the division is being sold and offer incentive bonuses to all employees who stay on through the divestiture and following acquisition.

Typically though, the parent company will form a senior management team whose sole function is to divest the division, occasionally even the top management of the division being divested doesn't know it is being sold. There are some reasons behind choosing an upper management team to do the divestiture. First, companies tend to divest in secret. Any leak of the news could cause any of the employee problems mentioned above. This is especially true in the case where finding a buyer may take a long time. (A longer time means more likelihood for a leak.) Second, the head of a division is never the right person to sell the division. No matter how the decision to divest is sugarcoated it is still an admission of failure. This makes it difficult for the managers to take an objective view of the business. It also impedes the decision on who is a suitable and qualified buyer of the company. Having the management team doing the divestiture also avoids or minimizes any conflict between those who may be responsible for the failure and those who were not. The third reason to appoint a top management team to do the divestiture is that it is simply not a job that would be welcomed by lower-level managers. It is a thankless task that brings little reward for a hard job well done and has no future. It is a dead-end job.

Because the job falls on senior management, this also creates a problem. Their time is limited, particularly during a period where the company is trying to recover. If the team has neither the time nor the inclination to do this divestiture, the job performed may be sloppy. The decision analysis could be approximate rather than one based on actual numbers, as may be the selling price. Also, if pressed for time the team may be restricted to dealing with only one buyer instead of negotiating with many suitors, which would improve the selling price and the return for the parent. This time pressure may be caused by the division's cash requirements rather than the divestiture team time constraints. If the parent can only support the cash drain of the division for a certain time period after the decision to divest, this puts a definite time constraint on the timing of the sale.

MEANS OF DIVESTITURE

After the initial planning of the divestiture comes the tricky part of approaching potential buyers. The trick involved is to present enough information to pique the interest but also present the need for confidentiality (if required by the situation). The usual technique is to sound out a few potential buyers at a time, to see if they would be interested in acquiring a business in your industry with sales potential of X dollars.

This is done via a short letter or a phone call to the CEO of the possibly interested firms. This communication, again, should just whet their appetite for information. If they express a desire for further dialogue, a prospectus should be sent. However, if after the prospectus has been reviewed, no further interest exists, this potential acquirer should be crossed off the list.

The other option, depending on the skills and time demands of the members of the divestiture team, is to use a third party (broker) to find suitable buyers and enter into negotiations. The use of the third party will, in many cases, provide a needed veil of secrecy, if needed. The third party is also useful in trying to market the division on a world wide scale. This can get exposure for the division. This is particularly important where the parent or division had no previous exposure.

VALUATION AND APPRAISAL IN DIVESTITURE

When the time comes to sell a division, an asking price needs to be determined. Valuation of a division is not an exact science and, in the final analysis, the value of a division is in the eye of the purchaser. While the expertise of an investment banker or business broker can and should be enlisted in setting the price of the division, some standard accounting methods can be used to estimate a division's value. A business broker will usually be very willing to help in the initial estimate phase in hopes that they will get the opportunity to act as your agent in selling the division.

There are basically four groups of methods of valuation or appraisal: (1) asset valuation methods, (2) sales and income methods, (3) market comparison methods, and (4) discounted cash flow methods. Although these methods vary in their applicability and depend on certain facts and circumstances, they can be used to determine a range of values for a division.

Asset Valuation Methods

Asset valuation methods are based on the asset value of a business segment. Four popular methods are described below.

Adjusted Net Book Value. One of the most conservative methods of valuation is the adjusted net book value, because it determines the value based on historical (book) value and not on market value. This can be adjusted to compensate for this shortage by adding in such items as favorable lease arrangements, and other intangible items such as customer lists, patents, and goodwill.

Replacement Cost. Another method is the replacement cost technique. It asks "What would it cost to purchase the division's assets new?" This method will give a higher division value than the adjusted net book value method and is therefore good for adjusting the book value to account for new costs. This figure can also be used as a basis for determining the liquidation value of the division's assets. The most reasonable value comes from adjusting the replacement value for depreciation and obsolescence of equipment.

Liquidation Value. The liquidation value is also a conservative estimate of a division's value since it does not consider the division's ongoing earning power. The liquidation value does provide the seller with a bottom line figure as to how low the price can be. The liquidation value is determined by estimating the cash value of assets assuming that they are to be sold in a short period of time. All the liabilities, real and estimated, are then deducted from the cash that was raised to determine the net liquidation value. Liquidation value can be determined based on fire sale prices or on a longer-term sales price. Obviously, the fire sale value would be lower.

Secured Loan Value. The secured loan value technique is based on the borrowing power of the division's assets. Banks will usually lend up to 90% of the value of accounts receivable and anywhere from 10%–60% on the value of inventory depending on the quantity of the inventory in the conversion process.

Sales and Income Methods

Using sales and/or income figures as the basis for valuation can be done in two different ways:

1. *Price-Earnings (P/E) Ratios.* The P/E ratios for publicly held companies are known and therefore valuation is made easy. The division's value can be determined by multiplying the P/E ratio by the expected earnings for the division. This will give a derived price that all suitors can readily understand. The earnings can be estimated from quarterly or annual reports published by the company.

   For privately held companies, however, it is difficult to determine a P/E ratio as the stock of the company is not traded and the earnings are rarely disclosed. However, the earnings can be estimated and an industry average P/E ratio can be used in the calculation to estimate the private company's sales value.

2. *Sales or Earnings Multiples.* There are many rules of thumb that can be used when estimating a division's value based on a multiple of sales or earnings. For example, insurance agencies sell for 200% of annual commissions or liquor stores sell for ten times monthly sales. Another example would be radio stations selling for eight times earnings or cash flow. These rules are fast and dirty and may result in a completely erroneous estimate of a division's value. Most business brokers will know these rule of thumb values to assist management in estimating the value of a division.

Market Comparison Methods

Every day that a public company is traded on the stock market a new value is assigned to it by the traders. Thus, the stock price can be compared to equivalent companies in terms of products, size of operations, and average P/E ratios. From these P/E ratios, an estimated sales price can be arrived at, as described earlier.

In the case of private companies, it is difficult for the buyer to determine the earnings of the company. However, they can compare the company to other companies that are publicly traded. Comparison to publicly traded companies is necessary as the sales price is typically disclosed in the sale or acquisition announcement.

Discounted Cash Flow Methods

Another method of determining value of a business segment is to use discounted cash flow (DCF) analysis. This bases the value of the segment on the current value of its projected cash flow. In theory, this method should result in a division's value being equal to that determined by one of the P/E ratio calculations, since both reflect the current worth of the company's earnings. In actuality, discounted cash flow is basing the value of the company on actual forecasted cash flows whereas the stock market is basing the stock price on other things including the market's perception of the company and its potential cash flow.

The DCF method requires information on:

- Forecasted actual cash flows.

- Assumed terminal (residual) value of the division at the end of the forecast period (book value, zero, or a multiple of earnings are frequently used).

- Discount rate.

Choosing the right discount rate is the key to the successful use of the DCF technique. It must take into account the following factors:

- Purchaser's expected return on investment (ROI).

- Purchaser's assessment of risk.

- Cost of capital.

- Projected inflation rates.

- Current interest rates.

In general, whichever method of evaluation is chosen it is wise to check the resulting value with at least one other method to see if it is a reasonable figure. We have to be careful of excessively high or low figures. It is also a good idea to determine the liquidation value of the company or division as this will set a floor for negotiations.

DISCOUNTED CASH FLOW ANALYSIS

Management will choose to divest a segment of their business if they perceive that the action will increase the wealth of the stockholders, as reflected in the price of the firm's stock. It can be further said that the price of the firm's stock will react favorably to a divestiture if the new present value of the transaction is perceived by the market to be positive.

Should a profitable business segment be retained and not divested, it would generate annual cash inflows for a particular or infinite number of years. Discounted cash flow analysis involves a comparison of initial incoming cash flows resulting from the sale of a business unit with the present value of the foregone future cash inflows given up by the firm. Foregone future cash flows refers to the cash flows that the business unit is anticipated to generate and will generate for the acquiring firm. The divesting firm gives up these cash inflows in exchange for the selling price of the business segment. For divestiture analysis to be of any value, the foregone future cash flow must be accurately estimated. The present value of these future inflows is found by discounting them at the firm's weighted average cost of capital k_0.

EXAMPLE 1: Exhibit 40-1 shows estimated cash inflows and outflows for a fictitious divestment candidate (FDC) over the next five years. The cash flows represent the best estimates by the managers of FDC's parent company and they further believe that FDC will be able to be sold at its residual value of $58.7 million in five years. The firm's cost of capital is assumed to be known and is 15%.

The net present value of the future cash inflows of FDC is $47.3 million. If FDC were to be divested, the managers of its parent company should only consider selling prices greater than this amount. This logic also assumes that the $47.3 million can be reinvested at a 15% rate of return.

Another way of looking at this valuing task makes use of the following equation for divestiture net present value (DNPV):

$$DNPV = P - \sum \frac{NCF_t}{(1-k)^t} \qquad (1)$$

where P = the selling price of the business unit and NCF_t = net cash flow in period t. If a $50 million offer was made by a firm for FDC, the DNPV from Equation 1 will equal $2.7 million, as shown below.

$$DNPV = 50 - \frac{9.8}{1.15} + \frac{.4}{(1.15)^2} + \frac{2.4}{(1.15)^3} + \frac{5.8}{(1.15)^4} + \frac{62.9}{(1.15)^5}$$

DNPV = 50 – 47.3 = $2.7 million

From a financial point of view, this divestment is acceptable. If the divestment candidate has an unlimited life, such as a division in a healthy industry, then cash flows must be forecasted to infinity. This task is made simple by treating the cash flows similarly to a constant growth stock and valuing accordingly. If the cash inflows are expected to remain constant (zero growth) to infinity, then the present value of the NCF can be determined in the same manner as for a preferred stock, or perpetuity. In this case, the DNPV will be:

$$DNPV = P - \frac{NCF}{k} \qquad (2)$$

Exhibit 40-1: FDC's Cash Flow Projections

Cash Inflows (in millions)	1	2	3	4	5
Net Operating Profit	$3.1	$3.6	$4.0	$5.1	$ 6.0
Depreciation	2.1	2.4	1.8	2.3	2.1
Residual Value					58.7
Total	$5.2	$6.0	$5.8	$7.4	$66.8
Cash Outflows (in millions)					
Capital Expenditure	$ 1.7	$1.3	$0.8	$2.1	$ 1.7
Increase (Decrease) in Working Capital	(6.3)	1.3	2.6	(0.5)	2.2
Total	$(4.6)	$2.6	$3.4	$1.6	$ 3.9
Net Cash Flow (NCF)	$ 9.8	$3.4	$2.4	$5.8	$62.9
T3*	0.8696	0.7561	0.6575	0.5718	0.4972
Net Present Value	$8.5	$2.6	$1.6	$3.3	$31.3
Total NPV:	$47.3				

* T3=Present value interest factor for the cost of capital of 15%.

For future cash flows that are expected to grow at an after-tax rate of g, the present value of those flows can be found using the constant-growth valuation model. In this case, the DNPV will be

$$ DNPV \; = \; P \; - \; \frac{NCF_1}{K-g} \qquad (3) $$

where

NCF_1 = the expected NCF in the next period.

A final situation encountered often when evaluating divestiture candidates is the case where the NCFs are expected to be uneven for a number of years followed by even growth. In this case, the DNPV can be found as:

$$ DNPV = R - \frac{NCF_1}{(1+k)} + \frac{NCF_2}{(1+k)} + \cdots + \frac{NCF_{0-1}}{(k-g)} * \frac{1}{(1+k)} $$

where NCF_1 and NCF_2 represent foregone cash flows in periods 1 and 2 and c = the first year in which constant growth applies.

Firms should only divest of assets with positive DNPVs. To do so will increase the value of the firm and, subsequently, the price of its stock. If two different candidates are mutually exclusive, the one with the highest DNPV should be chosen since this will increase the value of the firm the most. If divestiture is forced by the government, for example, and the firm finds it has a choice of candidates, all with negative DNPVs, it should divest the one whose DNPV is closest to zero, since this will reduce the value of the firm the least.

DIVESTITURE WITH UNCERTAINTY

Due to the difficulty in predicting the NCFs and also in knowing what kinds of prices will be offered for the divestment candidate, the divestment's net present value is normally uncertain.

For situations involving an unknown selling price (due to a lack of offers), the parent firm can either elect not to divest of the candidate or set its asking price such that the DNPV will equal zero. This should be the minimum they are willing to accept. They can also look for other divestment candidates that offer promising DNPVs.

Adjusting for uncertain NCFs is much more difficult. While there is no generally accepted method for accounting for this risk, a number of useful techniques borrowed from capital budgeting can be used.

Risk-Adjusted Discount Rate

Employing a risk-adjusted discount rate is one technique that can be used to account for the uncertainty of the expected NCFs. In the previous examples, the firm's weighted-average cost of capital was used to discount the NCFs to their present value. This is an appropriate choice when the divestiture candidate is as risky as the firm itself. When it is more risky, a higher discount rate can be used for adjustment. This will reduce the present values of the cash flows and increase the DNPV. This is logical since a relatively risky divestment candidate with uncertain cash flows will be of less value to the firm, in present dollars. The added benefit of divesting such a candidate will be reflected in the increased DNPV. On the other hand, when the NCFs are more certain than those of the rest of the firm, the discount rate should be lowered. This lowers the DNPV and makes the divestiture less attractive. Equation I can be rewritten as shown below:

$$\text{DNPV} = P - \sum \frac{\text{NCF}_t}{(1 + k')^t} \qquad (4)$$

where all terms are the same except for k' which now is the adjusted rate to be used for discounting the cash flows. Using data from Table 45-2 and assuming that the divestment candidate is less risky than the firm as a whole (lowering k from .15 to .14) shows:

$$DNPV \;=\; 50 \;-\; \frac{9.8}{1.14} \;+\; \frac{3.4}{(1.14)^2} \;+\; \frac{2.4}{(1.14)^3} \;+\; \frac{5.8}{(1.14)^4} \;+\; \frac{62.9}{(1.14)^5}$$

Using a lower discount rate lessened the DNPV by $1.6 million ($2.7 million – $1.1 million). This is reasonable in that the attractiveness of a divestment candidate at a certain selling price will be lessened as the candidate is found to be less risky.

Sensitivity Analysis

Sensitivity analysis is another technique that can be used in making divestiture decisions. In sensitivity analysis, the parent company evaluates the effect that certain factors have on the NCFs. For example, a divestment candidate's NCFs might be largely influenced by the price of copper, the U.S. Navy defense budget, and upcoming union contract talks. For these three influencing factors, a number of different scenarios or forecasts can be projected, each with their expected NCFs. For instance, the expected NCFs would be highest in the scenario where all three influencing factors are favorable. Having evaluated the NCFs and DNPVs for different scenarios, the parent firm has a better understanding of the range that the NCFs might fall in and also what factors influence them the most. Further, if the probability of the scenarios can be forecasted, statistical techniques can be used to give the probability of realizing a negative DNPV, the expected DNPV and the standard deviation, and coefficient of variation of DNPVs. This information would be very useful in making divestment decisions. It should be noted that the NCFs using sensitivity analysis are discounted at the firm's weighted-average cost of capital.

Simulation

Simulation is a technique used to account for the uncertainty of future cash flows. It is similar to but more sophisticated than sensitivity analysis. In simulation, the parent firm's managers first identify key factors which they believe are likely to influence the NCF's of a divestment candidate. Next they create a probability distribution describing the future outcome of each key factor. The managers finally must specify the impact of each key variable on the NCFs and ultimately the DNPVs. The firm's cost of capital is again used to discount the NCFs. Computer programs are available to assist managers in the simulation analysis. After the data have been input and the program run, the computer will estimate NCFs and corresponding DNPVs over the whole range of probabilities. From this distribution, the analyst can determine the expected DNPV and the probability that the actual DNPV will be above or below some critical value. The uncertainty associated with the DNPV can also be determined, as measured by the dispersion of possible DNPV value. It is important to note that this technique is only as good as the input it receives from managers, and even then it cannot make a firm's divestment decision. It does, however, provide a comprehensive evaluation of the divestiture proposal.

LIQUIDATION PROCESS

Divestment of a company or division is nearly always preferred to liquidation even though liquidation may provide the greatest potential for monetary gain. The reason why it is not the method of choice is that it usually takes longer to liquidate a business than it does to sell one outright. However, should the case exist where the value of the business is zero or less and no buyer can be found, liquidation becomes the obvious alternative. Liquidation may be so expensive that it is not feasible. This would be the result of the cost of getting out of leases, contracts, and possible salary continuation requirements; it may be cheaper to pay the existing management or an entrepreneur to take over the business. The other option is bankruptcy.

The liquidation can be accomplished by contacting a liquidation company and having them perform all of the work in the liquidation process such as asset valuation, advertising the sale, negotiating the sale prices, and collecting the money for the goods. From this they will take a prenegotiated sum of money for their services. Another technique involves doing all the work in-house that the liquidation company would do and contacting competitors and the various vendor representatives in the area and alerting them to the fact that you will be having a going out of business sale. They will typically already know you are about to go out of business since word has probably already spread in these circles.

LIQUIDATION BASIS

According to Accounting Standards Update (ASU) No. 2013-07 (April 2013), *Presentation of Financial Statements* (Topic 205), *Liquidation Basis of Accounting*, financial statements prepared using the liquidation basis of accounting should show the company's expected resources in liquidation by reporting assets at anticipated cash proceeds from liquidation. Disclosure should be made of the company's liquidation plan, methods, and assumptions used to measure assets and liabilities, type and amount of accrued costs and revenue, and the anticipated time period of the liquidation process.

ACCOUNTING

A gain or loss cannot be recorded on a corporate divestiture. However, footnote disclosure should be provided of the nature and provisions of the divestiture.

If there is an exchange of stock held by a parent in a subsidiary for stock of the parent company itself held by stockholders in the parent, there is a non-pro-rata split-off of the business segment because a reorganization is recorded at fair value. However, if there is a split-off of a targeted company distributed on a proportionate basis to the one holding the applicable targeted stock, it should be recorded at historical cost provided the targeted stock did not arise in contemplation of the later split-off. If the contemplated situation did in fact exist, then the transaction is recorded at fair value. In a split-off, there is a distribution of shares being exchanged on a proportionate basis for the shares of the new entity. In a split-off, the transaction is in effect the acquisition of treasury stock. Retained earnings are not charged.

In a spin-off, there is a distribution of the segment's shares to the investor's shareholders without the holders surrendering their shares.

In some instances, a split-off or spin-off may be treated as a discontinued operation of a business segment.

In a split-up, there is a transfer of the operations of the original entity to at least two new entities.

CHAPTER 41

FAILURE AND REORGANIZATION

CONTENTS

When a company fails it can be either reorganized or dissolved, depending on the circumstances. A number of ways exist for business failure to occur, including a poor rate of return, technical insolvency, and bankruptcy.

A company may fail if its rate of return is negative or poor. If there are operating losses, the company may not be able to satisfy its debt. A negative rate of return will result in a drop in the market price of its stock. When a company does not earn a return greater than its cost of capital, it may fail. If corrective action is not forthcoming, perhaps the company should liquidate. A poor return, however, does not constitute legal evidence of failure.

Technical insolvency means that the company cannot meet current obligations when due even if total assets exceed total liabilities.

In bankruptcy, liabilities are greater than the fair market value of assets. There exists a negative real net worth.

According to law, failure of a company can be either technical insolvency or bankruptcy. When creditor claims against a business are in question, the law gives creditors recourse against the company.

Under the Sarbanes-Oxley Act, some types of debt are not dischargeable in bankruptcy. These arise from violating federal or local securities law, or from fraud relating to buying or selling securities.

Some causes of business failure include poor management, an economic downturn affecting the company and/or industry, overexpansion, the end of the life cycle of the firm, lawsuit, and catastrophe.

VOLUNTARY SETTLEMENT

A voluntary settlement with creditors allows the company to save many of the costs that would occur in bankruptcy. Such a settlement is reached out of court. The voluntary settlement permits the company to either continue or be liquidated and is initiated to enable the debtor firm to recover some of its investment.

A creditor committee may elect to permit the company to operate if it is anticipated that the firm will recover. Creditors may also keep doing business with the company. In sustaining the company's existence, there may be:

- An extension.
- A composition.
- Creditor control.
- Integration of all of the above.

Extension

In an extension, creditors will receive the balances due but over an extended time period. Current purchases are made with cash. It is also possible that the creditors may agree, not only to extend the maturity date for payment, but also to subordinate their claims to current debt for suppliers providing credit in the extension period. The creditors expect the debtor will be able to work out its problems.

The creditor committee may mandate certain controls, including legal control over the firm's assets or common stock, obtaining a security interest in assets, and approval of all cash payments.

If there are creditors dissenting to the extension agreement, they may be paid immediately to prevent them from having the firm declared bankrupt.

Composition

In a composition, there is a voluntary reduction of the amount the debtor owes the creditor. The creditor obtains from the debtor a specified percent of the obligation in full satisfaction of the debt irrespective of how low the percent is. The agreement permits the debtor to continue to operate. The creditor may attempt to work with the debtor in handling the company's financial difficulties, since a stable customer may result. The benefits of a composition are that court costs are eliminated as well as the stigma of a bankrupt company.

If dissenting stockholders exist, they may be paid in full or they may be allowed to recover a higher percentage so that they do not force the business to close.

For an extension or composition to be practical, there should be an expectation that the debtor will recover, and present business conditions must be conducive to that recovery.

Creditor Control

A committee of creditors may take control of the firm if they are not pleased with current management. They will operate the business so as to satisfy their claims. Once paid, the creditors may recommend new management replace the old before further credit may be given.

Integration

With integration, the company and creditors negotiate a settlement involving a combination of extension, composition, and creditor control. For example, the settlement may provide for a 10% cash payment of the balance owed plus five future payments of 15%, usually in notes. Thus, the total payment is 85%.

The benefits of negotiated settlements are:

- They cost less, particularly in legal fees.
- They are easier to implement than bankruptcy proceedings.
- They are less formal than bankruptcy.

The drawbacks of a negotiated settlement are:

- If the troubled debtor still has control over its business affairs, there may occur further decline in asset values. However, creditor control can provide some protection.
- Unrealistic small creditors may drain the negotiating process.

BANKRUPTCY REORGANIZATION

If no voluntary settlement is agreed upon, the company may be put into bankruptcy by its creditors. The bankruptcy proceeding may either reorganize or liquidate the company.

Bankruptcy occurs when the company cannot pay its bills or when liabilities exceed the fair market value of the assets. Here, legal bankruptcy may be declared. A company may file for reorganization under which it will formulate a plan for continued life.

Chapter 7 of the Bankruptcy Reform Act of 1978 outlines the procedures to be followed for liquidation. Under Chapter 7, the company ceases all operations and goes completely out of business. A trustee is appointed to liquidate (sell) the company's assets and the proceeds are used to pay off the debt, which may include debts to creditors and investors. Chapter 7 is filed for when reorganization is not practical. Chapter 11 involves reorganizing a failed business. Under Chapter 11, the company can continue operations and control the bankruptcy process. The two kinds of reorganization petitions are as follows:

1. *Voluntary.* The company petitions for its own reorganization. The firm does not have to be insolvent to file for voluntary reorganization.

2. *Involuntary.* Creditors file for an involuntary reorganization of the company. An involuntary petition must establish either that the debtor firm is not meeting its debts when due or that a creditor or another party has taken control over the debtor's assets. In general, most of the creditors or claims must support the petition.

The five steps in a reorganization are:

1. A reorganization petition is filed under Chapter 11 in court.

2. A judge approves the petition and either appoints a trustee or allows the creditors to elect one to handle the disposition of the assets.

3. The trustee provides a fair plan of reorganization to the court.

4. The plan is given to the creditors and stockholders of the company for approval.

5. The debtor pays the expenses of the parties performing services in the reorganization proceedings.

The trustee in a reorganization plan is required to:

- Value the company.
- Recapitalize the company.
- Exchange outstanding debts for new securities.

Valuation

In valuing the company, the trustee must estimate its liquidation value versus its value as a going concern. Liquidation is called for when the liquidation value exceeds the continuity value. If the company is more valuable when operating, reorganization is the answer. Future earnings must be predicted when arriving at the value of the reorganized company. The going concern value represents the present value of future earnings.

> **EXAMPLE 1:** A petition for reorganization of a company was filed under Chapter 11. The trustee computed the firm's liquidation value after deducting expenses as $4.5 million. The trustee estimates that the reorganized business will generate $530,000 in annual earnings. The cost of capital is 10%. Assuming the earnings continue indefinitely, the value of the business as a going concern is:
>
> $$\$530,000/.10 = \$5,300,000$$
>
> Since the company's value as a going concern ($5.3 million) exceeds its liquidation value ($4.5 million), reorganization is called for.

Recapitalization

If the trustee recommends reorganization, a plan must be formulated. The obligations may be extended or equity securities may be issued in place of the debt. Income bonds may be given for the debentures. As noted in a prior chapter, with an income bond, interest is paid only when there are earnings. This process of exchanging liabilities for other types of liabilities or equity securities is referred to as recapitalization. In recapitalizing the company, the objective is to have a mixture of debt and equity that will allow the company to meet its debts and furnish a reasonable profit for the owners.

> **EXAMPLE 2:** The current capital structure of Y Corporation is presented below:

Debentures	$1,500,000
Collateral bonds	3,000,000
Preferred stock	800,000
Common stock	2,500,000
Total	$7,800,000

There exists high financial leverage:

$$\frac{\text{Debt}}{\text{Equity}} = \frac{\$4,500,000}{\$3,300,000} = 1.36$$

Assuming the company is deemed to be worth $5 million as a going concern, the trustee can develop a less leveraged capital structure having a total capital of $5 million as follows:

Debentures	$1,000,000
Collateral bonds	1,000,000
Income bonds	1,500,000
Preferred stock	500,000
Common stock	1,000,000
Total	$5,000,000

The income bond of $1.5 million is similar to equity in appraising financial leverage, since interest is not paid unless there is income. The new debt equity ratio is safer:

$$\frac{\text{Debt} + \text{Collateral bonds}}{\text{Income bonds} + \text{Preferred stock} + \text{Common stock}} = \frac{\$2,000,000}{\$3,000,000} = 0.67$$

Exchange of Obligations

In exchanging obligations to arrive at the optimal capital structure, priorities must be followed. Senior claims are paid before junior ones. Senior debt holders receive a claim on new capital equal to their prior claims. The last priority goes to common stockholders in receiving new securities. A debt holder typically receives a combination of different securities. Preferred and common stockholders may receive nothing. Typically, however, they retain some small ownership. After the exchange, the debt holders may become the company's new owners.

LIQUIDATION OWING TO BANKRUPTCY

When a company becomes bankrupt, it may be liquidated under Chapter 7 of the Bankruptcy Reform Act of 1978. The major elements of liquidation are legal considerations, claim priority, and dissolution.

Legal Considerations

When a firm is declared bankrupt, creditors have to meet between 10 and 30 days after that declaration. A judge or referee takes charge of the meeting in which the creditors provide their claims. A trustee is appointed by the creditors. The trustee handles the property of the defaulted firm, liquidates the business, maintains records, appraises the creditors' claims, makes payments, and provides relevant information of the liquidation process.

Claim Priority

Some claims against the company take precedence over others in bankruptcy. The following is the order in which claims are to be met:

1. *Secured claims.* Secured creditors receive the value of the secured assets in support of their claims. If the value of the secured assets is inadequate to meet their claims in full, the balance reverts to general creditor status.

2. *Bankruptcy administrative costs.* These costs include any expenses of handling bankruptcy such as legal and trustee expenses.

3. *Unsecured salaries and commissions.* These claims are limited to a maximum specified amount per individual and must have been incurred within 90 days of the bankruptcy petition.

4. *Unsecured customer deposit claims.* These claims are limited to a nominal amount each.

5. *Taxes.* Tax claims apply to unpaid taxes due the government.

6. *General creditor claims.* General creditors loaned the company money without specific collateral. Included are debentures and accounts payable.

7. *Preferred stockholders.*

8. *Common stockholders.*

Dissolution

After claims have been met in priority order and an accounting made of the proceedings, an application to discharge the bankrupt business may then be instituted. A discharge occurs when the court releases the company from legitimate debts in bankruptcy, with the exception of debts that are immune to discharge. As long as a debtor has not been discharged within the previous six years and was not bankrupt due to fraud, the debtor may then start a new business.

   EXAMPLE 3: The balance sheet of Ace Corporation for the year ended December 31, 2X11, follows:

Balance Sheet

Current assets	$400,000	Current liabilities	$475,000
Fixed assets	410,000	Long-term liabilities	250,000
		Common stock	175,000
		Retained earnings	(90,000)
		Total liabilities and stockholders' equity	
Total assets	$810,000		$810,000

The company's liquidation value is $625,000. Rather than liquidate, there could be a reorganization with an investment of an additional $320,000. The reorganization is expected to generate earnings of $115,000 per year. A multiplier of 7.5 is appropriate. If the $320,000 is obtained, long-term debt holders will receive 40% of the common stock in the reorganized business in substitution for their current claims.

If $320,000 of further investment is made, the firm's going-concern value is $862,500 (7.5 × $115,000). The liquidation value is given at $625,000. Because the reorganization value exceeds the liquidation value, reorganization is required.

EXAMPLE 4: Fixed assets with a book value of $1.5 million were sold for $1.3 million. There are mortgage bonds on the fixed assets amounting to $1.8 million. The proceeds from the collateral sale are inadequate to meet the secured claim. Therefore, the unsatisfied portion of $500,000 ($1,800,000 – $1,300,000) of the claim becomes a general creditor claim.

EXAMPLE 5: Land having a book value of $1.2 million was sold for $800,000. Mortgage bonds on the land are $600,000. The excess of $200,000 will be returned to the trustee to pay other creditors.

EXAMPLE 6: Charles Company is bankrupt. The book and liquidation values follow:

	Book Value	Liquidation Value
Cash	$ 600,000	$ 600,000
Accounts receivable	1,900,000	1,500,000
Inventory	3,700,000	2,100,000
Land	5,000,000	3,200,000
Building	7,800,000	5,300,000
Equipment	6,700,000	2,800,000
Total assets	$25,700,000	$15,500,000

The liabilities and stockholders' equity at the date of liquidation are:

Current liabilities

Accounts payable	$ 1,800,000	
Notes payable	900,000	
Accrued taxes	650,000	
Accrued salaries	450,000[a]	
Total current liabilities		$ 3,800,000

Long-term liabilities

Mortgage on land	$ 3,200,000	
First mortgage—building	2,800,000	
Second mortgage—building	2,500,000	
Subordinated debentures	4,800,000	
Total long-term liabilities		13,300,000
Total liabilities		$17,100,000

Stockholders' equity

Preferred stock	$ 4,700,000	
Common stock	6,800,000	
Retained earnings	(2,900,000)	
Total stockholders' equity		8,600,000
Total liabilities and stockholders' equity		$25,700,000

---

[a] The salary owed each worker is below the specified amount and was incurred within 90 days of the bankruptcy petition.

Expenses of the liquidation including legal costs were 15% of the proceeds. The debentures are subordinated only with regard to the two first-mortgage bonds.

The distribution of the proceeds follows:

Proceeds	$15,500,000	
Mortgage on land	$3,200,000	
First mortgage—building	2,800,000	
Second mortgage—building	2,500,000	
Liquidation expenses (15% × $15,500,000)	2,325,000	
Accrued salaries	450,000	
Accrued taxes	650,000	
Total		11,925,000
Balance		$ 3,575,000

The percent to be paid to general creditors is:

$$\frac{\text{Proceeds balance}}{\text{Total owed}} = \frac{\$3,575,000}{\$7,500,000} = 47.66667\%$$

The balance due general creditors follows:

General Creditors	Owed	Paid
Accounts payable	$1,800,000	$ 858,000
Notes payable	900,000	429,000
Subordinated debentures	4,800,000	2,288,000
Total	$7,500,000	$3,575,000

EXAMPLE 7: The balance sheet of the Oakhurst Company is presented below:

Assets

Current assets		
Cash	$9,000	
Marketable securities	6,000	
Receivables	1,100,000	
Inventory	3,000,000	
Prepaid expenses	4,000	
Total current assets	$4,119,000	
Noncurrent assets		
Land	$1,800,000	
Fixed assets	2,000,000	
Total noncurrent assets		3,800,000
Total assets		$7,919,000

Liabilities and Stockholders' Equity

Current liabilities		
Accounts payable	$180,000	
Bank loan payable	900,000	
Accrued salaries	300,000[a]	
Employee benefits payable	70,000[b]	
Customer claims—unsecured	80,000[c]	
Taxes payable	350,000	
Total current liabilities		$1,880,000

Liabilities and Stockholders' Equity

Noncurrent liabilities		
First mortgage payable	$1,800,000	
Second mortgage payable	1,100,000	
Subordinated debentures	700,000	
Total noncurrent liabilities		3,400,000
Total liabilities		$5,280,000
Stockholders' equity		
Preferred stock (3,500 shares)	$350,000	
Common stock (8,000 shares)	480,000	
Paid-in capital	1,600,000	
Retained earnings	209,000	
Total stockholders' equity		2,639,000
Total liabilities and stockholders' equity		$7,919,000

[a] The salary owed to each worker is below the specified amount and was incurred within 90 days of the bankruptcy petition.

[b] Employee benefits payable have the same limitations as unsecured wages and satisfy for eligibility in bankruptcy distribution.

[c] No customer claim is greater than the nominal amount.

Additional data are as follows:

1. The mortgages apply to the company's total noncurrent assets.
2. The subordinated debentures are subordinated to the bank loan payable. Therefore, they come after the bank loan payable in liquidation.
3. The trustee has sold the company's current assets for $2.1 million and the noncurrent assets for $1.9 million. Therefore, a total of $4 million was received.
4. The business is bankrupt, since the total liabilities of $5.28 million are greater than the $4 million of the fair value of the assets.

Assume that the administration expense for handling the bankrupt company is $900,000. This liability is not reflected in the foregoing balance sheet.

The allocation of the $4 million to the creditors follows:

Proceeds		$4,000,000
Available to secured creditors		
First mortgage—payable from $1,900,000 proceeds of noncurrent assets	$1,600,000	
Second mortgage—payable from balance of proceeds of noncurrent assets	300,000	1,900,000
Balance after secured creditors		$2,100,000

Next priority

Administrative expenses	$ 900,000	
Accrued salaries	300,000	
Employee benefits payable	70,000	
Customer claims—unsecured	80,000	
Taxes payable	350,000	1,700,000
Proceeds available to general creditors		$ 400,000

Now that the claims on the proceeds from liquidation have been met, general creditors receive the balance on a pro rata basis. The distribution of the $400,000 follows:

General Creditor	Amount	Pro Rata Allocation for Balance to Be Paid
Second-mortgage balance ($1,100,000 – $300,000)	$ 800,000	$124,031
Accounts payable	180,000	27,907
Bank loan payable	900,000	248,062[a]
Subordinated debentures	700,000	0
Total	$2,580,000	$400,000

[a] Because the debentures are subordinated, the bank loan payable must be satisfied in full before any amount can go to the subordinated debentures. The subordinated debenture holders therefore receive nothing.

EXAMPLE 8: Nolan Company is having severe financial problems. Jefferson Bank holds a first mortgage on the plant and has an $800,000 unsecured loan that is already delinquent. The Alto Insurance Company holds $4.7 million of the company's subordinated debentures to the notes payable. Nolan is deciding whether to reorganize the business or declare bankruptcy.

Another company is considering acquiring Nolan Company by offering to take over the mortgage of $7.5 million, pay the past due taxes, and pay $4.38 million for the firm.

Nolan's balance sheet follows:

Assets

Current assets	$ 2,800,000
Plant assets	11,700,000
Other assets	3,000,000
Total assets	$17,500,000

Liabilities and Stockholders' Equity

Current liabilities		
Accounts payable	$ 1,800,000	
Taxes payable	170,000	
Bank note payable	260,000	
Other current liabilities	1,400,000	
Total current liabilities		$ 3,630,000
Noncurrent liabilities		
Mortgage payable	$ 7,500,000	
Subordinated debentures	5,300,000	
Total noncurrent liabilities		12,800,000
Total liabilities		$16,430,000
Stockholders' equity		
Common stock	$ 1,000,000	
Premium on common stock	2,300,000	
Retained earnings	(2,230,000)	
Total stockholders' equity		1,070,000
Total liabilities and stockholders' equity		$17,500,000

The impact of the proposed reorganization on creditor claims is indicated below:

Outstanding obligations		$16,430,000
Claims met through the reorganization		
Mortgage payable	$7,500,000	
Taxes payable	170,000	
Total		7,670,000
Balance of claims		$ 8,760,000

The cash arising from reorganization is given as $4.38 million, which is 50% ($4,380,000/$8,760,000) of the unsatisfied claims. The distribution to general creditors follows:

General Creditor	Liability Due	50%	Adjusted for Subordination
Bank note payable	$ 260,000	$ 130,000	$ 260,000[a]
Subordinated debenture	5,300,000	2,650,000	2,520,000

General Creditor	Liability Due	50%	Adjusted for Subordination
Other creditors (accounts payable + other current liabilities)	3,200,000	1,600,000	1,600,000
Total	$8,760,000	$4,380,000	$4,380,000

[a] The bank note payable is paid in full before the subordinated debenture.

BANKRUPTCY ABUSE PREVENTION AND CONSUMER PROTECTION ACT OF 2005

The Bankruptcy Abuse Prevention and Consumer Protection Act of 2005 makes changes to both business and consumer bankruptcy law.

Per Section 546(c), there is a new federal right of reclamation enabling creditors to demand recovery of merchandise delivered within 45 days before the bankruptcy filing. Under this law, the debtor must return the reclaimed goods to the creditor rather than substituting an administrative claim on the debtor's assets.

Bankruptcy notices must be sent to the creditor at the address contained on the pre-bankruptcy notice.

Section 365 mandates that a debtor-in-possession be assigned to decide whether to assume or reject an unexpired lease of non-residential real property within 60 days after the initiation of the bankruptcy, unless such period is extended for cause. A debtor-in-possession has 120 days to make a decision regarding the acceptance or rejection of a lease. A court's power to grant an extension for cause is limited to 90 days.

Lessors of nonresidential real property can gain substantial leverage by not granting their approval for time extensions. However, if a debtor in error assumes a lease and later rejects it, the lessor's damages are limited to a claim for no more than two years rent after rejection.

The Act stipulates that if the trustee avoids a transfer made between 90 days and one year before the petition date to a noninsider creditor, the transfer can only be avoided as to the insider creditor.

The Act is very advantageous to vendors that sell merchandise on open credit. Goods may be reclaimed up to 45 days after receipt by the debtor. The Act allows vendors to submit a claim for the value of any goods sold to and received by a debtor within 20 days prior to the start of the debtor's bankruptcy case.

CHAPTER 42

BUSINESS STRATEGIES AND SHAREHOLDER VALUE ANALYSIS

CONTENTS

Critics of large corporations allege that corporate financial managers have too much power and that they act in ways that benefit themselves at the expense of shareholders. Many managers view corporate growth, survival, or personal ambition as taking precedence over shareholder interests. These misguided policies may be one of the reasons for the periodic surge in takeover activity. Corporate raiders are constantly searching for poorly managed companies, where aggressive changes in strategic direction and/or the redeployment of underutilized assets can dramatically improve the value of a stock.

There is, however, a growing number of business leaders who are realizing that the interests of the shareholder are of primary concern to the corporation, and are beginning to employ strategies designed to create shareholder value. They believe that value is not created by the manipulation of accounting statements, but by managing the real economic value of the firm. These financial executives feel that a stock's value is tied to the perceived present value of the firm's future cash flows and that value is added when they are able to invest at rates that exceed the firm's cost of capital.

To achieve rates of return above the cost of capital, management must select and implement strategies that will position the firm in such a manner as to give it the greatest sustainable competitive advantage. The value of a strategy can be determined by discounting the anticipated cash flows generated by the strategy by the firm's cost of capital. The technique known as Shareholder Value Analysis (SVA) is an offshoot of the Discounted Cash Flow (DCF) method used in capital budgeting. With a few modifications DCF can be adopted to evaluate strategies as well. SVA enables a firm to measure how alternative strategies will affect the firm's value. SVA also enables a firm to identify the specific operating factors that drive the value of a business. This chapter will explore SVA by first examining the shortcomings of traditional accounting measures, then introduce SVA through the use of a simplified example, then go on to address some of the limitations of SVA, and finally discuss its benefits to management.

SHORTCOMINGS OF ACCOUNTING MEASURES

Eventually, most strategic and long-term plans are translated into pro forma financial statements. Many financial managers use these statements to measure the financial implications of their strategies. Unfortunately, accrual-based accounting measures do not provide an accurate picture of the current or future economic performance of an organization. For example, earnings per share can grow as a company invests above its cost of capital. This happens because accrual-based accounting uses alternative methods to attempt to match costs with revenues. Arbitrary methods such as FIFO versus LIFO and straight line versus accelerated depreciation do not affect pretax cash flows, vary between companies, and change over time. These methods are arbitrary because there is no sound basis for choosing one method over another. Conventional earnings determination by the matching process does not, nor do accountants purport it to, measure changes in the value of a firm.

In addition to differing methods, accrual-based accounting does not assess changes in risk, dividend policies, time value of money and additional investment in working capital and fixed capital investment necessary to ensure growth. Further discussion of these factors follows.

Risk is of primary concern when establishing the economic value of any asset. The level of risk is determined by the nature of a firm's operations (business risk) and by the capital structure of the firm (financial risk). The higher the risk the greater the return an investor will expect.

Dividends are not included in earnings calculations. If a firm's objective was to increase earnings, then it could be argued that dividends should not be paid. However, the return to shareholders is a function of stock appreciation and dividends paid, therefore, dividends are a very important factor in calculating economic value.

Earnings measures also fail to take into consideration the time value of money. The economic value of an investment is determined by discounting anticipated cash flows. The discount rate used to determine the economic value of an investment not only determines the time value of money but inflation expectations as well.

Finally, accounting earnings fail to consider the additional investment in working capital and fixed capital investment needed for growth. As a business grows, its working capital increases because inventory swells to meet anticipated demand and receivables increase as sales outpace cash collections. Fixed investment also rises as firms increase capacity and invest in the latest technologies.

SHAREHOLDER VALUE APPROACH

The shareholder value approach estimates the economic value of an investment by discounting forecasted cash flows by the cost of capital. These cash flows, in turn, serve as the foundation for shareholder returns from dividends and share-price appreciation. Basic valuation parameters or value drivers are used in the shareholder value calculation. These drivers are forecast duration, sales growth rate, operating profit margin, cash income tax rate, incremental working capital investment, incremental fixed capital investment, and cost of capital.

Estimating Shareholder Value

The total value of a company is the sum of the values of its debt and its equity. The equity portion is called "shareholder value." The debt portion of corporate value includes the market value of debt, unfunded pension liabilities and other claims such as preferred stock. Therefore:

Shareholder Value = Corporate Value – Debt

Before shareholder value can be determined, corporate value must be calculated. Corporate value consists of the present value of forecasted cash flows from operations plus residual value plus short-term investments. Residual value represents the present value of cash flows beyond the forecast period.

Corporate Value	=	Present value of forecasted cash flows from operations
	+	Present value of the residual value
	+	Short-term investments

To show how Shareholder Value Analysis can be applied, a simple example will be used to explain the components of the calculation.

The management of Amercom, Inc., a manufacturing firm, has finished its long-term plan for the next five years. This plan was translated into the financial statements presented in Exhibit 42-1. Management feels that their strategy will increase earnings per share nearly 14% a year. The plan's impact on shareholder value will be assessed.

Cash Flows from Operations

The present value of forecasted cash flows from operations consist of cash operating inflows and outflows discounted back at the company's cost of capital. Each year the cash flow is calculated as follows:

Cash flow   =   [(Sales in prior year) (1 + Sales growth rate)
               (Operating profit margin) (1 – Cash income tax rate)]
          –   (Incremental fixed capital investment
          +   Incremental working capital investment)

The sales growth rate is simply the year-to-year increase in sales as a percent of the prior period's sales. In our example the sales growth rate is 10% a year.

Exhibit 42-1: Amercom, Inc.—Long-Term Business Plan

	Forecast ($) Thousands					
	2X14	2X15	2X16	2X17	2X18	2X19
Income Statement						
Sales	100,000	110,000	121,000	133,100	146,410	161,051
Cost of sales	75,000	82,500	90,750	99,825	109,807	120,788
Gross profit	25,000	27,500	30,250	33,275	36,602	40,263
SG&A expenses	18,000	19,800	21,780	23,958	26,354	28,989
Other income/(expense)	2,000	2,200	2,420	2,662	2,928	3,221
Interest expense	2,302	2,280	2,457	2,657	2,874	3,111
Income before taxes	6,698	7,620	8,433	9,322	10,303	11,384
Income taxes	2,679	3,048	3,373	3,729	4,121	4,553
Net income	4,019	4,572	5,060	5,593	6,182	6,830
Balance Sheet—Assets						
Short-term investments	7,000	7,000	7,000	7,000	7,000	7,000
Accounts receivable	20,000	22,000	24,200	26,620	29,282	32,210
Inventories	15,000	16,500	18,150	19,965	21,961	24,158
Total current assets	42,000	45,500	49,350	53,585	58,243	63,368
Property, plant & equip. (PP&E)	52,000	57,200	62,920	69,212	76,133	83,746
Accumulated depreciation	27,000	29,700	32,670	35,937	39,531	43,484
Net PP&E	25,000	27,500	30,250	33,275	36,602	40,263
Total assets	67,000	73,000	79,600	86,860	94,846	103,631
Balance Sheet—Liabilities & Equity						
Accounts payable	5,000	5,500	6,050	6,655	7,320	8,053
Short-term debt	0	2,476	5,139	7,951	10,925	14,075

Exhibit 42-1: Amercom, Inc.—Long-Term Business Plan

			Forecast ($) Thousands			
	2X14	2X15	2X16	2X17	2X18	2X19
Accrued liabilities	7,000	7,700	8,470	9,317	10,249	11,274
Total current liabilities	12,000	15,676	19,659	23,923	28,494	33,401
Deferred income taxes	7,943	8,705	9,548	10,480	11,510	12,649
Long-term debt	19,000	18,000	17,000	16,000	15,000	14,000
Total liabilities	38,943	42,380	46,207	50,403	55,004	60,049
Capital stock	9,000	9,000	9,000	9,000	9,000	9,000
Retained earnings	19,057	21,619	24,393	27,457	30,842	34,581
Total equity	28,057	30,619	33,393	36,457	39,842	43,581
Total liabilities & equity	67,000	73,000	79,600	86,860	94,846	103,631
Sales growth rate		10.0%	10.0%	10.0%	10.0%	10
Operating profit margin		9.0%	9.0%	9.0%	9.0%	9.0
Cash income tax rate		30.0%	30.0%	30.0%	30.0%	30.0
Incremental fixed capital investment		25.0%	25.0%	25.0%	25.0%	25.0
Incremental working capital investment		23.0%	23.0%	23.0%	23.0%	23.0
Debt to equity	67.7%	66.9%	66.3%	65.7%	65.1%	64.4
Current ratio	3.5	2.9	2.5	2.2	2.0	1.9

The operating profit margin is the ratio of preinterest, pre-tax operating income to sales. It is calculated:

Operating profit margin = (Sales – Cost of goods sold – SG&A expense
+ Other operating income) + Sales

Amercom's operating profit margin equals 9% of sales each forecasted year.

The cash income tax rate represents taxes on operating profit for a fiscal year that arc either paid during the year or are a liability (income taxes payable) at the end of the year. Cash income taxes are often less than the book income tax expense. This occurs because of deferred taxes which arise from temporary differences in the recognition of some revenue and expense items for book and tax purposes. Amercom's cash income tax rate was determined by subtracting the change in deferred taxes from the provision for income taxes and then dividing the difference by the pretax income resulting in a rate of 30%.

Incremental fixed capital investment is defined as capital expenditures in excess of depreciation expense, where the depreciation is assumed to approximate the cost of replacing equipment to maintain existing plant without adding capacity. Depreciation was not added back when calculating the operating profit margin. Depreciation, a noncash expense, is eliminated from the analysis by taking the capital expenditures over total depreciation. Therefore, the incremental fixed capital investment represents the portion of total expenditures for the capacity expansion necessary to support increased sales. That is:

Incremental fixed capital investment ratio = (Capital expenditures
– Depreciation expense)
+ Change in sales

Incremental working capital investment required for operations is defined as the increase in total current assets (excluding short-term investments) minus the increase in total current liabilities (excluding debt). It, too, is expressed as a percentage of sales and is calculated as follows:

Incremental working capital = (Increase in current assets – Increase in
investment ratio   short-term investments – Increase in
current liabilities + Increase in current
portion of long-term debt + Increase in
notes payable) + Change in Sales

Amercom's incremental fixed capital and working capital investment ratios are 25% and 23%, respectively.

Cost of Capital

To calculate the present value of the forecasted cash flows from operations, one needs the firm's cost of capital. The cost of capital is the weighted-average cost of debt and equity. The cost of debt is measured as the long-term rate or yield to maturity, which reflects the rate currently demanded by debtholders. It is important that the cost of new debt rather than existing debt be incorporated because the economic desirability of a perspective investment depends upon future costs and not past or sunk costs.

The cost of equity is the minimum expected return that will induce investors to buy a company's shares. The cost of equity is calculated as follows:

Cost of equity = Risk-free rate + [Beta (Expected return on market
                 - Risk-free rate)]

The assumption is made that investors will demand the risk-free rate as reflected in the current yields available on U.S. Treasury securities, plus an additional equity risk premium for investing in the company's more risky shares. The equity risk premium, in turn, is a function of the expected variability of the future yields of the stock.

In pricing common stocks the equity risk premium would depend on the market risk premium, adjusted by the stock's beta coefficient. The market risk premium can be estimated by taking the expected rate of return on a market index such as the S&P 500 and then subtracting the risk-free rate. A number of investment banking firms publish their estimates of the expected rate of return on the stock market using discounted cash flow models.

The beta coefficient reflects the volatility of a stock's price, relative to that of the market as a whole. If its beta is greater than 1, a stock is more volatile and therefore riskier than the market. A beta less than 1 is below average in risk, while a beta of zero would imply a risk-free security. The beta coefficient of a stock is calculated by performing a linear regression analysis between past returns for the stock and past returns on a market index such as the S&P 500. Services like *Value Line* regularly publish betas for publicly traded stocks.

When estimating the cost of capital it is important that the relative weights attached to debt and equity are based upon the firm's long-term targeted capital structure and not that of past levels of debt and equity. Amercom's management wants to maintain a debt-to-equity ratio of approximately 65%; therefore their cost of capital is estimated to be 20%.

Residual Value

The residual value is the amount of total corporate value that is attributable to the period after the forecast period. In most cases the residual value is the largest portion of the value of the firm. Its size is directly dependent upon the assumptions made for the forecast period. Unfortunately there are no unique formulas for calculating residual value. There are, however, several methods for estimating residual value that can be applied in different circumstances. For example, a liquidation value might be used if the strategy is to "harvest" the business. Most strategies assume a going concern and therefore require an appropriate estimating method. One such method is known as the perpetuity method. The expected earnings from a business arc assumed to behave like a perpetual annuity, so they can be capitalized. The assumption is made that any business able to generate returns greater than the minimum return required by its owners will eventually attract competitors whose entry into the industry will drive the returns of the company down to the owners' minimum rate of return.

Once the rate of return has been driven down to the minimum acceptable, period-by-period differences in future cash flows do not alter the value of the business. Therefore these future cash flows can be treated as if they were a "perpetuity" or an infinite stream of identical cash flows.

The present value of any perpetuity is simply the value of the expected annual cash flows divided by the rate of return. Using the perpetuity method, the present value of the residual value is therefore calculated by dividing the after-tax perpetuity operating profit by the cost of capital. That is:

Residual value = Perpetuity cash flow + Cost of capital

The perpetuity calculation is based on operating profit rather than cash flow because there is no need to take into account the additional investment in fixed and working capital during the postforecast period. Although investments in expansion projects in the postforecast period may help increase the future cash inflows, as long as the investment is earning only the cost of capital rate of return, any increase in cash inflows will be offset by the investment cash outflows required to expand capacity.

The perpetuity method for estimating residual value is not based on the assumption that all future cash flows will actually be identical. It simply reflects the fact that the cash flows resulting from future investments will not affect the value of the firm because the overall rate of return earned on those investments is equal to the cost of capital.

Shareholder Value Creation

From the financial statements prepared for the management of Amercom, Inc. the ratios explained in the foregoing were calculated and presented in Exhibit 42-2.

Exhibit 42-3 takes the ratios and calculates the shareholder value created by the strategy. For the sake of argument, it is assumed that the market value of Amercom's debt is equal to its current balance of $19 million. Short-term investments equal $7 million. Total economic value resulting from the strategy (shareholder value) is estimated to be $15.9 million. The value lost by the five-year strategy is $3.6 million. Clearly, the strategy proposed by management, while increasing earnings per share, will decrease shareholder value.

The year-by-year decrease in value is calculated by the annual change in the cumulative present value of the cash flows plus the present value of the residual value. For example, the decrease in year 3 of $0.714 million is equal to $29.157 million less $29.871 million. In other words, the value created or lost is the difference between shareholder value and prestrategy value.

Prestrategy value represents the value of the business today assuming no additional value created. In other words, it does not anticipate any value creation potential associated with the firm's prospective investments. Prestrategy value is calculated by applying the appropriate residual value method to the most recent period of historical data. Returning to the example, sales for the most recent year were $100 million. With an operating profit margin of 9% and a cash income tax rate of 30%, cash flow before new investment amounts to $6.3 million. Assuming the perpetuity method for estimating residual value, the prestrategy shareholder value is calculated as follows:

Exhibit 42-2: Shareholder Value Assumptions

$ Millions	
Number of periods in forecast	5
Sales (last historical period)	$100
Sales growth rate	10%
Operating profit margin	9%
Cash income tax rate	30%
Incremental fixed capital investment	25%
Incremental working capital investment	23%
Cost of capital	20%
Short-term investments	$7
Market value of debt & other obligations	$19

Exhibit 42-3: Shareholder Value Calculation

Cost of Capital = 20.0%
$ Millions

Year	Sales	Operating Profit Cash Flow	Incremental Fixed Capital Investment	Incremental Working Capital Investment	Total Cash Flow	Present Value of Cash Flow	Cumulative PV of Cash Flow	Future Value of Residual Value	Present Value of Residual Value	Cumulative PV CF + PV RV	Increase Value
0	100	6.300						31.500	31.500	31.500	
1	110	6.930	2.500	2.300	2.130	1.775	1.775	34.65	28.875	30.650	0.850
2	121	7.623	2.75	2.53	2.343	1.627	3.402	38.115	26.469	29.871	-0.779
3	133	8.385	3.025	2.783	2.577	1.491	4.894	41.926	24.263	29.157	-0.714
4	146	9.224	3.328	3.061	2.835	1.367	6.261	46.119	22.241	28.502	-0.655
5	161	10.146	3.66	3.367	3.119	1.253	7.514	50.731	20.388	27.902	-0.600
											-3.598

Present Value of Cash Flows   7.514
Present Value of Residual Value   20.388
Short-Term Investments   7.000
CORPORATE VALUE   34.902
Less: Market Value of Debt & Other   19.000
SHAREHOLDER VALUE   15.902

$$
\begin{aligned}
\text{Prestrategy value} \;=\; & \text{(After tax operating profit cash flow +} \\
& \text{cost of} \\
& \text{Capital) + Short term investments – Debt} \\
=\; & (6.3 + 20\%) + 7 - 19 \\
=\; & 31.5 + 7 - 19 \\
=\; & 19.5
\end{aligned}
$$

The value lost by the strategy of $3.598 million is the difference between the $15.9 million shareholder value and the $19.5 million prestrategy value.

Impact of Value Drivers

The management of Amercom, Inc. can also measure the impact on shareholder value from changes in the value drivers (e.g., sales growth rate, operating profit margin, cost of capital). Exhibit 42-4 shows the impact on shareholder value of a 1-percentage-point increase in each of the value drivers. If you compare the sales growth rate and operating profit margin, you can see that a 1-percentage-point increase in sales growth (10% to 11%) will decrease Amercom's value by about $400,000, whereas a percentage-point improvement in the operating profit margin will increase value $5.0 million. In other words, for this business, value is affected by improvements in margins, not sales growth. Therefore management's preoccupation with sales growth will reduce the firm's overall value.

Limitations

Shareholder Value Analysis (SVA) has a long list of limitations. At the top of the list is complexity and difficulty of use. SVA often frustrates business managers because accounting systems fail to provide the balance sheet and cost information the analysis requires. Another limitation is that managers seldom agree on the value drivers that influence the results, like the cost of capital and the duration of the forecast period. Still another limitation lies in the measure of residual value. This projection is the furthest in the future and therefore the least certain.

Many critics of SVA complain that using the method can lead to a preoccupation with calculating values and relative impacts at the expense of creative strategic thinking. Finally, how well SVA will estimate the value of a strategy designed to open markets whose possibilities are not known yet is questionable.

Exhibit 42-4: Relative Impact of Value Drivers

$ Millions		
A 1-Percentage-Point Increase in:	$	%
Sales growth rate	-0.4	2.7%
Operating profit margin	5.0	31.3%
Cash income tax rate	-0.6	-4.0%
Incremental fixed capital investment	-0.4	-2.2%
Incremental working capital investment	-0.4	-2.2%
Cost of capital	-1.9	-12.2%

BENEFITS OF SHAREHOLDER VALUE ANALYSIS

Shareholder value analysis has several important benefits for financial management. First, it provides a consistent basis for systematically evaluating and measuring internal and external capital allocation decisions and management performance. Second, it overcomes shortcomings of accounting measures that never were designed to evaluate future investment opportunities. Third, it reduces the corporate gamesmanship in submitting divisional plans and budgets. Fourth, it can provide a standard for investor communications that reflects how the market actually behaves.

CHAPTER 43

FINANCIAL AND EARNINGS FORECASTING

CONTENTS

Exhibits

Financial forecasting, an essential element of planning, is the basis for *budgeting* activities. It is also needed when estimating future financing requirements. The company may look either internally or externally for financing. Internal financing refers to cash flow generated by the company's normal operating activities. External financing refers to capital provided by parties external to the company. You need to analyze how to estimate *external* financing requirements. Basically, forecasts of future sales and related expenses provide the firm with the information to project future external financing needs.

The chapter discusses (1) the *percent-of-sales method* to determine the amount of external financing needed, (2) the CPA's involvement in prospective financial statements, and (3) earnings forecast. Earnings forecasts provide useful information concerning the expectations of a firm's future total market return. This is of interest to security analysts and investors.

THE PERCENT-OF-SALES METHOD FOR FINANCIAL FORECASTING

Percentage of sales is the most widely used method for projecting the company's financing needs. This method involves estimating the various expenses, assets, and liabilities for a future period as a percent of the sales forecast and then using these percentages, together with the projected sales, to construct pro forma balance sheets.

Basically, forecasts of future sales and their related expenses provide the firm with the information needed to project its future needs for financing. The basic steps in projecting financing needs are:

1. Project the firm's sales. The sales forecast is the initial most important step. Most other forecasts (budgets) follow the sales forecast.

2. Project additional variables such as expenses.

3. Estimate the level of investment in current and fixed assets required to support the projected sales.

4. Calculate the firm's financing needs.

The following example illustrates how to develop a pro forma balance sheet and determine the amount of external financing needed.

   EXAMPLE 1: Assume that sales for 2X14 = $20, projected sales for 2X15 = $24, net income = 5% of sales, and the dividend payout ratio = 40%. Exhibit 43-1 illustrates the step-by-step method. All dollar amounts are in millions.

Exhibit 43-1: Pro Forma Balance Sheet (in millions of dollars)

	Present (2X14)	% of Sales (2X14 Sales = $20)	Projected (2X15 Sales = $24)
ASSETS			
Current assets	2	10	2.4
Fixed assets	4	20	4.8
Total assets	6		7.2
LIABILITIES AND STOCKHOLDERS' EQUITY			
Current liabilities	2	10	2.4
Long-term debt	2.5	n.a.	2.5
Total liabilities	4.5		4.9
Common stock	0.1	n.a.	0.1

	Present (2X14)	% of Sales (2X14 Sales = $20)	Projected (2X15 Sales = $24)	
Paid-in-Capital	0.2	n.a.	0.2	
Retained earnings	1.2		1.92[a]	
Total equity	1.5		2.22	
Total liabilities and stockholders' equity	6		7.12	Total financing needed
			0.08[b]	External financing needed
			7.2	Total

[a] 2X15 retained earnings = 2X14 retained earnings + projected net income – cash dividends paid

= $1.2 + 5%($24) – 40%[5%($24)]

= $1.2 + $1.2 – 0$0.48

= $2.4 – $0.48

= $1.92

[b] External financing needed

= projected total assets – (projected total liabilities + projected equity)

= $7.2 – ($4.9 + $2.22)

= $7.2 – $7.12

= $0.08

The steps for the computations are outlined as follows:

Step 1. Express those balance sheet items that vary directly with sales as a percentage of sales. Any item such as long-term debt that does not vary directly with sales is designated "n.a.," or "not applicable."

Step 2. Multiply these percentages by the 2X15 projected sales = $24 to obtain the projected amounts as shown in the last column.

Step 3. Simply insert figures for long-term debt, common stock and paid-in-capital from the 2X14 balance sheet.

Step 4. Compute 2X15 retained earnings as shown in (b).

Step 5. Sum the asset accounts, obtaining total projected assets of $7.2, and also add the projected liabilities and equity to obtain $7.12, the total financing provided. Since liabilities and equity must total $7.2, but only $7.12 is projected, we have a shortfall of $0.08 "external financing needed."

Although the forecast of additional funds required can be made by setting up pro forma balance sheets as described above, it is often easier to use the following formula:

External funds needed (EFN)	=	Required increase in assets	–	Spontaneous increase in liabilities	–	Increase in retained earnings
EFN	=	$(A/S) \, \Delta S$	–	$(L/S) \, \Delta S$	–	$(PM)(PS)(1-d)$

Where

A/S = Assets that increase spontaneously with sales as a percentage of sales.

L/S = Liabilities that increase spontaneously with sales as a percentage of sales.

ΔS = Change in sales.

PM = Profit margin on sales.

PS = Projected sales.

d = Dividend payout ratio.

EXAMPLE 2: In Example 1:

A/S = $6/$20 = 30%
L/S = $2/$20 = 10%
ΔS = ($24 – $20) = $4
PM = 5% on sales
PS = $24
d = 40%

Plugging these figures into the formula yields:

$$EFN = 0.3(\$4) - 0.1(\$4) - (0.05)(\$24)(1-0.4)$$
$$= \$1.2 - \$0.4 - \$0.72 = \$0.08$$

Thus, the amount of external financing needed is $800,000, which can be raised by issuing notes payable, bonds, stocks, or any combination of these financing sources.

The major advantage of the percent-of-sales method of financial forecasting is that it is simple and inexpensive to use. One important assumption behind the use of the method is that the firm is operating at full capacity. This means that the company has no sufficient productive capacity to absorb a projected increase in sales and thus requires additional investment in assets. Therefore, the method must be used with extreme caution if excess capacity exists in certain asset accounts.

To obtain a more precise projection of the firm's future financing needs, however, the preparation of a cash budget may be required.

THE CPA'S INVOLVEMENT WITH PROSPECTIVE FINANCIAL STATEMENTS

Prospective financial statements encompass (1) financial forecasts and (2) financial projections; they do not include pro forma financial statements and partial presentations.

Financial forecasts are prospective financial statements that present, to the best of the responsible party's knowledge and belief, an entity's expected financial position, results of operations, and cash flows. They are based on assumptions about conditions *actually* expected to exist and the course of action expected to be taken.

Financial projections are prospective financial statements that present, to the best of the responsible party's knowledge and belief, an entity's expected financial position, results of operations, and cash flows. They are based on assumptions about conditions expected to exist and the course of action expected to be taken, given one or more hypothetical (i.e., "what-if") assumptions.

Responsible parties are those responsible for the underling assumptions. For example, if a client is negotiating with a bank for a large loan and the bank stipulates the assumptions to be used, the bank represents the responsible party. The responsible party, though usually management, may be a third party.

The CPA's Reporting Responsibilities

Statement on Standards for Attestation Engagements No. 10 (SSAE-10), *Attestation Standards: Revision and Recodification*, specifically precludes an accountant from compiling, examining, or applying agreed-upon procedures to prospective financial statements that fail to include a summary of significant assumptions. The practice standards in SSAE-10 are not applicable to the following types of engagements:

- Those involving prospective financial statements that are restricted to internal use.

- Those used solely in litigation support services (e.g., in circumstances where the practitioner is serving as an expert witness).

Use of Prospective Financial Statements

The intended use of an entity's prospective financial statements governs the type of prospective financial statements to be presented. When an entity's prospective financial statements are for general use (i.e., the statements will be used by persons not negotiating directly with the responsible party), only a financial forecast is to be presented (e.g., in a public offering of a tax shelter interest). When an entity's prospective financial statements are for *limited use* (i.e., situations where the statements are to be used by the responsible party alone or by the responsible party and those parties negotiating directly with the responsible party), either a financial forecast or a financial projection may be presented. For example, if a client is negotiating directly with a bank, either a forecast or a projection is appropriate.

Compilation of Prospective Financial Statements

Compilation procedures applicable to prospective financial statements are not designed to provide any form of assurance on the presentation of the statements or the underlying assumptions. They are essentially the same as those applicable to historical financial statements. Additional procedures are as follows:

- Inquire of the responsible party as to the underlying assumptions developed.

- Compile or obtain a list of the underlying assumptions and consider the possibility of obvious omissions or inconsistencies.

- Verify the mathematical accuracy of the assumptions.

- Read the prospective financial statements in order to identify departures from AICPA presentation guidelines.

- Obtain a client representation letter in order to confirm that the responsible party acknowledges its responsibility for the prospective statements (including the underlying assumptions).

Caution: An accountant is precluded from compiling forecasts and projections that do not present the summary of significant assumptions. Furthermore, the practitioner should not compile a projection that fails to identify the underlying hypothetical assumptions or describe the limitations on the utility of the projection.

The accountant's report on compiled prospective financial statements should include the following:

- Identification of the prospective financial statements presented.

- A statement as to the level of service provided and the fact that the prospective financial statements were compiled in accordance with attestation standards established by the AICPA.

- A statement describing the limited scope of a compilation and the fact that no opinion or any other form of assurance is being expressed.

- A warning that the prospective results may not materialize.

- A statement that the accountant is under no responsibility to update his or her report for conditions occurring after the compilation report is issued.

- The date of the report, which should coincide with the completion of the compilation procedures.

- The accountant's signature.

- In the case of a projection, a separate paragraph describing the limitations on the utility of the statements.

- When the statements present the expected results in the form of a range of values, a separate paragraph as to that fact.

- If the accountant is not independent, a statement as to that fact. (No disclosure should be made as to the reasons why the accountant feels that he or she is not independent.)

- When the prospective statements contain a departure from AICPA presentation guidelines or omit disclosures unrelated to the significant assumptions, an explanatory paragraph.

Exhibit 43-2 is a standard report on the compiled forecasts. Exhibit 43-3 presents a standard report on compiled projections.

Exhibit 43-2: Standard Report on Compiled Forecasts

I (We) have compiled the accompanying forecasted balance sheet, statement of income, retained earnings, and cash flows of Future Corporation as of December 31, 2X15 and for the year then ending, in accordance with attestation standards established by the American Institute of Certified Public Accountants.

A compilation is limited to presenting, in the form of a forecast, information that is the representation of management (or other responsible party) and does not include evaluation of the support for the assumptions underlying the forecast. I (We) have not examined the forecast and, accordingly, do not express an opinion or any other form of assurance on the accompanying statements or assumptions. Furthermore, there will usually be differences between the forecasted results and the actual results, because events and circumstances frequently do not occur as expected, and those differences may be material. I (We) have no responsibility to update this report for events and circumstances occurring after the date of this report.

Exhibit 43-3: Standard Report on Compiled Projections

I (We) have compiled the accompanying projected balance sheet, statements of income, retained earnings, and cash flows of Future Corporation as of December 31, 2X15, and for the year then ending, in accordance with attestation standards established by the American Institute of Certified Public Accountants.

The accompanying projection, and this report, were prepared for [*state special purpose (e.g., "the Takeover Corporation for the purpose of negotiating a buyout of the Company,")*] and should not be used for any other purpose.

A compilation is limited to presenting, in the form of a projection, information that is the representation of management (or other responsible party) and does not include evaluation of the support for the assumptions underlying the projection. I (We) have not examined the projection and, accordingly, do not express an opinion or any other form of assurance on the accompanying statements or assumptions. Furthermore, even if [*describe hypothetical assumption (e.g., "the buyout is consummated")*] there will usually be differences between the projected results and the actual results, because events and circumstances frequently do not occur as expected, and those differences may be material. I (We) have no responsibility to update this report for events and circumstances occurring after the date of this report.

EARNINGS FORECAST

For many years, financial analysts have predicted earnings per share and stock price performance. Considerable emphasis has been placed on such forecasts in order to provide guidance to investors. Recently, management forecast disclosures in financial statements have placed greater emphasis on the development of fore-casting methodology in this area. The accuracy of these earnings forecasts has been given much attention recently primarily due to the SEC's position on financial forecasts.

Security Analysts versus Time-Series Models

Forecasts of earnings per share (EPS) for business firms are published by both management and security analysts. Unfortunately, however, the accuracy of EPS forecasts by security analysts have been shown to be little if any better than that produced by some "naive" models such as extrapolating the past trend of earnings. Indeed, it increasingly appears that the change in EPS may be a random variable.

Projections of EPS are frequently made by independent security analysts. Examples of forecast sources include (1) Value Line Investment Survey, (2) Lynch, Jones and Ryan's Institutional Brokers Estimate System (IBES), and (3) Standard & Poor's The Earnings Forecaster.

Exhibit 43-4 summarizes the pros and cons of both approaches.

Exhibit 43-4: Pros and Cons of Security Analyst and Univariate Time-Series Model Approaches to Forecasting

Security Analysts Approach to Forecasting

Pros

1. Ability to incorporate information form many sources.
2. Ability to adjust to structural change immediately.
3. Ability to update continually as new information becomes available.

Cons

1. High initial setup costs and high ongoing cost to monitor numerous variables, make company visits, and so on.
2. Heavy dependence on the skills of a single individual.
3. Analyst may have an incentive not to provide an unbiased forecast (e.g., due to pressure to conform to consensus forecasts).
4. Analyst may be manipulated by company officials (at least in the short run).

Univariate Time-Series Model Approach to Forecasting

Pros

1. Ability to detect and exploit systematic patterns in the past series.
2. Relatively low degree of subjectivity in the forecasting (especially give the availability of computer algorithms to identify and estimate models).
3. Low cost and ease of updating.
4. Ability to compute confidence intervals around the forecasts.

Cons

1. Limited number of observations available for newly formed firms, firms with structural change, and so on.
2. Financial statement data may not satisfy distributional assumptions of time-series model used.
3. Inability to update forecasts between successive interim or annual earnings releases.
4. Difficulty of communicating approach to clients (especially the statistical methodology used in identifying and estimating univariate models).

Source: Foster, George, *Financial Statement Analysis,* 2nd ed., Prentice Hall, Englewood Cliffs, NJ, 1986, p. 278.

Exhibit 43-5 shows sources of earnings forecasting data preferred by financial analysts.

Exhibit 43-5: Preferred Sources of Earnings Forecasting Data

	Rank	*1*	*2*	*3*	*4*	*5*
Company contacts		56	28	24	8	9
Own research		55	15	5	1	
Industry statistics		19	14	14	7	
Other analysis		12	17	2	8	11
Historical financial data		8	12	8	5	4
Economic forecasts		7	7	10	3	
Competition		1	7	2	6	1
Computer simulation						2
Field trips			1			
Government agencies				2		
Industry & trade sources		1	7	17	3	5
Public relations of a promotional nature						1
Retired directors						1
Rumor						2

	Rank	1	2	3	4	5
Wall Street sources		1	4	9	3	4
Rank 1 = most preferred						
5 = least preferred						

Source: Carper, Brent W., Barton Jr., Frank M., Wunder Haroldene F., "The Future of Forecasting," *Management Accounting.* August, 1979, pp. 27-31.

This section compares various forecasting methods using a sample drawn from the Standard and Poor's 400. It also examines the ability of financial analysts to forecast earnings per share performance based on the relationship of past forecasts of future earnings by financial analysts and through the use of recent univariate time-series models.

Our sample of Earnings per Share (EPS) was drawn from the 2010 through 2012 time period using the quarterly *Compustat Industrial* data tapes available from S&P. Included in our sample are 30 firms randomly selected from the Standard & Poor's 400 index for manufacturing firms over the period January 2010 to July 2012, using monthly data as reported to the public security markets. To collect data on financial analyst forecasts, we have selected the *Value Line Forecasting Survey,* which is one of several reporting agencies that employ financial analysts and report their forecasts on a weekly basis.

To compare the forecasting ability of financial analysts with extrapolative models, seven time-series models were used to forecast earnings per share. The popular computer forecasting software RATS was used to estimate the models.

Data for the resulting sample of firms were used over the five-year time period studied (i.e., January 2010-July 2012) to estimate the models. This period was a relatively short time period to avoid the possibility of structural changes in the economy affecting the results of the study.

Next, forecasts were derived from July 2014 to June 2015 using monthly data. The accuracy of the forecasts from each of the models for the period was evaluated using two measures: (1) MAPE (mean absolute percentage error) and (2) MSE (mean square error).

Forecasting Methodology

The forecasting models presented relate to various models proposed by earnings forecasters in the accounting, finance, and forecasting literature. They are as follows:

- Exponential Smoothing Model with Additive Seasonal Effect.
- Single Exponential Smoothing Model
- Exponential Smoothing Model with Linear Trend and Seasonal Additive Effects.
- Exponential Smoothing Model with Exponential Trend and Seasonal Additive Effects.

- Box-Jenkins Analysis SARIMA (1,0,0) (0,1,0) s = 12

  A seasonal autoregressive integrated moving average (SARIMA) model is identified with first-order autoregressive parameters and a 12-month seasonal adjustment.

- Box-Jenkins Analysis SARIMA (1,0,0) (0,1,1) s = 12

  A seasonal autoregressive integrated moving average (SARIMA) model is identified with first-order autoregressive parameters and a 12-month seasonal adjustment. It also contains a seasonal moving average.

- Linear Trend Analysis.

- Value Line Forecast.

Forecasting Accuracy

In Exhibit 43-6, the Sample Average Forecast Error was estimated for each of 12 months, based on earlier data. From July 2014 through June 2015, the monthly forecast errors are presented using the MAPE measure. From this analysis, there is some variation in forecasting accuracy. The exponential forecasting methods performed well for methods 1, 2, and 3. The Box-Jenkins approaches for methods 5 and 6 and the linear trend analysis for method 7 were reasonably successful. Overall, however, the monthly Value Line forecast resulted in the largest forecast errors.

Exhibit 43-6: Sample Average Forecast Errors from 30 Companies' Mean Absolute Percentage Error (MAPE)

Method	1	2	3	4	5	6	7	8
2014:7	0.28	0.30	0.39	1.54	0.42	0.64	0.57	1.77
2014:8	0.24	0.23	0.29	1.51	0.72	0.95	0.58	1.39
2014:9	0.19	0.22	0.16	1.51	1.00	1.23	0.56	0.70
2014:10	0.19	0.22	0.16	1.55	1.28	1.54	0.56	0.70
2014:11	0.24	0.43	0.46	1.48	1.72	1.98	0.56	1.73
2015:12	0.27	0.71	0.71	1.48	2.09	2.35	0.69	4.28
2015:1	0.42	0.83	1.11	1.46	2.47	2.60	0.55	4.97
2015:2	0.42	0.83	1.11	1.46	2.47	2.60	0.55	4.97
2015:3	0.67	2.15	2.10	2.00	3.31	3.45	0.73	6.01
2015:4	0.78	3.17	1.48	1.72	3.53	3.65	0.73	9.00
2015:5	0.81	1.44	1.44	1.80	0.86	0.99	0.68	8.62
2015:6	0.81	1.44	1.44	1.80	0.86	0.99	0.68	8.62

Exhibit 43-6 presents the MSE results. Generally, the mean square error reflected similar conclusions (see Exhibit 43-7).

Exhibit 43-7: Sample Average Forecast Errors from 30 Companies'
Mean Square Error (MSE)

Method	1	2	3	4	5	6	7	8
2014:7	0.42	0.34	0.39	6.27	0.12	0.12	1.21	1.59
2014:8	0.31	0.23	0.40	6.17	0.13	0.13	1.26	1.63
2014:9	0.31	0.23	0.33	5.93	0.14	0.14	1.31	1.69
2014:10	0.31	0.21	0.33	5.93	0.14	0.14	1.31	1.69
2014:11	0.32	0.64	0.76	6.22	0.48	0.47	1.47	2.19
2014:12	0.34	0.78	0.87	5.93	0.55	0.53	1.62	2.39
2015:1	0.71	1.32	1.38	5.91	0.97	0.95	1.45	0.99
2015:2	0.71	1.32	1.38	5.91	0.97	0.95	1.45	0.99
2015:3	1.40	5.48	1.81	5.68	3.89	3.86	2.28	0.85
2015:4	1.20	6.10	1.40	5.33	3.45	3.43	1.95	0.82
2015:5	1.21	7.29	1.41	5.21	3.35	3.34	2.03	0.74
2015:6	1.21	7.29	1.41	5.21	3.35	3.34	2.03	0.7

PRO FORMA EARNINGS PER SHARE

Many companies are reporting pro forma EPS along with U.S. GAAP-based EPS in the financial information provided to investors. Pro forma earnings typically exceed GAAP earnings because the pro forma numbers exclude such items as restructuring charges, impairment of assets, R&D expenditures, and stock compensation expense. Following are GAAP-based EPS and pro forma EPS figures for several companies.

Company	GAAP EPS	Pro Forma EPS
Broadcom	(6.36)	(0.13)
Corning	(0.24)	0.09
Honeywell	(0.38)	0.44
International Paper	(0.57)	0.14
Qualcomm	(0.06)	0.20

Source: Company web site press releases.

The SEC has expressed concern that pro forma earnings may be misleading.

The SEC now requires companies that provide pro forma financial information to make sure that the information is not misleading. In addition, reconciliation between pro forma and GAAP-based information is required. [SEC Accounting and Enforcement Release No. 1499 (January 16, 2002); "SEC Proposes Rules to Implement Sarbanes-Oxley Act Reforms," SEC Press Release 2002-155 (October 30, 2002)]

CHAPTER 44

CASH FLOW FORECASTING AND CASH BUDGETING

CONTENTS

A forecast of cash collections and potential write-offs of accounts receivable is essential in *cash budgeting* and in judging the appropriateness of current credit and discount policies. The critical step in making such a forecast is estimating the cash collection and bad debt percentages to be applied to sales or accounts receivable balances. This chapter discusses several methods of estimating *cash collection rates* (or *payment proportions*) and illustrates how these rates are used for cash budgeting purposes.

The first approach, which is based on the Markov model, involves the use of a probability matrix based on the estimates of what are referred to as transition probabilities. This method is described on a step-by-step basis using an illustrative example. The second approach involves a simple average. The third approach offers a more pragmatic method of estimating collection and bad debt percentages by relating credit sales and collection data. This method employs regression analysis. By using these approaches, a financial planner should be able to:

- Estimate future cash collections from accounts receivable.
- Establish an allowance for doubtful accounts.
- Provide a valuable insight into better methods of managing accounts receivable.

MARKOV APPROACH

The Markov (probability matrix) approach has been around for a long time. This approach has been successfully applied by Cyert and others to accounts receivable analysis, specifically to the estimation of that portion of the accounts receivable that will eventually become uncollectible. The method requires classification of outstanding accounts receivable according to age categories that reflect the stage of account delinquency (e.g., current accounts, accounts one month past due, and accounts two months past due). Consider the following example.

EXAMPLE 1: XYZ department store divides its accounts receivable into the following two classifications:

1. 0 to 60 days old.

2. 61 to 120 days old.

Accounts that are more than 120 days old are declared uncollectible by XYZ. XYZ currently has $10,000 in accounts receivable broken down as follows:

- $7,000 from the 0 to 60-day category

- $3,000 from the 61- to 120-day category

Based on an analysis of its past records, it provides us with what is known as the matrix of transition possibilities, as shown in Exhibit 58-1.

Exhibit 44-1: Probability Matrix

From To	Collected	Uncollectible	0–60 Days Old	61–120 Days Old
Collected	①	0	0	0
Uncollectible	0	①	0	0
0–60 days old	.3	[0]	.5	.2
61–120 days old	.5	.1	.3	.1

Transition probabilities are nothing more than the probability that an account receivable moves from one age stage category to another. There are three basic features of this matrix. First, notice the squared element, 0 in the matrix. This indicates that $1 in the 0–60 days category cannot become a bad debt in one month's time. Now look at the two circled elements. Each of these is 1, indicating that, in time, all the accounts receivable dollars will either be paid or become uncollectible. Eventually, all the dollars wind up as either collected or uncollectible, but XYZ would be interested in knowing the probability that a dollar of a 0–60-day-old or a 61–120-day-old receivable would eventually find its way into either paid bills or bad debts. It is convenient to partition the matrix of transition probabilities into four submatrices, as follows:

$$\begin{bmatrix} I & O \\ R & Q \end{bmatrix}$$

so that

$$I = \begin{bmatrix} 1 & 0 \\ 0 & 1 \end{bmatrix} \quad O = \begin{bmatrix} 0 & 0 \\ 0 & 0 \end{bmatrix}$$

$$R = \begin{bmatrix} .3 & 0 \\ .5 & .1 \end{bmatrix} \quad Q = \begin{bmatrix} .5 & .2 \\ .3 & .1 \end{bmatrix}$$

Now we are in a position to illustrate the procedure used to determine:

- Estimated collection and bad debt percentages by age category.
- Estimated allowance for doubtful accounts.

Step by step, the procedure is as follows:

Step 1. Set up the matrix [I − Q].

$$[I - Q] = \begin{bmatrix} 1 & 0 \\ 0 & 1 \end{bmatrix} - \begin{bmatrix} .5 & .2 \\ .3 & .1 \end{bmatrix} = \begin{bmatrix} .5 & -.2 \\ -.3 & .9 \end{bmatrix}$$

Step 2. Find the inverse of this matrix, denoted by N.

$$N = [I - Q]^{-1} = \begin{bmatrix} 2.31 & .51 \\ .77 & 1.28 \end{bmatrix}$$

Note: The inverse of a matrix can be readily performed by spreadsheet programs, such as Microsoft's Excel, Lotus 1-2-3, or Quattro Pro.

Step 3. Multiply this inverse by matrix R.

$$NR = \begin{bmatrix} 2.31 & .51 \\ .77 & 1.28 \end{bmatrix} \begin{bmatrix} .3 & 0 \\ .5 & .1 \end{bmatrix} = \begin{bmatrix} .95 & .05 \\ .87 & .13 \end{bmatrix}$$

NR gives us the probability that an account will eventually be collected or become a bad debt. Specifically, the top row in the answer is the probability that $1 of XYZ's accounts receivable in the 0–60 days category will end up in the collected and bad debt category will be paid, and a .05 probability that it will eventually become a bad debt. Turning to the second row, the two entries represent the probability that $1 now in the 61–120 days category will end up in the collected and bad debt categories. We can see from this row that there is a .87 probability that $1 currently in the 61–120 days category will be collected and a .13 probability that it will eventually become uncollectible.

If XYZ wants to estimate the future of its $10,000 accounts receivable ($7,000 in the 0–60 days category and $3,000 in the 61–120 days category), it must set up the following matrix multiplication:

$$[7,000 \quad 3,000]\begin{bmatrix} .95 & .05 \\ .87 & .13 \end{bmatrix} = [9,260 \quad 740]$$

Hence, of its $10,000 in accounts receivable, XYZ expects to collect $9,260 and to lose $740 to bad debts. Therefore, the estimated allowance for the collectible accounts is $740.

The variance of each component is equal to

$$A = be(cNR - (cNR)_{sq})$$

where $c_i = b/\sum_{i=1}^{2} b_i$ and e is the unit vector

In our example, $b = (7,000 \ 3,000)$, $c = (.7 \ .3)$. Therefore,

$$A = [7,000 \quad 3,000]\begin{bmatrix} 1 \\ 1 \end{bmatrix}\left\{[.7 \quad .3]\begin{bmatrix} .95 & .05 \\ .87 & .13 \end{bmatrix} - [.7 \quad .3]\begin{bmatrix} .95 & .05 \\ .87 & .13 \end{bmatrix}sq\right\}$$

$$= 10,000[[.926 \ .074] \quad [.857476 \ .005476]]$$
$$= [685.24 \ 385.24]$$

which makes the standard deviation equal to $26.18 ($\sqrt{\$68 - 5.24}$). If we want to be 95% confident about our estimate of collections, we would set the interval estimate at $9,260 + 2(26.18)$, or $9,207.64 – $9,312.36, assuming t = 2 as a rule of thumb. We would also be able to set the allowance to cover the bad debts at $740 + 2(26.18)$, or $792.36.

SIMPLE AVERAGE

The most straightforward way to estimate collection percentages is to compute the average value realized from past data—that is:

$$P'_i = \text{AVE}(C_{t+i}/S_t)$$

$$= \frac{1}{N} \sum_{t=1}^{N} \frac{C_{t+i}}{S_t}, \ i = 0,1,2\ldots$$

where

P'_i = an empirical estimate of collection percentages,

C_{t+i} = cash collection in month $t + i$ from credit sales in month t,

S_t = credit sales in month t, and

N = the number of months of past data to compute the average.

LAGGED REGRESSION APPROACH

A more scientific approach to estimating cash collection percentages (or payment proportions) is to utilize multiple regression. We know that there is typically a time lag between the point of a credit sale and realization of cash. More specifically, the lagged effect of credit sales and cash inflows is distributed over a number of periods, as follows:

$$C_t = b_1 S_{t-1} + b_2 S_{t-2} + \ldots b_i S_{t-i}$$

where

C_t = cash collection in month t,

S_t = credit sales made in period t,

$b_1 b_2, \ldots b_i$ = collection percentages (the same as F_i,), and

i = number of periods lagged.

By using the regression method discussed previously, we will be able to estimate these collection rates. We can utilize "Regression" of Excel or special packages, such as SPSS, SAS, or Minitab.

It should be noted that the cash collection percentages ($b_1, b_2 \ldots b_i$) may not add up to 100% because of the possibility of bad debts. Once we estimate these percentages by using the regression method, we should be able to compute the bad debt percentage with no difficulty.

Exhibit 44-2 shows the regression results using actual monthly data on credit sales and cash inflows for a real company. Equation 1 can be written as follows:

$$C_t = 60.6\%(S_{t-1}) + 19.3\%(S_{t-2}) + 8.8\%(S_{t-3})$$

This result indicates that the receivables generated by the credit sales are collected at the following rates: first month after sale, 60.6%; second month after sale, 19.3%; and third month after sale, 8.8%. The bad debt percentage is computed as 6.3% (100–93.7%).

These collection and bad debt percentages are probabilistic variables (that is, variables whose values cannot be known with precision). However, the standard error of the regression coefficient and the 5-value permit us to assess the probability that the true percentage is between specified limits. The confidence interval takes the following form:

$$b \pm tS_b$$

where S_b = standard error of the coefficient.

Exhibit 44-2: Regression Results for Cash Collection (C_t)

Independent Variables	Equation 1	Equation 2
S_{t-1}	0.606[a]	0.596[a]
	(0.062)[b]	(0.097)
S_{t-2}	0.193[a]	0.142
	(0.085)	(0.120)
S_{t-3}	0.088	0.043
	(0.157)	(0.191)
S_{t-4}		0.136
	(0.800)	
R^2	0.754	0.753
Durbin-Watson	2.52[c]	2.48[c]
Standard error of the estimate (S_e)	11.63	16.05
Number of monthly observations	21	20
Bad debt percentages	0.063	0.083

[a] Statistically significant at the 5% significance level.
[b] This figure in parentheses is the standard error of the e estimate for the coefficient (S_b).
[c] No autocorrelation present at the 5% significance level.

EXAMPLE 2: To illustrate, assuming $t = 2$ as rule of thumb at the 95% confidence level, the true collection percentage from the prior month's sales will be:

$$60.6\% \pm 2(6.2\%) = 60.6\% \pm 12.4\%$$

Turning to the estimation of cash collections and allowance for doubtful accounts, the following values are used for illustrative purposes:

S_{t-1} = $77.6, S_{t-2} = $58.5, S_{t-3} = $76.4, and forecast average monthly

net credit sales = $75.2

Then, (a) the forecast cash collection for period t would be

$$C_t = 60.6\%(77.6) + 19.3\%(58.5) + 8.8\%(76.4) = \$65.04$$

If the financial manager wants to be 95% confident about this forecast value, then the interval would be set as follows:

$$C_t = tS_e$$

where S_e = standard error of the estimate.

To illustrate, using t = 2 as a rule of thumb at the 95% confidence level, the true value for cash collections in period t will be

$$\$65.04 \pm 2(11.63) = \$65.04 \pm 23.26$$

(b) the estimated allowance for uncollectible accounts for period t will be

$$6.3\% (\$75.2) = \$4.74$$

By using the limits discussed so far, financial planners can develop flexible (or probabilistic) cash budgets, where the lower and upper limits can be interpreted as pessimistic and optimistic outcomes, respectively. They can also simulate a cash budget in an attempt to determine both the expected change in cash collections for each period and the variation in this value.

In preparing a conventional cash inflow budget, the financial manager considers re various sources of cash, including cash on account, sale of assets, and incurrence of debt. Cash collections from customers are emphasized, since that is the greatest problem in this type of budget.

EXAMPLE 3: The following data are given for Erich Stores:

	September Actual	October Actual	November Estimated	December Estimated
Cash sales	$ 7,000	$ 6,000	$ 8,000	$ 6,000
Credit sales	50,000	48,000	62,000	80,000
Total sales	$57,000	$54,000	$70,000	$86,000

Past experience indicates net collections normally occur in the following pattern:

- No collections are made in the month of sale.
- 80% of the sales of any month are collected in the following month.
- 19% of sales are collected in the second following month.
- 1% of sales are uncollectible.

We can project total cash receipts for November and December as follows:

	November	December
Cash receipts		
Cash sales	$ 8,000	$ 6,000
Cash collections		
September sales		
50,000 (19%)	9,500	
October sales		
48,000 (80%)	38,400	
48,000 (19%)		9,120
November sales		
62,000 (80%)		49,600
Total cash receipts	$55,900	$64,720

THE CASH BUDGET

The budget preparation process begins with the sales budget and continues through the preparation of pro forma financial statements. The last schedule prepared before the financial statements is the cash budget, which is a schedule of estimated cash collections and payments. The various operating budgets and the capital budget are inputs to the cash budgeting process.

The cash budget is prepared for the purpose of cash planning and control. It presents the expected cash inflow and outflow for a designated time period. The cash budget assists management in maintaining cash balances in reasonable relationship to its needs. It provides information about the balance of cash currently existing in the company, thus assisting management in avoiding unnecessary idle cash and possible cash shortages. For example, if there is excess cash in the budget, the money may be invested in short-term securities such as U.S. Treasury bills and commercial paper to earn a return. If there is a cash shortage, management may decide to borrow money, cut expenditures, or sell assets. Thus, the cash budget ensures that sufficient funds are available to a business at all times.

The cash budget also allows a company to review its future cash receipts and payments to uncover possible *patterns of cash flows*. In this way, it can study its collection and disbursement efforts to ascertain if it is maximizing its net cash flows. In addition, the cash budget reveals the proper time and amount to borrow, as well as the timing regarding its ability to repay the loan. For example, if a cash budget indicates that a significant cash outlay is required to purchase assets (e.g., store equipment), the company may have to consider borrowing money and determine a debt repayment schedule. In order to obtain a line of credit, lenders typically require a company to issue a cash budget, along with its financial statements.

The cash budget should be prepared for the shortest time period for which reliable financial information can be obtained. It is often prepared monthly, but there are no strict rules for determining the length of the budget period. In the case of small businesses, a cash budget can be prepared in one week. However, predicting major cash receipts and cash payments for a specific day is also possible. As a general rule, cash budget preparation should be long enough to present the effect of a company's policies, yet short enough so that estimates can be made with reasonable accuracy. Exhibit 44-3 presents the major components of a cash budget.

Exhibit 44-3: Major Cash Flow Components of a Cash Budget

Cash Inflows	*Cash Outflows*
Operating:	**Operating:**
Cash sales	Payroll
Collections	Inventory purchases
	Insurance
	Payments to suppliers

	Cash Inflows	Cash Outflows
	Nonoperating:	**Nonoperating:**
	Royalties	Capital expenditures
	Rents	Interest
	Investments income	Loan repayments
	Sale of marketable securities	Tax payments
	Loan proceeds	Purchase of marketable securities

The basis for estimating cash receipts is *sales*, whether from cash sales or collections from customer balances. An incorrect sales estimate will result in erroneous cash estimates. Sales predictions also influence projected cash outlays for manufacturing costs, since production is tied to sales. The projection of operating expenses may be tied to the suppliers' payment terms. Exhibit 44-4 presents a monthly cash budget.

Exhibit 44-4: Monthly Cash Budget

	October (actual)	November (actual)	December (actual)	January	February	March
Expected Sales	$375,000	$457,500	$510,000	$545,000	$575,000	$610,000
Cash receipts:						
Cash sales	10%			54,500	57,500	61,000
Collection from sales:						
One month ago	75%			344,250	367,875	388,125
Two months ago	15%			61,763	68,850	73,575
Three months ago	8%			27,000	32,940	36,720
Bad debts	2%					
	100%			487,513	527,165	559,420
Other cash receipts				11,000	7,600	18,500
Beginning of month cash				80,000	4,513	15,878
Total available cash				578,513	539,278	593,798
Cash disbursements:						
Material				138,000	145,000	150,000
Labor and wages				172,000	110,000	169,000
Selling costs				175,000	169,000	181,000
General and administrative costs				46,000	49,500	48,000
Income taxes					28,500	
Capital equipment				28,000	5,200	21,200
Interest expense				15,000	16,200	17,500
Total cash disbursements				574,000	523,400	586,700

	October (actual)	November (actual)	December (actual)	January	February	March
Ending cash balance (deficiency) before additional borrowings/ (repayments) or (investments) redemptions				4,513	15,878	7,098
Bank borrowings/ (repayments)					–	–
(Investments)/redemptions						
Ending cash balance				$4,513	$15,878	$7,098

CASH VARIANCE ANALYSIS

Comparing estimated and actual cash figures allows the financial manager to investigate the reasons for any significant discrepancies and to take the necessary corrective measures. *Variance analysis* presents a clearer picture of a company's cash position and provides insight in improving cash estimates in the next budgeting period. In addition, it aids in the periodic revision of projections, which typically occurs at the beginning of each budget segment (e.g., the first day of a quarter for budgets prepared quarterly or the first day of the month for budgets prepared monthly). Budgets should be adjusted immediately for significant changes. Exhibit 44-5 presents an analysis of cash budget variances.

Exhibit 44-5: Cash Budget Variance Analysis

	Previous Week		Year-to-Date	
	Budget	Actual	Budget	Actual
Cash receipts				
Collection from customers	$111,000	$109,000	$ 990,000	$ 979,000
Investment income	$ 2,400	$ 2,500	$ 33,000	$ 32,500
Royalty	$ 3,000	$ 3,000	$ 60,000	$ 60,000
Total cash receipts	$116,400	$114,500	$1,083,000	$1,071,500
Cash disbursements:				
Material purchases	$26,300	$18,410	$176,000	$226,000
Payroll	27,500	29,000	400,000	412,800
Property taxes	5,500	5,540	5,500	5,500
Group insurance premium	13,000	13,200	39,000	39,600
Bank note-interest	4,320	4,320	15,000	12,960

	Previous Week		Year-to-Date	
	Budget	*Actual*	*Budget*	*Actual*
Lease payment-building	5,475	5,475	16,425	16,425
Dividend payment	1,232	1,232	3,696	3,696
Rent	6,897	6,897	20,691	20,691
Total disbursements	63,924	65,664	500,312	511,672
Net increase (decrease) in cash	$47,076	$43,336	$489,688	$467,328

CONCLUSION

Two methods of estimating the expected collectible and uncollectible patterns were presented. One advantage of the Markov model is that the expected value and standard deviation of these percentages can be determined, thereby making it possible to specify probabilistic statements about these figures. We have to be careful about these results, however, since the model makes some strong assumptions. A serious assumption is that the matrix of transition probabilities is constant over time. We do not expect this to be perfectly true. Updating of the matrix may have to be done, perhaps through the use of such techniques as exponential smoothing and time series analysis.

The regression approach is relatively inexpensive to use in the sense that it does not require a lot of data. All it requires is data on cash collections and credit sales. Furthermore, credit sales values are all predetermined; we use previous months' credit sales to forecast cash collections—that is, there is no need to forecast credit sales. The model also allows you to make all kinds of statistical inferences about the cash collection percentages and forecast values.

Extensions of these models can be made toward setting credit and discount policies. Corresponding to a given set of policies, there is an associated transition matrix in the Markov model, and associated collection percentages in the regression model. By computing long-term collections and bad debts for each policy, an optimal policy can be chosen that maximizes expected long-run profits per period.

CHAPTER 45

FORECASTING CORPORATE FINANCIAL DISTRESS

CONTENTS

The number of companies that file for bankruptcy is increasing. Will the company of the stock you own be among them? Will you go bankrupt? Will your major customers or suppliers go bankrupt? What warning signs exist and what can be done to avoid corporate failure?

Bankruptcy for a company is the final declaration of the inability to sustain current operations given the current debt obligations. The most firms require loans and, therefore, increase their liabilities during their operations in order to expand, improve, or even just survive. The "degree" to which a firm has current debt in excess of assets is the most common factor in bankruptcy.

If you can predict with reasonable accuracy ahead of time, for, say, a year or two, that the company you are interested in or your company is developing financial distress, you could better protect yourself. For example, loan institutions face a major difficulty in calculating the "degree of debt relative to assets" or the likelihood of bankruptcy, yet this is precisely what these institutions must accomplish prior to issuing a financial loan to a firm.

NEED FOR PREDICTION

Various groups of business people can reap significant rewards and benefits from a predictive model for their own purposes. For example:

1. *Merger analysis.* The predictive model can help identify potential problems with a merger candidate.

2. *Turnaround management.* The model can be used to develop emergency action plans and turnaround strategies to quickly correct a deteriorating situation.

3. *Insurance underwriting.* The model can be used to evaluate the potential credit risk of the proposed insured, including risk sharing and self-insured retentions.

4. *Corporate governance.* The predictive model is used for board of directors and audit committee analysis of going concern capability, consideration of corporate risk, and analysis of merger and acquisition scenarios.

5. *Investment analysis.* The model can help an investor selecting stocks of potentially troubled companies. It is also used by venture capitalists, investment bankers, and business valuation experts as they evaluate potential investment decisions.

6. *Auditing analysis.* External CPA auditors can use the model to evaluate whether a firm is a going concern and to consider opinion qualification and financial statement disclosures.

7. *Legal analysis.* Those investing or giving credit to your company may sue for losses incurred. The model can help in your company's defense.

8. *Loan credit analysis.* Bankers and lenders can use it to determine whether they should extend a loan. If bankers can identify companies in danger of failure sufficiently far in advance, corrective action can be taken. The banker can (a) decline to accept the company as a customer, (b) encourage the company to identify its problems and take steps to rectify those problems, (c) encourage the principals of the company to inject more capital into the business, and (d) encourage the company to seek other financing. Other creditors, such as vendors, have used it to determine whether to extend credit.

You should build early warning systems to detect the likelihood of bankruptcy. Investment bankers, financial analysts, security analysts, financial managers, auditors, and others have used financial ratios as an indication of the financial strength of a company. However, financial ratio analysis is limited because the methodology is basically *univariate*. Each ratio is examined in isolation and it is up to the financial manager to use professional judgment to determine whether a set of financial ratios is developing into a meaningful analysis.

In order to overcome the shortcomings of financial ratio analysis, it is necessary to combine mutually exclusive ratios into groups to develop a meaningful predictive model. *Regression analysis* and *multiple discriminant analysis* (MDA) are two statistical techniques that have been used to predict the financial strength of a company.

THREE BANKRUPTCY MODELS

This chapter evaluates three predictive bankruptcy models: (1) The well-known Z-Score Model, (2) The Degree of Relative Liquidity Model, and (3) The Lambda Index Model.

The *Z-score model* evaluates a combination of several financial ratios to predict the likelihood of future bankruptcy. The model, developed by Edward Altman, uses multiple discriminant analysis to give a relative prediction of whether a firm will go bankrupt within five years. The *Degree of Relative Liquidity Model*, on the other hand, evaluates a firm's ability to meet its short-term obligations. This model also uses discriminant analysis by combining several ratios to derive a percentage figure that indicates the firm's ability to meet short-term obligations. Third, the *Lambda Index Model* evaluates a firm's ability to generate or obtain cash on a short-term basis to meet current obligations and therefore predict solvency. These models are outlined and described in the following sections.

Z-Score Model

Using a blend of the traditional financial ratios and multiple discrimination analysis, Altman[1] developed a bankruptcy prediction model that produces a Z-score as follows:

$$Z = 1.2 * X_1 + 1.4 * X_2 + 3.3 * X_3 + 0.6 * X_4 + 0.999 * X_5$$

where

X_1 = Working capital/Total assets

X_2 = Retained earnings/Total assets

X_3 = Earnings before interest and taxes (EBIT)/Total assets

X_4 = Market value of equity/Book value of debt (or Net worth for *private firms*)

X_5 = Sales/Total assets

Altman also established the following guideline for classifying firms:

Z-Score	Probability of Short-term Illiquidity
1.8 or less	Very high
1.81–2.99	Not sure
3.0 or higher	Unlikely

The Z-score is known to be about 90% accurate in forecasting business failure one year in the future and about 80% accurate in forecasting it two years in the future. It has been found that with the many important changes in reporting standards since the late 1960s, the Z-Score model is somewhat out of date. A second-generation model known as *Zeta Analysis* adjusts for these changes, primarily the capitalization of financial leases. The resulting Zeta discriminant model is extremely accurate for up to five years before failure. Since this analysis is a proprietary one, the exact

[1] Edward I. Altman, *Corporate Financial Distress* (New York: John Wiley & Sons, 1983).

weights for the model's seven variables cannot be specified here. The new study resulted in the following variables explaining corporate failure.

X_1 = Return on assets—Earnings before interest and taxes to total assets.

X_2 = Stability of earnings—Measure by the "normalized measure of the standard error of estimate around a ten-year trend in X1."

X_3 = Debt service—Earnings before interest and taxes to total interest payments.

X_4 = Cumulative profitability—Retained earnings to total assets.

X_5 = Liquidity—Current assets to current liabilities.

X_6 = Capitalization—Equity to total capital.

X_7 = Size measured by the firm's total assets.

The Degree of Relative Liquidity Model

The degree of relative liquidity (DRL), developed by Skomp and Edwards,[2] has been proposed as an alternative method for measuring the liquidity of a small firm and can have significant applications for larger companies. It has been compared to the two common liquidity ratios, the current and acid-test (or quick) ratios, which are often used to evaluate the liquidity of a firm. However, under certain circumstances these two ratios sometimes provide incomplete and often misleading indications of a firm's ability to meet its short-term obligations and may be opposite to the trend at hand. A logical approach to evaluating several liquidity measures simultaneously is to consider how appropriately each measure responds to changes relative to direction and degree of sensitivity. Following are examples of instances where the current or acid-test ratio may give misleading indications.

Current—An obsolete or slow-moving inventory and uncollectible accounts receivable may distort this ratio.

Acid-test—Uncollectible receivables and the exclusion of inventories can provide an incomplete picture.

The DRL represents the percentage of a firm's cash expenditure requirements which could be secured from beginning working capital and from cash generated through the normal operating process. Emphasis is placed upon the availability of cash sources relative to cash needs, omitting sources and uses of cash such as:

• Capital expenditures and sale of fixed assets.

• Sale and extinguishment of capital stock.

• Receipt and repayment of long-term borrowings.

• Investments and liquidations in marketable securities and bonds.

The DRL is calculated by dividing the total cash potential by the expected cash expenditures. In equation form,

---

[2] Stephen E. Skomp and Donald E. Edwards, "Measuring Small Business Liquidity: An Alternative to Current and Quick Ratios," *Journal of Small Business Management* (April 1978): Vol. 16, 22. This and the Lambda model are not illustrated here. Please refer for details to Jae K. Shim and others, *Strategic Business Forecasting*, St. Lucie Press, 2000.

$$DRL = \frac{TCP}{E} \quad or \quad \frac{WC + (OT - SVI)}{NSV - [(NI + NON) + WCC]}$$

where

TCP	=	Total cash potential
E	=	Cash expenditures for normal operations
WC	=	Beginning working capital (Beginning current assets − Beginning current liabilities)
OT	=	Operating turnover, or

$$\frac{Sales}{(Accounts\ Receivable + Inventory) \times Sales/Cost\ of\ Sales}$$

SVI	=	Sales value of inventory (Inventory at cost × Sales/Cost of sales)
NSV	=	Net sales values
NI	=	Net income
NON	=	Noncash expenditures (such as depreciation and amortization)
WCC	=	Change in working capital

If the DRL ratio is greater than 1.00 (or 100%), the firm can meet its current obligations for the period and have *some* net working capital available at the end of the period. If the DRL is less than 1.00, the firm should seek outside working capital financing before the end of the period.

The DRL may be derived by dividing the total cash potential (TCP) by expected cash expenditures (E) in the operating period. The TCP is the sum of initial potential and the cash potential from normal operations. The initial cash potential is reflected in the beginning working capital (WC) assuming reported values can be realized in cash. The cash potential from operations can be determined by multiplying the operating turnover rate (OT) by the sales value of existing finished goods inventory (SVI). The operating turnover rate (OT) reflects the number of times the sales value of finished goods inventory (at retail) and accounts receivables (net of uncollectibles) is converted into cash in an operating period. The sales value of finished goods inventory (SVI) is the adjustment of inventory at cost to retail value.

The expected cash expenditures (E) are derived by subtracting cash flow from operations from net sales (NSV). Cash flow from operations can be derived by accrual net income (NI) plus noncash expenses (NON) plus the change in working capital (WCC).

Lambda Index Model

The Lambda Index, developed by Gary Emery and 1990 Nobel Laureate Merton Miller,[3] is a ratio that focuses on two relevant components of liquidity-short-term cash balances and available credit to gauge the probability that a firm will become insolvent. The index measures the probability of a company going bankrupt and it includes the key aspect of uncertainty in cash flow measurement by utilizing a sample standard deviation. In consequence, it can be used like a z value from the standard normal distribution table.

For a given period, Lambda is the sum of a company's initial liquid reserve and net flow of funds divided by the uncertainty associated with the flows:

$$\frac{\text{Initial liquid reserve} \quad + \quad \begin{array}{c} \text{Total anticipated net cash} \\ \text{flow during the analysis horizon} \end{array}}{\text{Uncertainty about net cash flow during the analysis horizon}}$$

Net cash flow is the balance of cash receipts less cash outlays. Unused lines of credit, short-term investments, and cash balances make up the initial liquid reserve. The uncertainty is based on the standard deviation of net cash flow. In order to calculate and utilize the Lambda index, a cash forecast should be used.

A worksheet can be prepared to contain 11 line items in the following order from top to bottom: short-term line of credit; beginning liquid assets; adjustments; initial liquid reserve; total sources of funds; total uses of funds; ending liquid assets; ending liquid reserve; standard deviation; the Lambda index; and, finally, additional cash required to maintain a Lambda of 3.

A firm's short-term line of credit may not change during the course of the forecast (i.e., 1 year), which simplifies calculations. Liquid assets, by definition, include marketable securities and cash at the start of the forecast summary. By having an adjustments line item one can see the result of decreasing or increasing the cash level. The initial liquid reserve is the total short-term line of credit with any adjustments. The total sources and uses of funds are forecasts by company management, resulting in a positive or negative net cash flow. The Lambda value should rise if a firm's short-term line of credit doesn't change and it has a positive net cash flow. Ending liquid assets is the sum of three values: beginning liquid assets, adjustments, and net cash flow. Ending liquid reserve is the sum of two values: short-term line of credit and ending liquid assets. The standard deviation is drawn from the net cash flows from period to period. Next, the Lambda index is calculated by dividing the ending liquid reserve by the standard deviation.

And, finally, the last line item is additional cash needed to hold a Lambda of 3. A negative number here indicates a Lambda value of greater than 3 and, hence, a safer firm financially. A high negative value here, assuming that management is confident of its forecasts, may point out that those funds could be better utilized somewhere else.

---

[3] As cited by Kelly R. Conaster, "Can You Pay the Bills," *Lotus,* January, 1991.

Once an index value has been determined using the equation, the pertinent odds can be found by referencing a standard normal distribution table (see Exhibit 17-4 in Chapter 17, "Cost-Volume-Profit Analysis and Leverage"). For example, a Lambda of 2.33 has a value of .9901 from the table, which says that there is a 99% chance that problems won't occur and a 1% chance that they will.

Generally, a firm with a Lambda value of 9 or higher is financially healthy. Companies with a Lambda of 15 or more are considered very safe. A Lambda value of 3 translates to one chance in a thousand that cash outlays will exceed available cash on hand. A Lambda value of 3.9 puts the probability at 1 in 20 thousand. A low Lambda of 1.64 is equivalent to a one in twenty chance of required disbursements exceeding available cash on hand. A worksheet that keeps a running tally of Lambda shows how changes in the financial picture affect future cash balances.

There are a number of positive aspects to using the Lambda index. The Lambda index focuses on the key factors of liquidity and available unused credit and cash flows, which by contrast are ignored by standard cash forecasts. Further, by including the standard deviation of cash flows, Lambda penalizes irregular cash flows. The result of higher changes in cash flows would be a lower Lambda.

A drawback to Lambda, however, is the fact that it's significantly tied to revenue forecasts, which at times can be suspect depending on the time horizon and the industry. A strong Lambda doesn't carry much weight if a firm isn't confident about its forecast.

Exhibit 45-1 summarizes guidelines for classifying firms under the three models.

VARIOUS USES OF THE Z-SCORE

The Z-Score may be used by different people for varying uses. The Z-Score offers an excellent measure of the probability of a firm's insolvency, but, like any tool, one must use it with care and skill. The Z-Score should be evaluated over a number of years and should not be the sole basis of evaluation.

The Z-Score may also be used to compare the stability of different firms. Care should be exercised when the Z-Score is used for this purpose. The firms must be in the same market offering the same, if not very similar, products. In addition, the measure must be taken across the same period of years. These similarities are requirements in order to eliminate external environmental factors which would be reflected in the score.

Exhibit 45-1: Classifying Guidelines under the Three Predictive Models

	Model	*Guidelines*
(1) Z-Score Model	*Z-score*	*Probability of Short-term Illiquidity*
	1.8 or less	Very high
	1.81-2.99	Not sure
	3.0 or higher	Unlikely

	Model	*Guidelines*
(2) Degree of Relative Liquidity (DRL) Model	*DRL score* Less than 1.00 Higher than 1.00	*Probability of Short-term Illiquidity* Very high Unlikely
(3) Lambda Index	*Lambda score*	*Probability of Short-term Illiquidity*
	1.64	1 in 20
	3.90	1 in 20,000
	9.00 or higher	Unlikely

The DRL is a more comprehensive measure of liquidity than the current ratio or the acid-test ratio. However, like the current and the acid-test ratios, the DRL is a relative measure and should be used only in relation to either the firm's own historical DRL or to those of other businesses. Since the DRL does not incorporate the timing and variances in cash flows (assumed to be uniform and continuous), comparing the DRL of two dissimilar firms is hazardous. It is important to note that the DRL does correctly identify an improved or deteriorated liquidity position. However, it does not suggest explicit causes of change. On the other hand, the DRL provides a basis from which to pursue an analysis and interpretation of those causes of change because the derivation of the DRL requires input for all the factors relevant to liquidity position.

As with DRL, the Lambda index is a method for gauging a firm's liquidity, but one should consider a firm's historical background and always use common sense in evaluating any calculated value. A weak point of this model is that in order to calculate the index, forecasted figures must be used, making the final Lambda value somewhat suspect in some cases.

CONCLUSION

The three models discussed in this chapter all point to early signs of financial distress. It is our contention, however, that the Z-score model is a more positive predictor for bankruptcy than the other two because it covers a wider range of financial ratios, especially retained earnings divided by total assets. Note that *retained earnings* (of course, backed by a cash balance) is primarily the one that will save the company in financial trouble especially in economic hard times.

All developers of prediction models warn that the technique should be considered as just another tool of the analyst and that it is not intended to replace experienced and informed personal evaluation. Perhaps the best use of any of these models is as a "filter" to identify companies requiring further review or to establish a trend for a company over a number of years. Companies whose downward trend continues over a number of years have problems that, if caught in time, can be corrected to allow the company to survive.

CHAPTER 46

CORPORATE VALUATIONS

CONTENTS

Corporate valuation, or, broadly, *business valuation* involves estimating the worth or price of a company, its operating unit, or its ownership shares. Valuations are required when purchasing or selling businesses, performing mergers or acquisitions, engaging in buyback agreements, expanding credit lines, or dealing with particular tax matters. Valuations may be used in litigation involving partner disputes and dissenting shareholder actions or when economies of scale encourage mergers and acquisitions to help maintain market share and ensure economic stability in a recessing economy.

When buying or selling a business, a valuation can be important for establishing an asking or offering price. Valuations can determine the worth of a company by examining its assets, earnings, customer base, or reputation. Other important items to consider include a company's major activities, industry conditions, marketing requirements, management possibilities, risk factors, earnings potential, and financial health.

The National Association of Certified Valuation Analysts lists business valuation opportunities as follows:

- Buy-sell agreements.
- Mergers, acquisitions, and spinoffs.
- Liquidation or reorganization of a business.
- Initial public offerings.
- Minority shareholder interests.
- Employee stock ownership plans.
- Financing.
- Return-on-investment analysis.
- Government actions.
- Allocation of acquisition price.
- Adequacy of life insurance.
- Litigation.
- Divorce action.
- Compensatory damage cases.
- Insurance claims.
- Estate and gift taxes.
- Incentive stock options.
- Charitable contributions.

Usually, *value* is determined by an interested party. Although no single value (or worth) can be associated with a business in all situations, a defendable value can be assigned to a business in most situations. To be a proficient valuation analyst, a chief financial officer (CFO) requires analytical and writing skills. More specifically, the CFO must be adept at financial analysis, economic forecasts, accounting and auditing fundamentals, income taxes, and legal and economic research.

The valuation process is subjective, as it is based on personal perception. Nevertheless, this chapter provides basic steps involved in valuation and various ways to determine the worth of a business.

To determine a company's value, the CFO must specify the purpose of the valuation and an appropriate perspective. The perspective might be that of a buyer, a seller, the IRS, or a court. Once this is decided, the CFO performs a business appraisal. Generally, the appraisal process determines the value of a business based on an asset, earnings (or cash flows), and market approach. In valuing a business, the following factors should be considered:

- History of the business.
- Nature of the company.

- Economic and political conditions.
- Health of the industry.
- Distribution channels and marketing factors.
- Financial position.
- Degree of risk.
- Growth potential.
- Trend and stability of earnings.
- Competition.
- Employee relationships.
- Location.
- Customer base.
- Quality of management.
- Ease of transferability of ownership.

MATCHING VALUE DEFINITIONS AND REASONS FOR VALUATION

To begin the business valuation process, the CFO must match the reason for, and perspective of, the valuation with an appropriate definition of value. In a given situation, several definitions might concurrently apply. Exhibit 46-1 provides the reasons for valuation and the value definitions that may be associated with them.

Exhibit 46-1: Reasons for Valuation and Associated Definitions of Value

	Definitions of Value			
	Fair Market Value	Liquidation Value	Replacement Value	Going Concern Value
Reasons for Valuation				
Purchase of business	X		X	X
Sale of business	X			X
Shareholder litigation	X			X
Bankruptcy, dissolution		X		
Recapitalization	X			X

Individuals perceive the value of a business differently and thus disagree on how that value should be determined. As a result, the definition of value varies. Common value definitions follow.

Fair Market Value

Fair market value is generally defined as the price at which property changes hands between a willing buyer and a willing seller, when neither is compelled to act and both have a reasonable knowledge of the relevant facts. With the asset approach, assets are valued (i.e., appraised) at fair market value.

Fair market value is often an important valuation definition in estate, gift, and other federal tax-related valuations. It is a well-accepted IRS and tax court concept. Generally, these groups will consider that a company's value is equivalent to its fair market value. Accordingly, a financial manager will need to consider this definition when performing valuations that may have the IRS as an interested party.

Replacement Value

Replacement value is the cost of replacing something. The use of the definition might be applicable for establishing damages in antitrust suits or condemnation proceedings. At times, the definition is used in a federal or state court. In some situations, replacement value might be determined to be a company's fair market value.

Liquidation Value

The lowest value associated with a business is its liquidation value. Liquidation value is, in effect, the value of an item (a business) sold to the highest available bidder. Typically, the seller is compelled to sell and the buyer is aware of the seller's need to sell; therefore, liquidation value is a depressed value. For a business, assets might be sold piecemeal. Usually, liquidation value is defined as the amount received by the seller after the sale and the payment of administrative expenses. At times, a company's liquidation value could be its fair market value.

Going Concern Value

Going concern value is the opposite of liquidation value, as it is based on the presumption that the business will continue as an operating entity and therefore not be liquidated. A company's going concern value is usually its fair market value.

GENERAL APPROACHES TO BUSINESS VALUATION

When a company is not publicly traded, willing buyers and willing sellers capable of establishing an independent, objective value for a business do not exist at most times when a valuation is needed. Accordingly, an estimate of the price at which the company might change hands between a willing buyer and a willing seller must be made. To do this, one or more of the following three approaches to valuation might be used.

Market Comparison

In this approach, values of comparable companies in the industry may provide useful norms. The idea is to establish the company's value based on actual sales that are indicative of the company's current value.

A basic requirement for using prior sales of a company's ownership interests in the appraisal of its current value is that each prior sale should be indicative of the existing circumstances of the company. If prior sales were made in the too distant past, or were of a form or substance not indicative of the subject company's current situation, use of the sales may not be appropriate for establishing the company's current worth. In particular, small sales of noncontrolling interests and sales between related parties might not indicate the value of the company and its related ownership interests at the time of the sale and thus would not be indicative of the company's current value.

When comparable company sales are evaluated, the requirements are greater. Comparable company sales should be used only when sales have occurred in the recent past and are of a sufficient size to appropriately establish a supportable value. Comparable companies should be in the same industry and have similar products and services, competitive positions, financial structures, and historical financial performance. Unfortunately, finding comparable companies is difficult because closely held company operating performance and sale information is frequently unavailable. However, business sales statistics are available from companies such as BizStats (www.bizstats.com).

Earnings (or Cash Flows)

The earnings approach considers a company's value to be equivalent to its ability to create income (or cash flow). The company's income is associated with a rate of return commensurate with the company's investment risk.

Assets

The assets approach to establishing the value of a business considers the value of a company to be equivalent to the value of its net tangible assets. For the dissolution of a business, company value might be based on the liquidated value of its assets. If the company is to be duplicated, its value might be based on asset replacement values. If the company is to continue as a going concern, its value might be based on the fair market value of its assets.

PERFORMING A GENERAL ANALYSIS OF THE COMPANY BEING VALUED

For appraisal purposes, the determination of a company's value is based primarily on a market earnings and assets approach to value. Various business valuation methods are associated with each approach. To understand and apply these methods, the CFO needs to understand various attributes about the company being valued, such as the industry, customers and markets, products and services, employees and management, assets, and historical and projected financial performance. Each of these areas significantly influences a business valuation and the use of various valuation methods.

STEPS IN VALUATION

Business valuations essentially involve five steps as shown in Exhibit 46-2. These steps are discussed below.

Analyzing Historical Performance

The first step in performing any valuation is accumulating and analyzing key financial information, which includes historical financial statements, projected financial statements, and tax returns. There must be a familiarity with the business, including the company's strategic position in the industry; and major assumptions of the valuation must be clearly spelled out. A variety of what-if scenarios must be investigated to reduce valuation errors.

Projecting Future Performance

After the CFO analyzes the company's historical performance, he or she can forecast its future performance. The key to projecting performance is to develop a point of view on how the company can or will perform the key value drivers of growth and return on investment. The CFO should evaluate the company's strategic position by considering the industry characteristics as well as the company's competitive advantages or disadvantages.

Industry Outlook. In assessing a company's industry, the CFO should evaluate the economic outlook for the industry, barriers to entry, government controls, and similar items. If the industry is expected to grow, companies in the industry might be perceived as valuable. In addition, the CFO needs to consider competition. In a highly competitive industry, companies may become less valuable because of competitive pressures or price discounting.

Customers and Markets. In assessing a company's customers and markets, the CFO should evaluate the company's key customers and customer strength. If the company has many customers and none of them represents a significant percentage of company sales, the company should be considered as stable and thus have a lower associated investment risk. If the company has only a few large customers, the CFO needs to consider the implications and likelihood of a decreased customer base.

Exhibit 46-2: Steps in a Valuation

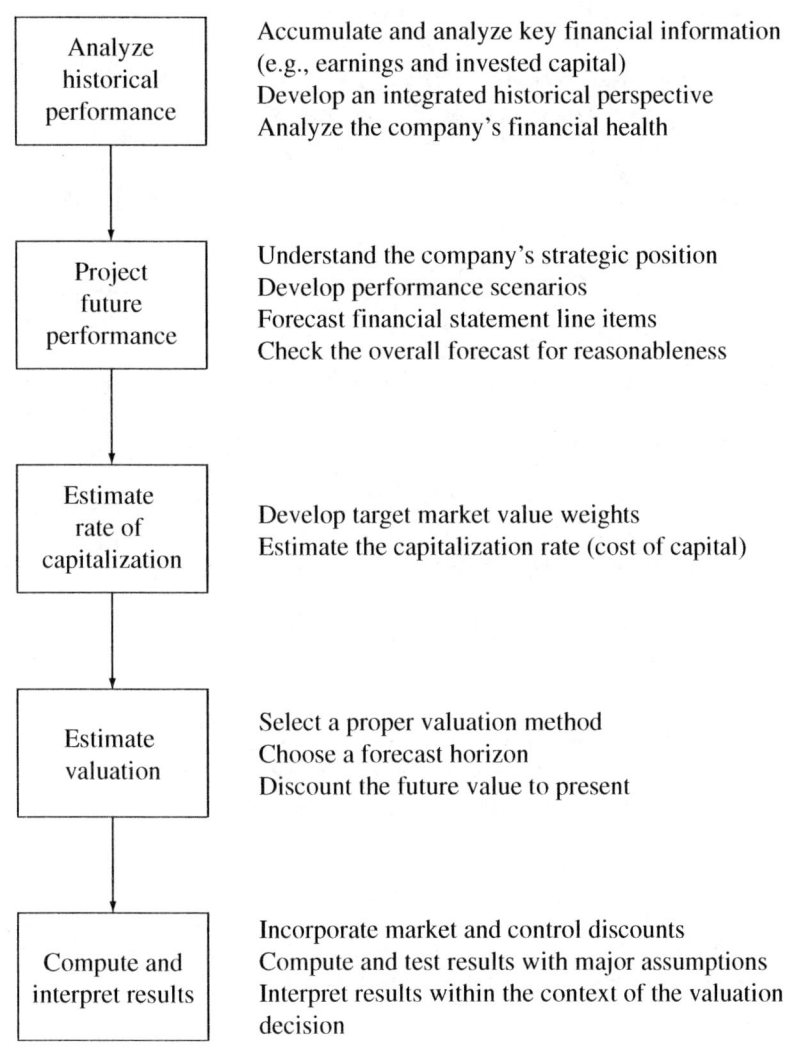

| Analyze historical performance | Accumulate and analyze key financial information (e.g., earnings and invested capital)
Develop an integrated historical perspective
Analyze the company's financial health |

| Project future performance | Understand the company's strategic position
Develop performance scenarios
Forecast financial statement line items
Check the overall forecast for reasonableness |

| Estimate rate of capitalization | Develop target market value weights
Estimate the capitalization rate (cost of capital) |

| Estimate valuation | Select a proper valuation method
Choose a forecast horizon
Discount the future value to present |

| Compute and interpret results | Incorporate market and control discounts
Compute and test results with major assumptions
Interpret results within the context of the valuation decision |

Products and Services. When evaluating a company's products and services, the CFO should inspect their quality and compare them with competitive products and services. In addition, the CFO should evaluate the company's investments in research and development and historical trends in sales and expenses of important products and services. The CFO should also consider the number of products and services the company offers and the extent to which the company relies on one or several products or services for most of its sales and profits. When a company has only one or a few products or services, the competitive risks associated with the products and services become a factor. Generally, diverse and stable product lines are associated with a stable company, and limited product lines imply an increased investment risk.

Employees and Management. Qualified management usually indicates that the company is stable. Thus, a company that employs qualified management will enhance its value. A company that has had a significant turnover in its management or employees might be considered a risky investment. In general, inexperienced management coupled with a high turnover rate is indicative of a high-risk company.

Assets. Typically, the value of a company's tangible assets is the minimum value associated with a business. For valuation purposes, a company's assets should be examined to ensure their worth. The CFO should scrutinize items such as obsolete inventory, old fixed assets, bad debts in accounts receivable, and capitalized expenses. For some assets, specific evaluations are necessary.

Historical and Projected Financial Performance. Evaluating a company's historical and projected financial performance can be time-consuming and complex. The CFO must establish the reliability of the company's historical financial statements and assess the implications of sales, expenses, and profits. Typically, for determining the value of a company, the company's operating performance should be evaluated. Accordingly, the CFO may have to remove the implications of a typical transactions and nonoperating transactions included in the company's financial statements.

A company's historical financial statements might include excess compensation and significant perks to owners. Frequently, the CFO needs to add excess compensation paid to owners back to the company's income to fully understand the profitability of the company. In addition, adjustments may need to be made to the financial statements to convert cash basis statements to accrual basis statements, as cash basis statements might not display accounts receivable, accounts payable, and accrued liabilities.

When evaluating a company's financial performance, the CFO should review expense ratios as a percent of sales and should review sales, income, and expense trends. In particular, the CFO should assess the financial statements to make assumptions about the future profitability of the company and should evaluate various company ratios and compare them with other companies in the industry. The CFO may also develop projected financial statements for the company for three or more years.

Estimating the Rate of Capitalization

Both creditors and shareholders expect to be compensated for the opportunity cost of investing their funds in one particular business instead of others with equivalent risk. The capitalization rate is used to calculate the time value of money, which, in turn, is used to convert expected future cash flow into present value for all investors. The capitalization rate (weighted-average cost of capital) is the discount rate. Estimating the weighted cost of capital involves developing market value weights and calculating the cost of each source of financing. Chapter 56, "Cost of Capital and Capital Structure Decisions," provides an in-depth discussion of this topic.

Estimating the Valuation

There are numerous ways of determining the value of a business and many possible combinations of methods. The CFO should select a proper valuation method. Popular valuation methods are discussed in the following paragraphs.

Adjusted Net Assets Method. The adjusted net assets valuation method presumes the value of a company is equivalent to the value of its net tangible assets. Asset values are often based on fair market values when the company is expected to continue as a going concern, liquidated values when the company is not expected to continue as a going concern, and replacement values when the costs of duplicating the company are being assessed.

The fair market value of a company's net tangible assets (including goodwill) may be based on an independent appraisal. For example, an investment banking firm that handles the purchase and sale of businesses may be hired to appraise the tangible property. In most cases, the fair market value of the assets exceeds their book value; for example:

Net tangible assets (at fair market value)	$12,000,000
Plus goodwill	6,000,000
Valuation	$18,000,000

An advantage of the adjusted net assets valuation method is that it is often an easy way to determine the value of a company's tangible net assets. A disadvantage of the method is that it ignores the important implications of company earnings. Therefore, in many instances, an adjusted net assets valuation is a conservative valuation because it measures the minimum value associated with a business.

Gross Revenue Multiplier Method. The value of a company may be determined on the basis of its revenue-generating capacity. For example, many Internet stocks that lose money in the short run but have great future earnings potential derive their value from their revenue-generating capacity or registered member subscriptions. The formula for this method is as follows:

Value of the business = Revenue × Gross revenue multiplier

The gross revenue multiplier that follows is customarily used in the industry. The industry norm gross multiplier is based on the average ratio of market price to sales typical in the industry. **Note:** CCH, a Wolters Kluwer business, publishes the *Almanac of Business and Industrial Financial Ratios*, by Leo Troy, which contains average industry ratios (http://CCHGroup.com/Books).

If reported earnings are suspect, this method may also be advisable.

Gross revenue	$32,500,000
× Gross revenue multiplier	.4
Valuation	$13,000,000

Capitalization of Earnings Method. The capitalization of earnings valuation method is in many ways the opposite of the adjusted net assets valuation method, as it uses income rather than assets to value a business. A variation of this method incorporates *cash flows* as opposed to earnings.

The capitalization of earnings valuation method is based on the notion that investors will acquire stock in a company only if they can earn a rate of return that is high enough to offset the risks associated with the investment. Thus, high-risk companies need to yield high rates of return to stimulate equity investments, whereas low-risk companies that produce lower rates of return still attract equity investors.

The formula for the capitalization of earnings method follows:

Value of the business = Earnings (or cash flow) ÷ Capitalization rate

Frequently, earnings or cash flow for this method is the current year's earnings (or cash flow), a simple average of two to five prior years, weighted-average adjusted historical earnings, or the company's projected profit for the following year. The method presumes the earnings value used is indicative of future earnings expectations on an ongoing basis. For this method, earnings can be one of the following:

- Before-tax earnings;

- After-tax earnings; or

- Earnings before interest and taxes (EBIT).

The capitalization rate is the rate of return an investor expects to receive for investing in the company, based on the company's perceived risk. It is typically a weighted cost of capital, with the weights being a target mix of different sources of financing, equity, or nonequity. For example:

Earnings (simple average)	$1,250,000
÷ Capitalization rate	10%
Valuation	$12,500,00

The following example uses weighted-average historical earnings, in which additional weight is given to the most recent years. The weighted average is more representative than a simple average, as current earnings reflect current prices and recent business activity. In the case of a five-year weighted average, the current year is assigned a weight of 5, and the initial year is assigned a weight of 1. The multiplier is then applied to the weighted-average, five-year adjusted historical earnings to derive a valuation.

Year	Historical Earnings	Weight	Total
2X15	$2,780,000	5	$13,900,000
2X14	$1,670,000	4	$ 6,680,000

Year	Historical Earnings	Weight	Total
2X13	$1,350,000	3	$ 4,050,000
2X12	$1,780,000	2	$ 3,560,000
2X11	$2,100,000	1	$ 2,100,000
		15	$30,290,000

Weighted-average 5-year earnings:
$30,290,000 ÷ 15 = $2,019,333

Weighted-average 5-year earnings	$ 2,019,333
÷ Capitalization rate (20%)	20%
Valuation	$10,096,667

When cash flow is used instead of earnings, it is *distributable* or *free cash flow*—a term gaining in popularity among financial analysts. Free cash flow is defined as the company's operating cash flows (before interests) *minus* cash outlays for the replacement of existing operating capacity, such as buildings, equipment, and furnishings. It is the amount available to finance planned expansion of operating capacity, to reduce debt, pay dividends, or repurchase stock.

Many analysts prefer to use accrual accounting earnings rather than cash flows in the belief that current accrual accounting earnings are more useful than measures of current cash flows in predicting future cash flows.

Price-Earnings Ratio Method. For publicly traded stocks, stock trading prices are often directly proportional to earnings. Often, within industries, there is a consistency among companies. The price-earnings ratio (P/E) method is predicated on the notion that price-earnings ratios of publicly traded stocks might be indicative of a closely held company's value. For example, if a closely held company were publicly traded, it would trade at a price similar to the price at which comparable companies trade. The formula for this method is as follows:

Value of the Business = Earnings per share ÷ Price-earnings multiplier

Typically, earnings for this method are the most recent year's earnings per share (EPS) or an average of two to five prior years. The price-earnings multiplier is usually a historical average based on comparable, actively traded stocks. A price-earnings ratio may be used based on the most current period rather than an average of prior years as follows:

Earnings after taxes	$ 1,000,000
Outstanding shares	250,000
Earnings per share	$4
P/E ratio	15
Estimated market price per share	$60
× Number of shares outstanding	250,000
Valuation	$15,000,000

Dividend Payout (or Dividend-Paying Capacity) Method. The dividend payout (or dividend-paying capacity) valuation method presumes that the compensation for stock ownership is dividends. The method is based on the notion that a stock's value is related to the company's ability to pay dividends and the yield investors expect.

The dividend payout method involves the following steps:

1. Company's dividend-paying capacity = Earnings × Dividend payout percentage

2. Value of business = Company's dividend-paying capacity ÷ Dividend yield rate

Typically, earnings for this method are an average of two to five prior years. Before-tax profits or after-tax profits may be used. The dividend payout percentage and dividend yield rate are established with reference to comparable, publicly traded stocks. A variation of this method would establish the company's dividend-paying capacity to be monies received by the owners of the closely held company as dividends, excess compensation, and perks.

Although this method is infrequently used, it incorporates some of the most defensible valuation principles of all the methods as follows:

Earnings after taxes	$1,000,000
Dividend payout percentage	40%
Dividend-paying capacity	$400,000
÷ Dividend yield rate	4%
Valuation	$10,000,000

Excess Earnings Return on Assets Method. The excess earnings return on assets valuation method implies that within an industry, a given level of company assets generate a particular level of earnings. To the extent a company has exceeded the expected level of earnings, the company is presumed to have an enhanced value. The enhanced value is attributed to goodwill (or intangible assets). The addition of the value of the goodwill and the fair market value of net tangible assets equals the total valuation.

The excess earnings return on assets method involves the following steps:

1. Industry expected earnings = Company assets × Industry expected return on assets

2. Excess earnings = Company earnings – Industry expected earnings

3. Goodwill (intangible assets) = Excess earnings ÷ Capitalization rate

4. Value of the business = Goodwill + Fair market value of net tangible assets

Regarding IRS Revenue Ruling 59-60, the IRS recommends this method to value a business for tax purposes. For example:

Year	Net Tangible Assets	Weight	Total
2X15	$10,000,000	1	$ 10,000,000
2X14	$14,000,000	2	$ 28,000,000
2X13	$18,000,000	3	$ 54,000,000
2X12	$19,000,000	4	$ 76,000,000
2X11	$18,500,000	5	$ 92,500,000
		15	$260,500,000

Weighted-average net tangible assets
$260,500,000 ÷ 15 = $17,366,667

Weighted-average earnings (5 years)— Assumed minus industry rate of return on weighted-average	$ 1,800,000
Net tangible assets ($17,366,667 × 10%)	1,736,667
Excess earnings	$ 63,333
÷ Capitalization factor (20%)	0.2
Plus goodwill (intangibles)	$ 316,667
Plus fair market value of net tangible assets	$ 16,000,000
Valuation	$ 16,316,667

Excess Earnings Return on Sales Method. The excess earnings return on sales valuation method values a company by its sales, earnings, and assets. Generally, this method implies that within an industry, a given level of sales will generate a given level of earnings. Earnings that exceed industry expectations are regarded as goodwill or intangible assets. The value of goodwill and the fair market value of net tangible assets are considered to be the value of the company.

The excess earnings return on sales method involves the following steps:

1. Industry Expected Earnings = Company Sales × Industry Expected Return on Sales

2. Excess Earnings = Company Earnings − Industry Expected Earnings

3. Goodwill (Intangible Assets) = Excess Earnings ÷ Capitalization Rate

4. Value of the Business = Goodwill + Fair Market Value of Net Tangible Assets

Variations in this method include the use of a company's current-year sales or a two- to five-year average for computing the industry's expected profits. For example:

Year	Sales	Weight	Total
2X15	$11,100,000	1	$ 11,100,000
2X14	$12,500,000	2	$ 25,000,000
2X13	$20,000,000	3	$ 60,000,000

Year	Sales	Weight	Total
2X12	$21,000,000	4	$ 84,000,000
2X11	$24,200,000	5	$121,000,000
		15	$301,100,000

Weighted-average sales
  $301,100,000 ÷ 15 = $20,073,333

Weighted-average earnings (5 years)— Assumed minus industry rate of return on weighted-average	$ 1,800,000
sales ($20,073,333 × 4%)	802,933
Excess earnings	$ 997,067
÷ Capitalization factor (20%)	0.2
Valuation of goodwill (intangibles)	$ 4,985,333
Plus fair market value of net tangible assets	$ 16,000,000
Valuation	$ 20,985,333

Discounted Cash Flow Method. The discounted cash flow (DCF) method equates the value of a business with its expected cash flows. The DCF method presumes that the purpose of a company is to generate cash flows or earnings where items, such as assets and distribution channels, are valued based on the cash flows they create.

This method is similar to the capitalization of the earnings valuation method except that in the DCF method, *projected* earnings or cash flows, as opposed to historical earnings or cash flows, are assessed. If the growth rate is used to project future earnings, the rate may be based on prior growth rate, future expectations, and inflation rate, whereas the discount rate may be based on the market interest rate of a low risk asset investment.

The formula for the discounted cash flow method follows:

Value of the business = Present value of the earnings (or cash flow) projection
    + Present value of terminal value (selling price)

Typically, cash flows are projected for at least five years, and a terminal value or selling price is established for the value of the business at the end of the term as follows:

Year	Cash Flows (7% Growth Rate)	Present Value Factor at a 10% Discount Rate	Total Present Value
2X15	$500,000	0.909	$454,500
2X14	$535,000	0.826	$441,910
2X13	$572,450	0.751	$429,910
2X12	$612,522	0.683	$418,352
2X11	$655,398	0.621	$407,002

Year	Cash Flows (7% Growth Rate)	Present Value Factor at a 10% Discount Rate	Total Present Value
Present value of future earnings			$2,151,674

If the anticipated selling price at the end of year 2X11 is $15,000,000, the valuation of the business equals:

Present value of future earnings		$2,151,674
Present value of selling price $18,000,000 × .621		$11,178,000
Valuation		$13,329,674

Abnormal Earnings Approach. The abnormal earnings approach is used when value is driven not by the level of earnings but by the level of earnings *relative to some benchmark* (i.e., the cost of capital or a minimum required rate of return). The rationale is that investors are willing to pay a premium for companies that earn more than the cost of capital, implying companies that produce *positive abnormal earnings*. The formula is

Value of the business = Book value of assets + Present value of expected future abnormal earnings (Actual earnings – Required earnings)

For example, if a company's book value of assets at the beginning of the year is $100 per share and the cost of capital is 13%, investors would require earnings of at least $13 per share ($100 × 13%). If the market expects the company to report earnings equal to benchmark earnings and the company exceeds the benchmark by earning $23 per share for the year, the value of the company (i.e., its stock price) increases to reflect its superior performance.

Combining Valuation Methods. Combining valuation methods establishes a more reasonable value for a business than any single method. In particular, earnings, assets, comparable companies, prior sales of company stock, and other important valuation concepts can be accounted for using this method.

In addition, the valuation of a company may be estimated based on the weighted-average value of several methods. The earnings method typically holds the most weight, whereas asset-type valuation methods carry the least weight. For example:

Method	Valuation Amount	Weight	Total
Adjusted net assets	$18,000,000	1	$18,000,000
Excess earnings on rate of return	$20,985,333	2	$41,970,666
		3	$59,970,666
Total/3 = $59,970,666 ÷ 3 = $19,990,222			
Valuation			$19,990,222

Generally, before a combination method is used, it should be established that the method results in a better valuation than any individual method, and that the use of each method in the combination supports the final valuation.

Earnings Surprise. Many valuation methods require estimates of future earnings, which may be misleading, resulting in an earnings surprise. For example, a positive earnings surprise (i.e., reported earnings exceed market expectations) tends to have an upward rift in stock value. Earnings estimates are reported by companies, such as *Zacks, First Call, IBES* and *Nelson's*—the leading trackers of analysis earnings projections. These companies constantly poll brokerages for their earnings estimates and publish the information, including the high, low, and mean prediction for a company's upcoming quarterly and fiscal year results.

Computing and Interpreting Results

The final phase of the valuation process involves calculating and testing the company's value, then interpreting the results in terms of the decision context involved. This phase includes incorporating market and control discounts.

Marketability Discounts. Generally, a business ownership interest that can be sold quickly is more valuable than a similar ownership interest that cannot be sold quickly. This implication may be considered in a business valuation method. When the implication is not considered, a marketability discount can be associated with the value of the ownership interest otherwise determined. A marketability discount is the reduced value of a company (or ownership interest) that takes considerable time to sell.

There are differences of opinion about marketability discounts. The IRS objects to them, arguing that the implications of marketability have been accounted for elsewhere in the valuation process. Yet, many state that statistics prove there is a depressed value for closely held company ownership interests and assign discounts as high as 25% to 45% to account for this finding.

In assigning a marketability discount, some analysts compute the cost of taking the company public and deduct the amount from the value of the company otherwise determined. The presumption is that if the company is taken public, its ownership interests will be marketable.

Control Premiums and Discounts. A business valuation does not have to be restricted to the valuation of an entire company. Frequently, partial ownership interests are valued, for example, for purchase or sale, divorce proceedings, or estate planning.

When a partial ownership interest is appraised, it is not necessarily true that its value is equivalent to its ownership percentage multiplied by the value of the company. Generally, an ownership interest has an enhanced value if it controls the activities of a company. Practitioners frequently account for this with control premiums and lack of control discounts.

For closely held companies, noncontrolling ownership interests can have a depressed value. The company might not be particularly marketable and the noncontrolling interests might be even less appealing because of their inability to influence the payment of dividends and the general operations of the company.

In developing control premiums and lack of control discounts, the circumstances of the ownership interests must be considered. Before a discount or premium is assigned, it should be determined that an ownership interest has an increased or decreased value based on control or lack of control implications. For example, in a company where the father is the controlling owner and the two children are the noncontrolling owners, circumstances indicate that the noncontrolling owners are receiving dividends commensurate with the value of their ownership percentages. Accordingly, depending on the purpose of the valuation, the assignment of a discount to the noncontrolling interests might not be appropriate. Before assigning premiums or discounts, the analyst should ensure that the control or lack of control implication is not accounted for in some other way in the valuation process.

PART VII

LIQUIDITY AND TREASURY

CHAPTER 47

WORKING CAPITAL AND CASH MANAGEMENT

CONTENTS

The ability to manage working capital will improve return and minimize the risk of running short of cash. There are various ways of managing working capital and cash to achieve success including using quantitative techniques to find optimal asset levels. The amount invested in any current asset may change daily and requires close appraisal. Improper asset management occurs when funds tied up in the asset can be used more productively elsewhere.

EVALUATING WORKING CAPITAL

Working capital equals current assets less current liabilities. Management of working capital involves regulating the various types of current assets and current liabilities. Involved are decisions on how assets should be financed (e.g., short-term debt, long-term debt, or equity). Managing working capital involves a tradeoff between return and risk. If funds go from fixed assets to current assets, there is a reduction in liquidity risk, greater ability to obtain short-term financing, and greater flexibility, because the company can more readily adjust current assets to changes in sales volume. But less of a return is earned because the yield on fixed assets is more than that on current assets. Financing with noncurrent debt has less liquidity risk than financing with current debt. However, long-term debt often has a higher cost than short-term debt because of the greater uncertainty, which detracts from the company's overall return.

What to Do: Use the hedging approach to financing where assets are financed by liabilities of similar maturity. In this way, there are adequate funds to meet debt when due. For instance, permanent assets should be financed with long-term debt instead of short-term debt.

Rule of Thumb: The longer it takes to purchase or manufacture goods, the more working capital is required. Working capital also applies to the volume of purchases and the cost per unit. For example, if the company can receive a raw material in two weeks, it needs less of an inventory level than if two months lead time is involved.

Tip: Purchase material early if materially lower prices are available and if the material's cost savings exceed inventory carrying costs.

CASH MANAGEMENT

Cash management refers to the collection, concentration, and payment of cash. Its purpose is to manage cash balances to maximize cash availability in order to avoid the risk of insolvency. Cash management is particularly important for new and growing businesses; and realistic cash flow projections are essential.

In a small company, the controller may be responsible for cash management. In a large company, cash management is typically the responsibility of the treasurer.

A centralized cash management system minimizes idle cash in the system and maximizes cash available for use. The cash management system should integrate all cash flows of the firm (e.g., domestic and international divisions and subsidiaries). A centralized system will identify situations where one subsidiary is borrowing at high interest rates while another subsidiary has excess, idle cash. The cash processes should be coordinated, such as investment, disbursement, and collection.

Cash should be made available to cash-using divisions from cash-generating ones of the company so as to keep borrowing at a minimum and to have sufficient funds available for investment. For example, foreign currency payments should be netted among divisions to eliminate currency conversion and reduce float time between operations. There should be an integration of foreign currency requirements between the parent and subsidiaries. An international company must use a bank known for quality international services including networking, cash concentration, and clearing. The financial manager should determine the average number of competitive quotations received before making a disbursement in a foreign country.

The purpose of cash management is to invest excess cash for a return and at the same time have adequate liquidity to meet future needs. A proper cash balance should exist, neither excessive nor deficient. For example, companies with many bank accounts may be accumulating excessive balances. Do you know how much cash you need, how much you have, where the cash is, what the sources of cash are, and where the cash will be used?

This is particularly crucial in recession. Proper cash forecasting is required to determine: (1) the optimal time to incur and pay back debt and (2) the amount to transfer daily between accounts. A daily computerized listing of cash balances and transaction reporting should be prepared. This lets the financial officer know the up-to-date cash balance so a decision can be made where it is best to put the funds into use. A listing of daily transactions enables one to find out if any problems exist so immediate rectification may be made.

Recommendation: The financial manager should establish, control, and report bank accounts, services, and activities. Are banking services cost effective? Analyze each bank account as to type, balance, and cost. What is the processing cost for checks, bank transfers, and direct debits? The adequacy of controls for intercompany transactions and transfers should be reviewed. When cash receipts and cash payments are highly synchronized and predictable, the company may keep a smaller cash balance. If quick liquidity is needed, invest in marketable securities.

General Rule: Additional cash should be invested in income-producing securities with maturities structured to provide the necessary liquidity.

Companies that arc strong financially and able to borrow at favorable rates even in problem financial markets can afford a lower level of cash and cash equivalents than companies that are highly leveraged or considered poor credit risks.

A high-tech company may want to have more cash on hand to weather unforeseen occurrences or problems in the financial markets. A company in a mature industry could have minimal cash on hand with short-term cash requirements met through short-term borrowing.

The minimum cash to hold is the greater of: (1) compensating balances (a deposit held by a bank to compensate it for providing services), or (2) precautionary balances (money held for emergency purposes) plus transaction balances (money to cover checks outstanding). The firm must hold enough cash to meet its daily requirements.

Factors in Determining the Amount of Cash to Be Held

- Use of effective cash management.
- Asset size.
- Financial philosophy and strength.
- Utility preferences regarding liquidity and business risks.
- Expected future cash flows, considering the probabilities of different cash flows under alternative circumstances. Because cash forecasting may result in errors, there should be some excess cash on hand or short-term debt capacity to cover such eventuality.

- Maturity period of debt.
- Ability to borrow on short notice and on favorable terms.
- Return rates.
- Possibility of unexpected problems (e.g., customer defaults).

Less cash needs to be kept on hand when a company can borrow quickly from a bank, such as under a line of credit agreement, which permits a firm to borrow instantly up to a specified maximum amount. However, make sure the line of credit is not excessive because of the associated commitment fee on the unused line (if any).

Watch the amount of the compensating balance, since the portion of a loan that serves as collateral is restricted and unavailable for corporate use. Are compensating balances too costly? Often, keeping compensating balances is more costly than paying fees for banking services provided. Is cash unnecessarily tied up in other accounts (e.g., loans to employees, insurance deposits)?

Warning: Liquid asset holdings are required during a downturn in a company's cycle, when funds from operations decline.

Excess cash should be invested in marketable securities for a return. Automatic short-term money market investments mean that excess cash is immediately deposited in money market securities so a return is earned on the funds. Holding marketable securities serves as protection against cash shortages. Companies with seasonal operations may purchase marketable securities when they have excess funds and then sell the securities when cash deficits occur. A firm may also invest in marketable securities when funds are being held temporarily in expectation of short-term capital expansion. In selecting an investment portfolio, consideration should be given to return, default risk, marketability, and maturity date.

Coupon and security collection is needed to assure that any interest the company is entitled to is gotten and that securities maturing or sold are properly collected and deposited.

Recommendation: Do not seek to fund peak seasonal cash requirements internally. Rather, borrow on a short-term basis to enable internal funds to be used more profitably throughout the year, such as by investing in plant and equipment. The thrust of cash management is to accelerate cash receipts and delay cash payments.

Acceleration of Cash Inflow

You should evaluate the causes and take corrective action for delays in having cash receipts deposited.

What to Do: Ascertain how and where cash receipts come, how cash is transferred from outlying accounts to the main corporate account, banking policy regarding availability of funds, and time lag between receiving a check and depositing it.

Types of Delays in Processing Checks
- Mail float—the time required for a check to move from debtor to creditor.
- Processing float—the time needed for the creditor to enter the payment.
- Deposit collection float—the time for a check to clear.

Exhibit 47-1 depicts the total float of a check.

Means of Accelerating Cash Receipts
- Use a lockbox arrangement where the optimum collection point is placed near customers. Customer payments are mailed to strategic post office boxes geographically situated to hasten mailing and depositing time. Banks collect from these boxes several times a day and make deposits to the corporate account. A computer listing is prepared of payments received by account and a daily total.

  Recommendation: Undertake a cost-benefit analysis to ensure that instituting a lockbox arrangement will result in net savings. Determine the average face value of checks received, cost of operations eliminated, reducible processing overhead, and reduction in mail float days. Because per-item processing cost is typically significant, it is most advantageous to use a lockbox when low-volume, high-dollar collections are involved. But the system is becoming increasingly more available to firms with high-volume, low-dollar receipts as technological advances (such as machine-readable documents) lower the per-item cost of lockboxes.

Exhibit 47-1: Float Due to a Check Issued and Mailed by Payer to Payee

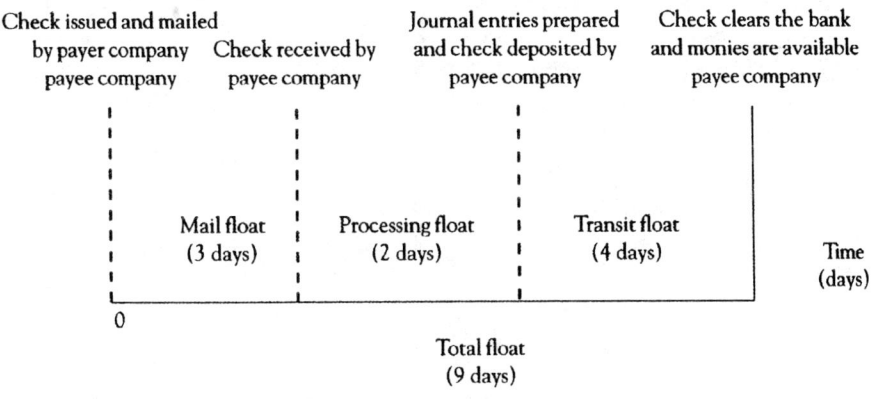

Tip: Compare the return earned on freed cash to the cost of the lockbox arrangement. A wholesale lockbox is used for checks received from other companies. The average cash receipt is large and the number of cash receipts is small. The bank prepares an electronic list of payments received and transmits the information to the company. A wholesale lockbox system aids in internal control because there is a separation between billing and receivables processing. Many wholesale lockboxes result only in mail time reductions of no more than one business day, and check clearing time reductions of only a few tenths of one day. Wholesale lockboxes are beneficial for companies with gross revenues of several million dollars or more. It is best when large checks are received from distant customers. A retail lockbox is best if the company is dealing with the public (retail consumers as distinguished from companies). Retail lockboxes typically have many transactions of a nominal amount. The lockbox reduces float and transfers workload from the company to the bank. The net effect should be improved cash flow and a reduction in expenses. In general, remittances are processed in an automated environment.

- Take advantage of concentration banking, where funds are collected in local banks and transferred to a main concentration account.

- Identify and monitor changes in collection patterns. Determine the reasons for any delays.

- On the return envelope for customer remission, use bar codes, nine-digit code numbers, and post office box numbers.

  Note: Accelerated Reply Mail (ARM) is the assignment of a unique "truncating" ZIP code to payments, such as lockbox receivables. The coded remittances are removed from the postal system and processed by banks or third parties.

- Send customers preaddressed, stamped envelopes.

- Obtain approval from a customer to have a preauthorized debit (PAD) automatically charged to the customer's bank account for repetitive charges. An example is an insurance company that has PADs charged to its policyholders for insurance premiums. These debits may take the form of paper preauthorized checks (PACs) or paperless automatic clearing house entries. PADs are cost effective because they avoid the process of billing a customer, receiving and processing a payment, and depositing a check.

  Note: Variable payments are not as efficient as fixed payments because the amount of the PAD must be changed each period and typically the customer must be advised by mail of the amount of the debit. PADs are best for constant, relatively nominal periodic (e.g., monthly, semiweekly) payments.

Transfer funds between banks by wire transfers or depository transfer checks (DTCs). Wire transfers may be used for intracompany transactions. Wire transfers may be made by computer terminal and telephone. A wire transfer allows for the same-day transfer of funds. It should be made only for significant dollar amounts because of the cost, since per-wire-transfer fees are assessed by both the originating bank and the receiving bank. Wire transfers are best for intraorganization transfers. Examples include making transfers to and from investments, placing funds in an account the day checks are expected to clear, and putting funds in any other account that requires immediate availability of funds. Two types of wire transfers are preformatted (recurring) and free-form (nonrepetitive). With preformatted wire transfers, there is not extensive authorization. This type is suitable for typical transfers such as for investments and other company accounts. The company specifies an issuing bank and a receiving bank along with the account number. There is greater control for nonrecurring transfers. The control includes written confirmation instead of confirmation only from telephone or computer terminal. Wire transfers may also be used to fund other types of checking accounts, such as payroll accounts. In order to control balances in the account, the account may be funded on a staggered basis. However, to prevent an overdraft, make sure balances are maintained in another account at the bank.

Paper or paperless depository transfer checks may be used to transfer funds between the company's bank accounts. No signature is required on depository transfer checks but of course the check is payable to the bank for credit to the company's account. However, control must exist to assure that an employee does not use depository transfer checks to transfer funds from an account on which he or she does not have signature authorization to an account in which he or she does. Depository transfer checks typically clear in one day. If manual depository transfer checks are used, preprinted checks include all information except the amount and date. Manual preparation is advisable if there are only a few checks prepared daily. If there are automated depository transfer checks, they are printed as needed.

Tip: Usually it is best to use the bank's printer since it is not cost effective for the company to purchase the printer. Automatic check preparation is advisable only when a large number of transfer checks are to be prepared daily.

- Accelerate billing.

- Require deposits on large or custom orders or progress billings as the work progresses.

- Charge interest on accounts receivable after a certain amount of time.

- Use personal collection efforts.

- Offer discounts for early payment.

- Have postdated checks for customers.

- Have cash-on-delivery terms.

- Deposit checks immediately.

- Make repeated collection calls and visits.

EXAMPLE 1: The financial officer is determining whether to initiate a lockbox arrangement that will cost $150,000 annually. The daily average collections are $700,000. The system will reduce mailing and processing time by two days. The rate of return is 14%.

Return on freed cash (14% × 2 × $700,000)	$196,000
Annual cost	150,000
Net advantage of lockbox system	$ 46,000

EXAMPLE 2: You currently have a lockbox arrangement with Bank A in which it handles $5 million a day in return for an $800,000 compensating balance. You are thinking of canceling this arrangement and further dividing your western region by entering into contracts with two other banks. Bank B will handle $3 million a day in collections with a compensating balance of $600,000. Collections will be half a day quicker than the current situation. Your return rate is 12%.

Accelerated cash receipts ($5 million per day × 0.5 day)	$2,500,000
Increased compensating balance	500,000
Improved cash flow	$2,000,000
Rate of return	× 0.12
Net annual savings	$ 240,000

Delay of Cash Outlay

The company should delay cash payments to earn a greater return. Evaluate who the payees are and to what extent one can reasonably stretch time limits.

Ways of Delaying Cash Payments

- Centralize the payables operation so that debt may be paid at the most profitable time and so that the amount of disbursement float in the system may be ascertained.

- Have zero balance accounts where zero balances are established for all of the company's disbursing units. These accounts are in the same concentration bank. Checks are drawn against these accounts, with the balance in each account never exceeding $0. Divisional disbursing authority is thus maintained at the local level of management. The advantages of zero balance accounts are better control over cash payments, reduction in excess cash balances held in regional banks, and a possible increase in disbursing float. Under the zero balance account concept the company only puts funds into its payroll and payables checking accounts when it expects checks to clear. This is an aggressive strategy.

  Caution: Watch out for overdrafts and service charges. In a zero balance account (ZBA) system, the bank automatically transfers funds from a master (concentration) account as checks are presented against the payroll and payables accounts. Therefore, payroll and payable accounts are retained at zero balances. Under ZBA, the financial manager does not have to anticipate clearing times on each account.

- Make partial payments.

- Request additional information about an invoice before approving it for payment.

- Use payment drafts, where payment is not made on demand. Instead, the draft is presented for collection to the bank, which in turn goes to the issuer for acceptance. A draft may be used to provide for inspection before payment. When approved, the company deposits the funds.

  Net Result: Less of a checking balance is required.

  Note: The use of drafts may require bank charges (e.g., fixed monthly fee) and the inconvenience of always having to approve the draft formally before payment.

- Draw checks on remote banks (e.g., a New York company using a Texas bank).

- Mail from post offices with limited service or where mail has to go through numerous handling points.

  Tip: If you utilize float properly you can maintain higher bank balances than the actual lower book balances. For instance, if you write checks averaging $200,000 per day and three days are necessary for them to clear, you will have a checking balance that is $600,000 less than the bank's records.

- Use probability analysis to determine the expected date for checks to clear.

  Suggestion: Have separate checking accounts (e.g., payroll, dividends) and monitor check clearing dates. For example, payroll checks are not all cashed on the payroll date, so funds can be deposited later to earn a return.

- Use a computer terminal to transfer funds between various bank accounts at opportune times.

- Use a charge account to lengthen the time between buying goods and paying for them.

- Stretch payments provided there is no associated finance charge or impairment in credit rating.

- Do not pay bills before the due date.

- Utilize noncash compensation and remuneration methods (e.g., stock).

- Delay the frequency of payments to employees (e.g., expense account reimbursements, payrolls).

- Disburse commissions on sales when the receivables are collected rather than when sales are made.

A cash management system is shown in Exhibit 47-2.

   EXAMPLE 3: Every two weeks the company disburses checks that average $500,000 and take three days to clear. The financial manager wants to find out how much money can be saved annually if the transfer of funds is delayed from an interest-bearing account that pays 0.0384% per day (annual rate of 14%) for those three days.

$$\$500{,}000 \times (0.000384 \times 3) = \$576$$

The savings per year is $\$578 \times 26$ (yearly) $= \$14{,}976$

The disbursement of cash is improved if based on controlled disbursement when the amount of money to be deposited on a daily basis to pay checks clearing that day is determined. Other effective means to disbursed cash are using a positive pay service to reduce the incidence of fraud, and using an accounts receivable reconcilement service.

Cash Models

William Baumol developed a model to determine the optimum amount of transaction cash under conditions of certainty. The objective is to minimize the sum of the fixed costs of transactions and the opportunity cost of holding cash balances. These costs are expressed as:

$$F \times \frac{(T)}{(C)} + i \frac{(C)}{2}$$

where

F = the fixed cost of a transaction

T = the total cash needed for the time period involved

i = the interest rate on marketable securities

C = cash balance

The optimal level of cash is determined using the following formula:

$$\frac{C^*}{2} = \frac{\$400{,}000}{2} = \$200{,}000$$

Exhibit 47-2: Cash Management System

Acceleration of cash receipts	Delay of cash payments
Lockbox system	Pay by draft
Concentration banking	Requisition more frequently
Preauthorized checks	Disburse float
Preaddressed stamped envelopes	Make partial payments
Obtain deposits on large orders	Use charge accounts
Charge interest on overdue receivables	Delay frequency of paying employees

A helpful graph follows:

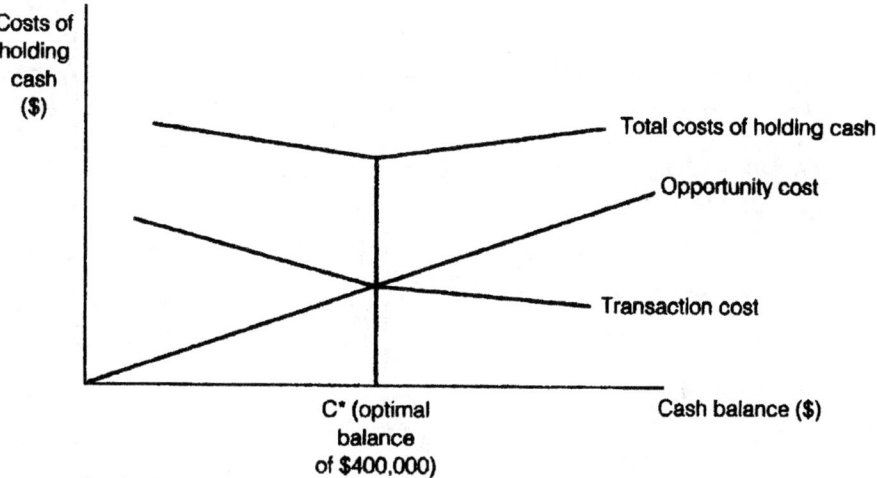

EXAMPLE 4: You estimate a cash need for $4,000,000 over a one-month period where the cash account is expected to be disbursed at a constant rate. The opportunity interest rate is 6% per annum, or 0.5% for a one-month period. The transaction cost each time you borrow or withdraw is $100. The optimal transaction size (the optimal borrowing or withdrawal lot size) and the number of transactions you should make during the month follow:

$$C^* = \sqrt{\frac{2FT}{i}} = \sqrt{\frac{2(100)(4,000,000)}{0.005}} = \$400,000$$

The optimal transaction size is $400,000.

The average cash balance is:

$$\frac{C^*}{2} = \frac{\$400,000}{2} = \$200,000$$

The number of transactions required is:

$$\frac{\$4,000,000}{\$400,000} = 10 \text{ transactions during the month}$$

You can use a stochastic model for cash management where major uncertainty exists regarding cash payments. The Miller-Orr model places an upper and lower limit for cash balances. When the upper limit is reached, a transfer of cash to marketable securities is made. When the lower limit is reached, a transfer from securities to cash takes place. A transaction will not occur as long as the cash balance falls within the limits.

Factors taken into account in the Miller-Orr model are the fixed costs of a securities transaction (F), assumed to be the same for buying as well as selling, the daily interest rate on marketable securities (i), and the variance of daily net cash flows (σ^2). The objective is to meet cash requirements at the lowest possible cost. A major assumption is the randomness of cash flows. The two control limits in the Miller-Orr model may be specified as d dollars at the upper limit and zero dollars at the lower limit. When the cash balance reaches the upper level, d less z dollars of securities are bought and the new balance becomes z dollars. When the cash balance equals zero, z dollars of securities are sold and the new balance again reaches z. Of course, practically speaking, you should note that the minimum cash balance is established at an amount greater than zero due to delays in transfer as well as to having a safety buffer.

The optimal cash balance z is computed as follows:

$$z = \sqrt[3]{\frac{3F\sigma^2}{4i}}$$

The optimal value for d is computed as $3z$.

The average cash balance will approximate $\dfrac{(z + d)}{3}$

EXAMPLE 5: You wish to use the Miller-Orr model. The following information is supplied:

Fixed cost of a securities transaction	$10
Variance of daily net cash flows	$50
Daily interest rate on securities (10.8%/360)	0.0003

The optimal cash balance, the upper limit of cash needed, and the average cash balance follow:

$$z = \sqrt[3]{\frac{3(10)(50)}{4(0.0003)}} = \sqrt[3]{\frac{3(10)(50)}{.0012}} = \sqrt[3]{\frac{1,500}{0.0012}} = \sqrt[3]{1,250,000}$$

The optimal cash balance is $108.

The upper limit is $324 (3 × $108).

The average cash balance is $136 $\dfrac{\$108 + \$324}{3}$

A brief elaboration of these findings is needed for clarification. When the upper limit of $324 is reached, $216 of securities ($324 – $108) will be purchased to bring you to the optimal cash balance of $144. When the lower limit of zero dollars is reached, $108 of securities will be sold to again bring you to the optimal cash balance of $108.

An informative graph follows.

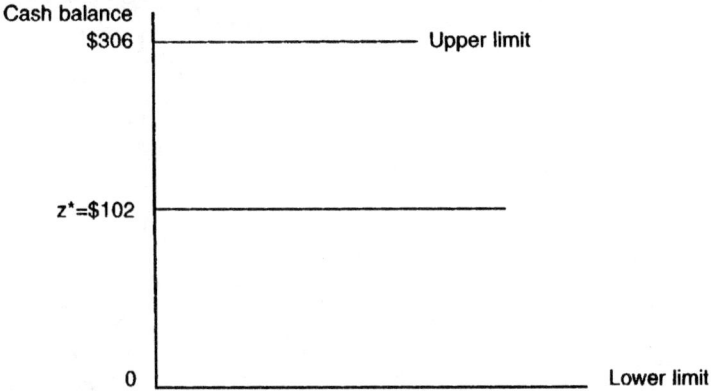

BANKING RELATIONSHIPS

The company may want to restrict the maximum total deposits at particular banks having financial problems to no more than the insurance provided by the Federal Deposit Insurance Corporation for commercial banks or the Federal Savings and Loan Insurance Corporation for savings and loan institutions.

Note: With a checking account, the maximum deposit may be exceeded on the bank's records but not on the company's books due to the clearing time required for checks and concentration entries.

A maximum deposit should be determined to keep at specific banks, which exceeds the insurance limit. Deposits of unlimited amounts should be authorized at given financial institutions.

Different banks can be used for different services depending on what is best for the company. In selecting a bank, the following should be considered:

- Location (affects lockboxes and disbursement points).
- Type and cost of services.
- Availability of funds.

An appraisal should be made of the financial soundness of the bank. Here, reference may be made to ratings provided by services tracking banks.

Undertake a bank account analysis by comparing the value of the company balance maintained at the bank to the service charges. Banks will provide such analysis, if you wish, but the bank's analysis must be closely scrutinized.

A balance reporting system may be used where the lead bank gathers relevant and essential information for all other banks. The information may then be transferred to the company via telecommunications. The cost effectiveness of the system should be evaluated periodically.

Most checks clear in one business day. Clearing time of three or more business days is rare. Try to arrange for the financial institution to give same-day credit on a deposit received prior to a specified cut-off time. However, if the deposit is made over the counter with a letter, immediate availability of those funds may not be received. However, if the deposit is made early enough, especially through a lock-box, immediate availability of those funds may be received.

It is usually financially better to pay a higher deposited item charge in return for accelerated availability of funds.

In doing an account reconciliation, the bank sorts checks into serial number order, lists all checks cleared, and matches issued checks provided by the company to paid checks so as to list outstanding checks and exception items. One purpose is to reconcile the cash balances on deposit at various banks for control purposes. If voluminous checks are issued, the services are cost effective.

A bank reconciliation is prepared by the company of each bank account to ensure the balance per books equals the balance per bank after adjusting for reconciling items. The bank reconciliation is done as an internal control of cash.

COUNTERPARTY RISK

Counterparty (default) risk is the risk to each contract participant that the counterparty will not abide by its commitments. Such risk applies to each individual or entity in an agreement such as a sales contract. Counterparty risk may be controlled by using a central counterparty.

In counterparty risk there is the risk that a company will not pay a bond, credit derivative, or other kind of transaction. It is also conceivable that a company that has bought credit insurance still has the risk that the insurer itself will not be able to pay because of financial difficulties.

An example of counterparty risk is when company X lends money to company Y. The default risk is that company Y will not pay back the loan or company X will stop providing additional loans. Another example is when a company fails to provide agreed-upon securities.

CHAPTER 48

MANAGEMENT OF ACCOUNTS RECEIVABLE

CONTENTS

Credit management falls under the responsibility of the controller or treasurer. Accounts receivable management directly impacts the profitability of the firm. It considers discount policy, whether to extend credit to marginal customers, ways of speeding up collections and reducing bad debts, and setting terms.

The financial manager should appraise order entry, billing, and accounts receivable activities to assure proper procedures and controls from the time an order is received until ultimate collection. What is the average time lag between completing the sales transaction and invoicing the customer?

Accounts receivable management involves two types of float-invoicing and mail. Invoicing float is the days between the time goods are shipped to the customer and the time the invoice is rendered. The company should mail invoices out on a timely basis. Mail float is the time between the preparation of an invoice and the time it is received by the customer. This mail float may be reduced by the following:

- Decentralizing invoicing and mailing.
- Coordinating outgoing mail with post office schedules.
- Using express mail services for large invoices.
- Enforcing due dates.
- Offering discounts.

In managing accounts receivable, the financial manager should consider that there is an opportunity cost associated with holding receivables. The opportunity cost is tying up money in accounts receivable resulting in losing the return that could be earned on having those funds invested elsewhere. Therefore, means to analyze and expedite collections should be undertaken.

A key concern is the amount and credit terms given to customers since this will affect sales volume and collections. For example, a longer credit term will probably result in increased sales. The credit terms have a direct bearing on the costs and revenue generated from receivables. If credit terms are tight, there will be less investment in accounts receivable and less bad debt losses, but there will also be lower sales, reduced profits, and adverse customer reaction. On the other hand, if credit terms are lax, there will be higher sales and gross profit but greater bad debts and a higher opportunity cost of carrying the investment in accounts receivable because marginal customers take longer to pay. Receivable terms should be liberalized when you want to get rid of excessive inventory or items near obsolescence. Longer receivable terms are appropriate for industries in which products are sold in advance of retail seasons (e.g., swimsuits). If products are perishable, short receivable terms or even payment on delivery is recommended.

In evaluating a potential customer's ability to pay, consider the customer's integrity, financial soundness, and collateral to be pledged. A customer's credit soundness may be appraised through quantitative techniques such as regression analysis. Such techniques are most useful when a large number of small customers are involved. Bad debt losses can be estimated reliably when a company sells to many customers and when its credit policies have not changed for a long time.

The financial manager has to consider the costs of giving credit including administrative costs of the credit department, computer services, fees to rating agencies, and periodic field investigations.

CREDIT REFERENCES

Reference may be made to retail credit bureaus and professional credit reference services in appraising a customer's ability to pay. One service is Dun and Bradstreet (D&B), which rates companies. D&B reports contain information about a company's nature of business, product line, management, financial statement information, number of employees, previous payment history as reported by suppliers, amounts currently owed and past due, terms of sale, audit opinion, lawsuits, insurance coverage, leases, criminal proceedings, banking relationships and account information (e.g., current bank loans), location of business, and seasonality aspects.

SETTING ACCOUNTS RECEIVABLE STANDARDS

To monitor and improve accounts receivable functional activities, we can establish unit credit standards to be accomplished. For invoice preparation, unit cost standards might be based on cost per invoice, order, or item. For credit investigation and approval, unit cost standards may include cost per account, sales order, or credit sales transaction. In looking at credit correspondence records, we may use cost per sales order, account sold, or letter. In terms of preparing customer statements, unit cost standards may be in terms of cost per statement or account sold. The standard for the computation of commissions on cash collections may be based on cost per remittance.

MONITORING RECEIVABLES

There are many ways to optimize profitability from accounts receivable and keep losses to a minimum. These include:

- "Cycle bill" to produce greater uniformity in the billing process.
- Mail customer statements within 24 hours of the close of the accounting period.
- Send an invoice to customers when the order is processed at the warehouse instead of when merchandise is shipped.
- Bill for services periodically when work is performed or charge a retainer.

  Tip: Bill large sales immediately.

- Use seasonal datings.

  Recommendation: When business is slow, sell to customers with delayed payment terms to stimulate demand for customers who are unable to pay until later in the season.

  What to Do: Compare profitability on incremental sales plus the reduction in inventory carrying costs, which have to exceed the opportunity cost on the additional investment in average accounts receivable.

- Carefully analyze customer financial statements before giving credit. Also, obtain ratings from financial advisory sources.
- Avoid typically high-risk receivables (e.g., customers in a financially troubled industry or region). Be careful of accounts in business less than one year (about 50% of businesses fail within the first two years).
- Modify credit limits based on changes in customer's financial health.
- Ask for collateral in support of questionable accounts.

  Tip: The collateral value should equal or exceed the account balance.

- Factor accounts receivable when net savings ensue. However, beware that confidential information may be disclosed.
- Use outside collection agencies where warranted.
- Consider marketing factors, since a stringent credit policy might result in a loss of business.
- Note that consumer receivables have greater risk of default than corporate receivables.
- Age accounts receivable to spot delinquent customers. Interest should be charged on such accounts. Aged receivables can be compared to prior years, industry norms, and competition. Bad Debt Loss Reports should be prepared showing cumulative bad debt losses detailed by customer, terms

of sale, size of account, and summarized by department, product line, and type of customer (e.g., industry).

Note: Bad debt losses are typically higher for smaller companies than for larger ones. Of course, the company should charge back to the salesperson the commission already paid on an uncollectible account.

- Accelerate collections from customers currently having financial problems. Also, withhold products or services until payment is made.

- Have credit insurance to guard against unusual bad debt losses.

  What to Consider: In deciding whether to get this insurance, take into account expected average bad debt losses, financial capability of the firm to withstand the losses, and the cost of insurance.

- Keep track of customer complaints about order item and invoice errors and orders not filled on time.

- Look at the relationship of credit department costs to credit sales.

The collection period for accounts receivable partly depends on corporate policy and conditions. In granting trade credit, competition and economic conditions have to be taken into account. In recession, the financial manager may relax the credit policy because additional business is needed. For example, the company may not rebill customers who take a cash discount even after the discount period has elapsed. On the contrary, in times of short supply, credit policy may be tightened because the seller is at an advantage.

Attributes of a Good Credit System

- Clear, quick, and uniform in application.

- Does not intrude on customer's privacy.

- Inexpensive (e.g., centralization of credit decisions by experienced staff).

- Based upon past experience, considering characteristics of good, questionable, and bad accounts.

  Tip: Determine the correlation between customer characteristics and future uncollectibility.

THE INVESTMENT IN ACCOUNTS RECEIVABLE

The financial executive often has to determine the dollar investment tied up in accounts receivable.

> **EXAMPLE 1:** A company sells on terms of net/30. The accounts are on average 20 days past due. Annual credit sales are $600,000. The investment in accounts receivable is:

$$\frac{50}{360} \times \$600,000 = \$83,333.28$$

EXAMPLE 2: The cost of a product is 30% of selling price, and the cost of capital is 10% of selling price. On average, accounts are paid four months after sale. Average sales are $70,000 per month.

The investment in accounts receivable from this product is:

Accounts receivable (4 months × $70,000)	$280,000
Investment in accounts receivable [$280,000 × (0.30 + 0.10)]	112,000

EXAMPLE 3: You have accounts receivable of $700,000. The average manufacturing cost is 40% of the sales price. The before-tax profit margin is 10%. The carrying cost of inventory is 3% of selling price. The sales commission is 8% of sales. The investment in accounts receivable is:

$$\$700,000\ (0.40 + 0.03 + 0.08) = \$700,000\ (0.51) = \$357,000$$

DISCOUNT POLICY

Should customers be offered a discount for the early payment of account balances? The financial manager has to compare the return on freed cash resulting from the customer's paying sooner to the cost of the discount.

EXAMPLE 4:

The following data are provided:

Current annual credit sales	$14,000,000
Collection period	3 months
Terms	net/30
Minimum rate of return	15%

The company is considering offering a 3/10, net/30 discount. We expect 25% of the customers to take advantage of it. The collection period will decline to two months.

The discount should be offered, as indicated in the following calculations:

Advantage

Increased profitability:

Average accounts receivable balance before a change in policy:

$$\frac{\text{Credit sales}}{\text{Accounts receivable turnover}} = \frac{\$14,000,000}{4} = \$3,500,000$$

Average accounts receivable balance after change in policy:

$$\frac{\text{Credit sales}}{\text{Accounts receivable turnover}} = \frac{\$14,000,000}{6} = \underline{\$2,333,333}$$

Reduction in average accounts receivable balance	$1,116,667
Rate of return	× .15
Return	$175,000

Disadvantage

Cost of the discount 0.30 × 0.25 × $14,000,000	$105,000
Net advantage of discount	$70,000

CREDIT POLICY

Should the company give credit to marginal customers? We have to compare the earnings on sales obtained to the added cost of the receivables.

Note: If the company has idle capacity, the additional earnings equal the contribution margin on the incremental sales because fixed costs are constant. The additional cost on the additional receivables results from the greater number of bad debts and the opportunity cost of tying up funds in receivables for a longer time period.

EXAMPLE 5:

Sales price per unit	$120
Variable cost per unit	80
Fixed cost per unit	15
Annual credit sales	$600,000
Collection period	1 month
Minimum return	16%

If you liberalize the credit policy, you project that

- Sales will increase by 40%.

- The collection period on total accounts will be two months.

- Bad debts on the increased sales will be 5%.

Preliminary calculations:

Current units ($600,000/$120)	5000
Additional units (5,000 × 0.4)	2000

The new average unit cost is now calculated:

	Units	×	Unit cost	=	Total cost
Current units	5,000	×	$95		$475,000
Additional units	2,000	×	$80		160,000
Total	7,000				$635,000

$$\text{New average unit cost} = \frac{\text{Total cost}}{\text{Units}} = \frac{\$635,000}{7,000} = \underline{\$90.71}$$

Note that at idle capacity, fixed cost remains constant. Thus, the incremental cost is only the variable cost of $80 per unit. This will cause the new average unit cost to drop.

Advantage

Additional profitability:

Incremental sales volume	2,000 units
× Contribution margin per unit (Selling price – variable cost)	
$120 – $80	× $40
Incremental profitability	$80,000

Disadvantage

Incremental bad debts:	
Incremental units × Selling price 2,000 × $120	$240,000
Bad debt percentage	× 0.05
Additional bad debts	$12,000

Opportunity cost of funds tied up in accounts receivable:

Average investment in accounts receivable after change in policy:

$$\frac{\text{Credit sales}}{\text{Accounts receivable turnover}} \times \frac{\text{Unit cost}}{\text{Selling price}}$$

$$\frac{\$840,000^{a}}{6} \times \frac{\$90.71}{\$120} \qquad \$105,828$$

^{a} 7,000 units × $120 = $840,000

Current average investment in accounts receivable:

$$\frac{\$600,000}{12} \times \frac{\$95}{\$120} \qquad \qquad 39,583$$

Additional investment in accounts receivable	$ 66,245
Minimum return	× 0.16
Opportunity cost of funds tied up	$ 10,599

Net advantage of relaxation in credit standards:

Additional earnings		$ 80,000
Less:		
Additional bad debt losses	$12,000	
Opportunity cost	10,599	22,599
Net savings		$ 57,401

The company may have to decide whether to extend full credit to presently limited credit customers or no-credit customers. Full credit should be given only if net profitability occurs.

EXAMPLE 6:

Category	Bad Debt Percentage	Collection Period	Credit Policy	Increase in Annual Sales if Credit Restrictions Are Relaxed
X	2%	30 days	Unlimited	$ 80,000
Y	5%	40 days	Restricted	600,000
Z	30%	80 days	No Credit	850,000

Gross profit is 25% of sales. The minimum return on investment is 12%.

	Category Y	Category Z
Gross profit		
$600,000 × .25	$150,000	
$850,000 × .25		$212,500
Less bad debts		
$600,000 × .05	−30,000	
$850,000 × .30		−255,000
Incremental average investment in accounts receivable		
$\frac{40}{360}$ × (0.75 × $600,000)	$50,000	
$\frac{80}{360}$ × (0.75 × $850,000)		$141,667
Opportunity cost of incremental investment in accounts receivable	× 0.12 −6,000	× 0.12 −17,000
Net earnings	$114,000	$(59,500)

Credit should be extended to category Y.

EXAMPLE 7: You are considering liberalizing the credit policy to encourage more customers to purchase on credit. Currently, 80% of sales are on credit and there is a gross margin of 30%. Other relevant data are:

	Current	**Proposal**
Sales	$300,000	$450,000
Credit sales	240,000	360,000
Collection expenses	4% of credit sales	5% of credit sales
Accounts receivable turnover	4.5	3

An analysis of the proposal yields the following results:

Average accounts receivable balance (Credit sales/accounts receivable turnover)

Expected average accounts receivable $360,000/3	$120,000
Current average accounts receivable $240,000/4.5	53,333
Increase	$66,667

Gross profit:

Expected increase in credit sales ($360,000 – $240,000)	$120,000
Gross profit rate	× 0.30
Increase	$36,000

Collection expenses:

Expected collection expenses 0.05 × $360,000	$18,000
Current collection expenses 0.04 × $240,000	9,600
Increase	$9,600

You would benefit from a more liberal credit policy.

EXAMPLE 8: The company is planning a sales campaign in which it will offer credit terms of 3/10, net/45. We expect the collection period to increase from 60 days to 80 days. Relevant data for the contemplated campaign follow:

	Percent of Sales Before Campaign	**Percent of Sales During Campaign**
Cash sales	40%	30%
Payment from		
1-10	25	55
11-100	35	15

The proposed sales strategy will probably increase sales from $8 million to $10 million. There is a gross margin rate of 30%. The rate of return is 14%. Sales discounts are given on cash sales.

	Without Sales Campaign		With Sales Campaign
Gross margin			
(0.3 × $8,000,000)	$2,400,000	0.3 × $10,000,000	$3,000,000
Sales subject to discount			
0.65 × $8,000,000	$5,200,000		
0.85 × $10,000,000		$ 8,500,000	
Sales discount	× 0.03 – 156,000	× 0.03	–255,000
Investment in average accounts receivable			

$$\frac{60}{360} \times \$8,000,000 \times 0.7 \qquad \$\,933,333$$

$$\frac{80}{360} \times \$10,000,000 \times 0.7 \qquad\qquad \$\,1,555,555$$

Return rate	× 0.14 – 130.667	× 0.14	–217,778
Net profit	$2,113,333		$2,527,222

The company should undertake the sales campaign, because earnings will increase by $413,889 ($2,527,222 – $2,113,333).

FACTORING RECEIVABLES

Factoring/selling receivables is a type of financial service in which a company transfers title to its accounts receivable to a factoring company who then acts as principal, not as agent. The receivables are sold with or without recourse. Factors also accommodate clients with advances, such as loans in expectation of sales, which permit inventory buildup before peak selling periods. Factoring is more prevalent in the garment industry.

OTHER THAN SALES

A significant amount of receivable transactions other than regular sales may result in losses. Examples include insurance claims and freight claims. The financial manager should develop a plan to handle these transactions. Unfortunately, some companies lack formalized record keeping in this area. In fact, some firms retain only pieces of correspondence.

EXPORT RECEIVABLES

Export receivables and foreign risk may be managed better by taking out export credit insurance coverage to assure payment for shipped goods. Credit coverage may be obtained via the U.S. Export-Import Bank or a letter of credit from a U.S. or foreign bank. Even though a letter of credit guards against customer default, it needs to be secured before each export transaction. In emerging markets, the multinational company should consider the following as part of its accounts receivable management program:

- Stability of the foreign country's banking system.
- Variability in foreign exchange rates.
- Variance in foreign payment schedules.
- Stability of political, economic and financial conditions.
- Astuteness of financial management by the country's trade representatives and other government officials.

CONCLUSION

The major decisions regarding accounts receivable are the determination of whether to give credit, to whom, the amount, and the terms. A useful ratio is sales to cash collections which may be looked at over a three-month period as an indicator of overall collections on sales.

CHAPTER 49

INVENTORY MANAGEMENT

CONTENTS

The purpose of inventory management is to develop policies that will achieve an optimal inventory investment. The optimal level of inventory varies among industries and among companies in a particular industry. Successful inventory management minimizes inventory at all stages of manufacturing while retaining cost-effective production volume. This improves profitability and cash flow. By operating with minimum inventory levels and with short production lead times, the company increases its flexibility. This flexibility is needed to respond immediately to changing market conditions.

Inventory files should contain inventory location, quantity on hand, and quantity committed. Adequate inventory must be maintained to meet customer orders, properly utilize machines, keep production schedules, and assure smooth production activity. By maintaining a functional inventory supply, a company will be able to protect itself against unplanned changes in supply. Some inventory must be held at the different manufacturing stages as hedges against the variabilities of supply and demand as well as hedges in the event problems surface in the manufacturing process itself. A sales forecast is the starting point for effective inventory management since expected sales determines how much inventory is needed.

Inventory records should provide information to satisfy the needs of the financial, sales, purchasing, and production managers. Inventory information may include the following by major type: unit cost, historical usage, quantity on order, minimum-maximum quantities, quantities in transit, delivery times, scheduling dates, and quantities set aside for specific contracts, production orders, and customers. With regard to minimum-maximum quantities, such a procedure is practical when stability exists in the rate of sale or the use of the product and where the order time is short. The minimum is a "cushion" to be used only in an emergency. The maximum is the "ceiling" of the desirable inventory. The reorder point is between the minimum and maximum.

There should be a master item file containing identification, description, and specifications of the item's raw material, component parts, and assembly relationship. An item specification should include up-to-date data about the part, production process, uses of the item, possible substitutions, demand information, competitive factors, and overall supply. Information may also be furnished about suppliers and relevant information that may affect the availability and price of the item.

The inventory balance is affected by many factors including the production cycle, product perishability and obsolescence, sales flexibility, cyclicality of business, liquidity, inventory financing available, and markdowns in the industry. The goal is to maximize sales with minimum inventory. Thus, inventory levels should be closely correlated to the selling cycle. A poor inventory management system may be revealed by failure to meet production plans, expediting of parts, slow-moving or obsolete goods, poor customer service, "rush" jobs in the factory, production bottlenecks, downtime, poor forecasts and deficient performance reporting, and internal conflicts between members of the organization such as production and marketing.

An advantage of a "bloated" inventory is the resulting reduction in production costs from larger production runs. It also provides a safety buffer if there is a nondelivery of raw materials or the prior department's manufacturing process breaks down.

Sales forecasting is crucial because an inaccurately high sales forecast can result in high inventory levels, markdowns, obsolescence, and inventory writeoffs. An inaccurately low forecast will result in low inventory and lost sales.

Suppliers should be evaluated in terms of fairness in pricing, meeting delivery times, quality of goods shipped (e.g., in accordance with product specifications), and ability to meet "rush" jobs.

The benefits to be obtained from proper inventory management include:

- Reduction of waste and cost arising from excess storage, handling, and obsolescence.

- Reduction of the risk of inventory theft.

- Reduction of production delays because needed raw materials are maintained. This results in lower production costs and longer runs.

- Improvement of customer service because needed materials are available.

Questions to ask with respect to a company's inventory health are as follows:

1. Are operating inventories broken down into the reporting levels of safety, replenishment, and excess or obsolete merchandise?

2. Is the optimal order or manufacturing frequency computed regularly as an element of a continual improvement process?

3. Is statistical analysis used in predicting sales, manufacturing lead times, and service levels?

4. Is root-cause appraisal on excess or obsolete merchandise performed?

5. Are safety stock levels recalculated regularly to assure they are current?

INVENTORY MANAGEMENT POLICIES

- Appraise the adequacy of the raw materials level, which depends on expected production, condition of equipment, supplier reliability, and seasonal considerations. Raw material requirements may be forecast using such techniques as statistical analysis of historical trends and cycles, econometric models, and Delphi methods.

  Recommendation: Have sound material management guidelines to specify what and how much should be stored. Manufacturing requires an appropriate balance of parts to produce an end item.

  What to Watch Out For: A situation in which you have four of five needed components, because this results in having four excess inventories when a stockout of the fifth occurs.

- Forecast future movements in raw materials prices, so that if prices are expected to increase, additional materials are bought at lower prices.

- Discard slow-moving products to reduce inventory carrying costs and improve cash flow.

- Stock-higher-profit margin items for quick sale.

- Guard against inventory buildup, since it is associated with substantial carrying and opportunity costs.

- Minimize inventory levels when liquidity and/or inventory financing problems exist.

- Plan for a stock balance that will guard against and cushion the possible loss of business from a shortage in materials. The timing of an order also depends on seasonal factors.

- Ensure that inventory is received when needed so that production runs smoothly.

  What to Do: Compare vendor and production receipts to promised delivery due dates.

- A long sales order entry process requires the stocking of additional inventory.

- Try to convince customers to keep higher stock levels to reduce the company's inventory of finished goods.

- Examine the quality of merchandise received. The ratio of purchase returns to purchases should be enlightening. A sharp increase in the ratio indicates that a new supplier may be warranted. A performance measurement and evaluation system should exist to appraise vendor quality and reliability (e.g., meeting promised delivery dates). If there is a problem with the vendor, problems will arise in production scheduling, imbalances in work-in-process, and "rush" purchase orders.

- Keep a careful record of back orders. A high back order level indicates that less inventory balances are needed. This is because back orders may be used as indicators of the production required, resulting in improved production planning and procurement. The trend in the ratio of the dollar amount of back orders to the average per-day sales will prove useful.

- Appraise the acquisition and inventory control functions. Any problems must be identified and rectified. In areas where control is weak, inventory balances should be restricted.

- Accuracy is needed for the bills of materials to indicate the parts and quantities received to produce an end product.

  What to Do: Conduct audits on the production floor when the parts are assembled.

- Have accurate inventory records and assign inventory responsibilities to managers. For example, assign to the engineering manager responsibility for the bills of material. Do you have the necessary inventory measurement tools (e.g., scales)?

- Closely supervise warehouse and materials handling staff to guard against theft and to maximize efficiency.

- Frequently review stock lines for poor earnings.

- Minimize the lead time in the acquisition, manufacturing, and distribution functions. The lead time is how long it takes to receive merchandise from suppliers after an order is placed. Depending upon lead times, an increase in inventory stocking may be required or the purchasing pattern may have to be altered.

What to Do: Calculate the ratio of the value of outstanding orders to average daily purchases to indicate the lead time for receiving orders from suppliers. The ratio indicates whether you should increase the inventory balance or change your buying pattern. Are vendors keeping their delivery date promises?

- Examine the time between raw materials input and the completion of production to see if production and engineering techniques can be implemented to hasten the production operation.

- Examine the degree of spoilage and take steps to reduce it.

- Prepare an inventory analysis report presenting the number of months of insurance coverage. The report should highlight items with excess inventory coverage resulting from such causes as changes in customer demand or poor inventory practices.

- Maintain proper inventory control, such as through the application of computer techniques. For example, a point-of-sale computerized electronic register may be used by a retail business. The register continually updates inventory for sales and purchases. These data facilitate the computation of reorder points and quantity per order.

- Look at the trend in the unit cost of manufactured items. Reasons for variations should be analyzed to see if they are due to factors within or beyond company control (i.e., increase in oil prices, managerial inefficiencies).

- Have economies in production run size to reduce setup costs and idle time.

- Have vendors consign inventory to you and invoice as used.

- Utilize computer techniques and operations research to control inventory properly. For example, statistical forecasting methods can be used to determine inventory levels related to a preset acceptability level of outage probability.

The purchasing department can assist in inventory management in the following ways:

- Have blanket orders for operating supplies.

- Have tight control over subcontracted operations.

- Determine a price for raw materials that will protect the company in volatile markets.

- Gradually increase purchase size as you get to know the supplier better.

- Schedule delivery of raw materials using statistical and just-in-time techniques.

SYMPTOMS OF PROBLEMS IN INVENTORY MANAGEMENT

- Periodic extension of back orders.

- Material shortages.

- Material inventory writedowns at the end of the accounting period.

- Uneven production and downtime.
- Order cancellations.
- Periodic lack of storage space.
- Frequent layoffs and rehirings.
- Differing rates of turnover among inventory items within the same inventory category.
- Significant differences between book inventory and physical inventory.

Good internal control over inventory is necessary to guard against theft or other irregularities. A surprise inventory count should periodically occur to assure agreement between the book inventory and physical inventory. Have controlled audit groups of work-in-process moving through the manufacturing process to see the accuracy with which work-in-process is documented.

Major shortages may take place and be unnoticed for a long time if satisfactory control is lacking. Inventory is vulnerable to theft. Good control is needed in the acquisition and handling phases. Segregation should exist in purchasing, receiving, storing, and shipping of inventories.

An inventory control system should accomplish the following objectives: (1) proper record keeping, (2) implementing inventory decision models, (3) reporting exceptions, (4) aiding in forecasting usage and needs, and (5) maintaining proper safeguards to prevent misuse. If there is a lack of internal control, inventory balances should be restricted.

INVENTORY ANALYSIS

Inventory analysis should include consideration of the following:

- Customer order backlog as a percent of the inventory balance.
- Inventory carrying cost by month and by year.
- Inventory months' supply on hand by period for the major product lines.
- Customer order backlog in weeks as a percent of the production process cycle (lead time).
- Safety stock and slow-moving (obsolete) inventory as a percent of cost of sales and of the inventory balance.

Try to have work-in-process processed into finished goods as soon as possible. Work-in-process should arise only from manageable variability in the production process.

In inflationary and tight money periods, flexibility in inventory management is needed. For example, the quantity to be ordered may have to be adjusted to reflect increased costs.

The financial manager must consider the obsolescence and spoilage risk of inventory. For example, technological, perishable, fashionable, flammable, and specialized goods usually have high salability risk. The nature of the risks should be taken into account in computing desired inventory levels. The marketing department should be held accountable for obsolete and slow-moving items that they originally recommended. Before a product design is changed at the insistence of marketing, it should be carefully reviewed.

Different inventory items vary in profitability and the amount of space they occupy. Inventory management involves a tradeoff between the costs of keeping inventory versus the benefits of holding it. Higher inventory levels result in increased costs from storage, casualty and theft insurance, spoilage, higher property taxes for larger facilities, increased labor requirements, and interest on borrowed funds to finance inventory acquisition. However, an increase in inventory lowers the possibility of lost sales from stockouts and the incidence of production slowdowns from inadequate inventory. Additionally, large volume purchases will result in greater purchase discounts. Inventory levels are also affected by short-term interest rates. For instance, as short-term interest rates increase, the optimum level of holding inventory will be reduced.

To reduce costs of handling inventory:

- Use several assembly lines and move crews to the next line which has already been set up.
- Hasten routing reproduction by using standardized forms.
- Keep materials at subassemblies, not final assemblies.
- Minimize seasonal stocking of material.
- Consolidate the number of inventory storage locations and/or warehouses.
- Simplify and standardize the product.
- Avoid shutting down the plant, such as by having varying vacations.
- Decrease the time between filling an order and replacing the stock sold.
- Stop supplying "old" service parts but rather give customers the blueprints so they may manufacture them internally.

The inventory balance to be held depends upon:

- Vertical integration of the product line as indicated by manufactured versus purchased parts.
- Accuracy of manufacturing documents (e.g., route sheets, bills of materials).
- Accuracy of inventory records considering the deviation between the books and physical amounts.
- Reliability in estimating customer needs. Here, consideration should be given to the forecasting error.

Inventory of raw materials depends upon:

- Expected level and seasonality of production.
- Reliability of supply sources.

Inventory of work-in-process typically varies the most. Inventory of work-in-process depends upon:

- Length and time of the production run.
- Number of stages in the production cycle, lot-sizing, quality problems, lead time, line balancing, and manufacturing scheduling.

Work-in-process inventory may be viewed as a liability by inventory managers. Work-in-process takes away essential production capacity and cash while increasing the risk of obsolescence and shrinkage. While high machine utilization is good, an associated buildup of work-in-process is bad.

The financial manager may have to decide whether it is more profitable to sell inventory as is, or sell it after further processing. For example, inventory can be sold as is for $40,000, or sold for $80,000 if it is put into further processing costing $20,000. The latter should be selected because further processing yields a $60,000 profit relative to $40,000 for the current sale.

Inventory should be counted at regular, cyclic intervals because this provides the ability to check inventory on an ongoing basis as well as to reconcile the book and physical amounts.

Recommendation: To lessen the time needed for counting, use standardized labeling procedures and quantity markings as well as orderly warehouse stocking.

Tip: Take the count during nonworking hours to guard against duplicate counting. Alternatively, warehouse pickers could carefully enter daily movement when the cycle count takes place. Cyclic counting has the following advantages:

- Permits the efficient use of a few full-time experienced counters throughout the year.

- Enables the timely detection and correction of the causes of inventory error.

- Does not require a plant shutdown, as does a year-end count.

- Facilitates the modifications of computer inventory programs, if needed.

MATERIALS REQUIREMENTS PLANNING

The manager can use materials requirements planning, which is a technique using bills of material, inventory information, and the production schedule to compute material requirements. It indicates when material should be replenished and how much to order.

Tip: Determine raw materials needed per item at each level.

Note: A particular component may be needed for a number of assemblies at different levels. It is a good approach to formulate and maintain appropriate due dates on orders. If the production schedule changes, the timing and amount of materials needed will also change. The production quantities (how much) are based on specific identifiable customer orders.

Note: Consider replacement (service) parts needs of customers. The amount ordered is based on periodic forecasts. There must be immediate feedback of changes in the production schedule (e.g., due to changes in priority) in order to adjust and control the planning and scheduling system. There should exist a master assembly schedule.

The computerized system should answer what-if questions. There is operational planning in units and financial planning in dollars.

There is a linkage of production planning, business planning, materials requirements planning, capacity requirements planning, and the support systems for material and capacity. The output generated by these systems should be linked with the financial reports. Financial reports include inventory forecasts, shipping budget, purchase commitment analysis, and the overall business plan. Materials requirements planning will aid in planning manufacturing resources.

Materials requirements planning requires information about bills of material, routing of parts through the production stages, lead times, and availability of material information and status.

In materials requirements planning, ascertain material requirements at what level and when to order to produce the needed finished goods. Materials requirements planning is involved with having sufficient materials when needed to manufacture quality products in a timely and efficient manner.

A production and inventory management system involves:

- A product structure, such as the materials needed and when to produce.
- The necessary sequence of production steps.
- The work centers involved in production and their functions.
- Managing product configuration and available parts.

The production schedule depends on the organization of the work centers, time-phased material requirements, production constraints (e.g., bottlenecks), and routing sequences.

In scheduling production, all constraints should be looked at simultaneously. Of course, the production schedule will influence the lead time needed.

Note: High machine utilization does not necessarily mean good production performance.

MANUFACTURING PROCESS DESIGN

Poor manufacturing process design may be indicated by:

- A high ratio of actual in-process time to standard process time.
- The scheduling of long production runs under lot-sizing systems.

A long setup time means a longer run and the resulting higher inventory balances. Long production runs may indicate poor quality output because machine settings often go out of place in long runs. Significant rework may be required to solve the problem.

The engineering department must work closely with the production and inventory management centers, otherwise design problems may occur resulting in production difficulties and unsuitable products. A change in product design should be reviewed and approved carefully because it may affect product quality, demand, and safety.

There should be good facilities design to avoid excess inventory or excess labor to move inventories around. Every move wastes time and increases the risk of damage. The longer the distance between sequential operations, the more inspection is needed and the greater is the loss of automated transfer to the next production point. A multidimension matrix model should be used in looking at the facilities design. An optimum layout should be formulated for the facility and product mix. Analysis of facilities is needed to identify and correct for flow problems, reduce inventory balances, and minimize move times with their related costs.

The cause of rejections occurring during the production process must be carefully analyzed.

DETERMINING CARRYING AND ORDERING COSTS

Inventory carrying costs include warehousing, handling, insurance, and property taxes. Further, the opportunity cost of holding inventory should be taken into account. A provisional cost for spoilage and obsolescence should also be included in the analysis. The more inventory is held, the greater is the carrying cost. Carrying cost equals:

$$\text{Carrying Cost} = \frac{Q}{2} \times C$$

where

$\dfrac{Q}{2}$ represents average quantity and C is the carrying cost per unit.

Inventory ordering costs are the costs of placing an order and receiving the merchandise. They include freight and the clerical costs to place the order. To minimize ordering costs, enter the fewest number of orders possible. In the case of produced items, ordering cost includes scheduling cost. Ordering cost equals:

$$\text{Ordering cost} = \frac{S}{Q} \times P$$

where

S = total usage, Q = quantity per order, and P = cost of placing an order.

The total inventory cost is therefore:

$$\frac{QC}{2} + \frac{SP}{C}$$

A tradeoff exists between ordering and carrying costs. A greater order quantity will increase carrying costs but lower ordering costs.

THE ECONOMIC ORDER QUANTITY

The economic order quantity (EOQ) is the optimum amount of goods to order each time so that total inventory costs are minimized. EOQ analysis should be applied to every product that represents a significant proportion of sales.

$$EOQ = \sqrt{\frac{2SP}{C}}$$

Some basic assumptions underlying the EOQ model are:

- Demand is constant and known with certainty.

- Depletion of stock is linear and constant.

- No discount is allowed for quantity purchases.

- Lead time, which is the time interval between placing an order and receiving delivery, is a constant, i.e., stockout is not possible.

The number of orders for a period is the usage (*S*) divided by the EOQ. Exhibit 49-1 is a graphic depiction of the EOQ point.

Exhibit 49-1: The Economic Order Quantity Point

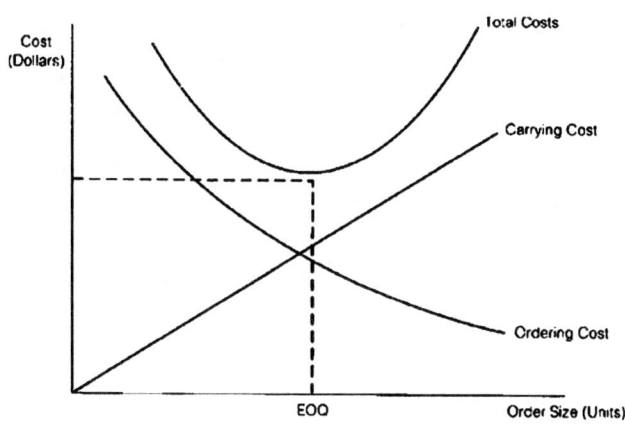

EXAMPLE 1: The manager wants to know how frequently to place orders. The following information is provided:

S = 500 units per month

P = $40 per order

C = $4 per unit

$$EOQ = \sqrt{\frac{2SP}{C}} = \sqrt{\frac{2(500)(40)}{4}} = \sqrt{10,000} = 100 \text{ units}$$

The number of orders each month is:

$$S/EOQ = 500/100 = 5$$

Therefore, an order should be placed about every six days (31/5).

EXAMPLE 2: A company is determining its frequency of orders for product X. Each product X costs $15. The annual carrying cost is $200. The ordering cost is $10. The company anticipates selling 50 of product X each month. Its desired average inventory level is 40.

$$S = 50 \times 12 = 600$$

$$P = \$10$$

$$C = \frac{\text{Purchase price} \times \text{carrying cost}}{\text{Average investment}} = \frac{\$15 \times \$200}{40 \times 15} = \$5$$

$$EOQ = \sqrt{\frac{2SP}{C}} = \sqrt{\frac{2(600)(10)}{5}} = \sqrt{\frac{12,000}{5}}$$

$$= \sqrt{2,400} = 49 \text{ (rounded)}$$

The number of orders per year is:

$$\frac{S}{EOQ} = \frac{600}{49} = 12 \text{ orders (rounded)}$$

The company should place an order about every 30 days (365/12).

For a detailed discussion of the EOQ model, see Chapter 27, "Decision Modeling in Corporate Financial Management."

AVOIDING STOCKOUTS

Stockout of raw materials or work-in-process can cause a slowdown in production. To avoid a stockout situation, a safety stock should be kept. Safety stock is the minimum inventory for an item, based on expected usage (demand) and delivery (lead) time of materials. This cushion guards against unusual product demand or unexpected delivery problems. The variability in demand of the item can be measured by the standard deviation or mean absolute deviation. The standard deviation measures the degree to which the actual level at the end of the cycle differs from the normal level. The trend period used in computing standard deviation should take into account market characteristics, demand volatility, and product maturity. A large standard deviation indicates that each period the inventory levels vary significantly. Therefore, the probability of being significantly out of stock at various times during the year is high if no safety stock exists. Safety stock helps to prevent the potential damage to customer relations and to future sales that can occur when there is a lack of inventory to fill an order immediately. The need for a safety stock increases the total inventory required. In effect, safety stock requires a balancing of expected costs of stockouts against the costs of carrying the additional inventory.

Rule of Thumb: A typical inventory management system uses a 5% stockout factor.

EXAMPLE 3: An order is placed when the inventory level reaches 210 units rather than 180 units. Thus, the safety stock is 30 units. In other words, one expects to be stocked with 30 units when the new order is received. The optimum safety stock is the point where the increased carrying cost equals the opportunity cost of a potential stockout. The increased carrying cost equals the carrying cost per unit multiplied by the safety stock.

$$\frac{\text{Stockout}}{\text{cost}} = \frac{\text{Number}}{\text{of orders}} \left(\frac{\text{Usage}}{\text{Order quantity}} \right) \times \frac{\text{Stockout}}{\text{units}}$$

$$\times \text{ Unit stockout cost} \times \text{Probability of a stockout}$$

EXAMPLE 4: A company uses 100,000 units annually. Each order is for 10,000 units. Stockout is 1,000 units; this amount is the difference between the maximum daily usage during the lead time less the reorder point, ignoring a safety stock factor. The stockout probability the manager wishes to take is 30%. The per unit stockout cost is $2.30. The carrying cost per unit is $5.

The stockout cost is:

$$\frac{100,000}{10,000} \times 1,000 \times \$2.30 \times .3 = \$6,900$$

The amount of safety stock needed is computed below:

Let X = Safety stock

Stockout cost = Carrying cost of safety stock

$\$6,900 = \$5X$

$1,380 \text{ units} = X$

EXAMPLE 5: A company uses 250,000 units per year. Each order is for 25,000 units. Stockout is 4,000 units. The tolerable stockout probability is 25%. The per unit stockout cost is $4. The carrying cost per unit is $8.

$$\text{Stockout cost} = \frac{250,000}{25,000} \times 4,000 \times \$4 \times 0.25 = \$40,000$$

$$\text{Amount of safety stock needed} = \frac{\text{Stockout cost}}{\text{Carrying cost per unit}}$$

$$= \frac{\$40,000}{\$8} = 5,000 \text{ units}$$

THE REORDER POINT

The reorder point (ROP) signals when to place an order. However, the reorder point requires knowledge of the lead time from placing to receiving an order. The reorder point may be influenced by the months of supply or total dollar ceilings on inventory to be held or inventory to be ordered.

Reorder point is computed as follows:

ROP = Lead time × Average usage per unit of time

This reveals the inventory level at which a new order should be placed. If a safety stock is needed, then add this amount to the ROP.

The more the vendor's backlog, the greater will be the ensuing work-in-process. This results in a longer and more inaccurate lead time. If a product is made to a customer's order, the lead time is the run time, queue time, move time, setup time, and procurement time for raw material.

EXAMPLE 6: A company needs 6,400 units evenly throughout the year. There is a lead time of one week. There are 50 working weeks in the year. The reorder point is:

$$1 \text{ week} \times \frac{6,400}{50 \text{ weeks}} = 1 \times 128 = 128 \text{ units}$$

When the inventory level drops to 128 units, a new order should be placed.

An optimal inventory level can be based on consideration of the incremental profitability resulting from having more merchandise to the opportunity cost of carrying the higher inventory balances.

EXAMPLE 7: The current inventory turnover is 12 times. Variable costs are 60% of sales. An increase in inventory balances is expected to prevent stockouts, thus increasing sales. Minimum rate of return is 18%. Relevant data follow:

Sales	Turnover
$800,000	12
890,000	10
940,000	8
980,000	7

(1) Sales	(2) Turnover	(3) [(1)(2)] Average Inventory Balance	(4) Opportunity Cost of Carrying Incremental Inventory[a]	(5) Increased Profitability[b]	(6) [(5)-(4)] Net Savings
$800,000	12	$ 66,667	—	—	—
890,000	10	89,000	$4,020	$36,000	$31,980
940,000	8	117,500	5,130	20,000	14,870
980,000	7	140,000	4,050	16,000	11,950

[a] Increased inventory × 0.18.
[b] Increased sales × 0.40.

The optimal inventory level is $89,000, because it results in the highest net savings.

SERVICE LEVEL

Service level can be defined as the probability that demand will not exceed supply during lead time. Thus, a service level of 90% implies a probability of 90% that demand will not exceed supply during lead time. To determine the optimal level of safety stock size, you might want to measure costs of not having enough inventory (stockout costs). Following are two cases for computing the safety stock, neither of which recognizes stockout costs.

Case 1: Variable Usage Rate, Constant Lead Time

For variable usage with constant lead time, the reorder point is computed as follows:

$$\text{ROP} = \text{expected usage during lead time} + \text{safety stock}$$
$$= \bar{\mu}LT + zLT(\sigma_\mu)$$

where

$$\bar{\mu} = \text{average usage rate}$$

$$LT = \text{lead time}$$

$$\sigma_\mu = \text{standard deviation of usage rate}$$

$$z = \text{standard normal variable as defined in Exhibit 42-2}$$

For a normal distribution, a given service level amounts to the shaded area under the curve to the left of ROP in Exhibit 49-3.

Exhibit 49-2: Computing Safety Stock—Values of Z_p for Specified Probabilities P

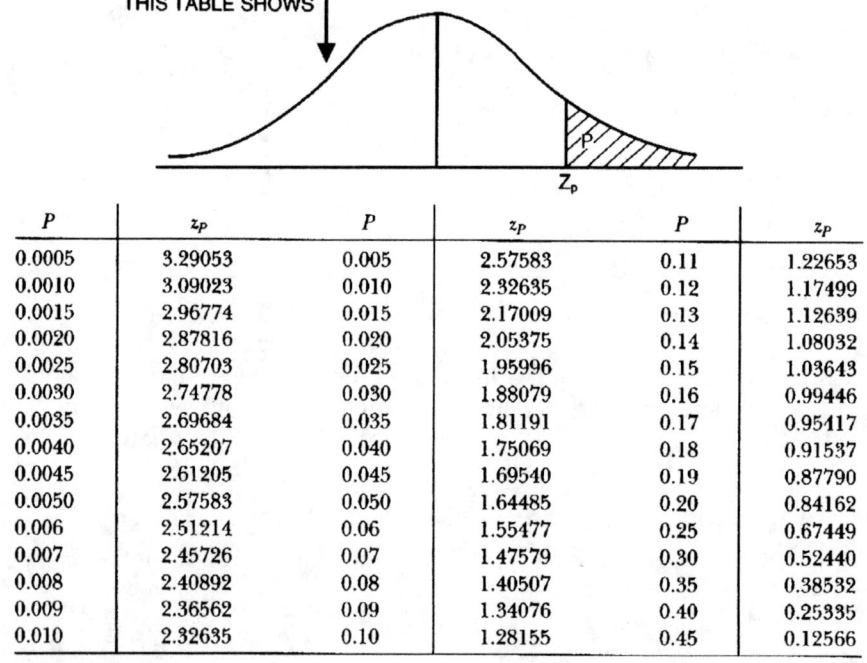

P	z_P	P	z_P	P	z_P
0.0005	3.29053	0.005	2.57583	0.11	1.22653
0.0010	3.09023	0.010	2.32635	0.12	1.17499
0.0015	2.96774	0.015	2.17009	0.13	1.12639
0.0020	2.87816	0.020	2.05375	0.14	1.08032
0.0025	2.80703	0.025	1.95996	0.15	1.03643
0.0030	2.74778	0.030	1.88079	0.16	0.99446
0.0035	2.69684	0.035	1.81191	0.17	0.95417
0.0040	2.65207	0.040	1.75069	0.18	0.91537
0.0045	2.61205	0.045	1.69540	0.19	0.87790
0.0050	2.57583	0.050	1.64485	0.20	0.84162
0.006	2.51214	0.06	1.55477	0.25	0.67449
0.007	2.45726	0.07	1.47579	0.30	0.52440
0.008	2.40892	0.08	1.40507	0.35	0.38532
0.009	2.36562	0.09	1.34076	0.40	0.25335
0.010	2.32635	0.10	1.28155	0.45	0.12566

z_P is the value of the standardized normal (mean = 0, standard deviation = 1) random variable z such that the probability of obtaining a sample z value at least as large as z_P is P. The value of P must be doubled if two-sided statements are made using the same z_P value.

Source: Croxton/Cowden/Bolch, *Practical Business Statistics*, 4th Ed., © 1969, p. 393. Reprinted by permission of Prentice-Hall, Inc., Englewood Cliffs, NJ.

Exhibit 49-3: Service Level

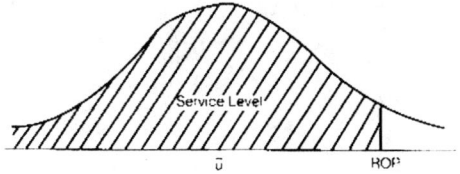

EXAMPLE 8: A company uses large cases of a product at an average rate of 50 units per day. Usage can be approximated by a normal distribution with a standard deviation of five units per day. Lead time is four days. Thus:

$$\bar{\mu} = 50 \text{ units per day}$$
$$\sigma_\mu = 5 \text{ units}$$
$$LT = 4 \text{ days}$$

For a service level of 99% (as shown in Exhibit 49-4), z = 2.33 (from Exhibit 49-2)

Thus:

$$\text{Safety stock} = 2.33 \, \sqrt{4}(5) = 23.3 \text{ cans}$$
$$\text{ROP} = 50(4) + 23.3 = 223.3 \text{ cans}$$

Case 2: Constant Usage Rate, Variable Lead Time

For constant usage with variable lead time, the reorder point is computed as follows:

$$\text{ROP} = \text{expected usage during lead time} + \text{safety stock}$$
$$= \bar{\mu}\overline{\text{LT}} + z_{\bar{\mu}}(\sigma_{\text{LT}})$$

where

$$\bar{\mu} = \text{constant usage rate}$$

$$\overline{LT} = \text{average lead time}$$

$$\sigma_{LT} = \text{standard deviation of lead time}$$

Exhibit 49-4: Service Level = 99%

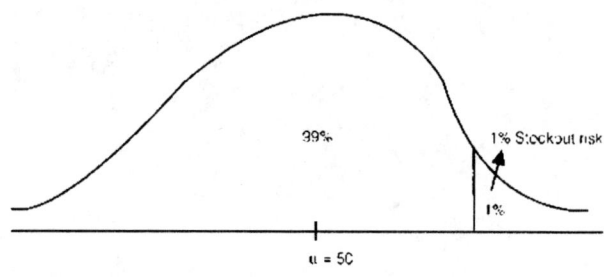

EXAMPLE 9: A company uses 10 gallons of product X per day. Lead time is normally distributed with a mean of six days and a standard deviation of two days. Thus,

$$\mu = \text{10 gallons per day}$$
$$LT = \text{6 days}$$
$$\sigma_{LT} = \text{2 days}$$
$$\text{Safety stock} = 2.33(10)(2) = 46.6 \text{ gallons}$$
$$\text{ROP} = 10(6) + 46.6 = 106.6 \text{ gallons}$$

Exhibit 49-5 shows the changes in level of inventory over time.

The product that results in the highest contribution margin per square foot should typically have the most priority in allocating space.

EXAMPLE 10: The following information pertains to product X:

Sales price	$ 15
Variable cost per unit	5
Contribution margin per unit	$ 10
Contribution margin per dozen	$120
Storage space per dozen	2 cubic feet
Contribution margin per cubic foot	$ 60
Number of units sold per period	4
Expected contribution margin per cubic foot	$240

STOCHASTIC INVENTORY MODELS

Stochastic inventory models are models which treat demands or lead times or both as random variables with specific probability distributions. A classic model is the single-period model with probabilistic demand whereby a single stocking decision is made for one time period for an item which is either perishable or salvageable. Examples are stocking of newspapers, magazines, food, and so on. Multiperiod periodic review models with stochastic demand represent another important class of models. Different approaches to solving stochastic inventory models are Markov process, dynamic programming, simulation, and classical methods such as statistics and calculus. Quantitative methods are discussed in Chapter 27, "Decision Modeling in Corporate Financial Management."

Exhibit 49-5: Changes in Level of Inventory over Time

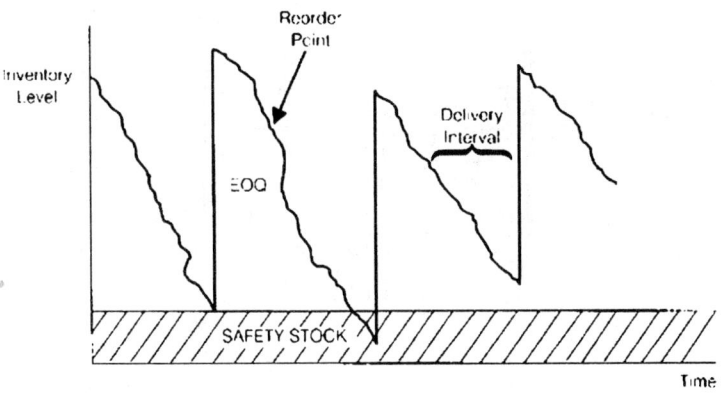

How to Use the ABC Inventory Control Method

ABC analysis focuses on the most critical items, looking at gross profitability, sensitive price or demand patterns, and supply excesses or shortages. The ABC method requires the classification of inventory into one of four groups, A, B, C, or D. The classification is according to the potential savings associated with a proper level of such control.

Perpetual inventory records should be maintained for "A" items because of the required accuracy and frequent attention, often daily. "A" items typically refer to one out of every ten items in inventory usually consisting of 70% of the dollar value of inventory. Group "B" items are less expensive than group "A" items but are still important and require intermediate level control. The group "B" items usually account for 20% of the inventory items and also 20% of the dollar value of the inventory. Group "C" designation is for most of the inventory items. Because they are usually less expensive and less used, there is less attention given to them. There is typically a high safety stock level for group "C" items. Blanket purchase orders should exist for "A" items and only "spot buys" for "Bs" and "Cs." Group "D" items are the losers. There has been no usage of "D" items for an extended time period (e.g., six months). "D" items should not be reordered unless special authorization is given. The ABC classification assigned should not be changed for at least six months. Items may be reclassified as need be. For instance, a fragile item or one being stolen can be reclassified from "C" to "A."

The higher the value of the inventory items, the more control is needed. For example, in looking at "A" items, carefully examine records, bills of material, customer orders, open purchase orders, and open manufacturing orders. The steps under the ABC method are:

1. A segregation is made of merchandise into components (e.g., varying models) based on dollar value.

2. Annual dollar usage is computed by inventory type (anticipated annual usage times unit cost).

3. There is a ranking given to inventory in terms of dollar usage ranging from high to low (e.g., "As" in top 30%, "Bs" in next 50%, and "Cs" in last 20%).

4. Inventory is tagged with the appropriate classifications so proper emphasis may be placed on them. A recording is made in the inventory records of the classifications.

EXAMPLE 11: An actual distribution in a manufacturing operation that the authors are familiar with shows that the top 15% of the line items in terms of annual dollar usage represents 80% of the total annual dollar usage. These items were classified as "A" items. The next 15% of the line items in terms of the annual dollar usage represent an additional 15% of the annual dollar usage and were classified as "B" items. The remaining 70% of the items in inventory account for only 5% of the total annual dollar usage. These were classified as "C" items.

Exhibit 49-6 depicts an ABC inventory control system. Exhibit 49-7 illustrates an ABC distribution.

Exhibit 49-6: ABC Inventory Control System

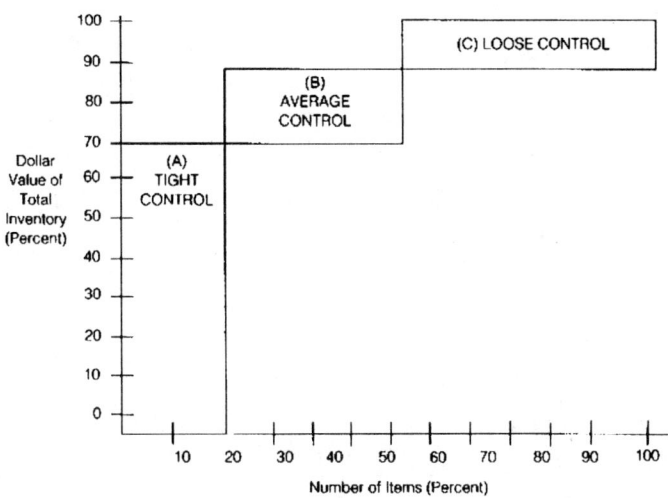

Exhibit 49-7: ABC Inventory Distribution

Classification	Population (Percent)	Dollar Usage (Percent)
A	20	80
B	30	15
C	50	5

RADIO FREQUENCY IDENTIFICATION SYSTEMS

Radio frequency identification (RFID) systems enable remote, real-time inventory tracking. With an RFID system, each inventory item can be treated individually. Every RFID system includes a radio frequency (RF) subsystem composed of electronic product code (EPC) tags and readers that enable users to conduct identification and related transactions by wireless communication. Tags may be read and written to, thereby allowing data to be exchanged in the supply chain. In deploying RFID technology, an appraisal should be made of the needs of the company and system requirements. RFID aids in data collection and improves business processes. When selecting a vendor, one should be chosen based on its familiarity with the company's business activities and information systems.

The decision about when and how to use RFID technology is based on several considerations, including possible interference in the environment, volume of data, transmission rate and range, and cost. Consideration should be given to the effect of RFID use on data communication, data storage, and information sharing within the company and associated companies.

In many RFID systems, the RF subsystem is supported by an enterprise subsystem, consisting of network infrastructure, data bases, application systems, and Web servers. Data is stored, processed, and analyzed. There is also an inter-enterprise subsystem consisting of Internet, object naming, and discovery services. Enterprise subsystems are connected when information must be shared between suppliers and customers.

Automated means should be implemented to monitor and manage RFID readers. Any potential system threats must be evaluated to avoid operational disruptions and loss of profitability. In deploying RFID, middleware may be required for the interface between RFID readers and a company's present application system.

SUPPLY CHAIN/JUST-IN-TIME

Just-in-time (JIT) inventory control is an approach that closely coordinates with suppliers to optimize the relationship between manufacturing and sales levels with inventory to reduce carrying costs. In many instances, JIT is linked with a computerized point-of-sale system. Inventory balances are maintained through an automated reordering system linked to suppliers in order to minimize stockouts.

INVENTORY IN A SERVICE BUSINESS

In a service business, inventories are less tangible than durable goods and they are perishable by nature. Examples of inventory in a service business are an empty hotel room, empty seat in an airplane, and empty table in a restaurant. In these cases, inventory is lost as time passes by and the empty condition persists. Inventory also includes service parts.

Inventory in a service business consists of the following levels:

- *Primary Level.* This level represents the capacity of the facility or equipment to provide the service.

- *Secondary Level.* This level is the variable capacity employed at different time periods to deliver the service.

Marginal pricing may be used to obtain income from otherwise lost opportunities. Examples are hotels offering "weekend specials" and airlines offering "offpeak" fares. The goal is to divert minimal income from the normal service customer by attracting lower-margin business. The profit of the service business may depend on the perishability of the service inventory.

The labor force should be such that labor costs are matched with the ability to sell the product.

CHAPTER 50

CORPORATE INVESTMENTS IN SECURITIES

CONTENTS

This chapter covers how to manage a company's surplus liquidity funds. A firm's surplus funds or idle cash are usually considered only of a temporary nature. The funds should be made available to cover a shortfall in cash flow or working capital or to serve as a reservoir for capital spending and acquisition. Many companies flush with cash have been redeploying surplus cash—not only in increased dividends and M&A activity, but also in share buybacks, debt payouts, and in some capital expenditures.

Most corporate financial officers are conservative (not speculative) when considering investing idle cash in financial securities since the money should be on hand without loss in value of the funds when needed. Securities cover a broad range of investment instruments, including common stocks, preferred stocks, bonds, and options. There are two broad categories of securities available to corporate investors: equity securities, which represent ownership of a company, and debt (or fixed income) securities, which represent a loan from the investor to a company or government. Fixed income securities generally stress current fixed income and offer little or no opportunity for appreciation in value. They are usually liquid and bear less market risk than other types of investments. This type of investment performs well during stable economic conditions and lower inflation. Examples of fixed income securities include:

- Corporate bonds.
- Government securities.
- Mortgage-backed securities.
- Preferred stocks.
- Short-term debt securities.

Fixed income securities such as bonds and preferred stocks have a twofold appeal to corporate investors: They are usually safer than equity securities such as common stocks and they typically generate a higher current return. It is important to realize that yields on bonds and their prices can be just as volatile as common stock prices and almost as risky. Bonds are subject to risks such as default risk, interest rate risk, and inflation risk. Preferred stock is a hybrid security since it has features of both common stock and bonds. In investing in fixed income securities, corporate investors should have an understanding of quality ratings, yields, safety, and risks associated with the securities.

Each type of security has not only distinct characteristics, but also advantages and disadvantages which vary by corporate investor. This chapter focuses on investing in fixed income (debt) securities—with especially short and intermediate-term maturity—normally utilized by corporate investors.

FACTORS TO BE CONSIDERED IN INVESTMENT DECISIONS

Consideration should be given to:

- *Security of Principal.* The degree of risk involved in a particular investment. The company will not want to lose part or all of the initial investment.

- *Yield and Risk.* The primary purpose of investing is to earn a return on invested money in the form of interest, dividends, rental income, and capital appreciation. However, increasing total returns would entail greater investment risks. Thus, yield and degree of risk are directly related. Greater risk also means sacrificing security of principal. A corporate investment officer (CIO) has to choose the priority that fits the corporation's financial circumstances and objectives.

- *Stability of Income.* When steady income is the most important consideration, bond interest or preferred stock dividends should be emphasized. This might be the situation if the company needs to supplement its earned income on a regular basis with income from its outside investments.

- *Marketability and Liquidity.* The ability to find a ready market to dispose of the investment at the right price.

- *Tax Factors.* Corporate investors in high tax brackets will have different investment objectives than those in lower brackets. If the company is in a high tax bracket, it may prefer municipal bonds (interest is not taxable) or investments that provide tax credits or tax shelters, such as those in oil and gas.

Additional factors to be considered include:

- Current and future income needs.
- Hedging against inflation.
- Ability to withstand financial loss.
- Ease of management.
- Amount of investment.
- Diversification.
- Long-term versus short-term potential.

Questions to Be Asked

In developing the corporation's investment strategy, it is advisable to ask the following questions:

- What proportion of funds does the company want safe and liquid?
- Is the company willing to invest for higher return but greater risk?
- How long a maturity period is the company willing to take on its investment?
- What should be the mix of its investments for diversification?
- Does the company need to invest in tax-free securities?

Types of Investment Instruments

There are many fixed income securities from which a CIO can choose. They can be categorized into short-term and long-term investments, as indicated in Exhibit 50-1.

CORPORATE BONDS

A bond is a certificate or security showing the corporate investor loaned funds to an issuing company or to a government in return for fixed future interest and repayment of principal. Bonds have the following advantages:

- There is fixed interest income each year.
- Bonds are safer than equity securities such as common stock. This is because bondholders come before common stockholders in the event of corporate bankruptcy.

Bonds suffer from the following disadvantages:

- They do not participate in incremental profitability.
- There are no voting rights.

Exhibit 50-1: Short- and Long-Term Investment Vehicle Categories

Short-Term Vehicles	*Long-Term Vehicles*
• U.S. Treasury bills	• U.S. Treasury notes and bonds
• Certificates of deposit (CDs)	• Corporate bonds
• Banker's acceptances (BAs)	• Mortgage-backed securities
• Commercial paper	• Municipal bonds
• Repurchase agreements (Repos)	• Preferred stock, fixed or adjustable
• Money market funds	• Bond funds
• Eurodollar time deposits	• Unit investment trusts

Terms and Features of Bonds

There are certain terms and features of bonds a corporate investment officer should be familiar with, including:

- *Par value.* The par value of a bond is the face value of the bond, usually $1,000.
- *Coupon rate.* The coupon rate is the nominal interest rate that determines the actual interest to be received on a bond. It is an annual interest per par value. For example, if a corporate investor owns a $1,000,000 bond having a coupon rate of 10%, the annual interest to be received will be $100,000.
- *Maturity date.* The maturity date is the final date on which repayment of the bond principal is due.
- *Indenture.* The bond indenture is the lengthy, legal agreement detailing the issuer's obligations pertaining to a bond issue. It contains the terms and conditions of the bond issue as well as any restrictive provisions placed on the firm, known as restrictive covenants. The indenture is administered by an independent trustee. Restrictive covenants include maintenance of (a)

required levels of working capital, (b) a particular current ratio, and (c) a specified debt ratio.

- *Trustee.* The trustee is the third party with whom the indenture is made. The trustee's job is to see that the terms of the indenture are actually carried out.

- *Yield.* The yield is different than the coupon interest rate. It is the effective interest rate the corporate investor earns on the bond investment. If a bond is bought below its face value (i.e., purchased at a discount), the yield is higher than the coupon rate. If a bond is acquired above its face value (i.e., bought at a premium), the yield is below the coupon rate.

- *Call provision.* A call provision entitles the issuing corporation to repurchase, or "call" the bond from its holders at stated prices over specified periods.

- *Sinking fund.* In a sinking fund bond, money is put aside by the issuing company periodically for the repayment of debt, thus reducing the total amount of debt outstanding. This particular provision may be included in the bond indenture to protect investors.

Types of Bonds

There are many types of bonds according to different criteria including:

- *Mortgage bonds.* Mortgage bonds are secured by physical property. In case of default, the bondholders may foreclose on the secured property and sell it to satisfy their claims.

- *Debentures.* Debentures are unsecured bonds. They are protected by the general credit of the issuing corporation. Credit ratings are very important for this type of bond. Federal, state, and municipal government issues are debentures. Subordinated debentures are junior issues ranking after other unsecured debt as a result of explicit provisions in the indenture. Finance companies have made extensive use of these types of bonds.

- *Convertible bonds.* These bonds are subordinated debentures which may be converted, at the investor's option, into a specified amount of other securities (usually common stock) at a fixed price. They are hybrid securities having characteristics of both bonds and common stock in that they provide fixed interest income and potential appreciation through participation in future price increases of the underlying common stock.

- *Income bonds.* In income bonds, interest is paid only if earned. They are often called reorganization bonds.

- *Tax-exempt bonds.* Tax-exempt bonds are usually municipal bonds where interest income is not subject to federal tax, although the Tax Reform Act (TRA) of 1986 imposed restrictions on the issuance of tax-exempt municipal bonds. Municipal bonds may carry a lower interest rate than taxable bonds of similar quality and safety. However, after-tax yield from these bonds is usually higher than that of a bond with a higher rate of taxable interest. Note that municipal bonds are subject to two principal risks—interest rate and default.

- *U.S. government and agency securities.* They include Treasury bills, notes, bonds, and mortgage-backed securities such as "Ginnie Maes." Treasury bills represent short-term government financing and mature in 12 months or less. U.S. Treasury notes have a maturity of one to ten years, whereas U.S. Treasury bonds have a maturity of 10 to 25 years and can be purchased in denominations as low as $1,000. All these types of U.S. government securities are subject to federal income taxes, but not subject to state and local income taxes. "Ginnie Maes" represent pools of 25- to 30-year Federal Housing Administration (FHA) or Veterans Administration (VA) mortgages purchased by the Government National Mortgage Association.

- *Zero-coupon bonds.* With zero-coupon bonds, the interest, instead of being paid out directly, is added to the principal semiannually and both the principal and accumulated interest are paid at maturity.

  Tip: This compounding factor results in the investor receiving higher returns on the original investment at maturity. Zero-coupon bonds are not fixed income securities in the historical sense, because they provide no periodic income. The interest on the bond is paid at maturity. However, accrued interest, though not received, is taxable yearly as ordinary income. Zero-coupon bonds have two basic advantages over regular coupon-bearing bonds: (1) a relatively small investment is required to buy these bonds; and (2) the investor is assured of a specific yield throughout the term of the investment.

- *Junk bonds.* Junk bonds, or high-yield bonds, are bonds with a speculative credit rating of Baa or lower by Moody's and BBB or lower by Standard and Poor's rating system. Coupon rates on junk bonds are considerably higher than those of better-quality issues. Note that junk bonds are issued by companies without track records of sales and earnings and therefore are subject to high default risk. Today, many nonmortgage-backed bonds issued by corporations are junk. Very recently, a large number of junk bonds have been issued as part of corporate mergers or takeovers. Since junk bonds are known for their high yields and high risk, many risk-oriented corporate investors including banks specialize in trading them. However, the bonds may be defaulted on. During periods of recession and high interest rates, when servicing debts is very difficult, junk bonds can pose a serious default risk to investors.

How to Select a Bond

When selecting a bond, corporate investors should take into consideration five factors:

1.   Investment quality—Rating of bonds
2.   Length of maturity—Short-term (0–5 years)
                                           Medium (6–15 years)
                                           Long-term (over 15 years)

3. Features of bonds—call or conversion features

4. Tax status

5. Yield to maturity

Investment Quality—Rating of Bonds. The investment quality of a bond is measured by its bond rating which reflects the probability that a bond issue will go into default. The rating should influence the investor's perception of risk and therefore have an impact on the interest rate the investor is willing to accept, the price the investor is willing to pay, and the maturity period of the bond the investor is willing to accept.

Bond investors tend to place more emphasis on independent analysis of quality than do common stock investors. Bond analysis and ratings are done, among others, by Standard & Poor's and Moody's. The following is an actual listing of the designations used by these well-known independent agencies. Descriptions on ratings are summarized. For original versions of descriptions, see Moody's Bond Record and Standard & Poor's Bond Guide.

*Description of Bond Ratings**

Moody's	Standard & Poor's	Quality Indication
Aaa	AAA	Highest quality
Aa	AA	High quality
A	A	Upper medium grade
Baa	BBB	Medium grade
Ba	BB	Contains speculative elements
B	B	Outright speculative
Caa	CCC & CC	Default definitely possible
Ca	C	Default, only partial recovery likely
C	D	Default, little recovery likely

* Ratings may also have + or – signs to show relative standings in each class.

Corporate investors should pay careful attention to ratings since they can affect not only potential market behavior but relative yields as well. Specifically, the higher the rating, the lower will be the yield of a bond, other things being equal. It should be noted that the ratings do change over time and the rating agencies have "credit watch lists" of various types. Corporate investment policy should specify this point: for example, the company is allowed to invest in only those bonds rated Baa or above by Moody's or BBB or above by Standard & Poor's, even though doing so means giving up about three-fourths of a percentage point in yield.

Length of Maturity. In addition to the ratings, an investment officer can control the risk element through the maturities to be selected. The maturity indicates how much the company stands to lose if interest rates rise. The longer a bond's maturity, the more volatile is its price. There is a tradeoff. Shorter maturities usually mean lower yields. A conservative corporate investor, which is typical, may select bonds with shorter maturities.

Features. Check to see whether a bond has a call provision, which allows the issuing company to redeem its bonds after a certain date if it chooses to, rather than at maturity. The investor is generally paid a small premium over par if an issue is called but not as much as the investor would have received if the bond were held until maturity. That is because bonds are usually called only if their interest rates are higher than the going market rate. Try to avoid bonds that have a call provision of companies that may be involved in "event risk" (mergers and acquisitions, leveraged buyouts, and so on.)

Also check to see if a bond has a convertible feature. Convertible bonds can be converted into common stock at a later date. They provide fixed income in the form of interest. The corporate investor also can benefit from the appreciation value of common stock.

Tax Status. If the investing company is in a high tax bracket, it may want to consider tax-exempt bonds. Most municipal bonds are rated A or above, making them a good grade risk. They can also be bought in mutual funds.

Yield to Maturity. Yield has a lot to do with the rating of a bond. How to calculate various yield measures is taken up later.

How to Read a Bond Quotation

To see how bond quotations are presented in the newspaper, let us look at the data for an IBM bond.

Bonds	Cur Y/d	Vol	High	Low	Close	Net Chg
IBM 9 3/8 15	11	169	84 5/8	84	84	–11/8

The column numbers immediately following the company name gives the bond coupon rate and maturity date. This particular bond carries a 9.375% interest rate and matures in 2015. The next column, labeled "cur yld," provides the current yield calculated by dividing the annual interest income (9 3/8%) by the current market price of the bond (a closing price of 84). Thus, the current yield for the IBM bond is 11% (9 3/8 divided by 84). This figure represents the effective, or real, rate of return on the current market price represented by the bond's interest earnings. The "vol" column indicates the number of bonds traded on the given day (i.e., 169 bonds).

The market price of a bond is usually expressed as a percent of its par (face) value, which is customarily $1,000. Corporate bonds are quoted to the nearest one-eighth of a percent, and a quote of 84 5/8 in the above indicates a price of $846.25 or 84 5/8% of $1,000.

U.S. government bonds are highly marketable and deal in keenly competitive markets so they are quoted in thirty-seconds or sixty-fourths rather than eighths.

Moreover, decimals are used, rather than fractions, in quoting prices. For example, a quotation of 106.17 for a Treasury bond indicates a price of $1,065.31 [$1,060 + (17/32 × $10)]. When a plus sign follows the quotation, the Treasury bond is being quoted in sixty-fourths. We must double the number following the decimal point and add I to determine the fraction of $10 represented in the quote. For example, a quote of 95.16+ indicates a price of $955.16 [$950 + (33/64 × $10)].

How to Calculate Yield (Effective Rate of Return) on a Bond

Bonds are evaluated on many different types of returns including current yield, yield to maturity, yield to call, and realized yield.

Current Yield. The current yield is the annual interest payment divided by the current price of the bond, which was discussed in the previous section ("How to Read a Bond Quotation"). This is reported in The Wall Street Journal, among others. The current yield is:

$$\frac{\text{Annual interest payment}}{\text{Current price}}$$

EXAMPLE 1: Assume a 12% coupon rate, $1,000 par value bond selling for $960. The current yield = $120/$960 = 12.5%.

The problem with this measure of return is that it does not take into account the maturity date of the bond. A bond with one year to run and another with 15 years to run would have the same current yield quote if interest payments were $120 and the price was $960. Clearly, the one-year bond would be preferable under this circumstance because you would not only get $120 in interest, but also a gain of $40 ($1000 – $960) with a one-year time period, and this amount could be reinvested.

Yield to Maturity (YTM). The yield to maturity takes into account the maturity date of the bond. It is the real return the investor would receive from interest income plus capital gain assuming the bond is held to maturity. The exact way of calculating this measure is a little complicated and not presented here. But the approximate method is:

$$\text{Yield} = \frac{I + (\$1,000 - V)/n}{(\$1,000 + V)/2}$$

where

V = the market value of the bond

I = dollars of interest paid per year

n = number of years to maturity

EXAMPLE 2: An investor bought a 10-year, 8% coupon, $1,000 par value bond at a price of $877.60. The rate of return (yield) on the bond if held to maturity is:

$$\text{Yield} = \frac{\$80 + (\$1,000 - \$877.60)/10}{(\$1,000 + \$877.60)/2} = \frac{\$80 + \$12,24}{\$938.80} = \frac{\$92.24}{\$93.80} = 9.8\%$$

As can be seen, since the bond was bought at a discount, the yield (9.8%) came out greater than the coupon rate of 8%.

Yield to Call. Not all bonds are held to maturity. If the bond may be called prior to maturity, the yield-to-maturity formula will have the call price in place of the par value of $1,000.

EXAMPLE 3: Assume a 20-year bond was initially bought at a 13.5% coupon rate, and after two years, rates have dropped. Assume further that the bond is currently selling for $1,180, the yield to maturity on the bond is 11.15%, and the bond can be called in five years after issue at $1,090. Thus if the investor buys the bond two years after issue, the bond may be called back after three more years at $1,090. The yield to call can be calculated as follows:

$$\frac{\$135 + (\$1,090 - \$1,180)/3}{(\$1,090 + \$1,180)/2} = \frac{\$135 + (-\$90/3)}{\$1,135} = \frac{\$105}{\$1,135} = 9.25\%$$

Note: The yield-to-call figure of 9.25% is 190 basis points less than the yield to maturity of 11.15%. Clearly, you need to be aware of the differential because a lower return is earned.

Realized Yield. The investor may trade in and out of a bond long before it matures. The investor obviously needs a measure of return to evaluate the investment appeal of any bonds that are intended to be bought and quickly sold. Realized yield is used for this purpose. This measure is simply a variation of yield-to-maturity, as only two variables are changed in the yield to maturity formula. Future price is used in place of par value ($1,000), and the length of the holding period is substituted for the number of years to maturity.

EXAMPLE 4: In Example 2, assume that the investor anticipates holding the bond only three years and that the investor has estimated interest rates will change in the future so that the price of the bond will move to about $925 from its present level of $877.70. Thus, the investor will buy the bond today at a market price of $877.70 and sell the issue three years later at a price of $925. Given these assumptions, the realized yield of this bond would be:

$$\text{Realized yield} = \frac{\$80 + (\$925 - \$877.70)/3}{\$925 + \$877.70)/2} = \frac{\$80 + \$15.77}{\$901.35} = \frac{\$95.77}{\$901.35}$$

$$= 10.63\%$$

Note: Use a bond table to find the value for various yield measures.

Equivalent Before-Tax Yield. Yield on a municipal bond needs to be looked at on an equivalent before-tax yield basis, because the interest received is not subject to federal income taxes. The formula used to equate interest on municipals to other investments is:

Tax equivalent paid = Tax-exempt yield/(1 – tax rate)

EXAMPLE 5: If a company has a marginal tax rate of 34% and is evaluating a municipal bond paying 10% interest, the equivalent before-tax yield on a taxable investment would be:

10%/(1 – .34) = 15.15%

Thus, the company could choose between a taxable investment paying 15.15% and a tax-exempt bond paying 10% and be indifferent between the two.

Determining Interest-Rate Risk

Interest-rate risk can be determined in two ways. One way is to look at the term structure of a debt security by measuring its average term to maturity—a duration. The other way is to measure the sensitivity of changes in a debt security's price associated with changes in its yield to maturity. We will discuss two measurement approaches: Macaulay's duration coefficient and the interest elasticity.

Macaulay's Duration Coefficient. Macaulay's duration (D) is an attempt to measure risk in a bond. It is defined as the weighted-average number of years required to recover principal and all interest payments. A simple example below illustrates the duration calculations.

EXAMPLE 6: A bond pays a 7% coupon rate annually on its $1,000 face value if it has three years until its maturity and has a YTM of 6%. The computation of Macaulay's duration coefficient involves the following three steps:

Step 1: Calculate the present value of the bond for each year.

Step 2: Express present values as proportions of the price of the bond.

Step 3: Multiply proportions by years' digits to obtain the weighted-average time.

(1) Year	(2) Cash Flow	(3) PV Factor @ 6%	(Step 1) (4) PV of Cash Flow	(Step 2) (5) PV as Proportion of Price of Bond	(Step 3) (6) Column (1) × Column (5)
1	$70	.9434	$66.04	.0643	.0643
2	70	.8900	62.30	.0607	.1214
3	1,070	.8396	898.37	.8750	2.6250
			$1,026.71	1.0000	2.8107

This 3-year bond's duration is a little over 2.8 years. In all cases, a bond's duration is less than or equal to its term to maturity. Only a pure discount bond—that is, one with no coupon or sinking fund payments—has duration equal to the maturity.

The higher the D value, the greater is the interest rate risk, since it implies a longer recovery period.

Excel has DURATION (settlement, maturity, couponyld, frequency, basis). In Example 6, we have:

= DURATION ("1/1/2010," "1/1/2013," 0.07,0.06,1,1) equals 2.8017

EXAMPLE 7: A bond has the following terms:

January 1, 2010, settlement date

January 1, 2015, maturity date

8% coupon

9.0% yield

Frequency is semiannual

Actual/actual basis

The duration (in the 2010 date system) is:

DURATION ("1/1/2010", "1/1/2015", 0.08,0.09,2,1) equals 5.993775

Interest Rate Elasticity

A bond's interest rate elasticity (E) is defined as:

$$E = \frac{\text{Percentage change in bond price}}{\text{Percentage change in YTM}}$$

Because bond prices and YTMs always move inversely, the elasticity will always be a negative number. Any bond's elasticity can be determined directly with the above formula. Knowing the duration coefficient (D), we can calculate the E using the following simple formula:

$$(-1)E = D \frac{YTM}{(1 + YTM)}$$

EXAMPLE 8: Using the same data in Example 6, the elasticity is calculated as follows:

$$(-1)\ E = 2.08107\ [0.6/(1.06)] = .1586$$

INVESTING IN A BOND FUND

It is possible that a corporate investor may decide to invest in a bond fund. The three key facts about the bonds in any portfolio are as follows:

1. *Quality.* Check the credit rating of the typical bond in the fund. Ratings by Standard & Poor's and Moody's show the relative danger that an issuer

will default on interest or principal payments. AAA is the best grade. A rating of BB or lower signifies a junk bond.

2. *Maturity.* The average maturity of your fund's bonds indicates how much a corporate investor stands to lose if interest rates rise. The longer the term of the bonds, the more volatile the price. For example, a 20-year bond may fluctuate in price four times as much as a four-year issue.

3. *Premium or discount.* Some funds with high current yields hold bonds that trade for more than their face value, or at a premium. Such funds are less vulnerable to losses if rates go up. Funds that hold bonds trading at a discount to face value can lose most.

Corporate investors must keep in mind the following guidelines:

- Rising interest rates drive down the value of all bond funds. For this reason, rather than focusing only on current yield, the investor should look primarily at total return (yield plus capital gains from falling interest rates or minus capital losses if rates climb).

- All bond funds do not benefit equally from tumbling interest rates. If a corporate investment officer thinks interest rates will decline and he or she wants to increase total return, he or she should buy funds that invest in U.S. Treasuries or top-rated corporate bonds. The investment officer should consider high-yield corporate bonds (junk bonds) if he or she believes interest rates are stabilizing.

- Unlike bonds, bond funds do not allow the corporate investor to lock in a yield. A mutual fund with a constantly changing portfolio is not like an individual bond, which can be kept to maturity. If the investor wants steady, secure income over several years or more, he or she should consider, as alternatives to funds, buying individual top-quality bonds or investing in a municipal bond unit trust, which maintains a fixed portfolio.

CONSIDERING UNIT INVESTMENT TRUSTS

Like a mutual fund, a unit investment trust offers to investors the advantages of a large, professionally selected and diversified portfolio. Unlike a mutual fund, however, its portfolio is fixed; once structured, it is not actively managed. Unit investment trusts are available of tax-exempt bonds, money market securities, corporate bonds of different grades; mortgage-backed securities; preferred stocks; utility common stocks; and other investments. Unit trusts are most suitable for corporate investors who need a fixed income and a guaranteed return of capital. They disband and pay off investors after the majority of their investments have been redeemed.

OTHER SHORT-TERM FIXED INCOME SECURITIES

Besides bonds and mortgage-backed securities, there are other significant forms of debt instruments from which corporate investors may choose, and they are primarily short-term in nature. They are:

- *Certificates of deposit (CDs).* These safe instruments are issued by commercial banks and thrift institutions and have traditionally been in amounts of $10,000 or $100,000 (jumbo CDs). CDs have a fixed maturity period varying from several months to many years. There is a penalty for cashing in the certificate prior to the maturity date, however.

- *Repurchase agreements (repos).* Repurchase agreements are a form of loan in which the borrower sells securities (such as government securities and other marketable securities) to the lender, but simultaneously contracts to repurchase the same securities either on call or on a specified date at a price that will produce an agreed yield. For example, a corporate investment officer agrees to buy a 90-day Treasury bill from a bank at a price to yield 7% with a contract to buy the bills back one day later. Repos arc attractive to corporate investors because, unlike demand deposits, repos pay explicit interest and it may be difficult to locate a one-day-maturity government security. Although repos can be a sound investment, it will cost to buy them (such as bank safekeeping fees, legal fees, and paperwork).

Accounting Standards Update (ASU) No. 2011-03 (April 2011), *Transfers and Servicing* (ASC Topic 860), *Reconsideration of Effective Control for Repurchase Agreements*, removes from the appraisal of effective control the criterion requiring the transferor to have the ability to repurchase financial assets on agreed terms, even when the transferee defaults. A transferor is deemed to have retained effective control over transferred financial assets (and therefore has to account for the transaction as a secured borrowing) for agreements that require the transferor to repurchase financial assets before their maturity date if all of the following criteria exist:

— The repurchase will be made before maturity at an ascertainable price.

— The contract is made in contemplation of the transfer.

— The repurchased financial assets are the same as those transferred.

This update withdraws the prior requirement that the transferor have adequate collateral to fund most of the cost to purchase replaced financial assets.

The update improves the accounting for repurchase agreements (repos).

Accounting Standards Update (ASU) No. 2014-11 (June 2014), *Transfers and Servicing (Topic 860), Repurchase-to-Maturity Transactions, Repurchase Financings, and Disclosures*, changes the accounting for repurchase-to-maturity transactions to secured borrowing accounting. Disclosure should be made of the carrying value of assets derecognized, gross amount of proceeds received by the transferor when derecognition of assets occurs, transferor's exposure from transferred financial assets, derivative contracts, gross obligation by collateral pledged, and risks associated with pledged assets.

- *Banker's acceptances (BAs).* A banker's acceptance is a draft drawn on a bank by a corporation to pay for merchandise. The draft promises payment of a certain sum of money to its holder at some future date. What makes BAs unique is that by prearrangement a bank accepts them, thereby guaranteeing their payment at the stated time. Most BAs arise in foreign trade transactions. The most common maturity for BAs is three months, although they can have maturities of up to 270 days. Their typical denominations are $500,000 and $1 million. BAs offer the following advantages as a corporate investment vehicle:

— Safety

— Negotiability

— Liquidity since an active secondary market for instruments of $1 million or more exists

— BAs offer several basis points higher yield spread than those of T-bills

— Smaller investment amount producing a yield similar to that of a CD with a comparable face value

- *Commercial paper.* Commercial paper is issued by large corporations to the public. It usually comes in minimum denominations of $25,000. It represents an unsecured promissory note. It usually carries a higher yield than small CDs. The maturity is usually 30, 60, and 90 days. The degree of risk depends on the company's credit rating.

- *Treasury bills.* Treasury bills have a maximum maturity of one year and common maturities of 91 and 182 days. They trade in minimum units of $10,000. They do not pay interest in the traditional sense; they are sold at a discount, and redeemed when the maturity date comes around, at face value. T-bills are extremely liquid in that there is an active secondary or resale market for these securities. T-bills have an extremely low risk because they are backed by the U.S. government.

Yields on discount securities such as T-bills are calculated using the formula:

$$\frac{P_1 - P_0}{P_0} \times \frac{52}{n}$$

where P_1 = redemption price, P_0 = purchase price, and n = maturity in weeks.

EXAMPLE 9: Assume that P_1 = $10,000, P_0 = $9,800, and m = 13 weeks. Then the T-bill yield is:

$$\frac{\$10,000 - \$9,800}{\$9,800} \times \frac{52}{13} = \frac{\$200}{\$9,800}$$
$$\times 4 = .0816 = 8.16\%$$

- *Eurodollar time deposits and CDs.* Eurodollar time deposits are essentially nonnegotiable, full liability, U.S. dollar-denominated time deposits in an offshore branch of an American or foreign bank. Hence, these time deposits are not liquid or marketable. Eurodollar CDs, on the other hand, are negotiable and typically offer a higher return than domestic CDs because of their exposure to sovereign risk.

- *Student Loan Marketing Association (Sallie Mae) securities.* Sallie Mae purchases loans made by financial institutions under a variety of federal and state loan programs. Sallie Mae securities are not guaranteed, but generally insured by the federal government and its agencies. These securities include floating-rate and fixed-rate obligations with maturities of five years or more as well as discount notes with maturities from a few days to 360 days.

INVESTING IN MONEY MARKET FUNDS

Money market funds are a special form of mutual funds. The investor can own a portfolio of high-yielding CDs, T-bills, and other similar securities of short-term nature, with a small amount to invest. There is a great deal of liquidity and flexibility in withdrawing funds through check-writing privileges. Money market funds are considered very conservative, because most of the securities purchased by the funds are quite safe.

Money market mutual funds invest in short-term government securities, commercial paper, and certificates of deposits. They provide more safety of principal than other mutual funds since net asset value never fluctuates. Each share has a net asset value of $1. The yield, however, fluctuates daily. The advantages are:

- Money market funds are no-load.

- There may be a low deposit in these funds.

- The fund is a form of checking account, allowing a firm to write checks against its balance in the account.

The disadvantage is that the deposit in these funds is not insured as it is in a money market account or other federally insured deposit in banks.

Exhibit 50-2 ranks various short-term investment vehicles in terms of their default risk.

Exhibit 50-2: Default Risk Among Short-Term Investment Vehicles

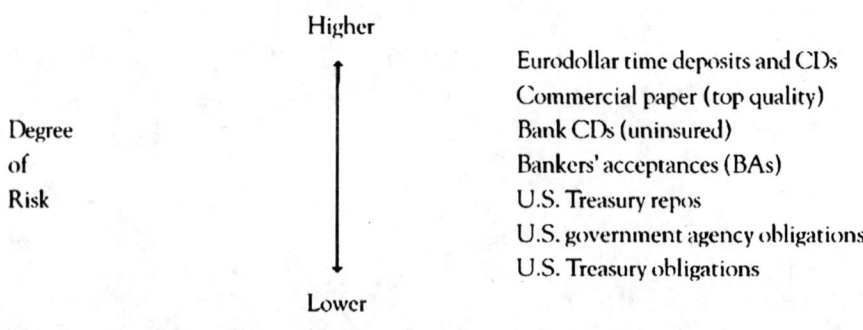

PREFERRED STOCK—A HYBRID SECURITY

Preferred stock carries a fixed dividend that is paid quarterly. The dividend is stated in dollar terms per share, or as a percentage of par (stated) value of the stock. Preferred stock is considered a hybrid security because it possesses features of both common stock and a corporate bond. It is like common stock in that:

- It represents equity ownership and is issued without stated maturity dates.

- It pays dividends.

Preferred stock is also like a corporate bond in that:

- It provides for prior claims on earnings and assets.

- Its dividend is fixed for the life of the issue.

- It can carry call and convertible features and sinking fund provisions.

Since preferred stocks are traded on the basis of the yield offered to investors, they are in effect viewed as fixed income securities and, as a result, are in competition with bonds in the marketplace.

Note: Corporate bonds, however, occupy a position senior to preferred stocks.

Advantages of owning preferred stocks include:

- Their high current income, which is highly predictable.

- Safety.

- Lower unit cost ($10 to $25 per share).

Disadvantages are:

- Their susceptibility to inflation and high interest rates.

- They lack substantial capital gains potential.

Preferred Stock Ratings

Like bond ratings, Standard & Poor's and Moody's have long rated the investment quality of preferred stocks. S&P uses basically the same rating system as they do with bonds, except that triple A ratings are not given to preferred stocks. Moody's uses a slightly different system, which is given in the following section. These ratings are intended to provide an indication of the quality of the issue and are based largely on an assessment of the firm's ability to pay preferred dividends in a prompt and timely fashion.

Note: Preferred stock ratings should not be compared with bond ratings as they are not equivalent; preferred stocks occupy a position junior to bonds.

HOW TO CALCULATE EXPECTED RETURN FROM PREFERRED STOCK

The expected return from preferred stock is calculated in a manner similar to the expected return on bonds. The calculations depend upon whether the preferred stock is issued in perpetuity or if it has a call that is likely to be exercised.

Moody's Preferred Stock Rating System

Rating Symbol	Definition
aaa	Top Quality
aa	High grade
a	Upper medium grade
baa	Lower medium grade
ba	Speculative type
b	Little assurance of future dividends
caa	Likely to be already in arrears

A Perpetuity. Since preferred stock usually has no maturity date when the company must redeem it, you cannot calculate a yield to maturity. You can calculate a current yield as follows:

$$\text{Current yield} = D/P$$

where

D = annual dividend, and P = the market price of the preferred stock.

    EXAMPLE 10: A preferred stock paying $4.00 a year in dividends and having a market price of $25 would have a current yield of 16% ($4/$25).

Yield to Call. If a call is likely, a more appropriate return measure is yield to call (YTC). Theoretically, YTC is the rate that equates the present value of the future dividends and the call price with the current market price of the preferred stock. Two examples are given below.

    EXAMPLE 11: Consider the following two preferreds:

Preferreds	Market Price	Call Price	Dividends	Term to Call	YTC
A	$8/share	$9	$1/year	3 years	16.06%
B	10	9	$1	3	6.89

Comparison to Bond Yields. The example shows that yields on straight preferreds are closely correlated to bond yields, since both are fixed income securities. However, yields on preferreds are often below bond yields, which seems unusual because preferreds have a position junior to bonds. The reason is that corporate investors favor preferreds over bonds because of a dividend exclusion allowed in determining corporate taxable income, which will be explained in the following section.

ADJUSTABLE RATE PREFERRED STOCK

Corporate treasurers with excess funds can make short-term investments in long-term securities such as long-term bonds and common and preferred stocks. They may be naturally averse to the price volatility of long-term bonds, especially when they put money aside for a specific payment such as income taxes. Perhaps for a similar reason, common and preferred stocks would be equally unattractive for short-term investments. But this is not quite true, since these securities provide an interesting tax advantage for corporations. For example, if the company invests its surplus funds in a short-or long-term debt, it must pay tax on the interest received. Thus, for $1 of interest, a corporation in a 46% marginal tax bracket ends up with only $0.54. However, companies pay tax on only 20% of dividends received from investments in stocks. [Under current tax laws, corporations are allowed to exclude 80% of the dividends they receive from a stock (either common or preferred) from their taxable income.] Thus, for $1 of dividends received, the firm winds up with $1 - (.20 × .46) = $0.91. The effective tax rate is only 9.1%.

The problem with preferred stocks is that since preferred dividends are fixed, the prices of preferred shares change when long-term interest rates change. Many corporate money managers are reluctant to buy straight preferred because of its interest risk. To encourage corporate investments in preferred shares, a new type of preferred stock was introduced in May 1982 by Chemical New York Corporation. These securities—the so-called adjustable rate (floating rate) preferreds—pay dividends that go up and down with the general level of interest rates. The prices of these securities are therefore less volatile than fixed-dividend preferreds, and they are a safer haven for the corporation's excess cash. Yields obtained from preferreds may be lower than the debt issue. The corporations buying the preferreds would still be happy with the lower yield because 80% of the dividends they receive escape tax.

Preferred Stock Quotation

If preferred stocks are listed on the organized exchanges, they are reported in the same sections as common stocks in newspapers. The symbol "pf" appears after the name of the corporation, designating the issue as preferred. Preferred stocks are read the same way as common stock quotations. Two companies are illustrated below.

Stock	Div	Y/d%	PIE Ratio	Sales 100s	High	Low	Close	Net Chg
(1) A can pf	13.75	11.8	—	5	117	117	117	–7/8
(2) Aetna pf	4.97e	9.3	—	10	53/	43 1/8	43/	–1/8

In stock (2), the e symbol after the dividend indicates a varying dividend payment; this issue is probably adjustable preferred.

INVESTING IN MONEY MARKET PREFERRED STOCK

The money market preferred stock (MMPS), also known as auction-rate preferred stock, is the newest and most popular member of the preferred stock group attractive to corporate investors since it offers the following advantages:

- Low market risk in the event of price decline.
- Competitive yield.
- Liquidity.

MMPS pays dividends and adjusts rates up or down, depending on the current market, every seven weeks. Unlike other adjustable preferreds, the market, not the issuer, sets the rate at the auction. If no bids are placed for a stock, MMPS' dividend rate is automatically set at the 60-day AA commercial paper rate quoted by the Federal Reserve Bank. There is a possibility, however, of a failed auction if no buyers show up at the auction. Corporate investors must take into account the credit quality of a money market preferred stock. Money market preferreds include:

- Short-term Auction-Rate Stock (STARS).
- Dutch-Auction-Rate Transferable Securities (DARTS).
- Market-Auction Preferred Stock (MAPS).
- Auction-Market Preferred Stock (AMPS).
- Cumulative Auction-Market Preferred Stock (CAMPS).

CORPORATE CASH MANAGEMENT: CURRENT TRENDS

The current business, economic and regulatory environments offer both opportunities and challenges for cash managers seeking to optimize their cash positions. Coupled with the aftermath of the Sarbanes-Oxley Act of 2002, which enforced stricter regulations around transparency and fiduciary oversight, cash managers or chief investment officers (CIOs) face a challenging environment that calls for a proactive approach to cash management. Given this environment, maintaining an optimal cash position is essential for CFOs, controllers, and treasurers, who have the opportunity to improve their companies' balance sheets through sound, flexible cash management strategies. This section addresses how companies are answering these issues, provides insight on key trends in liquidity management, and offers strategies for maximizing cash management.

Classifying Investments on the Balance Sheet

With the increased scrutiny and accounting changes that are occurring today, companies must be very careful about how they classify investments on their balance sheets. In the past, when a company classified assets on the balance sheet, they were classified as *cash and cash equivalents* and *short-term marketable securities*. The FASB is dropping "cash and cash equivalents" and redefining what "cash" means. Anything that is not considered "cash" now becomes a "short-term marketable security," effectively eliminating the classification of *cash equivalent*. IFRS (IAS 7) also defines:

- *Cash.* Comprises cash on hand and demand deposits with banks.
- *Cash equivalents.* Short-term, highly liquid investments that are readily convertible into known amounts of cash and that are subject to an insignificant amount of risk of changes in value.

Cash-Investment Policies on the Rise

A number of developments in recent years—including enactment of the Sarbanes-Oxley Act of 2002—have prompted many companies to adopt stricter liquidity management policies as part of improving financial controls. One of the obvious reasons for developing a written policy is that these companies have a fiduciary responsibility to their shareholders. Clearly delineating cash investment policies helps address today's more stringent transparency mandates and at the same time provides better controls for the company.

Diversification Not Fully Realized

While many organizations' policies allow for the use of a significant variety of investment vehicles for short-term investments, relatively few of those companies embrace the opportunity to fully diversify. The number of different investments in a company's short-term portfolio is often a function of an organization's relative level of sophistication and resources. For example, companies with fewer resources or limited internal expertise may not have the ability to perform credit research. They may lean toward *plain vanilla* or more conservative investments, thereby making use of only a small portion of the market. To achieve a much fuller range of diversification, many more organizations are enlisting an outside professional investment manager to administer at least some of their short-term portfolios.

Expanding Allowable Investments

One category of short-term investments that could provide additional return, but which companies are not turning to in very large numbers, includes investment-grade securities at the lower end of the ratings scale. Companies' investment policies often dictate the levels of investment quality that are required in order to invest in various corporate-debt or municipal-debt vehicles. Some policies ignore the potential viability of BBB or even A-rated investments. These ratings may not be the highest, but the investments they represent can actually offer excellent risk/reward characteristics. In effect, policies may establish credit-quality requirements that could be described as too conservative in certain instances. For instance, a policy that forbids investment in BBB-rated municipal bonds might impose an unnecessary opportunity cost, when one considers that such bonds have had lower historical default rates than some AAA-rated corporate debt. *Cash plus funds* could offer a similar opportunity for higher returns, but relatively few liquidity managers are including them in their portfolios. *Cash plus* indicates something beyond a simple money market fund, such as ultra-short bond funds with fluctuating net asset values, or even what are sometimes called *enhanced-cash* funds.

Investing Offshore

Another growing trend is for companies to invest cash outside the United States. Companies invest offshore for many reasons, such as to avoid certain U.S. taxes or to domicile an offshore insurance captive. However, CIOs must assess the foreign tax implications of maintaining cash offshore before making substantial investments.

Taking Control with Electronic Trading Portals

Another trend is the choice made by many businesses to use an electronic, multi-family fund trading portal to execute at least some of their short-term investment transactions, including money market mutual funds. This *self-service* approach is more common among large corporations with dedicated teams who trade frequently and can therefore more readily realize economic gains from an electronic trading portal. Frequently, companies that use an electronic, multifamily trading portal complement this approach by having a professional investment manager oversee a core portion of their portfolios. The way some companies approach liquidity management is to make overnight or money market investments—representing their primary liquidity—through the electronic, multifamily trading portal. They then outsource to a professional investment manager the responsibility of investing the other core cash balances in longer-term instruments.

Outsourcing Gaining Popularity

Outsourcing is gaining popularity in the corporate money management space. An increasing number of companies have been looking for advice and guidance from professional money managers. Outside money managers can provide companies with the market knowledge and insight needed to more effectively diversify their short-term investments while seeking to capture opportunities for higher returns than they currently achieve. Outsourced professional liquidity managers are expected to provide key ongoing services such as strategic consulting, investment policy development, delivery of consistent, informative and timely reports, and in-person investment reviews with the companies.

CHAPTER 51

PORTFOLIO DIVERSIFICATION AND FINANCIAL RISK MANAGEMENT

CONTENTS

Portfolio theory is concerned with the composition of an investment portfolio that is efficient in balancing the risk with rate of return. The core assumption of the theory is that rational investors behave in a way that reflects their aversion to taking increased risk without being compensated by an adequate increase in expected return. Further, for any given expected return, most investors will prefer a lower risk, and for any given level of risk, they will prefer a higher return to a lower return.

Most financial assets are not held in isolation, but instead as parts of portfolios. Therefore, risk/return analysis should not be confined to single assets only. Controllers should look at the gains from diversification and the portfolio's risk. The rationale behind portfolio diversification is the reduction of risk, and the main method of reducing that risk is the combining of assets, which are not perfectly positively correlated in their returns.

PORTFOLIO RETURN

The expected return on a portfolio (r_p) is simply the weighted-average return of the individual sets in the portfolio, the weights being the fraction of the total funds invested in each asset:

$$r_\rho = w_1 r_1 + w_2 r_2 + \cdots + w_n r_n = \sum_{j=1}^{n} w_j r_j$$

where r_j = expected return on each individual asset

w_j = fraction for each respective asset investment

n = number of assets in the portfolio

$$\sum_{j=1}^{n} w_j = 1.0$$

EXAMPLE 1: A portfolio consists of assets A and B. Asset A makes up one-third of the portfolio and has an expected return of 18%. Asset B makes up the other two-thirds of the portfolio and is expected to earn 9%. The expected return on the portfolio is:

Asset	Return (r$_j$)	Fraction (w$_j$)	w$_j$r$_j$
A	18%	1/3	1/3×18% = 6%
B	9%	2/3	2/3×9% = 6%
			r$_\rho$ = 12%

PORTFOLIO RISK

Unlike returns, the risk of a portfolio (σ_ρ) is not simply the weighted average of the standard deviations of the individual assets. It is smaller than the weighted average of the assets' standard deviations. In fact, a portfolio's risk is also dependent on the correlation coefficients of its assets. The correlation coefficient (ρ) is a measure of the degree to which two variables "move" together. It has a numerical value that ranges from –1.0 to 1.0. In a two-asset (A and B) portfolio, the portfolio risk is defined as:

$$\sigma_\rho = \sqrt{w_A^2 \sigma_A^2 + w_B^2 \sigma_B^2 + 2 \rho_{AB} w_A w_B \sigma_A \sigma_B}$$

where

σ_A and σ_B = standard deviations of assets A and B, respectively

w_α and w_β = weights, or fractions, of total funds invested in assets A and B

ρ_{AB} = the correlation coefficient between assets A and B

Incidentally, the correlation coefficient is the measurement of joint movement between two securities.

DIVERSIFICATION

As can be seen in the preceding formula, the portfolio risk, measured in terms of s is not the weighted average of the individual asset risks in the portfolio. We have in the formula a third term, (r), which makes a significant contribution to the overall portfolio risk. What the formula shows is that portfolio risk can be minimized or completely eliminated by diversification. The degree of reduction in portfolio risk depends on the correlation between the assets being combined. Generally speaking, by combining two perfectly negatively correlated assets (r = –1.0), the risk can be completely eliminated. In the real world, however, most securities are negatively, but not perfectly correlated. In fact, most assets are positively correlated. Still, portfolio risk can be reduced by combining even positively correlated assets. An example of the latter might be ownership of two automobile stocks or two housing stocks.

EXAMPLE 2: Assume the following:

Asset	σ	w
A	20%	1/3
B	10%	2/3

The portfolio risk then is:

$$\sigma_p = \sqrt{w_A^2 \sigma_A^2 + w_B^2 \sigma_B^2 + 2\rho_{AB}\, w_A\, w_B\, \sigma_A\, \sigma_B}$$

$$= \sqrt{[(1/3)^2\,(0.2)^2 + (2/3)^2(0.1)^2 + 2\rho_{AB}(1/3)(2/3)(0.2)(0.1)]}$$

$$= \sqrt{0.0089 + 0.0089\rho_{AB}}$$

(a) Now assume that the correlation coefficient between A and B is +1 (a perfectly positive correlation). This means that when the value of asset A increases in response to market conditions, so does the value of asset B, and it does so at exactly the same rate as A. The portfolio risk when ρ_{AB} = +1 then becomes:

$$\sigma_p = \sqrt{0.0089 + 0.0089\rho_{AB}} = \sqrt{0.0089 + 0.0089(+1)} = \sqrt{0.0178} = 0.1334 = 13.34\%$$

(b) If ρ_{AB} = 0, the assets lack correlation and the portfolio risk is simply the risk of the expected returns on the assets—that is, the weighted average of the standard deviations of the individual assets in the portfolio. Therefore, when ρ_{AB} = 0, the portfolio risk for this example is:

$$\sigma_p = \sqrt{0.0089 + 0.0089\rho_{AB}} = \sqrt{0.0089 + 0.0089(0)} = \sqrt{0.0089} = 0.0943 = 9.43\%$$

(c) If $\rho_{AB} = -1$ (a perfectly negative correlation coefficient), then as the price of A rises, the price of B declines at the very same rate. In such a case, risk would be completely eliminated. Therefore, when $\rho_{AB} = -1$, the portfolio risk is:

$$\sigma_p = \sqrt{0.0089 + 0.0089\rho_{AB}} = \sqrt{0.0089 + 0.0089(-1)} = \sqrt{0.0089 - 0.0089} = \sqrt{0} = 0$$

When we compare the results of (a), (b), and (c), we see that a positive correlation between assets increases a portfolio's risk above the level found at zero correlation, whereas a perfectly negative correlation eliminates that risk.

EXAMPLE 3: To illustrate the point of diversification, assume data on the following three securities are as follows:

Year	Security X (%)	Security Y (%)	Security Z (%)
2X08	10	50	10
2X09	20	40	20
2X10	30	30	30
2X11	40	20	40
2X12	50	10	50
r_j	30	30	30
σ_p	14.14	14.14	14.14

Note here that securities X and Y have a perfectly negative correlation, and securities X and Z have a perfectly positive correlation. Notice what happens to the portfolio risk when X and Y, and X and Z are combined, assume that funds are split equally between the two securities in each portfolio:

Year	Portfolio XY (50% = 50%)	Portfolio XZ (50% = 50%)
2X08	30	10
2X09	30	20
2X10	30	30

Year	Portfolio XY (50% = 50%)	Portfolio XZ (50% = 50%)
2X11	30	40
2X12	30	50
r_ρ	30	30
σ_ρ	0	14.14

Again, see that the two perfectly negative correlated securities (XY) result in a zero overall risk.

THE CAPITAL ASSET PRICING MODEL

An asset's risk consists of two components: (1) diversifiable risk and (2) nondiversifiable risk.

Diversifiable risk, sometimes called *company-specific risk, controllable risk*, or *unsystematic risk*, represents the portion of a security's risk that can be eliminated by diversification. This type of risk is unique to a specific company's operations—new products, patents, acquisitions, competition, for example—and thus is not priced.

Nondiversifiable risk, sometimes referred to as *market risk, noncontrollable risk*, or *systematic risk*, results from forces outside of the firm's control and cannot be eliminated by diversification. The relevant risk of an individual asset is its contribution to the riskiness of a well-diversified portfolio, which is the asset's market risk. Because market risk cannot be controlled by diversification, investors must be compensated for bearing it. The market risk is measured by the *beta* coefficient. Beta measures the extent to which the stock's returns move relative to the market.

The capital asset pricing model (CAPM) relates the market risk to the level of expected or required rate of return on a security. It answers the question: How much return is required to compensate investors for a given amount of risk?

The model is given as follows:

$$r_i = r_f + b(r_m - r_f)$$

where

r_i = the expected (or required) return on security I

r_f = the risk-free security (such as a T-bill)

r_m = the expected return on the market portfolio (such as Standard & Poor's 500 Stock Composite Index)

b = beta, an index of market risk.

In words, the CAPM equation shows that the required (expected) rate of return on a given security (r $_i$) is equal to the return required for securities that have no risk (r $_f$) plus a risk premium required by investors for assuming a given level of risk. The higher the degree of market risk (b), the higher the return on a given security demanded by investors.

A guide for reading betas follows:

Beta	Meaning
0	The security's return is independent of the market. An example is a risk-free security (e.g., T-Bill).
0.5	The security is half as volatile as the market.
1.0	The security is as volatile or risky as the market (i.e., average risk). This is the beta value of the market portfolio (e.g., Standard &Poor's 500).
2.0	The security is twice as volatile or risky as the market.

Beta measures volatility. Put another way, it is a measure of a security's return over time versus that of the overall market. For example, if ABC's beta is 1.5, it means that if the stock market goes up 10%, ABC's common stock goes up 15%; if the market goes down 10%, ABC goes down 15%. Beta of a particular stock is useful in predicting how much the security will go up or down, provided that investors know which way the market will go. The higher the beta for a security, the greater the return expected (or demanded) by the investor.

Note: A low beta, however, does not necessarily mean lower volatility—just that the fund does not have a high correlation with its benchmark. The beta is used for comparative purposes only. It should not be interpreted as a predictor or a guarantee of future performance.

EXAMPLE 4: Assuming that the risk-free rate (r_f) is 8%, and the expected return for the market (r_m) is 12%, if:

$b = 0$ (risk-free security)	$r_j = 8\% + 0(12\% - 8\%) = 8\%$
$b = 0.5$	$r_j = 8\% + 0.5(12\% - 8\%) = 10\%$
$b = 1.0$ (market portfolio)	$r_j = 8\% + 1.0(12\% - 8\%) = 12\%$
$b = 2.0$	$r_j = 8\% + 2.0(12\% - 8\%) = 16\%$

EXAMPLE 5: XYZ stock actually returned 9%. Assuming that the risk-free rate (e.g., return on a T-bill) = 5%, market return (e.g., return on the S&P 500) = 10%, and XYZ's beta = 1.5. Then the return on XYZ stock required by investors would be

Expected (required) return $= 5\% + 1.5 (10\% - 5\%) = 5\% + 7.5\% = 12.5\%$

Because the actual return (9%) is less than the required return (12.5%), investors would not be willing to buy the stock.

Betas for stocks (and mutual funds) are widely available in many investment newsletters, directories, and online financial sites (e.g., Google Finance and MSN Money Central Investor).

Exhibit 51-1 presents betas for some selected companies.

Exhibit 51-1: Betas for Some Selected Corporations

Company	December 11, 2013
Boeing (BA)	1.19
Google (GOOG)	0.87
Toyota (TM)	0.70
Nordstrom (JWN)	1.31
Intel (INTC)	0.93
Wal Mart (WMT)	0.41

Source: MSN Money Central Investor (http://money.msn.com)

THE ARBITRAGE PRICING MODEL

Arbitrage pricing model (APM) is based on the assumption that an asset's return is based on multiple systematic risk factors. This is an attempt to dispute the CAPM, which uses just one risk factor, the asset's *beta*, to explain the asset's return. The APM includes any number of risk factors:

$$r = r_f + b_1 RP_1 + b_2 RP_2 + \ldots + b_n RP_n$$

where

r = the expected return for a given stock or portfolio

r_f = the risk-free rate

b_i = the sensitivity (or reaction) of the returns of the stock to unexpected changes in economic forces ($i = 1, \ldots n$)

RP_i = the market risk premium associated with an unexpected change in the ith economic force.

n = the number of relevant economic forces.

The following five economic forces are often suggested:

1. Changes in expected inflation.
2. Unanticipated changes in inflation.
3. Unanticipated changes in industrial production.
4. Unanticipated changes in the yield differential between low-and high-grade bonds (the default-risk premium).
5. Unanticipated changes in the yield differential between long-term and short-term bonds (the term structure of interest rates).

In addition, industry factors, investor confidence, exchange rates, oil prices, and a host of other variables play a role. It appears, however, that the ability to describe with confidence the underlying reasons for cross-sectional differences in average returns, is a long way off.

EXAMPLE 6: A three-factor APM holds, and the risk-free rate is 6%. An investor is interested in two particular stocks: A and B. The returns on both stocks are related to factors 1 and 2 as follows:

$$r = 0.06 + b_1(0.09) - b_2(0.03) + b_3(0.04)$$

The sensitivity coefficients for the two stocks follow:

Stock	b_1	b_2	b_3
A	0.70	0.80	0.20
B	0.50	0.04	1.20

The expected returns on both stocks can be calculated as follows:

For stock A: $r = 0.06 + (0.07)(0.09) - (0.80)(0.03) + (0.20)(0.04) = 10.70\%$

For stock B: $r = 0.06 + (0.50)(0.09) - (0.04)(0.03) + (1.20)(0.04) = 14.10\%$

Stock B requires a higher return, indicating it is the riskier of the two. Part of the reason is that its return is substantially more sensitive to the third economic force than is stock A's return.

CHAPTER 52

SHORT-TERM FINANCING

CONTENTS

This chapter provides the financial manager with a "broad picture" of short-term financing sources including their advantages and disadvantages. Short-term refers to financing that will be repaid in one year or less. Short-term financing may be used to meet seasonal and temporary fluctuations in funds position as well as to meet permanent needs. For instance, short-term financing may be used to provide additional working capital, finance current assets (such as receivables and inventory), or provide interim financing for a long-term project (such as the acquisition of plant and equipment) until long-term financing may be issued. Long-term financing may not be appropriate at the present time because of, say, perceived long-term credit risk or excessively high cost.

When compared to long-term financing, short-term financing has several advantages including being easier to arrange, less expensive, and more flexible. The drawbacks of short-term financing are that interest rates fluctuate more often (also resulting in greater earnings sensitivity), refinancing is frequently required, there is greater risk of not being able to pay, and delinquent repayment may be detrimental to the company's credit rating. The financial manager can hedge interest rate risk by selling and later buying back interest rate futures contracts to offset an increase in interest expense with the corresponding profit from the futures transaction.

What sources of short-term financing can be tapped? They include trade credit, bank loans, bankers' acceptances, finance company loans, commercial paper, receivable financing, and inventory financing. A particular source may be more appropriate in a given circumstance. Some are more desirable than others because of interest rates or collateral requirements.

You should consider the merits of the different alternative sources of short-term financing. The factors bearing upon the selection of a particular source include:

- *Cost.*
- *Effect on financial ratios.*
- *Effect on credit rating.* Some sources of short-term financing may negatively impact the company's credit rating, such as factoring accounts receivable.
- *Risk.* Consider the reliability of the source of funds for future borrowing. If the company is materially affected by outside forces, it will need more stability and reliability in financing.
- *Restrictions.* Certain lenders may impose restrictions, such as requiring a minimum level of working capital.
- *Flexibility.* Certain lenders are more willing to work with the company, for example, to adjust periodically the amount of funds needed.
- *Expected money market conditions (e.g., future interest rates) and availability of future financing.*
- *Inflation rate.*
- *Profitability and liquidity positions.* A company must be liquid to pay its near-term obligations.
- *Stability and maturity of operations.*
- *Tax rate.*

If the company will be short of cash during certain times, the financial manager should arrange for financing (such as a line of credit) in advance instead of waiting for an emergency.

HOW TO USE TRADE CREDIT

Trade credit (accounts payable) are balances owed suppliers. It is a spontaneous (recurring) financing source since it comes from normal operations. Trade credit is the least expensive form of financing inventory. The benefits of trade credit are: it is readily available, since suppliers want business; collateral is not required; interest is typically not demanded or, if so, the rate is minimal; it is convenient; and trade creditors are frequently lenient if the company gets into financial trouble. If the company has liquidity difficulties, it may be able to stretch (extend) accounts payable; however, among the disadvantages of doing so are the giving up of any cash discount offered and the probability of lowering the company's credit rating. A report should be prepared analyzing accounts payable in terms of lost discounts, aged debit balances, aged unpaid invoices, and days to pay.

EXAMPLE 1: The company purchases $500 worth of merchandise per day from suppliers. The terms of purchase are net/60, and the company pays on time. The accounts payable balance is:

$$\$500 \text{ per day} \times 60 \text{ days} = \$30,000$$

The company should typically take advantage of a cash discount offered on the early payment of accounts payable because the failure to do so results in a high opportunity cost. The cost of not taking a discount equals:

$$\left(\frac{\text{Discount lost}}{\substack{\text{Dollar proceeds you} \\ \text{have use of by not} \\ \text{taking the discount}}} \right) \times \left(\frac{360}{\substack{\text{Number of days you have} \\ \text{use of the money by} \\ \text{not taking the discount}}} \right)$$

EXAMPLE 2: The company buys $1,000 in merchandise on terms of 2/10, net/30. The company fails to take the discount and pays the bill on the 30th day. The cost of the discount is:

$$\frac{\$20}{\$980} \times \frac{360}{20} = 36.7\%$$

The company would be better off taking the discount since the opportunity cost is 36.7%, even if it needed to borrow the money from the bank. The interest rate on a bank loan would be far less than 36.7%.

WHEN BANK LOANS ARE ADVISABLE

Even though other institutions (e.g., savings and loan associations, credit unions) provide banking services, most banking activities are conducted by commercial banks. Commercial banks give the company the ability to operate with minimal cash and still be confident of planning activities even in light of uncertainty.

Commercial banks favor short-term loans since they like to see their money back within one year. However, loans in excess of one year may be given. There is an intimacy between the company and the bank that is the case with typical supplier relationships. If the company is large, a group of banks may form a consortium to furnish the desired level of capital.

Bank loans are not spontaneous financing as is trade credit. One example is a self-liquidating (seasonal) loan used to pay for a temporary increase in accounts receivable or inventory. As soon as the assets realize cash, the loan is repaid.

The prime interest rate is the lowest interest rate applied to short-term loans from a bank charged the most creditworthy companies. The company's interest rate may be higher depending upon its risk.

Bank financing may take the following forms:

- Unsecured loans.
- Secured loans.
- Lines of credit.
- Installment loans.

Unsecured Loans

Most short-term unsecured (no collateral) loans are self-liquidating. This kind of loan is recommended if the company has an excellent credit rating. It is usually used to finance projects having quick cash flows. It is appropriate if the company has immediate cash and can either repay the loan in the near future or quickly obtain longer-term financing. Seasonal cash shortfalls and desired inventory build-ups are reasons to use an unsecured loan. The disadvantages of this kind of loan are that, because it is made for the short term, it carries a higher interest rate than a secured loan and payment in a lump sum is required.

Secured Loans

If the company's credit rating is deficient, the bank may lend money only on a secured basis. Collateral may take many forms including inventory, marketable securities, or fixed assets.

Tip: Even though the company is able to obtain an unsecured loan, it may still give collateral to get a lower interest rate.

Line of Credit

Under a line of credit, the bank agrees to lend money on a recurring basis up to a specified amount. Credit lines are typically established for a 1-year period and may be renewed annually. Determine if the line of credit is adequate for present and immediate future needs.

The advantages of a line of credit are the easy and immediate access to funds during tight money market conditions and the ability to borrow only as much as needed and repay immediately when cash is available.

Recommendation: Use a line of credit if the company is working on large individual projects for a long time period and obtain minimal or no payments until the job is completed. The disadvantages relate to the collateral requirements and the additional financial information that must be presented to the bank. Also, the bank may place restrictions upon the company, such as a ceiling on capital expenditures or the maintenance of a minimum level of working capital. Further, the bank typically charges a commitment fee on the amount of the unused credit line.

When the company borrows under a line of credit, it may be required to maintain a compensating balance (deposit with the bank that does not earn interest). The compensating balance is stated as a percentage of the loan and effectively increases the cost of the loan. A compensating balance may also be placed on the unused portion of a line of credit, in which case the interest rate would be reduced.

EXAMPLE 3: The company borrows $200,000 and is required to keep a 12% compensating balance. It also has an unused line of credit of $100,000, for which a 10% compensating balance is required. The minimum balance that must be maintained is:

$$(\$200,000 \times .12) + (\$100,000 \times .10) = \$24,000 + \$10,000 = \$34,000$$

A line of credit is typically decided upon prior to the actual borrowing. In the days between the arrangement for the loan and the actual borrowing, interest rates will change. Therefore, the agreement will stipulate the loan is at the prime interest rate prevailing when the loan is extended plus a risk premium.

Note: The prime interest rate is not known until you actually borrow the money.

The bank may test the company's financial capability by requiring it to "clean up," that is, repay the loan for a brief time during the year (e.g., for one month). If the company is unable to repay a short-term loan, it should probably finance with long-term funds. The payment shows the bank that the loan is actually seasonal rather than permanent.

Letter of Credit

A letter of credit is a conditional bank commitment on behalf of the company to pay a third party in accordance with specified terms and commitments. Payment may be made on submission of proof of shipment or other performance. The advantages are that the company does not have to pay cash in advance of shipment and funds could be used elsewhere in the business. Banks charge a fee and a rate for bankers' acceptances arising after shipment which approximates the prime interest rate.

Revolving Credit

With revolving credit, notes are short term (typically 90 days). The financial officer may renew the loan or borrow additional funds up to a maximum amount. Advantages are readily available credit and fewer restrictions relative to the line-of-credit agreement. A disadvantage is the bank restrictions.

Installment Loans

An installment loan requires monthly payments. When the principal on the loan decreases sufficiently, refinancing can take place at lower interest rates.

The advantage of this kind of loan is that it may be tailored to satisfy seasonal financing needs.

Interest

Interest on a loan may be paid either at maturity (ordinary interest) or in advance (discounting the loan). When interest is paid in advance, the loan proceeds are reduced and the effective (true) interest cost is increased.

EXAMPLE 4: The company borrows $30,000 at 16% interest per annum and repays the loan one year later. The interest is $30,000 × .16 = $4,800. The effective interest rate is 16% ($4,800/$30,000).

EXAMPLE 5: Assume the same facts as in the prior example, except the note is discounted. The effective interest rate increases as follows:

Proceeds = Principal-Interest = $30,000 − $4,800 = $25,200

$$\text{Effective interest rate} = \frac{\text{Interests}}{\text{Proceeds}} = \frac{\$4,800}{\$25,000} = 19\%$$

A compensating balance will increase the effective interest rate.

EXAMPLE 6: The effective interest rate for a one-year, $600,000 loan that has a nominal interest rate of 19%, with interest due at maturity and requiring a 15% compensating balance follows:

Effective interest rate (with compensating balance) equals:

$$\frac{\text{Interest rate} \times \text{Principal}}{\text{Proceeds, \%} \times \text{Principal}} = \frac{.19 \times \$600,000}{(1.00 - .15) \times \$600,000}$$

$$= \frac{\$114,000}{\$510,000} = 22.4\%$$

EXAMPLE 7: Assume the same facts as in the prior example, except that the loan is discounted. The effective interest rate is:

Effective interest rate (with discount) equals:

$$\frac{\text{Interest rate} \times \text{Principal}}{(\text{Proceeds, \%} \times \text{Principal}) - \text{Interest}}$$

$$\frac{0.19 \times \$600,000}{(0.85 \times \$600,000) - \$114,000} = \frac{\$114,000}{\$396,000} = 28.8\%$$

EXAMPLE 8: The company has a credit line of $400,000, but it must maintain a compensating balance of 13% on outstanding loans and a compensating balance of 10% on the unused credit. The interest rate on the loan is 18%. The company borrows $275,000. The effective interest rate on the loan is calculated as follows.

The required compensating balance is:

.13 × $275,000	$35,750
.10 × 125,000	12,500
	$48,250

Effective interest rate (with line of credit) equals:

$$\frac{\text{Interest rate (on loan)} \times \text{Principal}}{\text{Principal} - \text{Compensating balance}}$$

$$\frac{0.18 \times \$275,000}{\$275,000 - \$48,250} = \frac{\$49,500}{\$226,750} = 21.8\%$$

On an installment loan, the effective interest rate computation is illustrated below. Assuming a one-year loan payable in equal monthly installments, the effective rate is based on the average amount outstanding for the year. The interest is computed on the face amount of the loan.

EXAMPLE 9: The company borrows $40,000 at an interest rate of 10% to be paid in 12 monthly installments. The average loan balance is $40,000/2 = $20,000. The effective interest rate is $4,000/$20,000 = 20%.

EXAMPLE 10: Assume the same facts as in the prior example, except that the loan is discounted. The interest of $4,000 is deducted in advance so the proceeds received are $40,000 − $4,000 = $36,000. The average loan balance is $36,000/2 = $18,000. The effective interest rate is $4,000/$18,000 = 22.2%.

The effective interest cost computation may be more complicated when installment payments differ. The true interest cost of an installment loan is the internal rate of return of the applicable cash flows converted on an annual basis (if desired).

EXAMPLE 11: The company borrows $100,000 and will repay it in three monthly installments of $25,000, $25,000, and $50,000. The interest rate is 12%.

Amount of borrowing equals:

Installment loan	$100,000
Less: Interest on first installment ($100,000 × .25 × .12)	3,000
Balance	$97,000

Effective interest cost of installment loan equals:

$$0 = \$97,000 + \$25,000/(1 + \text{Cost}) + \$25,000/(1 + \text{Cost})2 + \$50,000/(1 + \text{Cost})3$$

= 1.37% on monthly basis

= 1.37% × 12 = 16.44% on annual basis

Bankers' Acceptances

A bankers' acceptance is a short-term non-interest-bearing draft (age to six months), drawn by the company and accepted by a bank, that orders payment to a third party at a later date. It is typically issued up to $1 million on a discount basis. The creditworthiness of the draft is of good quality because it has the backing of the bank, not the drawer. It is, in essence, a debt instrument created out of a self-liquidating business transaction. Bankers' acceptances are often used to finance the shipment and handling of both domestic and foreign merchandise. Acceptances are classed as short-term financing because they typically have maturities of less than 180 days.

Dealing with the Banker

Banks are anxious to lend money to meet self-liquidating, cyclical business needs. A short-term bank loan is an inexpensive way to obtain funds to satisfy working capital requirements during the business cycle. However, the financial officer must be able to explain what the company's needs are in an intelligent manner.

COMMERCIAL FINANCE LOANS

When credit is unavailable from a bank, the company may have to go to a commercial finance company. The finance company loan has a higher interest rate than a bank, and generally is secured. Typically, the amount of collateral placed will be greater than the balance of the loan. Collateral includes accounts receivable, inventories, and fixed assets. Commercial finance companies also finance the installment purchases of industrial equipment by firms. A portion of their financing is sometimes obtained through commercial bank borrowing at wholesale rates.

ISSUING COMMERCIAL PAPER

Commercial paper can be issued only if the company possesses a very high credit rating. Therefore, the interest rate is less than that of a bank loan, typically 1/2% below the prime interest rate. Commercial paper is unsecured and sold at a discount (below face value). The maturity date is usually less than 270 days, otherwise Securities and Exchange Commission (SEC) registration is needed. Since the note is sold at a discount, the interest is immediately deducted from the face of the note by the creditor, but the company will pay the full face value. Commercial paper may be issued through a dealer or directly placed to an institutional investor.

The benefits of commercial paper are that no security is required, the interest rate is typically less than through bank or finance company borrowing, and the commercial paper dealer often offers financial advice. The drawbacks are that commercial paper can be issued only by large, financially sound companies, and commercial paper dealings relative to bank dealings are impersonal.

EXAMPLE 12: A company's balance sheet appears below:

Assets

Current assets	$ 540,000
Fixed assets	800,000
Total assets	$1,340,000

Liabilities and Stockholders' Equity

Current liabilities:	
Notes payable to banks	$ 100,000
Commercial paper	650,000
Total current liabilities	$750,000
Long-term liabilities	260,000
Total liabilities	$1,010,000
Stockholders' equity	330,000
Total liabilities and stockholders' equity	$1,340,000

The amount of commercial paper issued by the company is a high percentage of both its current liabilities, 86.7% ($650,000/$750,000), and its total liabilities, 64.4% ($650,000/$1,010,000). Probably the company should do more bank borrowing because in the event of a money market squeeze, the company would find it advantageous to have a working relationship with a bank.

EXAMPLE 13: The company issues $500,000 of commercial paper every two months at a 13% rate. There is a $1,000 placement cost each time. The percentage cost of the commercial paper is:

Interest ($500,000 × .13)	$65,000
Placement cost ($1,000 × 6)	6,000
Cost	$71,000
Percentage cost of commercial paper	$= \dfrac{\$71,000}{\$500,000} = 14.2\%$

EXAMPLE 14: The company needs $300,000 for the month of November. Its options are:

1. A one-year line of credit for $300,000 with a bank. The commitment fee is 0.5%, and the interest charge on the used funds is 12%.

2. Issue two-month commercial paper at 10% interest. Because the funds are needed for only one month, the excess funds ($300,000) can be invested in 8% marketable securities for December. The total transaction fee for the marketable securities is 0.3%.

The line of credit costs:

Commitment fee for unused period	
(0.005) (300,000) (11/12)	$1,375
Interest for one month (0.12) (300,000) (1/12)	3,000
Total cost	$4,375

The commercial paper costs:

Interest charge (0.10)(300,000)(2/12)	$5,000
Transaction fee (0.003)(300,000)	900
Less interest earned on marketable securities	(2,000)
(0.08)(300,000)(1/12)	(2,000)
Total cost	$3,900

The commercial paper arrangement is less costly.

RECEIVABLES FOR FINANCING

In accounts receivable financing, the accounts receivable are the security for the loan as well as the source of repayment.

Financing of accounts receivable may generally take place when:

- Receivables are a minimum of $25,000.

- Sales are a minimum of $250,000.

- Individual receivables are at a minimum of $100.

- Receivables apply to selling merchandise rather than rendering services.

- Customers are financially strong.

- Sales returns are not great.

- Title to the goods is received by the buyer at shipment.

Receivable financing has several advantages, including avoiding the need for long-term financing and obtaining a recurring cash flow. Accounts receivable financing has the drawback of high administrative costs when there are many small accounts.

Accounts receivable may be financed under either a factoring or assignment (pledging) arrangement. Factoring is the outright sale of accounts receivable to a bank or finance company without recourse. The purchaser takes all credit and collection risks. The proceeds received are equal to the face value of the receivables less the commission charge, which is usually 2% to 4% higher than the prime interest rate. The cost of the factoring arrangement is the factor's commission for credit investigation, interest on the unpaid balance of advanced funds, and a discount from the face value of the receivables where high credit risk exists. Remissions by customers are made directly to the factor.

The advantages of factoring are immediate availability of cash, reduction in overhead because the credit examination function is no longer needed, obtaining financial advice, receipt of advances as required on a seasonal basis, and strengthening of the balance sheet position.

The disadvantages of factoring include both the high cost and the negative impression left with customers due to the change in ownership of the receivables.

Also, factors may antagonize customers by their demanding methods of collecting delinquent accounts.

In an assignment (pledging), there is no transfer of the ownership of the accounts receivable. Receivables are given to a finance company with recourse. The finance company usually advances between 50% and 85% of the face value of the receivables in cash. You are responsible for a service charge, interest on the advance, and any resulting bad debt losses. Customer remissions continue to be made directly to the company.

The assignment of accounts receivable has the advantage of immediate availability of cash, cash advances available on a seasonal basis, and avoidance of negative customer feelings. The disadvantages include the high cost, the continuance of the clerical function associated with accounts receivable, and the bearing of all credit risk.

The financial manager has to be aware of the impact of a change in accounts receivable policy on the cost of financing receivables. When accounts receivable are financed, the cost of financing may rise or fall under different conditions, for example: (1) when credit standards are relaxed, costs rise; (2) when recourse for defaults is given to the finance company, costs decrease; and (3) when the minimum invoice amount of a credit sale is increased, costs decline.

The financial officer should compute the costs of accounts receivable financing and select the least expensive alternative.

EXAMPLE 15: A factor will purchase the company's $120,000 per month accounts receivable. The factor will advance up to 80% of the receivables for an annual charge of 14%, and a 1.5% fee on receivables purchased. The cost of this factoring arrangement is:

Factor fee [0.015 × ($120,000 × 12)]	$21,600
Cost of borrowing [0.14 × ($120,000 × 0.8)]	13,440
Total cost	$35,040

EXAMPLE 16: A factor charges a 3% fee per month. The factor lends the company up to 75% of receivables purchased for an additional 1% per month. Credit sales are $400,000 per month. As a result of the factoring arrangement, the company saves $6,500 per month in credit costs and a bad debt expense of 2% of credit sales.

XYZ Bank has offered an arrangement to lend the company up to 75% of the receivables. The bank will charge 2% per month interest plus a 4% processing charge on receivable lending.

The collection period is 30 days. If the company borrows the maximum per month, should it stay with the factor or switch to XYZ Bank?

Cost of factor:

Purchase receivables (0.03 × $400,000)	$12,000
Lending fee (0.01 × $300,000)	3,000
Total cost	$15,000

Cost of bank financing:

Interest (0.02 × $300,000)	$ 6,000
Processing charge (0.04 × $300,000)	12,000
Additional cost of not using the factor:	
Credit costs	6,500
Bad debts (0.02 × $400,000)	8,000
Total cost	$32,500

The company should stay with the factor.

EXAMPLE 17: A company needs $250,000 and is weighing the alternatives of arranging a bank loan or going to a factor. The bank loan terms are 18% interest, discounted, with a compensating balance of 20%. The factor will charge a 4% commission on invoices purchased monthly, and the interest rate on the purchased invoices is 12%, deducted in advance. By using a factor, the company will save $1,000 monthly credit department costs, and uncollectible accounts estimated at 3% of the factored accounts receivable will not occur. Which is the better alternative for the company?

The bank loan, which will net the company its desired $250,000 in proceeds, is:

$$\frac{\text{Proceeds}}{(100\% - \text{Proceeds deducted})} = \frac{\$250,000}{100\% - (18\% + 20\%)}$$

$$\frac{\$250,000}{1.0 - 0.38} = \frac{\$250,000}{0.62} = \$403,226$$

The effective interest rate associated with the bank loan is:

$$\text{Effective interest rate} = \frac{\text{Interest rate}}{\text{Proceeds, \%}} = \frac{.18}{.62} = 29.0\%$$

The amount of accounts receivable that should be factored to net the firm $250,000 is:

$$\frac{\$250,000}{1.0 - 0.16} = \frac{\$250,000}{0.84} = \$297,619$$

The total annual cost of the bank arrangement is:

Interest ($250,000 × 0.29)	$72,500
Additional cost of not using a factor:	
Credit costs ($1,000 × 12)	12,000

Uncollectible accounts ($297,619 × 0.03)	8,929
Total cost	$93,429

The effective interest rate associated with factoring accounts receivable is:

$$\text{Effective interest rate} = \frac{\text{Interest rate}}{\text{Proceeds, \%}} = \frac{12\%}{100\% - (12\% + 4\%)}$$

$$= \frac{0.12}{0.84} = 14.3\%$$

The total annual cost of the factoring alternative is:

Interest ($250,000 × 0.143)	$35,750
Factoring ($297,619 × 0.04)	11,905
Total cost	$47,655

Factoring should be used since it will cost almost half as much as the bank loan.

EXAMPLE 18: A company is considering a factoring arrangement. The company's sales are $2,700,000, accounts receivable turnover is nine times, and a 17% reserve on accounts receivable is required. The factor's commission charge on average accounts receivable payable at the point of receivable purchase is 2.0%. The factor's interest charge is 16% of receivables after subtracting the commission charge and reserve. The interest charge reduces the advance. The annual effective cost under the factoring arrangement is computed as follows:

$$\text{Average accounts receivable} = \frac{\text{Credit sales}}{\text{Turnover}} = \frac{\$2,700,000}{9}$$

$$= \$300,000$$

The company will receive the following amount by factoring its accounts receivable:

Average accounts receivable	$300,000
Less: reserve ($300,000 × 0.17)	−51,000
Commission ($300,000 × 0.02)	− 6,000
Net prior to interest	$243,000
Less: Interest [$243,000 × (16%/9)]	4,320
Proceeds received	$238,680

The annual cost of the factoring arrangement is:

Commission ($300,000 × 0.02)	$6,000
Interest [$243,000 × (16%/9)]	4,320
Cost each 40 days (360/9)	$10,320
Turnover	× 9
Total annual cost	$92,880

The annual effective cost under the factoring arrangement based on the amount received is:

$$\frac{\text{Annual cost}}{\text{Average amount received}} = \frac{\$92,880}{\$238,680} = 38.9\%$$

USING INVENTORIES FOR FINANCING

Financing inventory typically takes place when the company has completely used its borrowing capacity on receivables. Inventory financing requires the existence of marketable, nonperishable, and standardized goods that have quick turnover. The merchandise should not be subject to rapid obsolescence. Good collateral inventory can be marketed apart from the company's marketing organization. Inventory financing should consider the price stability of the merchandise and the costs of selling it. The advance is high when there is marketable inventory. In general, the financing of raw materials and finished goods is about 75% of their value. The interest rate approximates 3 to 5 points over the prime interest rate.

The drawbacks to inventory financing include the high interest rate and the restrictions placed on inventory.

The types of inventory financing include a floating (blanket) lien, warehouse receipt, and trust receipt. With a floating lien, the creditor's security lies in the aggregate inventory rather than in its components. Even though the company sells and restocks, the lender's security interest continues. With a warehouse receipt, the lender receives an interest in the inventory stored at a public warehouse; however, the fixed costs of this arrangement are high. There may be a field warehouse arrangement where the warehouser sets up a secured area directly at the company's location. The company has access to the goods but must continually account for them. With a trust receipt loan, the creditor has title to the goods but releases them to the company to sell on the creditor's behalf As goods arc sold, the company remits the funds to the lender. A good example of trust receipt use is in automobile dealer financing. The drawback of the trust receipt arrangement is that a trust receipt must be given for specific items.

A collateral certificate may be issued by a third party to the lender guaranteeing the existence of pledged inventory. The advantage of a collateral certificate is flexibility because merchandise does not have to be segregated or possessed by the lender.

EXAMPLE 19: The company wants to finance $500,000 of inventory. Funds are required for three months. A warehouse receipt loan may be taken at 16% with a 90% advance against the inventory's value. The warehousing cost is $4,000 for the three-month period. The cost of financing the inventory is:

Interest [0.16 × 0.90 × $500,000 × (3/12)]	$18,000
Warehousing cost	4,000
Total cost	$22,000

EXAMPLE 20: The company shows growth in operations but is experiencing liquidity difficulties. Among its customers are six large financially sound companies, responsible for 75% of sales. On the basis of the below financial information for 2X11, should the financial manager borrow on receivables or inventory? Balance sheet data follow:

Balance Sheet

ASSETS		
Current assets		
Cash	$ 27,000	
Receivables	380,000	
Inventory (consisting of 55% of work-in-process)	320,000	
Total current assets		$727,000
Fixed assets		250,000
Yale/assets		$977,000
LIABILITIES AND STOCKHOLDERS' EQUITY		
Current liabilities		
Accounts payable	$260,000	
Loans payable	200,000	
Accrued expenses	35,000	
Total current liabilities		$495,000
Noncurrent liabilities		
Bonds payable		110,000
Total liabilities		$605,000
Stockholders' equity		
Common stock	$250,000	
Retained earnings	122,000	
Total stockholders' equity		372,000
Total liabilities and stockholders' equity		$977,000

Selected income statement information follows:

Sales	$1,800,000
Net income	130,000

Receivable financing can be expected since a high percentage of sales are made to only six large financially strong companies. Receivables thus show collectibility. It is also easier to control a few large customer accounts. Inventory financing is not likely, due to the high percentage of partially completed items. Lenders are reluctant to finance inventory when a large work-in-process balance exists since the goods will be difficult to process and sell by lenders.

USING OTHER ASSETS FOR FINANCING

Assets other than inventory and receivables, such as real estate, plant and equipment, cash surrender value of life insurance policies, and securities, may be used as security for short-term bank loans. Also, lenders are typically willing to advance a high percentage of the market value of bonds. Further, loans may be made based on a guaranty of a third party.

Exhibit 52-1 presents a summary of the major features of short-term financing coverage.

COMPARING SHORT-TERM AND LONG-TERM FINANCING

Short-term financing is easier to arrange, has lower cost, and is more flexible than long-term financing. However, short-term financing makes the borrower subject to interest rate swings, requires refinancing more quickly, and is more difficult to repay.

In short-term financing, the best financing tool should be used to meet the company's objectives. The financing instrument depends upon the company's particular circumstances. Consideration is given to such factors as cost, risk, restrictions, stability of operations, and tax rate. Sources of short-term financing include trade credit, bank loans, bankers' acceptances, finance company loans, commercial paper, receivables financing, and inventory financing.

Recommendation: Use short-term financing as additional working capital, to finance short-lived assets, or as interim financing on long-term projects. Long-term financing is more appropriate to finance long-term assets or construction projects.

Exhibit 52-1: Summary of Major Short-Term Financing Sources

Type of Financing	Source	Cost or Terms	Features
A. Spontaneous Sources			
Accounts payable	Suppliers	No explicit cost but there is an opportunity cost if a cash discount for early payment is not taken. Companies should take advantage of the discount offered.	The main source of short-term financing typically on terms of 1 to 120 days.
Accrued expenses	Employees and tax agencies	None	Expenses incurred but not yet paid (e.g., accrued wages payable, accrued taxes payable).
B. Unsecured Sources			
Bank loans		Prime interest rate plus risk premium. The interest rate may be fixed or variable. Unsecured loans are less costly than secured loans.	
1. Single-payment note	Commercial banks		A single-payment loan to satisfy a funds shortage to last a short time period.
2. Lines of credit	Commercial banks	Prime interest rate plus risk premium. The interest rate may be fixed or variable. A compensating balance is typically required. The line of credit must be "cleaned up" periodically.	An agreed upon borrowing limit for funds to satisfy seasonal needs.

Exhibit 52-1: Summary of Major Short-Term Financing Sources

Type of Financing	Source	Cost or Terms	Features
Commercial paper	Commercial banks, insurance companies, other financial institutions, and other companies.	A little less than the prime interest rate.	Unsecured, short-term note of financially strong companies.
C. Secured Sources			
Accounts receivable as collateral	Commercial banks and finance companies	2% to 5% above prime plus fees (usually 2%–3%). Low administrative costs. Advances typically ranging from 60% to 85%.	Qualified accounts receivable accounts serve as collateral. Upon collection of the account, the borrower remits to the lender.
1. Pledging			Customers are not notified of the arrangement. With recourse meaning that the risk of nonpayment is borne by the company.
2. Factoring	Factors, commercial banks, and commercial finance companies	Typically a 2%–3% discount from the face value of factored receivables. Interest on advances of almost 3% over prime. Interest on surplus balances held by factor of about 1/2% per month. Costs with factoring are higher than with pledging.	Certain accounts receivable are sold on a discount basis without recourse. Customers are notified of the arrangement. The factor provides more services than is the case with pledging.

Exhibit 52-1: Summary of Major Short-Term Financing Sources

Type of Financing	Source	Cost or Terms	Features
Inventory collateral	Commercial banks and commercial finance companies	About 4% above prime. Advance is about 40% of collateral value.	Collateral is all the inventory. There should be a stable inventory with many inexpensive items.
1. Floating liens			
2. Trust receipts (floor planning)	Commercial banks and commercial finance companies	About 3% above prime. Advances ranging from 80% to 100% of collateral value.	Collateral is specific inventory that is typically expensive. Borrower retains collateral. Borrower remits proceeds to lender upon sale of the inventory.
3. Warehouse receipts	Commercial banks and commercial finance companies	About 4% above prime plus about a 2% warehouse fee. Advance of about 80% of collateral value.	Collateralized inventory is controlled by lender. A warehousing company issues a warehouse receipt held by the lender. The warehousing company acts as the lender's agent.

CHAPTER 53

TERM LOANS AND LEASING

CONTENTS

This chapter considers intermediate-term loans, primarily from banks, and leasing arrangements to meet corporate financing needs. Intermediate-term loans include bank loans such as revolving credit, insurance company term loans, and equipment financing.

WHEN TO TAKE OUT AN INTERMEDIATE-TERM BANK LOAN

Intermediate-term loans are loans with a maturity of more than one year. They are appropriate when short-term unsecured loans are not, such as when a business is acquired, new fixed assets are purchased, and long-term debt is retired. If a company wants to float long-term debt or issue common stock but conditions are unfavorable in the market, it may seek an intermediate loan to bridge the gap until long-term financing can be undertaken on favorable terms. A company may use extendible debt when there is a continuing financing need. This reduces the time and cost of many debt issuances.

The interest rate on an intermediate-term loan is typically more than on a short-term loan due to the longer maturity period. The interest rate may be either fixed or variable (according to, for instance, changes in the prime interest rate). The cost of an intermediate-term loan changes with the amount of the loan and the company's financial strength.

Ordinary intermediate-term loans are payable in periodic equal installments except for the last payment, which may be higher (referred to as a balloon payment). The schedule of loan payments should be based on the company's cash flow position to satisfy the debt. The periodic payment in a term loan equals:

$$\text{Periodic Payment} = \frac{\text{Amount of loan}}{\text{Present value factor}}$$

EXAMPLE 1: The company contracts to repay a term loan in five equal year-end installments. The amount of the loan is $150,000 and the interest rate is 10%. The payment each year is:

$$\frac{\$150,000}{3.7908\,(a)} = \$39,569.48$$

(a) Present value of annuity for five years at 10%.

The total interest on the loan is:

Total payments (5 × $39,569.48)	$197,847.40
Principal	150,000.00
Interest	$47,847.40

EXAMPLE 2: The company takes out a term loan in 20 year-end annual installments of $2,000 each. The interest rate is 12%. The amount of the loan is:

$$\$2,000 = \frac{\text{Amount of loan}}{7.4694\,(a)}$$

Amount of loan = $2,000 × 7.4694 = $14.939.80

(a) Present value of annuity for 20 years at 12%.

The amortization schedule for the first two years is:

Year	Payment	Interest[a]	Principal	Balance
0				$14,938.80
1	$2,000	$1,792.66	$207.34	14,731.46
2	2,000	1,767.78	232.22	14,499.24

[a] 12% times the balance of the loan at the beginning of the year.

What restrictions does the company face? Restrictive provisions to protect the lender in an intermediate-term loan agreement may be:

- General provisions used in most agreements which vary depending upon the company's situation. Examples are working capital and cash dividend requirements.

- Routine (uniform) provisions that are employed universally in most agreements. Examples are the payment of taxes and the maintenance of proper insurance to assure maximum lender protection.

- Specific provisions tailored to a particular situation. Examples are the placing of limits on future loans and the carrying of adequate life insurance for executives.

Advantages of Intermediate-Term Loans

- Flexibility in that the terms may be altered as the company's financing requirements change.
- Financial information is kept confidential, since no public issuance is involved.
- The loan may be arranged quickly, relative to a public offering.
- Avoids the possible nonrenewal of a short-term loan.
- Public flotation costs are not involved.

Disadvantages of Intermediate-Term Loans

- Collateral and possible restrictive covenants are required, as opposed to none for commercial paper and unsecured short-term bank loans.
- Budgets and financial statements may have to be submitted periodically to the lender.
- "Kickers," or "sweeteners," such as stock warrants or a share of the profits are sometimes requested by the bank.

REVOLVING CREDIT

Revolving credit, usually used for seasonal financing, may have a three-year maturity, but the notes evidencing the revolving credit are short-term, usually 90 days. The advantages of revolving credit are flexibility and ready availability. Within the time period of the revolving credit agreement, the company may renew a loan or enter into additional financing up to a specified maximum amount. Relative to a line of credit, there are typically fewer restrictions on revolving credit but at the cost of a slightly higher interest rate.

INSURANCE COMPANY TERM LOANS

Insurance companies and other institutional lenders may extend intermediate-term loans. Insurance companies typically accept loan maturity dates exceeding ten years, but their rate of interest is often higher than that of bank loans. Insurance companies do not require compensating balances, but usually there is a prepayment penalty, which is typically not the case with a bank loan. A company may take out an insurance company loan when it desires a longer maturity range.

FINANCING WITH EQUIPMENT

Equipment may serve as collateral for a loan. An advance is made against the market value of the equipment. The more marketable the equipment is, the higher the advance will be. Also considered is the cost of selling the equipment. The repayment schedule is designed so that the market value of the equipment at any given time is in excess of the unpaid loan principal.

Equipment financing may be obtained from banks, finance companies, and manufacturers of equipment. Equipment loans may be secured by a chattel mortgage or a conditional sales contract. A chattel mortgage serves as a lien on property except for real estate. In a conditional sales contract, the seller of the equipment keeps title to it until the buyer has satisfied the terms; otherwise the seller will repossess the equipment. The buyer makes periodic payments to the seller over a specified time period. A conditional sales contract is generally used by a small company with a low credit rating.

Equipment trust certificates may be issued to finance the purchase of readily salable equipment. Preferably, the equipment should be general purpose and movable. A trust is formed to buy the equipment and lease it to the user. The trust issues the certificates to finance 75% to 85% of the purchase price and holds title to the equipment until all the certificates have been fully repaid at which time the title passes to the lessee.

LEASING

The parties in a lease are the lessor, who legally owns the property, and the lessee, who uses it in exchange for making rental payments. Of course, your company is the lessee.

The types of leases are as follows:

- *Operating (service) lease.* This type of lease includes both financing and maintenance services. The company leases property that is owned by the lessor. The lessor may be the manufacturer of the asset or it may be a leasing company that buys assets from the manufacturer to lease to others. The lease payments under the contract arc typically not adequate to recover the full cost of the property. Maintenance and service arc provided by the lessor and related costs are included in the lease payments. There usually exists a cancellation clause that provides the lessee with the right to cancel the contract and return the property prior to the expiration date of the agreement. The life of the contract is less than the economic life of the property.

- *Financial lease.* This type of lease does not typically provide for maintenance services, is noncancelable, and requires rental payments that equal the full price of the leased property. The life of the contract approximates the life of the property.

- *Sale and leaseback.* With this lease arrangement, the company sells an asset to another (usually a financial institution) and then leases it back. This allows the company to obtain cash from the sale and still have the property for use.

- *Leveraged lease.* In a leveraged lease, there is a third party who serves as the lender. Here, the lessor borrows a significant portion of the purchase price (usually up to 80%) to buy the asset and provides the balance of the purchase price as an equity investment. The property is then leased to the lessee. As security for the loan, the lessor grants the long-term lender a mortgage on the asset and assigns the lease contract to the lender. Leverage leasing is a cost-effective alternative to debt financing when the lessee cannot use the full tax benefits of asset ownership.

Advantages of Leasing

- Immediate cash outlay is not required.
- Provides for temporary equipment need and flexibility in operations.
- Typically, a purchase option exists, allowing the company to obtain the property at a bargain price at the expiration of the lease. This provides the flexibility to make the purchase decision based on the value of the property at the termination date.
- Lessor's expert service is available.
- Typically, fewer financing restrictions (e.g., limitations on dividends) are placed by the lessor than are imposed when obtaining a loan to purchase the asset.
- Obligation for future rental payment does not have to be reported on the balance sheet if the lease is considered an operating lease.
- Leasing allows the company, in effect, to depreciate land, which is not allowed if land is purchased.
- In bankruptcy or reorganization, the maximum claim of lessors is three years of lease payments. With debt, creditors have a claim for the total amount of the unpaid financing.
- Eliminates equipment disposal. Leasing may be more attractive than buying when a business cannot use all of the tax deductions and tax credits associated with the assets in a timely fashion.

Disadvantages of Leasing

- Higher cost in the long run than if the asset is bought. The lessee is not building equity.
- Interest cost of leasing is typically higher than the interest cost on debt.
- If the property reverts to the lessor at termination of the lease, the lessee must either sign a new lease or buy the property at higher current prices. Also, the salvage value of the property is realized by the lessor.
- May have to retain property no longer needed (i.e., obsolete equipment).
- Unable to make improvements to the leased property without the permission of the lessor.

EXAMPLE 3: The company enters into a lease for a $100,000 machine. It is to make 10 equal annual payments at year-end. The interest rate on the lease is 14%. The periodic payment equals:

$$\frac{\$100,000}{5.2161\,(a)} = 19{,}171$$

(a) The present value of an ordinary annuity factor for $n = 10$, $i = 14\%$ is 5.2161.

EXAMPLE 4: Assume the same facts as Example 3, except that now the annual payments are to be made at the beginning of each year. The periodic payment equals:

Year	Factor
0	1.0
1–9	4.9464
	5.9464

$$\frac{\$100,000}{5.9464} = \$16,817$$

The interest rate associated with a lease agreement can also be computed. Divide the value of the leased property by the annual payment to obtain the factor, which is then used to find the interest rate with the help of an annuity table.

EXAMPLE 5: The company leased $300,000 of property and is to make equal annual payments at year-end of $40,000 for 11 years. The interest rate associated with the lease agreement is:

$$\frac{\$300,000}{\$40,000} = 7.5$$

Going to the present value of annuity table and looking across 11 years to a factor nearest to 7.5, we find 7.4987 at a 7% interest rate. Thus, the interest rate in the lease agreement is 7%. The capitalized value of a lease can be found by dividing the annual lease payment by an appropriate present value of annuity factor.

EXAMPLE 6: Property is to be leased for eight years at an annual rental payment of $140,000 payable at the beginning of each year. The capitalization rate is 12%. The capitalized value of the lease is:

$$\frac{\text{Annual lease payment}}{\text{Present value factor}} = \frac{\$140,000}{1 + 4.5638} = \$25,163$$

The Lease-or-Purchase Decision

Often, a decision must be made as to whether it is better to buy an asset or lease it. Present value analysis may be used to determine the cheapest alternative (see Chapter 22, "The Use of Capital Budgeting in Decision Making").

CHAPTER 54

DECIDING ON LONG-TERM FINANCING

CONTENTS

Long-term financing generally refers to financing for more than five years. This chapter discusses the what, why, and how to of equity and long-term debt financing. Equity financing consists of issuing preferred stock and common stock, whereas long-term debt financing consists primarily of issuing bonds. Long-term financing is often used to finance long-lived assets (e.g., land, plant) or construction projects. The more capital intensive the business, the greater should be the reliance on long-term debt and equity. First, the role of the investment banker is mentioned. Also, a comparison of public versus private placement of securities is given. The advantages and disadvantages of issuing long-term debt, preferred stock, and common stock are presented. We will discuss what financing strategy is most appropriate under a given set of circumstances that your company is experiencing. The financing policies should be in response to the overall strategic direction of the company.

Your company may finance over the long term with debt or equity (preferred stock and common stock) funds. Each has its own advantages and disadvantages. The facts of a situation have to be examined to determine which type is best under the circumstances. For example, a rapidly growing company needs flexibility in its capital structure. While to sustain growth, a high debt position may be needed, it is important that periodic additions to equity are made.

A company's mix of long-term funds is referred to as the capital structure. The ideal capital structure maximizes the total value of the company and minimizes the overall cost of capital. The formulation of an appropriate capital structure should take into account the nature of the business and industry, strategic business plan of the company, current and historical capital structure, and planned growth rate.

INVESTMENT BANKING

Investment banking involves the sale of a security issue. Investment bankers conduct the following activities:

- *Underwriting.* The investment banker buys a new security issue, pays the issuer, and markets the securities. The underwriter's compensation is the difference between the price at which the securities are sold to the public, and the price paid to the issuing company.

- *Distributing.* The investment banker markets the company's security issue.

- *Advising.* The investment banker gives advice to the company regarding the optimal way to obtain funds. The investment banker is knowledgeable about the alternative sources of long-term funds, debt and equity markets, and Securities and Exchange Commission (SEC) regulations.

- *Providing funds.* The investment banker provides funds to the company during the distribution period.

When several investment bankers form a group because a particular issue is large and/or risky, they are termed a syndicate. A syndicate is a temporary association of investment bankers brought together for the purpose of selling new securities. One investment banker among the group will be selected to manage the syndicate (originating house) and underwrite the major amount of the issue. One bid price for the issue is made on behalf of the group, but the terms and features of the issue are set by the company.

The distribution channels for a new security issue appear in Exhibit 54-1. In another approach to investment banking, the investment banker agrees to sell the company's securities on a best-efforts basis, or as an agent. Here, the investment banker does not act as underwriter but instead sells the stock and receives a sales commission. An investment banker may insist on this type of arrangement when he or she has reservations about the success of the security offering.

In selecting an investment banker for a new issue of securities, the following are positive signs:

Exhibit 54-1: Distribution Channels for a New Security Issue

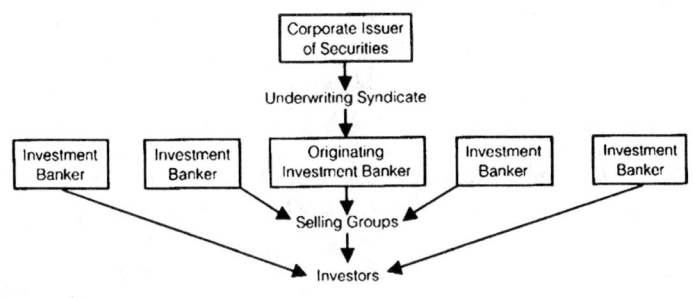

- Low spread.
- Good references.
- Able to float many shares at a good price.
- Institutional and retail support.
- Good after market performance.
- Wide geographic distribution.
- Attractive secondary markets.
- Knowledge of market, regulations, industry, and company.

SHOULD SECURITIES BE PUBLICLY OR PRIVATELY PLACED?

Equity and debt securities may be issued either publicly or privately. A consideration in determining whether to issue securities to the public or privately is the type and amount of required financing.

In a public issuance, the shares are bought by the general public. In a private placement, the company issues securities directly to either one or a few large investors. The large investors are financial institutions such as insurance companies, pension plans, and commercial banks.

Private placement has the following advantages relative to a public issuance:

- The flotation cost is less. Flotation cost is the expense of registering and selling the stock issue. Examples are brokerage commissions and underwriting fees. The flotation cost for common stock exceeds that for preferred stock. Flotation cost expressed as a percentage of gross proceeds is higher for smaller issues than for larger ones.
- It avoids SEC filing requirements.

- It avoids the disclosure of information to the public.
- There is less time involved in obtaining funds.
- There is greater flexibility.
- It may not be practical to issue securities in the public market if the company is so small that an investment banker would not find it profitable.
- The company's credit rating may be low, and as a result investors may not be interested in purchasing securities when the money supply is limited.

Private placement has the following disadvantages relative to a public issuance:

- There is a higher interest rate due to less liquidity of a debt issue relative to public issuance.
- There is typically a shorter maturity period than for a public issue.
- It is more difficult to obtain significant amounts of money privately than publicly.
- Large investors typically use stringent credit standards requiring the company to be in strong financial condition. In addition, there are more restrictive terms.
- Large institutional investors may watch more closely the company's activities than smaller investors in a public issue.
- Large institutional investors are more capable of obtaining voting control of the company.

Most private placements involve debt securities. In fact, only about 2% of common stock is placed privately. The private market is more receptive to smaller issues (e.g., several million dollars). Small and medium-size companies typically find it cheaper to place debt privately than publicly, especially when the issue is $5 million or less.

TYPES OF LONG-TERM DEBT AND WHEN EACH SHOULD BE USED

We now discuss the characteristics, advantages, and disadvantages of long-term debt financing. In addition to the various types of debt instruments, the circumstances in which a particular type of debt is most appropriate are mentioned. Sources of long-term debt include mortgages and bonds. The amount of debt a company may have depends largely on its available collateral. Bond refunding is also highlighted.

Mortgages

Mortgages are notes payable that have as collateral real assets and require periodic payments. Mortgages can be issued to finance the purchase of assets, construction of plant, and modernization of facilities. The bank will require that the value of the property exceed the mortgage on that property. Most mortgage loans are between 70% and 90% of the value of the collateral. Mortgages may be obtained from a bank, life insurance company, or other financial institution. It is easier to obtain mortgage loans for multiple-use real assets than for single-use real assets.

There are two types of mortgages: (1) a senior mortgage, which has first claim on assets and earnings, and (2) a junior mortgage, which has a subordinate lien. A mortgage may have a closed-end provision that prevents the company from issuing additional debt of the same priority against the specific property. If the mortgage is open-ended, the company can issue additional first-mortgage bonds against the property.

Mortgages have a number of advantages, including favorable interest rates, less financing restrictions, extended maturity date for loan repayment, and relatively easy availability. A drawback is the collateral requirement.

Bonds

Long-term debt principally takes the form of bonds payable and loans payable. A *bond* is a certificate indicating that the company has borrowed a given sum of money and agrees to repay it. A written agreement, called an *indenture*, describes the features of the bond issue (e.g., payment dates, call and conversion privileges, if any, and restrictions). The indenture is a contract between the company, the bondholder, and the trustee. The trustee makes sure that the company meets the terms of the bond contract. In many instances, the trustee is the trust department of a commercial bank. Although the trustee is an agent for the bondholder, it is selected by the company prior to the issuance of the bonds. The indenture provides for certain restrictions on the company such as a limitation on dividends and minimum working capital requirements. If a provision of the indenture is violated, the bonds are in default.

Note: Covenants should be flexible because of the quick changes in the financial world. The indenture may also have a negative pledge clause, which precludes the issuance of new debt taking priority over existing debt in the event of liquidation. The clause can apply to assets currently held as well as to assets that may be purchased in the future.

Tip: Try to avoid issuing a bond where there is a large Treasury financing because that can temporarily depress the private debt market. The price of a bond depends on several factors such as its maturity date, interest rate, and collateral. In selecting a maturity period for long-term debt, consider the debt repayment schedule which should not be overloaded at one time. Also, if a company's credit rating is expected to get better in the near term, short-term debt should be issued because the company will be able to refinance at a lower interest rate.

Bond prices and market interest rates are inversely related. For example, as market interest rates increase, the price of the existing bond falls because investors can invest in new bonds paying higher interest rates.

Types of Bonds. The various types of bonds that may be issued by a company are:

- *Debentures.* Because debentures are unsecured (no collateral) debt, they can be issued only by large, financially strong companies with excellent credit ratings.

- *Subordinated debentures.* The claims of the holders of these bonds are subordinated to those of senior creditors. Debt having a prior claim over the subordinated debentures is set forth in the bond indenture. Typically, in liquidation, subordinated debentures come after short-term debt.

- *Mortgage bonds.* These are bonds secured by real assets. The first-mortgage claim must be met before a distribution is made to a second-mortgage claim. There may be several mortgages for the same property (e.g., building).

- *Collateral trust bonds.* The collateral for these bonds is the company's security investments in other companies (bonds or stocks), which are given to a trustee for safekeeping.

- *Convertible bonds.* These may be converted to stock at a later date based on a specified conversion ratio. The conversion ratio equals the par value of the convertible security divided by the conversion price. Convertible bonds are typically issued in the form of subordinated debentures. Convertible bonds are more marketable and are typically issued at a lower interest rate than are regular bonds because they offer the conversion right to common stock. Of course, if bonds are converted to stock, debt repayment is not involved. A convertible bond is a quasi-equity security because its market value is tied to its value if converted rather than as a bond. The degree of importance of the reasons to issue convertible bonds appears in Exhibit 54-2. Convertible bonds are discussed in detail in Chapter 55, "Warrants and Convertibles."

- *Income bonds.* These bonds pay interest only if there is a profit. The interest may be cumulative or noncumulative. If cumulative, the interest accumulates regardless of earnings, and if bypassed, must be paid in a later year when adequate earnings exist. Income bonds are appropriate for companies with large fixed capital investments and large fluctuations in earnings, or for emerging companies with the expectation of low earnings in the early years.

- *Guaranteed bonds.* These are debt issued by one party with payment guaranteed by another.

- *Serial bonds.* A portion of these bonds comes due each year. At the time serial bonds are issued, a schedule shows the yields, interest rates, and prices for each maturity. The interest rate on the shorter maturities is lower than the interest rate on the longer maturities because less uncertainty exists regarding the future.

- *Deep discount bonds.* These bonds have very low interest rates and thus are issued at substantial discounts from face value. The return to the holder comes primarily from appreciation in price rather than from interest payments. The bonds are volatile in price. Since these bonds are typically callable at par, this reduces the refunding flexibility of the issuer.

- *Zero-coupon bonds.* These bonds do not provide for interest. The return to the holder is in the form of appreciation in price. Note: Lower interest rates may be available for zero coupon bonds (and deep discount bonds) because of the lack of callability and possible foreign tax laws.

- *Variable-rate bonds.* The interest rates on the bonds are adjusted periodically to changes in money market conditions (e.g., prime interest rate). These bonds are popular when there is uncertainty of future interest rates and inflation.

- *Deferred interest bonds.* The periodic interest payments are fully or partially deferred in the first few years. The deferred period allows the issuer to improve financial performance, sell underperforming assets, and refinance loan agreements.

- *Industrial revenue bonds.* The company offers tax-free interest to lenders. These bonds can be issued at a lower cost because of the resulting tax exemption. However, there are many conditions imposed by the government upon the company issuing these bonds. For example, the types of facilities that may be funded are restricted; usually these are public service facilities.

Exhibit 54-2: Degree of Importance of Reasons to Issue Convertible Bonds

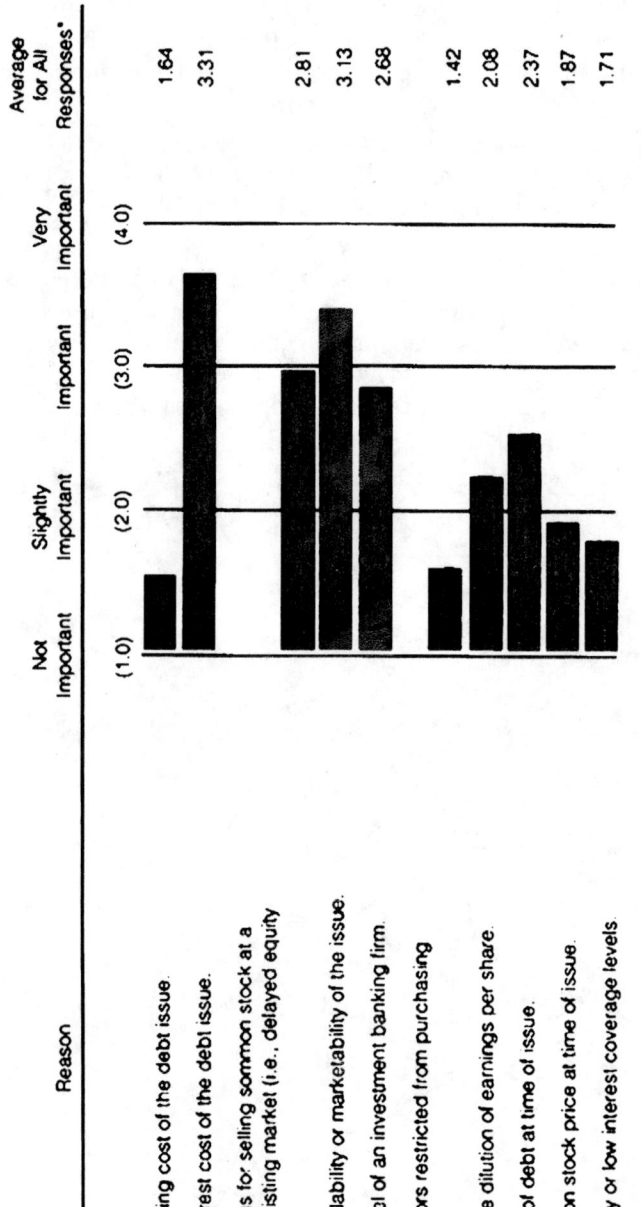

Reason	Not Important (1.0)	Slightly Important (2.0)	Important (3.0)	Very Important (4.0)	Average for All Responses[*]
1. To reduce the issuing cost of the debt issue.					1.64
2. To reduce the interest cost of the debt issue.					3.31
3. To provide a means for selling common stock at a price above the existing market (i.e., delayed equity financing).					2.81
4. To enhance the salability or marketability of the issue.					3.13
5. Advice and counsel of an investment banking firm.					2.68
6. Institutional investors restricted from purchasing common stock					1.42
7. To avoid immediate dilution of earnings per share.					2.08
8. High interest cost of debt at time of issue.					2.37
9. Depressed common stock price at time of issue.					1.87
10. High debt-to-equity or low interest coverage levels					1.71

Source: Ronald W. Melicher and J. Ronald Hoffmeister, "The Issue Is Convertible Bonds," *Financial Executive* (November, 1977), pp. 46–50.

- *Eurobonds.* Eurobonds are issued outside the country in whose currency the bonds are denominated. Eurobonds cannot be issued to U.S. investors but only to foreign investors. The reason is that Eurobonds are not registered with the SEC. The bonds are typically in bearer form.

Tip: Check to see if at the present time the Eurodollar market will give the company a lower-cost option than the U.S. market. These bonds typically can be issued only by high-quality borrowers.

A summary of the characteristics and priority claims associated with bonds appears in Exhibit 54-3.

If the company is small and emerging with an unproven track record, it may have to issue what are commonly referred to as "Junk bonds" (high-yielding risky bonds rated by Standard and Poor's as B+ or below or Moody's Investors Service as B+ or below). These are considered non-investment-grade bonds.

How Bonds Are Rated. Financial advisory services (e.g., Standard and Poor's, Moody's) rate publicly traded bonds according to risk in terms of the receipt of principal and interest. An inverse relationship exists between the quality of a bond issue and its yield; that is, low quality bonds will have a higher yield than high quality bonds. Hence, a risk-return tradeoff exists for the bondholder. Bond ratings are important because they influence marketability and the cost associated with the bond issue. Bond ratings are fully discussed in Chapter 50, "Corporate Investments in Securities."

Advantages and Disadvantages of Debt Financing

The advantages of issuing long-term debt include:

- Interest is tax deductible, while dividends are not.
- Bondholders do not participate in superior earnings of the company.
- The repayment of debt is in cheaper dollars during inflation.
- There is no dilution of company control.
- Financing flexibility can be achieved by including a call provision in the bond indenture. A call provision allows the company to pay the debt before the expiration date of the bond.
- It may safeguard the company's future financial stability, for instance, in times of tight money markets when short-term loans are not available.

Exhibit 54-3: Summary of Characteristics and Priority Claims of Bonds

Bond Type	Characteristics	Priority of Lender's Claims
Debentures	Available only to financially strong companies. Convertible bonds are typically debentures.	General creditor.
Subordinated Debentures	Comes after senior debt holders.	General creditor.
Mortgage Bonds	Collateral is real property or buildings.	Paid from the proceeds from the sale of the mortgaged assets. If any deficiency exists, general creditor status applies.
Collateral Trust Bonds	Secured by stock and/or bonds owned by the issuer. Collateral value is usually 30% more than bond value.	Paid from the proceeds of stock and/or bond that is collateralized. If there is a deficiency, general creditor status applies.
Income Bonds	Interest is paid only if there is net income. Often issued when a company is in reorganization because of financial problems.	General creditor.
Deep Discount (and Zero-coupon) Bonds	Issued at very low or no (zero) coupon rates. Issued at prices significantly below face value. Usually callable at per value.	Unsecured or secured status may apply depending on the features of the issue.
Variable-rate Bonds	Coupon rate changes within limits based on changes in money or capital market rates. Appropriate when uncertainty exists regarding inflation and future interest rates. Because of the automatic adjustment to changing market conditions, the bonds sell near face value.	Unsecured or secured status may apply depending on the features of the issue.

The disadvantages of issuing long-term debt include:

- Interest charges must be met regardless of the company's earnings.
- Debt must be repaid at maturity.
- Higher debt infers greater financial risk, which may increase the cost of financing.
- Indenture provisions may place stringent restrictions on the company.
- Overcommitments may arise due to forecasting errors.

How does issuing debt stack up against issuing equity securities? The advantages of issuing debt rather than equity securities are that interest is tax deductible whereas dividends are not; during inflation the payback will be in cheaper dollars; no dilution of voting control occurs; and flexibility in financing can be achieved by including a call provision in the bond indenture. The disadvantages of debt incurrence relative to issuing equity securities are that fixed interest charges and principal repayment must be met irrespective of the firm's cash flow position, and stringent indenture restrictions often exist.

The proper mixture of long-term debt to equity depends on company organization, credit availability, and after-tax cost of financing. Where a high degree of debt already exists, the company should take steps to minimize other corporate risks.

When should long-term debt be issued? Debt financing is more appropriate when:

- The interest rate on debt is less than the rate of return earned on the money borrowed. By using other people's money (OPM), the after-tax profit of the company will increase. Stockholders have made an extra profit with no extra investment!
- Stability in revenue and earnings exists so that the company will be able to meet interest and principal payments in both good and bad years. However, cyclical factors should not scare a company away from having any debt. The important thing is to accumulate no more interest and principal repayment obligations than can reasonably be satisfied in bad times as well as good.
- There is a satisfactory profit margin so that earnings exist to meet debt obligations.
- There is a good liquidity and cash flow position.
- The debt-equity ratio is low so the company can handle additional obligations.
- The risk level of the firm is low.
- Stock prices are currently depressed so that it does not pay to issue common stock at the present time.
- Control considerations are a primary factor so that if common stock were issued greater control might fall in the wrong hands.
- The firm is mature.
- Inflation is expected so that debt can be paid back in cheaper dollars.

- There is a lack of competition (e.g., barriers of entry in the industry exist).
- The markets for the company's products are expanding and the company is growing.
- The tax rate is high so there is a benefit from the tax deductibility of interest.
- Bond indenture restrictions are not burdensome.
- Money market trends and availability of financing are favorable.

Project financing is tied to particular projects and may be suitable for large, self-contained undertakings perhaps involving joint ventures.

Tip: If your company is experiencing financial difficulties, it may wish to refinance short-term debt on a long-term basis such as by extending the maturity dates of existing loans. This may alleviate current liquidity and cash flow problems.

As the default risk of your company becomes higher, so will the interest rate to compensate for the greater risk.

Recommendation: When a high degree of debt (financial leverage) exists, try to reduce other risks (e.g., product risk) so that total corporate risk is controlled. The amount of leverage in the capital structure depends upon the company's propensity for risk and the debt levels at competing companies.

The threat of financial distress or even bankruptcy is the ultimate limitation on leverage. Beyond a debt limit, the tax savings on interest expense will be offset by an increased interest rate demanded by creditors for the increased risk. Excessive debt will lower the market price of stock because greater risk is associated with the company.

Note: Smaller companies with thinly traded stocks often issue debt and equity securities together in the form of units. A company may elect to issue units instead of convertible debt if it desires to increase its common equity immediately.

Long-term financing may be from unexpected sources. Is governmental financing available in terms of grants, low-interest-rate loans, and tax relief? Is export financing available in foreign countries? Can the company use current and/or interest-rate swaps? Will the supplier or customer provide the company with financing?

EXAMPLE 1: Your company has $10 million of 12% mortgage bonds outstanding. The indenture permits additional bonds to be issued provided all of the following conditions are met:

1. The pretax times-interest-earned ratio exceeds 5.
2. Book value of the mortgaged assets is at least 1.5 times the amount of debt.
3. The debt-equity ratio is below 0.6.

The following additional information is provided:

1. Income before tax is $9 million.
2. Equity is $30 million.

3. Book value of assets is $34 million.

4. There are no sinking fund payments for the current year. (A sinking fund is money set aside to be used to retire a bond issue.)

5. Half the proceeds of a new issue would be added to the base of mortgaged assets.

Only $7 million more of 12% debt can be issued based on the following calculations:

1. The before-tax times-interest-earned ratio is:

$$\frac{\text{Income before tax and interest}}{\text{Interest}} = \frac{\$9,000,000 + 1,200,000^a}{\$1,200,000 + 0.12X} = 5$$

$$\frac{\$10,200,000}{\$1,200,000 + 0.12X} = 5$$

$$\$10,200,000 = \$6,000,000 + 0.60X$$
$$X = \$7,000,000$$
$$^a\text{Interest is } \$10,000,000 \times 0.12 = \$1,200,000$$

2.
$$\frac{\text{Book value of mortgaged assets}}{\text{Debt}} = \frac{\$34,000,000 + 0.5X}{\$10,000,000 + X} = 1.5$$

$$\$34,000,000 + 0.5X = \$15,000,000 + 1.5X$$
$$X = \$19,000,000$$

3.
$$\frac{\text{Debt}}{\text{Equity}} = \frac{\$10,000,000 + X}{\$30,000,000} = 0.6$$

$$\$10,000,000 + X = \$18,000,000$$
$$X = \$8,000,000$$

The first condition is controlling and hence limits the amount of new debt to $7 million.

Bond Refunding

Bonds may be refunded before maturity through either the issuance of a serial bond or exercising a call privilege on a straight bond. The issuance of serial bonds allows the company to refund the debt over the life of the issue. A call feature in a bond enables the company to retire it before the expiration date. The call feature is included in many corporate bond issues.

When future interest rates are expected to drop, a call provision is recommended. Such a provision enables the firm to buy back the higher-interest bond and issue a lower-interest one. The timing for the refunding depends on expected future interest rates. A call price is typically set in excess of the face value of the bond. The resulting call premium equals the difference between the call price and the maturity value. The company pays the premium to the bondholder in order to acquire the outstanding bonds prior to the maturity date. The call premium is usually equal to one year's interest if the bond is called in the first year, and it declines at a constant rate each year thereafter. Also involved in selling a new issue are flotation costs (e.g., brokerage commissions, printing costs).

A bond with a call provision typically will have a lower offering price, and will be issued at an interest rate higher than one without the call provision. The investor prefers not to have a situation where the company can buy back the bond at its option prior to maturity. The investor would obviously desire to hold onto a high-interest bond when prevailing interest rates are low.

EXAMPLE 2: A $100,000, 8%, 10-year bond is issued at 94%. The call price is 103%. Three years after the issue the bond is called. The call premium is equal to:

Call price	$103,000
Face value of bond	100,000
Call premium	$3,000

The desirability of refunding a bond requires present value analysis, which was discussed in Chapter 22, "The Use of Capital Budgeting in Decision Making."

EXAMPLE 3: Your company has a $20 million, 10% bond issue outstanding that has 10 years to maturity. The call premium is 7% of face value. New ten-year bonds in the amount of $20 million can be issued at an 8% interest rate. Flotation costs of the new issue are $600,000.

Refunding of the original bond issue should occur as shown below:

Old interest payments ($20,000,000 × 0.10)	$2,000,000
New interest payments ($20,000,000 × 0.08)	1,600,000
Annual savings	$400,000
Call premium ($20,000,000 × 0.07)	$1,400,000
Flotation cost	600,000
Total cost	$2,000,000

Year	Calculation	Present Value
0	-$2,000,000 × 1	-$2,000,000
1–10	$400,000 × 6.71 [a]	2,684,000
Net Present value		$ 684,000

[a] Present value of annuity factor for $i = 8\%$, $n = 10$

EXAMPLE 4: Your company is considering calling a $10 million, 20-year bond that was issued five years ago at a nominal interest rate of 10%. The call price on the bonds is 105. The bonds were initially sold at 90. The discount on bonds payable at the time of sale was, therefore, $1 million and the net proceeds received were $9 million. The initial flotation cost was $100,000. The firm is considering issuing $10 million, 8%, 15-year bonds and using the net proceeds to retire the old bonds. The new bonds will be issued at face value. The flotation cost for the new issue is $150,000. The company's tax rate is 46%. The after-tax cost of new debt, ignoring flotation costs, is 4.32% (8% × 54%). With the flotation cost, the after-tax cost of new debt is estimated at 5%. There is an overlap period of three months in which interest must be paid on the old and new bonds.

The initial cash outlay is:

Cost to call old bonds		
($10,000,000 × 105%)		$10,500,00
Cost to issue new bond		150,000
Interest on old bonds for overlap period		
($10,000,000 × 10% × 3/12)		250,000
Initial cash outlay		$10,900,000

The initial cash inflow is:

Proceeds from selling new bond		$10,000,000
Tax-deductible items		
Call premium	$500,000	
Unamortized discount		
($1,000,000 × 15/20)	750,000	
Overlap in interest		
($10,000,000 × 10% × 3/12)	250,000	
Unamortized issue cost of old bond		
($100,000 × 15/20)	75,000	
Total tax-deductible items	$1,575,000	
Tax rate	× 0.46	
Tax savings		724,500
Initial cash inflow		$10,724,500

The net initial cash outlay is therefore:

Initial cash outlay		$10,900,000
Initial cash inflow		10,724,500
Net initial cash outlay		$ 175,500

The annual cash flow for the old bond is:

Interest (10% × $10,000,000)		$1,000,000
Less: tax-deductible items		
Interest	$1,000,000	

Amortization of discount		
($1,000,000/20 years)	50,000	
Amortization of issue cost		
($100,000/20 years)	5,000	
Total tax-deductible items	$1,055,000	
Tax rate	0.46	
Tax savings		485,300
Annual cash outflow with old bond		$ 514,700

The annual cash flow for the new bond is:

Interest		$800,000
Less: tax-deductible items		
Interest	$800,000	
Amortization of issue cost		
($150,000/15 years)	10,000	
Total tax-deductible items	$810,000	
Tax rate	0.46	
Tax savings		372,600
Annual cash outflow with new bond		$427,400

The net annual cash savings with the new bond compared to the old bond is:

Annual cash outflow with old bond	$514,700
Annual cash outflow with new bond	427,400
Net annual cash savings	$ 87,300

The net present value associated with the refunding is:

	Calculation	Present Value
Year 0	–$175,500 × 1	–$175,500
Year 1–15	$87,300 × 10.38[a]	+ 906,174
Net present value		$730,674

[a] Present value of annuity factor for $I = 5\%$, $n = 15$

Since a positive net present value exists, the refunding of the old bond should be made.

Sinking fund requirements may exist in a bond issue. With a sinking fund, the company puts aside money to buy and retire part of a bond issue each year. Usually, there is a mandatory fixed amount that must be retired, but occasionally the retirement may relate to the company's sales or profit for the current year. If a sinking fund payment is not made, the bond issue may be in default.

In many instances, the company can handle the sinking fund in one of the following two ways:

1. It can call a given percentage of the bonds at a specified price each year, for instance, 10% of the original amount at a price of $1,070.

2. It can buy its own bonds on the open market.

The least costly alternative should be selected. If interest rates have increased, the price of the bonds will have decreased, and the open market option should be employed. If interest rates have decreased, the bond prices will have increased, and thus calling the bonds is preferred.

> **EXAMPLE 5:** Your company has to reduce bonds payable by $300,000. The call price is 104. The market price of the bonds is 103. The company will opt to buy back the bonds on the open market because it is less expensive, as indicated below:

Call price ($300,000 × 104%)	$312,000
Purchase on open market ($300,000 × 103%)	309,000
Advantage of purchasing bonds on the open market	$ 3,000

VARIABLE-COUPON RENEWABLE NOTES

Variable-coupon renewable notes are long-term financing vehicles with the prospect of significant cost savings to the issuing company. They are generally for 50 years and contain a put feature permitting note holders to accept a reduced coupon spread for the last three payments. The coupon is changed weekly based on a spread over the rates for three-month Treasury bills. Interest is paid quarterly. The issuing company may use this as a long-term financing source while paying short-term interest rates.

FEDERAL LOAN PROGRAMS

The company may elect to take advantage of federal loan programs, where appropriate. The three major loan agencies are:

1. *Small Business Administration* (SBA). The SBA will lend money only for a feasible project and where the security is adequate. Bond financing at a reasonable interest rate must not be available. The bank must confirm that it will not participate without an SBA guarantee.

2. *Economic Development Administration.* This agency provides financial assistance if the company is upgrading an area economically by providing well-paying jobs for local residents. The company must expand or locate new facilities in areas of high unemployment or low family income.

3. *Farmers Home Administration.* This agency encourages the creation and maintenance of employment in rural communities.

THE ISSUANCE OF EQUITY SECURITIES

The sources of equity financing consist of preferred stock and common stock. The advantages and disadvantages of issuing preferred and common are addressed, along with the various circumstances in which either financing source is most suited. Stock rights are also described.

When to Use Preferred Stock

Preferred stock is a hybrid between bonds and common stock. Preferred stock comes after debt but before common stock in liquidation and in the distribution of earnings. Preferred stock may be issued when the cost of common stock is high. The optimal time to issue preferred stock is when the company has excessive debt and an issue of common stock might result in control problems. Preferred stock is a more expensive way to raise capital than a bond issue because the dividend payment is not tax deductible. Many utilities offer preferred stock.

Preferred stock may be cumulative or noncumulative. Cumulative preferred stock means that if any prior year's dividend payments have been missed, they must be paid before dividends can be paid to common stockholders. If preferred dividends are in arrears for a long time, the company may find it difficult to resume its dividend payments to common stockholders. With noncumulative preferred stock, the company need not pay missed preferred dividends. Preferred stock dividends are limited to the rate specified, which is based on the total par value of the outstanding shares. Most preferred stock is cumulative.

Participating preferred stock means that if declared dividends exceed the amount typically given to preferred stockholders and common stockholders, the preferred and common stockholders will participate in the excess dividends. Unless stated otherwise, the distribution of the excess dividends will be based on the relative total par values. Nonparticipating preferred stock does not participate with common stock in excess dividends. Most preferred stock is nonparticipating.

Preferred stock may be callable, which means that the company can purchase it back at a subsequent date at a specified call price. The call provision is advantageous when interest rates decline, since the company has the option of discontinuing payments of dividends at a rate that has become excessive by buying back preferred stock that was issued when bond interest rates were high. Unlike bonds, preferred stock rarely has a maturity date. However, if preferred stock has a sinking fund associated with it, this, in effect, establishes a maturity date for repayment.

There are possible variations to preferred stock issues. Limited life preferred stock has a specified maturity date or can be redeemed at the holder's option. Perpetual preferred stock automatically converts to common stock at a given date. There are also preferred stocks with "floating rate" dividends so as to keep the preferred stock at par by altering the dividend rate.

In bankruptcy, preferred stockholders are paid after creditors and before common stockholders. In such a case, preferred stockholders receive the par value of their shares, dividends in arrears, and the current year's dividend. Any asset balance then goes to the common stockholders.

The cost of preferred stock usually follows changes in interest rates. Hence, the cost of preferred stock will most likely be low when interest rates are low.

When the cost of common stock is high, preferred stock issuance may be achieved at a lower cost.

A preferred stock issue has the following advantages:

- Preferred dividends do not have to be paid (important during periods of financial distress), whereas interest on debt must be paid.
- Preferred stockholders cannot force the company into bankruptcy.
- Preferred shareholders do not share in unusually high profits because the common stockholders are the real owners of the business.
- If the company is a growth one, it can generate better earnings for its original owners by issuing preferred stock having a fixed dividend rate than by issuing common stock.
- Preferred stock issuance does not dilute the ownership interest of common stockholders in terms of earnings participation and voting rights.
- The company does not have to collateralize its assets as it may have to do if bonds are issued.
- The debt-to-equity ratio is improved.

A preferred stock issue has the following disadvantages:

- Preferred stock requires a higher yield than bonds because of greater risk.
- Preferred dividends are not tax deductible.
- There are higher flotation costs than with bonds.

The advantages of preferred stock over bonds is that the company can omit a dividend readily, no maturity date exists, and no sinking fund is required. Preferred stock also has a number of advantages over common stock. It avoids dilution of control and the equal participation in profits that are afforded to common stockholders.

Disadvantages of preferred stock issuance compared to bonds are that it requires a higher yield than debt because it is more risky to the holder. Also, dividends are not tax deductible.

The Issuance of Common Stock

Common stock is the residual equity ownership in the business. Common stockholders have voting power but come after preferred stockholders in receiving dividends and in liquidation. Common stock does not involve fixed charges, maturity dates, or sinking fund requirements.

In a few cases, a company may issue different classes of common stock. Class A is stock issued to the public and typically has no dividends. However, it usually has voting rights. Class B stock is typically kept by the company's organizers. Dividends are usually not paid on it until the company has generated adequate earnings. Voting rights are provided in order for control to be maintained.

The price of common stock moves in the opposite direction as market interest rates. For example, if market interest rates increase, stock prices fall because investors will transfer funds out of stock into higher-yielding money market instruments and bank accounts. Further, higher interest rates make it costly for a company to borrow, resulting in lower profits and the resulting decline in stock price.

Common stock may basically be issued in one of the following ways:

- *Broad syndication.* This is the most common method because it gives the issuer the greatest control over distribution and thus probably achieves the highest net price. It also provides the most public exposure. The drawbacks are that it may take longer and there are high transaction costs.

- *Limited distribution.* There are a limited number of underwriters involved in the issuance.

- *Sole distribution.* Only one underwriter is used which may result in unsold shares. The company has less control in the distribution process. This will lower transaction costs and is fast.

- *Dribble out.* The company periodically issues stock over time resulting in an average price. This approach is not recommended because of the high associated costs, and it may depress stock price because of the constant issuance of shares.

In timing a public issuance of common stock, the following should be noted:

- Do not offer shares near the expiration date for options on the company's shares since the option-related transaction may affect share price.

- Offer higher-yielding common stock just before the ex-dividend date so investors will be attracted to it.

- Issue common stock when there is little competition of share issuance by other companies in the industry.

- Issue shares in bull markets and refrain from issuing them in bear markets.

A number of options exist for equity financing in the case of small businesses, including:

- Venture capital (investor) groups who typically invest in high-risk ventures.

- Issuances directly to institutional investors (e.g., insurance companies, banks).

- Issuances to relatives or friends.

- Issuances to major customers and suppliers.

A determination of the number of shares that must be issued to raise adequate funds to satisfy a capital budget may be needed.

EXAMPLE 6: Your company currently has 650,000 shares of common stock outstanding. The capital budget for the upcoming year is $1.8 million.

Assuming new stock may be issued for $16 a share, the number of shares that must be issued to provide the necessary funds to meet the capital budget is:

$$\frac{\text{Funds needed}}{\text{Market price per share}} = \frac{\$1,800,000}{\$16} = 112,500 \text{ shares}$$

EXAMPLE 7: Your company wants to raise $3 million in its first public issue of common stock, After its issuance, the total market value of stock is expected to be $7 million. Currently, there are 140,000 outstanding shares that are closely held.

We want to compute the number of new shares that must be issued to raise the $3 million.

The new shares will have 3/7 ($3 million/$7 million) of the outstanding shares after the stock issuance. Thus, current stockholders will be holding 4/7 of the shares.

140,000 shares = 4/7 of the total shares

Total shares = 245,000

New shares = 3/7 × 245,000 = 105,000 shares

After the stock issuance, the expected price per share is:

$$\text{Price per share} = \frac{\text{Market value}}{\text{Shares outstanding}} = \frac{\$7,000,000}{245,000} = \$28.57$$

A company that initially issues its common stock publicly is referred to as "going public." The estimated price per share to sell the securities is equal to:

$$\frac{\text{Anticipated market value of the company}}{\text{Total outstanding shares}}$$

For an established company, the market price per share can be determined as follows:

$$\frac{\text{Expected dividend}}{\text{Cost of capital} - \text{Growth rate in dividends}}$$

EXAMPLE 8: Your company expected the dividend for the year to be $10 a share. The cost of capital is 13%. The growth rate in dividends is expected to be constant at 8%. The price per share is:

$$\text{Price per share} = \frac{\text{Expected dividend}}{\text{Cost of capital} - \text{Growth rate in dividends}}$$

$$= \frac{\$10}{0.13 - 0.08} = \frac{\$10}{0.05} = \$200$$

Another approach to pricing the share of stock for an existing company is through the use of the price/earnings (P/E) ratio, which is equal to:

$$\frac{\text{Market price per share}}{\text{Earnings per share}}$$

EXAMPLE 9: Your company's earnings per share is $7. It is expected that the company's stock should sell at eight times its earnings. The market price per share is therefore:

$$\text{P/E} = \frac{\text{Market prices per share}}{\text{Earnings per share}}$$

Market prices per share = P/E multiple × earnings per share

$$= 8 \times \$7 = \$56$$

There are a number of different ways to determine the market value of your company's stock.

EXAMPLE 10: Assuming an indefinite stream of future dividends of $300,000 and a required return rate of 14%, the market value of the stock equals:

$$\text{Market value} \quad \frac{\text{Expected dividends}}{\text{Rate of return}} = \frac{\$300,000}{0.14} = \$2,142,857$$

If there are 200,000 shares, the market price per share is:

$$\text{Market value} = \frac{\$2,142,857}{200,000} = \$10.71$$

EXAMPLE 11: Your company is considering a public issue of its securities. The average price/earnings multiple in the industry is 15. The company's earnings are $400,000. There will be 100,000 shares outstanding after the issuance of the stock. The expected price per share is:

Total market value = Net income × Price/earnings multiple
= $400,000 × 15 = $6,000,000

$$\text{Price per share} \quad \frac{\text{Market value}}{\text{Shares}} = \frac{\$6,000,000}{100,000} = \$60$$

EXAMPLE 12: Your company issues 400,000 new shares of common stock to current stockholders at a $25 price per share. The price per share before the new issue was $29. Currently, there are 500,000 outstanding shares. The expected price per share after the new issue is:

Value of outstanding shares (500,000 × $29)	$14,500,000
Value of newly issued shares (400,000 × $25)	10,000,000
Value of entire issue	$24,500,000

$$\text{Value of share} = \frac{\text{Value of entire share}}{\text{Total number of shares}} = \frac{\$24,500,000}{900,000} = \$27.22$$

EXAMPLE 13: Your company is considering constructing a new plant. The firm has usually distributed all its earnings in dividends. Capital expansion has been financed through the issue of common stock. The firm has no preferred stock or debt.

The following expectations exist:

Net income	$23,000,000
Shares outstanding	5,000,000
Construction cost of new plant	$18,000,000

Incremental annual earnings expected because of the new plant are $2 million. The rate of return expected by stockholders is 12% per annum. The total market value of the firm if the plant is financed through the issuance of common stock is:

$$\frac{\text{Total net income}}{\text{Rate of return}} = \frac{\$25,000,000}{0.12} = \$208,330,000$$

The financial manager may want to compute the company's price-earnings ratio and required rate of return.

EXAMPLE 14: Your company has experienced an 8% growth rate in profits and dividends. Next year, it expects earnings per share of $4 and dividends per share of $2.50. The company will be having its first public issue of common stock. The stock will be issued at $50 per share.

The price-earnings ratio is:

$$\frac{\text{Market price per share}}{\text{Earnings per share}} = \frac{\$50}{\$4} = 12.5 \text{ times}$$

The required rate of return on the stock is:

$$\frac{\text{Dividends per share}}{\text{Market price per share}} + \text{Growth rate in dividends}$$

$$\frac{\$2.50}{\$50.00} + 0.08 \; = 0.13$$

If your company has significant debt, it would be better off financing with an equity issue to lower overall financial risk.

Financing with common stock has the following advantages:

- There is no requirement to pay fixed charges such as interest or dividends.
- There is no repayment date or sinking fund requirement.
- A common stock issue improves the company's credit rating relative to the issuance of debt. For example, the debt-equity ratio is improved.

Financing with common stock has the following disadvantages:

- Dividends are not tax deductible.
- Ownership interest is diluted. The additional voting rights could vote to take control away from the current ownership group.
- Earnings and dividends are spread over more shares outstanding.
- The flotation costs of a common stock issue are higher than with preferred stock and debt financing.

It is always cheaper to finance operations from internally generated funds because financing out of retained earnings involves no flotation costs. Retained earnings may be used as equity funding if the company believes its stock price is lower than the true value of its assets. Retained earnings are also preferred if transaction costs are high for external financing.

The company may make use of dividend reinvestment plans and employee stock option plans to raise financing and thus avoid issuance costs and the market impact of a public offering.

Stockholders are typically better off when a company cuts back on its dividends instead of issuing common stock as a source of additional funds. When earnings are retained rather than new stock issued, the market price per share of existing stock will rise, as indicated by higher earnings per share. Also, a company typically earns a higher rate of return than stockholders, so if funds are retained, the market price of stock should appreciate. One caution, however: Lower dividend payments may be looked at negatively in the market and may cause a reduction in the market price of stock due to psychological factors.

A summary comparison of bonds and common stock is presented in Exhibit 54-4.

STOCK RIGHTS

Stock rights are options to buy securities at a specified price at a later date. They are a good source of common stock financing. The preemptive right provides that existing stockholders have the first option to buy additional shares. Exercising this right permits investors to maintain voting control and protects against dilution in ownership and earnings.

Financial management decides on the life of the right (typically about two months), its price (typically below the current market price), and the number of rights needed to buy a share.

Exhibit 54-4: Summary Comparison of Bonds and Common Stock

Bonds	Common Stock
Bondholders are creditors.	Stockholders are owners.
No voting rights exist.	Voting rights exist.
There is a maturity date.	There is no maturity date.
Bondholders have prior claims on profits and assets in bankruptcy.	Stockholders have residual claims on profits and assets in bankruptcy.
Interest payments represent fixed charges.	Dividend payments do not constitute fixed charges.
Interest payments are deductible on the tax return.	There is no tax deductibility for dividend payments.
The rate of return required by bondholders is typically lower than that required by stockholders.	The rate of return required by stockholders is typically greater than that required by bondholders.

EXAMPLE 15: Your company has 500,000 shares of common stock outstanding and is planning to issue another 100,000 shares through stock rights. Each current stockholder will receive one right per share. Each right permits the stockholder to buy 1/5 of a share of new common stock (100,000 shares/500,000 shares). Hence, five rights are needed to buy one share of stock. Thus, a shareholder holding 10,000 shares would be able to buy 2,000 new shares (10,000 × 1/5). By exercising his or her right, the stockholder would now have a total of 12,000 shares, representing a 2% interest (12,000/600,000) in the total shares outstanding. This is the same 2% ownership (10,000/500,000) the stockholder held prior to the rights offering.

In a rights offering, there is a date of record, which states the last day that the receiver of the right must be the legal owner as reflected in the company's stock ledger. Because of a lag in bookkeeping, stocks are often sold ex rights (without rights) four business days before the record date. Before this point, the stock is sold rights on, which means the purchasers receive the rights.

The recipient of the rights can exercise them, sell them, or let them expire. Since stock rights are transferable, many are traded on the stock exchange and over-the-counter markets. They may be exercised for a given period of time at a subscription price, which is set somewhat below the prevailing market price.

After the subscription price has been determined, management must ascertain the number of rights necessary to purchase a share of stock. The total number of shares that must be sold equals:

$$\text{Shares to be sold} = \frac{\text{Amount of funds to be obtained}}{\text{Subscription price}}$$

The number of rights needed to acquire one share equals:

$$\text{Rights per share} = \frac{\text{Total shares outstanding}}{\text{Shares to be sold}}$$

EXAMPLE 16: Your company wants to obtain $800,000 by a rights offering. There are presently 100,000 shares outstanding. The subscription price is $40 a share. The shares to be sold equal:

$$\text{Shares to be sold} = \frac{\text{Amount of funds to be obtained}}{\text{Subscription price}} = \frac{\$800,000}{\$40}$$
$$= 20,000 \text{ shares}$$

The number of rights needed to acquire one share equals:

$$\text{Rights per share} = \frac{\text{Total shares outstanding}}{\text{Shares to be sold}} = \frac{100,000}{20,000} = 5$$

Thus, five rights will be required to buy each new share at $40. Each right enables the holder to buy 1/5 of a share of stock.

Value of a Right

The value of a right should, theoretically, be the same whether the stock is selling with rights on or ex rights.

When stock is selling with rights on, the value of a right equals:

$$\frac{\text{Market value of stock with rights on} - \text{Subscription price}}{\text{Number of rights needed to buy one share} + 1}$$

EXAMPLE 17: Your company's common stock sells for $55 a share with rights on. Each stockholder is given the right to buy one new share at $35 for every four shares held. The value of each right is:

$$\frac{\$55 - \$35}{4 + 1} = \frac{\$20}{5} = \$4$$

When stock is traded ex rights, the market price is expected to decline by the value of the right. The market value of stock trading ex rights should theoretically equal:

Market value of stock with rights on – Value of a right when stock is selling rights on

The value of a right when stock is selling ex rights equals:

$$\frac{\text{Market value of stock trading ex rights} - \text{Subscription price}}{\text{Number of rights needed to buy one new share} + 1}$$

EXAMPLE 18: Assuming the same information, the value of the company's stock trading ex rights should equal:

Market value of stock with rights on − Value of a right when stock is selling rights on

$$\$55 - \$4 = \$51$$

The value of a right when stock is selling ex rights is therefore:

$$\frac{\text{Market value of stock trading ex rights} - \text{Subscription price}}{\text{Number of rights needed to buy one new share} + 1}$$

$$\frac{\$51 - \$35}{4} = \frac{\$16}{4} = \$4$$

Note: The theoretical value of the right is identical when the stock is selling rights on or ex rights.

GOVERNMENTAL REGULATION

When securities are issued publicly, they must conform to federal and state regulations. State rules are referred to as *blue sky laws*. The major federal laws are the Securities Act of 1933 and the Securities Exchange Act of 1934. The 1934 Act applies to existing security transactions, while the 1933 Act deals with regulation of new security issues. The Acts require full disclosure to investors concerning the company's affairs. Prior to the issuance of a new security, the company must prepare a prospectus for investors containing a condensed version of the registration statement filed with the SEC. For a more detailed discussion of financial reporting to the SEC, see Chapter 2, "SEC Reporting."

FINANCING

Some companies obtain most of their funds from issuing stock and from earnings retained in the business. Other companies borrow as much as possible and raise additional money from stockholders only when they can no longer borrow. Most companies are somewhere in the middle.

The financial manager is concerned with selecting the best possible source of financing based on the facts of the situation. He or she has to look at the various circumstances to determine the mix of financing required.

In formulating a financing strategy in terms of source and amount, the company should consider the following:

- *The cost and risk of alternative financing strategies.*
- *The future trend in market conditions and how they will impact upon future fund availability and interest rates.* For example, if interest rates are ex-

pected to go up, the company would be better off financing with long-term debt at the currently lower interest rates. If stock prices are high, equity issuance may be preferred over debt.

- *The current debt to equity ratio.* A very high ratio, for example, indicates financial risk so additional funds should come from equity sources.

- *The maturity dates of present debt instruments.* For example, the company should avoid having all debt come due at the same time because in an economic downturn the company may not have adequate funds to meet all that debt.

- *The restrictions in loan agreements.* For instance, a restriction may exist placing a cap on the allowable debt-equity ratio.

- *The type and amount of collateral required by long-term creditors.*

- *The ability to change financing strategy to adjust to changing economic conditions.* For example, a company subject to large cyclical variations should have less debt because the company may not be able to meet principal and interest at the low point of the cycle. If earnings are unstable and/or there is a highly competitive environment, more emphasis should be given to equity financing.

- *The amount, nature, and stability of internally generated funds.* If stability exists in earnings generation, the company is better able to meet debt obligations.

- *The adequacy of present lines of credit for current and future needs.*

- *The inflation rate*, since with debt the repayment is in cheaper dollars.

- *The earning power and liquidity position of the firm.* For example, a liquid company is better able to meet debt payments.

- *The nature and risk of assets.* High-quality assets allow for greater debt.

- *The nature of the product line.* A company, for example, that has technological obsolescence risk in its product line (e.g., computers) should refrain from over-use of debt.

- *The uncertainty of large expenditures.* If huge cash outlays may be required (e.g., lawsuit, acquisition of another company), there should be unused debt capacity available.

- *The tax rate.* For example, a higher tax rate makes debt more attractive because there is a greater tax savings from interest expense.

- *Foreign operations.* If operations are in questionable foreign areas and foreign competition is keen, or if the exchange rate fluctuates widely, the debt position should be conservative.

What financing situations does the company face? What is it doing about it? You have to select the best possible source of financing based on the facts.

EXAMPLE 19: Your company is considering issuing either debt or preferred stock to finance the purchase of a plant costing $1.3 million. The interest rate on the debt is 15%. The dividend rate on the preferred stock is 10%. The tax rate is 34%.

The annual interest payment on the debt is:

$$15\% \times \$1,300,000 = \$195,000$$

The annual dividend on the preferred stock is:

$$10\% \times \$1,300,000 = \$130,000$$

The required earnings before interest and taxes to meet the dividend payment are:

$$\frac{\$130,000}{(1 - 0.34)} = \$196,970$$

If your company anticipates earning $196,970 without a problem, it should issue the preferred stock.

EXAMPLE 20: Your company has sales of $30 million a year. It needs $6 million in financing for capital expansion. The debt-equity ratio is 68%. Your company is in a risky industry, and net income is not stable. The common stock is selling at a high P/E ratio compared to competition. Under consideration is either the issuance of common stock or debt.

Because your company is in a high-risk industry and has a high debt-equity ratio and unstable earnings, issuing debt would be costly, restrictive, and potentially dangerous to future financial health. The issuance of common stock is recommended.

EXAMPLE 21: Your company is a mature one in its industry. There is limited ownership. The company has vacillating sales and earnings. Your firm's debt-equity ratio is 70% relative to the industry standard of 55%. The after-tax rate of return is 16%. Since your company is a seasonal business, there are certain times during the year when its liquidity position is inadequate. Your company is unsure on the best way to finance.

Preferred stock is one possible means of financing. Debt financing is not recommended due to the already high debt-equity ratio, the fluctuation in profit, seasonal nature of the business, and the deficient liquidity posture. Because of the limited ownership, common stock financing may not be appropriate because this would dilute the ownership.

EXAMPLE 22: A new company is established and it plans to raise $15 million in funds. The company expects that it will obtain contracts that will provide $1,200,000 a year in before-tax profits. The firm is considering whether to issue bonds only or an equal amount of bonds and preferred stock. The interest rate on AA corporate bonds is 12%. The tax rate is 50%.

The company will probably have difficulty issuing $15 million of AA bonds because the interest cost of $1,800,000 (12% × $15,000,000) associated with these bonds is greater than the estimated earnings before interest and taxes. The issuance of debt by a new company is a risky alternative.

Financing with $7.5 million in debt and $7.5 million in preferred stock is also not recommended. While some debt may be issued, it is not practical to finance the balance with preferred stock. In the case that $7.5 million of AA bonds were issued at the 12% rate, the company would be required to pay $900,000 in interest. In this event, a forecasted income statement would look as follows:

Earnings before interest and taxes	$1,200,000
Interest	900,000
Taxable income	$300,000
Taxes	150,000
Net income	$150,000

The amount available for the payment of preferred dividends is only $150,000. Hence, the maximum rate of return that could be paid on $7.5 million of preferred stock is .02 ($150,000/$7,500,000).

Stockholders would not invest in preferred stock that offers only a 2% rate of return.

The company should consider financing with common stock.

EXAMPLE 23: Your company wants to construct a plant that will take about 15 years to construct. The plant will be used to produce a new product line, for which your company expects a high demand. The new plant will materially increase corporate size. The following costs are expected:

1. The cost to build the plant, $800,000.
2. Funds needed for contingencies, $100,000.
3. Annual operating costs, $175,000.

The asset, debt, and equity positions of your company are similar to industry standards. The market price of the company's stock is less than it should be, taking into account the future earning power of the new product line. What would be an appropriate means to finance the construction?

Since the market price of stock is less than it should be and considering the potential of the product line, convertible bonds and installment bank loans might be appropriate means of financing, since interest expense is tax deductible. Additionally, the issuance of convertible bonds might not require repayment, since the bonds are likely to be converted to common stock because of the company's profitability. Installment bank loans can be gradually paid off as the new product generates cash inflow. Funds needed for contingencies can be in the form of open bank lines of credit.

If the market price of the stock were not at a depressed level, financing through equity would be an alternative financing strategy.

EXAMPLE 24: Your company wants to acquire another business but has not determined an optimal means to finance the acquisition. The current debt-equity position is within the industry guideline. In prior years, financing has been achieved through the issuance of short-term debt.

Profit has shown vacillation and, as a result, the market price of the stock has fluctuated. Currently, however, the market price of stock is strong.

Your company's tax bracket is low.

The purchase should be financed through the issuance of equity securities for the following reasons:

- The market price of stock is currently at a high level.

- The issuance of long-term debt will cause greater instability in earnings because of the high fixed interest charges. In consequence, there will be more instability in stock price.

- The issuance of debt will result in a higher debt-equity ratio relative to the industry norm. This will negatively impact the company's cost of capital and availability of financing.

- Because it will take a long time to derive the funds needed for the purchase price, short-term debt should not be issued. If short-term debt were issued, the debt would have to be paid before the receipt of the return from the acquired business.

EXAMPLE 25: Breakstone Corporation wants to undertake a capital expansion program and must, therefore, obtain $7 million in financing. The company has a good credit rating. The current market price of its common stock is $60. The interest rate for long-term debt is 18%. The dividend rate associated with preferred stock is 16%, and Breakstone's tax rate is 46%.

Relevant ratios for the industry and the company are:

	Industry	**Breakstone**
Net income to total assets	13%	22%
Long-term debt to total assets	31%	29%
Total liabilities to total assets	47%	45%
Preferred stock to total assets	3%	0
Current ratio	2.6	3.2
Net income plus interest to interest	8	17

Dividends per share are $8, the dividend growth rate is 7%, no sinking fund provisions exist, the trend in earnings shows stability, and the present ownership group wishes to retain control. The cost of common stock is:

$$\frac{\text{Dividend per share}}{\text{Market price per share} + \text{Dividend growth rate}}$$

$$\frac{\$8}{\$60} + 0.07 \ = \ 20.3\%$$

The after-tax cost of long-term debt is 9.7% (18% × 54%). The cost of preferred stock is 16%. How should Breakstone finance its expansion?

The issuance of long-term debt is more appropriate for the following reasons:

1. Its after-tax cost is the lowest.

2. The company's ratios of long-term debt to total assets and total liabilities to total assets are less than the industry average, pointing to the company's ability to issue additional debt.

3. Corporate liquidity is satisfactory based on the favorable current ratio relative to the industry standard.

4. Fixed interest charges can be met, taking into account the stability in earnings, the earning power of the firm, and the very favorable times interest-earned ratio. Additional interest charges should be met without difficulty.

5. The firm's credit rating is satisfactory.

6. There are no required sinking fund provisions.

7. The leveraging effect can take place to improve earnings further.

In the case that the firm does not want to finance through further debt, preferred stock would be the next best financing alternative, since its cost is lower than that associated with common stock and no dilution in the ownership interest will take place.

EXAMPLE 26: Harris Corporation has experienced growth in sales and net income but is in a weak liquidity position. The inflation rate is high. At the end of 2X11, the company needs $600,000 for the following reasons:

New equipment	$175,000
Research and development	95,000
Paying overdue accounts payable	215,000
Paying accrued liabilities	60,000
Desired increase in cash balance	55,000
	$600,000

Presented below are the financial statements for 2X11.

Harris Corporation—Balance Sheet—Dec. 31, 2X11

Assets

Current assets

Cash	$ 12,000
Accounts receivable	140,000

Harris Corporation—Balance Sheet—Dec. 31, 2X11

Notes receivable	25,000	
Inventory	165,000	
Office supplies	20,000	
Total current assets		$362,000
Fixed assets		468,000
Total assets		$830,000

Liabilities and Stockholders' Equity

Current liabilities

Loans payable	$ 74,000	
Accounts payable	360,000	
Accrued liabilities	55,000	
Total current liabilities		$489,000
Long-term debt		61,000
Total liabilities		$550,000

Stockholders' equity

Common stock	$200,000	
Retained earnings	80,000	
Total stockholders' equity		280,000
Total, liabilities and stockholders' equity		$830,000

Harris Corporation Income Statement for the Year Ended Dec. 31, 2X11

Sales	$1,400,000
Cost of sales	750,000
Gross margin	$ 650,000
Operating expenses	480,000
Income before tax	$ 170,000
Tax	68,000
Net income	$ 102,000

It is anticipated that sales will increase on a yearly basis by 22% and that net income will increase by 17%. What type of financing is best suited for Harris Corporation?

The most suitable source of financing is long term. A company in a growth stage needs a large investment in equipment, and research and development expenditure. With regard to 20X5, $270,000 of the $600,000 is required for this purpose. A growth company also needs funds to satisfy working capital requirements. Here, 45.8% of financing is necessary to pay overdue accounts payable and accrued liabilities. The firm also needs sufficient cash to capitalize on lucrative opportunities. The present cash balance to total assets is at a low 1.4%.

Long-term debt financing is recommended for the following reasons:

1. The ratio of long-term debt to stockholders' equity is a low 21.8%. The additional issuance of long-term debt will not impair the overall capital structure.

2. The company has been profitable and there is an expectation of future growth in earnings. Internally generated funds should therefore ensue, enabling the payment of fixed interest charges.

3. During inflation, the issuance of long-term debt generates purchasing power gains because the firm will be repaying creditors in cheaper dollars.

4. Interest expense is tax deductible.

EXAMPLE 27: On average over the past ten years, Tektronix's return on equity has not been sufficient to finance growth of the business, thus an infusion of new capital from outside sources has been required. Most of the additional capital has been in the form of long-term debt, which represented 13% of total capital in fiscal 2X11 and 21% of total capital in fiscal 2X15.

With expansion of the business expected to accelerate in the next few years after the current lull, but with return on equity likely to remain somewhat depressed because of competitive factors and costs associated with "preparing for the millennium," a need for additional capital is developing. Also, of the $146 million of long-term debt outstanding at the fiscal 2X15 year-end, nearly $65 million matures in the fiscal-2X16-to-fiscal-2X18 period. Thus, it is possible that as much as $100 million of capital may have to be raised to meet all requirements.

In anticipation of capital needs, Tektronix in fiscal 2X15 borrowed funds in the commercial paper market, and the company intends to replace these commercial paper borrowings at some future time with long-term financing.

Given the foregoing circumstances, and also given that Tektronix common stock currently is quoted on the New York Stock Exchange at 160% of book value and that the current interest rate on newly issued triple A industrial bonds of long maturity is 14%, evaluate on an immediate-and-longer-term basis each of the following options. Include in your answers economic and capital market assumptions: (a) Tektronix is selling two million shares of common stock at $50 per share, (b) Tektronix is selling a $100 million straight debenture issue maturing in 20 years, and (c) Tektronix is selling a $100 million bond issue convertible into common stock and maturing in 20 years. (CFA, adapted.)

Solution

(a) From the timing viewpoint, selling equity is attractive considering price-to-book rates (160%) and comparatively modest dilution (two million shares represents 11% of currently outstanding shares, less impact of after-tax cost of borrowing to be retired). However, price soon could move higher given a better economic environment, earnings recovery, and resultant stronger general stock market. Over the long term, selling equity is expensive, as continuing dividend service is with after-tax dollars. Also, immediate return on equity capital will diminish with reduced leverage as debt matures.

(b) Increasing debt, net of maturities, to a larger part of total capital is tolerable by most standards. According to the data provided, debt of about $146 million would increase to around $181 million ($146 + $100 – $65), and by 2X18 this sum presumably would not represent much more than the current 21% subject to earnings retention during the interim. However, this would be an appealing option only if interest rate assumptions indicate other than a rather meaningful decline over the next year or two, and if pro forma interest charge coverage and/or the current lull in the business do not seriously impact the rating and issue price of the bonds. The after-tax cost of debt service will be comparatively low, and so would be the net cost of capital. Another consideration will be sinking fund requirements and call restrictions and price.

(c) A convertible bond issue has certain disadvantages but it also has advantages: (1) it can be sold at a lower interest cost than a straight debt, and (2) the potential dilution is less than an issue of common reflecting the premium over the common market.

PRIVATE EQUITY

Private equity is an asset class consisting of equity securities in operating companies that are not publicly traded on a stock exchange. Private equities are generally illiquid and thought of as a long-term investment. Private equity investments are not subject to the same high level of government regulation as stock offerings to the general public. Private equity is also far less liquid than publicly traded stock. Types of private equity include the following:

1. **Venture Capital.** Venture capital refers to equity investments made, typically in companies in their early stages, to either launch, develop, and/or expand a new business. Venture capital investment is often associated with new ideas or products that have not yet been tested. The earlier the investment stage, the greater the risk/return characteristics for the investor. In other words, investing at the very beginning of what may become a profitable technology could offer substantial returns if successful, but the probability of success may not be high. Waiting until a business or idea has begun and just investing in the expansion of that business may provide a lower return, but the investor has a higher probability of success when compared to the start-up investor.

2. **Leveraged Buyouts (LBO).** At its most basic level, an LBO is a method of acquiring a company with money that is nearly all borrowed. This allows investors to make a large acquisition without committing a lot of capital. The acquirers of the target company often attempt to sell or take the target company public after five or ten years with the goal of making sizable profits. Doing an LBO can be expensive and complex, but if successful can provide considerable returns. One of the most famous LBOs was the $25 billion takeover of RJR Nabisco by private equity firm Kohlberg Kravis Roberts in 1989.

3. **Distressed or special situations.** This is a broad category referring to investments in equity or debt securities of financially stressed companies. As this area focuses on investing in entities that are in default, under bankruptcy protection, or headed in that direction, investors must evaluate not only the ability for the entity to make a comeback but also which class of securities might be more beneficial to hold during a restructuring process.

4. **Mezzanine capital.** These are typically structured as either a subordinate debt or preferred stock investment with claims below that of the other debt issued by the entity but above that of the common stockholders. Entities that obtain financing in this manner must pay a higher cost due to the investor's junior position.

5. **Other private equity strategies.** These may include real estate, energy and power, merchant banking, and infrastructure.

CHAPTER 55

WARRANTS AND CONVERTIBLES

CONTENTS

Warrants and convertibles are unique relative to other kinds of securities because they may be converted into common stock. This chapter discusses warrants and convertibles along with their valuation, presents their advantages and disadvantages, and discusses when their issuance is most appropriate.

WARRANTS

A warrant is the option given holders to purchase a given number of shares of stock at a specified price. Warrants can be either detachable or nondetachable. A detachable warrant may be sold separately from the bond with which it is associated. Thus, the holder may exercise the warrant but not redeem the bond if he or she wishes. A company may issue bonds with detachable warrants to purchase additional bonds if it wants to hedge the risk of adverse future interest rate movements since the warrant is convertible into a bond at a fixed interest rate. If interest rates rise, the warrant will be worthless, and the issue price of the warrant will partially offset the higher interest cost of the future debt issue. A nondetachable warrant is sold with its bond to be exercised by the bond owner simultaneously with the convertible bond.

A company may sell warrants separately (e.g., American Express) or in combination with other securities (e.g., MGM/UA).

To obtain common stock the warrant must be given up along with the payment of cash called the exercise price. Although warrants typically expire on a given date, some are perpetual. A holder of a warrant may exercise it by buying the stock, sell it on the market to other investors, or continue to hold it. The company cannot force the exercise of a warrant.

If desired, the company may have the exercise price associated with a warrant vary over time (e.g., increase each year).

If there is a stock split or stock dividend before the warrant is exercised, the option price of the warrant is usually adjusted for it.

Through warrants additional funds are received by the issuer. When a bond is issued with a warrant, the warrant price is typically set between 10% and 20% above the stock's market price. If the company's stock price goes above the option price, the warrants will, of course, be exercised at the option price. The closer the warrants are to their expiration date, the greater is the chance that they will be exercised.

Valuation of Warrants

The theoretical value of a warrant may be computed by a formula. The formula value is usually less than the market price of the warrant. This is because the speculative appeal of a warrant allows the investor to obtain a good degree of personal leverage.

$$\text{Value of a warrant} = (\text{Market price per share} - \text{Exercise price}) \times \text{Number of shares that may be bought}$$

EXAMPLE 1: A warrant for XYZ company's stock gives the owner the right to buy one share of common stock at $25 a share. The market price of the common stock is $53. The formula price of the warrant is $28 [($53 – $25) × 1].

If the owner had the right to buy three shares of common stock with one warrant, the theoretical value of the warrant would be $84 [($53 – $25) × 3].

If the stock is selling for an amount below the option price, there will be a negative value. Since this is illogical, we use a formula value of zero.

EXAMPLE 2: Assume the same facts as in Example 1, except that the stock is selling at $21 a share. The formula amount is: $4 [($21 – $25) 1]. However, zero will be assigned.

Warrants do not have an investment value because there is no interest or dividends paid on them nor voting rights given. Hence, the market value of a warrant is solely attributable to its convertibility value into common stock. However, the market price of a warrant is usually more than its theoretical value, which is referred to as the premium on the warrant. The lowest amount that a warrant will sell for is its theoretical value.

The value of a warrant depends on the remaining life of the option, dividend payments on the common stock, the variability in price of the common stock, whether the warrant is listed on the exchange, and the opportunity cost of funds for the investor. A high value is associated with a warrant when its life is long, the dividend payment on common stock is small, the stock price is volatile, it is listed on the exchange, and the value of funds to the investor is great (because the warrant requires a lesser investment).

EXAMPLE 3: ABC stock currently has a market value of $50. The exercise price of the warrant is also $50. Therefore, the theoretical value of the warrant is $0. However, the warrant will sell at a premium (positive price) provided there is the possibility that the market price of the common stock will exceed $50 before the expiration date of the warrant. The further into the future the expiration date is, the greater will be the premium, since there is a longer period for possible price appreciation.

Of course, the lower the market price compared to the exercise price, the less the premium is.

EXAMPLE 4: Assume the same facts as in Example 3, except that the current market price of the stock is $35. The warrant's premium in this instance will be much lower, since it would take a long time for the stock's price to increase above $50 a share. If investors anticipated that the stock price would not increase above $50 at a subsequent date, the value of the warrant would be $0.

If the market price of ABC stock rises above $50, the market price of the warrant will increase and the premium will decrease. In other words, when the stock price exceeds the exercise price, the market price of the warrant approximately equals the theoretical value causing the premium to disappear. The reduction in the premium arises because of the lessening of the advantage of owning the warrant relative to exercising it.

Advantages and Disadvantages of Warrants

The advantages of issuing warrants include the following:

- They allow for balanced financing between debt and equity.
- They permit the issuance of debt at a low interest rate.
- They serve as a "sweetener" for an issue of debt or preferred stock.
- Additional cash is received when the warrants are exercised.

The disadvantages of issuing warrants include the following:

- When exercised they will result in a dilution of common stock. This may result in a decline in the market price of stock.
- They may be exercised at a time when the business has no need for additional capital.

CONVERTIBLE SECURITIES

A convertible security is one that may be exchanged for common stock by the holder, and in some cases the issuer, according to agreed upon terms. Examples are convertible bonds and convertible preferred stock. A specified number of shares of stock are received by the holder of the convertible security when he or she makes the exchange. This is referred to as the conversion ratio, which equals:

$$\text{Conversion ratio} = \frac{\text{Par value of convertible security}}{\text{Conversion price}}$$

The conversion price applies to the effective price the holder pays for the common stock when the conversion is effected. The conversion price and the conversion ratio are set when the convertible security is issued. The conversion price should be tied to the growth potential of the company. The greater the potential, the greater the conversion price should be.

A convertible bond is a quasi-equity security because its market value is tied to its value if converted rather than as a bond. The convertible bond may be considered a delayed issue of common stock at a price above the current level.

EXAMPLE 5: A $1,000 bond is convertible into 30 shares of stock. The conversion price is $33.33 ($1,000/30 shares).

EXAMPLE 6: A share of convertible preferred stock with a par value of $50 is convertible into four shares of common stock. The conversion price is $12.50 ($50/4).

EXAMPLE 7: A $1,000 convertible bond is issued that entitles the holder to convert the bond into 10 shares of common stock. Hence, the conversion ratio is 10 shares for one bond. Since the face value of the bond is $1,000 the holder is tendering this amount upon conversion. The conversion price equals $100 per share ($1,000/10 shares).

EXAMPLE 8: Y Company issued a $1,000 convertible bond at par. The conversion price is $40. The conversion ratio is:

$$\text{Conversion ratio} = \frac{\text{Par value of convertible security}}{\text{Conversion price}}$$

$$= \frac{\$1,000}{\$40} = 25$$

The conversion value of a security is computed as follows:

Conversion value = Common stock price × Conversion ratio

When a convertible security is issued, it is priced higher than its conversion value. The difference is referred to as the conversion premium. The percentage conversion premium is computed in the following manner:

$$\frac{\text{Percentage}}{\text{Conversion premium}} = \frac{\text{Market value} - \text{Conversion value}}{\text{Conversion value}}$$

EXAMPLE 9: LA Corporation issued a $1,000 convertible bond at par. The market price of the common stock at the date of issue was $48. The conversion price is $55.

$$\text{Conversion ratio} = \frac{\text{Par value of convertible security}}{\text{Conversion price}}$$

$$= \frac{\$1{,}000}{\$55} = 18.18$$

Conversion value of the bond equals:

Common stock price × Conversion ratio = $48 × 18.18 = $872

The difference between the conversion value of $872 and the issue price of $1,000 constitutes the conversion premium of $128. The conversion premium may also be expressed as a percentage of the conversion value. The percent in this case is:

Percentage conversion premium equals:

$$\frac{\text{Market value} - \text{Conversion value}}{\text{Conversion value}} = \frac{\$1{,}000 - \$872}{\$872} = \frac{\$128}{\$872} = 14.7\%$$

The conversion terms may not be static but may increase in steps over specified time periods. Hence, as time passes fewer common shares are exchanged for the bond. In some instances, after a certain time period the conversion option may expire.

Typically, the convertible security contains a clause that protects it from dilution caused by stock dividends, stock splits, and stock rights. The clause usually prevents the issuance of common stock at a price lower than the conversion price. Also, the conversion price is reduced by the percentage amount of any stock split or stock dividend. This enables the shareholder of common stock to maintain his or her proportionate interest.

EXAMPLE 10: A 3-for-1 stock split occurs, which requires a tripling of the conversion ratio. A 20% stock dividend requires a 20% increase in the conversion ratio.

The voluntary conversion of a security by the holder depends on the relationship of the interest on the bond relative to the dividend on the stock, the risk preference of the holder (stock has a greater risk than a bond), and the current and expected market price of the stock.

Valuation of Convertibles

A convertible security is a hybrid security because it has attributes that are similar to common stock and bonds. The expectation is that the holder will ultimately receive both interest yield and a capital gain. Interest yield relates to the coupon interest relative to the market price of the bond when purchased. The capital gain yield applies to the difference between the conversion price and the stock price at the issuance date and the expected growth rate in stock price.

The investment value of a convertible security is the value of the security, assuming it was not convertible but had all other attributes. For a convertible bond, its investment value equals the present value of future interest payments plus the present value of the maturity amount. For preferred stock the investment value equals the present value of future dividend payments plus the present value of expected selling price.

Conversion value refers to the value of stock received upon converting the bond. As the price of the stock increases so will its conversion value.

EXAMPLE 11: A $1,000 bond is convertible into 18 shares of common stock with a market value of $52 per share. The conversion value of the bond equals:

$$\$52 \times 18 \text{ shares} = \$936$$

EXAMPLE 12: At the date a $100,000 convertible bond is issued, the market price of the stock is $18 a share. Each $1,000 bond is convertible into 50 shares of stock. The conversion ratio is thus 50. The number of shares the bond is convertible into is:

$$100 \text{ bonds } (\$100,000/\$1,000) \times 50 \text{ shares} = 5,000 \text{ shares}$$

The conversion value is $90,000 ($18 × 5,000 shares).

If the stock price is expected to grow at 6% per year, the conversion value at the end of the first year is:

Shares	5,000
Stock price ($18 × 1.06)	$19.08
Conversion value	$95,400

A convertible security will not sell at less than its value as straight debt (non-convertible security). This is because the conversion privilege has to have some value in terms of its potential convertibility to common stock and in terms of reducing the holder's risk exposure to a declining bond price (convertible bonds fall off less in price than straight debt issues). Market value will equal investment value only when the conversion privilege is worthless due to a low market price of the common stock compared to the conversion price.

When convertible bonds are issued, the business expects that the value of common stock will appreciate and that the bonds will ultimately be converted. If conversion does occur, the company could then issue another convertible bond. Such a financial policy is termed "leapfrog financing."

If the market price of common stock drops instead of rising, the holder will not convert the debt into equity. In this instance, the convertible security continues as debt and is termed a "hung" convertible.

A convertible security holder may prefer to hold the security instead of converting it even though the conversion value exceeds the price paid for it. First, as the price of the common stock increases so will the price of the convertible security. Second, the holder receives regular interest payments or preferred dividends. To force conversion, companies issuing convertibles often have a call price. The call price is above the face value of the bond (about 10% to 20% higher). This forces the conversion of stock as long as the stock price exceeds the conversion price. The holder would prefer a higher-value common stock than a lower call price for the bond.

The issuing company may force conversion of its convertible bond to common stock when financially advantageous such as when the market price of the stock has dropped, or when the interest rate on the convertible debt is currently higher than the prevailing market interest rates. An example of a company that has in the past had a conversion of its convertible bond when the market price of its stock was low was United Technologies.

> **EXAMPLE 13:** The conversion price on a $1,000 debenture is $40 and the call price is $1,100. In order for the conversion value of the bond to equal the call price, the market price of the stock would have to be $44 ($1,100/25). If the conversion value of a bond is 15% higher than the call price, the approximate market price of common stock would be $51 (1.15 × $44). At a $51 price, conversion is virtually guaranteed, since if the investor did not convert he or she would incur a material opportunity loss.

> **EXAMPLE 14:** ABC Company's convertible bond has a conversion price of $80. The conversion ratio is 10. The market price of the stock is $140. The call price is $1,100. The bondholder would rather convert to common stock with a market value of $1,400 ($140 × 10) than have his or her convertible bond redeemed at $1,100. In this instance, the call provision forces the conversion when the bondholder might be tempted to wait longer.

Advantages and Disadvantages of Convertibles

The advantages of issuing convertible securities are as follows:

- It is a "sweetener" in a debt offering by giving the investor a chance to take part in the price appreciation of common stock.
- The issuance of convertible debt allows for a lower interest rate on the financing relative to issuing straight debt.
- A convertible security may be issued in a tight money market, when it is difficult for a creditworthy firm to issue a straight bond or preferred stock.
- There are fewer financing restrictions involved with a convertible security issuance.
- Convertibles provide a means of issuing equity at prices higher than current market prices.
- The call provision enables the company to force conversion whenever the market price of the stock exceeds the conversion price.
- In the case the company issued straight debt now and common stock later to meet the debt, they would incur flotation costs twice, whereas with convertible debt, flotation costs would occur only once, with the initial issuance of the convertible bonds.

The disadvantages of issuing convertible securities are as follows:

- If the company's stock price appreciably increases in value, it would have been better off financing through a regular issuance of common stock by waiting to issue it at the higher price instead of allowing conversion at the lower price.

- The company is obligated to pay the convertible debt if the stock price does not rise.

Corporate Financing Strategy

When a firm's stock price is currently depressed, convertible debt instead of common stock issuance may be called for if the price of stock is anticipated to increase. Establishing a conversion price above the present market price of stock will involve the issuance of fewer shares when the bonds are converted compared to selling the shares at a current lower price. Also, less share dilution will be involved. Of course, the conversion will occur only if the price of the stock rises above the conversion price. The drawback is that if the stock price does not increase and conversion does not take place, an additional debt burden is placed upon the company.

The issuance of convertible debt is suggested when the company wants to leverage itself in the short run but desires not to incur interest cost and pay principal on the convertible debt in the long run (due to its conversion).

A convertible issue is often a good financing tool for a growth company with a low dividend yield on stock. The quicker the growth rate, the earlier the conversion will be. For instance, a convertible bond may act as a temporary source of funds in a construction period. It is a relatively inexpensive source for financing growth. A convertible issuance is not recommended for a company with a modest growth rate, since it would take a long time to force conversion. During such a time the company will not be able to issue additional financing easily. A long conversion interval may imply to the investing public that the firm is a prime consideration in determining whether convertibles are the best method of financing.

A company may also issue bonds exchangeable for the common stock of other companies. The issuer may do this if it owns a sizable stake in another company's stock and it wants to raise cash currently and intends to sell the shares at a later date because it expects the share price to rise.

In conclusion, a convertible bond is a delayed common equity financing. The issuer expects stock price to rise in the future (e.g., 2–4 years) to stimulate conversion. Convertible bonds may be suitable for smaller, rapidly growing companies.

Note: A company that has an uncertain future tax position can issue convertible preferred stock exchangeable at the option of the company (i.e., when it becomes a taxpayer) into convertible debt of the company.

CONVERTIBLES VERSUS WARRANTS

The differences between convertibles and warrants are as follows:

- Exercising convertibles does not typically provide additional funds to the company, while the exercise of warrants does.
- When conversion occurs the debt ratio is reduced. However, the exercise of warrants adds to the equity position with debt still remaining.
- Because of the call feature, the company has more control over the timing of the capital structure with convertibles than with warrants.

CHAPTER 56

COST OF CAPITAL AND CAPITAL STRUCTURE DECISIONS

CONTENTS

Cost of capital is defined as the rate of return that is necessary to maintain the market value of the firm (or price of the firm's stock). Financial managers must know the cost of capital (the minimum required rate of return) in: (1) making capital budgeting decisions, (2) helping to establish the optimal capital structure, and (3) making decisions such as leasing, bond refunding, and working capital management. The cost of capital is computed as a weighted average of the various capital components, which are items on the right-hand side of the balance sheet such as debt, preferred stock, common stock, and retained earnings. This chapter covers the following topics:

- How to compute costs of capital.
- EBIT-EPS approach to financial leverage.
- Capital structure decisions in practice.

COMPUTING INDIVIDUAL COSTS OF CAPITAL

Each element of capital has a component cost that is identified by the following:

- k_i = before-tax cost of debt
- $k_d = k_i (1 - t)$ = after-tax cost of debt, where t = tax rate
- k_p = cost of preferred stock
- k_s = cost of retained earnings (or internal equity)
- k_e = cost of external equity, or cost of issuing new common stock
- k_o = firm's overall cost of capital, or a weighted average cost of capital

Cost of Debt

The before-tax cost of debt can be found by determining the internal rate of return (or yield to maturity) on the bond cash flows.

However, the following short-cut formula may be used for approximating the yield to maturity on a bond:

$$k_i = \frac{I + (M - V)/n}{(M + V)/2}$$

where

I = annual interest payments in dollars

M = par value, usually $1,000 per bond

V = value or net proceeds from the sale of a bond

n = term of the bond in years

Since the interest payments are tax deductible, the cost of debt must be stated on an after-tax basis. The after-tax cost of debt is:

$$k_d = k_i(I = i)$$

where t is the tax rate.

EXAMPLE 1: Assume that the Carter Company issues a $1,000, 8%, 20-year bond whose net proceeds are $940. The tax rate is 40%. Then, the before-tax cost of debt, k_i, is:

$$k_i = \frac{I + (M - V)/n}{(M + V)/2}$$

$$= \frac{\$80 + (\$1,000 - \$940)/20}{(\$1,000 - \$940)/2} = \frac{\$83}{\$970} = 8.56\%$$

Therefore, the after-tax cost of debt is:

$$k_d = (1 - t)$$
$$= 8.56\% (1 - 0.4) = 5.14\%$$

Cost of Preferred Stock

The cost of preferred stock k_p, is found by dividing the annual preferred stock dividend d_p, by the net proceeds from the sale of the preferred stock p, as follows:

$$k_p = \frac{d_p}{p}$$

Because preferred stock dividends are not a tax-deductible expense, these dividends are paid out after taxes. Consequently, no tax adjustment is required.

EXAMPLE 2: Suppose that the Carter Company has preferred stock that pays a $13 dividend per share and sells for $100 per share in the market. The flotation (or underwriting) cost is 3%, or $3 per share. Then the cost of preferred stock is:

$$k_p = \frac{d_p}{p}$$

$$= \frac{\$13}{\$97} = 13.4\%$$

Cost of Equity Capital

The cost of common stock k_e, is generally viewed as the rate of return investors require on a firm's common stock. Three techniques for measuring the cost of common stock equity capital are available: (1) the Gordon's growth model, (2) the capital asset pricing model (CAPM) approach, and (3) the bond plus approach.

The Gordon's Growth Model. The Gordon's model is:

$$P_0 = \frac{D_1}{r-g}$$

where

P_0 = value of common stock

D_1 = dividend to be received in one year

r = investor's required rate of return

g = rate of growth (assumed to be constant over time)

Solving the model for r results in the formula for the cost of common stock:

$$r = \frac{D_1}{P_0} + g \text{ or } k_e = \frac{D_1}{P_0} + g$$

Note that the symbol r is changed to k_e to show that it is used for the computation of cost of capital.

EXAMPLE 3: Assume that the market price of the Carter Company's stock is $40. The dividend to be paid at the end of the coming year is $4 per share and is expected to grow at a constant annual rate of 6%. Then the cost of this common stock is:

$$k_e = \frac{D_1}{P_0} + g = \frac{\$4}{\$40} + 6\% = 16\%$$

The cost of new common stock, or external equity capital, is higher than the cost of existing common stock because of the flotation costs involved in selling the new common stock. If f is flotation cost in percent, the formula for the cost of new common stock is:

$$k_e = \frac{D_1}{P_0(1-f)} + g$$

EXAMPLE 4: Assume the same data as in Example 3, except the firm is trying to sell new issues of Stock A and its flotation cost is 10%. Then:

$$k_e = \frac{D_1}{P_0(1-f)} + g$$

$$= \frac{\$4}{\$40(1-0.1)} + 6\% = \frac{\$4}{\$36} + 6\% = 11.11\% + 6\% = 17.11\%$$

The CAPM Approach. An alternative approach to measuring the cost of common stock is to use the CAPM, which involves the following steps:

1. Estimate the risk-free rate r, generally taken to be the United States Treasury bill rate.

2. Estimate the stock's beta coefficient b, which is an index of systematic (or nondiversifiable market) risk.

3. Estimate the rate of return on the market portfolio such as the Standard & Poor's 500 Stock Composite Index or Dow Jones 30 Industrials.

4. Estimate the required rate of return on the firm's stock, using the CAPM (or SML) equation:

$$k_e = r_f + b(r_m - r_f)$$

Again, note that the symbol r_j is changed to k_e.

EXAMPLE 5: Assuming that r_f is 7%, b is 1.5, and r_m is 13%, then:

$$k_e = r_f + b(r_m - r_f) = 7\% + 1.5(13\% - 7\%) = 16\%$$

This 16% cost of common stock can be viewed as consisting of a 7% risk-free rate plus a 9% risk premium, which reflects that the firm's stock price is 1.5 times more volatile than the market portfolio to the factors affecting nondiversifiable, or systematic, risk.

The Bond Plus Approach. Still another simple but useful approach to determining the cost of common stock is to add a risk premium to the firm's own cost of long-term debt, as follows:

$$k_e = \text{Long-term bond rate} + \text{Risk premium}$$
$$= k_i(1 - t) + \text{Risk premium}$$

A risk premium of about 4% is commonly used with this approach.

> **EXAMPLE 6:** Using the data found in Example 1, the cost of common stock using the bond plus approach is:
>
> $$k_e = \text{Long-term bond rate} + \text{Risk premium}$$
> $$= k_i(1 - t) + \text{Risk premium}$$
> $$= 5.14\% + 4\% = 9.14\%$$

Cost of Retained Earnings

The cost of retained earnings k_s, is closely related to the cost of existing common stock, since the cost of equity obtained by retained earnings is the same as the rate of return investors require on the firm's common stock. Therefore:

$$k_e = k_s$$

Measuring the Overall Cost of Capital

The firm's overall cost of capital is the weighted-average of the individual capital costs, with the weights being the proportions of each type of capital used. Let k_0 be the overall cost of capital.

$$k_0 = \sum \left(\begin{array}{c} \text{\% of total capital} \\ \text{structure supplied by} \\ \text{each type of} \\ \text{capital} \end{array} \times \begin{array}{c} \text{Cost of} \\ \text{capital for} \\ \text{each source} \\ \text{of capital} \end{array} \right)$$

$$= w_d \cdot k_d + w_p \cdot k_p + w_e \cdot k_e + w_s \cdot k_s$$

where

w_d = % of total capital supplied by debt

w_p = % of total capital supplied by preferred stock

w_e = % of total capital supplied by external equity

w_s = % of total capital supplied by retained earnings (or internal equity)

The weights can be historical, target, or marginal.

Historical Weights

Historical weights are based on a firm's existing capital structure. The use of these weights is based on the assumption that the firm's existing capital structure is optimal and therefore should be maintained in the future. Two types of historical weights can be used—book value weights and market value weights.

Book Value Weights. The use of book value weights in calculating the firm's weighted cost of capital assumes that new financing will be raised using the same method the firm used for its present capital structure. The weights are determined by dividing the book value of each capital component by the sum of the book values of all the long-term capital sources. The computation of overall cost of capital is illustrated in the following example.

> **EXAMPLE 7:** Assume the following capital structure for the Carter Company:

Mortgage bonds ($1,000 par)	$20,000,000
Preferred stock ($100 par)	5,000,000
Common stock ($40 par)	20,000,000
Retained earnings	5,000,000
Total	$50,000,000

The book value weights and the overall cost of capital are computed as follows:

Source	Book Value	Weights	Cost	Weighted Cost
Debt	$20,000,000	40%	5.14%	2.06%
Preferred stock	5,000,000	10	13.40%	1.34
Common stock	20,000,000	40	17.11%	6.84
Retained earnings	5,000,000	10	16.00%	1.60
	$50,000,000	100%		11.84%

Overall cost of capital = k_o = 11.84%

Market Value Weights. Market value weights are determined by dividing the market value of each source by the sum of the market values of all sources. The use of market value weights for computing a firm's weighted-average cost of capital is theoretically more appealing than the use of book value weights because the market values of the securities closely approximate the actual dollars to be received from their sale.

> **EXAMPLE 8:** In addition to the data from Example 7, assume that the security market prices are as follows:

> Mortgage bonds = $1,100 per bond

> Preferred stock = $90 per share

> Common stock = $80 per share

$$\text{Mortgage bonds} = \frac{\$20,000,000}{\$1,000} = 20,000$$

$$\text{Preferred stock} = \frac{\$5,000,000}{\$1,000} = 50,000$$

$$\text{Common stock} = \frac{\$20,000,000}{\$40} = 500,000$$

The firm's number of securities in each category is:

Therefore, the market value weights are:

Source	Number of Securities	Price	Market Value
Debt	20,000	$1,100	$22,000,000
Preferred stock	50,000	$90	4,500,000
Common stock	500,000	$80	40,000,000
			$66,500,000

The $40 million common stock value must be split in the ratio of 4 to 1 (the $20 million common stock versus the $5 million retained earnings in the original capital structure), since the market value of the retained earnings has been impounded into the common stock.

The firm's cost of capital is as follows:

Source	Market Value	Weights	Cost	Weighted Average
Debt	$22,000,000	33.08 %	5.14%	1.70 %
Preferred stock	4,500,000	6.77	13.40%	0.91
Common stock	32,000,000	48.12	17.11%	8.23
Retained earnings	8,000,000	12.03	16.00%	1.92
	$66,500,000	100.00 %		12.76 %

Overall cost of capital = k_o = 12.76%

Target Weights

If the firm has determined that the capital structure is consistent with its goals, the use of that capital structure and associated weights is appropriate.

Marginal Weights

The use of marginal weights involves weighing the specific costs of various types of financing by the percentage of the total financing expected to be raised using each method. In using target weights, the firm is concerned with what it believes to be the optimal capital structure or target percentage. In using marginal weights, the firm is concerned with the actual dollar amounts of each type of financing to be needed for a given investment project.

> **EXAMPLE 9:** The Carter Company is considering raising $8 million for plant expansion. Management estimates using the following mix for financing this project:
>
> | | | |
> |---|---|---|
> | Debt | $4,000,000 | 50% |
> | Common stock | 2,000,000 | 25% |
> | Retained earnings | 2,000,000 | 25% |
> | | $8,000,000 | 100% |
>
> The company's cost of capital is computed as follows:
>
> | Source | Marginal Weights | Cost | Weighted Cost |
> |---|---|---|---|
> | Debt | 50 % | 5.14% | 2.57 % |
> | Common stock | 25 | 17.11% | 4.28 |
> | Retained earnings | 25 | 16.00% | 4.00 |
> | | 100 % | | 10.85 % |
>
> Overall cost of capital = k_o = 10.85%

Level of Financing and the Marginal Cost of Capital

Because external equity capital has a higher cost than retained earnings due to flotation costs, the weighted cost of capital increases for each dollar of new financing. Therefore, the lower-cost capital sources are used first. In fact, the firm's cost of capital is a function of the size of its total investment. A schedule or graph relating the firm's cost of capital to the level of new financing is called the weighted marginal cost of capital (MCC). Such a schedule is used to determine the discount rate to be used in the firm's capital budgeting process. The steps to be followed in calculating the firm's marginal cost of capital are:

1. Determine the cost and the percentage of financing to be used for each source of capital (debt, preferred stock, common stock equity).

2. Compute the break points on the MCC curve where the weighted cost will increase. The formula for computing the break points is:

$$\text{Break point} = \frac{\text{Maximum amount of the lower-cost source of capital}}{\text{Percentage financing provided by the source}}$$

3. Calculate the weighted cost of capital over the range of total financing between break points.

4. Construct an MCC schedule or graph that shows the weighted cost of capital for each level of total new financing. This schedule will be used in conjunction with the firm's available investment opportunities schedule (IOS) in order to select the investments. As long as a project's internal rate of return (IRR) is greater than the marginal cost of new financing, the project should be accepted. Also, the point at which the IRR intersects the MCC gives the optimal capital budget.

EXAMPLE 10: A firm is contemplating three investment projects, A, B, and C, whose initial cash outlays and expected IRR are shown below. IOS for these projects is:

Project	Cash Outlay	IRR
A	$2,000,000	13%
B	$2,000,000	15%
C	$1,000,000	10%

If these projects are accepted, the financing will consist of 50% debt and 50% common stock. The firm should have $1.8 million in earnings available for reinvestment (internal common). This firm will consider only the effects of increases in the cost of common stock on its marginal cost of capital.

1. The costs of capital for each source of financing have been computed and are given below:

Source	Cost
Debt	5%
Common stock ($1.8 million)	15%
New common stock	19%

If the firm uses only internally generated common stock, the weighted cost of capital is:

k_0 = Σ Percentage of the total capital structure supplied by each source of capital × Cost of capital for each source

In this case, the capital structure is composed of 50% debt and 50% internally generated common stock. Thus,

$$k_o = (0.5)5\% + (0.5)15\% = 10\%$$

If the firm uses only new common stock, the weighted cost of capital is:

$$k_o = (0.5)5\% + (0.5)19\% = 12\%$$

Range of Total New Financing (in Millions of Dollars)	Type of Capital	Proportion	Cost	Weighted Cost
$0–$3.6	Debt	0.5	5%	2.5%
	Internal common	0.5	15%	7.5
				10.0%
$3.6 and up	Debt	0.5	5%	2.5%
	New common	0.5	19%	9.5
				12.0%

2. Next compute the break point, which is the level of financing at which the weighted cost of capital increases.

$$\text{Break point} = \frac{\text{Maximum amount of source of the lower-cost source of capital}}{\text{Percentage financing provided by the sources}}$$

$$= \frac{\$1,800,000}{0.5} = \$3,600,000$$

3. The firm may be able to finance $3.6 million in new investments with internal common stock and debt without having to change the current mix of 50% debt and 50% common stock. Therefore, if the total financing is $3.6 million or less, the firm's cost of capital is 10%.

4. Construct the MCC schedule on the IOS graph to determine the discount rate to be used in order to decide in which project to invest and to show the firm's optimal capital budget. See Exhibit 56-1.

The firm should continue to invest up to the point where the IRR equals the MCC. From the graph in Exhibit 56-1, note that the firm should invest in projects B and A, as each IRR exceeds the marginal cost of captal. The firm should reject project C since its cost of capital is greater than the IRR. The optimal capital budget is $4 million, as this is the sum of the cash outlay required for projects A and B.

Exhibit 56-1: MCC Schedule and IOS Graph

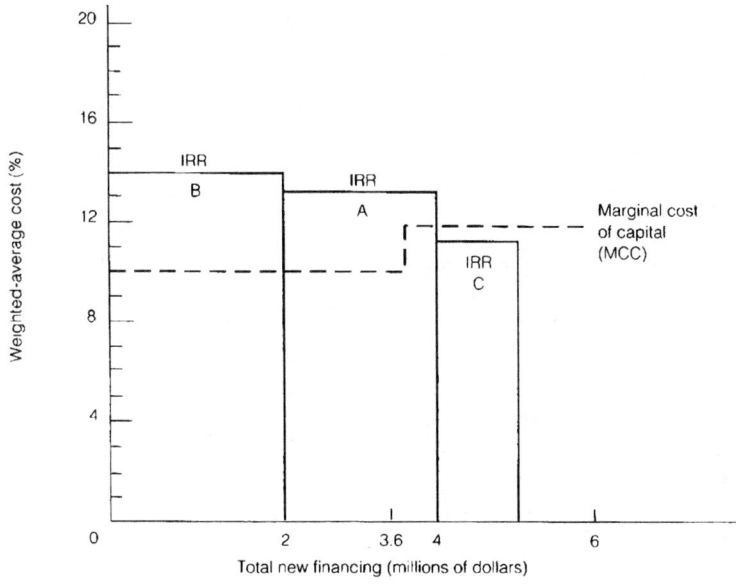

EBIT-EPS APPROACH TO CAPITAL STRUCTURE

The EBIT-EPS approach to capital structure is a practical tool for use by financial managers in order to evaluate alternative financing plans. This is a practical effort to move towards achieving an optimal capital structure which results in the lowest overall cost of capital.

The use of financial leverage has two effects on the earnings that go to the firm's common stockholders: (1) an increased risk in earnings per share (EPS) due to the use of fixed financial obligations, and (2) a change in the level of EPS at a given EBIT associated with a specific capital structure.

The first effect is measured by the degree of financial leverage. The second effect is analyzed by means of EBIT-EPS analysis. This analysis is a practical approach that enables the financial manager to evaluate alternative financing plans by investigating their effect on EPS over a range of EBIT levels. Its primary objective is to determine the EBIT break-even, or indifference, points between the various alternative financing plans. The indifference points between any two methods of financing can be determined by solving for EBIT in the following equality:

$$\frac{(EBIT - I)\,(1 - t) - PD}{S_1} = \frac{(EBIT - I)\,(1 - t) - PD}{S_2}$$

where

t = tax rate

PD = preferred stock dividends

S_1 and S_2 = number of shares of common stock outstanding after financing for plan 1 and plan 2, respectively.

EXAMPLE 11: Assume that ABC Company, with long-term capitalization consisting entirely of $5 million in stock, wants to raise $2 million for the acquisition of special equipment by: (1) selling 40,000 shares of common stock at $50 each, (2) selling bonds at 10% interest, or (3) issuing preferred stock with an 8% dividend. The present EBIT is $8 million, the income tax rate is 50%, and 100,000 shares of common stock are now outstanding. In order to compute the indifference points, we begin by calculating EPS at a projected level of $1 million.

	All Common	All Debt	All Preferred
EBIT	$1,000,000	$1,000,000	$1,000,000
Interest	200,000		
Earnings before taxes (EBT)	$1,000,000	$ 800,000	$1,000,000
Taxes	500,000	400,000	500,000
Earnings after taxes (EAT)	$ 500,000	$ 400,000	$ 500,000
Preferred stock dividend			160,000
EAC	$ 500,000	$ 400,000	$ 340,000
Number of shares	140,000	1,000,000	100,000
EPS	$ 3.57	$ 4.00	$ 3.40

Now connect the EPSs at the level of EBIT of $1 million with the EBITs for each financing alternative on the horizontal axis to obtain the EPS-EBIT graphs. We plot the EBIT necessary to cover all fixed financial costs for each financing alternative on the horizontal axis. For the common stock plan, there are no fixed costs, so the intercept on the horizontal axis is zero. For the debt plan, there must be an EBIT of $200,000 to cover interest charges. For the preferred stock plan, there must be an EBIT of $320,000 [$160,000/(I – 0.5)] to cover $160,000 in preferred stock dividends at a 50% income tax rate; or $320,000 becomes the horizontal axis intercept. See Exhibit 56-2.

In this example, the indifference point between all common and all debt is:

$$\frac{(EBIT - I)\ (1 - t) - PD}{S_1} = \frac{(EBIT - I)\ (1 - t) - PD}{S_2}$$

$$\frac{(EBIT - 0)\ (1 - 0.5) - 0}{140,000} = \frac{(EBIT - 200,000)\ (1 - 0.5) - 0}{100,000}$$

Rearranging yields:

$$0.5(EBIT)(100,000) = 0.5(EBIT)(140,000) - 0.5(200,000)(140,000)$$
$$20,000\ EBIT = 14,000,000,000$$
$$EBIT = \$700,000$$

Similarly, the difference point between all common and all preferred would be:

$$\frac{(EBIT - I)\ (1 - t) - PD}{S_1} = \frac{(EBIT - I)\ (1 - t) - PD}{S_2}$$

$$\frac{(EBIT - 0)\ (1 - 0.5) - 0}{140,000} = \frac{(EBIT - 0)\ (1 - 0.5) - 160,000}{100,000}$$

Rearranging yields:

$$0.5(EBIT)(100,000) = 0.5(EBIT)(140,000) - 0.5(160,000)(140,000)$$
$$20,000\ EBIT = 22,400,000,000$$
$$EBIT = \$1,120,000$$

Exhibit 56-2: EBIT-EPS Graph

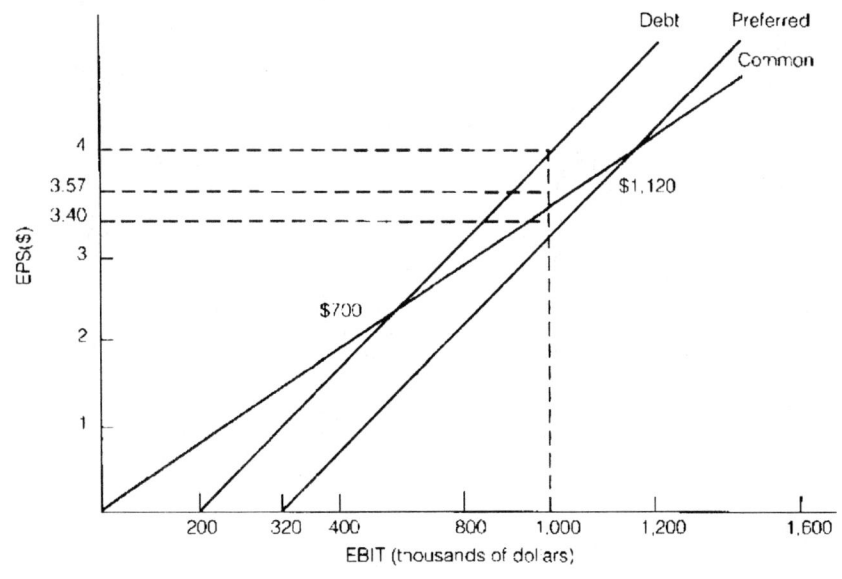

Based on the above computations, we can draw the following conclusions:

1. At any level of EBIT, debt is better than preferred stock.

2. At a level of EBIT above $700,000, debt is better than common stock. If EBIT is below $700,000, the reverse is true.

3. At a level of EBIT above $1,120,000, preferred stock is better than common. At or below that point, the reverse is true.

Financial leverage is a two-edged sword. It can magnify profits but it can also increase losses. The EBIT-EPS approach helps financial managers examine the impact of financial leverage as a financing method. It is important to realize that investment performance is crucial to the successful application of any leveraging strategy.

CAPITAL STRUCTURE DECISIONS IN PRACTICE

Many financial officers believe that there is an optimum capital structure for the corporation. How do companies decide which financing source to use? It is a complex decision, related to a company's balance sheet, market conditions, outstanding obligations, and a host of other factors. Surveys consistently point out that: (1) financial officers set target debt ratios for their companies and (2) the values of those ratios are affected by a prudent evaluation of the basic business risk to which the firm is exposed. The most frequently mentioned influence on the target debt ratio is the firm's cash-flow ability to service fixed charges. The greater the dollar amount of senior securities the firm issues and the shorter their maturity, the greater are the fixed charges of the firm. These charges include principal and interest payments on debt, lease payments, and preferred stock dividends. Before assuming additional fixed charges, the firm should analyze its expected future cash flows, for fixed charges must be met with cash. The inability to meet these charges, with the exception of preferred stock dividends, may result in insolvency. The greater and more stable the expected future cash flows of the firm, the greater is the debt capacity of the company.

Other factors identified as affecting the target debt ratio are:

- Providing adequate borrowing reserve
- Maintaining a desired bond rating
- Business risk to which the firm is exposed
- Exploiting the advantages of positive financial leverage (or trading on equity)
- Restrictive debt covenants
- Industry standard
- Voting control of the firm

Coverage Ratios

Among the ways we can gain insight into the debt capacity of a firm is through the use of coverage ratios. In the computation of these ratios, a corporate financial officer typically uses earnings before interest and taxes (EBIT) as a rough measure of the cash flow available to cover debt-servicing obligations. Perhaps the most widely used coverage ratio is times interest earned, which is simply:

$$\text{Times interest earned} \ = \ \frac{\text{EBIT}}{\text{Interest on debt}}$$

Assume that the most recent annual EBIT for a company were $4 million, and that interest payments on all debt obligations were $1 million. Therefore, times interest earned would be 4 times. This tells us that EBIT can drop by as much as 75% and the firm still will be able to cover its interest payments out of earnings.

However, a coverage ratio of only 1 indicates that earnings are just sufficient to satisfy the interest burden. While it is difficult to generalize as to what is an appropriate interest coverage ratio, a corporate financial officer usually is concerned when the ratio gets much below 3:1. However, it all depends. In a highly stable industry, a relatively low times-interest-earned ratio may be appropriate, whereas it is not appropriate in a highly cyclical one.

Unfortunately, the times-interest-earned ratio tells us nothing about the ability of the firm to meet principal payments on its debt. The inability to meet a principal payment constitutes the same legal default as failure to meet an interest payment. Therefore it is useful to compute the coverage ratio for the full debt-service burden. This ratio is

$$\text{Debt-service coverage} = \frac{\text{EBIT}}{\text{Interest} + \dfrac{\text{Principal payment}}{1 - \text{Tax rate}}}$$

Here principal payments are adjusted upward for the tax effect. The reason is that EBIT represents earnings before taxes. Because principal payments are not tax deductible, they must be paid out of after-tax earnings. Therefore, we must adjust principal payments so that they are consistent with EBIT. If principal payments in our previous example were $1.5 million per annum and the tax rate was 34%, the debt-service coverage ratio would be:

$$\text{Debt-service coverage} = \frac{\$4 \text{ million}}{\$1 \text{ million} + \dfrac{\$1.5 \text{ million}}{1 - .34}} = 1.22$$

A coverage ratio of 1.22 means that EBIT can fall by only 22% before earnings coverage is insufficient to service the debt. Obviously, the closer the ratio is to 1.0, the worse things are, all other things being equal. However, even with a coverage ratio of less than 1.0, a company may still meet its obligations if it can renew some of its debt when it comes due.

The financial risk associated with leverage should be analyzed on the basis of the firm's ability to service total fixed charges. While lease financing is not debt per se, its impact on cash flows is exactly the same as the payment of interest and principal on a debt obligation. Therefore, annual lease payments should be added to the denominator of the formula in order to properly reflect the total cash-flow burden associated with financing.

Trend Analysis and Industry Comparisons

Two types of comparison should be undertaken with coverage ratios. First, it should be compared with past and expected future ratios of the same company. The purpose is to determine if there has been an improvement or a deterioration in coverage over time. Another method of analyzing the appropriate capital structure for a company is to evaluate the capital structure of other companies having similar business risk. Companies used in this comparison may be those in the same industry. If the firm is contemplating a capital structure significantly out of line with that of similar companies, it is conspicuous to the marketplace. This is not to say, however, that the firm is wrong; other companies in the industry may be too conservative with respect to the use of debt. The optimal capital structure for all companies in the industry might call for a higher proportion of debt to equity than the industry average. As a result, the firm may well be able to justify more debt than the industry average. Because investment analysts and creditors tend to evaluate companies by industry, however, the firm should be able to justify its position if its capital structure is noticeably out of line in either direction.

Ultimately, a financial officer wants to make generalizations about the appropriate amount of debt (and leases) for a firm to have in its capital structure. It is clear that over the long run the source to service debt for the going concern is earnings. Therefore, coverage ratios are an important tool of analysis. However, they are but one tool by which a financial manager is able to reach conclusions with respect to the appropriate capital structure for the firm. Coverage ratios are subject to certain limitations and, consequently, cannot be used as a sole means for determining a capital structure. For one thing, the fact that EBIT falls below the debt-service burden does not spell immediate doom for the company. Often alternative sources of funds, including renewal of the loan, are available, and these sources must be considered.

CHAPTER 57

DIVIDEND POLICY

CONTENTS

A company's dividend policy is important for the following reasons:

- It influences investor attitudes. For instance, stockholders look negatively upon the company when dividends are cut, since they associate the cutback with corporate financial difficulties. Further, in establishing a dividend policy, management must determine and fulfill the owners' objectives. Otherwise, the stockholders may sell their shares, which in turn may lower the market price of the stock. Stockholder dissatisfaction raises the possibility that control of the company may be seized by an outside group.

- It impacts the financing program and capital budget of the firm.

- It affects the company's cash flow. A company with a poor liquidity position may be forced to restrict its dividend payments.

- It lowers stockholders' equity, since dividends are paid from retained earnings, and so results in a higher debt-to-equity ratio.

- If a company's cash flows and investment requirements are volatile, the company should not establish a high regular dividend. It would be better to establish a low regular dividend that can be met even in bad years.

COMPANY POLICY

A financial manager's objectives for the company's dividend policy are to maximize owner wealth while providing adequate financing for the firm. When a company's earnings increase, management does not automatically raise the dividend. Generally, there is a time lag between increased earnings and the payment of a higher dividend. Only when management is optimistic that the increased earnings will be sustained should they increase the dividend. Once dividends are increased, they should continue to be paid at the higher rate. There are different types of dividend policies that may be established, including the following four:

1. *Stable dividend-per-share policy.* Many companies use a stable dividend-per-share policy since it is looked upon positively by investors. Dividend stability implies a low-risk company. Even in a year that the company shows a loss instead of a profit the dividend should be maintained to avoid negative connotations to current and prospective investors. By continuing to pay the dividend, the shareholders are more apt to consider the loss as temporary. Some stockholders rely on the receipt of stable dividends for income. A stable dividend policy is also necessary for a company to be placed on a list of securities in which financial institutions (pension funds, insurance companies) invest. Being on such a list provides greater marketability for corporate shares.

2. *Constant dividend-payout ratio (dividends per share/earnings per share).* With this policy a constant percentage of earnings is paid out in dividends. Because net income fluctuates, dividends paid will also vary using this approach. The problem this policy causes is that if the company's earnings fall drastically or there is a loss, the dividends paid will be significantly reduced or nonexistent. This policy will not maximize market price per share since most stockholders do not want variability in their dividend receipts.

3. *A compromise policy.* A compromise between the policies of a stable dollar amount and a percentage amount of dividends is for a company to pay a lower dollar amount per share plus a percentage increment in good years. While this policy gives flexibility, it also results in uncertainty in the minds of investors as to the amount of dividends they are likely to receive. Stockholders typically do not like such uncertainty. However, this policy may be appropriate when earnings vary considerably over the years. The percentage, or extra, portion of the dividend should not be paid regularly, otherwise it becomes meaningless.

4. *Residual-dividend policy.* When a company's investment opportunities are not stable, management may wish to consider a vacillating dividend policy. With this type of policy the amount of earnings retained depends upon the availability of investment opportunities in a given year. Dividends constitute the residual amount from earnings after the company's investment needs are met.

EXAMPLE 1: Company A and Company B are identical in every respect except for their dividend policies. Company A pays out a constant percentage of its net income (60% dividends), while company B pays out a constant dollar dividend. Company B's market price per share is higher than that of company A because the stock market looks favorably upon stable dollar dividends. They reflect less uncertainty about the firm.

EXAMPLE 2: Most Corporation had a net income of $800,000 in 2X11. Earnings have grown at an 8% annual rate. Dividends in 2X11 were $300,000. In 2X12, the net income was $1,100,000. This was much higher than the typical 8% annual growth rate. It is expected that profits will be back to the 8% rate in future years. The investment in 2X12 was $700,000.

Assuming a stable dividend payout ratio of 25%, the dividends to be paid in 2X12 will be $275,000 ($1,100,000 × 25%).

If a stable dollar dividend policy is maintained, the 2X12 dividend payment will be $324,000 ($300,000 × 1.08).

Assuming a residual dividend policy is maintained and 40% of the 2X12 investment is financed with debt, the 2X12 dividend will be:

$$\text{Equity needed} = \$700,000 \times 60\% = \$420,000$$

Because net income exceeds the equity needed, all of the $420,000 of equity investment will be derived from net income.

$$\text{Dividend} = \$1,100,000 - \$420,000 = \$680,000$$

If the investment for 2X12 is to be financed with 80% debt and 20% retained earnings, and any net income not invested is paid out in dividends, then the dividends will be:

$$\text{Earnings retained} = \$700,000 \times 2\% = \$140,000$$

$$\text{Dividend} = \text{Net income} - \text{Earnings retained}$$

$$\$960,000 = \$1,100,000 - \$140,000$$

Theoretical Position

Theoretically, a company should retain earnings rather than distribute them when the corporate return exceeds the return investors can obtain on their money elsewhere. Further, if the company obtains a return on its profits that exceeds the cost of capital, the market price of its stock will be maximized. On the other hand, a company should not, theoretically, keep funds for investment if it earns less of a return than what the investors can earn elsewhere. If the owners have better investment opportunities outside the company, the firm should pay a high dividend.

Although theoretical considerations from a financial perspective should be taken into account when establishing dividend policy, the *practicality* of the situation is that investors expect to be paid dividends. Psychological factors come into play which may adversely impact the market price of the stock of a company that does not pay dividends.

FACTORS THAT INFLUENCE DIVIDEND POLICY

A company's dividend policy depends on many variables, some of which have already been mentioned. Other factors to be considered are:

- *Company growth rate.* A rapidly growing business, even if profitable, may have to restrict dividends to keep needed funds within the company for growth.

- *Restrictive covenants.* Sometimes there is a restriction in a credit agreement that will limit the dividends that may be paid.

- *Profitability.* Dividend distribution is keyed to the profitability of the company.

- *Earnings stability.* A company with stable earnings is more apt to distribute a higher percentage of its earnings than one with unstable earnings.

- *Maintenance of control.* Management that is reluctant to issue additional common stock because it does not want to dilute control of the firm will retain a higher percentage of its earnings. Internal financing enables control to be kept within.

- *Degree of financial leverage.* A company with a high debt-to-equity ratio is more likely to retain profits so that it will have the required funds to pay interest and principal on debt.

- *Ability to finance externally.* A company that is capable of entering the capital markets easily can afford to have a higher dividend payout ratio. Where there is a limitation to external sources of funds, more earnings will be retained for planned financial needs.

- *Uncertainty.* Payment of dividends reduces the chance of uncertainty in stockholders' minds about the firm's financial health.

- *Age and size.* The age and size of the company bear upon its ease of access to capital markets.

- *Tax penalties.* Possible tax penalties for excess accumulation of retained earnings may result in high dividend payouts.

Controversy

The dividend policy controversy can best be described by presenting the approaches put forth by various authors:

- Gordon et al. believe that cash flows of a company having a low dividend payout will be capitalized at a higher rate because investors will consider capital gains resulting from earnings retention to be more risky than dividends.

- Miller and Modigliani argue that a change in dividends impacts the price of the stock since investors will consider such a change as being a statement about expected future profits. They believe that investors are generally indifferent as to dividends or capital gains.

- Weston and Brigham et al. believe that the best dividend policy varies with the particular characteristics of the company and its owners, depending on such factors as the tax bracket and income needs of stockholders, and corporate investment opportunities.

STOCK REPURCHASES

The purchase of treasury stock is an alternative to paying dividends. Since outstanding shares will be fewer after stock has been repurchased, earnings per share will increase (assuming net income is held constant). The increase in earnings per share may result in a higher market price per share.

EXAMPLE 3: A company earned $2.5 million in 2X12. Of this amount, it decided that 20% would be used to buy treasury stock. Currently, there are 400,000 shares outstanding. Market price per share is $18. The company can use $500,000 (20% × $2.5 million) to buy back 25,000 shares through a tender offer of $20 per share.

Current earnings per share is:

$$\text{EPS} = \frac{\text{Net income}}{\text{Outstanding shares}} = \frac{\$2,500,000}{\$400,000} = \$6.25$$

The current P/E multiple is:

$$\frac{\text{Market price per share}}{\text{Earnings per share}} = \frac{\$18}{\$6.25} = 2.88 \text{ times}$$

Earnings per share after treasury stock is acquired becomes:

$$\frac{\$2,500,000}{375,000} = \$6.67$$

The expected market price, assuming the P/E ratio remains the same, is:

P/E multiple × New earnings per share = Expected market price

$$2.88 \times \$6.67 = \$19.21$$

The benefits from a stock repurchase include the following:

- If there is excess cash flow that is deemed temporary, management may prefer to repurchase stock than to pay a higher dividend that they feel cannot be maintained.

- Treasury stock can be used for future acquisitions or for stock options.

- If management is holding stock, they would favor a stock repurchase rather than a dividend because of the favorable tax treatment.

- Treasury stock can be resold in the market if additional funds are needed.

The disadvantages of treasury stock acquisition include:

- If investors believe that the company is engaging in a repurchase plan because its management does not have alternative good investment opportunities, a drop in the market price of stock may ensue. However, there are cases where this has not happened, such as when General Electric announced in 1989 its plan of periodic reacquisitions of stock because of a lack of more attractive investment opportunities.

- If the reacquisition of stock makes it appear that the company is manipulating its stock price, the company will have problems with the Securities and Exchange Commission (SEC). Further, if the Internal Revenue Service (IRS) concludes that the repurchase is designed to avoid the payment of tax on dividends, tax penalties may be imposed because of the improper accumulation of earnings as specified in the tax code.

CHAPTER 58

INTERNATIONAL FINANCIAL MANAGEMENT

CONTENTS

Exhibits

Many companies are multinational corporations (MNCs) that have significant foreign operations deriving a high percentage of their sales overseas. The controllers of MNCs require an understanding of the complexities of international finance to make sound financial and investment decisions. International finance involves consideration of managing working capital, financing the business, control of foreign exchange and political risks, and foreign direct investments. Most important, the controller has to consider the value of the U.S. dollar relative to the value of the currency of the foreign country in which business activities are being conducted. Currency exchange rates may materially affect receivables and payables, and imports and exports of the U.S. company in its multinational operations. The effect is more pronounced with increasing activities abroad.

When a company penetrates a foreign market it may use foreign brokers, foreign licensees, or joint ventures. Financial instruments to support foreign operations may be issued, such as Eurobonds. The tax structure in foreign countries also has to be considered. An unstable foreign exchange rate may lead to earnings fluctuations unless hedging activities are undertaken. Foreign currency translations and transactions have to be determined along with their financial effects.

FINANCIAL MANAGEMENT OF A MULTINATIONAL CORPORATION

- *Mutiple-currency problem.* Sales revenues may be collected in one currency, assets denominated in another, and profits measured in a third.

- *Various legal, institutional, and economic constraints.* There are variations in such things as tax laws, labor practices, balance of payment policies, and government controls with respect to the types and sizes of investments, types and amount of capital raised, and repatriation of profits.

- *Internal control problem.* When the parent office of an MNC and its affiliates are widely located, internal organizational difficulties arise.

POPULAR FINANCIAL GOALS OF MULTINATIONAL CORPORATIONS

A survey made of controllers of MNCs lists the financial goals of MNCs in the following order of importance:

1. Maximize growth in corporate earnings, whether total earnings, earnings before interest and taxes (EBIT), or earnings per share (EPS).

2. Maximize return on equity.

3. Guarantee that funds are always available when needed.

THE TYPES OF FOREIGN OPERATIONS

When strong competition exists in the U.S., a company may look to enter or expand its foreign base. However, if a company is unsuccessful in the domestic market, it is likely to have problems overseas as well. Further, the controller must be cognizant of local customs and risks in the international markets.

A large, well-established company with much international experience may eventually have wholly-owned subsidiaries. However, a small company with limited foreign experience operating in "risky areas" may be restricted to export and import activity.

If the company's sales force has minimal experience in export sales, it is advisable to use foreign brokers when specialized knowledge of foreign markets is needed. When sufficient volume exists, the company may establish a foreign branch sales office including salespeople and technical service staff. As the operation matures, production facilities may be located in the foreign market. However, some foreign countries require licensing before foreign sales and production can take place. In this case, a foreign licensee sells and produces the product. A problem with this is that confidential information and knowledge are passed on to the licensees who can then become competitors at the expiration of the agreement.

A joint venture with a foreign company is another way to proceed internationally and share the risk. Some foreign governments require this to be the path to follow to operate in their countries. The foreign company may have local goodwill to assure success. A drawback is less control over activities and a conflict of interest.

In evaluating the impact that foreign operations have on the entity's financial health, the controller should consider the extent of intercountry transactions, foreign restrictions and laws, tax structure of the foreign country and the economic and political stability of the country. If a subsidiary is operating in a high-tax country with a double-tax agreement, dividend payments are not subject to further U.S. taxes. One way to transfer income from high tax areas to low tax areas is to levy royalties or management fees on the subsidiaries.

THE FOREIGN EXCHANGE MARKET

Except in a few European centers, there is no central marketplace for the foreign exchange market. Rather, business is carried out over telephone or telex. The major dealers are large banks. A company that wants to buy or sell currency typically uses a commercial bank. International transactions and investments involve more than one currency. For example, when a U.S. company sells merchandise to a Japanese firm, the former wants to be paid in dollars but the Japanese company typically expects to receive yen. Due to the foreign exchange market, the buyer may pay in one currency while the seller can receive payment in another currency.

SPOT AND FORWARD FOREIGN EXCHANGE RATES

An exchange rate is the ratio of one unit of currency to another. An exchange rate is established between different countries. The conversion rate between currencies depends on the demand-supply relationship. Because of the change in exchange rates, companies are susceptible to exchange rate fluctuation risks because of a net asset or net liability position in a foreign country.

Exchange rates may be in terms of dollars per foreign currency unit (called a direct quote) or units of foreign currency per dollar (called an indirect quote). Therefore, an indirect quote is the reciprocal of a direct quote and vice versa.

$$\text{An indirect quote} = 1/\text{direct quote}$$
$$\text{Euro}/\$ = 1/(\$/\text{euro})$$

EXAMPLE 1: A rate of 1.5740/euro means each euro costs the U.S. company $1.574. In other words, the U.S. company gets 1/1.574 = .6353 pound for each dollar.

The spot rate is the exchange rate for immediate delivery of currencies exchanged, while the forward rate is the exchange rate for later delivery of currencies exchanged. For example, there may be a 90-day exchange rate. The forward exchange rate of a currency will be slightly different from the spot rate at the current date because of future expectations and uncertainties.

Forward rates may be greater than the current spot rate (premium) or less than the current spot rate (discount).

CROSS RATES

A cross rate is the indirect calculation of the exchange rate of one currency from the exchange rates of two other currencies. It is the exchange rate between two currencies derived by dividing each currency's exchange rate with a third currency.

EXAMPLE 2: Hypothetical dollar-per-pound and yen-per-dollar rates are given in Exhibit 58-1. For example, if dollars per pound is $1.5999/£ and yen per dollar is ¥110.66/$, the cross rate between Japanese yen and British pounds is:

$$\text{Cross rate between yen and pound} = \frac{\text{Dollars}}{\text{Pound}} \times \frac{\text{Yen}}{\text{Dollar}} = \frac{\text{Yen}}{\text{Pound}}$$
$$= \$/£ \times ¥/\$ = ¥/£$$

= 1.5999 dollars per pound × 11 0.66 yen per dollar

= 177.05 yen per pound

Because most currencies are quoted against the dollar, it may be necessary to work out the cross rates for currencies other than the dollar. The cross rate is needed to consummate financial transactions between two countries.

Exhibit 58-1: Example of Foreign Exchange Rates

Currency	Contract	U.S. Dollar Equivalent	Country per U.S. $
Britain	Spot	1.5740	.6353
(Pound)	30-day future	1.5731	.6357
	90-day future	1.5711	.6365
	180-day future	1.5676	.6379
Switzerland	Spot	.7416	1.3484
(Franc)	30-day future	.7421	1.3475
	90-day future	.7432	1.3455
	180-day future	.7447	1.3428
Japan	Spot	.009965	100.35
(Yen)	30-day future	.009996	100.04
	90-day future	.01009	99.070
	180-day future	.01024	97.670

EXAMPLE 3: On December 18, 2X15, assume that forward rates on the Japanese yen were at a premium in relation to the spot rate, while the forward rates for the British pound were at a discount from the spot rate. This means that participants in the foreign exchange market anticipated that the Japanese yen would appreciate relative to the U.S. dollar in the future but the British pound would depreciate against the dollar.

Exhibit 58-2: Example of Key Currency Cross Rates

	British Pound	Euro	Japanese Yen	U.S. Dollar
British Pound	—	0.6172	0.5653	0.6250
Euro	1.6203	—	0.9153	1.0129
Japanese Yen	177.05	109.25	—	110.66
U.S. Dollar	1.5999	0.9873	0.9037	—

Note: The *Wall Street Journal* routinely publishes key currency cross rates, as shown in the hypothetical rates. They are also available on www.bloomberg.com. A cross currency table calculator is widely available online.

The percentage premium or discount is computed as follows:

Forward premium (or discount) equals:

$$\frac{\text{Forward rate} - \text{Spot rate}}{\text{Spot rate}} \times \frac{\text{12 months}}{\text{Length of forward contracts in months}} \times 100$$

where if the forward rate > the spot rate, the result is the annualized premium (discount) in percent.

EXAMPLE 4:

1. On December 18, 2X15, a 30-day forward contract in Japanese yen was selling at a 3.72% premium:

$$\frac{.009996 - .009965}{.009965} \times \frac{\text{12 months}}{\text{1 month}} \times 100 = 3.11\%$$

2. On December 18, 2X15, a 30-day forward contract in British pounds selling at a .69% discount:

$$\frac{1.5731 - 1.5740}{1.5740} \times \frac{\text{12 months}}{\text{1 month}} \times 100 = -.69\%$$

THE CONTROL OF FOREIGN EXCHANGE RISK

Foreign exchange rate risk exists when the contract is written in terms of the foreign currency or denominated in foreign currency. The exchange rate fluctuations increase the riskiness of the investment and incur cash losses. The controllers must not only seek the highest return on temporary investments but must also be concerned about changing values of the currencies invested. You do not necessarily eliminate foreign exchange risk. You may only try to contain it. In countries where currency values are likely to drop, controllers of the subsidiaries should:

- Avoid paying advances on purchase orders unless the seller pays interest on the advances sufficient to cover the loss of purchasing power.

- Not have excess idle cash. Excess cash can be used to buy inventory or other real assets.

- Buy materials and supplies on credit in the country in which the foreign subsidiary is operating, extending the final payment date as long as possible.

- Avoid giving excessive trade credit. If accounts receivable balances are outstanding for an extended time period, interest should be charged to absorb the loss in purchasing power.

- Borrow local currency funds when the interest rate charged does not exceed U.S. rates after taking into account expected devaluation in the foreign country.

THREE DIFFERENT TYPES OF FOREIGN EXCHANGE EXPOSURE

MNCs' controllers are faced with the dilemma of the following three different types of foreign exchange:

1. *Translation exposure,* often called *accounting exposure,* measures the impact of an exchange rate change on the firm's financial statements. An example would be the impact of a French franc devaluation on a U.S. firm's reported income statement and balance sheet.

2. *Transaction exposure* measures potential gains or losses on the future settlement of outstanding obligations that are denominated in a foreign currency. An example would be a U.S. dollar loss after the franc devalues, on payment received for an export invoiced in francs before that devaluation.

3. *Operating exposure,* often called *economic exposure,* is the potential for the change in the present value of future cash flows due to an unexpected change in the exchange rate.

Translation Exposure

A major purpose of translation is to provide data about expected impacts of rate changes on cash flow and equity. In the translation of the foreign subsidiaries' financial statements into the U.S. parent's financial statements, the following steps are involved:

1. The foreign financial statements are put into U.S. generally accepted accounting principles.

2. The foreign currency is translated into U.S. dollars.

Balance sheet accounts are translated using the current exchange rate at the balance sheet date. If a current exchange rate is not available at the balance sheet date, use the first exchange rate available after that date. Income statement accounts are translated using the weighted-average exchange rate for the period.

ASC 830-10-45, *Foreign Currency Translation,* requires translation by the current rate method. Under the current rate method:

- All balance sheet assets and liabilities are translated at the current rate of exchange in effect on the balance sheet date.

- Income statement items are usually translated at an average exchange rate for the reporting period.

- All equity accounts are translated at the historical exchange rates that were in effect at the time the accounts first entered the balance sheet.

- Translation gains and losses are reported as a separate item in the stockholders' equity section of the balance sheet.

Translation gains and losses are included in net income only when there is a sale or liquidation of the entire investment in a foreign entity.

Transaction Exposure

Foreign currency transactions may result in receivables or payables fixed in terms of the amount of foreign currency to be received or paid. Transaction gains and losses are reported in the income statement.

Foreign currency transactions are those transactions whose terms are denominated in a currency other than the entity's functional currency. Foreign currency transactions take place when a business:

- Buys or sells on credit goods or services the prices of which are denominated in a foreign currency.

- Borrows or lends funds, and the amounts payable or receivable are denominated in a foreign currency.

- Is a party to an unperformed forward exchange contract.

- Acquires or disposes of assets, or incurs or settles liabilities denominated in a foreign currency.

Note: Transaction losses differ from translation losses, which do not influence taxable income.

Long Position versus Short Position. When there is a devaluation of the dollar, foreign assets and income in strong currency countries are worth more dollars as long as foreign liabilities do not offset this beneficial effect.

Foreign exchange risk may be analyzed by examining expected receipts or obligations in foreign currency units. A company expecting receipts in foreign currency units ("long" position in the foreign currency units) has the risk that the value of the foreign currency units will drop. This results in devaluing the foreign currency relative to the dollar. If a company is expecting to have obligations in foreign currency units ("short" position in the foreign currency units), there is risk that the value of the foreign currency will rise and it will need to buy the currency at a higher price.

If net claims are greater than liabilities in a foreign currency, the company has a "long" position since it will benefit if the value of the foreign currency rises. If net liabilities exceed claims with respect to foreign currencies, the company is in a "short" position because it will gain if the foreign currency drops in value.

Monetary Position. Monetary balance is avoiding either a net receivable or a net payable position. Monetary assets and liabilities do not change in value with devaluation or revaluation in foreign currencies.

A company with a long position in a foreign currency will be receiving more funds in the foreign currency. It will have a net monetary asset position (monetary assets exceed monetary liabilities) in that currency.

A company with net receipts is a net monetary creditor. Its foreign exchange rate risk exposure has a net receipts position in a foreign currency that is susceptible to a drop in value.

A company with a future net obligation in foreign currency has a net monetary debtor position. It faces a foreign exchange risk of the possibility of an increase in the value of the foreign currency.

Ways to Neutralize Foreign Exchange Risk. Foreign exchange risk can be neutralized or hedged by a change in the asset and liability position in the foreign currency. Here are some ways to control exchange risk:

- *Entering a money-market hedge.* The exposed position in a foreign currency is offset by borrowing or lending in the money market.

    EXAMPLE 5: XYZ, an American importer, enters into a contract with a British supplier to buy merchandise of 4,000 pounds. The amount is payable on the delivery of the goods, 30 days from today. The company knows the exact amount of its pound liability in 30 days. However, it does not know the payable in dollars. Assume that the 30-day money market rates for both lending and borrowing in the U.S. and U.K. are .5% and 1%, respectively. Assume further that today's foreign exchange rate is $1.7350 per pound.

    In a money market hedge, XYZ can take the following steps:

    Step 1.   Buy a one-month U.K. money market security, worth 4,000 (1 + .005) = 3,980 pounds. This investment will compound to exactly 4,000 pounds in one month.

    Step 2.   Exchange dollars on today's spot (cash) market to obtain the 3,980 pounds. The dollar amount needed today is 3,980 pounds × $1,7350 per pound = $6,905.30.

    Step 3.   If XYZ does not have this amount, it can borrow it from the U.S. money market at the going rate of 1%. In 30 days XYZ will need to repay $6,905.30 × (1 + .1) $7,595.83.

    Note: XYZ need not wait for the future exchange rate to be available. On today's date, the future dollar amount of the contract is known with certainty. The British supplier will receive 4,000 pounds, and the cost of XYZ to make the payment is $7,595.83.

- *Hedging by purchasing forward (or futures) exchange contracts.* A forward exchange contracts is a commitment to buy or sell, at a specified future date, one currency for a specified amount of another currency (at a specified exchange rate). This can be a hedge against changes in exchange rates during a period of contract or exposure to risk from such changes. More specifically, you do the following: (1) buy foreign exchange forward contracts to cover payables denominated in a foreign currency, and (2) sell foreign exchange forward contracts to cover receivables denominated in a foreign currency. This way, any gain or loss on the foreign receivables or payables due to changes in exchange rates is offset by the gain or loss on the forward exchange contract.

EXAMPLE 6: In the previous example, assume that the 30-day forward exchange rate is $1.7272. XYZ may take the following steps to cover its payable:

Step 1.   Buy a forward contract today to purchase 4,000 pounds in 30 days.
Step 2.   On the 30th day pay the foreign exchange dealer 4,000 pounds × $1.7272 per pound = $6,908.80 and collect 4,000 pounds. Pay this amount to the British supplier.

Note: Using the forward contract, XYZ knows the exact worth of the future payment in dollars ($6,908.80).

Note: The basic difference between futures contracts and forward contracts is that futures contracts are for specified amounts and maturities, whereas forward contracts are for any size and maturity desired.

  • *Hedging by foreign currency options.* Foreign currency options can be purchased or sold in three different types of markets: (a) options on the physical currency, purchased on the over-the-counter (interbank) market, (b) options on the physical currency, on organized exchanges such as the Philadelphia Stock Exchange and the Chicago Mercantile Exchange, and (c) options on futures contracts, purchased on the International Monetary Market (IMM) of the Chicago Mercantile Exchange.

    Note: The difference between using a futures contract and using an option on a futures contract is that with a futures contract, the company must deliver one currency against another or reverse the contract on the exchange, while with an option the company may abandon the option and use the spot (cash) market if that is more advantageous.

  • *Repositioning cash by leading and lagging the time at which an MNC makes operations or financial payments.* Often, money-and forward-market hedges are not available to eliminate exchange risk. Under such circumstances, leading (accelerating) and lagging (decelerating) may be used to reduce risk.

    Note: A net asset position (i.e., assets minus liabilities) is not desirable in a weak or potentially depreciating currency. In this case, you should expedite the disposal of the asset. By the same token, you should lag or delay the collection against a net asset position in a strong currency.

  • *Maintaining balance between receivables and payables denominated in a foreign currency.* MNCs typically set up "mutilateral netting centers" as a special department to settle the outstanding balances of affiliates of an MNC with each other on a net basis. It is the development of a "clearing house" for payments by the firm's affiliates. If there are amounts due among affiliates they are offset insofar as possible. The net amount would be paid in the currency of the transaction. The total amounts owed need not be paid in the currency of the transaction; thus, a much lower quantity of the currency must be acquired.

Note: The major advantage of the system is a reduction of the costs associated with a large number of separate foreign exchange transactions.

- *Positioning funds through transfer pricing.* A transfer price is the price at which an MNC sells goods and services to its foreign affiliates or, alternatively, the price at which an affiliate sells to the parent. For example, a parent that wishes to transfer funds from an affiliate in a depreciating-currency country may charge a higher price on the goods and services sold to this affiliate by the parent or by affiliates from strong-currency countries. Transfer pricing affects not only transfer of funds from one entity to another but also the income taxes paid by both entities.

Operating Exposure

Operating (economic) exposure is the possibility that an unexpected change in exchange rates will cause a change in the future cash flows of a firm and its market value. It differs from translation and transaction exposures in that it is subjective and thus not easily quantified.

Note: The best strategy to control operation exposure is to diversify operations and financing internationally.

Key Questions for Identifying Foreign Exchange Risk

A systematic approach to identifying an MNC's exposure to foreign exchange risk is to ask a series of questions regarding the net effects on profits of changes in foreign currency revenues and costs. The questions are:

- Where is the MNC selling? (Domestic vs. foreign sales share)
- Who are the firm's major competitors? (Domestic vs. foreign)
- Where is the firm producing? (Domestic vs. foreign)
- Where are the firm's inputs coming from? (Domestic vs. foreign)
- How sensitive is quantity demanded to price? (Elastic vs. inelastic)
- How are the firm's inputs or outputs priced? (Priced in a domestic market or a global market; the currency of denomination)

Accounting Standards Update (ASU) No. 2010-19 (May 2010), *Foreign Currency* (ASC Topic 830), *Foreign Currency Issues,* provides the following information.

In the case of a foreign company's financial statements in a highly inflationary environment, there should be a remeasurement assuming the functional currency is the reporting currency. If there is a difference existing before using the mandates of a highly inflationary accounting between the financial reporting balances and the U.S. dollar denominated balances, it should be reflected in the profit and loss statement.

Disclosure should be made of translation and remeasurement rates, why U.S. dollar denominated balances are different from financial reporting balances, and the reasons why different rates were employed for translation and remeasurement.

FORECASTING FOREIGN EXCHANGE RATES

The forecasting of foreign exchange rates is a formidable task. Most MNCs rely primarily on bank and bank services for assistance and information in preparing exchange rate projections. The following economic indicators are considered to be the most important for the forecasting process:

- Recent rate movements.
- Relative inflation rates.
- Balance of payments and trade.
- Money supply growth.
- Interest rate differentials.

INTEREST RATES

Interest rates have an important influence on exchange rates. In fact, there is an important economic relationship between any two nations' spot rates, forward rates, and interest rates. This relationship is called the interest rate parity theorem (IRPT). The IRPT states that the ratio of the forward and spot rates is directly related to the two interest rates:

$$\frac{F}{S} = \frac{1 + i\$}{1 + iF}$$

where

F = forward exchange rate ($/foreign currency)

S = spot exchange rate ($/foreign currency)

i$ = U.S. interest rate

iF = foreign interest rate

EXAMPLE 7: Assume the following data concerning U.S. and Japanese currency:

$$F = \$0.008349$$
$$S = \$0.008341$$
$$iF = 10\%$$

then

$$\frac{0.008349}{0.008341} = \frac{1 + i\$}{1.10}$$

so

$$i\$ = 0.1009 = 10.09\%$$

Note that the forward yen is selling at a premium and U.S. interest rates are higher than Japanese interest rates.

INFLATION

Inflation, which is a change in price levels, also affects future exchange rates. The mathematical relationship that links changes in exchange rates and changes in price level is called the purchasing power parity theorem (PPPT). The PPPT states that the ratio of the forward and spot rates is directly related to the two inflation rates:

$$\frac{F}{S} = \frac{1 + i\$}{1 + iF}$$

where

F = forward exchange rate (\$/foreign currency)

S = spot exchange rate (\$/foreign currency)

i\$ = U.S. inflation rate

iF = foreign inflation rate

> **EXAMPLE 8:** Assume the following data for the U.S. and Japan:
>
> Expected U.S. inflation rate = 5%
>
> Expected Japanese inflation rate = 10%
>
> S = \$0.008341/yen

then

$$\frac{F}{0.008341} = \frac{1.05}{1.10}$$

so

$$F = \$0.0079/yen$$

> **Note:** If Japan has the higher inflation rate, then the purchasing power of the yen is declining faster than that of the dollar. This will lead to a forward discount on the yen relative to the dollar.

ANALYSIS OF FOREIGN INVESTMENTS

Also called international capital budgeting, foreign investment decisions are basically capital budgeting decisions at the international level. Capital budgeting analysis for foreign as compared to domestic projects introduces the following complications:

- Cash flows to a project and to the parent must be differentiated.
- National differences in tax systems, financial institutions, financial norms, and constraints on financial flows must be recognized.
- Different inflation rates can affect profitability and the competitive position of an affiliate.
- Foreign exchange rate changes can alter the competitive position of a foreign affiliate and the value of cash flows between the affiliate and the parent.

- Segmented capital markets create opportunities for financial gains or they may cause additional costs.

- Political risk can significantly change the value of a foreign investment.

The foreign investment decision requires two major components:

1. *The estimation of the relevant future cash flows.* Cash flows are the dividends and possible future sales price of the investment. The estimation depends on the sales forecast, the effects on exchange rate changes, the risk in cash flows, and the actions of foreign governments.

2. *The choice of the proper discount rate (cost of capital).* The cost of capital in foreign investment projects is higher due to the increased risks of:

   a. *Currency risk (or foreign exchange risk).* This risk of changes in exchange rates may adversely affect sales by making competing imported goods cheaper.

   b. *Political risk (or sovereignty risk).* The possibility of nationalization or other restrictions with net losses to the parent company.

The methods of evaluating multinational capital budgeting decisions include net present value (NPV), adjusted present value (APV), and internal rate of return (IRR).

EXAMPLE 9: Here we will illustrate a case of multinational capital budgeting. We analyze a hypothetical foreign investment project in Korea by a U.S. manufacturing firm (called "Am-tel"). The analysis is based on the following data gathered by a project team.

Product. The company (to be called Ko-tel hereafter) is expected to be a wholly owned Korean manufacturer of customized integrated circuits (ICs) for use in computers, automobiles, and robots. Ko-tel's products would be sold primarily in Korea, and all sales would be denominated in Korean won.

Sales. Sales in the first year are forecasted to be won 26,000 million. Sales are expected to grow at 10% per annum for the foreseeable future.

Working capital. Ko-tel needs gross working capital (that is, cash, receivables, and inventory) equal to 25% of sales. Half of gross working capital can be financed by local payables, but the other half must be financed by Ko-tel or Am-tel.

Parent-supplied components. Components sold to Ko-tel by Am-tel have a direct cost to Am-tel equal to 95% of their sales price. The margin is therefore 5%.

Depreciation. Plant and equipment will be depreciated on a straight-line basis for both accounting and tax purposes over an expected life of ten years. No salvage value is anticipated.

License fees. Ko-tel will pay a license fee of 2.5% of sales revenue to Am-tel. This fee is tax deductible in Korea but provides taxable income to Am-tel.

Taxes. The Korean corporate income tax rate is 35%, and the U.S. rate is 38%. Korea has no withholding tax on dividends, interest, or fees paid to foreign residents.

Cost of capital. The cost of capital (or minimum required return) used in Korea by companies of comparable risk is 22%. Am-tel also uses 22% as a discount rate for its investments.

Inflation. Prices are expected to increase as follows.

Korean general price level:	9% per annum
Ko-tel average sales price:	9% per annum
Korean raw material costs:	3% per annum
Korean labor costs:	12% per annum
U.S. general price level:	5% per annum

Exchange rates. In the year in which the initial investment takes place, the exchange rate is won 1,150 to the dollar. Am-tel forecasts the won to appreciate relative to the dollar at 1% per annum.

Dividend policy. Ko-tel will pay 70% of accounting net income to Am-tel as an annual cash dividend. Ko-tel and Am-tel estimate that over a five year period the other 30% of net income must be reinvested to finance working capital growth.

Financing. Ko-tel will be financed by Am-tel with a $11,000,000 purchase of won 8,250,000,000 common stock, all to be owned by Am-tel.

In order to develop the normal cash flow projections, Am-tel has made the following assumptions:

1. Sales revenue in the first year of operations is expected to be won 26,000 million. Won sales revenue will increase annually at 10% because of physical growth and at an additional 9% because of price increases. Consequently, sales revenue will grow at (1.1) (1.09) = 1.20, or 20% per annum.

2. Korean raw material costs in the first year are budgeted at won 4,000 million. Korean raw material costs are expected to increase at 10% per annum because of physical growth and at an additional 3% because of price increases. Consequently, raw material cost will grow at (1.1) (1.03) = 1.13, or 13% per annum.

3. Parent-supplied component costs in the first year are budgeted at won 9,000 million. Parent-supplied component costs are expected to increase annually at 10% because of physical growth, plus an additional 5% because of U.S. inflation, plus another 1% in won terms because of the expected appreciation of the won relative to the dollar. Consequently, the won cost of parent-supplied imports will increase at (1.1) (1.05) (.99) = 1.14 or 14% per annum.

4. Direct labor costs and overhead in the first year are budgeted at won 5,000 million. Korean direct labor costs and overhead are expected to

increase at 10% per annum because of physical growth, and at an additional 12% because of an increase in Korean wage rates. Consequently, Korean direct labor and overhead will increase at $(1.1)(1.12) = 1.232$ or 23.32% per annum.

5. Marketing and general and administrative expenses are budgeted at won 4,000 million, fixed, plus 4% of sales.

6. As for liquidation value, at the end of five years, the project (including working capital) is expected to be sold on a going-concern basis to Korean investors for won 9,000 million, equal to approximately $10 million at the expected exchange rate of won 903.44/$. This sales price is free of all Korean and U.S. taxes, and will be used as a terminal value.

Exhibit 58-3: Multinational Capital Budgeting Example—Beginning Balance Sheet, Ko-tel

		Millions of Won	Thousands of Dollars
Assets			
1 Cash balance		650	565
2 Accounts receivable		-	-
3 Inventory		1,050	913
4 Net plant and equipment		7,000	6,087
5	Total	8,700	7,565
Liabilities and Net Worth			
6 Accounts payable		700	609
7 Common stock equity		8,000	6,957
8	Total	8,700	7,565

Won/$=	1150
Pro. Cost	-11000
Liq. Value	9000000

Exhibit 58-4: Multinational Capital Budgeting Example—Sales and Cost Data

Item	1	2	3	4	5
			Year		
1 Total sales revenue		26,000	31,174	37,378	44,816	53,734
2 Korean raw material		4,000	4,532	5,135	5,818	6,591
Components purchases from Am- 3 tel		9,000	10,291	11,767	13,455	15,385
Korean labor and 4 overhead		5,000	6,160	7,589	9,350	11,519
5 Depreciation		700	700	700	700	700
Cost of sales 6 [(2)+(3)+(4)+(5)]		18,700	21,683	25,191	29,323	34,196
Gross margin [(1)- 7 (6)]		7,300	9,491	12,186	15,493	19,538
License fee [2.5% of 8 (1)]		650	779	934	1,120	1,343
Marketing and general & 9 administrative		5,040	5,247	5,495	5,793	6,149
EBIT* [(7) – (8) – 10 (9)]		1,610	3,465	5,757	8,580	12,046
Korean income 11 taxes (35%)		564	1,213	2,015	3,003	4,216
Net income after Korean taxes [(10) – 12 (11)]		1,047	2,252	3,742	5,577	7,830
Cash dividend [70% 13 of (12)]		733	1,576	2,619	3,904	5,481

* EBIT= earnings before interest and taxes

Given the facts and stated assumptions, the beginning balance sheet is presented in Exhibit 58-3. Exhibit 58-4 shows revenue and cost projections for Ko-tel over the expected five-year life of the project.

Exhibit 58-5 shows how the annual increase in working capital investment is calculated. According to the facts, half of gross working capital must be financed by Ko-tel or Am-tel. Therefore, half of any annual increase in working capital would represent an additional required capital investment.

Exhibit 58-6 forecasts project cash flows from the viewpoint of Ko-tel. Thanks to healthy liquidation value, the project has a positive NPV and an IRR greater than the 22% local (Korean) cost of capital for projects of similar risk. Therefore Ko-tel passes the first of the two tests of required rate of return.

Does Ko-tel also pass the second test? That is, does it show at least a 22% required rate of return from the viewpoint of Am-tel? Exhibit 58-7 shows the calculation for expected after-tax dividends from Ko-tel to be received by Am-tel. For purposes of this example, note that Am-tel must pay regular U.S. corporate income taxes (38% rate) on dividends received from Ko-tel. However, the U.S. tax law allows Am-tel to claim a tax credit for income taxes paid to Korea on the Korean income that generated the dividend. The process of calculating the regional income in Korea is called "grossing up" and is illustrated in Exhibit 58-7, lines 1, 2, and 3.

Exhibit 58-5: Multinational Capital Budgeting Example—Working Capital Calculation

Item	1	2	3	4	5
1 Total revenue	26,000	31,174	37,378	44,816	53,734
2 Net working capital needs at year-end [25% of (1)]	6,500	7,794	9,344	11,204	13,434
3 Less year-beginning working capital	1,700	6,500	7,794	9,344	11,204
4 Required addition to working capital	4,800	1,294	1,551	1,860	2,230
5 Less working capital financed in Korean by payables	2,400	647	775	930	1,115
6 Net new investment in working capital	2,400	647	775	930	1,115

Exhibit 58-6: Cash Flow Projection—NPV and IRR for Ko-tel

Item	0	1	2	3	4	5
1 EBIT [Exhibit 29-7, (10)]		1,610	3,465	5,757	8,580	12,046
2 Korean income taxes (35%)		564	1,213	2,015	3,003	4,216
3 Net income, all equity basis		1,047	2,252	3,742	5,577	7,830
4 Depreciation		700	700	700	700	700
5 Liquidation value						9,000
6 Half of addition to working capital		2,400	647	775	930	1,115
7 Cost of project	(8,000)					
8 Net cash flow	(8,000)	(654)	2,305	3,667	5,347	16,415
12 IRR	33.09%	=				
13 NPV = PV (at 22%) - 1	$3,519.54					

This imputed Korean won income is converted from won to dollars in lines (4) and (5). Then the U.S. income tax is calculated at 38% in line (6). A tax credit is given for the Korean income taxes paid, as calculated in line (7). Line (8) then shows the net additional U.S. tax due, and line (10) shows the net dividend received by Am-tel after the additional U.S. tax is paid. Finally, Exhibit 58-8 calculates the rate of return on cash flows from Ko-tel from the viewpoint of Am-tel. Ko-tel passed the test because it had a positive NPV and an IRR above the 22% rate of return required by Am-tel.

What-If Analysis

So far, the project investigation team has used a set of "most likely" assumptions to forecast rates of return. It is now time to subject the most likely outcome to sensitivity analyses. The many probabilistic techniques are available to test the sensitivity of results to political and foreign exchange risks as are used to test sensitivity to business and financial risks. But it is more common to test sensitivity to political and foreign exchange risk by simulating what would happen to net present value and earnings under a variety of what-if scenarios. Spreadsheet programs such as Excel can be utilized to test various scenarios (see Exhibit 58-9).

Exhibit 58-7: After-Tax Dividend Received by Am-tel

Item	0	1	2	3	4	5
			Year			
In Millions of Won						
1 Cash dividend paid [Exhibit 29-4, (13)		733	1,576	2,619	3,904	5,481
2 A 70% of Korean income tax [Exhibit 29-7, (11)]		394	849	1,410	2,102	2,951
3 Grossed-up dividend [(1) + (2)]		1,127	2,425	4,030	6,006	8,432
4 Exchange-rate (won/$)	1,150	1,139	1,127	1,116	1,105	1,094
In Thousands of Dollars						
5 Grossed-up dividend [(3)/ (4) x 1000]		990	2,152	3,611	5,437	7,710
6 U.S. tax (38%)		376	818	1,372	2,066	2,930

Item	Year 0	1	2	3	4	5
7 Credit for Korea taxes [(2)/(4) x 1000]		346	753	1,264	1,903	2,698
8 Additional U.S. Tax due [(6) − (7), if (6) is larger]		30	65	108	163	231
9 Excess U.S. tax credit [(7) − (6), if (7) is larger		-	-	-	-	-
10 Dividend received by Am-tel after all taxes [(1)/(4) x 1000 − (8)]		614	1,334	2,239	3,371	4,780

Exhibit 58-10 depicts an NPV graph of various scenarios.

Exhibit 58-8: NPV and IRR for Am-tel

Item	Year 0	1	2	3	4	5
In Million of Won						
1 License fee from Ko-tel (2.5%) [Exhibit 29-7, (7)]		650	779	934	1,120	1,343
2 Margin on exports to Ko-tel [5% of (3) in Exhibit 29-4]		450	515	588	673	769
3 Total receipts		1,100	1,294	1,523	1,793	2,113
4 Exchange rate (won/$)	950	941	931	922	913	903
In thousands of Dollars						
5 Pre-tax receipts [(3)/(4) x 1000]		1,170	1,390	1,652	1,965	2,338
6 U.S. taxes (38%)		444	528	628	747	889
7 License fees and export profits, after tax		725	862	1,024	1,218	1,450
8 After-tax dividend [Exhibit 5, (10)]		614	1,334	2,239	3,371	4,780
9 Project cost	(11,000)					
10 Liquidation value						9,962
11 Net cash flow	(11,000)	1,339	2,196	3,263	4,589	16,192
12 IRR	25.99%	=				
13 NPV = PV (at 22%) - I	$1,432.29					

Exhibit 58-9: NPV Profiles for Ko-tel and Am-tel—Sensitivity Analysis

Discount rate (%)	0	4	8	12	16	20	22	24	28	32	36	40
Project pt of view (Ko-Tel)	$19,080.30	$14,825.10	$11,383.91	$8,576.47	$6,267.33	$4,353.58	$3,519.54	$2,756.24	$1,414.14	$279.48	$(685.41)	$(1,510.43)
Parent pt of view (Parent)	$16,578.90	$12,449.86	$9,105.75	$6,372.77	$4,120.33	$2,249.29	$1,432.29	$683.56	$(635.75)	$(1,754.67)	$(2,709.47)	$(3,528.94)

Exhibit 58-10: NPV Profiles for Ko-tel and Am-tel—Sensitivity Analysis Graph

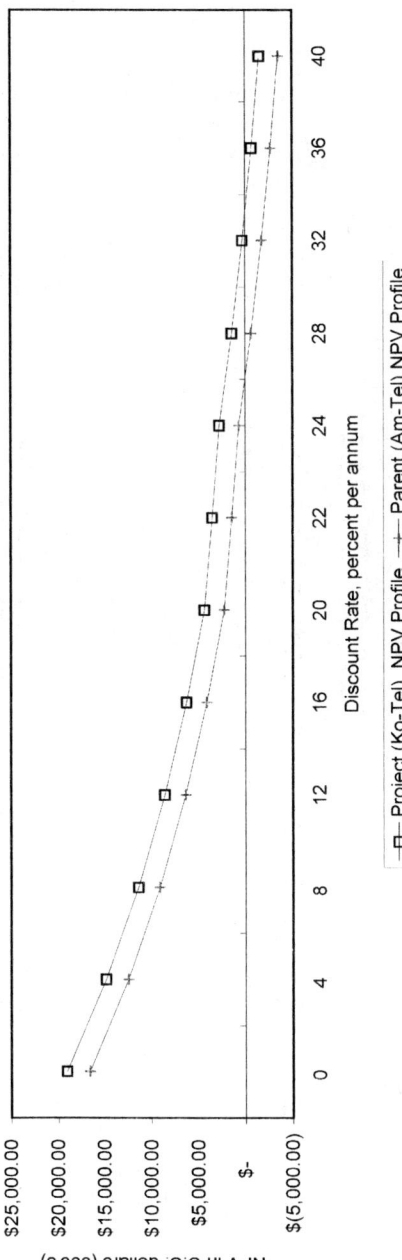

POLITICAL RISK

Multinational corporations are exposed to the following types of political risks:

- Expropriation of plants and equipment without compensation or with minimal compensation that is below actual market value.

- Nonconvertibility of the affiliate's foreign earnings into the parent's currency—the problem of "blocked funds."

- Substantial changes in the laws governing taxation.

- Government controls in the host country regarding wages, compensation to personnel, hiring of personnel, the sales price of the product, making of transfer payments to the parent, and local borrowing.

In addition, culture plays a key role in international business.

How to Measure Political Risk

Many MNCs and banks have attempted to measure political risks in their businesses. They even hire or maintain a group of political risk analysts. The following independent services provide political risk and country risk ratings:

- *Euromoney* magazine's annual *Country Risk Rating,* which is based on a measure of different countries' access to international credit, trade finance, political risk, and a country's payment record. The rankings are generally confirmed by political risk insurers and top syndicate managers in the Euromarkets.

- Ratings by the *Economist Intelligence Unit,* a New York-based subsidiary of the Economist Group, London, which are based on factors such as external debt and trends in the current account, the consistency of government policy, foreign-exchange reserves, and the quality of economic management.

- *International Country Risk Guide,* published by a U.S. division of *International Business Communications, Ltd.,* London, which offers a composite risk rating, as well as individual ratings for political, financial, and economic risk. The political variable—which makes up half of the composite index—includes factors such as government corruption and how economic expectations diverge from reality. The financial rating looks at such things as the likelihood of losses from exchange controls and loan defaults. Finally, economic ratings consider such factors as inflation and debt-service costs.

Methods for Dealing with Political Risk

To the extent that forecasting political risks is a formidable task, what can an MNC do to cope with them? The suggested methods are:

- *Avoidance.* Try to avoid political risk by minimizing activities in or with countries that are considered to be of high risk. Use higher discount rates for projects in riskier countries.

- *Adaptation.* Try to reduce risk by adapting the activities (for example, by using hedging techniques discussed previously).

- *Diversification.* Diversify across national borders, so that problems in one country do not severely damage the company.
- *Risk transfer.* Buy insurance policies for political risks.

> *EXAMPLE 10:* Most developed nations offer insurance for political risk to their exporters. Examples are:
>
> - In the U.S., the Eximbank offer policies to exporters that cover such political risks as war, currency inconvertibility, and civil unrest. Furthermore, the Overseas Private Investment Corporation (OPIC) offers policies to U.S. foreign investors to cover such risks as currency inconvertibility, civil or foreign war damages, or expropriation.
> - In the U.K., similar policies are offered by the Export Credit Guarantee Department (ECGD); in Canada, by the Export Development Council (EDC); and in Germany, by an agency called Hermes.

INTERNATIONAL FINANCIAL REPORTING STANDARDS VS. GENERALLY ACCEPTED ACCOUNTING PRINCIPLES

In most cases, financial statement preparation and disclosures between U.S. generally accepted accounting principles (GAAP) and international financial reporting standards (IFRS) are similar. However, differences do exist such as IFRS only mandates comparative information on each financial statement solely for the previous year, while GAAP has multi-year comparable financial figures. In consolidations, GAAP requires a parent company to issue consolidated financial statements, whereas IFRS permits exemptions when a parent is wholly owned.

Balance Sheet

IFRS permits offsetting of cash overdrafts, while GAAP does not. Under IFRS, receivables are initially reported at fair market value. Unlike GAAP, IFRS also includes marketing costs in cost of sales. LIFO (last in, first out) inventory valuation is not permitted under IFRS. Fixed assets are presented at fair market value less accumulated depreciation under IFRS. In the case of a contingent liability, IFRS records the estimated loss at the mid-point of the estimate range, while GAAP uses the more conservative low-end estimate. In the case of leases, IFRS excludes service costs from minimum lease payments.

Income Statement

IFRS generally recognizes revenue when there is probable economic benefit and reliable measurement exists. Under IFRS, gains are included with revenue, while under GAAP, gains are segregated from revenue. In construction contracts, IFRS only permits the percentage of completion method, while GAAP also allows for the completed contract method. IFRS permits the recovery of impairment losses on intangible assets in later years if a change in economic conditions occurs.

INTERNATIONAL SOURCES OF FINANCING

A company may finance its activities abroad, especially in countries it is operating in. A successful company in domestic markets is more likely to be able to attract financing for international expansion.

The most important international sources of funds are the Eurocurrency market and the Eurobond market. Also, MNCs have access to national capital markets in which their subsidiaries are located. Exhibit 58-11 presents an overview of international financial markets.

Exhibit 58-11: International Financial Markets

Market	Instruments	Participants	Regulator
International monetary system	Special drawing fights; gold; foreign exchange	Central banks; International Monetary Fund	International Monetary Fund
Foreign exchange markets	Bank deposits; currency; futures and forward contracts	Commercial and central banks; firms; individuals	Central bank in each country
National money-markets (short term)	Bank deposits and loans; short-term government securities; commercial paper	Banks, firms; individuals; government agencies	Central bank; other government agencies
National capital markets (long term)	Bonds; long-term bank deposits and loans; stocks; long-term government securities	Banks; firms; individuals; government agencies	Central bank; other government agencies
Eurocurrency market	Bank deposits; bank loans; Eurocommercial paper	Commercial banks; firms; government agencies	Substantially unregulated
Eurobond market	Bonds	Banks; firms; individuals; government agencies	Substantially unregulated

The Eurocurrency market is a largely short-term (usually less than one year of maturity) market for bank deposits and loans denominated in any currency except the currency of the country where the market is located. For example, in London, the Eurocurrency market is a market for bank deposits and loans denominated in dollars, yen, francs, marks, and any other currency except British pounds. The main instruments used in this market are CDs and time deposits, and bank loans.

Note: The term market in this context is not a physical marketplace, but a set of bank deposits and loans.

The Eurobond market is a long-term market for bonds denominated in any currency except the currency of the country where the market is located. Eurobonds may be of different types such as straight, convertible, and with warrants. While most Eurobonds have a fixed rate, variable-rate bonds also exist. Maturities vary, but 10–12 years is typical.

Although Eurobonds are issued in many currencies, you wish to select a stable, fully convertible, and actively traded currency. In some cases, if a Eurobond is denominated in a weak currency, the holder has the option of requesting payment in another currency.

Sometimes, large MNCs establish wholly owned offshore finance subsidiaries. These subsidiaries issue Eurobond debt and the proceeds are given to the parent or to overseas operating subsidiaries. Debt service goes back to bondholders through the finance subsidiaries.

If the Eurobond were issued by the parent directly, the U.S. would require a withholding tax on interest. There may also be an estate tax when the bond-holder dies. These tax problems do not arise when a bond is issued by a finance subsidiary incorporated in a tax haven. Hence, the subsidiary may borrow at less cost than the parent.

In summary, the Euromarkets offer borrowers and investors in one country the opportunity to deal with borrowers and investors from many other countries, buying and selling bank deposits, bonds, and loans denominated in many currencies.

Exhibit 58-12 provides a list of funding sources available to a foreign affiliate of an MNC (debt and equity).

Exhibit 58-12: International Sources of Credit

Borrowing	Domestic Inside the Firm	Domestic Market	Foreign Inside the Firm	Foreign Market	Euromarket
Direct, short-term	Intrafirm loans, transfer pricing, royalties, fees, service charges	Commercial paper	International intrafirm loans, international transfer pricing, dividends, royalties, fees		Eurocommercial paper
Intermediated, short-term		Short-term bank loans, discounted receivables	International back-to-back loans	Short-term bank loans, discounted receivables	Euro short-term loans
Direct, long-term	Intrafirm loans, invested in affiliates	Stock issue Bond issue	International intrafirm long-term loans, FDI	Stock issue Bond issue	Eurobonds
Intermediated, long-term		Long-term bank loans	International back-to-back loans	Long-term bank loans	Euro long-term loans

PART VIII

Tax Preparation and Planning

CHAPTER 59

How Taxes Affect Business Decisions

CONTENTS

The objective of companies is to maximize profits while simultaneously minimizing income taxes. Tax planning strategies are essential in satisfying this basic objective. The controller must: (1) be familiar with certain basic federal income tax rules, and (2) be aware of the complex tax implications of business combinations.

The company and the shareholders must be considered when planning and implementing tax strategies. The determination of whether a business should operate as a C corporation or an S corporation involves consideration of tax rates at both the entity and owner's levels. Further consideration should be given to Internal Revenue Code restrictions. long-term considerations, including liquidation possibilities are crucial. The selection of the cash or accrual basis of accounting must be based on a variety of factors including regulatory agency requirements, federal income tax provisions, and basic timing factors in accounting recognition. Where alternatives exist, the controller is called upon for analysis and recommendations.

TAX ACCOUNTING METHODS

The cash method of accounting results in the recognition of income when collected and expenses when paid. Under this method, constructive receipt of income results in recognition. The apparent advantage to the cash method of accounting is that careful planning can result in the deferral of income from the current period to the next. Billing and collection should therefore be timed carefully. Under Internal Revenue Code (IRC) Sec. 448, however, the cash method of accounting may be elected only by: (1) C corporations with average annual gross receipts of $5 million or less ($25 million or less for tax years beginning in 2018), (2) qualified personal service corporations, and (3) certain farming and timber businesses. Taxpayers failing to qualify for the cash method of accounting must use the accrual method of accounting, whereby income is recognized when earned and expenses are recognized when incurred.

INSTALLMENT SALES

Pursuant to IRC Sec. 453, the installment sale provisions prorate the gross profit on a sale over the years in which payments are to be received. Depending on current and potential tax rate changes, the installment sale provisions might be advantageous. The installment sale provisions are automatic; i.e., a taxpayer must elect not to be covered by the statutory provisions. The installment sale provisions are applicable to sales of real property and casual sales of personal property at a gain. Sales by dealers of personal or real property are generally not eligible for the installment sale provisions, nor are revolving credit sales and sales of publicly traded securities. The character of gain recognized will not be altered under the installment sale provisions; accordingly, the disposition of a capital asset will result in capital gain. Caution must be exercised in case of depreciable property since any depreciation that must be recaptured under IRC Sec. 1245 and IRC Sec. 1250 must be recaptured in the year of sale, regardless of the installment sale provisions.

DIVIDENDS-RECEIVED DEDUCTION

Corporations that receive dividends from unaffiliated domestic taxable corporations are generally entitled to a 70% dividends-received deduction. The deduction, however, is limited to 70% of the corporation's tentative taxable income, which is the taxable income of the corporation before consideration of the dividend-received deduction and any applicable net operating loss deduction. The 70% of tentative taxable income limitation is not applicable when the corporation sustains a net operating loss before or after the dividends-received deduction. Additionally, the deduction is increased to 80% in cases where the dividends are received from a 20%-or-more owned corporation.

Note that for tax years beginning after December 31, 2017, the 80% dividends-received deduction is reduced to 65%, and the 70% dividends-received deduction is reduced to 50%.

A corporation whose stock is included in a debt-financed portfolio will partially or totally lose the dividends-received deduction. The beneficial provisions will also not be applicable in cases involving the receipt of dividends from mutual savings banks, since such receipts in essence represent interest income.

Note that dividends received from affiliated corporations are generally entitled to a 100% dividends-received deduction.

The application of the general rule may be illustrated as follows:

Sales	$300,000
Dividend income received from a less than 20%-owned corporation	100,000
	400,000
Operating expenses	310,000
Tentative taxable income	90,000
Dividends-received deduction; limited to 70% of $90,000	63,000
Taxable income	$ 27,000

On the other hand, had the corporation sustained an operating loss of $90,000, the "70% of tentative taxable income limitation" would not be applicable; accordingly, the dividends-received deduction would be 70% of $100,000, or $70,000, effectively increasing the net operating loss to $160,000.

Further, the following example illustrates that the "70% of tentative taxable income limitation: does not apply if the corporation sustains a net operating loss after the dividends-received deduction:"

Sales	$300,000
Dividend income received from a less than 20%-owned corporation	100,000
	400,000
Operating expenses	390,000
Tentative taxable income	10,000
Dividends-received deduction; 70% of $100,000	70,000
Net operating loss	$ (60,000)

Investment strategies should be carefully monitored in order to secure the benefits of the dividends-received deduction. The wrong investment vehicles could easily result in the loss of the desired tax benefit. For example, the following dividends are not eligible for the dividends-received deduction:

- Dividends from mutual savings banks, which in essence represent interest on bank accounts.
- Dividends derived from real estate investment trusts.
- Capital gains dividends passed through from mutual funds.
- Dividends from money market funds which invest solely in interest-paying securities.

It should also be noted that the dividends-received deduction is allowed only if the dividend-paying stock is held at least 46 days during the 90-day period that commences 45 days before the stock became ex-dividend with respect to the dividend.

CHARITABLE CONTRIBUTIONS

The deduction for charitable contributions is generally limited annually to 10% of taxable income, computed without regard to the deduction for charitable contributions, and with taking into account: (1) the dividends-received deduction, (2) any net operating loss carryback, and (3) any net capital loss carryback. Furthermore, the charitable contribution deduction may not increase an existing net operating loss. Any charitable contributions which may not be deducted in the current year by virtue of the 10% limitation may be carried forward up to five years. Corporations using the accrual method of accounting may deduct charitable contributions authorized by the board of directors but paid after year-end as long as payment is made within two months after year-end. Otherwise, cash basis accounting is applicable.

With respect to contributions of property, the deduction is generally measured by the corporation's basis in the property. In the case of contributions of inventory and other ordinary income producing property for the care of the ill, the needy, or infants, the deduction is equal to the corporation's basis in the property increased by 50% of the property's appreciation. In no event, however, may the deduction exceed twice the property's basis. A contribution of a vehicle is generally limited to the gross proceeds the charitable organization receives upon subsequent sale of the vehicle. In the event that the vehicle is not sold by the charitable organization (donee), the donee must provide written certification of the vehicle and the duration of its use.

NET OPERATING LOSS DEDUCTIONS

In general, net operating losses of corporations may be carried back up to two years and carried forward up to 20 years.

An election may be made, however, to forego the carryback. This may be advisable when tax rates in future years render the loss deduction more valuable. IRS attention is drawn to the tax return for the year to which the carryback is claimed. Accordingly, it might be judicious to relinquish the right to a carryback claim since the prior year's tax return may be subject to IRS scrutiny. When calculating the net operating loss deduction, no deduction is allowed for net operating loss carrybacks or carryovers. The dividends-received deduction, however, is allowable.

Prior to enactment of the Tax Cuts and Jobs Act of 2017, net operating losses of corporations could be carried back up to two years and carried forward up to 20 years.

Under the 2017 legislation, the two-year carryback period and the 20-year carry forward period are repealed. Net operating losses may now be carried forward indefinitely. In addition, the net operating loss deduction is limited to 80% of taxable income (computed without regard to the net operating loss deduction).

ORGANIZATION COSTS

Organization costs are costs incurred in connection with creating a corporation. Organization costs include legal and accounting fees as well as filing fees and payments to temporary directors. Under current tax law, up to $5,000 of start-up costs and $5,000 of organization costs may be deducted in the year of commencement of business.

The available $5,000 deduction for organization costs must be reduced by the amount by which the cumulative start-up or organization costs exceed $50,000. Any remaining start-up costs and organization costs may be amortized over 15 years. An election may be made to capitalize and amortize all organization costs.

DEPRECIATION

With respect to tangible depreciable property placed into service after 1986, the modified accelerated cost recovery system (MACRS) of depreciation is applicable.

Under MACRS, assets are placed into recovery periods based on estimated economic lives specified in the Code.

The table below represents the recovery periods applicable to tangible personal property subject to depreciation recapture under IRC Sec. 1245.

Recovery Period	Qualifying Property
3 years	Assets with a life of 4 years or less
5 years	Assets with a life of at least 4 years and less than 10 years
7 years	Assets with a life of at least 10 years and less than 16 years
10 years	Assets with a life of at least 16 years and less than 20 years
15 years	Assets with a life of at least 20 years and less than 25 years
20 years	Assets with a life of at least 25 years

Examples of tangible personal property classified by recovery period are presented in the following table:

Recovery Period	Examples of Eligible Property
3 years	Special tools
5 years	Light duty trucks, automobiles, and computers
7 years	Office furniture and fixtures, and other equipment
10 years	Railroad tank cars
15 years	Industrial generation systems
20 years	Sewer pipes

Real property is classified into three recovery periods. Residential real property is 27.5-year recovery property while nonresidential real property is 31.5-year recovery property (if placed into service after 1986 and before May 13, 1993) or 39-year recovery property (if placed into service after May 12, 1993). Leasehold improvements made to nonresidential real property before 2006 may be depreciated over a 15-year recovery period.

Personal property in the 3-year, 5-year, 7-year, and 10-year recovery period categories is to be depreciated using the 200% declining balance method with a switch to the straight-line method at the point in time when deductions will be maximized (i.e., generally in the middle of the recovery period). The 150% declining balance method is applicable to 15-year and 20-year recovery property. The provision regarding the switch to straight line is also applicable. An election may be made to calculate the cost recovery deduction utilizing the straight line method. The election must be made for all assets placed into service in a particular class in each year.

In general, an additional first-year depreciation deduction is available. For assets placed into service through September 27, 2017, the additional deduction is equal to 50% of the property's basis. For assets placed into service after September 27, 2017, the additional deduction is equal to 100% of the property's basis. The adjusted basis of qualified property must be reduced by the additional deduction before computing the depreciation deduction otherwise allowable. Further, if the Section 179 deduction (discussed later) is claimed, it reduces the adjusted basis of the property eligible for the additional first-year deduction. The additional first-year depreciation deduction is automatic unless an election is made to forego the additional amount. The election to forego the additional deduction is required to be made for all assets acquired in a particular recovery class in each year.

Real property must be depreciated utilizing the straight-line method. Classification into residential and nonresidential categories is irrelevant.

Whether the accelerated method or the straight-line method is used for personal property, a half-year convention is applicable in the year the asset is placed into service and in the year the property is disposed of, if prior to the expiration of the recovery period.

The timing of asset purchases must be planned because the "mid-quarter convention" may be triggered. Under the "mid-quarter convention," if more than 40% of the aggregate value of personal property is placed into service during the last quarter of the year, the half-year convention must be replaced by the mid-quarter convention. With respect to real property, a mid-month convention is to be applied when the asset is placed into service and when the asset is disposed of prior to the expiration of the recovery period.

The *Alternative Depreciation System* (ADS) must be used for certain types of property including personal property used outside of the United States and property leased to tax-exempt entities. ADS, however, may be elected for any class of property placed into service. The recovery deduction will be based on the straight-line method and longer recovery periods. Personal property with no class life will be recovered over 12 years, nonresidential real property will be recovered over 40 years, and residential real property will be recovered over 30 years. All other property will be recovered over the applicable class life.

Automobiles are included in a special category of property referred to as "listed property."

The annual depreciation deduction for automobiles is dependent upon the year in which the auto was placed into service, because the Internal Revenue Service issues applicable tables annually.

If a business leases an automobile that is used 100% for business purposes, the full lease cost will generally be deductible. However, in order to prevent the avoidance of the "listed property" limitations, the IRS requires that an "add-back" be included in income each year of the automobile's use. The inclusion, which is based on the initial fair market value of the vehicle and the year in which the lease was effected, is adjusted annually for inflation.

The deductible amounts are periodically adjusted for inflation. Listed property not used more than 50% of the time for business must use the alternative depreciation system.

The Sec. 179 election allows the expensing of certain depreciable assets (and off-the-shelf computer software). Under the statute, in lieu of capitalizing the asset and depreciating it, the assets may be expensed in the year they are placed into service. The annual limitation is $510,000 for property placed into service in 2017 ($1,000,000 for 2018). This must be reduced (phased out) dollar-for-dollar by the amount for which the Sec. 179 property placed into service during 2017 exceeds

$2,030,000 ($2,500,000 for 2018). Additionally, the deduction cannot be used to create or increase a net operating loss. Furthermore, the deduction must be considered for depreciation recapture purposes. The Sec. 179 deduction is limited to $25,000 (to be adjusted annually for inflation) with respect to a sport utility vehicle.

CAPITAL GAINS AND LOSSES

Corporations cannot deduct capital losses against ordinary income. Capital losses can be offset only against capital gains. Capital losses that cannot be utilized in the year sustained may be carried back up to three years and then carried forward for up to five years. The net capital loss, if carried forward, is treated as a short-term loss. Capital gains are taxed at the corporation's ordinary tax rates.

MANUFACTURERS' DEDUCTION

A C corporation or an S corporation that is a U.S. manufacturer may be entitled to a deduction equal to 9% of its net income derived from qualified domestic manufacturing activities. For tax years beginning in 2010 and later, the applicable percentage is 9%. The deduction is allowed not only for regular tax purposes but for computing alternative tax liability and adjusted current earnings. The deduction is repealed for tax years beginning after December 31, 2017.

The applicable percentage is to be multiplied by the lesser of the entity's "qualified production activities income" or taxable income (before the manufacturers' deduction is taken into account). In no event, however, may the deduction exceed 50% of the entity's W-2 wages.

Qualified production activities include, but are not limited to:

- Manufacture, production, growth, or extraction of personal property, including computer software but not retail preparation of food or beverages.
- Extraction of natural gas, electricity, and potable water.
- U.S. construction relating to engineering and architectural services.

"Qualified production activities income" includes amounts received from:

- Sale, lease, rental, license, exchange, or other disposition of qualifying domestic production property.
- Construction performed in the United States.
- Engineering and architectural services performed in the United States relating to U.S. construction projects.

Qualifying income must, however, be reduced by the following:

- Cost of goods sold.
- Directly related expenses, including wages.
- Indirectly related expenses, including overhead.

FEDERAL TAX RATES

IRC Sec. 63 specifies the regular income tax rates as follows:

Taxable Income	Tax Rate
First $50,000	15%
$50,001-$75,000	25%
$75,001-$10,000,000	34%
$10,000,001 and above	35%

Personal Service Corporations, however, may not avail themselves of the preferential brackets. In such cases, a flat 35% rate is applicable.

When a corporation's taxable income is in excess of $100,000, it is liable for an additional tax in the amount of the lesser of: (1) 5% of such excess, or (2) $11,750. When a corporation's taxable income is in excess of $15,000,000, it is liable for a second additional tax equal to the lesser of: (1) 3% of such excess, or (2) $100,000.

For tax years beginning after December 31, 2017, the corporate tax rate is reduced to a flat 21%.

Generally, a corporation must make quarterly estimated tax payments if it expects its estimated tax to be $500 or more. In the case of a calendar year corporation, these estimated tax payments are generally due on April 15, June 15, September 15, and December 15.

FOREIGN TAX CREDIT

If a corporation pays income taxes to a foreign country, it may be entitled to a U.S. foreign tax credit. This credit, however, cannot be used to reduce the U.S. tax liability on income from U.S. sources. The tentative U.S. foreign tax credit is calculated using the following formula:

$$\text{Foreign tax credit} = \frac{\text{Foreign source income}}{\text{Total worldwide income}} \times \text{U.S. tax liability}$$

An unused foreign tax credit may be carried back one year and carried forward 10 years.

THE ALTERNATIVE MINIMUM TAX

The alternative minimum tax (AMT) calculation represents perhaps the most difficult provision of the IRC. The AMT is designed to prevent taxpayers from minimizing their tax liability through the deduction of preferential items. The AMT is based on the following formula:

    Regular taxable income (Before net operating loss deductions)

+ Tax preference items and adjustments

= Pre-net operating loss alternative minimum taxable income

– Up to 90% of alternative minimum tax net operating loss deductions

= Alternative minimum taxable income (AMTI)

- Exemption amount
= Balance
× 20%
= Alternative minimum tax
- Applicable credits
- Regular current year tax liability
= Alternative minimum tax liability

Some of the more common tax preference items are:

- Excess accelerated depreciation on real property.
- Excess percentage depletion for coal and iron ore.
- With respect to tangible depreciable personal property placed into service after December 31, 1986, the excess of accelerated depreciation over the amount calculated using the 150% declining balance method with the appropriate switch to straight line.
- Excess amortization of pollution control facilities.
- The Adjusted Current Earnings (ACE) Adjustment. The ACE adjustment is generally equal to 75% of the amount by which adjusted current earnings exceed AMTI. However, if AMTI exceeds adjusted current earnings, a reduction in AMTI equal to 75% of the difference is allowed. Accordingly, the ACE adjustment can be a positive or negative amount.

  Adjusted current earnings is equal to AMTI (before the ACE adjustment and the AMTI net operating loss deduction) plus or minus certain adjustments. The calculation of adjusted current earnings is based on tax concepts similar to those used in determining earnings and profits (i.e., E & P) for regular tax purposes. Accordingly, adjustments may be necessary for (1) depreciation, (2) certain items excluded from gross income but which are properly includible in E & P, and (3) items of deduction which are allowed in arriving at regular taxable income, but which are not allowed in arriving at E & P. For example, in determining adjusted current earnings: (1) all municipal bond interest is includible income, (2) all costs to purchase and carry municipal bonds are deductible, and (3) the 70% dividends-received deduction is not allowable but the 80% dividends-received deduction is allowable. Further, the method of depreciation for personal property placed in service after 1989 for determining ACE is governed by the Alternative Depreciation system. Accordingly, the straight line method must be used.

The main adjustment to be considered in the calculation of the AMT relates to depreciation. The depreciation adjustment is essentially equal to the depreciation of the assets placed into service after 1986 using the alternative depreciation system (discussed earlier) reduced by the company's regular depreciation expense.

The exemption amount is $40,000, but must be reduced by 25% of the AMTI in excess of $150,000.

If a corporation is deemed to be a small corporation, then it may not be subject to the alternative minimum tax. To be treated initially as a small corporation, the corporation's average annual gross receipts for the most recent three-year period beginning after 1994 must be less than $5,000,000. Treatment as a small corporation will be lost in a particular year if the entity's average gross receipts for the preceding three years is in excess of $7,500,000.

The calculation of the AMT is extremely complex. It is suggested that a tax advisor be consulted.

Note that the alternative minimum tax on corporations is repealed for tax years beginning after December 31, 2017.

THE PERSONAL HOLDING COMPANY TAX

The intent of the personal holding company tax is to compel corporations to distribute annually earnings derived from investments. Corporations subject to the personal holding company tax must pay an additional tax on undistributed personal holding company income. The tax is (1) in the nature of a penalty tax, (2) in addition to the company's regular income tax liability, and (3) imposed at the rate of 20% (15% for tax years beginning after 2002 and before 2013).

In order to be classified as a personal holding company, two tests must be satisfied. Generally, the income test requires that at least 60% of the corporation's adjusted ordinary gross income be derived from interest, dividends, certain royalties, certain types of rental income, as well as certain types of annuities and pass-through items from estates and trusts. The stock ownership test is essentially met if, during the last half of the tax year, more than 50% of the entity's stock is owned by five or fewer shareholders. For purposes of determining the five individuals, the rules of constructive ownership are applicable. Pursuant to the constructive ownership rules, stock owned, directly or indirectly, by or for a corporation, partnership, estate, or trust shall be considered as being owned proportionately by its shareholders, partners, or beneficiaries. Additionally, an individual shall be considered as owning the stock owned, directly, or indirectly, by or for his or her family or by or for his or her partner. For this purpose, family is limited to brothers, sisters, spouse, ancestors (i.e., grandparents) and lineal descendants (i.e., children and grandchildren).

The personal holding company tax is self-imposed; i.e., corporations must determine their status as a personal holding company and then file a Form 1120-PH along with their regular tax return.

The personal holding company tax is imposed on "undistributed personal holding company income," which is taxable income with the following adjustments, minus the dividends paid deduction:

- Deduction is allowed for federal and foreign income and excess profits taxes.
- Deduction is allowed for excess charitable contributions; in lieu of the normal 10% limit, the deduction may be as high as 50% of taxable income.
- Deduction is allowed for net long-term capital gain less related federal income taxes.
- The dividends-received deduction is not allowed.
- Other than a special one-year net operating loss carryover deduction, no deduction is allowed for a net operating loss.

Corporations may plan to mitigate the personal holding company tax by paying sufficient dividends to their stockholders. It should be noted that the deduction for dividends paid includes the following:

- Dividends actually paid during the tax year.

- Consent dividends, which represent amounts not actually paid out as dividends but that are includible in the shareholder's income because such an election was made by consenting shareholders on the last day of the corporation's tax year.

- With certain limitations, "late paid" dividends. "Late paid" dividends are dividends paid after year-end, but no later than the fifteenth day of the third month of the following year. In order to claim the deduction for "late paid" dividends, a proper election must be made.

ACCUMULATED EARNINGS TAX

The accumulated earnings tax, like the personal holding company tax, is in the nature of a penalty tax. Also imposed at the rate of 20% (15% for tax years beginning after 2002 and before 2013), this tax is in addition to the corporation's regular income tax liability. The imposition of the accumulated earnings tax forces corporations to distribute earnings and profits in the form of dividends. If not for the provisions of the accumulated earnings tax, the tax at the shareholder level (which is in addition to the corporate tax imposed on the entity's regular taxable income) could be avoided.

The accumulated earnings tax is imposed on the year's "accumulated taxable income," which is regular taxable income reduced by: (1) dividends paid to shareholders, (2) federal income taxes, (3) charitable contributions in excess of the 10% limitation discussed earlier, (4) net capital losses not deductible in calculating ordinary taxable income, (5) net capital gain for the year (reduced by the taxes attributed thereto), and (6) the accumulated earnings credit. The taxable base must be increased by the dividends-received deduction. The accumulated earnings credit is equal to the earnings retained for the reasonable needs of the business. The minimum accumulated earnings credit is $250,000 except for a personal service corporation, in which case the credit is reduced to $150,000.

As in the case of the personal holding company tax, careful tax planning can mitigate the imposition of the penalty tax. The payment of sufficient dividends to the shareholders can mitigate the tax. Dividends paid after year end but on or before the fifteenth day of the third month of the New Year may be considered in reducing the base subject to the accumulated earnings tax.

Unlike the personal holding company tax, the accumulated earnings tax is not self-imposed. Rather, the Internal Revenue Service must determine that a liability exists for the accumulated earnings tax.

CORPORATE REORGANIZATIONS

Generally, corporate reorganizations do not result in the imposition of income tax. IRC Sec. 368 defines the seven types of corporate reorganizations.

A Type A reorganization may be a statutory merger or consolidation. A merger is effected when there is a union between two or more corporations. Pursuant to the union, one corporation retains its existence while the other parties to the reorganization are absorbed. A consolidation, on the other hand, is effected when a new corporation is created and the other parties are absorbed.

A Type B reorganization involves the acquisition by one corporation, in exchange solely for all or part of its voting stock (or in exchange solely for all of the voting stock of a corporation which is in control of the acquiring corporation), of stock of another corporation if, immediately after the acquisition, the acquiring corporation has control (i.e., 80%) of such other corporation (whether or not such acquiring corporation had control immediately before the acquisition).

A Type C reorganization results in the acquisition by one corporation, in exchange solely for all or part of its voting stock (or in exchange for all or a part of the voting stock of a corporation which is in control of the acquiring corporation), of substantially all of the properties of another corporation, but in determining whether the exchange is solely for stock the assumption by the acquiring corporation of a liability of the other, or the fact that property acquired is subject to a liability, shall be disregarded.

A Type D reorganization is predicated on a transfer by a corporation of all or a part of its assets to another corporation if immediately after the transfer the transferer, or one or more of its shareholders (including persons who were shareholders immediately before the transfer), or any combination thereof, is in control of the corporation to which the assets were transferred; but only if, in pursuance of the plan, stock or securities of the corporation to which the assets are transferred are distributed to the shareholders in a tax-free or partially tax-free transaction.

A Type E reorganization, called a recapitalization, involves changes in the amount and/or character of the corporation's stock or paid-in capital. An exchange of stock for stock, for example, qualifies as a Type E reorganization.

A Type F reorganization entails a mere change in identity, form, or place of organization of one corporation, however effected.

A Type G reorganization results in a transfer by a corporation of all or a part of its assets to another corporation (under title 11 of the Bankruptcy Code) but only if, in pursuance of the plan, stock or securities of the corporation to which the assets are transferred are distributed to the shareholders in a tax-free or partially tax-free transaction.

In general, no tax gain arises in corporate reorganizations unless "boot" is involved. *Boot* is generally property in addition to the stock of the parties involved. For example, when cash in received in a statutory merger, it is treated as boot.

It is important to note that a stock redemption is not a corporate reorganization.

STOCK REDEMPTIONS

A stock redemption, which occurs when a corporation cancels or redeems its own stock, may afford shareholders beneficial tax treatment.

In general, a stockholder will recognize capital gain or loss in connection with a stock redemption if one of five conditions is satisfied:

1. The redemption is not essentially equivalent to a dividend; i.e., the redemption results in a meaningful reduction in the shareholder's voting power, interest in the earnings and assets of the corporation, etc.

2. The redemption is substantially disproportionate; i.e., immediately after the redemption (a) the ratio of the shareholder's voting stock to the total outstanding voting stock is less tan 80% of that ratio immediately before the redemption, and (b) the shareholder owns less than 50% of the corporation's outstanding voting stock.

3. The redemption results in the complete termination of the shareholder's interest.

4. The redemption is a redemption of a noncorporate shareholder's stock in partial liquidation of the corporation.

5. The redemption occurred in order to pay a decendent's death taxes and administrative expenses.

Distributions received in connection with redemptions not meeting one of the conditions above will be treated as dividends; accordingly, such distributions will be taxed as ordinary income.

CONTROLLED GROUP OF CORPORATIONS

There are two types of controlled groups of corporations.

The first type is known as a brother-sister controlled group. A brother-sister controlled group exists when (1) five or fewer persons (which may be individuals, estates or trusts) own at least 80% of the total voting stock (or value of shares) of each of two or more corporations, and (2) these same persons own more than 50% of the total voting power (or value of shares) of each corporation. For purposes of apportioning the preferential tax bracket amounts (discussed below), the accumulated earnings credit, and the minimum tax credit, a brother-sister controlled group exists when five or fewer persons own more than 50% of the total voting power *or* value of all stock. It should be observed that a particular person's stock is to be considered only to the extent that it is owned identically with respect to each corporation.

The second type of controlled group is known as the parent-subsidiary group. (See the discussion on affiliated corporations.)

It is important to recognize the existence of either type of controlled groups of corporations. A controlled group of corporations must generally apportion the preferential tax bracket amounts equally among all members of the group. However, a valid election may be made by all members of the group to an apportionment plan. For example, assuming Corporation A and Corporation B are brother-sister corporations, Corporations A and B may (1) apportion the first $50,000 of taxable income (subject to the preferential 15% tax rate) equally between themselves or (2) apportion the first $50,000 of taxable income between themselves in any manner that is most beneficial to the group. Under the latter election, if Company A sustained a net operating loss of $50,000 and Company B generated a $50,000 profit, it would probably be prudent to allocate the entire $50,000 tax bracket (subject to the preferential tax rate of 15%) to Company B.

Further, a controlled group of corporations must apportion other tax attributes. For example, the annual Section 179 election must be apportioned amongst the corporations in the controlled group. In this case, if the apportionment rules were not applicable, establishing multiple corporations could easily enable the intent of the law's annual limit to be overridden.

AFFILIATED CORPORATIONS

An affiliated group of corporations is created when one or more chains of includible corporations is connected through stock ownership with a common parent corporation which is an includible corporation, but only if (1) the common parent corporation owns at least 80% of the total voting power and at least 80% of the total value of the stock of at least one includible corporation, and (2) stock meeting the 80% requirement in each of the includible corporations (but not the common parent corporation) is owned directly by one or more of the other includible corporations.

An includible corporation is defined as any corporation other than:

- An exempt corporation.
- A life insurance or mutual insurance company.
- A foreign corporation.
- A corporation deriving at least 80% of its income from possessions of the United States.
- A regulated investment company.
- A real estate investment trust.
- Certain domestic international sales corporations.

If all of the corporations that were members of the affiliate group at any time during the tax year consent before the last day for filing the return, an election may be made to file consolidated tax returns for the period that they are affiliated. Accordingly, net operating losses of some members of the group may be used to offset taxable income of other group members; the net effect obviously results in a decrease in tax liability.

TAX-FREE EXCHANGE OF PROPERTY FOR STOCK

Under IRC Sec. 351, if property is transferred to a corporation by one or more persons (which includes individuals, trusts, estates, partnerships and corporations) solely in exchange for stock in that corporation, an immediately after the exchange such person or persons are in control of the corporation to which the property was transferred, then no gain or loss will generally be recognized by the transferor or transferee.

For the purposes of IRC Sec. 351, control means that the person or persons making the transfer (i.e., transferor(s)) must own, immediately after the exchange, 80% or more of the total combined voting power of all classes of voting stock and 80% or more of the total number of outstanding nonvoting shares.

"Property" includes cash or other property, but does not include services rendered to the corporation. If stock is received for services rendered, then a taxable event has occurred. The recipient will be required to recognize ordinary income measured by the fair market value of the stock.

In the event that a transferor receives cash or other property in addition to stock, then gain will be recognized by the transferor, but only to the extent of the cash and/or fair market value of the other property received in the exchange. However, a loss on the transaction may never be recognized.

If property encumbered by debt (e.g., a mortgage) is transferred to a corporation, gain will only be recognized to the extent that the debt assumed by the corporation is in excess of the adjusted basis of the property transferred.

The stockholder's basis in stock received is equal to the cash plus the adjusted basis of any property transferred to the corporation, increased by any gain to be recognized. The stockholder's basis is reduced by the cash and the fair market value of any property received by the shareholder as part of the exchange. Further, since debt assumed by the corporation is treated as cash, the shareholder's basis in the stock is reduced by any debt assumed by the corporation.

From the corporation's point of view, the basis of property it receives is generally equal to the shareholder's basis immediately prior to the transfer, increased by any gain recognized by the shareholder in connection with the transfer.

The corporation's basis in the property must generally be reduced to the property's fair market value if the shareholder's adjusted basis in the contributed property is greater that the property's fair market value. In lieu of this basis reduction, the corporation and the shareholder may elect to limit the basis in the shareholder's stock to the fair market value of the contributed property.

To illustrate the major points above, assume that on July 1 of the current year, Moose Inc. is formed by Katie and Michael. Katie transfers $200,000 in cash to Moose and Michael transfers land and a building that originally cost him 180,000, but have a fair market value of $250,000 on July 1. The building is subject to a $150,000 mortgage, which is assumed by Moose. Based on these facts, the following should be noted:

- No gain or loss is to be recognized by Katie, Michael, or Moose Inc.
- Katie's basis in her Moose stock is $200,000.
- Michael's basis in his Moose stock is $180,000 less $150,000, or $30,000.
- Moose's basis in the land and building received from Michael is $180,000.

CORPORATE LIQUIDATIONS

The tax consequences of complete liquidations are relatively straightforward. A shareholder will generally recognize capital gain or loss upon receipt of cash or other property in complete liquidation of the corporation. The gain or loss is measured by the difference between the cash and fair market value of property received reduced by the adjusted basis of the stock surrendered. The liquidating corporation must recognize gain or loss on its normal business transactions during the liquidation period. Additionally, gain must be recognized by the distributing corporation to the extent that the fair market value of any property distributed exceeds the adjusted basis of that property. In calculating the gain, assets subject to liabilities cannot have a fair market value less than the amount of the liability.

Liquidation of corporate subsidiaries can be effected tax free if: (1) the parent corporation owns at least 80% of the subsidiary, and (2) the basis of the assets in the hands of the parent corporation is the same as the basis to the subsidiary. It should be noted that cancellation of debt in exchange for assets will not result in a taxable transaction.

Partial liquidations are extremely complex and should be consummated only after consulting a tax advisor.

S CORPORATIONS

An S corporation is a corporation that has elected to be treated essentially as a partnership. Accordingly, an S corporation will generally not pay tax.

Election

To elect status as an S corporation, a Form 2553, which can be found on the Internal Revenue Service's Web site (www.irs.gov/pub/irs-pdf/f2553.pdf), generally must be filed on or before the fifteenth day of the third month of the corporation's tax year. An election which is filed late generally becomes effective the first day of the following tax year. All shareholders must consent to the election. In addition, three conditions must be satisfied:

1. The corporation is a domestic corporation (i.e., organized or incorporated in the United States).

2. The corporation has no more than 100 shareholders who are individuals, estates, or certain types of trusts. Other corporations, partnerships, non-qualifying trusts, and nonresident aliens may not be shareholders. Pursuant to the American Jobs Creation Act of 2004, an election may be made to treat all family members as one shareholder. A family includes a common ancestor as well as lineal descendants for six generations.

3. The corporation may have only one class of stock. Different voting rights associated with different shares of common stock will not be construed as a violation of the one class of stock rule.

An S corporation may own one or more 80%-or-more-owned C corporations. An S corporation, however, may not file a consolidated return with its affiliated C corporations. Further, an S corporation may own one or more qualified Subchapter

S subsidiaries (QSSS). A QSSS is a domestic corporation that qualifies as an S corporation and is 100% owned by another S corporation, which makes an election to treat it as a QSSS. It should be noted that the assets, liabilities, income, deductions, and credits of a QSSS are considered to be the assets, liabilities, income, deductions, and credits of the parent S corporation.

The decision to elect S corporation status should be based on the following:

- An extremely profitable C corporation will generally pay more income tax than the tax levied on the shareholders of an S corporation.

- Corporations that become S corporations at inception are not subject to corporate tax upon liquidation.

- S corporations are not liable for the alternative minimum tax.

- Small C corporations, which generally strip their profits by paying additional salaries to their owner-employees, may derive no additional benefit by electing S corporation status.

- Some states do not recognize S corporation status. Accordingly, there may be no savings of tax at the state level.

- Certain states that do recognize S corporation status require nonresident shareholders to report their respective pass-through items. Accordingly, nonresident tax returns may be required.

Computing Taxable Income

With certain exceptions, the computation of an S corporation's taxable income is similar to the computation of the taxable income of a C corporation. Since an S corporation is a flow-through entity, any items of income, deduction, gain, loss, or credit which would receive special handling or treatment on the returns of the shareholders are passed through and accounted for separately. All other items are considered in the computation of the corporation's taxable income. Some of the more common items that are passed through and accounted for separately are:

- Capital gains and losses.
- Ordinary gains and losses properly reported on Form 4797.
- Gains and losses on the disposition of tangible depreciable property used in the trade or business activity of the corporation.
- Donations to charitable organizations.
- Interest income derived from tax-exempt securities.
- Portfolio income such as interest and dividend income.
- Income and deductions attributable to passive activity.

Shareholders must report on their tax returns a pro rata portion of the items which are separately stated in addition to a pro rata portion of the corporation's taxable income which is not separately computed. Whether or not the shareholders received distributions is irrelevant.

S Corporations may not deduct net operating losses since they pass through to the shareholders on a pro rata basis. Ownership of stock at the end of the year is not necessary in order to deduct a portion of the corporation's net operating loss, because the proration of the loss is based on the days of ownership. Losses, however, may be deducted only to the extent of the shareholder's basis in: (1) the corporate stock held during the year, and (2) any indebtedness owed to the shareholder by the corporation. In the event that a net operating loss is not deductible because basis does not exceed zero, the shareholder may carry forward the losses indefinitely until basis does exist.

Distribution to Shareholders

With respect to distributions by an S corporation that has accumulated earnings and profits from its days as a C corporation, a four-level system is to be followed:

- *Level-one distributions* are treated as nontaxable returns of capital since these distributions are derived from the accumulated adjustments account (AAA). AAA is essentially the post-1982 taxable income of the S corporation reported by the shareholders, reduced by certain nondeductible expenses of the corporation.

- *Level-two distributions* are taxed as dividends since they are traced to the corporation's accumulated earnings and profits earned from operating as a C corporation.

- *Level-three distributions* reduce the basis of the shareholder's stock and accordingly represent tax-free distributions.

- *Level-four distributions* result in the recognition of capital gain.

Corporations that have elected S status from inception obviously need not be concerned with level two distributions.

Basis of S Corporation Stock

In determining the basis of S corporation stock, the starting point is either the price paid in a stock purchase or the initial contribution to capital in exchange for the stock. The shareholder's basis is then increased by his or her ratable share of separately stated and non-separately stated items of income. The shareholder's basis is reduced, in order, by: (1) distributions representing a return of capital (i.e., level-one and level-three distributions), (2) his or her ratable share of corporate loss and deductions, whether or not separately stated, and (3) all expenses not deducted in computing taxable income and not properly charged to the capital account. The fair market value of property distributions, it should be noted, reduces the shareholder's basis in stock. In no event may the basis in stock go below zero. Since the shareholder's deduction of net operating losses of S corporations is affected by the shareholder's basis in his or her stock, planning is crucial. If the shareholder's basis in stock is insufficient, loans to the corporation should be considered. Caution must be exercised because the payback of the loan might result in a taxable situation.

Shareholder/Employee Benefits

A problem arises in the case of fringe benefits paid to shareholders possessing more than 2% of the corporation's outstanding stock. If a shareholder, at any time during the year, actually or by virtue of the attribution rules of IRC Sec. 318, owned more than 2% of the corporation's outstanding stock (or more than 2% of the total voting power), then the following fringe benefits, while normally tax-free, will be taxable:

- The exclusion under IRC Sec. 105(b)-(d) of amounts paid pursuant to certain accident and health plans.

- The exclusion under IRC Sec. 106 of employer-paid accident and health insurance plans.

- The $50,000 group term life insurance premium exclusion under IRC Sec. 79.

The Internal Revenue Service has great latitude in defining fringe benefits. Accordingly, the above list of fringe benefits should not be construed as all inclusive.

Tax Year

An S corporation, in general, must adopt a calendar year. A fiscal year is available if it can be demonstrated that there is a bona fide business purpose for the fiscal year. Additionally, under IRC Sec. 444, an S corporation may adopt a fiscal year if the deferral period for the year is not more than three months. If a fiscal year is adopted, liability may exist for an annual "required payment" which essentially represents the prepayment of tax on the income attributable to the deferral period.

PITFALLS IN CONVERTING FROM A C CORPORATION TO AN S CORPORATION

The conversion from C corporation status to S corporation status may result in certain problems as discussed in the following:

Passive Investment Income Tax

The possibility of the passive investment income tax is only applicable to an S corporation that was previously a C corporation. Tax liability arises when the S corporation: (1) has Subchapter C earnings and profits, and (2) more than 25% of its income is in the form of passive investment income (which includes rents, royalties, interest, dividends, annuities, and capital gains resulting from the disposition of stock and securities). The tax is imposed at the highest rate of corporate tax. The base subject to tax is the lesser of: (1) excess net passive income, or (2) current taxable income, computed as if the corporation were a C corporation. Excess net passive income is equal to the entity's net passive investment income multiplied by a fraction (the numerator of which is the excess of passive investment income over 25% of gross income, the denominator of which is the passive investment income). It becomes obvious that in order to avoid the imposition of this tax, dividend distributions should be considered.

Built-In Gains Tax

The built-in gains tax is a corporate-level tax imposed under IRC Sec. 1374. The tax is imposed on the built-in gains attributable to assets disposed within five years after converting to S corporation status. An asset's built-in gain is its appreciation in value while held by the C corporation. The tax is imposed at the highest corporate

rate multiplied by the lesser of the current year: (1) recognized built-in gain, or (2) taxable income computed as if the corporation were a C corporation.

Termination and Revocation

Three situations may result in revocation or termination of the S corporation election:

1. Revocation by shareholders owning more than 50% of the outstanding stock of the corporation.

2. The corporation ceases to qualify as an S corporation.

3. The corporation has passive investment income in excess of 25% of its gross income for three consecutive years. Termination will result, however, only if the corporation has accumulated earnings and profits (from its days as a C corporation) at the end of each of these three years.

In the case of a revocation by shareholders owning more than 50% of the outstanding stock, the effective date is the first day of the year if the election is made on or before the fifteenth day of the third month of the tax year. Otherwise, the revocation becomes effective on the first day of the following tax year.

In the case of an election that is terminated because the corporation ceases to qualify as an S corporation, the effective date is the date of cessation of operations as an S corporation. This will require that the tax year be split into two short years, with a proration of tax due on the income attributable to the days as a C corporation.

The effective date of a termination due to the passive investment income limitation is the first day of the fourth year (i.e., after the three consecutive years rule is met).

SAMPLE FILLED-IN TAX FORMS

Presented in Exhibits 59-1 and 59-2 are (1) the adjusted trial balance and (2) filled-in Form 1120, U.S. Corporation Income Tax Return, for Karen, Katie and Michael Corp. for the year ended December 31, 2017 (i.e., the initial year of the corporation). In this example, the corporation is a C corporation, as opposed to an S corporation. Further, the machinery was placed into service on September 15, 2017.

Exhibit 59-1:   Sample Adjusted Trial Balance for a C Corporation

KAREN, KATIE AND MICHAEL CORP.
Adjusted Trial Balance
12/31/2017

No.	Description	Trial Balance Debit	Trial Balance Credit
1001	CASH IN BANK - CHECKING	257,100	
1031	ACCOUNTS RECEIVABLE	41,460	
1051	INVENTORY	6,830	
1521	MACHINERY	113,200	
1621	ACCUM DEPRECIATION		113,200
1801	DEPOSITS	150	
1821	PREPAID EXPENSES	127,620	
2200	PAYROLL TAXES PAYABLE		23,236
2205	NOTES PAYABLE - LONG TERM		126,803
2207	NOTES PAYABLE - SHAREHOLDER		82,630
2208	NOTE PAYABLE - CURRENT		8,749
2216	ACCRUED EXPENSES		17,473
2218	ACCOUNTS PAYABLE		15,374
3000	CAPITAL STOCK		6,000
4001	SALES		846,675
5001	PURCHASES	107,538	
5021	ENDING INVENTORY		6,830
6001	SALARIES - OFFICER	128,435	
6021	SALARIES - OTHERS	118,080	
6031	PAYROLL TAXES	15,890	
6041	ADVERTISING	3,336	
6051	AUTO EXPENSES	26,883	
6071	COMPUTER EXPENSES	4,879	
6091	DEPRECIATION/AMORTIZATION	113,200	
6101	DUES AND SUBSCRIPTIONS	462	
6121	EMPLOYEE BENEFITS	3,525	
6131	HOSPITALIZATION INSURANCE	2,586	
6141	INSURANCE - GENERAL	11,545	
6161	INTEREST	2,659	
6171	OFFICE EXPENSES	8,504	
6181	PROFESSIONAL FEES	7,990	
6201	REPAIRS AND MAINTENANCE	18,375	
6211	POSTAGE AND SHIPPING	7,477	
6221	STORAGE	2,700	
6241	STATE FRANCHISE TAX	1,325	
6251	MISCELLANEOUS TAXES	1,315	
6261	TELEPHONE	9,547	
6271	TRAVEL AND ENTERTAINMENT	1,882	
6281	UTILITIES	5,940	
6311	FINES AND PENALTIES	269	
6331	ROYALTIES	25,200	
8031	FEDERAL INCOME TAX	71,068	
	Total	1,246,970	1,246,970

Exhibit 59-2: Sample Filled-In Form 1120 for a C Corporation

Form **1120**	U.S. Corporation Income Tax Return	OMB No. 1545-0123
Department of the Treasury Internal Revenue Service	For calendar year 2017 or tax year beginning _____ , ending _____ ▶ Go to *www.irs.gov/Form1120* for instructions and the latest information.	**2017**

A Check if:
1a Consolidated return (attach Form 851) ☐
b Life/nonlife consolidated return ☐
2 Personal holding co. (attach Sch. PH) ☐
3 Personal service corp. (see instructions) ☐
4 Schedule M-3 attached ☐

TYPE OR PRINT	Name **KAREN, KATIE & MICHAEL CORP.**	**B** Employer Identification number **99-9999999**
	Number, street, and room or suite no. If a P.O. box, see instructions. **123 ANY STREET**	**C** Date incorporated **01/01/2017**
	City or town, state, or province, country, and ZIP or foreign postal code **ANY CITY NY 99999**	**D** Total assets (see instructions) **$ 433,160**

E Check if: (1) Initial return ☐ (2) Final return ☐ (3) Name change ☐ (4) Address change ☐

Income

1a	Gross receipts or sales	1a	846,675
b	Returns and allowances	1b	
c	Balance. Subtract line 1b from line 1a	1c	846,675
2	Cost of goods sold (attach Form 1125-A)	2	100,708
3	Gross profit. Subtract line 2 from line 1c	3	745,967
4	Dividends (Schedule C, line 19)	4	
5	Interest	5	
6	Gross rents	6	
7	Gross royalties	7	
8	Capital gain net income (attach Schedule D (Form 1120))	8	
9	Net gain or (loss) from Form 4797, Part II, line 17 (attach Form 4797)	9	
10	Other income (see instructions—attach statement)	10	
11	**Total income.** Add lines 3 through 10 ▶	11	745,967

Deductions (See instructions for limitations on deductions.)

12	Compensation of officers (see instructions—attach Form 1125-E) ▶	12	128,435
13	Salaries and wages (less employment credits)	13	118,080
14	Repairs and maintenance	14	18,375
15	Bad debts	15	
16	Rents	16	
17	Taxes and licenses	17	18,530
18	Interest	18	2,659
19	Charitable contributions	19	
20	Depreciation from Form 4562 not claimed on Form 1125-A or elsewhere on return (attach Form 4562)	20	113,200
21	Depletion	21	
22	Advertising	22	3,336
23	Pension, profit-sharing, etc., plans	23	
24	Employee benefit programs	24	3,525
25	Domestic production activities deduction (attach Form 8903)	25	
26	Other deductions (attach statement) SEE STMT	26	114,654
27	**Total deductions.** Add lines 12 through 26 ▶	27	520,794
28	Taxable income before net operating loss deduction and special deductions. Subtract line 27 from line 11	28	225,173
29a	Net operating loss deduction (see instructions)	29a	
b	Special deductions (Schedule C, line 20)	29b	
c	Add lines 29a and 29b	29c	

Tax, Refundable Credits, and Payments

30	**Taxable income.** Subtract line 29c from line 28. See instructions	30	225,173
31	Total tax (Schedule J, Part I, line 11)	31	71,068
32	Total payments and refundable credits (Schedule J, Part II, line 21)	32	71,068
33	Estimated tax penalty. See instructions. Check if Form 2220 is attached ▶ ☐	33	
34	Amount owed. If line 32 is smaller than the total of lines 31 and 33, enter amount owed	34	
35	Overpayment. If line 32 is larger than the total of lines 31 and 33, enter amount overpaid	35	
36	Enter amount from line 35 you want: Credited to 2018 estimated tax ▶ _____ Refunded ▶	36	

Sign Here
Under penalties of perjury, I declare that I have examined this return, including accompanying schedules and statements, and to the best of my knowledge and belief, it is true, correct, and complete. Declaration of preparer (other than taxpayer) is based on all information of which preparer has any knowledge.

Signature of officer _____ Date _____ Title _____

May the IRS discuss this return with the preparer shown below? See instructions. ☐ Yes ☐ No

Paid Preparer Use Only

Print/Type preparer's name	Preparer's signature	Date	Check ☐ if self-employed	PTIN
Firm's name ▶			Firm's EIN ▶	
Firm's address ▶			Phone no.	

For Paperwork Reduction Act Notice, see separate instructions.
DAA

Form **1120** (2017)

Exhibit 59-2: Sample Filled-In Form 1120 for a C Corporation *(Continued)*

Form 1120 (2017)   KAREN, KATIE & MICHAEL CORP.   99-9999999   Page **2**

Schedule C	Dividends and Special Deductions (see instructions)	(a) Dividends received	(b) %	(c) Special deductions (a) x (b)
1	Dividends from less-than-20%-owned domestic corporations (other than debt-financed stock)		70	
2	Dividends from 20%-or-more-owned domestic corporations (other than debt-financed stock)		80	
3	Dividends on debt-financed stock of domestic and foreign corporations		see instructions	
4	Dividends on certain preferred stock of less-than-20%-owned public utilities		42	
5	Dividends on certain preferred stock of 20%-or-more-owned public utilities		48	
6	Dividends from less-than-20%-owned foreign corporations and certain FSCs		70	
7	Dividends from 20%-or-more-owned foreign corporations and certain FSCs		80	
8	Dividends from wholly owned foreign subsidiaries		100	
9	Total. Add lines 1 through 8. See instructions for limitation			
10	Dividends from domestic corporations received by a small business investment company operating under the Small Business Investment Act of 1958		100	
11	Dividends from affiliated group members		100	
12	Dividends from certain FSCs		100	
13	Dividends from foreign corporations not included on line 3, 6, 7, 8, 11, or 12			
14	Income from controlled foreign corporations under subpart F (attach Form(s) 5471)			
15	Foreign dividend gross-up			
16	IC-DISC and former DISC dividends not included on line 1, 2, or 3			
17	Other dividends			
18	Deduction for dividends paid on certain preferred stock of public utilities			
19	Total dividends. Add lines 1 through 17. Enter here and on page 1, line 4 ▶			
20	Total special deductions. Add lines 9, 10, 11, 12, and 18. Enter here and on page 1, line 29b ▶			

Form **1120** (2017)

DAA

Exhibit 59-2: ***Sample Filled-In Form 1120 for a C Corporation***
(Continued)

Form 1120 (2017) KAREN, KATIE & MICHAEL CORP.		99-9999999		Page **3**

Schedule J   Tax Computation and Payment (see instructions)

Part I—Tax Computation

1	Check if the corporation is a member of a controlled group (attach Schedule O (Form 1120)). See instructions ▶ ☐		
2	Income tax. Check if a qualified personal service corporation. See instructions ▶ ☐	**2**	71,068
3	Alternative minimum tax (attach Form 4626)	**3**	
4	Add lines 2 and 3	**4**	71,068
5a	Foreign tax credit (attach Form 1118) **5a**		
b	Credit from Form 8834 (see instructions) **5b**		
c	General business credit (attach Form 3800) **5c**		
d	Credit for prior year minimum tax (attach Form 8827) **5d**		
e	Bond credits from Form 8912 **5e**		
6	**Total credits.** Add lines 5a through 5e	**6**	0
7	Subtract line 6 from line 4	**7**	71,068
8	Personal holding company tax (attach Schedule PH (Form 1120))	**8**	
9a	Recapture of investment credit (attach Form 4255) **9a**		
b	Recapture of low-income housing credit (attach Form 8611) **9b**		
c	Interest due under the look-back method—completed long-term contracts (attach Form 8697) **9c**		
d	Interest due under the look-back method—income forecast method (attach Form 8866) **9d**		
e	Alternative tax on qualifying shipping activities (attach Form 8902) **9e**		
f	Other (see instructions—attach statement) **9f**		
10	**Total.** Add lines 9a through 9f	**10**	
11	**Total tax.** Add lines 7, 8, and 10. Enter here and on page 1, line 31	**11**	71,068

Part II—Payments and Refundable Credits

12	2016 overpayment credited to 2017	**12**	
13	2017 estimated tax payments	**13**	71,068
14	2017 refund applied for on Form 4466	**14**	( )
15	Combine lines 12, 13, and 14	**15**	71,068
16	Tax deposited with Form 7004	**16**	
17	Withholding (see instructions)	**17**	
18	**Total payments.** Add lines 15, 16, and 17	**18**	71,068
19	Refundable credits from:		
a	Form 2439 **19a**		
b	Form 4136 **19b**		
c	Form 8827, line 8c **19c**		
d	Other (attach statement—see instructions) **19d**		
20	**Total credits.** Add lines 19a through 19d	**20**	
21	**Total payments and credits.** Add lines 18 and 20. Enter here and on page 1, line 32	**21**	71,068

Schedule K   Other Information (see instructions)

		Yes	No
1	Check accounting method: a ☐ Cash b ☒ Accrual c ☐ Other (specify) ▶		
2	See the instructions and enter the:		
a	Business activity code no. ▶ **334110**		
b	Business activity ▶ **MANUFACTURING**		
c	Product or service ▶ **COMPUTERS**		
3	Is the corporation a subsidiary in an affiliated group or a parent-subsidiary controlled group?		X
	If "Yes," enter name and EIN of the parent corporation ▶		
4	At the end of the tax year:		
a	Did any foreign or domestic corporation, partnership (including any entity treated as a partnership), trust, or tax-exempt organization own directly 20% or more, or own, directly or indirectly, 50% or more of the total voting power of all classes of the corporation's stock entitled to vote? If "Yes," complete Part I of Schedule G (Form 1120) (attach Schedule G)		X
b	Did any individual or estate own directly 20% or more, or own, directly or indirectly, 50% or more of the total voting power of all classes of the corporation's stock entitled to vote? If "Yes," complete Part II of Schedule G (Form 1120) (attach Schedule G)		X

Form **1120** (2017)

DAA

Exhibit 59-2:   Sample Filled-In Form 1120 for a C Corporation
(Continued)

Form 1120 (2017)   **KAREN, KATIE & MICHAEL CORP.**   99-9999999   Page **4**

Schedule K	**Other Information** *(continued from page 3)*

		Yes	No

5   At the end of the tax year, did the corporation:

a   Own directly 20% or more, or own, directly or indirectly, 50% or more of the total voting power of all classes of stock entitled to vote of any foreign or domestic corporation not included on **Form 851,** Affiliations Schedule? For rules of constructive ownership, see instructions. | | **X**

If "Yes," complete (i) through (iv) below.

(i) Name of Corporation	(ii) Employer Identification Number (if any)	(iii) Country of Incorporation	(iv) Percentage Owned in Voting Stock

b   Own directly an interest of 20% or more, or own, directly or indirectly, an interest of 50% or more in any foreign or domestic partnership (including an entity treated as a partnership) or in the beneficial interest of a trust? For rules of constructive ownership, see instructions. | | **X**

If "Yes," complete (i) through (iv) below.

(i) Name of Entity	(ii) Employer Identification Number (if any)	(iii) Country of Organization	(iv) Maximum Percentage Owned in Profit, Loss, or Capital

6   During this tax year, did the corporation pay dividends (other than stock dividends and distributions in exchange for stock) in excess of the corporation's current and accumulated earnings and profits? See sections 301 and 316 | | **X**
If "Yes," file **Form 5452,** Corporate Report of Nondividend Distributions. See the instructions for Form 5452.
If this is a consolidated return, answer here for the parent corporation and on Form 851 for each subsidiary.

7   At any time during the tax year, did one foreign person own, directly or indirectly, at least 25% of the total voting power of all classes of the corporation's stock entitled to vote or at least 25% of the total value of all classes of the corporation's stock? | | **X**
For rules of attribution, see section 318. If "Yes," enter:
(a)   Percentage owned ▶ ....   and (b) Owner's country ▶
(c)   The corporation may have to file **Form 5472,** Information Return of a 25% Foreign-Owned U.S. Corporation or a Foreign Corporation Engaged in a U.S. Trade or Business. Enter the number of Forms 5472 attached ▶

8   Check this box if the corporation issued publicly offered debt instruments with original issue discount   ▶ ☐
If checked, the corporation may have to file **Form 8281,** Information Return for Publicly Offered Original Issue Discount Instruments.

9   Enter the amount of tax-exempt interest received or accrued during the tax year ▶ $ 0

10 Enter the number of shareholders at the end of the tax year (if 100 or fewer) ▶

11 If the corporation has an NOL for the tax year and is electing to forego the carryback period, check here   ▶ ☐
If the corporation is filing a consolidated return, the statement required by Regulations section 1.1502-21(b)(3) must be attached or the election won't be valid.

12 Enter the available NOL carryover from prior tax years (do not reduce it by any deduction reported on page 1, line 29a.)   ▶ $

13 Are the corporation's total receipts (page 1, line 1a, plus lines 4 through 10) for the tax year **and** its total assets at the end of the tax year less than $250,000? | | **X**
If "Yes," the corporation is not required to complete Schedules L, M-1, and M-2. Instead, enter the total amount of cash distributions and the book value of property distributions (other than cash) made during the tax year ▶ $

14 Is the corporation required to file Schedule UTP (Form 1120), Uncertain Tax Position Statement? See instructions | | **X**
If "Yes," complete and attach Schedule UTP.

15a Did the corporation make any payments in 2017 that would require it to file Form(s) 1099? | | **X**
b   If "Yes," did or will the corporation file required Forms 1099? | | **X**

16 During this tax year, did the corporation have an 80% or more change in ownership, including a change due to redemption of its own stock? | | **X**

17 During or subsequent to this tax year, but before the filing of this return, did the corporation dispose of more than 65% (by value) of its assets in a taxable, non-taxable, or tax deferred transaction? | | **X**

18 Did the corporation receive assets in a section 351 transfer in which any of the transferred assets had a fair market basis or fair market value of more than $1 million? | | **X**

19 During the corporation's tax year, did the corporation make any payments that would require it to file Forms 1042 and 1042-S under chapter 3 (sections 1441 through 1464) or chapter 4 (sections 1471 through 1474) of the Code? | | **X**

Form **1120** (2017)

DAA

Exhibit 59-2:   Sample Filled-In Form 1120 for a C Corporation (Continued)

Form 1120 (2017)   **KAREN, KATIE & MICHAEL CORP.**   99-9999999   Page 5

Schedule L   Balance Sheets per Books

	Assets	Beginning of tax year (a)	(b)	End of tax year (c)	(d)
1	Cash				257,100
2a	Trade notes and accounts receivable			41,460	
b	Less allowance for bad debts				41,460
3	Inventories				6,830
4	U.S. government obligations				
5	Tax-exempt securities (see instructions)				
6	Other current assets (att. stmt.) STMT 2				127,620
7	Loans to shareholders				
8	Mortgage and real estate loans				
9	Other investments (attach stmt.)				
10a	Buildings and other depreciable assets			113,200	
b	Less accumulated depreciation			113,200	0
11a	Depletable assets				
b	Less accumulated depletion				
12	Land (net of any amortization)				
13a	Intangible assets (amortizable only)				
b	Less accumulated amortization				
14	Other assets (attach stmt.) STMT 3				150
15	Total assets		0		433,160
	Liabilities and Shareholders' Equity				
16	Accounts payable				15,374
17	Mortgages, notes, bonds payable in less than 1 year				8,749
18	Other current liabilities (att. stmt.) STMT 4				40,709
19	Loans from shareholders				82,630
20	Mortgages, notes, bonds payable in 1 year or more				126,803
21	Other liabilities (attach statement)				
22	Capital stock: a Preferred stock				
	b Common stock			6,000	6,000
23	Additional paid-in capital				
24	Retained earnings—Appropriated (att. stmt.)				
25	Retained earnings—Unappropriated				152,895
26	Adjustments to SH equity (att. stmt.)				
27	Less cost of treasury stock				( )
28	Total liabilities and shareholders' equity		0		433,160

Schedule M-1   Reconciliation of Income (Loss) per Books With Income per Return

Note: The corporation may be required to file Schedule M-3. See instructions.

1	Net income (loss) per books	152,895	7	Income recorded on books this year not included on this return (itemize):		
2	Federal income tax per books	71,068				
3	Excess of capital losses over capital gains			Tax-exempt interest $		
4	Income subject to tax not recorded on books this year (itemize):					
			8	Deductions on this return not charged against book income this year (itemize):		
5	Expenses recorded on books this year not deducted on this return (itemize):		a	Depreciation $		
a	Depreciation $		b	Charitable contributions $		
b	Charitable contributions $					
c	Travel and entertainment $ 941					
	STMT 5 269	1,210	9	Add lines 7 and 8		
6	Add lines 1 through 5	225,173	10	Income (page 1, line 28)—line 6 less line 9		225,173

Schedule M-2   Analysis of Unappropriated Retained Earnings per Books (Line 25, Schedule L)

1	Balance at beginning of year	0	5	Distributions: a Cash		
2	Net income (loss) per books	152,895		b Stock		
3	Other increases (itemize):			c Property		
			6	Other decreases (itemize):		
			7	Add lines 5 and 6		
4	Add lines 1, 2, and 3	152,895	8	Balance at end of year (line 4 less line 7)		152,895

Form **1120** (2017)

DAA

Exhibit 59-2:   Sample Filled-In Form 1120 for a C Corporation
(Continued)

Form **1125-A**		**Cost of Goods Sold**		
(Rev. October 2016) Department of the Treasury Internal Revenue Service		▶ Attach to Form 1120, 1120-C, 1120-F, 1120S, 1065, or 1065-B. ▶ Information about Form 1125-A and its instructions is at *www.irs.gov/form1125a.*		OMB No. 1545-0123

Name	Employer identification number
KAREN, KATIE & MICHAEL CORP.	99-9999999

1	Inventory at beginning of year	**1**	
2	Purchases	**2**	107,538
3	Cost of labor	**3**	
4	Additional section 263A costs (attach schedule)	**4**	
5	Other costs (attach schedule)	**5**	
6	**Total.** Add lines 1 through 5	**6**	107,538
7	Inventory at end of year	**7**	6,830
8	**Cost of goods sold.** Subtract line 7 from line 6. Enter here and on Form 1120, page 1, line 2 or the appropriate line of your tax return. See instructions	**8**	100,708

9a Check all methods used for valuing closing inventory:
   (i) ☐ Cost
   (ii) ☒ Lower of cost or market
   (iii) ☐ Other (Specify method used and attach explanation.) ▶

b Check if there was a writedown of subnormal goods .... ▶ ☐

c Check if the LIFO inventory method was adopted this tax year for any goods (if checked, attach Form 970) .... ▶ ☐

d If the LIFO inventory method was used for this tax year, enter amount of closing inventory computed under LIFO ..... | **9d** |

e If property is produced or acquired for resale, do the rules of section 263A apply to the entity? See instructions .... ☐ Yes ☒ No

f Was there any change in determining quantities, cost, or valuations between opening and closing inventory? If "Yes," attach explanation .... ☐ Yes ☒ No

For Paperwork Reduction Act Notice, see instructions.   Form **1125-A** (Rev. 10-2016)

DAA

Exhibit 59-2: Sample Filled-In Form 1120 for a C Corporation *(Continued)*

Form 1125-E
(Rev. October 2016)
Department of the Treasury
Internal Revenue Service

Compensation of Officers

▶ Attach to Form 1120, 1120-C, 1120-F, 1120-REIT, 1120-RIC, or 1120S.

▶ Information about Form 1125-E and its separate instructions is at *www.irs.gov/form1125e.*

OMB No. 1545-0123

Name	Employer identification number
KAREN, KATIE & MICHAEL CORP.	99-9999999

Note: Complete Form 1125-E only if total receipts are $500,000 or more. See instructions for definition of total receipts.

(a) Name of officer	(b) Social security number (see instructions)	(c) Percent of time devoted to business	Percent of stock owned		(f) Amount of compensation
			(d) Common	(e) Preferred	
1 MICHAEL LIGHTYEAR	999-99-9999	100.000 %	33.333%	%	128,435
		%	%	%	
		%	%	%	
		%	%	%	
		%	%	%	
		%	%	%	
		%	%	%	
		%	%	%	
		%	%	%	
		%	%	%	
		%	%	%	
		%	%	%	
		%	%	%	
		%	%	%	
		%	%	%	
		%	%	%	
		%	%	%	
		%	%	%	
		%	%	%	

2	Total compensation of officers	**2**	128,435
3	Compensation of officers claimed on Form 1125-A or elsewhere on return	**3**	
4	Subtract line 3 from line 2. Enter the result here and on Form 1120, page 1, line 12 or the appropriate line of your tax return	**4**	128,435

For Paperwork Reduction Act Notice, see separate instructions.

Form **1125-E** (Rev. 10-2016)

DAA

Exhibit 59-2: Sample Filled-In Form 1120 for a C Corporation
(Continued)

Form **4562**	**Depreciation and Amortization**	OMB No. 1545-0172
Department of the Treasury Internal Revenue Service (99)	**(Including Information on Listed Property)** ▶ Attach to your tax return. ▶ Go to *www.irs.gov/Form4562* for instructions and the latest information.	**2017** Attachment Sequence No. **179**

Name(s) shown on return: **KAREN, KATIE & MICHAEL CORP.**   Identifying number: **99-9999999**

Business or activity to which this form relates: **REGULAR DEPRECIATION**

Part I — Election To Expense Certain Property Under Section 179

Note: If you have any listed property, complete Part V before you complete Part I.

#		
1	Maximum amount (see instructions)	510,000
2	Total cost of section 179 property placed in service (see instructions)	113,200
3	Threshold cost of section 179 property before reduction in limitation (see instructions)	2,030,000
4	Reduction in limitation. Subtract line 3 from line 2. If zero or less, enter -0-	0
5	Dollar limitation for tax year. Subtract line 4 from line 1. If zero or less, enter -0-. If married filing separately, see instructions	510,000

6 (a) Description of property	(b) Cost (business use only)	(c) Elected cost
MACHINERY	113,200	113,200

#		
7	Listed property. Enter the amount from line 29	
8	Total elected cost of section 179 property. Add amounts in column (c), lines 6 and 7	113,200
9	Tentative deduction. Enter the smaller of line 5 or line 8	113,200
10	Carryover of disallowed deduction from line 13 of your 2016 Form 4562	
11	Business income limitation. Enter the smaller of business income (not less than zero) or line 5 (see instructions)	338,373
12	Section 179 expense deduction. Add lines 9 and 10, but don't enter more than line 11	113,200
13	Carryover of disallowed deduction to 2018. Add lines 9 and 10, less line 12 ▶ 13	

Note: Don't use Part II or Part III below for listed property. Instead, use Part V.

Part II — Special Depreciation Allowance and Other Depreciation (Don't include listed property.) (See instructions.)

#		
14	Special depreciation allowance for qualified property (other than listed property) placed in service during the tax year (see instructions)	
15	Property subject to section 168(f)(1) election	
16	Other depreciation (including ACRS)	

Part III — MACRS Depreciation (Don't include listed property.) (See instructions.)

Section A

#		
17	MACRS deductions for assets placed in service in tax years beginning before 2017	0
18	If you are electing to group any assets placed in service during the tax year into one or more general asset accounts, check here ▶ ☐	

Section B—Assets Placed in Service During 2017 Tax Year Using the General Depreciation System

(a) Classification of property	(b) Month and year placed in service	(c) Basis for depreciation (business/investment use only—see instructions)	(d) Recovery period	(e) Convention	(f) Method	(g) Depreciation deduction
19a 3-year property						
b 5-year property						
c 7-year property						
d 10-year property						
e 15-year property						
f 20-year property						
g 25-year property			25 yrs.		S/L	
h Residential rental property			27.5 yrs.	MM	S/L	
			27.5 yrs.	MM	S/L	
i Nonresidential real property			39 yrs.	MM	S/L	
				MM	S/L	

Section C—Assets Placed in Service During 2017 Tax Year Using the Alternative Depreciation System

20a Class life					S/L	
b 12-year			12 yrs.		S/L	
c 40-year			40 yrs.	MM	S/L	

Part IV — Summary (See instructions.)

#		
21	Listed property. Enter amount from line 28	
22	Total. Add amounts from line 12, lines 14 through 17, lines 19 and 20 in column (g), and line 21. Enter here and on the appropriate lines of your return. Partnerships and S corporations—see instructions	113,200
23	For assets shown above and placed in service during the current year, enter the portion of the basis attributable to section 263A costs	

For Paperwork Reduction Act Notice, see separate instructions.

DAA   THERE ARE NO AMOUNTS FOR PAGE 2   Form **4562** (2017)

Exhibit 59-2:   Sample Filled-In Form 1120 for a C Corporation
(Continued)

99-9999999	**Federal Statements**

Statement 1 - Form 1120, Page 1, Line 26 - Other Deductions

Description	Amount
AUTOMOBILE EXPENSES	$ 26,883
COMPUTER EXPENSES	4,879
DUES AND SUBSCRIPTIONS	462
GENERAL INSURANCE	11,545
HOSPITALIZATION INSURANCE	2,586
OFFICE EXPENSES	8,504
POSTAGE & SHIPPING	7,477
PROFESSIONAL FEES	7,990
ROYALTIES	25,200
STORAGE	2,700
TELEPHONE	9,547
UTILITIES	5,940
50% OF MEALS & ENTERTAINMENT	941
TOTAL	$ 114,654

Statement 2 - Form 1120, Page 5, Schedule L, Line 6 - Other Current Assets

Description	Beginning of Year	End of Year
PREPAID EXPENSES	$	$ 127,620
TOTAL	$ 0	$ 127,620

Statement 3 - Form 1120, Page 5, Schedule L, Line 14 - Other Assets

Description	Beginning of Year	End of Year
DEPOSITS	$	$ 150
TOTAL	$ 0	$ 150

Statement 4 - Form 1120, Page 5, Schedule L, Line 18 - Other Current Liabilities

Description	Beginning of Year	End of Year
ACCRUED EXPENSES AND TAXES	$	$ 17,473
PAYROLL TAXES PAYABLE		23,236
TOTAL	$ 0	$ 40,709

Statement 5 - Form 1120, Page 5, Schedule M-1, Line 5 - Expenses on Books Not on Return

Description	Amount
FINES AND PENALTIES	$ 269
TOTAL	$ 269

Presented in Exhibits 59-3 and 59-4 are (1) the adjusted trial balance and (2) filled-in Form 1120S, U.S. Corporation Income Tax Return for an S Corporation, for Karen, Katie and Michael Corp. for the year ended December 31, 2017 (i.e., the initial year of the corporation). In this example, the corporation is an S corporation, as opposed to a C corporation. It should be noted that (1) the trial balance in this example has been modified to eliminate any items specific to a C corporation, and (2) the machinery was placed into service on September 15, 2017.

Exhibit 59-3: Sample Adjusted Trial Balance for an S Corporation

KAREN, KATIE AND MICHAEL CORP.
Adjusted Trial Balance
12/31/2017

No.	Description	Trial Balance	
		Debit	Credit
1001	CASH IN BANK - CHECKING	257,100	
1031	ACCOUNTS RECEIVABLE	41,460	
1051	INVENTORY	6,830	
1521	MACHINERY	113,200	
1621	ACCUM DEPRECIATION		113,200
1801	DEPOSITS	150	
1821	PREPAID EXPENSES	127,620	
2200	PAYROLL TAXES PAYABLE		23,236
2205	NOTES PAYABLE - LONG TERM		126,803
2207	NOTES PAYABLE - SHAREHOLDER		82,630
2208	NOTE PAYABLE - CURRENT		8,749
2216	ACCRUED EXPENSES		17,473
2218	ACCOUNTS PAYABLE		15,374
3000	CAPITAL STOCK		6,000
4001	SALES		846,675
5001	PURCHASES	107,538	
5021	ENDING INVENTORY		6,830
6001	SALARIES - OFFICER	128,435	
6021	SALARIES - OTHERS	118,080	
6031	PAYROLL TAXES	15,890	
6041	ADVERTISING	3,336	
6051	AUTO EXPENSES	26,883	
6071	COMPUTER EXPENSES	4,879	
6091	DEPRECIATION/AMORTIZATION	113,200	
6101	DUES AND SUBSCRIPTIONS	462	
6121	EMPLOYEE BENEFITS	3,525	
6131	HOSPITALIZATION INSURANCE	2,586	
6141	INSURANCE - GENERAL	82,613	
6161	INTEREST	2,659	
6171	OFFICE EXPENSES	8,504	
6181	PROFESSIONAL FEES	7,990	
6201	REPAIRS AND MAINTENANCE	18,375	
6211	POSTAGE AND SHIPPING	7,477	
6221	STORAGE	2,700	
6241	STATE FRANCHISE TAX	1,325	
6251	MISCELLANEOUS TAXES	1,315	
6261	TELEPHONE	9,547	
6271	TRAVEL AND ENTERTAINMENT	1,882	
6281	UTILITIES	5,940	
6311	FINES AND PENALTIES	269	
6331	ROYALTIES	25,200	
	Total	1,246,970	1,246,970

Exhibit 59-4:   Sample Filled-In Form 1120 for an S Corporation

Form **1120S**		**U.S. Income Tax Return for an S Corporation**		OMB No. 1545-0123
Department of the Treasury Internal Revenue Service		▶ Do not file this form unless the corporation has filed or is attaching Form 2553 to elect to be an S corporation. ▶ Go to *www.irs.gov/Form1120S* for instructions and the latest information.		**2017**

For calendar year 2017 or tax year beginning _____ , ending _____

A S election effective date	**TYPE**	Name **KAREN, KATIE & MICHAEL CORP.**	**D** Employer identification number **99-9999999**	
B Business activity code number (see instructions) **334110**	**OR**	Number, street, and room or suite no. If a P.O. box, see instructions. **123 ANY STREET**	**E** Date incorporated **01/01/2017**	
C Check if Sch. M-3 attached ☐	**PRINT**	City or town, state or province, country, and ZIP or foreign postal code **ANY CITY NY 99999**	**F** Total assets (see instructions) $ **433,160**	

G Is the corporation electing to be an S corporation beginning with this tax year?   ☐ Yes   ☐ No   If "Yes," attach Form 2553 if not already filed

H Check if: **(1)** ☐ Final return   **(2)** ☐ Name change   **(3)** ☐ Address change   **(4)** ☐ Amended return   **(5)** ☐ S election termination or revocation

I Enter the number of shareholders who were shareholders during any part of the tax year   ▶   **3**

Caution. Include only trade or business income and expenses on lines 1a through 21. See the instructions for more information.

Income	**1a** Gross receipts or sales		**1a** 846,675	
	b Returns and allowances		**1b**	
	c Balance. Subtract line 1b from line 1a		**1c**	846,675
	2 Cost of goods sold (attach Form 1125-A)		**2**	100,708
	3 Gross profit. Subtract line 2 from line 1c		**3**	745,967
	4 Net gain (loss) from Form 4797, line 17 (attach Form 4797)		**4**	
	5 Other income (loss) (see instructions—attach statement)		**5**	
	6 **Total income (loss).** Add lines 3 through 5 ▶		**6**	745,967
Deductions (see instructions for limitations)	**7** Compensation of officers (see instructions—attach Form 1125-E)		**7**	128,435
	8 Salaries and wages (less employment credits)		**8**	118,080
	9 Repairs and maintenance		**9**	18,375
	10 Bad debts		**10**	
	11 Rents		**11**	
	12 Taxes and licenses		**12**	18,530
	13 Interest		**13**	2,659
	14 Depreciation not claimed on Form 1125-A or elsewhere on return (attach Form 4562)		**14**	
	15 Depletion (Do not deduct oil and gas depletion.)		**15**	
	16 Advertising		**16**	3,336
	17 Pension, profit-sharing, etc., plans		**17**	
	18 Employee benefit programs		**18**	3,525
	19 Other deductions (attach statement) **SEE STMT 1**		**19**	185,722
	20 Total deductions. Add lines 7 through 19 ▶		**20**	478,662
	21 **Ordinary business income (loss).** Subtract line 20 from line 6		**21**	267,305
Tax and Payments	**22a** Excess net passive income or LIFO recapture tax (see instructions)	**22a**		
	b Tax from Schedule D (Form 1120S)	**22b**		
	c Add lines 22a and 22b (see instructions for additional taxes)		**22c**	
	23a 2017 estimated tax payments and 2016 overpayment credited to 2017	**23a**		
	b Tax deposited with Form 7004	**23b**		
	c Credit for federal tax paid on fuels (attach Form 4136)	**23c**		
	d Add lines 23a through 23c		**23d**	
	24 Estimated tax penalty (see instructions). Check if Form 2220 is attached ▶ ☐		**24**	
	25 Amount owed. If line 23d is smaller than the total of lines 22c and 24, enter amount owed		**25**	
	26 Overpayment. If line 23d is larger than the total of lines 22c and 24, enter amount overpaid		**26**	
	27 Enter amount from line 26 Credited to 2018 estimated tax ▶ Refunded ▶		**27**	

Sign Here	Under penalties of perjury, I declare that I have examined this return, including accompanying schedules and statements, and to the best of my knowledge and belief, it is true, correct, and complete. Declaration of preparer (other than taxpayer) is based on all information of which preparer has any knowledge.				May the IRS discuss this return with the preparer shown below (see instructions)? ☐ Yes ☐ No
	▶ Signature of officer		Date	▶ Title	
Paid Preparer Use Only	Print/Type preparer's name	Preparer's signature	Date	Check ☐ if self-employed	PTIN
	Firm's name ▶			Firm's EIN ▶	
	Firm's address ▶			Phone no.	

For Paperwork Reduction Act Notice, see separate instructions.   Form **1120S** (2017)

DAA

Exhibit 59-4: Sample Filled-In Form 1120 for an S Corporation (Continued)

Form 1120S (2017)   **KAREN, KATIE & MICHAEL CORP.**   99-9999999   Page 2

Schedule B   Other Information (see instructions)

		Yes	No
1	Check accounting method: a ☐ Cash b ☒ Accrual c ☐ Other (specify) ▶		
2	See the instructions and enter the: a Business activity ▶ MANUFACTURING b Product or service ▶ COMPUTERS		
3	At any time during the tax year, was any shareholder of the corporation a disregarded entity, a trust, an estate, or a nominee or similar person? If "Yes," attach Schedule B-1, Information on Certain Shareholders of an S Corporation		X
4	At the end of the tax year, did the corporation:		
a	Own directly 20% or more, or own, directly or indirectly, 50% or more of the total stock issued and outstanding of any foreign or domestic corporation? For rules of constructive ownership, see instructions. If "Yes," complete (i) through (v) below		X

(i) Name of Corporation	(ii) Employer Identification Number (if any)	(iii) Country of Incorporation	(iv) Percentage of Stock Owned	(v) If Percentage in (iv) is 100%, Enter the Date (if any) a Qualified Subchapter S Subsidiary Election Was Made

		Yes	No
b	Own directly an interest of 20% or more, or own, directly or indirectly, an interest of 50% or more in the profit, loss, or capital in any foreign or domestic partnership (including an entity treated as a partnership) or in the beneficial interest of a trust? For rules of constructive ownership, see instructions. If "Yes," complete (i) through (v) below		X

(i) Name of Entity	(ii) Employer Identification Number (if any)	(iii) Type of Entity	(iv) Country of Organization	(v) Maximum Percentage Owned in Profit, Loss, or Capital

		Yes	No
6a	At the end of the tax year, did the corporation have any outstanding shares of restricted stock?		X
	If "Yes," complete lines (i) and (ii) below.		
(i)	Total shares of restricted stock ▶		
(ii)	Total shares of non-restricted stock ▶		
b	At the end of the tax year, did the corporation have any outstanding stock options, warrants, or similar instruments?		X
	If "Yes," complete lines (i) and (ii) below.		
(i)	Total shares of stock outstanding at the end of the tax year ▶		
(ii)	Total shares of stock outstanding if all instruments were executed ▶		
6	Has this corporation filed, or is it required to file, Form 8918, Material Advisor Disclosure Statement, to provide information on any reportable transaction?		X
7	Check this box if the corporation issued publicly offered debt instruments with original issue discount ▶ ☐		
	If checked, the corporation may have to file Form 8281, Information Return for Publicly Offered Original Issue Discount Instruments.		
8	If the corporation: (a) was a C corporation before it elected to be an S corporation or the corporation acquired an asset with a basis determined by reference to the basis of the asset (or the basis of any other property) in the hands of a C corporation and (b) has net unrealized built-in gain in excess of the net recognized built-in gain from prior years, enter the net unrealized built-in gain reduced by net recognized built-in gain from prior years (see instructions) ▶ $		
9	Enter the accumulated earnings and profits of the corporation at the end of the tax year. $		
10	Does the corporation satisfy both of the following conditions?		
a	The corporation's total receipts (see instructions) for the tax year were less than $250,000		
b	The corporation's total assets at the end of the tax year were less than $250,000		X
	If "Yes," the corporation is not required to complete Schedules L and M-1.		
11	During the tax year, did the corporation have any non-shareholder debt that was canceled, was forgiven, or had the terms modified so as to reduce the principal amount of the debt?		X
	If "Yes," enter the amount of principal reduction $		
12	During the tax year, was a qualified subchapter S subsidiary election terminated or revoked? If "Yes," see instructions		X
13a	Did the corporation make any payments in 2017 that would require it to file Form(s) 1099?		X
b	If "Yes," did the corporation file or will it file required Forms 1099?		

Form **1120S** (2017)

DAA

Exhibit 59-4:   Sample Filled-In Form 1120 for an S Corporation
(Continued)

Form 1120S (2017)	KAREN, KATIE & MICHAEL CORP.		99-9999999		Page 3

		Schedule K	Shareholders' Pro Rata Share Items				Total amount
Income (Loss)	1	Ordinary business income (loss) (page 1, line 21)			1	267,305
	2	Net rental real estate income (loss) (attach Form 8825)			2	
	3a	Other gross rental income (loss)	3a			
	b	Expenses from other rental activities (attach statement)	3b			
	c	Other net rental income (loss). Subtract line 3b from line 3a			3c	
	4	Interest income			4	
	5	Dividends: a Ordinary dividends			5a	
		b Qualified dividends	5b			
	6	Royalties			6	
	7	Net short-term capital gain (loss) (attach Schedule D (Form 1120S))			7	
	8a	Net long-term capital gain (loss) (attach Schedule D (Form 1120S))			8a	
	b	Collectibles (28%) gain (loss)	8b			
	c	Unrecaptured section 1250 gain (attach statement)	8c			
	9	Net section 1231 gain (loss) (attach Form 4797)			9	
	10	Other income (loss) (see instructions) Type ▶			10	
Deductions	11	Section 179 deduction (attach Form 4562)			11	113,200
	12a	Charitable contributions			12a	
	b	Investment interest expense			12b	
	c	Section 59(e)(2) expenditures (1) Type ▶		(2) Amount ▶	12c(2)	
	d	Other deductions (see instructions) Type ▶			12d	
Credits	13a	Low-income housing credit (section 42(j)(5))			13a	
	b	Low-income housing credit (other)			13b	
	c	Qualified rehabilitation expenditures (rental real estate) (attach Form 3468, if applicable)			13c	
	d	Other rental real estate credits (see instructions) Type ▶			13d	
	e	Other rental credits (see instructions) Type ▶			13e	
	f	Biofuel producer credit (attach Form 6478)			13f	
	g	Other credits (see instructions) Type ▶			13g	
Foreign Transactions	14a	Name of country or U.S. possession ▶				
	b	Gross income from all sources			14b	
	c	Gross income sourced at shareholder level			14c	
		Foreign gross income sourced at corporate level				
	d	Passive category			14d	
	e	General category			14e	
	f	Other (attach statement)			14f	
		Deductions allocated and apportioned at shareholder level				
	g	Interest expense			14g	
	h	Other			14h	
		Deductions allocated and apportioned at corporate level to foreign source income				
	i	Passive category			14i	
	j	General category			14j	
	k	Other (attach statement)			14k	
		Other information				
	l	Total foreign taxes (check one): ▶ ☐ Paid ☐ Accrued			14l	
	m	Reduction in taxes available for credit (attach statement)			14m	
	n	Other foreign tax information (attach statement)				
Alternative Minimum Tax (AMT) Items	15a	Post-1986 depreciation adjustment			15a	
	b	Adjusted gain or loss			15b	
	c	Depletion (other than oil and gas)			15c	
	d	Oil, gas, and geothermal properties – gross income			15d	
	e	Oil, gas, and geothermal properties – deductions			15e	
	f	Other AMT items (attach statement)			15f	
Items Affecting Shareholder Basis	16a	Tax-exempt interest income			16a	
	b	Other tax-exempt income			16b	
	c	Nondeductible expenses			16c	941
	d	Distributions (attach statement if required) (see instructions)			16d	
	e	Repayment of loans from shareholders			16e	

Form **1120S** (2017)

DAA

Exhibit 59-4:   Sample Filled-In Form 1120 for an S Corporation (Continued)

Form 1120S (2017)   KAREN, KATIE & MICHAEL CORP.   99-9999999   Page 4

Schedule K Shareholders' Pro Rata Share Items (continued)

			Total amount
Other Information	17a Investment income	17a	
	b Investment expenses	17b	
	c Dividend distributions paid from accumulated earnings and profits	17c	
	d Other items and amounts (attach statement)		
Recon-ciliation	18 Income/loss reconciliation. Combine the amounts on lines 1 through 10 in the far right column. From the result, subtract the sum of the amounts on lines 11 through 12d and 14l	18	154,105

Schedule L Balance Sheets per Books

	Assets	Beginning of tax year (a)	(b)	End of tax year (c)	(d)
1	Cash				257,100
2a	Trade notes and accounts receivable			41,460	
b	Less allowance for bad debts	( )		( )	41,460
3	Inventories				6,830
4	U.S. government obligations				
5	Tax-exempt securities (see instructions)				
6	Other current assets (attach statement) **STMT 2**				127,620
7	Loans to shareholders				
8	Mortgage and real estate loans				
9	Other investments (attach statement)				
10a	Buildings and other depreciable assets			113,200	
b	Less accumulated depreciation	( )		(113,200)	0
11a	Depletable assets				
b	Less accumulated depletion	( )		( )	
12	Land (net of any amortization)				
13a	Intangible assets (amortizable only)				
b	Less accumulated amortization	( )		( )	
14	Other assets (attach statement) **STMT 3**				150
15	Total assets		0		433,160
	Liabilities and Shareholders' Equity				
16	Accounts payable				15,374
17	Mortgages, notes, bonds payable in less than 1 year				8,749
18	Other current liabilities (attach statement) **STMT 4**				40,709
19	Loans from shareholders				82,630
20	Mortgages, notes, bonds payable in 1 year or more				126,803
21	Other liabilities (attach statement)				
22	Capital stock				6,000
23	Additional paid-in capital				
24	Retained earnings				152,895
25	Adjustments to shareholders' equity (attach statement)				
26	Less cost of treasury stock		( )		( )
27	Total liabilities and shareholders' equity		0		433,160

Form **1120S** (2017)

DAA

Exhibit 59-4:   Sample Filled-In Form 1120 for an S Corporation
(Continued)

Form 1120S (2017)   **KAREN, KATIE & MICHAEL CORP.**   99-9999999   Page 5

Schedule M-1   **Reconciliation of Income (Loss) per Books With Income (Loss) per Return**

Note: The corporation may be required to file Schedule M-3 (see instructions)

1	Net income (loss) per books		152,895	5	Income recorded on books this year not included
2	Income included on Schedule K, lines 1, 2, 3c, 4,				on Schedule K, lines 1 through 10 (itemize):
	5a, 6, 7, 8a, 9, and 10, not recorded on books this			a	Tax-exempt interest $
	year (itemize)				
3	Expenses recorded on books this year not			6	Deductions included on Schedule K,
	included on Schedule K, lines 1 through 12				lines 1 through 12 and 14l, not charged
	and 14l (itemize):				against book income this year (itemize):
a	Depreciation $			a	Depreciation $
b	Travel and entertainment $	941			
	STMT 5	269	1,210	7	Add lines 5 and 6
4	Add lines 1 through 3		154,105	8	Income (loss) (Schedule K, line 18). Line 4 less line 7	154,105

Schedule M-2   **Analysis of Accumulated Adjustments Account, Other Adjustments Account, and Shareholders' Undistributed Taxable Income Previously Taxed** (see instructions)

		(a) Accumulated adjustments account	(b) Other adjustments account	(c) Shareholders' undistributed taxable income previously taxed
1	Balance at beginning of tax year			
2	Ordinary income from page 1, line 21	267,305		
3	Other additions			
4	Loss from page 1, line 21	(		
5	Other reductions STMT 6	(114,410)(		
6	Combine lines 1 through 5	152,895		
7	Distributions other than dividend distributions			
8	Balance at end of tax year. Subtract line 7 from line 6	152,895		

Form **1120S** (2017)

DAA

Exhibit 59-4:   Sample Filled-In Form 1120 for an S Corporation *(Continued)*

Form **1125-A** (Rev. October 2016) Department of the Treasury Internal Revenue Service	**Cost of Goods Sold** ▶ Attach to Form 1120, 1120-C, 1120-F, 1120S, 1065, or 1065-B. ▶ Information about Form 1125-A and its instructions is at *www.irs.gov/form1125a.*	OMB No. 1545-0123

Name		Employer identification number
KAREN, KATIE & MICHAEL CORP.		99-9999999

1	Inventory at beginning of year	**1**	
2	Purchases	**2**	107,538
3	Cost of labor	**3**	
4	Additional section 263A costs (attach schedule)	**4**	
5	Other costs (attach schedule)	**5**	
6	**Total.** Add lines 1 through 5	**6**	107,538
7	Inventory at end of year	**7**	6,830
8	**Cost of goods sold.** Subtract line 7 from line 6. Enter here and on Form 1120, page 1, line 2 or the appropriate line of your tax return. See instructions	**8**	100,708

9a Check all methods used for valuing closing inventory:
　(i) ☐ Cost
　(ii) ☒ Lower of cost or market
　(iii) ☐ Other (Specify method used and attach explanation.) ▶

b Check if there was a writedown of subnormal goods .... ▶ ☐

c Check if the LIFO inventory method was adopted this tax year for any goods (if checked, attach Form 970) ..... ▶ ☐

d If the LIFO inventory method was used for this tax year, enter amount of closing inventory computed under LIFO .... **9d** |

e If property is produced or acquired for resale, do the rules of section 263A apply to the entity? See instructions .... ☐ Yes ☒ No

f Was there any change in determining quantities, cost, or valuations between opening and closing inventory? If "Yes," attach explanation .... ☐ Yes ☒ No

For Paperwork Reduction Act Notice, see instructions.　　　　　　　　　　　　　　　　　Form **1125-A** (Rev. 10-2016)

DAA

Exhibit 59-4:   Sample Filled-In Form 1120 for an S Corporation (Continued)

Form **1125-E** (Rev. October 2016) Department of the Treasury Internal Revenue Service	**Compensation of Officers** ▶ Attach to Form 1120, 1120-C, 1120-F, 1120-REIT, 1120-RIC, or 1120S. ▶ Information about Form 1125-E and its separate instructions is at *www.irs.gov/form1125e.*	OMB No. 1545-0123

Name KAREN, KATIE & MICHAEL CORP.	Employer identification number 99-9999999

Note: Complete Form 1125-E only if total receipts are $500,000 or more. See instructions for definition of total receipts.

(a) Name of officer	(b) Social security number (see instructions)	(c) Percent of time devoted to business	Percent of stock owned		(f) Amount of compensation
			(d) Common	(e) Preferred	
1 MICHAEL LIGHTYEAR	999-99-9999	100.000 %	33.333%	%	128,435
		%	%	%	
		%	%	%	
		%	%	%	
		%	%	%	
		%	%	%	
		%	%	%	
		%	%	%	
		%	%	%	
		%	%	%	
		%	%	%	
		%	%	%	
		%	%	%	
		%	%	%	
		%	%	%	
		%	%	%	
		%	%	%	
		%	%	%	
		%	%	%	
		%	%	%	

2	Total compensation of officers	2	128,435
3	Compensation of officers claimed on Form 1125-A or elsewhere on return	3	
4	Subtract line 3 from line 2. Enter the result here and on Form 1120, page 1, line 12 or the appropriate line of your tax return	4	128,435

For Paperwork Reduction Act Notice, see separate instructions.   Form **1125-E** (Rev. 10-2016)

DAA

Exhibit 59-4: *Sample Filled-In Form 1120 for an S Corporation (Continued)*

671117

☐ Final K-1	☐ Amended K-1 OMB No. 1545-0123

Schedule K-1
(Form 1120S)
Department of the Treasury
Internal Revenue Service

2017
For calendar year 2017, or tax year

beginning [ ]   ending [ ]

Shareholder's Share of Income, Deductions, Credits, etc. ► See back of form and separate instructions.

Part I   Information About the Corporation

A Corporation's employer identification number
   99-9999999

B Corporation's name, address, city, state, and ZIP code
   KAREN, KATIE & MICHAEL CORP.

   123 ANY STREET
   ANY CITY   NY   99999

C IRS Center where corporation filed return
   E-FILE

Part II   Information About the Shareholder

D Shareholder's identifying number
   111-11-1111

E Shareholder's name, address, city, state, and ZIP code
   MICHAEL LIGHTYEAR
   222 ANY BLVD.

   ANY CITY   NY   99999

F Shareholder's percentage of stock
   ownership for tax year .... 33.333300 %

For IRS Use Only

Part III   Shareholder's Share of Current Year Income, Deductions, Credits, and Other Items

#	Item	#	Item
1	Ordinary business income (loss) 89,102	13	Credits
2	Net rental real estate income (loss)		
3	Other net rental income (loss)		
4	Interest income		
5a	Ordinary dividends		
5b	Qualified dividends	14	Foreign transactions
6	Royalties		
7	Net short-term capital gain (loss)		
8a	Net long-term capital gain (loss)		
8b	Collectibles (28%) gain (loss)		
8c	Unrecaptured section 1250 gain		
9	Net section 1231 gain (loss)		
10	Other income (loss)	15	Alternative minimum tax (AMT) items
11	Section 179 deduction 37,733	16 C*	Items affecting shareholder basis 314
12	Other deductions		
		17	Other information

* See attached statement for additional information.

For Paperwork Reduction Act Notice, see the Instructions for Form 1120S.   www.irs.gov/Form1120S   Schedule K-1 (Form 1120S) 2017

DAA

Exhibit 59-4:   Sample Filled-In Form 1120 for an S Corporation
(Continued)

99-9999999   **Federal Statements**
                              MICHAEL LIGHTYEAR
                              111-11-1111

Schedule K-1, Box 16, Code C - Nondeductible Expenses

Description	Shareholder Amount
PAGE 1 MEALS/ENTERTAINMENT	$ 314
TOTAL	$ 314

Exhibit 59-4:   *Sample Filled-In Form 1120 for an S Corporation*
(Continued)

		671117

☐ Final K-1	☐ Amended K-1		OMB No. 1545-0123

Schedule K-1 **(Form 1120S)** Department of the Treasury Internal Revenue Service	**2017** For calendar year 2017, or tax year	**Part III**	**Shareholder's Share of Current Year Income,** **Deductions, Credits, and Other Items**		
		1	Ordinary business income (loss) 89,101	13	Credits
beginning ☐ ending ☐		2	Net rental real estate income (loss)		
Shareholder's Share of Income, Deductions, **Credits, etc.** ▶ See back of form and separate instructions.		3	Other net rental income (loss)		
Part I Information About the Corporation		4	Interest income		
A Corporation's employer identification number 99-9999999		5a	Ordinary dividends		
B Corporation's name, address, city, state, and ZIP code KAREN, KATIE & MICHAEL CORP. 123 ANY STREET ANY CITY NY 99999		5b	Qualified dividends	14	Foreign transactions
		6	Royalties		
		7	Net short-term capital gain (loss)		
C IRS Center where corporation filed return E-FILE		8a	Net long-term capital gain (loss)		
Part II Information About the Shareholder		8b	Collectibles (28%) gain (loss)		
D Shareholder's identifying number 222-22-2222		8c	Unrecaptured section 1250 gain		
E Shareholder's name, address, city, state, and ZIP code KAREN LIGHTYEAR 222 ANY BLVD. ANY CITY NY 99999		9	Net section 1231 gain (loss)		
		10	Other income (loss)	15	Alternative minimum tax (AMT) items
F Shareholder's percentage of stock ownership for tax year .... 33.333300 %					
		11	Section 179 deduction 37,733	16 C*	Items affecting shareholder basis 313
		12	Other deductions		
				17	Other information
For IRS Use Only					
			* See attached statement for additional information.		

For Paperwork Reduction Act Notice, see the Instructions for Form 1120S.	www.irs.gov/Form1120S	Schedule K-1 (Form 1120S) 2017

DAA

Exhibit 59-4:   Sample Filled-In Form 1120 for an S Corporation (Continued)

99-9999999	**Federal Statements** **KAREN LIGHTYEAR** **222-22-2222**

Schedule K-1, Box 16, Code C - Nondeductible Expenses

Description	Shareholder Amount
PAGE 1 MEALS/ENTERTAINMENT	$ 313
TOTAL	$ 313

Exhibit 59-4: Sample Filled-In Form 1120 for an S Corporation
(Continued)

671117

☐ Final K-1	☐ Amended K-1	OMB No. 1545-0123

Schedule K-1
(Form 1120S)
Department of the Treasury
Internal Revenue Service

2017
For calendar year 2017, or tax year

beginning _____ ending _____

Shareholder's Share of Income, Deductions, Credits, etc. ▶ See back of form and separate instructions.

Part I	Information About the Corporation

A Corporation's employer identification number
99-9999999

B Corporation's name, address, city, state, and ZIP code
KAREN, KATIE & MICHAEL CORP.

123 ANY STREET
ANY CITY   NY   99999

C IRS Center where corporation filed return
E-FILE

Part II	Information About the Shareholder

D Shareholder's identifying number
333-33-3333

E Shareholder's name, address, city, state, and ZIP code
KATIE LIGHTYEAR
222 ANY BLVD.

ANY CITY   NY   99999

F Shareholder's percentage of stock
ownership for tax year .... **33.333300 %**

For IRS Use Only

Part III	Shareholder's Share of Current-Year Income, Deductions, Credits, and Other Items		
1 Ordinary business income (loss)		**13** Credits	
	89,102		
2 Net rental real estate income (loss)			
3 Other net rental income (loss)			
4 Interest income			
5a Ordinary dividends			
5b Qualified dividends		**14** Foreign transactions	
6 Royalties			
7 Net short-term capital gain (loss)			
8a Net long-term capital gain (loss)			
8b Collectibles (28%) gain (loss)			
8c Unrecaptured section 1250 gain			
9 Net section 1231 gain (loss)			
10 Other income (loss)		**15** Alternative minimum tax (AMT) items	
11 Section 179 deduction	**37,734**	**16** Items affecting shareholder basis **C***	**314**
12 Other deductions			
		17 Other information	

* See attached statement for additional information.

For Paperwork Reduction Act Notice, see the Instructions for Form 1120S.   www.irs.gov/Form1120S   Schedule K-1 (Form 1120S) 2017

DAA

Exhibit 59-4:   ***Sample Filled-In Form 1120 for an S Corporation*** *(Continued)*

99-9999999	**Federal Statements**
	KATIE LIGHTYEAR
	333-33-3333

Schedule K-1, Box 16, Code C - Nondeductible Expenses

Description	Shareholder Amount
PAGE 1 MEALS/ENTERTAINMENT	$ 314
TOTAL	$ 314

Exhibit 59-4: *Sample Filled-In Form 1120 for an S Corporation (Continued)*

Form **4562**	**Depreciation and Amortization**	OMB No. 1545-0172
Department of the Treasury Internal Revenue Service (99)	**(Including Information on Listed Property)** ▶ Attach to your tax return. ▶ Go to *www.irs.gov/Form4562* for instructions and the latest information.	**2017** Attachment Sequence No. **179**

Name(s) shown on return	Identifying number
KAREN, KATIE & MICHAEL CORP.	99-9999999

Business or activity to which this form relates
REGULAR DEPRECIATION

Part I — Election To Expense Certain Property Under Section 179

Note: If you have any listed property, complete Part V before you complete Part I.

1	Maximum amount (see instructions)	1	510,000
2	Total cost of section 179 property placed in service (see instructions)	2	113,200
3	Threshold cost of section 179 property before reduction in limitation (see instructions)	3	2,030,000
4	Reduction in limitation. Subtract line 3 from line 2. If zero or less, enter -0-	4	0
5	Dollar limitation for tax year. Subtract line 4 from line 1. If zero or less, enter -0-. If married filing separately, see instructions	5	510,000

6	(a) Description of property	(b) Cost (business use only)	(c) Elected cost	
	MACHINERY	113,200	113,200	

7	Listed property. Enter the amount from line 29	7	
8	Total elected cost of section 179 property. Add amounts in column (c), lines 6 and 7	8	113,200
9	Tentative deduction. Enter the **smaller** of line 5 or line 8	9	113,200
10	Carryover of disallowed deduction from line 13 of your 2016 Form 4562	10	
11	Business income limitation. Enter the smaller of business income (not less than zero) or line 5 (see instructions)	11	267,305
12	Section 179 expense deduction. Add lines 9 and 10, but don't enter more than line 11	12	113,200
13	Carryover of disallowed deduction to 2018. Add lines 9 and 10, less line 12 ▶	13	

Note: Don't use Part II or Part III below for listed property. Instead, use Part V.

Part II — Special Depreciation Allowance and Other Depreciation (Don't include listed property.) (See instructions.)

14	Special depreciation allowance for qualified property (other than listed property) placed in service during the tax year (see instructions)	14	
15	Property subject to section 168(f)(1) election	15	
16	Other depreciation (including ACRS)	16	

Part III — MACRS Depreciation (Don't include listed property.) (See instructions.)

Section A

17	MACRS deductions for assets placed in service in tax years beginning before 2017	17	0
18	If you are electing to group any assets placed in service during the tax year into one or more general asset accounts, check here ▶ ☐		

Section B—Assets Placed in Service During 2017 Tax Year Using the General Depreciation System

	(a) Classification of property	(b) Month and year placed in service	(c) Basis for depreciation (business/investment use only—see instructions)	(d) Recovery period	(e) Convention	(f) Method	(g) Depreciation deduction
19a	3-year property						
b	5-year property						
c	7-year property						
d	10-year property						
e	15-year property						
f	20-year property						
g	25-year property			25 yrs.		S/L	
h	Residential rental property			27.5 yrs.	MM	S/L	
				27.5 yrs.	MM	S/L	
i	Nonresidential real property			39 yrs.	MM	S/L	
					MM	S/L	

Section C—Assets Placed in Service During 2017 Tax Year Using the Alternative Depreciation System

		(b)	(c)	(d)	(e)	(f)	(g)
20a	Class life					S/L	
b	12-year			12 yrs.		S/L	
c	40-year			40 yrs.	MM	S/L	

Part IV — Summary (See instructions.)

21	Listed property. Enter amount from line 28	21	
22	**Total.** Add amounts from line 12, lines 14 through 17, lines 19 and 20 in column (g), and line 21. Enter here and on the appropriate lines of your return. Partnerships and S corporations—see instructions	22	
23	For assets shown above and placed in service during the current year, enter the portion of the basis attributable to section 263A costs	23	

For Paperwork Reduction Act Notice, see separate instructions.

DAA

THERE ARE NO AMOUNTS FOR PAGE 2

Form **4562** (2017)

Exhibit 59-4:   Sample Filled-In Form 1120 for an S Corporation (Continued)

99-9999999	**Federal Statements**

Statement 1 - Form 1120S, Page 1, Line 19 - Other Deductions

Description	Amount
AUTOMOBILE EXPENSES	$ 26,883
COMPUTER EXPENSES	4,879
DUES AND SUBSCRIPTIONS	462
GENERAL INSURANCE	82,613
HOSPITALIZATION INSURANCE	2,586
OFFICE EXPENSES	8,504
POSTAGE & SHIPPING	7,477
PROFESSIONAL FEES	7,990
ROYALTIES	25,200
STORAGE	2,700
TELEPHONE	9,547
UTILITIES	5,940
50% OF MEALS & ENTERTAINMENT	941
TOTAL	$ 185,722

Statement 2 - Form 1120S, Page 4, Schedule L, Line 6 - Other Current Assets

Description	Beginning of Year	End of Year
PREPAID EXPENSES	$	$ 127,620
TOTAL	$ 0	$ 127,620

Statement 3 - Form 1120S, Page 4, Schedule L, Line 14 - Other Assets

Description	Beginning of Year	End of Year
DEPOSITS	$	$ 150
TOTAL	$ 0	$ 150

Statement 4 - Form 1120S, Page 4, Schedule L, Line 18 - Other Current Liabilities

Description	Beginning of Year	End of Year
ACCRUED EXPENSES AND TAXES	$	$ 17,473
PAYROLL TAXES PAYABLE		23,236
TOTAL	$ 0	$ 40,709

Statement 5 - Form 1120S, Page 5, Schedule M-1, Line 3 - Expenses on Books Not on Return

Description	Amount
FINES AND PENALTIES	$ 269
TOTAL	$ 269

1-5

Exhibit 59-4: Sample Filled-In Form 1120 for an S Corporation (Continued)

99-9999999	**Federal Statements**

Statement 6 - Form 1120S, Page 5, Schedule M-2, Line 5(a) - Other Reductions

Description	Amount
FINES AND PENALTIES	$ 269
MEALS & ENTERTAINMENT	941
SECTION 179 EXPENSE	113,200
TOTAL	$ 114,410

6

CONCLUSION

When making business decisions, a controller must consider both tax and nontax factors. The controller should possess a basic understanding of pertinent tax laws. When the need arises, it is prudent to consult a detailed tax information service. Commerce Clearing House and Research Institute of America are two publishers of such outstanding tax reports.

CHAPTER 60

PAYROLL TAXES

CONTENTS

Payroll usually represents the largest operating expense of a company. It is obvious then that the related payroll taxes become a significant consideration for the controller. The controller must be familiar with federal, state, and local payroll tax payment and filing requirements. In addition, attention must be given to workers' compensation and disability insurance.

The controller plays an important role in the payroll tax function. The controller is responsible for: (1) making timely tax deposits, and (2) filing tax reports when due. It is also important to establish whether a worker is an employee or an independent contractor since the former is subject to a variety of payroll taxes. Classification of workers as independent contractors may reduce the company's tax liability.

Tax forms referred to in this chapter are available from various governmental offices and have not been reproduced herein because they are constantly subject to change.

SOCIAL SECURITY AND MEDICARE TAXES

Social security and Medicare taxes are burdens to both employees and their employers. Social security was required to be withheld from the first $127,200 of employee wages in 2017 ($128,400 in 2018) at the rate of 6.2%.

The Medicare tax is imposed at the rate of 1.45% on all wages; there is no limitation on the amount of wages subject to the Medicare tax. Employers must remit to the Internal Revenue Service both the employer and employee portions of the social security and Medicare taxes. The employer's social security tax rate is 6.2% and the employer's Medicare tax rate is 1.45%. For withholding purposes, wages in excess of $200,000 are subject to an additional Medicare tax at the rate of 0.9%. It should be noted that the additional Medicare tax is not matched by employers.

Since cost reduction is an important function of the controller, he or she should attempt to minimize the social security and Medicare tax burdens by considering: (1) independent contractor status of workers, and (2) the common paymaster provisions of the Internal Revenue Code.

INDEPENDENT CONTRACTOR STATUS

The definition of an employee in IRC Sec. 3121 leaves much to be desired. The statute refers to a twenty-factor control test based on common law provisions, which have been subject to interpretation throughout the years. The overriding consideration seems to be whether the person rendering the services is under the control of the so-called "employer." If the worker can be supervised, guided, and told where the work is to be performed, control is presumed and employee status is generally mandated. Furthermore, employee status is usually presumed when work hours are fixed and when the individual is forbidden by contract to perform services for others. Similarly, participation in profit sharing plans is a good indication that employee status is present.

Clearly, from a company's point of view, the independent contractor status of an individual results in a savings of social security and Medicare taxes, since the independent contractor is responsible for the payment of his or her own taxes. An independent contractor is also responsible for his or her own worker's compensation and disability insurance.

To ensure that the taxing authorities do not successfully contest independent contractor status of a worker, an indemnification agreement should be drafted. In the agreement, the independent contractor should acknowledge his or her responsibility for social security, Medicare, federal, and state (and local, if applicable) income taxes as well as worker's compensation and disability insurance. It would be prudent to obtain a copy of the independent contractor's worker's compensation policy. This one document is often useful in sustaining independent status upon challenge by unemployment insurance agencies. It is important to provide a Form 1099-MISC to all independent contractors who were paid at least $600 during the year. A blank Form 1099-MISC can be found on the Internal Revenue Service website at www.irs.gov.

THE COMMON PAYMASTER PROVISION

If an individual performs services for two or more related companies, one of the corporations may serve as a common paymaster. In such instances, the common paymaster is responsible for the payment of all wages and pay-roll taxes. Failure on the part of the common paymaster to withhold and pay the appropriate taxes could prove to be costly, since all of the corporations involved would then become liable for the deficiencies.

For a particular calendar quarter, to be included in the group of corporations treated as a common paymaster for a particular quarter, at least one of the following tests must be satisfied:

1. The company is a member of either a brother-sister or parent-subsidiary controlled group, except that the 80%-ownership requirement of IRC Sec. 1563 is replaced with a 50%-ownership requirement.

2. At least 50% of one corporation's officers are officers of the other corporation(s) that is (are) included in the group.

3. At least 30% of the employees of one corporation are employed by one of the other corporations included in the group.

FEDERAL WITHHOLDING TAXES

Every employer is required to withhold federal withholding taxes from employee wage payments in accordance with the allowances claimed by the employee on Form W-4. A blank W-4 form and instructions can be found on the Internal Revenue Service's Web site: www.irs.gov.

TAX DEPOSITS

The amount of taxes owed by the company determines the frequency of required deposits. Every November, the Internal Revenue Service notifies each employer as to whether tax deposits must be made using a monthly or semiweekly schedule. The deposit schedule is determined from the total employment taxes reported on the quarterly Forms 941 in a four-quarter look-back period (i.e., July 1 through June 30). If $50,000 or less of employment taxes for the look-back period has been reported, then the monthly deposit schedule must be used. If more than $50,000 of employment taxes for the look-back period has been reported, then the semiweekly schedule must be used.

Under the monthly deposit schedule, employment taxes withheld on wages paid during a calendar month must be deposited by the fifteenth day of the following month.

Under the semiweekly deposit schedule, employment taxes withheld on wages paid on Wednesday, Thursday, and/or Friday must be deposited by the following Wednesday. Amounts accumulated on wages paid on Saturday, Sunday, Monday, and/or Tuesday must be deposited by the following Friday.

If an employer accumulates less than a $2,500 tax liability during a calendar quarter, no deposits are required and the liability may be paid with the tax return for the period.

Further, employers must make a deposit of taxes by the close of the next banking day if the undeposited tax liability (i.e., generally federal income tax withheld plus both the employee and employer social security and Medicare taxes) is $100,000 or more.

The liability for payment of federal withholding, social security, and Medicare taxes arises when the wages are paid, not when the payroll period ends.

A company's tax liability and deposits are reported quarterly on Form 941. Form 941, *Employer's Quarterly Federal Tax Return,* and instructions can be found on the Internal Revenue Service's Web site (www.irs.gov). These forms must be filed as follows:

Calendar Quarter Ending	Due Date
March 31	April 30
June 30	July 31
September 30	October 31
December 31	January 31

In general, a business must make all deposits (including payments for unemployment taxes and corporate income taxes) using the Electronic Federal Tax Payment System (EFTPS). Answers to questions on the enrollment and payment processes can be found at www.EFTPS.gov. Alternatively, questions may be directed to EFTPS customer service representatives. Failure to use EFTPS when required to do so may result in the imposition of a 10% penalty.

Sample Filled-In Tax Form

Presented below is Woody Corporation's payroll summary for the quarter ended December 31, 2017. Woody Corporation's sole employee is John Zurg, who lives in Florida, a state that does not impose an income tax. In this example, Woody Corporation is a monthly depositer.

Pay Date	Gross Wages	FICA Withheld	Medicare Tax Withheld	Federal Tax Withheld	Net Pay
10/7	$1,955.18	$121.22	$28.35	$480.00	$1,325.61
10/21	1,826.21	113.23	26.48	460.00	1,226.50
11/4	1,955.18	121.22	28.35	480.00	1,325.61
11/18	1,632.87	101.24	23.68	440.00	1,067.95
12/3	1,550.00	96.10	22.48	430.00	1,001.42
12/17	1,985.82	123.12	28.79	490.00	1,343.91
12/31	1,755.00	108.81	25.45	450.00	1,170.74
Total	$12,660.26	$784.94	$183.58	$3,230.00	$8,461.74

Woody Corporation made the following federal tax deposits for the quarter ended December 31, 2017.

11/15/17	$1,518.56
12/15/17	1,468.98
1/15/18	2,179.50
Total	$5,167.04

Presented in Exhibit 60-1 is Woody Corporation's filled-in Form 941 for the quarter ended December 31, 2017.

Exhibit 60-1:   Sample Filled-In Form 941

Form **941 for 2017:**   **Employer's QUARTERLY Federal Tax Return**   970117

(Rev. January 2017)   Department of the Treasury -- Internal Revenue Service   OMB No. 1545-0029

Employer Identification number (EIN)   99-9999999

Name (not your trade name)   WOODY CORPORATION

Trade name (if any) _____

Address   123 SPRINGFIELD STREET

ANY CITY, FL 11111

Report for this Quarter of 2017
(Check one.)

☐ **1:** January, February, March

☐ **2:** April, May, June

☐ **3:** July, August, September

☒ **4:** October, November, December

Instructions and prior year forms are available at www.irs.gov/form941.

Read the separate instructions before you complete Form 941. Type or print within the boxes.

Part 1: Answer these questions for this quarter.

1   Number of employees who received wages, tips, or other compensation for the pay period including: Mar. 12 (Quarter 1), June 12 (Quarter 2), Sept. 12 (Quarter 3), or Dec. 12 (Quarter 4)   .   **1**   1

2   Wages, tips, and other compensation **2**   12,660.26

3   Federal income tax withheld from wages, tips, and other compensation **3**   3,230.00

4   If no wages, tips, and other compensation are subject to social security or Medicare tax   ...   ☐   Check and go to line 6.

	Column 1		Column 2
5a Taxable social security wages	12,660.26	x 0.124 =	1,569.87
5b Taxable social security tips		x 0.124 =	
5c Taxable Medicare wages & tips ...	12,660.26	x 0.029 =	367.15
5d Taxable wages & tips subject to Additional Medicare Tax withholding .		x 0.009 =	

5e   Add Column 2 from lines 5a, 5b, 5c, and 5d **5e**   1,937.02

5f   Section 3121(q) Notice and Demand -- Tax due on unreported tips (see instructions) **5f**

6   Total taxes before adjustments. Add lines 3, 5e, and 5f **6**   5,167.02

7   Current quarter's adjustment for fractions of cents **7**   0.02

8   Current quarter's adjustment for sick pay **8**

9   Current quarter's adjustments for tips and group-term life insurance **9**

10   Total taxes after adjustments. Combine lines 6 through 9   ....   **10**   5,167.04

11   Qualified small business payroll tax credit for increasing research activities. Attach Form 8974   **11**

12   Total taxes after adjustments and credits. Subtract line 11 from line 10   ....   **12**   5,167.04

13   Total deposits for this quarter, including overpayment applied from a prior quarter and overpayments applied from Form 941-X, 941-X (PR), 944-X, or 944-X (SP) filed in the current quarter   **13**   5,167.04

14   Balance due. If line 12 is more than line 13, enter the difference and see instructions **14**

15   Overpayment. If line 13 is more than line 12, enter the difference   [_____] Check one: ☐ Apply to next return. ☐ Send a refund.

▶ You MUST complete both pages of Form 941 and SIGN it.   Next ▶

For Privacy Act and Paperwork Reduction Act Notice, see the back of the Payment Voucher.   DXA   Form **941** (Rev. 1-2017)

Exhibit 60-1: *Sample Filled-In Form 941 (Continued)*

970217

Form **941** (Rev. 1-2017) Page **2**

Name (not your trade name)	Employer identification number (EIN)
WOODY CORPORATION	99-9999999

Part 2: Tell us about your deposit schedule and tax liability for this quarter.

If you are unsure about whether you are a monthly schedule depositor or a semiweekly schedule depositor, see section 11 of Pub. 15.

16 Check one: ☐ Line 12 on this return is less than $2,500 or line 12 (line 10 if the prior quarter was the fourth quarter of 2016) on the return for the prior quarter was less than $2,500, and you didn't incur a $100,000 next-day deposit obligation during the current quarter. If line 12 (line 10 if the prior quarter was the fourth quarter of 2016) for the prior quarter was less than $2,500 but line 12 on this return is $100,000 or more, you must provide a record of your federal tax liability. If you are a monthly schedule depositor, complete the deposit schedule below; if you are a semiweekly schedule depositor, attach Schedule B (Form 941). Go to Part 3.

☒ You were a monthly schedule depositor for the entire quarter. Enter your tax liability for each month and total liability for the quarter, then go to Part 3.

Tax liability:	Month 1	1,518.56
	Month 2	1,468.98
	Month 3	2,179.50
Total liability for quarter		5,167.04	Total must equal line 12.

☐ You were a semiweekly schedule depositor for any part of this quarter. Complete Schedule B (Form 941), Report of Tax Liability for Semiweekly Schedule Depositors, and attach it to Form 941.

Part 3: Tell us about your business. If a question does NOT apply to your business, leave it blank.

17 If your business has closed or you stopped paying wages . . . . ☐ Check here, and

enter the final date you paid wages [   ] .

18 If you are a seasonal employer and you don't have to file a return for every quarter of the year . . . . ☐ Check here.

Part 4: May we speak with your third-party designee?

Do you want to allow an employee, a paid tax preparer, or another person to discuss this return with the IRS? See the instructions for details.

☐ Yes. Designee's name and phone number [   ] [   ]

Select a 5-digit Personal Identification Number (PIN) to use when talking to the IRS. [   ]

☐ No.

Part 5: Sign here. You MUST complete both pages of Form 941 and SIGN it.

Under penalties of perjury, I declare that I have examined this return, including accompanying schedules and statements, and to the best of my knowledge and belief, it is true, correct, and complete. Declaration of preparer (other than taxpayer) is based on all information of which preparer has any knowledge.

▶ Sign your name here [   ]

Print your name here [   ]

Print your title here [   ]

Date [   ]

Best daytime phone [   ]

Paid Preparer Use Only   Check if you are self-employed . . . . ☐

Preparer's name	[ ]	PTIN	[ ]
Preparer's signature	[ ]	Date	[ ]
Firm's name (or yours if self-employed)	[ ]	EIN	[ ]
Address	[ ]	Phone	[ ]
City	[ ]	State [ ]	ZIP code	[ ]

WORKERS' COMPENSATION AND DISABILITY INSURANCE

Workers' compensation insurance is intended to cover the cost of medical expenses incurred by employees who sustain injuries during the course of their employment. In addition, workers' compensation insurance reimburses an employee for the loss of income during the employee's convalescing period.

A company's premiums for workers' compensation insurance are dependent upon: (1) the nature of the employer's business, (2) the classification of the company's employees, (3) the wages paid to the employees, and (4) the volume of company claims filed by the company in the past.

Rules and regulations pertaining to premium calculations are normally dependent upon state statutes. However, to minimize premiums, an employer should exercise caution when classifying employees. For instance, employees who work with heavy-duty machinery are subject to higher premiums than those who are classified as clerical workers. Furthermore, employers should be careful not to overstate the payroll base subject to the premiums. Officers' salaries are usually capped at a maximum amount and overtime for other employees is often excluded.

Adequate and accurate records should be maintained by the controller in order to ensure that: (1) premiums are minimized, and (2) the company will not be liable for additional premiums upon audit by the insurance carrier.

Disability insurance is designed to compensate an employee for lost wages resulting from a "disabling" injury or illness which is not work related. Unlike the calculation of premiums for worker's compensation insurance, disability insurance premiums are not based on employee classification. Quite often, a uniform rate is applicable to a maximum wage base which is established by the insurer. Other times, the premium is set at a given dollar amount per employee in a given month. Many disability insurers establish premiums based on the gender of the employee. Depending upon the insurer, premiums could be due quarterly, semiannually, or annually.

UNEMPLOYMENT INSURANCE

State unemployment insurance coverage varies from state to state. Each year an employer is assigned an experience rating which determines the rate of tax to be imposed upon the employer. The maximum wage base also varies from state to state.

Rules pertaining to federal unemployment insurance tax, on the other hand, are uniform throughout the United States.

An employer must generally file an annual Form 940 by January 31, which covers the payroll of the prior year. If the amount of tax for the year is not more than $500, the tax may be paid with the return. If an entity's annual liability is in excess of $500, the tax must be deposited on a timely basis using EFTPS. Deposits must be made by the last day of the month following the close of the quarter when the liability is in excess of $500. At present, the tax is imposed on the first $7,000 of wages paid to each employee during the calendar year. The rate of tax is 6.0%. A maximum credit of 5.4% may be available if the employer has paid all required contributions to the state unemployment funds by the due date of Form 940. It is important to note that a state that has not repaid money it borrowed from the federal government to pay unemployment benefits is a "credit reduction state." The Department of Labor determines these states. If an employer pays wages that are subject to the unemployment tax laws of a credit reduction state, then the employer must pay additional federal unemployment tax when filing Form 940. Form 940, Schedule A, is used to report the additional tax resulting from the credit reduction.

Form 940 and instructions can be found on the Internal Revenue Service's Web site: www.irs.gov.

Sample Filled-In Tax Form

Following is Woody Corporation's payroll summary for the year ended December 31, 2017. For this illustration (1) Woody Corporation's sole employee is John Zurg and (2) the corporation has timely paid state unemployment insurance contributions to the State of Florida, which is not a "credit reduction state."

Quarter Ended	Gross Wages
3/31	$5,660.26
6/30	$5,660.26
9/30	$5,660.26
12/31	$5,660.26
Total	$22,641.04

Presented in Exhibit 60-2 is Woody Corporation's filled-in Form 940 for the calendar year 2017.

Exhibit 60-2:   Sample Filled-In Form 940

Form **940 for 2017:** Employer's Annual Federal Unemployment (FUTA) Tax Return   850113
Department of the Treasury -- Internal Revenue Service   OMB No. 1545-0028

Employer Identification number (EIN)	9 9 – 9 9 9 9 9 9 9

Name *(not your trade name)* WOODY CORPORATION

Trade name *(if any)*

Address 123 SPRINGFIELD STREET
Number   Street   Suite or room number

ANY CITY   FL   11111
City   State   ZIP code

Foreign country name   Foreign province/county   Foreign postal code

Type of Return
(Check all that apply.)

☐ a. Amended

☐ b. Successor employer

☐ c. No payments to employees in 2017

☐ d. Final: Business closed or stopped paying wages

Go to *www.irs.gov/Form940* for instructions and the latest information.

Read the separate instructions before you complete this form. Please type or print within the boxes.

Part 1:   Tell us about your return. If any line does NOT apply, leave it blank. See instructions before completing Part 1.

1a If you had to pay state unemployment tax in one state only, enter the state abbreviation. 1a F L

1b If you had to pay state unemployment tax in more than one state, you are a multi-state employer . . . . 1b ☐ Check here. Complete Schedule A (Form 940).

2   If you paid wages in a state that is subject to CREDIT REDUCTION . . . . 2 ☐ Check here. Complete Schedule A (Form 940).

Part 2:   Determine your FUTA tax before adjustments. If any line does NOT apply, leave it blank.

3   Total payments to all employees . . . . 3 | 22,641.04 |

4   Payments exempt from FUTA tax . . . . 4 | 15,641.04 |

Check all that apply: 4a ☐ Fringe benefits   4c ☐ Retirement/Pension   4e ☐ Other
                        4b ☐ Group-term life insurance   4d ☐ Dependent care

5   Total of payments made to each employee in excess of $7,000 . . . . 5 | |

6   Subtotal (line 4 + line 5 = line 6) . . . . 6 | 15,641.04 |

7   Total taxable FUTA wages (line 3 - line 6 = line 7). See instructions . . . . 7 | 7,000.00 |

8   FUTA tax before adjustments (line 7 x 0.006 = line 8) . . . . 8 | 42.00 |

Part 3:   Determine your adjustments. If any line does NOT apply, leave it blank.

9   If ALL of the taxable FUTA wages you paid were excluded from state unemployment tax, multiply line 7 by 0.054 (line 7 × 0.054 = line 9). Go to line 12 . . . . 9 | |

10 If SOME of the taxable FUTA wages you paid were excluded from state unemployment tax, OR you paid ANY state unemployment tax late (after the due date for filing Form 940), complete the worksheet in the instructions. Enter the amount from line 7 of the worksheet 10 | |

11 If credit reduction applies, enter the total from Schedule A (Form 940) . . . . 11 | |

Part 4:   Determine your FUTA tax and balance due or overpayment. If any line does NOT apply, leave it blank.

12 Total FUTA tax after adjustments (lines 8 + 9 + 10 + 11 = line 12) . . . . 12 | 42.00 |

13 FUTA tax deposited for the year, including any overpayment applied from a prior year 13 | |

14 Balance due. If line 12 is more than line 13, enter the excess on line 14.
    • If line 14 is more than $500, you must deposit your tax.
    • If line 14 is $500 or less, you may pay with this return. See instructions . . . . 14 | 42.00 |

15 Overpayment. If line 13 is more than line 12, enter the excess on line 15 and check a box below 15 | |
    ▶ You MUST complete both pages of this form and SIGN it.   Check one: ☐ Apply to next return. ☐ Send a refund.

Next ▶

For Privacy Act and Paperwork Reduction Act Notice, see the back of the Payment Voucher.
DXA

Form **940** (2017)

Exhibit 60-2: Sample Filled-In Form 940 (Continued)

850212

Name *(not your trade name)*	Employer identification number (EIN)
WOODY CORPORATION	99-9999999

Part 5: Report your FUTA tax liability by quarter only if line 12 is more than $500. If not, go to Part 6.

16 Report the amount of your FUTA tax liability for each quarter; do NOT enter the amount you deposited. If you had no liability for a quarter, leave the line blank.

16a **1st quarter** (January 1 -- March 31) **16a**

16b **2nd quarter** (April 1 -- June 30) **16b**

16c **3rd quarter** (July 1 -- September 30) **16c**

16d **4th quarter** (October 1 -- December 31) **16d**

17 Total tax liability for the year (lines 16a + 16b + 16c + 16d = line 17) **17**   **Total must equal line 12.**

Part 6: **May we speak with your third-party designee?**

Do you want to allow an employee, a paid tax preparer, or another person to discuss this return with the IRS? See the instructions for details.

☐ **Yes.** Designee's name and phone number

Select a 5-digit Personal Identification Number (PIN) to use when talking to IRS

☐ **No.**

Part 7: **Sign here. You MUST complete both pages of this form and SIGN it.**

Under penalties of perjury, I declare that I have examined this return, including accompanying schedules and statements, and to the best of my knowledge and belief, it is true, correct, and complete, and that no part of any payment made to a state unemployment fund claimed as a credit was, or is to be, deducted from the payments made to employees. Declaration of preparer (other than taxpayer) is based on all information of which preparer has any knowledge.

X **Sign your name here**

Print your name here

Print your title here

Date

Best daytime phone

Paid Preparer Use Only   Check if you are self-employed . . . . . . ☐

Preparer's name		PTIN	
Preparer's signature		Date	
Firm's name (or yours if self-employed)		EIN	
Address		Phone	
City	State	ZIP code	

Page **2**
DXA

Form **940** (2017)

EMPLOYMENT ELIGIBILITY VERIFICATION

All employees must submit a completed Form I-9, *Employment Eligibility Verification*, at the time of hire. The purpose of Form I-9 is to ensure that employees are legally entitled to work in the United States. Form I-9 must be retained by the employer rather than submitted to Immigration and Naturalization Service.

A blank Form I-9, along with related instructions, can be found on the Internal Revenue Service's Web site: www.irs.gov.

APPENDIX

Table A-1   Future Value of $1 = T1 (i,n)

Interest Rate

Number of Years	1%	2%	3%	4%	5%	6%	7%	8%	9%	10%	12%	14%	15%	16%	18%	20%	24%	28%	32%	36%
1	1.0100	1.0200	1.0300	1.0400	1.0500	1.0600	1.0700	1.0800	1.0900	1.1000	1.1200	1.1400	1.1500	1.1600	1.1800	1.2000	1.2400	1.2800	1.3200	1.3600
2	1.0201	1.0404	1.0609	1.0816	1.1025	1.1236	1.1449	1.1664	1.1881	1.2100	1.2544	1.2996	1.3225	1.3456	1.3924	1.4400	1.5376	1.6384	1.7424	1.8496
3	1.0303	1.0612	1.0927	1.1249	1.1576	1.1910	1.2250	1.2597	1.2950	1.3310	1.4049	1.4815	1.5209	1.5609	1.6430	1.7280	1.9066	2.0972	2.3000	2.5155
4	1.0406	1.0824	1.1255	1.1699	1.2155	1.2625	1.3108	1.3605	1.4116	1.4641	1.5735	1.6890	1.7490	1.8106	1.9388	2.0736	2.3642	2.6844	3.0360	3.4210
5	1.0510	1.1041	1.1593	1.2167	1.2763	1.3382	1.4026	1.4693	1.5386	1.6105	1.7623	1.9254	2.0144	2.1003	2.2878	2.4883	2.9316	3.4360	4.0075	4.6526
6	1.0615	1.1262	1.1941	1.2653	1.3401	1.4185	1.5007	1.5869	1.6771	1.7716	1.9738	2.1950	2.3131	2.4364	2.6996	2.9860	3.6352	4.3980	5.2899	6.3275
7	1.0721	1.1487	1.2299	1.3159	1.4071	1.5036	1.6058	1.7138	1.8280	1.9487	2.2107	2.5023	2.6600	2.8262	3.1855	3.5832	4.5077	5.6295	6.9826	8.6054
8	1.0829	1.1717	1.2668	1.3686	1.4775	1.5938	1.7182	1.8509	1.9926	2.1436	2.4760	2.8526	3.0590	3.2784	3.7589	4.2998	5.5895	7.2058	9.2170	11.703
9	1.0937	1.1951	1.3048	1.4233	1.5513	1.6895	1.8385	1.9990	2.1719	2.3579	2.7731	3.2519	3.5179	3.8030	4.4355	5.1598	6.9310	9.2234	12.166	15.916
10	1.1046	1.2190	1.3439	1.4802	1.6289	1.7908	1.9672	2.1589	2.3674	2.5937	3.1058	3.7072	4.0456	4.4114	5.2338	6.1917	8.5944	11.805	16.059	21.646
11	1.1157	1.2434	1.3842	1.5395	1.7103	1.8983	2.1049	2.3316	2.5804	2.8531	3.4785	4.2262	4.6524	5.1173	6.1759	7.4301	10.657	15.111	21.198	29.439
12	1.1268	1.2682	1.4258	1.6010	1.7959	2.0122	2.2522	2.5182	2.8127	3.1384	3.8960	4.8179	5.3502	5.9360	7.2876	8.9161	13.214	19.342	27.982	40.037
13	1.1381	1.2936	1.4685	1.6651	1.8856	2.1329	2.4098	2.7196	3.0658	3.4523	4.3635	5.4924	6.1528	6.8858	8.5994	10.699	16.386	24.748	36.937	54.451
14	1.1495	1.3195	1.5126	1.7317	1.9799	2.2609	2.5785	2.9372	3.3417	3.7975	4.8871	6.2613	7.0757	7.9875	10.147	12.839	20.319	31.691	48.756	74.053
15	1.1610	1.3459	1.5580	1.8009	2.0789	2.3966	2.7590	3.1722	3.6425	4.1772	5.4736	7.1379	8.1371	9.2655	11.973	15.407	25.195	40.564	53.358	100.71
16	1.1726	1.3728	1.6047	1.8730	2.1829	2.5404	2.9522	3.4259	3.9703	4.5950	6.1304	8.1372	9.3576	10.748	14.129	18.488	31.242	51.923	84.953	136.96
17	1.1834	1.4002	1.6528	1.9479	2.2920	2.6928	3.1588	3.7000	4.3276	5.0545	6.8660	9.2765	10.761	12.467	16.672	22.186	38.740	66.461	112.13	186.27
18	1.1961	1.4282	1.7024	2.0258	2.4066	2.8543	3.3799	3.9960	4.7171	5.5599	7.6900	10.575	12.375	14.462	19.673	26.623	48.038	85.070	148.02	253.33
19	1.2081	1.4568	1.7535	2.1068	2.5270	3.0256	3.6165	4.3157	5.1417	6.1159	8.6129	12.055	14.231	16.776	23.214	31.948	59.567	108.89	195.39	344.53
20	1.2202	1.4859	1.8061	2.1911	2.6533	3.2071	3.8697	4.6610	5.6044	6.7275	9.6463	13.743	16.366	19.460	27.393	38.337	73.864	139.37	257.91	468.57
21	1.2324	1.5157	1.8603	2.2788	2.7860	3.3996	4.1406	5.0338	6.1088	7.4002	10.803	15.667	18.821	22.574	32.323	46.005	91.591	178.40	340.44	637.26
22	1.2447	1.5460	1.9161	2.3699	2.9253	3.6035	4.4304	5.4365	6.6586	8.1403	12.100	17.861	21.644	26.186	38.142	55.206	113.57	228.35	449.39	866.67
23	1.2572	1.5769	1.9736	2.4627	3.0715	3.8197	4.7405	5.8715	7.2579	8.9543	13.552	20.361	24.891	30.376	45.007	66.247	140.83	292.30	593.19	1178.6
24	1.2697	1.6084	2.0328	2.5633	3.2251	4.0489	5.0724	6.3412	7.9111	9.8497	15.178	23.212	28.625	35.236	53.108	79.496	174.63	374.14	783.02	1602.9
25	1.2824	1.6406	2.0938	2.6658	3.3864	4.2919	5.2474	6.8485	8.6231	10.834	17.000	26.461	32.918	40.874	62.668	95.396	216.54	478.90	1033.5	2180.0
26	1.2953	1.6734	2.1566	2.7725	3.5557	4.5497	5.8074	7.3964	9.3992	11.918	19.040	30.166	37.856	47.414	73.948	114.47	268.51	612.99	1364.3	2964.9
27	1.3082	1.7069	2.2213	2.8834	3.7335	4.8223	6.2139	7.9881	10.245	13.110	21.324	34.389	43.535	55.000	87.259	137.37	332.95	784.63	1800.9	4032.2
28	1.3213	1.7410	2.2879	2.9987	3.9201	5.1117	6.6488	8.6271	11.167	14.421	23.883	39.204	50.065	63.800	102.96	164.84	412.86	1004.3	2377.2	5483.8
29	1.3345	1.7758	2.3566	3.1187	4.1161	5.4184	7.1143	9.3173	12.172	15.863	26.749	44.693	57.575	74.008	121.50	197.81	511.95	1285.5	3137.9	7458.0
30	1.3478	1.8114	2.4273	3.2434	4.3219	5.7435	7.6123	10.062	13.267	17.449	29.959	50.950	66.211	85.849	143.37	237.37	634.81	1645.5	4142.0	10143.
40	1.4889	2.2080	3.2620	4.8010	7.0400	10.285	14.974	21.724	31.409	45.259	93.050	188.88	267.86	378.72	750.37	1469.7	5455.9	19426.	*	*
50	1.6446	2.6916	4.3839	7.1067	11.467	18.420	29.457	46.901	74.357	117.39	289.00	700.23	1083.6	1670.7	3927.3	9100.4	46890.	*	66520	*
60	1.8167	3.2810	5.8916	10.519	18.679	32.987	57.946	101.25	176.03	304.48	897.59	2595.9	4383.9	7370.1	20555	56347	*	*	*	*

Table A-2   Future Value of Annuity of $1 = T2 (i,n)

Interest Rate

Number of Years	1%	2%	3%	4%	5%	6%	7%	8%	9%	10%	12%	14%	15%	16%	18%	20%	24%	28%	32%	36%
1	1.0000	1.0000	1.0000	1.0000	1.0000	1.0000	1.0000	1.0000	1.0000	1.0000	1.0000	1.0000	1.0000	1.0000	1.0000	1.0000	1.0000	1.0000	1.0000	1.0000
2	2.0100	2.0200	2.0300	2.0400	2.0500	2.0600	2.0700	2.0800	2.0900	2.1000	2.1200	2.1400	2.1500	2.1600	2.1800	2.2000	2.2400	2.2800	2.3200	2.3600
3	3.0301	3.0604	3.0909	3.1216	3.1525	3.1836	3.2149	3.2464	3.2781	3.3100	3.3744	3.4396	3.4725	3.5056	3.5724	3.6400	3.7776	3.9184	4.0624	4.2096
4	4.0604	4.1216	4.1836	4.2465	4.3101	4.3746	4.4399	4.5061	4.5731	4.6410	4.7793	4.9211	4.9934	5.0665	5.2154	5.3680	5.6842	6.0156	6.3624	6.7251
5	5.1010	5.2040	5.3091	5.4163	5.5256	5.6371	5.7507	5.8666	5.9847	6.1051	6.3528	6.6101	6.7424	6.8771	7.1542	7.4416	8.0484	8.6999	9.3983	10.146
6	6.1520	6.3081	6.4684	6.6330	6.8019	6.9753	7.1533	7.3359	7.5233	7.7156	8.1152	8.5355	8.7537	8.9775	9.4420	9.9299	10.980	12.135	13.405	14.798
7	7.2135	7.4343	7.6625	7.8983	8.1420	8.3938	8.6540	8.9228	9.2004	9.4872	10.089	10.730	11.066	11.413	12.141	12.915	14.615	16.533	18.695	21.126
8	8.2857	8.5830	8.8923	9.2142	9.5491	9.8975	10.259	10.636	11.028	11.435	12.299	13.232	13.726	14.240	15.327	16.499	19.122	22.163	25.678	29.731
9	9.3685	9.7546	10.159	10.582	11.026	11.491	11.978	12.487	13.021	13.579	14.775	16.085	16.785	17.518	19.085	20.798	24.712	29.369	34.895	41.435
10	10.462	10.949	11.463	12.006	12.577	13.180	13.816	14.486	15.192	15.937	17.548	19.337	20.303	21.321	23.521	25.958	31.643	38.592	47.061	57.351
11	11.566	12.168	12.807	13.486	14.206	14.971	15.783	16.645	17.560	18.531	20.654	23.044	24.349	25.732	28.755	32.150	40.237	50.398	63.121	78.998
12	12.682	13.412	14.192	15.025	15.917	16.869	17.888	18.977	20.140	21.384	24.133	27.270	29.001	30.850	34.931	39.580	50.894	65.510	84.320	108.43
13	13.809	14.680	15.617	16.626	17.713	18.882	20.140	21.495	22.953	24.522	28.029	32.088	34.351	36.786	42.218	48.496	64.109	84.852	112.30	148.47
14	14.947	15.973	17.086	18.291	19.598	21.015	22.550	24.214	26.019	27.975	32.392	37.581	40.504	43.672	50.818	59.195	80.496	109.61	149.23	202.92
15	16.096	17.293	18.598	20.023	21.578	23.276	25.129	27.152	29.360	31.772	37.279	43.842	47.580	51.659	60.965	72.035	100.81	141.30	197.99	276.97
16	17.257	18.639	20.156	21.824	23.657	25.672	27.888	30.324	33.003	35.949	42.753	50.980	55.717	60.925	72.939	87.442	126.01	181.86	262.35	377.69
17	18.430	20.012	21.761	23.697	25.840	28.212	30.840	33.750	36.973	40.544	48.883	59.117	65.075	71.673	87.068	105.93	157.25	233.79	347.30	514.66
18	19.614	21.412	23.414	25.645	28.132	30.905	33.99	36.450	41.301	45.599	55.749	68.394	75.836	84.140	103.74	128.11	195.99	300.25	459.44	700.93
19	20.810	22.840	25.116	27.671	30.539	33.760	37.379	41.446	46.018	51.159	63.439	78.969	88.211	98.603	123.41	154.74	244.03	385.32	607.47	954.27
20	22.019	24.297	26.870	29.778	33.066	36.785	40.995	45.762	51.160	57.275	72.052	91.024	102.44	115.37	146.62	186.68	303.60	494.21	802.86	1298.8
21	23.239	25.783	28.676	31.969	35.719	39.992	44.865	50.442	56.764	64.002	81.698	104.76	118.81	134.84	174.02	225.02	377.46	633.59	1060.7	1767.3
22	24.471	27.299	30.536	34.248	38.505	43.392	49.005	55.456	62.873	71.402	92.502	120.43	137.63	157.41	206.34	271.03	469.05	811.99	1401.2	2404.6
23	25.716	28.845	32.452	36.617	41.430	46.995	53.436	60.893	69.531	79.543	104.60	138.29	159.27	183.60	244.48	326.23	582.62	1040.3	1850.6	3271.3
24	26.973	30.421	34.426	39.082	44.502	50.815	58.176	66.764	76.789	88.497	118.15	158.65	184.16	213.97	289.49	392.48	723.46	1332.6	2443.8	4449.9
25	28.243	32.030	36.459	41.645	47.727	54.864	63.249	73.105	84.700	98.347	133.33	181.87	212.79	249.21	342.60	471.98	898.09	1706.8	3226.8	6052.9
26	29.525	33.670	38.553	44.311	51.113	59.156	68.676	79.954	93.323	109.18	150.33	208.33	245.71	290.08	405.27	567.37	1114.6	2185.7	4260.4	8233.0
27	30.820	35.344	40.709	47.084	54.669	63.705	74.483	87.350	102.72	121.09	169.37	238.49	283.56	337.50	479.22	681.85	1383.1	2798.7	5624.7	11197.9
28	32.129	37.051	42.930	49.967	58.402	68.528	80.697	95.338	112.96	134.20	190.69	272.88	327.10	392.50	566.48	819.22	1716.0	3583.3	7425.6	15230.2
29	32.450	38.792	45.218	52.966	62.322	73.689	87.346	103.96	124.13	148.63	214.58	312.09	377.16	456.30	669.44	984.06	2128.9	4587.6	9802.9	20714.1
30	34.784	40.568	47.576	56.084	66.438	79.058	94.460	113.28	136.30	164.49	241.33	356.78	434.74	530.31	790.94	1181.8	2640.9	5873.2	12940	28172.2
40	48.886	60.402	75.401	95.025	120.79	154.76	199.63	259.05	337.88	442.59	767.09	1342.0	1779.0	2360.7	4163.2	7343.8	22728	63977	*	*
50	64.473	84.579	112.79	152.66	209.34	290.33	406.52	573.76	815.08	1163.9	2400.0	4994.5	7217.7	10435	21813	45497	*	*	*	*
60	81.669	114.05	163.05	297.90	353.58	533.12	813.52	1253.2	1944.7	3034.8	7471.6	18535	29219	46057	*	*	*	*	*	*

Table A-3 Present Value of $1 = T3 (i,n)

Interest Rate

Number of Years	1%	2%	3%	4%	5%	6%	7%	8%	9%	10%	12%	14%	15%	16%	18%	20%	24%	28%	32%	36%
1	0.9901	0.9804	0.9709	0.9615	0.9524	0.9434	0.9346	0.9259	0.9174	0.9091	0.8929	0.8772	0.8696	0.8621	0.8475	0.8333	0.8065	0.7813	0.7576	0.7353
2	0.9803	0.9612	0.9426	0.9246	0.9070	0.8900	0.8734	0.8573	0.8417	0.8264	0.7972	0.7695	0.7561	0.7432	0.7182	0.6944	0.6504	0.6104	0.5739	0.5407
3	0.9706	0.9423	0.9151	0.8890	0.8638	0.8396	0.8163	0.7938	0.7722	0.7513	0.7118	0.6750	0.6575	0.6407	0.6086	0.5787	0.5245	0.4768	0.4348	0.3975
4	0.9610	0.9238	0.8885	0.8548	0.8227	0.7921	0.7629	0.7350	0.7084	0.6830	0.6355	0.5921	0.5718	0.5523	0.5158	0.4823	0.4230	0.3725	0.3294	0.2923
5	0.9515	0.9057	0.8626	0.8219	0.7835	0.7473	0.7130	0.6806	0.6499	0.6209	0.5674	0.5194	0.4972	0.4761	0.4371	0.4019	0.3411	0.2910	0.2495	0.2149
6	0.9420	0.8880	0.8375	0.7903	0.7462	0.7050	0.6663	0.6302	0.5963	0.5645	0.5066	0.4556	0.4323	0.4104	0.3704	0.3449	0.2751	0.2274	0.1890	0.1580
7	0.9327	0.8706	0.8131	0.7599	0.7101	0.6651	0.6227	0.5835	0.5470	0.5132	0.4523	0.3996	0.3759	0.3538	0.3139	0.2791	0.2218	0.1776	0.1432	0.1162
8	0.9235	0.8535	0.7894	0.7307	0.6768	0.6274	0.5820	0.5403	0.5019	0.4665	0.4039	0.3506	0.3269	0.3050	0.2660	0.2326	0.1789	0.1388	0.1085	0.0854
9	0.9143	0.8368	0.7664	0.7026	0.6446	0.5919	0.5439	0.5002	0.4604	0.4241	0.3606	0.3075	0.2843	0.2630	0.2255	0.1938	0.1443	0.1084	0.0822	0.0628
10	0.9053	0.8203	0.7441	0.6756	0.6139	0.5584	0.5083	0.4632	0.4224	0.3855	0.3220	0.2697	0.2472	0.2267	0.1911	0.1615	0.1164	0.0847	0.0623	0.0462
11	0.8963	0.8043	0.7224	0.6496	0.5847	0.5268	0.4751	0.4289	0.3875	0.3505	0.2875	0.2366	0.2149	0.1954	0.1619	0.1346	0.0938	0.0662	0.0472	0.0340
12	0.8874	0.7885	0.7014	0.6246	0.5568	0.4970	0.4440	0.3971	0.3555	0.3186	0.2567	0.2076	0.1869	0.1685	0.1372	0.1122	0.0757	0.0517	0.0357	0.0250
13	0.8787	0.7730	0.6810	0.6006	0.5303	0.4688	0.4150	0.3677	0.3262	0.2897	0.2292	0.1821	0.1625	0.1452	0.1163	0.0935	0.0610	0.0404	0.0271	0.0184
14	0.8700	0.7579	0.6611	0.5775	0.5051	0.4423	0.3878	0.3405	0.2992	0.2633	0.2046	0.1597	0.1413	0.1252	0.0985	0.0779	0.0492	0.0316	0.0205	0.0135
15	0.8613	0.7430	0.6419	0.5553	0.4810	0.4173	0.3624	0.3152	0.2745	0.2394	0.1827	0.1401	0.1229	0.1079	0.0835	0.0649	0.0397	0.0247	0.0155	0.0099
16	0.8528	0.7284	0.6232	0.5339	0.4581	0.3936	0.3387	0.2919	0.2519	0.2176	0.1631	0.1229	0.1069	0.0930	0.0708	0.0541	0.0320	0.0193	0.0118	0.0073
17	0.8444	0.7142	0.6050	0.5134	0.4363	0.3714	0.3166	0.2703	0.2311	0.1978	0.1456	0.1078	0.0929	0.0802	0.0600	0.0451	0.0258	0.0150	0.0089	0.0054
18	0.8360	0.7002	0.5874	0.4936	0.4155	0.3503	0.2959	0.2502	0.2120	0.1799	0.1300	0.0946	0.0808	0.0691	0.0508	0.0376	0.0208	0.0118	0.0068	0.0038
19	0.8277	0.6864	0.5703	0.4746	0.3957	0.3305	0.2765	0.2317	0.1945	0.1635	0.1161	0.0829	0.0703	0.0596	0.0431	0.0313	0.0168	0.0092	0.0051	0.0029
20	0.8195	0.6730	0.5537	0.4564	0.3769	0.3118	0.2584	0.2145	0.1784	0.1486	0.1037	0.0728	0.0611	0.0514	0.0365	0.0261	0.0135	0.0072	0.0039	0.0021
25	0.7798	0.6095	0.4776	0.3751	0.2953	0.2330	0.1842	0.1460	0.1160	0.0923	0.0588	0.0378	0.0304	0.0245	0.0160	0.0105	0.0046	0.0021	0.0010	0.0005
30	0.7419	0.5521	0.4120	0.3083	0.2314	0.1741	0.1314	0.0994	0.0754	0.0573	0.0334	0.0196	0.0151	0.0116	0.0070	0.0042	0.0016	0.0006	0.0002	0.0001
40	0.6717	0.4529	0.3066	0.2083	0.1420	0.0972	0.0668	0.0460	0.0318	0.0221	0.0107	0.0053	0.0037	0.0026	0.0013	0.0007	0.0002	0.0001	*	*
50	0.6080	0.3715	0.2281	0.1407	0.0872	0.0543	0.0339	0.0213	0.0182	0.0085	0.0035	0.0014	0.0009	0.0006	0.0003	0.0001	*	*	*	*
60	0.5504	0.3048	0.1697	0.0951	0.0535	0.0303	0.0173	0.0099	0.0057	0.0033	0.0011	0.0004	0.0002	0.0001	*	*	*	*	*	*

Table A-4   Present Value of an Annuity of \$1 = T4 (i, n)

Interest Rate

Number of Years	1%	2%	3%	4%	5%	6%	7%	8%	9%	10%	12%	14%	15%	16%	18%	20%	24%	28%	32%
1	0.9901	0.9804	0.9709	0.9615	0.9524	0.9434	0.9346	0.9259	0.9174	0.9091	0.8929	0.8772	0.8696	0.8621	0.8475	0.8333	0.8065	0.7813	0.7576
2	1.9704	1.9415	1.9135	1.8861	1.8594	1.8334	1.8080	1.7833	1.7591	1.7355	1.6901	1.6467	1.6257	1.6052	1.5656	1.5278	1.4568	1.3916	1.3315
3	2.9410	2.8839	2.8286	2.7751	2.7232	2.6730	2.6243	2.5771	2.5313	2.4869	2.4018	2.3216	2.2832	2.2459	2.1743	2.1065	1.9813	1.8684	1.7663
4	3.9020	3.8077	3.7171	3.6299	3.5460	3.4651	3.3872	3.3121	3.2397	3.1699	3.0373	2.9137	2.8550	2.7982	2.6901	2.5887	2.4043	2.2410	2.0957
5	4.8534	4.7135	4.5797	4.4518	4.3295	4.2124	4.1002	3.9927	3.8897	3.7908	3.6048	3.4331	3.3522	3.2743	3.1272	2.9906	2.7454	2.5320	2.3452
6	5.7955	5.6014	5.4172	5.1421	5.0757	4.9173	4.7665	4.6229	4.4859	4.3553	4.1114	3.8887	3.7845	3.6847	3.4976	3.3255	3.0205	2.7594	2.5342
7	6.7282	6.4720	6.2303	6.0021	5.7864	5.5824	5.3893	5.2064	5.0330	4.8684	4.5638	4.2883	4.1604	4.0386	3.8115	3.6046	3.2423	2.9370	2.6775
8	7.6517	7.3255	7.0197	6.7327	6.4632	6.2098	5.9713	5.7466	5.5348	5.3349	4.9676	4.6389	4.4873	4.3436	4.0776	3.8372	3.4212	3.0758	2.7860
9	8.5660	8.1622	7.7861	7.4353	7.1078	6.8017	6.5152	6.2469	5.9952	5.7590	5.3282	4.9464	4.7716	4.6065	4.3030	4.0310	3.5655	3.1842	2.8681
10	9.4713	8.9826	8.5302	8.1109	7.7217	7.3601	7.0236	6.7101	6.4177	6.1446	5.6502	5.2161	5.0188	4.8332	4.4941	4.1925	3.6819	3.2689	2.9304
11	10.3676	9.7858	9.2526	8.7605	8.3064	7.8869	7.4987	7.1390	6.8052	6.4951	5.9377	5.4527	5.2337	5.0286	4.6560	4.3271	3.7757	3.3351	2.9776
12	11.2551	10.5753	9.9540	9.3851	8.8633	8.3838	7.9427	7.5361	7.1607	6.8137	6.1944	5.6603	5.4206	5.1971	4.7932	4.4392	3.8514	3.3868	3.0133
13	12.1337	11.3484	10.6350	9.9856	9.3936	8.8527	8.3577	7.9038	7.4869	7.1034	6.4235	5.8424	5.5831	5.3423	4.9095	4.5327	3.9124	3.4272	3.0404
14	13.0037	12.1062	11.2961	10.5631	9.8986	9.2950	8.7455	8.2442	7.7862	7.3667	6.6282	6.0021	5.7245	5.4675	5.0081	4.6106	3.9616	3.4587	3.0609
15	13.8651	12.8493	11.9379	11.1184	10.3797	9.7122	9.1079	8.5595	8.0607	7.6061	6.8109	6.1422	5.8474	5.5755	5.0916	4.6755	4.0013	3.4834	3.0764
16	14.7179	13.5777	12.5611	11.6523	10.8378	10.1059	9.4466	8.8514	8.3126	7.8237	6.9740	6.2651	5.9542	5.6685	5.1724	4.7296	4.0333	3.5026	3.0882
17	15.5623	14.2919	13.1661	12.1657	11.2741	10.4773	9.7632	9.1216	8.5436	8.0216	7.1196	6.3729	6.0472	5.7487	5.2223	4.7746	4.0591	3.5177	3.0971
18	16.3983	14.9920	13.7535	12.6593	11.6896	10.8276	10.0591	9.3719	8.7556	8.2014	7.2497	6.4674	6.1280	5.8178	5.2732	4.8122	4.0799	3.5294	3.1039
19	17.2260	15.6785	14.3238	13.1339	12.0853	11.1581	10.3356	9.6036	8.9501	8.3649	7.3658	6.5504	6.1982	5.8775	5.3162	4.8435	4.0967	3.5386	3.1090
20	18.0456	16.3514	14.8775	13.5903	12.4622	11.4699	10.5940	9.8181	9.1285	8.5436	7.4694	6.6231	6.2593	5.9288	5.3527	4.8696	4.1103	3.5458	3.1129
25	22.0232	19.5235	17.4131	15.6221	14.0939	12.7834	11.6536	10.6748	9.8226	9.0770	7.8431	6.8729	6.4641	6.0971	5.4669	4.9476	4.1474	3.5640	3.1220
30	25.8077	22.3965	19.6004	17.2920	15.3725	13.7648	12.4090	11.2578	10.2737	9.4269	8.0552	7.0072	6.5660	6.1772	5.5168	4.9789	4.1601	3.5693	3.1242
40	32.8347	27.3555	23.1148	19.7928	17.1591	15.0463	13.3317	11.9246	10.7574	9.7791	8.2438	7.1050	6.6418	6.2335	5.5482	4.9966	4.1659	3.5712	3.1250
50	39.1961	31.4236	25.7298	21.4822	18.2559	15.7619	13.8007	12.2335	10.9617	9.9148	8.3045	7.1327	6.6605	6.2463	5.5541	4.9995	4.1666	3.5714	3.1250
60	44.9550	34.7609	27.8656	22.6235	18.9293	16.1614	14.0392	12.3766	11.0480	9.9672	8.3240	7.1401	6.6651	6.2492	5.5553	4.9999	4.1667	3.5714	3.1250

INDEX

A

Aatrix software . . . 6013

Abandonment value, capital budgeting . . . 22,028

ABC and ABM software . . . 6023-6024

ABC inventory control method . . . 49,019-49,021

ABM. *See* Activity-based management

Acceptable quality level (AQL) . . . 25,026, 26,002, 26,005

Accountants
. cloud computing, growth of . . . 7011-7012

Accountant's Trial Balance (ATB) . . . 6021-6022

Account Edge . . . 6013

Accounting
. changes in . . . 11,002-11,006
. divestitures . . . 40,013
. estimates, and income statement analysis . . . 31,037-31,038
. exposure . . . 58,008-58,011
. income statement analysis . . . 31,032-31,040
. in JIT system . . . 25,032
. key areas . . . 12,001-12,085
. policies, disclosure of . . . 11,008
. principle, changes in . . . 11,002-11,004
. prior-period adjustments . . . 11,006-11,008
. simple rate of return . . . 22,007-22,009
. software. *See* Accounting software
. tax planning . . . 59,002
. wireless technology . . . 7021-7022

Accounting changes . . . 11,002-11,006
. in accounting estimate . . . 11,005
. in accounting principle . . . 11,002-11,004
. in reporting entity . . . 11,005-11,006

Accounting disclosures . . . 11,001-11,020 *See also* Disclosure
. capital structure information . . . 11,014
. collaborative arrangements . . . 11,017-11,018
. derivatives . . . 11,015-11,016
. development-stage companies . . . 11,008-11,009
. environmental reporting . . . 11,018-11,020
. . accounting and reporting . . . 11,019

Accounting disclosures—continued
. environmental reporting—continued
. . business interruption insurance . . . 11,019
. . insurance contracts . . . 11,019-11,020
. . legislation . . . 11,018-11,019
. going concern . . . 11,020
. imputing interest on notes . . . 11,011-11,014
. inflation information . . . 11,016
. policies . . . 11,008
. prior-period adjustments . . . 11,006-11,008
. related parties . . . 11,014-11,015
. segmental . . . 13,004-13,007
. . attributes . . . 13,004-13,005
. . "chief operating decision maker," meaning of . . . 13,004
. . disclosures . . . 13,006-13,007
. . percentage tests . . . 13,005
. . reconciliation . . . 13,005
. . restatement . . . 13,005
. subsequent events . . . 11,016-11,017
. troubled debt restructuring . . . 11,009-11,011
. . creditor . . . 11,011
. . debtor . . . 11,010-11,011

Accounting estimates, and income statement analysis . . . 31,037-31,038

Accounting exposure . . . 58,008-58,011

Accounting (simple) rate of return (ARR) . . . 22,007-22,009

Accounting software . . . 4012-4018, 6008-6025 *See also* Database management software (DBMS); Software
. ABC and ABM software . . . 6023-6024
. accounts payable modules . . . 4015-4016, 6010
. accounts receivable modules . . . 4014-4015, 6009-6010
. advice and caveats . . . 6017-6018
. audit software . . . 6021-6022
. budgeting . . . 20,034-20,041
. compliance software . . . 6018-6019
. fixed asset modules . . . 4018, 6010-6011
. general ledger module . . . 4013-4014, 6009
. high-end packages . . . 6011-6012
. inventory modules . . . 4017-4018, 6010

ACC

ACC

ACC

ACT

ASC

ASC

BUS

COM

Computers.—continued
. fixed asset modules . . . 4018
. forecasting and statistical software . . .
4019-4020, 6004-6005
. general ledger module . . . 4013-4014
. graphics software . . . 4009-4010
. internal audit applications checklist . . .
28,029-28,034
. inventory modules . . . 4017-4018
. online risk management database
services . . . 34,010
. payroll modules . . . 4016-4017
. spreadsheet programs . . . 4005-4009,
22,023
. value chain management software . . .
4020-4024

Conditional promise for donation . . . 8046

Confidentiality of practitioners . . . 3042

Conflict of interest. *See also* Business ethics
. analyst . . . 3013-3015, 3021-3022
. control methods . . . 3044
. defined . . . 3044
. ethics . . . 3039-3045

Conglomerate mergers . . . 39,003

Consideration as element of contract . . .
36,011-36,012
. in suretyship and creditor's rights . . .
36,021

Consolidation . . . 12,003-12,008, 36,027

Constant dividend-payout ratio . . . 57,002

Consumer Credit Protection Act . . . 36,022

Consumer Leasing Act (CLA) . . . 36,023

Consumer products firm, balanced
scorecard . . . 24,020-24,021

Consumer Protection Act of 2005 . . . 41,013

Contingency planning . . . 5018-5019

Contingent business interruption
coverage . . . 11,019, 36,009

Contracts . . . 36,010-36,013
. costs . . . 8048-8049
. definition . . . 36,010
. elements . . . 36,011-36,012
. government . . . 8049
. legality . . . 36,012
. parol evidence rule . . . 36,013
. promissory estoppel . . . 36,012
. statute of frauds . . . 36,012
. types . . . 8047-8049, 36,010-36,011
. UCC . . . 36,010

Contribution income statement . . .
16,018-16,019

Contribution margin (CM) . . . 17,002-17,003
. cost-volume-profit analysis . . .
17,002-17,003
. income statement . . . 18,001-18,003
. short-term and nonroutine decisions,
analysis for . . . 18,001-18,016

Contribution price . . . 18,005

Contributions . . . 8046-8047, 59,004-59,005

Controllable costs . . . 14,008-14,009

Controllable risk . . . 51,005

Controlled group of corporations . . .
59,014-59,015

Controller
. database management systems . . .
5001-5019
. defined . . . 1002
. financial analysis . . . 1007-1008
. financing . . . 1008
. generally accepted accounting
principles . . . 1005-1006
. information technology . . . 4001-4026
. internal auditing and control . . . 1007
. investments . . . 1008
. management accounting . . . 1006-1007
. management of assets . . . 1008
. mergers and acquisitions . . . 1008
. reports of . . . 1005, 3001-3045
. responsibilities of . . . 1001-1009
. skills . . . 1004-1005
. tax preparation and planning . . . 1008
. treasurer vs . . . 1005

Controller reports . . . 1005, 3001-3045,
33,001
. analytical and control reports . . . 3003
. board of directors, reports for . . . 3004
. divisional managers, reports for . . . 3004
. to employees . . . 3004-3006
. exception reports . . . 3003
. financial forecasts . . . 3002
. financial projections . . . 3002
. financial reports . . . 3003-3004
. informational reports . . . 3003
. New York Stock Exchange (NYSE),
reporting to . . . 3006
. planning reports . . . 3002-3003
. prospective financial statements . . .
3001-3002
. senior management, special reports to . . .
3004
. to stockholders . . . 3006

Conversion costs . . . 14,004

Conversion spread . . . 9087

Convertible bonds . . . 50,005, 54,006, 54,008

CON

Fair market value . . . 9021-9025

Fair value measurements . . . 9066

Fair value of financial assets . . . 12,082-12,085

Fair value option . . . 9069-9074
. available-for-sale securities . . . 9074
. balance sheet . . . 9071-9072
. disclosures . . . 9072-9073
. electing fair value option . . . 9070
. eligible items at effective date . . . 9073-9074
. events . . . 9070
. held-to-maturity securities . . . 9074
. instrument application . . . 9070-9071
. statement of cash flows . . . 9072

Family and Medical Leave Act (FMLA) . . . 36,018

Farmers Home Administration . . . 54,017

FAS-123, Accounting for Stock-Based Compensation . . . 38,028

FAS-123(R), Share-Based Payment . . . 38,028

FAS-157-4, Determining Fair Value When the Volume and Level of Activity for the Asset or Liability Have Significantly Decreased and Identifying Transactions That Are Not Orderly . . . 9067

FAS-167, Amendments to FASB Interpretation No. 46(R) . . . 12,006

FASB. *See* Financial Accounting Standards Board

FASB Accounting Standards Codification . . . 1006

FCBA (Fair Credit Billing Act) . . . 36,023

FCPA. *See* Foreign Corrupt Practices Act of 1977

FDIC (Federal Deposit Insurance Corporation) Call Report System . . . 7005

Federal deficit, as monetary indicator . . . 37,023-37,025

Federal Deposit Insurance Corporation (FDIC) Call Report System . . . 7005

Federal Express . . . 4023, 25,024

Federal tax rates . . . 59,008-59,009

Federal withholding taxes . . . 60,003

FERF (Gartner and Financial Executives Research Foundation) . . . 4025

FIFO (First-in first-out) vs. weighted-average costing . . . 14,023-14,027

File controls . . . 4004-4005

FAI

Finance budget . . . 20,003

Financial accounting areas . . . 12,001-12,085
. annuity contracts . . . 12,057
. computer software . . . 6008-6025
. consolidation . . . 12,003-12,008
. decision making . . . 6001-6025
. derivatives . . . 12,077-12,083
. . bunny bonds . . . 12,081
. . covered option securities (COPs) . . . 12,081
. . dual-currency bonds . . . 12,081
. . Dutch auction notes . . . 12,081
. . embedded derivatives . . . 12,080-12,081
. . European currency bonds (ECUs) . . . 12,081
. . forward contract . . . 12,078
. . futures contract . . . 12,078
. . hedge accounting . . . 12,081-12,083
. . increasing-rate debt . . . 12,081
. . option contract . . . 12,079-12,080
. . pay-in-kind (PIK) preferred stock . . . 12,081
. . swap contract . . . 12,079
. . types of . . . 12,078-12,080
. . variable-coupon redeemable notes (VCRs) . . . 12,081
. . zero-coupon bond . . . 12,081
. fair value of financial assets . . . 12,017-12,018
. financial assets . . . 12,083-12,085
. foreign currency . . . 12,070-12,077
. . forward exchange contracts . . . 12,076-12,077
. . gains and losses excluded from net income . . . 12,076
. . hedges . . . 12,077
. . terminology . . . 12,070-12,073
. . transactions . . . 12,074-12,076
. . translation process . . . 12,073-12,074
. impairment guidance . . . 12,010-12,017
. income tax accounting
. . business combinations . . . 12,069
. . deferred tax liability vs. deferred tax asset . . . 12,066-12,067
. . ESOPs . . . 12,069
. . financial statement presentation . . . 12,065-12,066
. . indefinite reversal . . . 12,068
. . intraperiod tax allocation . . . 12,066
. . loss carrybacks and carryforwards . . . 12,066
. . multiple tax jurisdictions . . . 12,068
. . permanent differences . . . 12,065
. . quasi-reorganization . . . 12,069
. . share-based payment awards . . . 12,069

G

Internal control.—continued
. control environment . . . 28,011
. . information and communication . . . 28,012
. . monitoring . . . 28,012-28,013
. . risk assessment . . . 28,011-28,012
. control principles . . . 34,044-34,045
. COSO model . . . 34,043-34,044
. identifying deficiencies in . . . 28,013-28,015
. questionnaires. *See* Internal control questionnaires
. reports . . . 6019
. repository . . . 3031-3032

Internal control questionnaires . . . 28,016-28,066
. assessment form . . . 28,016-28,029
. computer applications checklist computer control environment . . . 28,029-28,034
. . hardware . . . 28,029-28,030, 28,031
. . outside computer service organizations . . . 28,034
. . software . . . 28,030, 28,031-28,032
. determining other areas for evaluation . . . 28,025-28,029
. financial reporting information systems and controls checklist . . . 28,034-28,066
. financing . . . 28,052-28,057
. inventory . . . 28,047-28,052
. payroll cycle . . . 28,061-28,066
. property, plant, and equipment . . . 28,057-28,061
. purchasing cycle . . . 28,042-28,047
. revenue cycle . . . 28,034-28,042
. understanding control environment . . . 28,016-28,027

Internal control reports . . . 6019

Internal rate of return (IRR) . . . 22,020-22,023
. modified . . . 22,025-22,026
. multinational capital budgeting . . . 58,014
. multiple . . . 22,023
. payback reciprocal . . . 22,011

Internal Revenue Code. *See* Tax planning

International budgeting decision . . . 58,013-58,023
. complications . . . 58,013-58,014

International financial management . . . 58,001-58,028
. cross rates . . . 58,004-58,006
. financial goals . . . 58,003
. financing sources . . . 58,025-58,028
. foreign exchange. *See* Foreign exchange

International financial management—continued
. foreign investment analysis . . . 58,013-58,023
. foreign operations, types of . . . 58,003
. inflation . . . 58,013
. interest rates . . . 58,012
. international capital budgeting . . . 58,013-58,023
. . complications . . . 58,013-58,014
. . what-if analysis . . . 58,020
. multinational corporations . . . 58,002
. political risks
. . dealing with . . . 58,024-58,025
. . measuring . . . 58,024
. . types of . . . 58,003
. reporting standards vs. GAAP . . . 10,020, 58,025
. spot and forward foreign exchange rates . . . 58,004

International Financial Reporting Standards (IFRS) . . . 10,020

International Monetary Market . . . 38,026

Internet
. financial reporting . . . 31,051-31,052 *See also* XBRL
. resources . . . 6002
. risk management database services . . . 34,010
. sources . . . 6024

Intraperiod tax allocation . . . 12,066

Intuit . . . 6013, 6017

Inventory . . . 9009-9016 *See also* Inventory management/planning
. balance sheet analysis . . . 31,009-31,010
. channel stuffing . . . 3009-3010
. dollar value LIFO . . . 9015
. ending inventory budget . . . 20,012
. financing . . . 52,014-52,016
. first-in, first-out (FIFO) . . . 9010
. inventory stated at market value in excess of cost . . . 9016
. inventory valuation difficulties . . . 9016
. last-in, first-out (LIFO) . . . 9010
. lower of cost and net realizable value (LCANRV) . . . 9009-9011
. lower of cost or market (LCM) . . . 9010, 9011-9012
. modules in accounting software . . . 4017-4018, 6010
. purchase commitments, losses on . . . 9015-9016
. retail LIFO . . . 9013-9015

MET

OPE

PPP